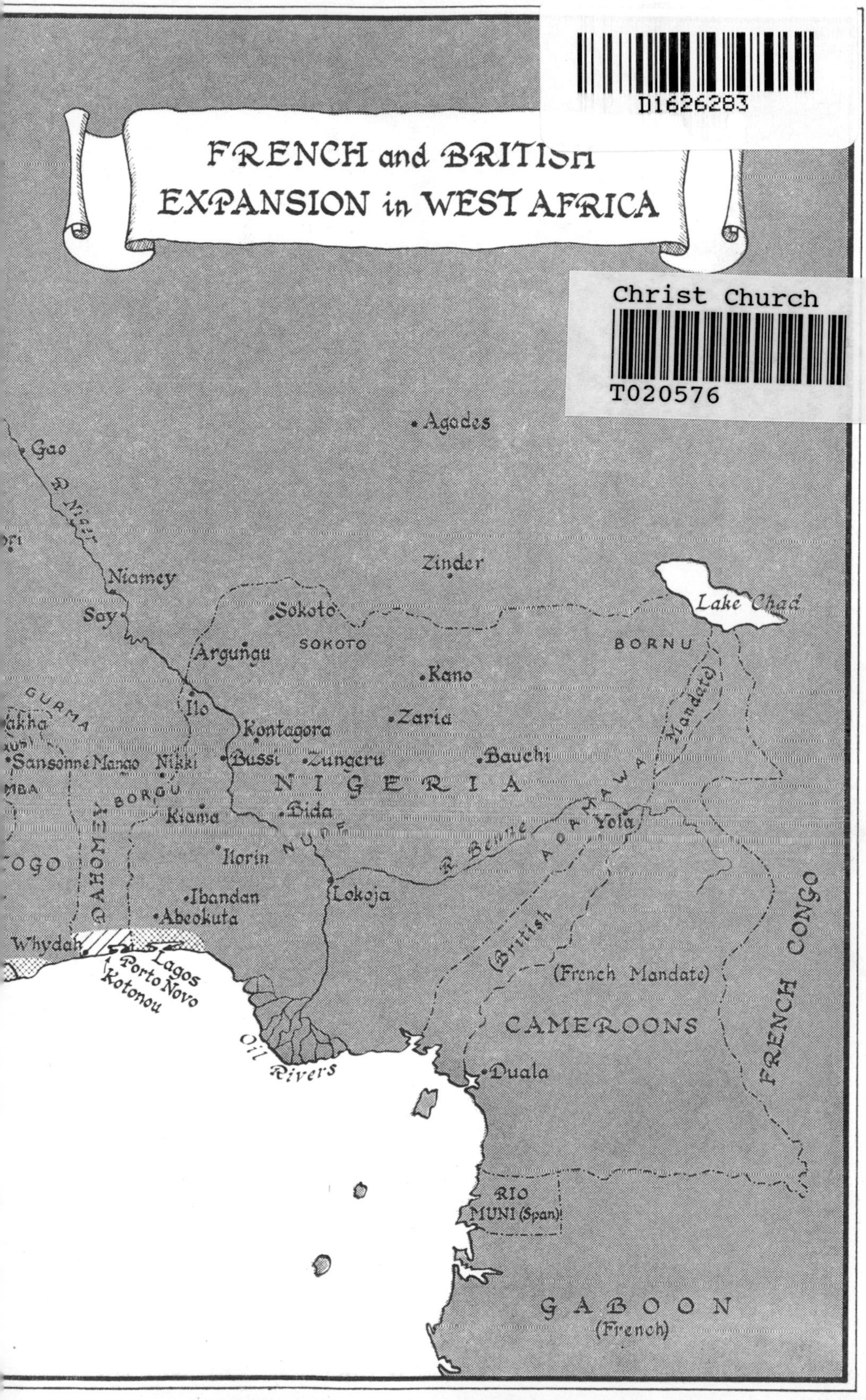

FRENCH and BRITISH EXPANSION in WEST AFRICA

Agodes
Gao
R. Niger
Zinder
Niamey
Say
Sokoto
SOKOTO
Lake Chad
BORNU
Argungu
Kano
GURMA
Ilo
Zaria
Kontagora
Sansonne Mango
Nikki
Bussi
Zungeru
Bauchi
NIGERIA
BORGU
DAHOMEY
Kiama
Bida
NUPE
ADAMAWA
Yola
(British Mandate)
R. Benue
TOGO
Ilorin
Ibandan
Lokoja
FRENCH CONGO
Abeokuta
Whydah
Lagos
Porto Novo
Kotonou
(French Mandate)
CAMEROONS
Oil Rivers
Duala
RIO MUNI (Span.)
GABOON
(French)

J/XVIII. 4. 35

FRANCE AND BRITAIN IN AFRICA

FRANCE AND BRITAIN IN AFRICA

Imperial Rivalry and Colonial Rule

edited by
PROSSER GIFFORD
and
WM. ROGER LOUIS

Yale University Press, New Haven and London

1971

Copyright © 1971 by Yale University.
All rights reserved. This book may not be reproduced, in whole or in part, in any form (except by reviewers for the public press), without written permission from the publishers.
Library of Congress catalog card number: 70-151574
International standard book number: 0-300-01289-6

Designed by John O. C. McCrillis and set in Caledonia type.
Printed in the United States of America by The Vail-Ballou Press, Inc., Binghamton, N.Y.

Distributed in Great Britain, Europe, and Africa by Yale University Press, Ltd., London; in Canada by McGill-Queen's University Press, Montreal; in Mexico by Centro Interamericano de Libros Académicos, Mexico City; in Central and South America by Kaiman & Polon, Inc., New York City; in Australasia by Australia and New Zealand Book Co., Pty., Ltd., Artarmon, New South Wales; in India by UBS Publishers' Distributors Pvt., Ltd., Delhi; in Japan by John Weatherhill, Inc., Tokyo.

CONTENTS

PART III *Bibliography*

MAPS

FOREWORD

The partitioning of Africa by the major European powers and the history of the European empires created on that continent are the history of less than a century, a short period by comparison with empires of the past which endured for hundreds of years. This brief history can be looked upon as a mere episode in the history of Africa as well as of Europe; its importance, on the other hand, for both areas remains a large one, even if it is still too early to assess its full significance.

In this present study scholars are concerned with the roles of France and Britain in Africa. At the time of partition these countries were both industrial states, in which democratic ideas were having a growing role. Some of these ideas, essentially anticolonial, went back not only to the thought developed during the French revolution and English Parliamentary struggles, but also to the American Declaration of Independence and, in particular, to Adam Smith.

It was a paradox that European countries should seek to establish colonies in the last quarter of the nineteenth century when the parliamentary climates of opinion still held that people should govern themselves and that the possession of colonies was indefensible on economic grounds, a great cost to the mother country. Acting on these older views many liberals were determined to give imperial promoters little or no financial support for such objectionable undertakings. The consequence was that private interests had to explore and administer the newly occupied territories by means of chartered companies and concessions, a principle of government that led to the worst type of colonial rule by placing African societies under the uncontrolled sway of their exploiters. The arrangement led to forced labor, taxation in kind, private armies, the seizure of lands from Africans, the ruthless exploitation of resources. That liberal humanitarians should have to share a responsibility for the worst type of colonial policy is one of the ugly but understandable facts of modern history. One is hardly surprised at the large number of rebellions against Europeans in Africa around 1900 and the hostilities toward Europeans that had their ultimate issue in the struggle for independence. The publicized evils of this colonialism outraged humanitarians in Europe and were, in some ways, to lead to demands for a better management of African affairs.

This humanitarian anticolonialism carried forward into the colonial debates of the First World War. President Wilson and certain European statesmen felt that all colonial rule was the selfish and cruel business of men concerned only with exploitation. The British and French eventually fell in line with President Wilson's proposal to place the former German colonies under international supervision. Under the mandates system of the League of Nations, Englishmen and Frenchmen regarded their African wards as a "sacred trust of civilization." The reality of this high principle is well discussed in several of the following essays.

The abolition of chartered companies, the French notion of association rather than assimilation, the concept of the Dual Mandate, the increased use of indirect rule—these were part of the effort to make the colonial system more palatable to critics in Europe, in the United States, and in Africa, as well as to reform and improve its actual practice. Part of the result was that Africans began in earnest after the First World War to organize their demands for a greater say in running the affairs of their countries. Initially, their requests were modest ones. As the years went by, their demands mounted and became more specific, and their backers became more numerous. They had good reason for increased apprehension in these decades. Despite President Wilson's hope after the signing of the armistice in 1918 that armed imperialism had ended, France and Spain were engaged in war for the conquest and partitioning of Morocco. Italy was fighting in Libya.

New needs faced Europe as a consequence of the First World War and as a result of altered tariff and immigration policies. The relative freedom of movement that people and goods had enjoyed in the latter part of the nineteenth century was severely curtailed. The world that called itself international because it had created the League of Nations had become most nationalistic with the adoption of these and other restrictive policies. Lacking the possibility of relatively easy expansion as in the 1870s and 1880s, countries were compelled to find solutions for their problems within their narrow borders. With economic depression the centralizing, regulatory state—Communist, Fascist, Nazi, and Socialist—gained acceptability in many countries. Although these were originally efforts to find local solutions within national economies, it was not long before nationalist leaders espoused again the common belief that solutions were to be found beyond their borders.

As the Western Allies had encouraged Africans to fight against other Europeans in the First World War, they did the same in the Second. Africans contributed manpower and resources to help the British and French achieve victory; and they were encouraged to believe that this aid would gain them more than they had obtained after the defeat of Germany in 1918. The promises made in the course of the Second World War were less vague than those made in the First. The Four Freedoms of President Roosevelt were to apply "everywhere in the world." In the Atlantic Charter of 1941 President Roosevelt and Prime Minister Churchill were agreed in their desire "to see no territorial changes that do not accord with the freely expressed wishes of the people concerned"; they respected "the right of all peoples to choose the form of government under which they will live; and they wish to see sovereign rights and self-government restored to those who have been forcibly deprived of them." At Brazzaville in 1944, Charles DeGaulle emphasized the increasing freedoms possible for French Africans within the French constitutional structure. In the Charter of the United Nations, it was agreed by the colonial powers in the new world organization that they recognized the paramountcy of the interests of the peoples living in the territories under their administration, that, among other things, they would assist in developing self-government, and that they would report regularly to the United Nations on the economic, social, and educational conditions in their colonies. The Trusteeship Council had far greater authority than the Permanent Mandates Commission of the League of Nations. This came close to fulfilling the ideals that President Wilson expressed in 1918–19. As will be seen in the essays of this symposium, the colonial problems of the First World War make an interesting contrast with the interaction of British and French policies during the Second World War.

In many instances, the real economic value of African territories to Europe was developed after 1920. Prior to that time the chief value of these areas to official Europe had been diplomatic rather than economic, a fact documented in the large number of accords and ententes involving African territories made by European states with one another. Some of these agreements became the basis for wartime alliances. It is doubtful that such agreements could have been made had it been known that the territories possessed resources of great economic and strategic value. Because African territories were sometimes regarded as diplomatic counters, it is possible to state that the possession of African territories as potential objects of barter without consulting their inhabitants was a factor for peace in Europe, a "safety valve" that enabled the European powers to readjust their alignments and resolve problems beyond their own confines. Mr. Fieldhouse's essay in this volume explodes many false economic theories, but, to go beyond his argument, it is perhaps worth noting that it is difficult in history to find a country that did not sooner or later feel compelled to move beyond confining borders in its effort to solve otherwise insoluble problems of more land, more resources, and more food. In the companion volume *Britain and Germany in Africa* (New Haven, 1967), Professor Henry Turner, forcefully argues that the partition of Africa occurred in part because of *Torschlusspanik*—the fear that other nations might benefit from the resources of Africa to turn the balance of power in Europe. Like the argument put forward by Fieldhouse, Turner's thesis points to the probable conclusion that, however internecine the European rivalries in Africa may have been, the evidence suggests that "imperialism" as a cause of war did not find its primary source in Africa.

As before the war, African interests were being sacrificed to the needs of European diplomacy. In addition to the realities of colonialism, there were signs of old attitudes continuing: Italy, Portugal, France, Britain, Belgium—all discussed sending more settlers into Africa; there was even talk of permitting Nazi and racist Germany to reacquire African territory. These facts and rumors made it clear to African leaders that the lofty promises implicit in the war aims of the First World War could not be relied upon; even the League of Nations offered little hope. The League could do little for the people of Southwest Africa mandated to South Africa. The League did nothing in Ethiopia. France and Britain were willing to give Italy a free hand despite Mussolini's formal agreement with Ethiopia to settle differences without resort to war. Colonial welfare and development schemes before and after the Second World War appeared to be more concerned with getting African resources for Europeans than with fostering the well-being of African populations. Then, when in the critical years of war against Germany, Italy, and Japan, the colonial powers made promises of self-government to all colonial subjects bearing no date for their fulfillment, African spokesmen made clear that the Trusteeship Council of the United Nations should wield far greater authority over Africa than the Mandates Commission of the League of Nations had possessed.

Within less than two decades the colonial powers had to grant the demands of African leaders, who could count on the support of the Soviet Union and often of the United States in the United Nations and on increasing political support at home. The powers whose victories in two world wars had led to the expulsion of Germany and Italy from Africa now found themselves being forced out of their own colonies by the same arguments they had used against their former enemies.

In the two decades that have elapsed since Libya gained independence through international agreement in 1951, African peoples have reclaimed their own history and have given evidence of a capacity for international action that shows few of the concerns that formerly informed French and British colonial policies in Africa. Because African and Asian nations are again threatened by the economic and strategic projections of Great Power rivalries, it is wise to recall the antecedents and consequences of the colonial era just ended.

It is against this kind of background that one must read the study of *Britain and Germany in Africa* and this new volume on *France and Britain in Africa*. Words of deep gratitude must be expressed to former colleagues, Professor Prosser Gifford of Amherst College and Professor Wm. Roger Louis of the University of Texas. Their labors organized the two conferences at Yale and provided scholars with two outstanding volumes.

Harry R. Rudin

☙ INTRODUCTION

In March 1965 the Concilium on International Studies at Yale University sponsored a conference on British and German Colonialism in Africa. The conference papers, intended from the outset to form a cohesive book, were published subsequently by the Yale University Press under the title *Britain and Germany in Africa: Imperial Rivalry and Colonial Rule.* The success of the conference and the enthusiastic reception of the book encouraged us to convene another conference designed to produce a companion volume comparing the imperial rivalry and colonial administration of France and Britain in Africa. The second conference, again sponsored by the Concilium on International Studies, was held at Yale in March 1968, and the present volume, again drawn from the papers delivered, represents our attempt to make certain comparisons between the overseas activities of the two preeminent African colonial powers.

The general sense of achievement and excitement that the conferences generated is attributable to several factors. First, the theme of both conferences was a discussion of the forces that caused the expansion of the three principal colonial powers and of the differences in their resulting colonial administrations. Bringing together students of the British, German, and French colonial experience, the conferences also bridged to some extent the gap that tends to exist between those who view the "scramble" for colonies from the imperial perspective of European archives and those who work in the archives of African countries on colonial policy and internal administration.

Second, we were able to bring younger scholars, who were about to complete or who had just completed their dissertations, together with some of the authorities of the field. The resulting discussions provided many fresh ideas, not to mention anecdotes. Participants debated the subtleties of colonial expansion and rule and, above all, suggested the directions that future research might take.

Third, the procedure of the conferences in regard to the presentation of papers contributed to the value of the scholarship in the first, and we hope in the second, volume. Before each conference the drafts of the papers were circulated, and the authors had the advantage of the conference discussions in revising their chapters for publication. Although the scheme of the two volumes had been planned as much as possible in advance, the authors did not give their chapters final form until after the criticism of the conference participants could be taken into account. Each, of course, wrote according to his own judgment and was free to accept or reject the suggestions put forward by his colleagues; we believe the positive value of the cooperative scholarship of the two conferences is manifest.

The idea to have two senior scholars responsible for the two concluding chapters (one for the imperial, the other for the administrative aspects) has aided greatly in giving focus and clarity to the conclusions of the two conferences. We are indebted to Jean Stengers and John Fage, who performed this duty in the first volume, and to Henri Brunschwig and Leonard Thompson for tying together the principal ideas discussed in the second conference and relating them to the main themes of the chapters.

The two parts of the second volume indicate to an extent greater than those of the first volume the present state of scholarship in relation to the partition of Africa and its subsequent administration. We feel that the first part, together with the chapters on imperial expansion in the German volume, brings us closer to a definitive study of the Scramble for Africa. Although the framework is essentially that of a symposium rather than a comprehensive volume, the essays do focus on the salient events and issues of European expansion into Africa in the late nineteenth and early twentieth centuries. In this volume, the story begins with a survey of Anglo-French relations throughout most of the nineteenth century and recognizes the landmarks of colonial diplomacy—Tunis, Egypt, the Congo, protectionist policies, the Berlin Conference, the competition in Western Africa, Fashoda, the Entente—and ends with the last major episode of Anglo-French colonial rivalry, that of the First World War. We regret that J. L. Miège of the Faculté des Lettres et Sciences Humaines, D'Aix, was unable, owing to illness, to present his chapter on Morocco, but this has been dealt with to some extent by Henri Brunschwig's conclusion.

Narrowly conceived, the chapters in the first part of the volume might be considered as a specialized branch of European diplomatic history; but we have done our best to try to avoid the pitfalls of specialization and have encouraged each of the authors to try to take into account the economic, social, and psychological aspects of European imperialism. These themes are particularly noticeable in the chapters by Brunschwig, Newbury, and Stengers. Collectively the chapters in the first half of the volume attempt not only to make the connection between problems of expansion and administration, but also to contribute fundamentally to an understanding of the problem of European imperialism by asking what caused the expansion of Europe into Africa, and, in an even more ambitious sense, what caused the First World War. These chapters ask, but perhaps do not answer, the question whether Europe's eruption into Africa has significance in the long view of African history.

The second half of the volume poses questions of an equally interesting but more tentative nature. Taken together, these chapters indicate some of the directions in which students of African administration will continue to move. Taken together, they also make plain why, in the study of internal African history, we still have a distance to go before attaining the perspective now available to historians of imperial rivalry.

The differences between the colonial policies of European powers is no longer a question of the seminal significance it once seemed. We now realize that from an African viewpoint the colonial era has many common characteristics, irrespective of the nationality of European rulers. What once appeared to be problems of "colonial policy"—an aspect of the expansion of Europe—can now also be examined as phases of African history. The complexities of interaction between African peoples and colonial administrators have less to do in many instances with putative European national characteristics than with the rooted realities of local and regional history. The chapters by Sidney Kanya-Forstner and Boniface Obichere document the importance of local context and decisions. In western Africa, French military commanders, no less than African rulers, had to deal with the African polities resulting from the turbulent internal history of the first half of the nineteenth century. To explain the consequences of colonial policies in Africa, knowledge of African conditions is as necessary as knowledge of the policies that the administrators were seeking to implement. Both Hubert Deschamps and Robert Heussler underline the importance of local conditions, even for the interwar years, the period of most self-confident colonial rule.

Yet the differences between the approaches and aims of French and British policy in their African colonies had significance, although not always the significance attributed to them at the time. The chapters by William Cohen, Ralph Austen, and David Fieldhouse put into perspective some of these differences as they were evident in recruitment, in attitudes toward mandates, and in economic practice. The differences in retrospect are often not the differences once alleged by colonial experts, although the long-run significance of French and British rule may turn upon the division of Africa into two major language groups incorporating European cultural values that to some extent have permeated African societies.

Careful comparison of colonial administration and its effects remains difficult, however, for several reasons. There has been less open access to archives bearing upon French administration than to the archives of either the Public Record Office or of some of the former British colonial territories. The result is an unevenness of documentation, particularly for the later years of colonial rule. Thus even where monographs delve into aspects of colonial administration, seldom is there an analysis in equal depth of both French and British practice. These conditions emphasize the value of bringing French, British, and American scholars together.

The conferences and consequent volumes owed much to the hospitality of Yale University. The discussion of ideas flourishes in informal as well as formal settings, and the combination of hard-working formal meetings with informal discussion proved very valuable indeed. The facilities provided by the Concilium on International Studies, by the Department of History, the Yale University Press, the Colleges, and by various faculty members played an important role in making the conferences of academic value. In particular we are especially grateful to Miss Casey Miller, Mrs. Ruth Davis Kaufman and Mrs. Marian Ash, Dean Georges May, and Professors Philip Curtin, Leon Lipson, Arthur F. Wright, and Howard R. Lamar. Professor Emeritus Harry R. Rudin inspired the first volume, and he has generously contributed a foreword to the second. Financial support from the Henry L. Stimson Fund for Research in World Affairs, administered by the Concilium, has made possible the publication of this volume.

The ultimate scholarly value of the project lies in the field of comparative history, though we could claim to make no more than a modest effort in this direction. The idea of comparative colonial studies was developed mainly in the 1930s by a few British and European scholars; only now have the archival resources—metropolitan and African—begun to become available for a systematic return to those issues. Although we are still probably one generation away from an adequate overview of the colonial era, we believe that cooperative scholarship has made advances in this direction. Given the variety of languages and archives involved, cooperation among scholars generates new ideas and tests individual research, which is the foundation for history itself. The chief importance of the colonial years in Africa will rest finally in the differing degrees to which Africans used them to gain the capacity and the will for viable independence. We hope that this volume brings us nearer to a full analysis of these manifold interactions between Europe and Africa.

Prosser Gifford
Wm. Roger Louis

PART I

Imperial Rivalry

⸎ 1. *Anglophobia and French African Policy*

⸎ HENRI BRUNSCHWIG

"Anglophobia" means fear of England. Did the French fear England in the nineteenth century? They would be surprised at the question today. At school they are told about the "Anglophilia" of French writers influenced by Walter Scott, Lord Byron, or Edgar Allan Poe, the American. Their history books note the "Anglophilia" of the "dandies." If you were to press the matter, they might just remember the Egyptian crisis of 1840, but their books in this matter put more emphasis on the quarrel between "Die Wacht am Rhein" and "The Marseillaise of peace" than on an exchange of notes between Palmerston and Thiers. The only phobia that remains firmly fixed in the memory of all French people is certainly that about Germany, whose menacing shadow darkened the horizon for three generations between 1870 and 1950.

If, nevertheless, as we shall see, it is possible to discern the germs of Anglophobia in certain circles from the start of the century, it is in no way comparable to the epidemic of "Germanophobia" that infected the French population after 1870. And since public opinion cannot, at the same time, become equally impassioned for diverse causes, and since, also, "Anglophobia" and "Germanophobia" were to all intents contradictory, the friendship of one being indispensable in order to face up to the other, it was inevitable that after 1870, when public opinion became sensitive to foreign affairs, it should choose friendship with Britain. In spite of Bismarck's efforts, in spite of humiliation over Fashoda, public opinion approved the Entente Cordiale in 1904. If it had been possible to carry out public opinion polls with modern methods in the nineteenth century, there is no doubt that they would never have shown general hostility toward Britain.

A microscope is necessary to discover the germs of "Anglophobia" among the French. Undoubtedly they can be found almost everywhere after the wars of the Empire. But they were far from being virulent, for the ground was not favorable. Under the Bourbon Restoration, succeeding British governments wished for the friendship of France and showed themselves understanding of the need of the ministers of Louis XVIII and Charles X for prestige. The British recognized the justice of French claims to the restitution of their former colonies. Frequently they hauled their representatives over the coals when they seemed reluctant to hand over their powers to the delegates of France. Real difficulties only occurred over the trading ports along the eastern coast of Madagascar. Sir Robert Farquhar, the British governor of L'Ile de France (Mauritius), claimed that the ports were dependent on him. "L'lle de France," which had been rebaptized in its former Dutch name, Mauritius, was the only exception to the principle of restitution of colonies. It became British under the Vienna Treaty, which made no mention of Madagascar. The French governor of Bourbon Island (Réunion), Admiral Bouvet, appealed to the principle of restitution, and London decided in his favor. The French reoccupied Sainte Marie Island. The rivalry between Bourbon (Réunion) Island and Mauritius for influence over the king of the Hovas, Radama, went on until 1828 when the king died, and the two competitors were sent packing. Queen Ranavalona wanted neither missionaries nor European counselors.

An attempt in 1829, under the command of Captain Gourbeyre of the French navy, to set foot once again on the great island failed in face of Hova resistance, for the Hovas claimed to dominate the whole island. So the French held to Sainte Marie Island, and after a few years both French and British lost interest in Madagascar.

On the other hand, French traders sometimes complained of British competition. But there were so few of them and the levels were so different that their complaints could not hope to arouse general "Anglophobia." French trade with black Africa represented hardly anything at all. When France reappeared on these coasts after 1840, she had seen that she could very well live without colonies. She "needed" neither trade outlets nor colonial products. The inquiries, which preceded taking possession of Grand Bassam, Assinie, and Gaboon in 1843, had shown that French industry could not furnish the trade articles the Negroes required. The major African product, palm oil, consumption of which increased considerably in Europe during the century, attracted the interest of the French only very late. They would not use the cheap yellow soap which became the rage in Anglo-Saxon countries. Large-scale imports of the oil only began after the chemist Rougier had found a way of making it colorless (1852). French industry was not sufficiently mechanized to create a need for lubricants, as was the case in England. Nor was the French peasant in a hurry to replace his tallow candle by one made of stearine. Until about 1870 French shipowners exported to England the greater part of the palm oil they treated at Whydah and at the mouth of the Niger. As for sugar produced in other colonies, such as Réunion or the Antilles, it raised more problems than it resolved, for the French economy turned toward sugar beet. No, the French economy did not need colonies, and the occasional ill humor of certain traders against the English never reached important levels of the population.

The fight against the slave trade brought the French and British together. In fact they collaborated, in spite of French reserve concerning the mutual right of search on the high seas. But such reserve on the part of the French navy was not the only reason for mediocre cooperation between the two countries. The main reason was that French public opinion remained comparatively indifferent to this crusade, which was passionately followed by the British masses. Except for a few small circles of liberals who cultivated the spirit of the Encylopaedia and the ideology of the Rights of Man, neither the rural masses nor the Catholic Church nor the middle classes concerned with the conflicts of home policy felt themselves involved in the issue of the slave trade. It would be entirely futile to pinpoint this or that individual appearance of Anglophobia. The great and evident fact was that there was no deep reason for hostility. The French and British lived in two different worlds, with only superficial contact between them.

The British, in fact, were far more concerned with what happened overseas. Many of them emigrated. Their mechanized industry needed overseas markets and tropical raw materials. Their navy ruled the waves. Nevertheless Britain remained faithful to the principle laid down by Secretary of State Lord Shelburne in 1783: "We prefer commerce to dominion." The "decolonization" of the United States reinforced the point, since it in no way injured the progress of trade. Britain, therefore, did not seek the costly prestige of acquiring new lands.

Liberal and soon Free Trading Britain linked its anti-slave-trade passion to its need for commercial expansion. None of these fundamental aspects of its policy clashed with France's essential interests. The liberalism of British policy, which was often invoked by the French, furnished them with as many reasons for Anglophilia as the quarrels over the return of trading posts on the rivalry of traders at the courts of Negro kings provided for Anglophobia.

It was not until the French navy was reconstituted under Louis-

Philippe that favorable ground occurred for cultivating the virus of Anglophobia. It was then that the first phenomenon appears in this story, which was to remain a constant until our day: Anglophobia developed at the same time as the navy and remained until 1870 the navy's prerogative. All its officers, juniors who served at sea or seniors who governed colonies or worked in the offices and ministries, all showed at every point an anti-British reflex, which no doubt owed its origin to eighteenth-century rivalries. Whatever files one may consult, the General Correspondence of the Directorate of Colonies; dispatches from the various colonies, which are preserved at "National Archives, Overseas section"; the "B B[4] Mouvements" series of the Naval Archives; "Memoirs and Documents, Africa" of the Foreign Ministry at the Quai d'Orsay; everywhere you will come across the same imperialistic attitude, mingled with an urge to expansion purely for reasons of prestige and a morbid suspicion of Britain. Humiliated by defeat at Trafalgar, the navy was deeply hurt by the loss of L'Ile de France, the best station on the route to India. As soon as enough ships were available, the sailors sought to compensate for this loss, and in general terms to acquire whatever they suspected the British might want. They continuously accuse Britain of imperialist aims, which she was far from showing.

Nothing is more revealing in this matter than the numerous treaties concluded between 1830 and 1880 with the Negro chiefs of the coast. Almost all British texts insist on four points: the abolition of the slave trade, freedom to trade for all white men, help for ships in peril and a share in wrecks, and the protection of missionaries. Cession of sovereignty is rare, and when it occurs it is dictated by local conditions: the need to repress smuggling in the slave trade, or the need to augment revenue by the control customs. This was so in the case of the annexation of Lagos in 1861 and of its extension to Badagri, Palma, and Lekki in 1863.

Franco-African agreements on the contrary always start by the granting of political sovereignty to France, and generally do not deal with slavery. They often seek a trade monopoly, which they frequently do not dare to claim openly from the Negro chief, who prefers British goods. It is clear from this comparison that the aims of the two countries were not the same; for the British they were material advantage and the satisfaction of a humanitarian ideal; for the French a thirst for political prestige.

This need for self-affirmation, for planting the flag and insisting that foreign vessels should salute it, this psychological complex of the defeated, explains the suspicion with which French sailors regarded their British opposite numbers. Judging others by themselves, they could not believe that Britain was not seeking new colonies in Africa, and thus accused her of hypocrisy. Britain's commercial and humanitarian interests appeared in their eyes as disguising a thirst for power. Personal rivalries with some particular British officer, who became caught up in the situation and showed himself in turn highly suspicious, did nothing but confirm their conviction.

Nothing is more characteristic of this passionate conviction than the ease with which the Ministry of Marine swallowed the revelations of a certain master mariner named Garnot. He arrived in Paris from Madagascar, with Queen Ranavalona's ambassadors. The queen had sent the ambassadors to Paris and London to inquire into what Europe was, for she judged its influence to be deleterious. Garnot asserted that the Queen was prepared to exchange Sainte Marie Island for Diégo-Suarez Bay, which she did not possess but which she, he asserted, would not claim. In fact, the ambassadors, about whom the archives tell us little, were not empowered to negotiate. We know little more about Garnot. But it would surely have been easy for the ministry to have checked up, as it did in similar circumstances later, on this individual. However, it did not do so. His story was accepted, and he was sent to Tananarive to prepare negotiations, which nevertheless it was judged prudent should be conducted by the governor of Bourbon (Réunion).

On April 18, 1837, minister for the navy Du Camp de Rosamel sent a long report to his colleague the foreign minister, Count Molé:

> Monsieur Garnot, who accompanies the Malagasy envoys, has communicated to your department, and to that of the Navy, information from which it follows that Queen Ranavalona Marejaka would be prepared to grant the French flag all the trade advantages which attract it to Madagascar, and has conceded, in exchange for our possessions on various points of this island, the territory that includes Diégo-Suarez Bay.

The Minister goes on to explain that this territory is inhabited by a Sakalava population, which cannot oppose the expansion of the Hovas who have not yet conquered the whole island. The present French possessions, which to all intents and purposes are confined to Sainte Marie Island, whose military post costs sixty thousand francs a year, are unhealthy. Diégo-Suarez "on the contrary offers one of the finest harbors in the world and would in this matter amply compensate us for the loss of L'Ile de France [Mauritius]. Its territory, besides, does not harbor the serious illnesses found on the rest of the Malagasy coast."

I must call your Excellency's attention to the stipulation that in ceding Sainte Marie Island to the Queen it will be necessary to insist that the Queen's armies should occupy it as soon as we evacuate. Without this clause it is to be feared that British forces would establish themselves on the island, and there are all manner of reasons for opposing such an outcome in advance. Queen Ranavalo [sic] Marejaka will have to give France guarantees against any disturbance in the possession of Diégo-Suarez, whether it come from the Sakalava or any other peoples who might claim it as their property; this clause is essential owing to uncertainty concerning the real rights of the Hovas over the territory in question.

This and other reasons which I have already indicated must imply that France recognizes that the sovereignty of Madagascar resides in the person of Queen Ranavalo Marejaka, thus there is no reason for not giving this Queen the title of Queen of Madagascar, which is that under which she appears to wish to treat with France.

I have taken no account in the preceding observations of any umbrage which the British government might take at the establishment of French forces at Diégo-Suarez.

Our office has on divers occasions discussed its views on Madagascar with the British Ministry which has never contested our rights to the possession of certain points on the coast of this island. Nevertheless, I think it would be advisable that the negotiations to be opened with Queen Ranavalo Marejaka should be kept secret until the moment that we are in effective possession of the territory which will have been ceded to us in the bay of Diégo-Suarez.[1]

Both regret for the loss of Mauritius, and an insistent Anglophobia appear in this letter. On the fourteenth of July the same minister announced that Captain Garnot was to negotiate the exchange and at the same time asked Post Captain de Hell, who had been appointed Governor of Bourbon Island (Réunion),

to dispatch a vessel, whose captain will have as special commission to make all necessary exploration of Diégo-Suarez. . . . The commander of this vessel will be instructed to make contact with

1. Archives National Section Outre-Mer [ANSOM hereafter], General Correspondence, *189*, 93.

Captain Garnot, to whom I shall write to this effect, and to inquire how the negotiations which the latter has undertaken are proceeding, as well as informing him of the results of his exploration. As he left Paris, Captain Garnot gave it as his opinion that the government should not wait until His Majesty the King had ratified the treaty, before occupying Diégo-Suarez. He fears the intrigues of British agents in Madagascar should they learn of the aim of the negotiations before we have taken possession of this new territory. He even fears that some British ship should hasten adventurously to plant the British flag on the territory, which would give rise to serious difficulties.[2]

The French Foreign Ministry delayed giving its agreement, and the naval minister wrote again on December 15. Then in February 1838 it was discovered that the chart of Diégo-Suarez Bay, drawn up in 1833 by the corvette *La Nièvre* and kept in the Ministry of Marine chart room, had "for the most part kept to the same names as those used on a chart of this bay printed in London in 1824 and titled 'British Sound on the North East Coast of Madagascar under the direction of Captain S. W. Owen.' "[3]

This, of course, does not mean that the French Government envisages the need to defend its rights of occupation at Diégo-Saurez against any claim that Britain might make, based on prior exploration or nomenclature. Nevertheless it is possible that the British Government might, by reference to the French Chart, ask embarrassing questions should it wish to contest the French right to a permanent establishment at Diégo-Suarez. . . . Thus the Minister has considered that it would be advisable to modify the published chart by substituting national names for those used by the British.[4]

The government agreed, and the following month the minister dispatched the corvette *La Dordogne* in support of the Garnot mission.

I have no information concerning the results which may have attended the new voyage to Madagascar undertaken by Monsieur Garnot, in command of "La Mathilde." But I suppose that the confidential note with which he was provided by the Minister for

2. Ibid., p. 180.
3. Ibid., p. 353.
4. ANSOM, General Correspondence, *190*, 59.

Foreign Affairs before his departure . . . must have allowed him access to the Hova Government. . . . On the other hand it has always been my thought that the Governor of Bourbon should be charged with the direction of the higher levels of this operation, and that he should be in charge of this projected establishment, as soon as it should be opportune. . . .

As you may see from the documents that have been communicated to you, Captain Garnot considered that we should occupy Diégo-Suarez immediately, even before the negotiations, which he was to begin, were completed. Such an occupation has obvious advantages, but the honor of the flag demands that it should take place explicitly only once it can be considered definitive. Until then, "La Dordogne," should you send her to Diégo-Suarez, must be considered as merely continuing the exploration begun by "La Nièvre" in 1832. Should it happen, though most unlikely, that "La Dordogne" should find British vessels in the Bay, the corvette should return immediately to Bourbon, and should not return to Diégo-Saurez until the British ships have left or after right to possession of the territory granted by Treaty with the Queen of the Hovas becomes effective. . . . The greatest secrecy must be maintained at Bourbon concerning "La Dordogne's" expedition to Diégo-Suarez. The commander of this corvette will only be informed of his mission under circumstances defined by this dispatch. You will easily understand the need for these reservations.[5]

In spite of careful preparation, the project was abandoned in March 1839, after de Hell had informed the minister that the queen had no desire to negotiate. The minister then dropped Garnot as lightly as he had welcomed him. On March 27, 1839, he approved de Hell's decision not to negotiate with the Hovas and told him: "Monsieur Garnot has landed at Bordeaux but it does not seem that he has come to Paris, and for my part I saw no usefulness in summoning him, considering the information you supplied me with in the matter." [6]

But de Hell, since he saw that it was impossible to form an alliance with the Hovas, suggested that it might be possible to form an alliance against them, with the Sakalavas. The reasons were always the same. Admiral Duperré, the naval minister, on the first of October pleaded in favor of de Hell's case with the foreign minister, Marshal Soult:

5. Ibid., *190,* August 10 and Carton 4 N.208.
6. Ibid., *191,* 455.

My predecessor [he explained], had authorized the governor of Bourbon to occupy Diégo-Suarez. It was believed that the Queen would accept the proposed exchange. However as a result of Captain de Hell's report of June 10th last concerning the mission undertaken by "La Dordogne," it does not seem that there is the least chance of coming to such an arrangement. Captain Garnot, for his part, who returned to France after having been thrown out by the Galmaches [sic] chiefs, did not conceal from me that he considered all negotiation of the kind he had hoped to undertake, would be vain.

A French trader who succeeded Garnot in the confidence of the Malagasy Chiefs, named Delastelle, told me that the Hova Government would never consent to cede any of its territory to a foreign power, any more than it would allow France to regain possession of its former establishments on the East Coast.

Under such circumstances it will be necessary for the King's Government to examine whether to abandon without compensation French possessions on the East Coast, retaining only Sainte Marie Island, in spite of the grave inconvenience of such a situation, or whether, in conformity with the views of the Governor of Bourbon to occupy Diégo-Suarez with the determination to install a military establishment which would defend the territory with the assistance of the fighting tribe of the Salavas [sic] and chief or prince Ramanatika, both of whom would require arms or money.

Your ministry and mine know how well founded is all that Monsieur de Hell says on the complete absence of any British intervention in our troubles in Madagascar, and on the flagrant usurpation by the Hova tribe of the Diégo-Suarez territory.

After having expatiated on the salubrious climate of the bay, the goodwill of the "Salavars," and the economical nature of de Hell's plan, he concludes:

"Deprived, by the ever regrettable loss of Mauritius, of its only port beyond the Cape of Good Hope, France would derive, in Peace as in War, immense advantages in the possession of Diégo-Suarez bay." [7]

The Egyptian crisis of 1840 caused the postponement of the great Diégo-Suarez operation. De Hell, with his minister's approval, confined himself to preparatory work. A new exploration of the bay was undertaken by Captain Passot, contacts were undertaken with the Sakalava leaders, and finally, in April 1840, *La Prévoyante* was sent to Nossi

7. Ibid., p. 525.

Bé in order to find "a small military harbor." Roussin, the minister of marine, soon obtained Foreign Minister Guizot's agreement (on September 19)[8] and de Hell was able to give rein to his Anglophobia in his order concerning taking possession of Nossi Bé and Nossi Cumba islands, dated St. Denis, the thirteenth of February 1841.

> Whereas, the rights of France over Madagascar and its dependant islands are based on its anteriority in taking possession and occupying a part of this great island, at a time when other nations entertained few, if any relations with this country, and maintained there no stable establishment:
>
> Whereas, France has never renounced its rights in this matter, since on each occasion when circumstances required she repeated or proclaimed them:
>
> Whereas, in the same way as Britain bases its sovereign rights over the continent of New Holland on the fact that she took possession of Botany Bay, it would be impossible to deny France's claim to the whole island of Madagascar, based on the same principle, and in consequence of her taking possession and occupying diverse parts of the East Coast, and in particular, Fort Dauphin, Foulpointe, Tamatave and the Bay of Antongil:
>
> Whereas, the cession made by the Queen of the Sakalavas and the chiefs placed under her authority, cannot but be considered as a new recognition of France's anterior rights over that part of Madagascar, formerly or actually occupied by the tribe of the Sakalavas. . . .
>
> We order and command the following . . .[9]

It would require too many pages to give the full history of this question. Anglophobia is constantly apparent in it. Scarcely was Nossi Bé occupied than de Hell, now promoted to rear admiral and still consumed by the great Diégo-Suarez operation, discovered the value of Mayotte Island, one of the Comoro group, which the British would certainly occupy if the French did not precede them.

Mayotte "has all that is necessary to build one of the finest harbors in these parts. . . . it is superior, from a military and naval point of view, to Nossi-Bé"[10] writes Admiral Duperré in confirmation to de

8. Ibid., *193*, 123–27, and Archives du Ministère des Affaires Etrangères, Mémoires et Documents [MAE MD hereafter], 69, Iles de l'Océan Indien I, pp. 9, 10, 11.

9. MAE MD, 69, pp. 14–18 and 43–44.

10. ANSOM, *195*, 459–69.

Hell in April 1841. "The setting up a French establishment on Nossi-Bé, to be completed later by the occupation of Mayotte, is a most useful measure . . . and can . . . give us a much more favorable starting point [than Sainte Marie Island], should the project for occupying the northern part of Madagascar be revived." However, Guizot feared that the imam of Muscat might protest, for he was an ally of the British, and, so it appeared, suzerain lord of the Comoros. De Hell, however, was insistent.

> Both from a military and a maritime point of view [he wrote to Duperré on February 28, 1841], the possession would almost compensate us, I am assured, for the loss of Mauritius. The possession of Mayotte is indispensable, not only because of the immense utility of the harbor which this island encloses, but also because a British occupation, which would probably be the consequence of our establishing ourselves at Nossy-Bé, would result in the British dominating our position and would put an end to all our efforts on the northwest coast of Madagascar.[11]

Duperré, in his correspondence with Guizot, showed himself as Anglophobe as de Hell. In a long report dated October 8, 1841, he notes that an establishment at Nossi Bé "would be of no real importance, if the British, or any other maritime power, should establish themselves at a more important point, such as Mayotte Island appears to be."

> Monsieur de Hell emphasizes the urgency of taking a definitive decision in the matter, in view of the preparations being undertaken by the governor of Mauritius, either to occupy the island before us, or to exploit the influence which Britain exercises over the chiefs of the two other islands of the Comoro group, Anjouan and Mohéli, by way of the Imam of Muscat.
>
> British ambitions are not confined to getting in ahead of us on this matter. While, owing to successive postponements since 1833, projects conceived by the Navy Department for the reestablishment of French power in Madagascar, have not been followed up, British commercial speculation has turned toward this island. Further it seems as though the views of that government were now turned toward the occupation of the most important harbor of this island, that is to say the Bay of Diégo-Suarez, which has been described by our hydrographical explorations as suitable, in the hands of a

11. Ibid., *196*, 317, 323, 437, and MAE MD.

powerful nation, to becoming in a short time, the most formidable port of seas beyond the Cape of Good Hope.

The coincidence of information arriving at the same time from London, Mauritius and India, make it impossible for the French government to delay any longer in finding a solution to this question. Recent examples show us clearly enough what happens in similar circumstances to a country that deliberates when faced with a government that knows how to act.

Since 1814 France has allowed the entire occupation of New Holland by Britain, when at least half of this great continent could now belong to us, if the Government of the Restoration, preoccupied by other matters, had not discarded the project submitted to it, of founding a colony on the Swan River. Today all the parts of the coast of New Holland, discovered and described by French navigators, are being covered with British establishments which preserve their French names. More recently New Zealand also has come almost entirely under British domination. I do not need to recall the sorry issue of the expedition which left our ports in 1839 for those vast possessions. But here at least, if France was outdistanced, she was neither supplanted nor beaten as she would be in Madagascar, if, after having occupied so many important points on the great island, her flag should be excluded in peacetime by that of Britain, in territories which she has never ceased to own. Such an outcome would produce a deplorable effect in France and would become, it must be said, the subject of eternal reproach for the government that allows it to happen.[12]

Finally Guizot agreed. De Hell had returned to France and had been succeeded by Rear Admiral Bazoche.[13] The latter received secret instructions from the minister of marine, Roussin, dated February 16, 1843. Should the British have arrived on Mayotte before him, he was to emphasize France's anterior rights, which were based on a treaty obtained by Captain Passot from the local chief. "If however it was not possible to carry out this operation [a landing] except in conditions that might bring about a clash, he should abstain from any form of disembarkation, and on withdrawal, content himself with lodging a formal protest." [14]

The British made no protest, and Bazoche undertook to extend French domination to the other Comoro Islands, beginning with

12. ANSOM, General Correspondence, *196,* 437–44, *69,* 47 ff.
13. ANSOM, General Correspondence, *200,* 137, and MAE MD, 69, p. 68.
14. ANSOM, General Correspondence, *199,* 691.

Anjouan. De Hell, meanwhile, was drawing up a plan for the conquest of Madagascar from a base on Diégo-Suarez Bay. Duperré submitted this plan to the cabinet, which rejected it. In spite of this he revealed it in Parliament, which provoked a strong reaction from Guizot. In his speech of March 31, 1843, Guizot sought to limit French actions to the acquisition of supporting points.[15]

There is no room in this essay, however, for a detailed account of the story of Madagascar,[16] in which Anglophobia on the part of the navy constantly appears. The navy was also responsible for the setting up of establishments in the Gulf of Guinea. But here opposition came less from their British opposite numbers than from British traders who were perturbed at the appearance of a foreign sovereignty.

As it is known, Edouard Bouët-Willaumetz,[17] a member of the French squadron cruising out of Gorée on an anti-slave-trade patrol, managed to have carried out a survey of the coast south of Senegal, the plans for which had been drawn up by the slave traders. He obtained a commission to carry out a trade prospection in association with Broquant, a master mariner of Bordeaux. *La Malouine* made a first voyage in 1836–39, then set out again to offer protectorate treaties, while Paris studied the reports sent by Bouët and Broquant. The final outcome showed that French industry could not provide the Negroes with articles of trade as mediocre and as cheap as British manufactures. On the other hand, there were few French traders. Local chambers of commerce when consulted showed little enthusiasm, and the government therefore decided not to ratify the treaties. Then, in August 1842, a Select Committee of the House of Commons on the abolition of the slave trade recommended that treaties should be signed with Negro chiefs, and that forts, abandoned after abolition, should be reoccupied in order to make enforcement more effective. When this was learned in Paris, the navy's imperialist reflexes came into play. The director of colonies, Henri Galos, claimed for France the same advantages as those Britain would enjoy. He obtained that possession should be taken, as a matter of urgency, of points mentioned in the nonratified treaties. In 1843 a fort, a small garrison of about twenty-five men, and the French flag were set up at Grand Bassam, Assinie, and Gaboon.

Serious difficulties were only encountered in Gaboon, where British

15. MAE MD, 69, p. 127.

16. Ibid., pp. 63–67, 70, and ANSOM, General Correspondence, *199*, 675–89, 726–60, 969–74, 983, 1005, etc.

17. Bernard Schnapper, *La politique et le commerce français dans le Golfe de Guinée de 1838 à 1871* (Paris, 1961), pp. 15 ff.

traders had long frequented the villages of King Louis and King Glass, on the north coast of the estuary. Bouët first ally, King Denis, was on the sandy south coast. Fort Aumale was built near Louis' village. A little further upstream, an American Protestant mission was established on King Glass' territory by a Reverend Wilson. King Glass signed a protectorate treaty on March 28, 1844, which was proposed by Lieutenant Commander Darricau, in the presence of a master mariner from Nantes named Amouroux. Then under the influence of one Dyer, the master of the trader *Englishman,* Glass and 112 of the leading villagers put their x's to a protest, written in English, which assured King Louis-Philippe that they had signed the protection treaty under duress. This petition, signed on the fifth of April, was followed on the twenty-fifth of July by another addressed to the minister of foreign affairs and sent to Queen Victoria. It was published in Britain, and when the French ambassador lodged a protest against the masters of British trading vessels for not recognizing French jurisdiction, the British foreign minister used it as a reply.

The details of the affair are picturesque. Behind the political conflict it shows the irritation felt by the British at France's lack of energy in the repression of the slave trade. We have not the space to develop this theme,[18] but, for example, the protectorate treaties made no mention of this matter. Things might have taken a turn for the worse after Commander Eastcourt of the British naval steamship *Eclair* was sent to make a report. The report was not favorable to France, and during the whole of 1845, British and American merchantmen passed "within gunshot of the fort, without either saluting the French flag, or showing their own colour." Guizot protested against the *Eclair's* report, and at the same time (a matter we shall return to later), reassured the British concerning the commercial and humanitarian consequences of French occupation.[19] Neither Lord Aberdeen nor Guizot considered that such mediocre conflicts between mediocre traders were of sufficient importance to compromise the "entente cordiale" which was reestablishing itself after the 1840 crisis.

There were other conflicts and other inevitable clumsiness on the part of Anglophobe sailors. Lieutenant Commander Leps could certainly have avoided firing into the shrouds of a British merchantman which had not shown the color in the presence of a French warship.[20] Mackau, the navy minister, would have been well advised in 1844 if

18. See MAE MD Afrique 58.
19. MAE MD, 58, Congo, Gabon I. pp. 106–09.
20. MAE MD Afrique 51, p. 16.

he had refrained from warning Guizot that the British had their eyes on Principe Island. Count de St. Aulaire, French ambassador to the Court of St. James's, gave an account of his mission on December 24:

> You had also asked me to obtain some information concerning the British Navy taking possession of a part of Principe Island, with the declared intention of turning it into a coaling station. Lord Aberdeen, when I asked directly about the matter, confessed that he knew nothing about it. He knew neither where Principe Island was situated nor to whom it belonged. All that he remembered was that a few months ago there had been much talk of the difficulty of finding coal for the Navy on the West Coast of Africa, and of the excessive cost of coaling in these circumstances. He willingly promised to furnish me with the information I had requested when he had received it from his colleague at the Admiralty.[21]

The French navy was also no doubt wrong in pressing the government to establish a protectorate over Porto-Novo in February 1863, on the pretext that the British intended to establish themselves there. When France, because of the hostiliy of Dahomey, had to evacuate the territory in December 1864, the British made no move.[22]

Except for variations of time and place, it is always the same picture that appears. Because of the conviction on the part of the French navy that they are going to be tricked by the British, they fail in part in their duty to defend the honor of the flag.

There is one more African theater in which the Anglophobia of the navy was violently expressed before 1870—the Red Sea. We will not recount here the history of French exploration in Ethiopia, or the various projects for the recruitment of labor on the coast of the Red Sea, which were planned under the patronage of the Governor of Réunion. The ships of the Indian Ocean squadron regularly carried out missions which took them from Réunion to the Somali Coast, the Red Sea, Aden, and Bombay. Their commanders, on occasion, obtained information on the possibilities of the recruitment of labor. No project, in fact, came to fruition, and neither the foreign ministry or even the navy dreamed of setting up establishments in this area.

Offers sent in at almost the same moment by a Captain Méquet and Henri Lambert, French consular agent at Aden, would never have been considered by the foreign minister, but the Colonial Office had

21. MAE MD Afrique 58, p. 84.
22. Schnapper, *Le politique et le commerce français*, pp. 194–99.

been transferred from Foreign Affairs to the Ministry of Algeria and the Colonies which had been formed by Prince Napoleon, the emperor's cousin. Méquet had met the king of Tigré, who said he was ready to authorize the recruitment of labor and had formally asked for a French protectorate. Lambert transmitted a similar request in August, on behalf of a chief on the Obock Coast, Abu Bekr, who was in dispute with the Turkish Pasha of Hodeida, his overlord.

Count Walewski, the foreign minister, was reticent when consulted on the matter by Prince Napoleon. He requested his colleague Hamelin, at the Ministry of Marine, to open an inquiry. This showed that Lambert's statements concerning Obock were wildly overenthusiastic. Prince Napoleon insisted, however, and finally sent the emperor, on the twenty-third of August, a long report which is a monument to Anglophobe imperialism.

> Sire, the massacre at Jedda, the grave events in the Far East, the project to cut through the Isthmus of Suez, the progressive movement drawing trade toward India and China and finally France's position in the Mediterranean, which is now no more than a terminus, seem to make it imperative that the Emperor's government should not only make its presence felt in the Red Sea, but also its power, before this sea falls entirely under British power.
>
> I am engaged in laying the bases of a convention which would result in constant and regular communication by French packets, between Metropolitan France and its colonies in the Indian Sea. If this combination succeeds, thanks to these packets and the cruisers of the Imperial Navy, our colors will float uninterruptedly from the Nile Delta to the Coast of Madagascar. Under their watchful care, under their aegis, our political and commercial influence will spread rapidly through the neighboring regions, where friendly memories of our country are ineffaceable, and where Imperial France has a great work of civilization to accomplish. But if our relations are to spread and consolidate themselves; if your warships and merchantmen are to sail the Red Sea under equal conditions to those enjoyed by the British Navy; and finally, if we are to take advantage of present resources, and profit from those that will appear in the near future, it is imperiously necessary that we should possess a base in these parts.
>
> Britain, not content with exercising a sort of preponderance at Alexandria and Suez, and with the creation of another Gibraltar at Aden, has quite recently occupied Perim, and is busily preparing to make this place into a redoutable military position.

> When so many first-class interests wave from beyond the Indian Sea, toward the uttermost confines of the Asiatic world, France must not hesitate, in her turn, to set foot on this Canal which still remains neutral, which links the French waters of the Mediterranean with the French waters of Madagascar, of the Comoros, of Réunion and her establishments in India, and, perhaps soon, in Cochin China.

He then summarizes the two protectorate requests and insists on the need to "establish a halting place on the military line from the West to the East, along which Britain has strung, with characteristic forethought and cleverness, so many coaling stations, lighthouses, batteries and fortified positions."

And he states that he has commissioned an officer

> to carry out a complete exploration in the Red Sea, in order to establish the positions, which for three reasons, political, maritime and commercial, it would be of real interest to us to occupy. . . .
>
> I have therefore prayed the Emperor to let me know whether, in view of these considerations, he authorizes the occupation, by pacific means, of a point on the Red Sea which could give shelter to our ships; could store coal and water for our packets; could be a center for the recruitment of free labor; could serve as a pivot for our commercial operations and finally as a support for our coreligionaries and our adherents.[23]

The minister for foreign affairs had no reason to fear a British or Turkish protest, but could see no "serious advantage" in the operation. The prince then sent an officer friend of his, Commander Russel, who in December 1859 acquired, from the king of Tigré, the coast of Adulis Bay and Dissée Island, as well as a protectorate along the whole Ethiopian coast from Alula to Zeila and the right to recruit labor. As we shall see the government did not ratify.

It would be easy to multiply quotations, showing Anglophobia, in matters concerning the slave trade, in conflicts between traders around the Gulf of Guinea, in reprisals against Negro chieftains who had been guilty of pillage. Whether they were inspired by the compensation complex aroused by the loss of Mauritius insofar as Madagascar was concerned, or by the ill-humor of British traders who were hostile to the establishment of French sovereignty in the Gulf of Guinea, or by the attraction of a world policy equivalent to that of Britain, these statements allow us to assert that Anglophobia existed in France's African policy between 1830 and 1870. But it is necessary, before ex-

23. ANSOM, Océan Indien, I7.

amining the next period, to set rigorous limits to the extent of this sentiment.

The Anglophobia of maritime and colonial circles was circumscribed by the Anglophilia of the Quai d'Orsay and the aristocracy. It is striking that throughout the nineteenth and twentieth centuries, both when relations between the two countries were tense, owing to deep divergences of interest, and during the periods of entente and military alliance, the Quai d'Orsay constantly subordinated France's activity in black Africa to solicitude in avoiding a conflict with Britain.

As long as the navy alone was imperialistic, and since public opinion as a whole cared little for foreign policy, this was comparatively easy. The principles of African policy were laid down by Guizot and scrupulously followed thereafter. Guizot allowed the navy a free hand as long as there was no risk of involving France in a costly war or of embroiling France with Britain. He allowed de Hell and the ministers who supported him, Duperré and Roussin, to occupy Nossi Bé and Nossi Cumba and, after having assured himself that Britain did not support the claims of the imam of Muscat, Mayotte. But when de Hell and Duperré sought to launch a long and costly campaign for the conquest of Madagascar, he reacted and made his famous speech of March 31, 1843, on the policy of outlying stations. It is famous today, for at the time public opinion was not interested. A politician as important as Rémusat, who in his memoirs wrote of parliamentary history, cabinet by cabinet, breathes no word of it.[24] Guizot carried the day and found in Mackau a navy minister who was more interested in building ships than in acquiring colonies.

When Bouët had ordered the occupation of posts on the West African coast, and the Glass affair in Gaboon brought France into opposition to Britain, he only gave his navy minister moderate support. He seems clearly to have understood that the spheres of interest were not the same. When Aberdeen asked for information on the occupation of Assinie, which was close to the British trading post of Appolonia, Guizot wrote to the French ambassador in London that France's sovereignty was "exterior," and excluded all interference in the "interior" affairs of the country. He added, "the King's Government, with regard to the new trading posts which it has just founded, has so little idea of being exclusive, that they are freely open to European trade." [25]

The treaties signed between 1839 and 1843 were revised at the be-

24. Charles de Rémusat, *Mémoires de ma vie* (4 vols. Paris, 1962), *4*, 38 ff.
25. MAE MD Afrique 51, pp. 59–61 (November 27, 1843).

ginning of 1844 on the occasion of a voyage of inspection undertaken by Bouët, who had become governor of Senegal. Instructions drawn up by Mackau, and revised by Guizot, insisted on a "regime of unlimited freedom" of trade, and on "external sovereignty,"[26] instructions intended to reassure the British and prevent the navy from planning conquests of the Madagascar type. If the successive treaties are compared it will be found that there was no longer any question of French monopoly at Assinie, and that the protection of missionaries was included for Grand Bassam.

As for Gaboon, after Commander Eastcourt's inquiries, Guizot allowed Bouët to send the gunboat *L'Alsacienne* from Gorée, which threatened to blockade Glass' village and thus obtained submission from the chief. Then, since there had been no British reaction, he sent a note to Lord Cowley, the British ambassador in Paris, on October 25, 1845, in which he undertook that freedom of trade would be "full and complete" at Gaboon, which had become an adjunct of Gorée. He also protested against the procedure of the inquiry: "His Majesty's Government never having refused honest explanations when they were asked for, has some right to expect that, should a similar situation arise in the future, Her Britannic Majesty would address itself directly to this government."[27] Almost at the same moment (October 15) the Commander of the Western Station of Africa and Gorée promulgated a "Declaration made to the Chiefs of Gaboon, with the aim of informing them that the slave trade for export must cease completely in the said river, as in all the lands, islands, peninsulas or capes which this river touches, full and complete sovereignty of these parts being conceded to His Majesty, the King of the French."[28]

One final incident occurred in 1846. Commander Bosanquet of the British brig *Alert* conducted himself at Gaboon as though French sovereignty did not exist. In reply to Guizot's protests, Aberdeen on July 15 promised to issue the necessary instructions. Nevertheless Mackau was not satisfied.

> I cannot read, without regret, the various passages in which allusion is made to rights of French sovereignty. . . . that Lord Aberdeen should have expressed himself with a reserve such, that up to a certain point it is permissible to deduce that French sovereignty is not recognized to its full extent by the British Gov-

26. Ibid., p. 65 (December 18, 1843).
27. Ibid., p. 119.
28. Dakar, Archives Série G-G 11.

ernment. . . . you will no doubt judge, like me, that it would be most regrettable if Lord Aberdeen's caution should imply any mental reservation concerning our rights. It is therefore most desirable that further explanations between the French and British governments should leave no doubts about our sovereignty over Gaboon.

A note, penciled in the margin, gives Guizot's reply: "I believe there would be greater inconvenience than advantage in the present state of affairs if we insisted on further explanation." [29]

Guizot's African policy was not Anglophobe. Rather it seems to follow closely the imperatives of British policy. By restricting conquest (exterior sovereignty), by ensuring freedom of trade, and by supporting the repression of the slave trade, he respected the principles Britain held dear. The British, who did not wish for sovereignty, might be irritated by French claims, but not sufficiently to oppose them. After all they were able to enjoy practical advantages which derived from the situation. They traded, and the cost of sovereignty was not theirs. This policy survived Guizot. The 1844 treaties served as models to Captain Souriau, Captain Serval, and Lieutenant Aymès when they added Cape Lopez and Fernan Vaz to French Gaboon in 1862 and 1868.[30]

Neither Walewski nor Thouvenel nor the emperor himself gave support to Prince Napoleon's schemes in the Red Sea. The Russel treaties were finally rejected in a note written by Thouvenel on April 9, 1860:

> The true, if not the only importance of the question, is in my opinion the inevitable effect in Britain of our taking possession on so wide a scale. We must not hide from ourselves, that in our present delicate circumstances, we could not accept these proposals and put them into execution without expecting serious difficulties on the part of the British.[31]

When the assassination of Consular Agent Lambert brought into question the honor of the French flag, however, the Quai d'Orsay acquiesced to the demands of the navy. Captain Fleuriot de Langle was sent on a mission that resulted in the acquisition of the Obock territory. But there was no question of ratifying the Russel treaties, which were still extant. The aim was only to reestablish the honor of

29. MAE MD Afrique 58, Congo Gabon I., pp. 127–28.
30. Ibid., pp. 168, 179, 208, 225.
31. MAE MD, 63, Mer Rouge 1, p. 123.

the flag. The Treaty of March 11, 1862, failed to define exactly the limits of the territory acquired, and that part of the coast which had become French remained unoccupied until 1884.

From one end of this period to the other, it appears that French activity, in Africa, was subordinated to the British Alliance which under the Second Empire enabled action in common to be taken in the Crimea in 1854 and in China in 1860. In spite of the navy's Anglophobia, France's African policy, as defined by Guizot, appears if anything Anglophile rather than Anglophobe when looked at objectively.

The picture becomes more complicated after 1870. The whole of public opinion became Germanophobe, and nationalism, until then the preserve of the navy, became common to all Frenchmen. Less humiliated by the military defeat of the Empire than by the contempt shown for the right of peoples to self-determination, which the Alsatians and the Lorrainers had invoked in vain, the French refused to consider themselves defeated. Compensation was sought, not for the loss of Mauritius, but for that of Alsace and Lorraine. The psychological complex, however, is the same and expresses itself in the same way. France must prove to the world that she remains a great power. The whole nation cherished prestige and glory. The army, like the navy, wished to show its prowess. In Africa they met the British and considered them as rivals, who must be fought. But this did not affect the fact that the only true enemy, the one which became in literature France's hereditary foe, was Germany. If impatience for revenge was palliated by conquests in Africa, the one and only objective remained Alsace-Lorraine, which Gambetta counseled should be "thought of always and spoken of, never."

In a climate of nationalist fever, public opinion took a greater interest in the African exploits of its soldiers and sailors. But this was a civilian public opinion which had new ideas on colonization. It was influenced by economists, such as Paul Leroy-Beaulieu; it preferred colonization by administrators and capital investment to that of emigration; it was scornful of armed conquests. But traditional French colonization of Africa was also that of administrators and capital, and Leroy-Beaulieu's liberalism was largely inspired by British example. The new school's Anglophobia was rather a patriotic desire to see France demonstrate its prowess than a fear and hate of Britain. Fear and hate were reserved for Germany.

On the other hand, these civilians, whose ideas were also adopted by young army engineer officers or naval medical officers, had been particularly impressed by the technical achievements of 1869. The Suez Canal had been opened in 1869 and the first transcontinental railway had linked New York to San Francisco in 1872. Nothing henceforward seemed impossible to these budding technocrats, who dreamed of becoming, like Ferdinand de Lesseps, great Frenchmen and at the same time the benefactors of humanity. We cannot here recall all the canal projects that preoccupied public opinion between 1870 and 1880. Some, like that of Denis de Rivoyre, who in 1880 planned to "change the course of the Nile and thus sterilize Egypt, should Britain seek to take possession of the country," [32] undoubtedly had some Anglophobe inspiration. But most of the time these technocrats, without capital, hoped, like de Lesseps, to found universal companies to finance their projects.

Neither can we retrace all the railway projects, though certain stages must be noted, for they paralleled the progress of expansion, and it seems likely that at times such projects inspired the aims of the military and the diplomats. It began with plans for a trans-Saharan railway proposed by Duponchel, an engineer, Soleillet, an explorer, and the Commission for the Trans-Saharan Railway, set up in 1879 by Freycinet, minister for public works. The line was to link Algeria with Senegal, by way of Timbuktu and the Sudan. This presupposed a military advance, which the governor of Senegal undertook toward the "toucouleur" empire of Segu. The project was abandoned after the massacre of the Flatters mission, which was prospecting the line in 1881. At almost the same time another civilian proposed a rail link between the coast of Guinea and the Niger River, across the Fouta Djallon range. After the Franco-British agreement of 1890, which fixed the limits of the French advance from the north on the Say-Barroua line, the Chad became the objective of Radiot, a Parisian lawyer. He proposed an extension to the Congo and a branch line to the Rio Nunez. This project would have at the same time provided the various territories of French Africa with a rapid means of communication and, by allowing passengers to reach the "Atlantic Narrows" rapidly, would have provided the world with a new means of communicating with South America.[33] The former members of the Trans-Saharan Commission, and particularly Georges Rolland, the engineer, abandoned Duponchel's Nigerian line (Algiers to Timbuktu) and substituted a

32. MAE MD Afrique, Mer Rouge 2, Min. de la Guerre à Min. A.E. November 24, 1881.

33. *La Géographie,* December 4 and 11, 1890, ANSOM, Guinée XII.

"Central African" line toward the Chad. A branch line would have linked Agades to Say and the Nigerian Sudan. A continuation was provided to Ubangui and the Congo. The aim was to weld the various parts of French Africa together, and the project in no way concerned Britain.[34] Another engineer, Amédée Sébillot, developed these ideas and wished to replace the trans-Saharan by a trans-African line, to be financed by a universal company. The scope of this project makes one dream of the plans of Léonce Lagarde who projected an Ethiopian mission to meet Marchand. The Sébillot project, published in 1893, aimed first to link Algiers to Ighargar in the Sahara. A branch line was to go on to Obock. The main line would then continue toward the Chad, where a second branch would proceed to Ouiddah, and beyond toward the Congo and Johannesburg, already linked to the Cape by rail.[35]

Until 1914 numerous other projects were elaborated by Leroy-Beaulieu and by a Major Roumens; both recognized that it would be advantageous to build two lines, one toward the Nigerian Sudan, the other toward the Chad. These schemes were Anglophobe, insofar as their authors came up against real or imagined British hopes; they were of course aware of the Cape to Cairo railway dreams. On the other hand, they were always ready to emphasize the Latin character of links that would bring South America closer to the Mediterranean.

The civilian newcomers had pens but no real means of action. Some managed to obtain small grants from the Foreign Ministry or from scientific societies. On the spot, they were dependent on the military and in general did not get on well with them. Nevertheless, once the treaty which Savorgnan de Brazza, acting on his own initiative, had concluded with Makoko, king of the Bateke, had been ratified, and Brazza had been sent to the Congo as commissioner of the Republic in West Africa in 1883, a new field of action opened up in which the civilians were on top. Not only were the British not interested in the Congo, but those who were exploring the region, recruited by Brazza, were much less concerned with the British than the military in the Sudan. Brazza himself had resigned from the navy and was attached to the Ministry of Education. Thus if we are to determine the part played by Anglophobia in black Africa under the Third Republic, we must distinguish between the two theaters of action and the two kinds of actor. In the Sudan and along the coast of the Gulf of Guinea, the army and the navy had the upper hand. They continued as in the past

34. Georges Rolland, *Le Trans-Saharien: Un an après* (Paris, 1891).
35. Amédée Sébillot, *Le Transafricain* (Paris, 1893).

to be Anglophobe. In the Congo, the representative of the new colonial school had little occasion to adopt an attitude for or against, and we can leave them aside.

The military—who, after Colonel Brière de L'Isle had been appointed to the government of Senegal, revived Faidherbe's project for making Senegal or the French posts on the "Southern Rivers" (Guinea) an outlet for the Sudan trade—were always up against the British. Rivalry between Senegal and Sierra Leone for the control of the Guinea coast, and that which, in the Fouta Djallon, opposed Dr. Bayol and Gouldsbury, the Englishman, are well known. John Hargreaves [36] has told the story without giving importance to the expressions of Anglophobia and Francophobia that abound in the correspondence.[37] Bayol, for instance, wrote to Bareste, the French vice-consul at Freetown, to announce that he had on "the 14th July 1881 signed a protectorate treaty with the Almamys of Fouta Djallon, in spite of the efforts of the British."

> The part played by France in Northern Sudan is increasing; we are now certainly in advance of the British. I am profoundly happy to have been able, in spite of obstacles and calumnies, to hold the flag of the Republic high and steady. I fairly beat Dr. Gouldsbury, the envoy of the British Government. The written promises of Almamy Ibrahima will be of no use to the British Ambassador. . . . A letter from the Almamy to Sierre Leone remained unanswered. You will find enclosed a letter in Arabic which you will kindly see is forwarded to His Excellency the Governor of Freetown. Almamy Ibrahima in this way is teaching the British government a lesson in politeness.
>
> The role of the British in the Fouta is now terminated.[38]

The same note is heard in Dahomey, where Admiral Ribourt and agents at Whydah suspected the British, when the port was blockaded in 1876, of preparing a decisive blow "and of taking by force a country where their influence has little chance of establishing itself in a friendly fashion." [39]

The detailed history of the "Blockade of Whydah [1876–77] and

36. John D. Hargreaves, *Prelude to the Partition of West Africa* (London, 1963), pp. 196–97.

37. MAE MD Afrique 49 and 50.

38. ANSOM, Missions, 54 Bayol, Freetown, August 4, 1881.

39. Archives Marine, BB4 1059, Admiral R. Court to the Minister, Dakar, Feb. 10, 1876, May 12, 1876.

Franco-British rivalry in Dahomey" has been told by Madame Coquery.[40]

When Louis Binger was preparing his great exploration on the Ivory Coast (1887–89) he chose the land route from Senegal instead of sailing from one of the French ports on the coast. He gave his reasons: "It is impossible to reach Assinie or Grand Bassam except by British steamer; it would have been injudicious to arouse British interest in my plans to penetrate into an area which they have long coveted." [41]

Mizon's troubles with the British Niger Company in 1890–93 and, later, the steeplechase between Sir Frederick Lugard and Captain Decœur for Borgou (1894–95), gave rise to occasions that were definitely hostile to Britain, such as the banquet offered to Mizon in Paris, and a number of impassioned newspaper articles. John Flint has summarized these events, basing his work on British sources.[42] Also to be consulted are the French archives and the press of the period, due attention being paid to circulation figures. It is clear, however, that the diplomats were not overimpressed, and that this Anglophobia did not correspond to any profound wave of public opinion. Even the banquet, attended by a number of official personalities, was no more than a ceremonial rite of welcome to a successful explorer.

At Obock, also, plans for a coaling station, alarmist dispatches from French consulate agents at Aden, the outburst of petty local chiefs, now under the more or less effective dominion of Egypt, gave rise to innumerable reports through which runs the web of rivalry with Britain. Neither the navy nor the Quai d'Orsay lost their heads. When in 1884 Léonce Lagarde was sent to negotiate the boundaries of what was to become the French Somali Coast, his instructions did not involve opposition to Britain.[43]

It would be easy to make a manual of French Anglophobia with extracts from the press between 1890 and 1898, to which could be added as an appendix some of the projects considered by the Colonial Missions Commission, instituted in 1883 at the Navy Ministry.[44] One might add also some of the imperative demands that were made at the time, such as that of the "patriot" Frémicourt addressing the Minister of Foreign Affairs. In 1880, among other demands, he insisted that

40. "Cahiers d'Etudes Africaines," 2 (1962), 373–419.

41. *Du Niger au Golfe de Guinée par le pays de Kong et le Mossi 1887–1889* (Paris, 1892), *1*, 3.

42. John E. Flint, *Sir George Goldie and the Making of Nigeria* (London, 1960), pp. 168 ff. and 222 ff.

43. See MAE MD Afrique 65, Mer Rouge 111.

44. ANSOM, Missions 100.

Gambia and the Portuguese trading posts of the Rio Grande should be bought or exchanged. He enclosed a hastily drawn sketch map on which were underlined the points evacuated by France on the Ivory Coast, on occasion to the advantage of the House of Swanzy in London (Assinie), and concluded angrily, "It is a disgrace!" [45]

It was at the beginning of the scramble for Africa that colonialist circles were most active in Paris. And, of course, when they drew up their plans they first of all came up against British rivalry. There are many documents to which one might refer. We shall, however, limit ourselves to one of the most characteristic. Under the signature of two personalities well known for their work on the trans-Saharan railway, General Philibert and the mining engineer Rolland, it contains all the most frequently used arguments. In May 1890, three months before the Franco-British convention, it notes that various European nations claim "zones of influence" in Africa and continues: "As always Britain is getting the lion's share." It then mentions the Cape to Cairo project and the wait-and-see attitude of the French who allowed themselves "to be supplanted by Britain in Egypt."

"There is no vacant place left for France except in West Africa"; the basins of the Niger and Chad should enter wholly into "France's legitimate sphere of influence," along with the Haussa States, Sokoto, Damergou, Bornou, and Bagirmi.

> But over the past ten years, owing to lack of support from public opinion and owing to the absence of a program in colonial matters, we have allowed what should have been the *intangible* part of the future to be seriously whittled away. Britain, the great and insatiable Britain, not content with its Asiatic Indies, with its Dominion of Canada, with its Australian Empire, with its vast possessions in South and East Africa, wishes to snatch from us Central Sudan and dreams of establishing its economic supremacy not only northward from the Great Lakes to Egypt and southward to the Cape, but westward also to Timbuctoo.

In order to put a brake on these ambitions it is necessary to go beyond Timbucktu, from the Sudan; to go to Sokoto, to Bornou, to Bagirmi, to the Oudaz and the Chad, and to link the latter to the Congo and the Dahomey coast to the Sudan. It is necessary "*to make a single whole of Algeria, Senegal and the Congo by way of Tuareg*

45. MAE MD Afrique 50, pp. 255–58.

Sahara and Central and western Sudan." The line of the railway to be built was then sketched in.[46]

All this goes to show that under the Third Republic a part of public opinion was won over to Anglophobia, and the development of nationalism, in a general way, had made public opinion xenophobic. In Africa, wherever the French are neighbors of the British (which more or less excludes the Congo and Equatorial Africa) they become Anglophobe. Meanwhile in Europe, specialized periodicals, such as the *Bulletin of the Society for Colonial and Maritime Studies* and those of the French African Committee and the Colonial Union, the *Colonial Fortnightly* and the *Colonial Dispatch,* multiplied, and the articles they published were picked up by the influential dailies *Journal des Debats, Figaro, Le Temps,* etc. One might well suppose, on such evidence, that popular Anglophobia was the loom on which explorers and diplomats wove the new colonial empire. But before being able to make the assertion, once again we must try to define this Anglophobia.

We are far from the fine balance of jousts between navy and colonies, on the one hand, and the Quai d'Orsay, on the other, which took place in the midst of public indifference and which were resolved by the arbitration of Guizot's African policy.

At the very beginning of the Third Republic that balance still remained. The conflict between Senegal and Sierra Leone corresponded curiously with those of the preceding period. The treaties concluded by Captain Boilève, Brière de l'Isle's representative, with the chiefs of the Southern Rivers are similar to the revised treaties of 1844: French sovereignty, but equality in trade for all, an annual rent paid by France, and rules concerning wrecks and stranded vessels. The Waddington-Salisbury combination is homologous to that of Guizot-Aberdeen, with one slight improvement—Waddington had been at Oxford with Salisbury!

When Jauréguiberry, the minister of marine, submitted the treaties to Waddington's approval on May 15, 1878, the latter emphasized

> Our conduct in these parts cannot be too circumspect if we are to avoid embarrasing complications with the authorities in British possessions adjoining our establishments. It is obvious that prudence on our part should not go so far as the abandonment of rights which

46. All the above, Général Philibert and Georges Rolland, *La France en Afrique et le Trans-Saharien* (Paris, 1890), pp. 20, 21, 22.

have been recognized and established by long usage. But while resisting unjustifiable pretensions, it is necessary that the officers sent by Monsieur Brière de L'Isle to Benty should know how to link the firmness needed to preserve our interests with much moderation. They must be most exactly informed of the conditions created by the treaties, so as to avoid any well-founded claim by the Sierra Leone government.

Thus, I cannot but approve the wisdom of your reservations concerning the military action proposed by the Governor of our colony, the object of which appears to be to induce native chiefs who are still hesitant to accept our sovereignty.

I do not reject a concept, the utility of which, no more than you, I am far from underrating and the application of which does not appear to raise objections in principle as far as you are concerned. On the other hand I feel it my duty to insist that all precautions should be taken in order to avoid all false interpretations, which the appearance of our forces in Mellacoree might give rise to, and the anxiety which they might provoke.[47]

The precautions were not taken. When Brière de L'Isle ordered the occupation of Matacong Island, at the mouth of the Melakori, London protested. Waddington arranged with Salisbury for the nomination of a mixed commission which was to fix the respective boundaries of the zones of influence of Senegal and Sierra Leone. Brière de L'Isle was forced to send Captain Gallieni to evacuate the island and impose the status quo ante while the commission was at work.

The commission concluded in 1881, and its report resulted in the agreement of 1882. Thus once again the Quai d'Orsay held the navy in leash. The policy of Franco-British "entente," which was active at the Congress of Berlin in 1878 and in Egypt with the setting-up of financial condominium in 1879, was more important than the rivalry between Dr. Rowe and Colonel Brière.

The Quai d'Orsay remained faithful to its function as a brake, which had become traditional, and to the subordination of expansion in Africa to good understanding with Britain. When the great treaty that divided up West Africa was being negotiated, the Quai d'Orsay never even dreamed of calling in experts from the Undersecretariat for the Colonies. The treaty signed on August 4, 1890, halted the movement from Senegal southward on the line Say-Barroua. These negotiations, which followed closely on an Anglo-German agreement on the first of

47. MAE MD Afrique 49, Sénégal et Dépendances, May 15, 1878.

July, were part of international policy. The Quai d'Orsay's principle, which was to draw an ideal line on the map and then leave to commissions the business of fixing exact boundaries on the spot, was accepted. What it amounted to was that colonial differences should always be settled on an amicable basis. It would have been folly to quarrel with Britain when faced by Germany, who in 1875, in 1882, and in 1887 had been threatening and whose future conduct was far from discernible on the morrow of Bismark's fall. Besides which, the German government was Anglophobe. Bismark had always been and William II was to be. If French policy had been the same, then it would have accepted the few advances made by Germany. Thus, whereas Jules Ferry had agreed to invite the powers to the Berlin West Africa Conference "conjointly" with Bismark, he never, in the long term, gave up the intention of winning back Alsace-Lorraine.

A minister of foreign affairs' horizon allowed for no doubt at all about African policy, since Russia had no part to play there. When a question of choice arose, the answer could never be anything but the "Entente Cordiale." This was made clear enough in 1898.

Historians, basing themselves on press polemics, may have been led to believe that the Fashoda incident brought France and Britain to the edge of war. But in fact it produced the "Entente Cordiale of 1904. This agreement was negotiated by the former Anglophobe colonial minister, Delcassé, who had become an Anglophile foreign minister since he could not be anything but a Germanophobe. Recent research into the archives has shown clearly that at no moment of the crisis did either the British Foreign Office or the Quai d'Orsay ever seriously envisage a diplomatic rupture. G. N. Sanderson has demonstrated this.[48] Marc Michel, with complementary French documents, arrived at an identical conclusion.[49] As before, the Quai d'Orsay brake came into play over Fashoda, but it remains to be explained why it did not do so earlier and so prevent the crisis.

And this leads us to a closer consideration of the notion of Anglophobia. The civilians tended to substitute a more reasoned patriotism for the pure and simple nationalist reflexes of the soldiers and the sailors. They were neither Anglophobe nor Anglophile; they were French and easily became xenophobe. Their theses often sought

48. G. N. Sanderson, *England, Europe and the Upper Nile, 1882–1899* (Edinburgh, 1965).

49. Marc Michel, "La Mission Marchand," a manuscript thesis using files which were lost and found again in the Archives National, Section Outre-Mer, and Liotard's private papers.

inspiration in British and Dutch sources. The press campaign in favor of the Charter Companies orchestrated by Undersecretary of State Etienne, and the violent criticism of traditional colonial administration that obstructed private initiative launched by such men as Olivier Pastré de Sanderval, Binger, and how many "rapporteurs" of the Colonial office budget in the Chamber of Deputies, broke down the Anglophobe front, diversified attitudes, and multiplied internal rivalries. Civilians at last stormed the fortress so long occupied by the army and navy; the Directorate for Colonies was transformed into an undersecretaryship, sometimes attached to the Ministry of Commerce, and became a Ministry of Colonies for Delcassé in 1893. From then on strict rules and the habits of discipline that had maintained the Anglophobe front against the Quai d'Orsay began to weaken. When Borgnis-Desbordes captured Mourgoula in 1882, in spite of instructions issued by Jauréguiberry, the minister of marine; when Lieutenant Colonel Archinard conquered Koundian in 1889, in spite of the orders of Etienne, undersecretary of state for the Colonies, there arose an atmosphere of distrust between the military command and the ministerial departments that corroded the latent Anglophobia in both. The policy of squaring off and nibbling at the Sudan, which is proved by sketches preserved in the archives at Dakar,[50] was never discussed at a cabinet meeting in Paris.

The discontent aroused at the Pavillon de Flore, home of the undersecretaryship for colonies, by the Treaty of August 4, 1890, negotiated between the British Foreign Office and the Quai d'Orsay, incited the undersecretaryship to encourage, unofficially, private exploration by associations such as the Committee of French Africa, the aim being to engage the country before consulting the Quai.[51]

Under such circumstances it becomes difficult to speak of a "French African policy" such as had existed at the time of Guizot. When an operation was undertaken, the aims might not have been the same in the minds of all those concerned. And so Fashoda. Its distant origins are to be found in the desire to open up the question of Egypt once again. Delcassé, colonial minister in 1893, planned the Monteil mission to that end. Marchand was a member, but the mission was stillborn. When Marchand returned to France and put forward his plan to Hanoteaux, the foreign minister, the latter was at first definitely hostile.

50. Archives Dakar, Série 13G 10. Unpublished thesis by Yves de Saint Martin on diplomatic relations between France and the "toucouleur" state.

51. Marcel Blanchard, "Français et Anglais au Niger, 1890–1898," *Le Monde Français* (1948), pp. 409–23.

Nevertheless at the Colonial Ministry, Archinard, "director of colonial defense" and leader of the expansionist military, gave his former subordinate full support.

He had in mind, just as Léonce Lagarde, the founder of Djibouti (1886) and secretary general of the Colonial Ministry after André Lebon had come to power in June 1898, the dream of French east-west rail links across Africa as a counter to Cecil Rhodes' Cape to Cairo. The Germans at the same time were talking of a *Mittelafrika* linking the Cameroons to German East Africa. If one adds up the more or less explicit mental reservations of some, the hesitation of others, the false appreciations of men who were unable to measure the responsibilities undertaken in an operation which was, in relation to the whole of foreign policy, of secondary importance, it is easy to understand how the crisis broke out without its having been intended.

We shall not go into the details of an affair which is well known today. Those who have studied it recently agree that neither Paris nor London wished to alter their general policy because of the incident. Sanderson has shown clearly that France did not wish to come closer to Germany against Britain, and that public opinion in general was very far from being bellicose.[52]

Thus it seems that Anglophobia, coming from restricted groups in the navy and army, had reached a wider range of public opinion where it dissolved like a drop of strong black coffee in a cup of milk. In spite of appearances, under the Third Republic, Anglophobia had even less influence on France's African policies than formerly.

The conclusion of this study, therefore, is more negative than might have been foreseen at its beginning. All nationalism is xenophobic, and French xenophobia could not but be aimed at its most powerful neighbors. Until 1870 the only states close to France were Spain and Britain. But up to about 1840 only the navy was nationalistic. Navy men practiced an effective Anglophobe policy in Africa as long as they were their own masters.

For the Ministry of Foreign Affairs, however, Africa was of only minor interest. Its nationalism required that France hold her place in the Concert of Europe among the Great Powers, which were Britain, Austria-Hungary, Russia, and slightly in the background, Prussia. France could not call its own tune. She had to ensure, with allies, a certain equilibrium that guaranteed peace. The best ally, whose liberal regime was the closest to her own, was Britain. From then on, Franco-British understanding, in the face of the autocratic powers, appeared as

52. Sanderson, *Upper Nile,* pp. 328 ff. and 359 ff.

the best international arrangement. From time to time it was destroyed, but both sides sought at once to reestablish it. This happened after the Egyptian crisis of 1840 as it did after Fashoda. The feelings of the navy could do nothing against this principle, and the Quai d'Orsay never hesitated to sacrifice colonization in Africa with a light heart in favor of the Entente Cordiale. Guizot in 1843 fixed the limits within which the Navy might act, and these limits were the very principles the British observed: free trade, the repression of the slave trade, the protection of missionaries. The limits did not forbid the acquisition of political sovereignty in regard to which the British for long remained indifferent.

After 1870, the accession of Germany to the status of a great power made British friendship even more precious in the eyes of the French. But Britain was also extending her sovereignty over black Africa, and numerous occasions for rivalry occurred and were passionately followed by a public opinion that had become nationalistic. But this French nationalism was in the first place Germanophobe. The Quai d'Orsay would always sacrifice its grievances against its British rival to the nation's general feeling of the constant German threat. Thus we are forced to conclude that after 1870, as before, the French African empire was constituted with the explicit or implicit agreement of Britain.

⚘§ 2. *France, England, and the Tunisian Affair*

⚘§ JEAN GANIAGE

Ten years after the fall of the Empire, the establishment of the French protectorate over Tunisia marked the end of France's policy of *recueillement* and her return to an active foreign policy. At the Congress of Berlin, the French delegates were offered the Regency of Tunis as a part of the spoils in the partition of the Ottoman Empire. England's initial goodwill and Bismarck's constant encouragement in many ways explain the success of a policy that had been put off to no good end during three years of indecision. The Tunisian affair, therefore, can be seen as a direct result of the Berlin Congress as well as the starting point for a new colonial policy which eventually gave France a vast African empire.

At first, England took France's side in the matter, but a change in government was accompanied by a noticeable reversal in attitude toward France. Only after considerable vacillation did the liberal government resign itself to the occupation of the Regency which a conservative cabinet had offered France three years earlier.

With the French conquest of Algeria and the transformation of Tripolitania into an Ottoman province, Tunis remained the last of the three regencies to keep its independence during the nineteenth century. Nevertheless, this independence was a juridically contestable fact, for the bey of Tunis had not formally disassociated himself from the sultan's protection, and the Porte continued to consider the bey's kingdom as one of the Empire's provinces. Well aware of their weakness, the Tunisian princes tried to steer a course between the demands of their powerful neighbors at the cost of repeated concessions, in order to prolong the life of their tiny state of one million people. Thus, the Regency had slipped into a situation halfway between autonomy and complete independence, which allowed the European powers, according to their interests, to treat the beys either as independent princes or as vassals of the Ottoman Porte.

After the sixteenth century, the bonds that linked Tunisia to the Ottoman Empire had been progressively loosened. Sinan Pasha, the commander of the Turkish expeditionary corps that had definitively chased the Spanish from Tunis and Goletta in 1574, had organized the country into a pashalik, similar to those in Algiers and Tripoli. In other words, Tunisia became a Turkish province governed by a pasha who was supported by janissaries recruited in the East. But the pasha was soon deprived of his power by the commander of the militia, the dey, who was in turn supplanted by a civil functionary, the bey.

The sultan recognized these changes by according the title of pasha to the bey and giving him the right to transmit his authority to his descendants. The first beylical dynasty, the Muradites, did not succeed in establishing themselves in the country, however. In 1705, the commander of the militia, Hussein ben Ali, a soldier of Greek origin, profited from widespread civil strife to seize power. He was recognized by the Porte and founded a dynasty that lasted two and a half centuries. In spite of quarrels between princes, and even assassinations, the rule of succession by age rank was finally established by the middle of the eighteenth century.[1] In this way, Bey Muhammad succeeded his cousin Ahmad in 1855, before leaving the throne to his younger brother, Muhammad es-Sadek (1859–82). (See the accompanying genealogy.)

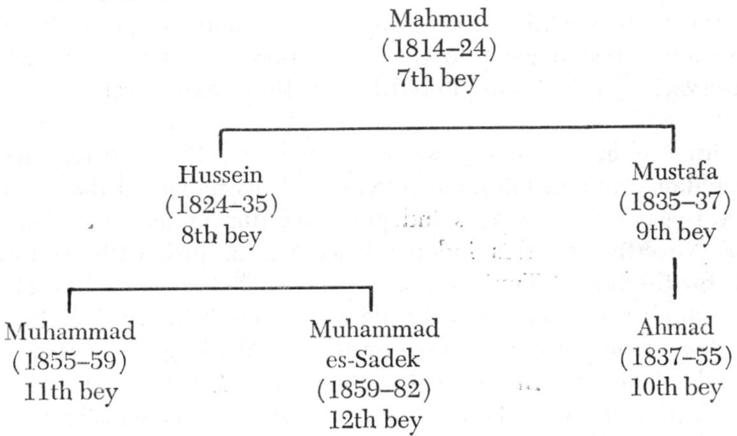

The Princes of the Husseinite Dynasty (1814–82)

1. The system, known as "tanistry," or Muslim seniority, had previously been adopted by the Vandal kings to avoid the danger of an infant's coming to power.

At the time of Muhammad es-Sadek's accession in 1859, the Husseinite dynasty had been strengthened by a century and a half of hereditary transmission of power and traditions of independence which gave the beys the authority of sovereign princes. The Tunisian princes were fully autonomous: they legislated as they wished and governed with the councillors they themselves had chosen. They had even more exalted prerogatives which gave them the appearance of being sovereign: they had their own army and navy, they coined money, maintained diplomatic relations, declared war, signed treaties. Although the beys had neither legations nor embassies abroad, they could conduct political affairs in Tunis with the consuls of the principal European powers. These prerogatives of sovereignty were emphasized by the fact that even the Porte recognized the existence of a Tunisian flag.

Nevertheless, these hereditary princes continued to carry the titles of pasha and bey, which gave them the same rank as the governors of the large provinces of the Ottoman Empire. In Tunis, prayers continued to be recited in the name of the sultan and money coined with his mark. Upon his accession, each bey sent an ambassador to Constantinople to so inform the sultan and to receive from him a firman of investiture, which was a mark of his dependance. Tunisian contingents periodically participated in the wars Turkey was led to wage. Tunisian warships were sunk in the ranks of the Turkish squadron at Navarino. Ahmad Bey sent a corps of troops to participate in the Crimean War in 1854. It was not clear whether the beys were fulfulling the duties of a good vassal, or voluntarily acting the part of friendly princes defending Islam. Anyway, since the Tunisian princes had not formally declared their independence, no foreign power disputed the nominal suzerainty that the sultan exercised over the Regency, and it was as vassal princes of the Porte that the beys were treated by European courts.

Paradoxically, the conquest of Algeria brought about a rapprochement between France and Tunisia and accentuated the latter's detachment from Turkey. The French expedition had been well received in the Regency, where everyone had been delighted by the fall of hated rivals. Nevertheless, extension of the conquest into the Constantine region raised some delicate border questions; but the French danger was nothing compared to the threat of an Ottoman reconquest. In 1835, the Porte had taken advantage of a civil war between two Tripoli princes of the Caramanli family in order to intervene in that Regency and to bring it again under its direct authority.

Tunis was afraid it might share the fate of Tripoli, and the bey realized he could scarcely fare better than his neighbor in resisting the intervention of the Ottoman squadron. His awareness of his weakness inclined him to rely on those of his neighbors who seemed to hold lesser danger for the immediate future. Ahmad Bey called on France for protection to discourage the Turks from any offensive probings. Every time an Ottoman squadron sailed out of the Sea of Marmara, the Toulon squadron's show of force and the remonstrances of the French ambassador in Constantinople would cause the sultan's ships to turn tail. Finally, Tunisia ended up by becoming a kingdom in semivassalage to France, a buffer state on the eastern borders of Algeria.

The French Imperial government, well satisfied with this situation, never dreamed of annexing the Regency. However, it was led to intervene more directly in Tunisia's affairs in 1867 when the bey found himself bankrupt, thanks to the wasteful policies and peculation of his entourage. Weak in character and dissolute in his habits, Muhammad es-Sadek had completely abandoned the management of his affairs to his minister, Mustafa Khaznadar, a mameluke of Greek origin who had been in power for thirty years and who thought mainly of enriching himself.

England's and Italy's protests prevented France from establishing exclusive control over the country under the guise of financial reorganization. After considerable discussions, the three powers agreed to subject the bey to tripartite control. In July 1869, an international commission of nine members was established. Its president was General Khérédine, who was a son-in-law of Khaznadar, but at odds with him. The person in charge of day to day operations was Victor Villet, an official of the French treasury, who held the title of vice-president. Thanks to the cooperation between these two men, the commission was able to draw up a balance sheet of assets and liabilities, reduce and consolidate debts, and impose strict control over the bey's finances.

This system made official a tripartite protectorate over the Regency. However, the presence of a French civil servant at the heart of the commission emphasized France's privileged role. The personality of "Bey Villet" and his friendly relations with Khérédine did even more. Thanks to his exceptional personal power, France was able to maintain her influence at the Tunisian court after 1870, in spite of her defeats on the Continent.

The war of 1870 was a heavy blow to French influence in all of North Africa. Italy, a rising power with many nationals in the Regency, tried to profit from the war by substituting its influence for that of its neighbor. But its agents' blunders mainly helped the English, whose active and effective consul, Richard Wood, had been in Tunis for fifteen years and had become one of the closest councillors of Prime Minister Khaznadar.[2]

Until then England had had few immediate interests in the Regency. Its only subjects were a handful of Jews and seven to eight thousand Maltese, all equally ignorant of the Queen's English. They were a miserable colony which, according to the consulate, reflected little credit on Great Britain. However, Tunisia was a good market for British products because the Capitulation agreements limited taxation to 3 percent on imported articles. Through its regular sales of cotton stuffs, England provided more than a third of Tunisian imports, even more than France (24 percent) which had lost ground to its rivals.

What mainly interested the English was freedom of communication in the Mediterranean, a sea that had taken on vital importance since the opening of the Suez Canal. The strategic position of Bizerte had been recognized for a long time. Everyone knew the advantages a great power could gain from its shelter. If France were to occupy Tunisia, it could transform Bizerte into an African Toulon. It could control the passage between the two Mediterranean basins and neutralize Malta, which the Admiralty was making the base of operations for its squadrons. Moreover, English interests compelled them to prevent as far as possible Tunisia's being controlled by any European power, whether France or Italy, since its location would sooner or later lead it to play a large role in the Mediterranean. Under Tunisian or Turkish control, the Regency could not be a threat, since it was clear that neither the bey nor the sultan would for a long time to come have the resources to create a serious military base.

The British consuls had tried to consolidate the fragile bonds that still linked Tunis to the Ottoman Empire. They wanted to prevent France from extending her Algerian possessions to the Regency, and to maintain the integrity of Turkey, one of the tenets of British policy from the beginning of the century. That policy gained more success after 1871, because of the French defeats on the Continent. At the bey's court Wood pleaded the cause of reconciliation with Turkey, the only means, he thought, for safeguarding Tunisian independence. The con-

2. Sir Richard Wood, born in Constantinople in 1806, died in Bagni di Lucca in 1900. He belonged to a Syrian Jewish family converted to Catholicism which had anglicized its oriental name of Rhattab. He had played an important role alongside the Turks in the second Syrian war before being appointed consul in Damascus in 1846.

quest of Algeria was now over, and the Regency ought to have its turn sooner or later. On the contrary, a weakened Turkey could no longer be a threat for the bey.

At the same time, Wood tried to develop the influence of his country by attracting British companies to Tunisia. England was not short of money. Thanks to Mustafa's goodwill, it was easy to obtain concessions. The opportunity had come for employing a wretched colony of Maltese which could afford a staff of foremen for British enterprises. Supported by its general policy in the Near East, the British influence would uphold an autonomous Tunisia despite French and Italian eagerness.

Wood did not receive much support from the Foreign Office, but he was free to do as he liked. He scored for the first time in 1871, when a Tunisian delegation, led by General Khérédine, brought back from Constantinople an imperial firman that regularized the bey's situation. An English company built the first Tunisian railway, the T.G.M., which linked Tunis, Goletta, and La Marsa; another built a gas works. At the same time, an English bank was established in the capital. British merchants took an interest in Tunisian esparto grass. Unfortunately, none of these enterprises succeeded. The gas company failed, and the bank shut its doors after three years. As for the railway company, it went on laboriously operating under a deficit. The fall of Khaznadar, expelled from government through a harem intrigue in October 1873, dealt another blow to the influence Wood had long exercised over the Tunisian court.[3]

For several years, Mustafa ben Ismaïl, a minion whom Khaznadar had not got rid of in due time, had been exercising more and more influence over the mind of the senile prince. To overthrow the prime minister, whose corrupt administration compromised financial recovery, Villet and Khérédine set up the favorite against him. After his fall, Khaznadar was emprisoned and his possessions confiscated. Although he had succeeded in transferring the greater part of his wealth to Europe, he never recovered it because the Jewish managers who were to hide the money took advantage of the situation to appropriate it for themselves. Khaznadar died five years later during 1878.

His successor was none other than General Khérédine, who governed the Regency for four years, from October 1873 to July 1877. His administration helped heal old wounds, and thanks to several good crops,

3. Jean Ganiage, *Les origines du protectorat français en Tunisie, 1861–1881* (Paris, 1959), pp. 415–36.

Tunisia experienced a relatively tranquil period. During this time, Khérédine tried to carry out a centrist policy. He claimed that Tunisian autonomy was guaranteed by the 1871 firman. "Le vasselage de la Tunisie," he said, "est une garantie d'indépendance. Tant que l'empire turc sera debout, les états tributaries ou vassaux n'auront rien à craindre, parce que leur existence touche à la solution de la question d'Orient."[4] At home, he carried out a policy of equilibrium. "The English already have privileges and concessions. Let us also give some to the French and Italians." It was in this light that he granted to the French the concession for the Medjerda railroad between Tunis and the Algerian frontier, a line the English had not been allowed to construct. In 1877, the Medjerda line was conceded to the Compagnie française du Bône-Guelma, which was already exploiting a network in the Constantine region. This was a personal success for the French consul, Roustan, who had been in Tunis since the end of 1874.

Khérédine was not liked by the bey, and his policy aroused considerable criticism. He was denounced simultaneously as a Francophile and as a Turcophile—which seemed rather contradictory. It is true he had great sympathy for France and that he had very close ties with Inspector Villet. But even if he wished for the development of French influence, he understood it should be balanced off by drawing Tunis closer to the Ottoman Empire. In turn, Khérédine was overthrown by intrigues of the favorite, and he was obliged to present his resignation in July 1877 before withdrawing to Constantinople. Mustafa ben Ismaïl, the new prime minister, took up again the beylical court's traditional policy of lavish spending and corruption.

Through a curious conjunction of circumstances, the fate of Tunisia was decided in Berlin, in the corridors of a congress that had met to end the Balkan crisis simmering since 1875. France, in effect, was encouraged to abandon the policy of "recueillement," which she had been following since her defeats in 1870, and to launch a policy of colonial expansion whose first act was the establishment of a protectorate over the Regency.

England offered Tunis to France as compensation for the occupation of Cyprus, and Bismarck agreed because he hoped to make the French forget about their loss of Alsace-Lorraine. The conversations in Berlin were the result of negotiations that had been going on for three years between the great powers. France benefited from the clumsiness of

4. "Documents sur Khérédine," *Revue tunisienne,* 1936, p. 229.

Italy, which had annoyed England by refusing to take sides against Russia and had irritated the central powers by its untimely claims against Austria-Hungary.

England's offer of Tunis to France implied a departure from her traditional policy in the Near East. From the time of Pitt, under Canning and particularly under Palmerston, England had stoutly defended the integrity of the Ottoman Empire because of its access routes to India but also, thanks to the Capitulations, because it was an excellent market. In order to defend Turkey. England had not hesitated to come to the side of the sultan against Mahamet Ali in 1840 nor against Russia in the Crimean War. Its agents, its ministers in Tunis as well as in Cairo had continually fought against any attempts at independence on the part of local rulers. But the opening of the Suez Canal suddenly shifted commercial and strategic routes to Egypt. The failure of the policy of reforms carried on at Constantinople since the Crimean War, the disorder of Turkish administration, the bankruptcy discouraged the English from supporting a state that seemed about to collapse by itself. As early as 1875, the British ambassador in Berlin, Lord Odo Russell, confided to Bismarck that "England has completely abandoned her traditional policy" in the Eastern question.[5] "Personne," wrote the French chargé d'affaires in London, "ne songe plus à sauver la Turquie de sa ruine. . . . La question se réduit donc à préserver dans le cataclysme inévitable, la route de l'Inde, ce canal qu'un Français a ouvert à travers l'Egypte malgré l'Angleterre." [6]

The Bulgarian atrocities, publicly condemned by Gladstone, horrified the whole country. The foreign secretary, Lord Derby, stated at the time that "if Russia declared war on Turkey, H.M's Government considered it practically impossible to take part in the defense of the Ottoman Empire." [7] Disraeli realized that a partition of Turkey could no longer be avoided. Salisbury, who was to succeed Derby at the head of the Foreign Office, was particularly hostile to the Turks. He considered their alliance a misfortune for England. Time had come for defending the English interests in a more direct way "by some territorial rearrangement." [8] Bismarck offered a settlement based on the partition of the Ottoman Empire. He periodically encouraged the

5. *Die Grosse Politik, 1871–1914* (Berlin, 1922), 2, 30.

6. To Decazes, London, November 19, 1875, Archives du Ministère des Affaires Etrangères [MAE hereafter] Angleterre, 770.

7. Quoted by Seton-Watson, *Disraeli and Gladstone,* pp. 62–63.

8. Lady Gwendolen Cecil, *Life of Robert, Marquis of Salisbury* (4 vols. London, 1921–32), 2, 130.

English to occupy Egypt. But the conservative cabinet was thinking rather about seizing some eastern Mediterranean island that could be a "place of arms," another Gilbraltar to protect entry to the Suez Canal and the new route to India.[9]

Even were England resigned to Turkey's dismemberment, it could not agree to a breakdown in the balance of power in the Mediterranean and Near East. Beaconsfield was ready to accept considerable extension of Austrian influence in the Balkans, but he particularly feared any Russian expansion which in the Mediterranean and Armenia, as in Central Asia, could make Russia a dangerous rival for British interests. He could not tolerate Russian hegemony over half the Balkans, nor the scarcely concealed occupation of Constantinople which could be foreseen in the provisions of the San Stefano treaty.

To apply pressure on the czar, Beaconsfield would like to have won Austria-Hungary to England's side, but Andrassy stuck to the Three Emperors Entente. Andrassy wanted European Turkey divided into two zones of influence, Russian and Austrian, under the benevolent patronage of Bismarck. It had been known for quite a long time that Austria had reserved for herself the occupation or annexation of Bosnia, and intended to gain recognition for the extension of her influence over the western half of the Balkans. Nevertheless, Andrassy refused to be tied down to specific declarations. Rather than taking a step against Russia in the defense of essentially English interests, he preferred to negotiate secretly with Gortchakoff to bargain for new concessions for Austria.[10]

England remained isolated. She could no longer count on France who was weakened by her defeats and, since 1871, was following a policy of withdrawal. Disraeli did not believe that France would recover. "Nor do I see," he wrote to Lady Bradford in September 1875, "any prospect of the revival of France as a military puissance. She is more likely to be partitioned than to conquer Europe again." [11] Moreover, French policy remained uncertain. Until the end of 1877, the Quai d'Orsay, with Duke Decazes in charge, had been favorably disposed toward Russia. Even at the beginning of 1878, Lord Lyons, the English ambassador in Paris, described France's hesitation between a rap-

9. Dwight E. Lee, *Great Britain and the Cyprus Convention Policy of 1878* (Cambridge, Mass., 1934), pp. 31–32; Salisbury to Derby, Berlin, November 23, 1876, Cecil, *Life of Salisbury, 2,* 96; Münster to Bismarck, London, April 20, 1878, *Politique extérieure de l'Allemagne* [PEA hereafter], 2, No. 405.

10. Decazes to Harcourt, Versailles, November 26, MAE, Angleterre, 770; Vogüé to Waddington, passim, January–April 1878, MAE Autriche, 522.

11. G. E. Buckle, *Life of Disraeli, 6,* 13.

prochement with Germany and an understanding with Russia.[12] England also turned naturally toward Italy, which having achieved unity and freed itself from French tutelage, seemed impatient to play an important role in the Mediterranean. Henceforth promoted to the rank of a great power, Italy was looking toward Tunis and the Balkans, and seemed ready to take over from France in the Near East. She could well be the ally England was looking for.

At the beginning of March 1878, Derby instructed Paget to sound out Depretis, the Italian premier as to whether he would be willing to enter into an understanding with Great Britain for the maintenance of "their commercial and political interests in the Mediterranean and the Straits." [13] Derby dreamed of a Mediterranean league which would prevent Russian incursions in the Balkans, but since the Depretis cabinet had just resigned, Paget had to put off his approach until a new ministry was constituted.

The reopening of the Eastern question offered Italy particularly favorable circumstances for its entry into the concert of major powers. It was easy for Italy to make its Mediterranean ambitions known when the Ottoman Empire was about to collapse. Ever since 1876, Andrassy had been trying to turn the attentions of the Italian government towards Tunis. In order to calm the irredentist turmoil that was taking place on the peninsula, he renewed his proposals in February 1878: "Wir sind gerne bereit einen Wunsch Italiens nach einer Kompensation, sei es einer Insel, eines Hafens, Tunis oder Tripoli in Freundenschaft zu prüfen und sogar gegebenen Falles beiden Kabinetten zu unterstützen." [14] Bismarck, for his part, advised Italy to reach an understanding with Austria about Tunis, Tripoli, or Albania as to eventual compensation for the occupation of Bosnia. The Russians were no less generous. Gortchakoff let the Italians know in March 1878 that they would receive northern Albania as reward for their acceptance of Austria's annexation of Bosnia.

Italy had a choice: Albania, Tunisia, or Tripoli, but she still had to define a foreign policy and take on the responsibilities of a great power. Unfortunately, she was in the midst of a ministerial crisis at

12. Lyons to Derby, Paris, January 25 and February 12, 1878, FO 27/2304/2305.

13. Derby to Paget, March 13, 1878, FO 45/337. According to Giolitti, *Memorie della mia vita* (Milan, 1922), *1,* 131. The price of Italian cooperation was to be Tunisia, but the fact is not mentioned in the English and Italian archives.

14. Andrassy to Haymerle, February 2, 1878, Archives, Vienna.

this decisive moment. The Cairoli government, which had been constituted with some difficulty on March 24, 1878, was mainly preoccupied with Italy's claims over Istria and Trentino. Lack of money and domestic difficulties created other problems. The new foreign minister, Count Corti, was a timid man who did not dare accept the English proposals and instead hid behind a policy of abstention.

On March 28, 1878, when Paget went to Corti with the proposal prepared by Derby for a Mediterranean entente, Corti refused to bind his government "by any engagements which might perhaps lead into war." [15] Italy thereby withdrew from the diplomatic game that was to lead to the partition of the Turkish spoils. In Bismarck's eyes the Roman cabinet, which had just rejected new Austrian offers of cooperation, was falling back into the deadly sin of irredentism. In Berlin as in Vienna what was only weakness and hesitation was immediately seen as duplicity, and from then on Bismark ranked Italy among the nations disturbing European order. Diplomatically isolated, without allies and without a policy, Italy could only cut a rather sorry figure at the Congress of Berlin.

On the other hand, in the spring of 1878, France appeared as a moderating element, a power which, in spite of its cautious attitude, could take up that traditional role in Mediterranean and Near East policy that Italy failed to assume. The strengthening of a moderate and liberal Republic reassured Bismarck, who, warmly welcomed the new French ambassador to Berlin, Count Saint-Vallier, at the end of December 1877. The failure of the "16 mai" affair and the success of the moderate republicans brought back into power a conservative bourgeoisie more interested in law and order and good economic management than in foreign adventure.

For several years Bismarck had been thinking about a rapprochement with France. To make France forget Sedan, he was ready to encourage French expansion in the Mediterranean and in all areas where there was no risk of harming German interests. "It is not for us a disadvantage, nor a tendency to be fought," he wrote to Hohenlohe as early as January 1875, "that French policy is seeking in North Africa a field for her activity." [16] However, he had not yet had a chance to show his goodwill toward France. The subsiding of religious passions, Waddington's entrance into office, and the appointment of Saint-Vallier to Berlin all immediately made Franco-German relations much easier.

15. Paget to Derby, March 28, 1878, FO 45/337.
16. *PEA, 1,* 167.

The Berlin talks and the Tunisian and Egyptian affairs gave the chancellor the opportunity to inaugurate a policy of reconciliation with France which he was to follow for several years.

For its part, the English conservative cabinet was looking kindly on the new directions that Waddington gave to French foreign policy in the spring of 1878. Waddington drew closer to England, siding with her in the Balkans by asking that the San Stefano treaty be submitted to a European congress. He seemed to show no hostility toward the British cabinet's proposal to acquire Mytilene, as long as the status quo was maintained in Egypt and Syria.

After Italy's refusal, it was natural that England look toward France for an understanding on a new balance of power in the Mediterranean. In exchange for their freedom of action in the eastern Mediterranean, the English were ready to compensate France in Syria or Tunisia. The word "Tunis" was mentioned for the first time in April 1876 by Lord Odo Russell, during a conversation with his French colleague at Berlin, Gontaut-Biron.[17] British intentions were clarified in the spring of 1878. The German ambassador, Count Münster, in a talk with Lord Salisbury on the Egyptian question in April, stated French ambitions in the Regency: "What France is striving for in Africa, and what is regarded as necessary for the consolidation of her power in Algeria, is Tunis, the old Carthage and the wonderful harbour of Cape Bon [sic]."[18]

Salisbury heartily welcomed these overtures. He immediately informed Lord Lyons that England no longer intended to oppose French penetration into Tunisia and asked to be kept informed of France's true intentions in this matter. "It is of course an extension of territory and influence of which we should not have the slightest jealously or fear."[19] It seemed as if Tunis would be the price England would pay for French agreement to the acquisition of Cyprus that Britain had already decided upon. Moreover, the English government hoped to get France out of Egyptian affairs and put an end to the financial

17. During a conversation bearing on the disruption of the Ottoman Empire, Russell had broached the subject with Gontaut-Biron: "Pour nous, dit lord Odo en riant, nous sommes prêts pour le cas d'effondrement! Nous avons mis la main sur l'Egypte! . . . Quant à vous, Français, j'imagine que la Tunisie pourrait bien vous aller! . . . Je ne dis pas non, repris-je sur le même ton." Gontaut-Biron to Decazes, Berlin, April 15, 1876, MAE Allemagne, *18*.

18. Münster to Bismarck, London, April 20, 1878, *PEA*, *3*, 253.

19. Salisbury to Lyons, May 11, 1878, in Lord Newton, *Lord Lyons, a Record of British Diplomacy* (2 vols. London, 1913), *2*, 139.

condominium established in 1876. Perhaps, the English believed, France would be more easily resigned to this if she received a Tunisian compensation.

In any case, Tunisia was destined one day or another to fall under French or Italian protection. England had little interest in the Regency and preferred that France rather than Italy be established in Tunis because the latter, in holding both banks of the Sicilian straits, could at will block the Mediterranean and the Suez route which had become essential for the British Empire.

Thus, before the Congress of Berlin had convened, even before England had settled the acquisition of Cyprus with Turkey, British statesmen were seriously thinking of offering Tunis to France as reward for her agreement to English policy in the eastern Mediterranean, and as part of the spoils from the dismemberment of the Ottoman Empire.

The Congress opened in Berlin on June 13, 1878. Waddington had agreed to French participation on condition that only questions stemming directly from the war were to be discussed. Nothing was to be said about the West, Egypt, Syria, or the Holy Land.

The French delegates in Berlin, Waddington, Saint-Vallier, and Desprez, graciously accepted Austria's occupation of Bosnia.[20] They offered their services to reconcile Russian and English viewpoints regarding Bulgaria. But the English diplomats waited more than three weeks before publicizing the Cyprus convention which they had concluded with Turkey on June 4. Waddington learned of it on July 6, one week before the closing of the Congress and only the day before the official text was unveiled by the *Daily Telegraph.*

The news provoked an outburst of bad feeling in France, and violent articles appeared in the Parisian press. But as Salisbury had expected, members of the French diplomatic circle confined themselves to "epigram." Waddington did not hide his surprise and annoyance from Salisbury. He could have formally protested at the congress and emphasized France's opposition by leaving Berlin at once, but rather than risk a quarrel with England, he preferred to accept the fait accompli

20. F. Desprez was director of political affairs at the Quai d'Orsay. The other plenipotentiaries were, for Germany, Bismarck; State Secretary of Foreign Policy Bernhard von Bülow; the Prince of Hohenlohe, ambassador in Paris; for England, Disraeli, Count of Beaconsfield; Salisbury; and the ambassador in Berlin, Lord Odo Russell. The Austrian delegation was supervised by Count Andrassy; the Russian, Italian, and Turkish ones respectively by Prince Gortchakoff, Count Corti, and Caratheodory Pasha.

and to negotiate with Salisbury for a new balance of power in the Mediterranean.

These negotiations produced an Anglo-French agreement that prepared a new balance of power among the great nations. France accepted the occupation of Cyprus. In return, she received the maintenance of the status quo in Syria and the Holy Land and the recognition of the catholic protectorate she traditionally exercised in those regions. The two powers mutually recognized their interests in Egypt and agreed to collaborate in the financial restoration of the country. Finally, and most importantly, Lord Salisbury, soon joined by Bismarck, unequivocally invited Waddington to seek compensation in Tunisia for the occupation of Cyprus.

" 'Prenez Tunis, si vous voulez,' Lord Salisbury told me, 'L'Angleterre ne s'y opposera pas et respectera vos décisions. D'ailleurs,' he added in another conversation, 'vous ne pouvez laisser Carthage aux mains des barbares.' " This was how Waddington reported his talks with the British statesman to the ambassador in London.[21] Bismarck, obviously in agreement with the English, added his entreaties to Salisbury's in assuring Waddington that he gave his complete consent.[22] In turn, Edward, the Prince of Wales, who was visiting the International Exposition in Paris, brought his approval on July 21.

Waddington immediately realized all he could gain from the Anglo-German suggestions. Although he rejected the idea of an immediate direct annexation of Tunis to Algeria, he raised the possibility of French action at a later date. "What we are determined to have," he

21. Salisbury's words were "Do what you like there," and on another occasion, "You will be obliged to take it, you cannot leave Carthage in the hands of the Barbarians." Waddington to Harcourt, Paris, July 21, 1878, MAE Angleterre, 777.

22. The Anglo-German agreement would have been concluded before the congress, according to the indication given by the interviews of April 1878 between Münster and Salisbury. As a matter of fact, it was confirmed as soon as the first talks in Berlin. Blowitz, a journalist who did not believe in Bismarck's words (one of the sallies he sometimes indulged in), when referring to one interview with the chancellor, wrote: "He himself told me: 'On first seeing Lord Beaconsfield, I said to him, you ought to have an understanding with Russia instead of thwarting her. You might leave her a free hand at Constantinople and yourselves take Egypt, which would compensate you for your complaisance. France would not be so vexed as may be imagined, and, in any case, Tunis or Syria might be given to her as an equivalent.' I took this at the time and still take it for a jest, but the Prince had previously spoken in the same strain to Lord Salisbury and M. Waddington." *The Times,* April 5, 1881, p. 5; quoted in *France and Tunis; Memoirs . . . ,* p. 140.

told Salisbury, "is the formal recognition of the protectorate which we in fact exercise in that country, and to be entirely at liberty to extend our influence and to develop our interests as we see fit, without clashing with rival pretentions." [23]

Italy, however, could still make trouble. To Waddington's objections on that score, Salisbury answered that the Italians could take Tripoli.[24] The French in Tunis, the Italians in Tripoli, it was a good bargain for France. However, the Italians had not yet been consulted, and no one knew what they would think of it. But the French delegates were anxious to keep the proposal secret since it had not yet been submitted to their government. They stayed clear of their transalpine colleagues.

Salisbury, for his part, was not particularly anxious to arbitrate a Franco-Italian conflict over Tunisia. Unquestionably he preferred France, but at this moment he was only concerned with getting all the other powers to accept the occupation of Cyprus. Without informing the Italians of the suggestion he had just made to Waddington, he spoke about compensations to Italy and evoked prospects of African expansion.[25] He expressed himself in rather vague terms, so that the Italian diplomats could have thought he was indicating Tunis or Tripoli equally as objects of their ambitions.[26]

Until then the Italian delegates, particularly Corti, had attended the Congress's deliberations as observers. Italy was treated as a negligible quantity, and her delegation was the only one not to be informed by the English about the occupation of Cyprus. Corti learned about it only from the newspapers on July 7. He was finally informed by Salisbury the same day, as the Cyprus convention was made public, and he showed his displeasure. To soothe Italian feelings, the English evoked in rather vague terms the idea of African compensation for Italy, and in this were soon followed by the Germans. Salisbury hinted to de Launay, the second ranking Italian delegate, that Italy could think about expansion toward Tripoli or Tunis. It seems likely

23. Waddington to Harcourt, Paris, July 21, 1878, MAE Angleterre, 777.

24. Ibid.

25. Salisbury admitted to Menabréa only on August 13, 1878, that he had talked to Waddington about Tunis, but had received little enthusiasm. Gorrini, *Tunisi e Biserta:* p. 24.

26. Gorrini insists on this point. He thinks that Salisbury and Disraeli acted more unthinkably than with an intent to deceive in order to extricate themselves from a momentary difficulty without taking into account the long-range effects of their words. *Tunisi e Biserta,* pp. 20 ff.

that Corti received more direct encouragement to take Tunisia from Bülow.[27] These were kind words, doubtless, but they were lost in the uproar of the end of a congress where everyone was straining to offer others territories that were not theirs to distribute. The Italian diplomats paid only scant attention to them and did not think of having them made more explicit. But shortly after the conference, when the unsuspected offer of Tunis to France was specified, the Italian diplomats remembered the encouragement they had received from many sides. Thereby was born the story of Bismarck's simultaneous offer of Tunis to France and Italy, a story that worried people in France spread in order to denounce a Machiavellian plot to set France against Italy and to lure the latter into a German alliance.[28]

After the congress, while Corti went back to face an irritated and greatly disappointed Italian public, Waddington hurried home to take note of the English proposals. As soon as he had informed his ministerial colleagues and President MacMahon of his Berlin conversations, he sent to the ambassador to London, the Marquis d'Harcourt, two long dispatches in which he emphasized the clarity of Lord Salisbury's declarations concerning Tunisia. Without prejudicing French intentions, he requested d'Harcourt to ask the head of the Foreign Office for official confirmation of Lord Salisbury's words. He wrote:

27. "Vous voulez donc nous brouiller avec la France," answered Corti; quoted in Luigi Chiala, *Pagine di storia contemporanea,* (Torino, 1892), *2,* 91.

28. The hypothesis of a simultaneous offer of Tunis to France and Italy is based on Corti's statements which Alexander M. Broadley, *The Last Punic War: Tunis, Past and Present* (London, 1882) *1,* 169, Billot (*La France et l'Italie, Histoire des années troubles 1881–99* (Paris, 1905), Vol. 2, p. 53, and many other authors have taken up. The Berlin talks were scrupulously studied by William Langer in a well-documented article that appeared in 1925, "The European Powers and the French Occupation of Tunis" (*American Historical Review,* pp. 55–78, 251–65). Langer, who remained very skeptical about an actual German offer, stressed the difficulties in coming to a conclusion. Without denying Bülow's words, he suggests an explanation of this conversation: that Bülow was not up to date on the final developments of the congress which were taking place by individual conversations. At any rate, his words were binding only to himself and, after Corti's refusal, Bismarck could have turned to France to offer her the Regency.

The word "Tunis" was perhaps not even pronounced by Bülow, according to Gorrini's study on the Tunisian question drawn up for Crispi in 1890 using Italian documents. This study, published in 1940, was entitled *Tunisi e Biserta* (*Part I, Tunisi: leggenda e storia, 1878–1881*). Gorrini states that no document proved that Italy had been offered Tunis during the congress (p. 16). He calls the simultaneous offer to France and Italy a myth, and the opening of the Italian archives allows us today to confirm his opinion.

It is my opinion that we must take advantage of the opportunity being offered to obtain from the English their formal agreement to anything we may want to do in Tunis, *including annexation*. . . . In fact, it could well happen that three months from now the English would have changed their minds. If need be, you will therefore insist on a categorical reply: the English government must commit itself to giving us *a free hand* in Tunis. What we will do in Tunis, we do not yet know. The question is being studied.[29]

The marquis d'Harcourt approached Lord Salisbury on July 23, 1878, and found him reserved, embarrassed, and above all anxious not to have revealed the talks in which he had already gone far.[30] Salisbury did not hide his displeasure at seeing in an official dispatch the words he had used in Berlin. "We cannot give away other people's property," he said to Harcourt. Without denying the accuracy of Waddington's recollections, he suggested that the French dispatch should be put in a more diplomatic form.[31]

Waddington readily agreed. Following the wishes of the English prime minister, on July 26 he drew up a new letter in which he related less crudely what had been said in Berlin. Salisbury answered on August 7 in a long letter in which he witnessed to France's great work of civilization and in moderate terms called for a possible French expansion into Tunisia which England did not intend to obstruct.

The presence of France on those shores, supported as it is by an imposing military force, must have the effect of giving to her the

29. Waddington to Harcourt, Paris, July 21, 1878, MAE Angleterre, 777.

30. Salisbury's embarrassment is obvious in the letter he wrote to Lord Lyons on July 20, 1878: "If France occupied Tunis tomorrow, we should not even remonstrate. But to promise that publicly would be a little difficult, because we must avoid giving away other people's property without their consent, and also because it is no business of ours to pronounce beforehand on the considerations which Italy would probably advance upon that subject"; quoted in Newton, *Lord Lyons, 2,* 155.

31. From Harcourt, London, July 24, 1878, MAE Angleterre, 777. To Lyons, secret FO, July 24, 1878, FO 27/2300. "The general tenor is quite accurate, but his vivacious French by no means renders the tone of my communication, and what is of more importance, to the rights and claims of other Powers, Turkey and Italy especially. What I told him was that if a state of things should arise in which there was no other obstacle to his occupying Tunis but our objection, that objection would not be made. . . . But he makes me talk of Tunis and Carthage as if they had been my own personal property and I was making him a liberal wedding present." Salisbury to Lyons, July 24, 1878; quoted in Newton, *Lord Lyons, 2,* 158.

> power of pressing with decisive force upon the Government of the neighbouring province of Tunis. This is a result which [the British Government] has long recognized as inevitable and has accepted without reluctance. England has no special interests in this region which could possibly lead her to view with apprehension or distrust the legitimate and expanding influence of France.[32]

All this was not done without reservation or reticence. Salisbury emphasized the private nature of his conversations with Waddington.[33] He ended with a warning to the French about possible Italian ambitions. But the essential had been said: England accepted French influence in the Regency without setting limits to its development. Salisbury announced the British had no interests at stake, and he assured Waddington, without making his statement sound like an offer, that politically England was withdrawing from Tunisian affairs.

Thus France had a free hand in Tunisia, and Waddington prepared to go ahead. Even before receiving the English reply, he had already sketched out the general lines of his program in talks with French politicians and in his letters to Roustan. He fixed the goals and limits of French intervention by the use of the word "protectorate."

It took France nearly three years of indecision and half-measures before she moved into action in 1881 and, as if half-heartedly, sent out an expedition to impose a protectorate on the bey. In 1878, international conditions were favorable, but French politicians were afraid of the public's rather hostile reaction to colonial expeditions. Colonies were generally considered to be as expensive to administrate as to conquer. The Mexican expedition had left unfortunate memories, and the latest Algerian uprising showed that pacification was always an uncertain thing. There seemed no reason to renew the overseas expansion carried out under the Second Empire. France was not forced to it either out of commercial need or out of demographical impera-

32. Salisbury to Lyons, August 7, 1878, FO 27/2300.

33. The conversations with M. Waddington "were of a private character and did not differ in their circumstances from those which daily took place between the various plenipotentiaries. I did not, therefore, at the time, make any note of them, or transmit any summary of them to Y. Exc. as it is usual to do after conversations of importance taking place at the Foreign Office. I am consequently unable to affirm that M. Waddington has reproduced the precise words made use of then, either by himself or me. . . . So far, and without being able to confirm the exact phrases attributed to me, I have great pleasure in bearing witness to the general justice of his recollections." Ibid.

tives. For most politicians, colonial expansion was nothing but a luxury which could dissipate the country's strength just when she was most concerned with her continental security.

Furthermore, the struggle between the republican Chamber and monarchist Senate caused an instability in French politics that was scarcely conducive to bold ventures. Success in Tunisia could give added prestige to President MacMahon who, since the abortive "16 mai" coup d'etat, faced the latent hostility of the republicans. Gambetta had come out strongly against the project, and many politicians dreaded unfavorable Italian reactions.

Even the most determined thought mainly of avoiding the cost of a military expedition. In spite of Roustan's warnings, the people in Paris hoped that the Tunisian protectorate could be settled amicably and that the bey could be persuaded to sign an accord with France. On two occasions, Waddington gave the bey agreements on the protectorate, but these were brushed aside. Then, in December 1879, de Freycinet took Waddington's place at the Quai d'Orsay. Months and years passed while French rivalry with Italy grew more and more heated.

Waddington, upon his return from Berlin, found his colleagues had little enthusiasm for the Tunisian affair. He overcame their objections, however, and persuaded them to take advantage of the promises made in Berlin. At the beginning of August, Waddington, Roustan, and the governor of Algeria, Chanzy, worked out a protectorate agreement planning for the occupation of a certain number of strategic points such as Bizerte, Le Kef, Goletta, and Gabes, and for the installation of a French resident in the bey's court. France was not to take over local administration. She would only reorganize the police and gendarmerie and agreed to place the civil list under the bey's control during his lifetime.

Roustan was given the task of presenting this treaty to the bey under the guise of a friendly agreement. Should he refuse, a naval demonstration supported by troop movements across the border would oblige him to come to terms. Pretexts were readily available. The French could open their file on border incidents. They could demand the punishment of the Khrumirs whose latest misdeed, the pillage of a French ship cast up on Tunisian shores at the end of January 1878, still went unpunished. To disarm Italy, Waddington hoped to offer it Tripoli.[34]

Just as Lord Salisbury had said, Italy was the main obstacle to

34. Telegram to Roustan, July 19, 1878, MAE Tunis, *46*.

France's plans, but the situation was not favorable for opening Franco-Italian talks on North Africa. The Italian public had been greatly disappointed and displeased by the results of the Berlin Congress. The Cairoli cabinet, in full disarray, appeared to be on the verge of dissolving. It seemed advisable to wait until calm was restored in the peninsula before talking about Tunisia. A French declaration, even one paired with suggestions about Tripoli, would once again have hurt Italian pride. It was well known in Paris that Italy intended her expansion toward Tunis, rather than toward Tripoli.

During a conversation in France at the beginning of September, Waddington asked Salisbury whether he could not get Turkey to cede Tripoli to Italy. But Salisbury refused to get into such a scheme. Finally, Waddington had to abandon his plans temporarily because of French domestic difficulties and the lack of support from England. Roustan had not had time to act. On September 1, a telegram from Paris ordered him to suspend his action in the bey's court.

The Tunisian affair therefore remained for awhile in abeyance. Waddington hoped to take advantage of this lull to begin talks with Italy and to ease the rivalry between the English and French consuls in Tunisia. In October, the French ambassador to Rome, the marquis de Noailles, was told to present the Quai d'Orsay's views on the Tunisian problem. The French government considered the Regency a country destined to move in the French orbit and to be under its influence. "Italy could not cherish dreams of a Tunisian conquest without clashing with the French and risking a conflict with them." [35]

French claims were clearly stated. Nevertheless, Waddington did not intend to close the door to Italy's expansion into Africa. He advised her to turn her hopes toward "the district of Barka and the port of Tobruk." De Noailles was not to take any initiative. Moreover, Waddington thought that the settlement of the Greek affair would provide France with a fine opportunity to set forth her claims and talk about compensation with Italy.[36]

Waddington tried to obtain from the English improved relations between the consuls of their two countries in Tunisia. Roustan continued to complain about Wood, and the foreign minister repeated these complaints first to Lyons, then to Salisbury whom he met in France at the end of summer 1878. Salisbury reaffirmed his good will and promised to calm French feelings on this score. But his solution,

35. Secret instructions from Waddington, Paris, October 13, 1878, MAE Italie, *53*.

36. To Roustan, Paris, September 7, 1878, MAE Tunis, *46*.

the honorable retirement of Wood, was delayed for several months, and Roustan continued to complain about the difficulties caused by his English and Italian colleagues.

As Waddington had written to Roustan in September 1878, the question of a Tunisian protectorate had merely been postponed. Three months later, the French government found a pretext to take it up again much more vigorously, thanks to the Sidi Tabet affair, a private conflict between the bey and a Frenchman named Sancy.

Ferdinand Veillet-Devaux, who claimed to be "Count de Sancy," had obtained in 1866 the concession of 3,000 acres near Tunis in order to raise horses and cattle. After much difficulty with the bey, Sancy had arranged in July 1877 to extend his land to 7,500 acres. However, being short of money, he was unable to put the land to use, and at the end of a year it appeared that he had not the number of animals provided for by the contract. Therefore, the bey decided to cancel the concession, with the agreement of a commission of control which had been created for the occasion.[37]

Sancy's cause was not tenable, but the incident came at the right moment, because Roustan had just received the go-ahead from Paris. He immediately saw what he could gain from the incident and bent all his energies to force a break. In December 1878, a commission sent by the bey to repossess the land found a janissary of the French consulate in Sidi Tabet who forbade it to set foot on that "French land." The bey's protests gave Roustan a chance to enlarge the crisis. He immediately prepared a list of reparations to demand from the bey, in drawing up a proposal for an ultimatum. Muhammad es-Sadek could certainly not cede, and the break would provide the occasion for a military show of force which would permit France to impose her protectorate over the country.

Waddington appeared firmly set on this course, and at the beginning of January 1879 the rupture seemed inevitable. France could act freely; England had lost interest in the affair and showed no inclination to intervene. More explicit encouragement came from Berlin. Waddington had instructed Saint-Vallier to sound out the chancellor. Bismarck replied with great warmth: "I believe the Tunisian pear is ripe and that the time has come for you to pick it."[38] He also told the French ambassador he had informed the Italians that, as far as he was concerned, Tunis was within the French sphere of influence. Moreover, he asked Disraeli for explanations of Wood's behavior toward France.

37. J. Ganiage, *Les origines du protectorat français en Tunisie,* pp. 533–40.
38. Saint-Vallier to Waddington, Berlin, January 5, 1879, MAE Allemagne.

Bismarck expressed the hope that the British consul's actions "should not endanger relations between France and Great Britain." In sum, Germany had decided to lend moral support to France in its Tunisian policy.

On January 7 and 8, Waddington informed Roustan that all preparations had been made in Toulon for the immediate departure of the Mediterranean squadron and for active measures should the ultimatum be rejected. Saint-Vallier was delighted. "Je désire," he wrote on January 7, "que le bey nous refuse satisfaction parce que jamais nous ne retrouverons une pareille occasion d'établir notre prépondérance dans la Régence." [39]

However, French hopes were dashed. The bey, frightened by the turn of events, gave in all along the line.[40] On January 9, at the expiration of the time limit, he accepted the French demands. The prime minister officially apologized on behalf of the Tunisian government. The Sancy concession was confirmed, and several Tunisian officials who were made responsible for the crisis were dismissed.

This was only a partial success for France. Waddington had shown a lack of determination. Taken by surprise at the capitulation of the bey, he had not thought of including in his ultimatum any political guarantees for the future, and the question of the protectorate, taken up again too late, dragged on inconclusively. In spite of the intervention of Mustafa ben Ismaïl, a favorite of the bey who was then completely devoted to Roustan, Muhammad es-Sadek rejected the Franco-Tunisian alliance agreement that had been prepared by Waddington (February–July 1879). The policy of persuasion had failed. While waiting for the French government to decide on a policy of force, Roustan was not idle. He laid the basis for a program of economic penetration which was greatly facilitated by the departure of his old adversary, the British consul.

Wood's retirement was the great event of the spring of 1879. Since the preceding summer, Waddington had protested at great length about the British consul's conduct, sometimes to Salisbury himself, but most often to Lyons who complained to London about French insistence.[41] Salisbury several times advised Wood to maintain the

39. Berlin, January 7, 1879, ibid.; *Mémoires et documents, 166.*

40. The bey asked Wood whether he would guarantee Tunisian territory in case he should reject the French ultimatum. The British consul could not provide this assurance. He announced that he had no formal authority to give any formal guarantee. FO 102/126.

41. Waddington "made his life a burden to him in connection with the proceedings of the British consul general in Tunis"; quoted in Newton, *Lord Lyons,* 2, 164.

strictest neutrality in local affairs, but what the French wanted was the removal of an adversary experienced in intrigue and used to acting independently, who could never resign himself to inactivity. France herself had recalled one of her agents from Egypt for similar reasons.

In January 1879, Waddington made another move by writing personally to Salisbury. But, it was difficult to remove without adequate cause an agent who had more than half a century of good service. The Foreign Office tried to retire him by resurrecting an age limit of seventy which until then had been only theoretical. Wood who was seventy-three, claimed to be sixty-seven.[42] The ministry then used the pretext of a reorganization of the service to notify Wood of his retirement on February 24. Wood was not fooled, but he could only give in.[43] On March 31, he turned the office over to the vice-consul, and in June embarked for France where he retired to Nice.

Fifty-five years of activity and continuous struggles for English prestige and interests ended suddenly in a rather discourteous dismissal. The agent who was no longer useful had been sacrificed to an understanding with France with only brief regrets for "his valuable services." A new leaf was rapidly turned over. As soon as Wood had been informed of his retirement, the ministry worked only to hasten his departure. Not only was Consul Wood leaving, but his going marked the end of an era, the end of a tradition. Wood's retirement destroyed the network of information, interests, and intrigues that for over twenty years had made the British consulate a real power. Salisbury, in reducing the consulate's personnel and in naming a nonentity to Tunis, showed England's willingness to withdraw from Tunisian affairs.[44] Wood's retirement tolled the knell for English influence in Tunisia. For Roustan as for Waddington, this was a real success, a success which could somewhat soften the failure of their plans for a Tunisian protectorate.

Wood's retirement delivered the French consul from one dangerous opponent, but Roustan was confronted by another rival who, although less flexible than Wood, was equally active and tenacious. This was

42. He was born in 1806. "Having reported himself as 67 years of age, he entered the services 55 years ago and, therefore, must have begun his public duties at a precocious age," Salisbury wittily commented to Lyons, March 6, 1879; quoted in Newton, *Lord Lyons, 2,* 173.

43. "It is superfluous for me," he wrote on the twenty-sixth, "to dwell on the mental distress which the sudden resolution of H. M.'s Government has caused me." FO, 102/125.

44. "We have hot water enough elsewhere without desiring to boil any in Tunis." To Lyons, March 6, 1879; quoted in Newton, *Lord Lyons, 2,* 174.

Licurgo Macciò, the new Italian consul who, right from the beginning, announced his determination to carry out an energetic fight against French encroachment.

The collision between French and Italian ambitions in Tunis soon took on the allure of a personal rivalry between Roustan and Macciò, a desperate duel between "deux consuls de combat" [45] as an English publicist of the time called it. The European society split into angrily opposed cliques. Conflict of interests, rancor, and personal enmity inflamed and aggravated the differences between the French and the Italian party, if we can give such a name to clans where the French partisans of Macciò were as numerous as the Italians who supported Roustan. The two consuls' entourages were further compromised by a court of Jews, suspicious Levantines, and informers or middlemen looking for a piece of the action.

Roustan let himself be taken over by the family Mussalli. The husband, a Syrian Catholic of Egyptian origin, who was undersecretary at the foreign affairs ministry, faithfully served France in the bey's court. No one in Tunis could ignore the liaison between Roustan and Madame Mussalli, a Genoan who, although in her forties, had remained astonishingly beautiful. At ceremonies she was treated officially as first lady of the French colony. Her salon was the meeting place for important members of the French party. The opposing clique was to be found at the Traverso salon where the household orbited abound Macciò. Pietro Traverso, the brother of Madame Mussalli, was dominated by his wife, the intriguing Marietta who kept discreet her liaison with the Italian consul. False accusations exchanged between the two salons were immediately picked up by the correspondents of the Marseilles and Cagliari newspapers. The ups and downs of this little local war ended by making everyone nearly forget the political and economic stakes in the rivalry between the two countries.

For Roustan as well as for Macciò, the rivalry was mainly based on the issue of economic penetration. The two adversaries, taking up the program formerly advocated by Wood, were at daggers drawn over the quest for concessions. The Italians had an advantage in the size of their colony. The French on their side had money and the support of Mustafa ben Ismaïl who had become all powerful at the Bardo palace.

In the spring of 1880, the Italians appeared to gain a point in the T.G.M. affair. For years, the English company had been trying to get rid of a debt-ridden railroad that had brought them only disap-

45. Alexander M. Broadley, *The Last Punic War, 1,* 174 (in French).

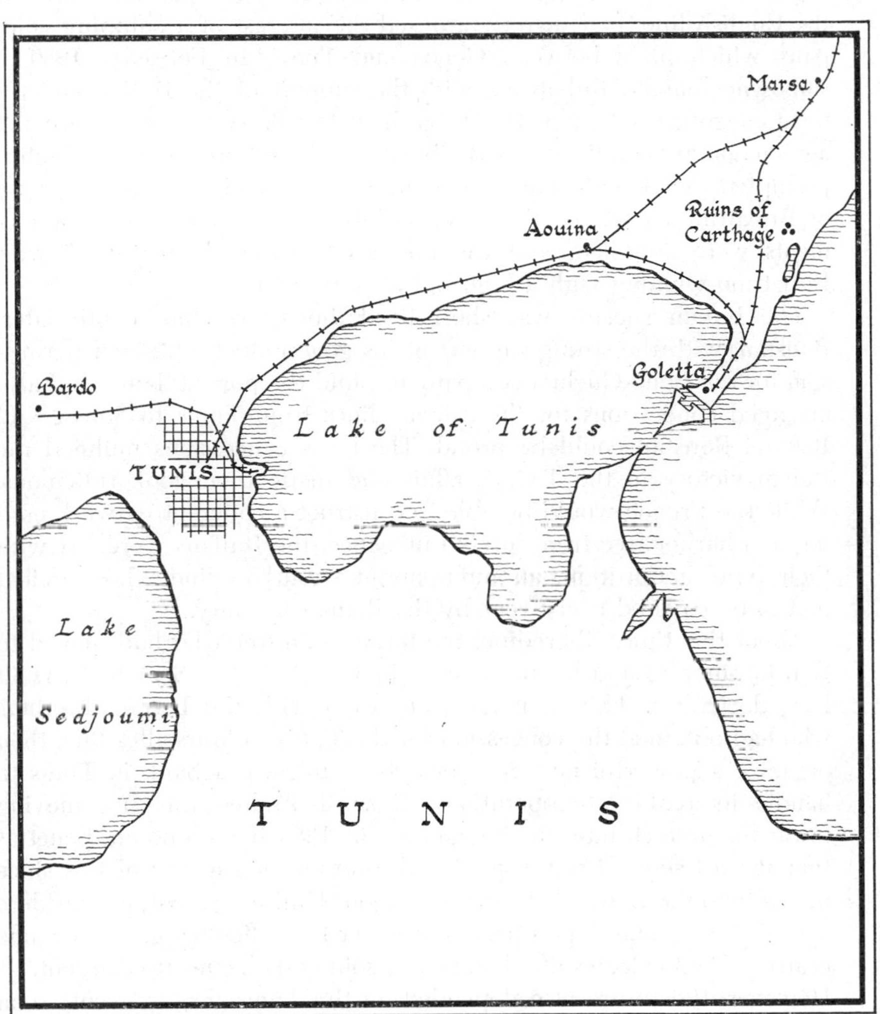

The Tunis-Goletta-Marsa railway

pointment. But, the only possible buyer, the Bône-Guelma company, was waiting for the English to lower their price. They had cause to regret this because Macciò, who had recognized the political value of the English line, had secretly aroused the interest of a shipping company which plied between Genoa and Tunis. In February 1880, a shipowner named Rubattino, with the support of the Italian government, negotiated to pay the English £90,000. However, before the agreement was ratified, a deliberate indiscretion by the English prompted the Bône-Guelma company to make a higher offer. Because of Rubattino's protests, the affair was brought to court. Both agreements were annulled, and the line was auctioned on July 7 with Rubattino winning with a high bid of £165,000.

The Italian success was short lived, however. One month later, Roustan, with the strong support of his government, obtained permission for the Bône-Guelma company to build the port at Tunis and also arranged concessions for the railway lines from Tunis to Sousse and Bizerte. Roustan could be proud. The bey's concessions nullified the Italian victory in the T.G.M. affair and made them look ridiculous. While the French would be able to construct a coherent network ending in a harbor free from foreign influence, the Italians were left with their puny acquisition, an unimportant suburban line whose deficit had to be covered every year by the Roman treasury.

About this time, Khérédine, the former minister who had moved to Constantinople, sold his possessions in Tunisia to the Société Marseillaise de Crédit. This bank, in association with the Péreire brothers who had obtained the concession for the Tunis to Marseilles line, then organize a powerful financial consortium to form a bank in Tunis to handle its real-estate operations. Even if France was not moving toward a protectorate, in the summer of 1880 her economic penetration at least seemed to be successful. Roustan was aware of this since he wrote to the Baron de Courcel: "Aujourd'hui seulement, je considère ma mission comme à peu près achevée et les difficultés graves comme écartées. Pour cela, il suffit d'un peu de soin et de beaucoup d'argent." [46] However, the future also depended on the Tunisians, as events soon showed.

Contrary to all expectations, the French program of economic penetration did not succeed. During the autumn of 1880, relations between Mustafa and Roustan appeared to be cooling. Mustafa had been displeased by the French bank's purchase of Khérédine's possessions since he had hoped to acquire them at no expense. What he coveted par-

46. Roustan to Noailles, Tunis, August 17, 1880, MAE, Papiers Noailles.

ticularly was the vast Enfida domain, a province of 96,000 hectares which extended between Sousse and Tunis along the Hammamet Gulf. At the end of the year, Mustafa broke off with Roustan to draw closer to Macciò. To prevent the Société Marseillaise from taking over Enfida, Mustafa set up a straw man, a British subject from Sousse by the name of Levy who claimed an imaginary right of preemption on the domain. This was a good opportunity for Italy to drag England into a quarrel with France, particularly since the 1880 elections had been won by Gladstone, who seemed less well disposed to France than Disraeli.

From then on Macciò seemed to triumph. With his encouragement, Mustafa systematically went after the French enterprises in the Regency. Any pretext was used to prevent construction of the Sousse line and to refuse the French use of the rights obtained in the last concessions. Slowly but surely, in Tunis as in Europe, the situation deteriorated. "The French," Bismarck said in January, "are now forgetting the moral of the fable and letting go of the prey for the shadow; they are wasting on the Greek sparrows the powder they ought to save for the Tunisian pigeon[47] . . . In politics as in gambling, one has to take advantage of opportunity. The French have had three years to seize it, and they have not been able to do it. The good cards have changed hands. Italy holds them today."[48]

Bismarck's warnings were justified. New difficulties were already threatening France in Tunisia. The Italo-Tunisian party had raised the Enfida question, drawing in Levy and his lawyer, Broadley, who in turn drew in his friend Thomas Reade, the English consul. In one way or another they tried to get support from the British cabinet, but the latter had too many problems in Ireland, Transvaal, and Afghanistan to want to create new difficulties for itself with France. In spite of Reade's and Broadley's activities, which included a vigorous campaign in the press, the Foreign Office remained reserved and showed no desire to get involved. From the beginning, Lord Granville had listened to those who counseled prudence; he wished it to remain a local affair and reserved his opinion until he was better informed.

However, it soon became apparent that Levy's claims were going to be difficult to uphold. Lord Lyons, the ambassador in Paris, did not conceal his skepticism. The British interest in Tunisia, he wrote to

47. Rectification of the Greco-Turkish frontier in Thessaly, one of the consequences of the Congress of Berlin.

48. Saint-Vallier to B. Saint-Hilaire, Berlin, January 15, 1881, MAE, Allemagne, Mémoires et documents, 167.

Granville on January 18, "is not worth a quarrel or even a coolness with France." [49] The assistant undersecretary of state for foreign affairs, Julian Pauncefote, was more trenchant: "Can it be said that Mr. Levy has a *bona fide* interest and that his proceedings are not vexations? It is stated that he is an instrument in the hands of the Italian party at Tunis, to thwart French interests. . . . It appears to me that though Levy may have the law on his side, H. M.'s Government may properly decline to assist him in playing the cards of Italy against France." [50] Granville himself adjudged the explanations provided by the consulate in Tunis as insufficient, perhaps even biased.[51]

Under these circumstances, the foreign secretary could do nothing but welcome French suggestions that they take the matter out of the hands of the local agents and have the affairs studied by the two governments. On January 17, Barthélemy Saint-Hilaire talked directly about it to Lord Lyons, who gave his approval. He then requested the ambassador in London to keep the Foreign Office informed. On January 31, Granville and Challemel-Lacour agreed on the need to put off discussion until more complete information arrived.

It was at this point that France made an unfortunate attempt at intimidation which nearly called everything into question again. Barthélemy Saint-Hilaire, who had decided to wind up the Tunisian affair, in a cabinet meeting on January 29, upheld the need for intervening by force in the Regency. His colleagues, however, did not go along with him. For want of stronger measures, they agreed to send a battleship into Tunisian waters. In Constantinople, the rumor went round that the sultan was preparing to depose the bey and to appoint the former grand vizier, Khérédine, as pasha of Tunis. These poorly founded rumors could serve as a pretext, but the real reason for the dispatch of the *Friedland,* which was the most powerful ship in the Mediterranean squadron, was none other than the Enfida affair, as Barthélemy Saint-Hilaire was innocently to confess to Lord Lyons.[52] The idea came from the minister himself. Courcel could barely hide his skepticism as to the wisdom of such a maneuver.[53]

As might have been expected, the English reacted angrily. If the *Friedland* were not immediately recalled, Granville wrote on February 3, Her Majesty's Government would be constrained to send a squadron off Tunis. Then, Barthélemy Saint-Hilaire denied that the dispatch of

49. Lyons to Granville, Paris, January 18, 1881, Granville papers, 171.
50. Pauncefote's note. January 23, 1881, FO 102/143.
51. Granville's notes. January 1881, FO 102/143.
52. Lyons to Granville, Paris, February 4, 1881, Granville papers, 171.
53. Courcel to Noailles, Paris, January 30, 1881, MAE, Papiers Noailles.

the *Friedland* had any connection with the Levy affair. On February 4, contradicting his statement of the previous day to Lord Lyons, he assured the English that the French demonstration was only directed at preventing a Turkish attack against the Regency. Moreover, the *Friedland* would remain only a short while. The cabinet in London could be reassured and give up the idea of a counterdemonstration.[54]

Granville, however, did not intend to be satisfied with such a "vague" reply. He asked the prime minister to send one or two ships rather than a squadron off Goletta. Gladstone, who had been irritated by the "foolish escapade" of the French, agreed to it without calling a cabinet meeting. On February 5, the Admiralty sent out the battleship *Thunderer.* "We did not want to keep the French out of Tunis," asserted Sir Charles Dilke, undersecretary of state, "but we could not have ironclads used to force Tunisian law courts into giving decisions hostile to British subjects." [55] Under these circumstances, Barthélemy Saint-Hilaire had to give in. On February 8, he announced the departure of the *Friedland,* which was followed without delay by that of the *Thunderer.*

The British success did not solve anything, however, because the recall of the two ships still left the thorny question of Enfida. On February 7, Dilke declared to the House of Commons that the affair should be settled by the Tunisian courts. Barthélemy Saint-Hilaire immediately protested. The French government, in fact, wanted the question entrusted to "an impartial arbitration." Like it or not, Granville was gradually brought around to this point of view.

The negotiations dragged on interminably without progress. Granville found himself harassed by the press, by parliamentary questions, by France's moves, and even by Italy who was always trying to create confusion for its rival. The foreign secretary did not conceal his difficulties. With more perseverance than success, he tried to define a coherent policy, namely, to defend Levy's rights without prejudice to the issue and to use his influence with France without arousing local rivalries. The English government, he said to Count Menabrea, the Italian ambassador, of February 4, intends to maintain a complete separation between the Levy affair and other Tunisian problems.[56] He categorically refused to have the sultan intervene in the Regency's affairs. Reade had been exulting ever since the appearance

54. Note remise à Lord Lyons le 4 février 1881, MAE, Angleterre, 789; *DDF, 3,* n. 563.

55. G. M. Tuckwell and S. Gwynn, *The Life of . . . Sir Charles W. Dilke* (2 vols. London, 1917), *1,* 380.

56. Granville to Paget, FO 45/424.

of the *Thunderer,* and Granville tried in vain to calm him. "I am afraid [he] has been too impulsive," Granville wrote to Lyons on February 10, and, a month later, he added: "I wish Reade had never been sent to Tunis." [57]

In spite of the prime minister's reticence, it was obvious that Great Britain, by interfering with the Levy affair, could not avoid looking like France's opponent, and thereby playing Italy's game. England's hesitant and uncertain policy gave France the impression of unmitigated ill will. "Je vous ai dit et je vous répète que le gouvernement anglais est notre adversaire à Tunis," Challemel-Lacour wrote bitterly on February 14.[58] Lord Granville, after equivocating for a long time, ended up by simply withdrawing from the debate. On April 21, he decided that the English government should not intervene in a private dispute—a prudent measure that had long been counseled by Lord Lyons who acidly suggested that he could "wash his hands of the whole affair." [59]

French troops were already entering Tunisia. Granville's decision came too late to have any influence. In fact, his equivocation had worried the Quai d'Orsay enough to encourage its intervention in the Regency, but it had not provided a sufficient threat to lead France to renounce the operation it was contemplating.[60]

The decision to intervene, made in Paris at the end of March 1881, was precipitated by the Enfida crisis and Italian provocations. The man who finally made the decision was not Jules Ferry or his foreign minister, but the Baron de Courcel, director of political affairs at the Quai d'Orsay.

For a long time Courcel had been lobbying in the foreign affairs ministry. Freycinet had withdrawn without having done anything, and Courcel had to work to convince his successor in the Jules Ferry cabinet, Barthélemy Saint-Hilaire. In order to succeed, he confided in all the ambassadors who were known to favor intervention, asking them to use their influence with the minister. On January 26, the ambassador in Berlin wrote to Barthélemy Saint-Hilaire:

> Vous me dites qu'on veut laisser passer les élections et qu'on agira ensuite. . . . Quelle imprudence et quel aveuglement! Dans dix

57. To Lyons, February 10 and March 16, 1881, Granville papers, 202.

58. Challemel-Lacour to B. Saint-Hilaire, London, February 14, 1881, MAE Angleterre, 789 (*DDF, 3,* 358, n. 375).

59. Lyons to Granville, Paris, February 25, 1881, Granville papers, 171.

60. André Raymond, "Les libéraux anglais et la question tunisienne (1880–1881)," *Cahiers de Tunisie,* 1955, p. 446.

mois, vous serez en face d'une alliance secrète organisée et conclue contre nous, et vous devrez reculer de nouveau, car ce ne sera plus comme au jour où nous sommes, une promenade militaire à accomplir, mais une guerre européenne à soutenir pour sauver notre colonie algérienne. Ah! mon cher ministre, vous êtes bon patriote. M. Gambetta l'est aussi; voyez-le, entendez-vous avec lui, et faites en sorte que notre pays n'ait jamais à subir la nouvelle humiliation, le nouvel amoindrissement dont il est menacé; j'en suis si affecté, si inquiet, si malheureux que si je m'écoutais je partirais pour Paris, y passer quarante-huit heures, vous conjurer, conjurer M. Gambetta, M. Ferry, M. Grévy, la Chambre entière de faire ce que commandent impérieusement l'honneur et l'intérêt de la patrie. . . . Un acte de fermeté, d'énergique volonté, sans danger sérieux, sans effusion de sang, et nous reprenons notre rang dans l'estime des nations; une nouvelle preuve de faiblesse et nous achevons de nous reléguer au rang de l'Espagne.[61]

However, even if Barthélemy Saint-Hilaire ended up by coming around to his colleagues' point of view, he did not think of getting involved in a distant undertaking. Jules Ferry was mainly occupied with educational questions, and elections were coming up. Moreover, the Elysée gave the project a frigid reception, and Grévy thought the Tunis affair was not worth "un cigare à deux sous." The monarchists in Parliament advocated the policy of "recueillement," and the radical extreme left took the same position. The opportunist majority remained indifferent or hostile. Gambetta was reported to have said that the Tunisian question should be "chloroformed" for a few years. Nevertheless, on January 28, 1881, Saint-Hilaire, who had been duly lectured by Courcel, submitted the Tunisian question at a ministerial council and asked for strong measures. His proposition was rebuffed by all but three of his colleagues, who decided to wait. "Une expédition à Tunis, dans une année d'élections," added Ferry, "mon cher Saint-Hilaire, vous n'y pensez pas!"

On March 23, Courcel, at Saint-Vallier's suggestion, went to see Gambetta. The interview was decisive, for the president of the Chamber of Deputies, quickly convinced, agreed to the project. The battle was won. Shielded on that side, Ferry in turn made up his mind, and once convinced, he acted vigorously.

Gambetta's contemporaries were amazed at his change of mind, since they had long considered him a friend of Italy and an opponent to the Tunisian project. The opposition tried to explain away this sud-

61. MAE Allemagne, Mémoires et documents, 167 (*DDF, 3,* 330).

den change by business relations with suspect financiers. They denounced "une guerre pour les affaires" in which Enfida, Bône-Guelma, and speculation on Tunisian securities became the real reasons for French intervention. In the press campaign which began in the autumn of 1881, Rochefort distinguished himself by his outrageous remarks. Most of the polemicists, badly informed about Tunisian affairs, accepted unverified rumors as gospel truth and published the most improbable allegations in the opposition press. However, the Société Marseillaise did have a good case in the Enfida affair; the Bône-Guelma company was a serious enterprise whose interests had nothing mysterious about them. Of course, it is true that there was speculation on Tunisian securities. Certain bankers, such as the well-known Erlanger, could certainly have been informed by Gambetta's friends that the decision had been made and could have speculated on the eve of the expedition. But even if this maneuver seems to be an immediate result of French intervention, it is hard to present it as one of its causes.

Anyhow, the decision had been made at the top, but a pretext for intervention still had to be found, a task that was not very difficult. Roustan had been working hard to show this for months. "Nous devons attendre et préparer nos motifs d'agir avant nos moyens d'action. La sottise du gouvernement tunisien nous y aidera," he wrote to Courcel in May 1880. A few months later, he added, "Soyez bien convaincu que nous avons chaque semaine un *casus belli* sur la frontière. Il dépend de nous de le faire valoir."[62] The denials of justice and the effronteries that French enterprises had had to suffer at the hands of Mustafa and his friends ever since the beginning of 1881 could give the government other pretexts for justifying intervention in the Regency. In Roustan's eyes, however, nothing could equal a good border incident which would allow the French to send out a land expedition.

At this moment, a band of Khrumirs appeared on the Algerian border. An encounter between French troops and Tunisian tribes on March 30 and 31 provided the pretext Roustan was looking for. A last glance at the diplomatic situation showed Germany still favorable, England hesitant, and Italy powerless in her isolation. France was therefore free to do as she intended. Although Bismarck did not express himself in the picturesque way he had two years earlier in referring to the "Tunisian pear," his support was nonetheless just as strong.

62. Roustan to Courcel, Tunis, May 21 and September 24, 1880, MAE Tunis, 50, 51.

In Tunis, Roustan had at his disposal a substitute prince in case the bey should remain obstinate. Prince Taieb, one of the younger brothers of Muhammad es-Sadek, offered to come to France in order to return to Tunisia with the French troops.

On April 4, Ferry informed Parliament about the Tunisian incident. After expounding the need for an expedition whose sole avowed object was the punishment of border tribes, he received by unanimous vote of the Chamber on April 7, 1881, the five million francs he had requested for military operations.

At the end of April, thirty thousand men in two columns under the command of General Bréart and General Forgemol entered Tunisia while a squadron disembarked eight thousand men at Bizerte. Despite Italy's and Turkey's fitful attempts to intervene, the bey was diplomatically isolated and could do nothing. Like it or not, the Tunisian army had to be placed at the disposition of the French troops who, after a three-week march, arrived at the gates of Tunis. "Nous ne sommes pas et nous ne voulons pas être en guerre avec le bey. . . . C'est en alliés que nous entendons entrer et opérer sur le territoire tunisien pour la répression des désordres," repeated Barthélemy Saint-Hilaire.[63] Officially, it was simply a question of helping the bey put down traditionally insubordinate tribes.

As for the Khrumirs, they were soon no longer mentioned. While some Parisian journalists found this good material for levity,[64] France on the international level confronted serious opposition that might have been transformed into a coalition but for Bismarck's open support of France.

Granville had at first glumly resigned himself to a sullen neutrality, but the occupation of Bizerte provoked a wave of ill humor in England. Turkey, as well as Italy, urged the British government to intervene. The Saint Petersburg cabinet announced that it was ready to act in conjunction with London. On May 5, a desperate plea came from Tunis.

On May 6 the Foreign Office debated the possibility of English intervention. Granville, who favored European mediation, proposed circulating a letter to the great powers, but he ran into the opposition of his colleagues, Dilke and Tenterden, and so finally gave up this idea. Others called Granville's attention to the fact that neither Germany nor Austria would respond to Britain's overtures, and that the "concert of Europe" would be reduced to Russia, Italy, and England,

63. B. Saint-Hilaire to Roustan, Paris, April 13, 1881, MAE Tunis, 57.
64. H. Rochefort, "Cherchez le Khroumir!" *L'Intransigeant,* April 21, 1881.

"a curious league . . . and a queer concert."[65] Finally the Foreign Office limited itself to offering its services to France to help it settle rapidly its dispute with Tunisia.[66]

Barthélemy Saint-Hilaire politely declined the English offer of mediation, repeating that France did not intend to annex Tunis, that the occupation of the country was temporary, and that the treaty to be concluded with the bey would respect the Regency's previous commitments. The fate of Tunisia was sealed. While Granville was brushing aside the last steps from the Italians and Turks, the French troops arrived before Tunis. Roustan, in accord with General Bréart, presented the protectorate convention for the bey's immediate signature. On May 12, 1881, the treaty of Bardo was signed at the Kassar-Saïd Palace, and it was ratified twelve days later by the Chamber of Deputies. Ferry's operation seemed to have met with complete success.

However, at the end of June, while the French command was busy reembarking troops, it was surprised by an insurrection in central and southern Tunisia. Sfax and Gabes revolted, while nomadic tribes entered the fray. Hammama, Zlass, Methellith, Swassi, and Beni Zid assembled under the command of a caid of the Neffat, Ali ben Khalifa, who expected support from Ottoman troops of Tripoli. Westward, too, Majeur, Frechich, and Uled Ayar tribes were on a war footing. The French had to carry out a campaign during the summer and send for reinforcements of fifty thousand troops from the French and Algerian garrisons. Sfax was bombarded by the squadron before being stormed by the marines on July 26.

Ferry, taking advantage of the summer vacation, tried to minimize the affair. He urged the generals to act and bring him victory before the reopening of Parliament. On October 26, Kairouan was occupied without a fight by three columns converging from Tebessa, Tunis, and Sousse. Gafsa and Gabes were captured during November. The principal insurgent tribes, the Hammama, Zlass, Neffat, and Swassi, comprising more than one hundred thousand nomads, fled the French

65. Tuckwell and Gwynn, *Sir Charles Dilke, 1,* 380.

66. Gladstone and his colleagues felt bound by Salisbury's agreement with Waddington to give the French a free hand. But "the main consideration was that the French in Tunis did not seem to present any threat to the vital interest of maintaining British influence in Egypt"; Ronald Robinson and John Gallagher, with Alice Denny, *Africa and the Victorians: The Official Mind of Imperialism* (London, 1961), p. 94. However, Bismarck's intervention cannot be passed over in silence. Turkish documents bring to light new evidence about it. See Abdurrahman Tchaidjè, *La Question tunisienne et la politique ottomane (1181–1913)* (Erzeroum, 1963), pp. 48–67.

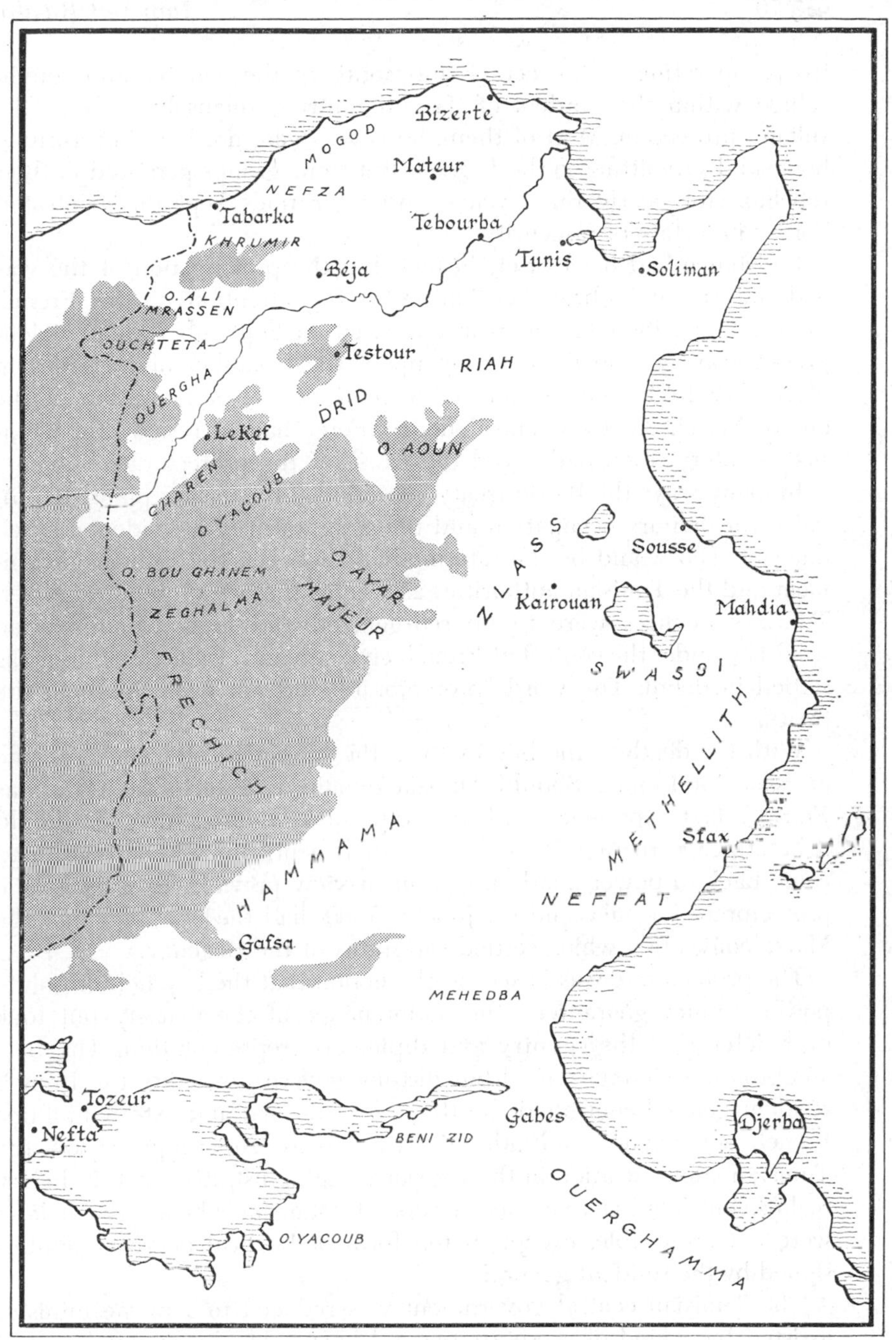

The Tunisian tribes in the mid-nineteenth century

troops operating in the center and south of the country and sought refuge within the borders of Tripoli, putting themselves under the sultan's protection. Most of them, however, were not long in returning home and submitting to the French. But some groups persisted in their rebellion for nearly three years, and their raids kept this contested border in a state of insecurity.

Resistance had been brief, in fact, but the prolongation of the war had unfortunately brought Tunisia to the attention of the French public. Opposition to the war appeared in September in a violent press campaign and then sprang up in the Chamber of Deputies in November 1881. The session of the ninth was a prefiguration of the one of March 30, 1885. The defeated Ferry had to resign, but Gambetta's intervention had saved the cause of the protectorate.

In many ways the Bardo treaty reproduced the earlier plans. It provided for military occupation and the assignment of a resident French minister who would be the intermediary between the French government and the Tunisian authorities as well as the bey's foreign minister. Tunisia's finances were to be reorganized and local administration would be under the control of French civil servants. In fact, nothing was settled in detail. The word "protectorate" did not even figure in the treaty.

With the death of the bey in 1882, the fate of the Regency became an issue for France. Should Tunisia remain a protectorate (this was France's first experience with this type of administration), or should it be attached to Algeria as a new department? Jules Ferry, who had come back to power, made his point of view prevail. He stuck to the protectorate formula, and on June 8, 1883, had the new bey sign the Marsa convention which settled the status of the Regency.

The protectorate was based on the fiction that the bey held absolute power. France guaranteed the maintenance of the dynasty but took over defense of the country and diplomatic representation. The bey, an absolute sovereign, ruled but did not govern. In reality the French resident general controlled the Regency's internal and external affairs. French sovereignty and administration were superimposed on the Tunisian administration in the legislative, administrative, and judiciary realms, but Tunisia remained a separate state in which French laws were not applicable, except in the form of beylical decrees countersigned by the resident general.

The Tunisian central government was reduced to a prime minister assisted by a kind of secretary-general known by the quaint name of "ministre de la Plume." All the newly created services were assigned French directors. The old administration, although simplified and transformed, remained on the local level with its hierarchy of caids, khalifas, and sheikhs. The number of districts was reduced, and about forty caids were put under the supervision of French officials known as "contrôleurs civils." The courts and treasury were also quickly reorganized.

Because of its flexibility, the protectorate arrangement was easily accepted in Tunisia. The restoration of order and a better administration favored economic development. On the eve of the First World War, Tunisia was cited in French political circles as a model colony. In any case, the country profited from a prosperity it had not known for many years.

The opposition's newspaper campaign had discredited the Tunisian expedition. The French public remembered only questionable deals, and intrigues plotted in a corrupt little Eastern court, not a conquest attained without a fight. The renewal of colonial expansion, one of the major events of modern French history, was accomplished indirectly by a campaign that had been too easy, and that lacked the military encounters that would have gratified national pride.

Ferry soon started talking about foreign bases, trade outlets, and industrial and commercial expansion. He tried vaily to show that in a world on the move the greatness of France was closely tied to the greatness of its enterprises, and if the country ceased to develop, it would inevitably go down the road to decadence. Ferry, however, could not sweep along the French public, which remained indifferent to the larger problems of foreign policy. Tunis did not make the French forget Strasbourg; the renewal of colonial expansion still left the whole German problem. The French did not forget, as Bismarck had hoped, their desire for revenge, which was rendered more and more improbable as each year went by.

The resolution of the Tunisian crisis was in keeping with the commitment Lord Salisbury had made three years earlier. But Granville's hesitations and the liberal cabinet's ambivalent attitude had made England lose all the advantages of its final acquiescence to the protectorate. The Liberals, when they took office, given the agreement between Salisbury and Waddington, could have chosen between two courses of action. In the name of political principles, they could have repudiated their predecessor's commitments. However, if it seemed important to hold on to Cyprus and to maintain the continuity of English policy, they had no alternative other than to stick to the 1878 agreement.

Granville, however, proved incapable of choosing sides and adopting a coherent policy. In deciding to keep Cyprus, which contradicted the principles and declarations of the Liberal party, the cabinet made it impossible to reject the Tunisian counterpart of the Anglo-Turk agreement. Granville continued to equivocate, and his difficulty came to light in the spring of 1881. The rapid French intervention left the major powers with a fait accompli, since Bismarck's attitude prevented an appeal to the concert of Europe. England, which for a half-century had played an important role in the Regency, was therefore reduced to a powerless state at the decisive moment. After giving up his plans for mediation on the recommendation of his colleagues, Granville became resigned and, with rather ill grace, accepted a solution that he was in no position to prevent.

Even though Salisbury's declarations had prepared the way for a reconciliation with France in which the Tunisian and Egyptian affairs were both to play a role, Granville's inconsistent policy could only have displeased the French. From this, it seems difficult to establish a parallel between Granville's attitude in the spring of 1881 and that of Freycinet toward the Egyptian problem a year later. There seems no justification for the idea that France received Tunisia as part of a bargain in exchange for which she was to stay out of the eastern Mediterranean basin.

☙ 3. *Great Britain and France in Egypt 1876–1882*

☙ AGATHA RAMM

The British military occupation of Egypt in July 1882 is, in retrospect, a glaring fact. It was not the fact, however, that was decisive at the time. In the wider context of contemporary Anglo-French relations, the institution of the Dual Control in November 1879 and its end in December 1882 were both more significant. This discussion is concerned, therefore, with the institution and the end of the Anglo-French condominium in Egypt. It lasted three years. It brought to an end a French dominance in Egypt that had been largely cultural: the French language was that most used after Arabic; Egyptians brought up to know something of Western Europe, knew chiefly France and French literature. Its beginning marked the beginning of a British dominance that was financial and political. Its end made this British dominance exclusive. In short, the end of the Dual Control gave political meaning to the military occupation.

The Dual Control was a product more of British than of French policy. It was caused ultimately by the Palmerstonian policy adopted by Disraeli. "Palmerstonian" is not, it must be admitted, a precise description. Palmerston was only the most famous exponent of a policy that was followed with singular consistency by Pitt the Younger, Lord Castlereagh, Canning, and Lord Salisbury. Nor is it precise to speak as if Disraeli conducted foreign policy. This was from 1874 to 1878 the business of Lord Derby, who, however, resigned because he could not carry his views with the prime minister and the cabinet; he then in disgust called their policy one of "occupy, fortify, grab & brag." [1] After 1878 it was the business of Lord Salisbury, who taking his inspiration from Disraeli, yet carried prime minister and cabinet with him in a policy that was essentially his own. But it is Disraeli's imagined picture of what a British policy should be that has stamped

1. A. Ramm, ed., *The Political Correspondence of Mr. Gladstone and Lord Granville,* 1876–1886 (2 vols. Oxford, 1962) [hereafter *Gladstone-Granville*], *1,* No. 476.

the national memory of the period 1874 to 1880. His view was realist and related foreign policy to a struggle for ascendancy among units of organized power. It was clear-headed and thoroughly defined. It found warrants for action in the defense of British interests. The word "interests" had a precise and not a generalized meaning. It did not mean mere advantage. Interests were capable of tabulation: for example, the neutrality of Belgium, the closure of the straits of the Bosphorus and Dardanelles, the freedom of the Suez Canal. They were assumed to be constantly jostling against the interests, equally definable, of the other European Great Powers. The aim of foreign policy was to keep the jostling equal: to prevent any one Power, by its absolute ascendancy, from making the struggle one of life or death for the others; to avoid its leading to war; to keep it a *game* of power poiltics.

Similarly the end of the Dual Control was caused ultimately by the pacifist foreign policy of Gladstone. "Pacifist" is as much a makeshift word to describe Gladstone's foreign policy as "Palmerstonian" is to describe Disraeli's policy. For want of a better word it will do to describe a view of foreign policy that did not relate policy to power and did not assume the existence of a struggle for ascendancy among organized units of power. Nor did Gladstone, any more than Disraeli, conduct foreign policy. That was the responsibility of Lord Granville, the foreign secretary from 1880 to 1885. He was not, however, an original or constructive thinker, and he took his ideas from Gladstone. He was a skillful negotiator and an intelligent critic and conciliator, an admirable executant of the other man's ideas. All the achievements of the period—the great work of political construction in Egypt, where Britain created an army and institutions as if it were another India, and the final stabilization of Egyptian finances by the convention of 1885—were, for better or worse, the product of Gladstonian ideas. When Gladstone failed to provide the ideas, because he was preoccupied or had no ideas appropriate to the situation, confusion descended. Thus naval and military measures were taken and Egypt occupied by a cabinet that could only reconcile this action with its pacifist policy by the confused argument of war today for a better peace tomorrow.[2] Gladstone's view of foreign policy assumed that the notion of jostling interests was nonsense: what was the legitimate interest of one Great Power was equally the interest of them all, as, for example, the peaceful use of the Suez Canal. Such a view of foreign policy found warrants for action in general ideas. Liberals defined

2. Gladstone, in trying to dissuade John Bright from resigning from the cabinet after the bombardment of Alexandria, ibid., *1*, 393, n. 3.

these as precisely as the holders of the contrary view of foreign policy tabulated "interests." Thus they justified action by considerations such as the well-being of populations; the saving of public money and the payment of public debts; justice conceived as the rule of law or, more precisely, as the sanctity of treaty obligations; the responsibility of the Great Powers to assure these things, erroneously assumed to be discernible by all men of goodwill, for the small states; European Concert and general European utility erroneously believed to be promoted by national self-determination rather than disrupted by it.

It would satisfy one's taste for symmetry if one could trace a similar alternation in French policy. Under the Third Republic there was a succession of policies but no such alternation. Nor do the changes key in with the British alternation. The two contrasting British policies met a series of different responses from successive French ministers. It was this relationship of initiative and response that, with one exception, ultimately governed the institution and end of the Dual Control. The succession in France went as follows: from the cautious Anglophile policy of Waddington to the policy of European Concert adopted by Freycinet; continuing with a return to an Anglophile policy under Barthélemy Saint-Hilaire, vigorous assertion under Gambetta, and a return to European Concert during Freycinet's second term of office; ending with the Anglophile policy pursued by Duclerc.

William Henry Waddington (1829–94) was minister for foreign affairs from 1877 to November 1879 and later a successful ambassador in London (1883–93). Jules Barthélemy Saint-Hilaire (1805–95) was minister for foreign affairs from September 24, 1880, to November 14, 1881. Charles Duclerc (1812–88) was foreign minister from August 1, 1882, to January 1883. Though none of them belonged to the Right, they were not distinctively identified with the Republic: the first was a man of mixed English and French blood married to an English wife; the second a philosopher born under Napoleon, a friend of Thiers, a man whose mind was shaped by antagonism to the Bourbons and by life under the Orleanist monarchy; the last also was born under the first Empire and educated under monarchies. Their policy was conciliatory, based upon an acceptance of French weakness and an attempt to exploit it. Under them France held herself open to such overtures as came to her, whether from Germany or England. If her policy was on the whole Anglophile, it was so because Britain (when Salisbury sought to strengthen her Mediterranean position or Gladstone to gain the execution of the Treaty of Berlin) most needed French support and hence made the overtures. A different policy was pursued by Léon

Gambetta (1838–82) or later by Jules Ferry (1832–93). These were younger men, bred in the tradition of Republican opposition to Napoleon III. They were wholly identified with the *future* of the Third Republic and disowned that especial respect for Thiers which both Barthélemy Saint-Hilaire and Freycinet repeatedly expressed. Léon Gambetta was prime minister and foreign minister in his *grand ministère of* November 14, 1881, to January 27, 1882. He claimed and took initiative for France Under Gambetta, France chose her own course and did not wait to respond to decisions made elsewhere. But Gambetta's policy was cut short before it developed, so that it is impossible to descry its objective. This was the exceptional period in the Anglo-French relationship that governed the institution and end of the Dual Control. During these three months what happened over Egypt was ultimately determined by the initiative of France and the response of Britain, and not contrariwise.

A third position, as different from that of Waddington, Barthélemy Saint-Hilaire, and Duclerc as it was from that of Gambetta, was occupied by Charles de Saulces de Freycinet (1828–1923). He was foreign minister from January to September 1880, for a second time when he was also prime minister from January 28 to July 31, 1882, and for a third time in 1886. He was distinctively identified with the Third Republic, for as a young man of twenty he had played a part in the events of 1848–49. Yet as a scientist and engineer by training he had little taste for the art of exercising personal power over other men as Disraeli or Gambetta understood it. His first period at the foreign office was notable for a reform that released it from the aristocratic paternalism that had long prevailed there. He united the diplomatic and consular services and put entry, promotion, and retirement under known and fixed rules, removing them from the personal patronage by which they had hitherto been governed. His policy at the time was said to be colorless—Freycinet was known as the white mouse—but it was not without character. He tried to do what public opinion, as he encountered it in the Chamber of Deputies, wanted. To please it he attempted a policy that was both inexpensive and yet carried prestige. It was anti-German, but not pro-English; it involved initiative, but not independent initiative, since the Chamber was not likely to tolerate the expense that might be involved in isolated action by France. The Chamber might, on the other hand, welcome a French initiative that appeared to give France the lead in the European Concert and to tolerate expense where failure to do so would mean withdrawal from the other five Powers and a loss of prestige. Freycinet promoted action by the European Concert. Yet over Egypt he would not go to the point of working with the European Powers to isolate Britain and counterwork her policy, since that would have been tantamount to the expensive policy of isolated assertion.[3] Thus the relationship continued to be one in which Britain took the initial decisions and France responded to them.

The ultimate causes of the establishment and of the end of the Dual Control in Egypt lay in the foreign policies of the Great Powers. The immediate causes lay in Egypt itself. The contemporary view that the Egyptian people were the victims of a corrupt, effeminate Orientalism and that Britain and France brought to them honesty and virility or civilization and freedom is too simple. Robinson and Gallagher have drawn attention to the national and Muslim revolt in both Tunis and Egypt against alien and Christian rule.[4] France, be it said, was at the time alive to this. Britain was more sceptical.

There is more to be said. The decisions of successive viceroys—viceroys of the sultan of the Ottoman Empire—had brought Egypt into European politics and caused her to live her life among European ideas. Under Mehemet Ali (who died in 1849) she had appeared in Greece as a military Power on the European scene. Some forty years later—by 1876—she had borrowed European capital to such an extent that Ismail Pasha had a consolidated debt of some 68 million pounds and a floating debt of some 26 million pounds, and on her territory was the Suez Canal, partly built by European capital, largely owned and entirely administered by Europeans. Such absolute power wielded by the viceroy or khedive was incompatible with the European notions among which Egypt by 1876 lived. Secondly, the Mohammedan character of the country meant that it had no political, judicial, or administrative institutions such as would enable it to play a part on an equal footing in the European world, a world which was becoming increasingly rationalist and democratic in its general ideas and more and more dependent on materialist and scientific techniques. Thirdly, Egypt was a country of agriculture and crafts where the cultivation of the soil was the dominant and governing factor. The dependence of the

3. This reading of Freycinet's policy is based on the whole correspondence in Archives du Ministère des Affaires Etrangères, Paris [MAE hereafter], Correspondance Politique [CP hereafter], Egypte, and in the Foreign Office archives in the Public Record Office, France [hereafter FO 27]; but one dispatch especially confirms it: see Lyons to Granville, No. 709 Secret, July 11, 1882, FO 27/2566.

4. Ronald E. Robinson and John Gallagher, "The Partition of Africa," *New Cambridge Modern History, 11* (Cambridge, 1962), 594.

peasant, or fellah, upon the landowner was absolute and his methods of cultivation irreceptive to capital investment. An expanding economy on European lines was an impossibility. Unless Egypt withdrew herself from Europe, to which she was now too deeply committed for such a step to be easy, she must sooner or later have accepted some degree of European tutelage in order to acquire the government by law, the democratic institutions, the rational administration, and the capitalized economy that would alone enable her to hold her own as an organized unit in a Europeanized world.

Egypt fell under this tutelage in a series of financial crises. These were the consequence of the interplay of the conduct of the khedive Ismail with the foreign policies of Britain and France. The first crisis happened in April 1876. On April 8, 1876, Ismail Pasha suspended the payment of interest on his debt. An account into which Egyptian revenues, assigned to the servicing of the public debt, were to be paid was then opened. It was placed under the control of three commissioners: E.-G. de Barbier Comte de Blignières, Von Kremer, and Baravelli, the nominees respectively of France, Austria-Hungary, and Italy. This was the beginning of what was later known as the *Caisse de la Dette Publique*. The debt in the same month, May 1876, was consolidated. Britain, though she declined representation on the commission of the public debt, was yet in a strong position. She had no responsibility but, since her advice was accepted at Cairo, had a controlling voice. Indeed, before the year 1876 was out, George J. Goschen, acting on behalf of the British creditors of Egypt,[5] cooperated with Joubert, acting in the same capacity for French creditors, to induce the khedive to improve these arrangements. Certain debts were separated from the consolidated debt for special treatment; a number of Europeans, mostly English (Englishmen claiming to have financial qualifications and ready to work abroad seemed easier to find) were intruded into the Egyptian administration in order to ensure that the estimated revenues were realized; and a British commissioner was nominated, not by the British government, but by George Goschen, acting on behalf of the British creditors, to serve on the commission of the public debt. Charles Rivers Wilson, a Treasury official, was the British commissioner. Among the British and French officials imported into the Egyptian service were two who, under the khedivial decree of November 18, 1876, exercised the functions and bore the title of

5. Goschen was the son of a partner in the banking house of Frühling and Goschen through whom the loan of 1862 had been put on the English market; see D. S. Landes, *Bankers and Pachas* (1958), p. 167.

controllers of finance. The British controller of receipts, Romaine, was a private person employed by the Egyptian government; the French controller of expenditure, the Baron de Malaret, was the nominee of the French government. The Egyptian question had become a financial question and European tutelage had begun.

Two years later the second crisis happened. Given the Egyptian accounting system and the arbitrary method of taking money haphazard used by the government and its agents, given the nature of the Egyptian economy and the small size of the actual revenue, the interest on the debt, paid with difficulty in 1877, would be impossible to meet in the spring of 1878. On French insistence payment was nevertheless made. The consequence was a new breakdown, much more far-reaching in its effects than the first. The khedive instituted a European commission of inquiry into his affairs and virtually handed over his proper business to Europeans. Out of these events emerged the so-called system of August 28, 1878. The khedive surrendered his personal property and accepted a civil list. He gave up absolute power and accepted the principle of ministerial responsibility. The principle could have no other meaning in a nonparliamentary country than a *transfer* of power. Absolute power was transferred from the khedive to the Ministry, that is to Nubar Pasha, a Christian and an Armenian with no knowledge of Arabic; to the two European ministers, Rivers Wilson, minister of finance, and de Blignières, minister of public works; and to Riaz Pasha, minister of the interior. Wilson and de Blignières were replaced by substitutes on the commission of the debt, and the commission of inquiry continued its work. The French government, but not the British government, had been involved in these arrangements.

The third crisis happened on February 18, 1879. Its principal consequence was to cause the British government to be as fully involved as the French. When it began there existed an Anglo-French entente, which was soon to be confirmed and strengthened. Salisbury had brought to the Foreign Office in March 1878 a positive policy based on a vigorous definition of British interests and a clear-headed understanding of the elements of power. He had cooperated with Austria-Hungary before the Congress of Berlin to check Russia; at the Congress itself he turned to France. He was met more than halfway by Waddington, seeking to develop the policy, in which Louis Decazes had gained a notable success in 1875, of gaining friends. An informal understanding, that Britain, having taken Cyprus, would not demure if France took Tunis and that France would accept the British lead in

Egypt, was established.[6] The understanding was developed by an exchange of dispatches in September 1879. The most formal version was contained in Salisbury's dispatch to Edward Malet, then British agent and consul general in Egypt, September 19, 1879, and in Waddington's dispatch to Admiral Pothuau, his ambassador in London, of September 30, 1879.[7]

These documents recorded a conversation between Salisbury and Waddington at Puys, in France, where Salisbury had a house. Gladstone and Granville claimed they acquiesced in the French occupation of Tunis because they were bound by the secret commitment of Salisbury to Waddington.[8] Similarly they contended in 1882 that the dispatch of September 19 constituted a secret and unbreakable commitment that bound them to a particular Egyptian policy. Gladstone called it an "outrage" because it was secret and yet left him no freedom of action.[9] It constituted, he claimed, a triple pledge to support the government of the khedive, to keep European Powers other than France out of Egypt, and to act entirely with France. The Dual Control and this pledge were alike legacies from Salisbury and alike, Gladstone claimed, responsible for the military occupation of Egypt. Salisbury never accepted Gladstone's contention that he had no freedom of action over Egypt.[10] It is certain that the meaning and implications of the entente in Salisbury's day were imprecise. It was less a program for execution than an assertion that Britain and France had certain interests in common and, more important, that these interests were exclusive to themselves. The entente worked as long as it meant an exclusive friendship and did not become a bargain in which Tunis was offset by Egypt in a chaffering spirit. It is equally certain that Gladstone and Granville destroyed it by first merging it in the Concert of Europe and then executing it as if it were a bargain.

At the time of the third Egyptian crisis all this lay in the future, and Anglo-French relations were based on the cordial understanding of July 1878. This already implied that France should fall behind Britain. H. C. Vivian was British agent and consul general in Egypt, and

6. Lyons to Salisbury, No. 572 Very Confidential, July 19, 1878, FO 27/2311 Salisbury to Lyons, No. 492, August 7, 1878, FO 27/2300; PRO 30/29/143; Waddington to d'Harcourt, October 4 and 10, 1878, *Documents diplomatiques français* [*DDF* hereafter], 1st series, 2, Nos. 347, 350.

7. *Parliamentary Papers* [*PP* hereafter] (1884), LXXXVIII, 385; *DDF*, 1st series, 2, No. 470.

8. *Gladstone-Granville, 1,* Nos. 474, 490, 491.

9. Ibid., No. 809; cf. Nos. 788–90, 924.

10. *Hansard Parliamentary Debates,* CCLXXI, 1498.

Godeaux, Monge, and Tricou succeeded each other as French representatives. Vivian took the lead in advising the khedive, and Godeaux took care that his audiences happened after those of Vivian and that he made them the occasion for reinforcing Vivian's advice.[11] The Egyptian army had been cut down and some 2,500 officers placed on half pay with the arrears of pay, still due to them, unpaid. The good object of cutting down state expenditure caused individual poverty and despair.[12] The crisis of February 18, 1879, was produced by a demonstration of army officers in Cairo. It was a crisis of authority. The government's failure to cope with the demonstration showed that, if the khedive had abdicated power, Nubar Pasha and his European ministers had not acquired it.

But this crisis was turned. A repair of the system of August 28, 1878, was botched together. Nubar Pasha was replaced as prime minister by Tewfiq Pasha, the khedive's son, who was soon to succeed him. The European ministers remained and were strengthened by being given a veto on all decisions, and Riaz Pasha was kept in office in defiance of the khedive's wish to dismiss him. The khedive remained powerless. This botched-up settlement did not long survive. In April 1879 the khedive staged a coup d'état. He declared that he would henceforth rule as before August 28, 1878, appointed Cherif Pasha his chief minister, dismissed the European ministers (though they were later invited to resume office in a consultative capacity), and produced his own plan for paying off his European debt. The result was the first direct intervention of the British government in Egypt.

In the early summer of 1879 the British government joined with that of France to bring about the deposition of the khedive. The two Powers acted together to gain the cooperation of the European Powers and action by the sultan.[13] Ismail himself, by refusing voluntary abdication, prevented Britain's share of responsibility for this Egyptian event from being disguised. Tewfiq acceded on June 27, 1879. In the autumn of the same year the measures recommended by the commission of inquiry were adopted and embodied in a khedivial decree of November 15, 1879. The British government shared with the French the responsibility for this decree and acknowledged that it did so.

11. See for example Godeaux to Waddington, No. 10, January 2, 1879, MAE CP Egypte, 62.

12. Godeaux to Waddington, telegram, February 18, 1879, ibid.

13. The steps in this cooperation may be followed in Salisbury to Lyons, FO 27/2358, and Lyons to Salisbury, April 12–June 26, 1879, FO 27/2366, 2367, 2368, 2369.

The chief of the institutions thus established was the Dual Control. Great care was taken to maintain continuity with the control of 1876 despite the break during the period of European ministers. Salisbury's whole policy and most deliberately adopted intention was to maintain the exclusiveness of the Anglo-French position in Egypt. He told Waddington that to abolish the control of 1876 and to institute a new one was to run the risk of provoking other Powers to ask why Britain and France should exercise exclusive supervision over the affairs of Egypt.[14] Salisbury intended that this was precisely what Britain and France should exercise, and in that order of precedence. The Dual Control should be established without opposition and appear incontestable because it had never been contested. The decree of November 15, 1879, therefore, followed the wording of that of November 18, 1876. There was to be a controller of receipts and a controller of expenditure; they were to share in the making of the budget, though the ultimate decision on the distribution of expenditure was to be left with the Egyptian minister of finance; they were to have wider powers of inspection than their predecessors; above all, one was to be British and the other French. The essential difference, that is between a control that had been exercised by European ministers and one under which the controllers were allowed no executive powers, did not appear in the decree. The change was effected by instructions to the controllers communicated to the khedive.

Salisbury had taken the initiative in masking the fact that the Dual Control constituted an innovation. But Waddington was equally firm in pursuing the purpose of this initiative: to maintain the exclusive character of the Anglo-French position. Austria-Hungary did demand European participation in the control. She proposed the nomination of a third controller who should represent the interests of Austria-Hungary, Germany, and Italy, and should be nominated by each of these states in turn. France took the lead in repelling this demand. Austria-Hungary abandoned it (in December) in face of the unbroken front presented by Britain and France.[15] Sir Evelyn Baring, who was appointed controller general by the British government, was a man of proconsular stature. The French acknowledged his combination of

14. Salisbury to Lyons, Nos. 1012, 1018, July 28, August 2, 1879, FO 27/2359; Lyons to Waddington, July 29, 1879, MAE CP Egypte, 64.

15. Negotiation summarized in Waddington to Ring, No. 45, December 8, 1879, MAE CP Egypte, 64, in the part not printed in *DDF*, 1st series, 2, No. 482; cf. Lyons to Salisbury, No. 1127 Very Confidential, November 11, 1879, FO 27/2375; for Waddington's attitude to Russia, see Lyons to Salisbury, No. 781 Confidential, July 23, FO 27/2371.

ability and authority, and from November 1879 to July 1880, when he was replaced by Sir Auckland Colvin, the control was exercised generously and tactfully but nonetheless with remorseless steadiness, as the virtual dictatorship of one man. Blignières, appointed by France, was a man of standing and authority in his own way, but he took the policy of cooperation with Britain to the point of placing Baring on a pedestal, "se contentant de poser lui-même à demi l'ombre sur le gradin de support." [16]

In addition to the Dual Control, the decree of November 15, 1879, established an international commission of liquidation with the task of framing a law of liquidation laying down clear prescriptions about the interest due to the creditors and the several uses to which the meager resources of the Egyptian government, now exactly known, might be put. On this body Britain and France had each two representatives and Austria-Hungary, Germany, and Italy one each. Britain and France, united, thus had a permanent majority. The greatest care was taken that the four, Auckland Colvin, Rivers Wilson, Bellaigue de Bughas, and Liron d'Airoles, should speak with one voice. Baring and Blignières acting together saw to this in the first instance, and if they failed, the diplomatic representatives, Edward Malet and Baron de Ring, then brought their influence to bear. The regularity with which Britain and France determined the decisions of the liquidation commission is evinced by the consternation when on one occasion they did not. Rivers Wilson, assertive and financially pedantic, separated himself from Colvin in insisting that any surplus of Egypt's revenue over expenditure in any one year should be devoted to increasing the interest payable to her creditors. He refused to accept a compromise and carried his own view against his British and French colleagues by means of the Austrian, German, and Italian votes. Malet and Ring both appealed to their governments to bring pressure on Wilson. Baring, Blignières, Malet, and Ring made their views plain to him. The night brought counsel to Wilson, and he contrived during subsequent meetings of the commission to undo his work.[17] The law of liquidation when signed by the khedive on July 17, 1880, substantially represented the successful operation of an exclusive Anglo-French entente. In July 1880 Baring was replaced by Sir Auckland Colvin, and in March 1882 Blignières was replaced by Léon Brédif. The control by then had solved the financial problem in its worst phase.

16. Ring to Barthélemy Saint-Hilaire, No. 135, December 11, 1880, MAE CP Egypte, 67

17. Ring to Freycinet, No. 83, May 24, 1880, ibid., 66.

During 1880 a third international body was set to work in Egypt. This was the commission representing ten, later fifteen, nations, with one representative each, who were concerned in the establishment of the so-called Mixed Tribunals (or Tribuneaux de la Réforme) in Egypt. These dealt with cases involving foreigners or foreign-protected persons, since justice was otherwise largely administered by the religious authorities. The commission was charged with the task of reforming these institutions and elaborating a code which they should apply. The five years for which the tribunals had been established in 1875 was about to end. The commission repeatedly suspended its work, and the period of the tribunals' existence was twice extended (leaving them in existence and unreformed until February 1883) before the British occupation of Egypt finally brought it to an end. In this commission Anglo-French paramountcy was also assured, for the small states attached themselves to Britain and France and enabled them to outvote Austria-Hungary, Germany, and Italy.

In November 1879 an Anglo-French condominium had been established in Egypt. Both controllers were the nominees of their government. A new phase had been opened in the Egyptian question. This was recognized when both Britain and France appointed men of standing to the post of agent and consul general in Egypt. H. C. Vivian had been replaced by Frank Lascelles in April 1879. He still only had the rank of secretary of embassy. In October he was sent as minister to Sofia and replaced by a senior man, Edward Baldwin Malet. Lascelles was no less able than Malet, whom he was to succeed in 1895 as ambassador in Berlin, but it was important to signalize the greater part henceforward to be played in Egyptian affairs by the British government. On the French side, Monge remained as second in command, but the Baron de Ring was put over him in December 1879.

The institution of the Dual Control marked an increase in Egyptian dependence. The enactment of the law of liquidation on July 17, 1880, ended the period when the Egyptian question was primarily financial. Resources were henceforward as well known as the debt. It was impossible that Egypt's arrangements with her creditors should be again overset by the disclosure of new deficiencies in the revenue or in the machinery for collecting it. A new breakdown would not be a financial one, but a collapse of authority. The Egyptian quesion had become a question of who was to be master in Egypt. From 1880 to 1881 it was nominally the khedive and his ministers; to the more discerning eye it was Britain and France; to the most acute eye it was already Britain.

A third result of the establishment of the Dual Control was a loss of position by France. Her political influence declined. Waddington had already conceded paramountcy to Britain when he accepted the appointment of Rivers Wilson to the Ministry of Finance and that of Blignières to the Ministry of Public Works. The post of minister of finance was one both of power in itself and of opportunity, since it allowed penetration into other departments. Englishmen by July 1879 headed the government of the Sudan, the Railway Administration, the Telegraph Office, the Post Office, the khedive's private secretariat, the Lighthouse and Port administration for the Mediterranean and the Red Sea, the administration of the Port of Alexandria, and the Customs administration. Frenchmen were installed in the Bulgah Museum and the Khedivial Library but were thrown back for any increase of influence upon a plan for the establishment of a School of Egypt on the lines of the School of Rome or Athens. The Ministry of Public Works had the chance of gaining contracts for French firms but was not especially successful in doing so. There were also ministries with Frenchmen in the second place to Englishmen. But as de Ring recorded in his first dispatch, "il n'y a donc dans le pays aucune administration purement française." [18] When in 1881 the English language was for the first time recognized as a permissible language in the courts and administration, the French lost their remaining political advantage. While French was the only language permissible in addition to Arabic, some Frenchmen were necessary in all administrations, and, in mixed administrations they had an advantage that balanced their subordinate position. The French foreign minister on at least three occasions [19] urged his agent in Cairo to seek to increase French representation in the Egyptian administration, and when it did not grow, the French controller, Blignières, was made the scapegoat. He could point to a handful of successes—some five—and could take comfort in the good quality of French officials.[20] But de Ring's remark, "il n'y a donc pas, je le répète, égalité de situation entre les deux pays" [21] was as incontestable in 1882 as it already was in 1879.

The financial stake of France in Egypt also declined. De Ring recorded in 1880 that the British took up Egyptian securities with greater eagerness than the French. This was so marked that he was

18. Ring to Waddington, No. 1 Confidential, December 27, 1879, ibid., 64; for return of Europeans employed in Egypt, see *PP* (1882), LXXXII 89, 189.

19. Waddington in December 1879, MAE CP Egypte, 64; Freycinet to Ring, No. 2, Confidential, January 13, 1880, and Private, February 8, 1880, ibid., 65; Freycinet to Ring, May 25, 1880, ibid., 66.

20. Blignières to Freycinet, May 30, 1880, ibid., 66.

21. Ring to Waddington, No. 1 Confidential, December 27, 1879, ibid., 64.

convinced that it was because the British government was more successful than the French in creating confidence in these securities, and he begged his own government to outdo the British here. Freycinet penciled in exasperation: "Quel moyen *pratique* indique M. de Ring pour [cet] objet." [22] French trade dropped. The overall increase in Egyptian imports during 1880 was estimated at 31 percent but the increase in French imports at 24 percent only. The trade of France in Egypt had for three years been stationary, and in 1880 "il a pris un développement exceptionel," [23] but the fact remained that it had not increased as much as the British. The French colony had declined because of the poor success of Frenchmen in gaining concessions. Egypt enjoyed a good year, but the French colony had done badly. "Notre colonie tend à diminuer numériquement et malgré l'essor général du commerce égyptien celui que font ici nos nationaux languit." [24] British trade already represented in 1881 70 percent of Egyptian trade and was increasing. When in September 1880 Barthélemy Saint-Hilaire succeeded Freycinet, the decline of the French position was accentuated. He relaxed the pressure upon Blignières to gain the appointment of Frenchmen to administrative positions, though he renewed anxious inquiries about French trade and influence. In February 1881 de Ring was first rebuked and then sharply recalled when, in circumstances to be described presently, he went ahead of his British colleague in attempting to prepare the way for the succession of his own nominee to Riaz Pasha.[25] There was, then, joint control, but there was no doubt about its being more British than French.

Egyptian opposition to foreign control introduced yet another factor into the situation. Its earliest spokesmen were the seventy-five members of the Chamber of Notables or the *Chambre des Délégués*. These men were elected: either one or two for each constituency according to its population, by electors nominated by the headmen or sheikhs of the villages. They were Muslim Arab landowners of standing elected by Muslim Arab landowners of somewhat lower standing. The foreign communities of businessmen and merchants were wholly alien to them. They were first called together in December 1878 and were in session from January to April 1879. They became increasingly restive at the failure of Nubar Pasha's Ministry to consult them; they

22. Ring to Freycinet, No. 28, February 14, 1880, ibid., 65.

23. Blignières to Barthélemy Saint-Hilaire, April 23, 1881, ibid., 66, with documents of 1880.

24. Ring to Barthélemy Saint-Hilaire, No. 135, December 11, 1880, ibid., 67.

25. Barthélemy Saint-Hilaire to Ring, telegram, telegram drafted by himself, and further telegram, February 18, 19, and 22, 1881, ibid., 68.

were ready to rally to the khedive but, conscious of their own independent strength, they defied the Ministry when it decreed the end of the session.

At about this time, the spring of 1879, the sheikhs in the villages, outside and apart from the Chamber of Notables, became the spokesmen of anti-European and particularly of anti-British feeling. Rivers Wilson made no secret of his contempt for Egyptian corruption, dishonesty, and misgovernment. He had made a tour through Egypt in an endeavor to assure the tax revenue. The sheikhs were provoked to protest to the Ministry of Finance that the areas for which they were responsible could not pay what was demanded. Wilson had not hesitated to replace Egyptian employees in the Ministry of Finance by Englishmen, commanding higher salaries and able to exact payment of them while Egyptian officials were unpaid. He was preparing to engage forty Europeans in the cadastral survey, about to be undertaken as a preliminary to the reassessment of the land tax, when there were French-trained Egyptian soldiers capable of doing the work.[26] London supported Rivers Wilson. The reason Vivian had been replaced by Lascelles in April 1879 was because he had criticized Wilson's methods. Yet these officials, since Britain's colonial and Indian services took the cream of her able men, could not always justify privilege by ability. The excessive employment of Europeans and tax discriminations in their favor were recognized by Sir Auckland Colvin, when he replaced Baring in 1880, and by Gladstone and Granville in 1882, as genuine grievances and as causes of the anti-foreign sentiment.[27] In the third place, Nubar Pasha, as a Christian and an Armenian, French-speaking and French-educated, provoked between August 1878 and April 1879 widespread Egyptian hostility which the army officers clearly expressed. This was reflected in his want of authority throughout the country. Yet his position was ambiguous, since by 1881 he was as much opposed to the khedive as the army officers were. Phrases such as "great unrest in Upper Egypt" or "widespread effervescence throughout the country" recur in the British and French reports. Even the khedive's coup d'état of April 1879 appeared to the French representative as a cession to "le sentiment national."[28]

26. This unfavorable view of Wilson is based on the French correspondence, see e.g. Godeaux to Waddington, No. 25, January 21, 1879, No. 41, February 20, 1879, ibid., 62.

27. Mem. by Colvin enclosed in Malet to Granville, No. 389 Confidential, December 26, 1882, FO 78/3326. *Gladstone-Granville, 1,* Nos. 849, 919, 924.

28. Godeaux to Waddington, No. 76, April 9, 1879, MAE CP Egypte, 63.

After June 1880, although Tewfiq consolidated his power on the basis of cooperation with his Anglo-French advisers and the long-lived Ministry of Riaz Pasha (September 21, 1879, to September 13, 1881), unrest worsened. The legitimate grievances of the army officers remained unredressed. Simultaneously in the Sudan the khedive's authority, represented by an Englishman as governor-general (General Gordon, whose destiny was already connected with the Sudan), yielded in 1880 before the national and religious force of the Mahdi. In Cairo discontent was openly voiced again on May 23 and 24. A newspaper, published in Cairo in French, had been suppressed for printing an alleged incitement not to pay taxes. The Egyptian government appealed for support to its British and French advisers. Since the posting of certain army officers to distant garrisons, the dismissal of certain officials, the retirement of Nubar Pasha to take the waters at Bad Kissingen and of Cherif Pasha to plant cotton on the Nile Delta quietened this agitation, the British were inclined to dismiss it as factitious.[29] It was thought real enough in retrospect. Even at the end of May 1880 it was impossible not to notice that the village headmen were still centers of disaffection, and that "l'opinion est très monté." [30] The suppression of the Moukabala tax, thought to work in favor of the foreign element, the constant evidence of higher salaries going to foreign than to Egyptian officials, and, in August, the enactment of universal military service created real grievances.

A revolutionary situation was being created during that annus mirabilis of Egyptian prosperity, 1880. Prosperity and the knowledge of what was due from him in tax, military service, or labor released the fellah from the apathy that years of arbitrary oppression had induced. The harvests were good and the operation of the Nile flood favorable. The peasant was inclined to listen to the local headman who promised him even better conditions if the regime were changed. Above all the position in the army deteriorated. The reduction of its size continued. For some four to five hundred officers on active service there were some thirteen hundred on half pay. Every three months those on active service were supposed to be replaced by a new batch of those on half pay. But the system was worked so that privileged Circassians, Turks, and others were always on active service while native Egyptians were unable to keep themselves and their families in food and shelter. Moreover a group of leaders was emerging.

All this was made plain by the mutiny of the colonels on February 1,

29. Ring to Freycinet, No. 94, June 12, 1880, ibid., 66.
30. Ring to Freycinet, No. 84, May 31, 1880, ibid., 66,

1881. The Arab colonel of a regiment of cavalry had been dismissed and replaced by a Circassian, a member of the privileged element in the army; the Arab officers petitioned the prime minister, Riaz Pasha, for the reinstatement of the Arab; the government answered by the arrest of the three colonels to whose regiments the petitioners belonged. The officers mutinied and forced the release of the three colonels. The outcome was a very considerable weakening of the authority of Riaz Pasha, so much so that de Ring now began to prepare the way for a successor. The minister of war was now changed, some attempt was made to reemploy the half-pay officers in other work; their pay, and later that of all officers, was raised; a commission of inquiry was set up to devise other remedies. These concessions further weakened the authority of the khedive and his government. The two necessary elements of a revolutionary situation were there: on one side, subjects who were gradually becoming convinced that anything was possible to them; on the other side, authority that had come to distrust itself and ceased to exact any respect. But the movement was still directed only to the removal of particular grievances, privileges, and injustices. When in May 1881 the French occupied Tunis, the movement found a general purpose which included all particular and local causes.[31] The French action gave point and meaning to all that had gone before. The explanation of Egyptian bankruptcy, of the penetration of foreigners into the Egyptian government, and of the deflection of Egyptian money into foreign pockets was that Egypt was destined to the same fate as Tunis. In the secret meetings by night of the army officers, which continued throughout the summer, Arabi Bey had a subject for his harangues and a basis on which he could build his leadership. He bade his followers be on their guard ready to defend Egyptian independence; for the occupation of Egypt by Britain was about to follow that of Tunis by France.

Egypt had already passed through three crises. Each had been followed by a strengthening of the European control and a widening of the range of discontent. The climax of the autumn of 1881 was devastating in its consequences. On September 6, 1881, news from Cairo was that the army was relatively quiet but that colonels were touring the villages to rouse the population against the Europeans.[32] Three days later, like a clap of thunder from a clear sky, came Arabi Bey's demonstration. On September 9, four regiments besieged the

31. Monge to Barthélemy Saint-Hilaire, No. 57, June 30, 1881, ibid., 69.

32. Sienkiewiz to Barthélemy Saint-Hilaire, No. 22, September 6, 1881, ibid., 70.

khedive in the Abedin Palace, demanding the dismissal of Riaz Pasha, the reinstatement of Cherif Pasha, and the redress of grievances. The khedive telegraphed for help to the sultan, asking him for twenty battalions, a small army. The French representative telegraphed for a naval division to be sent to the eastern Mediterranean.[33] Malet, returning from leave as chance would have it, was in Constantinople, and the French believed the worst. The event of September 9 was more than a demonstration of the army: but its purport was not clear. Arabi was fumbling for remedies that would put right what he and his followers obscurely felt to be wrong. He might find a *point d'appui* in the cry of Egypt for the Egyptians, but he had no alternative regime to offer. Cherif Pasha was not a national leader. He was a pure Turk who had come early in life to Egypt from Constantinople. He was well-versed in French thought and ways, and he did not hate the foreigner. The Egyptians he treated as a conquered people. In demanding his appointment the army tacitly confessed that it did not know what the root of trouble was or where the remedy lay. There was, in short, a complete vacuum of power in the whole Nile valley.

There were three possible ways in which the vacuum might be filled. The first—that it should be filled by Turkey—was especially attractive to the legalist mind of Gladstone: the more so since he was too preoccupied with the Irish question for any checks on this legalism, which more thorough reflection might have suggested, to occur to him. It seemed possible of achievement: since the khedive had appealed for troops to the sultan; Malet urged intervention upon him; and Sienkiewiz, the new French agent in Cairo, favored Turkish troops acting under the direction of a British and a French general.[34] The British position was that Turkish troops were preferable to any others, if armed action became necessary, and meanwhile Britain proposed the dispatch to Cairo of Turkish generals with orders to disband the mutinous regiments. The French government's response was outright rejection of Turkish intervention of any kind. Turkish intervention would be "funeste à l'œuvre de civilisation et de progrès que la France et l'Angleterre poursuivent en commun au bord du Nil." "Toute intervention de la Porte Ottomane sous quelque forme et quelque pré-

33. Sienkiewiz to Barthélemy Saint-Hilaire, telegram, September 10, 1881, ibid., 70, *DDF*, 1st series, *4*, No. 119

34. Malet to Granville, No. 246 Confidential, September 21, 1881, FO 78/3324; Sienkiewiz to Barthélemy Saint-Hilaire, telegram, September 12, 1881, MAE CP Egypte, 70.

texte qu'elle se produisît . . . serait désastreuse pour l'Egypte." Barthélemy Saint-Hilaire developed his theme at length, rejected Sienkiewiz' own view, and concluded that any revival of Turkish authority in Egypt would be a reversal of the policy France had followed for more than half a century. Two days later he wrote to Sienkiewiz: "Je vous prie d'écarter absolument tout projet de recours à la Porte Ottomane." Britain bowed to this opposition, disowned Malet's proceedings in Constantinople: he had in fact not committed his government; withdrew the proposal of Turkish generals: it was anyhow uncertain whether Rivers Wilson was right in thinking they would be obeyed.[35] In the event, two Turkish emissaries arrived in Cairo—on October 5, after the play was over—and the khedive under British and French guidance gave no opening for any assertion of Turkish authority.[36] The emissaries left on October 19, 1881. The notion of an assertion of Turkish power was quite unreal, and even Granville remarked that it might be thought incompatible with the previous Liberal attitude to Turkey.

The second way in which the vacuum might have been filled was by Arabi himself. The inauguration of the new Ministry, at his bidding, under Cherif Pasha on September 13, the great activity of the new Ministry in coping with immediate distress, and the decision to re-convene the Chamber of Notables seemed signs of success for the dogma that Egypt must save herself out of her own resources. It seemed that the new regime, with Arabi Bey behind it, might capture the movement and lead it along the path of orderly reform. Behind the appearance lay unfortunate realities. Cherif Pasha's position was false: in the last analysis he was too proud to dedicate himself to the cause of a people he despised. Arabi's position was equally false: Sir Auckland Colvin had guided him in the formulation of his demands, and their satisfaction, therefore, put him in a false position with his own followers. The French response to the development of British policy that had taken place, not by decisions in London but by Colvin's action in Cairo, was to propose to take it to its logical conclusion. Barthélemy Saint-Hilaire suggested the institution of a military control by British and French generals which might become the counterpart of the financial control, reform the army, strengthen its authority,

35. Barthélemy Saint-Hilaire to Sienkiewiz, telegrams, September 11, 13, 20, 1881, ibid., 70. *Gladstone-Granville, 1,* Nos. 528, 529, p. 292 nn. 4 and 5.

36. Sienkiewiz to Barthélemy Saint-Hilaire, No. 43, October 10, 1881, MAE CP Egypte, 70.

but keep it in leading strings.[37] This proposal met the temporizing opposition of Britain and was dropped when the situation improved. It was accepted, however, to the extent that identical instructions were sent to Malet and Sienkiewiz to assure the khedive of British and French support in retaining Cherif Pasha's Ministry.[38] No progress had in fact been made toward a normal regime: the khedive remained without power or authority; Arabi Bey did not acquire power through the existence of Cherf's Ministry; Cherif himself had no independent power but was dependent upon Arabi and the army. "C'est impossible de dire," wrote Sienkiewiz, "où réside le pouvoir effectif." [39]

The third solution was that Britain and France should themselves fill the vacuum of power. Both were clear that their primary need was for each other on the basis of the entente of September 1878. Britain was equally clear that any extension of Anglo-French control was to be avoided. France, however, was less clear. Her response to the British insistence on the closest concert was to propose the mission of two ships to be present off Alexandria at the time when the Turkish emissaries arrived. Barthélemy Saint-Hilaire's pretext for making the proposal was that the ships were needed for the protection of British and French nationals if the arrival of the Turks provoked an outburst of Muslim fanaticism. Granville and Gladstone accepted the proposal on that basis. The French ship *Alma* arrived on October 10, H.M.S. *Invincible* on October 20. They left together on the following day. This inexpensive demonstration of Anglo-French amity was deliberately intended by Barthélemy Saint-Hilaire. In a private letter to Sienkiewiz he acknowledged that the protection of nationals had been a mere pretext, that the initiative had been French and not British, and that the earlier arrival of the French ship had not been accidental but contrived. "Pour moi," he concluded, "le résultat considérable de la démonstration navale, c'est précisément d'avoir montré au monde la bonne et réelle intelligence des deux gouvernements au bord du Nil." [40] It chimed exactly, however, with the British mood. Gladstone wrote to Granville at this time, "I shall be glad if you can arrange for some

37. Barthélemy Saint-Hilaire to Sienkiewiz, telegram, September 14, 1881, ibid., 70.

38. Barthélemy Saint-Hilaire to Sienkiewiz, telegram, October 7, 1881, ibid., 70; Granville to Lyons, No. 952A Most Confidential, October 1, 1881, FO 27/2422.

39. Sienkiewiz to Barthélemy Saint-Hilaire, No. 40, October 4, 1881, MAE CP Egypte, 70.

40. Barthélemy Saint-Hilaire to Sienkiewiz, Private, holograph, October 27, 1881, ibid., 70.

joint act with France which may have the effect of discouraging Bismarck's intrigues." Granville telegraphed to Malet asking whether he could suggest any "useful or harmless action that we can take with France." [41] This line of policy led nowhere, however, as long as neither Power was prepared to take over the government of Egypt. The failure of the two to do anything to fill the vacuum of power in Egypt created in September 1881 was a turning point. It was the last hour at which this might have been done deliberately. When Britain eventually acted and took over the government of Egypt, she did so without premeditation and in response to immediate circumstances.

The next phase in the question should have been clarification in Egypt. That it was not so was due to the accident of a change of government in France. On November 14 Léon Gambetta became both prime minister and minister for foreign affairs. He was still, at 43, a relatively young man at the height of his powers; he carried with him all the authority derived from his leadership of the resistance to the Germans after Sedan; he attracted the support of all those who valued the French Revolutionary tradition; he had behind him the more recent triumph of the August elections; his party of about 200, though not enough to dominate an assembly of 533 deputies, was considerable as French parliamentary parties went. But his was a ministry of one man: he could not gain colleagues of standing and talent. Gambetta at the Quai d'Orsay meant a positive policy of assertion. In relation to Egypt it meant the joint note, dated January 7, 1882, and read to the khedive on January 8. By this communication Britain and France briefly declared that the maintenance of the khedive on the throne of Egypt was the best guarantee of good order and material progress, that they wished to assure the khedive of their support in the maintenance of the existing order of things so as to parry (parer à) all causes of domestic or foreign complications. The pretext for the demarche was the imminent meeting of the Chamber of Notables.

The origin of the particular form which Gambetta's initiative took was threefold. First, it originated in the British wish to take some useful or harmless action with the French, already alluded to. This explains the British response to a proposal which was out of key with the normal British policy, as Granville was later to recognize, of avoiding provocation.

Second, it originated in a French misunderstanding of the British dispatch of November 4, 1881. This document, cast in high-sounding

41. *Gladstone-Granville, 1,* 298; Granville to Malet, telegram No. 58, October 4 and reply telegram No. 75, October 5, 1881, FO 78/3327.

generalities, was intended for domestic consumption. It was published at once—in *The Times,* since Parliament was not sitting—as a statement of British policy in Egypt to quiet the Liberals' own supporters in the country.[42] It was understood by the French as a manifesto for foreign consumption. Sienkiewiz drew attention to its reference to the bond between Turkey and Egypt as having value only in keeping other European Powers out of Egypt. He especially drew attention to its reservation of British liberty of action in the event of anarchy in Egypt. He added: "Lorsequ'un gouvernement ne fait dépendre son action que d'une condition dont il s'institue seul juge, c'est qu'il tient évidemment à ce que cette condition se produise."[43] Gambetta, in his first dispatch to Sienkiewiz, referred to his having read his No. 69 of November 14 which discusses the effect of the dispatch of November 4. It is perhaps a sign of Gambetta's interest that No. 69 is missing from the archives and only the telegram summarizing it is there.

In the third place the form of the note originated in an increasing French suspicion that Britain was working toward intervention, whether British or Turkish. Sienkiewiz made this one of his principal themes in surveying the state of the Egyptian question for the benefit of the new arrival at the Quai d'Orsay.[44] Again and again he drew a distinction between official British policy, which maintained the entente with France, and the tendencies of decisions and actions on the spot which always increased Britain's influence at the expense of that of France.[45] Sienkiewiz proposed, as a way of counteracting these tendencies, that yet another change of khedive should be attempted. Halim Pasha might replace Tewfiq and be kept under French influence. The departmental note referred to later begins by rejecting this project, and the joint note itself contains, in its reference to keeping Tewfiq on the throne, a sentence that can only be understood in the light of Sienkiewiz's proposal.

The intention of the joint note, though Britain did not understand this, was, within the general purpose of making heard the voice of France, to procure from Britain some statement that would bind her about intervention. There survives at the Quai d'Orsay a French de-

42. *The Times,* November 25, 1881, p. 6a; Granville to Malet, No. 261, November 4, 1881, FO 78/3320; *PP* (1882), LXXXII, 1.

43. Sienkiewiz to Barthélemy Saint-Hilaire, telegram, November 9, 1881, and to Gambetta, No. 77, November 28, 1881, MAE CP Egypte, 71.

44. Sienkiewiz to Gambetta, No. 73, November 21, 1881, ibid., 71.

45. E.g. Sienkiewiz to Barthélemy Saint-Hilaire, No. 55 Confidentielle, November 8, 1881; to Gambetta, Private, November 27, 1881, No. 94, December 12, 1881, ibid., 71.

partmental note that "le ministre pense . . . qu'il y aurait lieu de poser dès à présent une question formelle à l'Angleterre sur ce qu'elle compte faire, de concert avec nous le jour où une nouvelle émeute militaire mettrait le pouvoir du Khédive en peril." It lists three possibilities: Turkish intervention; Anglo-French intervention; no intervention. It ends: "Il faudrait que le cabinet anglais s'explique clairement là dessus." [46]

The justification for judging the intention of the note wholly from the French side is that both the initial proposal and the final text were French. Granville was passive. He recognized that the meeting of the Chamber of Notables would be a turning point. "We shall be in a scrape, if we are not prepared with any policy," he wrote, but added, "I am not prepared to propose anything." [47] Gambetta, however, acted at once in accordance with the departmental note of December 12 and made a formal proposal to Lord Lyons.[48] In London there were no regular cabinet meetings since Parliament stood adjourned. Granville wondered whether it should not be summoned but did not press his suggestion, though Gladstone would have adopted it. He did, however, consult Malet who saw no objections. He then accepted (December 27) Gambetta's proposal. Gambetta then drafted the text, and after two further conversations with Lyons it was ready on December 30 and sent to London on December 31. The cabinet was then summoned for the following Friday, January 6. Granville asked it to accept Gambetta's text as it stood. Chamberlain demurred at this and insisted on adding the reservation "that it did not commit Britain to any particular subsequent course." [49] One notes that this reservation which, if taken seriously would have completely traversed Gambetta's intention, came from Chamberlain the future imperialist. Granville accepted it but also, in putting it to Gambetta, explained it away. The reserve did not exclude Anglo-French action and meant that Britain kept her freedom "sur le mode d'action seulement." Thus the note as read to the khedive on January 8 was a wholly Gambettist measure, the reflection of his intentions.

Although the clarification in Egypt, owing to the advent of

46. Note signed R.M. dated December 12, 1881, ibid., 71.

47. *Gladstone-Granville, 1,* No. 588.

48. Lyons to Granville, No. 1122 Confidential, December 15, 1881, FO 27/2499.

49. *Gladstone-Granville, 1,* 321, n. 1, 326, n. 4; Granville to Lyons, Nos. 1228, December 19 and 27, 1881, FO 27/2487; Malet to Granville, telegram No. 123, December 27, 1881, FO 78/3327; Lyons to Granville, Nos. 1161, 1162, 1172, 1180, December 24, 29, 31, 1881, FO 27/2499.

Gambetta, attracted little attention, it did happen after the Chamber of Notables met on December 23. The movement in Egypt became more definite. It was a coalescence of the army, whose spokesman was Arabi Bey, the landowners, speaking through the Chamber of Notables, and the Mohammedan element, speaking through the ulema and the university of Al Azhar. One of Arabi's earliest measures after he became minister of war was to attach a sheikh to each regiment responsible for preserving its Muslim character. One recognizes the elements of the "natural Right" as it existed in industrialized Europe, after the growth of an urbanized revolutionary Left. What in Europe represented a survival from an earlier agrarian society was in non-industrialized Egypt (where those concerned with business and industry tended to be foreigners) the natural governing class of a native agrarian society. The future might not lie with it, given the process of economic change, but in the circumstances of the time it represented the only active political power in the country.

It posed an insoluble problem to the English Liberals who belonged, by their practices and interests, to the midnineteenth century business world of economic capitalism and, by their convictions and ideals, to the supporters of national self-determination. Both Britain and France recognized that, if they accepted it, they must surrender not only political, but also financial control of Egypt. If they combatted it they must surrender their ideals. The tendency of the British in these circumstances was to be sceptical of the national character of the Egyptian movement. An extreme position was that its members were misguided, self-seeking, or ignorant men, the victims of Arabi Bey's criminal disloyalty to his sovereign. The tendency of the French was to maintain complete reserve, to play for time, and meanwhile to cultivate such relations with the leaders of the movement as would give them confidence in France. Both governments lived from hand to mouth.

The proceedings of the Chamber of Notables began with a speech by Cherif Pasha in which the members were invited to debate and decide on their powers on the basis of a *projet de règlement* presented to them. The Chamber chose a committee of sixteen from itself to deal with details and in a businesslike way set to the task of gaining a very considerable enlargement of its powers. Before the *règlement organique* was finally enacted on February 9, 1882, the Chamber and Cherif's Ministry had each drafted three projects or counterprojects, the controllers general had intervened with an eminently wise set of proposals, and Cherif's Ministry had been replaced by one nominated by the Chamber and composed of its leaders. The Egyptian movement had been moderate, responsible, and successful in its purposes. The Chamber had sought to transform the meaningless Article 18 about ministers being "solidairement responsable vis à vis de la Chambre" into a real power to turn out a ministry in whom it had lost confidence and replace it by another. This it achieved when on February 2 Cherif Pasha resigned and the khedive, under the guidance of Malet and Sienkiewiz, asked the Chamber to name either a list of ministers acceptable to it or else a president of the council who would then name his colleagues. The new Ministry, the so-called Ministry of February 2, under Mahmoud Samy Baroudi, included Arabi Bey, as minister for war. In the second place, the Chamber demanded real legislative power. This involved a strengthening of the articles that allowed it to discuss and vote projects of law coming to it on the initiative of the Ministry, and laid it down (Article 28) "que nul impôt nouveau, direct ou indirect, foncier, mobilier ou personnel ne peut être établi en Egypte sans une loi votée par la Chambre des Délégués." These articles would be strengthened to give it the right to initiate legislation. A compromise, the work of Sir Auckland Colvin, withheld legislative initiative but, referring to the special knowledge and position of the Notables in relation to the affairs of the villages, public works, irrigation, and education, assured them of special consideration on these subjects. Finally and most important the Chamber claimed the right to vote the budget. Article 22 of the original *projet de règlement* allowed it to express "des avis sur le budget" and Article 35 to do this for the budget of each department. Article 34 excluded from their advice money set aside for the tribute to Turkey, the servicing of the public debt, and any other funds governed by the law of liquidation or international obligations. The claim to control the budget was for two months the crux of a prolonged conflict in which the fate of the Anglo-French control was clearly at stake. The final settlement carefully preserved the text of the all-important Article 34, but otherwise made a concession largely designed by Malet but influenced also by Colvin and Blignières. The whole budget was to continue as before to be decided by the Council of Ministers in consultation with the controllers general. The budget for the interior, covering public works, irrigation, education, and village police, was to be decided and voted by a commission composed in equal parts of members of the Chamber and of the Ministry. This settlement was not made without a considerable strain on the Anglo-French entente, but it survived.

There were also other causes of strain. Britain entertained a project for a note supplementary to and explanatory of the joint note of January 7. France found it inacceptable. Granville in London, Malet in Cairo, and Lyons in Paris, to a less degree, were all taken by surprise when the Egyptian government regarded the joint note as a declaration heralding a tightening of the Anglo-French control; when the Chamber of Notables, since the note came down so heavily on the side of the status quo, considered it as a proclamation of opposition to them; and when Austria-Hungary, Germany, and Italy, since it was such a clear affirmation of Anglo-French exclusiveness, thought it a demarche against *them.* Malet, on the evening of January 9 in Cherif Pasha's presence, proposed to Sienkiewiz an explanatory note to counteract these misunderstandings. Granville, without any view of his own, referred the proposal, when it came to him, through Lyons to the French. It met the sharpest possible opposition from Gambetta. Malet, however, pursued his course at Cairo proposing in face of this opposition that the khedive should reply to the joint note in such a way that the explanation could be given in response to his reply. This also the French sharply opposed.[50] From Gambetta's point of view the joint note had achieved its purpose and he wished now to be silent. Granville, dilatory and only looking for a reasonable attitude to take, was scarcely aware of what was involved and ended by giving Malet instructions that left him discretion to make an explanation or not as he thought fit, while he gave to the French ambassador in London, Challemel Lacour, the strongest assurances of his loyalty to the union with France.[51] Sienkiewiz succeeded in dissuading the khedive from replying to the joint note so that Malet had no chance to make his explanation, while Gambetta, with much cleverness, limited himself to making the most of the assurances given to Challemel Lacour.

France on her side strained the entente by continually playing with the idea of a naval demonstration. Ever since Barthélemy Saint-Hilaire had caused the *Alma* and H.M.S. *Invincible* to come to Alexandria in October 1881, Sienkiewiz had harped on the effectiveness of a strong French force in the eastern Mediterranean. Gambetta, therefore, proposed to send a cruiser to show that the French were serious in resisting the demands of the Chamber of Notables. Sienkiewiz now

50. Sienkiewiz to Gambetta, telegrams, January 9, 10, 11, and dispatch No. 117 confidentielle, January 12, 1882; Gambetta to Sienkiewiz, telegrams, January 10 and 11, 1882, MAE CP Egypte, 72; Malet to Granville and Granville to Malet, telegrams, January 9–16, 1882, FO 78/3448, FO 78/3446; Granville to Lyons, telegrams, Nos. 1 and 2, January 11, 1882, FO 27/2574.

51. Challemel Lacour to Gambetta, January 16, 1882, DDF, 1st series, 4, No. 233; Gambetta to Sienkiewiz, January 17, 1882, MAE CP Egypte, 72.

drew back. Whereupon Gambetta telegraphed: "Veuillez me dire si à votre avis l'envoi d'un ou plusieurs navirs vous paraît utile." [52] He also asked for guidance about the precise moment when they should be sent, if they were desired. While the tide of national sentiment was rising, Sienkiewiz believed, the Egyptians would resent being treated like Turkey at the time of the naval demonstration off Montenegro in 1880, and recommended only the strengthening of French forces at the Piraeus.[53] Gambetta did this. When the more temporizing Freycinet succeeded him, the policy was adopted of keeping single French warships, on their way through the Canal to the Far East, at Port Said as long as possible. The frigate *Victorieuse* lingered at Port Said until the cruiser *Alma* arrived at the Piraeus from Toulon. Later the *Reine Blanche* called at Alexandria, and Freycinet fell in with Sienkiewiz' view that another should replace it quickly, "pour habituer les Egyptiens à voir flotter pavillon sans appréhension." [54]

Much the most important cause of strain was that Gambetta was stiffer than Malet, Granville, or Gladstone in wishing to resist the demands of the Chamber of Notables. The controllers general had wished to present a stiff memorandum denying all right to vote any part of the budget in any circumstances. Sienkiewiz opposed this as a naked assertion of foreign power and preferred to "traîner les choses en longueur." Malet believed that the Ministry, which Cherif Pasha still led, must resist the demand, but he feared that a conflict between the Ministry and the Chamber might cause a new crisis. Both Sienkiewiz and Malet were determined that international rights should not be impaired, but this fear led Malet to search for a compromise. His first suggestion was that one might be found by promising the right to control the budget for the future, say, for the budgets of 1884 and 1885. Gambetta and Granville were, however, united in thinking this postponed the difficulty and did not solve it. Thenceforward Gambetta was unshakable in stiffening Cherif Pasha's opposition to the Chamber. Granville, however, in rejecting Malet's proposal, told him that he might hold out the hope of some part of their demands being considered later.[55] At the same time Gladstone wrote, "the demand of the Chamber to deal with the non-assigned revenues is not on the

52. Gambetta to Sienkiewiz, telegram, January 16, 1882, MAE CP Egypte, 72.

53. Sienkiewiz to Gambetta, No. 18, January 18, 1882, ibid.

54. Sienkiewiz to Freycinet, telegram, February 22, 1882, ibid.

55. Malet to Granville, telegrams, FO 78/3448; Granville to Malet, telegrams, FO 78/3446; Lyons to Granville, telegrams, FO 27/2574; Granville to Lyons, telegrams, FO 27/2573.

surface of it unreasonable. . . . If in this country, there were given me the Spirit, Tobacco and Beer Duties, I should not mind undertaking to provide for the National Debt leaving all other Revenue & Charge to the House of Commons." Again, in urging a compromise he wrote, "think of Bismarck & the Turk fighting the battle of representative and popular principles against us!" He was shocked that Gambetta was so determined to withhold power from the Chamber of Notables. "I am a little disappointed at not finding in Gambetta any sign that he counts popular principles for any thing in the matter." On January 31 he could not but "be struck by the total absence from Gambetta's Memorandum on the Notables of any indication of the spirit of a true Liberal." [56] Granville was advised throughout, perhaps disastrously, by Rivers Wilson who was attached to Nubar Pasha and entirely unsympathetic to the Egyptians. It was Gladstone who pressed forward with insistence, and constructive ideas, to the discovery of a compromise that gave the Chamber of Notables the measure of control it won over domestic expenditure. Malet formulated and carried it through in Cairo. Gambetta remained uncompromising. "Ne conseillez pas de concessions; ne parlez pas d'intervention; gagnez du temps," he telegraphed, though Sienkiewiz might point out what large powers the *projet de règlement* already gave the Notables. "Gagner du temps sans engager toutefois mon gouvernement" was the line Sienkiewiz took.[57] Gladstone, in developing his policy in a characteristic direction, had so strained the entente that had Gambetta remained in office it must have broken. Freycinet's advent and the accession of the nationalist Ministry enabled the "settlement" of February 1882 to be achieved.

Gladstone was at the same time seeking to Europeanize the Egyptian question. At Cairo Malet, when the constitutional question first caused him to fear a conflict between the Ministry and the Chamber, had ventilated the idea of a demonstration by all the Great Powers as a way of calming excitement. The French, seeing every proposal while Gambetta was in office as improving or depressing France's position in relation to that of Britain, opposed the idea. Britain would have a favored position among the Great Powers and would not share it with France, or, as Sienkiewiz later wrote, France would have been again in the position in which she was in 1840. Malet, however, had meanwhile telegraphed his proposal home, and Gladstone responded with

56. *Gladstone-Granville, 1,* Nos. 600, 606, 614, and 620.

57. Gambetta to Sienkiewiz, telegram, January 23, 1882; Sienkiewiz to Gambetta, January 29, 1882, MAE CP Egypte, 72.

alacrity. "Should you be very averse," he asked Granvlle, "to extending the Anglo-French concert in Egypt to an European concert?" Granville simultaneously formulated a different version of the same idea: that Britain and France, while continuing to act together, should do so as "the mandatories of Europe." The proposal, however, met the decided and ably argued opposition of Lord Lyons. His main ground of dissent was that Britain would lose her freedom of action, while still probably bearing the brunt of anything that might be done; since she alone had such large financial and commercial interests that she must defend them and she alone had the naval power to do so effectively.[58] But Malet continued to work in Cairo in the direction in which Gladstone and Granville were thinking. "M. Malet," reported Sienkiewiz, "fasse que la France et l'Angleterre pourrait agir par délégation des grandes puissances." [59] Gladstone and Granville embodied their proposal in a draft to Lyons and it, together with Lyons' letters, was put before the cabinet. Lord Spencer, the lord president, and an old ally of Granville, and Lord Kimberley, colonial secretary, alone gave it their support. Hartington, secretary of state for India, was strongly opposed. "Whether it has ever been acknowledged in words or not," he wrote, "the joint action of England and France seems to be the simple and logical consequence, in case of necessity, of the present arrangement which we have accepted and which all Europe conceives we reaffirmed by the late joint note." Harcourt, the home secretary, supported Hartington. Bright and Chamberlain, for opposite reasons, abstained from expressing opinions. A variety of self-contradictory suggestions were made by others. Gladstone and Granville were reduced to formulating a general principle: namely, that, if the need for intervention arose, Britain wished that it should represent the united action and authority of Europe and that the sultan should be a party to any proceedings or discussions.[60] It was this policy that was so reprehensible to Gambetta. It was also the declaration of intentions

58. Sienkiewiz to Gambetta, telegram, January 14, dispatch No. 118 Confidentielle, January 16, 1882, ibid.; Sienkiewiz to Freycinet, No. 152, March 6, 1882, ibid., 73; Malet to Granville, telegram No. 17, January 14, 1882, FO 78/3448; *Gladstone-Granville, 1,* No. 606; Granville to Lyons, private, January 17, 1882, PRO 30/29/203, printed together with reply, January 19, Lord Newton, *Lord Lyons* (2 vols. London, 1913) *2,* 270–71.

59. Sienkiewiz to Gambetta, telegram and dispatch No. 123, January 21, 1882, MAE CP Egypte, 72.

60. Granville to Lyons, No. 110A Confidential, January 30, 1882, FO/2552, printed *PP* (1882), LXXXII; for cabinet opinions, see PRO 30/29/143; Granville to Lyons, telegram No. 144, February 6, 1882, FO 27/2573.

about intervention that his joint note had been intended to provoke. On the basis of this principle, an approach was made to the European Powers by Britain and France for the opening of discussions on the Egyptian question.[61] That the entente was thus maintained and that France accepted British policy, abandoned Gambetta's struggle for parity, and reconciled herself afresh to British paramountcy was due to the advent of Freycinet.

Gambetta had fallen (on January 27) over the choice between *scrutin de liste* and *scrutin d'arrondissement.* The return of solid blocs of Gambettist supporters from single departments was suspected to be his object in trying to introduce the former. The French Chamber showed that, under Thiers, it had had enough of the dictatorship that greater party cohesion was thought likely to cause, and Gambetta fell. Freycinet came in with the acknowledged mission of paying greater attention than Gambetta to the opinion of the Chamber. Action by France, concealed by the action of Europe, seemed to Freycinet to be a way of satisfying both the Chamber's wish to repudiate a strong Gambettist policy and his own inclination to maintain the influence and power of France. He fell in, therefore, with the Gladstone-Granville policy of Europeanization. It is significant of his wish to conceal initiative that when he explained his policy to the Chamber he said that Britain and France had *received* communications from the Great Powers, claiming the Egyptian question as the responsibility of Europe, not the truth that they had *approached* the Powers.[62]

The overture to the Powers of February 8–12 explains the presence, throughout the culminating crisis of the Egyptian question, of a conference of ambassadors at Constantinople. It discussed a variety of proposals for intervention in Egypt. These were reduced in the end to a proposal for Turkish intervention, and the ambassadors were engaged in the task of devising the conditions under which Turkish troops might be allowed to act in Egypt when the British occupation took place. The *formal* proposal for the conference came from France when the breakdown of May 12 provided the occasion for it. The first meeting was on June 23. Its deliberations had reached the point, on July 2, where it agreed to invite Turkey to send troops to Egypt and, on July 6, where it agreed on the text of the invitation and decided to

61. Granville to the British ambassadors at Berlin, Rome, St. Petersburg, and Vienna, February 8, 1882, FO 27/2532; the French circular was dated February 12, 1882, *DDF,* 1st series, *4,* No. 254.

62. See draft of his speech in MAE Freycinet papers *1,* dossier B, Egypte, pièce 1.

embody the conditions in a military convention between the European Powers on one side and Turkey on the other. On July 15 the British landing took place at Alexandria. The French expected the conference to restore the status quo ante, but it made no move to do so. The sultan, who had at first refused to take part in the conference, thought it wiser after the British landing to accept representation, but his participation brought the signature of the military convention no nearer. During the deadlock on the main question, the conference discussed, also ineffectually, measures for the protection of the Suez Canal. By August 18 the terms of the military convention had been adopted. Then the sultan's refusal to proclaim Arabi a rebel caused the whole project of Turkish intervention to be dropped. In the first week of September the conference died a natural death.

The Great Powers understood neither the relationship of Turkey to Egypt nor that of Turkey to themselves. Turkey had no objection to Egyptian opposition to European control; she was not opposed to Arabi's movement until the dismissal of the Circassian officers, and she was prepared to deal with that as an isolated event; she had no particular goodwill toward the khedive, a nominee of the European Powers and not a success in maintaining Turkish authority in Egypt; and she was resolved, anyhow, not to be the mere instrument of European action in Egypt.

While the conference was still in the future, discussions in Egypt centered on a strengthening of Article 34 in the *règlement organique* enacted in February. Britain and France agreed with some difficulty on a new text (March 14) but suspended their demand for its adoption by the Chamber, lest it should upset the precarious peace that had been established.[63] On March 26 the Chamber was adjourned for the summer. The French controller general had made no secret of his view that the constitutional settlement was a disastrous impairment of the control and offered his resignation to Freycinet (February 6). Colvin, to keep him in countenance, offered his to Granville. After over a month's delay Freycinet accepted de Blignière's resignation, and on March 31 he left the country with which he had identified himself. Granville did not accept that of Colvin. The appointment by the French of Léon Brédif, who had been in the accounts department at the Quai d'Orsay and had no Egyptian experience, was yet another

63. Granville to Lyons, Nos. 194 and 195, February 22, 1882, FO 27/2552; telegram No. 75, March 7, 1882, dispatches Nos. 262, 294, March 10, 16, FO 27/2553; Lyons to Granville, No. 183, March 3, 1882, FO 27/2561; Lyons to Freycinet, March 14, 1882, MAE CP Egypte, 73.

sign that Britain and France were ceasing to march in step, and that France had abandoned Gambetta's struggle for parity.[64]

The national movement in Egypt was feeling its strength and more and more asserting itself against foreign privilege whether European or Turkish. Circassian officers were dismissed wholesale, and means were found to bring prominent men among them, including Osman Pasha Rifki, who had been minister of war in the Ministry of February 1881, to trial for treasonable conspiracy. A court martial delivered sentences of deportation. Turkey remonstrated (on May 6) and, as the khedive's suzerain, forbade the execution of the sentence. The Ministry was brought by Malet to take a step that would simultaneously remove the ground for Turkish intervention and restore harmony between itself and the khedive: it addressed a formal request to him to act on his prerogative and convert the sentence of deportation into one of banishment (May 7). Turkey would lose her ground for intervention; since the firmans only allowed it if the officers suffered personal degradation. The khedive, however, unwisely replied that since the sultan had intervened, the affair was out of his hands. Malet and Sienkiewiz, following their instructions, argued for three hours with the khedive on the morning of the ninth and induced him at last to use his prerogative and to sign a decree commuting the sentence.[65] That the khedive had yielded to Europeans what he had refused to them was no satisfaction to his ministers, who on the following day (May 10) took matters into their own hands and reconvened the Chamber of Notables. Legally only the khedive could do this. The Council of Ministers was now acting as a revolutionary government, having broken off relations with the khedive, whose word was nowhere any longer respected.

It was careful to give a full assurance of safety to all Europeans. During the three weeks while the conflict lasted (May 2 to 26) there was complete order, and no violence was used either in Cairo or Alexandria; all taxes were paid, and everyone went about his ordinary business. The Chamber, when it met under the guidance of Sultan Pasha, its president, Mahmoud Pasha Sami, and Arabi Bey, appealed

64. Blignière's and Colvin's note, signed by both, was telegraphed to Paris by Sienkiewiz, MAE CP Egypte, 72, and to London by Malet, February 6, 1882, FO 78/3448; Freycinet to Sienkiewiz, telegrams, March 11 and 13, 1882, MAE CP Egypte, 73.

65. Freycinet to Sienkiewiz, telegram, May 8, 1882; Sienkiewiz to Freycinet, telegram, May 9, 1882, ibid., 74; Malet to Granville, telegram, May 9, 1882, FO 78/3448. The story of the events from May 2 to 26 is based on the telegrams in MAE CP Egypte, 74, and FO 78/3448.

to the khedive to legalize its reassembly. Although this would have helped to end the crisis and was supported by Malet and Sienkiewiz, the khedive refused. Malet and Sienkiewiz then proposed that Mahmoud Pasha Sami should resign and another man take his place at the head of the Ministry to whom the khedive would grant the request to legalize the Chamber. This the Ministry refused, declaring that it stood or fell together. On May 15 the khedive was induced by Malet and Sienkiewiz to renew relations with Mahmoud Pasha Sami and the existing Ministry. On May 16 there were protestations of loyalty and goodwill on both sides, and the Chamber of Notables continued its sessions. But late on the following day an Anglo-French squadron consisting of two ships from each Power, under Admirals Seymour and Conrad, arrived off Alexandria.[66]

They came in support of the khedive in answer to telegrams from Malet and Sienkiewiz who decided that the political advantage outweighed the danger of provoking an outburst of fanaticism. Malet and Sienkiewiz, acting on instructions from their governments, for which Malet had been responsible, declared the object of the Anglo-French intervention to be the maintenance of the status quo, urged the khedive to dismiss the Ministry, to compose a new Ministry under Cherif Pasha or "another person who offered equivalent guarantees," and to decree the banishment of the leaders of the army at the same time promising them retention of their salaries and rank and issuing a general amnesty. It took, however, a week for agreement on this demarche between Cairo, London, and Paris to be effective. Malet and Sienkiewiz acted on May 25. The khedive as usual found European pressure irresistible. On May 27 the Ministry resigned in protest at the interference of the controlling Powers in the internal affairs of Egypt. There were now demonstrations in Arabi's favor in Cairo and Alexandria. On May 29 the khedive reinstated the Ministry with Arabi Bey at its head and with dictatorial powers. He had already on May 28 appealed to Turkey for the dispatch to Egypt of a Turkish emissary.

Since the beginning of March the Egyptian army, raised as quickly as possible by Arabi from 12,000, to which it had been reduced, to 15,000 men, had been preparing fortifications and defensive works with the clear intention of resisting armed action. Just before Arabi Pasha, as we must now call him, finally established his dictatorship, defensive preparations were renewed (May 23) and thenceforward continued without real interruption.

The cabinets in London and Paris lost control of the situation in

66. Malet to Granville, telegram, May 14, 1882, FO 78/3448.

Egypt. This happened because they assumed that divisions existed in the Egyption movement that would cause it to break up at a show of force. The Chamber of Notables was a moderate and independent element, but it was not ready to side with European diplomats and the controllers general against the Ministry and army leaders. Arabi's Ministry might submit to the advice of the controllers general and the European officials, when it needed it, but it was not prepared to be isolated from the Chamber of Notables nor to be reconciled with the khedive, except on its own terms. Divisions seemed to exist among three parties: those of the Notables, of the army, and of the khedive. But this was because the leaders were fumbling after short-term objectives as they went along. They were united in their long-term wish to make the Dual Control their servant instead of their master. Freycinet's belief that Arabi could be managed by playing on the vanity in his "nature orgueilleux et puérile" was matched by Gladstone's belief that he was a criminal.[67] Britain and France seriously underestimated the unity and strength of the national movement.

Another reason why the cabinets lost control was that they failed to keep in step with each other. The British cabinet followed the direction indicated by Malet. The French cabinet kept its representatives in Egypt on a different course. Malet during January and February had given his chief support to Cherif Pasha and the Ministry; he had then taken the lead in formulating concessions to the Chamber; but by mid-May he was giving his chief support to the khedive as the only legally constituted authority. Freycinet in Paris and Sienkiewiz on the spot consistently withheld full support from the khedive and cultivated the confidence of the *parti militaire,* as Sienkiewiz, abandoning in March the phrase *parti national,* came to call it. Freycinet for the first time on February 11 and on several subsequent occasions instructed him to maintain an attitude of benevolent reserve and retain the confidence of the national leaders. Over the affair of the Circassians, Malet's relations with him came near to the breaking point. Malet, on instructions from London, framed a khedivial revision of the sentence more strongly asserting the khedive's prerogative than Sienkiewiz was allowed to do. When during May 2 to 26 Malet, while seeking means of reconciliation, gave his support more and more to the khedive, Sienkiewiz pressed upon his government the possibility

67. Freycinet to Sienkiewiz, telegram, No. 45 matin, May 20, 1882, MAE CP Egypte, 74; *Gladstone-Granville, 1,* Nos. 798, 855, 857. Arabi reciprocated Gladstone's disparagement by an appeal for his support, July 2, *The Times,* July 24, 1882.

of a change of khedive. He virtually broke off relations with the khedive and only saw him when he went with Malet to read to him the note of May 25. Colvin, as controller general, continued to attend the meetings of the Ministry; Brédif ceased to attend. Throughout May, in short, Malet and Colvin pursued a positive policy while Sienkiewiz and Brédif adopted a position of reserve in the background.[68] They recognized their isolation as the representatives of Germany, Austria-Hungary, and Italy drew together on the other wing.

The third reason why the British and French cabinets lost control was that they acted as if the naval demonstration was a *terminus ad quem.* It could only be effective if the two Powers were decided on the purpose it was intended to achieve. It was enough to provoke a hardening of the national movement but did not by itself cause a transfer of power from Arabi's hands to those of any other authority, since Britain and France had not agreed which authority this should be. After the arrival of the ships, the real decisions all remained to be taken. As far as the French were concerned, these were forced upon the government by the Chamber of Deputies. As far as the British were concerned, they were forced upon the government by the action of the men on the spot: Malet, until he withdrew, and Admiral Seymour.

There were debates in the French Chamber on May 12, June 2, and June 19.[69] On the first occasion Freycinet had attempted a chauvinist speech, but it was so ill received that he knew he could not sanction belligerent action at Alexandria. The French admiral was debarred from firing a shot unless his ships were fired upon. Yet Freycinet recognized, too, that the Chamber would make his position impossible if French lives were lost in an outbreak of violence in Cairo or Alexandria. He was easily convinced, therefore, by Sienkiewiz' constant assertions that the landing of Turkish or European troops in Egypt would provoke an outbreak of Muslim fanacticism and put Frenchmen in danger of their lives in Tunis, Algiers, and Syria as well as Egypt. On June 2 Freycinet was attacked from the Right for allowing common action with Britain to lead to oblique action by Britain alone nullifying the common action. The Right deplored both Freycinet's sending the fleet to Alexandria and his failure to defend the honor of France. It seemed to think this could be done by Turkish action. He

68. Freycinet to Sienkiewiz, telegrams, February 11, May 5, 1882, MAE CP Egypte, 73 and 74; Sienkiewiz to Freycinet, telegrams, May 10, 12, 23, 1882, ibid., 74; Lyons to Granville, No. 646 Secret, June 30, 1882, FO 27/2565, reports Freycinet's inclination to come to terms with Arabi.

69. *Débats parlémentaires,* May–June 1882, pp. 567 ff., 754 ff.

was equally attacked from the Left. Gambetta, however, found little support in calling for a forward policy, and it was asserted as an accusation that he was preparing troops for Egypt when he left office. Georges Clemenceau found more support in repudiating the action recommended by Gambetta and at the same time what he called the weakness of Freycinet. France must be strong and must retain her freedom of action but must also, it seemed, refrain from measures of force. The vote on the order of the day which followed was tantamount to withholding support from the government without indicating any alternative policy. On June 19 the Right took up the attack again. Casimir Périer's suggestion that the Chamber would not refuse in certain contingencies the means of "enabling France to play her part in Egypt, provoked long continued murmurs." It was quite clear that the Chamber would not tolerate the dispatch of troops to Egypt—now an imminent possibility. Freycinet, characteristically responding to its mood, made a round declaration that no French troops would be sent. The mood of country and Chamber was one of "aplatissement." [70] Both complacently accepted the French withdrawal that gradually took place after May 16. Although Freycinet secured a vote on July 19 for the credits he asked for to defray the costs of the naval expedition and a vote of confidence on the next day, the further vote on July 29 against the Suez Canal credits bill finally clinched the decision against France's continuing side by side with Britain. The Chamber voted against what Freycinet offered: the maintenance of the British alliance within and subordinate to the European Concert.

On the British side policy was the consequence of decisions taken at Cairo and Alexandria. These decisions were the response to the events of June. The khedive's appeal to the sultan brought to Egypt on June 5 a substantial Turkish mission headed by Dervish Pasha and Labitte Effendi and comprising fifty-six hangers-on of various kinds. They were even less effective than the two Turkish emissaries of October 1881. But while they were in Cairo the first violence occurred in what had so far been a silent revolution of ideas. On June 11 a riot broke out at Alexandria in which some forty-six Europeans or European-protected persons lost their lives. It made plain the unreality of Turkish sovereignty. Arabi now sent three Egyptian regiments into Alexandria (June 12) and no further disorder occurred. Thus it also made plain that he controlled the situation. This the sultan recognized when he withdrew his mission and asserted his authority by bestowing

70. Lyons to Granville, June 19, 1882, FO 27/2565.

a high honor on Arabi. On June 21 a new Ministry under Rhageb Pasha, a leader of the national movement of the forties but now an old man, with Arabi Pasha still at the War Office, seemed to consolidate the latter's power. It was exercised by the continued rearming of Alexandria's puny fortifications, as an act of defiance to the considerable Anglo-French naval force (reinforced after May 31) anchored in the roads. Malet decided to find a way of breaking off relations without formally doing so. He fell ill, was for several days incommunicado, and then withdrew (on June 15) to one of the British ships. Sienkiewiz and the representatives of the other Powers busied themselves with the matter of compensation for the loss of lives and property in the Alexandria riot. But Sienkiewiz received no dispatches and only brief telegrams form Freycinet during May and June. When, lacking anything else to do, he wrote long disquisitions on how Egypt might be put under the protection of the six Great Powers by the Constantinople Conference, he was first rebuked by Freycinet for meddling in "la politique générale" and then abruptly recalled (June 28) [71] and replaced at once by Dormet de Vorges.

Malet's withdrawal and Seymour's holding of the British ships at Alexandria while Arabi defied them put the British government into an attitude of hostility that it had either to accept and act upon or break. It decided to act. On June 27 it inquired what troops could be supplied at once to Seymour. On July 3 it instructed Seymour, after summoning Arabi to dismantle the Alexandria batteries, to silence them. Seymour summoned Arabi to *surrender* the forts[72] and so practically, if not actually, committed his government to take power out of Arabi's hands into his own. After the bombardment on July 11, however, he had no troops to land. On July 12 fire broke out and the town was pillaged, it was said, by Arabi's retreating forces. Seymour then telegraphed for two battalions from Cyprus. On July 15 the town was policed by eight hundred British soldiers, Arabi's forces having withdrawn into the interior. On July 17 Seymour, in a proclamation posted in Alexandria, announced that "with the permission of the Khedive" he alone was responsible for the maintenance of order in the town. Seymour had now fully committed his government, for to maintain his position and assure it against attack from Arabi, considerable reinforcements and the complete reorganization of authority in Egypt

71. Freycinet to Sienkiewiz, telegrams, June 24, 25, 28, 1882, MAE CP Egypte, 74.

72. *Gladstone-Granville, 1,* 385, n. 1 and No. 746.

would be necessary. Gladstone's and Granville's hands were now further forced by the service ministers, who conceived it their duty to back Seymour. On July 24 the House of Commons voted the credits necessary for the military occupation of Egypt and the protection of the Suez Canal. On the same day the cabinet took the decision to send Indian troops to Egypt. On July 25 and 26 troops from Malta and Gibraltar landed, and on July 27 they occupied and fortified Ramleh. No British army was in Egypt until a fortnight after the bombardment, and no military action happened until six weeks afterward. Sir Garnet Wolseley only arrived from Britain with the main British force on August 4. Operations did not begin until August 18 when troops were taken through the Canal and landed at Ismailia and Port Said. The advance from Ismailia began on August 20 and continued its slow, inexorable pressure until the final destruction of the Egyptian army on September 13 at Tell-el-Kebir.[73]

When did the French withdraw and precisely from what sort of action? It is clear that France had exercised no influence upon events at Cairo or Alexandria since the beginning of May. The presence of her ships side by side with the British in the roads of Alexandria was a continuing of the policy that had led her to keep the *Victorieuse* or *Reine Blanche* in Egyptian waters as long as possible to ensure respect for the members of the French colony and to keep the idea of French power present in Egyptian minds. The recall of Sienkiewiz on June 28 was the sign of a decision. On July 1 Admiral Conrad disengaged his ships from the formation in which they had stood with the British, although he kept them in Egyptian waters. On July 5, as Lyons intimated to his government, the French cabinet met and decided not to join the British in the bombardment of the forts. The French ships, which had by then evacuated all French nationals and protected persons who wished to leave, remained in Egyptian waters. They now turned their attention to the protection of the Suez Canal. On June 24 Freycinet repelled a British overture for an exclusive Anglo-French agreement about measures to be taken for the protection of the Canal. But he made it clear that he would not refuse a proposal that came from the Constantinople conference.[74] Freycinet was confirmed in this attitude by the appearance of Italian ships at Port Said and an Italian

73. The most succinct reports of the British movements were the French, MAE CP Egypte, 75. The story is more difficult to follow from FO 78 but is the same.

74. Freycinet to Tissot (London), June 24, 30, 1882, *DDF*, 1st series, 2, Nos. 408, 417.

offer to join with Britain in the protection of the Canal.[75] By July 16 Britain and France had hammered out a proposal to be put to the Constantinople conference that they should be jointly charged with the protection of the Canal.

Measures on the spot as usual forestalled the ponderous machine of international agreement. France took her share in these, but Britain determined what was done. The day before the bombardment British ships were advised not to use the Canal until the following day when a convoy system would be instituted. Admiral Hoskins, in command of ships in the Red Sea, organized the gunboat convoy and the patrol of the Canal. The French admiral Conrad was instructed to join with Hoskins in policing the Canal. On July 24 Conrad reported that French ships were policing the Canal as if Hoskins had left the scene. Meanwhile the proposal made to the conference on July 19 had failed. Britain then proposed that she and France should declare themselves ready to protect the Canal either alone or together with any Power willing to join them. A joint Anglo-French invitation then went forward to Italy. Italy, indeed, was also invited to cooperate in military movements into the interior. By July 26 an arrangement for the occupation of the Canal, with ships and troops, if necessary, at Port Said, Ismailia, and Suez, was embodied in a protocol. All now depended on the money being voted by the French Chamber. On July 29 it rejected the Suez Canal Credits Bill. The unfortunate Italians had meanwhile accepted the Anglo-French invitation. They got out of a scrape by adding the condition that their participation depended on the institution of a regular defense system in which all the Powers could participate. There was, in effect, no further international action. The truth that Britain, after the action of July 11, was master of the Canal was acknowledged when on August 18 she declared it temporarily closed during the landing of her army at Ismailia.

Throughout July a lively controversy was conducted between newspapers, believed to be respectively the mouthpieces of Gambetta and Freycinet, on the assumption that French armed action was still possible in Egypt. They only differed about whether this should be in cooperation with Britain or in cooperation with the European Powers

75. For overtures to and from Italy for participation in active intervention, see, Granville to Paget, Nos. 155, 246A, telegram 260, No. 250, May 11, July 22, 24, 26, FO 45/450, FO 45/451; Paget to Granville, No. 248 Confidential, No. 260, No. 325 Most Confidential, July 5, 29, August 2, 1882, FO 45/455, FO 45/456. Cf. G. M. Tuckwell and S. Gwynn, *The Life of Sir Charles Dilke* (2 vols. London 1912), *1*, 464

"pour y surveiller, y contrôller et y limiter" the action of Britain.[76] Least of all did the French intend to withdraw Frenchmen from the several Egyptian administrations in which they were employed. De Vorges immediately on his arrival at Alexandria wrote privately to Freycinet that in the circumstances his main task would be "d'empêcher les Anglais de nous expulser de toutes les positions." [77] This was no easy task, since the French representative on the *Caisse de la Dette Publique* had left its archives, funds, and employees all in the charge of his English colleague—the Austrian and Italian members were on leave—while he took refuge like all the chief French officials on the *Hirondelle.* Moreover, one of the earliest British actions was to take over completely the Railway Administration. Freycinet would give no precise instructions about how the Frenchmen were to regain their places in the administration of the Domaines, the Daira, and the Ministry of Finance. Even the controller general, Brédif, found himself with nothing to do when he returned to Cairo. But they were never formally withdrawn.

As long as the Constantinople conference was still sitting the French could well claim to be disassociating themselves from nothing more than an illegal act of war on the part of Britain. She acted in contravention of the solemn declaration of the Constantinople conference that no member would seek individual advantage in Egypt, and contrary to her own disclaimer of any intention to land troops or occupy the country. Britain on more than one occasion recognized that she had no right other than *force majeure* to act. The financial control did not of itself give the controllers any right to prevent the Egyptians from arming forts if they wished. Gladstone acknowledged that Seymour had no right to act when he insisted on the demand for the "surrender" of the forts being modified to a demand for "surrender for the purpose of disarmament." But it was a change of form without a change of substance. Again the reluctance to land troops and Gladstone's insistence that the battalions from Cyprus should go in as a police force only bespeaks his embarrassment at the position in which he found himself. Indeed, he wrote to Granville that he would be puzzled to answer the question "*que diable faisait-il dans cette galère?* What was the exact title of our fleet to remain in Alexandrian waters after we had drawn off our own people?" [78] Finally the closure of the Suez Canal

76. Lyons to Granville, Nos. 690, 691, 709 Secret, 741, July 7, 11, 17, 1882, FO 27/2566.

77. De Vorges to Freycinet, telegram, July 2, 1882, MAE CP Egypte, 75.

78. *Gladstone-Granville, 1,* Nos. 747, 764, 775.

on August 18 fully merited Vorges' stricture that Britain was taking actions which if done by a small nation would have scandalized her.[79]

There is some truth in the French view that the British had taken the initiative in Europeanizing the Egyptian question, but when France, repudiating Gambetta, made this policy her own, Britain departed from it and adopted a policy of undisguised aggrandizement. The profounder truth is that events were not the consequence of policy formulated by Gladstone, Granville, or the cabinet in London, but the result of decisions taken in Cairo or off Alexandria. This was bound to be so because Gladstone, Granville, and the cabinet were formulating a policy unrelated to power and power politics. But what was at stake in Egypt was precisely the question of where should power and authority rest. The professional interest and the self-confidence of British officials, investors, and traders had built up after 1875 an administrative empire, financial and commercial interests that were closely interelated and, gathering a momentum of their own, demanded the habits of order and security which Seymour, on orders from the cabinet, eventually bombarded the forts to assure. But the cabinet had to order this action because Seymour, having embarked British nationals, had kept the fleet off Alexandria and challenged the defiance of Arabi.

By means of a telegram and dispatch of July 28 and 29 to her ambassador at Constantinople, Britain assumed full responsibility for reconstruction in Egypt and announced this to the conference. Both Chamberlain and Granville had drafted versions of these documents, and they were amended and modified by Childers, Northbrook, Hartington, Harcourt, and Gladstone. The assumption of sole responsibility was a cabinet decision. Britain announced that she had been obliged to take a more prominent position in regard to the measures for restoring order in Egypt than had originally been her intention or desire, but that she had now made further preparations which she believed would "be sufficient of themselves for the restoration of the authority of the Khedive and the establishment of settled order in Egypt."[80] Yet even now Britain spoke with two voices. Alongside this clear assumption of responsibility was an invitation to any Power who cared to do so, to join with her and a declaration of readiness to accept Turkish

79. De Vorges to Freycinet, telegrams, August 16, 20, 1882, MAE CP Egypte, 75.

80. Granville to Dufferin (Constantinople) telegrams 444 and 445, July 28, 29, 1882, FO 78/3395; for different versions and cabinet opinions on them, see PRO 30/29/143.

troops provided the sultan would proclaim Arabi a rebel. This the sultan refused to do, and the invitation to the Powers was heard in silence. On the other hand, Britain steadily discharged the responsibility she had assumed. The sphere of her action gradually grew. This is well illustrated by her attitude toward the trial of Arabi, who was taken prisoner after Tell-el-Kebir, and other leaders, captured in July. Gladstone was ready at that time to insist that "anyone [in Egypt] apparently implicated in crime should have a fair trial by native judges impartially chosen." When this looked like involving Britain in representation at the trial, however, he thought it would be enough to specify "equitable trial according to civilised usage." [81] When Arabi's trial eventually took place in December, not only did Sir (as he became in 1880) Charles Rivers Wilson attend the trial, but its outcome had been carefully arranged in advance after consultation with the law officers, negotiation with the Egyptian Ministry, and between Octave Borelli, a French lawyer employed in the Egyptian Ministry of Finance, and A. M. Broadley, a British lawyer also employed by the Egyptians, who acted as prosecuting and defense counsels. The accusation was framed in the most general terms, Arabi pleaded guilty and was deprived of his rank and fortune and banished. A general amnesty was then issued, and on December 27 Arabi and his associates sailed for Ceylon. The Queen was shocked that "innocent Christianity should remain unavenged."

During August to December the decisions taken in Cairo under Britain's advice steadily widened the area of her control. Malet, acting entirely without his French colleague, made a new Ministry under Cherif Pasha (August 28).[82] It was decided that a new constitution, planned by Cherif Pasha, should not be decreed, but that the Chamber of Notables should be allowed to revise its own organic law; that Egypt must pay the interest due on her debt before she paid all that was due in salaries to her officials; [83] that her primary need was for a police force and army and that her secondary need was for a Westernized administrative machine. Thus it came about that a *gendarmerie* was organized by Sir Samuel Baker; that British officers began to organize an Egyptian army—by November 20 under Sir Evelyn Wood

81. *Gladstone-Granville, 1,* Nos. 787 and 813.

82. De Vorges to Duclerc, Nos. 10 and 13, August 14 and 18, 1882, MAE CP Egypte, 75. De Vorges describes Malet as "mettant une certaine coquetterie à me faire savoir *ce qui est fait,* après m'avoir caché autant qu'il a pu, ses démarches pour ce qui *était à faire.*"

83. Granville to Malet, telegram No. 463, September 13, 1882, FO 78/3447.

as commander-in-chief; and that the Chamber of Notables lost all rights in relation to the initiation of legislation and to the budget, whereas in the localities municipal councils were organized and increasingly used in governing the interior. Three days after Tell-el-Kebir Gladstone had already decided in his own mind to send Lord Dufferin, who had been governor-general of Canada and ambassador in St. Petersburg and was then ambassador in Constantinople, to report on the institutional and administrative needs of Egypt. A variety of difficulties were surmounted, and within six weeks (October 29) his appointment as special commissioner was approved. On November 4 he arrived in Cairo and began with great rapidity and understanding to build a new state. Gladstone had in fact shouldered in Britain's name the burden of "preparing Egypt for a self-governing future." [84] Nor did he demur when the French ambassador was said to have replied "naturally" to a remark dropped in conversation that England would now acquire predominance in Egypt, though he paused to insist that "naturally" must mean "inevitably," and if it were so it was the result "of effort and sacrifice crowned by success." [85]

Duclerc, within three weeks after coming into office, even before the battle of Tell-el-Kebir, had taken the first tentative step in trying to restore the entente with Britain. Joubert, who had been Goschen's partner in investigating the khedive's financial affairs in 1876, was a close friend of Duclerc. The latter suggested an approach to the British government through Goschen. This Joubert declined to make, but he did approach Plunkett, who was in charge of the Paris embassy while Lyons was on leave.[86] Then before sending Tissot back to London, Duclerc had two long conversations with him in which he developed the theme of the French need for the entente with Britain. After the battle of Tell-el-Kebir, Tissot in London and Duclerc in Paris both took the opportunity of broaching the subject of its renewal. Tissot thought Granville was responsive. In fact Duclerc and Granville were both hatching projects that would make renewal impossible. Duclerc was thinking toward compensation for French withdrawal from Egypt; Granville was thinking how to abolish the Dual Control without a formal request to the French to withdraw. Granville prepared a minute on September 18, trusting that he was not departing too far "from the paths of virtue and self abnegation." Gladstone hesitated to

84. *Gladstone-Granville, 1,* No. 826; for Dufferin's special mission, see FO 78/3453, 3454, 3455

85. *Gladstone-Granville, 1,* No. 818.

86. Plunkett to Granville, No. 955 Secret, August 30, 1882, FO 27/2568.

accept it, looking backward to the policy of Europeanizing the Egyptian question. "So far as the immediate or financial objects of the control are concerned," he wrote, "is it not the fact that the interests of all the European nations in regard to them are identical?" When Granville replied, "no, because the object of the control was the good of the country,—an object not so strongly entertained by the other powers," he referred Gladstone to another acceptable warrant for action, the general idea of the good of the population. By September 29 Gladstone was decisive: "There is nothing I think more clear in the Egyptian matter than that the *dual action* must be abolished." [87]

Meanwhile, on September 25, a new French consul general, V. Raindre, had arrived in Egypt. More than a fortnight before he had had a long conversation with Duclerc, who designated as the objectives of French policy both the restoration of the Dual Control, or the status quo ante, and the renewal of the entente with Britain. But Duclerc, recognizing that his second objective was incompatible with his first, also instructed Raindre to cultivate close relations with other representatives in Cairo, by which he meant those of Austria-Hungary and Germany, "qu'il nous sera peut-être un jour utiles de nous avoir ménagés." [88] Duclerc was preparing to put up a fight to gain some compensation for France if the Dual Control were not restored.

There were at this time eight groups in the French Chamber of Deputies. The extreme Right—the royalists, imperialists, and conservatives—and the extreme Left—the *Gauche Intransigeant* led by Clemenceau—constituted a permanent and a permanently divided opposition. They could, however, muster 245 votes at their maximum strength. The groups upon which Duclerc could rely mustered on their side 270 votes. But they were also divided. If Gambetta drew off his supporters, Duclerc could lose as many as 210 votes, and his position would become untenable. If the Freycinet group drew off it might also be untenable, for to lose as many as a dozen votes made Duclerc dangerously dependent upon a full muster of his divided supporters for victory. The Independent Republicans, his most reliable supporters, only numbered some fifty men. In short, Duclerc needed to show some compensation for leaving Egypt in order to keep the Gambettists. But behind his policy there was never a strong body of convinced personal supporters to give it drive.

Granville had prepared the French ambassador for a proposition,

87. Gladstone-Granville, *1,* Nos. 827, 829, 847.

88. Duclerc to Raindre, No. 49, September 12, 1882, MAE CP Egypte, 75.

and on October 2 a long discussion as to its substance opened between him and Gladstone. On October 20 it was extended to the rest of the cabinet. Throughout the period of the proposal's incubation and the subsequent negotiations upon it, reports from Paris encouraged Britain to withhold compensation. "The French," Plunkett reported, "generally seem to believe England means to treat them with consideration. They wish naturally to be put aside as little and as gently as possible; but practically they seem reconciled beforehand to whatever fate may have in store for them and to be prepared to yield to circumstances against which they have no longer the energy to struggle."[89] When the Chamber reassembled in November it constantly tempted Duclerc to stand out for compensation in order to placate the Gambettists, yet never gave him the steady support he needed in order to gain it.

In London discussion in the cabinet centered on the formula needed to conceal the awkward fact that Britain had no right to abolish by unilateral action something instituted by international action. The Dual Control could not be said to have lapsed while the decree of November 15, 1879, remained unrepealed; nor could it, strictly speaking, be said to have failed. It had to be described as a *provisional* arrangement which had been found wanting and could not be maintained. Thus came into being the preamble to the dispatch (No. 1198, Confidential, of October 23) instructing Lyons to open negotiations for the abolition of the Dual Control and to propose alternative arrangements. Gladstone had drafted it, but it was discussed with Lyons who was in London on leave. The first part of the alternative plan proposed a single financial adviser appointed by the khedive for a term of years; dismissible not upon permission gained from the European Powers but only upon proof of malversation by a regular and public judicial investigation; endowed with the right of being present at any meetings of the Ministry concerned with revenues assigned to the servicing of the debt, but having no executive powers; to be British in the first instance and always a national of a country principally interested in Egypt's provision for meeting the interest due to her creditors. The new arrangement, it was proposed, should form the substance of a khedivial decree. A second khedivial decree would at the same time abolish the Dual Control. The second part of the alternative plan involved the neutralization of Egypt, by European

89. Plunkett to Granville, No. 1099 Confidential, October 17, 1882, FO 27/2570.

act if need be, and a new firman from the sultan to the khedive granting him greater freedom. The second part was held in reserve and not at once communicated to the French.[90]

Duclerc, one is bound to admit, had right on his side when he tore away the flimsy decencies of the preamble and told Lyons crudely that it was not the abolition of the Control that was in question but the abolition of the French controller.[91] In the course of the negotiation, which then ensued, Duclerc insisted upon the compensation for which he had prepared the way. He avoided at first using the word and gained thereby the appointment of a Frenchman as president of the *Caisse de la Dette Publique,* but Granville successfully resisted his pressure for an enlargement of its functions. He then insisted upon a return to the position as it existed in June 1882 and the reinstitution of the Dual Control in working order before it was replaced by any alternative arrangements. Brédif in Cairo was abruptly instructed to fill the same place which his English colleague still occupied in Egyptian affairs and to attend the meetings of the Ministry as if the Control were still working. Britain refused to renew the Control and avoided becoming entangled in a legal argument with the French about whether, if she repudiated the decree of November 15, 1879, it still remained valid for France. The difficulty Gladstone and Granville had had with their own legal advisers on this matter and, indeed, in convincing themselves that the law was on their side, was fortunately not known in Paris. Nor would they consider compensation. They refused even to recognize that the idea of compensation was relevant to the situation. They refused "to buy the French out of Egypt." [92] The unvarnished truth was that Britain was in possession: she was exercising a single control and only force could eject her. She adjusted the rights in the case to suit these facts.

The negotiations with France failed. Duclerc announced that the British proposals were inacceptable. Britain then communicated them to the Powers without the preliminary agreement with France upon which she had counted in order to gain European sanction for them.

90. *Gladstone-Granville, 1,* Nos. 829, 832, 835, 841, 855–57; the draft of No. 1198 to Lyons is in FO 27/2557, and PRO 30/29/143 has cabinet opinions on the new arrangements in Egypt.

91. Duclerc to Tissot, October 28, 1882, DDF, 1st series, 4, No. 551.

92. Granville to Lyons, Nos. 1347, 1514, November 27, December 30, FO 27/2558; Duclerc to Tissot, December 13, *DDF,* 1st series, 4, No. 576; Duclerc to Raindre, December 16, 1882, ibid., No. 580. Dufferin reported Brédif's return to control business, telegram 48, December 18, 1882, FO 78/3455; *Gladstone-Granville, 1,* Nos. 904, 907, 908, 912, 917, 923, 924, 928, 936, 939, 941, 943.

France if she had not gained compensation had gained revenge. The Egyptian question became at this point what it was to continue to be for the rest of the century: the material which other Powers could use to fashion an instrument for withholding something from Britain that she needed. Germany, drawing Austria-Hungary, Italy, and Russia behind her, combined with France to withhold from England the international sanction she sought for the new administrative and financial arrangements in Egypt. The international financial conference on Egypt in 1883 was to be a failure, and it was not until March 1885 that Britain was at last able to put the financial arrangements on a stable basis. But between December 1882 and March 1885 the main lines of the partition of Africa had been drawn. Germany took the initiative in this, but one reason why she felt strong enough to do so was that the Dual Control had ended in the breakup of the Anglo-French entente. Thus the partition of Africa took place in the context of Anglo-French ill feeling. Bismarck was able to embark upon a colonial policy with a much greater degree of freedom than he would have enjoyed had the Anglo-French entente and the Anglo-French condominium in Egypt continued to exist.

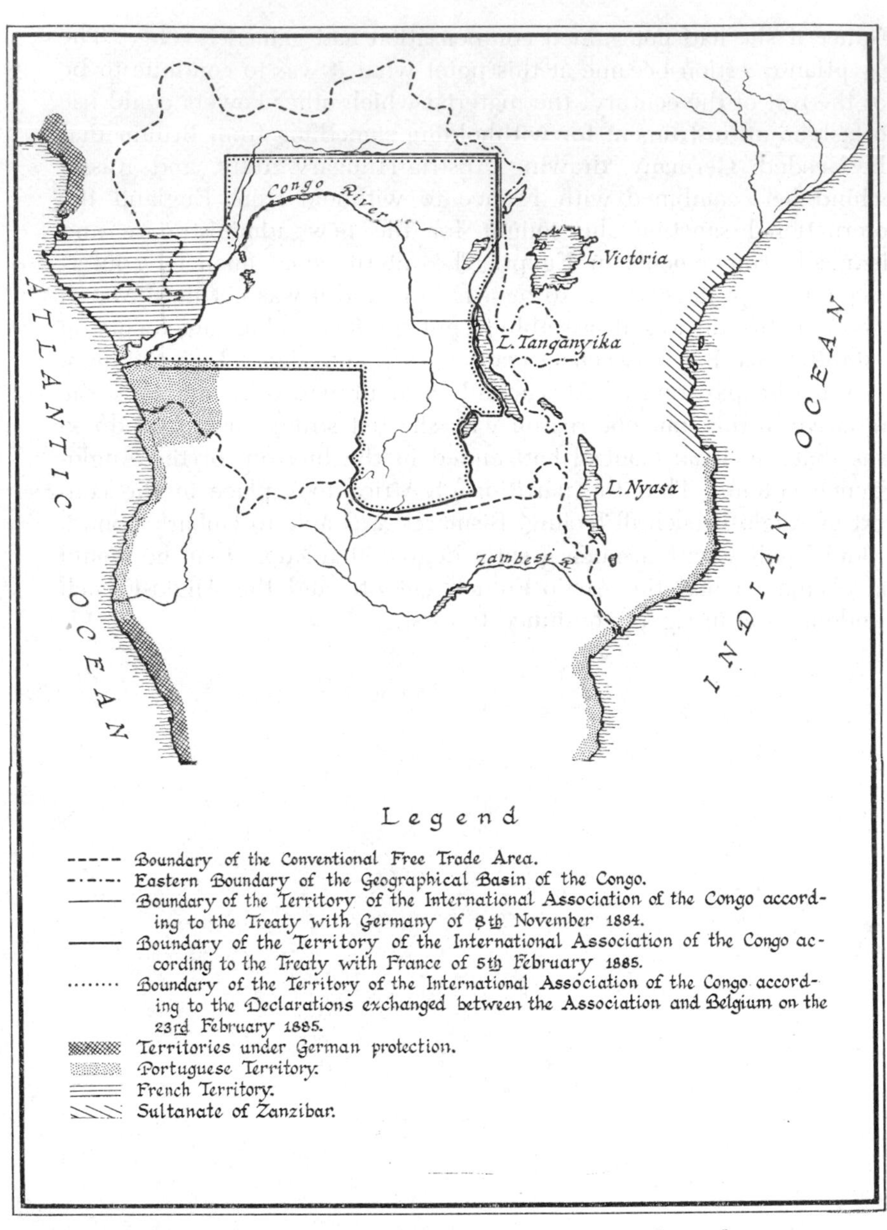
Congo River
L. Victoria
L. Tanganyika
L. Nyasa
Zambesi
ATLANTIC OCEAN
INDIAN OCEAN
Legend
Boundary of the Conventional Free Trade Area.
Eastern Boundary of the Geographical Basin of the Congo.
Boundary of the Territory of the International Association of the Congo according to the Treaty with Germany of 8th November 1884.
Boundary of the Territory of the International Association of the Congo according to the Treaty with France of 5th February 1885.
Boundary of the Territory of the International Association of the Congo according to the Declarations exchanged between the Association and Belgium on the 23rd February 1885.
Territories under German protection.
Portuguese Territory.
French Territory.
Sultanate of Zanzibar.

The Boundaries of Central Africa in 1885, based on the map by L. Friederichsen

☙ 4. *King Leopold and Anglo-French Rivalry, 1882–1884*

☙ JEAN STENGERS

The extraordinary success of Leopold II, King of the Belgians, dates between August 1879 and February 1885. In August 1879, a small expedition organized by King Leopold landed on the coast of Africa, at the mouth of the Congo. The expedition under the orders of Henry M. Stanley, numbered about ten Europeans. Its progress toward the interior of the continent was slow in the beginning, and it did not reach Stanley Pool until the end of November 1881. By February 1885, or scarcely more than three years after these relatively modest beginnings, King Leopold had become a head of state in Africa. At the conclusion of the Berlin Congo Conference, his sovereignty had been recognized by practically all the Powers. The two principal continental Powers, France and Germany, recognized his sovereignty over a territory covering approximately one-tenth of black Africa or one-fifth of the area of Europe.

One might think that this tremendous success was at least the reward for a definite plan, for an effort followed through with perseverance toward the goal that the king finally achieved. But it was nothing of the kind. There is a world between what the king sought in August 1879 and what he achieved in February 1885. In fact, if King Leopold had remained faithful to his initial objective, he would have merited complete failure. He succeeded only because he deviated from his original plan. Initially, the king wanted to start in Africa a large commercial company whose prosperity would be assured by preferential tariffs and monopolies, a business that would avoid any political tie with European powers. If he had persevered in this way, his chances would have been absolutely nil. He owed his success to the substitution of the idea of a state for that of a commercial company, and that of full liberty of trade for monopolies and preferential tariffs; finally—and this was essential in the territorial recognition he obtained from France and Germany—he formed a bond with France by a particular agreement, the agreement on the right of preemption. His success was due to this triple change of course.

Each time the king changed course, he did so in response to an initiative either from France or from Britain. Each one of these initiatives, whether French or British, was itself dictated fundamentally by the rivalry of the two powers in Africa. Without being paradoxical—and the aim of this essay is to show that it is not a question of a paradox—it can be said that King Leopold's success depended to a great extent on the vicissitudes of Anglo-French rivalry.

The question of how King Leopold conceived his large African enterprise in 1878–79, when he sent Stanley to the Congo, is not easy. The writings of King Leopold—and notably his private letters—to which one can turn are numerous, but in using them one must navigate between two snags. These obstacles are encountered again in nearly every period of the king's life. On the one hand, there are documents where, addressing certain correspondents, the king dissimulates his thought more than he reveals it. When, during the summer of 1879, he confided in a Belgian journalist and explained to him that in central Africa, "for the present, only scientific explorations are intended," [1] one is obviously faced with a misleading statement. But the manner in which the king succeeded in cloaking himself in an artificial fog was sometimes much more subtle, and consequently more difficult to uncover. On the other hand, one occasionally finds documents of such spontaneity—these are in many cases the memorandums the king wrote for himself which were later found in his papers—that the idea seems to gush forth as if from a spring; but the difficulty, in this case, is knowing whether the thought is really mature, considered, or if it is not one of those innumerable improvisations the king jotted down on paper only to forget the next day. Few men are as difficult to understand as when they are, like King Leopold, at the same time secretive and imaginative. It is very hard in such cases to determine with certainty the main line of their thought.

Moreover, in order to reconstruct the king's ideas at a given time in his career, one is forced to follow, at least in part, what appears to be the general structure of his thought. This results in interpretations that can be dangerous. For the beginnings of the Congolese enterprise,

1. "The Whitehall Review and the King of the Belgians," *The Whitehall Review*, August 2, 1879, p. 269. This interview was granted to the Belgian journalist Max Sulzberger: see *L'Etoile Belge* of August 4, 1879, and the account of Sulzberger by E. Nys in *Biographie Nationale, 24* (Brussels, 1926–29), cols. 265–66.

his ideas, when he attempted to influence opinion. They were fruitless efforts. From the beginning of his reign, the king had to bow to the facts: never, in colonial matters, could he count on a direct action by Belgium. Consequently, he was obliged to act on his own resources. In this respect, he had at his disposal a considerable asset: money. His personal fortune was extensive, and he was ready to risk it in an overseas enterprise. Nevertheless, as he did not want to supply all the capital himself, he was counting on the collaboration of Belgian and foreign capitalists who would join in his enterprise.

In the Far East, where the whole first phase of his efforts was situated, the king had sought above all to buy or lease either an existing colony or at least a politically organized territory. More than anything else he dreamed of obtaining the Philippines from Spain. An operation of this kind would take only money. The first move—purchase or lease—would have demanded a big capital outlay, but immediately afterward the king and his partners would have been able to begin a remunerative exploitation of the colony or territory.

But when the king turned toward central Africa, he faced radically different conditions. There was no colony to take over, no political organization on which to rely. An extensive territorial occupation consequently appeared at first sight excluded. It would require a real conquest, which the king could not consider. King Leopold, let us reemphasize, had no military forces at his disposal. He would be short of money if he attempted political occupation: what European capitalist would be foolish enough to join him and pledge his capital in an operation of conquest?

What could be done? Before settling on a precise formula, the king proceeded tentatively. He first wanted to work out a preliminary step. Africa still contained vast unknown areas. In the Congo basin in particular the map was almost entirely blank. It was thus necessary above all else to become more familiar with the "dark continent," to explore it, "open" it as the king put it. In order to succeed, King Leopold believed—and believed very sincerely, without any doubt—that it was necessary to organize an international collaboration: this took shape in 1876 with the meeting of the Geographical Conference, and with the creation of the Association Internationale Africaine. This African Association, after rather promising beginnings, was rapidly shipwrecked, through no fault of the king. With great enthusiasm, he had done his best to make it succeed. The documents we possess today prove that indisputably. What is also beyond question is that the African Association, in the king's mind, constituted only the first stage of his action.

Even if it had succeeded, he would have passed to the second. The second stage for him would have been to create in Africa—possibly under the wing of the African Association—a "private enterprise," with himself as the owner, which would be destined above all to reap profit from the riches of the continent.

When it was a matter of defining the form this enterprise would take, King Leopold hesitated. At the start, he thought of founding trading stations or posts somewhere in Africa. For several months in 1877, he considered setting up these stations in the Cameroons.[4] Then, at the announcement of Stanley's discoveries, his attention focused on the Congo basin—on the Congo and on Stanley himself, whom he thought of immediately engaging. "If I like Stanley," he wrote in November 1877, "I will raise the money for him to have several regions on the Congo and its tributaries thoroughly explored and to start trading posts there. Depending on the circumstances, I will try to transform these posts into some Belgian settlement or station either on water or on land which would belong to us." [5] In a note of May 1878, still using "if," the king repeated: "If I like Stanley, I am all for making a contract with this resourceful American, for agreeing to supply him with 100,000 dollars per year over five years to found a settlement on the Congo and from there to branch out as far as possible around this great river." [6] "Posts," "settlement," [7] "station": all this vocabulary is obviously rather vague—and it certainly reflects the lack of precision of the king's ideas—but it places us very far, in any case, from the idea of political occupation of a vast territory. When Stanley "branched

4. L. Greindl, "Quelques documents sur un projet d'expédition au mont Cameroun en 1877," *Bulletin de l'Académie Royale des Sciences coloniales,* 5 (1959), 864–84. See also a very illuminating text by Emile Banning, who was closely involved in formulation of the plan; it leaves no doubt about the fact that the end in view in the Cameroons was the establishment of stations; cf. J. Stengers, *Textes inédits d'Emile Banning* (Brussels, 1955), p. 34, and extracts published in A. Roeykens, *Les débuts de l'œuvre africaine,* pp. 332 ff.

5. Pierre van Zuylen, *L'Echiquier congolais ou le secret du Roi* (Brussels, 1959), pp. 43–44.

6. Note, no date, publ. in A. Roeykens, *La période initiale de l'œuvre africaine. de Léopold II. Nouvelles recherches et documents inédits, 1875–1883* (Brussels, 1957), pp. 92–93. As Father Roeykens has correctly observed, comparison with other texts proves that this note must be dated later than May 12, 1878; on the other hand it must be prior to June in view of the terms the king used to speak of events of June 1877.

7. The king also used the term "establishments" in the note of May 1878 to designate the trading posts on the Lower Congo owned by the Afrikaansche Handelsvereeniging of Rotterdam.

out" in the Congo basin, one could imagine the various possibilities before him: he might obtain from native leaders "leases" and "contracts" that would permit the development of economic activities;[8] he might even succeed in signing political accords with the leaders; but there was never any question of his subjecting extensive regions to the king's authority. This would have implied the possible use of force, and force, we repeat, was exactly what King Leopold could not resort to.

With direct contacts between Stanley and King Leopold in June 1878, more precise plans were elaborated. Stanley arrived in Brussels in June 1878 with a definite proposal—the creation of a large railway and trading company in the Congo. A "Société internationale de Commerce" would be formed with the object of "connecting the two navigable parts of the Livingstone [i.e. the Congo] by a short-run railway, establishing steamer navigation on the river, and setting up stations on the islands of the upper river to serve as centers and depots for European trade." The capital necessary to realize this program: 27 million francs. Anticipated net annual profit: 5 million francs, that is, a return of more than 18 percent.[9]

The king was interested from the start: he liked Stanley. From June 1878 on, the "Société internationale de Commerce" constituted his essential objective. He began a campaign to collect the money. But, in this connection the obstacles soon proved to be insurmountable: even those who desired to remain in the king's favor refused when asked millions for an enterprise that appeared to them—without their daring to say so openly—rather senseless.[10] There was thus no alter-

8. This is one of the hypotheses that Lambermont considered in a memorandum to the King of June 11, 1878; A. Roeykens, *Les débuts de l'œuvre africaine*, p. 325.

9. Facts taken from a report stating Stanley's proposals, which was completed in late June or early July 1878. In spite of our efforts, up to the present we have not managed to find this text, which constituted the real launching of the Congolese enterprise. It is only known to us through the résumés and excerpts given by two journalists who had it in their hands: one, an associate of the Parisian newspaper *Le Voltaire* ("La Mission Stanley," in *Le Voltaire* of October 23, 1882), the other, a socialist journalist of *Le Peuple*, of Brussels, who found the document among his papers from the banker Bischoffsheim (see *Le Peuple* of March 3, 1895, and March 4, 1895).

10. Bischoffsheim's correspondence with his son-in-law, the Baron de Hirsch, published in *Le Peuple* from March 2, 1895, to March 7, 1895, is extremely revealing in this regard. "*Stuss*" and "*Unsinn*" were the words that best suited Baron de Hirsch to express the feelings of devastation inspired by "*diese schöne Unternehmung*" (letters to Bischoffsheim of July 18 and July 22, 1878, in *Le Peuple* of March 5 and March 7, 1895); but one also senses the high value de Hirsch attached to not antagonizing the king.

native but to start with a preliminary study phase. Therefore the creation, at the end of 1878, of the Comité d'Etudes du Haut-Congo to which the Belgian and foreign capitalists who were solicited limited their pledges to a sum ranging from 5,000 to 50,000 francs each. The Comité, thanks to the funds thus gathered, was able to send Stanley to the Congo, instructing him to study the establishment of a line of communication between the Lower Congo and Stanley Pool—a region in which Stanley agreed to set up three stations—and to explore the commercial possibilities of the Upper Congo. If these studies yielded a "satisfactory result," the articles of the Comité provided the subscribers would be called on to form "two companies . . . one for the construction and exploitation of the communication route, the other for the establishment of navigation on the Upper Congo and to perform there all the business operations whose possibilities will have been or will be recognized." [11]

The Comité d'Etudes, in itself, was only of minor importance in the history of the Congolese enterprise (at the end of one year, its capital exhausted, it was dissolved),[12] but the documents concerning it have particular interest in that they show us where King Leopold decided to move in 1878. Once this direction was taken, the king abided by it for four years. Everything done in the Congo—where Stanley set up stations and negotiated treaties with native leaders—was done at the outset in the perspective of the large trading company the king intended to found.

To lay the foundations of such a company, the king thought it necessary first to obtain solid economic privileges. This was the object of the first treaty concluded by Stanley in the Congo. That first treaty, of

11. November 25, 1878, statutes of the Comité d'Etudes. The original text of these statutes was published in L. Guebels, "Rapport sur le dossier J. Greindl," *Bulletin de l'Institut Royal Colonial Belge, 24* (1953), 33–38. This text underwent some slight alterations in the course of 1879, with no modification of the date November 25, 1878 (the alterations consisted mainly in the elimination of the names of Pincoffs and Kerdyk, two directors of the Afrikaansche Handelsvereeniging who went bankrupt, and in the addition of the names of four new subscribers, two of whom were Hutton and Mackinnon); the altered version was published in the *Deutsches Kolonialblatt* of December 15, 1917, in an article later taken up again in the volume *Aus den Archiven des belgischen Kolonialministeriums* [*ABK* hereafter], 1. Folge (Berlin, 1918), pp. 53 ff.

Only two contributions to the Comité d'Etudes were over 50,000 francs: one from a company, the Afrikaansche Handelsvereeniging (130,000 fr.), and one from the banker Lambert (265,000 fr.), who served under the circumstances as a figurehead for King Leopold.

12. Robert Stanley Thomson, *Fondation de l'Etat Indépendant du Congo* (Brussels, 1933), pp. 74–75.

Vivi, on June 13, 1880, granted the Comité d'Etudes (a defunct organization, as we just said, but whose name continued to serve as a label covering the king's enterprise) all the monopolies that could possibly be reserved: "The sole and exclusive right of all foreigners and strangers to open any part of Vivee district by the making of roads, paths, constructing bridges or any other improvement required for freer communication in the district"; "The sole and exclusive right of all foreigners and strangers to cultivate any portion of Vivee district excepting that required by the natives themselves for their own subsistance and use"; "The sole and exclusive right of all foreigners and strangers to trade in any part of Vivee district," etc.[13] That was the model to follow, Leopold and his advisers explained to Stanley the year afterwards, in instructions dated January 31, 1881, of which we unfortunately possess no more than the résumé. Let us quote this text, for among all others it is probably the one that best conveys the spirit of King Leopold's enterprise at the beginning:

> Mr. Stanley will proceed to Stanley Pool as quickly as the men's strength allows. He will bring with him the *En Avant* (a small steamer which he is to launch at Stanley Pool). . . .[14]
>
> Once at Stanley Pool, Mr. Stanley will look for a favorable site to establish a station and will negotiate the lease of all the territory that the district leader is willing to yield. . . .
>
> As soon as everything has been arranged, Mr. Stanley will embark on the *En Avant* and sail up the Congo. . . . He will be exclusively interested in looking for the most advantageous points above the Pool for the purpose of establishing stations. . . . Everywhere Mr. Stanley lays the foundations of a station, he will negotiate, as at Vivi and Stanley Pool, the lease of as much land as possible; in contracting with the leaders, he will make sure that these leases grant exclusive privileges to the A.I.C.,[15] such that no other foreigner would have the right to settle in the domain. . . .

13. Brussels, Archives de l'ancien Ministère des Colonies, Fonds des Affaires indigènes [AAMC, FAI hereafter]. Subsequently King Leopold sent the United States a superbly falsified text of this treaty, adding a surrender of sovereignty clause, but carefully omitting everything referring to exclusive rights; this false text was the one printed in 1884 in the publications of the American Senate (*United States Senate, Report No. 393, 48th Congress, 1st Session,* p. 48).

14. On the story of the *En Avant,* see André Lederer, *Histoire de la navigation au Congo* (Tervuren, 1965), pp. 12 ff.

15. This mention of the A.I.C., the Association Internationale du Congo (mention of it is made again later in the text) unquestionably resulted from a misapprehension. For a reason that escapes us—mere inadvertence, perhaps—the

The whole success of the undertaking depends on the exclusive possession of a continuous zone from Stanley Pool to Vivi,[16] and of vast territories in the richest, most fertile and most populous regions of the Upper Congo. . . . The European capitalists will not be so eager to risk their money on operations planned in such far away and little known countries as those of equatorial Africa. . . . The promoters will not be able to create a railway without proving: (1) that it will not suffer the effects one day of ruinous competition; (2) that it is destined to develop vast lands belonging to the A.I.C. in its own right or placed under its exclusive jurisdiction.

To create a large trading company and railway, it is necessary to own immense lands, and not only to have established stations but also to secure from the leaders advantageous treaties which assure the A.I.C. of priority in exploiting mines, forests, in cultivating ownerless territories, in trading with the natives and buying their crops, to the exclusion of any competitor, etc., etc.

When we try to issue bonds for the trading, agriculture, and railway enterprise, we have to be able to advertise the extent, nature, diversity and advantages of the concessions which the A.I.C. has obtained and which alone will attract the subscribers we need. Subscribers will buy bonds only if they know from a reliable source that the A.I.C. has lands and concessions.[17]

---

author of the analysis substituted the name of the A.I.C., totally anachronistic to the date of January 31, 1881, for the name of the Comité d'Etudes, which must have appeared in the original text. The first authentic mention of the A.I.C., we note, was in October 1882: King Leopold to Strauch, October 9, 1882; Brussels, Archives du Ministère des Affaires Etrangères [MAE hereafter], Strauch papers.

16. This continuous zone was the route of the road connecting the Lower Congo to Stanley Pool (and later of the railway).

17. Brussels, Archives de l'ancien Ministère des Colonies, Document Notte [AAMC, "DN" hereafter]; cf. E. Van Grieken, "H. M. Stanley au Congo," *Bulletin de l'Institut Royal Colonial Belge,* 25 (1954), 1148–52. (The text is wrongly dated "late January—early February 1881"; to be very exact, it is from January 31, without any doubt.)

Again, we quote two equally characteristic texts of February and March 1881: King Leopold to Strauch, February 14, 1881: "I think that all the officers we send to Africa must know what our objective is: (1) to establish stations; (2) to obtain the largest concessions possible; (3) to conclude treaties with the chiefs ensuring us *special* advantages for our settlement, our trading, and the laborers we would need"; Brussels, Musée de la Dynastie [MD hereafter], Strauch papers. Strauch to Lindner, March 30, 1881: "The success of our enterprise depends entirely on the promptness with which we will occupy before all other competitors the most favorable sites for trade and conclude with the native chiefs

From that time on, the "exclusive treaties," loaded with the enumeration of monopolies and economic privileges, followed one after another. In 1882, one was signed in Isanghila (May 8),[18] in Manyanga (August 13),[19] in Ngombi (September 24),[20] in Leopoldville (October 12),[21] in Ndandanga, near Manyanga (October 14),[22] in Msuata (October 19),[23] in Lufuntchu, also near Manyanga (October 20).[24]

treaties of friendship which will secure us large territorial concessions and special commercial advantages. . . . It is only when we will have cast on the Upper Congo the basis of important establishments that we may begin the work which will put those establishments in communication with the Atlantic Ocean"; Marcel Luwel, *Otto Lindner, 1852–1945. Een weinig bekend medewerker van Leopold II in Afrika* (Brussels, 1959), p. 174.

18. AAMC, FAI.

19. Ibid. On the conclusion of this treaty, see Dr. Pechuel-Loesche, *Kongoland. I. Amtliche Berichte und Denkschriften über das Belgische Kongo-Unternehmen* (Jena, 1887), pp. 65–66. This treaty was likewise communicated to the American Senate in a falsified version, greatly reducing the clauses relating to economic privileges. See *United States Senate, Report No. 393,* p. 50.

20. AAMC, FAI.

21. Ibid.

22. Tervuren, Musée Royal de l'Afrique Centrale, 50-47-175; notebook of the missionary Comber.

23. AAMC, FAI.

24. Ibid. This is one of the treaties that brought King Leopold the most difficulties. In the course of a trip to Stanley Pool in 1883, Greshoff, the Rotterdam company's manager in Boma, succeeded in obtaining the text of the treaty and of two other agreements signed with native chiefs. On Greshoff's role, see C. Magalhães, *Le Zaïre et les contrats de l'Association Internationale* (Lisbon, 1884), pp. 17–18, and Lievin Van de Velde's letter to Stanley of May 28, 1883, in the Van de Velde papers, Eugene, University of Oregon Library. As he was very opposed to King Leopold's enterprise, Greshoff hastened to forward copies of these treaties to the Portuguese who, naturally, published them. Hence, they passed into a British Blue Book; *Africa No. 5, 1884,* C 4023, pp. 1–4. Copies were also sent to the Congo, to the French lieutenant-commander Cordier, who sent them to Paris with indignant comments; see Cordier to Brun, Naval Minister, June 30, 1883, with three enclosures, in Paris, Archives du Quai d'Orsay, *Mémoires et Documents. Afrique* [MDA hereafter], *88,* folio 101 ff.; this dispatch, with only one of its enclosures, was published in L. Jadin, "Informations du lieutenant L. Cordier sur l'Association Internationale Africaine," *Bulletin de l'Académie Royale des Sciences coloniales, 5* (1959), 301–07. As we will see later, King Leopold had to use a lot of ingenuity to palliate the effect of this unfortunate divulgation.

With regard to the "exclusive treaties" we have just reviewed, it will be noted that, if they had their inspiration in common, their clauses were not always worded in the same way; thus the size of the territory which the exclusive privileges applied to varied from one treaty to another; sometimes it was a matter of all the territory of the chief or chiefs signatories to the treaty, sometimes the clauses were applicable only to the lands ceded to the Comité d'Etudes.

In addition, while preparations for trade were being made, certain lucrative operations could just as well be started immediately: Stanley was therefore urged, repeatedly to make ivory purchases. "I am desirous," the king wrote him on December 31, 1881, "to see you purchase all the ivory which is to be found on the Congo." [25]

All things considered, how was the large trading company to be started? The king was still at the planning stage in this regard. In November 1881, for example, he jotted down a plan that occurred to him: he thought—for a moment at least—of entering into a partnership with the Dutch trading company of Rotterdam, which had posts on the Lower Congo. He noted how this could be done in a memorandum:

> Amalgamation of the Handelsvereeniging and the Comité d'Etudes du Congo, on the basis of leaving to each partner what it had established separately and uniting for ulterior developments, the Comité d'Etudes retaining political direction.
>
> *Société Internationale du Congo, Headquarters in Brussels, Branch in Rotterdam.*

The present owners keep their properties, which constitute separate shares, and pool together the proposed extensions. The Handelsvereeniging's settlements and those of the Comité du Congo will be enumerated. . . . The shareholders of the Handelsvereeniging, those of the Comité d'Etudes and the free Congo stations will have the right to subscribe 3 million florins each to the extension of the enterprise and the net revenues of the extension will be shared proportionally among the subscribers. By extension of the enterprise is understood every financial, commercial, industrial, agricultural operation increasing its yields." [26]

25. F. Hird, *Stanley,* p. 183. Abundant data on the subject of ivory purchases are in both the résumé of the correspondence between Stanley and Brussels furnished by the "DN" (cf. E. Van Grieken, "H. M. Stanley au Congo," passim), and in Stanley's letters of 1881–82 preserved in his letter-book (Tervuren, Musée Royal le l'Afrique Central) which were published in large part in Albert Maurice, *H. M. Stanley: Unpublished Letters* (London, no date). In his book on the Congo, Stanley later carefully crossed out everything relating to these commercial operations; cf. J. Stengers, "Quelques observations sur la correspondance de Stanley," *Zaïre,* 9 (1955), 920–21.

26. MD, Strauch papers. This note by the king has no date but was almost certainly included in a letter to Strauch of November 1, 1881. ("If Stanley prevents the Dutch from settling at Stanley Pool, they will speak to us. I wonder and would like your opinion on whether or not it is necessary to invite them to merge with us on the bases outlined on the other side.")

One is clearly very far from the idea of a state. If the king had continued in this direction, if he had tried to collect capital, if he had "exposed to the public" the commercial leases and monopolies he had procured in the Congo, it is certain that his enterprise would have ended as a total, irremediable failure. King Leopold was saved and finally achieved success only because he completely changed direction, abandoning his commercial objective.

In October 1882, Stanley returned to Europe, the object of international curiosity. To the journalists who assailed him, he made known the results of the work he accomplished in the Congo. It goes without saying this was a version of the facts destined for the general public, in which Stanley carefully conformed to King Leopold's instructions. The king made a point of appearing essentially in the guise of the sovereign philanthropist, founder of the African Association, which was conducting a disinterested operation in Africa. The founding of the African Association actually was for scientific, unselfish purposes and had indeed resounded throughout Europe. The Comité d'Etudes, however, had been practically a secret undertaking. King Leopold wanted above all to maintain the facade of the African Association, and Stanley collaborated. "In this matter of the Congo," he explained to a journalist, "the King is only a royal philanthropist." [27]

But, despite everything, Stanley hinted at the commercial idea in his first interviews of early October 1882. In the Congo, I was, he declared, "the representative of an international, civilizing, scientific and commercial association." [28] However, he deemphasized the commercial aspect. "We trade only in order to support our settlements without being obliged to have recourse constantly to subsidies from Europe." [29]

Trade: this word was condemned and disappeared one or two weeks later. The Comité d'Etudes never had any business transactions in Africa: such was the new official truth proclaimed as of the second half of October 1882. Stanley, with self-discipline, obeyed orders. "It is easy," he wrote, "to prove that the company is not commercial for

27. Interview of October 7, published in the *New York Herald,* October 30, 1882.

28. Interview of October 5, published in *Le Voltaire,* October 8, 1882.

29. Ibid. In his interview with the *New York Herald,* to the question: "Has the Belgian expedition no commercial objects in view?" Stanley replied: "They are commercial, in a sense, because it is necessary that the stations should endeavor to be self-supporting. . . . With this end in view we appoint a man at each station to look after commerce in a restricted way."

it has not exported a single product from Africa."[30] King Leopold declared emphatically in November 1882 that the association he directed "had no commercial character; it did not carry on trade."[31] Furthermore, it never had done so: "No one," wrote Emile Banning, "could point to a single mercantile operation performed on behalf of the Comité d'Etudes du Congo, from its origin up to this day."[32]

How do we explain—when in September 1882, detailed instructions sent to the Congo still insisted on the way to organize ivory trade[33]—that the line followed until then was abruptly broken? How do we explain that it was even judged necessary to disguise the past retrospectively (which the honest Banning did, moreover, in all innocence since he was not in on the instructions of a commercial nature sent to the Congo)? The reason was that an enterprise whose rivals could accuse it of being commercial would be unable to face on even terms the acute political danger represented by France and Savorgnan de Brazza. To be able to defend itself with some chance of success against the French flag, the opposition's flag had to be not that of a commercial enterprise but of a political organization. To affirm his political rights, and distinct privileges, without weakening them by commercial overtones: that, in King Leopold's judgment, was the only possible way of salvation, in view of the French menace.

Here, though, we must look back: it would be completely wrong to think that during the first phase of his enterprise King Leopold had ignored the political problems posed by his installation in Africa. On the contrary, he was greatly preoccupied with the political aspect from the start. A large trading company, he realized, could function in central Africa only if its bases of operation remained free, and if they did not fall into the hands of a European power. Thus, from a political standpoint, means had to be found of procuring a shield. What were these means? The king's ideas in this regard were not immediately de-

30. Letter to the *Daily Telegraph,* reproduced in *La Gazette,* October 28, 1882.

31. Memorandum "giving the King's views" delivered to the British minister in Brussels, November 15, 1882; cf. Lumley to Villiers, November 15, 1882, with enclosure, in Foreign Office [FO hereafter] 84/1802.

32. *L'Association Internationale Africaine et le Comité d'Etudes du Haut-Congo. Travaux et résultats de décembre 1877 à octobre 1882, par un de leurs coopérateurs* (Brussels, 1882), p. 27. This booklet by Banning appeared in late November (cf. *Echo du Parlement,* November 25, 1882). On its preparation, see A. Roeykens, *La période initiale de l'œuvre africaine,* pp. 213 ff.

33. Pechuel-Loesche, *Kongoland,* pp. 20–22; instructions of September 14, 1882.

termined; he had to grope. The first scheme he fancied for a moment in June 1879 consisted in creating in the Congo a "republican and independent confederation" of native chiefs, a "Black State" whose president the king would designate. "Of course," he made it clear "there is no question of granting the slightest political power in this project to Negroes. That would be absurd"; full powers would be in the hands of the white station managers, who would be responsible to the "Président de la confédération."[34] Stanley immediately cut all that short because it sounded improvised: the plan, he replied in July 1879, appeared to him totally impracticable. "It would be madness for one in my position to attempt it. . . . We must leave the petty tribes as we found them." On the other hand, Stanley thought it an excellent idea to turn each post in the Congo into "a little commonwealth." We could even go further, he wrote, "and say that though each station is a little sovereign commonwealth, yet it is but part and parcel of a large commonwealth, which is ruled over by the manager appointed by those who founded, promoted and sustained the unique enterprise."[35]

Abandoning his "Black State," the king was at once convinced by this idea. The instructions to Stanley in August 1879 were: "When the three stations are founded, they can be established as a free state to be joined by the stations set up later beyond the falls on the Congo."[36] From then on, and for years to come, the king cherished the idea of securing the "independence" of the stations so that they could become "free cities" and form a "confederation."[37]

34. The king's note, no date, in MAE, Strauch papers, which certainly must have been enclosed in the letter of June 27, 1879, from the king to Strauch ("memo enclosed concerning the points to discuss with Stanley"). Strauch made it the subject of instructions which he gave to Stanley at Gibraltar early in July. These instructions are known to us only through excerpts that Stanley quoted in his reply to Strauch: Stanley to Strauch, July 8, 1879, in H. M. Stanley, *The Congo and the Founding of its Free State* (2 vols. London, 1886), *1*, 52–54.

35. Stanley to Strauch, July 8, 1879, ibid.

36. Résumé of these instructions in "DN" (cf. E. Van Grieken, "H. M. Stanley au Congo," p. 1129); publ. in A. Roeykens, *Les débuts de l'œuvre africaine*, pp. 397–99. Father Roeykens pointed out very well that these instructions must date from August 16–17, 1879.

37. "As soon as our stations are large enough to assume their independence with some chance of success"; King Leopold to Strauch, July 10, 1880; MAE, Strauch papers. "Our plan: concessions, railway, treaties with the chiefs, formation of stations and their outbuildings into a free confederation having its own flag and placed under a governmental commission with headquarters in Brussels"; King Leopold to Strauch, February 14, 1881; MD, Strauch papers. "It would be especially necessary to report the fact that Vivi and Isangila were founded on concessions obtained from the chiefs, and to express the hope that these are the

In late 1881, he added another idea: it is necessary, wrote the king, to place the native chiefs surrounding our stations "under our suzerainty."[38] It is indispensable, he instructed Stanley on December 31, 1881, "that you place successively under the suzerainty of [the] Comité, as soon as possible and without losing one minute, all the chiefs from the mouth of the Congo to the Stanley Falls."[39] This keynote—making the chiefs accept the "suzerainty" of the Comité—was repeated in instructions of March and September 1882.[40]

There were then, unquestionably, clear political preoccupations. But to place them and weigh their importance accurately, it is necessary, in our opinion, to consider three observations.

First of all, the political formulas were not, in the king's mind, ends in themselves, but, as we said a moment ago, means of ensuring his

---

seeds of two free cities"; King Leopold to Strauch, May 3, 1881; MAE, Strauch papers. "The stations would be free cities whose influence would extend over the neighboring territories"; instructions to Stanley of October 14, 1881, after the résumé of the "DN"; cf. E. Van Grieken, "H. M. Stanley au Congo," pp. 1167–69; see also the king's letter to Strauch of October 6, 1881, and King Leopold's preparatory note concerning instructions to give Stanley quoted below, p. 136 and n. 41. "The Comité will not succeed in founding something durable in the Congo valley . . . as long as it does not hold independent territories with prerogatives to control them"; instructions to Stanley of March 27, 1882, after the résumé of the "DN"; E. Van Grieken, pp. 1176–77.

38. "Our greatest interest is in extending the supremacy of our stations over the native chiefs. We must try to have them accept our protectorate and our alliance", note by the king entitled "Instructions for Stanley," no date; MD, Strauch papers; this is obviously a preparatory note for the instructions of October 14, 1881. "Mr. Stanley has inspired the native chiefs with confidence; it will not be difficult for him . . . to convince them they have nothing to fear and everything to gain by concluding a treaty of alliance with the Comité, by accepting its guardianship, at least for their foreign affairs, by investing it with the right to represent them, to speak in their name and defend their cause before civilized nations"; instructions to Stanley of October 14, 1881, after the résumé in the "DN".

39. F. Hird, *Stanley*, p. 183.

40. The instructions of March 27, 1882, are known to us through two documents: (1) the résumé provided by the "DN"; (2) the instructions sent to Pechuel-Loesche on September 14, 1882, which clearly borrowed, word for word, long passages of the March 27 text; the copy of these passages makes it apparent that the "DN" résumé is quite incomplete and a bit inaccurate; see Pechuel-Loesche, *Kongoland*, pp. 15 ff.

Pechuel-Loesche, unfortunately, published his instructions in German translation. What they asked—and this is unquestionably a repetition of the March 27 text—was that the natives agree to "*sich selbst unter unseren Schutz zu stellen,*" "*unsere Oberleitung anerkennen,*" "*unsere Schutzherrschaft anerkennen*"; *Kongoland*, pp. 18–19.

security. The king's major objective was always economic. Nothing is more revealing in this regard than the letter he addressed to Strauch on October 6, 1881. He told him to write Stanley and "insist on the necessity of having the supremacy of our stations recognized by the native chiefs, so that we can have these same stations recognized by the powers in Europe as free cities, founding ourselves upon the natives' free consent." Where did this all lead? The king stated: "If our stations were recognized as free communities extending as far as possible on the banks of the Congo, we would have taken a first and large step toward the establishment of a trade and transport enterprise. We would have a base of operations assured."[41]

Second, the idea of setting up a "suzerainty" over the native chiefs —which marked a step beyond the idea of "free cities"—remained submerged for a certain time in the flood of instructions from Brussels, and probably made no particular impression on Stanley and his associates. It was only in March 1882 that, for the first time, this theme was really insisted upon and brought to the forefront. But then it was necessary to wait until August 1882 for the first treaty signed to the Congo along the lines of those instructions.[42]

Finally—and this is an essential point—even with the idea of "suzerainty" (a fuzzy notion, and a bit strange, we must confess; but King Leopold did not have a legal mind and often juggled with odd terms), the king by no means contemplated confiscating the so-called sover-

41. MAE, Strauch papers. See also, in the king's handwriting, his note, no date, "Instructions for Stanley," already quoted, which must be dated slightly later than this letter of October 6: "Our stations must become free cities, chief towns (sic) of the regions bordering the Congo River. That is of the utmost urgency. As soon as we have grouped a sufficient number of chiefs and small native tribes around our stations, thanks to your good offices, we will endeavor to have the Powers recognize the confederation of Congo free cities." And again, as in the letter of October sixth, there is a clue to the future: "It would be the first step permitting us to launch out safely into business undertakings and construction of the railway. In order to pursue this end, we must be *certain* not to be hindered by any foreign domination"; MD, Strauch papers.

42. Manyanga treaty of August 13, 1882 (cited above p. 130 and n. 19): "The chiefs and all their subjects, their villages and plantations, their domestic animals, their canoes and fishing implements shall be under the protection of the expedition. In accordance herewith all the public affairs of the acquired and protected district of Manyanga, quarrels among the chiefs themselves, elections of successors of defunct chiefs, questions of contention with the neighbouring tribes . . . must be settled at the station of Manyanga and put under the arbitration of such members of the expedition as are present at the station"; articles 2 and 3 of the treaty.

eignty of the native chiefs for his own profit. The March 1882 instructions, which were repeated in September, stated clearly: "Far from wanting to deprive the natives of their independence, we come to offer them the means to preserve it." [43] And the king again evoked, as he did in June 1879, the creation of a "model native State" which would safeguard the Africans' rights. Of course, in such a plan—which was just as vague in June 1882 as it had been in June 1879—the natives' sovereignty and independence would be nominal, but officially, at least, the king announced his intention to respect them.

It is in the psychological extension of everything we have just observed that the first parries attempted by the king were placed when the French menace appeared. What did the danger consist of on the French side? Brazza returned to France in 1882 brandishing the treaty he had concluded in 1880 with Chief Makoko, north of Stanley Pool. This treaty installed France on a territory which, though very small, was of fundamental strategic importance because of its location on the threshold of the navigable Congo basin. The question was whether the French government would ratify the agreement. If it did, that meant it accepted the creation of a French colony in the Congo. Brazza would be able to start out from his base at Stanley Pool to take over a vast part of the river basin.

King Leopold's first parry aimed at stressing all the disadvantages and dangers that ratification of the Brazza-Makoko treaty would present, so as to prevent, if possible, its ratification. The king pleaded that one should avoid annexations and acquisitions in the Congo that would transplant to Africa dangerous European political rivalries. "We think," King Leopold wrote to Ferdinand de Lesseps in September 1882, "that what is best for commerce, for peace and for civilization is to maintain the autonomy of the native states of the Congo while creating several free settlements to serve them as guides and direct them gradually in the way of progress." [44] In a note delivered to British leaders in the beginning of October, the king pleaded the same cause. The posts founded in Africa, he explained, "are small

43. Pechuel-Loesche, *Kongoland*, p. 19.

44. Letter of September 18, 1882. Original in Brussels, Bibliothèque Royale, Cabinet des MSS, II 7023; (copy) MDA, 59. When King Leopold wrote this letter, he contemplated using the same arguments with Brazza, having him told: "We believe that the interest of civilization and trade is in maintaining the native States and in laying there a certain number of free settlements, costing nothing to anyone and rendering a service to all"; the king to Strauch, September 17, 1882; MD, Strauch papers.

free communities." "By planting them in the midst of the native states, the Association expects to promote the welfare and strengthen the independence of these states and thinks this is the best that can be done in the interest of civilization as well as in the interest of commerce in general."[45]

No annexations, rather respect for the autonomy of the native states: that was the first policy, the first parry. A second one was added, but it is not known whether King Leopold actually employed it. In any case he considered it. Why not, he wondered, in order to win the favor of both Brazza and the French, have them take part in our business? "We will do well," he wrote to Strauch on September 10, 1882, "to consult Brazza on the best way to invite French capital to participate in our work and take whatever part in it they would like. This will be a way of leading up to an invitation to Brazza to become interested in our enterprises and direct some of them."[46] The scheme was still that of an association in the framework of a trading company.

Alas! In the face of Brazza's ardent patriotism and the talent with which he roused the enthusiasm of French opinion, King Leopold was powerless. In the first days of October, he still nourished the hope that France would perhaps hesitate to ratify the Brazza-Makoko agreement.[47] On October 8, he wrote to Henry Solvyns, the Belgian minister in London: "I am almost certain[48] that the Paris Cabinet will, in the end, ratify. . . . Brazza has very cleverly taken hold of

45. Memorandum deposited at the Foreign Office by Solvyns, the Belgian minister in London, October 5, 1882; FO 84/1802. The king had also sent this text personally to Gladstone and Granville; see Gladstone's acknowledgment of receipt of October 10, 1882, in Brussels, Archives des Palais Royaux, Fonds Congo [APR, FC hereafter], No. 100; the king subsequently made reference to this dispatch in his letters of October 12 to Gladstone and Granville: Public Record Office [PRO hereafter] 30/29/156. Another copy of the memorandum is in Brussels, A.G.R., Banning papers, No. 122. The King also tried to spread this theme in the press; see for example an article that obviously came from the Palace, in the *Journal de Bruxelles,* October 7, 1882: "The International African Association . . . does not proceed by annexation. . . . It was commissioned to avoid private annexations that necessarily provoke discord, struggles, and that would compromise or delay the final result, which is penetration of central Africa."

46. MAE, Strauch papers.

47. See in particular his letter of October 5, 1882, to Baron Beyens, Belgian minister to Paris; MAE, Lambermont papers, No. 175, and—for the postscript of the letter—No. 165.

48. In his minute, the king had first written: "I am afraid." Then he crossed out these words and replaced them with "I am almost certain." This was the moment his hopes were dimmed.

the national fiber, all the press is for him."[49] On October 13 or 14 the ax fell: the king received Ferdinand de Lesseps' reply to his September letter, and Lesseps informed him of the intentions of the French Président du Conseil to propose approval of the treaty to the French Chambers.[50]

At that moment, the king seemed to experience an hour of confusion. Brazza, in fact, risked ruining his work. "His dream," the king wrote on October 8, "is not only to see the treaty ratified but after that to take the whole Congo basin for France."[51] What could be done? Some rather foolish ideas crossed the king's mind at this time. He asked Solvyns to approach the Foreign Office and induce the British to take military measures: they should send a warship toward the coast of Africa, north of the Congo estuary, making sure that it got press coverage; in this manner everything could be saved. "A very small ship would suffice to foil Brazza's plans."[52] Solvyns, a sober diplomat, was wary of taking this step. If I had done it, he told Baron Lambermont, "I would have deserved to be immediately recalled."[53] But Solvyns suggested a solution of his own in his correspondence with the king: since the game seemed lost on the political level, why not be content with forming a company in the Congo that would merely have economic activities?[54]

Without knowing it, Solvyns echoed the formula the king had contemplated all along. Consequently, in mid-October, the king jotted down a draft of statutes for the "Congo company." Let us welcome this document because it was the last time the idea of the big trading

49. APR, FC, No. 100 (minute).

50. Lesseps to King Leopold, October 12, 1882. Original in APR, FC, No. 38; (copy) MDA, 59. The king had surely received this letter by October 14, to judge by the memo he wrote on that date for his negotiator in Paris, Lambert; publ. in A. Roeykens, *La période initiale de l'œuvre africaine*, pp. 212–13.

51. Letter to Solvyns, already cited.

52. Ibid.

53. Solvyns to Lambermont, October 12, 1882; MAE, *Afrique. Association Internationale du Congo, 1*, 1878–82, document 42.

54. See letter of October 10 to this effect from Solvyns to Jules Devaux, the king's secretary, accompanied by notes for the king, and the letter of the following day from Solvyns to King Leopold; APR, FC, No. 100. In his correspondence with Lambermont, Solvyns disclosed some of his ideas even more frankly: "I persist in believing . . . that formation of a Company is the best possible solution. It would be a disappointment, but at least it would be a way out. To continue with Stanley as agent and de Brazza as adversary would be pure foolishness"; letter of October 12, already cited. "The establishment of a business is in my view the only means of getting out of this unfortunate and costly adventure"; letter of October 24, APR, FC, document 52.

company, that until then had nourished his thought, appeared under his pen.

> The company would be incorporated. Its initial capital would consist of everything we have in the Congo, which would be divided into shares of stock. . . . It would have the right to increase its capital in order, among other things, to issue shares to its member or members who would meet the company's expenses.
>
> The company would be organized for business purposes, to fulfill the diverse obligations contracted with the native chiefs and kings and to enjoy the privileges they grant.[55]

But suddenly—this turning point was crucial and decisive—the king corrected himself. What would his company be worth if it were subject to France? To preserve what he created in the Congo, he had to prevent Brazza at all cost from coming there and planting the French flag. The only way to oppose extension of France's sovereignty was to set another sovereign organization's priority rights against it. There could be no more trading from then on, as that would compromise political resistance. The king's efforts would have to concentrate on the acquisition of political rights, of sovereignty. In his opinion this was the only way of salvation, and he committed himself to it with determination.

It would therefore be necessary to obtain a formal transfer of sovereignty in the treaties with the native chiefs in the Congo. Starting in late October, Stanley's instructions reflected this policy: he was told that circumstances having imposed "a change of procedure in Africa, we must bind the natives to us by regular treaties, blank forms of which are herewith sent." [56] Stanley and his associates used these "blank forms," of different types, during the following two years, getting the native chiefs to sign hundreds of treaties relinquishing

55. MAE, Strauch papers, note, no date, which was undoubtedly attached to the king's letter to Strauch of October 16, 1882: "Herewith a kind of an outline to use in drawing up a plan of statutes for the Congo Company"; publ. in A. Roeykens, *Jules Malou et l'œuvre congolaise de Léopold II, 1876–1886* (Brussels, 1962), p. 15, n. 2.

56. Instructions of November 1, 1882, cited in Stanley's Journal (Stanley papers) on November 5. These instructions had been completed during discussions between King Leopold and Stanley in late October (cf. the king's letter to Strauch of October 31, 1882, MAE, Strauch papers); hence their date of October 30 in the "DN" résumé; cf. E. Van Grieken, "H. M. Stanley au Congo," 2nd part, *Bulletin de l'Académie Royale des Sciences coloniales,* 25 (1954), pp. 1435–38.

sovereignty.[57] This was done without much difficulty, as the chiefs did not understand much in the text at the bottom of which they marked their X's.[58] But in Brussels, only the texts were read: King Leopold thus saw his sovereignty spread around the posts to increasingly vast areas.

Once launched on the political level, the movement expanded ac-

57. What was really new in this series of treaties, which began with Stanley's return to the Congo, was the *complete* surrender of sovereignty to which the native chiefs agreed. Indeed, in a preceding phase—which appears in a way as an intermediary step—the chiefs were asked to renounce their sovereignty over the *part* of their territory that they ceded by treaty. The instructions sent to Stanley in March 1882, and repeated to Pechuel-Loesche in September (see above, n. 40) indicated clearly what this clause should be. In Brussels they had even prepared a treaty-type form providing for the *partial* surrender of sovereignty. The terms of the form began with "After close examination . . . "; it was found in the Lindner papers (cf. M. Luwel, *Otto Lindner*, pp. 214–16, and reproduction in the back of the book). The first agreement we know of that was written according to this form was the treaty concluded by Parfonry with chiefs of Isanghila on November 15, 1882 (AAMC, FAI). Parfonry had left Belgium on August 15, and it is not unreasonable to think that the "After close examination . . . " form had been sent to the Congo at that time. In the Lindner papers, this form was attached to instructions from Strauch of November 30, 1881, but it is evident, as M. Luwel has very well pointed out, that there was a chronological error of classification: cf. *Otto Lindner*, pp. 120–21. Not so very long ago, I myself defended the validity of the November 1881 date, contradicting M. Luwel—see J. Stengers, "Un collaborateur de Léopold II, Otto Lindner," *Zaïre*, 13 (1959), pp. 422–23—but in my comparison of documents, I was naïvely relying upon a treaty sent by King Leopold to the United States Senate that is, as we know today, a false document.

Two more remarks concerning the treaties: (1) although the "After close examination . . . " form was conceived specifically for a *partial* surrender of sovereignty, it was subsequently used on many occasions, and contrary to all logic, in treaties arranging *complete* surrender of sovereignty. King Leopold's agents in the Congo, let us recall, were not legal experts; (2) of the treaties we know, one anticipated the instructions given Stanley at the end of October, and it stipulated that the chiefs who signed the treaty "recognized the sovereignty" of the Comité d'Etudes: this was the treaty concluded by Valcke, on October 29, 1882, with chiefs of the Inkissi region, between Manyanga and Leopoldville (AAMC, FAI; it was one of the treaties copied in 1883 by Greshoff, and consequently known in its own day: see above n. 24). But this is not at all surprising since Brussels had asked that the chiefs accept the "suzerainty" of the Comité (see above p. 136 and nn. 38 to 40). How would a worthy officer like Valcke have distinguished between "suzerainty" and "sovereignty" in drawing up the treaty?

58. Here we are alluding to the notion of sovereignty which they evidently must have failed to understand; when it was, on the other hand, a question of the cession of lands, the black chief most often grasped very well the full significance of the contract, and the negotiation was then very serious and cautious.

cording to a genuine internal logic, in which the steps automatically followed one after the other. They can be traced in the king's correspondence. Before the fall of 1882, King Leopold had evoked the possible political aspects of his work only in private correspondence with his associates. Having passed the turning point in October 1882, he brought the problem to everyone whose help he could hope for in Belgium and especially abroad. His requests grew larger and larger. In the first stage, the king asked that the independence and neutrality of the stations set up in Africa be recognized, so that they might become "free cities" (this is still the vocabulary of the preceding period). "We formed miniature free cities," he wrote, "so let them expand freely. . . . Bremen, Lubeck, Hamburg were free cities for a long time, why would there not be some in the Congo?" [59] But given the extension of sovereignty beyond the stations, the notion of "free cities" gave way to one of "free stations *and territories.*" As of February 1883, it was a matter of the "confederation of our stations and territories." [60] Cannot "free stations and territories" be regarded instead as so many small states, in view of their territorial expansion? This was the next stage in King Leopold's thought and in his demands; he asked that the "Congo free States" [61] be recognized. The final stage was passage from

59. Letter from Eugène Beyens, attaché to the king's cabinet, communicating the king's instructions to Léon Lambert, November 3, 1882; Brussels, Archives de la Banque Lambert.

60. Letter from Jules Devaux, February 1, 1883 (copy), in the Granville papers, PRO 30/29/156. The expression "free stations and territories" was used for the last time in April 1884 in the exchange of statements with France concerning the right of preemption; the International Association of the Congo there claimed to speak "in the name of the free stations and territories that it established in the Congo and in the Niadi-Quillou valley" (April 23, 1884).

61. This was essentially the vocabulary used in the negotiation with the United States. In a letter to President Chester Arthur, finished in early November 1883, the king wrote: "Entire territories ceded by sovereign chiefs have been constituted by us into independent States"; R. Stanley Thomson, "Leopold II et Henry S. Sanford," *Congo* (October 1930), p. 303; François Bontinck, *Aux origines de l'Etat Indépendant du Congo. Documents tirés d'archives américaines* (Louvain, 1966), p. 135. Writing to the United States afterward, he spoke continually and principally of the "Etats libres," the "Free States." See King Leopold's letters to Strauch of November 8 and November 9, 1883 (MAE, Strauch papers) and instructions delivered to Sanford on November 15, 1883 (F. Bontinck, *Aux origines,* pp. 138–39). In his proceedings and publicity in the United States, Sanford almost always used this expression. The April 22, 1884, declaration, in which the United States recognized the flag of the Congo Association, described the latter as "the International Association of the Congo, administering . . . the interests of the Free States there established."

the plural to the singular. The "free States," as King Leopold saw them on the map, would continue to grow larger and certain ones would soon meet to form a single block. We can direct our agents, he wrote in January 1884, "to ensure the joining of our possessions."[62] Consequently, one State, in the singular, took form. And for the first time, in January 1884, the king wrote in his own hand these words which were the culminating point of his political thought: the "new State."[63]

This materialization in January 1884 resulted directly from the machinery set in motion in October 1882.

As dedicated as he was to his political creation, the king did not lose sight of the necessity of organizing economic activity in the Congo, in order to give his enterprise a direction. During 1883, he actively urged the formation of an "Anglo-French-Belgian"[64] trading company, grouping British, French, and Belgian capitalists.[65] But it was no longer a question of a company merged into his Congo enterprise, as in the preceding phase. A political power was in position in the Congo and it would simply take the trading company under its wing. We could, King Leopold noted, "grant it facilities,"[66] "rent our lands"[67] to it, "grant it a lease."[68] Henceforth the separation between the political and the commercial spheres was established.

62. The king to Strauch, January 18, 1884; MD, Strauch papers.

63. The king to Strauch, January 3, 1884; MAE, Strauch papers. The king to Lord Wolseley, February 24, 1884: the "new Free State we have founded in the Congo"; Marcel Luwel, "Léopold II et son ami Lord Wolseley," *Africa—Tervuren, 11* (1965), p. 33. Jules Devaux to Sanford, February 25, 1884; "the new State"; R. S. Thomson, "Léopold II et Henry S. Sanford," p. 324. Jules Devaux to Sanford, March 6, 1884: "The Association will not delay much longer to emancipate the territories and to settle them into an Independent State"; F. Bontinck, *Aux origines,* p. 177. The king's memo of April 27, 1884: "We want to create and we are creating the Independent State of Central Africa"; APR, FC, No. 98. The memo of April 27 prescribed the terms of a letter to be written to Sanford; see this letter in F. Bontinck, *Aux origines,* pp. 202–03.

64. Strauch to the king, February 22, 1883; MD, Strauch papers.

65. On this subject we will see Roger Anstey, *Britain and the Congo in the Nineteenth Century* (Oxford, 1962), pp. 186–87, and A. Roeykens, *Jules Malou,* pp. 15–20.

66. "You know I have always offered British capital a large share in my African enterprises. The presence of the Dutch formerly prevented the formation of an Anglo-Belgian company. It has become much easier now that our stations exist and can grant it facilities"; the king to Mackinnon, March 4, 1883; APR, FC, No. 2.

67. The king to Strauch, March 17, 1883; MD, Strauch papers.

68. "formation of the large trading company we dream of as soon as we have progressed enough to grant such a concession"; the king to Strauch, February 2, 1884; MAE, Strauch papers.

If the International Association of the Congo (such was the new name taken by King Leopold as of the end of 1882) declared itself foreign to all commercial activity, it could still define its commercial and economic policy: by doing this with a certain degree of skill, King Leopold would bring into play what would constitute beyond question his major asset. This was his second change of course—the promise of free trade.

The moment he abandoned his immediate commercial objectives, King Leopold could bring out more than ever the unselfish nature of his efforts in the Congo. His talents as a propagandist in this connection inspired him with admirable formulas.

> The International Association of the Congo [he wrote], is an association of rich philanthropists and men of science who, with a disinterested goal of civilization and for love of progress, seek to open the Congo basin. The Association has constructed, at its own expense and without any aid, a free road from the sea to the upper basin of the Congo, and it is endeavoring to establish posts on the river destined to become centers of civilization; and to do this legally, it obtained from certain native chiefs surrender of their sovereign rights, as well as large concessions from many other chiefs.[69]

"The International Congo Association," he had written in *The Times* in March 1883, "as it does not seek to gain money, and does not beg for aid of any State, resembles in a measure, by its organization, the Society of the Red Cross; it has been formed by means of large voluntary contributions, and with the noble aim of rendering lasting and disinterested services to the cause of progress." [70]

Today these texts might seem amusing, but the historian has to take them very seriously. They help to clarify the atmosphere that King Leopold managed to create around his enterprise. By what he said

69. Memorandum of November 1882 cited above, n. 31.

70. "The International Congo Association," article from a "Belgian correspondent," *The Times,* March 28, 1883. This "Belgian correspondent" was none other than Jules Devaux, the king's private secretary, who merely recopied a text written by the king, supplying only slight emendations; cf. on this publication APR, FC, No. 1, documents 23, 26, 27, 34, and 46. In his minute, the king bluntly called the Congo Association "a kind of African Red Cross." Devaux corrected and wrote in a more covered way: "Quite similar in its organization and principles to the Society of the Red Cross."

and allowed to be spread abroad, through his correspondence, through his personal contacts—and King Leopold could be admirably persuasive in private conversation—he succeeded until very late in life in preserving the *aura* of nobility and philanthropy which his earliest African initiatives had won for him. A good many of his contemporaries, among them some very distinguished personalities, actually believed in him. To understand their attitude, the praises they addressed to the king should probably not be taken literally all the time. "The great undertaking set on foot by your Majesty," Lord Wolseley wrote to him, "is one in which every lover of the human race must be interested." [71] Your Majesty's work, Henry Sanford wrote for his part, is "the most beneficent work of the century." [72] We obviously have to make allowances for flattery in these remarks. But there were occasional remarks exchanged outside the king's presence that afford a measure of the warm feelings held for him. From Sir Bartle Frere, for example, came these very significant lines in February 1883: "I had been much interested in the King of the Belgians' undertaking, from the time he first explained his views to me, when I was his guest at Brussels, some years ago; and though H.M. has not proceeded exactly as I should have thought prudent, his designs are most philanthropic and are amongst the few schemes of the kind, which seem to me entirely free from any selfish commercial or political object." [73] And two years later, in February 1885, William Mackinnon spoke with clear conviction of the "noblest and most self-sacrificing scheme for Africa's development that has ever been or ever will be attempted." [74]

But if he had been able to count on the support of only those who admired his philanthropy, King Leopold undoubtedly would not have achieved much. His stroke of genius was to understand that besides conserving this emotional support, he had at the same time to win at

71. Letter of February 20, 1884; M. Luwel, "Léopold II et son ami Lord Wolseley," p. 33.

72. Sanford to Leopold, May 2, 1884; APR, FC, No. 98.

73. Sir Bartle Frere to Lord Northbrook, February 22, 1883; FO 84/1803. Jacob Bright for his part wrote to Emile de Laveleye: "The generosity and public spirit of your King are admirable. It is a rare thing for a person in his position to make such sacrifices for the benefit of humanity"; March 15, 1883; APR, FC, No. 1. Laveleye, a professor at the University of Liège, was intimately acquainted with British liberals; see in particular Robert Demoulin, "Laveleye et Gladstone," in the volume *Chronique de l'Université de Liège*, published by M. Florkin and L. E. Halkin (Liège, 1967).

74. F. Bontinck, *Aux origines*, p. 276.

all costs the infinitely more powerful financial support if he wanted to succeed. The price he paid was the promise of free trade.

While carefully observing events in Britain, the king had what appears to us, in retrospect, his great inspiration.

The British government, we know, also had reacted to ratification of the Brazza-Makoko treaty, and to all that this action seemed to foretell on the French side.[75] They were particularly fearful in London lest France expand toward the Lower Congo—this was the direction in which France was expected to carry her effort[76]—and lest certain regions, to which Britain exported her products without any hindrance until then, consequently pass under French customs control. Britain wanted none of that, at any price: French protectionism, in her eyes, was a curse on British interests. It would be better to let the Portuguese rather than the French establish their sovereignty on the shores

75. For all that follows, we refer generally to R. Anstey, *Britain and the Congo,* pp. 100 ff., and to Eric Axelson, *Portugal and the Scramble for Africa, 1875–1891* (Johannesburg, 1967), pp. 54 ff.

76. In this connection Banning was an excellent witness of the opinion prevailing among thoughtful observers. He wrote in a note of December 4, 1882: "France just paved the way for herself . . . by taking possession of a few leagues of territory on the right bank of Stanley Pool. Materially, this possession is insignificant . . . but if the French get a foothold on this side, they will inevitably tend to expand along the right bank to the Atlantic, about one hundred leagues [250 miles] away, thus embracing, with the entire Ogoué basin, the whole area between the Gabon and the Congo"; J. Stengers, *Textes inédits d'Emile Banning,* p. 59.

It would take too long to consider here in detail what Brazza's and France's plans actually were. It will be noted simply that a first plan of action, prepared by Brazza in late October 1882, did foresee, as one could imagine, a French occupation on the Lower Congo; memorandum of October 28, 1882; MDA, 59. Afterward, though, prudence prevailed in Paris, where they feared a clash with the Portuguese in the Lower Congo. Instructions to Brazza in February 1883 therefore forbade him any action south of latitude 5° 12′, that is in the region claimed by Portugal. (This did not figure in the text of the official instructions. See this text in MDA, 59, folios 105 to 117, publ. in "L'Epopée de Savorgnan de Brazza. Documents inédits," *Cahiers Charles de Foucauld,* 2nd trimester [1952], pp. 56–58. But explicit mention of it must have been made either in secret instructions or in verbal instructions conveyed to Brazza; a whole series of subsequent allusions admit no doubt on the subject: see for example Duclerc to Jules Ferry, April 26, 1884, in MDA, 89.) But this abstention did not at all mean that France renounced the Lower Congo: everything leads us to think that the Quai d'Orsay plan consisted in coming to an understanding with Portugal so that France could expand along the right bank of the river; this plan for an agreement hoped for with Portugal was evoked particularly in a letter from Ferry to Brazza of June 26, 1883 (MDA, 88) and in a memo by Dutreuil de Rhins of February 1884 (ibid., 89, folio 150).

of the Lower Congo. As Sir Charles Dilke, one of the principal artisans of British policy, said, "in order to keep out France, we were glad to put forward Portugal." [77] Thus began negotiations between London and Lisbon at the end of 1882 concerning recognition of Portuguese sovereignty on the Lower Congo.

But we also know to what extent British trading circles took alarm as soon as they found out about the negotiations with Lisbon. In these circles, the reputation of the Portuguese—whom Stanley spiritedly called "that fearful tariff-loving nation, the Portuguese" [78]—was as bad as possible. The Chambers of Commerce sent one petition after the other to the Foreign Office opposing Portuguese dominion over the Lower Congo and warning Britain to maintain full freedom of trade in this region. In the beginning of April 1883, the treaty draft was attacked head on in the House of Commons. Representatives from Manchester, Bradford, Liverpool, came to speak forcefully all the ill they thought of the Portuguese. "The Portuguese have a method of making trade impossible," declared Jacob Bright; "they have passports, papers, tolls, fines, and fees—fees at every corner." [79] Portuguese domination, he also emphasized, was "a curse" on the natives everywhere in Africa.[80] Other voices would be raised again in the course of the debate, stressing this moral aspect, but the leitmotif remained, in spite of everything, the defense of free trade in the Congo against Portuguese claims.

From Brussels, King Leopold had his eyes riveted on London throughout this period. The prospect of the Anglo-Portuguese treaty was obviously crushing for him. For a certain time, he even feared complete disaster: he dreaded that the Portuguese, by means of the treaty and their installation on the Lower Congo, might attack some of his posts and take possession of them.[81] Even when he received

77. Memorandum of December 14, 1884, Windsor, Royal Archives, P 19, No. 128a.

78. *Manchester Chamber of Commerce. Special Meeting of Members held on Tuesday, October 21st, 1884. . . . Address of Mr. H. M. Stanley* (Manchester, 1884), p. 21.

79. *Hansard, 277,* col. 1286.

80. Ibid., col. 1292.

81. Hence the king's plan—which showed the extent of his anxieties—to put his imperiled possessions under the name of a British person, acting as a figurehead. "I am going to try to find a Briton under whose name I can put those of my stations threatened by the Portuguese," he wrote to Strauch on February 4, 1883; MAE, Strauch papers. A few days later, the king decided to write to the Rothschilds of London. On February 15, 1883, he sent them a note through

assurances in this connection from London,[82] there remained the very dark prospect of seeing his settlements cut off from the sea by a Portuguese territory, something that would risk causing the worst possible difficulties. His best hope was therefore that those in Britain who took a stand against the very principle of the treaty would prevail. Moreover he encouraged their action very eagerly and even surreptitiously took part in it.[83]

Lambert in which he explained: "The Anglo-Portuguese treaty will contain a clause assuring British subjects of proprietorship and free enjoyment of all their establishments and creations on the territory turned over to Portugal. The King would like to profit by this clause by finding in Britain a friend in whose name he may list those of his possessions threatened to fall into Portuguese territory. . . . The King thought of Messrs. de Rothschild to possibly do him this favor"; APR, FC, No. 1. On February 28, King Leopold informed Strauch of Rothschild's negative reply: "he does not want to lend me his name"; MD, Strauch papers.

In any case, the king's idea had found its direct application early in February when it was the basis for instructions sent to the Congo. On February 5, 1883, Strauch sent the following instructions to the manager of the Vivi station: "If the Portuguese appear at your station or try to settle on the lands belonging to it, you will inform them that they are in a free city and on free territory; that the British have been co-proprietors of it since the beginning of our operations, for a considerable and perhaps even absolutely preponderant share; that you cannot surrender it to any one except on the order of the International Association of the Upper Congo; that in the meantime you claim for the city and territory the immunities stipulated by the treaty in behalf of the British settlements." Eugene, University of Oregon Library, Van de Velde papers.

82. By writing to the Prince of Wales, King Leopold succeeded in obtaining assurances in March 1883. The king "implored" his *dear Bertie* "to use his influence with Mr. Gladstone's Government to prevent any robbery by Portugal of his new African possessions"; Sir Sidney Lee, *King Edward VII. A Biography* (London, 1925), *1*, 630–31. The prince spoke of the matter to Granville, who wrote to him on March 12, 1883: "It might please the King of the Belgians if you were to inform him that Your Royal Highness has been informed by me that it is proposed to limit the Portuguese territory, or rather not to admit Portuguese sovereignty beyond Embomma. This will not comprise the Belgian settlements, and as free navigation and transit will be received, it is probable that the King will be satisfied." This text was immediately sent to Brussels, and the king found great consolation in it; Sir Francis Knollys to Jules Devaux, March 12, 1883, and King Leopold to the Prince of Wales, March 13, 1883, APR, FC, No. 1.

83. Here for example is the plan the king laid before Lambert on April 25, 1883, "to ask the Rothschilds to have M. Gladstone and Sir Charles Dilke, etc. speak to this effect": "Clearly the Portuguese yoke would ruin all the posts and enterprises in that country [i.e. the Lower Congo] and it would be entirely nominal in all other respects. As in Egypt, and despite all the laws and fine promises, foreigners would move away and slavery would flourish—who does not recall what Cameron said on this subject? . . . Civilization, Christianity, the

The debate in the House of Commons in early April delighted the king. The concluding speech by William Forster, an influential liberal, particularly impressed him.[84] Forster questioned why the Portuguese were so anxious to establish themselves on the Lower Congo. It is, he answered, because "the Congo has become a valuable country." Trade has started there "and the Portuguese wish to gain something by it." Nevertheless, if Britain was going to negotiate with Portugal, she should obtain the most trustworthy guarantees in order to safeguard her own commercial interests. "We must first of all make it clear that there shall be no toll-bar, that there will be no dues exacted on the river; that it will be a free highway." But, Forster added slyly, "if this be done, the motive of the Portuguese will be gone."[85]

This kindled the spark for King Leopold. According to Forster's reasoning, the idea of "no toll-bar" on the Lower Congo virtually condemned to death the Anglo-Portuguese treaty draft by depriving it, on the Portuguese side, of its raison d'être. Now what better means could there be for King Leopold to contribute to the triumph of this idea than to show how it was applied a little farther up on the Congo? At the same time—and this, too, was a principal factor—freedom of trade in the Congo, which the debate in Commons had proven the commercial circles to be especially sensitive about, could serve King Leopold as a lure, and a powerful lure, to obtain recognition of his settlements. The king made his decision at once: this was the card he would play.

Here the chronology is very illuminating. The debate in the Chamber of Commons took place on April 3, 1883. The report appeared the next morning, April 4, in *The Times,* and the king in all probability read it the same evening.[86] On April 6, he reached his decision. Ad-

trade and industry of the world and consequently of Britain, in particular, are interested in the Congo's being African and not Portuguese"; APR, FC, No. 82. "Christianity" is particularly odd here under the pen of a Catholic sovereign who asks Jews to caution a Protestant government against a Catholic power.

84. "The King was delighted at the excellent speeches of Messrs. Bright, Forster and Bourke and at those of Lord Fitzmaurice and of Mr. Gladstone. Nothing could be more clever than the way in which Mr. Forster ended the debate"; Devaux to Mackinnon, April 5, 1883; London, School of Oriental and African Studies, Mackinnon papers.

85. *Hansard, 277,* col. 1330–31.

86. The king's copy of *The Times* reached Brussels in the afternoon by the Ostend-Basel express. On passing in front of the little station at Laeken, the mail officer would throw the case containing the newspaper onto the platform. It was picked up by a footman and immediately brought to the Royal Palace. See Baron Carton de Wiart, *Léopold II. Souvenirs des dernières années, 1901–*

dressing his most influential British contact, Sir John Kirk, he had his private secretary, Jules Devaux, write: "His Majesty wants me to tell you confidentially that if England, alone or with other powers, were willing to proclaim the neutrality of the mouths of the Congo and to acknowledge the neutrality of our stations, we would take the engagement not to establish customs or any tax on our roads." [87]

Mackinnon—another valuable ally of the king—was likewise informed in the days that followed, and in a letter from Strauch to Mackinnon dated April 29, the promise took its full form: "His Majesty requests that you kindly explain to some of the influential members of Parliament, after coming to an understanding with Sir John Kirk, the importance and urgency of recognizing the neutrality of our stations. . . . As you and Sir John know, our stations would take the engagement not to establish any customs in the whole area of their possessions or any taxes for use of the international road connecting them." [88]

Early in May, writing to the banker Gerson von Bleichröder (who had close ties with Bismarck), the king stated precisely:

> The Congo is bordered with free stations and vast territories that belong to us. It would be well to neutralize them by an agreement among some or all the powers. . . . A bill of neutralization is an official act that entails neither expense, nor duty, nor responsibility for the States passing it. We would respond to it by a formal promise not to put any customs around our stations, or any tax on our international road.[89]

The change was complete: the contrabandist had become a gendarme. The man who had done his best to obtain the strictest monopolies in Africa became the champion of free trade.

1909 (Brussels, 1944), p. 44, and G. Stinglhamber and P. Dresse, *Léopold II au travail* (Brussels, 1945), p. 38. The reading of *The Times,* his correspondence shows, was a veritable daily ritual of the king

87. APR, FC, No. 1; Pierre van Zuylen, who published this text in French translation, mistakenly made of it a letter addressed to Mackinnon; see *L'Echiquier congolais,* p. 70

88. School of Oriental and African Studies, Mackinnon papers. The king's instructions to Strauch which originated this letter were dated April 28: "Write to Mackinnon tomorrow. . . . Tell him to try, in harmony with Sir J. Kirk, to plant the idea of proclaiming the neutrality of our stations (which would pledge not to have any customs) in the mind of several well placed Members of Parliament who could bring it up at the right moment"; MD, Strauch papers.

89. May 4, 1883 letter; Marcel Luwel, "Gerson von Bleichröder, l'ami commun de Léopold II et de Bismarck," *Africa-Tervuren, 11* (1965), pp. 96–97.

The king assumed this new role in such a way that it soon became the fundamental element in his policy. Negotiations with the United States, which began at the end of 1883, were based on assurances of free trade. The Congo "Free States," specified the instructions delivered to Henry S. Sanford on November 15, 1883, with a view to the negotiations, had a flag "under which there would be neither slavery, nor privileges for anyone, nor customs barrier." [90] The promise was so remarkable, so exceptional, that the king foresaw questions it could provoke. He defended himself in advance instructions: "If they were to ask: but without customs how will the Free States defray the cost of their administration?, we would answer: the philanthropic International Association of the Congo is engaged in subsidizing them." [91] In actual fact, this indiscreet question does not seem to have arisen during negotiations, and on April 22, 1884, emerged a formal agreement endorsed by the Association in exchange for recognition by the United States: the Association and the Congo "Free States" "have resolved to levy no custom-house duties upon goods or articles of merchandise imported to their territories or brought by the route which has been constructed around the Congo cataracts; this they have done with a view of enabling commerce to penetrate into Equatorial Africa."

90. F. Bontinck, *Aux origines,* p. 139.

91. This seems to be the first appearance of what developed into a significant theme of the king's propaganda in 1884: there is no need to worry about the financial future of the new Independent State for it will be "endowed." "*Eine Dotation solle seine Zukunft sicherstellen,*" the king said to the German minister in Brussels in May 1884; ABK, *1.* Folge, p. 71. "The new State," repeated Stanley, "has an endowment fund by which it is supported until it is well nigh matured and become fixed and stable"; *Manchester Chamber of Commerce. Special Meeting,* p. 18. In still greater detail, the Congo Association published a document entitled "Manifesto of the International Association" in October 1884 affirming: "The Association possess a capital at their disposal of which the interest has sufficed hitherto to cover the expenses of their work. As soon as the State shall have been recognised by the civilised nations, and its political existence assured, this capital will be employed to endow the new State. . . . The interest derived from this endowment fund will be equal to the revenue which might be obtained by a system of custom-house duties. It will suffice to defray all expenses of the new State until such time as the increase of public wealth, and the natural increase in the white population, will allow of its fulfilling all its engagements"; FO 84/1817, and as a supplement in *Manchester Chamber of Commerce. Special Meeting,* pp. 37–38. This wonderful "endowment," it will be noted, was not imaginary, but it consisted in nothing other than a part of King Leopold's personal fortune; cf. Jean Stengers, "Note sur l'histoire des finances congolaises: le *trésor* ou *fonds spécial* du Roi-Souverain," *Bulletin de l'Institut Royal Colonial Belge,* 25 (1954).

In 1884, when he arrived at the phrase "Independent State," King Leopold insisted vigorously on the fact that the state he created was "an Independent State without customs or taxes."[92] These simple words led him to triumph.

One of the king's problems after his metamorphosis was that he had not been able to erase all traces of his former state. Some of the first treaties signed in the Congo had been conveyed in 1883 to the Portuguese,[93] who, in publishing them, made a point of drawing attention to the "exclusive" clauses that figured in them prominently. But King Leopold's dialectical ingeniousness permitted him to find the answer: it was necessary, he declared, that the treaties make the Association exclusive mistress, in order to give it "without any question the right to offer free access to its territories to all peoples."[94] In fact, the promises for the present were so solemn and generous that, fortunately for King Leopold, hardly anyone lagged behind to examine the past too closely.

The promise of freedom of trade explained the recognition of the Congo Association by the United States. Probably this lure, notable in itself and skillfully handled as well, would have been sufficient to obtain similar recognition from other powers. But if such recognition allowed the Association to affirm its sovereign nature, it specified nothing as to which territory this sovereignty was exercised over.

92. "An Independent State without customs or taxes"; Jules Devaux to Sanford, March 6, 1884, publ. in F. Bontinck, *Aux origines,* p. 177. "The State without customs"; the king to Strauch, May 29, 1884; MAE, Strauch papers. "The International Association is trying to establish an independent state without customs"; from Borchgrave d'Altena, the king's private secretary, to Auguste d'Anethan, Belgian minister in The Hague, July 18, 1884; Brussels, d'Anethan papers. "We should like to see the new independent state without customs extend as far as the end of the mouth of the Congo"; Borchgrave to d'Anethan, ibid., July 30 ,1884; this text in the form of a memo was sent through d'Anethan to the Dutch foreign minister: see his letter of July 31, 1884 to The Hague, MAE, A 106, *Kongo Kwestie,* No. 2, January–August 1884. "Stanley asked me to make him an outline of the speeches he will have to make in Britain. . . . He has only to tell the story of what he has done . . . and explain that we seek to found an independent State without customs"; the king to Strauch, August 5, 1884; MAE, Strauch papers. "Stanley simply ought to explain the advantages that Britain and her trade derive from the creation of an independent State without customs in the Congo"; Borchgrave to Sanford, August 31, 1884, publ. in R. Stanley Thomson, "Léopold II et le Congo révélés par les notes privées de Henry S. Sanford," *Congo* (February 1931), p. 196, and F. Bontinck, *Aux origines,* p. 222; etc., etc.

93. See above, n. 24.

94. The king to Strauch, October 8, 1883; MAE, Strauch papers.

Now what King Leopold obtained successively from Germany and France, in addition to recognition of sovereignty, was recognition of the Association's frontiers: this was an unparalleled success—one tenth of tropical Africa bestowed upon a small monarch who so far could depend on only a very modest, effective occupation. At the time Germany accorded him the immense reaches of the Upper Congo, above Stanley Pool, he still had only about twenty European agents in all lost in that vastness.[95]

King Leopold would not have achieved this major success by means of the commercial attraction alone. It was only possible thanks to the special agreement he concluded with France in April 1884.

This agreement once again marked a departure from his original path. One of the king's guiding principles in his African enterprise had been to keep his hands entirely free, from a political standpoint. Yet in April 1884, he bound himself especially with France. Why?

Here again the king's tactics were dictated first of all by the perspectives opened by the Anglo-Portuguese treaty. This treaty had finally been concluded in February 1884 after prolonged negotiations. In accordance with her promises,[96] Britain had considered King Leopold's interests and had seen to it that the Association's posts remained outside the Portuguese zone. But passage between these posts and the sea—or, more precisely, the river ports accessible to seagoing ships—would henceforth be across Portuguese territory. It would therefore be necessary to negotiate a transit agreement with Lisbon. This was a grave matter, all the more difficult since the Portuguese were as ill-disposed as possible toward the Association. With a view to these negotiations, which promised to be very hard, King Leopold wanted an arm, a means of intimidation he could use to bring the Portuguese to reason. The means he conceived was the right of preemption.

To understand how King Leopold inserted this provision in his agreement with France, we must expose in a more general way where he stood in his relations with Paris in the beginning of 1884. The subject is not easy to treat. The sources indeed are very few and are some-

95. Cf. A. J. Wauters, *Les Belges au Congo* (Brussels, 1885), pp. 16 and 21–22. Add to the posts mentioned by Wauters that of Mpala, on Lake Tanganyika, run by Storms; R. Heremans, *Les établissements de l'Association Internationale Africaine au Lac Tanganika et les Pères Blancs. Mpala et Karéma, 1877–1885* (Tervuren, 1966), p. 53. The total number of Congo Association agents in Africa at the time we are speaking of—that is in November 1884—must have been about 160 (Wauters, ibid. and p. 24), but the great majority of them were in the Lower Congo, in the Niari-Kwilou region and on Stanley Pool.

96. See above, n. 82.

times deficient. This scarcity of sources resulted from the way negotiations with Paris were conducted. The main part was done through direct contacts at the Quai d'Orsay, between Jules Ferry and an unofficial representative of King Leopold, who had nothing of the diplomat about him but who was very widely known and well respected in Parisian society, the great picture dealer Arthur Stevens.[97] In Brussels, the regular diplomatic advisers, Lambermont and Banning, were not kept well informed; nor was the Belgian minister in Paris. Consequently no sources are to be found among Belgian diplomatic documents. Jules Ferry, for his part, did not consult his colleagues of the Navy and the Colonies: thus there was no correspondence between the Quai d'Orsay and the Colonial Office.[98] Even in the Quai d'Orsay almost nothing was saved by way of documents relating to the negotiation; in particular one finds practically no résumé of the Ferry-Stevens conversations. Stevens' correspondence with the king's cabinet no longer exists except in a very incomplete state; not one document has been found for the period from November 1883 to May 1884.[99] All this points to the historian's state of destitution and suffices to explain his occasional perplexity.

On the whole, though, when we put the remaining pieces of the puzzle together, we manage to see fairly clearly. The first interviews between Stevens and Ferry took place in late November and early December 1883.[100] The general theme was the conclusion of an understanding between France and the Association, so as to head off all possible clashes in Africa. From these first contacts and the ones that followed, a clear idea progressively emerged for the king of what France refused to grant him under any circumstances, what she would

97. "I am very pleased that your talks with Mr. Stevens were successful," the king wrote to Jules Ferry on April 23, 1884; MDA, *89*. On Arthur Stevens —whose two brothers, Joseph and Alfred, were well-known painters (Alfred Stevens painted with much refinement elegant Parisian women of the Second Empire)—see the account by L. Solvay in the *Biographie Nationale, 23* (Brussels, 1921–24), cols. 850–54, and G. Vanzype, *Les frères Stevens* (Brussels, 1936).

98. A memo from the colonial director, attached to a letter drafted by the colonial undersecretary of state to Jules Ferry on July 3, 1884, stated with regard to the agreement on the right of preemption: "the agreement that the department of Foreign Affairs concluded with the International Association—without consulting us"; Paris, Archives Nationales [AN hereafter], SOM, Afrique VI/41/a.

99. APR, FC, No. 103.

100. Note in MDA, *88*, folio 315, and letter from Stevens to Jules Devaux of November 23, 1883, APR, FC, No. 103.

eventually be ready to concede, and the price she would demand in exchange.

France refused under any circumstances to allow the Association or the Congo posts any statute of sovereignty whatever. Jules Ferry was very firm on this point. In 1883, before going into the Quai d'Orsay—he then had the problem before him as Président du Conseil—Ferry had written: "The Comité [he was still referring to the Comité d'Etudes du Haut-Congo] is and always will be only a private association, it is neither Belgium, nor the King of the Belgians, it can have neither a recognized flag, nor regular forces, nor sovereign rights of any kind." [101] He had not modified his opinion by the beginning of 1884, and it does not seem that King Leopold made any great effort to sway it; [102] he probably felt it would have been useless to try.

What could be obtained from France, on the other hand, was a good neighbor ("bon voisinage") agreement by which she engaged to "respect" the Association's possessions.

But what was the price to be paid for this? Actually it was rather reasonable: France demanded above all the Association's assurance not to sell its possessions. They simply said "sell," but each side understood it to mean, sell to Britain. Indeed, what Paris dreaded most was learning one fine day that King Leopold had disappeared from the African scene and that Britain had taken his place. This fear can be very easily explained. They were convinced that King Leopold—in whom they really wanted to see a philanthropist, but whom they also

101. Personal letter from Ferry to Brazza, June 26, 1883; MDA, *88*. In this letter Ferry defined his position following approaches made simultaneously to him and to the foreign minister, Challemel-Lacour, by Auguste Couvreur, a Belgian politician sent to Paris by King Leopold. Cf. on those approaches, in addition to the June 26 letter, the memorandum of June 9, 1883, in the same volume of MDA, folios 4 to 7 and 8 to 12. In a letter of August 14, 1883, to Couvreur, Ferry repeated that he saw in the Comité d'Etudes "a Company which will never, whatever happens, be anything but an institution of a private nature"; ibid., folios 120 to 122; the addressee of the letter was not named, but could only be Couvreur. The phrase "whatever happens" indicates the determined character of his position.

102. The theme of recognition was not even touched upon in a first draft agreement between France and the Association—drawn up in Brussels, of course —which Stevens submitted to Ferry, probably in late January 1884 or a little later: King Leopold undoubtedly realized it would have been labor lost; "Première proposition de M. Stevens," MDA, *89;* the document is attached to a letter of January 24, 1884, from Stevens to Ferry, but that resulted from a classification of documents in the file which appears quite unreliable; it was probably written later than January 24.

considered an incurably naïve "dreamer" [103]—was in the process of ruining himself in a foolish adventure. The experts waited for the time that would inevitably come when he would break his back.[104] At that moment, to whom would he give a chance, if not to Britain? Although the head of his expedition, Stanley, was of American nationality, he was British at heart. Ever since late 1882, agents recruited in Great Britain had been flocking to the Congo—an actual "British wave." [105] Was this not an indication that the enterprise could easily become British?

The minister of France in Brussels, Count Montebello, forewarned the Quai d'Orsay against this danger. As early as March 1883, he wrote: "It is not impossible to foresee the day when the International Association, left to the personal resources of the King of the Belgians or losing in him its only support, would surrender to some British company the fruit of its efforts which it could no longer maintain." [106] In December 1883 and March 1884 Montebello repeated these warnings.[107]

103. "The disease of the imagination to which the King of the Belgians is a prey," "a dreaming King," the "speculations and reveries of the King of the Belgians": these were the terms used by Jules Ferry speaking about King Leopold. See Ferry to Courcel, December 16, 1884; Geoffroy de Courcel, *L'Influence de la Conférence de Berlin de 1885 sur le droit colonial international* (Paris, 1935), pp. 78–79 and 98–99.

104. "No one supposes the Association is likely to last long, even if it be intended that it should do so"; memo by Lister concerning a dispatch from Malet to Granville of February 5, 1885; FO 84/1821.

105. "From 1882 onwards what we called the *great British wave* broke," Valcke wrote in his memoirs; L. Valcke, "L'idée coloniale et Léopold II," Chap. IV, *Le Vingtième Siècle,* January 13, 1932. The figures are very striking: at the time of Stanley's return to Europe in 1882, of forty-three European agents serving in the Congo, three were British (list in the A.G.R., Banning papers, No. 122); in November 1883, out of a hundred and seventeen agents, there were forty-one British (R. S. Thomson, "Léopold II et Henry S. Sanford," p. 305). It will be noted here that the massive recruitment of British agents had been linked in a large degree to political preoccupations. King Leopold was contemplating the most effective way possible to resist foreign enterprises—those of the Portuguese and of Brazza—and it seemed to him that Britons would make the most impression on the eventual adversary. "I do not need to explain to you the importance of finding some Britons and employing them in the Congo, that would be perhaps the only means of preventing the French from upsetting us," he wrote to Strauch in April 1883; letter of April 20 in MD, Strauch papers.

106. Dispatch of March 8, 1883; Quai d'Orsay, *Correspondance politique. Belgique 75.*

107. "The resources at the King's disposal do not allow us to think that he can . . . continue for a long time without more real support. The situation

From the depth of Africa, Brazza expressed the same fears. In late December 1883, he wrote to the Foreign Secretary: "May I call to your attention my anxiety concerning the introduction and increase of a British element around Stanley. It is to be feared that Belgium is being duped in this affair and that Britain is trying to start again here what she did in Egypt. She would then hold the whole center of Africa by means of the Niger, the Congo, and the Nile Rivers."[108] In May 1884 Father Augouard of the Fathers of the Holy Spirit reported for his part (he was at one and the same time the servant of God and of France) "According to what I have said, it seems to me that this expedition will become British in the near future, because the Belgian element today is being successively eliminated to make place for the British."[109]

Curiously, King Leopold himself had done nothing for some time to destroy this impression and these fears in Paris. In September 1883, when a personal letter from Stanley was published in Britain in which, in his British enthusiasm, he went as far as to wish for a protectorate of Britain over the Congo,[110] the king wrote to Strauch in the manner of

---

[meaning the financial situation] can become critical from one moment to the next. . . . One may assume that he would look to Britain for the basis for a settlement which some important syndicate would carry through at first, and then the British government would become involved; ibid., December 29, 1883. "Reliable sources have assured me that the King of the Belgians never intended, as has been insinuated, to make any transfer to Britain and he never even had such a notion at the back of his mind. Nevertheless we may expect that, tired at last of the considerable personal cost to himself of an operation which meets nothing but constant opposition, King Leopold will perhaps finish one day by accepting offers that would free him from the responsibility and the burdens of an enterprise that he is supporting alone today"; ibid., March 29, 1884.

108. Brazza to the Foreign Minister, "Poste au confluent Alima-Leketi," December 27, 1883; MDA *88*. In the same connection, see also the personal letter which Brazza wrote the same day to Jules Ferry: "I have the same misgivings as Dr. Ballay concerning the introduction and increase of the British element around Stanley, and I wonder what Belgium's role is. Is it a voluntary role of dupe that conceals other designs?"; ibid.

109. Augouard to Félix Faure, colonial undersecretary of state, May 13, 1884; Paris, ANSOM, Afrique IV/40/a.

110. See, on this letter and its psychological explanation, Jean Stengers, "Stanley, Léopold II et l'Angleterre," *Le Flambeau* (1954), pp. 383–85, and Roland Oliver, "Six unpublished letters of H. M. Stanley," *Bulletin de l'Académie Royale des Sciences coloniales, 3* (1957), pp. 344–46. The complete text of the letter, which was addressed to Johnston, is in R. Oliver, pp. 352–56. We point out that King Leopold did not take the affair too seriously. He wrote to Strauch on September 26: "Stanley's letter to Johnston urges the British to uphold their treaties with the chiefs of the Mouths of the Congo for the repression of slavery,

a Machiavellian calculator: "It is my judgment not to attempt a rectification. It does no harm for Paris to fear that a British protectorate could be established in the Congo." [111] Undoubtedly he saw there a way of bringing Britain into play against France.

But early in 1884, Jules Ferry wanted the speculating ended and any danger of possible surrender to Britain averted. He demanded therefore, as we said, that the Association formally promise not to sell its possessions to a foreign power.[112]

Accessorially, since the British danger was symbolized by Stanley, whom France considered an indomitable enemy (they never forgot in France that Stanley treated Brazza like a barefoot tramp, nor would they ever forgive him for that), Ferry also expressed the wish that Stanley be recalled.[113]

King Leopold complied in April 1884 with both the demand and the wish (Stanley's recall being treated only unofficially, of course).[114] But, by a sudden inspiration—here everything clearly bears the mark of improvisation—he went further: he *offered* France (who by no

---

and, since they are such an expansive people, not to block their own access to the magnificent Congo by handing its mouth over to the Portuguese. He reproaches Johnston with his Portuguese inclinations. There is nothing to find fault with in this letter, except where he urges the British to proclaim their protectorate. That word goes too far"; MD, Strauch papers. Nonetheless Stanley was admonished so he would not repeat the offense: "Mr. Stanley detracts from his own work by writing in such a way that one might believe . . . a British protectorate was necessary. The King begs him earnestly not to write that again to any one"; letter from Strauch to Stanley of October 1, 1883 (summary) "DN"; cf. E. Van Grieken, "H. M. Stanley au Congo," 2nd part, pp. 1453–54.

111. Letter of September 26, 1883; MD, Strauch papers.

112. "The truth is that France demanded from the Association the promise not to sell to any power"; the king's note of May 23, 1884; APR, FC, No. 98.

113. This was not mentioned explicitly in any document, but was implied in King Leopold's promise to recall Stanley.

114. "The King of the Belgians has sent me assurances that Stanley's recall is already a settled matter"; Jules Ferry to Brazza, April 25, 1884; MDA, 89. The question of the nationality of the Association's "officials" was probably brought up in a more general way in the Paris negotiations also. In any case, Jules Ferry stressed this theme in an official letter to King Leopold the day after the agreement was concluded: "Your Majesty will permit me to add that the happy agreement whose foundations we just sealed will be, in its daily application, all the easier to ensure as the African Association pays more particular attention to choosing its officials in the same spirit which dictated the convention. Anything that can make more manifest and tangible, as it were, the Association's neutral character will advance its credit in the world, and it seems to me from this standpoint that the collaboration of such distinguished officers borrowed from the Belgian army is most desirable and most appropriate to that end"; April 25, 1884; MDA, 89.

means asked for it) a right of preemption.[115] He sent the following formula to Paris:

> The International Congo Association, in the name of the free stations and territories it has established in the Congo and in the Niadi-Quillou valley, formally declares that it will not cede them to any power, reserving any special conventions which might be arranged between France and the Association, such as the delimitations of their territories or mutual concessions [this was the pledge France demanded].
>
> At the same time [this was King Leopold's addition] the Association desires to give fresh proof of its friendly sentiments toward France and engages to give her the right of preemption if unforeseen circumstances contrary to its goal should lead the Association to realize on its possessions.[116]

115. The king himself affirmed very clearly that he *offered* France the right of preemption. He had it written to Sanford on April 27, 1884, then he himself wrote him a few days later. Jules Devaux to Sanford, April 27: "We have had this accepted by Paris"; F. Bontinck, *Aux origines*, p. 212; Devaux's letter was based on one of the king's memos of the same date; he simply translated what the latter wrote concerning the right of preemption: "We have had this accepted by Paris," APR, FC, No. 98. The king's private letter to Sanford, written a few days later, so far has not been found; we know about it through an allusion by Sanford of May 22 (Bontinck, *Aux origines*, p. 210) and particularly through what the French minister to Washington said of it: "Mr. Sanford," wrote Roustan, "sent me in strict confidence a long, handwritten letter he received from King Leopold. Speaking of the clause which stipulates a privilege in France's favor in case of surrender, His Majesty says that this clause was inserted at his request to spare him difficulties with Portugal"; dispatch of June 13, 1884, Quai d'Orsay, *Correspondance politique. Etats-Unis 161.* In all probability this was the same letter sent to the German minister in Washington; he claimed in fact to have seen a handwritten letter by the king, and he quoted word for word the following passage from it: "The clause which gives France a right of preemption was introduced at our request to prevent Portugal from harassing us with attacks that could, if they discouraged us, secure France as her neighbor; thus it also has as a goal consolidation of the operation"; ABK, 1. Folge, p. 71. When he received the German minister in Brussels on May 13, King Leopold emphasized that the right of preemption clause had been "included in the exchange of statements in consideration of the Association's wish and not on France's suggestion nor under pressure from her"; R. S. Thomson, *Fondation de l'Etat Indépendant du Congo,* p. 167; ABK, 1. Folge, p. 71.

116. MDA, 89, folio 143. The date of "January 24, 1884" that was later inscribed on the document in a different hand is definitely incorrect; given the improvised nature of the right of preemption, it is practically certain that the formula must have been proposed at almost the last minute and must therefore be dated April 1884.

This text, slightly modified,[117] was the object of the final, official exchange of letters between Jules Ferry and Strauch dated April 23 and 24, 1884.

The king's own initiative and improvisation characterized the right of preemption. The advisers to the Belgian foreign secretary, Lambermont and Banning, knew nothing about the April agreement until it was communicated to them.[118] The only associate of the king who could have possibly helped him by his advice—but we do not know whether he did—was his private secretary, Jules Devaux.[119] The document proposed to Paris, which was accepted, was in any case written with as much levity as lack of foresight. The author did not even consider the hypothesis (which, nevertheless, obviously corresponded to the King's intentions, at some point) of a surrender of the Congo to Belgium. The oversight was almost absurd, but—the fact exists—it escaped the king's attention in the handling of his scheme. Consequently, each time there would be a question of an annexation of the Congo by Belgium, and when the annexation would be finally made, France would bring up her right of preemption and interfere in an

117. "Reserving *any* special conventions" was replaced in the final version by "reserving *the* special conventions"; "such as the delimitations of their territories or mutual concessions," by "to fix limits and conditions to their respective activities." These corrections resulted undoubtedly from a polishing of the text at the Quai d'Orsay; they are also found in the document cited in the preceding note, entered in the margin of the form sent out by the Association.

118. "The decision was made in the King's Cabinet without any participation by the Department of Foreign Affairs which only learned of it as an established bill"; Emile Banning, *La Belgique et l'Etat Indépendant du Congo. Histoire de leurs rapports, 1892–1895,* p. 169 of the typewritten copy, A.G.R., Banning papers, No. 156; see also E. Banning, *Mémoires politiques et diplomatiques* (Brussels, 1927), p. 8. In 1894, Lambermont explained to the British minister in Brussels that "the King had given the original engagement without previously consulting either him or any other of his usual councillors, and apparently without appreciating the possible consequences of the act. The only persons who knew beforehand of the King's intentions in this respect were Monsieur Devaux and Colonel Strauch"; dispatch by Plunkett, June 2, 1894; FO 10/615.

119. Devaux—through whom all the correspondence with Stevens passed (APR, FC, No. 103)—undoubtedly followed the negotiations from beginning to end; furthermore he informed the French minister in Brussels of their development (cf. in this regard Montebello's dispatch of May 10, 1884; Quai d'Orsay, *Correspondance politique. Belgique 75*). But did he advise the king? We have on this point only a vague assertion by Baron Beyens ("I have reason to believe that [the agreement] was suggested to King Leopold by M. Jules Devaux"; see "Souvenirs sur Léopold II et la Cour de Belgique," *Revue Générale,* June 15, 1932, p. 708), who was an attaché to the king's cabinet in 1884, but whose recollections of this problem are unfortunately tainted in other respects by confusion and many mistakes.

extremely annoying and disagreeable way.[120] During almost a quarter of a century, that was the price paid for a moment of inadvertence. Banning, who represented the traditions of prudent, cautious diplomacy, would never get over it.[121]

But what was the aim of the king's maneuver? He explained it very plainly himself in conversations and private letters. He put it briefly to Lambermont in a letter of May 13, 1884: "The clause reserving our right to sell is aimed at the Portuguese to oblige them to treat us with consideration." [122] He explained it more fully to Lord Granville on May 15: "Your lordship knows of the Portuguese attacks against us and their efforts to thwart our plans. . . . By reserving our power to liquidate our holdings and by granting France the right of preemption, we wanted to make some of our adversaries aware that, if successful, their efforts to injure us could finally turn against themselves." [123]

To translate this into less diplomatic terms, King Leopold would henceforward be able to say to the Portuguese in his negotiations with them: if you do not give me acceptable conditions, I will concede the game, and, given my agreement with France, consider who will become your neighbor in my place. That would make them think twice. "The Portuguese will probably be less hostile when they see that their opposition to us, if successful, would only result in giving them the French as neighbors," the king wrote to Francis de Winton, Stanley's successor in the Congo.[124]

In a conversation with the German minister in Brussels,[125] and in a

120. Banning, *La Belgique et l'Etat Indépendant du Congo,* Chap. V; P. van Zuylen, *L'Echiquier congolais,* Chaps. XI, XVII, and XXI; Jean Stengers, "La première tentative de reprise du Congo par la Belgique, 1894–1895," *Bulletin de la Société Royale Belge de Géographie, 73* (1949), 67 ff.

121. "Ill-considered promise," "fatal error," he wrote until the end of his life; *La Belgique et l'Etat Indépendant du Congo,* pp. 178 and 235.

122. MAE, *Afrique. Association Internationale du Congo, 3* (January–May 1884), document 82 bis.

123. Granville papers, PRO 30/29/156; publ. after the minute preserved in the royal archives, by P. van Zuylen, *L'Echiquier congolais,* pp. 87–88.

124. May 26, 1884; Marcel Luwel, *Sir Francis de Winton, Administrateur Général du Congo, 1884–1886* (Tervuren, 1964), p. 222.

125. On May 13 the king told the German diplomat that the Association "feared for its future existence, and dreaded especially the hostile attitude of Portugal, which . . . would try to make conditions for its existence as difficult as possible, and would work at its destruction as long as it could hope to profit from this policy. The clause that gives France a right of preemption . . . ruins Portugal's prospect. She will not try to bring about the ruin of a free State if she has to fear seeing France, a more powerful and more dangerous neighbor, take the place of the first one"; R. S. Thomson, *Fondation de l'Etat Indépendant du Congo,* p. 167; ABK, 1. Folge, p. 71.

personal letter to Sanford,[126] the king explained the sense of his tactics in the same way. Everything indicates that these were sincere explanations: the king demonstrated the maneuver he had conceived with the intention of making an impression on the Portuguese. Nothing leads us to think that he had further motives or more cleverly calculated objectives.

In other words, the weapon he found was not, in his mind, a grand strategy, but a tactical weapon for immediate use in a battle for which he was preparing.

But on the tactical level, which he envisaged, the results of the April 1884 agreement were disastrous. In London, the right of preemption granted to France provoked genuine fury:[127] it was a severe blow to the credit and popularity of the king, whom the Foreign Office accused of having played "a shabby and mischievous trick."[128] As for King Leopold's weapon, it proved completely useless because the negotiations in view of which it was conceived never took place: since the Anglo-Portuguese treaty never went into effect, no transit convention with Lisbon was necessary. For lack of an encounter, the weapon was left unused.

But, without King Leopold's having anticipated it in the slightest, the right of preemption produced major results of much longer fruition on the strategic level.

Results of two orders (we leave aside here France's interventions in the process of recovery of the Congo by Belgium, because as unpleasant as they may have been for Belgium, their importance was almost negligible if we take into account their influence on the general evolution of events): extraordinarily profitable results for King Leopold in the establishment of his frontiers; and, on the contrary, dreadful results when he then tried leaving his boundaries to extend his territorial occupation in Africa.

Frontiers first of all: from the moment King Leopold drew the

126. See above, n. 115.

127. R. Anstey, *Britain and the Congo,* pp. 171–72; J. Stengers, "Rapport sur le dossier: Correspondance Léopold II—Strauch," *Bulletin de l'Institut Royal Colonial Belge, 24* (1953), 1195–96 and 1203–09. The Belgian minister in London, Solvyns, was stupefied. Dilke related in his memoirs that "Solvyns came to the Foreign Office and told an Assistant Undersecretary what he thought of 'the folly of Belgium mixing herself up in such matters and running the risk of losing the friendship of England.' He said he had not the slightest idea what had induced his King to throw himself and his Congo Association into the hands of France"; London, British Museum, Add. MSS, 43.929, folio 26.

128. Lister's note of May 20, 1884; Granville papers, PRO 30/29/198.

boundaries he claimed in a bold outline on the map—he did so for the first time in the beginning of August 1884[129]—he showed himself extremely greedy: his pencil stroke penetrated as far as the heart of Africa. Yet, as we have said, the king succeeded in having such ambitious and all but unreasonable frontiers recognized successively by Germany and France. Germany—that is, Bismarck did so in November 1884, France (which even granted King Leopold an extension of territory in comparison with what Germany had accepted), in February 1885.

Bismarck played a major role by his gracious condescension. How is his attitude to be explained? His conversation with the ambassador of France, the Baron de Courcel, in late August 1884, no doubt enlightens us more than anything else. The chancellor was in Varzin at the time. He had just received from King Leopold the map of Africa interpreting the latter's ambitions. On August 27 he spoke to the French ambassador about it. This is the Baron's account:

> The Prince of Bismarck showed me a map King Leopold sent him on which were represented the boundaries of the territory where the Belgian association aspires to form a sovereign state: it is an immense quadrilateral including the whole sweep of the upper Congo, that is the whole course of the river from the cataracts on the West to the great lake region on the East, we might as well say all central Africa, the very core of the continent.
>
> It is indeed vast, the Prince-Chancellor said to me, but it is not for us to bridle those ambitions, seeing that the Company guarantees our trading freedom and that the benefit to us from application of this principle increases with the size of the Company's operations. I do not know just what this Belgian Association is, nor what will become of it, but all the same it would not succeed in establishing itself very seriously, and it is always useful for diverting troublesome rivalries and claims that we could handle less easily ourselves. We can give it our backing to clear the way.[130]

These loose, rather cynical remarks give us the key to Bismarck's attitude. He had hardly any confidence in King Leopold's success—moreover who did at the time?—but since this philanthropic king

129. Jean Stengers, "Léopold II et la fixation des frontières du Congo," *Le Flambeau* (1963), pp. 175–76.

130. Dispatch from Courcel, August 30, 1884; Quai d'Orsay, *Correspondance politique; Allemagne, 58.*

wanted to open Africa at his own expense and to everyone's gain, they might as well let him forge ahead; why stop him?

But if, after some hesitation, Bismarck finally went so far as to recognize formally the boundaries claimed by King Leopold, it was for still another essential reason: he knew that France—with whom he was engaged in politics of reconciliation—would make no objection to it. In his correspondence with King Leopold, he explicitly mentioned this favorable factor: "My conversations with the baron de Courcel permit me to think that France would not be opposed to the area indicated on the map which Your Majesty kindly sent me."[131] This was really a fundamental factor: Bismarck said yes only because France said yes, and France said yes on account of the right of preemption.

When King Leopold turned to France after reaching a satisfactory agreement with Bismarck, he hustled things on still more briskly. Negotiations with Paris most certainly presented some very delicate matters, but on one point at least there was no difficulty: King Leopold asked for even more far-reaching frontiers than Germany conceded him,[132] and Paris agreed, almost without argument. The right of preemption clearly underlay the whole affair: like a true heir apparent, France could only be very happy to see the territorial expansion of an association whose spoils she hoped to inherit one day.

In Berlin, the right of preemption was the condition sine qua non; in Paris, it was the reason for King Leopold's astounding success.[133]

Eventually, after the harvest of big profits, came the era of great drawbacks. It began the moment King Leopold directed his efforts to the Upper Nile. We know what that policy represented for the king: it soon constituted his major preoccupation, or more exactly, his obsession. The Congo, which he considered "prosaic," was not enough for him. He needed the Upper Nile, which fascinated him, at all cost. But his efforts in this direction—considerable efforts that at a certain time consumed the best of his resources—came up against Britain's watchful guard. Britain was the biggest obstacle in the king's path, and

131. Bismarck to King Leopold, September 4, 1884, APR, FC, No. 116; publ. in Pierre Daye, *Léopold II* (Paris, 1934), pp. 212–14.

132. J. Stengers, "Léopold II et la fixation des frontières," pp. 180–84.

133. As for Britain, she normally should have found in the right of preemption an objection—and even a major one—to recognizing the boundaries of a state to which France was named possible heir. But things did not happen normally: King Leopold obtained British recognition through a mistake made in the Foreign Office; see J. Stengers, "Léopold II et la fixation des frontières," pp. 188 ff. In Berlin and Paris, political logic had worked; in London, it was an accident of history.

it was she who made him fail in the end. But if Britain so firmly opposed him, the reason was that King Leopold was not alone, but rather accompained in the background by France, a possible successor. The right of preemption was a fatal handicap for him vis-à-vis Britain.

"Dreadful results," "fatal handicap": this is the vocabulary that King Leopold probably would have been inclined to use himself, pondering the way his policy on the Nile was weighed down by the right of preemption. But from another standpoint than his own, let us note that it is not forbidden to adopt a different perspective. Objectively considered, the Nile policy was in any case a piece of folly that could have no serious, positive result. To hinder the king in the unfolding of this policy was thus actually to do him a favor. King Leopold himself ought to have judged that the right of preemption would be his undoing on the Upper Nile. Perhaps an objective consideration of things allows one to say that here, too, in spite of everything, this particular failure was fortunate for him.

Strauch, who was King Leopold's continual collaborator in the creation of the Congo, wrote to an African agent in 1881: "Every new enterprise undergoes many vicissitudes. It is necessary to know how to bow to circumstances, and as they say, trim our sails to the wind." [134] The turn of phrase could have been signed by the king, for it conveys his policy admirably. King Leopold showed in his ventures a perseverance, an obstinacy that nothing discouraged, but he was very adaptable. We have seen it throughout this study, and we have also seen that this adaptability saved him.

From 1882 to 1884, each time King Leopold made a major change of direction, he did so in sympathy with either French or British policy in Africa. The first change: Brazza. The second: the Anglo-Portuguese treaty threat. The third: the treaty itself.

But under the circumstances, French policy and British policy were related. What King Leopold reacted to, the initiatives whether from Paris or London to which he had to adjust, were basically actions emanating from Anglo-French rivalry in Africa.

Yet the issues did not come to a head on the same level in all three cases: in the case of Brazza and ratification of the Makoko treaty, Anglo-French rivalry was felt on the level of public opinion; after that, for the Anglo-Portuguese treaty, the rivalry worked principally on the government level.

A few words, first of all, very briefly, on the meaning ratification of the Brazza-Makoko treaty had in France. A neutral, cool observer, the

134. Strauch to Lindner, October 31, 1881; M. Luwel, *Otto Lindner,* p. 210.

minister of the Netherlands in Paris, synthesized the development of the affair in a report of November 27, 1882, in these terms: "Initially, the French government was not very inclined to take the treaty seriously, but public opinion, roused by newspapers of every bent, forced, so to speak, its attention on the matter more than was its original intention."[135] This was a completely accurate interpretation. The minister, theoretically qualified to consider the problem of ratification, adopted a negative attitude and was ready to bury the affair;[136] the naval secretary, Jean Jauréguiberry, was even openly opposed to Brazza's undertaking.[137] But a big wave of enthusiasm coming from the press and breaking into public opinion carried the day: the government had to move in the direction necessitated by a public opinion literally obsessed by the Congo.[138] This patriotic, chauvinistic fever, which in the long run determined everything, had multiple psychological causes, but on the deepest level, it was primarily a will to affirm French grandeur after the humiliation suffered in Egypt. At the heart of it was the need to take revenge on Britain.[139] Here, Anglo-French rivalry was the great, basic psychological reality.

The rivalry also worked, only this time essentially on the governmental level—needless to bring it up again as it is very clear—in the negotiation of the Anglo-Portuguese treaty.

The winds that Anglo-French rivalry blew over Africa were the ones King Leopold, an ever watchful helmsman, "trimmed his sail" to; his frail skiff, which everything predisposed to shipwreck, thus came majestically into port.

135. The Hague, MAE, A 106, *Kongo Kwestie,* No. 1, 1876–83.

136. Henri Brunschwig, *L'avènement de l'Afrique noire du XIXe siècle à nos jours* (Paris, 1963), pp. 149 ff.

137. This hostility was openly spoken of in the meetings of the committee of the Chamber of Deputies charged to investigate approval of the treaty; see the committee's proceedings in AN, C 3393, dossier 2070. The chairman, Rouvier, proposed not mentioning the fact in the report. "It will be useless," he said, "to state in the report that the Naval Minister is opposed to the enterprise. But it must be clearly understood that this opposition will be rendered powerless."

138. Jean Stengers, "L'impérialisme colonial de la fin du XIXe siècle: mythe ou réalité," *Journal of African History,* 3 (1962), 474 ff.

139. Ibid., p. 476.

☙ 5. *The Berlin Congo Conference*

☙ WM. ROGER LOUIS

In reevaluating the history of the Berlin Conference of 1884–85, two dominant and neglected themes become apparent: the agitation of the British and French press over the questions of the Congo and Niger in relation to the major issues of international security and commerce in the late nineteenth century; and the legalistic approach of the Gladstone Government to colonial questions. Spurred by public opinion, the Foreign Office sought to establish British claims on the Niger and to protect British trade on the Congo; harnessed with the legal precepts of the lord chancellor, the British government espoused mid-Victorian juristic concepts that were imposed on the Conference and became embodied in the General Act. A new evaluation of the Berlin Conference from the perspective of Britain vis-à-vis France therefore must attempt to determine the nature of "public opinion" and its influence on the policy-making process, and the legalistic preconceptions of the policy makers. This smacks of jargon, but deliberately so, for this essay, basically historical in approach, attempts to reexamine the work of Britain at the Berlin Conference by drawing occasionally on the disciplines of political science and international law. It also aims to give the deathblow to the persisting myth recently restated by none other than Kwame Nkrumah, that "the original carve-up of Africa [was] arranged at the Berlin Conference of 1884." [1]

1. Kwame Nkrumah, *Challenge of the Congo* (New York, 1967), p. x. The mythology of the Berlin Act is traced in part by J. Stengers. "A propos de l'Acte de Berlin, ou comment naît une légende," *Zaïre, 8* (1953), 839–44.

In writing this chapter I have been indebted to Jean Stengers for placing at my disposal a large number of notes on the French press for 1884–85, which I have supplemented with my own research. Since in the preceding chapter he writes on a closely related topic from the perspective of France and Belgium, this essay relies essentially on British archives and newspapers in approaching the "Berlin Congo Conference" (its popular title in the press, which in my opinion it deserves to retain since the major discussions concerned that region). I have nevertheless studied the relevant unpublished as well as published French

Conspiratorial theories were rife in 1884–85, and contemporary misconceptions about the nature of the Conference help to explain the mythology of the European powers plotting Africa's fate only two years after Britain had occupied Egypt. Egypt remained foremost in the public's mind. A mere glance at the newspapers of 1884 strike the reader with the importance of the continuing Egyptian emergency. But was there a causal connection between the British occupation of Egypt and the subsequent "partition of Africa" with which the Berlin Conference is usually associated? Robinson and Gallagher in *Africa and the Victorians* argue forcefully that the British intervention sparked the "Scramble" for Africa.[2] Their book is a landmark in the history of the

---

documents and have attempted to survey the French press. In attempting to come to grips with that elusive concept, "public opinion," I have decided after much thought that it is best employed in accordance with its usage in 1884–85; in the words of the head of the African Department of the Foreign Office, it meant merely news and opinion *"published in the principal newspapers."* These are the French newspapers that occasionally had relevant passages: *Echo de Paris, Economiste Français, Evénement, Figaro, Français, France, Gaulois, Intransigeant, Journal des Débats, Liberté, Messager de Paris, National, Revue des Deux Mondes, Temps, Télégraphe, Republique Française, Soleil,* and *Voltaire.* The British press debated the issues of the Conference much more extensively. Some—but by no means all—of the newspapers I consulted are: *Daily Chronicle, Daily News, Daily Telegraph, Economist, Glasgow Herald, Globe, Leeds Mercury, Liverpool Courier, Liverpool Daily Post, Manchester Examiner and Times, Manchester Guardian, Morning Advertiser, Morning Post, Observer, Pall Mall Gazette, St. James Gazette, Saturday Review, Spectator, Standard, Sunday Times, The Times,* and *Truth.* The major problem facing the historian of the press is governmental influence on the news and editorial opinion, but that topic is irrelevant to the use I have attempted to make out of the press for this paper: to investigate European preconceptions of Africa in 1884–85. Anyone who works in the field of *Publicity and Diplomacy* is indebted to Oron James Hale who wrote a pioneer work of that title (New York, 1940), and to several works by E. Malcolm Carroll, of which the most relevant to this topic is *French Public Opinion and Foreign Affairs, 1870–1914* (New York, 1931).

2. Ronald Robinson and John Gallagher, with Alice Denny, *Africa and the Victorians: the Official Mind of Imperialism* (London, 1961); important reviews related to western Africa and the Congo by C. W. Newbury and Jean Stengers, *Journal of African History,* 3 (1962), 469–501. Robinson and Gallagher glide over the problems of the Conference and dismiss its importance by pointing out that "At no time before, during or after the Berlin Conference was there a parliamentary debate about its aims or its results" (p. 177). For the details of the Conference and the significance of the Berlin Act, one must rely on the two most important works on the subject, both of which were written over a quarter of a century ago: S. E. Crowe, *The Berlin West African Conference* (London, 1942), and Geoffroy de Courcel, *L'Influence de la Conférence de Berlin de 1885 sur le droit colonial international* (Paris, 1935). See also especially Rob-

expansion of Europe, above all because it demonstrates the crucial role of the Egyptian crisis in the grand strategy of British statesmen in the rest of Africa and, indeed, in the entire eastern hemisphere. Yet their single, basic explanation—Egypt—is as unsatisfactory as the answer given by British journalists and officials of the 1880s, who thought in a more general way that France conspired against England not only in Egypt but throughout the world.

Englishmen on the whole did not view Egypt's occupation as the decisive event that determined the course of the partition; and Robinson and Gallagher do not investigate why the English public held France responsible for the colonial rivalries that became the central theme of international relations in the 1880s and 1890s. The same observation (not criticism) applies to S. E. Crowe's book on the Berlin Conference, which will continue to remain the definitive study of official British policy. She also did not attempt to study the history of the era in relation to public opinion. This essay, in a sense, begins where both Robinson and Gallagher and Crowe stop—by asking these questions: docs a study of the British and French press as well as of the official documents throw light on what "caused" the Scramble, or, in a broader and more ambitious sense, the First World War? Does an examination of the publicity as well as the diplomacy of the Conference reveal further the development of European attitudes toward Africa—Europe's image of Africa in the mid-1880s? Does this sort of

---

ert Stanley Thomson, *La Fondation de l'Etat Indépendant du Congo* (Brussels, 1933); K. O. Diké, *Trade and Politics in the Niger Delta, 1830–1885* (Oxford, 1956); J. E. Flint, *Sir George Goldie and the Making of Nigeria* (London, 1960); Henri Brunschwig, *Mythes et Réalités de l'Impérialisme colonial français, 1871–1914* (Paris, 1960); Roger Anstey, *Britain and the Congo in the Nineteenth Century* (Oxford, 1962); and John D. Hargreaves, *Prelude to the Partition of West Africa* (London, 1963). A standard French work that deserves special mention is by Maurice Baumont, *L'Essor Industriel et l'Impérialisme Colonial* (Paris, 1937). Chapter nine of William L. Langer's *European Alliances and Alignments* (New York, 1956 ed.) has a valuable bibliography; see also Jacques Willequet, "Die Geschichte des Belgisch-Kongo 1876–1960: Eine bibliographische Orientierung," *Jahresbibliographie Bibliothek für Zeitgeschichte, 32* (1960), 357–82. Otherwise dated monographs that still have occasional points of interest include: A. B. Keith, *The Belgian Congo and the Berlin Act* (Oxford, 1919); Georg Königk, *Die Berliner Kongo-Konferenz 1884–1885* (Essen, 1938); J. S. Reeves, *The International Beginnings of the Congo Free State* (Baltimore, 1894); José Gonçalo Santa Ritta, *Conferência de Berlim de 1885* (Lisbon, 1916); Robert H. Wienefeld, *Franco-German Relations, 1878–1885* (Baltimore, 1929); and Howard E. Yarnall, *The Great Powers and the Congo Conference in the years 1884 and 1885* (Göttingen, 1934).

investigation have any relevance for African as well as European history? The answer may be negative; but the questions are worth asking, if only to take a step toward the main task yet to be accomplished by the historian of the expansion of Europe: to recapture, as Felix Frankfurter once said in quite a different context, "that impalpable thing, what was in the air" when Europe scrambled for colonies.

Who started it? "The kettle began it, but who lighted the fire which started the kettle?" asked the *Glasgow Herald* surveying the Scramble. "we fear the solution will be as difficult as in the old game of Blackcap and Bluecap. Germany says England, England says France, France says Germany, and Spain says everybody." [3] The quotation accurately depicts British attitudes. For reasons that Englishmen failed to attribute to economic gain, the French "colonial appetite" seemed to grow, in British eyes, with every new morsel of territory swallowed up in Africa and Asia. Glory and mischief, not profit, motivated the French in Tunis, Senegal, Madagascar, and Tonkin. According to *The Times* in May 1883:

> It has been said that France is always peeping through the keyhole to see what Prince Bismarck is doing; and that if at any time when she finds him looking the other way she sets off to amuse herself in her own old fashion in some unoccupied corner of the world. First it was Tunis, then the Congo, then Tonquin, and now the Madagascar adventure is in full activity.[4]

Over a year later the *Daily Chronicle* reiterated the theme that summarizes the general English interpretation of French expansion from 1881: "France, largely out of consideration for her reverses fourteen years ago and her decline as a European Power, has been allowed a free hand—a too free hand, indeed—in divers quarters of the globe, and she has shown her gratitude to the Powers that have left her free to pursue a 'spirited foreign policy' by ruthlessly trampling upon their interests when it has suited her to do so." [5]

When the *Daily Chronicle* voiced that typical indictment of French policy, Britain and France had been joined in the struggle for colonial supremacy by another major power, Germany. The colonial balance of power was shifting, but in which direction? Would English interests be damaged by the advent of Germany as a colonial power? Was England's "natural ally" Germany or France? The following excerpt

3. January 9, 1885.
4. May 25, 1883.
5. June 4, 1884.

from the *Manchester Guardian* reflects the consensus of English opinion at the time of the Berlin Conference, when Anglo-German colonial rivalry was most bitter:

> Are we to continue to regard the friendship of France as the keystone of our foreign policy, even though, as in Egypt and in most other parts of the world at present, our interests are opposed to hers; or are we to maintain our traditional friendship with Germany, whose interests in Europe are identical with our own? So long as the Continental Powers were entirely absorbed in their own revolutions or unifications it was possible for England to go her own way, gradually building up a colonial empire, and paying little or no regard to the disputes by which the unsettled commonwealth of Europe was agitated.
>
> Those days are over. The other Powers seek to gratify a natural ambition for colonial extension. It is impossible for us to resist them all, and we should be wise to make up our minds without delay which is the Power whose interests lie nearest to our own, and which is the Power whom we should prefer in case of need to find upon the same side with ourselves.[6]

France had provoked a colonial scramble; Germany had entered the race; and England's stance was indecisive. So ran the prominent ideas through the English press.

"Stands England where she did?" The question resounded throughout the years 1884–85. With the "capitalists of Europe" ready to advance into the non-European world, would England be able to maintain her commercial supremacy of the nineteenth century? Possibly drifting toward war with France over Egypt, and facing recurrent crises with Russia over Afghanistan, Englishmen questioned whether the "immortal lyric" of having ships, men, and money continued to hold true. "Britain still rules the waves," commented the *Globe,*[7] a newspaper that closely followed naval and colonial issues; but could England withstand an assault by a European alliance?

The industrial revolution led by England now seemed to be working against her as the European nations emerged as her competitors overseas and as they threatened her with alignments challenging her colonial supremacy. According to the Liberal newspaper most sensitive to colonial issues, the *Pall Mall Gazette:* "Day by Day the world perceptibly shrinks before our eyes. Steam and electricity have brought all

6. January 2, 1885.
7. March 21, 1884.

the world next door. We have yet to re-adjust our political arrangements to the revolution that has been wrought in time and space." [8] The issue of England's ability to adjust to a changing world in turn gave rise to another fundamental question. Was the British Empire in a state of "decline and decay"? In jingo tone the *Morning Post* answered unequivocally:

> England is still a great Power. Nay, more, in a very comprehensive sense, she is the greatest of Powers and the mother of great Powers both present and future. England has an empire in every quarter of the globe. Her fleet still commands the seas. Her fleet is saluted by all the world. She would fain go on calmly in the majesty of her strength, ready to welcome all in the paths of peace and progress. But if she be struck at she will strike back. Not once, nor twice, but until right be done. At least she can strike with a heart which has never quailed, and with an arm which does not know the meaning of defeat.[9]

Such bluster might not seem surprising from such a conservative organ as the *Morning Post,* but similar effusions throughout the English press indicate the pangs of insecurity felt by the nation as a whole.

Frenchmen of course viewed the issues of overseas rivalry quite differently. Their attention in this regard mainly focused on Egypt, to a lesser degree on British "obstruction" in the Far East and West Africa. These insults hurled at the British during the abortive Anglo-French Egyptian Conference of June 1884 typified French sentiments: the *Journal des Débats* referred to the "chimerical time" when British troops would withdraw from the Nile and labeled English promises as "soapbubbles"; the *Télégraphe* entitled a leading article "Egypt for the English"; the *National* accused prime minister Jules Ferry of "excessive condescension" toward Gladstone; the *Gaulois* called the French ambassador in London "blind and incapable" in his dealings with the English; the *Messager de Paris* denounced the French policy of "capitulation"; and the *France* caught the general polemical tone of the press by attacking the English as "clever traders" who did not hesitate to take advantage of French interests throughout the world. A few journals such as the *Liberté* and the *Voltaire* expressed more moderate opinion, but all in all the French attitude toward England in mid-1884 was hostile, and by no means only because of Egypt. The *Journal des Débats* saw this as the heart of the matter: "Not content

8. July 30, 1884.
9. August 12, 1884.

with seizing the Nile, the English want to get their hands on the Congo and the Niger, those grand commercial routes."[10] To prevent British domination of those rivers, the French public generally supported the idea of Franco-German cooperation in colonial questions.

The French publicists who wrote on colonial questions in 1884–85 recognized that the Franco-German entente was a colonial understanding and not an entente in the sense of a permanent alignment designed to change or stabilize the European balance of power. Despite alarmist reports that Jules Ferry had been tricked by Bismarck into compromising France's security by again becoming embroiled in overseas ventures, the press on the whole emphasized that the two governments had merely reached an accord on the affairs of western Africa, and that this agreement was relatively insignificant. The chronological evolution of the issue in the public eye reflects this view. From April 1884, when Bismarck broached the subject of naval and colonial cooperation with France against England,[11] to August of the same year, when he concluded the entente with Ferry,[12] the French press continued to be engrossed in the Egyptian question. Not until shortly before the convocation of the Berlin Conference did other African issues become the main topic of discussion.

An editorial in the *Republique Française* of October 10 is a good example of a typical analysis of the Franco-German rapprochement and its implications for Europe and the colonial world:

> For our part we have never attached importance to the report of a Franco-German alliance against England. That there exists between France and Germany a community of interests sufficiently important

10. October 12, 1884.

11. See Courcel to Ferry, April 25, 1884, *Documents diplomatiques français* [*DDF* hereafter], 1st series, 5, 267–71, No. 249. Bismarck's approach to France coincided with his commitment to protect German merchants in South-West Africa.

12. See *DDF,* 1st series, 5, 365 ff. The unpublished documents at the Ministère des Affaires Etrangères [MAE hereafter] and in the Section d'Outre-Mer, Archives Nationales [ANSOM hereafter] add but little to the published documents on Franco-German collaboration. For different interpretations see Pearl B. Mitchell, *The Bismarckian Policy of Conciliation with France, 1875–1885* (Philadelphia, 1935), A. J. P. Taylor, *Germany's First Bid for Colonies, 1884–1885* (London, 1938), and a thorough, critical reexamination of the problem by Henry Ashby Turner, Jr., "Bismarck's Imperialist Venture: Anti-British in Origin?" in *Britain and Germany in Africa: Imperial Rivalry and Colonial Rule,* eds. Prosser Gifford and Wm. Roger Louis (New Haven, 1967). The fullest account of French policy in the Berlin Conference era is by Thomas F. Power, Jr., *Jules Ferry and the Renaissance of French Imperialism* (New York, 1966 ed.).

> to give rise to an accord implying common diplomatic action is quite natural. But an alliance is quite another affair. . . . France and Germany do not gravitate in the same political orbit.

"The bulk of public opinion," concluded the newspaper, was "dead against this alliance, arrangement, or understanding" if it meant a permanent agreement about Europe. But the *Republique Française* admitted that there could be united action in tropical Africa. Most Frenchmen conscious of foreign affairs probably agreed. According to the *Journal des Débats* on October 6: "When certain newspapers talk of a *German alliance* it is impossible to ignore the fact that this is merely a play on words." A permanent political alignment would be impossible; but there were certain places where Germany and France had common interests to defend, and it would be no sign of weakness or humiliation if France joined Germany in righting English wrongs in Egypt or restraining English "annexationist tendencies" in other parts of Africa. "We can even make concessions to German colonial policy in the rest of Africa and support German colonial and commercial schemes where they do not run counter to ours." [13] Generally, Franco-German colonial cooperation would act as a check against Britain's maritime supremacy and would maintain equal access to territories not yet occupied; specifically, the French looked for German goodwill in Egypt and in return would support Bismarck's colonial ventures in western Africa.

The Frenchman who publicly voiced his opinion on western Africa with greatest authority was the publicist-parliamentarian, Gabriel Charmes.[14] An expert on the affairs of Egypt, he resented Britain's occupation in 1882 and since then, in signed editorials in the *Journal des Débats,* had repeatedly sounded alarms at British overseas activity elsewhere. He gave sustained attention to colonial issues, and the pattern of his thought makes him a representative of doctrinaire French "imperialism" in the 1880s. He believed that the French government's preoccupation with Europe prevented the public from seeing that France could recover from the reverse of 1870 only by colonial expansion. Lagging in industrial development, France needed

13. *Journal des Débats,* October 6, 1884

14. See his book, *Politique Extérieure et Coloniale* (Paris, 1885); also *L'Egypte* (Paris, 1891). For Charmes' background see *Le Livre du Centennaire du Journal des Débats, 1789–1889* (Paris, 1889), the article by Etienne Lamy, pp. 376–83; also Agnes Murphy, *The Ideology of French Imperialism* (Washington, 1948), Chap. 5. The other prominent publicist was Paul Leroy-Beaulieu, whose views are discussed below.

raw material and markets abroad. Colonial expansion would provide an outlet for surplus capital; moveover, it would give France the opportunity to mobilize the manpower of Africa and Asia, thereby perhaps eventually compensating for France's inferior size and growth of population. In a word, the power and glory of France in his opinion depended on overseas development.

Charmes' more specific views illustrate the temper of French opinion shortly before the Berlin Conference. One of the main purposes of colonial enterprise, he thought, was to improve France's economy and strategic potential against her continental rival; but overseas she found herself frustrated by Britain. Charmes wrote in October 1884:

> If we were always to remain separated from Prince von Bismarck, we ought to be united to England as her ally. For some years we were so united, and so long as this lasted, it was easy for us to hold aloof from Germany, because we had no interest to connect us with her. But everyone knows how the English alliance came to an end. . . . We have explained why we no longer have an alliance with England, and why, in China as in Egypt, we shall perhaps be compelled to accept the support of Germany, which will cost us much more and will be less useful to us.

Charmes thus adjusted his ideas to changing circumstances. French patriotism would not be compromised, he stated, if France and Germany worked together in western Africa. But French statesmen should be cautious in their dealings with Bismarck, whose overseas aims differed from France's. According to Charmes, Bismarck's colonial policy until 1884 consisted of being clever enough to profit from the colonies of others while Germany had none herself. Since Germany had "neither the cash nor inclination" to establish colonies in savage areas, the solution was to let others create colonies and make sure that German merchants had trading rights. That explained Bismarck's motive in wanting to collaborate on the Congo and Niger, and France clearly had less reason to be enthusiastic.[15]

"Regarding the Congo," Charmes wrote, "France, thanks to the courage and skill of M. de Brazza, possesses above the cataracts a vast tract of territory extending along both banks, we believe one as well as the other, but in any case a territory extensive enough so that we have nothing to fear from our neighbors." French rights to the Upper Congo as well as to other areas in Africa rested on the basis of effective occupation. "One can well understand how it is in Germany's

15. *Journal des Débats*, October 7, 1884.

interest to try to suppress these rights as well as those possessed by other nations that have long fought on the seas. In this way a tabula rasa would be created that would efface history." [16] Germany might be permitted to advance in regions where no French interests existed, but why should free trade be established in territory claimed by France? Charmes therefore urged limited Franco-German cooperation, but saw that the aims of the two countries differed fundamentally. He demanded to know whether the Ministry of Foreign affairs saw the dangers of Bismarck's proposals.

Bismarck's scheme essentially consisted of applying the principle of free trade to as much of western Africa as the French would agree to.[17] "The German proposal," wrote Ferry, "aims to provide for German goods and products free access, free traffic and free trade in regions not yet explored in central Africa." The main territory in question was the Upper Congo, commonly believed to have the greatest potential for trade. France had access to that region via the Ogooué River and Brazzaville, and if a differential tariff were established, French commerce would be protected and would profit. But the Ogooué unfortunately was not the best entrance to the interior. The Congo River provided a shorter and easier route to Brazzaville; if a railway could be built around the cataracts to the beginning of the Upper Congo (Stanley Pool), the trade of the interior could be much more easily tapped. France therefore had an interest in seeing that railway privileges should be nondiscriminatory and in securing as free an access to the Congo River as other nations; in short, there were good reasons for applying the principle of free trade to the Congo and in cooperating with Bismarck in this regard—even though Germany would benefit from the pioneering of other countries. Bismarck's ideas about refusing to recognize new annexations without concomitant guarantees of free trade were obviously more problematical; there were advantages to be gained from the principle when foreign trading interests were predominant, disadvantages when French trade was supreme. Thus the French government had ambivalent feelings about espousing Bismarck's Free-Trade proposals, but in any case his support could be used to wrench concessions from the British. To the Niger, concluded Ferry, should be extended the same principles as applied to the Congo.[18]

16. Ibid., October 13, 1884.

17. See Ferry's memorandum of August 22, 1884, *DDF*, 1st series, 5, No. 376; supplementary material of interest in MAE Afrique 86 ff., 108–09, and Allemagne 59–62; and ANSOM Afrique VI/43–44.

18. Ferry, *DDF*, 1st series, 5, No. 376.

The idea that the Niger was anything other than an "English river" aroused indignation in England, where the issues of rivalry in western Africa were discussed with much greater intensity and frequency than in France. According to the *Globe:* "The Niger has been a British possession in all but the form of having been declared such, and in all the essentials of dominion it is as much part of our Colonial Empire as Natal or the Cape." [19] In the same vein the *Leeds Mercury* commented: "the Niger is now to all intents and purposes an English river. Its mouths have been formally annexed by England; the river itself has been opened up by English explorers and English traders; peace is kept among the peoples on its banks by the patrolling of English gunboats, and it is the English Consul who is the recognized arbiter of all disputes." [20]

In other words, the Niger was as English as the Senegal was French, and if the Niger became the subject of an international conference, why should not the Senegal also be discussed? With "French logic" Ferry and Bismarck seemed bent on "internationalizing" the wrong river:

> It is difficult to see how France can justify her claim to undivided rights on the Senegal by arguments which England may not with equal force apply to her own position on the greater river. We do not mean that England should imitate her neighbour's use of her opportunities. In the Senegal and the wide territories which it waters French trade enjoys exclusive privileges. In the Niger trade is as free to French and Germans as it is to Englishmen, as free as it is on the Hooghly or the Mersey. . . . The Niger cannot be rendered more free than it is at present.[21]

"The demand for free navigation," complained the *Standard,* "could be put forward much more cogently with respect to the Senegal; but . . . this magnificent stream is to remain under the exclusive dominion of France, as well as the entire Upper Niger from its source as far as Timbuctoo, over which France assumes a shadowy protectorate." [22] The same point was also often made in camparing the Niger with the Congo: "The claims of France in respect of the Congo are doubtful, shadowy, and a subject for future ambition. Those of this country in respect of the Lower Niger are real and actual." [23] No doubt existed in the public's mind about British dominance on the Niger.

19. October 17, 1884.
20. October 16, 1884.
21. *Daily News,* October 20, 1884.
22. November 15, 1884.
23. *Globe,* December 1, 1884.

The doctrine of Free Trade—trade "without restrictions, without preferential duties or private advantages of any sort"[24]—governed British attitudes and policy on both the Niger and Congo. As stated by the *Leeds Mercury,* "The policy of England in this matter is summed up in the good old phrase 'A fair field and no favour.'"[25] In the words of the *Standard:*

> "The object [of the Berlin Conference]" we are told, "is to extend the blessings of Free Trade and equality of rights to all nations interested in the trade of West Africa." It would be impossible to frame a policy more distinctly in accordance with British views and interests. Our complaint is that all the world over the Governments that are called civilised are building up walls of hostile tariffs, to keep out the legitimate commercial enterprise of this country. Our ambition is to find markets, not to assert dominion; we do not want to extend our Empire, but to find outlets for our industries and avenues for our trade.[26]

In that regard the main point was that the Niger stood on an entirely different footing from the Congo. The Niger had been opened up by English explorers and traders. It was under the protection of the English government. By contrast the Congo had only recently been explored and had become a cockpit of international rivalry. The English guaranteed Free Trade on the Niger, while the French threatened to seal off the Upper Congo by protective tariffs. Now, in collusion with Bismarck, the French also were attempting to introduce some sort of international regime on the Niger that would interfere with English trade and protection. According to the *Standard,* "Prince Bismarck and M. Ferry wish to oust British jurisdiction from a region where it has hitherto been indisputably exercised."[27] The *Daily Chronicle* thundered that for France and Germany to demand that Britain "give up an administration it has cost her much time and wealth to build up, and in which fair treatment is meted out is, to the trader and native alike, not only an absurdity, but almost an impertinence."[28]

24. *Manchester Examiner and Times,* October 18, 1884. This apepars to have been the popular conception of Free Trade at the time, but for its reality see the chapter below by Colin Newbury. I have capitalized such phrases as Free Trade and Scramble because that is the way they appeared in the press when they were meant to convey a concept beyond the literal meaning of the words.

25. October 16, 1884.

26. October 11, 1884.

27. November 15, 1884.

28. December 6, 1884.

The *Globe* most cogently stated the difference between the two cases in a leading article entitled "The Congo and the Niger":

> Surveillance over the exercise of free commerce, navigation, and so forth, should not be made the business of an International body, that being the duty and privilege of England, as the chief, if not sole proprietary Power on the Lower Niger. . . . There is . . . [a] failure to recognise the different international positions of the two rivers—that is to say, the main principle involved in the whole contention, so far as England is concerned. The equal neutrality of the two rivers, and their equal control by the same Association, would be tantamount to a refusal to recognise English rights; and should no strongly marked difference be made, then all the advantage we have obtained on the Niger will simply have been thrown away. . . .
>
> Before we accommodate our position on the Niger to the commercial requirements of the world, we must at least have assurance that we shall not be sufferers by the transaction. Any other course would be the folly of Lear, who gave away all he had, and, having thenceforth to depend on charity, was refused even the modicum of rights that he nominally retained.

There was, the *Globe* concluded, an "essential separation between the Congo and the Niger—between the territory which does, and the territory which does not, call for international administration."[29] If the editorials of English newspapers reflect the public's opinion, Englishmen were willing to establish an international regime to safeguard Free Trade on the Congo but were prepared to resist firmly, perhaps bellicosely, any attempt to place the Niger under international supervision.

English aversion to "internationalization" explains why news of an impending conference in Berlin was greeted with such hostility by certain organs of the press. Taking the most extreme position, the *Morning Post* denounced any form of international control on either the Niger or Congo and stated with alarm that English participation in an African conference convened by France and Germany would signify the decline and imminent fall of the British Empire:

> The summoning of a European Conference to take counsel upon the future destination of Africa is, under the circumstances, one of the gravest warnings which have ever been uttered in the ear of a

29. December 1, 1884.

torpid and self-forgetful people. . . . [The] African Conference is the most cruel, the most contemptuous, and the most dangerous blow to the reputation and influence of the British Government in a sphere which used up to yesterday to be pre-eminently British.[30]

The *Pall Mall Gazette* responded on the same day to that nearly hysterical view by pointing out that application to the Niger of the principles of the Congress of Vienna would not impair British sovereignty at the mouth of the river. "Roumania is the undisputed Sovereign of the territory through which the mouths of the Danube find their way to the sea, but there is an International Commission of the Danube, and our ownership of the delta is no bar to the establishment of an International Commission of the Niger." [31]

The *Standard* similarly ridiculed the idea "that the Congo Conference is, in some occult fashion, the handwriting on the wall announcing the downfall of the English Colonial Empire, and the erection on its ruins of a Franco-German cosmopolitan understanding by which the world is to gain benefits not yet computed." [32] Other newspapers such as the *Manchester Examiner and Times* interpreted the scheme of establishing an international commission on the Congo and Niger as a check to France:

French merchants are to be treated no better than the merchants of other nations. . . . It is proposed to apply to the navigation of the Congo and the Niger the principles adopted at the Congress of Vienna in order to ensure the freedom of navigation of several navigable rivers and afterwards applied to the Danube. France has assented to these proposals, but we do not gather that they were made by her, and there are some signs that she acceded to them with no exuberant willingness. The plain fact is that they effectually checkmate any policy which she might have contemplated carrying out for her own special advantage.[33]

Despite such informed opinion, confusion existed about the precise form of "internationalization" to be applied to the two rivers. Much of this confusion can be traced to the mystery surrounding the "In-

30. October 15, 1884.
31. October 18, 1884.
32. October 18, 1884.
33. October 18, 1884.

ternational Association" [34] founded by Leopold II, King of the Belgians, to bring "civilization and the blessings of free trade" to the natives of tropical Africa.

The ambivalence toward King Leopold and his Association manifested itself by the repeated usage of the words "philanthropic and beneficent," and "shadowy and artificial." There was widespread admiration at the king's attempt to introduce trade and civilization into tropical Africa; but how could an "Association" become a state? The United States on April 22, 1884, had recognized the flag of the Association as the flag of a friendly government, and on the following day King Leopold signed the "preemption" agreement with France whereby that country would acquire the territories of the Association in the event of the Association's demise.[35] The two transactions caused consternation in England. Later in the year, when Bismarck threw his support behind the Association by granting recognition from the German government on November 8, the British public continued to regard the Association with a mixed attitude of suspicion and enthusiasm. Was it wise to encourage the formation of a state that might fall to France? Or would the guarantee of Free Trade and chances of King Leopold's success protect British commerce in that part of the world? As the *Morning Post* summarized Britain's apparent dilemma: "Either the proposed Congo State is to be a mere despotism of irresponsible foreign traders—and in that case it could not be tolerated—or it must be the dependency of some foreign Power or Powers, and in that case England could not tolerate it without most serious guarantees." [36]

The *Morning Post* repeatedly denounced the agents of the Association as a gang of unscrupulous adventurers. But the mainstream of British opinion tended to hold the Association in higher esteem, above all because of King Leopold's reputation as a philanthropic Free

34. In the English press only the most informed newspapers such as *The Times* and the *Morning Post* drew a distinction between the International African Association (founded in 1876) and one of King Leopold's subsequent creations, the International Association of the Congo. Usually the press merely referred to the "International Association," which I use for convenience sake here. For a discussion of the evolution of King Leopold's various bodies that emerged finally as the Etat Indépendant du Congo, see especially Thomson, *Fondation de l'Etat Indépendant.*

35. For clear chronology of these events see Crowe, *Berlin West African Conference,* Chap. 8.

36. November 19, 1884.

Trader. The following extract from the *Daily Telegraph* typifies the praise the king received in 1884:

> Leopold II . . . has knit adventurers, traders, and missionaries of many races into one band of men, under the most illustrious of modern travellers [Henry M. Stanley], to carry into the interior of Africa new ideas of law, order, humanity, and protection of the natives. There can be no doubt that from his initiative will arise a free State of the Congo, and that we shall see the new nationality neutralised like Belgium itself. Deprived, as the King by position is, of an opportunity of playing a great part in European politics, he takes his revenge nobly, applying his mind and money to a lofty end, and becoming the *Scipio Africanus* of our time.[37]

Curiously enough, the *Morning Post* proved to be the best prophet when it stated that the Congo was being "opened not to peace and progress, but to the most horrible reprisals and massacres." [38]

Again, the leading Tory newspaper was accurate when it described the Association as essentially a commercial enterprise. Although there is no doubt exaggeration in the following quotation from the *Morning Post,* it is of interest because it represents virtually the only vitriolic criticism of the Association in the English press in 1884 and is identical with the attacks by the same newspaper when twenty years later it took the lead in the Congo reform campaign.

> There is really not the slightest essential difference between such a pretension [to territorial sovereignty by the Association] and the practice of Captain Kidd and other "sea kings" who set up their picturesque ensign on one or another of the islets of the Carribean and the Gulf of Mexico. The private ensign of sovereignty of the bold sea-rovers was, indeed, the Black Flag with the customary emblems and their large-minded operations were directed against all kinds of property which happened to suit them. The private ensign of the so-called "International Association" sports nothing more terrifying than a star, and we understand that the operations of the adventurers are strictly confined for the moment to the acquisition of the property of the African tribes by no means more violent . . . than the threat of "burning their villages over their heads." [39]

37. October 22, 1884.
38. December 13, 1884.
39. November 7, 1884.

Yet that sort of caustic remark was never made at the time about King Leopold or the leader of the Association in the Congo, Henry M. Stanley. By their enthusiasm and propaganda they managed to persuade British traders and philanthropists of the altruistic aims of the Association, despite disquieting reports in the press of what was actually happening in the Congo.[40] In the interest of Free Trade and science, and under the philanthropic sponsorship of the King of the Belgians, Stanley would strike *A White Line across the Dark Continent.*[41] From the Atlantic to the Indian Ocean, in the recurrent phrase, "peace, civilization, and the blessings of Free Trade will be brought to the dusky millions of the Congo." Countless times King Leopold's publicists drove home that point, and it probably did much to conceal the real situation in the Congo, where his agents were concluding monopolistic treaties with native chiefs that alienated not only sovereignty but also the land and its produce to the Association. Stanley appeared in the public eye as the champion of Free Trade struggling against French and Portuguese adversaries; in reality he helped to give birth to a state whose system of monopolies became the most vicious in Africa's history.

Except in general commentaries on French designs in central Africa, the issues of rivalry between Stanley and the French officer Savorgnan de Brazza for control of the Upper Congo aroused little comment in the English press of 1884. But publicists and statesmen alike recognized that the claims of the two explorers would shape in large part the political configuration of central Africa and would indirectly play an important role in the Berlin Conference. The reasons may be explained briefly. De Brazza's treaties in 1880 with Chief Makoko claimed for France a sphere on the Upper Congo, in particular the right bank of Stanley Pool (where the Congo river becomes navigable). The French Parliament approved the treaties in 1882, setting off a chain of reactions in England and in the Congo. The British Foreign Office perceived a French threat to the Congo and renewed negotiations with the Portuguese to protect British commerce. English businessmen connected with the International Association felt indignantly that de Brazza had "stolen a march" on Stanley when Stanley himself was performing the service of building a road around the cataracts. Stanley retaliated by claiming for the Association a rich area on the north bank of the Lower Congo called the Kwilu district, which, if left to the

40. See for example the *Manchester Examiner and Times*, November 28, 1884.

41. The title of King Leopold's propagandistic pamphlet published anonymously in 1884. For sharp criticism see the *Pall Mall Gazette*, April 24, 1884.

Association, would block the growth of French influence from the Gaboon to the Upper Congo.

In French eyes Stanley wholly responsible for this check to legitimate French territorial aims, and, because of his connections with English traders, he symbolized a danger to the growing French colonial empire. His efforts to "Anglicize" the Association raised fears that were not dispelled even by the Franco-Congolese preemptive agreement of April 1884. Common phrases in the French press of that year referred to the "peaceful" efforts of de Brazza and the "brutal" activities of Stanley. Various French newspapers such as the *Journal des Débats* began to maintain that de Brazza's treaty extended to both sides of Stanley Pool since Makoko's subjects resided there also and therefore were French subjects. In October 1884 the economist Paul Leroy-Beaulieu, author of the celebrated *Colonisation chez les peuples modernes,* wrote in the *Economiste Français* that the French government should not relinquish "one atom of sovereignty over the territory on the Congo placed under French protection by King Makoko, or over any station where the French flag waves." Although admitting that Danubian principles might be applied to the lower waters of the Congo and Niger, Leroy-Beaulieu felt that not only the Upper Congo but also the Upper Niger were "peculiarly and wholly French." That idea was most disturbing to Englishmen. To them de Brazza's treaties generally represented, in the words of the *Daily Telegraph,* "the old trick of tri-coloured pocket-handkerchiefs." [42] To the Foreign Office the Tricolour planted on the Congo signified so great a danger that it might be worth letting the Portuguese in to keep out the French—a sentiment definitely not shared by Stanley and the International Association.

Stanley played a crucial role in arousing English opinion against Portuguese claims on the Congo. The negotiations leading to the abortive Anglo-Portuguese Treaty of February 1884 can be summarized so as to illuminate his connection with its aftermath as well as the more well-known aspects of its failure caused by the International Association, France, and Germany. The scheme of recognizing Portugal's ancient claims to the mouth of the Congo in return for guarantees of free trade and other concessions originated in the 1870s, but the Foreign Office did not regard the matter as urgent until after the conclusion of de Brazza's treaties with Makoko. As the *Manchester Examiner and Times* succinctly described the ensuing events in retrospect:

> It was obvious that our negotiations with Portugal were entered upon with a desire to forestall the action of other Powers. Our chief

42. October 22, 1884.

> object was to put forward Portugal as a breakwater against the supposed designs of France, but Germany . . . had a West African policy, and our stealthy proceedings offended both Powers. The result was that Germany and France came to an understanding with each other on the West African question, and thenceforth took the lead. There is no doubt that we sustained a rebuff. The tables were turned.[43]

Bismarck's refusal to recognize the Anglo-Portuguese treaty in June 1884 precipitated the events leading to the Berlin Conference. Germany and France refused to recognize Portuguese sovereignty over the Lower Congo despite the guarantees of free trade; yet Portugal persisted in her claims, and it remained an open question whether the International Association could be made into a sovereign state.

In the three months preceding the Conference, the English climate of opinion turned enthusiastically in favor of the Association. Stanley, back from the Congo, gave interviews, wrote articles, and, most significantly, spoke before Chambers of Commerce. He denounced Portuguese maladministration and oppressive commercial policies, and emphasized that Portugal remained the only western European nation trafficking in slaves. He presented facts about commerce on the Lower Congo: of the 163 European traders there, 25 were English, 24 Dutch, 1 Italian, 6 German, 12 Swedish, 22 Belgian, 8 French, and 67 Portuguese. Despite the comparatively large number of Portuguese nationals, three-fourths of the imports came from England, and only Portuguese table wine was imported from Portugal for the consumption of Portuguese officials. In short, the Portuguese had done absolutely nothing since their discovery of the Congo four hundred years before except to ruin or injure trade. On the other hand, Stanley argued, the noble and disinterested King of the Belgians, with unbound liberality and earnest devotion, was attempting to introduce civilization and plant commerce among the millions in the unknown interior who thirsted for English trade. But his philanthropy would be frustrated if the Portuguese held the lower river. Those ideas Stanley reiterated before numerous audiences, and his speeches received widespread attention.[44] The *Daily Telegraph* caught the mood of the English public when it proclaimed:

> It may be that the founders of the International Association are dreamers: but should it prove so, the blame will not rest on men

43. November 22, 1884.

44. Most notably his addresses before the London and Manchester chambers of commerce were later published as pamphlets and reviewed extensively in the press.

> who sought to light up the Dark Continent by the vivifying fires of peace instead of the destructive flames of war. It will fall upon the communities, and their rulers, who will have shown that they could not rise from the low grounds of rivalries to support and stimulate an enterprise which had for its sole aim the benefit of all.[45]

To the English public one of the main points of the Conference in Berlin would be to determine whether King Leopold's idealistic experiment would succeed or fail.

There remains only one important point to make before passing on to British official policy toward the Niger and Congo and discussing the Conference itself. It is the vision of the Congo valley as projected by Stanley and perceived by the English public. The reason for the importance of this image is that it provides the key to understanding the setting and main issues at Berlin. There as in England Stanley was lionized. He spoke authoritatively as one of the great explorers of the nineteenth century. One newspaper referred to him as "himself a Sovereign Power to be reckoned with" and the International Association was often identified as "Stanley's Association." His herculean efforts on the Congo and unsurpassed knowledge of central Africa demanded respect; when he spoke, people listened. His message can be summed up in one word: trade.

Echoing Stanley's remarks made before the London Chamber of Commerce in September, the *Standard* commented:

> Here, according to Mr. Stanley, is a River which is the great inlet to Africa, draining one million three hundred square miles of country, permeated by vast waterways, peopled by forty million of tribesmen, some fierce cannibals, but the majority ready for civilization and eager for trade, abounding in ivory, cane-wood, india-rubber, and other wild products of the tropics, and capable of growing almost any crop suitable to such a climate.[46]

Introducing Stanley before the Manchester Chamber of Commerce, the president of the Chamber, J. F. Hutton (one of the Association's prominent supporters) said that the explorer "is here to tell us that these millions on the Congo are eager for our trade; he is here also to show us how the complete freedom of commerce may be established, and how all customs houses and all vexatious and impediments to trade may be utterly abolished and swept away from the banks of the Congo (Cheers)." Speaking at a time when England feared a depression in

45. September 19, 1884.
46. September 19, 1884.

the cotton industry, Stanley pitched his remarks at the growing manufacturing capacity and slackness of trade:

> Well, then, I come to you with at least one market where there are at present, perhaps, 6,250,000 yards of cheap cottons sold every year on the Congo banks and in the Congo markets. I was interested the other day in making a curious calculation, which was, supposing that all the inhabitants of the Congo basin were simply to have one Sunday dress each, how many yards of Manchester cloth would be required; and the amazing number was 300,000,000 yards, just for one Sunday dress! (Cheers). Proceeding still further with these figures I found that with Sunday dress and four-every-day dresses would in one year amount to 3,840,000,000 yards, which at 2d. per yard would be of the value of £16,000,000.[47]

Although a few scoffed at Stanley's statistics,[48] to most Englishmen he portrayed an overseas market that could have an adverse affect on England's industrial development if England were excluded. Since this issue would be decided at the Conference in Berlin, the English press could state without hyperbole that "To-day the Congo occupies a place in men's thoughts second only to the Nile," [49] and that the Conference represented a "turning point in the history of our Empire." [50]

47. *Manchester Examiner and Times*, October 22, 1884.

48. The *Glasgow Herald* of October 21, 1884, carried a most incisive critique of Stanley's optimistic views on the Congo market: "While one may enjoy the wonder of such visions as Mr. Stanley indulged in [at Manchester] one may doubt their practical value. There are unquestionably several millions of people in Central Africa who are naked. It does not follow that they desire clothes, or even that they need clothes, or that they would wear clothes if they had them, or that they could pay for them if they wanted them. And as for the moral influence of Manchester cotton, we must gauge it by the amount of sizing contained in the fabric, and the relation between the number of yards on the invoice and those in the bale. In sober earnest, there is a great deal of very unbusinesslike talk about trade in Central Africa. Some people seem to think that the only thing to do is to "annex" or "open up" a country, and that orders will at once flow out in ceaseless streams to Manchester and Glasgow and Birmingham and Sheffield. Trade is elastic, but it has no such balloon-like capacity of rapid expansion. It must grow, and, as a rule, the more slowly it grows the sounder it is. It is possible, although we are not sanguine, that all the cotton which the vivid imagination of Mr. Stanley depicted may some day be saleable in the Congo Basin. But the day must be in the dim future, and before it can arrive there are a good many preliminaries to arrange. The old saying that 'trade follows the flag' has been heretofore known as true only in connection with a national flag. We doubt its applicability to an international one."

49. *Leeds Mercury*, October 24, 1884.

50. *Globe*, October 17, 1884.

Much more is known about the British Foreign Office's policy in the months preceding the Conference that about the attitudes of the press, so the diplomatic prelude to "the extraordinary spectacle . . . at Berlin" [51] can be more succinctly surveyed. The main point to be made is that French as well as British statesmen felt the pressure of "public opinion," and that the prejudices coloring official views coincided with those expressed in the newspapers. In May 1884 the British ambassador in Paris, Lord Lyons, wrote, "So far as I can judge by the English Papers, the irritation in England against France is not less than that against England in this Country. The Newspapers on both sides of the channel seem to do all they can to fan the flame." [52] Later in the year he wrote again on the same subject:

> Ferry complained bitterly of the English Press. He said in particular that the irritating lecturing tone of the "Times" goaded the French to Madness; it used the same tone towards the Government of its own Country. I said that the Press on both sides of the Channel seemed to work as if for the express purpose of producing ill-will between the two Countries, but that certainly the English Government had no power to restrain it.[53]

Thus emerges one of the dominant themes in British documents relating to the origins of the First World War: the baleful influence of the press. Yet the Francophobe sentiments publicly expressed at this time hardly differed in substance or tone from the minutes written in the Foreign Office. Assistant undersecretary T. V. Lister once commented about French expansion:

> The feeling in France at this moment appears to be much in favour of Colonial expansion and enterprise. The French are jealous and bad colonists, they oppress the natives, repel foreign capitalists and have to fall back upon Slavery, slightly disguised, for the labour required on their plantations. They are monopolists and protectionists and judge all other nations by their own standard.[54]

Though less politely expressed, Lister's ideas were the same as those of most other British officials. The thoughts in his minutes well illustrate

51. *Morning Post,* November 19, 1884.

52. Lyons to Granville, Private, May 30, 1884, Public Record Office [PRO hereafter] 30/29/174.

53. Lyons to Granville, Private, October 17, 1884, ibid.

54. Minute by Lister, March 13, 1884, Foreign Office [FO hereafter] 84/1683.

the Foreign Office's low esteem of the French as colonizers and the tendency to hold them responsible for the Scramble.

So far as the British Cabinet considered the general affairs of tropical Africa at this time, they saw mainly the necessity of protecting the hinterlands of British territories on the west coast and safeguarding British trade on the Niger and Congo. They recognized the danger of French expansion, but did not detect a grand strategy whereby France would attempt to dominate the African continent. Like the editors of *The Times,* Gladstone and his colleagues perceived a French "feverish restlessness . . . on the Congo, in Tunis, in Tonquin, and in Madagascar . . . [that] have no relation to one another . . . [and] do not form part of any general scheme."[55] But in the Foreign Office and the Colonial Office, where experts gave prolonged attention to the details of the partition, the pieces of the puzzle seemed to fall into a comprehensible pattern. Apart from de Brazza's treaty with Makoko, one event in particular appeared to signal the dangers of French imperialism in western Africa—the proclamation of the protectorate over Porto-Novo in Dahomey in January 1883.

That event provoked a comprehensive memorandum on Anglo-French rivalry written by the head of the African Department, Percy Anderson. Anderson warned that, unless immediate action were taken, British trade would be imperiled on the Oil Rivers and the Lower Niger:

> If we remain passive, we shall see our trade stifled, we shall find our traders furious, and we shall hardly escape grave complications with the French as successive Protectorates produce fresh irritation till, when the field is finally closed against us, we shall have to deal with chronic grievances and complaints.

To protect British commerce, Anderson argued that a general settlement with France should be reached in which the Gabon would become British, France would acknowledge British rights on the Lower Niger and withdraw from the Gold Coast, and Britain in return would cede the Gambia. Such a policy would check the French scheme of ousting Britain from some of the most commercially valuable parts of western Africa. Of the scheme itself Anderson had no doubt. "If there is one thing clearer than another," he wrote, "it seems to be that the French have a settled policy in Africa, both on the East and West

55. June 21, 1883. The best succinct discussion of Gladstone's foreign policy is Agatha Ramm's introduction to *The Political Correspondence of Mr. Gladstone and Lord Granville, 1876–1886* (2 vols. Oxford, 1962).

Coast, and that policy is antagonistic to us. The progress of this policy is sometimes sluggish, sometimes feverish, but it never ceases."[56] In that conclusion lay the idea that governed British policy during the partition: France was the main enemy. Where British and French aims directly collide, such as on the Niger, British claims would have to be consolidated; where France threatened to take over territories where Britain had no traditional claims, such as on the Congo, minor powers such as Portugal would have to be put forward as a buffer.

Between July and October 1884 Consul E. H. Hewett concluded a series of treaties on the Oil River and the Lower Niger that successfully placed those territories under British protection.[57] On the Congo, however, British plans misfired. The basic idea had been to allow Portugal to assert her authority over the mouth of the river in return for guarantees of free trade. The plan was intensely unpopular. In England the philanthropists and trading community attacked it because of Portugal's tolerance of slavery and oppressive, corrupt colonial administration. Abroad Portugal was denounced as a cat's paw of Britain. To make the treaty more palatable, the Foreign Office demanded that Portugal limit her claims to the southern bank of the Congo and agree to the establishment of an Anglo-Portuguese commission to ensure free trade. According to a British official at Lisbon, "The idea of the Commission is distasteful to the Portuguese as they think it savours of foreign tutelage, the very mention of which makes them frantic."[58] Nevertheless the Portuguese acquiesced. Their concessions made the treaty, in Anderson's words, "an exceptionally liberal one, but . . . not . . . good enough for us."[59]

So strong was anti-Portuguese sentiment that not even stringent guarantees of free trade could save the agreement. "Manchester is up in arms," reported the *Examiner*. So also was the House of Commons, where the Foreign Office detected King Leopold's effective lobbying against the treaty.[60] Granville protested to a peer active in west African trading circles: "The agitation is being formented by the King of the Belgians, which is not fair after the pains we are taking to safeguard

56. Memorandum by Anderson, "On the French Occupation of Porto Novo," copy in FO 84/1806.

57. See especially Hargreaves, *Prelude to the Partition*, Chap. 7.

58. Baring to Sanderson, Private, June 23, 1883, PRO 30/29/183. For the Anglo-Portuguese negotiations, see Anstey, *Britain and the Congo*.

59. Minute by Anderson, July 13, 1883, FO 84/1806.

60. "The King is agitating to upset the Treaty in the House." Minute by Anderson, February 20, 1884, PRO 30/29/198.

his association."[61] Granville wrote to King Leopold himself that Britain had acted "in the general interest of the civilized world," and threatened to reveal publicly what the Foreign Office knew about the monopolistic nature of the Association if the king did not cease his efforts to upset the treaty. It was an empty threat. King Leopold had the upper hand, as was gradually recognized by the Foreign Office in the spring of 1884. When Bismarck refused to assent to the treaty in June, Leopold merely played another card in the Congo game that had already, in Anderson's words, been going "dead against us."[62] Bismarck intervened decisively by refusing to accept the Anglo-Portuguese treaty and by working with France in convening the Berlin Conference. But it is King Leopold, not Bismarck, who deserves the epithet of wheeler-dealer in the whole affair.

King Leopold's tactics irritated the Foreign Office. The description of his Congo organization as a philanthropic, free-trading association fooled no one in official circles. "The King of the Belgians' Co.," Anderson wrote, ". . . [is] a gigantic commercial monopoly."[63] When the King began to put forward his plans of transforming the Association into an independent and sovereign state, Lister retorted that the proposal was absurd,

> [that] the "Internat. African Assn." has not, as far as we know, any recognized position, and that it does not appear to be controlled by, protected by or responsible to any govt. That it can have no right to make treaties which can claim to be respected by legitimate govts. That the offl. recogn. of the priv. flag wd. create a very dangerous precedent. That the treaties made by the "Assoc" are drawn up in a spirit of the strictest monoply. That the K of the B has bound himself to give the refusal of all the possessions of the "Assoc" to one of the most exclusive and protectionist Govts in the world. And that it is therefore incumbent upon all Govts that value freedom of trade to abstain from recognizing the Assoc its treaties and its flag.[64]

Lister held to his opinion that King Leopold's proceedings were "absurdly irregular," but his colleagues came around to the view that Britain had no alternative to supporting the Association.

61. Granville to Aberdare, Confidential (copy), February 20, 1884, PRO 30/29/148.

62. Minute by Anderson, May 18, 1884, PRO 30/29/198.

63. Memorandum by Anderson, March 2, 1884, FO 84/1807.

64. Minute by Lister, May 16, 1884, PRO 30/29/198.

With the disaster of the Anglo-Portuguese treaty and France and Germany threatening to interfere jointly, the Foreign Office had to yield the initiative on the Congo in order to defend the Niger. Besides, King Leopold might be forced by international agreement to live up to his promises of free trade, and the Association might be buoyed up successfully as a buffer against France. The preemptive agreement consequently worked to King Leopold's advantage; given the collapse of the Anglo-Portuguese treaty, the Foreign Office had an interest in the success of the Association so as to keep it out of the hands of France. As usual Anderson plotted the main strategy in this regard. Writing shortly after Bismarck issued invitations on October 8 to come to Berlin to talk about the Congo and Niger, Anderson wrote: "it seems incontrovertible that . . . as regards the Congo, we can appear at the Conf. as one of many Powers interested, as regards the Niger we shld. take our seat as *the Niger Power*." [65] Thus affairs were turning to King Leopold's favor, but not necessarily to Britain's. There was no guarantee that the other powers would permit England to preempt the Niger seat. For that reason the permanent undersecretary, Sir Julian Pauncefote, wrote, "The Conference *may* end in smoke." [66]

The Conference opened on Saturday November 15, 1884. Fourteen nations were represented. Of them only Britain, France, Germany, Portugal, the Association, and to a lesser extent the Netherlands, were directly concerned with west African questions. The rest were Austria-Hungary, Belgium, Denmark, Italy, Russia, Spain, Sweden and Norway, Turkey, and the United States—powers with such insignificant colonial interests that the *Morning Post* blasted the idea that Britain would condescend as "the greatest colonial Power in the world . . . [to sit] at the board of the West African Conference like the simplest and least concerned of States, while half a score of Powers with colonial possessions often insignificant enjoy each an equal representation." [67] But even the *Morning Post* agreed with the rest of the press that it was a "brilliant assemblage." The delegates met at Bismarck's official residence in the Wilhelmstrasse, where the last great international Congress had assembled six years earlier. Sitting at a large, horseshoe-shaped table whose open end overlooked the garden, the representatives could remind themselvs of their immediate duties by

65. Memorandum by Anderson, October 14, 1884, FO 84/1813.
66. Minute by Pauncefote, October 30, 1884, FO 84/1814.
67. November 19, 1884.

gazing at a large map of Africa drawn by Kiepert. From this setting derived the myth that the Berlin Conference partitioned Africa.

At two o'clock Bismarck opened the first session and accepted the chairmanship. He stated that the purpose of the Conference was to promote the civilization of the African natives by opening the interior of the continent to commerce. He then attempted to define three specific goals: (1) freedom of commerce on the Congo; (2) freedom of navigation on the Congo and Niger; and (3) agreement about the formalities of valid annexation of territory in the future. Negatively, he said, the Conference would not concern itself with questions of sovereignty. Emphasizing that the Conference would serve the cause of peace and humanity, Bismarck ended his brief oration.[68] His remarks conveyed the impression of uncertainty and ambiguity. On the one hand he appeared to put the Niger and the Congo on the same footing. On the other, a close study of his phraseology left it unclear exactly what he had intended. As the Foreign Office analyzed what Bismarck had said, Lister wrote that his "speech is extremely vague and it leaves it doubtful whether the Conference is to do more than register a few platitudes about freedom of commerce and navigation." [69]

Bismarck's speech drew a rejoinder from the British ambassador, Sir Edward Malet. His remarks set the tone and substance of British policy during the rest of the Conference. He said first of all that commerce was not the exclusive subject of the Conference: "While it is desirable to secure a market in the Congo country, the welfare of the natives is not to be neglected." [70] Coming to his main point, he em-

68. First Protocol of the Conference. The proceedings are most conveniently available in *Accounts and Papers, 55, United States Senate Executive Document, 196* (49th Congress, 1st Session), and the French Yellow Book, *Affaires du Congo et de l'Afrique Occidentale, 1884–85* (Paris, 1885).

69. Minute by Lister, November 19, 1884, FO 84/1815. For a contemporary French interpretation of Bismarck's motives during the Conference, see especially the analysis by the French ambassador in Berlin: "Le prince de Bismarck a porté dans la politique coloniale où il se jette la même énergie d'impulsion, la même hauteur d'aspirations dont il a donné les marques dans sa politique continentale. On ne peut guère douter qu'il ne croie le moment venu de déposséder l'Angleterre de son hégémonie maritime, comme il a dépossé dé il y a quinze ans la France de l'hégémonie politique et militaire en Europe. Bien des indices tendent à prouver qu'il prépare contre la puissance anglaise une attaque à fond, calculée pour l'atteindre dans ses parties vitales, et pour la ruiner au profit de la grandeur industrielle et commerciale de l'Allemagne." (Courcel to Ferry, January 19, 1885, *DDF,* 1st series, 5, No. 528.)

70. First Protocol of the Conference.

phasized that the situation on the Congo was "entirely different" from that on the Niger. Her Majesty's government would consent to the appointment of an International Commission to regulate the Congo, but a Commission on the Niger would be "impracticable." The lower and upper reaches of the river, he argued, were distinct geographical entities, and the Lower Niger was exclusively a British concern where Britain accepted responsibilities of administration. He stated flatly that the British government would regulate the affairs of the Niger but would adhere to the principle of free navigation. Thus, to the public at least, the battle lines appeared to be drawn at the first session of the Conference. Britain refused to discuss the Niger on the same basis as the Congo. "If in the course of a few days," commented the *Liverpool Daily Post*, "we do not hear that Sir E. Malet has withdrawn from the Conference, we may conclude that the English protest has done its work." [71]

In fact the British hold over the Niger was so strong that it was hardly contested by the other powers. In the months immediately preceding the Conference British commercial and political influence on the river had become supreme. On November 1, George Goldie-Taubman of the National African Company wrote to the Foreign Office that the two French trading houses had sold out and that Britain stood "alone on the Niger"—such welcome information that Granville greeted it with "Hurrah." [72] With British commercial paramountcy and the political claims established by Hewett's treaties, Ferry's proposal to establish an International Commission became little more than empty words. Why had the French government permitted the sellout of the two trading firms? [73] The commercial expert of the Foreign Office, Joseph Archer Crowe (who attended the Conference as one of the British delegates), quoted from published French documents to prove that the French did not hope to exploit the Lower Niger, but rather to

71. November 18, 1884.

72. Minute by Granville c. November 3, 1884.

73. "There is a mystery here." (Robinson and Gallagher, *Africa and the Victorians,* p. 176 n. 5). "There is no 'mystery' . . . about the French government's indifference to the fate of the companies bought out by Goldie before the opening of the Berlin Conference. Throughout 1884 and 1885, Félix Faure, as Under-Secretary for Colonies, and Jules Ferry were concerned solely with the question of untariffed access through the Delta to the Upper Niger. . . . All that mattered was freedom of communication with the coast." C. W. Newbury, "Victorians, Republicans and the Partition of West Africa," *Journal of African History,* 3 (1962), 496.

gain control of the upper reaches of the river. Geographically, the Lower Niger was blocked from the interior by rapids; moreover the Niger delta was unhealthy and infested with British commercial houses; therefore the French would have to abandon their usual tactic of utilizing the mouth of the river in favor of attempting to tap the trade of the Upper Niger via the Senegal. "It seems clear," Crowe speculated, "that if France comes into the Conference with these views . . . we need hardly expect much discussion from her as to our claims of preponderance in the Lower Niger."[74] He guessed well. Compared with the French designs on the Upper Niger, their aim on the lower river in 1884 appears merely as a jab in the British belly.

In any case the move to internationalize the Lower Niger began to collapse when Bismarck gave his support to Britain on the day before the Conference. At that time Malet read his instructions from Granville, which included the passage about an international commission on the Niger being "impracticable."[75] Bismarck made no objection. The French ambassador began to surmise that France would receive little support for the scheme to internationalize the Niger. Thus the Franco-German entente began to crumble even before the Conference began. Bismarck increasingly saw that Germany's goal of free trade coincided with Britain's and diverged from France's. In short, to achieve the most liberal extension of free trade on the Congo, he supported Britain on the Niger. This changing partnership resulted in British victory. Within two weeks after the convening of the Conference, Britain emerged preeminent on the Niger, with no threat of international interference. "VICTORY ON THE NIGER"—as the English press emphasized in captions to leading articles—at once transformed

74. Memorandum by Crowe, November 7, 1884, FO Confidential Print 5033. It is noteworthy, however, that Antoine Mattei, who sold most of the comptoirs, and General Faidherbe vehemently held that the sale of the commercial houses in no way transferred exclusive political rights in the Lower Niger to Britain. They argued that this was merely a normal business transaction and did not mean that France had lost political rights in the region. See Faidherbe, "La Question du Niger," *Revue Scientifique, 3* (January 17, 1885), 67; and Antoine Mattei, *Bas Niger, Benoue, Dahomey* (Grenoble, 1890), pp. 49–63. See also C. W. Newbury, "The Development of French Policy on the Lower and Upper Niger, 1880–1898," *Journal of Modern History, 31* (1959). Also K. Vignes, "Etude sur la rivalité d'influence entre les puissances europées en Afrique équatoriale et occidentale depuis l'acte général de Berlin jusqu'au seuil du XXe siècle," *Revue française d'histoire d'outre-mer, 48* (1961).

75. The instructions are in Granville to Malet, No. 59 Africa, November 7, 1884, FO 84/1814.

a conference designed by Germany and France against Britain's interests into a congress in which Britain emerged as triumphant as in 1878.[76]

British diplomacy was almost as successful in the major problem facing the Conference—the future of the Congo. Here again Stanley played a crucial role. He attended the Conference as an American delegate, though in fact he was King Leopold's agent. He believed the aims of the Association should not conflict with the free trade policy of Britain. Speaking before the Conference "in his own racy, humorous and vivacious English," he dwelt on the natural wealth of the Congo region, "where Europeans could thrive as well as in their own temperate zone if they adopted their habits to the African climate." [77] Emphasizing that free trade would benefit Africans and Europeans alike, he urged the desirability of establishing a free trade zone that was as large as possible. On November 21 he proposed to delimit the "Geographical and Commercial" basin of the Congo by drawing the northern boundary as a line running from Fernando Vaz on the coast up the Ogooué and the southern from Coanza inland—thus including slices of territory claimed by France and Portugal. Seeing no reason why this geopolitical exercise should not be continued, the American delegate, John A. Kasson, on the next day proposed extending the line to the eastern coast of Africa from 5 degrees north to the Zambezi, a proposal supported by the Germans as well as the British on grounds that "the greater the territory to which the principle is applied the greater will be the future advantage to [German] trade." [78]

This wild geographical interpretation of the Congo basin—an enormous chunk of territory running smack through the middle of the continent—astonished the British Foreign Office. One official said that it was geographically so confused that it would be comparable to drawing a map putting the Rhine in the basin of the Rhone.[79] Lister complained of "these fancy definitions of the 'basin of the Congo'" (which he regarded as "absurd") and had a telegram sent to Malet

76. "The British delegation came back from Berlin . . . nearly as happy as Disraeli had been seven years before. The difference was that they had not the same gift as Disraeli for the immortal historical phrase." Jean Stengers, "British and German Imperial Rivalry: A Conclusion," in *Britain and Germany in Africa*, p. 338. Stengers is not entirely correct. In his own prosaic way, Granville stumbled on exactly the right word: Britain got on "swimmingly."

77. *The Times*, November 19, 1884.

78. See Malet to Granville, No. 21 Africa telegram, November 25, 1884, FO 84/1815. See also Yarnall, *The Great Powers and the Congo Conference.*

79. Minute by Kennedy, c. November 22, 1884, FO 84/1815.

saying that Her Majesty's Government saw "grave objections to definitions of the Congo which do not accord with geographical facts." [80] The response from the British ambassador in Berlin must have been enlightening. It was *Anderson* who had drawn the line and had put the American delegation up to presenting it to the Conference.[81]

The scheme amounted to reserving as much of the interior as possible for free trade. Since most of the interior was unclaimed, none of the powers had legitimate grounds for protest. The British refused to mention the source of the Nile (an interesting reservation at such an early date in the partition) and insisted that the free trade guarantees would not affect the sovereignty of the sultan of Zanzibar in his mainland possessions. The French and Portuguese, on the other hand, were forced into a defensive position and had to fight to get the line pushed away from their spheres on the west coast. In final form the French and Portuguese acquiesced in a free-trade area beginning at Sette Camma in the north and at the Loge River in the south, thence looping in artistic ecstasy into the interior. The Foreign Office continued to protest against the "fantastic" definition of the Congo basin, but finally yielded feebly in the argument that it was a "commercial" as well as geographical area. Engineered by Anderson, it was a clever move that immediately caused the French to wonder why they had agreed to attend the Conference in the first place.

The commentaries in the press well illustrate French disillusionment with the results of the Conference as early as the beginning of December. Paul Leroy-Beaulieu complained that France "has everything to lose and nothing whatever to gain from the proceedings of the Conference." He went on:

> Having already large dominions and larger claims in Africa, France will find, if the Conference has its way, that the claims will be denied, and that the dominions will be thrown open to the commerce of all the world. France will only have acquired colonies and dependencies in order to be forbidden to make any more use of them than any foreign nation which may choose to utilize them for commerce and trade.[82]

80. Granville to Malet, telegram, November 25, 1884 (draft by Lister), ibid.

81. "I and the gentlemen whom your Lordship has associated with me at the Conference thought that it would come with much greater weight before the members of the Commission if it were proposed by Mr. Stanley than if it were submitted by one of the British Delegation . . . we have thought it right to waive any credit which might ultimately attach to Great Britain as the originator of the line." Malet to Granville, No. 92 Africa, November 22, 1884, ibid.

82. *Economiste Français,* December 7, 1884.

That typical comment from Paris indicates the sudden and unexpected adroitness of British policy, inspired not from London but from the delegation in Berlin. Even the *Morning Post*, antagonistic from the beginning, stated that the results of the Conference by early December were "amazing"—in a favorable sense.

At this stage of the Conference—late November to mid-December—issues of territorial expansion and sovereignty that had been expressly excluded from the agenda nevertheless formed the background of the deliberations. Ultimately these questions of sovereignty proved of much greater importance than the proclamation of free trade on the Congo and Niger, because the sovereign power, despite international agreement, could throw aside trade restrictions almost with impunity. Both the Niger and the Congo basins later became notorious as centers of monopoly—and in the latter the monopolistic system of exploiting wild rubber gave rise to some of the worst atrocities in colonial history.

On the Niger, Britain assumed jurisdiction without international interference, and the Foreign Office attempted to hold British and other nationals responsible for their actions. On the Congo the Conference made provisions for the creation of an International Commission to regulate the affairs of the region, but it was never established. Europeans in the Congo were responsible to no one other than an independent and irresponsible despotism known in history as the Congo Free State. The Berlin Conference did not formally give birth to this bizarre child, but its delegates certainly sanctioned it. In Berlin, in the corridors outside the conference room, the delegates negotiated a series of bilateral treaties with the agents of the Association, transforming it into an independent and sovereign state. By taking the lead in their respective agreements of April 22 and November 8, the American and German governments were instrumental in its creation. But British support was also necessary. Recognition at precisely the right time led to the British victory on the Niger. The British side of this story has never been fully told, and its telling makes a good study in the decision-making process of the Foreign Office in 1884 as well as in the history of the creation of the international monstrosity with which the formal Conference usually is erroneously identified.

On November 19 Bismarck asked the British ambassador to help the Association "in its endeavour to become a State." This was the critical moment of the Conference. British refusal would leave the Congo open to territorial rivalry in which France and Portugal would probably be the winners at the expense of Free Trade; and Bismarck probably would not support Britain on the Niger. On the other hand British recognition might secure commercial liberty on the Congo and might gain Germany's help on the Niger. But recognition carried with it a significant departure from traditional international law that grated against the conservative outlook of the Foreign Office and the lord chancellor. Moreover the Foreign Office had no reason to be favorably disposed toward the Association, despite its trumpeting of Free Trade. The discovery of the treaties of monopoly, the preemptive agreement with France, and King Leopold's agitation against the Anglo-Portuguese treaty all deepened the Foreign Office's suspicion, in Anderson's words, of "the *bona fides* of the Association." Nevertheless, on December 16 Britain granted recognition. Why? Who made the decision? To answer those questions it is necessary to know precisely who was involved in the decision-making process during the Conference—who made the decisions in the delegation at Berlin, who in the Foreign Office, the interchange between those two groups, and the role of the lobbying groups and public opinion.

To begin, both the delegation and the Foreign Office were bombarded with memorials by British traders and missionaries who were hostile to France and Portugal and who were intensely devoted to the ideals advertised by King Leopold. A trading delegation including the firms of Hatton and Cookson, John Holt and Company, and the Elder Dempster Company actually went to Berlin. They claimed they represented British "public opinion." They pressed their views on the official delegation. It was no secret that some of them were making a profit by investing in King Leopold's enterprise.[83] And it was also not hard to guess that if the delegation flouted their wishes the press would erupt in London, Manchester, and Liverpool, and Britain's Congo policy would be condemned at the same time that the Foreign Office was being virulently denounced for caving in to the Germans in Africa and the Pacific. Thus in this instance "public opinion" was a tangible part of the policy-making process.

How were decisions made within the delegation? It consisted of Sir Edward Malet, the ambassador; H. Percy Anderson, the head of the African Department of the Foreign Office; Robert Meade, assistant undersecretary of the Colonial Office; A. W. L. Hemming, principal clerk of the Colonial Office; Joseph A. Crowe, commercial attaché for Europe; and an unofficial delegate, a jurist, Sir Travers Twiss. Meade acted as Granville's private correspondent and liaison with

83. See especially Lister's minutes on British traders "making large profits by supplying the Assocn. with goods" in FO 84/1815.

Bismarck.[84] But the strongest members of the team were Twiss and Anderson. Twiss was fully won over to King Leopold and actually drafted the Congo State's constitution. An elderly gentleman who often lost the train of his thought when speaking, Twiss carried great weight with the permanent undersecretary, Sir Julian Pauncefote, and with the lord chancellor. The three of them determined the legal aspects of British policy at the Conference.

Anderson was important in a different sense. He, not the ambassador, was the real British spokesman at the Conference. As Malet himself admitted the following February, "I have been an automaton of which he has made the works." [85] Anderson reasoned with the British traders, missionaries, and journalists in Berlin; he drafted the dispatches to the Foreign Office that later appeared in the Blue Books under Malet's signature; he represented the British delegation in the sessions where the real work was done, in the commissions; and he plotted the political strategy of Britain at the Conference. His motivation basically was Francophobe. He feared that France's expansion in Africa would cut off potential markets and increase her political and military power. To him any neighbor in Africa, even the Germans, would be better than the French. To win German support against France he was prepared to acquiesce in the Anglo-German disputes in South-West Africa, the Cameroons, and New Guinea—a policy labeled as "complete surrender" and "Bismarckized" by some of his colleagues. He willingly followed Bismarck's lead in making the Association into a state, hoping that with sufficient guarantees it would keep the Congo open to free trade and frustrate French ambitions. Above all Anderson wanted to prevent France from meddling on the Niger, and this required Bismarck's support. To win it he pushed hard in favor of the Association, despite his awareness of its sham philanthropic goals.

The actual decision to recognize the Association was made in London, not without strong protest by Lister. As assistant undersecretary (Anderson's immediate superior) he closely followed the actions of

84. The private correspondence about the Conference is in PRO 30/29/147, but it contains little of interest.

85. "He has been the moving spirit and my guide throughout the proceedings," wrote the ambassador. "He has conciliated the traders and missionaries who have been here. . . . I fancy that if we have the Niger now, de facto, in our possession it is mainly due to the pains which he has bestowed upon the question long previous to the meeting of the Conference, and . . . victory in regard to it has been the touchstone of our success." Malet to Granville, January 3, 1885, FO 343/6, Malet papers, and No. 129 Africa, February 21, 1885, FO 84/1822.

the Association and was outraged at King Leopold's "mischievous and shabby" behavior. His subordinates at the time of the Conference were a senior clerk, Clement Hill, and a junior clerk, H. Austin Lee. Hill during this time occupied himself with larger strategic and commercial aspects of the Scramble,[86] and had little to say about the Congo. Lee was too junior an official to influence policy, but nevertheless played an important role because he passed on the Foreign Office's secrets to Sir William Mackinnon, the director of the British and India Steam Navigation Company, who, as one of King Leopold's staunchest English supporters, in turn informed the Association's agents.[87]

In matters of routine Granville followed Lister's advice and usually acted as a rubber stamp, casually approving the draft dispatches and telegrams. Lister, with his influence as a permanent official, perhaps would have been able to thwart Britain's recognition of the Association had it not been for Sir Julian Pauncefote, and to a lesser extent the parliamentary undersecretary, Lord Edmond Fitzmaurice. Pauncefote, in his capacity as permanent undersecretary, attempted to give Granville's policy direction and precision. He overrode Lister's protests in almost every instance, and his voice was decisive. Two times in particular he spoke out in a way that paved the path toward recognition. First, on the opening date of the Conference, November 15, a dispatch drafted by Pauncefote was sent to Malet in which the ambassador was told:

> the Association under existing circumstances does not present the conditions which constitute a State. But it no doubt possesses elements out of which a state may be created. . . . The Association is still in its infancy; but having regard to the noble aims of its founder and to the liberal and enlightened principles which it is understood to advocate, Her Majesty's Government will watch with great interest and sympathy its effort to develop itself into a new State.[88]

This exchange had preceded the final draft of that dispatch:

> Lister: I think your [Pauncefote's] compliments to the Assocn. at the end of the Drt. go rather too far. The only evidence I have ever seen of its endeavours to promote freedom of Commerce & Naviga-

86. See his memorandum of December 9, 1884, FO Confidential Print 5051.

87. The papers of Sir William Mackinnon at the School of Oriental and African Studies, University of London, reveal much about King Leopold's English connections.

88. Granville to Malet, No. 78 Africa, November 15, 1884, FO 84/1814.

> tion are the treaties it has made with the chief by wh. it secures to itself an absolute monopoly.[89]

> Pauncefote: I cannot say that I concur. . . . The passage can do us no harm as it stands & nobody doubts the aim which the King of the Belgs. has had in view. Besides the Assocn. will only be recognised on the condons. of free navigation & trade etc.[90]

Pauncefote wrote to Granville, "I don't think we could steer a safer course."

The second instance of Pauncefote's decisive influence came on November 20, the day after the Foreign Office had received Malet's telegram stating Bismarck's request to help the Association become a state. Lister made this notation on the telegram:

> It is one thing to "assist the Assocn. in its endeavour to become a State" and another to recognise it as being one. It is, I imagine, usual in recognising a new state to have a clear idea of its boundaries and even perhaps some proof of the validity of its claims to its territories. I shd. have thought that the proper mode of proceeding wd. have been for the Assn. to prove its title, to explain its constitution, to give assurances of its intentions as regards personal, religious and comml. freedom &c. &c. and then to petition the Confce. to recognise its sovereignty.[91]

Pauncefote retorted:

> Prince Bismarck has declared that the "status" of the Association is not to be brought before the Conference & I doubt the expediency of urging that it should be discussed there. . . . outside of the Conference . . . the Association might be recognised not as an actual State, but as a State *in course of formation* & on certain defined conditions as to consular jurisdiction, religious liberty, freedom of trade &c &c. . . . On those conditions it might be provisionally recognised for all practical and necessary purposes as an *inchoate State*. It would be a new feature in the practice of Nations, but I do not see any great objection to it under all the circes.[92]

Granville as usual merely noted "I agree," on Pauncefote's minute.

Although Pauncefote succeeded in leapfrogging the legal obstacles,

89. Lister to Pauncefote, November 14, 1884, ibid.

90. Minute by Pauncefote, ibid.

91. Minute by Lister of November 19 on Malet to Granville, No. 4 Africa telegram, November 19, 1884, FO 84/1815.

92. Minute by Pauncefote, November 20, 1884, ibid.

the British government nevertheless continued to dawdle until directly threatened by Germany. On December 1 Bismarck told Malet that unless Britain recognized the Association there would be "a generally unfriendly attitude of Germany on matters of the greatest importance to us"—implying not only the Niger but also the Nile. Granville brought the matter before the members of the cabinet. All favored recognition. Their comments were brief, with the exception of the lord chancellor's. Stating that he did not want to stand out for "mere form" and would acquiesce "for practical reasons," he wrote that he was not "among those who expect that, in this or in any other matter in which we may yield to pressure from Prince Bismarck and deviate from the exact line of our own policy for the sake of conciliating him, we shall succeed in obtaining from him, as to Egypt or any other subject in which we have special interests, any equivalent." Granville noted: "On several occasions I have urged concessions to a spoiled child, who happens, through Egypt, to have us a great deal in his power. In this case I think it is our policy as well as that of Germany, to strengthen the Association against France."[93] On December 2 at 5:45 P.M. the Foreign Office telegraphed Malet that Britain would recognize the Association.[94] The delegation in Berlin was greatly relieved. Malet immediately informed Bismarck and wrote to Granville: "The announcement of the intended recognition of the International Association has come at a very useful moment for us in the Conference, as it assures us the cooperation of the German, Belgian and United States Representatives in securing what we desire with regard to the Niger."[95]

During the rest of the Conference the Association fought for its political survival against the two powers with territorial claims on the Lower Congo, France and Portugal. Like the line of the conventional basin, the boundary of the Association was easy to draw in the interior, difficult to define along the coast and at the mouth of the river. France claimed the northern bank, Portugal the southern. If they realized their territorial ambitions, the new state would be cut off from the sea—"strangled at birth," as the representatives of the Association complained. After acrimonious negotiations the French finally offered to limit their claim to 5 degrees 12 minutes, which included the Kwilu district on the northern bank but gave the Association a thin strip of

93. Minute by Granville, December 1, 1884, PRO 30/29/144; see also Pauncefote's memorandum of December 2, 1884, FO 84/1816.

94. The agreement between Great Britain and the Association was finally signed on December 16. See Crowe, *Berlin West African Conference,* p. 147.

95. Malet to Granville, December 5, 1884, FO 343/6.

territory running to the sea. King Leopold thought the French were dealing harshly with him. The British nevertheless urged him to capitulate. Malet wrote to the King:

> I would give the French the line they ask, that is the parallel of 5°12′. They will not diminish their claim because they are sure that no pressure will be brought to bear on them to induce them to do so. The Germans will do nothing, and we shall do nothing beyond giving those platonic expressions of good will, which are often more irritating than expressions of hostility.[96]

Thus King Leopold was left to fend for himself. To Englishmen who had questioned the value of the Conference from the beginning, the situation now appeared ironical. According to the *Morning Post:* "if France 'recognises' Mr. Stanley's Association, it will be in exchange for many a thousand square kilometres of African soil. But apparently England has 'recognised' the International Association from pure goodness of heart, and just to prove once more that the interests of the Empire are the very last consideration of a truly humanitarian statesmanship." [97] The delegation at Berlin responded to similar criticism by pointing out that the establishment of the Association as a legitimate power at least had the merit of temporarily preventing a French take-over of the Congo.

From the point of view of the French press the unofficial results of the Conference also appeared paradoxical. Francis Charmes in the *Journal des Débats* attacked the Foreign Ministry for "giving away" to the Association territories that rightly belonged to France:

> Because the Association has established a certain number of stations in the north at 5°12′ it looks upon itself as the owner or, perhaps, the sovereign of the soil. Nothing could be more erroneous. The Association . . . is a mere tenant, and cannot claim any right of ownership. We contest that these territories belong to France, as far as the southern boundary of 5°12′. Moreover the treaty signed by M. de Brazza with King Makoko transferred to us a region near Stanley Pool extending along both banks of the great river. The International Association proposes an exchange of territories. We should give up what belongs to us on the left bank of the Congo,

96. Malet to King Leopold, Private and Confidential, December 20, 1884, FO 343/4.
97. December 19, 1884.

> and the Association would give in barter what? Why the land it owns in the north at 5°12′. But it owns nothing at all! [98]

Of course the argument in favor of French recognition was the preemption agreement. When the Association eventually collapsed—as was commonly assumed—the property would fall to France. Nevertheless the French drove a hard bargain. Finally on February 5, 1885, France signed a convention with the Association that drew the boundary at Manyanga, a little more than midway up the Lower Congo. It was unsatisfactory from King Leopold's viewpoint because he failed to get compensation for the Association's stations in the Kwilu district. But he did gain limited access to the sea.

The Association did better with the French than with the Portuguese, who as usual were obstinate. They demanded even more than they would have received in the Anglo-Portuguese treaty. King Leopold, who had "his heart set on getting both banks," [99] had to stand alone against the "preposterous" Portuguese claims that extended not only to the Cabinda enclave but also to the port of Banana at the mouth of the river and the territory along the southern bank up to Vivi instead of Noki. The King threatened to throw over the whole affair, burning his Congo boats and permitting France and Portugal to scorch the Lower Congo between them. According to his henchman, Henry S. Sanford of the American delegation:

> I consider the Association as practically abandoned by its friends, or those who should be. . . . Great Britain has shown good will, but no power. She has apparently no influence in Portugal. Germany [is] now satisfied with what she has secured. . . . If Portugal takes forcible possession today of Banana, Boma, Vivi—none will resist her—Your [British] Govt. will look on! [100]

Britain indeed had little reason to intervene on behalf of the Association. When the question arose before the Cabinet in early February whether Britain should exert pressure on Portugal to come to terms with the Association, Charles W. Dilke, President of the Local Government Board, wrote in a minute that reflected the cabinet's annoy-

98. January 13, 1885; see also his article of February 6, 1885.

99. H. S. Sanford to Mackinnon, January 12, 1885, Mackinnon papers. Sanford was King Leopold's American agent who secured recognition of the Association by the United States government. His Congo correspondence has been meticulously edited by François Bontinck, *Aux Origines de l'Etat Indépendant du Congo* (Louvain, 1966).

100. Sanford to Mackinnon, February 2, 1885, Mackinnon papers.

ance with the king: "The K. of the Belgians has behaved badly throughout . . . —& deserves in my opinion no consideration from us. I shd. stand aloof & not put prejudice on Portugal, but wash our hands of the bad business."[101] Granville and the delegation at Berlin, however, continued to be sympathetic to the Association. Britain joined Germany and France in presenting an ultimatum to Portugal.[102] On February 15 the Portuguese finally consented to have the boundary drawn at Nokki. "Harmless Portuguese authority," as the English press referred to it, thus became formally instated on the southern bank of the Congo and brought to a close the territorial negotiations at the Conference. In that way the delegates created a nascent state whose boundaries resembled a gigantic funnel, its narrow spout emptying into the sea, and its cone encompassing an enormous tract in the interior. The *Morning Post* commented that between France and Portugal the new state was "almost hermetically sealed off from external intercourse."[103] But King Leopold *did* have access to the Atlantic; and in the interior the boundaries of the Congo State stretched to Lake Tanganyika. In the words of the British ambassador, the King now had "an empire . . . sufficient for the grandest human ambition."[104]

Dedicated to the ideals of Free Trade and the introduction of civilization in central Africa, the new state hoped to bring peace to the Congo. The notion was enthusiastically supported by the American delegate, John A. Kasson, who simplistically thought that peace could be achieved by avoiding war. He proposed to the Conference that the entire free-trade area be neutralized.[105] From the Association's point of view this suggestion was eminently sensible, for practical as well as idealistic reasons. In its precarious existence the new state in the event of war would fall before the onslaught of even the puniest power—even Portugal. According to Stanley: "we though a State are not strong, we cannot fight—because if we did the greatest harm would befall the natives"—and, needless to say, the new state. Stanley went on: "We must be protected—how?—by a mutual agreement among the Powers that the territories of the Association shall be inviolate and considered neutral. Then and not till then shall I consider we are

101. Minute by Dilke of February 4 on Malet to Granville, No. 22 Africa telegram, February 3, 1885, FO 84/1821.

102. See Crowe, Part II, Chap. 5 for the best account of these negotiations.

103. January 31, 1885.

104. Malet to King Leopold, Private and Confidential, December 20, 1884, FO 403/4.

105. Protocol 4 of the Conference.

safe."[106] The goal, then, would be to make the Congo State neutral in the tradition of its sovereign, the King of the Belgians.

Cui bono? Obviously the Congo State. But proximity gave France and Portugal every reason *not* to remain neutral. Bismarck favored neutrality because in wartime German ships in African waters would be vulnerable to British sea power. For Britain neutrality was a double-edged sword—useful if it checked France, annoying if it restricted British action in a general war. The Foreign Office was perplexed. Lister wrote: "Why shd. one bit of W. Africa be exempt from warlike operons.? If the principle is good and practical why not extend it to all Colonies? Wd. it be advantageous to Engd. that such a principle shd. be partially or generally established?"[107] The Admiralty answered that in the case of the Congo neutrality would probably be desirable if belligerent ships could be prevented from coaling there.[108] The delegation at Berlin accordingly took that line, for reasons well analyzed in broad perspective by Anderson:

> It seems clear that it would be dangerous for England if an enemy should have the power of using the Congo as a base of operations in the flank of what would be, in case of the closing of the Suez Canal, our sole communication with the East, and that it is consequently advantageous to us to place those waters under the neutral régime; but that this advantage would be more than counterbalanced if we surrendered the right of following an enemy into the waters without ample security against his making indirect use of them to our detriment.[109]

With reservations the British delegation therefore supported the proposal to neutralize all of the conventional basin. But France and Portugal would not agree, on grounds that it would be "an infringement on their sovereign rights."[110]

Finally late in the Conference the delegates agreed to a compromise whereby a power possessing territory in the Congo basin had the option to proclaim itself neutral. Thus in a much watered-down form, neutrality found its way into the General Act and created confusion

106. Stanley to Mackinnon, December 16, 1884, Mackinnon papers.

107. Minute by Lister on Malet to Granville, No. 5 Africa telegram, November 19, 1884, FO 84/1815.

108. Minute by Northbrook, November 26, 1884, PRO 30/29/140.

109. Memorandum by Anderson on Neutrality enclosed in Malet to Granville, No. 218 Africa Confidential, December 13, 1884, FO 84/1817.

110. See Malet to Granville, No. 104 Africa, February 14, 1885.

in the public mind about what the Conference had accomplished in this regard. To take one of many examples, the *Manchester Examiner and Times* commented that the "neutralisation of the Congo Basin is . . . a decided gain to the world."[111] In fact the Berlin Act did not neutralize the Congo basin but merely created, in the words of the French delegate, "a moral obligation" on the part of the signatories to respect the neutrality of any state that proclaimed it. The Foreign Office noted that the clause was "innocuous" because it merely stated the truism that any state in time of war could claim neutrality.[112] In the aftermath of the Conference only the Congo State invoked the neutrality clause. During the First World War it was disregarded by Belgians and Germans alike.[113] But at the time of the founding of the Congo State, King Leopold's "Declaration of Neutrality" contributed significantly to the myth reiterated at the close of the Conference—that he was sovereign of "a neutral State given over to the world's free trade."

The problem of neutrality played an important part in the third and final transaction of the Conference. Having established free trade on the Congo and Niger as the first two bases of the general Act, the delegates now in January attempted to formulate a third base regulating the procedure of acquiring new territory in Africa. The main point hinged on the concept of "annexation" and, the idea gaining popularity at the time of the Conference, "protection." The legal adviser of the British delegation, Twiss, wrote:

> if the newfangled Protectorates are to come into fashion in the place of annexations, what is to be the status of a Protected State in time of War? Is it to follow the fortunes of the Protecting Power or is it to enjoy a Neutral character and to be exempt from hostile assault and if so, is the Protecting Power debarred from making it a base of belligerent operations and if so may the subjects of the enemy continue to trade with it as with any other State. . . . these Protectorates are looming in the future as Neutral Coaling Stations![114]

If the term protectorate merely meant a neutral annexation, then British sea power might be jeopardized in time of war. "'Protection'

111. February 28, 1885.

112. See Pauncefote to Granville, February 2, 1885, FO 84/1822.

113. See Jonathan E. Helmreich, "The End of Congo Neutrality, 1914," *Historian*, 28 (August 1966).

114. Twiss to Pauncefote, January 14, 1885, FO 84/1817.

is a honeyed word," Twiss concluded, "but a honeyed edge of the Cup does not guarantee the contents of the Cup to be innocent." [115]

The Foreign Office drew no clear distinction between annexations and protectorates. Nor did British officials have any precise ideas about the manner in which territories could or should be acquired. The answers to four questions that Lister posed to the Librarian of the Foreign Office, Sir Edward Hertslet, indicate the pragmatic and undoctrinaire way in which the British government regarded these issues:

1. T. V. L. Is there any generally recognised form for taking possession of an uninhabited island or district?
   Hertslet: There is no generally recognised form
2. T. V. L. In cases of an annexation on the mainland, proclaimed only on the coast, how far inland does the annexation extend?
   Hertslet: There is no general rule on this point.
3. T. V. L. In cases of annexation of a coast, must the formalities take place on shore? And, if so, at how many points along a long line of coast?
   Hertslet: This formality has certainly not been gone through as a rule.
4. When the countries to be annexed are inhabited, is the consent of the natives in any way necessary to the validity of the annexation?
   Hertslet: Such consent would not appear to be necessary on all occasions. But there is a great difficulty in these days in making a clear distinction between annexation and protection.[116]

On one point at least, the lord chancellor, the Earl of Selborne, had a definite answer. His view determined the outcome of the last major business of the Conference. "*Annexation,*" he wrote, "is the direct assumption of territorial Sovereignty. *Protectorate* is the recognition of the right of the aboriginal or other actual inhabitants to their own country, with no further assumption of territorial rights than is necessary to maintain the paramount authority & to discharge the duties of the Protecting Power." [117]

France and Germany, who resented British protectorates as "dogs in the mangers," urged that protectorates as well an annexations should

115. Ibid.

116. "Memorandum on the Formalities necessary for the effective Annexation of Territory," December 18, 1884, FO 84/1818.

117. Memorandum by Selborne (italics by Pauncefote), January 3, 1885, FO 84/1819.

carry with them *jurisdiction*—in other words, not only authority but also responsibility. Although perhaps anti-British in sentiment, this proposal otherwise was made in good faith by delegates who wanted to curtail the rampant annexationist craze by ensuring that new territorial acquisitions were real, not sham. The British delegation supported the idea (with a few reservations on the part of Sir Travers Twiss). They reported that the scope of the legislation would be limited, so as to avoid controversy. Malet pointed out on January 7 that the proposal was already so emasculated that nothing would be required but notification of new acquisitions on the coasts of Africa, which already were mostly under European control ("there will hardly be any territory to which the Declar. of the Confn. will attach," Pauncefote noted).[118] The Foreign Office also favored the idea. According to Pauncefote, "The 3d basis is clearly intended to prevent the secret acquisition of new territories without occupation."[119] Clearly Britain had as great an interest as the other powers in preventing "paper protectorates." By refusing to accept the responsibilities flowing from protectorates, the British, again in Pauncefote's strong words, would "incur great odium and suspicion."[120] Malet put forward the same point: "refusal on our part [to accept the article on protection] would look as if we were resolved to maintain the Dog in the manger policy of simply giving Protection for the purpose of keeping other Powers out of certain territories which we cannot use ourselves, but do not like anyone else to use."[121]

Nevertheless Britain, solely because of Selborne's objections, refused to adhere to the principle that protectorates involved administrative and judicial responsibility. In a manner unthinkable in a Salisbury government, England's participation in the partition of Africa under Gladstone in this instance was determined by the lord chancellor. The Foreign Office circulated almost every important dispatch, instruction, and telegram to him for approval; Granville deferred to him absolutely, probably for the astute reason that feeble diplomacy could be more easily defended if it had juridical sanction. For perhaps the only time in the history of the Scramble, the lord chancellor of England guided its course.

Selborne probably had as good a grasp over colonial and imperial

118. Minute by Pauncefote on Lister's draft telegram to Malet, Africa No. 7, January 17, 1885, FO 84/1820.

119. Minute by Pauncefote, January 1, 1885, FO 84/1818.

120. Pauncefote to Hill, January 10, 1885, FO Confidential Print 5080.

121. Malet to Granville, January 17, 1885, FO 343/6.

constitutional issues as any other lord chancellor in the history of the British Empire.[122] He certainly devoted more attention to them than most lord chancellors. He regarded the law of the Empire as unique, radically different in nature from that of the French or the embryonic German colonial system. In his view it probably made little difference to the French or Germans whether they designated their overseas territories "annexations" or "protectorates"; but to the British Empire the failure to make that distinction would have momentous and undesirable consequences.

> there is no substantial obstacle, in their case, to their treating the distinction between Protectorate and annexation as purely nominal, so that by Protectorate they mean . . . annexation under another name. But it is otherwise with us; and that for reasons, some of which are of peculiar force in Africa. If we annexed any territory, slavery must at once cease to exist. I am not aware that any other Power is embarrassed with this difficulty.[123]

The abolition of slavery was only one of many difficulties. In a protected state Britain constitutionally *could not* exercise authority or jurisdiction because such a territory technically was not part of the Queen's dominions. As a "Little Englander" and a most conscientious authority on constitutional law, Selborne saw every reason why Britain should fight against any declaration made by an international conference that would impose the duties of annexation in territories that Britain wished only to control and not to govern.

By refusing to apply jurisdiction to protectorates, British policy gave the impression of rejecting the principle of "effective occupation." In European eyes Britain wanted to remain free to proclaim protectorates merely to prevent the legitimate advance of other powers. The British delegation quickly found themselves isolated on this point and feared that the negotiations over the third base for the Act might rupture merely because of their "captious objections."[124] Britain would receive the blame. Moreover the delegation thought there were other good reasons for accepting the protectorate clause: European suspicions of British territorial ambitions would be proved wrong, and "effective occupation" would check French and German designs. In London Pauncefote championed the proposal and was distressed at

122. For Selborne's political views, see Roundell, Earl of Selborne, *Memorials Personal and Political, 1865–1895* (London, 1898).

123. Selborne to Pauncefote, January 23, 1885, FO 84/1820.

124. Malet to Granville, Africa No. 4 telegram, January 7, 1885, FO 84/1819.

the lord chancellor's intransigence. "I cannot see the danger of adopting this Rule *in Africa,*" he wrote, "—and indeed I think it a salutary one for it would prevent *Paper* Protectorates in those Regions." [125]

Selborne did not regard his objection as "captious" but as fundamental. "It appears to me to be neither necessary, nor reasonable, nor expedient, that, in every case of a Protectorate, the Protecting Power should take upon itself an obligation 'to establish and to maintain,' in and throughout the protected territory, 'a jurisdiction.'" [126] He denounced "our diplomatists at Berlin [who] place the smooth working of the Conference . . . upon a higher level than all other considerations connected with the question at issue." [127] He attacked Pauncefote for not seeing the worldwide ramification of the issue:

> I always feel great respect for Sir Julian Pauncefote's opinions: but, in this case, I cannot but think, that it would be most fallacious and dangerous to assent to the rules & principles of the "Projet" as to Africa, without being prepared to admit their application, practically, in other parts of the world also. If, in Africa, occupations & Protectorates mean the same thing, and are to carry with them the same obligations, why not in the rest of the world also? Can we assent to such a principle there, where *possibly* it might work in our favour, and deny it, where it might work against us? [128]

In the lord chancellor's view the words "recognise the obligation"—the crucial phrase of the proposal—would establish a principle applicable to all parts of the world and could not be restricted to Africa. The administrative and judicial burdens would be intolerable, especially to a Gladstonian government.

Curiously enough, that staunchest of all "Little Englanders," Sir William Harcourt, the home secretary, challenged Selborne's opinion:

> I cannot concure. . . . If a Protectorate is meant to carry with it the right to exclude other Powers from the territory, it in my judgment involves as a matter of course the obligations to do for other Powers what they could otherwise do for themselves, viz., protect their own rights and subjects within the territory. To appear to dispute this proposition, or to seek to cut it down, would in my opinion be at variance with the principles of international law, and would be highly inexpedient in regard to the question now so occupying

125. Pauncefote to Hill, January 9, 1885, ibid.
126. Memorandum by Selborne, January 8, 1885, ibid.
127. Selborne to Pauncefote, January 23, 1885, FO 84/1820.
128. Note by Selborne, January 11, 1885, FO 84/1819.

> the attention of Europe. . . . Any other view would lead to indefinite *"Paper Protectorates."* . . .
>
> We should, I think, justly have all European opinion against us. The Powers would say England wants to engross the globe, to take just such advantages as she thinks fit, and to repudiate the corresponding duties. This I conceive at the present moment would be most unwise.[129]

Harcourt accurately perceived the prevailing sentiment in Berlin. On the same day he wrote those lines, January 24, Bismarck warned the British ambassador that he might adjourn the Conference without agreement on the third basis of the Act. Britain would be stigmatized with obstruction. British "territorial greed," "colonial hegemony," "dog in the manger policy," and other such phrases would again echo in the European press. Granville consequently summoned a special meeting of the Cabinet. They overrode the lord chancellor's views. The Foreign Office on January 26 telegraphed Malet to acquiesce. Nevertheless Selborne triumphed. In the meantime Bismarck had changed his mind. In an abrupt about-face he dictated that the protectorate phrase should be modified. In final form the clause appeared nearly meaningless to many, merely requiring notification of occupations along the African coasts. The British ambassador thus could truly say in summary that the Conference had not been so bold as to attempt any daring innovations in international law. No "new rules" were adopted. Selborne's "Little Englander" philosophy emerged victorious over Sir William Harcourt's. Great Britain in accordance with the law of the Empire could have the advantages of controlling protectorates and remain untrammeled by the administrative and judicial responsibilities of the Crown's jurisdiction.

Why did Bismarck yield? Perhaps the answer is simple: with the Scramble at its height during the Conference, there would be virtually no territories along the coast to which the declaration would apply. The British delegates, however, attributed his change of policy to their persistent efforts to prove that his suspicions of British territorial aims were unfounded, and that Britain did not envy German colonial ambitions; they attempted to convince him of the difficulties of discharging precise administrative and judicial responsibilities in places such as South-West Africa. Would Germany be prepared to admit a direct and absolute responsibility under all circumstances for offences of the natives or crimes committed by Europeans? What was the

129. Memorandum by Harcourt, January 24, 1885, FO 84/1820.

purpose and function of German administration in a "protected state"? Those questions gave force to the lord chancellor's argument that the world had gone along well enough in the past without the complication of turning protectorates into annexations, and probably gave Bismarck cause for thought.[130] In any case the British delegation took full credit for bringing Bismarck around. Anderson wrote to Pauncefote:

> Dropping water will pierce the hardest stone, and so our unceasing efforts, public and private, in season and out of season, pierced Bismarck's understanding, though he shewed no sign of yielding till the last moment.
>
> We have scored a triumph, the more precious as it is a triumph of common sense.[131]

It was an appropriate note on which to leave Berlin. "Common sense" from the British point of view had won out in every major issue: free trade on the Congo; British control over the Niger; and the maintenance—at least in British eyes—of a sharp distinction between "protectorates" and "annexations."

During the Conference Stanley wrote that war might break out between the European powers if they could not settle the Congo issue. Preoccupied with Africa, he misinterpreted the temper of the time. *Revanche,* not the Congo or any other colonial question, remained the central French concern. Europe, not Africa or the Pacific, continued to govern Bismarck's policy. Even for England, the Congo and Niger were secondary regions compared to places of highest imperial importance; Egypt, the Cape, India, and Australia—the key points of the "Southern British World," as the press had already begun to refer to it in 1884–85. With remarkable insight the *Economist* placed the rivalry in western Africa in perspective and detected the main historical significance of the Conference on its opening day:

> The English public is not interested in the Congo. The majority of the electors know little about the area and are completely unaware of any bearing it may have on British trade. Among the more informed, there is a certain disgust with the colonies and particularly with the African enterprises from the Egyptian expedition to the operations in Bechuanaland. They watch the Congo affair with more curiosity as to the machinations of Germany than anything else.

130. Bismarck's views are most fully expounded by Turner in "Bismarck's Imperialist Venture."

131. Anderston to Pauncefote, January 31, 1885, FO 84/1820.

> Nonetheless, to those with an historical eye, the Conference is an important incident. It represents the first time that Europe as an informal group has assumed any jurisdiction over a large, uncivilized area. . . . This distribution of land is perhaps the last to be made, the remainder of the globe being already parcelled out. Any further changes . . . will probably be the result of war.[132]

For the next three decades the European powers continued to settle African disputes by diplomacy. When war broke out in 1914, the "concert of Europe" that had effectively regulated European activities overseas failed to function in Europe itself.

Yet it is also true that African issues exacerbated European relations and created intense suspicion. According to a typical French view, that of Francis Charmes in the *Journal des Débats:*

> Prince von Bismarck does not desire wars and boulversements: but he would nevertheless like to see . . . everybody well occupied in the Sudan, Afghanistan, the Red Sea, the Balkans, and Tonkin, while Germany remains severely and impassively presiding over the destinies of Europe with an eager eye to all profits or "brokerage" likely to accrue.[133]

Bismarck, as is well known, suspected that Britain tried to "close in," "encircle," wherever Germany attempted to colonize. But to the British, territories such as South-West Africa, the Cameroons, and New Guinea were traditional spheres of British influence being devoured by "a boy who eats too much." During the last two months of the Conference, Anglo-German colonial relations were extraordinarily bitter. The English press lampooned the Conference in such articles as "Dinner at Berlin." According to the *Glasgow Herald* the feast included "pickled Kangaroo from North New Guinea, lean (exceptionally lean) mutton from the Cameroons, and a barrel of very astonishing natives . . . from Wallfisch Bay." [134] Englishmen ridiculed Germany's advent as a colonial power but welcomed her in preference to France. They blamed the English "jellyfish politicians" as much as Bismarck for England's "eating humble pie" in Africa and the Pacific. Although there was some debate whether Granville was "a philistine or a sly diplomatic fox," most agreed that he should be held responsible for the "open boot kissing" of the Foreign Office and the "imbecility of English policy." A few responsible organs of the press restrained their

132. November 15, 1884.
133. March 11, 1885.
134. January 19, 1885.

criticism of the Foreign Office and emphasized that Germany's overseas empire would not threaten Britain's security because, in the words of the *Liverpool Daily Post*, "Germany is no match for England at sea. . . . every distant colony . . . is a vulnerable point at which any enemy that commands the sea can strike." [135] Along the same lines the British ambassador in Paris wrote a perceptive commentary that establishes the relevance of the colonial rivalries of the Berlin Conference era to the origins of the First World War: "Bismarck used to say that Germany and England were like a wolf and a shark, both dangerous animals, but unable to get at each other. His new Colonial Policy is very much as if the wolf should put his paws into the water so as to bring them within reach of the shark." [136] With empires go supporting navies; Bismarck's colonial policy launched Germany on a course of *Weltpolitik*.[137]

To Frenchmen the Scramble was as much a race for markets as a struggle for strategic position. At the beginning of the Conference France appeared to have the upper hand. With Bismarck's concurrence, Ferry refused absolutely to discuss the application of the free-trade principle to the Gabon, Guinea, or Senegal, and insisted that the Niger be considered along with the Congo. The Conference accomplished two-thirds of its major work by establishing freedom of navigation on the two rivers with freedom of trade on the Congo. But France emerged from the Conference having gained very little. Britain on the other hand succeeded in establishing a vast free-trade zone in central Africa and in beating off the French attempt to impinge on British control of the Niger. In retrospect the work of the Conference appears hollow in view of the commercial monopolies established despite the Berlin Act. But at the time the accomplishments of the Conference appeared substantial, especially in British eyes because of the reverses suffered by France. All in all the major achievement appeared to be that in the Congo "a vast European, and especially British, trade will be opened." [138] Compared with such jubilant comments, the tone of the French press was subdued. In one of the few lengthy commentaries on the results of the Conference, the *République Française* expressed the general feeling of French colonial circles when it unenthusiastically congratulated the government for securing

135. January 13, 1885.

136. Lyons to Granville, No. 101 Africa, Very Confidential, December 2, 1884, FO 84/1816.

137. See Turner, "Bismarck's Imperialist Venture," p. 82.

138. *Standard*, March 3, 1885.

the Ogooué and the right bank of the Upper Congo as "our exclusive property."[139]

The third basis of effective occupation proved to be as ineffective in regulating the partition of the continent as the first two bases were in preventing monopolies on the Congo and Niger. Yet the popular image of the Conference then as now is that it "partitioned Africa." Many captions in the press ran along the lines of "Setting the Rules of the Grab." Writers since then have assumed that because the Conference met during one of the Scramble's hottest phases, the delegates gave the partition momentum and "plotted Africa's fate." Since the Conference did not deal formally with questions of sovereignty, the interpretation is erroneous. But since the Conference did informally give birth to that bastard child, the Congo Free State, it can be said in a loose sense that the Conference gave the Scramble "international sanction," a vague phrase perhaps implying that Africa should be partitioned peacefully and in accordance with the principle of Free Trade.

Historians have often been sceptical about the Berlin Act either as an effective political instrument or as a legal precedent. Writing in 1942, Sybil Crowe stated that the events of the Scramble that were taking place at the time of the Conference "must not be confused with any far-reaching effect which the conference may have had, even indirectly, on international rivalry in Africa during the next fifty years or so. This appears to have been negligible."[140] By contrast a French scholar and diplomat, Geoffroy de Courcel, seven years earlier in an important book overlooked by many writers on the subject (including Crowe), concluded:

> Au point de vue économique et juridique, on a parfois voulu considérer l'Acte de Berlin comme une Charte coloniale universelle. Cette conception s'était même manifestée au cours des débats et explique certaines des dispositions adoptées.
>
> Sans avoir cette portée, l'Acte de Berlin a tenté une expérience libérale intéressante et il a consacré, au double point de vue économique et juridique, l'abandon du système de Pact colonial: l'exploitation de la colonie ne devait plus se faire au profit exclusif de la métropole, mais avant tout au profit de la colonie elle-même, en y étendant la puissance, l'influence et la civilisation de la métropole. . . .

139. April 14, 1885.
140. Crowe, *Berlin West African Conference*, p. 5.

> L'œuvre de la Conférence de Berlin a eu en définitive pour buts la paix, la prospérité et la civilisation.[141]

Which of the two writers held the more accurate view?

In a sense neither was wrong. They viewed the Berlin Act differently from their respective disciplines of history and international law. As a historian, Crowe held that the provisions of the Act were flouted and proved totally ineffective. She argued cogently that the historical significance of the Conference lay in the preceding events rather than its influence on the Scramble. With equal force de Courcel proved that the Berlin Act reflected a consensus of the family of nations on a "multiplicity" of issues that included, in addition to the three bases, protection of the natives, the slave trade, religious liberty, arbitration, and even the Universal Postal Union. The Foreign Office lamented the inadequacy of these minor clauses, and some sections of the press attacked the Conference for its "hollow humanitarianism" and "philanthropic gabble." Nevertheless the Berlin Act, as de Courcel emphasized, did broach major questions and established precedents later elaborated in the Brussels Antislavery Act, the Convention respecting Liquors in Africa, and the conventions of St. Germain-en-Laye. It should be added, on the basis of evidence not accessible when Crowe and de Courcel wrote, that the Berlin Act *did* have a relevance to the course of the partition and has a newly proven significance as precedent. At the height of the Congo reform controversy from 1906 to 1908 there was considerable talk of reconvening the Berlin Conference to consider the maladministration of the Congo State. The Foreign office prepared a 265-page brief against King Leopold for having violated the "spirit of the Berlin Act."[142] Had Belgium not annexed the Congo in 1908, the Congo probably would have become the subject of another international conference that would have judged whether the Congo State had violated the Berlin Act. Proved guilty, the Congo State might have been partitioned between Germany, France, and Britain. The other revelation is concrete, not "might have been." The recently released documents of the Foreign Office establish beyond doubt that the precedent in the minds of British statesmen as they established the mandates system was the Berlin Act.[143] The

141. Courcel, *L'Influence de la Conférence de Berlin,* p. 161. Cf. Boniface I. Obichere, *West African States and European Expansion: The Dahomey-Niger Hinterland, 1885–1898* (New Haven, 1971).

142. FO 371/117.

143. Wm. Roger Louis, *Great Britain and Germany's Lost Colonies* (Oxford, 1967), Chaps. 3 and 4.

Trusteeship System of the United Nations thus descends from the Conference of 1884–85.

In the phrase "the spirit of the Berlin Act" the historian perhaps finds the clue to the meaning of the Conference for African as well as European history. When African historians at some remote date re-examine Europe's relations with Africa, they will probably look upon the Berlin Conference as a curiosity. At no other time were European attitudes toward Africa more marked with confidence, enthusiasm, and idealism. The reformer E. D. Morel twenty years later described the spirit of the Conference:

> Now, although international jealousies contributed very largely to the Berlin Conference of 1885, it is unquestionable that the spirit displayed at that Conference and the policy it laid down were alike inspired by humanitarian motives—*practical* humanitarian motives. . . . there was throughout the deliberations which took place in the course of the framing of the clauses of the Act, a desire to protect the natives of Africa from injustice and expropriation; to guarantee them in the peaceful possession of their land and property; to check, as far as possible, inter-tribal warfare and the slave-raiding operations of Arab half-castes and to maintain and develop trade. Particular stress was laid upon the latter point, it being universally recognised that commercial intercourse is, above all things, the surest medium for the advancement of arts and crafts, and generally speaking to a higher conception of life.[144]

At the Berlin Conference, so the myth developed, King Leopold was appointed as Europe's "trustee" to introduce trade and civilization into the heart of the continent. With unbounded optimism the English press reported on the success of his mission and on the conditions of the Congo. There were of course a few sceptics who jeered at the thought of Manchester's cotton being peddled to Congo cannibals, but this description by the *Standard* might be fairly taken as representative of Europe's image of the Congo in 1885:

> The Congo affords 4000 miles of navigable waterway, and on either side stretches a country of the most exuberant fertility. Palm oil, rubber, gums, coffee, copper—already smelted by the natives—ivory, camwood and orchella weed (both valuable for dyeing purposes), palm fibre, and hides are amongst a few of the chief articles

144. Edmund D. Morel, *King Leopold's Rule in Africa* (London, 1904), pp. 3–4.

> of native trade, and there are besides vast areas covered with the most valuable timber such as ebony, mahogany, lignum vitre, teak, and redwood . . . there are 30,000,000 cubit feet of timber which will command the highest prices in the European market when the railway is made, and means of transport thus afforded. All kinds of European vegetables will grow luxuriantly, and both sugar and cotton are indigenous to many parts of the country.

Not only the products of the soil but also the animal life filled Europeans with enthusiasm:

> The greater part of the Free State is new country, and should be the paradise of sportsmen, containing as it does enormous numbers of elephants, lions, buffalos, hippopotami, crocodiles, antelopes, water bucks, lynxes and many other species of animals.

Above all the Africans hungered for European commerce:

> The wants of the natives are still more varied than their own products, and there is scarcely any branch of European industry which may not expect to benefit by the opening of this vast market. Cotton goods, blankets, crockery, muskets, gunpowder, hardware of all kinds, and cheap finery of every description are but a few amongst the goods in constant demand amongst them.[145]

The press referred to the inspirer of those lines, Stanley, as "the Clive of Africa," and quoted King Leopold in such rapturous phrases as "I speak of Africa and golden joys." "In the name of Almighty God" the "Congo Conference" had proclaimed the advent of civilization in the Dark Continent. Toasts were made to King Leopold, "that noble-minded Sovereign who had the wisdom and the courage to begin the enterprise of the Congo which will be the bright centre to the new Federation of Freedom and Peace." Having inspired such lofty sentiments, the Berlin Congo Conference should rightly be remembered in European colonial history as "the most remarkable Conference that has ever been assembled." [146]

145. March 2, 1885.
146. *Leeds Mercury*, February 28, 1885.

6. *The Tariff Factor in Anglo-French West African Partition*

C. W. NEWBURY

It is amusing to see how the French think we are going to take their trade, while our merchants are clamouring exactly the opposite.

A. W. L. Hemming, Minute, December 9, 1892 [1]

Si vous n'étiez pas si acharnés protectionnistes, vous ne nous trouveriez pas si gourmands de territoires.

Lord Salisbury, January 18, 1897 [2]

International rivalry in the African market is an ancient theme. Partition is a late variation on that theme, made infinitely complex by shifts in the European power balance and by political and economic changes in Africa. On the whole, historians of partition would reject any simple single-factor explanation of the division of the African continent in the late nineteenth century. Nor would they give much of a hearing to any argument from "economic imperialist" premises. Investment and development were the legacies of occupation, not its motivation. Trade and capital followed the flag.[3]

But not quite all trade or all capital. Some was present before the annexation of the interior, in sufficient quantities to help supply the New World with slaves and the Old World with exotic products.[4] Such trade was highly competitive; the capital was mostly private and inadequately protected in markets that were subject to inter-

1. Minute on Elder Dempster to Colonial Office [CO hereafter], December 8, 1892, CO 267/399.

2. Cited in Courcel to Hanotaux, January 18, 1897, Ministère des Affaires Etrangères [MAE hereafter] Grande-Bretagne 11; and *Documents diplomatiques français* [*DDF* hereafter], 1st series, *13*, 117.

3. See especially Ronald E. Robinson and John Gallagher, with Alice Denny, *Africa and the Victorians: The Official Mind of Imperialism* (London, 1961), Chap. 13.

4. K. G. Davies, *The Royal African Company* (London, 1957); Abdoulaye Ly, *La Compagnie du Sénégal* (Paris, 1958); Allan McPhee, *The Economic Revolution in British West Africa* (London, 1926).

ference by Africans and Europeans with very different ideas of redress and control. On the western coast of Africa these markets expanded slowly in the decades before partition; on the east coast they hardly expanded at all till partition was over. By the time Augustus Hemming wrote the comment cited above, British imports from the African continent were valued at about nineteen and a half million pounds.[5] But the Cape and Egypt accounted for most of that, while the markets of western Africa supplied only 1.8 million pounds and the east coast very much less.

Colonial Office officials, then, could flippantly make notes on the antics of those who thought West African trade worth shouting for. On the other hand, Hemming and his colleagues were not oblivious to the pressures of foreign competition in the 1890s; and Hemming as much as anyone had played a part in resisting them in diplomatic negotiations. Such things were taken seriously, even if many items in the mercantile *cahiers de doléances* were not.

In the same year, Lord Salisbury—no great champion of West African traders—included the following passage in his instructions to Lord Dufferin, then British ambassador in Paris:

> I should wish your Excellency to draw . . . special attention to the importance of the British commercial interests involved in the various [West African] demarcation negotiations. . . . Wherever, in West Africa, Great Britain has undertaken the task of developing and civilizing the interior, French trade profits equally with that of this country; but the tendency of French arrangements with the natives is to obtain exclusive commercial privileges for French commerce. Her Majesty's Government have no evidence that the trade of any of the British Colonies has as yet suffered from diversion of trade routes in consequence of Treaty obligations with France; they are aware that the Chiefs of the interior would not easily be compelled to abandon roads leading to favourable markets; but they cannot ignore the fact that British merchants [6] are apprehensive that attempts may be made to exclude them from sources of trade in territories under French influence, and they observe that these apprehensions are to some extent justified by the stipulations of the

5. Based on statistics in Public Record Office [PRO hereafter] Customs 4/87, and Customs 8/133.

6. More particularly the Liverpool Chamber of Commerce: see *Report of the Committee of the African Trade Section of the Liverpool Chamber of Commerce* (Liverpool, 1892), 12.

> VIIIth. Article of the French Treaty with Samadu of 1889.[7] No effort should, consequently, be spared to obtain an understanding that in territories under French, as in those under British influence, there shall be no differential treatment; and, as far as possible, to secure agreements as to Tariffs.[8]

Admittedly this was a piece for public consumption. It contrasts markedly with Salisbury's more peremptory replies to merchants' petitions at that period.[9] But the Foreign Office was certainly alive to their case, seen in the context of wider commercial and diplomatic developments. And it perhaps goes some way toward explaining Salisbury's extraordinary outburst, as reported by the French ambassador, Baron de Courcel, five years later,[10] when African partition was nearing its climax and there were greater international tensions to bear.

An impressive list of such quotations could be made to illustrate British apprehensions of French threats to commercial predominance in the tropical world. They would include, on the eve of the Berlin Conference, *The Times* leader that promised equal treatment for all in the Lower Niger, in contrast to the selfish aims of other Powers: "France, in particular, is as exclusive in her commercial policy on the Senegal, and in the Gaboon as in the Indo-Chinese peninsula."[11] And they would include, from a higher level of decision-making, the minute of Gladstone's cabinet which in November 1883 agreed to send Consul Edward Hewett back to the Niger Delta with power to annex "certain [ports?] offered to the British Power in Western Africa, with a view to the maintenance of an unfettered trade, which unhappily is not favoured by the arrangements of the French in those latitudes."[12]

7. Article 8 of Colonel Archinard's treaty with Samori, February 21, 1889, reads: "L'Almamy s'engage à favoriser le commerce des caravanes venant du Haut Sénégal et à faire son possible pour que les marchandises provenant de son pays soient dirigées sur les escales françaises." And cf. Article III of L. C. Binger's treaty at Kong, January 10, 1889: "Les Français seuls pourront faire le commerce dans les États de Kong"; and there were similar clauses in Binger's other Ivory Coast treaties and in J. S. Gallieni's treaty at Kendugu, June 18, 1888. Copies enclosed in FO to CO, July 3, 1890, CO 879/32, African 387.

8. Salisbury to Dufferin, March 30, 1892, *Parliamentary Papers* [*PP* hereafter], C.6701 (1892), *56*, 778.

9. For example, Salisbury to the Liverpool Chamber of Commerce, December 30, 1891, Report of the Committee of the African Trade Section (1892), 6.

10. See note 2 above.

11. "The Lower Niger a British River," *The Times*, October 15, 1884.

12. PRO Cabinet 41/17, November 22, 1883.

But they are not, of course, conclusive evidence about the state of African trade conditions, though they tell us something about the state of mind of British merchants and officials with interest in that region. Above all, they raise questions. What substance was there in talk of "exclusion" from African markets? What, at the period of partition, was meant by that elusive concept "Free Trade"?

In the fullest sense of the term—the unrestricted passage of goods, persons, and vessels—free trade was never completely accepted in British and French posts on the coast of Africa. True, the ramshackle prohibitions of the Navigation Acts, as far as they applied to Sierra Leone, the Gambia, and the Gold Coast, had been dismantled by 1835 and were replaced by port and customs regulations which aimed at raising revenue, rather than protecting national trade and shipping.[13] Such developments were carefully watched in the Ministry of Commerce and Agriculture.[14] But there was a considerable time-lag before foreign traders were allowed to reside in French African posts, or before the spirit of the Cobden Treaty of 1860 was felt in the import duties of Senegal or the export duties of the dependencies of Gorée.[15] In any case, differential tonnage duties still applied to foreign shipping (indeed, they were increased at Senegal in 1880).[16] And even for those foreigners who paid their *droits et actes de francisation,* the Senegal, Casamance, and Gabon rivers remained closed.

Free trade, then, was far from reciprocal in western Africa. Opinion among French manufacturers and merchants tended to keep it that way. On the one hand the metropolitan chambers of commerce at the great ports were partisans of commercial liberalism at home; on the other, many of the agents of their firms favored more restrictive policies abroad.[17] Lukewarm "free traders" or patriotic protectionists, they

13. Under the Order in Council of October 12, 1829, and the Sierra Leone Duties Act, November 8, 1884. C. W. Newbury, *British Policy Towards West Africa.* Vol. 1, *Select Documents 1786–1874* (Oxford, 1965), pp. 80–97.

14. "Note: Côte-Ouest Africa [sic] Possessions Anglaises. Régime Commerciale," Archives Nationales [AN hereafter] F[12]6460

15. B. Schnapper, "La fin du régime de l'exclusif: le commerce étranger dans les possessions françaises d'Afrique tropicale (1817–1870)," *Annales Africaines* (1959), 164–69; and for the background policy, see his *La politique et le commerce français dans le Golfe de Guinée de 1838 à 1871* (Paris, 1961), pp. 185–245.

16. Archives Nationales Section Outre-Mer [ANSOM hereafter], Sénégal IX/21/c.

17. For an analysas of the commercial policies of the metropolitan chambers and French firms in West Africa, see C. W. Newbury, "The Protectionist Revival in French Colonial Trade: The Case of Senegal," *Economic History Review, 21* (1968).

resented the return of the Gold Coast forts to the British Crown (1842–43), the purchase of the Dutch forts, and the annexation of Lagos, just as British traders complained about the restoration of Senegal and Gorée to the French and the establishment of French posts west of the Gold Coast, in Dahomey, and in the Melakori.[18]

There was more to this rivalry than the natural antipathies of competitors in distant and difficult markets. Much of the French traders' antagonism was directed against the fiscal policies of British settlements which levied high duties on spirits, arms, powder, and leaf tobacco, compared with the generally low ad valorem duties on other items of European manufacture—particularly the universally necessary British calicoes, prints, hardware, and woolen stuffs. Even in the Gambia, where they won most of the groundnut (peanut) trade, they resented duties that were higher than at St. Louis or Gorée.[19] At Lagos, British customs drove French firms to carve out an enclave for themselves at Whydah and Porto-Novo.[20] In short, French traders were completely unreconciled to the British conception of free trade: they felt the Senegal River should remain restricted; they demanded new French posts to counter the "Gibraltar" of Bulama Island; they protested at British surtaxes on shipping arriving from coastal ports near Lagos, at British blockades of the Gold Coast and Dahomey, and, above all, at high specific duties on French brandies and wines.[21]

Fundamentally, commercial rivalry was a reflection of the unequal trading positions of Britain and France in western Africa. In markets from Senegal to the Congo the two countries accounted for about four-fifths of Europe's exports and imports which rose in annual value from about four million pounds to six and one-half million pounds in the period 1850–70.[22] Perhaps one-quarter to one-third of this value

18. Traders' petitions in AN F[12]7208 and F[12]7209; Schnapper, *La politique et le commerce français*, pp. 185–240; Newbury, *British Policy*, pp. 97–98, 419–20, 443.

19. Petition to the Ministry of Commerce and Agriculture, October 9, 1863, enclosed in Régis to Chamber of Commerce, October 9, 1863 (with nineteen signatures), Chamber of Commerce Archives, Marseille [CCM hereafter], series OK, "Commerce avec les colonies françaises, 1857–1883."

20. C. W. Newbury, *The Western Slave Coast and Its Rulers*, 2nd ed. (Oxford, 1966), pp. 67–71.

21. Petitions in CCM, series OK; Bordeaux Chamber of Commerce to Ministry of Marine and Colonies [MMC hereafter], December 10, 1864, Chamber of Commerce Archives, Bordeaux [CCB hereafter], Minutes (1864), pp. 540–46; MAE to Ministry of Commerce and Agriculture, July 14, 1865, June 16, 1875, AN F[12]6460; Newbury, *The Western Slave Coast*, pp. 103–04.

22. Returns of trade in Customs 4/45–65, Customs 88/71–112; G. Hervet, *Le commerce extérieur de l'Afrique occidentale française* (Paris, 1911); ANSOM,

was handled by French firms operating mainly in Senegal and its dependencies. By contrast, United Kingdom trade with British possessions on the coast was only 30 percent of her total trade with western Africa in 1870. A decade later it was still only 32 percent.[23] And in the possessions themselves foreign trade expanded at exactly the same rate as British trade, accounting for slightly over half of import and export values.[24] The main commercial interest of Britain in the region lay in markets outside formal British control. On the other hand, the proportion of French national trade with Senegal and the Casamance was relatively high at 68.5 percent in the period 1863–80.[25] In addition, there was a steady increase in the value of products exported by French firms from the Scarcies and Melakori markets, the Ivory Coast and southern Dahomey—worth an estimated one million pounds by 1875. But these were marginal areas of groundnuts and palm products whose European prices were on the decline in the 1870s—a factor that contributed in no small measure to competition for available supplies and to French fears of the extension of British customs to the unregulated markets.[26] Moreover, the amount of French trade with British possessions other than the Gambia (commercially part of Senegal) was relatively small at about £200,000 annually, and showed a tendency to decline, particularly at Lagos, as British tariffs rose.[27] Victor Régis, who had most to lose in this area, explained why to the Ministry of Commerce and Agriculture:

> L'eau de vie à 50° vaut en France en ce moment 28 centimes le litre; le droit imposé à Lagos équivaut à 53 centimes le litre, soit presque deux fois la valeur de sorte qu'il faudrait envoyer à la Côte d'Afrique 200 mille francs d'espèces pour acquitter les droits d'une cargaison valant 100 mille francs. En agissant ainsi plus de la moitié de la valeur des produits de cette contrée passerait au profits de la caisse coloniale.[28]

Sénégal *9* and *13;* Ernest Fallot, *Histoire de la colonie française du Sénégal* (Paris, 1884).

23. Returns of trade in Customs 4/75 and Customs 8/121.

24. Statistical returns in *PP*, C.4519 (1884–85), C.4520 (1884–85), *83*, C.5507 (1888), *105*, C.7144 (1893–94), C.

25. Hervet, *Le commerce extérieur*, p. 143.

26. Schnapper, *La politique et le commerce français*, pp. 140–41; H. Muller, *Le commerce du globe* (Havre, 1872), p. 644; *Chambre de Commerce de Marseilles. Compte-rendu de la situation commerciale et industrielle de la circonscription de Marseille*, 1877–82, 1883–88, CCM.

27. Statistical returns in *PP*, C.4520 (1884–85), *83*.

28. Memorandum by Régis: "Sénégal-Gambie. Factoreries françaises de la Côte occidentale d'Afrique. Notes sommaires," in Régis to Ministry of Commerce, November 21, 1875, AN F[12]7209.

It was this kind of consideration that led to French annexation of Cotonou in 1878—an action defended by the French Foreign Minister in the name of free trade: "Les taxes de la nature de celles qui frappent à Lagos les marchandises de provenance plus spécialement française ne sort compensées dans nos possessions par aucune mesure fiscale analogue atteignant dans une proportion égale les produits Britanniques." [29]

This drew the predictable reply from the Colonial Office that duties at Lagos were "in no way differential . . . the same amount is levied on all taxable articles from whatever countries they may come or by whomsoever they may be imported." Their purpose was strictly fiscal: "to defray the cost of that protection which is afforded both to British and foreign traders alike, not only within the actual limits of the Colonial jurisdiction but in the neighbouring territories and waters." [30]

But it was precisely this protection in "neighbouring waters" that French traders preferred to do without, whether north of Sierra Leone or near Lagos and the Gold Coast, if it meant high duties on their staple imports. Conversely, the French Ministry of Foreign Affairs (misled to some extent by the Department of Colonies) was wrong about duties in French possessions. By 1879 there was a significant movement for a return to protection in national and colonial trade in France; and differential duties had been levied since 1877 on certain cloths of foreign manufacture in Senegal.

These two features of French and British customs administration—high specific rates on spirits and the revival of a discriminatory colonial tariff—were major irritants in Anglo-French relations in West Africa. All the more so because precise information about colonial customs was difficult to obtain; and the different senses of free trade, as employed by either side, were frequently misunderstood.

The situation was further complicated by the fact that the home ports of most French West Africa traders were no less in favor of free trade in the 1870s than Liverpool or Bristol. There is no evidence that Régis of Marseille, or his countrymen from Bordeaux, supported tariff protection to combat British predominance in the African trade. On the contrary, the pressure for the adoption of a discriminatory tariff on foreign cloth imports into Senegal in 1877 came from Rouen manufacturers and Pondicherry cotton interests, in combination with a few commission agents at St. Louis and officials in the Senegal adminis-

29. Waddington to Lyons, March 24, 1879, enclosed in CO to FO, April 12, 1879, CO 147/39.

30. CO to FO, April 12, 1879, CO 147/39.

tration.[31] The Bordeaux and Marseille chambers of commerce fought the measure, just as they fought the protectionist movement in the *Conseil supérieur du commerce* and the revision of the General Tariff in favor of French industry in 1881.[32] Clearly, there were issues at stake that were much more important than the trade of a few firms in West Africa. A general attack on colonial commercial autonomy had been launched in 1875; the first phase was not ended till 1885, when free-trading privileges were withdrawn from Guadeloupe, Réunion, and Martinique. By comparison, the Senegal "Guinea cloth" tariff, revised and reinforced after much debate in 1880, was the thin edge of a very big protectionist wedge. Just how big was revealed when a project of Governor Brière de L'Isle for a crushing anti-British tariff in Senegal was approved by both the minister of marine and the minister of commerce.[33] But this move to extend the range of differential duties in the colony was postponed for a decade by the creation of an antiprotectionist *conseil général* at St. Louis in 1879. The Senegal administration was then obliged to wait till the local assembly and the metropolitan chambers of commerce fell into line with the tariff reformers of 1892.[34] It had been a close thing. In the meantime the Guinea differential remained in force as an example of what was yet to come.

The significance of these developments in French economic policy was not lost on British merchants, the Foreign Office, or the Board of Trade. As early as 1875, Thomas Brown, an exceptionally well-informed Gambia trader, warned of impending differentials on British

31. Rouen Chamber of Commerce to Bordeaux, March 18, 1867; Bordeaux Chamber of Commerce to Rouen, March 22, 1867, CCB, Minutes (1867), 161–62; Vallière to MMC, May 22, 1876; Brière de L'Isle to MMC, June 22, 1876, ANSOM, Sénégal IX/27/b. And the circulars to merchants and officials and debates in the *Conseil supérieur du commerce*, 1875, in *Enquête sur le régime commercial des colonies françaises* (Paris, 1877), pp. 7–49, 96–98.

32. Newbury, "The Protectionist Revival"; and for the background to changes in French national tariffs, 1877–81, see L. Amé, *Etude sur les tarifs de douane et sur les traités de commerce* (2 vols. Paris, 1876); Percy Ashley, *Modern Tariff History* (London, 1904); A. von Brandt, *Beiträge zur Geschichte der französischen Handelspolitik* (Berlin, 1896); cf. Arthur Girault, *The Colonial Tariff Policy of France*, John Bates Clark, ed. (Oxford, 1916), pp. 80–91.

33. Brière de L'Isle to MMC, April 2, 1877, and October 7, 1878; Roussin to Brière de L'Isle (draft), October 4, 1877; MMC to Ministry of Commerce, April 8, 1873, and June 26, 1878; Ministry of Commerce to MMC, July 24, 1878, ANSOM, Sénégal IX/21/b.

34. Which had taken place by 1887. See Bordeaux Chamber of Commerce to Ministry of Finance, March 23, 1887, CCB, Minutes (1887), p. 168.

shipping and "blue bafts" (Guineas) in his argument against cession of the Gambia to France.[35] The Manchester Chamber of Commerce took up the case without success, when the new decrees were in force.[36] By 1884, the Foreign Office had received from its commercial attaché in Paris a complete analysis of the Guinea tariff and anchorage dues in Senegal, a 20 percent differential in Gabon, the use of fictitious bonding by French firms, the closure of French rivers, the reservation of trade for Frenchmen in the Casamance, the granting of exclusive mining rights in Upper Senegal, and, finally, the rumored privileges obtained by treaty in the Fouta Djallon in 1881.[37] Taken in conjunction with recent knowledge that British shipping was being excluded from Réunion, Nossi Bé, Mayotte, and Madagascar; that customs duties had been restored in the Old Colonies; and that Félix Faure, as under-secretary for colonies, had just launched an appeal for further tariff measures to assist national industries in France's colonial trade, all this was a fairly depressing list for a nation of free traders.[38]

For their part, the French had to face increased duties in British possessions, levied to remedy the financial crisis of the 1870s. At Freetown, for example, customs, expressed as a percentage of gross import values, had risen steeply from 7 percent in 1865 to 13 percent in 1875.[39] Moreover, they had been extended to the Iles de Los in the French commercial sphere in 1874; and as it became clear that revenues would continue to lag behind expenditure, an interdepartmental committee in London approved Governor Samuel Rowe's plans for further customs jurisdiction elsewhere in the river markets north of the colony and toward the Liberian border. The Colonial Office rejected a Treasury idea to make Freetown into a free port ("a black Hamburg"), but agreed to establish customs posts in the Scarcies, before the French did.[40] Such a move (in Rowe's strategy) would cordon off the Melakori.[41] At the same time old claims to the Sherbro

35. Brown to CO, September 24, 1875, *PP*, C.1409 (1876), 52, 56–58.

36. Manchester Chamber of Commerce to Ministry of Finance, August 10, 1877, enclosed in MMC to MAE, August 11, 1877, ANSOM, Sénégal IX/27/g.

37. Crowe to Lyons, June 20, 1884; Granville to Lyons, June 2, 1884, FO Confidential Print 4992.

38. Félix Faure, circular to colonial governors, January 24, 1884, enclosed in Crowe to Lyons, June 27, 1884, FO Confidential Print 4992.

39. See especially the Report of the Interdepartmental Committee, July 20, 1877, CO 879/11 African 189; and tables of trade enclosed in Rowe to CO, October 13, 1879, CO 879/17 African 206.

40. Treasury to CO, September 7, 1878; and minutes by Hemming, September 12, 1878, CO 267/336.

41. Rowe to Meade, August 14, 1876, CO 879/10 African 106.

and to Turner's Peninsula were revived; and a customs official was sent into the Scarcies in February 1879.[42] The French replied by moving into Samu Bullon in 1877 and taking Matacong in 1879.[43]

This competition for elbowroom along the coast could only be settled rationally by removing the causes of hostility—perhaps by territorial exchange. But the cession of the Gambia was made impossible in 1874 by British traders' opposition and by unacceptable British demands for compensation in the Gold Coast and Lagos areas. In any case, fiscal conditions in Senegal were about to change. Both the French Ministry of Foreign Affairs and the Ministry of Marine might well have sacrificed Marseille interests on the Slave Coast, in return for some guarantee about the restriction of Lagos customs. But in any exchange agreement, account had to be taken of possible alterations to the Senegal tariff—and its extension to the Gambia "au cas où le Gouvernement croirait devoir donner à l'Industrie française les satisfactions qu'elle réclame." [44]

That is to say, Thomas Brown's warning was essentially correct. The inquiry into Senegal and other tariffs was still in progress in 1876 and could still result in a decision for the protectionists in the *Conseil supérieur du commerce,* the Ministry of Commerce, and the administration at St. Louis. Moreover, the knowledge that differential tariffs were a possibility, if the Gambia were exchanged, kept the price (as fixed by Sir Robert Herbert in the Colonial Office) very high.[45]

Failing exchange of posts, customs might be equalized. But this proposal was twice rejected by Governor Rowe on the grounds that it would entail lower duties, and therefore loss of revenue, unless fiscal jurisdiction were enlarged to compensate. Hemming in the Colonial Office was inclined to agree.[46] The merits of the case, however, were lost in the acrimony that followed the extension of British customs into the Scarcies.[47]Attention was drawn away from the main issue, which

42. Rowe to Carnarvon, May 13, 1876, CO 267/329; CO to Rowe, October 31, 1878, and January 24, 1879; Rowe to CO, November 16, 1878, CO 879/14 African 159.

43. For the background to these maneuvers see J. D. Hargreaves, *Prelude to the Partition of West Africa* (London, 1963), Chaps. 5 and 6.

44. D'Azy, "Note pour le Ministre," February 1876, ANSOM Afrique VI/17/a.

45. CO to FO, March 10, 1876, and March 15, 1876; minutes by Herbert, March 10, 1876, CO 87/109; and CO 879/9 African 92.

46. Memorandum by Rowe, October 18, 1879, CO 879/17 African 206; minutes by Hemming, November 17, 1879, CO 267/338.

47. CO to FO, October 11, 1879, CO 379/17 African 206; Jauréguiberry to MAE, April 9, 1879, and July 28, 1879; MAE to MMC, August 19, 1879, and October 20, 1879; MMC to MAE, November 4, 1879, MAE Afrique/56.

was how to translate differing conceptions of commercial liberty into diplomatic agreement. Consequently, a French *Projet de règlement,* delivered in June 1879, was returned to Paris in September with accusations about differential duties, but no constructive suggestions about equalization.[48] And for his part, the French ambassador in London, Admiral Pothuau, did little more than attack the level of Sierra Leone customs—"augmentée de droits différentiels applicables aux produits étrangers, mais frappant pour ainsi dire uniquement le commerce français, c'est ainsi que les vins, les alcools etc., ont à payer à la douane anglaise plus de 50% de leur valeur." [49]

A second reason for the indeterminate character of discussion on equalization was the unauthorized extension of Lagos Protectorate to Katanu on the Porto-Novo creeks, which effectively reduced the value of the French position at nearby Cotonou.[50]

The French ambassador in London warned Salisbury that this move compromised the talks on tariffs.[51] The Foreign Office, however, took the view that the possible extension of Lagos duties should be linked with "other questions of Customs Duties at places North of Sierra Leone which are already under discussion between the two countries and that some arrangement securing in both localities the greatest practical freedom for European commerce may be obtained by common agreement." [52] But the Ministry of Marine did not see things that way and demanded guarantees for French traders in British fiscal areas, as well as recognition of claims to Matacong, Melakori, and Samu.[53] By April 1880, when French customs had also been extended to the South Rivers, the minister, Admiral Jean Jauréguiberry, excluded the Melakori from the area of negotiable territory. He then agreed to an Anglo-French conference to arrange a demarcation, but with complete reservations about accepting its decisions.[54]

These decisions were embodied in the unratified Convention of 1882 which delimited British and French spheres of interest in the disrupted

48. FO to CO, September 17, 1879, CO 879/17 African 206.

49. Pothuau to Salisbury, October 30, 1879, ibid.

50. Newbury, *The Western Slave Coast,* p. 94.

51. Montebello to Salisbury, November 27, 1879; Salisbury to Lyons, January 17, 1880, and January 21, 1880, FO 27/2418; FO to Pothuau (draft), December 20, 1879, CO 147/89.

52. FO to CO, December 20, 1879, CO 147/39.

53. MAC to MAE, February 9, 1880, MAE Afrique/56; FO to CO, April 16, 1880, CO 879/17 African 206; MMC to Ministry of Commerce, November 11, 1879, AN F[12]6460.

54. MMC to MAE, April 17, 1880, and May 15, 1880, MAE Afrique/56.

coastal area between Senegal and Sierra Leone.[55] From a comparison of the minutes drawn up by the two sets of delegates (not entirely the same in their respective versions), one might conclude that the Anglo-French discussions were more noteworthy for what they could not solve, namely, the opposed views of free trade held by either side. In fact the settlement of the boundary between the Mclakori and the Scarcies was easy enough. It was in the second session on May 18, 1881, when the line was provisionally accepted, that a major hitch occurred on the matter of "equal" rights in respective spheres. The French minutes record this point as equal rights *in all ports open to foreign flags* (which automatically excluded river ports in Senegal, the Casamance, and Gabon). The British minutes omit this phrase. In the next session on May 23 the discrepancy was only too clear: the French government accepted all the demarcation proposals, but limited the meaning of commercial equality to the subjects and not the goods of the two nations in ports already open. The argument put forward by Brière de L'Isle and Jules Roy, the French delegates, was that they could not change tariff laws in Senegal or the Gabon, where there was no complete equality. Hemming and Sir Arthur Havelock, therefore, were at a loss to find any compensation for a promised cession of the Iles de Los to the French. The conference was on the point of collapse.

To save the agreement the British ambassador, Lord Lyons, visited the foreign minister, St. Hilaire, the next day to make clear to him that although his government might tolerate the Senegal Guinea-cloth tariff, it was "essential that British manufactures should be assured against the continuance and possible extension of the system."[56] Without this assurance, talks would have to begin afresh some other time. St. Hilaire left the decision to the minister of commerce, and the minister of marine, Admiral Cloué. The latter summed up the French position in this delicate impasse and refused to yield:

> Je ne saurais vous dissimuler en effet que la concession douanière demandée par le Gouvernement Britannique serait, de notre part, absolument hors de proportion avec les très faibles avantages qui nous sont proposés en échange. Pour que nous puissions y consentir,

55. For accounts of the 1882 convention, see Hargreaves, *Prelude,* pp. 247–51; Robinson and Gallagher, *Africa and the Victorians,* p. 165; Newbury, *The Western Slave Coast,* p. 107; and for the commissioners' reports, MAE Afrique/57; CO 879/18; FO 27/2551.

56. Lyons to Granville, May 24, 1881, CO 879/18 African 233.

il faudrait qu'on nous octroyat des compensations bien autrement sérieuses. Mais, des propositions plus acceptables fussent elles faites, je verrais de grosses difficultés à conclure sur cette manière dans le sens d'une égalité de traitement pour les produits des deux puissances. Il y a lieu de remarquer, en effet, que les droits différentiels existant au Sénégal, et qui ne portent quant à présent que sur une seule marchandise (les Guinées), n'atteignent pas seulement ceux de ces tissus qui viennent d'Angleterre, mais tous ceux qui sont originaires des pays étrangers.

Cette taxe protectrice a été reclamée avec instance par les représentants de l'industrie nationale; elle n'a été récemment maintenue qu' après un long examen dans une commission spéciale où tous les intérêts ont été entendus. Enfin, elle ne pourrait être modifiée sans la participation des Ministres des Finances et du Commerce, qui ont contresignés le décret qui l'a établie. Or, je suis à peu près convaincu que l'agrément de ces deux départements ne serait pas obtenu. Voilà pour la situation présente. Mais la prétention émise va plus loin; en nous demandant de consentir à une clause établissant le même régime douanier pour les produits des deux pays, elle touche à l'avenir, et ne tend à rien moins qu'à nous lier les mains et à introduire un engagement ayant un caractère définitif et perpétuel, et qu'il est impossible de donner à une convention douanière quelconque.

Je suis persuadé qu'après avoir pris connaissance de ces observations vous comprendrez qu'il ne m'est pas possible de céder sur une question qui engage non-seulement les finances de nos possessions de la Côte d'Afrique, mais en quelque sorte le régime économique de la métropole et de nos colonies.[57]

In London, the Colonial Office, faced with this *non possumus,* fell back on the maintenance of territorial rights as a first line of defense:

as the French system of placing differential duties on foreign trade in the territories over which their influence extends must cause serious injury to British interests and renders it in Lord Kimberley's opinion incumbent on Her Majesty's Government to counteract as far as possible further encroachment on the part of the French in

57. Cloué to St. Hilaire, May 25, 1881, MAE, Afrique/57; and enclosures in FO to CO, May 27, 1881, CO 879/18 African 233.

these regions, and to endeavour to keep open every channel of trade which is at present under British control.[58]

Against the intransigence of protectionist policy something more than "gentlemen's agreements" was needed.

But for the moment the British government backed down and consented to exclude the tariff issue and the Isles de Los cession as a way of salvaging the territorial demarcation. The rest was anticlimax. The Convention was not signed till June 28, 1882. It was ratified by the Senate and rejected by a subcommittee of the Chamber, mainly on the ground that the open-ended boundary surrendered the country behind Senegambia to British commercial penetration.[59] In the Colonial Office there were also regrets, for opposite reasons, about the terms of "so one-sided an arrangement."[60] But on the whole it was a defeat for British commercial policy in West Africa in the face of French protectionism. The big issue of disagreement over tariffs had not been solved.

The Convention of 1882 had other consequences as well. When published in March 1883, its terms were misunderstood in the German Foreign Office as a partition of Anglo-French interests on the coast—to the exclusion of German trading rights. The Hamburg Chamber of Commerce exploited this confusion, which was an important factor behind Bismarck's decision to intervene in West Africa.[61]

Clearly, the 1882 demarcation was a temporary measure that failed to touch the real reasons for disagreeement between Britain and France (but gives us an indication as to where the basic trouble lay); it aroused German suspicions; and it was rendered nugatory by other

58. CO to FO, May 28, 1881, CO 879/18 African 233. The Senegal Guinea tariff was being considered for the Melakori: but it was not "new"; cf. Hargreaves, *Prelude*, p. 251.

59. Gasconi to MMC, October 26, 1883, ANSOM, Afrique IV/34/a; AN C 3393, dossier 2071 (information from A. Sydney Kanya-Forstner); there is a good discussion of the reasons for the committee's attitude, reflecting the views of Gasconi and Dureau) in FO to CO, August 17, 1883, and October 23, 1883, CO 879/18 African 233; Hargreaves, *Prelude*, pp. 289–93 and note.

60. Herbert to FO, November 1, 1883, CO 879/18 African 233.

61. Hans-Peter Jaeck, "Die deutsche Annexion," in *Kamerun unter deutscher Kolonialherrschaft*, ed. Helmuth Stoecker (East Berlin, 1960), p. 53; and Denkschrift, July 6, 1883, in Hamburg to Prussian Ambassador, July 20, 1883, Staatsarchiv, Hamburg, CL. vi. 15/6/4, cited in Newbury, *The Western Slave Coast*, p. 111 and note. An estimate of this influence on Bismarck is given by Henry Ashby Turner, Jr., "Bismarck's Imperialist Venture: Anti-British in Origin?" in *Britain and Germany in Africa: Imperial Rivalry and Colonial Rule*, ed. Prosser Gifford and Wm. Roger Louis (New Haven, 1967), pp. 54–58.

events. News of French progress toward the Upper Niger and in the Fouta Djallon reached the Colonial Office at the beginning of 1882. The feelings of "jealousy" confessed to in the minutes of Herbert and Kimberley were equalled only by their concern at a French outflanking movement in the interior.[62] Kimberley's only remedy, however, was to revive an outdated treaty of trade and friendship with the almamy of Timbo and pay up his arrears of stipend as a means of securing Sierra Leone's trade. For this was the sole justification for the British settlements, concluded the colonial secretary, "to open trade and communications with the interior. Whereever the French can get a footing, they endeavour to exclude all trade but their own. It is our direct interest by all peaceful means to counteract their policy." [63]

But would these "means" be sufficient? They were little more than a copy of the method used to defend British rights under the Tunis Convention of 1875 which had set a limit to the scale of duties that could be imposed on British manufactures. An exchange of notes with France had preserved these rights in 1881.[64] For a nation that had no wish to counter French advances by carving out hinterland territories of her own, treaties of trade with African states looked like a doubtful second best.

The treaty gambit was used again on the Lower Niger, when the British government finally made up its mind to allow consul Hewett in 1884 to give a paper basis to British claims.[65] Here, too, Jauréguiberry had been at work to secure a French sphere against the advance of British customs and to open a way to the markets of the Benue, Bornu, Adamawa, and Chad.[66] While Consul Mattei tried to carry out this policy and two warships showed the flag in 1883, Jules Ferry and Admiral Peyron changed its emphasis. In view of the weakness of French firms and the superior resources of the National African

62. Havelock to Kimberley, February 3, 1882; and minute by Herbert, February 25, 1882; minute by Kimberley, March 7, 1882, CO 267/348; *The Times*, February 3, 1882.

63. Minute by Kimberley, February 12, 1882, on Havelock to CO, January 13, 1882, CO 267/348.

64. Edward Hertslet, ed., *The Map of Africa by Treaty*, 1st ed. (2 vols. London, 1894), *2*, 548–53.

65. Robinson and Gallagher, *Africa and the Victorians*, pp. 171–72.

66. C. W. Newbury, "The Development of French Policy on the Lower and Upper Niger, 1880–1898," *Journal of Modern History, 31* (1959), 20; Jean Stengers, "L'impérialisme colonial de la fin du XIXe siècle: mythe ou réalité," *Journal of African History, 3* (1962), 479.

Company, they cared less for posts and more for "freedom" of navigation on an "international" waterway. The position of the two nations, compared with their situation north of Sierra Leone, was reversed.

By June 1884 the question of free trade on the Lower Niger was linked with the problem of access to the Congo. The origins and results of the Berlin Conference are well enough known.[67] But as in other areas of African partition, it is easy to lose from sight the economic factors that brought the main protagonists to engage in high-level diplomacy for relatively small gains. The twists and hesitations of British policy in the two years between the ratification of Brazza's Makoko treaty in November 1882 and the signing of the Berlin protocols in 1885 look like an attempt to avoid possible French and certain Portuguese restrictions on riverine navigation and trade. For, in Paris, Lord Lyons had warned that Brazza's treaty would bring France onto a navigable part of the Congo. And it can be argued that it was this threat of monopolies "detrimental to British commerce" that moved the Foreign Office to use Portuguese claims to the Congo mouth as a way of guaranteeing low customs and shipping dues.[68] The abortive Anglo-Portuguese treaty of February 26, 1884, however, aroused international objections. And British confidence in it was soon undermined by news of a new "trade-crushing Tariff" applied in Mozambique to destroy British Indian commerce, and by dire warnings of differential duties already in force in Portuguese ports on the southwest coast.[69]

As the Portuguese treaty looked less and less credible, the British government was hard put to it to find a counter to the threat posed by Brazza. Direct negotiation with France for a demarcation of interests on the Niger and the Congo was ruled out on the advice of Lyons that the 1882 convention was before the Chamber.[70] Decision became a cabinet matter; and after a year's delay, Hewett was given his instructions in May 1884. In June more complete evidence on French tariff policies in Africa came to hand from Crowe, the commercial attaché at the Paris embassy. And in the same month Bismarck laid

67. Robinson and Gallagher, *Africa and the Victorians,* p. 173; S. E. Crowe, *The Berlin West African Conference, 1884–1885* (London, 1942); and for a fresh interpretation, see Wm. Roger Louis, "The Berlin Congo Conference" (in the present volume).

68. FO to CO, November 25, 1882; Holt to FO, December 11, 1882, FO Confidential Print 4785.

69. O'Neill to Granville, November 27, 1882; d'Antas to Granville, January 10, 1883, FO Confidential Print 4785.

70. CO to FO, January 6, 1883, CO 879/20 African 259.

down his weighty objections to the Anglo-Portuguese arrangement which would be administered by untrustworthy officials in conditions that made "the suggestion to fix the duties at 10 percent ad valorem . . . even less valuable if some of the chief articles of import, such as tobacco, brandy, arms and ammunition are to be taken out of this limitation." [71]

There were features of the German argument that could not fail to appeal to the French (hostile to specific duties on arms and spirits), or to British merchants such as James F. Hutton, conducting his own private diplomacy in Berlin against the Portuguese and their methods.[72] Bismarck, too, had even harder things to say in private about them ("worse than the Russians"), and about French tariff policy in Gabon.[73]

But to gang up against Portugal was one thing; to prevent French restrictions on trade was something else. The most frustrating aspect of the Berlin Conference, from the British point of view, lay in Ferry's instructions to Courcel to limit the discussion of free trade to the Congo and the Niger:

> Par la liberté du commerce nous entendons le libre accès pour tous les pavillons, l'interdiction de tout monopole ou traitment différentiel; mais nous admettons l'établissement de taxes qui pourront être perçues comme compensation de dépenses utiles pour le commerce.
>
> Il est bien convenu qu'en poursuivant l'institution, dans le bassin du Congo, du régime de la liberté commerciale, et en se déclarant prêt à y contribuer pour sa part, le Gouvernement Français ne se propose pas d'étendre l'application de ce régime à ces établissements coloniaux du Gabon, de la Guinée, ou de Sénégal.[74]

British diplomacy faced the same kind of impasse that had been implicit in the results of the Paris talks in 1881. Some areas of French African policy were not open for discussion. There was no lack of

71. Bismarck to Münster, June 7, 1884, FO Confidential Print 5023.

72. Hutton to Granville (Private), December 12, 1884, FO Confidential (unnumbered: December 1884).

73. Memorandum by Meade, December 24, 1884, FO Confidential Print (unnumbered: December 1884).

74. Courcel to Bismarck, September 29, 1884, enclosed in Lyons to Granville, October 15, 1884, FO Confidential Print 5023. For a discussion of Ferry's instructions, see Kenneth Vignes, "Etude sur la rivalité d'influence entre les puissances européennes en Afrique équatoriale et occidentale depuis l'acte général de Berlin jusqu'au seuil du XXe siècle," *Revue française d'histoire d'outre-mer,* 48 (1961), 25.

angry comment on the "quite one-sided and somewhat contradictory" nature of Courcel's definition of free trade.[75] But nothing could be done about it. The Gabon tariff (which had just been raised even higher against foreign goods) could not be touched. The conference was, therefore, forced to accept the limitation of the Congo Conventional Basin to the area between Sette Camma and the River Loge.[76]

On the other hand, Lord Granville at the Foreign Office also shied away from a precise definition of the main issue at stake:

> The expression "freedom of trade" is commonly used in so many different senses, varying from a mere absence of prohibition to trade up to a complete exemption from all duties and charges, that Her Majesty's Government assume that the German Government agree with them that duties should be moderate in amount, and that there should be complete equality of treatment for all foreign traders.[77]

Perhaps it was all that could be said under the circumstances. For, if French rivers and the Portuguese Zambezi were excluded from the discussion, the Niger was not. It was a major achievement, therefore, that in an area where British trade was already important the practical interpretation of the meaning of "freedom of navigation" was to remain a British responsibility.

A similar situation arose during the Brussels Conference in 1890, when the level of tariffs for the Conventional Zone was fixed. Leopold's state needed revenue; France needed freedom of fiscal action. A compromise was found by which import duties were not to exceed 10 percent (by the Congo Tariff Agreement of 1891 they were in fact as low as 6 percent). But the Foreign Ministry could not accept the pretension of the conference to make the tariff binding on French Congo territory as well, or to put any limit other than the 10 percent maximum on French rights to change their tariffs without reference to an international convention. A private letter from the British ambassador to Salisbury makes it clear, too, that the Foreign Ministry was unwilling to antagonize the protectionist majority in the Chamber by committing France to any international commercial agreements beyond the operation of current commercial treaties.[78] Méline's tariff law was too near.

75. Cohen to Hill, October 17, 1884; memorandum by Hemming, October 16, 1884, FO Confidential Print 5023.

76. Crowe, *The Berlin West African Conference,* pp. 110–12.

77. Granville to Plessen, October 8, FO Confidential Print 5023.

78. Lytton to Salisbury, November 27, 1890 (Private), Salisbury papers A/58.

The growth of protectionism which had been foreshadowed in Senegal at an early date undoubtedly continued to have an influence on Anglo-French negotiations in the period 1885–98.[79] But a sense of proportion is needed. The French ministries had no well-articulated colonial theory that exactly reflected French economic theory. In both fields there were conflicting voices to be heard. One can detect, however, a gradual acceptance in the 1880s of the moderate viewpoint put forward by Félix Faure during a debate on Gabon customs in 1884: African colonies were not "fermes à exploiter . . . ce sont surtout des étapes qui permettent à nos produits de s'étendre à des marchés plus éloignés, des moyens de rayonnement et de distribution pour les industries nationales."[80]

This was the kind of stuff that even the antiprotectionist *conseil général* could accept; and after holding up a project for a 50 percent *détaxe* on goods of French origin for nearly a decade, it finally agreed to outright surcharges on foreign imports in 1890.[81] The same change is evident in the minutes of the chambers of commerce. It was helped along by the initiative of merchant planters, such as A. Verdier on the Ivory Coast, who persuaded the *Conseil supérieur du commerce* and the Ministry of Commerce to agree to sweeping differential duties in 1889, as a means of protecting his concessions.[82] And it was given expression in the restrictive clauses of treaties arranged with African states by Binger and Galliéni in 1888–89.

On the whole, the British government was more concerned about the effects of French national tariffs on United Kingdom foreign trade than these distant examples of colonial protection. Even Algerian cabotage was more important than exclusion from the Ogooué.[83] And it was obvious by 1891 that the adoption of a double tariff system in France would not be applied to all overseas territories. In the event, only the French Congo and Madagascar adopted metropolitan duties

79. For a different view of the early strength of the protectionist movement, see Hargreaves, *Prelude,* p. 228; Henri Brunschwig, *Mythes et réalités de l'impérialisme colonial français, 1871–1914* (Paris, 1960), Chap. 6.

80. *Procès-verbaux du conseil supérieur des colonies* (Paris, 1884), p. 26.

81. *Sénégal et dépendances. Procès-verbaux et délibérations du conseil général. Sessions extraordinaires* (Paris, 1894), pp. 174, 365–69, 386–90.

82. Ministry of Commerce to Council of State, April 4, 1889, ANSOM Sénégal IX/22/e; and see Paul Atger, *La France en Côte-d'Ivoire de 1843 à 1893. Cinquante ans d'hésitations politiques et commerciales* (Dakar, 1962), pp. 186–87.

83. French debates and British official reactions are covered exhaustively in FO Confidential Prints 6185, 6211, 6289; see also Shepard Bancroft Clough, *France: A History of National Economics 1789–1939* (New York, 1939), Chap. 7; memorandum by Crowe, January 31, 1890, Salisbury papers A/60; PRO Cabinet 37/29 (1891).

under the Méline Tariff Law of 1892, though Senegal continued to levy its 7 percent surtax on foreign goods, in addition to a general ad valorem of 5 percent.[84] It was still an open question, however, how far the Senegal or Congo systems might be applied elsewhere.

This element of uncertainty coincided with unfavorable trading conditions in Africa. The period 1884–90 was one of depression and falling commodity prices. Total trade in British possessions, for example, slumped from about 3.3 million pounds in 1883 to 2.2 million pounds in 1887.[85] Imports and exports recovered only slightly before the next downturn, 1892–93.

Moreover, in areas under British control these conditions produced revenue difficulties and a search for ways to offset the loss of customs without recourse to parliamentary grants. But the options for territorial expansion along the coast were much fewer than in the 1870s. Traders and their spokesmen began to look more to the interior and showed less patience with the unsettled politics or petty tolls of African states.[86] At Lagos, local initiative began to seek ways of preserving the markets of Yorubaland from foreign intervention. In Sierra Leone, Governor Rowe had to raise the customs duties in 1886, as tentative plans were made for a protectorate administration in the hinterland.[87] In the Gambia, too, there were efforts to change the tariff structure and reduce dependence on imperial grants.[88]

All this was made so much worse by French advances in the interior. By August 1887, the Colonial Office had some idea of the French treaty with Samori, suspecting that like Jean Bayol's compact of 1881 in the Fouta Djallon it aimed at the exclusion of British trade.[89] But the Foreign Office was content to rest the British case on past agreements with African states: for these were supposed to invalidate any French exclusive clauses. The issue at stake, however, was not merely French political control in the Sierra Leone interior,

84. J. Duché de Bricourt, *L'Evolution de la question douanière au Sénégal et dans ses anciennes dépendances* (Paris, 1902); Armand Touce in *Législation et finances coloniales,* ed. Louis Rolland and Pierre Lampué (Paris, 1960), pp. 271–88.

85. *Statistical Abstracts of the British Empire,* Cmd. 8665 (London, 1897), pp. 28–29, 34–35.

86. The best analysis of the influence of economic factors on expansion in West Africa at this period is given in A. G. Hopkins, "An Economic History of Lagos, 1880–1914" (unpublished Ph.D. thesis, London, 1964), Chap. 2.

87. Rowe to Granville, April 29, 1886; and memorandum, December 21, 1886, CO 879/24 African 323.

88. Rowe to Granville, June 8, 1886, *PP,* C.4978 (1887), 29–33.

89. War Office to CO, November 10, 1887, CO 879/23 African 318.

as opposed to British treaties, "d'ordre purement commercial." [90] The price was thought to be the whole pattern of caravan traffic, which had been expanding in the 1870s and was directed to markets near Freetown and the Gold Coast. Any extension of Senegal tariffs into this area, or further east into the Salaga-Gaman complex, was viewed with dismay in the Colonial Office.

But as long as British policy was on the defensive, the French ministries were not in a hurry to come to terms or give precise information (if they had any) about French relations with Samori. It was not until the end of 1887, when the commandant of the French Sudan, J. S. Gallieni, had a firmer hold on the Upper Niger, that Undersecretary Etienne thought there might be a general settlement of Anglo-French differences on the coast, including a cession of the Gambia.[91] An indeterminate series of exchanges with the Ministry of Foreign Affairs left these proposals in suspense. Two years later, when Binger had secured much of the Ivory Coast interior, Assinie and Grand Bassam were not for sale.

Insistence on a boundary settlement came from the Colonial Office and led to the Anglo-French agreement of August 10, 1889. But the mere demarcation of territory was not the main reason for that accord. It was clear by 1888 that a cession of the Gambia would be no way to tackle the problem of French advances in the interior: the Gambia could not save the caravan routes. For, "wherever the French obtain exclusive influence British trade is practically obliterated in consequence of the hindrances and differential treatment to which it is exposed." [92] Consequently, argued Hemming, if the Gambia were ceded, the price would have to be very high—no less than complete evacuation by France from the area between the Rio Pongas and Lagos; and "if we agree to the line being brought south of the Rio Pongas, we should demand, in return, an undertaking that there should be no differential treatment of British trade at the Gambia or in any other parts of the sphere reserved to French influence." [93] The demarcation of territory, or even its exchange, was only a means to the end that had eluded British diplomacy in 1881—to preserve West African markets from the threat to free trade.

But from the French point of view it was sufficient to seal the Gambia and avoid a general exchange. When discussions began in

90. Vignes, "Etude sur la rivalité d'influence," p. 25.
91. MMC to MAE, December 10, 1887, MAE Afrique/86.
92. Memorandum by Hemming, November 1888, CO 879/29 African 357.
93. Memorandum by Hemming, March 5, 1889, CO 879/29 African 365.

Paris, the French delegates achieved just this and refused to debate Senegal customs in relation to the British enclave.[94] The Sierra Leone boundary was extended further inland to the tenth degree of north latitude, but still left open-ended as in 1882. The reason for this, explained the British envoy to Salisbury, was the need felt by the British delegates to leave a way open to the Fouta Djallon (just as the French Parliamentary Committee had feared in 1882), "bearing in mind that our Colonial Policy cannot, in the interest or our producers, remain of the Manchester epoch when trade came without an effort into our mouths." [95]

There was trouble, however, over the Gold Coast–Ivory Coast boundary at the Tandoe River—an important exit for trade routes from Gaman and the interior markets. In return for allowing a British customs post at the mouth, the French commissioners demanded equalization of duties. Governor Bayol pressed E. H. Egerton, British chargé d'affaires, hard for this concession in private conversations, claiming that the only way to avoid submitting the Assinie tariff to the Senegal *Conseil général* for approval was to write it into an agreement with a foreign power, when "it could be imposed without further to-do." [96] Some of this was bluff: the tariff for Assinie had a generally high ad valorem duty of 10 percent with 20 to 30 percent on cotton goods and would probably not have been approved at St. Louis. In any case, equalization was not accepted by Governor Griffith of the Gold Coast. The critical deadlock was only broken after a hurried trip to London by Hemming, when Lord Knutsford agreed to the Tandoe as a boundary, provided the French would raise the scale of duties for spirits and lower the massive duty on British manufactures. These terms were written into the final draft.[97]

Finally, the Dahomey-Lagos frontier was laid down as far as the ninth parallel, again for guarantees of free navigation on the creeks and the "neutralization from a Customs point of view" of the trade route from Lagos to Porto-Novo, "until such time as a definitive Customs Agreement can be arrived at."

Tariffs, then, were the issue on which much of the 1889 Anglo-

94. The minutes of the 1889 talks are to be found in MAE Afrique/128 and CO 879/29 and 31 African 354, 360, 377.

95. Egerton to FO, May 11, 1889, CO 879/31 African 377.

96. Egerton to Salisbury, June 4, 1889, CO 879/29 African 354.

97. Hertslet, *The Map of Africa by Treaty, 2,* 558–63. France agreed to adopt for the Ivory Coast a higher duty on spirits and tobacco and a maximum 15 percent ad valorem on cotton goods: cf. Vignes, "Etude sur la rivalité d'influence," p. 48.

French discussions turned. The French felt that by proposing duties for Assinie that were considerably higher than those in most of their territories they had made an important concession. In June 1889, advised Egerton, equalization "was the only direction in which a settlement could be looked or hoped for." [98] Even after the draft agreement had been signed, it was nearly wrecked by a mistake in the tariff decreed for Bassam and Assinie in October 1889. But when this was cleared up, both sides were reasonably satisfied: the French had kept open their field for maneuver by limiting the British enclave in the Gambia; the British had some guarantee that the Senegal system would not be applied to the Ivory Coast or Porto-Novo.

In reality, the British position in the West African interior continued to weaken, as long as the Foreign Office and the Colonial Office followed the policy of relying on paper treaties as safeguards against a military campaign that threatened to cut off the hinterland of British settlements. The position was summed up by the administrator of the Gambia (and acting governor of Sierra Leone), Captain J. S. Hay:

> It seems to me, my Lord, that we shall find ourselves in this position. The French Government, whilst admitting our right to freedom of trade, will probably at once take advantage of their protectorate over [the Fouta Djallon] to impose prohibitory duties not only on British manufactures, but also on the products of the country which may be sent to this place from Foutah, or which may have to pass through it, and in these circumstances we should find the substance of our commercial relations with Foutah Djallon destroyed, although the shadow of the British traders' rights to freedom of trade would still exist.[99]

Other warnings came from Liverpool, where the Chamber of Commerce laid "prior claim" to Samori's empire and the Ivory Coast.[100] The War Office, too, took to heart Gallieni's announcement of a great military and commercial empire on the Middle Niger which would encircle Sierra Leone and drive away trade.[101]

The Foreign Office hardly reacted at all to this clamor. Discussions

98. Through Hemming who made a trip to London, June 8, for fresh instructions. CO to FO, June 11, 1889, CO 879/29 African 354.

99. Hay to Knutsford, February 1, 1889, CO 879/31 African 377.

100. *Report of the Committee of the African Trade Section of the Liverpool Chamber of Commerce* (1892), p. 12.

101. War Office to CO, November 29, 1889, CO 879/32 African 387.

with Paris were preoccupied with French insistence on a revision of the Anglo-Tunisian Convention and the implications of this *démarche* for Egypt, Zanzibar, and Madagascar. Both the French foreign Minister, Ribot, and the French ambassador, Waddington, seem to have lost touch with some of the realities of the West African situation in July 1890 by concentrating on a wide sphere of influence around Chad.[102] In Paris, the British ambassador, Lord Lytton, was sure they would give way on Tunis for compensation in Madagascar.[103] In London, Waddington got Salisbury to recognize a French zone from the Mediterranean possessions of France to the vague Say-Barroua line, somewhere north of the Niger Company marchland. The agreement of August 1890 acknowledged this claim and, implicitly, that of the company.[104]

For reasons of broader diplomacy the details were left to be filled in later. But these were the details that were hardest to settle in 1890s. There was already plenty of evidence that trade was being diverted away from Sierra Leone, as Hay had foreseen, while the Colonial Office still clung to the view that old treaties would make exclusive policies by the French "inoperative."[105] This optimism was belied by the statements of African traders, by instructions to an official mission to the Fouta in 1891, and by changes in the tariffs in the South Rivers posts the same year.[106] The Colonial Office was brought to see once more that the "real danger which arises from the extension of French influence and jurisdiction is the exclusive commercial policy which they force upon the countries over which they

102. Kenneth Vignes, "Etude sur les relations diplomatiques franco-britanniques qui conduisirent à la convention du 14 juin 1898," *Revue française d'histoire d'outre-mer,* 52 (1965), 358–60; Ribot to Waddington, July 10, 1890, MAE Angleterre/851; Ribot to Waddington, July 19, 1890, *DDF* 8, No. 124.

103. Lytton to Salisbury, July 24, 1890, Salisbury papers A/58.

104. Hertslet, *The Map of Africa by Treaty,* 2, 571–72; and see the analysis in Vignes, "Etude sur les relations diplomatiques," p. 365.

105. Herbert to FO, February 7, 1890, CO 879/32 African 387.

106. See African traders' evidence in Hay to Knutsford, April 2, 1890, and June 16, 1890; and for the new scale of duties in the Melakori (with a rumor of a 20 percent duty on British manufactures), Hay to Knutsford, October 4, 1890; CO to FO, October 29, 1890, CO 879/32 African 387. The policy of diverting caravan traffic away from Sierra Leone is attested (among other sources) in Cousturier to de Beeckmann [1891]: "et cette mesure aura de plus l'avantage de donner satisfaction au commerce des Rivières du Sud, qui sera d'autant plus disposé à favoriser les caravanes Foulah." *L'Expansion française en Afrique occidentale. De Beeckmann au Fouta-Djallon. Coppolani et la Mauritanie.* J. Quinquaund and Lieut. d'Otton Loyewski eds. (Paris, n.d.), pp. 12–13.

acquire authority."[107] Accordingly, when discussions continued about territorial demarcation north and west of the 1889 boundary, Knutsford suggested that the recognition of French claims be made conditional "upon the cancellation of the articles in the French treaties restricting freedom of trade, and upon an undertaking by the French Government that the commerce of the territories in question should be open to all."

But the French, too, taking heart from German complaints, were no less ready to debate restrictions on trade imposed by the Royal Niger Company. And in the field, Etienne's pincer movement from the Sudan and the Benue toward Chad challenged its unique position. It was no longer possible, as it had been in 1889, for British officials in Paris to turn "a deaf ear" on any discussion of the company, because as the British ambassador said then, "its ways are not our ways, it is a monopoly."[108] The monopoly lay in the path of a French advance.

Thus, when in November 1890, Egerton and Crowe met with the foreign minister Gabriel Hanotaux and Jacques Haussmann of the Colonial Department to carry out the provisions of the 1889 and 1890 agreements, the interests at stake were more sharply defined. The British commissioners wished to concentrate on Sierra Leone and obtain guarantees for British trade; the French were concerned more with the Niger territories. Hanotaux went so far as to hint that in return for any commercial concessions in the west, France might have to ask for concessions from the company.[109] Failing agreement along these lines, the commissioners were obliged to make another delimitation of the eastern boundary of Sierra Leone and the western Gold Coast frontier to the ninth parallel.[110] On the matter of a Porto-Novo–Lagos customs tariff (as promised in 1889) there was no discussion at all. Although the British embassy pressed for this, Etienne resisted any arrangement that might sacrifice the commercial position of his new colony.[111]

French conquests in Dahomey, British and French agreements with Germany in 1893 and 1894, and the wider considerations of Egypt and the Nile powerfully influenced the strategy and the priorities in Anglo-French negotiations in the decade after 1890. The details of expeditions and rival treaty claims which were increasingly used as

107. CO to FO, September 4, 1890, CO 879/32 African 387.

108. Egerton to Salisbury, June 27, 1889, Salisbury papers A/15.

109. Egerton to Lytton, November 13, 1890, CO 879/32 African 389; Vignes, "Etude sur les relations diplomatiques," pp. 370–81.

110. Agreement, June 26, 1891, Hertslet, *The Map of Africa by Treaty*, 2, 573–74.

111. Etienne to MAE, October 3, 1891, MAE Afrique/129.

bargaining counters for a general settlement do not concern us here. But in the midst of French military imperialism in the Sudan and British commercial monopoly on the Lower Niger, the theme of free trade and free navigation was still relevant. Indeed, the question of tariffs became even more important for Sierra Leone, after the closing of the interior frontier by the agreements of 1891 and 1893. The colony was surrounded by the possessions of a protectionist Power, and the Gold Coast was likely to go the same way.

Or so it seemed to the deputation of representatives from British chambers of commerce which arrived at the Colonial Office in December. The fiscal and tariff argument was put by G.F. Fisher, the delegate from Manchester:

> So serious has the matter appeared that a special committee has been appointed by the Board of Directors for the purpose of considering it. The exports of British manufactures principally cotton goods to the colony amount to about £350,000 per annum, and the trade is a steadily increasing one, affording the prospect of important further extension, if it is allowed to grow naturally and without the intervention of fiscal obstacles. The encroachments of French military and political agents upon the trading routes leading to Sierra Leone were not, for some time, regarded by the merchants of Sierra Leone with apprehension, because the effect of the encroachments, although entailing heavy loss to the revenue of the colony, was simply to cause the trade to reach Freetown through the French rivers instead of directly; and also because French and English merchandise hitherto have received equal treatment in those rivers, where three-forths of the trade is still in the hands of British merchants . . . . The policy now gaining ground in France of establishing differential duties in French colonies, in favour of French goods, threatens the very existence of the trade now carried on between Sierra Leone and the interior, through the adjacent French rivers. It is estimated that should these threatened duties be imposed, the export of British goods will be diminished to the extent of more than half of their present amount.[112]

Lord Knutsford's reply was not very reassuring: the French could not be removed from an area regarded as partitioned under the 1882

112. Proceedings of the delegation from Liverpool, Manchester, Glasgow, and London at the CO, December 8, 1891, CO 879/35 African 421.

convention. But the points raised by the merchants were not forgotten by Lord Salisbury in his instructions to the British ambassador, Lord Dufferin, on the eve of new talks in 1892.[113]

Meanwhile, reports of caravan diversions continued to come in; the War Office worried about French railway strategy which threatened to channel off more trade.[114] At the Foreign Office Lord Rosebery followed Salisbury's lead in stressing prior treaty rights: the chargé d'affaires in Paris, E. C. H. Phipps, was instructed to get a formal acknowledgment from Hanotaux of the justness of the British claim to traffic with the Fouta Djallon and the western Soudan.[115] But while officials debated the legal niceties of privileges accorded in agreements with African rulers, the French occupied more important posts in the interior during operations against Samori.

In Paris a critical stage was reached in June 1893, when Dufferin and Phipps made any Middle Niger boundary settlement depend on free access to French areas and cancellation of the restrictive commercial clause in the Samori treaty.[116] After first conceding this quid pro quo on the lines of the Congo Conventional tariff, Hanotaux suddenly stiffened his terms:

> Monsieur Hanotaux observed that there could be no question of according to British commerce, a régime precisely identic with that enjoyed by French traders. On reflection (meaning after consultation with the French Colonial Office) he found that the comparison he had made with the taxes in the Conventional basin of the Congo as laid down at Brussels and those provided for under Article III of the arrangement of 1889 at Assinie was not a correct one . . . inasmuch as in those two localities the tariffs were identic and not differential. Now he reminded me that he had pointed out that it was just that foreign commerce should, in the first instance, bear the cost of the sacrifices made, to ensure order as well as the organisation of every new colony. Consequently, British commerce, now the only one excepting French in those regions, must pay taxes higher than those to which French commerce would be subjected. But the exact rate at which these taxes should be placed could be

113. See above note 8.

114. Fleming to Ripon, October 22, 1892; War Office to CO, July 15, 1892, CO 879/37 African 433.

115. FO to CO, December 29, 1892, CO 879/37 African 433; CO to FO, January 16, 1893, CO 879/37 African 447.

116. CO to FO, July 25, 1893, CO 879/37 African 447.

examined in such a spirit that British commerce would not regard the rate as excessive and would acquiesce in it.[117]

This assumption that British trade should be taxed to pay for French conquests spread gloom in the Foreign Office. But Phipps saw that Hanotaux and his advisers in the Ministry of Commerce meant that something analogous to the national minimum (or conventional) tariff should be applied in French African territory through an international agreement. The Sudan would have its own conventional tariff—at a differential rate. He pressed instead for a single ad valorem duty—say 10 percent on British goods entering Samori's dominions or the Fouta Djallon. But Hanotaux would not be drawn into details until the French Department of Colonies was satisfied by the concession of a route south of the Fouta Djallon from the Melakori to the Sudan.

There the matter rested until near the end of 1894, when the basis of an agreement on the boundary between the western watershed of the Niger and the Franco-Liberian frontier was laid down. The French got their road. But nothing was said about commercial concessions in the final draft.[118] In fact, Phipps had quietly come to terms with Haussmann at the Ministry of Colonies: the eighth clause of the Samori treaty would lapse; trade would not be diverted and routes would remain open under the terms of past British treaties; no Senegal duties would be levied at present on goods coming into the French Sudan or the Fouta Djallon from British territory; finally, Phipps understood that duties on exports from the French zone would not exceed 7 percent ad valorem and would only be levied at certain points on the coast. There was still a point of doubt: "Monsieur Haussmann said that in view of the present policy in vogue in France under Monsieur Méline's influence, the French Government could not bind themselves (without the consent of the Chambers) that at some time the general tariff might not be applied to the imports into Senegal, &c . . . as had been done in the case of Indo-China." Nevertheless, Phipps recommended acceptance of these terms.[119]

Both sides agreed to leave this bargain out of the official text of

117. Phipps to Rosebery, June 20, 1893, ibid.

118. A draft dispatch from Kimberley (via the FO) to Dufferin, August 1897, makes it clear that the CO expected Hanotaux to make good a verbal promise to settle commercial difficulties, in return for recognition of French conquests in Dahomey. In September Hanotaux said he would "impose" his views on the Colonial Department; in October the British cabinet approved the terms of the commercial clauses. PRO Cabinet 37/37.

119. Phipps to Dufferin, December 21, 1894, CO 879/41 African 472.

the Anglo-French Agreement of January 21, 1895.[120] An exchange of notes was sufficient. But because the conditions were not made public, Phipps found himself in the position of having to defend the arrangement in the face of criticism from the Liverpool Chamber of Commerce. In an able (and openly Francophile) dispatch, he explained why it was "impossible to expect the French Government to abandon in its Colonies the doctrines on which the complete French commercial system is based, and which are in vogue in the mother country." In any case, a guarantee against differential duties in the future, as demanded by Liverpool, could only be given by the French Parliament; and this much the government dared not ask. The essential of Salisbury's instructions—access to sources of trade in the Fouta Djallon and the Sudan—had, he concluded, been obtained.[121]

But Phipps and Dufferin had failed to settle the problem of the Upper Niger. The talks on this area were called off in October 1894 and did not resume till the beginning of 1896. The details of the partition which was finally embodied in the Anglo-French Convention of 1898 have been partially covered by several historians, though little attention has been paid to the questions of free trade and free navigation that underlay the tedious wrangles about treaties, territory, and the politics of Gourma and Borgu.[122] Such things were means to ends. For the French, the end was access to the navigable Niger, made more necessary by the company regulations of 1891 and the fate of the French explorer Mizon.[123] For the Niger Company the prospect of French posts on the west bank with unrestricted passage to the sea meant (according to Sir George Goldie) an arms and spirits traffic

120. Nothing was said of Senegal either: "in order to ensure that no duties should be imposed on goods passing from the British Colony into French Possessions, unless such duties are actually in force in the immediately adjoining Colony of French Guinea. Otherwise such imposition in Senegal might be held to justify duties being levied on the inland frontier." Phipps to Dufferin, January 19, 1895, CO 879/42 African 481.

121. Phipps to Dufferin, ibid.

122. Vignes, "Etude sur les relations diplomatiques," pp. 381–403; John E. Flint, *Sir George Goldie and the Making of Nigeria* (London, 1960), Chap. 12; Margery Perham, *Lugard* (2 vols. London, 1956, 1960). Vol. 1, *The Years of Adventure, 1858–1898.* The most detailed analysis of the negotiations is given by Boniface I. Obichere, "Britain, France and the Dahomey-Niger Hinterland, 1885–1898" (unpublished D.Phil. thesis, Oxford, 1966), Chap. 7.

123. Flint, *Sir George Goldie,* pp. 168, 172–79. Regulations No. XL (1894) prohibited the import of spirits and limited ports of entry on the Niger Delta. CO 879/82 African 615; and for the customs duties, Newbury, "The Development of French Policy," p. 25 and note.

that would upset the political stability of Sokoto and reduce revenue.[124] For Salisbury's government there were wider considerations in the Egyptian Sudan; but once that important issue had been abstracted from the Niger negotiations in December 1897,[125] the old worry about French tariffs still nagged. In the new French empire from Dakar to Chad how could a place be preserved for British trade?

As early as May 1896, it was clear that both sides held incompatible views about the line to be drawn from Dahomey toward Say. Commissioners Roume and Larrouy admitted that the territory in that area was worthless. The only reason for clinging to their claims on the right bank was "to obtain access to the Niger. Access to the Niger in the north was, they said, to them a matter of minor importance; what they really desired was, access to that river in the immediate neighbourhood of the 9th parallel of north altitude, so as to connect their Colony of Dahomey with the Niger." [126]

The British commissioners refused. But Commissioner Henry Howard correctly estimated the importance of this point in Paris. So did the Chamber of Deputies during debates on colonial estimates in August 1896, when the minister of colonies, André Lebon, was committed to securing a right of passage in the same way as Britain had secured navigation rights from Portugal on the Zambezi.[127] The subject was, therefore, taken up again, when talks resumed in October 1897. This time French insistence on the stringency of the Niger regulations extracted a British offer to "provide every facility for trade and commerce on the Niger and for passing Boussa rapids." [128]

But that was not enough. And the procrastination of British diplomacy in making known this vague concession by Chamberlain (in order to give time for military preparations in West Africa) nourished the suspicions of Hanotaux.[129] In early November the French priorities for a settlement and territorial concessions to Great Britain were: a guarantee of communications under the Berlin Act, a tariff agreement similar to the Conventional Basin of the Congo, and some compensa-

124. Goldie to FO, July 27, 1897, enclosed in FO to CO, August 28, 1897, CO 879/48 African 529.

125. Monson to Hanotaux, December 10, 1897, cited in Vignes, "Etude sur les relations diplomatiques," p. 393.

126. Howard and Everett to Dufferin, May 23, 1896, CO 879/45 African 506.

127. Memorandum by Howard, August 5, 1896, ibid.; Monson to Salisbury, December 8, 1896, CO 879/48 African 529.

128. Gosselin and Everett to Salisbury, October 29, 1897, FO 403/251.

129. Monson to Salisbury, October 22, 1897, Salisbury papers A/115.

tion to French pride for evacuation of Bussa.[130] But in December Chamberlain still refused any suggestion of a port on the river; and Salisbury thought it unlikely the British cabinet would concede this point (with or without Zambezi-type regulations), though he was prepared to alter the Niger transit rules, if necessary.[131]

It is not generally realized how near the talks came to breaking down because of this negative attitude of the British government.[132] To find a compromise, the British commissioners embodied in a memorandum Hanotaux's proposals for a corridor from Nikki to the Niger. This, too, was rebuffed by Chamberlain in January, though he made a counterproposal by taking up Hanotaux's suggestion for a reciprocal tariff in West African territories, and offering revised regulations, lease of land for a port, and the recognition of French rights to Say, Gourma, Nikki, and the greater part of Borgu.[133]

The tariff question was now closely linked with the territorial delimitation of French and British spheres. It was reported to the French commissioners that "Her Majesty's Ambassador had proposed to the Minister for Foreign Affairs that, if a settlement of the territorial question were arrived at, both nations should agree to an identic Tariff on all the frontiers of their West African possessions, sea frontiers included." [134]

The reason for Chamberlain's offer is not entirely clear. But it is probable that it was put forward to counter the effects of a new discriminatory set of customs regulations for the Ivory Coast (contrary

130. Memorandum by Gosselin (Secret), enclosed in Gosselin to Salisbury (Private), November 7, 1897, Salisbury papers A/115. "Could not, asked His Excellency, some agreement be come to for a limited term, guaranteeing a general minimum tariff? I asked in which Colonies he proposed to apply this arrangement, and whether it was to be in the nature of a Zollverein or of a Customs Agreement on the lines of those drawn up in December 1890 and July 1891, for the Eastern and Western States within the Conventional Basin of the Congo. M. Hanotaux replied that he was not alluding to anything so ambitious as a Customs Union but rather something analagous to the Congo Agreements."

131. Minutes, by Chamberlain, of a conversation with Baron de Courcel, December 10, 1897, Salisbury papers A/92. But he agreed to revised regulations and "free access from the mouths of the Niger to the Rapids." Salisbury to Gosselin, December 30, 1897, FO 403/251.

132. Monson to Salisbury, January 14, 1898, Salisbury papers A/116; but he had also used the term "wrecked" about the negotiations earlier in October. Monson to Salisbury, October 22, 1897, Salisbury papers A/115.

133. PRO Cabinet 37/46; Salisbury to Monson, January 25, 1898, FO 27/3416.

134. Gosselin and Everett to Monson, February 1, 1898, FO 403/251.

to the 1889 agreement) which had been brought to his notice by the Foreign Office and the Bristol and Liverpool chambers of commerce in November 1897. This development gave rise to a not very accurate Foreign Office memorandum on the whole subject of differential customs in the region.[135] The timing of the colonial secretary's insertion of reciprocity into the Niger talks, however, predated both this document (which may have gone to the cabinet) and Salisbury's meeting with a deputation from the Chambers on February 23. But whatever its immediate origins, the new clause featured prominently in the important draft of instructions and terms sent by the Foreign Office to Monson, February 15, 1898:

> The fiscal arrangement proposed by Her Majesty's Government is that the Tariffs of the British and French territories respectively should apply to all merchandise alike, irrespective of origin, and that no charges should be imposed on British merchants in a French Colony, or on French merchants in a British Colony, beyond those payable by the nationals of either Colony. The same duties would thus be levied on goods of British and of French origin in British and French territories respectively, but the rates in the two territories would not necessarily be identical. The arrangement would apply to all the British and all the French possessions from the western frontier of the Ivory Coast to the eastern frontier of the Niger Coast Protectorate, to possessions on the coast as well as to those in the interior. It would embody the special commercial arrangements between the two countries already existing in West Africa, and would be drawn up by Commissioners selected by the respective Governments.[136]

In addition to this and to a territorial division of the Upper Niger, the company regulations would be changed and land leased, if needed, for a port on the navigable river.

Hanotaux favored these terms; but in the Council of Ministers, Méline fought the tariff proposal "tooth and nail" and threatened to block the convention in the Chamber.[137] For this reason the negotiations dragged on into March and April 1898, as the French commis-

135. *Report of the African Trade Section of the Liverpool Chamber of Commerce 1897–1898* (1898), p. 6; FO memorandum, "French Duties in West Africa," February 22, 1898, FO 27/3437. The terms agreed to were probably revealed confidentially to the Merchants' deputation from Bristol, February 23.

136. Bertie to Monson, February 15, 1898, FO 27/3408.

137. Monson to Salisbury, February 25, 1898. Salisbury papers A/116.

sioners tried to restrict the region in which the fiscal agreement would apply by excluding "Mossi and the countries to the eastward [which] were, they said, administered by the Lieutenant-Governor of the French Soudan, the whole of the supplies being imported through Senegal, the government of which controls the fiscal arrangements of the interior." [138] Once more, as in 1894, the inflexibility of the Senegal system of protective customs had to be taken into account.

But it was Salisbury who had his way on this point: Mossi was included in the fiscal zone that stretched from Calabar to Chad and across northern Nigeria to Wagadugu and the Ivory Coast.[139] The terms were to remain in force for thirty years. For Guinea there was already the confidential commercial agreement of 1895. But Senegal and the Sudan were excluded, as they always had been from arrangements that would have entailed a complete revision of their customs laws. And Salisbury accepted this, because he took the view that commercial rights on the Niger could not be denied to the French "as long as we adhere to free trade." [140] It was a view that assumed the disappearance of the Niger Company, by then an obstacle to Lagos traders no less than to the French.

With the fiscal clause accepted in Paris, Chamberlain told the cabinet early in May that agreement on the territorial demarcation would be reached.[141] An essential principle of British West Africa diplomacy had been gained—one which the French commissioners complained had raised against their government "the entire commercial class of France including the Directors of the three Navigation Companies trading in West Africa." [142] But this was probably an exaggeration to cover a diplomatic retreat, dictated by the imminent departure of Hanotaux from office and by knowledge of British military preparations in the field. Various quibbles remained—the Zambezi regulations (as adapted to the Niger case), Bona, and Ilo—but these did not add or subtract much from the final text which completed the Anglo-French demarcation of interests in the West African region.

138. Gosselin and Everett to Monson, April 30, 1898, enclosed in Monson to Salisbury, May 1, 1898, FO 27/3413.

139. Salisbury to Monson, May 6, 1898: "and . . . although it may be unlikely that British merchants will do any trade with Mossi, yet it will go towards justifying the surrender of the claims of Her Majesty's Government to the territory if they can include Mossi in the fiscal arrangement." FO 403/251.

140. Salisbury to Monson, May 1, 1898, FO 27/3413.

141. PRO Cabinet 41/24, Minutes May 4, 1898.

142. Gosselin and Everett to Monson, May 15, 1898, FO 27/3413.

The case for reconsidering the place of economic factors in West African partition is a strong one. Both Vignes and Stengers have drawn attention to the fear of exclusion from regional markets as a motive for territorial expansion.[143] Such a motive, it might be argued, was peculiar to localized interest groups and a handful of mad patriots. But it was certainly not absent either from the saner considerations of a Bismarck, a Salisbury, or a Hanotaux—if only because it might be politically important at home, rather than economically decisive abroad. Salisbury's exclamation to Courcel, cited at the head of this essay, is difficult to place in an imperial context (the ambassador's account of the conversation leaves it unclear which territories the British were "greedy" for, as a consequence of French protectionism). But it would fit the West African interior well enough. And it is consistent with his phrase about "facility for trade," or with his observation that the basis of Anglo-French difficulties over Madagascar lay in the loss of British guarantees against high duties.[144]

It was precisely when such rights were felt to be threatened in West African markets that British control was extended. The sense of security that had been shaken only by the Ashanti war began to be seriously undermined in the early 1880s, particularly in the Lower Niger and in the vicinity of Sierra Leone. From a British point of view, the predominant position of the nation's traders on the coast owed nothing to "favouring tariffs or exclusive privileges," and everything to "superiority in enterprise, capital and skill."[145] By the 1880s, this laissez-faire doctrine was no longer tenable. And the important place given to tariffs in the discussions leading to the agreements of 1882, 1889, 1895, and 1898 partially explains why.

Only partially, because the tariff clauses were not in themselves causes of partition, but symptoms of the need for the rationalization of European relations with West Africa. If it is true, as Robinson and Gallagher have persuasively argued, that the "Old Coast System" was breaking down prior to partition,[146] it was by no means clear to the Old Coasters or to African rulers what was to replace it. In the uncertainty, a whole complex of credit structures, petty monopolies, over mighty chiefs and consuls, and underdeveloped communications

143. Vignes, "Etude sur les relations diplomatiques," pp. 385–86, 393–94, 398, 401; Stengers, "L'impérialisme colonial de la fin du XIXe siècle, p. 487.

144. Salisbury to Monson, January 28, 1898, cited in Robinson and Gallagher, *Africa and the Victorians*, p. 386; Salisbury to Monson, August 19, 1899, Salisbury papers A/119.

145. *The Times*, October 15, 1884.

146. Robinson and Gallagher, *Africa and the Victorians*, pp. 381–88.

and resources, began to be questioned. Between the moral investment of the Niger expedition in 1841 and the economic investment of the railway loans in 1895, the frontier moved inland. There was nothing new in Chamberlain's theory of "underdeveloped" estates, only more knowledge of the estates themselves. France had already pioneered public works for the political conquest of the Niger heartland: and the Niger Company had made good administrative use of a natural highway to the interior. These were steps in the modernization of the African market, in charting the frontier, in answering the uncertainties about the location of authority.[147]

The official French and British answers to the question marks of West Africa, however, were very dissimilar. French military imperialism after 1870 went far beyond the brief campaigns against Ashanti; the differential customs policy begun in Senegal in 1877 was not merely fiscal in purpose, but aimed at reserving a place for French national and colonial trade. Both were a challenge to an old colonial power, unwilling to incur expense, unwilling to retire. As late as 1895, Salisbury still claimed possession of the valleys of the Nile, the Niger, and the Mekong: "& one of the beatitudes of the *possidentes* is that it is to their interest to hold their tongues."[148] But silence was not enough, when the assumptions on which British West African policy rested—minimum interference and free trade—were openly debated by France.

So it was that tariffs formed part of the great territorial settlements, because the reason for them was basically the same at the reason for the demarcation of frontiers—a need to insure in legal form against the expected illegalities of rivals. As such, they were moderately useful. The clauses of the 1895 and 1898 conventions did prevent the extension of the Senegal system, or the Congo tariff to Guinea, the Ivory Coast, or Dahomey. On the other hand, the 1898 convention was flouted by both sides during the First World War.[149] And the

147. These ideas are developed more fully in my article, "Trade and Authority in West Africa, 1850–1880," in *Colonialism in Africa, 1870–1960*, vol. 1, *The History and Politics of Colonialism, 1870–1914*, ed. Lewis Gann and Peter Duignan (Cambridge University Press, 1969).

148. Salisbury to Dufferin, July 26, 1895, Salisbury papers A/119.

149. The French administration in Dahomey and the Ivory Coast tried to reduce the quantity of palm products exported to British ports by the selective issue of licenses; the Colonial Office and the Board of Trade (in opposition to the views of the Foreign Office) imposed a differential duty on palm kernels shipped from British West Africa to foreign ports. The duty was upheld in 1919 as necessary to secure Germany's prewar kernel-crushing industry for the United

very size of the inland frontiers made nonsense of attempts to push this rationalization further toward customs unions. There could be no *Zollverein* in the administrative conditions of the nineteenth century in West Africa—not even in French West Africa which unified its customs in 1905 by paying revenues into a central fund.[150]

Nor was much achieved by the Franco-German customs agreement, 1887–90, for Togo and Dahomey which was sundered by the complaints of German and French traders.[151] The Anglo-German arrangement for the eastern Gold Coast and Togo lasted longer, 1894–1904, but was not renewed when German duties had to be increased for revenue. The promised Dahomey-Lagos adjustment of tariffs never took place, and it was left to the British administration to provide a special system of drawbacks to keep palm products moving out through the British port. In the Congo widespread smuggling helped to even out the fiscal absurdities of the low-tariff conventional zone and the high-tariff Gabon.[152]

By the end of the century the main features of the West African tariff structure were the heavy differentials in Senegal which levied 15 percent ad valorem on foreign goods; the generally high British specific duties on spirits, unmanufactured tobacco, powder, and arms; and the generally low duties of the German and Portuguese colonies. The Congo was a special case. The tariffs of the Ivory Coast and Dahomey closely resembled those of the Gold Coast and Lagos. But everywhere administrators were less concerned with favoring national manufactures than with raising taxes to support increasing costs of administration.

What difference did partition agreements with their tariff clauses make to the pattern of West African trade? This kind of question is

---

Kingdom. PRO Board of Trade/11 C.15654; FO to CO, July 3, 1917; minutes of the Commercial Department, Board of Trade, June 4, 1917; Board of Trade to CO, July 7, 1917; *Report of a Committee on Trade and Taxation for British West Africa*. Cmd. 1600 (1922), pp. 59–60.

150. Though some administrators had pressed for the unification of tariffs, as well as the payment of duties into the Government General budget. De Trentinian, "Réformes nécessaires dans nos possessions de l'Afrique occidentale," 1899, National Archives, Dakar, Government General 18/6/2. See too Henry Chevans, *La mise en valeur de l'Afrique occidentale française* (Paris, 1907), p. 261.

151. Newbury, *The Western Slave Coast*, p. 159; Fabre to Ministry of Commerce, February 18, 1889, AN F[12]6427.

152. Fernand Rouget, *L'Expansion coloniale au Congo français* (Paris, 1906), p. 583.

hard enough to answer in the case of the Méline Tariff, where metropolitan statistics are reasonably good. It can have no final answer for West Africa, where trade records are concerned above all with the coastal ports, rather than the interior.

But if there was any correlation between tariff policies and colonial trade, one might expect that Senegal and the French Congo would show higher percentage ratios in their trade with France than with other countries; while, on the other hand, the free-trading British areas would demonstrate less national commercial bias. In the case of Britain that is not entirely so. The total value of imports and exports in British possessions in West Africa for the period of partition, 1880–1900, more than doubled from 3.0 million pounds to 7.9 million. Britain's share of this trade increased from about half to some 65 percent.[153] The picture, however, is different if one looks at the statistics for Britain's trade with western Africa as a whole in this period. For that trade, in fact, is much less than the total trade of British possessions on the coast and rose from 1.7 million pounds to 5.8 million pounds for imports of African products and exports of United Kingdom products and manufactures.[154] Before 1890, British trade with non-British areas greatly exceeded trade with British possessions in West Africa. As partition proceeded, the proportions were exactly reversed. Thus, some of the increased percentage in British trade with British possessions, after 1890, is simply a recognition of the transfer of the Niger to formal control. If, on the other hand, the possessions are examined separately, the importance of foreign national trade in some of them (France in the Gambia, or Germany in southern Nigeria) is appreciable. But these individual differences do not outweigh the overall increase in the British share of British West Africa's imports and exports.

Conversely, in the case of France, there is a remarkable decline in the small national share of trade with British possessions on the coast. French traders did not prosper, as they had done in the 1870s, in Sierra Leone, and French trade with the Lower Niger remained pitifully small. The provisions of the Convention of 1898 for lease of land were never needed.

Part of the explanation for this may be that French firms moved into areas under national control (though they later established branches at British ports as larger enterprises were formed). But even for the

153. *Statistical Abstracts of the British Empire.* Cmd. 8665 (London, 1897), pp. 28–29, 34–35, 46–47, 52–53; *PP*, cd. 4954 (1909), CII.

154. PRO Customs 8/121–140; Customs 4/75–94.

whole of French West Africa total trade with France amounted to only 1.8 million pounds by 1898—or some 40 percent of the import and export values of French possessions. Throughout the period there was a tendency for the imports of foreign countries into French possessions to rise, proportionally, against a rising percentage of French West African products sent to France.[155] Senegal, as a discriminatory tariff area, resisted this tendency, as might be expected: by 1900 foreign national trade accounted for no more than 25 percent of total trade values in the colony. On the other hand, France had an extremely small percentage of the trade of Guinea, the Ivory Coast, or Dahomey.

Thus, it appears that during the period of partition there was some polarization of national trade in the respective colonies of France and Britain. The tendency was strongest in Senegal and somewhat less strong in the British possessions as a whole. The reverse was true of French territories in the 1898 conventional zone. But it would be facile to attribute this to tariff demarcations on the coast. For, to upset this theory, the highly protected French Congo, where all French goods had free entry, enjoyed a trade with foreign countries which far exceeded that with France.[156] Trade followed the flag—but not necessarily the national flag.

To these general conclusions some reservations must be added. There were other ways to influence trade patterns than by tariffs. Bordeaux merchants never wearied of explaining that it was impossible to do business on the coast of Africa without importing a great variety of goods from Britain and Germany, as well as France; but this concession to free trade did not stop them from pressing for a government-subsidized shipping line. We need to know more about the operation of shipping monopolies during and after the partition period, currency questions, the issue of trading licenses, and the ways in which larger French and British commercial enterprises were formed from small firms at the end of the century. The economic effects of investment in internal communications have yet to be assessed for West Africa. There is no thorough analysis of the market history of any of the major staples.

But however one judges the importance of tariffs in the subsequent

155. *Bulletin économique et politique de l'Afrique occidentale française* (Dakar, 1922); André Lefebvre, *De la création de l'outillage publique dans l'Afrique occidentale française* (Paris, 1904), pp. 368–371; cf. Constant Southworth, *The French Colonial Venture* (London, 1931), Tables III, IV, pp. 43, 56.

156. But foreign trade dropped sharply after 1904. Rouget, *L'Expansion coloniale,* p. 580.

economic development of West Africa, their imposition for revenue and, in some cases, protection, was a factor in the partition of the region from the end of the 1870s. And if British traders did not flock to Timbo or Wagadugu, African traders carrying British imported cottons did.

7. *British and French Imperialism in West Africa, 1885–1898*

JOHN D. HARGREAVES

"The colonial policy of Great Britain and France in West Africa has been widely different," wrote Lord Salisbury on March 30, 1892. In an often-quoted exposition he proceeded to contrast a French policy that had secured control of the Upper Niger basin "by a large and constant expenditure, and by a succession of military expeditions" with Great Britain's "policy of advance by commercial enterprise." [1] There were good reasons why a diplomatic dispatch destined for publication should emphasize such a contrast at that time. The chambers of commerce and other political pressure groups which were becoming interested in West African affairs were bemoaning the way in which Anglo-French agreements of 1882, 1889, and 1891 had excluded Sierra Leone from access to its markets in the northern rivers of Guinea and from the Niger sources (where one of its agents had proudly hoisted the Union Jack in 1890).[2] Yet Salisbury's dispatch authorized further negotiations that would certainly make this exclusion permanent; and its publication coincided with the dissolution of Parliament and the opening of an election campaign in which one minor but contentious issue would be Frederick Lugard's provocative policy toward French interests in Uganda.[3] As in his famous reference to the "light soil" conveyed to France by the Declaration of 1890, Salisbury was thus anxious to show that the apparently striking advance of French power in West Africa had been secured at a cost disproportionate to any benefits it would bring. By ironically contrasting their policy with the British government's hard-headed pursuit of commercial interest, he

1. *Parliamentary Papers* [*PP* hereafter], 1892, *56*, 777–78. C.6701 *Papers Relating to . . . West Africa,* June 1892. Salisbury to Dufferin, March 30, 1892.
2. Public Record Office [PRO hereafter], London, Colonial Office [CO hereafter] 879/35 Confidential Print African 421. Proceedings at a Deputation on the Boundaries of the West African Colonies, December 8, 1891; Liverpool Chamber of Commerce, *Affairs of the West African Colonies* (Liverpool, 1892).
3. Margery Perham, *Lugard* (2 vols. London, 1956, 1960), Vol. 1, *The Years of Adventure* pp. 327–35.

sought to excuse those sacrifices of territories of secondary interest to which a minority of critics were beginning to object.

Although Europeans involved in the scramble for Africa frequently tended thus to emphasize the unique nature of their own nation's purposes (contrasting them with inferior varieties of imperialism practiced by "lesser breeds without the law"), the thrust of the French military into the Sudan, and the campaigns against Amadu and Samori to which Salisbury referred, did represent a form of imperialism rarely paralleled elsewhere. The youngish professional officers who assumed the mission of realizing General Louis Faidherbe's hopes of an empire in the Sudanese interior—Borgnis-Desbordes, Combes, Archinard—came from a professional group not wholly at ease inside the civilian Third Republic. Their priorities, described in terms of national and personal honor and glory, were not those of the unenterprising, pacific merchants established in the Senegal, nor even those of the organized colonial pressure groups that developed in France after 1890; their code of values was autochthonous to their service. Of course, military officers followed similar codes elsewhere in Europe; what was unique about *Soudan français* was the way in which relatively junior military commanders were able in practice to secure a very remarkable freedom of initiative, independent of the government machine in Paris, and so were able largely to determine the pattern and timing of territorial expansion (as well as the initial form and style of administration in conquered territories). This sector of the imperialist front makes an interesting study (and a perplexing one for those committed to narrowly defined theories of economic imperialism); [4] it is easy to see why Salisbury—and others—should regard French behavior here as freakish and irrational.

But the military thrust to the interior was not the only element in French imperialism in West Africa; nor was it, up to the time at which Salisbury was writing, the one that caused most trouble to the British. The general pattern of Anglo-French relations in nineteenth-century West Africa was of two civilian governments seeking to balance concrete but limited interests (largely created by traders) against broader official appreciations of the policies needed to maintain the prosperity, power, and influence of their states in the world. Insofar as governments in Europe could control the African situation, they normally tried to protect local interests by locally improvised expedients, which at the diplomatic level implied open cooperation or reciprocal self-restraint. In both Paris and London, official thinking was normally

4. A. S. Kanya-Forstner, *The Conquest of the Western Sudan* (Cambridge, 1969). See also his paper in the present collection (Chap. 12).

inspired by foreign ministries that saw tropical Africa as a subordinate theater within a Eurocentric system of world politics. When—as was generally the case until the early 1880s—the imperatives of high policy indicated Anglo-French friendship, the two governments collaborated in maintaining conditions that would permit their citizens to coexist under African sovereignties. There might be fairly sharp differences in the nature of their respective local interests, and in the style of policies used to protect them; but it was only when Anglo-French relations broke down in Europe that these led to serious conflicts in Africa.

It is the purpose of this paper, in reviewing the record of Anglo-French relations in West Africa after 1885, to consider how far such conflicts really represented an encounter of incompatible imperialisms, how far an interaction between broadly comparable forces. It represents a still-incomplete attempt to discover how far the leitmotifs of the "prelude" remain discernible through the sound of percussion and brass that accompanied the European partition of West Africa.

Although one of the purposes of the Berlin Conference was to define the formalities to be observed in order that occupation of the coasts of Africa should be effective, the appropriation by European powers of the West African coastline south of the Senegal was in fact very largely completed by the time the final act was signed. The problems that remained consisted either of the detailed delimitation or adjustment of claims by normal diplomatic processes, or of the settlement of disputes arising from the extension of European claims to inland districts. The distribution of the coastline at first sight appeared arbitrary and irrational. French control extended southward from the Senegal to the watershed between the Melakori and Great Scarcies rivers (the line of the Anglo-French agreement of June 28, 1882, though unratified by the French Chamber, was in practice respected by both governments) but with two important and vexatious interruptions caused by the British settlements on the Gambia and by Portuguese Guinea. The limits of neither had yet been finally defined. The British also held the Iles de Los off Conakry. British authority in Sierra Leone extended from the Melakori-Scarcies watershed to the Mano River—a line Britain finally imposed on Liberia by a convention signed in 1885. The extent of French authority on the western Ivory Coast remained uncertain until 1892, but it was disputed by Liberia rather than Great Britain;[5] the starting point of the eastern boundary with the Gold

5. Paul Atger, *La France en Côte-d'Ivoire de 1843 à 1893* (Dakar, 1962), pp. 151–58.

Coast was accepted as far as the coastline itself was concerned, though its subsequent direction was proving difficult to delimit. The British had consolidated their position on the Gold Coast proper by the agreement with the Dutch in 1871 and the annexation of the "Colony" after the Ashanti war of 1873–74, but in the east French and German claims had spoiled their chances of uniting what in the 1870s were called "the two parts of the Gold Coast Colony." The rival claims of France and Germany to protectorates in the Popos states were settled by their agreement of December 24, 1885. Further east the French remained somewhat precariously installed in the state of Porto-Novo and at Cotonou; their boundary with British Lagos remained uncertain until 1889, and zealous agents of each power maneuvered for vantage points on the creeks around Katanu. The future of the Dahomean kingdom remained uncertain; French governments still hesitated to accept the logical consequences of their occupation of its main port at Cotonou, and between 1885 and 1887 the Portuguese, who precariously occupied a "fort" at Whydah, actually claimed a protectorate over the whole state. Finally, and most important, the Anglo-German exchange of notes in April and May 1885 effectively completed the recognition by interested powers of Britain's control of the whole coastline between the Porto-Novo–Lagos border and the frontier of German Kamerun at the elusive Rio del Rey. The way was thus prepared for breaking the administrative link between Lagos and the Gold Coast and the ultimate emergence of the new unity of British Nigeria.[6]

This checkered pattern of the coastline may well appear an arbitrary one from the point of view of European, let alone of African, interests; and so far as governments in Europe were concerned, some of these claims had indeed been originally staked "in a fit of absence of mind." Yet the failure of attempts during the 1860s and '70s to rationalize the arrangement of European interests by a comprehensive redistribution suggested that every territorial toehold represented the interests of at least some Europeans, and perhaps of their African associates too. In some cases these interests were recognized by the home governments as so substantial that there could hardly be any question of ceding them to European rivals. French Senegal and British Gold Coast were well-established colonies; within these colonial

6. For the various international agreements, see Edward Hertslet, ed., *The Map of Africa by Treaty* (3 vols. 3rd ed. London, 1909). For the background to many of them, John D. Hargreaves, *Prelude to the Partition of West Africa* (London, 1963).

societies and on their frontiers Europeans and mulattoes had established rights and interests which their imperial overlords acknowledged as legitimate. Sierra Leone was a liberated African settlement to which British philanthropists (though a declining force) were strongly attached; moreover, when the Carnarvon Defense Commission of 1879 recommended its fortification and development as the navy's intermediate coaling station between Gibraltar and the Cape, Sierra Leone became the one place in British West Africa of imperial strategic importance.[7] In Lagos and its Yoruba hinterland, in the Oil Rivers around the Niger delta, and in the sphere of operations secured by Goldie's National African Company there was a considerable British investment, at least of expectations.

Moreover, these interests did not concern only European and African residents in the coastal colonies. All the European settlements had established bonds of mutual interest—usually originating in commercial relationships—with some neighboring African states (and bonds of antagonism with others); the pattern of these often followed traditional African alignments, and sometimes even transcended divisions of the recent past. It is a curious paradox that whereas earlier European commercial activities had often encouraged, if not actually caused, schisms within African states, imperialists might aspire to restore ancient unities. Competition to trade with Europeans in the fifteenth century accelerated the breakup of Wolof political unity, which would only be restored with the French conquest of Senegal. (If the Gambia Wolofs were then excluded, it was not for want of effort by the French.) Britain's maladroit interventions in Yoruba affairs during the nineteenth century frequently tended to exacerbate internecine conflicts originating after the disintegration of the Oyo Empire; yet a common aim, and ultimately an effect, of the more spirited frontier policies pursued by governors of Lagos was to "promote Yoruba unity."[8] Thus the shape of the informal empires which these established coastal colonies now began to acquire frequently followed intelligible lines derived from earlier European and African activities.

Other claims by Britain and France might seem to have less solid

7. CO 879/26 C.P. African 334, No. 121. Note by General Brackenbury, 27 June 1887. For the Carnarvon Commission, see E. A. Benians, et al, ed., *Cambridge History of the British Empire, 3* (Cambridge, 1959), 232–35.

8. CO 879/26. C. P. African 334, No. 166, Moloney to Meade, Pte., July 15, 1887. For the general history of Anglo-Yoruba relations, see A. A. B. Aderibigbe, "Expansion of the Lagos Protectorate: 1863–1900" (Ph.D. thesis, University of London, 1959).

foundations. On the Ivory Coast, French interests had for twenty years been simply those of one trading house, Verdier of La Rochelle; although their range expanded during the 1880s, they remained restricted to the general area of Assinie. France's interest in Dahomey, and the protectorate she reestablished in 1883 at Porto-Novo, originally reflected the interest of three Marseille companies, one of whose spokesmen, Victor Régis, showed considerable skill over more than forty years in manipulating official policy to serve his personal ambitions. British traders in the Gambia, though somewhat longer established, might on more than one occasion have been induced by a moderate cash offer to bequeath their interests in this tiny colony to France. From the broader viewpoint of British or French world policy, none of these latter colonies had any very great intrinsic importance, and most official opinion favored attempts to rationalize their territorial distribution by a comprehensive exchange, such as was discussed in 1869–70 and 1875–76. Yet the failure of these attempts showed how even such marginal points of Afro-European contact could influence attitudes and decisions in Europe. Small localized pressure groups—Marseille merchants with influence in the Chamber of Commerce and with the local deputy; African residents of Bathurst, appealing to missionary allies and imperial sentiment in Britain—were able to obstruct plans for "comprehensive dealing," even when the climate of international politics was favorable during the 1870s.[9]

During the early 1880s the climate in the English Channel certainly became much cooler, in large part because of French opposition to the British occupation of Egypt. Robinson and Gallagher go so far as to argue that this question "gave the powers both incentive and opportunity to break the traditional understandings about tropical Africa," and stimulated French attempts to compel British evacuation "by loosing their pro-consuls against exposed British interests in unclaimed Africa."[10] In 1883–84 some junior French "proconsuls" did secure more freedom of action, though whether there was any expectation of such consequences in Egypt is more doubtful; hence sharp local conflicts developed in which the French and British governments participated more fully and actively than ever before.[11] Some of the

9. See Hargreaves, *Prelude*, esp. Chap. 4.

10. Ronald E. Robinson and John Gallagher, "The Partition of Africa," in *New Cambridge Modern History, 11* (Cambridge, 1962), 602; cf. their *Africa and the Victorians* (London, 1961), pp. 162, 166, 188–89.

11. Hargreaves, *Prelude*, pp. 278–301, 310–13; Jean Stengers, "L'impérialisme colonial de la fin du XIXe siècle: mythe ou réalité," *Journal of African History, 3* (1962).

people concerned saw themselves embarking on a great continental scramble for empire. In January 1884, Governor Bourdiaux of Senegal argued that the British were seeking compensation for their setbacks in the Nilotic Sudan by scheming to turn Samori against the French, hoping to establish their influence on the Niger in partnership with him and to make France experience her own "Khartoum" at Bamako.[12]

In the light of the British archives these fears seem ludicrously exaggerated, or at least premature (Samori at this date had had no contact with the British for more than three years, and when his messengers reappeared at Freetown in 1885, Governor Samuel Rowe's attitude was extremely reticent); but British agents may certainly be discovered thinking in comparable terms. The ultimate intentions of George Goldie and William Mackinnon at this period remain rather inscrutable; but on the other side of Africa, for example, young Harry Johnston was rejoicing to have found "a land eminently suited for European colonization, situated near midway between the Equatorial Lakes and the Coast. Within a few years it must be either English, French or German." [13] Given the "wild and irrational spirit" which Gladstone noted during the period of the Berlin Conference, it would not have been surprising if the scramble for coastal territories had been followed at once by a similarly fevered race to seize physically at least those inland territories which, like the Sokoto caliphate, were believed to represent the richest prizes.

Contrary to legend, this did not take place. Between 1885 and 1890 both French and British governments generally tried, with some success, to keep their proconsuls on the leash. The abatement in tempo was doubtless affected by the economic circumstances of these years; the fall in prices for African produce caused by the international economic recession seems generally to have discouraged governmental agents from investing in forward policies (except when, as in Johnston's deposition of Jaja, a relatively junior official without budgetary responsibilities succeeded in making good some independent initiative). Private interests were equally restrained. Immediately after the Berlin conference Goldie's Niger Company did sponsor one modest but crucially important expedition—Joseph Thomson's northern journey, which produced treaties, dated respectively June 1 and 13,

12. Archives du Ministère des Affaires Etrangères [MAE hereafter] Paris. Mémoires et Documents Afrique 84, enclosure in MMC to MAE, February 4, 1884.

13. Roland Oliver, *Sir Harry Johnston and the Scramble for Africa* (London, 1957), p. 67, Johnston to Fitzmaurice, July 10, 1884.

1885, conferring exclusive rights on the company in the names of the sultan of Sokoto and the emir of "Gandu." But these seem to have attracted curiously little public attention, and the company did nothing to follow them up by establishing even a commercial presence beyond the actual valleys of the Niger and Benue.[14]

French business, too, never conspicuously eager to invest in an imperial future in tropical Africa, was particularly cautious during these depression years. This was noted by Edouard Viard, an ardent imperialist who, after spending some years representing Count Charles de Semellé's Compagnie française de l'Afrique Equatoriale on the lower Niger, obtained an audience with Jules Ferry in November 1884 to urge the importance of establishing a French presence in that region.[15] Bitterly disappointed at the loss of the Lower Niger, Viard secured an interview with Charles de Freycinet, premier and foreign minister, early in 1886 and offered to try to forestall British designs on Sokoto (Thomson's treaty not yet being known) by leading an expedition from Porto-Novo by way of Boussa.[16] The Foreign Ministry (not being itself responsible for controlling operations in the area) was anxious to peg out claims against Britain on the Upper Niger. De Freycinet, who had been involved in launching the Niger railway scheme, offered Viard a grant of twenty thousand francs toward his estimated expenses of one hundred thousand, the balance to be raised from commercial firms. Six weeks later Viard submitted a depressing report:

> For forty days I have done nothing but pay visits, make representations and requests, and write letters to the French business world, which is undergoing such difficulties, and has such a need for new impetus. I tried to rouse it from its torpor and interest it in my journey and the advantages which it would bring; I made requests to everybody, not for merchandise but merely for collections of samples. I obtained no response; or those replies which I did receive drove me to despair. Some told me that it was the State which

14. Texts in Hertslet, *The Map of Africa,* 3rd ed. *1,* 122–24. Thomson gave accounts of Hausaland and its economic prospects in papers to the British Association, the Royal Geographical Society, and the Manchester Geographical Society; but the only account of his actual treaty-making appeared in *Good Words,* 27 (1886), 24–29, 109–18, 249–56, 323–30, in the form of edited "letters to a friend."

15. See the publisher's introduction to Edouard Viard, *Au Bas-Niger* (Paris [1885], 3rd ed. 1886).

16. MAE Afrique 85, Viard to Freycinet, February 12, 1886, enclosing Report.

ought to take complete responsibility for the expenses of the expedition; others that they did not know the country through which I was to travel, and that consequently it did not interest them. I left the world of commerce and directed my inquiries to that of banking and finance. That was even worse; I saw nothing but dirty schemes of avarice, and unmentionable appetites.[17]

Viard did his best to remain optimistic about French enterprise. "Although I have had no success, I do not despair of my countrymen. They fall back too much upon the State because they are ignorant, because they are still too timid. But who knows the limits of the energy they will display when they find before them great new productive markets, secured for their profit by the State." [18]

For the moment, however, the only sign of energy on the part of French business in West Africa was a request by a group of Bordeaux merchants, working with the firm of contractors that had built the Dakar–Saint Louis railway, for concessionary freight charges in return for a promise to develop further the transport facilities of Senegal.[19]

This modest subsidy to Viard, however, represented the limit of the state's financial commitment to new initiatives in West Africa. Economic stringency apart, the political climate after France's military setback in northern Vietnam in March 1885 did not favor imperial ambitions. The political director at the Quai d'Orsay from November 1885 until 1889 was Francis Charmes, an influential journalist who as a deputy had moved the resolution hostile to Ferry after Lang Son.[20] In the Ministry of Marine too, political caution prevailed over the desire of many officials to fortify France's position in Africa. During the parliamentary session of 1885–86, for example, each of these ministries urged the other to bring forward for ratification the Sierra Leone boundary agreement of 1882, which a committee of the previous Chamber had refused to support; but although ratification was felt to be urgently necessary to prevent the British from resuming the right to impede France in her fragile protectorate in the Guinea rivers, neither department was prepared to accept responsibility.[21]

17. Ibid., Viard to Freycinet, March 26, 1886.

18. Ibid., Viard to Charmes, March 26, 1886.

19. Ibid., Cmdt. Soulé to Freycinet, June 15, 1886.

20. M. Prevost and R. d'Amat, eds., *Dictionnaire de Biographie française, 8* (1959), s.v. Charmes, M. J. J. F.

21. Their correspondence may be followed in MAE Afrique 86; cf. Hargreaves, *Prelude,* pp. 289–94.

French officials did recognize the importance of securing their future position within the Niger basin. The Ministry of Marine regretted that in 1884 French diplomacy had failed to prevent British control of the Lower Niger (to secure which they would have accepted the political neutralization of the whole course of the river); as a second-best course they sought to prepare evidence of their own treaty rights in the upper basin of the river to document a notification of their protectorate to the other signatories of the Berlin Act. Their immediate object was "on the one hand, to cover our possessions in Senegambia; on the other to secure the route which leads to Algeria by way of Timbuktu." They wanted to forestall the supposed designs of Sierra Leone and the Gambia, but without giving rein to military expansionism; as the Foreign Ministry noted with disappointment, Samori was to be left in possession of the right bank of the Niger.[22] Disillusionment about the slow progress and mounting costs of the Niger railway and apprehension about the unexpected strength of African resistance had made the Ministry of Marine very cautious about military action in the Sudan. In May 1885 Combes' attack on Samori's gold-bearing province of Bouré produced such spirited resistance that the French, their lines of communication jeopardized near base by Lat-Dior, had to withdraw; in March 1886 there began an even more inhibiting campaign against Mamadu Lamina in the upper Senegal.

J. S. Gallieni, appointed to command in 1886, was the odd man out among the "Sudanese" military. His method of penetration was to secure protectorate treaties by devious diplomacy, where Desbordes and Archinard looked for military confrontations and glorious victories; and his geographical priorities were different too. By the end of this tour of duty he has come to believe that "the richest parts of French Sudan were to be found to the southward, in the upper valley of the Niger and its tributaries and in the lands separating them from the southern rivers";[23] earlier he tried to swing the axis of imperial advance away from the upper Senegal valley. Although he inherited the plan to push French influence down the Niger to Timbuktu with the help of gunboats constructed at Bamako, Gallieni wanted to achieve at least a temporary basis for collaborating with the Tokolor state—whose hostility might in any case have had disastrous consequences on the campaign against Mamadu Lamina. In the upper basin

22. MAE Afrique 122, de la Porte to Freycinet, March 1, 1886. Cf. Colin W. Newbury, "The Development of French Policy on the Lower and Upper Niger, 1880–1898," *Journal of Modern History, 31* (1959), 22–26.

23. J. S. Gallieni, *Deux Campagnes au Soudan français* (Paris, 1891), p. 620.

of the Niger, his prior aim was to exclude British influence from Samori's empire by a protectorate treaty "*restreint aux relations extérieures*" which the British would recognize.[24] Tournier's treaty of 1886 was not judged adequate for that purpose, but on March 23, 1887, Etienne Péroz secured a more satisfactory text.

There were, however, still other areas from which Britain would have to be excluded before the French monopoly of the Upper Niger was juridically or practically secure: Fouta Djallon and the neighboring districts (where existing French treaties seemed somewhat less than watertight), and also the much vaster area, hardly known to Europeans, to the south of the great Niger bend. If Britain secured a treaty with some chief whose lands turned out to border a navigable affluent of the Niger, the possibility of establishing an exclusively French regime over the upper basin would be lost; if on the other hand a route could be found through the fabulous mountains of Kong, France's possessions on the Ivory Coast might be "destined to become important outlets for our Niger trade." [25] In January 1887 Lieutenant Gustave Binger, a young protégé of the aging General Faidherbe, secured grants of 17,500 francs from each of the interested ministries to finance an exploration in this direction—and with unusual speed, thanks to the personal intervention of the minister of Marine, Admiral Aube, who had served under Governor Faidherbe in Senegal and married Faidherbe's wife's sister.[26] Although his journey represented only one subsidiary aspect of Gallieni's new strategy, its eventual success had important effeects on France's territorial priorities.

French policy under Gallieni, while temporarily renouncing military imperialism in favor of a more cautious policy of peaceful penetration in the western Sudan, did thus aim at extending the national influence, and in some new directions. What were the effects of these new

24. The phrase is taken from de la Porte to Genouille, October 20, 1886 (copy in MAE Afrique 85), a dispatch probably drafted with Gallieni's assistance.

25. Archives National Section Outre-Mer [ANSOM hereafter], Missions 12, Dossier Binger, "Projet d'un Voyage d'Exploration dans la Boucle du Niger," December 18, 1886.

26. Ibid., Binger to Aube, December 19, 1886, minute by Aube; Faidherbe to de la Porte, December 27, 1886; Binger to Aube, January 3, 1886 (sc. 1887), minute by Aube, January 3, 1887. Cf. MAE Afrique 85, Note pour le Ministre, January 24, 1887, with minute by Flourens, approving a grant of 17,000 fr. from the departmental budget, and adding "Lieutenant Binger will have to be provided with the necessary powers for concluding treaties."

priorities on relations with Britain? Lord Salisbury's attitude toward imperial expansion continued to be characterized by scepticism and restraint, but also by an increasing recognition that some British interests at least required to be protected by diplomacy. Temperamentally he was always interested in the possibility of some comprehensive settlement of the obscure and intractable problems of West Africa. Comprehensive dealing, however, might be on a small or large scale: either a linked settlement of disputed boundaries, where concessions of a few miles in one colony could be compensated by gains in another, or as an actual redistribution of spheres of influence, involving reciprocal withdrawals from whole colonies of secondary importance. If in the end only the more limited type of agreement proved possible in West Africa, it was not so much on account of the repercussions of the Egyptian question as because even the secondary colonies were becoming more difficult to abandon.

The shift of emphasis away from Senegambia meant that British Gambia—the key to former attempts at a broad exchange agreement—dropped in the scale of French priorities, especially after the death of Mamadu Lamina in December 1887 made it somewhat less of an operational nuisance to the military. The British Colonial Office on their side were not eager to put it on offer; Sir Henry Holland, Salisbury's unenterprising colonial secretary, could well remember the political complication that had disturbed his earlier career as a senior official. On the British side. Porto-Novo had lost some of its value, since even if the French were to withdraw, the presence of the Germans in Togo would prevent the establishment of fiscal control of the littoral between Lagos and the Gold Coast. French ambitions in these years were largely restricted to the reconstitution of the old kingdom of Porto-Novo under their protectorate;[27] without undertaking the conquest of Dahomey they could have little space for any advance toward the Niger. When Viard belatedly arrived in March 1888 he disobeyed instructions by signing a treaty at Abeokuta, where Catholic missionaries had been tacitly encouraging an anti-British party to hope for French support against Britain and Dahomey.[28] But the French authorities refused to approve this intrusion upon a recognized sphere of British influence, which would have upset the good working relationship recently established with Lagos.[29]

27. MAE Afrique 86, Etienne to Flourens, December 10, 1887.

28. Viard's reports are in ANSOM, Sénégal III/17/b.

29. ANSOM, Sénégal III/17/b, report by lieutenant-Governor Ballot, 25 April 1888. Cf. E. A. Ayandele, *The Missionary Impact on Modern Nigeria* (London, 1966), pp. 49–51.

Both French and British governments, in short, were quite ready to overrule their more hawkish citizens and to seek means of rationalizing the confused situation around the lagoon. Nor did there seem any reason why, given political determination, they should not settle the longstanding irritant of the Ivory Coast boundary. Although French residents there were beginning to realize that their colony had great possibilities for northward expansion, the discouraging impression the Colonial Department had formed was not dispelled until the arrival of Binger and Treich-Lapleine at Grand Bassam on March 20, 1889. They were therefore willing to consider concessions there, though apparently only minor ones, if Britain would cede the Gambia and the Iles de Los.[30]

It was in the area of Guinea and Sierra Leone that each power felt the need for agreement most urgently in 1887–88. French officials feared that the British of Sierra Leone might be tempted to abandon the agreement of 1882 and, besides seeking an agreement with Samori (as in fact they did, though tardily), try to interfere with France's still precarious control of the rivers, and of Fouta Djallon. To help consolidate French power along Gallieni's new axis, the cession of the Iles de Los was highly desirable, but the final delimitation of a boundary in the Fouta Djallon area was most urgent of all. Curiously enough the British, who rated their own power in the area less highly than the French, felt the same way. For several years they had been unconcerned about French advances in the Sudan, trusting that the French government would "soon get tired of throwing their money away." [31] Since 1885 however, Sierra Leone had become aware of the striking increase in Samori's power; Freetown merchants and professional men favored collaboration with him in order to secure the long-desired contact with the resources of the West African interior. Not only would a French protectorate over his dominion ruin this dream; it would bring French military influence dangerously close to the coaling station.

There was additional alarm when in 1888 it became known that Péroz' treaty referred to Samori's present and *future* conquests; three years earlier Samori's forces had seemed poised to move as far as Port Loko.[32] It suddenly became a matter of imperial importance to

30. MAE Afrique 86, Etienne to Flourens, December 10, 1887, February 13, 1888.

31. Derby's minutes on two reports of their activities in CO 87/121, FO to CO February 24 and July 7, 1883.

32. Sierra Leone Archives, M.P. 1400/85, Impha Allieu to Rowe, August 10, 1885; Lawson to Rowe, August 20, 1885.

settle the limits of French influence in the interior of Sierra Leone. To do so the War Office was willing to concede a favorable settlement of the disputed boundary at Porto-Novo (definitely abandoning hope of securing the Dahomean coastline) and apparently to cede the Gambia. Salisbury, always disposed to consider bold diplomatic solutions of minor disputes, welcomed the prospect of comprehensive dealing; and on January 4, 1888, the British ambassador, discussing the range of West African disputes with the French foreign minister, Flourens, suggested "some general arrangement for the collective settlement of the whole group of questions." Flourens, hoping that the Gambia and the Iles de Los might be included, accepted the need for such an arrangement "by means of exchange or otherwise." [33]

Those who already had clear conceptions of African empire wished to make such an agreement as comprehensive as possible. In the spring of 1888, J. F. Hutton, the ubiquitous Manchester merchant, sounded the opinion of F. Bohn, managing director of the Compagnie française de l'Afrique Occidentale, and reported that there was still hope of securing a comprehensive partition of spheres by extending far to the eastward the Sierra Leone boundary line fixed in 1882. In the opinion of Bohn—who was of course an interested party—France might still be induced to withdraw from Dahomey and the Ivory Coast by an offer of the Gambia.[34] Soon afterward Hutton's friend Johnston, fresh from disposing of Jaja, spent his famous weekend at Hatfield, where he urged Salisbury to use France's desire for the Gambia to promote a visionary partition of the entire continent.[35]

The authors of these schemes assumed that French and British imperial policies were sufficiently complementary to permit negotiation on a basis of mutual interest; as long as Gallieni kept the emphasis of French interior policy on peaceful penetration through Fouta Djallon, both powers could be expected to bargain on the basis of more or less rational commercial calculations. The year 1888 may thus have offered the last real chance of a truly comprehensive

33. CO 879/24, C.P. African 265, War Office [WO hereafter] to FO December 17, 1886; CO 879/26, C.P. African 334, No. 121, Memo by Capt. Davies, June 20, 1887. Note by Brackenbury June 27; No. 165, FO to CO August 12, 1887. CO 879/27, C.P. African 345, No. 63, Lytton to Salisbury, January 4, 1888.

34. CO 879/27, C.P. African 345, Nos. 89, 97; Hutton to CO March 19, April 6, 1888. CO 879/28 C.P. African 355 No. 44 Hutton to CO October 10, 1888.

35. Roland Oliver, *Sir Harry Johnston,* pp. 132–44; cf. Johnston's article in *The Times,* August 22, 1888.

adjustment of interests between the forces confronting each other in West Africa. Unfortunately, neither government was sufficiently determined to take it. The external action of the French government in 1888 was inhibited by the effects of the internal Boulangist crisis. The British for their part did not want to begin real negotiations until they knew whether or not Samori had indeed placed himself under French protection; until Major Festing returned from visiting Samori at Sikasso in May 1888, they wished to avoid having to accept or challenge Péroz' treaty.[36] Holland, too, could still not make up his mind to contemplate including the Gambia, although Hutton assured him that his mercantile colleagues would no longer oppose a favorable exchange agreement, and Augustus Hemming of the Colonial Office argued that "Without the cession of the Gambia it is doubtful whether the French will consent to negotiate at all, and even if they do, we shall have so little to offer them in exchange for the concessions we desire that no really desirable or permanent settlement is likely to be arrived at."[37]

Ultimately Holland reluctantly agreed that the Gambia might be discussed if the French raised the question, and in March 1889 Hemming drew up alternative schemes for comprehensive settlements on a large and a small scale. His proposals for the former case were ambitious and unrealistic (he hoped to get France out of the Melakori and regarded her total withdrawal from Dahomey and the Ivory Coast as the minimum compensation acceptable for the "valuable property" of the Gambia);[38] yet they were hardly more unreasonable than the views of French colonial officials at the same period.

The ideas of the two governments as to what would constitute a basis for a large comprehensive deal were still far apart. The demands of colonial officials were inflated beyond all reasonable expectations of success, and the Foreign Ministries now lacked the resolution to impose more reasonable views. Rational men in Paris and London thus had to confine themselves to comprehensive dealing on the small scale. In April 1889 detailed negotiations opened in Paris between Hemming and Egerton of the British embassy on the one side, and on the

36. CO 879/27, C.P. African 345, No. 88, CO to FO March 13, 1888; No. 92, FO to CO March 27, 1888; No. 95, CO to FO March 31, 1888; No. 110, FO to CO April 24, 1888.

37. CO 879/28, C.P. African 355, Hutton to CO October 15, 1888; No. 66, Manchester Chamber of Commerce to CO November 28; No. 74, London C. of C. to CO December 11, 1888. CO 879/29 C. P. African 357, Memo by Hemming, November 1888.

38. CO 879/28 C.P. African 355, No. 48 CO to FO October 16, 1888; CO 379/29, C. P. African 365. Memo by Hemming, March 5, 1889.

other Nisard and D'Estournelles of the Quai d'Orsay, stiffened by the excitable lieutenant-governor Jean Bayol, who took the leading role in discussions of detail. At the first meetings Egerton suggested the desirability of "clearly defining the French and English spheres in that part of the interior of Africa" and drew a demarcation line along the tenth parallel as far as 4 degrees west. But the French were no longer eager to jump at the implication that the Gambia could at last be theirs. The success of recent campaigns in Senegal led the colonial department to the conclusion that "this river will become French through force of circumstances, like Ziguinchor in the Casamance";[39] and more important still, the Ivory Coast, which would have to be offered in exchange, had taken on new importance since Binger's demonstration of its prospects of northward expansion. Bayol indeed had anticipated these prospects when he was in the Ivory Coast in 1886; for him there could be no question of abandoning the Ivory Coast, only of drawing a frontier that would secure against British encroachments that route to the northeast along which he had dispatched Treich-Lapleine in 1887.[40] He and his colleagues therefore insisted on discussing the various frontier problems seriatim, examining their respective merits within the context of the negotiation as a whole. Discussion proceeded on this restricted basis; the resulting agreement of August 10, 1889, settled the boundaries in the immediate vicinity of the coast at the Gambia, Assinie, and Porto-Novo, and laid down a demarcation line in the interior of Sierra Leone.[41]

Given the assumption that colonies once established would continue to exist, this was a sensible piece of horse-trading, which does not seem to represent much "vicarious generosity" by the British.[42] True, the French Foreign Ministry drew up a summary claiming great successes on all fronts: security in Saloum, Rip, and Bondou; the definitive exclusion of British influence from the Guinea rivers; a clear route from Assinie to the northern Ivory Coast; and at Porto-Novo such an access of strength as would secure France's future influence in

39. MAE Afrique 128; *Note aux Affaires Etrangères,* Ministry of Commerce, Industry and Colonies, April 25, 1889.

40. Atger, *La France en Côte-d'Ivoire,* pp. 110–26.

41. Records of the proceedings may be found in MAE Afrique 128; and in CO 879/29, C.P. African 360.

42. Robinson and Gallagher, "The Partition of Africa," p. 611. Compare this very British view with Kenneth Vignes, "Etude sur la rivalité d'influence entre les puissances européennes en Afrique équatoriale et occidentale depuis l'acte général de Berlin jusqu'au seuil du XXe siècle," *Revue française d'histoire d'outre-mer, 48* (1961), 47.

Dahomey and on the route to Mossi.[43] Yet only at Porto-Novo were the perils said to have been averted real, and even here the establishment of Germany in Togo had removed any real incentive for the British to squeeze out the French. Britain's sense of weakness had not been fully appreciated in Paris; what London had feared was that Bathurst or Freetown might be strangled by the arrival of France on the lower Gambia or at Port Loko, and these dangers at least were finally averted. The French memorandum was clearly written to provide ammunition against political critics who might understand what Britain had gained. Both Foreign and Colonial officials remembered the vicissitudes of the 1882 agreement, and later agreed that this one should be ratified by presidential decree, rather than submitted to "the inconvenience of reopening a political discussion upon questions which the Plenipotentiaries have only been able to resolve with the help of their professional experience, and [to] the danger of exposing to possible failure the results of negotiations that have required several years of study."[44]

Although the 1889 agreement thus brought old Anglo-French rivalries on the coasts of West Africa to a rather tame denouement, the references in the Foreign Ministry summary to Dahomey, Mossi, and the Sudan showed that a new chapter was beginning—a race to the interior in which popular forces of chauvinistic imperialism would eventually become more heavily engaged. Its first phase—Archinard's attack on Koundian on February 18, 1889—was no "involuntary imbroglio" with a "fighting Muslim theocracy" but a deliberate act of aggression by an ambitious and unscrupulous commander.[45] Thus began the great era of the *officiers soudanais,* during which rational officials in Paris would often deplore the foolhardy and unprincipled initiatives of officers in the field, yet feel themselves powerless to discipline or censure those whom the public hailed as national heroes upholding French honor in distant and barbarous places. Paris did retain more control over military operations launched from the coastal colonies, yet these too contributed to the imperialistic euphoria. In 1890 France became involved in hostilities against Dahomey which

43. MAE Afrique 128, "Résumé de la Situation Respective de la France et de l'Angleterre à la Côte Occidentale d'Afrique, avant et après l'arrangement définitif signé le 10 août 1889."

44. Ibid., Note pour le Ministre, December 20, 1889.

45. Kanya-Forstner, *The Conquest of the Western Sudan;* cf. Robinson and Gallagher "Partition," p. 609.

two years later culminated in the occupation of Abomey. Here again the new Fon king, Behanzin, although determined to defend the integrity and sovereign independence of his state, was by no means intransigently anti-French; imperceptive and obtuse proconsuls, notably Bayol, allowed themselves to be drawn into conflict by the intrigues of their ambitious protégé, Tofa of Porto-Novo. Such imbroglios were involuntary only in that responsibility rested with representatives on the spot rather than with any considered decision by French governments.[46]

Yet conditions in Paris were changing too. Eugène Etienne, who began a three-year stint as colonial undersecretary in February 1889, wished to establish French power more securely in the Bight of Benin, and to expand it inland. Under his direction new expansionist strategies began to develop, despite a political climate where fears of incurring financial or military commitments still tended to inhibit decision. Meanwhile interested sections of the French public began to organize themselves into colonial pressure groups, which sometimes reflected to the nation the interests and priorities of official policy makers, sometimes brought pressure to bear upon them. The exact relationship between these groups and France's established African interests remains to be demonstrated. The original committee of the Comité de l'Afrique française included deputies representing important business centers (as well as Borgnis-Desbordes and Binger); its objectives were "to acquire in central Africa the rights of the first occupant, and then to develop our trade within the regions placed under French influence."[47] Established African merchants from Bordeaux and Marseille, who during the 1880s had shown tendencies to combine in more heavily capitalized units, emerge as an open pressure group only three years later in the Union coloniale française;[48] previously they seem to have been more concerned to secure protection for localized interests than to promote a long-term colonial strategy. One unifying basis for these new colonial programs was the old romantic myth of a

46. David Ross, 'The Autonomous Kingdom of Dahomey, 1818–94" (Ph.D. thesis, University of London), 1967.

47. *Bulletin du Comité de l'Afrique française,* No. 1 (January 1891).

48. Henri Brunschwig, *Mythes et Réalités de l'imperialisme colonial français, 1871–1914* (Paris 1960), Chap. 8. Recent discussion of the French colonial party was greatly stimulated by the appearance of Brunschwig's pioneering essay, but much basic research in this field remains to be done. Among later contributions to the discussion, see G. N. Sanderson, *England, Europe and the Upper Nile, 1882–1899* (Edinburgh, 1965), and Kanya-Forstner, *The Conquest of the Western Sudan.*

rich and highly organized African interior, retold in somewhat more commercial terms, but still not underwritten by the entrepreneurs most directly concerned. The vision of a great transcontinental empire, hingeing somewhat implausibly on the unalluring marshlands around Lake Chad, proved to have a certain political effectiveness. By 1894 the colonial movement had acquired such momentum that Goldie saw in its "purely ideal" schemes for territorial continuity the culmination of a more or less coherent policy which he believed had begun with Gambetta's sponsoring of Verminck's Senegal Company in 1882.[49] This analysis was oversimplified, as was Salisbury's equation of French imperialism with the military expeditions. Britain was now faced with an imperialist movement much more broadly based than formerly, in which popular nationalism was excited both by military exploits and anticipations of economic gain; she responded, somewhat tardily, by producing a similar movement of her own.

There was, however, a time lag during which the "policy of advance by commercial enterprise" was not particularly effective. Liverpool merchants, and Sierra Leonean expansionists attracted by E. W. Blyden's vision of partnership between the Christian coast and the Muslim interior, regretted the renunication of access to the Sudan which the 1889 agreement implied. In January 1892 A. L. Jones's Sierra Leone Coaling Company made a treaty with Samori providing for railway construction and general assistance in the defense and development of his state; but Salisbury refused to recognize this unusually bold stroke of commercial enterprise.[50] The Gold Coast government, agreeing to make the running for British commerce, sponsored G. E. Ferguson's treaty-making operations to the northward in 1892–94; but these were unable to oppose any effective barrier to the occupation of the principal Mossi states by the French military after 1895.[51] In one crucial area, however, British commerce and diplomacy performed a successful holding action. In April 1890 Goldie, still intent on the supposed great prize of Sokoto, obtained through a Sierra Leonean agent documents purporting to confirm Thomson's treaties of 1885; on August 5 Salisbury obtained France's agreement to the famous Say-Barroua line (which he proceeded imprudently to

49. Sir George Taubman Goldie, "French Ambitions in Africa," *Asiatic Quarterly Review* (April 1894). Cf. Hargreaves, *Prelude*, p. 276 n.

50. Christopher H. Fyfe, *A History of Sierra Leone* (Oxford, 1962), pp. 503–04.

51. George E. Metcalfe, ed., *Great Britain and Ghana: Documents of Ghana History, 1807–1957* (Legon, 1964), Chap. 28.

celebrate by the indiscreet reference already mentioned). The Quai d'Orsay, anxious to maintain their priorities and avoid delay as a result of tiresome objections by their Colonial colleagues, made the agreement without properly consulting Etienne's department; yet, as Kanya-Forstner has shown, this was not at first regarded as a setback to imperial hopes. Apart from gains in Madagascar, France protected Algeria against the (remote) danger of being outflanked in the south, secured the possibility of access to Lake Chad for the missions in preparation, and set a limit to Britain's advance up the Niger (though at a point which the Niger Company had no immediate hope of reaching).[52] Later the French colonial party became disillusioned; Mizon's attempts to break the Niger Company's monopolistic position produced a great deal of reciprocal acrimony. Yet for three or four years the main thrusts of French imperialism—the military advances in the Sudan, the reconnaissances toward Lake Chad, the conquest of Dahomey, the tentative beginnings of northward expansion from the Ivory Coast—proceeded without drawing any violent British reaction. During these years there was a certain basis for Salisbury's view that French and British imperialists operated by different methods in different sectors of West Africa.

France's conquest of Dahomey, however, opened the possibility of participating in the famous "steeplechase" toward the navigable waters of the Middle Niger. In 1894 a new phase of Anglo-French West African rivalry opened, in which the popular chauvinism excited in France by the colonial party came to be reciprocated in Britain. Government departments became more actively concerned to frustrate the French; the Earl of Rosebery was a more convinced imperialist than Salisbury, and in January 1894 Sir Percy Anderson, whose "grand design" had long been the blocking of French expansion, became assistant undersecretary in the Foreign Office.[53] Most important of all, Joseph Chamberlain, who arrived at the Colonial Office in 1895, was a convinced imperialist, capable of pursuing political prestige with an uncommercial irrationality fully equal to that of any French chauvinist. When in 1898 Lugard—regarded in France and elsewhere as the very prototype of irresponsible "hare-brained *militaire*"—suggested that if Britain restricted her claims in Nigeria to the line of 12 degrees "we

52. John E. Flint, *Sir George Goldie and the Making of Nigeria* (London, 1960), pp. 163–68. A.S. Kanya-Forstner, "French African Policy and the Anglo-French Agreement of 5 August 1890," *Historical Journal, 12* (1969), 628–50.

53. Wm. Roger Louis, "Sir Percy Anderson's Grand African Strategy," *English Historical Review, 81* (1966).

shall have all the trade and France will have the capitals of Sokoto &c to deal with,"

> J. C. scouted the idea vehemently and angrily, saying he would *never* be a party to giving up our country in order to get what is already ours. . . . we could always have more money behind us than the French and hence spend double and have a larger force till they gave in—the Birmingham "Screw Policy!"[54]

Historians lack techniques for measuring public opinion, and it is well to be cautious in evaluating its effects. As Brunschwig points out in his paper in this volume, both French and British diplomatists remained anxious to contain the repercussions of African rivalries and find compromise solutions for the sake of their broader national interests. But between 1894 and 1898 they often found themselves powerless to do so; and this it seems was primarily because popular chauvinism—exerting itself in Parliament, in the press, and through the pressure groups—strengthened the hands of imperially minded colleagues, reduced their freedom to maneuver in negotiation, and swung governmental decisions in favor of forward policies of prestige. In 1894 attempts to settle the Middle Niger question collapsed, along with the abortive discussions over the Nile; in 1895–96 there was just sufficient détente to permit the remission of this matter to commissioners; the dispute was settled in 1898, only after armed confrontations on the spot compelled both governments seriously to consider the implications of war.[55] In this final phase, Anglo-French relations in West Africa represented, more clearly than ever before, a conflict between broadly comparable forces—the expansive imperialism of nation-states with broad electorates. Although both might have defined their long-term purposes as the securing of future commercial advantages, more immediately each seemed suddenly more ready to use military forces to assert the intangible force of prestige, both toward the Africans and toward one another.

In the end there was a certain anticlimax. The Middle Niger dispute, like its predecessors, was settled by another piece of horse-trading, though this time clearly in Britain's favor. Truly comprehensive dealing—that rationalization of the imperial interests of the

54. *The Diaries of Lord Lugard*, ed. Margery Perham and Mary Bull, *4* (London, 1963), 334; March 13, 1898.

55. G. N. Sanderson, *England, Europe and the Upper Nile, 1882–1899* (Edinburgh, 1965); John D. Hargreaves, "*Entente Manquée:* Anglo-French Relations, 1895–1896," *Cambridge Historical Journal, 11* (1953), 65–92.

two countries which the more far-sighted statesmen had repeatedly desired—seemed further away than ever in the year of Fashoda. But once that crisis was over, the political climate was changed by the ominous east winds from Berlin; and in the Entente of 1904 the principle of comprehensive dealing on the grand scale was applied to North Africa. For West Africa it was too late for anything more than marginal readjustments in a map whose general features had long been becoming apparent.

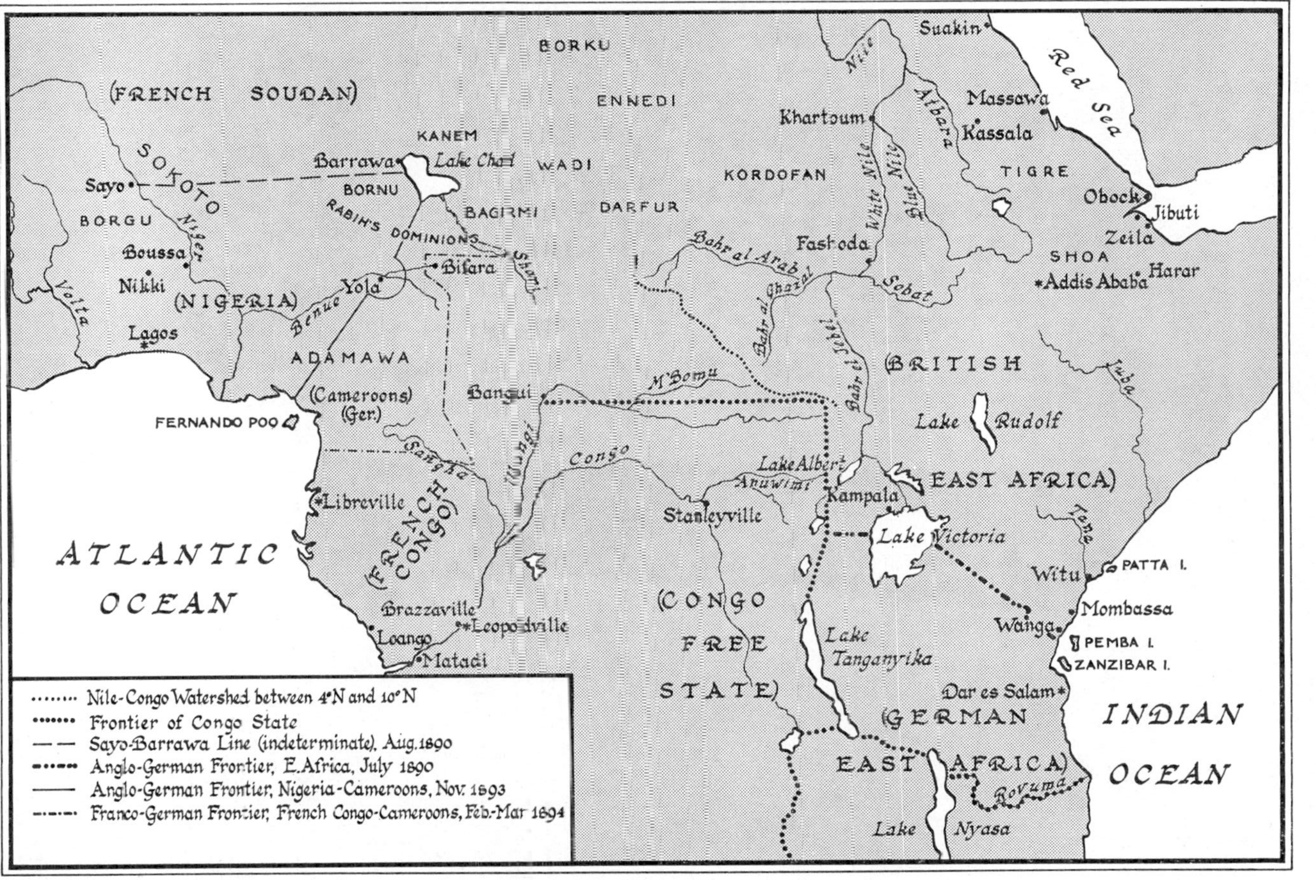

Boundaries and "spheres" of middle Africa in March 1894

⥼ 8. *The Origins and Significance of the Anglo-French Confrontation at Fashoda, 1898*

⥼ G. N. SANDERSON

"Jamais on ne prévit qu'on pût être amené à quitter le terrain diplomatique."[1] This rueful comment by the French publicist J. Darcy presents in its simplest form the essence of the Fashoda confrontation. Those responsible for the sending of Captain Jean-Baptiste Marchand there had calculated that his presence at Fashoda would provoke a conference of the Powers in which "la question de l'évacuation de l'Egypt découlerait tout naturellement de celle du Soudan égyptien."[2] When the time came, the other Powers showed no interest in a conference, and the British declined to negotiate at all until Marchand was under orders to retire from Fashoda. Even after he had left, they insisted by an implicit threat of war that the French flag should not fly "in any part of the water basin of the Nile."[3] The French, isolated diplomatically and lacking sufficient naval strength for the prosecution of war with England, had no rational alternative but to yield. Moreover, they had to stand impotently by while Britain transformed the status of the Egyptian Sudan, asserting her own de facto control with scant regard for treaty obligations or for international law.[4]

At this level, the crisis and its upshot can be analyzed in quite simple terms. It is also possible, at much the same level, to construct fairly simple models of the motives of the antagonists. The French could and did argue—though perhaps rather speciously—that the British occupation of Egypt tilted the Mediterranean balance against

1. J. Darcy, *France et Angleterre, Cent Années de Rivalité Coloniale* (Paris, 1903), p. 389.

2. *Documents diplomatiques français,* 1st series [*DDF* hereafter], *12,* No. 192, Note du capitaine Marchand, November 10, 1895.

3. [Public Record Office], Foreign Office [FO hereafter] 27/3454, Salisbury to Monson No. 40a, February 9, 1899.

4. In 1897 and 1898 it had been an important object of French policy to prevent the setting up of a "régime d'exception" in the Sudan. Cf. *DDF, 13,* No. 360; *14,* Nos. 11, 197.

France. Alexandre Ribot remarked in January 1892 that "l'occupation de cette partie de l'Empire ottoman par les troupes d'une puissance déjà établie à Gibraltar, à Malte et à Chypre . . . met en cause à la fois l'intégrité de la Turquie, l'équilibre de la Méditerranée et la liberté des communications de l'Europe avec l'extrême Orient." Even more galling to French opinion, however, was the loss of political influence in Egypt itself, which in its turn threatened a steady decline in what Ribot called "l'influence morale acquise à la France dans la vallée du Nil par une longue suite de services." [5] "La France est grande par le rayonnement des idées"; [6] it was inadmissible that this radiance should be obscured by the political success of a rival whose traditions of culture were at best provincial. France, "depuis la chute de l'empire romain . . . le foyer principal des grands événements qui ont ébranlé l'univers," [7] owed it to her own self-respect to find some means of resuming the task, bequeathed to her by the first Napoleon, of "enlightening" and "modernizing" Egypt.

The political ejection of France from Egypt was the more intolerable in that its circumstances had been humiliating. Fearful of weakening her position in Europe above all against Germany, France had shrunk from an operation which the British had carried out with spectacular ease and success. "Les Français pardonnent difficilement aux Britanniques de n'avoir pas partagé leur pusillanimité." [8] Indeed, so painful was the memory of Tell-el-Kebir that French publicists and even French diplomatists were often tempted to explain away the British victory by far-fetched legends in which "la cavalerie de Saint-Georges" played a major part.[9] In the 1890s, especially after the collapse of *Boulangisme,* the humiliation of 1871 was evidently irreparable within the foreseeable future. There was all the greater temptation to believe that the humiliation of 1882 might be wiped out by a bold stroke on the Upper Nile combined with a favorable diplomatic situation in Europe.

"Strategy" and "prestige" do not, indeed, exhaust the range of

5. *DDF, 9,* No. 180, Ribot to Paul Cambon, January 30, 1892.

6. Delcassé, Speech in the Chamber, November 30, 1891. He immediately added that material power was a great help in this process.

7. J. Cocheris, *Situation Internationale de l'Egypte et du Soudan* (Paris, 1903), p. 560.

8. J. Chastenet, *Histoire de la Troisième République: II, La République des Républicains* (Paris, 1954), p. 119.

9. For examples, cf. G. N. Sanderson, *England, Europe and the Upper Nile, 1882–1899* (Edinburgh, 1965), p. 115. The allusion is, of course, to golden sovereigns, with their reverse design of St. George and the Dragon.

French motives. From about the beginning of 1897 both the colonial and the foreign ministry (though probably not the foreign minister himself) were anxious to use the Marchand Mission as a means of acquiring territory in the southwestern Sudan. Nor can the personal motives of Captain Marchand be left out of account, in view of the major part he played in initiating the mission and defining its objectives. *Officiers soudanais* of Marchand's stamp were always ready to promote forward policies in West Africa in the well-founded belief that successful "faits de guerre" would accelerate their promotion.[10] Marchand's Upper Nile scheme was more subtle in that his original plan explicitly ruled out "faits de guerre." But he may well have considered that the successful "reopening of the Egyptian Question" could hardly have been less generously rewarded than success in some obscure West African campaign. However, it would probably be unjust to emphasize unduly Marchand's desire for personal advancement. No one resented more than Marchand the eclipse of French influence in Egypt; and he evidently felt that in Africa as a whole France was overshadowed by the "greedy and hypocritical" hereditary enemy, who sought at every turn to stifle the development of "la plus grande France."[11]

Simplifying still further, French activity in the Upper Nile may be presented as a specimen, as pure as one is likely to encounter in practice, of "the imperialism of prestige." When territory in the Sudan was sought, it was not for its intrinsic value, but as a tangible mark of success in competition with the British. As for the French claim to a "débouché sur le Nil," through the virtually impenetrable Bahr al-Ghazal *sudd,* for their nonexistent commerce on the Upper Ubangi, this was not so much a motive as a debating point, or a fig leaf to cover other motives less avowable within the conventions of diplomatic dialogue. As a genuine motive, only strategy can really compete with prestige; and although doubtless to France "Egypt meant more than prestige,"[12] it was in terms of prestige rather than of strategy that in the later 1890s French diplomatists discussed Egypt with the British, with other European Powers, and among themselves. Thus in February 1896 the French ambassador Alphonse de Courcel told Lord

10. A. S. Kanya-Forstner, *The Conquest of the Western Sudan: A Study in French Military Imperialism* (Cambridge, 1969), passim.

11. Cf. Marchand's published correspondence, esp. M.-A. Ménier, ed., Lettres du commandant Marchand à Guillaume Grandidier," *Revue d'Histoire des Colonies, 45* (1958), pp. 61–108.

12. A. S. Kanya-Forstner, review of *England, Europe and the Upper Nile* in *The Historical Journal,* 9, 2 (1966), 251–54.

Salisbury that in Egypt France sought no more than a psychological satisfaction by the removal of troops "under the British flag," and that she was prepared to accept an Anglo-French "condominium of influence" after the evacuation.[13] Doubtless the emphasis on this line of argument owed much to Courcel's diplomatic tact. But Gabriel Hanotaux, in attempting to rally Russian support in May 1896, takes the line that Egypt's abnormal situation was a standing affront, to France indeed but also to Europe as a whole; and that the practical French interest in Egypt was not so great as to justify the burden of isolated action by France. "Si elle [that is, Europe] veut me laisser tout le fardeau, je m'abstiens." [14] One might suspect that this threat of abstention was a tactical one, intended to spur Russia into action; but in an internal minute of January 1898 Hanotaux expresses much the same view, and declines to take the initiative "so long as Europe has not opened her eyes." [15]

It is indeed doubtful whether France had much to gain, strategically, from a mere ending to the British military occupation of Egypt. As the British director of Military Intelligence pointed out in October 1896, "We keep in Egypt only a sufficient garrison of British troops to maintain internal tranquillity. Its security depends to a great extent upon the maintenance of naval supremacy in the Red Sea [which] enables us to support Egypt from India." [16] So long as Britain retained her preponderance in these waters, the strategic situation of France would hardly be much improved. And this preponderance was based, in the Levant upon Malta, in the Red Sea upon Aden and Bombay; not upon Egypt, where Britain at that time maintained neither a naval base nor even a naval coaling station.

If, on the other hand, the British were to be expelled from Egypt as a result of a general collapse of their position in the Near East, France might profit strategically even less. The likely gainer would be Russia; and though France and Russia were allies, their competing interests in the Levant were, as French diplomatists recognized, "le grand défaut dans la cuirasse de l'alliance." Hanotaux in particular was always deeply anxious to avoid anything remotely approaching a

13. *DDF, 12,* No. 306, Courcel to Hanotaux, February 19, 1896. Cf. Salisbury Papers [SP hereafter], Egypt, Salisbury to Cromer, February 20, 1896.

14. *DDF, 12,* No. 386, Hanotaux to Montebello (St. Petersburg), May 13, 1896.

15. *DDF, 14,* No. 11, Minute by Hanotaux on Cogordan's dispatch of January 13, 1898.

16. D.M.I. Memorandum on Naval Policy, printed A. J. Marder, *The Anatomy of British Sea-Power* (New York, 1940), Appendix III, at p. 572.

Franco-Russian confrontation in this region; in his view, even slight friction here might be very dangerous to the Franco-Russe.[17] The friction following a collapse of British preponderance would hardly have been slight. Alphonse de Courcel showed his usual penetration when in January 1897 he admitted to Salisbury that the French had to avoid being "poussés par la considération puissante, mais accessoire, de nos idées sur l'Egypte à prendre parti au jour de la liquidation ottomane dans un sens peût-être contraire ou préjudiciable à nos intérêts généraux."[18] Strategically, the French gain from a British evacuation would have been marginal at best; at worst, it would have been non-existent or even negative. But the gain for France in prestige and *considération* would have been great even if the evacuation were amicably negotiated and qualified by safeguards. From an evacuation brought about by direct French pressure the prestige gains would have been enormous. They would in fact have reversed the position of the two countries in the Great Power "league."

For Britain too, therefore, a major question of prestige was involved in the Fashoda confrontation. To regard the Fashoda crisis (and still more the general "Nile Valley Crisis" of 1898–99) as "simply the climax to an old policy of imperial defence" is to ignore an important dimension. It was not the needs of a merely defensive strategy that prompted the aggressive speeches of Michael Hicks Beach, of Lord Rosebery, and even of Henry Campbell-Bannerman; nor did these needs inspire the bellicose jingoism of the British press. Although during the crisis Théophile Delcassé wisely refrained from attempting to "re-open the Egyptian Question," the presence of Marchand at Fashoda, and the initial reluctance of Paris to withdraw him, were rightly seen as a challenge to Britain's ability to assert her will in a region where she had for some time claimed a monopoly of influence. Ultimately, the quarrel was not about Fashoda, or about the fate of the Sudan, or even about the security of the Nile waters and of Egypt; it was about the relative status of Britain and France as Powers. When Paris offered as a bargain the withdrawal of Marchand in return for minor territorial concessions that could not have threatened the Nile waters, London was not placated; on the contrary, the pressure on France was increased. The British demand was that Marchand should be withdrawn at once and unconditionally, without even the promise of a negotiation to follow his withdrawal. The French

17. *DDF, 12,* No. 88, Courcel to Hanotaux, July 12, 1895; No. 410, same to same, June 20, 1896; No. 418, Hanotaux to Paul Cambon, July 1, 1896.

18. *DDF, 13,* No. 77, Courcel to Hanotaux, January 27, 1897.

challenge had, in the British view, not only to be defeated; it had to be defeated in the most unequivocal way possible. "This country," said Hicks Beach, "has put its foot down." [19]

Of course, this is not to deny the importance of strategy. Britain needed a presence in Egypt, not primarily to counterbalance France in the Mediterranean, but as a fall-back position from which to defend her influence in the Levant and her communications with India in the event of the seizure of the Straits and the establishment of a Mediterranean base by Russia. In the 1870s and 1880s the solution had been to forbid Constantinople to the Russians, ideally by getting there first if a threat developed, at all events by assisting the Turks to resist. From 1887, when French and Russian influence deterred the sultan from ratifying the Drummond Wolff Convention—thereby inspiring Salisbury to remark that "for all practical purposes, Turkey has become the 'Janitor' of Russia" [20]—this solution was gradually abandoned as impracticable. The contrary factors are well known: Turkey's growing weakness and growing unpopularity with British opinion; the sultan's distaste for "protection" by an infidel Power whose Muslim subjects outnumbered his own; the development of Russian naval strength; the Anglo-French tension, consequent on the occupation of Egypt, which even before the conclusion of the Franco-Russe forced the British to include in their calculations the French as well as the Russian fleet. Between 1887 and 1897, though not without hesitations and even retrograde movements, the policy of defense at Constantinople, or at least at the Dardanelles, gradually gave way to a policy of defense at Cairo. By 1889 at the latest, Salisbury had decided that Egypt must be retained at any rate as a second line of defense. This did not of course imply that the Straits were then abandoned: as late as November 1895 Salisbury was deterred from sending the fleet through the Dardanelles only by the adamant opposition of the first sea lord, backed by the cabinet. But it did imply that from 1889 the security of Egypt, and of the Nile waters without which that security could not exist, became "a separate and dominating factor" in Salisbury's diplomacy.[21] It was certainly no less dominant in the policy of Rosebery during the "Liberal Interlude" of 1892–95.

Egypt's "new frontiers of insecurity" were soon seen to be at least coterminous with the Nile basin, extending to the Ethiopian massif,

19. Public Speech by Hicks Beach, October 19, 1898.

20. Salisbury to Alfred Austin, July 3, 1887, printed Lady G. Cecil, *Life of Robert, Marquis of Salisbury* (4 vols. London, 1921, 1931, 1932), *4*, 48.

21. Cecil, ibid., pp. 139–40.

the northern half of the Great Lakes region, and the Nile-Congo divide. To the defense of these "frontiers" the British official mind was to devote itself with zeal and ingenuity for some ten years. The formulation of a defensive strategy to meet the changing flux of events was an immensely complicated process. It was not merely a matter of outwitting (or outbluffing) foreign rivals, or of taking calculated risks in Africa. Regional strategy had to be reconciled with the general pattern of British interests in Africa—not always an easy task when the Colonial Office, excluded from East Africa by a historical accident, defended the more tenaciously its West African preserves. African strategy, both general and regional, had constantly to be reviewed against the fluctuating diplomatic balance in Europe. The strategists had to make assumptions, which could often be no more than ill-informed guesses, about what was actually going on in the interior of the continent they were partitioning on paper. They had to take into account the views of the man on the spot—especially if he happened to be Evelyn Baring. On the one flank they were sniped at by "little Englanders" and Radicals; on the other by expansionist interests which were often "over-mighty collaborators," capable of creating not only faits accomplis in Africa but political difficulties at home. Moreover, with a Chamberlain at the Colonial Office, or a Wolseley as commander in chief, or a Goschen or a Hicks Beach at the Treasury, major strategy often had to accommodate itself to the exigencies of interdepartmental diplomacy.

The unraveling of this monstrous tangle is a task that has fascinated historians ever since the archives have been open. Doubtless the complex strategic puzzle was even more fascinating for those privileged to take part in its solution. But for them, of course, it was much more than a mere puzzle. As the movement from defense at the Straits to defense in Egypt became more clearly defined, the security of the Empire and the greatness of England seemed increasingly at stake on the Upper Nile. By 1896 the Admiralty had finally written off any prospect even of preventing Russia egress from the Dardanelles. Moreover, "in time Asia Minor will become Russian or at least entirely subject to Russian influence." When that day came, Britain could not hope to maintain her Mediterranean hegemony unless she had "3 fleets and 3 bases—Gibraltar, Malta and Alexandria." The conclusion was inescapable: Britain must "hold Egypt against all comers." [22] By

22. Marder, pp. 246–50, citing D.N.I. memoranda of November 12, 1895, and February 29, 1896; Appendix IV, pp. 578–80, D.N.I. memorandum on Naval Policy, October 28, 1896.

January 1897 Salisbury had finally accepted this conclusion, dismissing the defense of Constantinople as an impracticable and therefore obsolete policy. In October he spelled out the inevitable corollary: "to strengthen our position on the Nile" all the way to its source.[23]

Given the intrinsic fascination of the African strategic game, and the growing importance of winning it, it is small wonder that "the papers left by the policy-makers" [24] are almost invariably written in strategic terms. After all, most of these papers are simply the responses of the official mind to the problems posed by day-to-day changes in the strategic picture. To deal with these problems was occupation enough for ministers and senior officials. They rarely had the leisure, or the need, to expatiate on nonstrategic motives, especially when to do so would often have been merely to spell out those considerations which "went without saying." British public opinion, whose pressure might have prompted more explicit formulations, was (apart from a lively flurry early in 1895) comparatively quiescent until the spring of 1898. The doctrine of "the primacy of strategy" relies rather heavily on a quantitative method of evaluating the evidence; but given the kind of work the policy makers had to do, and the situation in which they did it, one authoritative statement of a nonstrategic motive can reasonably be equated with a large volume of material devoted to strategy. It therefore seems worth while to attempt an assessment of the fluctuating relative importance of strategic and nonstrategic motives; to examine the extent to which both the "official mind" and public opinion regarded the abandonment of even a materially worthless "sphere" as an inadmissible humiliation; and to assess the influence of individuals or groups who, with whatever motives, regarded territorial expansion as positively desirable.

The policy makers, it is admitted, rarely discussed the nonstrategic motives for their actions. Rarely; but not quite never. As early as 1887 Salisbury admitted the "prestige" difficulty of relinquishing Egypt, at a time when he was anything but convinced of its strategic value—indeed, when he still regarded the occupation, with its consequence of excessive dependence on Bismarck's goodwill, as a distasteful burden. "I heartily wish we had never gone into Egypt. Had we not done so, we could snap our fingers at all the world. But the national, or

23. *British Documents on the Origins of the War* [*BD* hereafter], 9 (i), 775–76, Salisbury to Rumbold (Vienna), January 20, 1897; SP, Salisbury to Currie (Constantinople), October 19, 1897.

24. Cf. Ronald E. Robinson and John Gallagher, with Alice Denny, *Africa and the Victorians* (London, 1961), p. 464.

acquisitional feeling has been roused; it has tasted the fleshpots and it will not let them go." [25] This "feeling" was to grow even stronger, especially in Salisbury's own party, during the next dozen years. Quite apart from the strategic importance of Egypt, a large and increasing section of opinion would have heartily endorsed Queen Victoria's robust and simple axiom: "Giving up what one has is always a bad thing." [26]

Salisbury himself, an archstrategist who despised and distrusted "feelings" as a basis for policy, normally regarded acquisition on the Upper Nile as an unwelcome last resort when other expedients proved unworkable. In 1890 he would, it appears, have originally been content simply to exclude Germany from the Upper Nile, without claiming for Britain anything so positive as a "sphere." [27] But once the sphere had been claimed and had been recognized by Germany, Italy, and the Congo State, its diplomatic defense against France became an important matter of prestige. If defensive strategy had been crucial for the policy makers, they could in October 1894 have accepted the proposal of mutual nonintervention in the sphere that Gabriel Hanotaux then offered to Edmund Phipps, the British negotiator at Paris. As recently as June 1894 the foreign secretary, Lord Kimberley, had told the Austrian ambassador that Britain's only serious interest in the Upper Nile was "to prevent any foreign Power from establishing itself there and so being in a position to threaten Egypt" through the Nile waters.[28] Yet Rosebery rejected Hanotaux' proposal. The loss of prestige implied in a de facto renunciation of an internationally recognized sphere was unacceptable, especially after the recent humiliating collapse of the Anglo-Congolese Agreement of April–May 1894 under French and German pressure.

Rosebery was a convinced ideological imperialist who believed that not only Britain's interest, but her "racial" duty, demanded the maximum possible program of overseas expansion.[29] Even he, however, showed some interest in the self-denying proposal and was perhaps

25. Salisbury to Wolff, February 23, 1887, printed in Cecil, *4*, 41–42. Cf. Salisbury to Malet, February 23, 1887, printed ibid., pp. 40–41: "Our position in Egypt is one that public opinion here will not allow us to abandon altogether, but it is a disastrous inheritance."

26. *Letters of Queen Victoria*, 3rd series, *1*, 615, the Queen to Salisbury, June 12, 1890.

27. Sanderson, *Upper Nile*, pp. 63–64, 395.

28. Deym to Kálnoky, 28 June 1894, cited M. P. Hornik, *Der Kampf der Grossmächte um den Oberlauf des Nil* (Vienna, n.d.), pp. 118–19.

29. Cf. his speech to the Colonial Institute in March 1893.

secretly tempted by it. Doubtless even to him the southern Sudan seemed a rather unpromising field for imperial enterprise. But Sir Percy Anderson, the head of the African Department at the Foreign Office, was made of sterner stuff. Invoking "the interest of the Empire," he would waive formal recognition of the sphere by France only if (1) the French would agree not to enter it, and (2) Britain were enabled to administer the whole of the sphere—if not directly, at least indirectly through Egypt. At the same time he was anxious not to be tied down "to any definite admission as to how far the claims of Egypt may subsequently be admitted." Anderson of course recognized the strategic value of the Upper Nile; but his minutes do not touch on this. Instead, they dwell not merely on the prestige value of maintaining the sphere but on territorial possession and expansion as in themselves desirable goals.[30] It was of course Anderson's official business to press for the maximum British claims almost irrespective of the consequences; and there are some signs that Rosebery's own views were, when it came to the point, slightly less extreme. All the same, Anderson was allowed to determine British policy. Phipps, who persistently tried to convince the Foreign Office that territorial self-denial would be a reasonable price to pay for the major strategic achievement of keeping France out of the Nile valley, was punished for this lukewarmness by a posting to Buenos Aires.

For all his importance as a policy maker in 1894, Anderson's appetite for acquisitions was hardly representative at that time. Even in the flurry of public excitement and alarm that preceded (and elicited) the Grey Declaration of March 1895, there is little sign of any acquisitive urge. The concern of press and Commons was impeccably and well-nigh exclusively strategic—to protect the Nile waters from malicious interference by the French. There was, however, for the first time a serious demand for a British military presence on the Upper Nile: gunboats to patrol "as far as Lado and even Fashoda"; "a small force to place the British flag at the junction of the Bahr el Ghazal and the Bahr el Jebel."[31] Public opinion was now far more alert than it had been in the summer of 1894, when it had greeted with surprising stolidity both the conclusion and the destruction of the Anglo-

30. Sanderson, pp. 193–203, affords a fully documented analysis of Anderson's attitudes and policy. Cf. especially FO 27/3209, memoranda by Anderson, October 9 and 16, 1894; FO 27/3187, minute by Anderson, October 10; FO 27/3188, minute by Anderson, October 11, 1894.

31. Speeches in the Commons by Sir E. Ashmead-Bartlett and Major Darwin, March 28, 1895.

Congolese Agreement. Moreover, the Grey Declaration, together with the Opposition statements that preceded and followed it, created the impression, even in circles which were by no means "imperialist," that Britain had "by right" a special position on the Upper Nile. Courcel warned Hanotaux of the consequences: the British public, "une fois son amour-propre national engagé . . . ne reculera plus d'une semelle dans la défense de ce qu'il croit être son droit acquis." [32]

The Upper Nile had for the time being ceased to be a diplomatists' preserve and had become a region where public opinion believed that British prestige was at stake. Yet active interest did not survive the passing away of the ephemeral scare that had provoked the Grey Declaration. The months flowed by, nothing spectacular happened on the Upper Nile, and the demand for action died away. Nor was there, in 1895 and 1896, any discernible appetite for territorial acquisition in the northern Sudan. Whatever the motives for the "Anglo-Egyptian" advance in March 1896, enthusiasm for reconquest, whether official or popular, was certainly not one of them. The prevailing mood, both in the cabinet and (so far as one can judge) among the public, was rather one of misgiving. The ghosts of Hicks and Gordon still walked: Chamberlain warned Salisbury that "the Government would be deserted by its own followers" if British troops had to be sent to the rescue of the Egyptians.[33] By the spring of 1898, with British troops at last actively engaged and the press writing up the battle of the Atbara as a "British victory," public enthusiasm was rapidly mounting. But it was of course now concentrated on the *northern* Sudan; the "British sphere" in the southern Sudan attracted little attention until the Fashoda confrontation,

The policy makers were therefore left very largely to their own devices in 1896 and 1897. With Anderson now dead, and Chamberlain's acquisitive itch pretty effectively confined to western and southern Africa, policy making was for the most part a dialogue between Lord Cromer and Salisbury. Cromer had never been happy about the Sudan campaign, and he had no serious plans for using it to increase British influence even in the northern Sudan. In October 1897, when Kitchener was held up at Berber, he rejected a War Office proposal that the advance to Khartoum should be resumed with the aid of British troops. He did so on the grounds that "no sufficiently important British interest is involved to justify the loss of life and money."

32. *DDF, 11,* No. 429, Courcel to Hanotaux, April 2, 1895.

33. Chamberlain to Salisbury, March 11, 1896, cited J. L. Garvin, *Life of Joseph Chamberlain,* 3 (London, 1932), 169–70

As for the southern Sudan, his major objective was to avoid being saddled with these "large tracts of useless territory which it would be difficult and costly to administer properly."[34] By January 1898 he had grudgingly admitted that "sooner or later we shall have to put up an Egyptian [sic] flag at Fashoda"; but he continued to insist that operations south of Khartoum should be confined to the "absolutely necessary" minimum.[35]

Salisbury could not treat the southern Sudan so cavalierly; but throughout 1896 and 1897 his interest in it remained purely strategic. True, the Macdonald Mission to the southern Sudan, launched by Salisbury in June 1897, looks at first sight like a typical land-grabbing expedition. In fact, it was a hastily improvised strategic move, designed to forestall a junction between Marchand and the French expeditions from Ethiopia. Deserted for once by his usual sceptical coolness, Salisbury had mistakenly believed this junction to be imminent.[36] But once he had recovered from this scare, he showed no enthusiasm for the acquisition of territory in the southern Sudan. In October 1897 he was content to describe the "British sphere," vaguely and negatively, as "whatever, in the valley between Lado and Khartoum, is not Egyptian."[37] A day or so later Hicks Beach reminded him of the difficulties and expense likely to be involved in "the conquest and administration of all the territory that used to be dependent on the Khedive in Ismail's time."[38] Salisbury needed no reminding. He never seems to have doubted that the southern Sudan, as territory, was worthless. At the very height of the Fashoda crisis he dismissed as "wretched stuff" a glowing report on the alleged wealth of the Bahr al-Ghazal.[39]

Nor did Salisbury in 1897 contemplate any change in the status of the northern Sudan. In November 1897 Hicks Beach could still take it for granted that this region was not expected to become British territory. He was indeed frankly puzzled about its future: "But

34. SP, Cabinet Memoranda, Cromer to Salisbury, October 22, and November 5, 1897.

35. Cromer to Salisbury, January 28, 1898, cited by the Marquess of Zetland, *Lord Cromer* (London, 1932), pp. 260–61; SP Cabinet Memoranda, Cromer to Salisbury, June 15, 1898.

36. For the origins of the Macdonald Mission, see Sanderson, *Upper Nile,* pp. 254–58; Robinson and Gallagher, *Africa and the Victorians,* pp. 361–63.

37. SP, Egypt, Salisbury to Cromer, October 29, 1897.

38. SP, Hicks Beach, Hicks Beach to Salisbury, November 1, 1897, cited Robinson and Gallagher, pp. 363–64.

39. FO 78/5051, minute on a report by Gleichen, October 20, 1898.

suppose [Khartoum] taken . . . what then? Can we stop [i.e., remain] there? I think not."[40] In June 1898 Salisbury solved this puzzle by the abandonment of the separate British sphere and the assertion of a joint Anglo-Egyptian right of conquest over "the whole of the Mahdi state from Halfa to Wadelai."[41] This revolutionary change of policy was indeed originally prompted, in part at least, by strategic motives. It enabled Salisbury to "shake free of a good deal of diplomatic hamper." There was a threat of joint Franco-Ottoman diplomatic intervention; this would fall to the ground if it could be established that the Sudan was no longer part of the Ottoman dominions but an independent and sovereign "Mahdi state." Again, Salisbury evidently believed, quite erroneously, that the conquest of a capital city carried with it a valid title to the whole of the territory of which it was capital; and therefore thought that his right-of-conquest thesis would be useful against the French. In fact, if the former Egyptian right were extinguished—a necessary corollary of the right-of-conquest argument—Marchand's right of conquest at Fashoda was as good as Kitchener's at Omdurman; and Salisbury tacitly admitted this when he abandoned his original argument during his discussions with Courcel.[42]

The right-of-conquest argument did not in fact serve the more specialized strategic purposes for which it had originally been devised. The threatened Ottoman intervention never materialized, and as against France the effect of the argument was to force Salisbury to take on "diplomatic hamper" rather than to enable him to shake free of it. It did, however, enable Salisbury to shake free of the historic rights of Egypt in the Sudan, and so give him a legal tabula rasa on which to construct his own settlement. It also extinguished Ottoman rights and so deprived the Powers, as guarantors of the Ottoman Empire, of any right to be consulted in that settlement. Egypt, stripped of her historic rights in the Sudan, was left alone in the arena with Britain. The right-of-conquest thesis not only contained the germ of the Condominium Agreement, with its de facto British annexation of the Sudan; it also shook free of the "diplomatic hamper" that might have impeded this consummation. Of course the mere dumping of the "diplomatic hamper" was not in itself enough. The French, and the

40. Hicks Beach to Salisbury, November 1, 1897, cited Robinson and Gallagher, pp. 363–64.

41. FO 78/5050, Salisbury to Cromer tel. No. 47, June 3, 1898. Cf. SP, Private Secretary, Salisbury to the Law Officers of the Crown, June 30, 1898.

42. Cf. Robinson and Gallagher, pp. 367–68; Sanderson, *Upper Nile*, pp. 266–68, 344–47.

Powers, were warned off the Sudan settlement by the British naval mobilization, which reached its peak in the second half of January 1899 and was countermanded only when it became clear that nobody was prepared to challenge the Condominium Agreement.[43]

The right-of-conquest thesis may indeed have been designed from the outset with a view to acquisition, as well as to defensive strategy. A week or two before Salisbury revealed this policy to Cromer, he had already applied a similar theory, but in an even more far-reaching form, not only to the Sudan but to Egypt itself. Salisbury asserted that in 1882 the khedive Tawfīq had been deprived of his sovereign rights over Egypt by 'Urābī Pasha. These rights had then been "wrested from ['Urābī] by British victory at Tell-el-Kebir, and England has never parted with the rights over Egypt which she won at that battle. H. M. Government *acquired then by conquest* complete control over the actions of the Khedivial Government." The khedive was also reminded that "it still remains for H. M. Government to determine how far the Soudan . . . shall be re-united to the Khedivial Government, and under what conditions and limitations"—indeed, "whether we should give back [sic] . . . the reconquered Soudan at all."[44]

Certainly by September 1898, probably as early as May and June, defensive strategy as a motive for policy was playing second fiddle to a positive acquisitiveness of a kind that Salisbury had never previously contemplated. What prompted this radical change? At all events, not a belief that the territory was intrinsically valuable. It has, however, been suggested that Salisbury's acquisitiveness was itself strategic, in that its main object was "to prevent the Powers from exercising in the Sudan the privileges they still enjoyed in Egypt."[45] This was of course a very useful gain; but there could be only two possible motives for making it a determinant of policy. One was to smooth the path of the future administrators of the Sudan. On this it is perhaps sufficient to say that Salisbury was not the man to subordinate major questions of policy to administrative convenience. The second possible motive is that the privileges of the Powers would have been a serious *political* danger in the Sudan. But even in Egypt itself these privileges, though a perennial irritant to Cromer, were no

43. As Cromer put it, "No one was prepared to bell the cat." The Earl of Cromer, *Modern Egypt* (2 vols. London, 1911), 2, 118. Cf., for full analysis, Sanderson, pp. 266–68, 364–69.

44. FO 141/336, Salisbury to Cromer, tels. No. 41 and 43, of May 15 and 25, 1898.

45. Kanya-Forstner, review in *Historical Journal*, 9, 251–54.

longer an effective political weapon. Indeed, in March 1897 Cromer had experienced some difficulty in dissuading Salisbury from agreeing to an increase of French influence on the *Caisse de la Dette Publique:* Salisbury had wished in this way "to enable Hanotaux to boast in the Chamber that his diplomacy has extorted a satisfaction from the English Government." [46]

By the summer of 1898 the time for such delicate gestures had long gone by. Salisbury now needed a political success which should not merely be sound, but spectacular. In the Sudan, this implied both territorial acquisition and, at Fashoda, complete intransigence toward the French. The demand for acquisition, or at least unequivocal British control, of the Sudan was well-nigh universal. Intransigence at Fashoda was dictated not merely by strategic or even acquisitive motives, but by grave misgivings about the recent course of British foreign policy and about Salisbury's capacity to direct it. Particularly since the rather feeble British reaction to the Russian occupation of Port Arthur in March 1898, the public had been increasingly uneasy about Salisbury's "graceful concessions." In July, *Punch* had published a cruel cartoon in which, above the title "The Open Door," Chamberlain showed Salisbury an open door labeled "Exit from Office." Rumor had it that Salisbury had become a senile invalid and had quite lost his grip on affairs; even his own colleagues are said to have been "alarmed lest some untoward event should occur." [47] In the Fashoda crisis and the Sudan settlement, Salisbury's personal position was at stake.

After the victories of the Atbara and Omdurman, which had been written up by the press as almost entirely British operations, large sections of opinion would not have tolerated any settlement that did not provide for direct control of territories apparently conquered by British blood and treasure. Opinion in Salisbury's own party went further. It fully expected that the reconquest of the Sudan would be crowned by the proclamation of a protectorate over Egypt, perhaps with the khedive "kept on for some years as a sort of Indian maharajah." As George Wyndham put it, "we don't care whether the Nile is called English or Egyptian, or what it is called, but we mean to have

46. FO 78/4895, Salisbury to Cromer, tels. No. 27 and 30, of March 1 and 4, 1897.

47. Sanderson, pp. 324, 396, 400. Zara Steiner, "The Last Years of the Old Foreign Office," *Historical Journal,* 6, 1 (1963), pp. 59–60. Anon., "The Failure of our Foreign Policy," *Contemporary Review,* April 1898. "Diplomaticus," "Fashoda and Lord Salisbury's Vindication," *Fortnightly Review,* December 1898.

it."[48] Moreover, even Radicals and humanitarians who normally shrank from acquisition shrank still more from the alternative of restoring the conquered territory to Egypt, whose record as ruler of the Sudan was widely believed to have been a chapter in the history of crime.[49] The Churches and missionary interests would have bitterly opposed the restoration of the Sudan to a Muslim government. The Church Missionary Society, which was particularly active, had managed to convince itself that the Muslim northern Sudan offered a favorable field for evangelism, and was already planning its campaign there.[50] To some, control of the Sudan was the prize of victory; to others, a humanitarian or religious obligation.

The British, not untypically, combined expansionist euphoria with an austere sense of duty. To a people in this mood, the mere presence of Marchand at Fashoda seemed an intolerable affront. The southern Sudan, which had for long attracted very little attention, now became one of the valuable "fruits of victory," which the French were attempting, by "covert and deceitful operations," to filch from under the noses of the deserving but unwily British.[51] But there was more to the situation than a mere squabble about territory. There was an implicit challenge to Britain (or so it seemed) to enforce her will if she dared: "Mr. Punch" implied as much when he maliciously enquired "what 'graceful concession' the Government will make to MARCHAND to induce him to evacuate Fashoda."[52]

British opinion was in a mood to respond vigorously to this challenge. Excited by the Khartoum campaign, it also recalled with resentment earlier French "pin-pricks" in West Africa, which had culminated in February 1898 with the news of a French "invasion" of Sokoto.[53] Kitchener further inflamed opinion by his tendentious reporting of the Fashoda situation; and as he denied to Marchand any

48. W. S. Blunt, *My Diaries* (London, 1919, reprint, 1932), pp. 299–300. For the expectation of a protectorate over Egypt, cf. the reaction of Salisbury's audience to his speech at the Lord Mayor's Banquet on November 9, 1898.

49. Sanderson, p. 399. Even Blunt abandoned as hopeless any attack upon the Condominium Agreement (*My Diaries*, pp. 313, 317, 319–25).

50. L. M. Sanderson, "Education in the Southern Sudan, 1898–1948" (unpublished Ph.D. dissertation, London, 1966), p. 46.

51. W. S. Churchill, *The River War* (London, 1899; references are to the reprint of 1951), pp. 318–20. Churchill doubtless reflects much contemporary opinion.

52. *Punch,* October 1, 1898.

53. For the origins of this "invasion" see Archives du Ministère de la France d'Outre-Mer [Outre-Mer hereafter], Afrique III Missions, 25, Mission Cazemajou. It caused a genuine, if minor and transient, war scare toward the end of

facilities for communication through Omdurman and Cairo, he made sure that the Kitchener version should have a very long start. According to Kitchener, the Marchand Mission consisted of a band of destitute and half-starved explorers marooned in darkest Africa, and saved from certain annihilation at the hands of the Dervishes only by his own timely victory at Omdurman.[54] To the French sins of aggression and deceit was thus added the even blacker sin of ingratitude. But perhaps the most intolerable provocation was the not ill-founded belief that Marchand was counting upon Ethiopian support. Here the polemic developed frankly racialistic overtones; some commentators urged that such a situation would in itself fully justify a war of retaliation. For Sir Edward Grey, it was "devilry." Campbell-Bannerman was no jingo; but, as he pointed out, "even the quietest amongst us were filled with hot indignation" at the prospect of Menelik's "warlike hordes" being called in, by fellow Europeans, to frustrate Kitchener's "civilising mission." [55] Courcel had no illusions about the vehemence of British feeling on this matter. On October 29 he told Delcassé, as an obvious truth and without stopping to argue the point, that if there were a junction between Marchand and the Ethiopians "c'est naturellement la guerre avec l'Angleterre." [56]

Emotional responses aside, there remained the cold political fact that France, so long as she maintained Marchand at Fashoda, was presenting a challenge to which anything but the most vigorous response would injure Britain's standing as a Power. It was widely felt, both inside and outside the Foreign Office, that this standing had already been considerably depreciated since the beginning of 1898; [57] and that unless Britain now enforced her will to the uttermost, she would suffer a permanent and grievous loss of status. This "now-or-never" attitude was indeed not unjustified. Had Britain followed a less intransigent policy in the circumstances of October 1898, there would certainly have been a temptation, not only in Paris but also in

February 1898. Cf. G. N. Sanderson, "Anglo-French Competition for the Control of the Upper Basin of the Nile" (unpublished Ph.D. dissertation, London, 1959), pp. 934–35, and references there cited.

54. FO 141/336, Kitchener to Rodd, tel., September 24, 1898. FO 141/333, Kitchener to Rodd, dispatch, September 21, 1898. Sanderson, *Upper Nile,* pp. 335–39.

55. Robinson and Gallagher (citing Grey), p. 337; Garvin, 3, 233–34 (citing Campbell-Bannerman). Cf. for a still more violent reaction, Anon., "France, Russia and the Nile," *Contemporary Review* (December 1898).

56. *DDF, 14,* No. 465, Courcel to Delcassé, October 29, 1898.

57. Sanderson, *Upper Nile,* pp. 324, 396.

St. Petersburg and Berlin, to write her off as a Power who would never risk a war, however great the provocation.

It was the misfortune of France that an expedition whose major objective was still to seek a diplomatic solution to the problems of the Nile valley should have precipitated the crisis at the very moment when British opinion was both rampantly acquisitive and more than usually sensitive to Britain's status as a Power. It was doubly unfortunate that the circumstances of Marchand's presence at Fashoda, and Kitchener's reporting of them, should have enabled British opinion to take a high moral line about a "bogus" occupation established by "deceit" and maintained after September 19 only thanks to the Sirdar's forbearance. Marchand's local position, for what it was worth, would have been much stronger had he been confronted, not by Kitchener disposing of overwhelming forces along a comparatively easy line of communication, but by an isolated expedition similar to his own—the Macdonald Mission, or the mythical "Colvile Mission" whose supposed activities caused so much uneasiness to Paris in 1894–96.[58]

Here again, Marchand and the French were simply unlucky. Until January 1898, when Kitchener reluctantly called for British reinforcements, no one in London or Cairo had ever thought it possible that the advance from the north would play any part in the denouement of the Upper Nile question.[59] It was indeed for precisely this reason that Salisbury was pushing ahead as fast as he could (though not nearly fast enough) with the Mombasa railway. In January 1898 British troops were indeed sent to the front, but not in order to hasten Kitchener's advance toward the southern Sudan. This policy had been suggested by General Wolseley in October 1897; but Salisbury, Cromer, and Lansdowne had unanimously rejected it. The troops were dispatched to enable Kitchener to resist a threatened Mahdist advance upon his very precarious position at Berber. The khalifa soon called off this operation; but without the reinforcements this scare had gained for Kitchener, it is very unlikely that he would have resumed his own advance in time to catch the 1898 Nile flood—the only season when his river transports and gunboats were able to pass the Sabaloka cataract immediately north of Khartoum. Had Kitchener missed the

58. Colvile was in fact invalided home at the end of December 1894, and did not return to East Africa; but as late as August 1896 Marchand was still worrying about the "Mission Coolville."

59. At least, hardly ever. In November 1896 Salisbury did fleetingly glance at this possibility; SP, Egypt, Salisbury to Cromer November 16 and 27, 1896. This hope was based on an overoptimistic appreciation by Kitchener and Cromer, and was soon abandoned.

1898 flood, the fall of Omdurman and presumably the Fashoda confrontation would have been delayed by a full year—a delay that could hardly have been other than favorable to the French.[60]

However much one may elaborate and qualify the oversimple model of the Fashoda confrontation as merely the climax to an old policy of imperial defense, no model can account for the devious ways in which policy works itself out. The course of events, too, has an irony of its own, which may devalue apparently major decisions and greatly enhance the importance of minor ones; or, as in January 1898, a decision may turn out to be critical for reasons quite other than those that prompted it at the time. No analysis of the Fashoda crisis can ignore the fortuitous elements, which as it happened worked mainly to the disadvantage of the French.

However, all fortuitous factors aside, any French advance to the Upper Nile in the later 1890s was certain to provoke a severe, even a dangerous crisis—a crisis in which national prestige as well as strategic defense would be at stake. As early as December 1894, d'Estournelles de Constant, a French diplomatist at London, observing the increasing "engagement" of even moderate British opinion in the Upper Nile question, had predicted the outcome with almost uncanny foresight.

> Car, personne ne s'y trompe, cette question du Soudan fixe l'attention générale: la solution qu'elle recevra ne sera pas seulement importante en elle-même, elle sera significative, décisive peut-être: elle donnera la juste mesure de la puissance britannique. C'est la grandeur même de l'Angleterre peut-être qui se trouve en jeu, c'est une question par conséquent de vie ou de mort.

D'Estournelles therefore urged that "il est temps maintenant de nous arrêter, de borner notre champ d'action de peur d'en faire à la longue, bientôt peut-être, un champ de bataille." [61]

Hanotaux, if his minutes be any guide, did not disagree with d'Estournelles' evaluation. But these views had little detectable in-

60. Salisbury believed that any forward move in the north would at once *provoke* a French advance to the Upper Nile, which he would be unable to challenge until the railway was finished (Sanderson, *Upper Nile,* pp. 240, 246). For the latter part of this paragraph, cf. ibid., pp. 264–65, 396; G. N. Sanderson, "Contributions from African Sources to the History of the European Competition in the Upper Valley of the Nile," *Journal of African History, 3,* 1 (1962), pp. 69–90.

61. *DDF, 11,* No. 303, d'Estournelles de Constant to Hanotaux, December 3, 1894.

fluence on the development of French policy. They might have had more effect had other French diplomatists shared d'Estournelles' clarity of insight and frankness of expression. In fact, most French diplomatic writing on this issue is marked by what seems in retrospect almost a willful refusal to see the situation as it was. But if French diplomatists failed to warn the Quai d'Orsay, British politicians cannot be reproached with that omission. The Grey Declaration of March 1895, though not intended at the time as the "bellicose manifesto" that later commentators saw in it,[62] was nevertheless a serious warning. It went unheeded. So did the more forthright though less publicized warning, transmitted by Salisbury in December 1897, which expressly denied that "any other European Power than Great Britain has any claim to occupy any part of the valley of the Nile." [63]

In April 1896 Georges Cogordan at Cairo had suggested that a "prise de possession" in the Bahr al-Ghazal was the best method of "re-opening the Egyptian Question." He rather airily dismissed the possible consequences with the reflection that when the British "asked for explanations," "notre réponse serait facile, car sans doute il nous coûterait peu . . . d'évacuer ces lointaines provinces, du jour où les troupes anglaises quitteraient le Delta." [64] Cogordan evidently did not take seriously the possibility that the British might "ask for explanations" at the pistol's point: witness his remark in March 1897 that Marchand's expedition, if it reached Fashoda, "formeraient une barrière que l'Angleterre ne pourrait franchir qu'au prix *d'une guerre qui n'est guère à craindre* ou de concessions qu'il nous appartiendrait d'apprécier." [65] Cogordan, from his specialized and rather peripheral viewpoint, can perhaps be excused for reasoning along these lines. It is, however, astonishing that as late as July 18, 1898, when the tide of British truculence was already strongly rising, the *Direction politique* at the Quai d'Orsay could complacently remark that, Marchand having reached Fashoda, "nous pourrons attendre, munis d'un excellent gage, l'heure des pourparlers" [66]

How did this enormous miscalculation come to be made? One of the objects of foreign policy in the late nineteenth century was to reduce all conflicts except those of life and death to the status of a *game* of

62. For argument on this controversial point, Sanderson, *Upper Nile,* pp. 213–17.

63. FO 27/3336, Salisbury to Monson, No. 406, December 9, 1897.

64. *DDF, 12,* No. 373, Cogordan to Léon Bourgeois, April 16, 1896.

65. *DDF, 13,* No. 154, Cogordan to Hanotaux, March 17, 1897.

66. *DDF, 14,* No. 258, Note du Département, July 18, 1898.

power politics, a game in which the moves and countermoves were purely diplomatic. Of course, force was there as the *ultima ratio*—without it the game would have been meaningless—but the actual use of force within the game of minor conflicts would almost always have been self-defeating and could therefore be safely ruled out. Nowhere was the "game" status of international relations better developed than in African questions: though here the game had an additional and fascinating, if potentially dangerous, dimension: it could, in unpartitioned regions, be played on the territorial as well as on the diplomatic chessboard. The fundamental mistake of the French was their failure to take seriously d'Estournelles' warning that the question of the Upper Nile could in certain circumstances become for England "une question . . . de vie ou de mort," to which the rules of the diplomatic-territorial African "game" would necessarily cease to apply.

Yet this is not the whole of the answer. Between January and September 1898, it became increasingly clear, both from the general trend of British policy and from the harder line adopted by London in West Africa down to the settlement of June,[67] that a confrontation on the Upper Nile would be taken very seriously in England. Yet the Quai d'Orsay remained unperturbed. The reflexions of Cogordan, when in November 1898 he ruefully surveyed the total collapse of French policy in the Nile valley, suggest that French diplomatists believed that they had in any case a reliable guarantee against anything more than the mere *threat* of force:

> Les hommes intelligents n'avaient jamais pensé que nous irions jusqu'à faire la guerre pour le Nil, quand nous ne la faisons pas pour le Rhin; mais presque tous admettaient comme une vérité démontrée, que jamais l'Angleterre n'ouvrirait les hostilités; que ses vaisseaux n'étaient destinés qu'à effrayer, que ses intérêts commerciaux l'empêcheraient toujours de s'exposer à voir ses communications avec le continent interrompues par l'état de guerre.[68]

In a "game" like that which the French believed themselves to be playing, close and unified central control was indispensable. In the absence of such control it was virtually certain that somebody, sometime, would make a move so dangerous that it might disrupt the game itself. It would also be almost impossible to withdraw or modify moves which, apparently legitimate enough when they were originally made, had become dangerously disruptive under altered circumstances. But

67. Cf. Sanderson, *Upper Nile*, pp. 320–22.
68. *DDF, 14,* No. 531, Cogordan to Delcassé, November 21, 1898.

the Marchand Mission, and indeed the French Nile project as a whole, was at best only intermittently and imperfectly under central control. The development of policy was a process of remarkable complexity, involving many different pressures and initiatives which neither ministers nor permanent officials could fully control and coordinate. Major decisions tended to emerge from the interplay of departmental and even personal substrategies; and those decisions were rarely, if ever, evaluated against an estimate of French resources or against the prospects offered by the European and African situations.

Those whose business it was to do this, and to restrain the excessive zeal of irresponsible "experts" with narrowly departmental interests, simply failed in their task. Armand Nisard, the *Directeur politique* at the Quai d'Orsay, who might be expected to have interested himself in the coordination of policy, took no action that can be detected in the published French documents. He seems to have regarded Africa as essentially a specialists' field, and was in any case engrossed with European affairs, especially with Franco-Russian relations.[69] Marcellin Berthelot, the distinguished chemist who as foreign minister gave official approval to the Marchand Mission in its original form, was almost certainly precluded by ignorance and inexperience from fully understanding what he was about. Hanotaux, who well understood the dangerous implications of the project, found himself faced by a fait accompli which he was unable or unwilling to undo. Instead, he attempted to modify it by removing some of its more dangerous elements. Early in 1897, however, the Colonial Ministry was able to override or evade the safeguards Hanotaux had introduced, and thereafter the foreign minister had little influence over French activity on the Upper Nile.

Failure of control did not end here. From about the beginning of 1898 the Colonial Ministry itself began to lose its grip on both its official and its semiofficial agents on the Upper Nile and in Ethiopia. This was in part due to practical difficulties of communication; but the *Colonies* was all too ready to condone rather than to rebuke even the more harebrained initiatives of its local agents, and to patronize shady adventurers over whom it had virtually no control at all. When the crisis broke in September 1898 the situation was little short of anarchic; perhaps not surprisingly, the main preoccupation of the

69. At the turn of 1895–96 these relations were particularly difficult, especially in the Near East. In December 1898 Monson described Nisard as "timid and fearful of responsibility . . . also exceedingly deaf." FO 27/3398, Monson to Salisbury, No. 703, December 23, 1898.

Colonial Ministry was now to transfer all responsibility back to the Quai d'Orsay. On September 15, 1898, the colonial minister pointed out to Delcassé that in 1895 "mon Département, en se plaçant au point de vue purement colonial, aurait été 'porté à restreindre au strict nécessaire' notre occupation du Haut-Oubangui," and demurely reminded him that "l'action de la France dans le Soudan égyptien, vous ne l'ignorez pas, n'a été qu'une des manifestations de notre politique générale."[70] Even for an official statement, this was a remarkable travesty of the truth.

Although the Marchand Mission was not inaugurated until the summer of 1895, the idea of sending a mission to the Upper Nile had been in the air for many years. In 1893 and again in 1894 unsuccessful attempts had been made actually to launch a mission. This long "prehistory" of the Marchand Mission helps to explain why the project of an aggressive junior officer was adopted by the Pavillon de Flore apparently without any serious examination of its diplomatic assumptions and implications; it also helps to explain why Hanotaux found it so difficult to keep the whole affair under control. During this prehistory there had developed an administrative "style" in dealing with Upper Nile affairs—a style that gave a lavish tolerance to uncoordinated and indeed secretive departmental and personal initiatives and in which interministerial liaison was either very weak or totally absent. The anarchy into which French Upper Nile policy fell during 1897 and 1898 becomes more explicable in the light of earlier events, especially those of 1893–95.

In May 1887, within a month of the cession to France by the Congo State of its territories on the right bank of the Ubangi, the then foreign minister Emile Flourens had pointed out to his colleague at the *Colonies* that the northern affluents of this river "pourraient . . . offrir des voies d'accès intéressantes vers le Soudan égyptien." Gabriel Hanotaux, as *sous-directeur des Protectorats* in 1888–89, and Savorgnan de Brazza, as governor of the French Congo in 1891, had seen similar possibilities. De Brazza had indeed explicitly suggested that a French occupation on the Upper Nile "peut . . . nous donner une situation qui . . . nous permettrait d'entrer avec l'Angleterre en pourparlers au sujet de concessions réciproques dans le règlement de la question égyptienne." In 1891 the colonialist deputy François Deloncle pointed out to the Chamber, though without much emphasis, that France now

70. *DDF, 14,* No. 352, Trouillot to Delcassé, September 15, 1898. The phrase cited within the quotation is from Berthelot's original letter of approval, November 30, 1895.

had "une ouverture sur le Nil"; and in mid-1892 there was a discussion of the Nile project both in the press and in the Chamber. It was indeed this discussion which first aroused the apprehensions of London.[71]

Yet in spite of these initiatives (and in spite of later legends about Liotard's "Upper Nile Mission" of 1890),[72] no action was taken until 1893. The priorities of Brazza and of Eugène Etienne (colonial undersecretary from 1889 to January 1892, but very influential even when not in office) lay elsewhere—in the drive northward from the lower Ubangi toward Lake Chad. The Upper Ubangi was starved of men and money, and from about 1890 the French agents there could make no headway against the calculated hostility of King Leopold's representatives. Leopold also influenced the development of French policy in other ways. Harry Alis, the secretary-general of the *Comité de l'Afrique Française,* was secretly in the king's pay from 1891; the French colonialist movement had been very effectively "penetrated." But this was certainly not the only reason for the very feeble French reaction to Congolese hostility on the Upper Ubangi. The anxiety of French capitalists concerned to protect their investments in the Congo State certainly counted for something. More important, however, was the widespread impression, at first shared by Etienne, that the Congo State was doomed to early financial collapse and that France, through her *droit de préférence,* would then reap the fruit of Leopold's work.[73]

In spite of the discussions of 1892, this apathy on the Upper Ubangi does not seem to have been counteracted by any popular demand for action on the Upper Nile; the recognition of the connection between the Upper Nile and Egypt does not then seem to have been at all widespread. Insofar as there was any popular enthusiasm for African expansion in this period, it seems to have been directed, like the policy of Etienne, toward Lake Chad.[74] Indeed, by a remarkable paradox, in

71. Flourens to Aube, May 16, 1887, cited M.-A. Ménier, "La marche au Tchad de 1887 à 1891," *Bulletin d'Etudes Centrafricaines,* 5 (1953), 6–7. G. Hanotaux, *Fachoda: Le Partage d'Afrique* (Paris, 1909), p. 71. Outre-Mer, Gabon-Congo I/37a, Brazza to Etienne, April 18, 1891; and monthly report, June–July 1891; *Journal Officiel,* Débats, Chambre, June 24, 1891. FO 84/2202, Gosselin to Salisbury, No. 53, June 17, 1892.

72. Cf. Sanderson, *Upper Nile,* pp. 121–22.

73. Ibid., pp. 123–38, for full discussion and sources.

74. H. Dehérain, "La Succession de l'Egypte dans la Province Equatoriale," *Revue des Deux Mondes* (May 1894). Dehérain lamented that popular enthusiasm for Lake Chad had distracted attention from the Upper Nile.

1892 the most powerful influence prompting a French expedition to the Upper Nile was that of King Leopold! Leopold hoped, by mobilizing the French, to frighten the British into abandoning their opposition to recent Congolese encroachments on the "British sphere." He also calculated that the French, in order to launch an expedition, would first have to settle their territorial dispute with the Congo State on terms favorable to himself.[75]

In January 1893, working through Harry Alis, Leopold resumed his pressure for a French expedition.[76] In the same month Théophile Delcassé, whose "grand tourment" had always been Egypt, became colonial undersecretary. Also in January 1893 the hydrologist Victor Prompt presented to the *Institut Egyptien* his notorious paper "Soudan Nilotique," in which he drew attention to the possibility of ruining Egypt by "opérations dues à la malveillance" on the Upper Nile.[77] It seems clear that Delcassé was influenced by this idea, the more fantastic in that there was no building stone (or indeed any kind of stone) within very many miles of Prompt's proposed site for a dam.[78] But Delcassé had no need of any prompting by Harry Alis. Nor had he any illusions about collaboration with the Congolese. Almost alone among French colonialists at this time, Delcassé adopted, and did not deviate from, a hard line toward King Leopold. Indeed, the expedition Delcassé projected was almost as much anti-Congolese as it was anti-British. He was determined to overcome, if necessary by force, the Congolese opposition on the Upper Ubangi; an opposition whose preponderance had recently been demonstrated by the humiliating detention, under Congolese guard, of a small French expedition under Victor Liotard.[79]

Delcassé developed his plans in great secrecy. Unaware of the full extent of Leopold's penetration, he confided in the *Comité de l'Afrique Française* rather than in his own permanent officials, or—astonishingly in view of the international implications of his project—in

75. J. Stengers, "Aux Origines de Fashoda: l'Expédition Monteil," *Revue Belge de Philologie et d'Histoire, 36* (1958), 436–50; *38* (1960), 366–404, 1040–65.

76. Stengers, *38*, 383–94.

77. V. Prompt, "Soudan Nilotique," *Bulletin de l'Institut Egyptien,* Series 3, *4* (1893), 71–116.

78. Outre-Mer, Afrique III Missions, 19a, Monteil to Maurice Lebon, March 7, 1894. Cf. Marchand's sardonic comment to Maskens, Belgian consul in Cairo, in November 1898. Maskens' report is printed by T. Simar, "Léopold II et le Soudan," *Congo* (1924), at p. 521.

79. Sanderson, *Upper Nile,* pp. 127–28, 142. Cf. Outre-Mer, Gabon-Congo I/40b, Delcassé to Chavannes, February 20, 1893.

the foreign minister, Jules Develle.[80] He did, however, confide in the president of the Republic, Sadi Carnot, who not only exerted his authority to prevail upon the reluctant Captain Parfait-Louis Monteil to undertake the mission to the Upper Nile, but also played an important part in initiating closer relations with the negus Menelik in the hope of obtaining Ethiopian support.[81] The Monteil Mission, and its Ethiopian ancillary operation, was thus not the official policy of the French government; it was rather an official conspiracy in the margin of policy. It was frustrated, partly at least, by a counterconspiracy: Monteil, wittingly or unwittingly under the influence of Leopold, refused to leave France without a *prior* territorial settlement with the Congo State; and this was not available on any terms that Delcassé was willing to consider.[82] Early in 1894 the mission seemed to receive its quietus. Jean Casimir-Périer, since December 1893 prime minister and foreign minister, strongly resented President Carnot's extraconstitutional incursions into the field of foreign policy. He gave the Nile project no support whatever. Indeed, he evidently intended to bury the whole question by making territorial concessions to Leopold on a scale which would close the French "ouverture sur le Nil."[83]

The publication of the Anglo-Congolese Agreement in May 1894 was immediately followed by the fall of Casimir-Périer. Delcassé returned to the Pavillon de Flore; Hanotaux became foreign minister. The publication of the agreement stimulated, apparently for the first time, a serious demand for action on the Upper Nile "to safeguard the interests of France." The Monteil Mission was at once revived with great publicity.[84] But during July, in profound secrecy, Monteil was given revised instructions that forbade him "to send a troop or even

80. Stengers, "Aux Origines de Fashoda," *Revue Belge, 36,* 448–49.

81. P.-L. Monteil, *Souvenirs Vécus: Quelques Feuillets de l'Histoire Coloniale* (Paris, 1924), pp. 65–68. C. Maistre, "Le Président Carnot et le plan français d'action sur le Nil en 1893," *Afrique Française* (March 1932), pp. 156–57. *DDF, 11,* No. 5, footnote, citing Sadi Carnot to Menelik, September 22, 1893.

82. Sanderson, *Upper Nile,* pp. 145–51. Cf. Outre-Mer Afrique III Missions, 19a, Monteil to Maurice Lebon, March 7, 1894.

83. Maistre, *Afrique Française,* 1932, pp. 156–57. Cocheris, p. 394. Archives du Ministère des Affaires Etrangères [MAE hereafter], Mémoires et Documents Afrique 139, Casimir-Périer to Hanotaux and Haussmann No. 2, April 16, 1894. Cf. FO 10/614, Plunkett to Kimberley No. 54, April 27, 1894, reporting van Eetvelde on Casimir-Périer's exceptionally "conciliatory spirit."

84. *Journal Officiel,* Débats, Chambre, speech by Hanotaux, June 7, 1894.

a single man" into the Nile valley.[85] This revision was the work of Hanotaux who wanted, not a head-on collision with Britain, but some kind of compromise settlement that could plausibly be represented as a diplomatic victory for France, and which would leave the Egyptian question open for future negotiation. No doubt Hanotaux had been impressed by the British ambassador's warning (which was, ironically enough, disapproved by London) that if Monteil entered the Nile basin "it would simply mean war between the two countries." [86] But once Hanotaux' diplomatic pressure upon the Congo State had on August 14 forced Leopold to relinquish his leases under the Anglo-Congolese Agreement and accept a frontier satisfactory to France, Monteil's revised and limited program had no attractions for Delcassé. Without consulting Hanotaux, Delcassé promptly diverted Monteil and the bulk of his troops to a campaign against Samori in the Ivory Coast hinterland.[87]

It did not, however, take Delcassé long to revive the fully fledged Nile project. By October 1894, and this time with the knowledge and support of his permanent officials, he was opposing the Phipps-Hanotaux plan for "mutual abstention" no less vehemently than Anderson in London.[88] He seems to have suspected that Phipps' eager acceptance of this solution concealed a British plan to steal a march on the French by pushing forward the (nonexistent) "Colvile Mission"; and he insisted that a mission under Liotard could reach the Upper Nile before Colevile.[89] On November 17, 1894, the Liotard Mission was approved by the French cabinet on the proposal of Delcassé and against the strong opposition of Hanotaux. It was approved because Casimir-Périer, in the chair as president of the Republic, now gave his full support to the precise policy which he had so bitterly opposed a few months earlier. His support in November, like his earlier oppo-

85. *DDF, 11,* No. 191, Delcassé to Monteil, July 13, 1894. Hanotaux personally interviewed Monteil and made him give his word of honor to obey this restriction. Hanotaux, minute of July 12, 1894; *DDF, 11,* No. 191, footnote.

86. Sanderson, *Upper Nile,* pp. 170–71, 181–84, 191–92. FO 27/3185, Dufferin to Kimberley No. 173a, June 30, 1894. This threat scandalized Harcourt, who successfully insisted that Dufferin redraft this portion of his dispatch. Cf. for details Stengers, "Aux Origines de Fashoda," *38,* 1044–51.

87. This abrupt decision disconcerted and angered Hanotaux: MAE, Mémoires et Documents Afrique, 139, Hanotaux to "mon cher ami" (probably Haussmann), August 21, 1894.

88. *DDF, 11,* No. 260, Note du Ministre, October 30, 1894.

89. Ibid., No. 260; No. 285, Note du Ministre, November 17, 1894.

sition, does not seem to have been based on any judgment of the intrinsic merits of the policy. So far as the evidence goes, Casimir-Périer seems merely to have wished to "faire acte d'autorité" by snubbing Hanotaux, who was, in his view, not keeping the Elysée adequately informed on foreign policy. To support Delcassé's project against Hanotaux, in a field relevant to the foreign minister's functions and on an issue about which he felt strongly, was simply a convenient way of doing this.[90]

In this oddly fortuitous and "personal" way the Nile project at last became the official policy of the French government. But the "Liotard Mission" was in fact hardly a "mission" at all. In organizing the French penetration from Dahomey to the Middle Niger, Delcassé had recognized that the "mission" must be a specialized and autonomous unit, led by an officer free from routine administrative responsibilities. The missions thus organized were a brilliant success.[91] Surprisingly, on the Upper Nile Delcassé departed from this principle, entrusting the "mission" to an administrative officer whose resources were already barely adequate for his routine tasks. In this situation Liotard, who was in any case wedded to a policy of cautious expansion and careful consolidation, made very little progress. He made even less after Emile Chautemps had replaced Delcassé as minister in January 1895. Chautemps, whose main principle of policy seems to have been to reverse Delcassé's decisions, at once placed the Upper Ubangi on a "care and maintenance" regime, posting reliefs only and no reinforcements. By the spring of 1895 Liotard was virtually marking time; ironically, Sir Edward Grey was moved to make his "Declaration" at a moment when the Nile project seemed to have been indefinitely postponed. As Pierre Renouvin has pointed out, "Pour que les difficultés soulevées par 'l'avertissement Grey' s'apaisent, il suffirait de laisser les événements suivre leur cours." [92]

90. Ibid., No. 285; No. 305, Hanotaux to Delcassé, December 5, 1894. G. Hanotaux, *Carnets* (Extracts, ed. G.-L. Jaray), *Revue des Deux Mondes* (April 1949), at p. 402.

91. M. Blanchard, "Théophile Delcassé au Pavillon de Flore," *Le Monde Français, 16* (1949), 3–34. Their success extorted the reluctant admiration of Sir Percy Anderson: "It is impossible not to be struck by the admirable way in which the numerous French expeditions are conducted by capable officers." (FO 27/3232, minute on Dufferin to Salisbury No. 250, September 14, 1895).

92. Blanchard, *16*, 3–34. *DDF, 12*, No. 152, Chautemps to Hanotaux, September 21, 1895. P. Renouvin, "Les Origines de l'Expédition de Fachoda," *Revue Historique, 200*, 408 (1948), 180–97.

It seemed that events would indeed be "allowed to take their course." On June 18, 1895, Chautemps told the Budget Commission that "la prétention d'agir sur le Haut-Nil à l'aide des troupes est une idée folle. Une action sérieuse sur le Haut-Nil est à écarter." [93] Yet very shortly after making this forthright declaration he had authorized Captain Marchand to study "l'extension plus large de notre sphère d'influence, en particulier dans la direction du Nil." True, when in September Marchand reappeared, having drafted "un intéressant rapport traçant tout un plan de mission," Chautemps told him to go and see Hanotaux, and left to the Quai d'Orsay the final decision on "une question qui touche plus encore à la politique générale extérieure qu'à des intérêts purement coloniaux." [94] But Marchand had won an important victory over the minister's *immobilisme.*

This was a remarkable achievement for a mere junior officer on leave from West Africa. Marchand had an excellent reputation in the French (Niger) Sudan as a fighting soldier and a military explorer; but so far as is known he lacked the social and political connections that might have made him influential at Paris. The documents do little or nothing to solve this problem. Marchand was of course a man of extraordinary strength of character, "une personnalité torrentielle"; [95] but (as he himself was to discover in due course) [96] bureaucratic inertia can be a well-nigh immovable object. It seems unlikely that Marchand's project would have got very far without backing from some of Chautemps' permanent officials, who may well have been dissatisfied with Liotard's lack of progress. The most important of these officials seems to have been Ernest Roume, the head of the commercial and administrative section, who was in November to play a leading part in importuning the Quai d'Orsay for a speedy and favorable decision. Another who may have helped is Colonel Louis Archinard, director of defense at the Ministry. Archinard had been from 1884 to 1893 successively *commandant-supérieur* and governor of the French Sudan, where Marchand had served under him and had attracted his favorable attention.

93. Cited Kanya-Forstner, *Historical Journal,* 9, 251–54, from Archives Nationales, C.5548.

94. *DDF, 12,* No. 152. Cf. Marchand's account in *Le Matin,* June 20, 1905.

95. I am indebted for this phrase to Hubert Deschamps.

96. He was intensely irritated by the Ministry's delays in the drafting of his instructions and the preparation of his mission. Cf. Sanderson, *Upper Nile,* pp. 276–79.

Marchand's project called for a nonmilitary and almost unofficial mission, "sans pavillon et sans mandat," which should make no annexations but rather take "territorial pledges" in the southern Sudan. This activity would, it was suggested, cause England to accept, perhaps even to request, a conference of the Powers to settle the fate of the Sudan and possibly that of Egypt also.[97]

Technical details and safeguards aside, such a plan involved some very hazardous assumptions about the state of international politics at some date in the future not precisely predictable. It assumed either that France would be able to obtain sufficient diplomatic support to impose her desire for a conference upon Britain, or that Britain would not proceed to extremities against France even if that support were not forthcoming. A man of Hanotaux' intelligence and diplomatic experience can hardly have taken this political crystal-gazing seriously; but when he interviewed Marchand in the course of September–October 1895, he was content merely to emphasize the military difficulties the mission was likely to encounter in Africa, and offered no criticism of the political assumptions upon which it was based.[98] He neither approved the expedition nor vetoed it; he hedged. He was still hedging when in the last week of October the Ribot government fell, to be replaced by a Radical cabinet under Léon Bourgeois.

Hanotaux' position was not an easy one. His authority in African affairs had already been seriously undermined by his unsuccessful confrontation with Delcassé and Casimir-Périer over the Liotard Mission. He was moreover a "nonpolitical" minister, sitting neither in the Chamber nor in the Senate, and lacking close links with any of the parties whose precarious coalitions supported French cabinets. If he made a move that aroused the hostility of some influential section of the Chamber, he could be dropped without serious political penalty. To veto the Marchand Mission might have raised such a storm. Moreover, Hanotaux may not have been entirely out of sympathy with some of the objects of the expedition; there are signs, both earlier and later in his career, that he saw some diplomatic value in a French "presence" in or near the Bahr al-Ghazal, though hardly in a direct Anglo-French confrontation on the Upper Nile.[99]

97. *DDF, 12,* No. 192, Note du capitaine Marchand, November 10, 1895 (reproducing extracts from an earlier note of September 11).

98. *DDF, 12,* No. 153, undated minute (September–October 1895) by Brice, of Hanotaux' secretariat.

99. Sanderson, *Upper Nile,* pp. 190–92, 284–85. Cf. infra, pp. 319–20.

But in October 1895 he apparently preferred to evade a decision. His evasion was ultimately to cost him dear.

Hanotaux was invited to retain office under the Radicals, but refused.[100] Their substitute was the totally inexperienced "vieux chimiste" Berthelot. At the Colonial Ministry was another newcomer, also a scholar, the mathematician and Egyptologist Paul Guieysse. The permanent offiicals did not neglect this opportunity. Roume at once began to press for a decision on the Marchand Mission as a matter of the utmost urgency. He was strongly supported by the *Direction* at the Quai d'Orsay. "The *Direction,*" in African affairs, meant Georges Benoit, *sous-directeur des Protectorats,* an ardent expansionist and a man who attached great importance to scoring successes against Britain in Africa. Under this pressure the Marchand Mission was approved on November 30, 1895, by Berthelot, perhaps the most Anglophile minister in what was certainly the most Anglophile French cabinet to hold office in the 1890s.[101]

The "Egyptian" side of the mission, and its potentially dangerous diplomatic implications, seem to have been studiously concealed from Berthelot. It was presented to him as a completely nonmilitary, almost nonpolitical expedition designed solely to secure for France a ticket of entry to a future conference on the southern Sudan. It was not, at this stage, even a mission to Fashoda; its operations were to be restricted to the Bahr al-Ghazal.[102] The overwhelming urgency which the officials had pleaded seems to have been factitious—at all events, it took the Colonial Ministry another three months to draft Marchand's instructions. One cannot but suspect that the real object of all this bustle was to commit Berthelot before he began to make inconvenient inquiries. The Marchand Mission was no doubt impeccably "official"; but its origins, like those of the Monteil Mission, have a slightly conspiratorial air. In the field of general policy, Berthelot was at this time striving, not unsuccessfully to bring about a rapprochement with

100. In order to avoid sullying his political purity by associating with revolutionaries who wished to introduce an income tax.

101. *DDF, 12,* No. 190, Note du Ministère des Colonies (to the *Direction Politique* at the Quai d'Orsay), November 8, 1895; No. 197, Note pour le Ministre (i.e. Berthelot), by the *Direction Politique,* November 13; No. 210, Note de M. Guieysse (to Berthelot), November 21 and footnote printing Roume to *Direction Politique,* November 22; No. 219, Berthelot to Guieysse, November 30, 1895. Cf. Sanderson, *Upper Nile,* pp. 273–76.

102. *DDF, 12,* No. 197, No. 219.

England;[103] and Georges Benoit, who briefed Berthelot and who doubtless drafted the letter of approval, must have been well aware of this.

In the letter put up for Berthelot to sign, the Quai d'Orsay not only assumed full responsibility for the mission, but in effect absolved the Colonial Ministry of any initiative in the matter.[104] The *Colonies* exploited its lack of responsibility. Marchand's instructions, signed on February 24, 1896—a time when Anglo-French relations were for a moment perhaps more friendly than at any time since 1882—abandoned many of the safeguards embodied in Marchand's original project. Marchand was instructed to acquire "dans la région du Nil blanc des alliances sérieuses et des titres indiscutables," and the mission was described as a "raid" (the English word was used—doubtless an echo of Jameson's recent exploit), with Fashoda as its goal.[105] These instructions were apparently drawn up without reference to the Quai d'Orsay. However, in April 1896, Léon Bourgeois, who had recently taken over the Foreign Ministry from Berthelot, interviewed Marchand. Irritated by the recent Anglo-Egyptian advance in the Sudan, under heavy Russian and domestic pressure to react strongly to this "provocation," and deluded by the erroneous belief that France could henceforward rely upon Russian support in the Nile valley, Bourgeois gave the mission his blessing.[106]

When Hanotaux returned to office at the end of April the Marchand Mission was thus a fait accompli; indeed, Marchand's advance party had already sailed for Africa.[107] Any attempt to countermand it now could have raised a storm that might have been fatal to a rather shaky government [108]—or to Hanotaux' career. Hanotaux therefore attempted to guard against the more obvious dangers of the mission by insisting

103. Sanderson, *Upper Nile,* pp. 228–32. J. D. Hargreaves, *"Entente Manquée:* Anglo-French Relations, 1895–1896," *Cambridge Historical Journal, 11,* 1 (1953), 65–92.

104. *DDF, 12,* No. 219. It remarked to Guieysse: "en se plaçant au point de vue exclusivement colonial, votre Département serait porté à restreindre au strict nécessaire les effectifs qui seraient envoyés sur le Haut-Oubangui."

105. *DDF, 12,* No. 312, Guieysse to Liotard, February 24, 1896. Similar instructions, the full text of which has been lost, were issued to Marchand: cf. André Lebon, *La Politique de la France en Afrique, 1896–1898* (Paris, 1901), pp. 3, 9–10.

106. Sanderson, *Upper Nile,* pp. 279–80. Renouvin, *Revue Historique, 200,* 180–97.

107. On April 25, 1896.

108. For the initial shakiness of the Méline government, in spite of its long innings, cf. FO 27/3267, Monson to Salisbury No. 388, December 11, 1896.

on the amendment of Marchand's instructions. The revised instructions, signed on June 23, omitted all reference to Fashoda and to the territorial annexations implied in the words "titres indiscutables." Marchand was enjoined to follow Liotard's policy of cautious advance and careful consolidation, with "notre établissment dans le bassin du Nil" as a rather distant goal.[109] The Colonial Ministry soon broke through this flimsy barrier. Early in 1897, apparently without consulting either Hanotaux or the cabinet, it ordered Marchand to push ahead to Fashoda as quickly as possible, making treaties of annexation as he went.[110] The mission which reached Fashoda in July 1898 was thus a very different mission from that which Marchand had originally proposed, and Berthelot approved.[111]

In September 1896 the Colonial Ministry began to revive the potentially very dangerous Ethiopian side of the project. In this they were supported by Hanotaux' own *Direction;* but Hanotaux fought back and withheld his agreement from anything more than the most tentative action in Ethiopia.[112] Undeterred, the Pavillon de Flore privately instructed Léonce Lagarde at Djibouti to make a treaty with Menelik partitioning the southern Sudan between France and Ethiopia.[113] In the course of March 1897, Hanotaux challenged in cabinet the contention of the colonial minister, André Lebon, that it was "indispensable" to persuade Menelik to push his frontier to the White Nile. But he allowed himself to be overruled and does not appear to have attempted to enforce his views by a threat of resignation.[114] On

109. *DDF, 12,* No. 411, Lebon to Liotard, June 23, 1896. Cf. Hanotaux, *Fachoda,* pp. 108–09, which gives a misleading account of this episode.

110. For the evidence, Sanderson, *Upper Nile,* pp. 285, 287–89. In the course of 1897 the Pavillon de Flore began to organize a general occupation of the Bahr al-Ghazal in support of Marchand's spearhead.

111. The mission was warlike: it fought a victorious battle with a Mahdist flotilla on August 25, 1898. It was political: the *reth* of the Shilluk accepted French protection by a formal treaty of September 3; and Marchand faced Kitchener with the claim that both Fashoda and the Bahr al-Ghazal were French protectorates.

112. Outre-Mer, Côte Française des Somalis, Lebon to Hanotaux, September 6, 1896; Hanotaux to Lebon, September 30; Lebon to Hanotaux, November 1; Lebon to Lagarde, Instructions (countersigned by Hanotaux), December 3, 1896. *DDF, 13,* No. 35, Hanotaux to Lebon, November 30, 1896; and footnote printing *Direction Politique* to Hanotaux, September 30, 1896.

113. Outre-Mer, Côte Française des Somalis, Note Spéciale d'Instructions pour M. Lagarde, December 18, 1896. *DDF, 13,* No. 149, Lebon to Lagarde, March 14, 1897; No. 159, *Convention pour le Nil Blanc* (between France and Ethiopia), March 20, 1897.

114. *DDF, 13,* No. 137, Lebon to Hanotaux, March 5, 1897; minute by

May 24, 1897, the partition treaty with Menelik was ratified by the president of the Republic.[115] This act implied the acceptance of Lebon's views on the objectives of the Marchand Mission; and in this typically roundabout way Lebon's policy became the official policy of the French government. Yet, as later events were to prove, President Félix Faure was fundamentally opposed to any policy likely to precipitate a crisis on the Upper Nile.

In February 1897, just before Hanotaux' defeat by Lebon on Ethiopian policy, his own *Direction* put up to him a detailed project for the use of the Marchand Mission as a means of obtaining territorial as well as diplomatic advantages in the Nile valley. The French objectives were to be the evacuation of an "Egypt" extended southward as far as the Fifth Cataract near Berber, and the outright annexation of the southwestern Sudan bounded by the Nile and the tenth parallel. Britain would be compensated by being permitted to acquire the remainder of the Sudan.[116] There is no evidence in Hanotaux' published correspondence which would suggest that he adopted this proposal. Indeed, in a letter to Cogordan of November 16, 1897, he seemed to renounce all acquisitive aims by explicitly declaring his support for the rights of the sultan and the khedive throughout the Sudan. In the same letter he looks forward to the day when a changed pattern of European alignments would permit an amicable diplomatic settlement of the whole complex of Nile problems.[117] Three weeks earlier he had described his Egyptian policy to the Russian ambassador as "non cassante mais vigilante." [118] And in January 1898 be minuted, on a dispatch from Cogordan concerning the situation in Egypt, that "la continuation de l'état de choses actuel est ce que nous devons désirer, aussi longtemps que l'Europe n'aura pas ouvert les yeux. . . . Donc, prolongeons et négocions." [119]

Hanotaux remained aloof from the Colonial Ministry's various schemes to set the Nile on fire—schemes that increasingly proliferated after Gustave Binger became *Directeur des affaires d'Afrique* in December 1896. He steered clear of the eccentric or shady adventurers

---

Nisard recording Hanotaux' opposition; No. 149, minute recording the cabinet decision.

115. *DDF, 12,* No. 159, footnote.

116. *DDF, 14,* No. 258, *Note du Département,* July 18, 1898, incorporating part of a *Note pour le Ministre,* February 10, 1897.

117. *DDF, 13,* No. 360, Hanotaux to Cogordan, November 16, 1897.

118. Ibid., No. 343, *Note du Ministre,* October 23, 1897.

119. *DDF, 14,* No. 11, minute on Cogordan to Hanotaux, January 13, 1898.

whom the Colonial Ministry increasingly patronized: the unbalanced Hungarian ex-officer Karl Inger who claimed to have secured for France the diplomatic and military support of the khalifa 'Abdallāhī;[120] the Russian "buccaneer" Nicolai Leontiev whose "governorship" of the (nonexistent) "Equatorial Provinces of Ethiopia" was expected in some quarters to be "un puissant élément d'équilibre" against the British on the Upper Nile.[121] And when Lagarde at Addis Ababa, on his own initiative but with the retrospective approval of Lebon, offered a French flag and French protection to the khalifa, Hanotaux administered a stinging rebuke to his colleague at the Pavillon de Flore.[122]

How was the Marchand Mission to be reconciled with Hanotaux' expectant and quiescent policy? Given the form which the mission finally took, that of a "raid" on Fashoda coupled with treaties implying territorial annexation, this reconciliation was evidently impossible. And yet from time to time, in his correspondence with Cogordan at least, Hanotaux hints fairly broadly that the mission might be a favorable factor in bringing about the diplomatic settlement for which he hoped. In January 1897 he attempts to encourage Cogordan by reference to the "marche sur le Bahr el Ghazal." (*Not,* be it noted, "sur Fachoda.")[123] In November, in a more elaborate passage, he sets out the factors which in his view tend "à accentuer encore le caractère européen de la question d'Egypte." In this context, he mentions the interests of "tous les Etats qui, à divers degrés et à divers titres, ont pris pied dans le bassin du Haut-Nil," and again to "l'extension de certaines possessions européennes"—oblique but unmistakable allusions to the Marchand Mission, especially as they occur in connexion with "la force croissante de l'Empire abyssin."[124] Hanotaux can hardly have believed that a direct confrontation with the British on the Upper Nile would produce the results he expected. But a more discreet French "presence" in the Bahr al-Ghazal might not be without value;

120. G. N. Sanderson, "'Emir Suleyman ibn Inger Abdullah,'" *Sudan Notes and Records, 35,* 1 (1954), pp. 22–74. Inger does claim to have seen Hanotaux' *sous-chef de Cabinet,* but this meeting had no traceable consequences.

121. Sanderson, *Upper Nile,* pp. 302–04. C. Jésman, *The Russians in Ethiopia* (London, 1958), pp. 110–25.

122. Sanderson, *Upper Nile,* pp. 299–300; "Contributions from African sources . . . ," pp. 69–90; and "'Emir Suleyman . . . ,'" pp. 22–74. *DDF, 14,* No. 55, Hanotaux to Lebon, February 17, 1898. The rebuke elicited a coolly insolent reply, probably drafted by Binger.

123. *DDF, 13,* No. 61, Hanotaux to Cogordan, January 10, 1897.

124. Ibid., No. 360, same to same, November 16, 1897.

and this was, after all, the object of the revised instructions upon which Hanotaux had insisted in June 1896.

True, these instructions had been overridden by the Colonial Ministry; but the practical difficulties in Africa might prove more effective than Hanotaux' rather cautious opposition. In this sense, at least, those critics may have been right who alleged that Hanotaux had hoped that "Marchand n'arriverait pas." [125] In his own apologia, Hanotaux remarked that the real object of the mission "n'était pas même un objet d'échange, un gage ou une matière à négociation, c'était la négociation elle-même." [126] This statement, on the face of it, is untrue and almost incomprehensible; but it makes some kind of sense if Hanotaux believed that local difficulties would after all force the mission to play the part which he, and not the Colonial Ministry, had written for it. This belief was not necessarily absurd; anyone but Marchand might well have abandoned the fantastically difficult passage of the Bahr al-Ghazal *sudd.*[127] But in dealing with this "personnalité torrentielle" it was very unwise to rely on local difficulties as a substitute for positive control.

However, in his last hours of office, indeed a week after he had become a caretaker minister on the fall of the Méline government, Hanotaux suddenly and unexpectedly reversed his Upper Nile policy —a reversal so sudden as to surprise and shock President Félix Faure. To Cogordan on June 21, 1898, he pointed out that Marchand was believed to be at or near Fashoda and that his arrival, combined with the forthcoming fall of Khartoum, would lead to negotiations in which "toutes les Puisances qui ont des intérêts en Egypte auront également à prendre part." The French objectives in this negotiation are not explicitly stated but are quite clearly indicated: the reestablishment of the "autorité de droit du Sultan et du Khédive" in the northern and Central Sudan, and the partition of the southern Sudan between France and Ethiopia. This was an extraordinary program, which went far beyond the proposals of the *Direction* in February 1897: England, which would have conquered the whole of the northern Sudan, would not receive a morsel of compensation. Some of the "favourable factors" cited by Hanotaux can hardly be taken seriously: the expected arrival of "certains émissaires de Ménélik" at Fashoda (although effective

125. E.g. Bonvalot (one of the French agents in Ethiopia), "Les Affaires du Nil," *Le Matin,* October 23, 1898.

126. Hanotaux, *Fachoda,* p. 137.

127. Sanderson, *Upper Nile,* pp. 285–87. For eyewitness accounts, see J. Emily, *Mission Marchand* (Paris, 1913); A.-E.-A. Baratier, *Souvenirs de la Mission Marchand, Fachoda* (Paris, 1941).

Franco-Ethiopian cooperation was already known to be a broken reed); the peace between Greece and Turkey which would free the hands of the sultan for intervention in the Nile valley![128] Moreover, Hanotaux had made no diplomatic preparations whatever to meet a crisis on the scale which his dispatch foreshadowed; in particular, he had long been aware that it was hopeless to expect effective Russian support in the Upper Nile.[129] It is difficult to know what to make of Hanotaux' motives in sending this dispatch. Was it simply a piece of rather meaningless panache by a retiring minister who would not have to answer for its consequences;[130] or was it a deliberate attempt to queer the pitch for Hanotaux' successor Delcassé, whom he despised and disliked to the point of refusing to give him a proper handover?

French political journalists were sadly mistaken when throughout the first half of 1898 they confidently asserted that Hanotaux would never have "sent Marchand to Fashoda" without making the necessary adjustments "sur l'échiquier européen." But then Hanotaux did not "send Marchand to Fashoda." Who, in fact, did send him? Berthelot bears the formal responsibility for "sending" him to the Upper Nile, though hardly to Fashoda. But the real responsibility lies with certain permanent officials—Roume, Benoit, Archinard, and, for the developments of 1897–98, Binger. What motives prompted these men? Anxious as they were to "solve the Egyptian question" by the discomfiture of England, it is difficult to believe that Mediterranean strategy was in the forefront of their minds. In the protracted Anglo-French West African negotiations of 1894–98, Roume and Benoit had been particularly aggressive and intransigent. To men like these, successes against Britain in Africa had in themselves a very high prestige value for France. They had particularly relished the dismay of the British as the French expeditions progressively revealed the falsity of George Goldie's paper claims. As one of the British negotiators remarked, Benoit though it "a huge joke to occupy all that we claim."[131] Binger,

128. *DDF, 14,* No. 236. Hanotaux to Cogordan, June 21, 1898. Cf. an evidently "inspired" article in *Le Matin,* June 19. Memorandum by Félix Faure on the Fashoda crisis, printed under the title "Fachoda (1898)," *Revue d'Histoire Diplomatique* 69 (1955), 29–39.

129. Cf. Sanderson, *Upper Nile,* pp. 282–83, 293, 304, 314.

130. On October 25, 1898, Hanotaux told Wilfrid Blunt that "no war would be popular in France, that nobody know where Fashoda was, or cared three straws about the Marchand Mission." Blunt, *My Diaries,* p. 303.

131. FO 27/3231, Howard (Paris) to Anderson, private, May 14, 1895. Cf. Sanderson, *Upper Nile,* pp. 231–32.

if collateral evidence relating to the Cazemajou Mission be any guide,[132] was even more combative toward Britain than Benoit and Roume. It was indeed immediately after his appointment as *directeur d'Afrique* in December 1896 that the Pavillon de Flore embarked upon its more aggressive, and openly acquisitive, policy toward the Upper Nile.

To men with these attitudes, there was a very strong temptation to strike a blow against Britain in the sphere where France had suffered her greatest humiliation since 1871. Their status as "specialists" would preoccupy them with the "game" of European rivalry in Africa, and would tend to insulate them from feeling much responsibility for the international consequences of their acts. No doubt, too, as Cogordan suggests, they believed that the "nation of shopkeepers" would never risk its profits by going to war.

"Nous avons été comme des fous en Afrique, entraînes par ces gens irresponsables qu'on appelle les coloniaux."[133] This considered verdict of Félix Faure on the Marchand Mission was not quite a true bill. It applied only to those "coloniaux" who were primarily interested in an imperialism of prestige. The business and economic colonialists, organized in the *Union Coloniale Française* whose growing influence Marchand himself recognized and detested, were from start to finish hostile to the Marchand Mission and the policy that it represented. Already strongly opposed to the expensive and economically worthless military imperialism in West Africa, they saw in Marchand simply another *officier soudanais* whose operations would convert the Upper Nile into "a new [Niger] Soudan with the additional aggravation of the proximity of the Mahdists." They predicted expensive and fruitless campaigns whose net result might well be a Mahdist invasion of the Upper Ubangi, and scoffed openly at the idea that the mission might hasten a solution of the Egyptian question.[134] Indeed, during the crisis of 1898 it was not so much the colonialists as the extreme anti-Dreyfusards, usually hostile to colonial expansion, who most vehemently demanded that Marchand be maintained at Fashoda even at the cost of war. They stood by Marchand's exploit, not because he was a

132. Outre-Mer, Afrique III Missions, 25, passim; and especially Lebon to Hanotaux, May 9, 1898 (drafted by Binger and signed unamended by Lebon).

133. Faure, *Revue d'Histoire Diplomatique,* pp. 29–39.

134. Kanya-Forstner, *The Conquest of the Western Sudan,* pp. 206–08; cf. pp. 255–57. Sanderson, *Upper Nile,* pp. 374–76. Cf. Marchand to Grandidier, November 25, 1897, *Revue d'Histoire des Colonies, 45;* and *La Politique Coloniale* (organ of the Union Coloniale), esp. for December 1895, and June and September 1896.

successful colonial pioneer, but because he was a symbol of the idolized army—a soldier who had successfully defied "perfide Albion" only to be betrayed by politicians sold to the British and (of course) to the Jews.[135]

Kitchener bitingly remarked that Marchand's presence at Fashoda was "more worthy of Opéra-Bouffe than of the outcome of the maturely considered plans of a great Government." [136] The sneer apart, his verdict was not altogether unjust. If the "raid" on Fashoda and the creation of a French protectorate were, since March (or perhaps May) 1897, the formally approved policy of the French government, they had become so by a backstairs route which had effectually prevented any "mature consideration" of either their practical utility or their probable consequences. The Marchand Mission was not, either in its origin or in the form which it finally took, the policy of Gabriel Hanotaux, the minister who was officially responsible for it during most of its existence. It was strongly supported by the *Comité de l'Afrique Française;* but it was in essence the policy of military officers and, more important, of high permanent officials who were by the tradition of their service extremely combative toward England and overready to assert French prestige by intensifying competition between the two countries. As Sir Edmund Monson complained in 1899, the French system too often permitted "questions of serious international moment" to become "dependent upon the manipulation . . . of irresponsible officials." [137] The history of the Marchand Mission is an extreme example of this tendency. The loss of control by Hanotaux early in 1897, and his inability or unwillingness to make any serious effort to regain it, left a clear field for the bureaucrats of the Pavillon de Flore, who accepted no responsibility for questions of general foreign policy. Nor did their minister, André Lebon. Indeed, Lebon seems to have done little more than sign the drafts prepared by Binger. And for Binger, the main function of the Quai d'Orsay was evidently to provide diplomatic backing for the policies of the Colonial Ministry however reckless those policies might be.[138]

135. Sanderson, *Upper Nile,* pp. 359–60, 373. R. Arie, "L'Opinion publique en France et l'affaire de Fachoda," *Revue d'Histoire des Colonies, 41* (1954), pp. 329–67. Cf. the abortive attempt, in the summer of 1899, to set up Marchand as a military "savior of society," a second (and less defective) Boulanger.

136. FO 141/333, Kitchener to Rodd, September 21, 1898.

137. FO 27/3455, Monson to Salisbury, No. 48, January 27, 1899.

138. Outre-Mer, Afrique III Missions, 25, Binger's draft of May 9, signed by Lebon. Binger crowned a defiant and indeed insolent letter with the observation that, should Hanotaux' diplomacy fail to secure the claims of France, "mon dé-

It was not only the bureaucrats at Paris who had a free hand. By 1898, subordinate agents in the field were making policy on their own account, doubtless encouraged by the very permissive attitude of the Colonial Ministry toward vigorous local initiative. The most reckless of these moves—Lagarde's offer of the French flag to the khalifa and Marchand's attempt to summon Ethiopian troops to Fashoda [139]—would have led direct to war if they had been successful. No wonder British warnings were ignored, or seemed to be ignored. Hanotaux, the responsible minister, was well aware—at all events after the beginning of 1898—that there was a sharp limit to London's willingness to remain within the conventions of the "game." But he was virtually powerless to intervene. The "game" was being played, for all it was worth, indeed for more than it was worth, by irresponsible agents both in France and in Africa. Lack of effective central control had marked the Nile project from first to last; and the "game" had now become a bizarre caricature, in which critical moves could often be made on the margin of policy, and sometimes even by dubious "secret agents" and adventurers. The melodramatic incidents—not so much "Opéra-Bouffe" as "James Bond"—which so frequently crop up in the story of the Nile project [140] should not be dismissed as mere light relief, unworthy of the attention of the serious historian. Properly understood, they go far to explain the French debacle at Fashoda.

The complex and even confused background of the Anglo-French confrontation at Fashoda does not encourage confident judgments about the "general nature" of British and French imperialism on the Upper Nile. Some light may, however, have been thrown upon this problem by the foregoing discussion of two rather more specific questions: why was the British reaction—of government and people

---

partement sans doute ne manquerait pas de le déplorer, mais avec le sentiment certain de n'avoir rien négligé, quant à lui, pour sauvegarder les intérêts de la France dans l'Afrique occidentale." And cf. Lebon's reply to Hanotaux' rebuke on the "French flag" affair, *DDF, 14,* No. 55, footnote.

139. Sanderson, *Upper Nile,* pp. 291, 343. C.-M.-E. Mangin, "Lettres de la Mission Marchand, 1895–1899," *Revue des Deux Mondes* (September 1931), pp. 241–83. Outre-Mer, Afrique III Missions, 34b, Mangin to Colonies, December 14, 1898.

140. E.g. the career and death of Harry Alis; the atmosphere of conspiracy and counterconspiracy that surrounds the Monteil Mission; the exploits of Inger, of Leontiev, of Lagarde, sometimes even of Marchand himself. And, in the background, the sinister yet absurdly impracticable threat of "opérations dues à la malveillance"—which was still in Marchand's mind in November 1898.

alike—so intransigent and even truculent during the Fashoda crisis; and, how did the French manage to play themselves into a position which seems, in retrospect, to have been foredoomed to failure?

Both these questions involve some exploration of the unexpressed assumptions that lie behind overt policy; and the first of them has to be answered at least partly by an assessment of British public opinion in 1898–99. The hazards of such a discussion are obvious. "Public opinion," in particular, is notoriously treacherous ground. Data are plentiful; but no generally satisfactory technique for weighing and interpreting these data seems yet to have been devised. Studies in "public opinion" are therefore apt to seem intolerably conjectural and subjective, especially when placed beside the findings of "pure" diplomatic history. But these hazards must be faced where the course of events does not seem to be fully explicable otherwise.

In assessing the British governmental reaction to the crisis, it is essential to reunite two episodes which the divergent interests of specialist historians have tended to put asunder: the Fashoda crisis and the Condominium Agreement.[141] It must be recognized that the assertion of British control over the whole of the Sudan was not a mere incidental coda to the Fashoda confrontation, but had become a major objective of British policy even before the opening of the crisis. Early in June 1898 Salisbury's abandonment of the doctrine of the "British Sphere" and his assertion of a joint Anglo-Egyptian right of conquest made direct British control of the northern Sudan a possibility; sometimes between June and September this possibility hardened into a policy. Strategically, however, this takeover of the whole Sudan was an unnecessary elaboration. Diplomatically, it carried with it at least potential risks. Cogordan called the Condominium Agreement "un défi lancé à l'Europe"; [142] and Europe was indeed entitled to resent, not only the takeover itself, but the arrogant nonchalance with which the British concocted an Anglo-Egyptian agreement of very dubious legality and then refused to communicate it formally to the Powers.[143] No doubt the immediate risk was very slight.

141. The Fashoda crisis has been the preserve of diplomatic historians; the Condominium Agreement that of specialists in Anglo-Egyptian relations and of historians of the Sudan.

142. *DDF, 15,* No. 29 footnote, Cogordan to Delcassé, January 21, 1899; cf. No. 33, same to same, January 20.

143. The legal weaknesses of the agreement are unsparingly exposed by Cocheris, pp. 505–09. Cf. Sanderson, *Upper Nile,* p. 367. For Salisbury's flat refusal to communicate the agreement to the Powers ("What have they to do with it?"), cf. FO 78/5025, Salisbury to Cromer, tel. No. 13, January 18, 1899.

No Power other than France had either prestige or serious material interests at stake in the Sudan; and the progressive British naval mobilization, continued until February 1899, effectively discouraged any "protest on principle." But diplomatists have long memories; and Salisbury was normally very reluctant to incur even long-term risks by giving unnecessary offence to the Powers.

The question therefore remains: why did Salisbury pursue a course whose acquisitiveness and doubtful legality were sure to arouse resentment, when no major strategic interest was at stake and when he certainly had no illusions about the intrinsic value of the territory concerned? It is at this point that those usually inscrutable entities, "the spirit of the times" and "the pressure of public opinion," can no longer be ignored. But in this case it seems clear that both the historical background and the immediate circumstances of the Fashoda confrontation prompted a demand for effective British control of the whole Sudan from almost every articulate section of public opinion—including, for special reasons, groups who were normally opposed in principle to territorial acquisition. It is no less clear that Lord Salisbury could not have rejected this demand without sacrificing his political reputation, and quite possibly his tenure of office.

It seems very likely that Salisbury had foreseen this demand, and was making preparations to meet it even before the crisis broke. It is, however, very difficult to follow in any detail the evolution of Salisbury's thought between his first formal enunciation of the right-of-conquest doctrine on June 3, 1898, and Cromer's submission of the first draft of the Condominium Agreement on November 10.[144] Cromer produced this draft without traceable instructions; he must have been briefed, either orally or otherwise informally, during his summer leave in England. On July 25 he attended a cabinet at which the decision was taken that Britain should, in practice, have undisputed control over the Sudan.[145] How this control was to be exercised was perhaps still an open question. On September 4 British intentions were communicated to the Egyptian government in very ambiguous terms, which seemed to leave the option open between either some form of "indirect rule" through Egypt or a radical change in the status of

144. FO 78/5050, Salisbury to Cromer tel. No. 47, June 3, 1898; FO 78/4957, Cromer to Salisbury, Separate and Secret No. 1, November 10, 1898.

145. Cf. FO 78/5050, Salisbury to Cromer, No. 109, August 2, 1898. This instruction was actually drafted by Cromer himself, on the basis of the cabinet (and possibly other) discussions.

the Sudan.[146] It is impossible to say whether these options were really still open, or whether this ambiguity was merely a soporific for Egyptian consumption. On September 22, however, Salisbury forbade Rennell Rodd at Cairo to publish this communication lest its ambiguity should "give rise to embarrassing comment." [147] By this time, if not before, the decision to adopt the more drastic solution had probably been taken. When Cromer left for Cairo a few days later, he was evidently empowered to alter the status of the Sudan.

The difficulty of following the development of Salisbury's thinking is increased by the fact that he does not seem to have confided his views on the future of the Sudan to anyone other than Cromer. On his own confession, Salisbury could never see the point of "talking things over" with colleagues or subordinates. Having collected the information he needed, he preferred to reach his decisions undistracted by "the intrusion of other men's thoughts." [148] Nor did he do much of his thinking on paper. The typical Salisbury document, of this period especially, is the terse, unargued instruction rather than the "policy paper" or the explanatory dispatch. Information to subordinate agents was restricted to what they needed to know in order to perform their tasks.[149] Nobody but Cromer needed to know what Salisbury intended to do about the Sudan; nobody at all needed to know how far Salisbury's views were being influenced by the demands of public opinion. The record is therefore silent. The motives and development of Salisbury's policy must be inferred from an examination of his overt acts against the background of his normal policy-predilections and of the political pressures upon him.

Analysis of French policy, especially in the origins and development of the Marchand Mission, is beset with even greater difficulties. The

146. FO 78/5050, Rodd to Salisbury, No. 134, September 4, 1898. The note asserted the British claim to "a predominant voice" in the Sudan, and warned Cairo that H.M.G. expected their advice on Sudan affairs to be followed without question. But it added that "this decision will have no reference to the manner in which the occupied countries are to be administered in the future."

147. FO 141/336, Salisbury to Rodd, tel. No. 82, September 22, 1898.

148. Cecil, *4*, 282, quoting Salisbury's own words.

149. On September 9, 1898, in an instruction of almost military brusqueness, Salisbury ordered Monson to assert the right of conquest in "all the territories which were subject to the Khalifa," and not to admit any discussion of this right; FO 141/336, Salisbury to Monson, unnumbered tel., September 9. On September 26 Monson was instructed to read Kitchener's Fashoda telegram to Delcassé. Thereafter Monson was sent virtually no information other than suitably edited versions of what Salisbury and Courcel had said to one another.

most fundamental of these is the serious defectiveness of the Colonial Ministry archives. Much material has been removed from the "Mission Marchand" dossiers, notably by the then Minister Georges Mandel in 1938 and 1939. In 1955 these dossiers contained no papers prior to March 1897, and none of any importance prior to the Fashoda crisis itself,[150] when the Colonial Ministry was little more than an ill-informed spectator. Less serious perhaps is the failure of *Documents diplomatiques français* to throw much light upon Hanotaux' very ambiguous attitude toward the Marchand Mission and the Upper Nile question in the critical period between January 1897 and June 1898. Since the publication of the relevant volumes of the *Documents,* the archives for this period are generally accessible.[151] It remains to be seen how far they will elucidate the apparently calculated ambiguity of Hanotaux' published correspondence down to June 1898, and his sudden adoption in that month of a bold and decided, but to all appearances quite impracticable, policy.

One consequence of these deficiencies is a recurrent difficulty in establishing who precisely was the initiator of any particular act of policy. This difficulty is particularly acute from the beginning of 1897, when the Colonial Ministry escaped from the control of the Quai d'Orsay, and when local agents (notably Lagarde) began to launch forth on initiatives of their own, sometimes without reference to Paris. Information upon these local substrategies is indeed particularly scanty in the Paris archives. Thus for Lagarde's offer of the French flag to the khalifa the most useful information comes from a Mahdist source; and Lagarde's dealings with Karl Inger seem to be traceable only in Inger's statements preserved in the Intelligence archives of the Egyptian army.

A less technical difficulty, but a very real one, besetting both the study of the Marchand Mission and a more general evaluation of the nature of French imperialism, is the almost complete absence of detailed analyses of the various interest groups and "schools of thought" which cooperated or conflicted within the French colonialist movement. The task of merely identifying these groups is evidently still incomplete; the full dissection of their various motives and approaches has scarcely begun, though A. S. Kanya-Forstner's study of French

150. Some of these losses have since been recovered. I have not seen the recovered papers.

151. These documents were however "weeded" by Delcassé in March 1904. (*DDF, 14,* Avant-propos, viii–ix.)

military imperialism in West Africa [152] is a very important pioneer contribution. For not dissimilar reasons, it is also difficult to gain a clear impression of some of the personalities involved. Of all those concerned, other than Marchand himself, Ernest Roume and Georges Benoit seem to bear the greatest responsibility for promoting the Marchand Mission. They have very successfully preserved their bureaucratic quality of "faceless men." But even some of the ministers involved in the history and prehistory of the mission—Develle, Jamais, Guieysse, the two Lebons (Maurice and André) [153]—still remain mere names rather than recognizable figures of flesh and blood.

Generalization about the nature of French imperialism can therefore at this stage be little more than an impressionistic sketch based upon defective and fragmentary materials. Indeed, the attempt to reconstruct the origins and development of a single episode—such as the Marchand Mission—involves a disconcerting amount of conjecture if the available facts are to be presented in a self-consistent and rationally satisfying pattern. As further material comes to light, the "rationally satisfying pattern" will doubtless turn out to be, at least in places, a crude oversimplification. Nevertheless, two elements in the pattern seem to be dominant enough to resist considerable critical erosion: the importance of the permanent officials as policy makers; and the preoccupation of the French "official mind" with national prestige as a motive for imperial expansion, at any rate within the Nile valley.

When the crisis came, the British refused to play the diplomatic-territorial "game" which had become the norm of international behavior in African affairs. In British eyes, far too much was at stake for the rules of the game to apply. Partly for long-term reasons which d'Estournelles de Constant had elucidated as early as December 1894, partly because of the particular circumstances of the Fashoda confrontation, the crisis was seen in England as a conflict whose upshot would indicate Britain's real strength or weakness as a Power. It was, in d'Estournelles' prescient words, "une question par conséquent de vie ou de mort." [154] That the British would react to it in this way

152. A. S. Kanya-Forstner, *The Conquest of the Western Sudan.*

153. Even so distinguished a historian as Pierre Renouvin confuses Maurice with André Lebon; *Revue Historique, 200,* 181. This is doubtless a mere slip—but surely a significant one.

154. *DDF, 11,* No. 303, d'Estournelles de Constant to Hanotaux, December 3, 1894.

was evidently a complete surprise to the French, and especially to the permanent officials who were so often the real policy makers. Whether their surprise ought to have been so complete is another question. But the flat refusal of the British to negotiate, and their evident willingness to back that refusal by force of arms, at once threw French policy into a disarray from which it was quite unable to recover.

The precise time at which the Fashoda confrontation took place was particularly favorable to the British and unfavorable to the French. This timing was largely fortuitous. Had Marchand's unforeseen local difficulties been less severe, he might have arrived a year earlier. Had Kitchener not been reinforced by British troops early in 1898—a reinforcement prompted solely by an unfounded belief in the khalifa's ability to mount a counteroffensive—the fall of Omdurman, and the Fashoda confrontation, would almost certainly have been postponed by a year. In either case, the course of the crisis, and perhaps even its upshot, might well have been very different.

However, once Kitchener had received his British reinforcements, it became increasingly probable that the crisis would erupt before the end of 1898. Salisbury was quick to see this; and he had already recognized in October 1897 that an Anglo-French confrontation on the Upper Nile would be "something to remember," a naked trial of strength in which "the technical considerations will not go for very much."[155] He therefore began carefully to mend his diplomatic fences. He sharply reined in Milner, who was "inclined to work up to a crisis" in South Africa. He took great pains to improve his relations with Berlin, now fortunately somewhat estranged from Russia by the German occupation of Kiaochow. Above all, he refused to quarrel with St. Petersburg over Port Arthur[156]—a humiliating "climb down" which for a time seriously damaged his political reputation.[157] The French reaction to the gathering storm was much more hesitant—indeed, almost nonexistent. There was hardly any sense of urgency; until September 1898 there seems to have been little inkling of either the imminence or the severity of the forthcoming crisis.[158] Hanotaux him-

155. SP, Egypt, Salisbury to Cromer, October 29, 1897.

156. Specifically because "in six months' time . . . we shall be on the verge of war with France; I can't afford to quarrel with Russia now." Memorandum of conversation, by Lady G. Cecil, cited A. L. Kennedy, *Salisbury 1830–1903* (London, 1953), p. 276.

157. Thereby making it the more necessary for Salisbury to "vindicate himself" by intransigence at Fashoda. Cf. supra, p. 299.

158. Cf. *DDF, 14,* No. 258, *Note du Département,* July 18, 1898; Nos. 176, Geoffray (London) to Hanotaux, April 30, 1898; Nos. 305, 330, Geoffray to

self was probably less complacent than the bureaux and embassies; but after 1897 he does not seem even to have attempted to modify the reserve which both Russia and Germany showed toward the affairs of the Upper Nile. Delcassé was equally passive until the beginning of September 1898.[159] So long as any illusion persisted of a settlement within the rules of the diplomatic-territorial "game," the difficulties, and the dangers, of attempting seriously to influence German or Russian policy doubtless seemed prohibitive. The Quai d'Orsay therefore yielded to the temptation to let matters drift; while Salisbury, "the one man who had got his eye in,"[160] hazarded his own political credit in order to reinforce good fortune by good management.

POSTSCRIPT

I should now wish to modify certain statements in this paper in the light of research completed since its submission, notably that of Marc Michel in his unpublished thesis "La Mission Marchand" (Paris, 1968).

1. The extent and political influence of Marchand's circle of acquaintances at Paris has been underestimated.

2. The account of the relations between Marchand, Roume, and Archinard is misleading. Roume does seem to have given some assistance at the outset of Marchand's campaign to convince the Ministries, while Archinard was not "converted" until September 1895. But thereafter Archinard became Marchand's principal supporter; and Roume showed increasing hostility to Marchand's project, not least because Archinard intended to use it as a means of transferring the Upper Ubangi from civilian to military control. The Roume-Archinard dispute was at least partly responsible for the delay in drafting Marchand's instructions.

Michel sees Hanotaux as a convinced and consistent supporter of Marchand's Fashoda strategy from October 1895 to June 1898. The new evidence which he adduces in support of this contention seems to me far from conclusive. But this is not the place to discuss it.

Delcassé, August 25, September 7, 1898; No. 246, Trouillot (Colonies) to Delcassé, July 4, 1898.

159. Ibid., No. 315, Delcassé to Montebello (St. Petersburg), September 1, 1898. Delcassé's approach to Berlin was not made during the crisis itself, but early in December 1898, when he feared a preemptive naval strike by Britain; cf. Sanderson, *Upper Nile,* pp. 377–78.

160. D. R. Gillard, review of Sanderson, *Upper Nile,* in *English Historical Review, 82,* 322 (1967), 194–95.

9. *The Entente of 1904 as a Colonial Settlement*

PIERRE GUILLEN

When France and England signed the 1904 agreements, they decided to bury their ancient quarrels. The settlement of the colonial disputes which had so long opposed the two powers was made possible because both parties desired a rapprochement. This colonial settlement became the cornerstone of a policy of close and long-lasting collaboration which had a vast influence on the European political situation. Therefore, it is a question with implications that go beyond Africa. Also, before studying the colonial aspect of these agreements, it would be appropriate to review the underlying factors that led to them.

At the end of the nineteenth century, France was experiencing increasing difficulty in conducting simultaneously a policy of colonial expansion in conflict with England and a European policy based on a latent antagonism toward Germany. Confronted with this problem as soon as he became foreign minister, Théophile Delcassé took upon himself the task of reconciling colonial and European imperatives. Two paths were open to him. An entente with Germany would make it possible to escalate colonial rivalry with England without fear of retaliation. An agreement with England based on mutual concessions would define the areas in which French expansion could be carried forth free of English intervention and would reinforce France's position in Europe vis-à-vis Germany. Did Delcassé, from the very beginning, opt for England? It is difficult to ascertain the motivations of a minister who was not prone to self-explanation.[1] Nonetheless, one has the general impression that Delcassé was undecided until June of 1902. Of course he declared, as early as 1899, that he desired "a sincere and lasting entente" with England, provided that she make

1. The archives of the Quai d'Orsay and the Delcassé papers are disappointing in that respect.

"legitimate concessions to our interests and our sensitivities." [2] However, during the Boer War, at a time when French public opinion supported the Boer cause and denounced England as the hereditary enemy, Delcassé's policies became decidedly anti-British. As a result of the latter's intervention, Count Michael Mouravieff failed to act upon a request by the Bank of England to the Russian banks for a gold loan.[3] At a cabinet meeting on February 28, 1900, the hypothesis of an armed conflict with England was discussed; Delcassé urged that the defenses of Bizerte, Diégo-Suarez, and Indochina be put in a state of readiness. He was also responsible for the decision to create a committee composed of the principal ministers and the commanding officers of the army and the navy. This committee drew up contingency plans in case war became unavoidable: landings in England, an expedition to Egypt, an attack on Burma from Indochina which would coincide with a Russian attack on India.[4] Delcassé also solidified the alliance with Russia. The General Staff Protocol of July 1900 provided for a Franco-Russian military collaboration against England.[5]

Throughout the year 1901, the Quai d'Orsay's attitude was contradictory. Upon several occasions, Paul Cambon, the French ambassador in London, insisted to the Foreign Minister, Lord Lansdowne, that it was necessary to reach an amicable settlement of the Moroccan and Newfoundland questions.[6] But at the same time Delcassé turned toward Germany and resumed the feelers, first sent out in December 1898, leading to a Franco-German colonial settlement, primarily with regard to Morocco.[7] Renewed efforts were made in that direction from October 1902 to January 1903,[8] but this time as a policy to be kept in reserve in case the Foreign Office maintained its disinterest toward

2. Delcassé to Cambon, March 7, 1899, *Documents diplomatiques français* (*DDF* hereafter), 1st series, *15;* Delcassé to Cambon, August 13, 1899, Archives du Ministère des Affaires Etrangères, Paris [MAE hereafter], Great Britain, new series [GB NS hereafter], 12.

3. Notes from the Political Direction, December 14 and 18, 1899, MAE GB NS 12.

4. Note from Delcassé, February 28, 1900, ibid.

5. If England attacked France, Russia would move to India; if England attacked Russia, France would concentrate 150,000 soldiers along the coast of the Channel.

6. G. W. Monger, *The End of Isolation: British Foreign Policy, 1900–1907* (London, 1963), pp. 38–44.

7. P. Guillen, *L'Allemagne et le Maroc de 1870 à 1905* (Paris, 1967), pp. 572–76.

8. Ibid., pp. 658–67.

the proposals delivered by Cambon in July 1902. In early summer of 1902, Delcassé had, in fact, made his choice: England was to be won over. What motives dictated this decision?

To offset the humiliation of the Fashoda incident, Delcassé sought a spectacular success in colonial policy. He thought he would obtain it by settling the Moroccan question to France's advantage; his purpose assumed England's acquiescence because Germany had displayed disinterest when approached on the matter. Moreover, since Russia was involved in the Far East, where a conflict with Japan seemed probable, the Franco-Russian alliance would lose value; a rapprochement with England would compensate for this weakening of the French position in Europe. The government also had to take into account a gradual shift in public opinion away from its traditional Anglophobia to the desire for an entente; many Frenchmen considered improved relations with England the best means to prevent her from drawing closer to Germany, a possibility greatly feared in France during the Anglo-German negotiations of 1898–1901. Abandoning their traditional positions, the colonial party chiefs henceforth considered that French expansion could not continue if England's hostility persisted. For their part, financial circles were also urging a rapprochement; considering dangerous a new increase in Russian securities invested in France, they wished to open the London market to Russian loans.[9]

The British leaders, too, hesitated for a long time. Their motives are now well known, thanks to Monger's research.[10] During the year 1900, the majority of them became convinced that an isolationist policy was no longer appropriate. To maintain her positions throughout the world while confronted with a hostile France, a hostile Russia, and a Germany that made no secret of her ambitions, Britain would have to exert efforts beyond her financial and naval capabilities. The pessimistic reports of the Admiralty and of the chancellor of the Exchequer played a decisive role in this respect. As Lord Salisbury refused to modify his policies, the cabinet rebelled against him, and he was forced to give up his position as foreign minister in November 1900. The government turned toward Germany, since it would be easier and cheaper to make an agreement with her than with France. Confronted with the failure of the conversations, certain politicians,

9. Radolin to Holstein, Private, May 18, 1903, Auswärtiges Amt [AA hereafter], Marokko 4/s.

10. Monger, *End of Isolation.* This book is based on many unprinted documents.

Joseph Chamberlain in particular, proposed a colonial settlement with France as an alternative solution. But the partisans of a rapprochement with Germany refused to capitulate; this tendency, represented principally by Arthur Balfour and Lansdowne, now foreign minister, prevailed within the cabinet until the end of 1901. When Ambassador Cambon tried to open discussions on Morocco and Newfoundland, his proposals fell upon deaf ears.[11] In 1902, the end of the Boer War, the alliance with Japan and the United States' support in the Far East renewed Lansdowne's confidence. He also hoped to maintain good relations with Germany. If he seemed inclined, as a result of Cambon's insistence, to examine certain minor colonial problems, he refused, on the other hand, to discuss important questions such as Siam and Morocco.[12]

The idea of an entente with France came to the fore toward the end of 1902. An anti-German faction appeared within the Foreign Office. Sir Francis Bertie, Sir Charles Hardinge, and Sir Edward Malet believed effective self-protection against Germany to be essential because the Weltpolitik constituted a grave threat.[13] The influence of this group grew because it enjoyed the support of Edward VII. Chamberlain was in complete agreement with their point of view and tried to so convince the cabinet. As he confided to Lord Cromer in Egypt, the Germans' Anglophobia and their commercial rivalry with the British made any agreement impossible; an entente with Russia was out of the question, and so, there remained France.[14] As for the Admiralty, it was worried about the growth of the German fleet. In a memorandum of October 1902, the Admiralty stressed the impossibility of achieving parity against the combined fleets of the three great naval powers, France, Russia, and Germany. Therefore, a change in foreign policy was mandatory. Relations with Russia were also a matter of concern. How could they arrest the Russian expansion toward Persia and Afghanistan and counter the permanent menace that the Russian Black Sea fleet constituted to the Straits? The government decided to carry on simultaneous negotiations to settle its disputes with France and Russia. It was, however, divided as to the meaning of this initiative. For Chamberlain and the anti-German faction in the Foreign Office,

11. Ibid., pp. 38–39, 44.

12. Ibid., pp. 72–73.

13. "She is false and grasping and our real enemy commercially and politically . . . We have nothing to fear from Germany if we remain on good terms with France. She cannot, without the active support of a naval power such as France, injure us." Bertie's letter quoted by Monger, *End of Isolation,* p. 100.

14. La Boulinière to Delcassé, December 12, 1902, MAE GB NS 13.

a colonial settlement with France would lead to close political cooperation in a broadened area and form a diplomatic combination against Germany. On the other hand, Balfour and Lansdowne considered rivalry with Germany as of secondary importance. In their minds, a rapprochement with France would serve only to neutralize the Russian menace. Their objective was to appease France by accepting her proposals for a colonial settlement, and then, using her as an intermediary, bring Russia to conclude an agreement.

The cabinet hesitated for several months before coming to a decision. Negotiations were opened only in July 1903 when there suddenly loomed the threat of a Russo-Japanese war which could well have involved England, an ally of Japan, in a conflict with Russia and France; an entente with the latter seemed to be the only way to avert war. The conversations deadlocked several times. However, at each meeting the heightening of Russo-Japanese tensions and the subsequent outbreak of war led the British government to make concessions and to press for the conclusion of a colonial agreement with France. Balfour and Lansdowne negotiated, always conscious of the Russian presence. The concept of an Anglo-French diplomatic front directed against the Germans was totally foreign to them at that time.

Such is the conclusion one draws from Monger's book, a book that, however, can be criticized for having studied British policy solely as a function of its leaders' concepts and for having overlooked a factor that plays an important role in a country like Great Britain, public opinion. The majority opinion of the day favored a rapprochement with France well before the government, and this attitude was dictated by fear of Germany. As early as 1900, *The Times* and the *Observer* had launched a campaign denouncing the German danger. Businessmen felt that any conflict with France would benefit Germany, their principal rival.[15] In the following years, antipathy toward Germany and its corollary, the desire for cordial relations with France, continued to grow.[16] Financial considerations also played a role. Shaken by the crisis of 1900–01, which coincided with the Boer War, the London market was sustained thanks to the numerous investments made in England by the large French banks.[17] These banks, however, began to withdraw their capital in the autumn of 1902. London financial circles became alarmed, and Cambon recommended to Delcassé that he take advantage of the situation to exert pressure on British

15. Cambon to Delcassé, April 2, 1900, *DDF,* 1st series, *16.*
16. Cambon to Delcassé, April 23 and May 9, 1903, *DDF,* 2nd series, *3.*
17. Cambon to Delcassé, June 19, 1902, MAE GB NS 33.

policies.[18] The withdrawal of French capital, arrested in the spring of 1903 (French banks had underwritten most of the Transvaal loan), recommenced in early summer and provoked a general drop in the value of English securities. To avoid a crisis, London financial circles were convinced that the reinvestment of French capital in London must be achieved.[19] It is quite likely that a political rapprochement with France seemed the best means to attain this end,[20] and in all probability these circles made their views known to the government.

On both sides of the Channel, the necessity of maintaining good relations became increasingly apparent. That is the reason for the decision to end colonial rivalries. The principal points of friction were in Africa where, in Egypt and Morocco, the policies and interests of the two powers had traditionally clashed.

Since the Anglo-Moroccan treaty of 1856 had opened Morocco to European penetration, Great Britain had enjoyed a solidly established position of influence in that country.[21] She owed it to the two principles that had constantly guided her policies: to defend the independence and territorial integrity of Morocco against the designs of France and Spain, and to advise the makhzen to pursue a policy of prudent reforms which would strengthen the government against foreign perils while at the same time serving British interests. Morocco had a considerable strategic and commercial importance for the British. The northern coast commanded the western entrance to the Mediterranean, where a French presence at Tangier would menace Gibraltar, thus threatening British mastery of the Mediterranean. This situation was noted by the first lord of the Admiralty in May 1901.[22] As for the Atlantic coast, the occupation of these ports by a great naval power would endanger maritime links with West Africa and South America. The Foreign Office had finally shelved the idea of an agreement with Germany on Morocco, negotiated between 1899–1901, primarily because the Ger-

18. Cambon to Delcassé, October 11, 1902, ibid.

19. Cambon to Delcassé, June 25, September 24 and 30, 1903, ibid.

20. As soon as the talks took a favorable turn, London financial circles announced the creation of an Anglo-French financial syndicate to support the value of those securities which had fallen in price. The London market immediately picked up again. Cambon to Delcassé, October 23, 1903, MAE GB NS 33.

21. J. L. Miège, *Le Maroc et l'Europe 1830–1894* (4 vols. Paris, 1961–63).

22. Mentzingen to Bülow, May 5, 1901, AA, Marokko 4. Lord Selborne was on a visit at Gibraltar.

mans demanded bases on the Atlantic coast.[23] Without dominating the Moroccan market as exclusively as in the past, British trade had by far the largest share. At the beginning of the twentieth century, Britain controlled 48 percent of the Moroccan market, as compared to 22 percent for France and 14 percent for Germany. By 1903, the percentage of the market controlled by Britain remained unchanged, but the absolute value of its trade had risen from £1,500,000 in 1898 to £2,000,000 in 1903.[24] More than a third of Morocco's exports went to London or Liverpool, while England provided more than half of her imports; 90 percent of the cotton goods (40 percent of total Moroccan imports), tea, and candles were imported from England. This preponderance is explained by the importance of maritime links (with 38 percent of the ships and tonnage, the British flag held first place in Moroccan ports), by the long-standing commercial ties maintained by some hundred firms in Manchester, Liverpool, London, and Birmingham, and by the activity of the British colony in Morocco, second in numbers (1,200) after the Spanish, but first in dynamism. This colony was composed of the staffs of prosperous businesses, usually branches of large British firms, and supplemented by several thousand local employees and commercial or agricultural agents. They were reinforced by a well-established consular network, their own newspaper, and representatives in business and parliamentary circles in England. This group looked upon Morocco as Britain's private preserve and the French as its most dangerous rival.

British policy, wedded for a long time to the maintenance of the status quo, began to change in 1900, a development that led to increasing rivalry with France. The latter defined her aims and moved her Algerian-based troops toward the border, and the sultan increased his appeals for help.[25] The British government, of course, was in no position to contemplate a serious conflict with France while bogged down in the Boer War; therefore, it simply made a mild representation to Delcassé. This timidity was denounced in the House of Commons

23. Memorandum from Bertie, November 9, 1901, *British Documents on the Origins of the War* [*BD* hereafter], 2. As early as 1899, Salisbury had categorically refused a German plan to partition the Atlantic coast of Morocco; Guillen, *L'Allemagne et le Maroc,* pp. 579–80.

24. *Diplomatic and Consular Reports on trade and finance to Morocco,* London, annual series.

25. Ba Ahmed to Queen Victoria, April 21, 1900; Abd el Aziz to Queen Victoria, September 20, 1900, January 21, 1901, Foreign Office [FO hereafter], 99/369 and 380.

where several members demanded a forceful diplomatic initiative to counter the threat of a French protectorate.[26] At the same time, the death of the grand vizir, Ba Ahmed, who had been a determined adversary of European penetration, changed the entire aspect of the Moroccan problem. The young sultan, Abd el Aziz, a modernist, henceforth listened to new advisers who wished to transform the old Morocco on the European pattern, and he announced his intention of bringing about fundamental changes in his domain. For England, this provided an opportunity to be seized. To assist and advise the sultan by suggesting reforms, to offer British financial and technical assistance in improving administration, building a communications system, and developing its resources would serve a double purpose: increase British political and economic dominance and reduce French influence while consolidating the sultan's position. This was the new policy line defined by Sir Arthur Nicolson, then the minister in Tangier, and approved by the Foreign Office.[27]

Nicolson held a number of trump cards: the presence of several British agents at the Sherifan court who had won the sultan's confidence; the support of that part of the makhzen in which the faction headed by El Menebhi, minister of war and a favorite of Abd el Aziz, saw in the British proposals the only means of escaping France's grasp; and, lastly, the assistance of the German legation because the British and German foreign offices, in order to defeat France, had decided to collaborate in launching a program of reforms.[28] This program, which was defined in the course of conversations with Menebhi in London and Berlin in June and July 1901, and during Nicolson's mission to Rabat in January 1902,[29] was barely inaugurated.[30] Many observers felt that Morocco would unavoidably fall under an Anglo-German condominium. In this situation, why did the British government finally decide to bow to France? The stakes were too high to admit overall considerations for a rapprochement with France as the sole explanation. The essential fact is that the situation in Morocco did not evolve in the manner the British had hoped for.

First of all they came up against the determined opposition of the

26. FO 413/33, Confidential Print.

27. Nicolson to Salisbury, May 22, 1900, FO 99/367; Nicolson to Lansdowne, April 1, 1901, FO 800/134.

28. Guillen, *L'Allemagne et le Maroc,* pp. 596–622.

29. Several memorandums from Nicolson and Lansdowne, FO 99/380, 413/33, 800/134.

30. Nicolson to Lansdowne, August 26, 1901, FO 99/381.

French government, which had been alerted by its agents in Tangier [31] and by Paul Cambon. In January 1902, a urgent letter from the ambassador [32] led Delcassé to counterattack on two fronts. In London, Cambon was instructed to warn Lansdowne "that the steps the Sultan is being encouraged to take cannot be considered by us as anything but unfriendly, and we will not countenance them." [33] In Morocco, the French legation stepped up its overtures to the makhzen, using threats and intimidation: if the sultan continued to listen to the British agents and accept their proposals, France would make "serious and immediate decisions" and "would take action." [34] It was decided to hold a Franco-Russian naval demonstration in Tangier, and the General staff drew up plans for military operations.[35] The makhzen, alarmed by these French initiatives, was forced to suspend the program proposed by Nicolson.[36] The policy defined in London could thus only be pursued if France's opposition were overcome, which would entail a bitter crisis with her. Paralyzed by the Boer War and isolated in Europe, the English government became aware of the contradiction between the Moroccan situation, which required action, and the general situation, which required restraint, and it decided to back down. On Lansdowne's instructions, Nicolson abandoned his schemes and thereupon spoke to the Moroccan leaders in quite different terms: any hasty action, any sign of preference for England, such as concessions for public works or the conclusion of a loan, would provoke a dispute with France, which was to be avoided at all costs.[37] The

31. Saint-René Taillandier to Delcassé, December 31, 1901, *DDF*, 2nd series, *1*.

32. "I have received alarming news from Morocco about the Anglo-German penetration. We must give the British no concessions. It would be most unfortunate for you to lose ground when you are doing so well." Cambon to Delcassé, January 13, 1902, MAE Delcassé papers 3.

33. Delcassé to Cambon, January 17, 1902, *DDF*, 2nd series, *1*.

34. Delcassé to Saint-René Taillandier, January 15, February 8, and Saint-René Taillandier to Delcassé, February 12, 1902, *DDF*, 2nd series, *1* and *2*.

35. This plan, delivered to Delcassé in December, provided for two combined operations: a 15,000-man column would advance on Fez from the Algerian-Moroccan frontier; a 12,000-man column would debark at Mazagan (now El-Jadida) with the mission of capturing Marrakesh, using secondary landings in Rabat and Mogador as a cover. Note for the Minister, December 16, 1902, MAE Delcassé papers 16.

36. Saint-René Taillandier to Delcassé, February 26, 1902, *DDF*, 2nd series, *2*.

37. Lansdowne to Nicolson, December 25, 1901, FO 800/134; Nicolson to Lansdowne, January 23, February 2, and Lansdowne to Nicolson, February 26, 1902, FO 99/384, 394, 400.

makhzen, worried about the French thrust, sought vainly to reinaugurate a program of reforms under British tutelage; its proposals fell upon deaf ears.[38] Financial considerations also forced England to be prudent. Morocco was in the throes of a serious financial and monetary crisis and was seeking a loan. Moreover, foreign capital was needed to finance the reform program at a time when the London market, facing serious difficulties itself, lacked resources. In addition, the English banks needed French financial assistance and couldn't contemplate competing with the French banks in Morocco, a country which the latter already considered their private bailiwick.[39] Forewarned by Harry MacLean, an Englishman in the sultan's entourage, London financial circles withdrew.[40] The makhzen was forced to accept the offers of a French consortium.

Moreover, the reform proposals only succeeded in precipitating an internal crisis in Morocco. Within the makhzen, the pro-British faction had to face the combined attacks of the Conservatives and the pro-French group, who won out in the end. British agents were snubbed and Menebhi fell into disgrace, whereas the influence of his rival, the minister of foreign affairs, Ben Slimane, chief of the pro-French group, immediately increased. A divided makhzen and a weak and irresolute sultan condemned Nicolson's efforts to failure, and he concluded that it was impossible to transform Morocco.[41] Furthermore, the majority of the Moroccan population was definitely opposed to innovations which could be interpreted as the beginning of foreign domination. Abd el Aziz, discredited, saw his influence undermined by a growing state of anarchy. The announcement of a reform of the fiscal system crystallized the discontent. In November 1902 an uprising broke out in eastern Morocco, and the subsequent defeat of the army encouraged further revolts. The conclusion in London was that Nicolson had taken the wrong path and brought British policy to an impasse.[42] Given these conditions, continuance of opposition to France

38. In a letter sent to Edward VII on September 10, the sultan asked England to guarantee the integrity of Morocco and to provide a large loan. In exchange England would receive railroad concessions. The British government refused. Memorandums from Nicolson, September 24 and 25, October 3 and 8, 1902, FO 99/395 and 396.

39. P. Guillen, *Finance et diplomatie. Les emprunts marocains de 1902–1904* (Paris, in the press).

40. Cambon to Delcassé, October 7 and 23, 1902, *DDF*, 2nd series, 2.

41. Nicolson to Lansdowne, August 23, October 10, 1901, March 2, 1902, FO 99/381, 382, 394.

42. Guillen, *L'Allemagne et le Maroc*, pp. 616–20.

appeared to be a conflict without hope. On the contrary, necessity dictated the conclusion of an agreement that would give France a free hand while at the same time protecting British interests and obtaining the best possible terms for this disengagement. The longer they delayed, the more France would strengthen her grip on Morocco and England's trump cards would lose their value.

The necessity for an entente with Great Britain became apparent to the French government at the same time. The latter had always considered the growth of any foreign influence in Morocco a menace to Algeria. Abandoning this purely defensive attitude, French policy had, at the turn of the century, taken the offensive. Blocked in Egypt, she transferred her expansionist ambitions to Northwest Africa. In turning toward Morocco, a country considered potentially rich, Delcassé wanted to offset the Fashoda incident and create a French North Africa.[43] The "colonial party," especially its chief, Eugene Etienne, a deputy from Oran, held the same point of view. Business circles expected to realize substantial profits from the exploitation of the Moroccan market; they wished to take advantage of the internal difficulties of the country to gain control of its finances and to control its development.[44] The joint English-German policy, which since 1900 had called for the reform of Morocco under English-German tutelage, was considered a grave menace to French interests and led to Quai d'Orsay to precipitous intervention.[45]

A military penetration from the east was recommended by the Algerian authorities. The first stage of this plan was the occupation of the oasis of Touat, in the spring of 1900. The French, however, were forced to abandon the plan because of the reactions of the British and German governments.[46] Subsequently, Delcassé decided to pursue a twofold policy: in Morocco, a policy called "peaceful penetration," i.e. to develop all means of influence, political, economic, and

43. "If France must seek a complement to its Algerian-Tunisian empire, that complement lies to the west. Laborers, water, and a subsoil as rich as and perhaps even richer than the topsoil can be found there." Delcassé's marginal note on a letter from Noailles, May 28, 1900, *DDF,* 1st series, *16.*

44. P. Guillen, "Les milieux d'affaires français et le Maroc à l'aube du XXe siècle," *Revue Historique* (1963), pp. 397–422.

45. Cambon to Delcassé, November 28, 1899, MAE GB NS 12; January 13 and February 27, 1902, MAE Delcassé papers 3; Révoil to Delcassé, June 2, 1900, MAE Delcassé papers 16; La Martinière to Delcassé, December 31, 1901, Saint-René Taillandier to Delcassé, January 11 and 17, March 5 and 9, 1902, *DDF,* 2nd series, *1* and *2.*

46. Monson to Salisbury, October 17, 1900, *BD, 2;* Münster to Bülow, May 3 and 5, 1900, AA, Marokko 4/s.

financial, which France had at her disposal in a manner designed to place the Moroccan government under French tutelage.[47] In Europe, a diplomatic offensive would be launched to effect the withdrawal of the other involved powers.[48] Obtaining England's consent, at the lowest possible price, presented the principal difficulty. Before confronting the obstacle, Delcassé tried to circumvent it. He concluded an agreement with Italy,[49] sounded out Germany, and opened negotiations with Spain, after which France would be "in a good position to have useful conversations with England, which she apparently desires."[50] But the German Foreign Ministry turned a deaf ear[51] and the Spanish cabinet, which had at first accepted a secret treaty of partition, refused to ratify it when the Foreign Office protested.[52] Therefore, a tête-à-tête with England became necessary.

During the year 1902, the Moroccan situation had evolved in the following manner. Faced with the aggravation of the internal crisis, England and France no longer considered possible the maintenance of the status quo. Her hopes dashed, England henceforth simply waged a rearguard action against France and sought a price for her withdrawal. France considered England the main obstacle to the penetration of her influence and to the diplomatic settlement that would assure her preponderance in the Moroccan Empire; this was a major objective of her colonial policy and was, therefore, worth great sacrifices. What remained to be found was some major concession to satisfy the British. The logic of a barter agreement involving Morocco and Egypt became apparent to both parties.

Although England had controlled Egypt since the 1882 expedition, in actuality her freedom of action there was seriously hampered by international control of Egyptian finances and by the legacy of the Anglo-French condominium. France regretted having yielded to her rival and attempted by all means possible to maintain her traditional influence. This situation nourished a permanent antagonism between the two powers, "England always trying to free herself from international ties which she sought to present as hampering her work of

47. Delcassé to Saint-René Taillandier, July 27, 1901, *DDF,* 2nd series, *1.*

48. Delcassé to Saint-René Taillandier, August 23, 1902, *DDF,* 2nd series, *2.*

49. Agreements of December 1900 and June 1902, by which France and Italy gave each other carte blanche in Morocco and Tripolitania.

50. Delcassé to Saint-René Taillandier, September 11, 1902, *DDF,* 2nd series, *2.*

51. Guillen, *L'Allemagne et le Maroc,* pp. 574–77.

52. Delcassé to J. Cambon, January 8, and J. Cambon to Delcassé, February 1, 1903, *DDF,* 2nd series, *3.*

reorganization, while France, on the other hand, held to those ties to defend her position and halt the encroaching progress of her old partner."[53] What were French interests and powers at the beginning of the twentieth century?[54]

French cultural influence, the heritage of a considerable past, was still strong: the Administration of Excavations and Egyptian Museums, the French Institute for Oriental Archaeology, the French Law School with 150 Egyptian students, and the protection of Catholic religious orders. Although the teaching of French in the public schools continued to lose ground to English,[55] the French religious congregations still taught 15,000 students in eighty-nine schools. In the economic sector, France retained a solid position in spite of constant British progress. Thanks to the activity of the French Chamber of Commerce of Alexandria, French business improved, advancing from sixty million francs in 1897 to seventy million in 1902, amounting to 12 percent of the foreign business of Egypt. French nationals owned large tracts of land, managed prosperous businesses, and directed important industrial enterprises founded by French capitalism.[56] In spite of the opposition of England, French industry (Fives-Lille and the Société des Batignolles) built public works projects for the Egyptian government. In order to defend its interests, assessed in 1902 at five hundred million francs, the French colony controlled several newspapers, some printed in Arabic, which were financed by the large banks and the Quai d'Orsay.[57] But the financial interests were the strongest weapon. The French banks controlled a large share of the Egyptian market. They included the Suez Canal Company and the Crédit Lyonnais, which enjoyed a limited monopoly for transactions with the Caisse de la Dette, the Société des Monts de Piété, and especially the Crédit Foncier Egyptien, with a capital of eighty million francs. Its securities, accepted at the Paris price, rose to three hundred million francs in 1902. This establishment "contributed heavily to the maintenance of [the French] political and economic situation in Egypt."[58] Above all, French stockholders were in possession of the major part of the Egyptian foreign debt, one and a

53. La Boulinière to Delcassé, November 11, 1903, MAE Egypte NS 21.

54. Note from the Political Direction, December 8, 1898, MAE Egypte NS 20; La Boulinière to Delcassé, November 25, 1903, MAE GB NS 14.

55. La Boulinière to Delcassé, June 29, 1904, MAE Egypte NS 21.

56. Sucreries et Raffineries d'Egypte, Société Lebon d'Eclairage, Société des Moulins, d'Egypte, Cie des Tramways d'Alexandrie, Cie des Eaux du Caire, Brasseries Karché, etc.

57. Cogordan to Delcassé, February 19, 1901, *DDF*, 2nd series, *1*.

58. Delcassé to Cogordan, December 20, 1901, MAE Egypte NS 80.

half billion francs, or 62.5 percent. The sum of all these interests represented one-fifteenth of all French capital invested abroad, which placed Egypt in sixth place. "The rights of France in Egypt are based on over two billion francs of French capital invested in the country. This special situation, while creating obligations for France, should also assure her of special consideration." [59]

To maintain her position France wielded effective weapons. She had never recognized the British occupation nor the Anglo-Egyptian condominium in the Sudan. In the Suez Canal question, strengthened by her investments and her many agents employed in the Canal administration, France tried to thwart Britain, periodically requesting application of the Treaty of 1888 on free use of the Canal.[60] Sixty French officials, remaining from the old condominium, still held important positions in different Egyptian ministries. England tried to eliminate them, but France had made their retention "a fundamental article of her political program in Egypt." [61] Moreover, almost two hundred French officials worked in the various international institutions. The significance of these institutions in the life of Egypt and the position France held there constituted the principal obstacle to British policy. England attempted to limit the powers of the Sanitary and Quarantine commissions of Alexandria and Suez, which were systematically used by the French agents to impede British commerce.[62] England protested the extension of the authority of the Mixed Courts, where French judges were in the majority, since they were considered "one of the most serious obstacles to the complete obsorption of Egypt by England." [63]

The British were also irritated at the retention of the three mixed Franco-British administrations created to guarantee the repayment of the debt. The Property Administration managed vast amounts of Egyptian government land as the security for the property loan, which was to be amortized by the sale of land in annual amounts of £300,000. The French officials delayed these sales in order to prolong the existence of the mixed administration, while the British capitalists hastened to gain for themselves the use of these hundreds of thousands

59. La Boulinière to Delcassé, November 25, 1903, MAE GB NS 14.

60. "The free use of the canal depends solely on the goodwill of England. It is useless to insist on the problems that such a state of affairs presents for France, a maritime and colonial power." Note from the Political Direction, December 8, 1898, MAE Egypte NS 20.

61. La Boulinière to Delcassé, November 25, 1903, MAE GB NS 14.

62. Note from the Political Direction, December 8, 1898, MAE Egypte NS 20.

63. Ibid.

of acres. The Administration of the Daira Sanieh managed the khedive's former domain with its large sugar factories, given to the creditors as the security for the Daira Sanieh loan. The French administrators were in the majority and entrusted the equipping of the factories to French industry. When England asked for a rapid repayment of the loan, which would abolish the joint administration, France opposed the request all the more firmly because of a prior arrangement with the khedive in 1897 these lands would revert to a British consortium. The Joint Administration of the Railroads, Telegraph, and Port of Alexandria also brought the two governments into opposition. The allocation of railroad profits to repaying the debt prevented the modernization and expansion of the rail system. In addition, British capital hoped to gain possession of the railroads, whose revenues increased annually.[64]

The powers of the Debt Commission constituted the major subject of discord. Established to ensure the strict enforcement of international decrees relating to the Egyptian financial system and to protect the profits used to repay the several loans, this commission had reached the point where it controlled the entire financial life of the country. It had limited Egyptian government expenses to the unchangeable figure of £5,237,000. Income beyond that amount was divided into two parts: the special reserve fund, returned to the government, and the general reserve fund, administered by the commissioners, who could authorize its use for "great expenses of general interest." Thus the Egyptian government could not freely dispose of its extra earnings, which were increasing with the improvement in the country's finances. England complained of the absurdity of this situation, whereas France held to the letter of the agreement. On the other hand, in 1890 the Great Powers had granted Egypt a reduction in the interest rate of the debt. France had inserted the clause that the savings resulting from this change would form a special fund, entrusted to the Debt Commission which could not use it without the consent of the Powers. France continually refused her consent. This fund, which increased by three hundred thousand pounds per year, reached a total of five and one-half million pounds in 1903, but it was still immobilized. England wanted to use the money to improve the technical level of the nation's economy, but France intended to keep that card in its hand.[65]

Until 1902 France freely used different means of creating problems

64. MAE Egypte NS 69 and 70, passim.

65. La Boulinière to Delcassé, November 25, 1903, MAE GB NS 14.

for British policy. The replacement of Gabriel Hanotaux by Delcassé and the agreement of March 1899 settling the Fashoda crisis did not at all change the approach of the Quai d'Orsay.[66] During the Boer War several official demonstrations strongly supported the French presence in Egypt.[67] Delcassé considered at that time reminding the British that they should evacuate Egypt.[68] He sounded out the other capitals on the advisability of requesting the application of the 1888 treaty on the Suez Canal,[69] as well as opposing a railroad loan by the Cassel group in Britain and supporting the concurrent offers of the Crédit Lyonnais.[70] Delcassé forbade the Egyptian government to use the savings from the lowered interest rate[71] and also refused it any credits for the Sudan from the general reserve fund.[72] However, as early as 1900 Delcassé realized that sooner or later he would have to abandon his policy of "resistance and obstruction" by giving way to Britain, but not without a quid pro quo.[73] His decision was made, it appears, during the summer of 1902. An indication of this decision was the simultaneous recall of two men who had long and successfully defended the French position in Egypt, Emile Cogordan, consul general in Cairo, and Georges Louis, Commissioner of the Debt Commission. Both were replaced by lesser men. Cogordan's appointment as director of political affairs in the Quai d'Orsay, and Louis' position first as director of commercial affairs and then as director of Delcassé's cabinet, showed on the other hand that Egyptian matters would be at the heart of the Franco-British negotiations which had just begun. How can we explain this new orientation?

First of all, the French leaders realized that time was working against them. Over the years the situation favoring England as a result of the occupation of 1882 had tended toward the establishment of a true protectorate. From that time on, any evacuation seemed out

66. Marginal note on a letter from Cogordan, December 20, 1899, *DDF,* 1st series, *16.*

67. The celebration of Bastille Day with unusual fervor, grandiose dedications of a statue of Lesseps, a monument to the dead, and a French hospital, MAE Egypte NS 20, passim.

68. Delcassé to the chargé d'affaires at St. Petersburg, January 25, 1900, *DDF,* 1st series, *16.*

69. Cogordan to Delcassé, January 29, 1900, *DDF,* 1st seires, *16.*

70. Georges Louis and Cogordan to Delcassé, May 5 and 14, and Delcassé to Cogordan, May 11, 1900, MAE Egypte NS 70.

71. Delcassé's marginal note on a letter from Cogordan, June 18, 1900, ibid.

72. Georges Louis to Delcassé, February 14, 1901, ibid.

73. Note from Delcassé, June 18, 1900, ibid.

of the question.[74] By requiring strict enforcement of the financial rules, France had hoped to place the Egyptian treasury in serious trouble and to obtain a means of exerting pressure on British policy. These weapons were now losing their strength.[75] The British government had given the khedive considerable money, and British investors looked to Egypt in growing numbers. Founded by the Rothschild and Cassel groups, the National Bank of Egypt gave rise to the creation of numerous companies and successfully multiplied its securities on the London market.[76] Moreover, as the financial situation in Egypt improved, the amount of budgetary excess returned to the government was increasing, reaching £462,455 in 1899 and £763,814 in 1901. "This increase rendered the Egyptian government more and more independent of the Caisse de la Dette." [77]

Also, France was faced by the 1905 deadline. At that time the five-year period for the Joint Courts would expire. In particular, Egypt would be able to repay in advance the major part of its debt, which would cause the disappearance of the joint administrations and then, shortly thereafter, that of the Debt Commission.[78] This possibility threatened to become a certainty. The Cassel group had redeemed in advance the Daira Sanieh and would repay the creditors starting in 1905. The property loan, already largely amortized, would be easily liquidated. If Egypt could not envisage repaying the privileged and unified loans because of the large amount, eighty million pounds, the Cassel group would try to organize a huge financial syndicate. It would obtain a loan in 1905 to end the debt and would obtain for itself, in exchange, most of Egypt's revenues.[79] This project took shape during 1903. It gained the support of Lord Cromer, who dreamed of crowning his long career in Egypt with the elimination of the international status of the country.[80] The French government became alarmed. Not only would it lose all its means of influence in the financial sector, but also the anticipated repayment would harm the stockholders, two-thirds of whom were French. The government could expect sharp reactions in political and business circles. Al-

74. Delcassé to Cambon, October 24, 1903, MAE GB NS 14.
75. Cogordan to Delcassé, June 18, 1900, MAE Egypte NS 70.
76. Cogordan to Delcassé, May 6, 1899, July 4, 1900, MAE Egypte NS 80.
77. Cogordan to Delcassé, January 8, 1902, MAE Egypte NS 70.
78. Query to Delcassé, November 25, 1903, MAE Egypte NS 21.
79. La Boulinière to Delcassé, September 6, 1902, and Delcassé to La Boulinière, March 12 ,1903, MAE Egypte NS 70 and 71.
80. "He is thinking of pushing us completely out of Egypt." La Boulinière to Delcassé, February 12, 1903, *DDF*, 2nd series, 3.

ready, after the revelations in the British press, numerous sales caused a drop in Egyptian securities in the Paris Bourse.[81] Delcassé was convinced that he could wait no longer to arrange a final settlement with England on the question of Egypt. "We have a clear interest in accepting in a general agreement with England the loss of privileges and rights which each year, as England consolidates its position in Egypt, tend to become purely theoretical. The longer we wait the less important will be the advantages for which we will be able to exchange them." [82]

For its part, the British government could not avoid a discussion with France. The project foreseen by Lord Cromer (issuing a loan of two billion francs to repay the Egyptian debt, thus putting an end to international control) was too vast for the London market and implied the agreement of the Parisian market, and thus an understanding with the French government, "which can prevent the realization of the loan by closing the Paris market." [83] On the other hand, the legal experts consulted by Cromer had stated that although legally nothing prevented Egypt from repaying its debt after 1905, in practice the Caisse de la Dette and the Great Powers could "raise a thousand quibbles and problems." Moreover, this repayment would not put an end to the Caisse de la Dette, which would still be responsible for administering the general capital reserves.[84] Consequently, Cromer reached the conclusion that in order to realize his goals it was necessary "to seek an understanding and friendly cooperation with France." In a memorandum addressed to the Foreign Office he emphasized the necessity for gaining complete liberty of action in the Egyptian financial realm. Initially France would agree to ending the Debt Commission and the mixed administrations.[85] In order to persuade his government of the importance of the matter and bring it to grant the necessary concessions to France, he sent Tigrane Pasha and Sir Eldon Gorst, the financial adviser to the khedive, to London. For their part the financial circles interested in the affair became excited. Sir Ernest Cassel inspired a press campaign and had several conversations with King Edward VII, of whom he was a close friend.[86] Lord Rothschild declared himself ready to facilitate the redemption of the Egyptian

81. Note from the Political Direction, June 29, 1903, MAE Egypte NS 71.
82. Delcassé to Cambon, October 24, 1903, MAE GB NS 14.
83. La Boulinière to Delcassé, April 15, 1903, *DDF*, 2nd series, 3.
84. La Boulinière to Delcassé, May 20, 1903, MAE Egypte NS 71.
85. Memorandum Cromer, August 7, 1903, *BD*, 2.
86. Cambon to Delcassé, August 28, 1903, MAE Egypte NS 71; Cambon to Geoffray, September 19 and 29, 1903, MAE GB NS 14.

debt, "but our cousins in Paris want to act only with the agreement of the French Government." [87] Under these pressures the cabinet decided to exert its influence to soften French attitudes in Egypt. This implied a favorable hearing to Cambon's propositions on Morocco. Therefore, independently of the general trends pushing Britain and France to settle their colonial problems, evolution of the Moroccan and Egyptian questions imposed on the two parties an understanding on the basis of a Moroccan-Egyptian exchange.

In the beginning of 1901, in order to end British opposition to an extension of French influence beyond the Algerian-Moroccan frontier, Cambon had proposed to Lansdowne the utility of talks on Morocco: England was primarily interested in the coast, France in the interior. Thus an agreement could be made. Lansdowne replied negatively.[88] A year later Joseph Chamberlain, disappointed by Germany, recommended an understanding with France and proposed to abandon to France the greater part of Morocco, except for the area around Tangier, but he was no more listened to than Cambon.[89] However, the Quai d'Orsay decided to make specific propositions.[90] On July 27, 1902, Cambon met Lansdowne and proved to him the necessity for settling a question that could provoke a conflict between the two countries.[91] On August 6 Cambon explained to Lansdowne the views of his government: "Morocco is like an extension of Algeria. It is the open door to our African empire. Not for any price can we permit the establishment there of a force which would escape our influence." Aside from the strategic importance of Tangier, England had only economic interests in this region. Thus Delcassé proposed the neutralization of Tangier, the definition of a zone in the north of the country devolving to Spain, and promises to maintain commercial freedom. "In this way all of England's interests in Morocco would be safeguarded, and she would not have to worry about the legitimate extension of French influence." Lansdowne replied that other powers, especially Germany, would consider themselves involved. Any effort to end the Morocco question prematurely would cause serious complications. Nevertheless, he promised to take up the conversations again

87. Declaration of Lord Rothschild's son to Cromer and quoted by La Boulinière to Delcassé, April 15, 1903, MAE Egypte NS 71.

88. Monger, *End of Isolation*, pp. 38–39.

89. J. Amery, *The Life of Joseph Chamberlain, 4* (London, 1951), 180–82.

90. Note from the Political Direction, July 15, 1902, *DDF*, 2nd series, 2.

91. Cambon to Delcassé, July 23, 1902, MAE Delcassé papers 3.

the following autumn.[92] When Cambon tried again in October, the answer was negative: "We are not prepared to discuss a possible liquidation of Morocco." [93]

Lansdowne had discussed the matter with the cabinet. The Admiralty remarked that it would be dangerous to let France control the Moroccan ports. The War Office was also opposed, for strategic reasons, to a French take-over. At the most it envisaged a division of the country, France taking the east, England the coast from Tangier to Casablanca, and Germany the southern coast.[94] On the other hand, several leaks of the proposed negotiations had occurred. While traveling through London Walter B. Harris, a British national in the service of the sultan, had benefited from the calculated indiscretions of those who opposed the retreat of British influence from Morocco. Warned, the sultan wrote to Edward VII to protest strongly; if England put the French offers into effect he would turn toward Germany. This letter, carried by Harry MacLean, made a strong impression on the king, who knighted its bearer.[95] Ending the tête-à-tête with France, which had stimulated so much opposition, the Foreign Office seemed ready to make a place for Germany at the end of autumn. The three powers would give a loan to the Moroccan government for railroad construction, thus setting the stage for a division of the country into three zones of influence, the solution recommended by the chiefs of the army and navy. "It is to our advantage to interpose a German sphere of influence between the French sphere in Algeria and its extension westwards." [96] As for the French government, it decided to await the outcome of negotiations with Spain before initiating a new effort.[97]

These negotiations took place at the end of December. The new Spanish government had just rejected the proposed French treaty.

92. Cambon to Delcassé, August 9, 1902, *DDF,* 2nd series, *2;* Cambon to Delcassé, August 12, 1902, MAE Delcassé papers 3; Lansdowne to Monson, July 23, August 6, 1902, *BD,* 2.

93. Lansdowne to Monson, October 15, 1902, *BD,* 2; Cambon to Delcassé, October 23, 1902, *DDF,* 2nd series, 2.

94. Monger, *End of Isolation,* p. 79.

95. Memorandums Nicolson, September 24 and 25, October 8, 1902, FO 99/395, 396; Saint-René Taillandier to Delcassé, October 17, Cambon to Delcassé, October 23, 1902, *DDF,* 2nd series, *2;* A. J. P. Taylor, "British Policy in Morocco, 1886–1902," *English Historical Review, 66* (1951), 371.

96. Memorandums from the Direction of Military Intelligence, October 28, November 22, 1902; memorandum from the Direction of Naval Intelligence, October 28, 1902, quoted by Monger, *End of Isolation,* p. 81.

97. Cambon to Delcassé, December 10, 1902, MAE Delcassé papers 3.

Alarmed by the activity of British agents, the French legation in Tangier concluded that it was impossible to delay calling the British to account any longer. After a trip to Tangier which convinced them of the gravity of the situation, Cambon and the governor-general of Algeria succeeded in convincing Delcassé that the key to the problem was in London.[98] Therefore, on December 29 Cambon called on Lansdowne. The French government desired to settle the Moroccan problem exclusively with England and Spain. Lansdowne had just received bad news from Morocco: an uprising had occurred, the Sherifian army was in flight, and an intervention by the Great Powers seemed inevitable. "The Moroccan question will be opened in a most complicated form." German relations at that time were bad, and Russia continued to pose a threat. In this delicate situation Lansdowne had to resign himself to listening to the French ambassador.[99]

In the opinion of the British officials it was not a matter of giving free rein to France, but only of collaboration to avoid the collapse of Morocco.[100] They sought to impose this collaboration in the matter of the loans. The Quai d'Orsay meant France to be the sole creditor of Morocco, but the Foreign Office opposed this idea. At the instigation of the Foreign Office, the Montagu and Cassel groups proposed to the consortium directed by the Banque de Paris et des Pays-Bas a joint loan to the Moroccan government. It would have been of considerable size, guaranteed by the two countries in the hope of large profits from reorganizing the customs administration with French and British personnel.[101] Delcassé reacted strongly: "The installation of an Anglo-French control over the customs apparatus would lead to the internationalization of Morocco. This would destroy the gains French policy has taken more than twenty years to make." [102] Cambon warned Lansdowne that an Anglo-Franco guardianship over Moroccan finances was out of the question.[103] Delcassé summoned the President

98. P. Cambon, *Correspondances, 2* (Paris, 1940), letter written on February 3, 1903; Comte de Saint-Aulaire, *Confessions d'un vieux diplomate* (Paris, 1953), pp. 71–72.

99. Monger, *End of Isolation,* pp. 111–12.

100. Ibid., pp. 113–14; see also Cambon to Delcassé, January 29, 1903, *DDF,* 2nd series, *3*.

101. Note from Georges Louis, January 3, 1903, ibid.

102. Note from Georges Louis, February 3, Delcassé to Cambon, February 26, 1903, MAE Maroc 206.

103. Delcassé to Cambon, February 3, and Cambon to Delcassé, February 4, 1903, *DDF,* 2nd series, *3*. Since Lansdowne insisted that the two governments recognize an arrangement between the British and French banks on the subject

of the Banque de Paris et des Pays-Bas and indicated to him his total opposition to the idea of an Anglo-Franco loan.[104] Lansdowne did not give up. Since veto of the Quai d'Orsay prevented the proposed loan, English finance would go it alone. At the strong request of the government and Edward VII, the Cassel and Stern groups granted to the sultan in March 1903 a loan of £300,000.[105] In general during the first months of 1903, Anglo-France rivalry seemed more intense than ever. England tried to install a radio station at Cape Spartel, and France encouraged the sultan to resist the proposal. When the Moroccan government ordered the Europeans to leave Fez, England kept her agents there. France protested and then decided to leave her military mission in Fez. When disturbances occurred in the area around Tetuán, the British Admiralty sent a squadron to the port, as did the French.[106] Clearly Great Britain was trying to improve her position before entering into decisive negotiations with France.

Conversations began in July 1903, on the occasion of the visit of President Loubet to London. It was agreed that Lansdowne and Delcassé would examine in depth the disputes in question.[107] Both sides seemed to want a rapid conclusion. As a result of the worsening situation in the Far East, Lansdowne wanted Delcassé to exert a moderating influence on Russia.[108] In France the colonial circles emphasized the urgency for settling the Moroccan question with England.[109] On July 7 Delcassé asked that France alone have the right to "regenerate" Morocco. He offered three conditions: neutralization of the Mediterranean coast; recognition of the interests of Spain; and the protection of British commerce. France could then be conciliatory on the other questions raised by Lansdowne, especially that of Egypt. "But the point of departure in French opinion was the settlement of the Moroccan question." [110]

---

of the Moroccan loans, Delcassé agreed to proceed to an exchange of letters, limiting himself to stating the conformity of views of the two governments, which committed him to nothing; Cambon to Lansdowne, February 7, 18, 19, and 26, 1903, and Delcassé to Cambon, February 17 and 25, 1903, MAE Maroc 206.

104. Georges Louis to Cogordan, March 7, 1903, MAE Maroc 206.

105. Monger, *End of Isolation,* p. 113; Saint-René Taillandier to Delcassé, April 2, 1903, MAE Maroc 206.

106. Delcassé to Saint-René Taillandier, February 10; Cambon to Delcassé, April 27; and note from the Department, May 14, 1903, *DDF,* 2nd series, 3.

107. Cambon to Delcassé, July 1, 1903, MAE Delcassé papers 3.

108. Monger, *End of Isolation,* pp. 128–29.

109. Chailley-Bert to Delcassé, June, 1903, MAE Delcassé papers 14.

110. Delcassé to Cambon, July 21, 1903, *DDF,* 2nd series, 3. See also Lansdowne to Monson, July 7, 1903, *BD,* 2.

For several months the negotiations marked time. Lansdowne, with the support of the cabinet, had approved Delcassé's propositions in principle. The Colonial Office raised no objections. When consulted, Cromer observed that England should accept the inevitable ("Morocco will become before long a French province") and obtain its compensation in Egypt.[111] But the army and navy had other ideas. Recognizing French preponderance in Morocco would require that Great Britain renounce all influence and ruin its commerce there. Moreover, the neutralization of Tangier and the extension of Spanish holdings were illusory guarantees. Sooner or later France would install herself on the Mediterranean coast and Britain would be unable to prevent her.[112] Lansdowne insisted that the Far Eastern situation made urgent an understanding with the French. In Morocco, France would continue to gain territory, whereas British positions were gradually crumbling. If Britain waited too long, she would not even be able to exact a price for her withdrawal. The navy rallied to this point of view, but the army maintained its opposition. It was finally necessary to appeal the matter to Edward VII, who decided in favor of Lansdowne.[113]

On the other hand, divisions had appeared between Paris and London. Delcassé wanted to settle the Moroccan question first. ("The settlement of the other questions will depend on England's favorable or unfavorable attitude toward Moroccan affairs.") Lansdowne wanted to negotiate all points at the same time and include them in the same agreement. When the French memorandum of July 27 made no reference to Egypt, Lansdowne issued a protest. Cambon replied that the introduction of the Egyptian question constituted a new subject. France, in that case, would be more demanding over Morocco: total liberty to reform the country, and, for a limited time only, an "open door policy."[114] To obtain satisfaction, Delcassé was counting on the importance to the British of an Egyptian settlement. His estimate was proven correct on October 1 when a memorandum from Lansdowne took up the basic points of the French demands.[115] Two aspects were still in dispute: the approval of a French monopoly to reorganize Morocco and the neutralization of the coasts.

In a second memorandum of October 24 Delcassé specified his new

111. Monger, *End of Isolation,* p. 129.

112. Memorandums from War Office and Direction of Naval Intelligence, quoted by Monger, pp. 130–31.

113. Monger, pp. 132–34.

114. Cambon to Delcassé, July 22 and 31, 1903, and Delcassé to Cambon, August 2, 1903, MAE GB NS 14.

115. Memorandum Lansdowne, October 1, 1903, *BD,* 2.

demands. The first was the removal of the paragraph on maintaining the political and territorial status quo in Morocco. He also asked that the term "intérêt singulier" be replaced by "intérêt exclusif de la France" to undertake not merely "améliorations" but rather "toutes les réformes" that were imperative in the administrative, economic, financial, and military aspects of the country. He also asked that commercial liberty for other nations be limited to fifteen years.[116] Lansdowne was very embarrassed, for at the same time a campaign was developing protesting the abandonment of Morocco to France. Under the leadership of the shipper Forwood, a Committee for the Defense of British Interests in Morocco had been created. Meetings of interested businessmen were taking place in London and Manchester at the same time as motions in Parliament, requests to the Foreign Office, and delegations to Lansdowne. London financial circles became excited, inspiring the campaign undertaken by the *Morning Post* and the *Standard* to demand the continuance of an independent Morocco. Pointing out the present and especially the future importance of the Moroccan market, business circles opposed giving unilateral control to France. Instead, they suggested the two countries should jointly assure the economic and industrial development of Morocco.[117]

To take into consideration these attitudes, Lansdowne, after discussions with the Cassel and Baring groups, again proposed the idea of an Anglo-Franco loan of two million pounds. This loan would be issued simultaneously in London and Paris and would be based on the customs system, which would be placed under the control of French and British officials. In spite of his strong insistence, he could not overcome Delcassé's categorical opposition. At the same time, Delcassé was laying plans for a deal with the Banque de Paris et des Pays-Bas which would place Morocco under the financial tutelage of France. Consequently, he replied that Lansdowne's proposals were untimely: concurrently with negotiations for French predominance in Morocco, it was out of the question to consider the involvement of British lenders and of joint control. Cambon denounced an effort, inspired by Sir Ernest Cassel, for the British to obtain financial advantages in Egypt later on. "They offer to end British control over Moroccan customs in exchange for the Egyptian debt. That would be a ridiculous trade, which we must decline." [118] Since Delcassé was intransigent in respect

116. Cambon to Lansdowne, October 26, 1903, *DDF*, 2nd series, *4*.

117. Cambon to Delcassé, October 21 and 22, November 9, 1903, ibid; Metternich to Bülow, October 19, November 10, 1903, AA, Marokko 4/s; *Bulletin du Comité de l'Afrique française* (1903), p. 368.

118. Geoffrey to Delcassé, October 10, and Cambon to Delcassé, November 4,

to finances, Lansdowne, in his memorandum of November 19, called for serious guarantees concerning the economy of Morocco; i.e. maintaining commercial freedom even in the event France should annex the country and permitting British participation in major public enterprises, such as the ports and railroads. The Quai d'Orsay remained inflexible, with the result that the Foreign Office had to give in, on condition that Great Britain would receive a similar monopoly in Egypt.[119] However, at the last moment Lansdowne demanded that "exclusively" be replaced by "especially" in the sentence reserving to France the responsibility for reforming Morocco. Delcassé opposed this change, then, since Lansdowne would not concede, agreed to remove the adverb altogether.[120] This concession was a mere formality, which really changed nothing, and was intended to reassure British public opinion.

The other ardently debated point was the neutralization of the Moroccan coast. Lansdowne had warned Cambon that it was up to the Admiralty to examine this question and to delimit the neutralized zone.[121] Anxious to assure Britains strategic positions, the chiefs of the army and navy demanded neutralization of the coastline from the Algerian border to El-Jadida (then called Mazagan). France would thus be unable to erect fortifications or establish a naval base on over half the Atlantic coast. The French countered with a proposal that the right bank of the Sebou River be the southern limit.[122] Lansdowne suggested as a compromise that the coast be neutralized as far as Rabat. Delcassé rejected this proposal, since the port of Rabat commanded one of the principal routes of French penetration.[123] Under pressure from the Admiralty, the cabinet maintained its point of view. It did not give in until March 11, 1904, and then only to avoid the failure of all the negotiations.[124]

The French government had finally obtained satisfaction on all

---

1903, MAE Maroc 206; Cambon to Delcassé, October 22, November 11, and Delcassé to Cambon, November 5 and 10, 1903, *DDF*, 2nd series, *4*.

119. Delcassé to Cambon, December 6, and Cambon to Delcassé, December 10 and 11, 1903, *DDF*, 2nd series, *4*.

120. Cambon to Delcassé, March 28, 29, 30, 31, and Delcassé to Cambon, March 29, 31, 1903, MAE GB NS 16.

121. Cambon to Delcassé, July 31, August 6, 1903, MAE GB NS 14.

122. British memorandum, October 1, and French memorandum, October 24, 1903, ibid.

123. Cambon to Delcassé, November 22, and Delcassé to Cambon, December 6, 1903, *DDF*, 2nd series, *4*.

124. Cambon to Delcassé, December 10 and 11, 1903, January 14, 1904, *DDF*, 2nd series, *4;* Cambon to Delcassé, March 11, 1904, MAE GB NS 15.

points. Faced with protests from business circles and criticism from the military leaders, Lansdowne had tried to limit the freedom of action permitted to France. The unyielding stance of the Quai d'Orsay accepted no such strictures. The French position gained its strength from the international situation, which required the fastest possible settlement, and from the role of such influential men as Cromer and Cassel, who gave priority to the Egyptian question. Delcassé knew how to exploit the situation, gaining maximum benefit from his holdings in Egypt.

As early as February of 1903 Lansdowne let it be known that the Moroccan question was tied to that of Egypt.[125] Delcassé understood this fact, in spite of his denials before the Chamber of Deputies.[126] The matter was first taken up at the time of President Emile Loubet's visit to London.[127] Supported by the cabinet and by the king, Lansdowne, who had taken Cromer's advice, drew up in his memorandum of October 1 a certain number of demands presented as the counterpart to an agreement on Morocco.[128] He asked that the British occupation of Egypt be recognized as permanent, as well as for several changes in financial administration. These would consist of free use of the profits from the new interest rate, the disappearance of the general reserve fund, and the end of the control exerted by the Debt Commission over the Egyptian budget. Because of financial hardships in England, Cromer had in fact abandoned for the time being his vast projects for totally liquidating the Egyptian debt. He satisfied himself instead, as a first step, "with less radical changes." [129] As for the Quai d'Orsay, it regarded the occupation of Egypt as an irreversible fact and agreed to give up the majority of French control over Egyptian finances.[130] Under such conditions the agreement should have been concluded easily. The discussions, however, were quite bitter.

125. Cambon to Delcassé, February 4, 1903, *DDF*, 2nd series, 3. Cromer had insisted on this point in his letters to Lansdowne, who realized that the suppression of the Caisse de la Dette would be "an immense thing"; Monger, *End of Isolation*, p. 128.

126. Delcassé's categorical answers to the questions of the deputies, meetings of March 10 and 11, 1903. However, Delcassé noted on the margin of a report from Cairo concerning Cromer's financial projects: "Speak to Mr. Cogordan about it. Compensations. Morocco"; La Boulinière to Delcassé, April 15, 1903, MAE Egypte NS 71.

127. Delcassé to Cambon, July 21, 1903, *DDF*, 2nd series, 3.

128. Monger, *End of Isolation*, p. 129.

129. La Boulinière to Delcassé, November 22, December 3, 1903, *DDF*, 2nd series, 4.

130. Note from the Political Direction, June 29, 1903, MAE Egypte NS 71.

In order to gain the greatest possible advantages in Morocco, the French government moved carefully. It began by denying that France could surrender its holdings in Egypt because of the size of its investment and of the sensitiveness of public opinion.[131] The French next tried to show that the exchange was unequal. In Morocco, French freedom of action was "a hope, not an immediate and tangible reality." Thus the British would be giving what they did not possess "while at the same time asking us to abandon rights and advantages of which we are in full possession in Egypt."[132] French public opinion, claimed Cambon, would consequently not permit "an immediate surrender of the French position in Egypt." The Quai d'Orsay proposed "progressive withdrawals balanced by compensations," which would constitute a "correlation between our progress in Morocco and our withdrawal in Egypt."[133] Cambon calculated that Lansdowne would finally accept this principle of "*pari passu.*" He emphasized to Lansdowne the need to profit from a situation that might not occur again. ("You may be certain that no political figure in France, with the exception of Mr. Delcassé, will have the daring to settle the Egyptian question.") Cambon also resorted to extortion: "Suppose that we were to refuse all concessions in Egypt and that, relying on Russia and Germany, we should try to place England under pressure. How would you escape from such a situation?"[134] The Quai d'Orsay decided to concede nothing and to take its time. "We have the right to be difficult. The British have more interest in gaining our cooperation in Egypt than do we with them in Morocco."[135] In fact, bombarded with letters from Cromer, the British government accepted the French point of view: France could not immediately retire from Egypt, since French liberty of action in Morocco would not be immediate. A compromise was required.[136]

131. Cambon to Delcassé, July 31, August 6, and Delcassé to Cambon, August 2, 1903, *DDF*, 2nd series, *3*.

132. "It was good to indicate from the outset our intention to sacrifice none of our holdings without receiving a valid counterpart in return." Cambon to Delcassé, October 11, 1903, *DDF*, 2nd series, *4*. Irritated, Lansdowne replied that England was already in Egypt, that there was not the slightest prospect of an evacuation, and that England could not wait indefinitely for recognition of the permanent nature of the British occupation.

133. Cambon to Delcassé, October 22; Delcassé to Cambon, October 24; and Cambon to Lansdowne, October 26, 1903, *DDF*, 2nd series, *4*.

134. Cambon to Delcassé, October 23, 1903, MAE GB NS 14; Cambon to Delcassé, October 28, November 4, 1903, *DDF*, 2nd series, *4*.

135. Cambon to Delcassé, November 18, 1903, *DDF*, 2nd series, *4*.

136. Cambon to Delcassé, November 11, *DDF*, ibid; La Boulinière to Delcassé, November 11, 1903, MAE GB NS 14; Monger, *End of Isolation*, pp. 137, 144.

The questions of free use of the Suez Canal and of the French officials serving in Egypt were easily settled.[137] Financial arrangements were the subject of numerous discussions. In a memorandum of November 19, Lansdowne accepted the continuance of the Caisse de la Dette, but it would be deprived of most of its functions. The Egyptian government would recover its financial autonomy, consisting of the liberty to conclude loans, to modify the fiscal administration, and to convert and repay its debt. In addition, the joint administration, the general reserve fund, and the fund of profits from the change in interest would all be terminated. Cambon and the French representative in Cairo advised Delcassé to refuse, since the creditors of Egypt would lose all. The protests of these stockholders would reach Parliament, which would refuse to ratify the convention. But Delcassé, satisfied with British concessions on Morocco, decided to accept, on condition that new guarantees would be assured to the stockholders. The British government agreed to this stipulation.[138] On two occasions Gorst, the financial adviser to the khedive, went to Paris to confer with Cogordan, Georges Louis, and Delcassé to draft the khedive's decree which would outline the new financial administration in Egypt. The Quai d'Orsay gave its approval to the British projects. In exchange it obtained for French stockholders the following guarantees:

1. The Caisse de la Dette would be provided with a reserve fund of £1,800,000 and a working capital of £500,000, to assure the payment of debts in case of a delay in deposits from the Egyptian government.

2. The property tax would be used to repay the debt, in order to replace the former revenues for this purpose which were now to be ended.

3. The date after which Egypt could convert or reimburse privileged, guaranteed, and unified loans would be advanced from 1905 to 1910.

4. The joint administration would be continued for the railroads until 1910 and for real estate until 1915.[139]

137. As far as free access to the Suez Canal is concerned, Great Britain accepted the enforcement of the 1888 convention, except for Article 8, which involved the creation of an international control commission. It was also understood that French officials serving in Egypt would retain the same status as that of the British functionaries.

138. Cambon to Delcassé, November 22, December 10, 1903, *DDF*, 2nd series, *4;* La Boulinière to Delcassé, November 27, December 1 and 3, and Lansdowne to Cambon, December 23, memorandum Gorst, December 24, MAE GB NS 14.

139. Cogordan to La Boulinière, January 4, note from Georges Louis, March 19; and Cambon to Delcassé, March 23 and 26, 1904, MAE GB NS 15 and 16.

These arrangements were well received by financial circles, where their announcement caused a rise in the values of Egyptian securities on the Paris Bourse. It would also be appropriate to point out that throughout the negotiations the large French banks exerted no pressure at all on the Quai d'Orsay, which is remarkable in view of the size of French financial holdings in Egypt. How can this fact be explained? Once the entente was concluded, freeing Egyptian finances, a rapid development of the country's resources could be expected. The great financiers of France counted on profiting from this development, for British business circles would not fail to ask for French assistance. In fact, during the months following the Entente Cordiale, the Land Bank of Egypt and the Union Foncière d'Egypte were founded, which combined British groups and the Société Marseillaise. The Banque de l'Union Parisienne entered into the Caisse Hypothécaire d'Egypte and founded several branches. At the time of the liquidation of the Daira Sanieh an agreement was signed between the Cassel group and the Crédit Foncier Egyptien. In November of 1905 the Quai d'Orsay noted that the total of securities issued during the past six months by businesses in Egypt and sold on the Paris market had reached 215 million francs.[140] In addition, there were one and one-half billion francs of Egyptian government funds invested in France. However, these securities were held by a great number of small investors. Convinced that the British would take over Egyptian finances sooner or later, the large Parisian banks had long since resold their stocks.[141]

Having settled the financial question, one last difficulty arose at the end of March 1904. In order to justify the withdrawal from Morocco to British public opinion, the Foreign Office asked the Quai d'Orsay to recognize formally the permanent occupation of Egypt. Delcassé refused, for this provision should not appear in the declaration on Morocco, where France could not publicly question the political status quo without angering other countries and alienating the Moroccan government. The French Parliament would oppose this difference between the position granted Great Britain in Egypt and that of France in Morocco. But the British government did not want to give in. To avoid a complete break in negotiations, Delcassé proposed a compromise, which was finally accepted in London: "France

140. Notes from the Political Direction, August 5, 1904, May 3, 1905, October 16, November 29, 1905, and La Boulinière to Delcassé, May 29, 1905, MAE Egypte NS 80.

141. J. Bouvier, "Les intérêts financiers et la question d'Egypte," *Revue Historique* (1960), pp. 75–105.

will not hamper British actions in the country by requiring that a fixed term be set for the occupation of Egypt." [142]

Although the joint agreements on the Moroccan and Egyptian questions were not reached without difficulties, deliberately magnified by the negotiators to gain concessions from the opposing country, these problems never really endangered the outcome of the discussions. It was an apparently minor dispute, that of Newfoundland, which set the two governments at odds with the greatest bitterness.

In 1901 Great Britain had set as a condition to any agreement that France relinquish its fishing rights in Newfoundland. The Quai d'Orsay announced that it was amenable to this proposal, but requested territorial compensation in Africa. The French choice was for the Gambia, to end that British enclave into Senegal. Lansdowne refused and asked Cambon to formulate new proposals.[143] The Quai d'Orsay thought of Sokoto, in order to assure communications with Chad.[144] The question was taken up again during the summer of 1903, but England offered only a narrow strip of land in the Nigerian desert.[145] The Quai d'Orsay, in this situation, again demanded the Gambia with the greatest insistence. Cromer favored giving in, but the Colonial Office categorically opposed losing the Gambia.[146] The negotiators then examined the map of Africa in the area of the Niger River. The Quai d'Orsay hoped to restudy the Convention of 1898, which had been very unfavorable to France, and to obtain greater access to the right bank of the river, south of the rapids, by the cession of Bussa and the Nikki-Badjibo-Illo triangle, territories France had sought unsuccessfully in 1898. The Foreign Office considered these claims as "quite unreasonable" and again offered a rectification of the frontier north of Sokoto.[147]

The Quai d'Orsay reacted sharply. "This is sand where the French

142. Cambon to Delcassé, March 23, 25, 28, and April 6, and Delcassé to Cambon, March 26 and 31, 1904, MAE GB NS 16.

143. Cambon to Delcassé, August 9, 1902, *DDF*, 2nd series, *2*.

144. Cambon to Delcassé, August 12, 1902, MAE Delcassé papers 3.

145. Cambon to Delcassé, August 6, 1903, MAE GB NS 14.

146. Cambon to Delcassé, October 22, 26, and 28, November 4 and 22, 1903, MAE GB NS 14. Delcassé asked only for the hinterland of Gambia, England keeping the coast; the Colonial Office rejected this compromise; Delcassé to Cambon, December 6, and Cambon to Delcassé, December 10, 1903, *DDF*, 2nd series, *4*.

147. Cambon to Delcassé, December 11, and Cambon to Lansdowne, December 27, 1903, MAE GB NS 14.

rooster could scratch at his ease. Now as for that sand, public opinion is that the Treaty of 1898 has already given up too much of it." Cambon's talks with Lansdowne turned sour. Delcassé expressed his feelings quite firmly to the British ambassador in Paris and then decided to suspend all negotiations. "Since all our affairs are mutually dependent, we cannot continue to discuss Egypt usefully until we are in agreement on the territorial compensation for Newfoundland." He warned Cromer of the situation, asking him to put pressure on his government. Cromer telegraphed to London immediately: a halt to the negotiations would be a calamity.[148] At a meeting on January 23, 1904, the British cabinet decided to hold firm on the question of the Middle Niger, but to propose to France a right of passage on the river, and border rectifications in the Gambia, to the north of Sokoto, and near Lake Chad. Delcassé thought these concessions insufficient and asked additionally for the Iles de Los, opposite Conakry. Lansdowne wanted to haggle. "We are not disposed to throw these islands into the bargain unless the French Government, for its part, adds something else to the scales. We suggest that to make the transaction equal France should accept the British protectorate over the New Hebrides."[149] The Quai d'Orsay refused. Moreover, the British Admiralty opposed the cession of the Iles de Los because of their strategic value. As a result of the significance French opinion attached to the Newfoundland question, Delcassé believed that an "appropriate compensation" was indispensable. He deemed it essential to demand substantial gains near Sokoto as well as the Iles de Los. The attitude of the British Admiralty was particularly painful to him. "At the time when we are trying, with the best faith in the world and in the most friendly spirit, to end the sources of conflict between our two countries, the Admiralty seems to want to keep the Iles de Los which will certainly lead to future problems." Discouraged, he seriously anticipated the failure of all the negotiations. "We are consequently reaching an extreme limit." Cambon did not hide from Lansdowne that they were close to breaking off the discussions.[150] This prospect alarmed the British government, for the Russo-Japanese War had just broken out. Cromer was

148. Cambon to Cogordan, January 7; Cambon to Delcassé, January 13, 14, and 18; Delcassé to La Boulinière, January 19; and La Boulinière to Delcassé, January 20, 1904, all *DDF*, 2nd series, *4*.

149. Cambon to Delcassé, January 24, and Delcassé, to Cambon, January 26, 1904, ibid.; Cambon to Delcassé, January 27, February 4, and Lansdowne to Cambon, February 5, 1904, MAE GB NS 15.

150. Cambon to Delcassé, February 11 and 18, and Delcassé to Cambon, February 16, 1904, MAE GB NS 15.

continuing to press the government when Edward VII intervened: "We should have no bone of contention at present with the French." On February 25 the cabinet accepted the cession of the Iles de Los and placed under study a new delineation of Nigeria's northern frontier.[151] It was understood that the frontier would pass to the south of the Say-Zinder road. But how far south? The Foreign Office proposed 500 meters and the Quai d'Orsay 10 kilometers, for the trail frequently changed. They agreed upon 5 kilometers, but then realized that the trail was not marked in the same place on the British and French maps. Finally it was decided that the tribes under the jurisdiction of the sultanates of Tessaoua, Maradi, and Zinder would be "left to France as much as possible." [152]

Access to the navigable part of the Gambia River and cession of the Iles de Los were of no great interest to France. On the other hand, the revision of the 1898 convention on the Niger had the advantage of assuring henceforth satisfactory communications between the Sudan and Chad. Nevertheless, it seems surprising today that the relinquishing of fishing rights in Newfoundland in exchange for minor concessions in Africa could have delayed for several months the settlement of far more important matters in Morocco and Egypt, as well as the overall political rapprochement between the two countries. Each of the two governments seems to have been concerned mainly with not making a bad bargain and not giving more than it received. It was essential to satisfy public opinion and lead it to accept the necessary sacrifices. In particular, the diplomats remained prisoners of the principle of a balance of power in colonial settlements, a sort of reciprocal give and take which had dominated international relations throughout the nineteenth century. The Entente Cordiale was born without grandeur in the midst of bargains.

The agreements of 1904 contained the first sign of a developing political collaboration. This was the famous article that dealt with mutual diplomatic support to assure the execution of those clauses pertaining to Morocco and Egypt. In actuality this stipulation was added at the last moment, without the two governments' realizing the implications of such an agreement. In November 1903 Cromer, who feared Germany's reaction, commented that the consent of all the

151. Monger, *End of Isolation*, pp. 157–58; Cambon to Delcassé, February 25, 1904, *DDF*, 2nd series, *4*.

152. Cambon to Delcassé, February 27 and 29, March 1, 4, and 11, 1904, MAE GB NS 15.

Great Powers was necessary before the British would be able to introduce administrative reforms in Egypt. France should promise to support the diplomatic efforts of England, so as to obtain the adherence of the Great Powers to the khedival decree. Lansdowne incorporated this clause in his memorandum of November 19, but the Quai d'Orsay refused.[153] Lansdowne, who thought the point unimportant, overlooked it during the negotiations. It was discussed again in March 1904, because of Cromer's strong insistence. Delcassé again refused and observed that France had not asked for British aid in Morocco. "It is up to each government to carry out those clauses which are favorable to it."[154] Since Balfour was immovable on this subject, the Quai d'Orsay finally gave in, but requested "British support in Morocco as the necessary counterpart." Lansdowne immediately accepted, without realizing how far this clause threatened to lead him. In his view, it was merely a question of "moral support."[155] Nevertheless, at the time the agreements were published the two governments hailed the beginning of a new era in Franco-British relations and asserted their willingness to act henceforth in concert on the great questions of world politics.[156] The application of the convention concerning Morocco and Egypt activated what was previously only a declaration of intention.

In Egypt the French government let the British use the freedom of action she had just granted them without raising the slightest difficulty. By the end of April Cromer was able to send to London a vast construction program for the improvement of Egypt and the Sudan (railroads, dams, and reservoirs permitting the irrigation of over two and one-half million acres). It was to be financed by the money put at Egypt's disposal through the arrangement concluded with France.[157] France provided its good offices to hasten acceptance of the khedival

153. Cambon to Delcassé, November 22, 1903, *DDF*, 2nd series, *4;* Cambon to Delcassé, December 11, 1904, MAE GB NS 14; Monger, *End of Isolation,* pp. 144–45.

154. Delcassé to Cambon, March 20; Cambon to Delcassé, March 23; note from the Political Direction, March 25, 1904, all MAE GB NS 15 and 16; Monger, *End of Isolation,* pp. 157–59.

155. Cambon to Delcassé, March 25, 26, and 31, and Delcassé to Cambon, March 26, 1903, MAE GB NS 16.

156. Statements from Lansdowne to the French chargé d'affaires, Geoffray to Delcassé, April 13, 1904, MAE GB NS 17; from the parliamentary undersecretary of the Foreign Office before the House of Commons, Cambon to Delcassé, June 2, 1904, MAE GB NS 18; from Delcassé in a communique to the embassies, April, 1904, MAE GB NS 16.

157. Cambon to Delcassé, August 10, 1904, MAE GB NS 18.

decree by the Great Powers. Strengthened by this support, England was able to gain the unconditional acceptance of Italy and reject disdainfully Germany's request for compensation.[158] Fearing complications with Russia, Lansdowne asked the French to support him in St. Petersburg. Thanks to the intervention of Delcassé, who put pressure on both governments, an agreement was reached: Russia accepted the khedival decree, and in exchange England promised not to establish a protectorate over Tibet.[159] Thus was begun the process that was to lead to the Triple Entente, as desired by certain British politicians and by King Edward VII, who felt the colonial settlement with France should facilitate a similar agreement with Russia.[160]

The Entente Cordiale became particularly important in regard to the Moroccan question. Even though freed of hindrance from the British, France still did not enjoy full control of Morocco. It was necessary to seek understanding with Spain, overcome Germany's hostility, and surmount the resistance of the Moroccan government. In spite of the agitation of the British colony in Tangier and the protests of British businessmen interested in Morocco, which were echoed by several major newspapers and by Lord Rosebery in a meeting of the Imperial Liberal League,[161] the British government carried out the agreement faithfully. It refrained from hampering French progress toward the "peaceful penetration" of Morocco and disavowed the anti-French attitude of its old agents in the sultan's court. Deprived of their legation's support, these individuals turned toward Germany.[162] During its difficult negotiations with Delcassé, the Spanish government, acting on German advice, sought support in London. Lansdowne undoubtedly told the Spanish and German ambassadors that he did not wish to see France acquire the Mediterranean coast in the area coveted by Spain. Consequently Germany could support the Spanish cabinet on this point. But at the same time Lansdowne calmed their fears, saying that Spain would soon receive satisfaction.[163] When in July the Spaniards raised new difficulties, the British ambassador in Madrid pressed them to come to an understanding with France, since their claims seemed

158. Monger, *End of Isolation*, pp. 161–62.

159. Cambon to Delcassé, April 7 and 20, May 13; Georges Louis to Cambon, April 20; and Nelidoff to Delcassé, April 18, 1904, MAE GB NS 16, 17, 18.

160. Crozier to Delcassé, April 12, and Cambon to Delcassé, April 13 and 21, 1904, MAE GB NS 17.

161. Guillen, *L'Allemagne et le Maroc*, pp. 878–79.

162. Ibid., pp. 624–25, 817.

163. Metternich to Bülow, June 1, 1904, AA, Marokko 4/s.

exaggerated and untimely to him.[164] For its part the German government considered opening a diplomatic campaign to oblige France to respect the open door principle and asked the Foreign Office what its attitude would be. Lansdowne replied that if Germany sought to oppose French policy in Morocco, England would support France.[165]

In fact, from the beginning of the crisis caused by Wilhelm II's trip to Tangier, the British government and public opinion reacted sharply. To preserve the entente with France and to keep Germany from acquiring a base on the Moroccan coast, the cabinet decided to support the French point of view unreservedly. On April 11 it joined the French in rejecting the German proposal of an international conference.[166] On May 18 and 25 Lansdowne confirmed to Cambon in writing that he wanted "to see the two governments undertake a careful and complete discussion . . . with a view to considering in advance any complication which could be feared during the somewhat unsettling period we are experiencing at this time."[167] When the Algeciras Conference was finally held, the new Liberal cabinet upheld the French position without hesitation, warning Germany that in the event of a Franco-German war Great Britain could not remain neutral.[168]

The German leaders had hoped by their intervention in the Moroccan question to nip the Franco-British entente in the bud. In fact, they contributed heavily to strengthening it. The agreement of 1904, by ending the long rivalry between the two great colonial nations, had created the conditions favorable for a rapprochement. Certainly on both sides of the Channel there were already politicians thinking of going further. But the two governments had not yet planned for closer relations.[169] They were led by a general fear of the German

164. Radowitz to Bülow, July 20, 1904, AA, Marokko 4/s.

165. Metternich to Bülow, August 13, 1904, AA, Marokko 4/s.

166. Monger, *End of Isolation,* pp. 186–91.

167. Cambon to Delcassé, May 29, 1905, MAE Delcassé papers 3.

168. Monger, *End of Isolation,* pp. 256–80; S. L. Mayer, "Anglo-German Rivalry at the Algeciras Conference," in *Britain and Germany in Africa: Imperial Rivalry and Colonial Rule* (New Haven, 1967), pp. 215–44.

169. In regard to Balfour and Lansdowne, this fact has already been demonstrated by Monger. As for Delcassé and Cambon, it is generally accepted that they were looking for an alliance with Great Britain. This point of view should be considered carefully. When in May 1905 Lansdowne proposed a close diplomatic collaboration, Cambon was quite reserved and explained his uncertainty to Delcassé. "To keep silent would discourage genuine goodwill and

menace. The British declared with annoyance that the Weltpolitik had chosen Morocco as its new front, constituting a grave threat for the strategic positions of the British Empire. The French understood that they could not overcome German opposition to the establishment of their protectorate without the total support of Great Britain.

---

give the impression that we are hesitant. To accept this proposed conversation would lead us toward a general understanding which would actually constitute an alliance. I do not know if the Government of the Republic would be disposed to approve such agreements." Cambon suggested informing Lansdowne that the two governments were already working together and should "limit themselves to declaring that an agreement existed between them on certain matters without discussing proposals for any more general agreements." Cambon to Delcassé, May 29, 1905, MAE Delcassé papers 3.

10. French War Aims in Africa 1914–1919

ANDRÉ KASPI

It is still impossible to study completely the question of French aims in Africa during World War I. First of all, political memoirs are disappointing on this aspect of the war,[1] and the officials who would have had interesting recollections wrote nothing.[2] French government archives, moreover, are not yet available.[3] Beyond any doubt, from the French point of view, a study of this subject will be more profitable in a few years. It is still valuable, however, to survey the problem now.

Are foreign materials available? Wm. Roger Louis has published a book under the title *Great Britain and Germany's Lost Colonies* (Oxford, 1967). The book relies upon important and original British materials which furnish us with a great amount of valuable information on the colonial policy of Great Britain, and also that of France insofar as the same question concerned both countries. The author was kind enough to let me read a typescript of the book before its publication, which has been most helpful.

In the United States, the Wilson administration did not give much consideration to the colonial expansion of France. There are few indications of any concern with this issue before 1917 and only a few more during the preparations for the Peace Conference.[4] The Department of State has published the minutes of the meetings of

1. See Raymond Poincaré, *Au service de la France* (10 vols., Paris, 1926–33); Georges Suares, *Briand, sa vie, son œuvre* (6 vols., Paris), *4* (1940) for this period; Abel Ferry, *Les carnets secrets* (Paris, 1957); Paul Cambon, *Correspondance, 1870–1924* (Paris, 1946).

2. Minister of Colonies Henri Simon (in Clemenceau's cabinet), Governor-General Merlin, etc., should have known much interesting information.

3. Regarding archives pertaining to French war aims, see Pierre Renouvin, "Les buts de guerre du gouvernement français, 1914–1918," *Revue Historique, 235* (January–March 1966), 1–38.

4. The Inquiry started its studies at the beginning of 1918. The role of U.S. colonial expert George L. Beer is discussed in Wm. Roger Louis, "The United States and the African Peace Settlement of 1919: The Pilgrimage of George Louis Beer," *Journal of African History, 4* (1963), 413–34.

the Council of Ten in the series *Papers Relating to the Foreign Relations of the United States.*[5]

Therefore, most of the problems involved in this discussion must be posed without the hope of definite answers. From 1914 to 1919, France was faced with this alternative: neutralization of all colonial possessions or the conquest of the German colonies in Africa. If the German colonies were to be conquered, should they have been annexed or considered as pawns in the future peace negotiations? How could the French position be adapted to the Wilsonian position characterized, at the Versailles conference, by the mandates system?

In 1914, France and her colonies extended over ten million square kilometers; her colonial empire, second only to that of the British, had a population of sixty million, the majority of which was in Africa. It would be rather difficult to imagine that she was not interested in the German territories. But, compared with her neighbor, France was a satisfied power. The dispute with Britain had been settled since 1904. Great Britain had accepted French interests in Morocco and, then, the Protectorate. France had recognized the British authority in Egypt. Neither Italy, which had just expanded into Libya, nor Spain, which had received the northern section of Morocco, could maintain any dangerous rivalry with France. And Germany? The agreement of November 4, 1911, had theoretically settled the Franco-German dispute. France had ceded part of her Congolese possessions for the recognition of her protectorate over Morocco.

The eastern border of the Cameroons, therefore, reached the Logone River; in the south it included Muni, without Spanish Guinea, in other words, a section of northern Gabon. In addition, the "antennae" resembled two arrows pointing toward the southeast, the first one including the Sangha River valley up to the Congo, the other the Lobaye up to the Ubangi River below Bangui.[6] As a result of this partition, French Equatorial Africa was cut into three sections, the central one being connected with the interior and the sea by a river that was controlled by the Germans. Freedom of navigation, however, was ensured in tropical and equatorial Africa, even in wartime, by the Act of the Congo signed at the Berlin Conference.

5. *The Paris Peace Conference, 1919* (13 vols. Government Printing Office, Washington, D.C., 1943).

6. There are very useful maps in F. J. Moberly, *Military Operations—Togoland and the Cameroons 1914–1916* in the series History of the Great War Based on Official Documents (London, 1931).

The ratification of the Caillaux agreement had passed the Chamber of Deputies by a vote of 393 to 36, with 14 abstentions.[7] Who formed this small opposition? Mainly conservative deputies, e.g. Denys Cochin and Albert de Mun; the latter had desired to voice his opinion although he was very ill. What arguments were advanced by opponents of the treaty? Indeed, the agreement gave France Morocco, but she lost territories with which she could have created a French axis in West Africa, an imitation of the Cape-to-Cairo axis dreamed of by the English. With more energy, France could have obtained Morocco and kept all of her Congolese territories.

In the Senate, the debate was a little more heated. Clemenceau revealed that Prime Minister Caillaux had conducted personal negotiations and had too often neglected the advice of the ambassador to Berlin, Jules Cambon, and of the minister of foreign affairs, de Selves. This disclosure brought the resignations of de Selves (January 9, 1912) and then Caillaux (January 12) but the treaty was ratified by a vote of 212 to 42, the opposition coming from the right and the radical socialist groups.

These debates indicate that French public opinion, on the whole, was glad to observe the disappearance of the German dispute. The "few acres" lost in Africa were replaced by Morocco; peace, all things considered, continued; and the national honor had been saved. It was not a new Fashoda crisis. In 1919, the minister of colonies was right to declare that France did not enter the war to acquire colonies. Public opinion never wished any kind of hostilities to unmake the 1911 agreement.[8]

On the other hand, when war broke out, would France have had, by herself, the means for an expansionist policy? Naval supremacy belonged to the British, and the French relied upon their allies to keep their lines of communication secure. It was unthinkable, therefore, to follow a policy that could have alarmed Great Britain; for, with her dominion of South Africa, Britain had considerably greater interests at stake than France in southwest and east Africa. Thus a cautious French policy was necessary.

7. See Edouard and Georges Bonnefous, *Histoire politique de la Troisième République* (5 vols. Paris), *1* (1956), 258–84.

8. According to *L'Afrique Française, 29* (September–October 1919), Simon declared to the deputies: "Ni la Grande-Bretagne, ni la France, ni l'Italie, riches en territoires coloniaux, n'éprouvaient le besoin de les agrandir et n'avaient fait la guerre dans ce but."

Another question seems to me still more important. Did France wish to follow such a policy? Two German colonies were in her sphere of action: Togoland and the Cameroons.

Togoland extended over 88,000 square kilometers, with a population of one million natives and less than five hundred Germans.[9] French colonial circles considered that it "could not be placed among the rich colonies" and that "the soil is generally rated as not very fertile."[10] Its capital, Lomé, was a harbor that could have been of some importance, mainly for Dahomey, the eastern neighbor. Railways were not developed. In addition to palm oil, rubber and cotton were the main products.

The Cameroons, with an area of over 790,000 square kilometers, had a population of 2,700,000 natives with a little more than 2,000 whites. Here rubber was more abundant and was produced along with palm and cocoa products. The main harbor, Douala, is one of the few anchorages along this marshy coast. Three railroad lines had been built which converged at Douala. The southern line would one day reach East Africa, but, at this time, it was only 120 miles long. Some trails led to the north, i.e. to Lake Chad. Most observers agreed in noting that these colonies were expensive to Germany and supplied only 3 percent of the colonial products required by her economy.[11]

In some circles of the French government, colonies were considered a dead weight on the country's war potential. According to this point of view, France had to concentrate all her strength on the continental war and, if necessary, remove troops from her empire. Abel Ferry, undersecretary of state in charge of North African Affairs in the first Viviani cabinet, wrote on July 27, 1914: "En cas de guerre continentale, tous vos efforts doivent tendre à ne maintenir au Maroc que le minimum des forces indispensables. Le sort du Maroc se règlera en Lorraine."

Another indication of this attitude was the surprising statement of the same period made by Jules Cambon:

> sorte de cardinal édenté, fin et habile, (qui) vint me voir et me dit qu'il avait beaucoup étonné Viviani en lui disant que l'affaire

9. Statistics given by George L. Beer, *African Questions at the Paris Peace Conference,* ed. L. H. Gray (New York, 1923). Beer borrowed them from *Statistiches Jahrbuch* (1915), p. 457.

10. Camille Martin, in *L'Afrique Française* 23 (October 1913).

11. G. Beer, pt. I. See also Henri Hauser, *Le problème colonial* (Paris, 1915), pp. 30–52.

marocaine était finie et que le seul événement politique de la diplomatie future était le partage de l'Afrique centrale.[12]

Others besides Viviani, including Abel Ferry, must have been surprised by this opinion. Ferry, moreover, had been raised by an uncle who had been the apostle of French colonialism.

As far as public opinion was concerned, the colonies were not an interesting issue at the beginning of the war. The public knew nothing of the developments in the French territories prior to 1914, and the subsequent African victories were to remain relatively unknown. For most of the French people, Lomé, Yaoundé, or the Sangha River were not evocative names. How could they have been with the Germans at the Marne, or, once repelled, still on the national soil?

Politicians, moreover, did not seem eager to make the public aware of the African victories. The colonial question did not excite either public opinion or parliamentary deputies. Albert Sarraut remarks:

> "L'action du Parlement est manifestement insuffisante. Les débats réservés aux questions coloniales sont trop rares ou trop hâtifs. La discussion du budget des colonies, plus ou moins vite expédiée au milieu du grand labeur budgétaire, n'obtient que l'avare crédit de quelques heures de séance." [13]

Most of the French doubted that the colonies would support France; and, in some official circles, it was believed that French colonial troops would be paralyzed by the limitations of the fleet and external and internal threats and unrest.[14] Did one think mainly of Morocco? It is possible; the report of General (later Marshal) Lyautey contemplated a dangerous situation in that protectorate.[15] As of yet, there is insufficient information for the other colonies; but the situation would not have been the same in Indochina or central Africa.

The conquest of the German territories was, therefore, an issue of some debate. Those who viewed the German colonies as unsuitable for white settlement and of only a mediocre value generally felt that France should limit herself to the maintenance of order in her own colonial empire. Others, however, considered that France could not be

12. Ferry, *Les carnets secrets,* pp. 250 and 20. See also cablegram from Ferry to General Lyautey, July 27, 1914), in Ferry, pp. 244–45.

13. Albert Sarraut in foreword to François Pierre-Alype, *La provocation allemande aux colonies* (Paris, 1915).

14. This opinion is reported by Hauser, *Le problème colonial,* p. 89.

15. Ferry, p. 244.

inactive in Africa, if colonies were to be acquired and defended between the Somme and the Vosges.[16] This latter group constituted a "colonial party" about which we should like to know more, but whose existence is indicated by various signs. Charles Mangin, then a lieutenant colonel, had published in 1911 his book on "la force noire" as a palliative for the insufficient French birthrate.[17] Few measures to enlist Africans had been taken before 1914.[18]

Others, or perhaps the same men, were uneasy about the German presence in Africa and were disposed to conquer Togoland and the Cameroons—provided, of course, Great Britain agreed and the European war were not neglected. In fact, it is difficult not to be surprised if we note that, precisely when Abel Ferry appeared to express the government's position, French troops were fighting in Africa. How had this policy of conquest developed? Our purpose is not to describe the West African campaigns[19] but to determine to what extent they indicate a colonial policy.

In Togoland, first of all, the French and the British initiated hostilities. The Germans, surrounded on three sides, possessing few troops, and inadequately supported by their navy, would have preferred not to fight. In fact, on August 4, the governor of Togoland, Major Von Doering, proposed to Dahomey the neutralization of African colonies, German and Allied. On the following day, the same proposal was made to the Gold Coast. The lieutenant governor of Dahomey forwarded the proposal to Dakar and immediately took measures against the German inhabitants of his territory. On August 6, London rejected the idea of neutralization and sent a spokesman to Lomé to demand the capitulation of German troops. But as early as July 29, the Gold Coast governor had taken "precautions," and on August 4, the French minister of colonies had wired to the governor-general of French West Africa: "Prenez les dispositions prévues pour cas de guerre."[20]

In Dahomey, staff plans had been prepared to occupy Lomé and the

16. The minister of colonies said to the deputies, on July 9, 1918: "Ce n'est pas sur leur sol que nous avons à les défendre, c'est sur le sol français que leur sort se jouera." Reported in *L'Afrique Française, 28* (July–August 1918).

17. Charles Mangin, *La force noire* (Paris, 1911).

18. "Le développement de l'armée noire était depuis quelques années à l'ordre du jour; en présence de la crise des effectifs dont souffrait la France, on avait songé à demander au réservoir d'hommes de l'Afrique Noire des ressources nouvelles." Albert Lebrun, lecture given at Toulouse on June 24, 1916, published under the title "L'effort colonial français" (Paris, 1916), p. 17.

19. There is a very good analysis of military operations in Moberly, passim.

20. All the foregoing, *L'Afrique Française, 25* (supplément 3, 1915), 82.

Togo coast in order to prevent the Germans from receiving support by sea. On August 7, the Germans evacuated the capital and a 120-kilometer zone which the British then occupied. The French crossed the border on the eighth, occupying Petit Popo (Anécho) and Porto Séguro, and appealed to the British for their cooperation. The English colonel, Bryant, then received the command of allied troops, who obtained the capitulation of Kamina (the radio station had been destroyed) and completed the conquest of Togoland before the end of August.[21]

The most obvious motive for this conquest was the radio station at Kamina, which was "en communication avec Berlin," [22] or, in any case, powerful enough to reach German ships. The objective was mainly military. After having acted independently, the French proposed the coordination of French and English forces, accepting a British commander in view of the numerically inferior French troops. It is interesting to note, in light of the staff plans relating to the Togoland conquest, that the French were preceded by their British allies in the conquest of Lomé.

In the Cameroons, the Germans followed a similar policy. Referring to Article 11 of the Act of the Congo, they asked the United States to intercede in order to neutralize "the conventional zone of free trade." [23] The United States had not signed the Congo convention and refused to become involved. In September, Germany could only obtain the forwarding of her proposal to France and England. Both countries rejected the German note, "Germany having taken the initiative in hostilities against the French and British possessions in the conventional basin of the Congo." Indeed, at the end of June some incidents had occurred on the Congo at the German post of Bonga.[24] But, in French territory, troops were concentrated at Mossaka to prepare for the advance on Wesso. In fact, French troops outnumbered German; but the length of the border and extent of French territories made a strategic attack necessary (e.g. on the "antennae") if war broke out.

21. The agreement on the provisional administration was signed on August 30, 1914.

22. Lebrun, p. 11. This is the usual explanation. The same argument will be used many times. In fact, the station had been completed in June, and, according to a French military report, the French did not even know it existed: see *L'Afrique Française, 25* (supplément 3, 1915), 99., and Moberly, p. 21.

23. Cablegram from the ambassador in Berlin, State Department files, 763. 72/631, August 22, 1914.

24. Etienne Antonelli, *L'Afrique et la paix de Versailles* (Paris, 1921), notes complémentaires.

The American consul general at Boma (Belgian Congo) reported on this theater of operations in a cablegram: the French advance followed the Sangha and the Lobaye. But, as in Togoland, the British and French rapidly cooperated, first by organizing a landing near Douala in September 1914, then in conquering the country slowly and painfully.[25] Terrain, vegetation, and German military defenses constituted difficult obstacles. Once again, in view of his experience, the English general, Dobell, was in command of the allied troops. Yaoundé was taken in January 1916; and, in late March, the Germans signed an armistice.[26]

Apparently, the main objective of the conquest of the Cameroons was the maintenance of free navigation on the Congo and the prevention of any possible unrest that the Germans, or Muslim chiefs supported by them, could have created along the border of French colonies. The French had acted under the impression that the Germans were going to attack. The bombing of Bône and Philippeville on August 4, 1914, and various incidents along the Congolese border could have strengthened this impression. But strategic considerations were the most important.

A European tradition existed that a war fought in Europe between colonial powers must be extended to the colonies. Lord Robert Cecil, undersecretary of state for foreign affairs, stated: "I do not pretend we have attacked the German colonies in order to free the natives from an oppressive government. We did it as part of the war against Germany."[27] It is unlikely that the French and British would have suddenly discarded this tradition, so advantageous in 1914, only because of a threat to white prestige. The only prestige that could have been undermined was that of Germany.

Another result of this allied military victory could have been to keep the neighboring colonies quiet: a display of power was an element of every colonial administrator's arsenal.[28] Moreover, the neutralization proposed by the Germans was an attempt to conceal the weakness of

25. State Department files, 763. 72/1103, September 1914.

26. Provisional agreement of March 4, 1916; letters exchanged between Cambon and the British government in May 1916.

27. Before the House of Commons on May 16, 1917. Quoted in *L'Afrique Française*, 27 (May–June 1917).

28. Discussing the results of the military policy in Togoland and the Cameroons on French colonies, Lebrun said, "[elle] a atteint ce double but d'y maintenir la tranquillité et de conquérir, d'accord avec nos Alliés, les territoires voisins où flottait encore le drapeau ennemi." Lebrun, p. 16.

their own colonial position; the Allies were right to refuse the German offer.

But other factors are still obscure. Was France directed solely by military considerations? It must have been very tempting to retake the "antennae," ceded "sous la menace." Since northern Gabon was on the verge of becoming economically dominated by the Cameroons, and since Dahomey needed Togolese outlets,[29] it was virtually inevitable that a defensive policy was followed by an offensive one that was considered relatively inexpensive. Indeed, the governor-general of French West Africa wrote that the results obtained in the Cameroons were due to "l'esprit de décision dont firent preuve l'administration locale, M. Estèbe, alors gouverneur-général par intérim, le général Aymerich, commandant supérieur des troupes,"[30] but this was only a matter of style employed to praise the executors of a policy decided in Paris. Why weren't the directions sent to French West Africa wired to French Equatorial Africa as well? It is possible that staff plans had been considered canceled by the treaty of 1911[31] but not the desire to erase the German military and economic threat in Africa.

These suppositions, no matter how plausible, should be confirmed and completed by official files which will presumably increase present knowledge regarding the conquest of the Cameroons and Togoland. We should also like to know what mental reservations the French had while negotiating the borders of provisional zones with the British. Louis' book is very useful concerning British intentions, but what about the French? Did they believe this agreement was really provisional? Did they expect to exchange territories with Great Britain? Was the government unanimous? Had the government formulated a precise policy regarding these territories?

In discussing the origins of the French attitude toward the German African colonies at the Peace Conference, let us note, first of all, that the African operations were quite unknown in 1914 and only a little less so in 1915 and 1916. Without any doubt, the German colonies

29. See Governor-General Merlin's remarks in a report quoted in *L'Afrique Française, 23* (April 1913).

30. *L'Afrique Française, 25* (supplément 3, 1915).

31. Moberly, p. 21, wrote that the 1911 agreement canceled all the French staff plans. But is it possible that nothing would have been prepared in a period of three years?

were of low priority. Those interested were too few and the countries involved too far away to inspire any passion in the French. The French colonials complained of the general apathy of the public, especially when they compared it with the imperial consciousness of the British.[32]

The government did not seem to know what France should do with the conquered territories. In an exchange of letters between Paul Cambon and th British government in 1916, for example, it is stated that the borders drawn by English and French administrators would be maintained if the Cameroons were not returned to Germany. Thus, it is probable that France was moving cautiously toward a policy of annexation. But no official statement was made before the summer of 1918. Although the British government announced its position as early as 1917, and kept on repeating it, France never mentioned Togoland and the Cameroons as a war aim. Neither Aristide Briand, in his letter to Paul Cambon on January 12, 1917, nor the resolution adopted by the Chamber of Deputies in June 1917, nor Paul Painleve in his introductory statement of September 18, 1917, indicated that the German territories were considered a war aim.

Lloyd George, however, included the following statement on the German colonies in his declaration of January 5, 1918: "With regard to the German colonies, I have repeatedly declared that they are held at the disposal of a conference whose decisions must have primary regard to the wishes and interests of the native inhabitants of such colonies. . . . The German treatment of their native populations in their colonies has been such as amply to justify their fear of submitting the future of those colonies to the wishes of the natives themselves." [33] This program, more Wilsonian than the "Fourteen Points," received Clemenceau's approval. But was this approval really an indication of a colonial policy?

How is this silence explained? The French government was anxious to avoid giving the war expansionist or imperialistic implications. Public opinion accepted a war for Right and Justice: the return of Alsace-Lorraine to France, the destruction of German militarism. But it would not accept a war to extend the French empire in Africa. In

32. Maurice Besson, in *L'Afrique Française 28* (September–October 1918), complained of this general apathy. The same attitude is found in Camille Fidel, *La paix coloniale française* (Paris, 1918).

33. In *Official Statements of War aims and Peace Proposals, December 1916 to November 1918,* prepared under the supervision of James Brown Scott (Carnegie Endowment for International Peace, Division of International Law, Washington D.C., 1921).

fact, France was primarily interested in Europe. There seemed ample time to deal with the colonies while conveniently leaving England and the Dominions with the propaganda. Finally, and this hypothesis does not exclude the first two, when peace returned it might have been necessary to make concessions. In such a case, France could have held Togoland and the Cameroons as pawns during the negotiations. Thus, until 1918 France did not really have war aims in Africa, although some spoke of an African Alsace-Lorraine (the ceded territories of 1911); but this propaganda was not effective.

Notwithstanding the general apathy, however, there was a party of men, both in and outside of Parliament, who were particularly interested in the colonial question. These circles had never been silent; [34] but, after 1915, through books, lectures, and primarily newspaper articles, they began to take a position on the future of Togoland and the Cameroons. Two examples of the books on this subject were Henri Hauser's *Le problème colonial* and François Julien Pierre-Alype's work on "*La provocation allemande aux colonies*" with a foreword by Albert Sarraut.[35]

Albert Lebrun, deputy and former minister of colonies, gave a lecture at Toulouse on June 24, 1916, which was printed under the title, "*L'effort colonial français.*" [36] Lebrun had been introduced by Eugène Etienne, a deputy and former minister of war and one of the founders and propagandists of French colonial thought. Finally, *L'Afrique Française,* the monthly bulletin of the Committee for French Africa and the Committee for Morocco, seemed to enjoy a widespread influence.[37] Both of these committees were centered in Paris and represented a politically influential group, including such men as Jules Siegfried, Etienne Jonnart, Eugène Etienne, J. Charles-Roux, Denys Cochin, Paul Deschanel, Paul Doumer, Gabriel Hanotaux, Joseph Reinach, Christian Schefer, Generals Gouraud and Lyautey, and im-

34. 'Le comité de l'Afrique française" (Committee for French Africa) was created in 1891, and the review has been published since that date.

35. Indeed, other books were published on this subject, and even a few articles in newspapers or magazines, e.g. "Les troupes coloniales, nos forces ignorées," *Revue de Paris* (September 15, 1915).

36. A special committee, named "L'effort de la France et de ses alliés," published Lebrun's lecture (Paris, 1916)

37. The main purpose of this committee was "organiser et appuyer des missions d'explorations, et d'études dans les régions africaines soumises ou à soumettre à notre influence; développer l'influence française dans les pays indépendants d'Afrique; encourager les travaux politiques, économiques et scientifiques relatifs à l'Afrique."

portant colonial administrators such as Governor-General Merlin. In addition to editorials, the review published articles on colonies, extracts from the British and German press concerning Africa, and approximately ten supplements annually, containing statistical information and reports on colonial questions. The origins of the French attitude regarding colonial matters are to be found in this review, since former, present, and future ministers sat in these committees along with deputies, generals, government officials, and businessmen. Their common bond was a mutual interest in anything that concerned French Africa.

But what were the sources of financial support for this review? Who were its readers? What economic interests were represented? From the political viewpoint, the review tended to be conservative, which meant that traditional concepts of colonization were supported; Wilsonian principles and socialist colonial ideals were not appreciated.[38] Because of the war, the review was anti-German. Its pro-British attitude was in vogue; and page after page cited the annexationist plans of Wilhelm II and his advisers. Primarily, however, the review concerned itself with the defense of French interests in Africa. When German-British discussions about Portuguese colonies were revealed shortly before the beginning of the war, the bulletin assumed a hostile position, deeming the discussions dangerous to the French possessions.[39]

Groups related to the committees of *L'Afrique Française* were La Société de Géographie à Paris, La Fédération des industriels et commercants, La Société de Géographie commerciale, L'Union Coloniale française, La Ligue coloniale française, La Société des Etudes coloniales et maritimes. Together, these groups constituted the colonial party.[40] Yet, while it is easy to understand their common concerns, we know virtually nothing about their members or the various organizational differences.

If we remember the background of the members of the Committee for French Africa, we can easily understand how their influence was exerted. When the minister of colonies needed advice, he asked the members of the committee because they were experts. Indeed, *L'Afrique Française* proclaimed it. In reporting what it knew of current negotiations, it reported in January 1919 that the minister of

38. See reports on the socialist conferences in various issues of *L'Afrique Française* in 1918.

39. *L'Afrique Française*, 23 (November 1913).

40. The expression was used in, and the list quoted from, *L'Afrique Française*, 28 (supplément 10, 1918).

colonies had formulated his policy with the aid of the interministerial commission, which will be discussed below, of the reports sent by geographical and propaganda societies, and the opinions expressed by the Committee for French Africa. But among the members of the above commission, we find the names of Eugène Etienne, Paul Doumer, Peretti de la Rocca. Another example: Jonnart was governor-general of Algeria in 1918.

If we take into account Lebrun's lecture, various books, and this particular magazine, *L'Afrique Française,* we can perhaps outline some aspects of the colonialist position on the German territories. To begin with, no precise claim on Togoland and Cameroons appeared in *L'Afrique Française* before 1915. In 1913, for example, it concerned itself primarily with Morocco and only slightly with equatorial Africa. The 1911 agreement, although it had provoked some protests, had been accepted; its positive aspects had been stressed more often than its negative ones. The conquest of Togoland and the operations in the Cameroons were not reported until the first issue of 1915. Debates over the future of the German colonies appeared in the second issue of that year. After 1915, the same themes are debated with varying frequency and intensity. Until 1918 (i.e. until President Wilson presented his "Fourteen Points"), propagandists insisted on two points: colonies were useful to France, even in wartime; and Togoland and the Cameroons should not be returned to Germany.

The best illustration of the first point can be found in Albert Lebrun's lecture, which contains all the arguments of the colonial party. The former minister was discussing the position of the French colonies in the war. "Dans une parfaite unanimité, elles se sont toutes rangées aux côtés de la métropole," he declared, listing all the loyalist manifestations coming from Algeria, Morocco, Tunisia, and Indochina. It was true that sometimes there had been "quelques tentatives de rebellion that sometimes there had been "quelques tentatives de rebellion locale," but these were not significant in terms of either their causes or effects.

Lebrun then described the fighting in Togoland and the Cameroons and ended his narrative with an equivocal sentence in which he spoke of the provisional allied administration and the organization and the development of both territories. In the last section of his lecture, Lebrun cataloged the efforts of the colonies to aid France through military, economic, and financial participation. "La France doit être légitimement fière du concours qu'elle rencontre chez tous ses sujets et protégés." But, he concluded, after the war France would have to follow a more liberal policy and encourage colonial economic development.

The second theme of this colonial propaganda specifically concerned Togoland and the Cameroons, namely, the opposition to their return to Germany. This theme was developed in great detail, and this development itself proves that the government had not yet made its decision. There was still time to influence it.

The first justification given for retention was moral The Germans, the argument went, did not behave properly in Africa. They followed a brutal policy aimed at the enslavement and, in some cases, the extermination of the natives. They did not deserve their civilizing mission. The natives, it was also claimed, had been subjected to forced labor; their numbers had declined due to alcoholism; their lands had been stolen by German colonists and exploitative companies.[41] In 1917, *Documents relatifs aux atrocités et aux violations du droit de la guerre commises par les Allemands en Afrique* were published. Sadly evocative pictures were accompanied by numerous written statements.[42]

The propagandists desired to demonstrate that the Allies were fighting the same evil in Africa that they were in Europe. The brutality which in Europe was called Prussian militarism was, in Africa, called colonial exploitation. With this goal in mind, George L. Beer, in his study for the Inquiry, cites from twelve to fifteeen thousand casualties among the Hereros whom the Germans had subdued in South-West Africa between 1904 and 1906.[43] After fifty years, we are less sensitive to this press campaign. It is, in fact, difficult not to remain cautious while dealing with the "atrocities question," for it was not limited to Africa but primarily involved the war in Europe. From August 1914 to March 1917, while the United States was still neutral, the State Department received dozens of protest letters. The French, the Germans, the English, the Turks, the Bulgars, the Serbs, the Austrians, the Montenegrins, etc.—all were compaining or accused. Every army was represented in this depressing pageant of photographs, real or fake, of more or less debatable statements that evidenced the necessarily bad faith of nations at war.[44]

41. G. L. Beer, Pt. I.
42. *L'Afrique Française,* 27 (supplément 1–2, 1917).
43. Beer, Pt. I.
44. An entire roll of microfilmed documents in the State Department files. Texts, quoted as a proof for the accusation, are often violent, especially regarding the black troops.

But the variety of sources—English, Belgian, French—and the types of witnesses—soldiers, civilians, members of religious missions—would lead us to accept the evaluation of socialist Jean Longuet, who wrote in 1919: "L'Allemagne . . . tout comme les autres nations capitalists—plus brutalement encore peut-être—maltraitaient et exploitaient ses indigènes." [45] One could also note that the Hereros had been massacred eight years before the war broke out, more than ten years before newspaper articles would try to create a general movement of indignation.

After 1915, a second justification for the annexation appeared. The Germans, we read, intended to build up a huge African empire, a *Mittelafrika,* which would have corresponded to their idea of a *Mitteleuropa.* Eugène Etienne, for example, recounted that, in March 1913, while he was minister of war, the French military attaché in Berlin informed him of the German disappointment over the Congo agreement.[46]

In addition, the conversation between Bethmann-Hollweg and the British ambassador to Berlin of July 29, 1914, was frequently cited.[47] The chancellor was trying to obtain English neutrality in the coming conflict; he indicated he would not touch European borders but was unable to give similar assurances about the French colonies. When informed, Sir Edward Grey nobly repulsed this overture. But the dialogue proved to colonists and natives that they were defending not only the mother country but also their own "country." [48] It also proved that Germany entertained important colonial ambitions in 1914 that constituted an essential, although neglected, motive for war.[49]

To strengthen this opinion, *L'Afrique Française* cited the Pan-German press: the explorer Emile Zimmermann had written that Germany must create a great colonial empire in the center of Africa; former colonial governor Albrecht von Rechenberg demanded the Belgian and French Congo for his country and proposed an exchange with England: Kiaochow, New Guinea, and the Pacific possessions

45. *L'Afrique Française,* 29 (supplément 11, 1919), in review of the parliamentary debates on the peace treaty.

46. *L'Afrique Française,* 25 (March 1915): note by the French military attaché in Berlin, March 15, 1913, sent also to the minister of foreign affairs on July 30, 1913.

47. This conversation was published by the Birtish as early as August 1914.

48. *L'Afrique Française,* 25 (March 1915).

49. The same idea proposed in Hauser, *Le problème colonial,* and in an article by Christian Schefer, professor at the Law School, member of the Comité de l'Afrique française, printed in *Revue des Sciences Politiques* (April 15, 1915).

for English East Africa and Uganda.[50] The German commanding officer at Lodz was reported to have said in 1915: "A victorious war would give us the French Congo, the Belgian Congo; and if Portugal continues to translate her hostile intentions toward us into action, it would also give us the Portuguese colonies on the east and west coasts of Africa. We should then have a colonial empire of which our fathers could never have dreamed."[51] Another example was the image of "provocation allemande aux colonies." A French publicist wrote: "Si cette guerre mondiale a été engagée et imposée par l'Allemagne, il est avéré aujourd'hui que c'est avec le projet audacieux et longuement mûri de s'emparer de nos possessions lointaines qui sont les fondements les plus certains de l'avenir de notre nation."[52] This argument was to become one of the foundations of French African policy. The minister of colonies used it in January 1919 before the Council of Ten and, more emphatically, before the Chamber of Deputies: "La création d'un grand empire africain, déclare-t-il, a été un des buts de guerre avoué de l'Allemagne."[53]

A third justification for the annexation of the German colonies was their economic value for Dahomey and French Equatorial Africa. Generally long reports tell us of palm oil in the Cameroons, the Douala harbor, or Lomé.[54] But this reasoning was dangerous for the allied cause. First of all, it contradicted the 1913 description and the judgments of writers such as Henri Hauser and George L. Beer.

After January 1918, there was a protest movement that tried to prevent Germany from being deprived of raw materials, i.e. her colonies. German colonials were, of course, the principal supporters of this cause, but the French socialists also supported it for very different reasons.[55] For President Wilson, the retention of German colonies could not be justified if such a solution were to ruin Germany. His colonial expert George Beer, however, had concluded that Germany would not suffer from the loss of her colonies.

50. A special section of the review was reversed for extracts of this press.

51. Quoted in Benjamin Brawley, *Africa and the War* (New York, 1918), p. 27.

52. Foreword by Albert Sarraut to Pierre-Alype, *La provocation*, p. xxxvi.

53. Papers relating to the foreign relations of the United States [FR hereafter], Paris Peace Conference 1919, *3*, meeting of January 28, 1919. See also *l'Afrique Française, 29* (September–October 1919).

54. *L'Afrique Française, 28* (January–March 1918); *27* (March 1917 and May–June 1917).

55. Statement by the Conseil National du Parti Socialiste Français, February 18, 1918.

This leads us to examine the development of colonial propaganda after the publication of Wilson's "Point Five." After January 1918, the emphasis was placed on the political wishes of the natives, the aggressive intentions of Germany, the colonizing methods and pledges of France, and the orientation of British public opinion. The aim was the same: Togoland and the Cameroons were to be annexed, but the rationale must please public opinion.

What were the wishes of the natives? Some, such as the editorialist of *L'Information,* viewed this subject ironically: "M. Wilson, toujours fidèle à son idéal et à ses principes soutient que les peuples—même les plus primitifs, les plus barbares, les moins aptes à user de la liberté—doivent pouvoir disposer de leur destin et garder, s'ils de désirent, leur entière indépendance." [56]

Others changed their arguments to fit the new situation. Lebrun had said in 1916 that the military, economic, and financial participation of the colonies should make France proud. In 1918, it was noted that the peoples of the Togoland and the Cameroons welcomed the allied armies, that there had been no problem in maintaining order since 1914, that the Germans were universally unpopular, with the exception of some Muslim chiefs and a few warlords. In January 1919, the minister of colonies spoke of "manifestations spontanées intéressantes à mentionner au moment où sont assemblés les membres de la Conférence de la Paix." [57] He also mentioned that the natives had been glad to see the Allies "et notamment le sultan de Garoua (Cameroun) et les grands dignitaires musulmans des régions islamisées de ce pays" and spoke of "leur vœu de demeurer sous la domination française."

The aggressive intentions of Germany in Africa no longer threatened the construction of a *Mittelafrika* but rather the recruitment of an immense black army which would help her wage a new war in Europe. It seems that General Smuts, in his lecture of January 1918, was the source of this propaganda. It is not necessary to stress that German colonial circles confirmed this propaganda; but, paradoxically, the Germans realized the importance of such an army only after they had observed the efficiency of French African troops. They had protested the use of Negroes in Europe as late as 1917.[58]

56. *L'Information,* January 28, 1919. Quoted in *L'Afrique Française,* 29 (January–February 1919).

57. Ibid.

58. See a German note, quoted in *L'Afrique Française,* 27 (January–February 1917): "L'emploi des troupes de couleur en Europe et l'extension de la guerre dans les colonies africaines, qui s'est produite contrairement aux traités existants

In 1913, the July Fourteenth parade afforded the opportunity to applaud the black troops, "des défenseurs débonnaires mais incapables de faillir, des compagnons d'armes prêts a accourir, innombrables et implacables, sur les champs de bataille de la mère-patrie." [59] In his 1916 lecture, Albert Lebrun clearly indicated the situation: "Le développement de l'armée noire était depuis quelques années à l'ordre du jour; en présence de la crise des effectifs dont souffrait la France, on avait songé à demander au réservoir d'hommes de l'Afrique noire des ressources nouvelles." And he cited the thousands of men that the colonies had given to the French army.

Henri Hauser explained that the colonials believed Africa to be an inexhaustible source of soldiers. George Beer gives some interesting statistics: five thousand natives in the German East African army and police, and thirty thousand in French West and Equatorial Africa. Ninety-two battalions of Senegalese and Malagasy infantrymen served with the French army (i.e. 200,000 men from 1914 to 1918). In 1919 there were still 133,000 black soldiers who, according to the report on the military budget for colonies, "participeront, tout au moins pendant la belle saison, à notre occupation militaire en Allemagne. Ils auront ainsi une claire notion de la victoire complète que nous avons remportée sur nos ennemis, et, rentrés dans leur pays natal, ils pourront en répandre le témoignage autour d'eux." [60] Compared with the large numbers of Negroes in the French army, the East African Askaris must have seemed numerically negligible.

When Arthur Balfour pointed out the menace of these German troops, a member of the House of Commons observed that France had been the first to use African troops on a large scale.[61] Balfour replied that the French native troops were used for pacific purposes whereas Germany pursued aggressive policies. On January 30, 1919, Lloyd George agreed with Clemenceau on this same point.[62]

The French used still another argument against the return of the German colonies. After 1915, some in France stressed the necessity of

---

et qui diminue le prestige de la race blanche dans cette partie du monde, ne sont pas moins inconciliables avec les principes du droit international et de la civilisation." The chamber of Deputies replied on January 18 by voting an order of the day which praised the loyalty of the colonial troops.

59. Louis Sondet in *L'Afrique Française, 23* (July 1913).

60. Report of Deputy Landry on the colonial military expenses from 1914 to 1918, in *L'Afrique Française, 29* (March–April 1919).

61. *L'Afrique Française, 28* (September 1918).

62. FR, Paris Peace Conference 1919, 3, meeting of January 30, 1919.

making, and upholding, financial commitments to the colonies. Such commitments were made in increasing amounts in 1918 and especially in 1919, a fact that indirectly justified the annexation of Togoland and the Cameroons, as well as the expenses encountered by France: "France has spent nine billion francs on the Mediterranean, 626 million in West Africa, and 272 million in Equatorial Africa." [63] Thus, neglect of her African possessions could not be charged of France as it had been of Germany.

Since 1917, British public opinion has assumed that the decision not to return the German colonies was indisputable.[64] Government statements in Great Britain and in the Dominions indicated that even if France did not support this attitude, she would not be able to oppose and would lose all benefits deriving from a partition. *L'Afrique Française* often cited declarations of English colonials, journalists, or ministers. General Smut's lecture was carefully analyzed.

The colonial party, however, did not limit its interests to established French territories and the German colonies. This group wished to obtain a "remembrement des territoires de l'ouest africain," that is, a coherent empire.[65] Reports on Gambia, Sierra Leone, and the Gold Coast, therefore, were not unbiased.[66] It was necessary, however, to know whether the British were ready to negotiate an exchange:

> "Depuis la disparition du Togo allemand, la France et L'Angleterre sont les deux seules grandes puissances europeénnes intéressees à l'Afrique Occidentale. Leur entente . . . nous garantit une solution facile et équitable de toutes les questions politiques et économiques qui viendront évidemment en discussion après l'armistice: du moins importe-t-il que de notre côté, ces questions communes soient, dès à présent, envisagées et étudiées sous leur double aspect." [67]

On the contrary, the colonial party was on its guard against allied covetousness. According to the treaty of 1915, Italy had to receive compensation in Africa, but the road to Chad and the territory of Djibouti or French interests in Abyssinia were not to be ceded to

63. Ibid., meeting of January 28, 1919.

64. Fidel, *La paix coloniale, française,* p. 52.

65. Maurice Besson cited "tous les avantages d'un empire africain d'un seul tenant." *L'Afrique Française, 28* (September–October 1918).

66. *L'Afrique Française, 27* (suppléments 5–6, 7–8, 9–12, 1917).

67. Ibid. (supplément 5–6, 1917), p. 120.

her.[68] Japan seemed to have ambitions in Indochina; and some American circles seemed to be interested in the French West Indies.[69]

The mandates system was not well understood, but the socialist projects for the internationalization of all colonies, at least those of Germany, were well publicized. *L'Afrique Française* was very hostile toward internationalization because it would have deprived France of all the advantages she could have expected from colonies. The review preferred a simple annexation, made more rational by negotiations with England and Italy. In short, even in 1918 colonial circles tried to obtain the German colonies as a war aim along with Alsace-Lorraine or the left bank of the Rhine. They hoped Maurice Barrès' opinion would be that of France's future commissioners to the Peace Conference: "Tout change de face. La politique coloniale s'absorbe dans la politique générale, et la question du Rhin est en étroite connexité avec celle du Congo." [70]

Government policy seemed singularly cautious. The only decision that had been made before 1918 was to transfer the Congolese territories ceded in 1911 to the administration of the governor of Equatorial Africa.[71] France indicated by this decision that she intended to keep what she had been compelled to cede "sous la menace." The best indication that no colonial policy had been arrived at was the documentary commission convened in October 1917 by the minister of colonies.[72] This commission, composed of high officials, prepared a list of questions to be studied and discussed. Ideas of the colonial party had a considerable effect on the commission. Although we know little about its deliberations, it seems that it opposed an extension into east Africa to avoid alarming the British. The commission also desired more adequate borders and naval outlets, which again posed the problem of exchanging territories with England, Portugal, and Spain.

A second commission met at the beginning of February 1918, this

68. Extensive debates in the columns of *L'Afrique Française* in 1918 between Camille Fidel and the Italian colonials.

69. See, for example, State Department file 851.d0144, March 11, 1919. J. P. Myers informed the State Department regarding a proposal under consideration to turn over Fernch Guiana with several islands in the West Indies to the United States as part of the payment of the debt which the French Republic owed the United States. The State Department replied that this proposal would receive "attentive consideration."

70. Maurice Barrès, in a foreword to Fidel's book, *La paix coloniale française*.

71. *L'Afrique Française*, 27 (January–February 1917).

72. See Antonelli, pp. 205 ff.

time with officials from other ministries. The minister of colonies presided, assisted by Gaston Doumergue and Eugène Etienne, also members of the Committee for French Africa. This commission was much more cautious about annexations and more interested in economics, customs, and native problems. It rejected a suggestion from the minister of trade to associate French industries with colonial development and accepted a special tariff schedule for the colonies. Traditional views emerged victorious.

Nothing was said about Togoland and the Cameroons, but in October, a report was published in *Journal Officiel* on the treatment of natives in these two German colonies.[73] The conclusion was clear: "C'est qu'il est impossible que les indigènes délivrés d'une telle tyrannie retombent un jour sous la domination de leurs anciens maîtres qui se sont révélés si indignes de la civilisation." As *L'Afrique Française* observed, it was the "first official French declaration." It is evident that after 1914 there was a shift in official circles and public opinion, but documentation indicates that this change in public opinion was slower in France than in Britain. However, when the Peace Conference opened, the minister of colonies possessed well-documented, if unoriginal, files.

We know that it was convenient for the victorious powers to start debate with a discussion of colonial questions. To begin with, President Wilson had not intended to demand the return of all former German colonies. All the Allies were agreed on this point.[74] This agreement undoubtedly represented a victory for colonial propaganda, and even more so, for the Dominions, which were concerned about their security. *L'Afrique Française* could claim a certain victory, but it realized that its role had been essentially secondary.

The Council of Ten, moreover, did not question the interests of France in Togoland and the Cameroons. Of course it would discuss "revendications equitables des gouvernements dont les titres sont examinés"; but the French wanted some border arrangements and realized that bilateral negotiations would be sufficient to settle the problem. Therefore, the new colonial problems of the future League of

73. "Comment les Allemands traitaient les indigènes dans leurs colonies africaines du Togo et du Cameroun." This report is quoted in *L'Afrique Française, 28* (supplément 11, 1918)

74. "President Wilson said that he thought all were agreed to oppose the restoration of the German colonies." Meeting of the Council of Ten, January 28, 1919, in FR, Paris Peace Conference 1919, 3.

Nations were discussed, i.e. the institution of the mandates system.

Colonial groups had rejected internationalization, but it was not suggested in January 1919. It was expected that the peacemakers would have to choose between simple annexation and the return of German colonies. In fact, most discussion centered on finding a regime that would satisfy the "interests of the local populations." French commissioners took a secondary role because New Zealand, South Africa, Australia, and, therefore, Great Britain had considerably greater interests at stake. The Dominions emerged as energetically opposed to any mandates idea when Henri Simon, the French minister of colonies, appeared before the Council on January 28.[75] The French minister's intervention was directed toward two main questions: French interest in Togoland and the Cameroons and the French preference regarding annexation or mandate.

Simon's arguments, although strong, were not original. It would be very interesting to know what role Governor-General Merlin had in their elaboration.[76] France, he claimed, limited her colonial ambitions to the two former German colonies in western Africa. She had sent the first explorers to this area and had signed the first treaties. If Germany had extended her Cameroon possessions, it was by threat of war. Such changes as Germany obtained under threat were no longer valid. French troops had actively participated in the campaigns of 1914–16, which were justified by the aggressive German attitude, particularly in the Congo basin.

From the political point of view, Simon went on, French ambitions were backed by the desires of the natives. Native tribes wished the French to remain. From the ethnic point of view, Dahomey was linked to Togoland because both countries shared the same traditions and were inhabited by the same tribes. As for the Cameroons, it was the natural outlet for equatorial Africa: "La politique de l'Allemagne, qui a abouti à l'accord de 1911, avait consisté à couper de la mer les possessions françaises, pour chasser par la suite les Français sur la plan économique. La côte maritime, étendue, du Cameroun, et le port de Douala sont indispensables au développement de l'Afrique équatoriale française." [77]

These justifications seemed so obvious to the Ten that they were

75. See Wm. Rogers Louis, *Great Britain and Germany's Lost Colonies* (Oxford, 1967).

76. Merlin was advising Simon from the beginning of 1919. *L'Afrique Française* was pleased.

77. FR, Paris Peace Conférence 1919, 3, meeting of January 28, 1919.

not commented upon; even the contention that the natives supported the French administration was not doubted. In fact, the second part of the speech was expected to be more interesting.

Without any hesitation, Simon declared that France adhered to the position of the Dominions: nothing was better than annexation. A mandate could be revoked, and that was an obstacle to investment and, therefore, to the territory's development. On the other hand, if a small nation were entrusted with a mandate, Germany would be able to carry on her intrigues. The trustee had to be a great nation with colonial experience and with resources to develop such territories. France qualified on both counts. If France were chosen, the League of Nations could be sure that natives would not suffer maltreatment and that the colonial market would not be closed. Therefore, French goals conformed to Point Five of the Wilsonian principles.

Simon did not clearly state that the open door policy would be applied. Perhaps he intended, as was suggested by the colonial party, to obtain Togo and Cameroon trade as a means of recovering from the destruction of the war. It is only certain that he was not very precise on this point. Possibly he feared that Germany, which was expected to enter the League within a few months or years, would benefit from the economic advantages promised to the Leagues members. In such a case, she would not have been punished and would again be dangerous. In any event, Simon did not accept the time limit attached to a mandate or the obligation to report to the League of Nations. In the following debates, Lloyd George pointed out that Simon agreed with the principles of a mandate but not the name, but this would seem to be an oversimplification of the minister's thesis.

Clemenceau's intervention, on the contrary, proved that the entire government did not share Simon's views. The prime minister stated that his minister was ready to make concessions; and, once Lloyd George had accepted the idea of the mandate, Clemenceau would rally to the general opinion. Togoland and the Cameroons, he indicated, were not worth a dispute between allies. When, on January 30, he was given the assurance that nothing would prevent France from recruiting troops in mandates of the B class for purposes of maintaining order and defense of the territory, he completely accepted the compromise as elaborated by General Smuts.

How is Clemenceau's conciliatory attitude to be explained? It is useful to note that during his entire political career he had opposed colonial expansion in order to prepare "La Revanche." Even if his views had changed somewhat, the two former German colonies were not particularly important at a time when the essential war aims of France were being discussed. It was most important to remain on good terms with Great Britain and the United States.

Clemenceau's policies did not please everyone, however. Paul Cambon, for example, wrote to his son:

> L'horreur de Clemenceau pour la politique coloniale m'ennuie. Le Cameroun, ou au moins la partie que l'Angleterre nous abandonne, nous est nécessaire. Quant au Togo, il serait bon de le partager avec l'Angleterre pour la sécurité de notre Dahomey. Il faut que ton oncle s'entende bien avec Tardieu pour empêcher Clemenceau de se livrer à des déclarations d'abandon sur lesquelles il est difficile de revenir ensuite.

Simon's policy seemed a little better to him:

> Notre ministre des Colonies . . . dont je ne connaissais même pas le nom, a fort bien exposé la question du Cameroun et du Togoland. Mais tout cela c'est du bavardage, et l'on ne voit pas une ligne directrice. C'est le reproche qu'on peut faire à Clemenceau qui, sur toutes ces questions spécials, ne s'est pas reseigné. [78]

France finally accepted the principle of mandates with mental reservations which we will find also in *L'Afrique Française.* The territories given to Germany in 1911 were definitely annexed to French Equatorial Africa by a decision of the Council of Four on May 6.[79] On May 7, an unofficial note was published at the end of a meeting of the Four: "Pour ce qui concerne le Togo et le Cameroun, la Grande-Bretagne et la France détermineront elles-même le régime futur de ces colonies et le recommander-ont à l'adoption de la Société des Nations." [80]

What did this note mean? On May 12, *Le Temps,* well informed, gave the following explanation: "On sait qu'en raison du partage prévu pour ces territories, le système du mandat ne sera appliqué ni au Togo ni au Cameroun." [81] At the same time, the chancellor of the exchequer declared before the House of Commons: "None of these territories will become a colony." [82]

78. Paul Cambon, *Correspondance,* 300, letter of January 23, 1919.

79. See Paul Mantoux, *Les délibérations du Conseil des Quatre* (2 vols. Paris, 1955), *1,* 325.

80. *L'Afrique Française,* 29 (May–June 1919), 133.

81. *Le Temps,* May 12, 1919. Quoted in *L'Afrique Française,* 29 (May–June 1919).

82. Meeting of May 14, 1919. Report given in *L'Afrique Française,* 29 (May–June 1919).

What were the reactions of the colonial party during these months as represented by *L'Afrique Française?* The magazine was pleased to note that due to the victory in Europe and a strong press campaign, the colonies would not be returned to Germany. It trusted Henri Simon to defend a policy elaborated by the commissions of 1917 and 1918. But the mandate proposal met "a less complete approbation,"[83] especially when the review realized that the system had been adopted as a result of British acceptance. It indicated that France and even England were not satisfied and that, in the United States, Wilson's policy was being criticized because that country could be involved in the Near East and Africa. Neither the pacifying declarations of Balfour or Lord Curzon, nor Lloyd George's speech of February 13, succeeded in reassuring *L'Afrique Française*.

Commenting upon Article 19 of the Covenant (Article 22 in the final text), *L'Afrique Française* noted that the prohibition of the slave and arms trades, the limitation of alcohol traffic, and the assurance of individual and religious freedoms were long-established principles in French colonies. The effects of the military stipulations would depend upon what the League would become; but equality of trading privileges in the mandates was bad. Gaston Doumergue expressed the same opinion in an article in *Le Soir* (February 7, 1919); France must be opposed to the open door policy because she had been "plus touchée que les autres nations par la guerre, et sa production est pour longtemps menacée et réduite par les ruines qu'elle a supportées en tant que frontière de la civilisation."

But the note of May 7 still left a few hopes. France received the harbor of Lomé from England, ceding some sections of northern Togoland.[84] Morocco was no longer subjected to the Capitulations, but Tangiers remained an international harbor. The review no longer speculated about an exchange of colonies with Great Britain. For some time it reminded its readers of the French colonial cause in Mauritius Island,[85] but the English opposition immediately stopped its efforts. *L'Afrique Française* was more eager to destroy Italian claims over Djibouti. On the whole the colonial party was satisfied, primarily because it believed the mandate system would not be applied to Togoland and the Cameroons.

When the ratification of the peace treaty entered into discussion at the Chamber, a deputy concluded, after having expressed his joy at the new French conquests in Africa: "Mais je n'ai pas pu savoir si

83. *L'Afrique Française,* 29 (May–June 1919).
84. After the Milner-Simon agreement, arrived at in July 1919.
85. *L'Afrique Française,* 29 (May–June 1919).

c'était avec ou sans mandat de la Société des Nations."[86] We must agree with him that the explanations heard, or to be heard, were not clear. On September 5, Minister of Finances Klotz stated: "Une part des colonies allemandes est placée sous le mandat de la France." René Besnard, in charge of the special report on German colonies, affirmed that France "obtient deux nouvelles colonies." André Tardieu defended the treaty: "Vous vouliez des résultats territoriaux: vous avez l'Alsace et la Lorraine, le Maroc, le Cameroun, le Togo, le Congo."[87] The minister of colonies was supposed to give the definitive answer. Referring to the May seventh note, he stated: "J'en conclus d'une façon nette que nous n'avons pas de mandat et j'aurais bien d'autres raisons dans le même sens." What were these other reasons? Had he received verbal or written assurances from Great Britain?

The future regime of Togoland and the Cameroons which the Minister described was not that of traditional colonies. He accepted the open door principles for all the members of the League—which excluded Germany—if it were possible to associate the older and newer territories in customs and economic matters. He noted that France would continue to recruit colonials troops to defend her own territory as well as the colonies. The conclusion: "Nous pretendons administrer sans mandat, mais dans l'esprit du mandat."

Rene Besnard had previously explained that the open door policy could be applied, but that it would be limited "as much as possible." He had also expressed an opinion very similar to that of the minister: "L'autorité territoriale doit garder la plus grande liberté et sa pleine souveraineté pour l'organisation de ces deux pays et leur incorporation tant au point de vue fiscal qu'au point de vue administratif et economique aux colonies voisines qui sont déjà en notre possession."

The appreciation of *L'Afrique Française* for this report was another indication that the mandate concept was accepted with mental reservations and that the colonial party was satisfied with the peace treaty. Besnard himself explained such a position. "General principles" would not be avoided and "une partie importante de notre domaine africain entre dans le bassin conventionnel du Congo et se trouve par conséquent soumise à ce régime de la Porte Ouverte." It was not impossible, moreover, that negotiations with the British might have led

86. The parliamentary debates on the peace treaty are reported in *L'Afrique Française,* 29 (supplément 11, 1919).

87. Louis Marin, a conservative deputy, pointed out that Morocco had not been obtained as a result of the war. In fact, Tardieu was placing very different territories into the same category.

to some territorial adjustments. Finally, only the Socialists opposed the colonial clauses of the treaty because they viewed the mandate concept as a hypocritical system which deprived Germany of indispensable raw materials.[88]

In the Senate, Lucien Hubert, in charge of the report, emphasized the obligations France assumed before the League of Nations in acquiring new territories. Leon Bourgeois' intervention gives a pretty accurate summary of the dangers threatening the mandates system: "Si, comme nous en avons l'espoir, et la ferme volonté, la SDN devient une réalité, si elle exerce rigoureusement le contrôle supréme dont elle est chargée, ce n'est pas l'esprit de civilisation et d'humanité." No one indicated more clearly that the mandates would be what the League made of them.

We can draw several conclusions from this study, which, of necessity, remains incomplete:

First of all, did France obtain her war aims in Africa? We have seen that she had waited until the last month of the war to declare them officially and that the arguments of the colonial party were undoubtedly the origins of the minister's attitude. She obtained Togoland with Lomé, four-fifths of the Cameroons with Douala, and the territories ceded in 1911. The Congo would no longer be "notre Cendrillon coloniale," and she was completely satisfied with Morocco. The Italians received minor concessions. France, of course, renounced an exchange of territories with Great Britain, perhaps because such a policy no longer seemed indispensable and, moreover, because English public opinion would have opposed it. *L'Afrique Française* and its friends were satisfied.

Second, was the mandates system considered menacing by the colonials? Certainly the answer would be yes at the beginning of 1919 because the concept had been confused with internationalization. When the concept had been more precisely defined, it remained unpopular because of the open door policy. But the French gave the mandate concept a very restricted meaning, first by obtaining the concession that native troops could be raised to defend the colonies (January) and then by contemplating strong limitations to the proposed commercial equality even for members of the League. There remained the necessity to report to the League, but, even at the end of spring and much more so at the beginning of autumn, colonials

88. A socialist deputy added that Germany, stripped of her colonies, would turn toward the East in order to find indispensable resources.

observed that Wilson's policies were opposed in the United States: the idea of a League of Nations was no longer as disturbing to the partisans of "réalisme politique." The French Parliament accepted the colonial clauses of the treaty because the mandate was considered primarily a vague moral responsibility rather than a real limitation of French sovereignty.

Finally, the preceding considerations indicate that official circles lacked both originality and generosity with regard to the colonies. They had not really understood that the native participation in the war had transformed the relationship between the colonies and France. In spite of their pledges, they were ready to follow a conservative policy. And, finally, the majority of the public, more interested in European problems, would not push them in the opposite direction.

☙ 11. Conclusion

☙ HENRI BRUNSCHWIG

In considering the scope of Anglo-French rivalries in Africa in the nineteenth century, one is struck by their limitations in time and space. In time, for the conflicts multiplied on the coasts and in the interior only after 1882, even though it is true that the French navy had not ceased its opposition to the British since the time France regained her former colonies after the Napoleonic era. These conflicts became increasingly volatile, arousing public opinion and even threatening the peace which existed between the two Powers, whose traditional entente had come to an end at the time of the English occupation of Egypt. The appearance of the new participants, King Leopold II and Bismarck, further complicated Anglo-French relations. This atmosphere of crisis persisted until the reestablishment of the Entente Cordiale in 1904.

In space, the rivalries occurred in two well-defined theaters of operation: North Africa from the Magreb to Egypt, and sub-Saharan Africa from the Atlantic coast to the vast Sudanese interior of Niger and Tchad. In the remainder of the continent—South Africa, East Africa, Central Africa—there were practically no conflicts, if Madagascar, whose history differs significantly from the rest of Africa, is excepted.

A close analysis of the reasons for these temporal and spacial limitations leads to a problem fascinating many of the authors of the preceding chapters: that of the origins of the Scramble. The solution of origins becomes more apparent, as they have indicated, when one tries to define more rigorously the meaning of the phrase "scramble" in the late nineteenth century. And this also leads to a keener understanding of the agreement which brought the rivalries to an end.

The two theaters in which the rivals confronted each other differed profoundly. Until about 1882 they had neither the same actors nor the same audience, nor were they even the setting for the enactment of the same play. North Africa was Mediterranean, white, and Moslem. Here the Near Eastern question was raised. Prerogative of the diplomats, who attempted to reserve all the roles for themselves, this play was followed by an attentive and informed public. Since the unification of Italy and Germany which, for all effects and purposes, had been resolved in 1871, the Near Eastern question had become the first order of business of foreign policy of the Great Powers. It was a basic chapter in secondary and college textbooks, the pet subject of candidates for examinations and for competitions, and the supreme test of the abilities of diplomats. The problem aroused the passions of public opinion mainly because of the legacy of the Greek war of independence at the beginning of the century and the serious Egyptian crisis of 1840. Three conflicts occupied, each in its turn, the center of the stage: the struggle of the Balkan peoples for national independence, encouraged alternately by the Russians and the Austrians; the control of navigation in the Straits, disputed by Russia and England; and the rivalry between the khedive of Cairo and the sultan of Constantinople—the latter, as Miss Ramm properly reminds us, formerly complicated by an ardent Anglo-French rivalry.

That period was over by the time of the era with which the preceding essays are mainly concerned. Since the agreement concluded between Guizot and Aberdeen in 1845, since the campaign of Crimea under the Second Empire, and because France had been provided in 1871 with another "hereditary enemy," the Entente had predominated. It had become indispensible in the eyes of the Quai d'Orsay, grateful for the discreet support that the British Foreign Office had given it when Bismark had threatened France in 1875. It had been strengthened at the Congress of Berlin of 1878, when France had not objected to the English occupation of Cyprus and Britain had promised a benevolent neutrality if France intervened in Tunisia. And it was finally embodied in the Egyptian Condominium. Since the opening of the Suez Canal, France had achieved a moral and cultural position of the first order in Egypt. She also dominated the "Public Debt Commission" created under her aegis in 1876 to watch over the interests of the creditors of Khedive Ismail. When, in 1878, the khedive once again suspended payments, France and Britain assumed joint control of the Egyptian administration through the agency of the Englishman Rivers Wilson, now minister of finance, and of the Frenchman de Blignières, now minister of public works. Then, when the first troubles broke out in Cairo, the two ministers of foreign affairs, Waddington and Salisbury, arranged to replace Ismail by his son Tewfik and to establish the dual financial control of November 15, 1879, which displaced the other powers from the administration of the Egyptian debt. Miss Ramm has accurately demonstrated that this Condominium obscured a much less flattering reality: although French was always the best-known foreign language, the English occupied dominant positions in economic, technical, and financial matters as well as in their role as political advisers. From just before the crisis of 1882, the Condominium became a sort of British protectorate—and those Egyptian nationalists were not the least mistaken who announced, immediately following upon the intervention of the French in Tunisia, the forthcoming occupation of Egypt by the English.[1] But the French did not acknowledge this. Tunisia was the reward that Bismark and Salisbury offered to France for having effectively played an unrewarding role in the "Congress of Berlin." Jean Ganiage's chapter clearly points out that Bismarck was also inciting the British to intervene in Egypt at the same time as the French in Tunisia. If the Republic had immediately seized its opportunity, perhaps Urabi and the Egyptian nationalists would not have drawn the parallel between Tunisia and Egypt.

At the beginning of 1882 the scene was exactly the same. French and English diplomats were playing the same roles in the comedy of the entente before the European participants. And that comedy figured in all the diplomatic programs—that of the Egyptian Condominium, that of Mediterranian policy, that of the Near Eastern question in the broad sense of the term and of the international relations of which it was the expression.

The other theater was that of Black Africa, coastal or Sudan, "animist" or Islamic. Here the principal actors were the sailors of the Royal Navy and the *Marine nationale.* At their side, merchants and missionaries—more numerous in the British troupe than the French—sought to raise themselves to principal roles. Frenchman and Englishman rivaled each other since the beginning of the century in a tragic-comedy that could have been entitled "ôte-toi de là pour que je m'y mette." Finally the actors took themselves seriously and enflamed each other to the point of disturbing public order. The diplomats then intervened and delegated some dramatic authority from the principal theater. Each actor was recalled to his script. Indeed, the play which played before a thinly scattered audience of colonial administrators was submitted to a sort of a posteriori censure which kept it at its

1. Chapter 3 in this volume, "Great Britain and France in Egypt," by Agatha Ramm.

level of minor theater. This was apparent on several occasions in the course of the century and, for the last time, in the affair of the rivers of the South, where the rival governors of Senegal and Sierra Leone, backed up by the rival ministers of the marine, failed to disturb the entente jealously preserved by the ministers of foreign affairs. Waddington and Salisbury kept it in good order. A truce was imposed on the combattants, and Brière de L'Isle had to send Captain Gallieni to effect the evacuation of the post of Matacong occupied by the French in 1879. A bipartisan commission was charged with fixing the limits of the respective zones of influence, and before it had ended its work the two fiery governors were recalled.[2]

It was not that the Guinean theater was without interest or that it was disregarded. Rather it was kept in its place, which was relatively minor. It was the one scene, besides Algeria, in which the subordinate ministries—Navy, War, Interior—were on center stage and were allowed to act as they wanted. Their roles were not negligible, since the colonial ministers could acquire territories and conclude treaties that became incumbent upon the ministers of foreign affairs to ratify by decree. Obviously, nobody would have dreamed of proposing to Parliament the ratification of a treaty signed by an "X" by some Amatifou, Lobenguela, or other illiterate Black chief. All of this was far from the Near Eastern question and the subtleties of international politics. The rivalries which, in the rivers of the South, at Fouta Djallon, at Dahomey, or in the delta of the Niger, set the French and English administrators, the navy, the merchants, and the missionaries in opposition, were not Franco-British national rivalries, but rivalries of the French and British military, explorers, or merchants. They had hardly any effect on the relations between the two states which depended on the ministries of foreign affairs who traditionally practiced a policy of entente.

This was also true of the relations with those few other powers with interests in Africa. The Gulf of Guinea and, in a general way, Black Africa were not considered part of the sphere of foreign affairs by the Portuguese, the Germans, the Belgians, the Dutch, or the other founders of settlements on the coast, where free trade reigned at least in principle.

This state of affairs must be taken into account in measuring the significance of African events in public opinion. Thus the issue of the rivers of the South could not have compared to that of the French

2. John D. Hargreaves, *Prelude to the Partition of West Africa* (London, 1963), pp. 214–52.

intervention in Tunisia or the outcome of the Egyptian crisis. Around 1880 Black Africa still did not exist in the same way as the Rhine, the Straits, or China in the average French or English mind.

At this point we approach the vexing question of public opinion. It is difficult to know exactly how to cope with it. Consider the press. But what press? Should specialized journals with limited circulation be ignored in favor of the nationally circulated popular press and the provincial papers? No doubt they should if what is sought is the assessment of public opinion at the level of the average citizen. But in this case Black Africa did not intrude into the news of these dailies. Another question: do newspapers reflect opinion, or are they used by their proprietors as a means of arousing public opinion? And in this latter case, are they successful? Even if distrustful of them, one cannot neglect the press accounts, by means of which Roger Louis has shown that the Egyptian question clearly preoccupied more people's minds, in France and in England, than did the question of the Congo on the eve of the convocation of the Berlin Conference of 1884–85.

In July 1882 the entente to which all of the foreign policy of France of forty years had remained faithful broke up. That the French had been humiliated by British intervention, even though they had deliberately refused to join in with the action and to follow a policy of condominium, was not taken for granted. After all, in questions of prestige there is no reality. Prestige does not reside in one plan and is not necessarily absent from another. Political prestige is found where it is placed. The Third Republic envisaged its prestige as equivalent to territorial aggrandizement; it acquired it by colonial expansion. Recently General de Gaulle attached prestige to withdrawal from the colonies, and France acquired it by decolonization. The harangue of the successive governments against the British—whom they had the bad grace to reproach for having acted alone when France could have joined Britain and when, on a moral level, the operation of Tunisia was no more defensible than that of Cairo—is explained by the fact that intervention revealed the truth. It tore away the mask of condominium. It revealed that in reality Egypt was already Anglicized, that England was alone in the process of modernizing it, and that the French presence appeared there especially in museums and in mundane receptions. It put a damper on the declarations about the civilizing mission which the French willingly misused, and it made apparent their real weakness, the timidity of their bankers, the mediocrity of their merchants, the vanity of their intellectuals. It was for this reason that the French had been humiliated and had searched for compensations; as if they had not just taken Tunis and as if they could not hope for British support in Morocco.

That compensation, which was immediately desired, Pierre Savorgnan de Brazza provided when he returned from his exploration of the Congo, just after the English intervention in Egypt. Charles Duclerc, successor of Freycinet, endeavored to turn the ratification of treaties signed with Makoko into a national success. In an unheard of manner for a minister of foreign affairs, he resorted to the solemn procedure of ratification by Parliament instead of merely issuing a decree: he staged in the great theater a show brought from the secondary scene. The press, fully informed, saturated public opinion with a philanthropic-chauvinistic ideology, and the legend of Brazza flourished. Could France have ratified these treaties, to which the minister of the navy, Admiral Jauréguiberry, was hostile because Brazza had acted on his own initiative, and to which the experts on the Quai d'Orsay denied all appreciable economic value, without a break in the Entente Cordiale? The matter is not certain. But she might have ratified them more discreetly, on the secondary stage. Is it necessary then to agree with Robinson and Gallagher and place the origin of the "Scramble" in that rupture of the entente cordiale? [3] We do not think so, for King Leopold was already on the spot, and the Scramble is characterized essentially by the substitution of multiple rivalries for the single Franco-British rivalry.

The word "scramble" was in current usage in England in the late nineteenth century, and the *Oxford English Dictionary* gives examples of its use in explications of territorial rivalries well before 1870. It does not seem that politicians or journalists had particularly resorted to it in discussions of the competition of French and English explorers in Fouta Djallon, for example, or in the rivers of the South. Technically, however, their activity did not differ from that of later expeditions organized by different countries: explorations were made, treaties were signed, posts were set up. Nor does the term seem to have been applied to the conflicts between naval personnel of the two countries at Dahomey or at Gabon. But if it had been used with respect to such a dual rivalry, it was not done at all in the same sense as after 1885.

3. Ronald Robinson and John Gallagher, with Alice Denny, *Africa and the Victorians* (London, 1961).

The matter is easier resolved on the French side, because it there appears as a new term. Speaking of colonial rivalries subsequent to the Berlin Conference, Jules Ferry in his book *Le Tonkin et la mère patrie* wrote in 1890:

> An irresistible movement carries the large European nations to the conquest of new lands. It is like an immense steeplechase on an unknown route. This steeplechase is scarcely five years old and, year by year, accelerates, like dust pushed by acquired speed.[4]

Littré informs us that a type of race like a steeplechase had been introduced in France at the beginning of the century, and in fact Alfred de Musset described it charmingly in 1832 in "A Quoi rèvent les jeunes filles" (scene IV):

> Have you ever seen the races in England?
> There are four jockeys—four saddled horses.
> The point is to finish, no matter the fashion.
> One choses a ravine—another a well-trodden path—
> This one will win if he doesn't run into a river;
> That one will do better, if he doesn't break his neck.

From a comparison of these texts it would appear that a sort of rivalry had begun between the European powers *scarcely five years* before 1890—that is to say around 1885. That rivalry is comparable to a race which was at least originally run by four riders on saddled horses. If that definition were still in effect in 1885, the four rivals were already designated: the four protagonists of the Berlin Conference—England, France, Germany, and King Leopold.

The Berlin Conference was not called to partition Africa. It only incidentally disposed of a territory—of some size it is true—by absorbing the negotiations followed elsewhere between King Leopold and the other states in order to recognize the Independent State of the Congo. The rules it enunciated—notification and effective occupation, rendering more difficult the acquisitions of sovereignty—tended more to limit than to favor a general partition. Nevertheless the legend more and more subscribed to that dates the partition of Africa from the Berlin Conference contains some elements of truth. Berlin was an innovation, not only because the major powers implicitly verified the British claim to the Lower Niger, as has been shown by Roger Louis, or because the right of first option conceded by King Leopold to France would direct future negotiations to come, as was explained

4. Jules Ferry, *Le Tonkin et la mère patrie* (Paris, 1890), p. 37.

by Jean Stengers; but because for the first time the major powers were assembled for the single purpose of discussing Black Africa.

Bismark used Black Africa in his efforts to achieve rapprochement with France. Metaphorically speaking, the actors of the major theater came to play on the minor stage. It was the last gala presentation that they gave there. For, from now on, there was only a single theater. Berlin marked the fusion between major international diplomacy conducted by the foreign ministries and the minor African diplomacy of the navy and the military. Henceforth, all diplomacy had to recognize African problems as well as the Near Eastern question. The partition of the dark continent, begun long before, was accelerated as a result. Diplomatic relations, the game of territorial exchange and compensation which, for example, tied up the fortunes of Uganda and Heligoland or of the Congo and Morocco, resulted from it. What was new was essentially the shift from dual rivalry to multinational rivalry, from a simple competition to a multiple steeplechase, a scramble, a melee.

If this was the case, the Scramble is defined by the multitude of competitors and thus dates from 1884. It was at that time that Bismarck put Germany on the starting line and King Leopold began to have his colonial undertaking recognized as a state in international public law. This much said, one can look for those responsible for the enlargement of the game.[5] It might be argued that without the intervention of King Leopold there would not have been the rivalry between Stanley and Brazza and perhaps not the Makoko treaties. Or that without the unilateral intervention of the British in Egypt there would not have been the ratification of the Makoko treaties which caused Portuguese protests and led to the Anglo-Portuguese treaty of February 26, 1884, the pretext for the meeting at Berlin. Or again that if Bismarck had not intervened, King Leopold would have remained out of it or returned to his essentially commercial projects, and that only the traditional rivalry between France and Britain would have been manifested in the Congo as in Dahomey or in Guinea. One could propose as godfathers of the "Scramble" Leopold II, Duclerc, Bismarck, or Granville, a little conjecture of the historian might move the origin back from 1884 to 1882 or even 1880. The important fact remains, however, the entry of Black Africa into the realm of international affairs, a fact which became evident when the powers of the whole world united to consult about it at Berlin.

5. Jean Stengers, "L'Impérialisme colonial de la fin du xixe siècle: mythe ou réalité," *Journal of African History, 3,* No. 2 (1962)

If the Berlin Conference is considered as one of the performances given by the International Relations repertory company, after that of the Congress of Berlin of 1878 and before that of the Conference of Brussels of 1889, it becomes clear that the chapters on the consecutive "partitions" at these meetings are essentially studies of diplomatic history. John Hargreaves stresses this fact well by the detail and the precision of his commentary on how the Anglo-French rivalry turned into an international steeplechase. But, paradoxically—and this emerges clearly from the contribution of Pierre Guillen—it was the diplomats involved in world politics who restored the two powers to the Entente Cordiale of 1904. The mitigation of disputed colonial claims was not the end but the condition of the Anglo-French accord, of which the essential object was the preservation of "European balance" in the period of "armed peace."

In the same way the studies of G. N. Sanderson on the crisis of Fashoda, and André Kaspi on French military objectives, place the European preoccupations, the questions of prestige and the personalities of diplomats, in the foreground and reveal that public opinion was less severely exercised than had been imagined.

It thus appears that the partition was completely achieved by Europeans living, thinking, and reacting within their European framework.

This internationalization of Africa came to accelerate its partition as it did that of the rest of the world. And this partition, functioning according to the principle of compensation in an international framework, came to neglect the particular characteristics of the assigned regions. There is general outrage at the cavalier attitude with which the powers divided up peoples and territories. But it is too often forgotten that the stipulations of the major treaties of partition were in reality only directives to territorial commissions already provided for. There was here something analogous to our *loi-cadres* which establish the principles the specialists are then to apply and work out in detail. The commissions worked on the local scene, often for several years, and they took local realities into account. The number of documents they have left behind and which have been studied will allow an appreciation of the degree to which they had been guided by differing existing factors of geography, strategy, economics, ethnography. They, no more than the treaties, respected the principles of nationalities, or the right of people to take care of themselves. There is still considerable indignation expressed over it, as if there had been nations or people united throughout Africa; as if these principles had always been respected in Europe; as if they were even today. It appears certain that the interests of the mother countries had always been considered by the commissions before those of the Africans. But it is no less certain that the European powers were incapable of judicious appraisal of their own interests. They had all more or less been influenced by the double obsession which appears to explain in full the policy of Bismarck: [6] to acquire colonies was to become more powerful and, in the eyes of public opinion, to acquire national prestige; not to acquire them, on the other hand, was to jeopardize the future. When all was divided up, it would be too late to intervene. For the future would doubtlessly reveal sources of riches and power in those scarcely known territories which were now being casually partitioned. One took a chance on them as on a lottery ticket. That was without doubt the most general and original feature of the partitions after 1885. The winning numbers turned out to be Katanga and Rhodesia.

6. Henry Ashby Turner, "Bismarck's Imperialist Venture" in *Britain and Germany in Africa,* edited by Prosser Gifford and Wm. Roger Louis with Alison Smith (New Haven, 1967), pp. 47–82.

PART II

Colonial Rule

12. *Military Expansion in the Western Sudan—French and British Style*

A. S. KANYA-FORSTNER

"The colonial policy of Great Britain and France in West Africa," wrote Lord Salisbury with evident satisfaction in March 1892, "has been widely different. France . . . has pursued steadily the aim of establishing herself on the Upper Niger . . . by a large and constant expenditure, and by a succession of military expeditions. Great Britain, on the other hand, has followed a policy of advance by commercial enterprise. She has not attempted to compete with the military operations of her neighbour."[1] It was an apt comment. By the 1890s France was committed to the military conquest of the Western Sudan and the destruction of those African polities that lay in her path. Segu and Nioro, the twin capitals of the Tukulor empire, had been captured in 1890 and 1891. Masina, the last refuge of the Sultan Ahmadu, was occupied in the spring of 1893. In January 1894 French expeditionary forces entered Timbuktu. Meanwhile, Samori was driven out of his territories on the Upper Niger eastward into the hinterland of the Ivory Coast. By 1894 the conquest of Dahomey had cleared the way into Borgu, and Commandant Monteil had moved north from the Ivory Coast to cut off the hinterlands of the Gold Coast and Togo.[2] Virtually the whole of the West African interior now seemed destined to pass under French sway.

British governments, unwilling to bear the cost of a more active West African policy, did little to stem this tide. They did not remain oblivious to the dangers of French expansion, but their responses were limited by a traditional concern for economy and a reluctance to commit themselves in areas of marginal strategic importance. The hinterlands of the Gambia and Sierra Leone had been surrendered

1. Salisbury to Dufferin, March 30, 1892, C. 6701, *Parliamentary Papers* [*PP* hereafter] [1892], *56*, 777–78.

2. This was the most important objective of the unsuccessful expedition to Kong. Delcassé to Monteil, Instructions, September 24, 1894, Archives Nationales Section Outre-Mer [ANSOM hereafter], Afrique III/19/b.

without much of a fight in 1889 and 1891. To protect the hinterland of the Gold Coast, Ferguson, the Native Agent, was twice sent to negotiate treaties with Mossi, Gurunsi, and Dagomba, but his efforts were as ineffective as they were cheap. In March 1895, Lord Ripon finally gave in to the appeals of the Gold Coast authorities and agreed to consider the possibility of an armed expedition against Ashanti; but he insisted that the cost would have to be met entirely from local funds.[3] Attempts to keep the French out of the Niger territories by diplomacy fared no better. Paris did not accept the British interpretation of the agreement of August 5, 1890, and the Anglo-German agreement of November 1893 had no sooner been signed than the Franco-German agreement made it quite meaningless. The more favored tactic of relying on George Goldie to safeguard British interests "without the expenditure of Imperial funds or the sacrifice of the life of a single British soldier" was also coming unstuck. Although the Royal Niger Company had the resources to contain filibustering expeditions like those of Mizon, the French military advance from Dahomey posed a much more serious challenge. To forestall the threat, Goldie mended his diplomatic fences in Borgu; but the French soon knocked them down. By the spring of 1895 Captain Decoeur had extorted his own treaties from Nikki and Kiama; a detachment from his expedition had temporarily occupied Say; and Captain Toutée had built Fort d'Arenberg below Bussa. Whitehall merely lodged a diplomatic protest. At the time, Britain's African policy still revolved around the security of Egypt; if the French could be kept off the Upper Nile, she was prepared to be more than reasonable in West Africa.[4]

After 1895, however, British policy underwent an apparently revolutionary transformation. Traditional prejudices against government intervention and expenditure were momentarily cast aside. For a time, West Africa became much more than a pawn in the Egyptian strategy, and the old hesitancy in the face of the French advance gave way to a new determination which was to bring the two countries to the brink of war. In November 1895 an expedition was sent against Ashanti and paid for initially out of the imperial exchequer. In 1896 expeditions were sent into the disputed territories north of the Gold

3. Ripon to Maxwell, Instructions, March 15, 1895, C. 7918, *PP* [1896], 58, 762.

4. E.g. d'Estournelles to Hanotaux, Confidential, September 22, 1894, Ministère des Affaires Etrangères, [MAE hereafter], Correspondance Politique, Angleterre 897; same to same, Most Confidential, November 1, 1894, MAE Angleterre 899.

Coast, and Goldie was pressured into an invasion of Nupe and Ilorin on the Niger. In 1897 reinforcements were sent to the Gold Coast and Lagos, and plans were drafted for the creation of the West African Frontier Force. By 1898 the military balance had been reversed, and the French chargé d'affaires in London could report with only slight exaggeration: "Quoi qu'il en soit des nouvelles souvent fantaisistes qui nous viennent de l'Afrique Occidentale, il n'est pas moins certain que les forces militaires des Anglais y sont actuellement très considérables et dépassent dans des proportions écrasantes le chiffre de nos troupes.[5] Eighteen months after the Anglo-French agreement of June 1898, the Crown assumed the rights and responsibilities of the Royal Niger Company in northern Nigeria, and Colonel Lugard took office as high commissioner for the new Protectorate. Just three years later, Lugard's forces took Kano and Sokoto, and Britain became mistress of a Sudanese empire as imposing in size and far more impressive in economic potential than its French counterpart on the Upper Niger.

Without a doubt, Joseph Chamberlain was the man most responsible for this "marvellous change" in British policy.[6] He was the most influential and energetic colonial secretary of the nineteenth century, and as the leader of the Liberal Unionists in the Salisbury government he enjoyed, within his chosen sphere of interest, an unprecedented freedom of action which he did not hesitate to exploit.[7] Chamberlain had no use for the "tact . . . discretion . . . patience . . . [and] non-interference" which had marked his predecessors' conduct of West African affairs. Instead, he set out "to deal with a strong hand with those questions which [they] . . . allowed to drift."[8] He launched the expedition against Ashanti and forced Goldie to stake the future of the Niger Company on the conquest of Nupe and Ilorin. His, too, was the new policy of firmness toward the French. To protect the northern territories of the Gold Coast from French and German in-

5. Geoffray to Hanotaux, April 30, 1898, encl. in MAE to Ministère des Colonies [MC hereafter], Confidential, May 6, 1898, ANSOM Afrique VI/149/c.

6. Flora Shaw [Lady Lugard], cited in J. L. Garvin, *The Life of Joseph Chamberlain* (3 vols. London, 1932–34), 3, 11: "The change at the Colonial Office was marvellous; it was a total transformation; the sleeping city awakened by a touch." In *A Tropical Dependency*, published in 1906, however, Lady Lugard was to take a less optimistic view about the effects of this change on British policy toward Northern Nigeria.

7. See Ronald E. Robinson and John Gallagher, with Alice Denny, *Africa and the Victorians: The Official Mind of Imperialism* (London, 1961), pp. 425–26.

8. Commons, March 18, 1901, *Hansard*, 4th series, *91*, cols. 350, 362.

cursions, he sent expeditions to occupy Buna and Gambakha, to visit Wa, and to confirm Ferguson's treaty with Wagadugu. To match the military resources of France here and on the Niger, he brought the West African Frontier Force into being. In future, the French were to be played and beaten at their own game. Only effective occupation, Chamberlain told Governor Maxwell of the Gold Coast in June 1897, could make good Britain's claims in West Africa. Since previous surrenders had thrown doubt upon her resolution, "the best evidence of our determination to adopt a different course . . . will be the presence of a force superior to [that of the French]." If the French could not be persuaded to evacuate British positions in Mossi and Bussa, they must be forced out "by what will in effect be a small West African army." Accordingly, Chamberlain authorized the governor to occupy, regardless of the financial cost, any point in the disputed territory not covered by previous agreements or actually in French hands. Six weeks later, he issued similar instructions to Governor McCallum of Lagos, promising to subsidize a force of 2,000 men and to provide the regular officers needed to command it.[9]

The colonial secretary took the game of "effective occupation" in deadly earnest. His choice of Lugard—the scourge of the Catholic party in Uganda and Decoeur's antagonist in Borgu—to command the West African Frontier Force was not calculated to soothe French susceptibilities. His instructions were even more provocative. Lugard was to "occupy the country which is already occupied by the French, . . . to cut off their communications, to prove to the natives that we are as good or better than they, and to show them that their policy of effective occupation is futile." The British were on no account to be the aggressors; "but if through them [the French] a clash occurs *tant mieux,* and we can go for them."[10] This was no bluff. "We ought —even at the cost of war—to keep the hinterland for the Gold Coast, Lagos and the Niger territories," Chamberlain had told his undersecretary in September 1897, and he meant what he said.[11] Maxwell had already been allowed to seize Bonduku, indisputably in

9. Chamberlain to Maxwell, June 4, 1897, encl. in Colonial Office [CO hereafter] to Foreign Office [FO hereafter], July 14, 1897; Chamberlain to McCallum, July 23, 1897, encl. in CO to FO, July 28, 1897, Foreign Office Confidential print [FO C.P. hereafter] 7004, Nos. 15, 38.

10. Lugard, Diary, March 13, 1898 [account of his conversation with Chamberlain, November 12, 1897], Margery Perham and Mary Bull, eds., *The Diaries of Lord Lugard* (4 vols. London, 1963), *4*, 332.

11. Chamberlain to Selborne, September 29, 1897, cited in Garvin, *Chamberlain, 3,* 211.

the French sphere, and in October Colonel Northcott was sent to occupy strategic points in Mossi and Gurunsi, with permission to defend himself against French attack. Northcott was given full support during the crisis that inevitably ensued, and in February 1898 Chamberlain specifically reminded him of his freedom to act in self-defense.[12] On the Niger, the colonial secretary wanted to occupy those French positions that were only held by native troops, and he gave Governor McCallum "authority to prevent violation of territory by resort to force if it should be absolutely necessary."[13] The arrival of the W.A.F.F. in the spring of 1898 raised temperatures even higher; by early summer war in Borgu seemed only a stray rifle shot away.

On the diplomatic front which opened with the resumption of the Anglo-French negotiations in October 1897, the colonial secretary was determined to "take the offensive and attack the French position."[14] Any thought of concessions was contemptuously rejected. The French, he claimed, were simply offering "to abandon doubtful claims in exchange for the surrender by us of undoubted rights. . . . They assume the position of a man who, after stealing my purse should then ask for my watch in consideration of a promise that he will not strip me of my clothes."[15] Chamberlain was not going to suffer any such indignity. Dragging the reluctant Salisbury in his wake, he charged at the French on every point in dispute, threatening to break off the talks whenever their progress was in any way impeded. By June 1898 only the possession of Buna and Ilo remained unsettled, but still he would not yield an inch. With great reluctance, he agreed that Buna might be given up in return for serious concessions; but he absolutely refused to abandon Ilo, and in the end he had his way.

Although the agreement of June 14, 1898, gave Chamberlain virtually everything he wanted from the French, it did not bring his interest in West Africa to an end. Undoubtedly, the need to protect British spheres of influence from French incursions was a crucial factor in his decision to pursue a more robust West African policy; but his conduct of the dispute with France was also a reflection of his general views about the value of African empires and the role of

12. Chamberlain to Maxwell, Instructions for Northcott, October 15, 1897, encl. in CO to FO, October 19, 1897, FO C.P. 7017, No. 48; CO to FO, February 7, 1898; FO to CO, February 7, 1898, FO C.P. 7144, Nos. 122, 125.

13. CO to FO, August 20, 1897; Chamberlain to McCallum, September 28, 1897, encl. in CO to FO, September 28, 1897, FO C.P. 7004, Nos. 62, 173.

14. CO to FO, November 10, 1897, FO C.P. 7017, No. 134.

15. Chamberlain, Memorandum, December 1, 1897, encl. in CO to FO, December 2, 1897, FO C.P. 7017, No. 239.

the state in their acquisition and development. Chamberlain was the one who inaugurated the era of fully fledged British imperialism in West Africa.[16] He had a Radical's conviction in the efficacy of strong government and in its role as the agent of progress and social improvement. "Government," he had once declared, "is the organised expression of the wishes and wants of the people; . . . [and] it is our business to see in what way its operations could be usefully enlarged." [17] He also possessed a fervent belief in the future of the empire and in Britain's imperial mission which would have done credit to the stoutest Jingo. He believed "in the British empire, and . . . the British race . . . [as] the greatest of governing races that the world has ever seen." And in an age when "the tendency of the time is to throw all power into the hands of the greater empires," he believed in Britain's duty to fulfill her "national mission" and to secure her own future by defending and extending her imperial estates.[18] The development of the empire by the direct efforts of the state was the core of Chamberlain's doctrine. It had a particular relevance to West Africa; for the tropical empire, so long the province of the private trader, was most clearly in need of government's more efficient care. "I regard many of our colonies as being in the condition of underdeveloped estates, and estates which can never be developed without Imperial assistance," Chamberlain declared on his arrival at the Colonial Office.[19] In too many cases, "progress [had] been delayed" and "Crown estates of immense extent and undoubted intrinsic value" neglected because private enterprise was unable to carry out the necessary improvements. Government therefore had to take a greater hand in "opening up new fields for private enterprise and new markets for British industry"; for government alone could "make the roads and the railways." [20]

Much of Chamberlain's doctrine was not new. Official support for trade was a well-established feature of British foreign policy; "to open and secure the roads for the merchant" was a recognized function of government. Nor was Chamberlain the first to think in the longer term; "pegging out claims for the future" was Lord Rosebery's phrase.

16. The following paragraphs owe much to Robinson and Gallagher, *Africa and the Victorians*, pp. 395–402.

17. Speech to the Eighty Club, April 28, 1885, C. W. Boyd, ed., *Mr. Chamberlain's Speeches* (2 vols. London, 1914), *1*, 164.

18. Speech at a dinner in honor of the Governor of Western Australia; speech to the Royal Colonial Institute, March 31, 1897, ibid. *1*, xxi; *2*, 5.

19. Commons, August 22, 1895, *Hansard*, 4th series, *36*, col. 641.

20. Colonial Office Memorandum, November 25, 1895, cited in Garvin, *Chamberlain*, *3*, 176–77.

But in some respects the colonial secretary's approach was revolutionary. He no longer expected local revenues to bear the total cost of development nor the prospect of immediate returns to justify expenditure. Instead, he tried to finance colonial development through government loans, confident that his investments would eventually bear fruit.[21] Whereas government intervention in the past had been limited to the protection of British trade against "unfair" foreign competition, to the creation of "a fair field and no favour," Chamberlain was concerned with much more than the guarantee of equal opportunity.[22] Development was the keystone of his policy, and no area of tropical Africa could be developed until it had been effectively occupied, until peace, order, and security had been imposed. Chamberlain was ready to impose order by military means, and he was prepared to invest men as well as money in West Africa. "Expeditions, punitive or otherwise," he believed, were "the only way we can establish peace between contending native tribes in Africa . . . the only system of civilising and practically of developing the trade of Africa." [23] Defense against foreign rivals was not the sole objective of his military policy; the satisfactory settlement of boundaries and spheres of influence was merely the first step. "From the moment we undertook responsibility for those spheres of influence," he later declared, "it became necessary . . . [and] we made it our business to establish once and for all that great Pax Britannica which we established in India." [24] This, perhaps, was his greatest contribution to the new imperialism.

Northern Nigeria provided Chamberlain with an ideal opportunity for putting his doctrine into practice. Here was a perfect example of the tropical African estate. The land was reputedly rich and heavily populated; indeed, the legendary wealth of the Western Sudan had exerted considerable influence on the course of British African policy for more than half a century after the 1780s.[25] Since the 1880s,

21. Commons, March 18, 1901, *Hansard,* 4th series, *91,* col. 363: "It has been said that the [Gold Coast] colony is a burden to the United Kingdom, that this vote of £400,000 which the [Ashanti] war has cost must be borne by the Imperial Exchequer. I have not the slightest doubt but that the whole of it will be repaid."

22. For a general discussion of the relationship between trade and British foreign policy, see D. C. M. Platt, *Finance, Trade, and British Foreign Policy, 1815–1914* (Oxford, 1968). Anglo-French commercial rivalry in West Africa is discussed in C. W. Newbury's paper, above

23. Commons, August 22, 1895, *Hansard,* 4th series, *36,* col. 640.

24. Commons, March 18, 1901, *Hansard,* 4th series, *91,* col. 363.

25. A. A. Boahen, *Britain, the Sahara, and the Western Sudan, 1788–1861* (Oxford, 1964).

moreover, it had been in the sphere of the Royal Niger Company, by far the most energetic and successful private commercial venture in tropical Africa. Yet the estate remained undeveloped and its markets largely untapped. Chamberlain therefore set out to bring it under imperial control. As far as he was concerned, the R.N.C. was merely a caretaker to be bullied into the defense of British interests until the superior resources of the state could be brought to bear, and discarded once it had served its purpose. "[Realizing] with his usual keenness that the greatest possibilities in the Empire lie in Nigeria," Goldie's friend Lugard commented bitterly, ". . . Joe determined to play the role of Ahab with this Naboth's vineyard. Having got the thing into his own hands from the F.O. it only remained to oust the Company." [26]

Once the French had been dealt with and the company evicted, the next objective was to establish the Pax Britannica. In Chamberlain's view, the development of his new estate had to rest on more solid foundations than the company's treaties with Sokoto. "As regards the future," he had told the anxious Salisbury in June 1898, "it is becoming clear that the so-called empire of Sokoto is in a state of dissolution like that of the Great Mogul in the time of Clive. I imagine that in accordance with that precedent a small European force, with perhaps Indian auxiliaries and modern armaments, will be able to establish our authority." [27] The colonial secretary was reluctant to begin the advance until the agreement with France had been concluded, and thereafter the need for military action became less urgent.[28] But the ultimate fate of the Fulani empire was no less surely decided. In August 1898 the departmental committee set up to consider the future status of the Niger territories concluded that Sokoto's power would eventually have to be broken, and even Salisbury accepted the need for some show of British force along the Anglo-French frontier.[29] By 1900 it was clear that Britain intended to assert much

26. Lugard, Diary, March 13, 1898, Perham and Bull, *Diaries, 4,* 342.

27. Chamberlain to Salisbury, June 2, 1898, cited in Garvin, *Chamberlain, 3,* 219.

28. Chamberlain to Lugard, June 9, 1898, encl. in CO to FO, June 10, 1898, FO C.P. 7297, No. 189: "You should . . . defer any movement . . . which might involve us in military operations in Sokoto until we have finally concluded arrangements at Paris. When this has been done, it will be possible to deal with Sokoto without any danger of interference on the part of the French." Chamberlain to Willcocks, October 17, 1898, cited in M. Perham, *Lugard* (2 vols. London, 1956, 1960). Vol 2, *The Years of Authority, 1898–1945,* 89: "Her Majesty's Government strenuously desire to avoid collision with Sokoto at present."

29. Selborne, Report, August 4, 1898, encl. in CO to FO, August 10, 1898, FO C.P. 7317, No. 60; FO to CO, June 25, 1898, FO C.P. 7297, No. 231.

more than a loose claim of influence over its new Protectorate. Lugard was armed with sovereign powers of jurisdiction and had 3,000 men under his command. British imperialism, embodied in Chamberlain's doctrine of tropical African estates, had set the stage for the conquest of Northern Nigeria.

Twenty years before, however, French policy makers, acting on the same premises and seeking the same objectives, had launched their colonial troops upon the conquest of the Western Sudan. Frenchmen in the early nineteenth century had accepted the legends of Sudanese wealth as eagerly as any of their contemporaries across the Channel.[30] For fifty years the Ministry of Marine strove to extend French civilization and trade into the West African interior and to create a vast commercial empire embracing both Senegal and Algeria, with the fabled city of Timbuktu at its heart.[31] Meanwhile, Senegal's energetic governor, Louis Faidherbe, drafted more concrete proposals for the extension of French military power to the Niger and the creation of a second India in the Western Sudan.[32] Few tangible results were achieved. In the decade after 1865, Muslim rebellion in southern Algeria and fear of Tukulor opposition in the Western Sudan, the diversion of resources to the Far East and Mexico, and then the disasters of war and revolution in Europe, all combined to dim the vision of an African empire. But by the late 1870s France was on the road to recovery, and a new, more confident generation of statesmen was beginning to assume the direction of her African policy.

Charles de Freycinet, the minister of public works, was one of the first to rediscover the attractions of the Western Sudan. An engineer

30. Minister of Marine and Colonies [MMC hereafter] to Schmalz, December 31, 1818, cited in C. Schefer, *Instructions Générales données aux Gouverneurs et Ordonnateurs des établissements français en Afrique occidentale* (2 vols. Paris, 1921), 2, 280: "A moins de vingt journées de distance de nos ports, plusieurs millions le bras peuvent être, en peu d'années, acquis à la culture des denrées coloniales, plusieurs millions de consommateurs peuvent être procurés au sol et aux fabriques de la France."

31. MMC to MAE, September 18, 1852, Ministère des Affaires Etrangères, Mémoires et Documents [MAE MD hereafter] Afrique 46; MMC to Minister of Public Instruction, April 10, 1855, ANSOM Afrique/III/9. For a discussion of French policies toward the Western Sudan during the early nineteenth century, see A. S. Kanya-Forstner, *The Conquest of the Western Sudan: A Study in French Military Imperialism* (Cambridge, 1969), pp. 24–28.

32. Faidherbe, Memorandum, October 1, 1858, ANSOM Sénégal I/45/a; Faidherbe to MMC, January 18, 1864, ANSOM Sénégal I/50/b; Extrait des délibérations du conseil d'administration, May 21, 1864 [copy], MAE MD Afrique 47.

by training and a railway-builder by vocation, Freycinet had been hard at work on his grandiose *Programme des Travaux Publiques* since 1877. By the end of 1878 the plan had been extended to include the reorganization of the Algerian railway system. The development of communications with the African interior was the next step. The minister eagerly seized the opportunity provided by the momentary popularity of schemes for building a trans-Saharan railway. In May 1879 he convened a departmental committee to study its feasibility, and that of a line from Saint-Louis to the Niger as well. Its report was favorable, and in July the minister set up a full *Commission Supérieure* to investigate "la mise en communication, par voie ferrée, de l'Algérie et du Sénégal avec l'intérieur du Soudan." [33]

Freycinet had no doubts about the benefits to be gained. The Sudan was the most noteworthy part of the central African interior; it was accessible both from Senegal and from Algeria; it had the Niger; its population was estimated at more than 100,000,000; the inhabitants were industrious, and "les éléments d'un trafic international paraissent y exister à un haut degré." [34] It was through railways, too, that the markets of the interior were to be opened up, the last traces of the shameful slave trade eradicated, and the benefits of civilization carried to the African. Fears of foreign rivalry provided the element of urgency. The scramble for Africa, Freycinet and his colleagues believed, was about to begin, and France could not afford to remain idle. She had to guarantee her future on the African continent, and government had to take the lead. "Il est du devoir du Gouvernement," Freycinet declared on becoming prime minister in December 1879, "de porter ses regards hors des frontières et d'examiner quelles conquêtes pacifiques il pourrait entreprendre. . . . L'Afrique, à nos portes, réclame plus particulièrement notre attention." [35] These were not merely stirring phrases. By the end of 1879 the Ministry of Public Works was planning to send a mission from Algeria toward Sokoto in order to open the Fulani empire to French trade and influence.[36] The government was also ready to shoulder the financial burdens of expansion.

33. Freycinet to Pérouse, May 10, 1879, Archives Nationales [AN hereafter] F14 12437; Rapport de la commission préliminaire, June 12, 1879, ibid.; Freycinet, Rapport au Président de la République, July 12, 1879, *Journal Officiel de la République Française* [*JO* hereafter], July 14, 1879, pp. 6633–35.

34. Freycinet, Rapport au Président de la République, July 12, 1879, ibid.

35. Freycinet, Rapport au Président de la République, December 31, 1879, p. 11700.

36. Projet d'instructions complémentaires [Flatters expedition], encl. in Ministry of Public Works to MAE, January 16, 1880, MAE MD Afrique 75.

Although the trans-Saharan railway never got past the planning stage, estimates for the Senegal-Niger line were submitted to Parliament in February 1880. Total public expenditure on the project was set at 54,000,000 francs, to be paid directly out of the Exchequer.[37] Not even Chamberlain with his preference for development loans was to go this far.

How to expand was the next issue to be settled. Peaceful penetration was the keynote of Freycinet's policy;[38] its objective was the traditional one of gradually extending trade and influence. But the minister of marine and colonies, Admiral Jean Jauréguiberry, had more definite objectives. Since 1877 his ministry had been preoccupied by the danger of British penetration into the Upper Niger. By 1881 Jauréguiberry himself was proclaiming to the Senate: "Nous avons des rivaux, des rivaux acharnés, qui luttent constamment contre l'influence que nous exerçons déjà au Sénégal. Ils cherchent à nous contrarier par tous les moyens. Ils veulent arriver avant nous au Niger."[39] French influence alone could not forestall this threat; only effective occupation could guarantee the future of the new empire. Accordingly, the blueprints which the minister approved were not those of Freycinet but those of Faidherbe. Despite his lip service to the principles of peaceful commercial penetration, Jauréguiberry's motives for adopting the Senegal-Niger railway project were political: the extension of French power to the Niger; and he was prepared to achieve this end by military means.[40] As a professional officer and a former governor of Senegal, the minister was more concerned than his civilian colleagues about the problems of security which the proposed advance was bound to create, and he was more inclined than they to favor military solutions. Since 1876, the ministry had also been under strong pressure from the Senegalese authorities to adopt more forceful policies along the Upper Senegal. Jauréguiberry needed little urging. In 1879 he authorized the construction of a new fort at Bafoulabé,

37. Projet de Loi, February 5, 1880, *JO Documents Parlementaires, Chambre,* No. 2266, pp. 2028–29. The line (including a branch from Saint-Louis to Dakar) was to be built in three sections, two of them by private enterprise. The total cost of the whole project was estimated at 120,000,000 francs.

38. Freycinet to Flatters, Instructions, November 7, 1879, AN F[14]12436.

39. *JO Débats Parlementaires, Sénat,* séance du 16 février 1881, p. 107. See also Michaux [Director of Colonies] to MAE, January 19, 1878, March 22, 1878, MAE MD Afrique 49.

40. Jauréguiberry to Freycinet, November 8, 1879, ANSOM Sénégal XII/76/a; Michaux, Note pour le Ministre, January 6, 1880, ANSOM Missions 15, Carrey 1880.

eighty miles beyond the advance post of Médine. Although Parliament slashed his railway estimates and allowed him only 1,300,000 francs to carry out further surveys, he used part of the money to pay for a new battalion of *tirailleurs sénégalais,* and in July 1880 he authorized the construction of a second fort at Kita, a hundred miles beyond Bafoulabé. Finally, in September 1880 he created the Upper Senegal Military Command and so placed the Sudan firmly under military control. This was the crucial decision that opened the era of French imperialism in the Western Sudan. Fifteen years before Chamberlain, the French had formulated their own doctrine of tropical African estates. In their essentials and their consequences, the two doctrines were the same; the only major difference between them was one of timing.[41]

The adoption of imperialist policies in London and Paris, it is true, did not automatically lead to military conquests in the Western Sudan. In pressing for the development of the tropical African estates, Chamberlain had to fight hard and by no means always successfully against established traditions of minimal government intervention and expenditure in West Africa. Even the colonial secretary was at one point forced to admit that *Festina lente* might, after all, be "a just motto in the development of colonies in the possession of barbarous tribes."[42] Whatever the emphasis on development, moreover, the principal reason for the intensification of British activity in West Africa after 1895 was the need to deal with the immediate threat of French expansion. Once this threat passed, West Africa ceased to be a major item on the government's list of African priorities. In the years after 1898, Chamberlain and his colleagues had far more important matters on their minds than the future of Northern Nigeria. No sooner had the Anglo-French conflict over the Niger been settled than a far more dangerous crisis broke on the Upper Nile. Scarcely a year later, Mafeking, Kimberley, and Ladysmith had been invested, and Kumasi too was under siege. Faced with a major war in South Africa and a minor one in Ashanti, Whitehall had no desire for yet another military confrontation on the frontiers of the empire. "We must not have another native war," commented Chamberlain in August 1900.[43]

41. For a fuller discussion of these developments in French policy and their significance for the partition of West Africa, see C. W. Newbury and A. S. Kanya-Forstner, "French Policy and the Origins of the Scramble for West Africa," *Journal of African History, 10* (1969), 253–75.

42. Cited in Robinson and Gallagher, *Africa and the Victorians,* pp. 401–02.

43. Minute by Chamberlain on Lugard to Chamberlain, August 23, 1900, cited in Perham, *Lugard,* 2, 89.

The chastening effects of the South African war did nothing to alter this conviction. In December 1902 Chamberlain's undersecretary, Onslow, was still reminding Lugard that "His Majesty's Government are anxious to avoid military operations in West Africa."[44]

French policies were marked by similar hesitations. Not even Jauréguiberry had ever intended the officers of his Upper Senegal Command to carve out a specifically military empire in the Western Sudan; their principal task was to provide the security essential for railway-building. Nor was massive expenditure on colonial development any more popular than it was in England. The parsimony of the French Chambers killed the Senegal-Niger railway project before it was born; in the end, only work on the first section between Medine and Bafoulabé was approved. Even this proved far more difficult than the politicians had anticipated. The railway soon became an expensive farce and a growing embarrassment to the government. By the mid-1880s the railway project had been abandoned in the face of mounting parliamentary opposition, and the policy makers had become thoroughly disillusioned with the whole Sudanese enterprise. The political repercussions of the retreat from Lang Son made them all the more anxious to avoid additional military complications in the Senegal-Niger valley.[45] By the late 1880s the role of the military in the Western Sudan was coming under ever more critical scrutiny. "La période de conquête doit être considérée comme terminée," declared the Sudan Commission in 1890, and this was to be government's constant refrain for the next decade.[46]

But the military paid no heed, and they were the ones who now held the initiative. Although the problems of occupation in the Western Sudan had forced them to adopt a defensive posture during the mid-1880s, they moved on to the attack as soon as conditions improved. Disregarding their instructions, they launched an all-out assault on the empires of Ahmadu and Samori. In 1889 the ambitious *commandant-supérieur,* Louis Archinard, stormed the Tukulor fortress of Koundian. In 1890 he maneuvered Paris into approving his expedition against Segu. His campaign against Samori the following year, Under-secretary Etienne exclaimed, was "une violation formelle de mes in-

44. Onslow to Lugard, December 19, 1902, Cd. 1433, *PP* [1903], *45,* 792.

45. See Kanya-Forstner, *Conquest of the Western Sudan,* pp. 130–41.

46. Rapport de la Commission, January 22, 1890, ANSOM Soudan VII/1/a; Jamais to Archinard, Instructions, September 12, 1892, ANSOM Soudan I/4/a; Delcassé to Grodet, Instructions, December 4, 1893, ANSOM Soudan I/6/a; Guillain to Governor-General, A.O.F., Instructions for Trentinian, November 10, 1898, ANSOM Soudan I/9/d; Procès-Verbaux de la Commission [on the reorganization of the Sudan], séance du 8 septembre 1899, ANSOM A.O.F. VII.

structions." [47] The conquest of Masina in 1893 was undertaken without the approval or even the knowledge of the government. The capture of Timbuktu was planned and executed "par les colonels Archinard et Bonnier en dépit des instructions formelles du gouvernement absolument contradictoires." [48] At the end of 1893 Undersecretary Delcassé placed the Sudan under civilian control because "l'administration des colonies n'[y] avait [plus] . . . la haute main sur les opérations ni sur les dépenses," [49] but by 1895 the military were back in power. In the end, Paris could break their stranglehold only by breaking up the Sudan itself. As the head of the Bureau d'Afrique concluded: "Il n'y avait pas d'autre moyen de supprimer en Afrique O[ccidentale] cette sorte d'Etat dans l'Etat." [50]

The British government found its military agent just as difficult to control. As in the Western Sudan, conquest did not immediately follow the establishment of a military presence. During the first few years Lugard had little opportunity to mount a major campaign. When he took up his new command, many of his officers were already being called to service in South Africa, and in the spring of 1900 he had to send 1,200 men to the Gold Coast for the Ashanti expedition. His own campaign against Bida and Kontagora had to be postponed until their return. In 1901 more troops were sent to Ashanti, and a contingent of 300 men was dispatched to take part in the Aro campaign. Lugard himself spent much of the year in England; the expedition against Yola was led by Colonel Morland. The extension of British power during this period is more aptly described as an occupation than as a conquest. Ibrahim, the Sarkin Sudan and emir of Kontagora, tried to defend his capital; but the emir of Bida fled without a fight. Although Zubeiru of Adamawa and later Mallam Jibrilla in Gombe put up a sterner resistance, the emir of Gombe joined the British. In 1902 the emir of Zaria sought British aid against the raids of the Sarkin Sudan; Umaru of Bauchi abandoned his emirate; and Bornu was occupied without a shot being fired. So far, the question of metropolitan control hardly arose; but the crucial battles were to be fought in the northern emirates, and here Lugard slipped the leash as easily as did the *officiers soudanais*. Although the high commissioner's plans for a campaign against Kano and Sokoto were common knowledge

47. Etienne to Governor of Senegal, April 14, 1891, ANSOM Sénégal I/91/b.

48. Havas note, published in *La Politique Coloniale,* February 17, 1894.

49. Procès-Verbaux de la Commission du Budget, séance du 18 juin 1894, AN C 5447, pp. 172–73.

50. Binger, Note pour le Ministre, n.d., ANSOM A.O.F. VII.

in Nigeria by the summer of 1902, he deliberately misled his superiors and kept them ignorant of his preparations. By the time Whitehall was fully informed, it was too late to halt the expedition.[51]

Governments could do little in the face of such determination; the military held the trumps and played them. The officers of the *infanterie* and *artillerie de marine* who planted the *tricolore* on the Upper Niger were perpetuating a tradition of military independence dating back to the conquest of Algeria and beyond. Like their Algerian predecessors, they were supremely confident of their own ability and knowledge of the local situation. Like them, they were contemptuous of ignorant officials in Paris whom they considered manifestly unfit to give them orders. "Prendre l'initiative," was the motto of the colonial officers, "cocevoir et entreprendre sans attendre les ordres d' 'En Haut,' lesquelles n'arrivent jamais ou n'arrivent que négatifs." [52] Their position as the men on the spot gave them ample scope for the exercise of this initiative. They were the experts on whose advice the policy makers had to rely; they supplied the information on which policy had to be based. During their periods of leave, they returned home to press their proposals directly on their ministers. When their tours of duty were over, they were often seconded to the Colonial Department where they became an integral part of the policy-making structure.[53]

The confused state of French politics in the late nineteenth century also worked to the officers' advantage. Precarious Republican ministries were reluctant to grasp the nettle of military indiscipline; for their enemies on the Right were only too anxious to inflate criticism of the *officiers soudanais* into an attack upon the whole sacrosanct military structure. Few politicians were prepared to stir up a major controversy over the emotionally charged issue of civilian-military relations. Even Delcassé waited until the government was about to fall before he dismissed the insubordinate Archinard in November 1893, and the scandal his action provoked did not encourage his successors to exercise the same firmness. The confused state of French

51. The most critical account of Lugard's actions is D. J. M. Muffett, *Concerning Brave Captains* (London, 1964); the most sympathetic is Perham, *Lugard, 2,* Chaps. 3, 5.

52. Marshal Lyautey, speech on the occasion of General Archinard's eightieth birthday, April 1930, *Revue de l'histoire des colonies françaises,* 18 (1930), 132–33.

53. The two most famous *commandants-supérieurs,* Borgnis-Desbordes and Archinard, both served in the Colonial Department, the latter as director of defense in the Ministry of Colonies.

military administration at the time strengthened the officers' influence still further. Before the creation of the Colonial Army in 1900, the administration of the Marine Corps was split between various government departments, and effective control tended to remain in the hands of the permanent inspectors general. During the crucial period of expansion both these men were *vieux soudanais*.[54] Through a web of intimate personal ties and through their control over postings and promotions, they commanded the loyalty of their subordinates in the Sudan and could exercise "un pouvoir occulte auquel certains commandants de troupes se sont complètement inféodés." [55] The pressures they exerted on the Colonial Department could at times be just as great; it was on their insistence alone that Archinard was reappointed to the Sudan command in 1892.[56]

British officers shared the same desire for freedom of initiative. In the matter of independence, Lugard owed little to the *officiers soudanais*. He was "not at all inclined to sacrifice my independence of judgement or to bow my knee to [Chamberlain] in order to obtain any possible honours he could give"; and he refused to take command of the W.A.F.F. when the Colonial Office tried to subordinate him to the governor of Lagos.[57] Similarly, his second in command, Willcocks, welcomed a posting "where responsibility would take the place of routine, and freedom of action would be given full play." [58] As men on the spot they enjoyed the same advantages as their French counterparts. During his periods of leave, Lugard, too, exercised considerable influence over the Nigerian policies of the Colonial Office; his failure to enlarge this influence and place it on a sound institutional footing contributed a great deal to his eventual resignation.[59] The loyalty of his subordinates, although he commanded it more through his personal magnetism than through his position in a military hierarchy, could be as fierce as that of any young *officier soudanais*. And if the political structure was less rickety in England than it was in France, Lugard still had his connections in the upper reaches of the political establish-

54. General Brière de L'Isle (governor of Senegal, 1876–81) for the *infanterie de marine;* General Borgnis-Desbordes (*commandant-supérieur,* 1880–83) for the *artillerie de marine.*

55. Lucien Hubert, Projet de Résolution, December 22, 1899, *JO Documents Parlementaires, Chambre.* No. 318, p. 414.

56. Archinard to Jamais, June 15, 1892, ANSOM Soudan I/2/f; Etienne Bonnier to Archinard, July 3, 1892, Archinard papers.

57. Perham and Bull, *Diaries, 4,* 348, 352–53.

58. Sir J. Willcocks, *From Kabul to Kumassi* (London, 1904), p. 161.

59. Perham, *Lugard, 2,* 280.

ment. His relations with Chamberlain, if not always cordial, were at least marked by mutual respect. He enjoyed the colonial secretary's confidence and had powerful friends in the latter's entourage. One of the most influential, Flora Shaw, married him in 1902, and through her indefatigable efforts he later gained the support of many leading figures in both parties.[60]

In the end, however, the military, French and British alike, found their greatest source of strength in the nature of their governments' own African policies. Politicians had to accept the consequences of their decision to establish a military presence. From the start, they were forced to give their officers wide powers of initiative and to recognize their freedom to act when the situation demanded it. Even Delcassé had to authorize military measures "pour repousser [une] aggression manifeste," and Lugard was given the same authority to take up arms if, in his judgment, "military operations . . . are absolutely necessary for defensive purposes."[61] Having introduced the military factor in the interests of security, the politicians were also forced to recognize the maintenance of security as the overriding objective. No matter how much they emphasized the importance of commercial development or deprecated the use of force, they dared not ignore reports of unrest on the frontiers or of imminent attacks that might threaten the very existence of their colonies. The argument of security was the most potent weapon in the military's armory, and the one they trained most frequently on the harassed officials. When attempts to bully them into approving military operations failed, the officers could always resort to the tactics of the fait accompli, and do so with relative impunity. For it was difficult for politicians to attack the military servants of the Republic or of the Crown who were risking their lives in the defense of their nation's interests. Only when insubordination ended in disaster did the *officiers soudanais* become the target for general criticism.[62] Lugard, too, was immune from public censure. Even after the Kano expedition, Austen Chamberlain (standing in for his father) had to reaffirm the government's "full confidence in that most experienced administrator."[63] And once

60. Ibid. Chap. 11.

61. Delcassé to Grodet, August 11, 1894, ANSOM Télégrammes Afrique, Soudan 1894, Départ No. 50; Onslow to Lugard, December 19, 1902, Cd. 1433, *PP* [1903], *45*, 792.

62. Most notably when Bonnier's column was massacred by Tuaregs after the unauthorized expedition to Timbuktu. For the political repercussions, see Kanya-Forstner, *Conquest of the Western Sudan*, pp. 221–23.

63. Commons, February 17, 1903, *Hansard*, 4th series, *118*, 120–21.

an expedition was under way, it could not be halted; no government would risk the consequences for security. Lugard could well afford to ask "whether you desire that I should stop advance of expedition started already"; he knew the answer that Onslow had to give.[64] French governments were equally powerless. Archinard's attack on Samori, Etienne ruefully admitted to the Quai d'Orsay, was "un fait accompli que je ne peux que regretter mais qui rend inévitable la continuation de la lutte." [65]

But the conflict between the military and their employers was not as fundamental as it appeared. Their quarrels were over the pace, the extent, and the timing of military expansion; there was no basic disagreement over its necessity. Once governments had decided to transform informal empires of trade into formal empires of rule, the imposition of such rule, by force of arms in the last resort, became the inescapable corollary of their plans. After 1880 the establishment of effective occupation was the constant objective of French Sudanese policy. The reluctance of Paris to authorize military action was more the product of the logistic and physical problems encountered in the colony and of the financial stringency experienced at home than of any desire to avoid conflict. "Si on peut faire les dépenses d'une campagne de guerre," commented Undersecretary Rousseau in 1885, "il serait puéril d'avoir recours à la diplomatie contre Ahmadou." [66] Although the maintenance of the peace required for economic development was given much greater emphasis after 1890, the maintenance of political supremacy remained the first priority. Paris, not the Sudanese authorities, rejected Samori's final offer of peace and held out for his complete subjugation in 1898.[67] Whitehall's attitude to military expansion after 1900 was somewhat more ambiguous; but in the end its policies, too, were governed by the same principles. "His Majesty's Government," Onslow told Lugard as the Kano expedition set out, ". . . have not concealed from themselves that the measures that they authorised you to take to suppress slave-raiding would probably bring us into conflict sooner or later with the Sultan [of Sokoto]. It is

64. Lugard to Onslow, January 15, 1903; Onslow to Lugard, January 19, 1903, Cd. 1433, *PP* [1903], *45*, 798–99.

65. Etienne to MAE, April 17, 1891, MAE MD Afrique 123.

66. Minute by Rousseau on Governor of Senegal to MMC, May 28, 1885, ANSOM Sénégal I/73/a.

67. Ballay to MC, August 31, 1898, ANSOM Télégrammes, Bureau d'Afrique 1898, Arrivée No. 110; MC to Ballay, September 2, 1898, September 26, 1898, ibid, Départ Nos. 129, 142.

necessary, in the interests both of humanity and of trade, that slave-raiding . . . should be met by force and suppressed so far as this can be done with the troops at your disposal." [68] The conquest of the Western Sudan depended as much upon the adoption of imperialist policies at home as it did upon the particular ambitions and strategies of the military on the ground.

The military agents of European imperialism determined the timing and the nature of the conquest. In many respects, Lugard and his subordinates differed sharply from the French colonial officers. Lugard himself was hardly a professional soldier in the conventional sense of the term. His connection with his regiment, the East Norfolks, was no more than nominal, and he spent much of his active career outside regular military employment.[69] The West African Frontier Force was a new creation and lacked an established regimental tradition. Its European officers and N.C.O.s were a mixture of old Royal Niger Constabulary hands and regular soldiers seconded for short periods from metropolitan regiments. The officers did share some common characteristics. Lugard chose most of the original ones himself, and the qualities he looked for were those of the typical public school man. Many, Lugard included, had seen previous service in India, or later in South Africa. All were volunteers who chose to serve overseas for fairly predictable reasons. The impecunious found life cheaper than at home or were attracted by the higher rates of pay and allowances. The adventurous disliked the boredom of garrison duty and wanted to see active service. The sporting types were attracted by the opportunities for hunting or polo.[70] One of them summed up the prevailing attitude very well: "The very romance of the life drew men from all branches—Cavalry, Artillery, Guard and Line regiments. The possibilities of active service, and the prospects of sport, when weighed against the monotony of home duty after the prolonged struggle in

68. Onslow to Lugard, January 28, 1903, Cd. 1433, *PP* [1903], *45*, 801.

69. E.g. Lugard, Diary, March 13, 1898, Perham and Bull, *Diaries, 4*, 338: "They [the War Office] said that I didn't care a curse for the W.O. and soldiering and had other interests—which is true."

70. E.g. inter alia, A. W. H. Haywood, *Sport and Service in Africa* (London, 1926); B. R. M. Glossop, *Sporting Trips of a Subaltern* (London, 1906). Some made a fetish of the healthy outdoor life. Willcocks, for example, wrote: "A day's healthy sport does more for a white man in such lands than weeks of imaginary hard labour without it. Moreover, I have always found that those of our officers who never missed the chance of a day's shooting when it could be legitimately had, were almost invariably those who never failed to do right well whatever job fell to them."

South Africa, were great inducements to the very best of fellows." A few officers were bloodthirsty, but men like Crozier, who looked forward to "a fight at last—some slaughter—much fun," were rare.[71] Others were merely hoping for some action. Coldie was afraid that some of Lugard's officers might seek to pressure him into unnecessary campaigns,[72] and Abadie, the resident at Zaria and one of Lugard's favorites, did press hard for the expedition against Kano. But it is doubtful whether his influence was decisive.[73]

The *officiers soudanais* were almost a different breed of men. For the most part they belonged to the *infanterie* or *artillerie de marine*—the colonial army in fact if not in name—a tightly knit military caste with an intense and exclusive esprit de corps.[74] They were the odd men out in the French military structure. Despised and discriminated against for much of the nineteenth century by the navy, of which they technically formed a part, they in turn despised the "metropolitans," civilians and soldiers alike.[75] Before the 1880s, colonial officers were often those graduates of the military academies who had failed to secure a more prestigious posting in one of the Algerian or metropolitan regiments. Thereafter, as the pace of military expansion in the colonies accelerated, those who joined the corps were the ambitious, dissatisfied with the limited prospects for promotion in the metropolitan army—"les éléments les plus énergiques, les plus aventureux de la nation et de l'armée."[76] What drew them to the Sudan was not love of sport[77] but the desire for a rapid and brilliant career, for only on colonial battlefields could they hope for the *faits*

71. H. C. Hall, *Barrack and Bush in Northern Nigeria* (London, 1923), p. 523 and F. P. Crozier, *Five Years Hard* (London, 1932), p. 148.

72. Perham, *Lugard, 2,* 89.

73. E.g. Lobb [Abadie's assistant] to his mother, cited in A. O. Anjorin, "The British Conquest and Development of Northern Nigeria" (unpublished Ph.D. dissertation, London, 1966): "We [Abadie and I] were burning to dash up and do the job [the taking of Kano] ourselves with the M.I. To our intense disgust, our alarmist reports had the unexpected effect of delaying the expedition because the people downcountry took them very seriously."

74. For a fuller discussion, see Kanya-Forstner, *Conquest of the Western Sudan,* pp. 8–15.

75. Borgnis-Desbordes to Félix Faure, May 1885, cited in M. Blanchard, "Correspondance de Félix Faure touchant les affaires coloniales, 1882–1898," *Revue de l'histoire des colonies françaises, 42* (1955), 159.

76. Godefroy Cavaignac, Projet de Loi, July 9, 1895, *JO Documents Parlementares, Chambre,* No. 1488, p. 1313.

77. Characteristically, Willcocks considered this lack of passion for sport the most important difference between the French and British officer serving in the colonies. Willcocks, *Kumassi,* p. 224.

de guerre that were the surest way to break the shackles of the seniority system.[78] On strictly professional grounds, the *officiers soudanais* had a strong incentive to perpetuate or if necessary to provoke military conflict, and few resisted the temptation. Major Archinard, for example, timed his attack on Koundian to coincide with the drafting of the *tableau d'avancement* at the Ministry of Marine. Although its capture failed to gain him his promotion, the capture of Segu was not similarly unrewarded. Even his unauthorized attack on Samori earned him a recommendation for promotion to full colonel.[79]

British and French officers also had different assumptions about the nature of the opposition they expected to encounter in the Sudan. Although Lugard considered Islam a religion "incapable of the highest development," [80] one "which renders Africans liable to wild bursts of religious frenzy," [81] and although he had a profound antipathy toward *militant* Islam "with its disregard for life and its selfish appropriation by the powerful of all that was desirable," [82] his attitude was not undiscriminating. He professed "a great respect for the Mohammedan religion" and a reluctance "to see the annihilation of a central and long-established system of rule, however bad, until another has been provided to replace it." [83] He also believed the Fulani, whatever their shortcomings, to be "born rulers and incomparably above the negroid tribes in ability." [84] Nor was Lugard by any means unique; his senior resident, Burdon, almost became more pro-Fulani than the Fulani themselves.[85] As a result, the British did show some readiness to extend their sovereignty by peaceful means if they could. After the capture of Kano, Lugard sent a conciliatory message to Sokoto and

78. E.g. Klobb to Archinard, November 25, 1893, Archinard papers.

79. These incidents are discussed in Kanya-Forstner, *Conquest of the Western Sudan*, pp. 177–86.

80. Lord Lugard, *The Dual Mandate in British Tropical Africa* (5th ed. London, 1965), p. 78.

81. *Annual Reports, Northern Nigeria,* 1900–01, Cd. 788–16, *PP* [1902] *45*, 503.

82. Lugard, *Dual Mandate,* p. 362.

83. Lugard to Chamberlain, June 13, 1898, encl. in CO to FO, September 23, 1898, FO C.P. 7317, No. 92.

84. *Annual Reports, Northern Nigeria,* 1900–01, Cd. 788–16, *PP* [1902], *45*, 489.

85. On one occasion, Burdon even asked Lugard to acknowledge the spiritual suzerainty of the sultan to Sokoto; E. A. Ayandele, *The Missionary Impact on Modern Nigeria, 1842–1914* (London, 1966), p. 142. Burdon, admittedly, was a rather extreme case.

was prepared to order the return of the expeditionary column if he received a satisfactory reply.[86]

The French on the other hand had a much more intimate knowledge of the dangers of concerted Muslim resistance. In North Africa they had felt the full impact of an anti-European jihad, and this experience had instilled in them both a pathological fear of Muslim hostility and a ferocious determination to eradicate every center of independent Muslim power. Faidherbe, while not unsympathetic to the religion itself, carried these feelings with him to Senegal. "Malheur à nous," he exclaimed in 1855, "si nous voyons se développer ici comme en Algérie, où j'ai servi six ans, la guerre sainte contre les Chrétiens." The destruction of the Tokolor empire was thus a definite if at times distant objective of his policy.[87] His successors exhibited the same fears and determination in a much more intense fashion. Muslims, one of them wrote, "sont nos ennemis naturels . . . opposés a toute idée de progrès et de civilisation." The animist Bambaras and Mandinkas were seen as the natural allies of the French. "C'est aux Bambaras qu'appartient l'avenir," Colonel Borgnis-Desbordes declared in 1883, "c'est sur eux qu'il faut s'appuyer." [88] And since Muslims were bound by the very nature of their religion to resist the advance of European civilization, there could be no peaceful occupation. From the start, the French military were convinced that "la guerre est la conséquence forcée de notre marche en avant." [89]

Yet in more important respects British and French officers shared a similar outlook. They were all soldiers on active service in an alien and potentially hostile environment. Military security was their most immediate concern, and they were understandably hypersensitive to the dangers that threatened it. European prestige, they believed, had to be maintained at all costs, for "prestige is another word for self-preservation in a country where millions are ruled by a few score." For the same reason, Europeans had to demonstrate their determina-

86. Lugard to Flora Lugard, February 28, 1903, cited in Perham, *Lugard*, 2, 119. The fact that the Colonial Office, much against Lugard's wishes, had appointed Colonel Kemball to command the expeditionary force may well have some significance for this decision.

87. Faidherbe to Governor of the Gambia, May 31, 1855 [copy], MAE MD Afrique 47; Faidherbe, Memorandum, October 1, 1858, ANSOM Sénégal I/45/a.

88. Gallieni to Brière, December 24, 1880, ANSOM Missions 16, Gallieni 1880; Desbordes to Bayol, Instructions, March 31, 1883, cited in Desbordes, Rapport . . . 1882–83, n.d., Chap. 6, ANSOM Missions 50, Borgnis-Desbordes 1882–83.

89. Desbordes, Rapport . . . 1880–81, July 6, 1881, pp. 4–5, 510, ANSOM Sénégal IV/73 bis.

tion to rule. "Our hesitation to settle once and for all who was to be suzerain," Lugard explained after the Sokoto campaign, confirmed "the old belief that we had not come to stay and would shortly leave our friends in the lurch . . . and gave grounds for belief that Government itself feared the power of Sokoto, and dared not assert itself."[90] The French acted on the same assumptions. "Notre autorité n'est pas suffisamment assise," wrote Commandant Combes in November 1884; "elle est discutée par de belliqueux voisins. Nos premiers succès leur ont inspiré une crainte salutaire, mais ils s'enhardissent peu à peu et nous attaqueront si nous ne les attaquerons pas."[91]

The military, however, were motivated by more than simple aggressiveness or an exaggerated preoccupation with security. In fact, the dangers they faced were much less alarming than they pictured them. By the late nineteenth century Segu and Sokoto were no longer the militant, powerful, and expansive empires they had been under their original leaderships. When the French began their advance in the 1880s, the Tukulor state no longer embodied the early spirit of the religious crusade and had been rent by succession disputes, factional strife, and Bambara unrest. Ahmadu had lost control over much of the original empire and was finding it increasingly difficult to cope with the rebellions that were threatening his hold over the remainder.[92] The Fulani empire was somewhat more stable. The nominal religious and political primacy of Sokoto was still unquestioned, and the sultan could on occasion determine the succession in subordinate emirates. Most of the emirates continued to acknowledge Sokoto's suzerainty; many sent contingents to participate in the sultan's campaigns and helped in the suppression of rebellions. But by the 1890s there was also clear evidence of Sokoto's growing weakness. Abd al-Rahman, who came to power in 1891, was not a popular ruler. His expedition against Argungu in 1892 ended disastrously; the ignominious failure of his attempt to intervene in the Kano dispute of 1893–94 sharply underlined the limitations of his influence over his emirs. In the east, the growing power of Rabih in Bornu and the Mahdist agitation of Hayatu and Mallam Jibrilla all posed a threat, if not a major one, to the security of the empire. Then in October 1902, just as

90. *Annual Reports, Northern Nigeria,* 1902, Cd. 1768–14, *PP* [1904] *47,* 168–70.

91. Combes to Governor of Senegal, November 1, 1884, ANSOM Sénégal IV/81/c.

92. See A. S. Kanya-Forstner, "Mali-Tukulor," in Michael Crowder, ed., *West African Resistance: The Military Response to Colonial Occupation* (London, 1971), pp. 53–77.

the final crisis with the British was about to break, Abd al-Rahman died and was succeeded by Muhammad Attahiru who was apparently not much more popular.[93]

The internal problems of these empires were bound to affect their responses to European expansion. Both Ahmadu and Abd al-Rahman appreciated the European danger; but they put up no military resistance to the piecemeal loss of their empires before the final confrontations. Ahmadu tried to hamper the French military advance by imposing trade bans which complicated an already serious problem of supply, and he sought to limit the extension of French influence by diplomacy. But he was far from intransigent. Indeed, he looked on the French as potential allies against his own rebellious subjects, and he offered them generous concessions in return for their empty promises of military aid. Abd al-Rahman was equally prudent. After the conquest of Nupe and Ilorin he broke off relations with the Niger Company and threatened war; but he soon adopted a more conciliatory tone.[94] He did not reply to Lugard's proclamation of the Protectorate, nor did he accept the offer to let him nominate the new emir of Kontagora. But his famous declaration of war, received in May 1902, was quickly followed by a much more moderate reply to Lugard's letter about the seizure of Bauchi.[95] The Fulani showed little real desire to fight the British, and many of their leaders, despairing in advance of the outcome, advocated a policy of mass emigration. Attahiru himself favored a *hijra,* and the Emir Ali of Kano, Lugard's bugbear, was one of those who pressed most strongly for it.[96] When faced with a bald choice between unconditional surrender and war, both Ahmadu and Attahiru stood and fought. But their resistance was pitifully ineffective.

The military, moreover, were aware of their opponents' weaknesses. They made great play with the danger of African resistance, but they were careful not to alarm their officials too much. As early as 1881 Colonel Borgnis-Desbordes assured Paris that the Tukulors were too

93. The most recent account of Sokoto in the nineteenth century is M. Last, *The Sokoto Caliphate* (London, 1967), which describes the empire as more stable than has hitherto been supposed. H. A. S. Johnston, *The Fulani Empire of Sokoto* (London, 1967), presents a more pessimistic view.

94. Goldie to FO, November 15, 1897, FO C.P. 7017, No. 156; Goldie to CO, December 20, 1897, encl. in CO to FO, December 31, 1897, FO C.P. 7144, No. 3.

95. The most balanced account of Lugard's relations with Sokoto is Johnston, *Fulani Empire,* App. 3.

96. Sarkin Kano to Waziri Muhammadu Buhari, H. F. Backwell, ed., *The Occupation of Hausaland, 1900–1904* (Lagos, 1927), Letter No. 125.

weak to oppose his advance effectively, and Archinard gave the same assurances when pressing for the attack on Segu in 1889. Lugard also issued dire warnings about Kano's hostile intentions, but he too proclaimed himself absolutely confident of his ability to deal with any resistance which the Fulani might offer.[97] The military were not "dragged into vast imperial conquests" by African opposition, imagined or real.[98] They were driven on by the same considerations that had led the policy makers to inaugurate the era of military expansion. Like the policy makers, they considered the imposition of unchallenged political control essential for economic development and for security from foreign rivals.[99] They too considered treaty rights a poor substitute for domination, and nothing less than domination was their goal. It made little difference whether Lugard wished to take Sokoto peacefully or by force; his objectives were the same: the establishment of British suzerainty, the installation of a garrison, and the appointment of a Resident.[100] As far as the military were concerned, dominion based on conquest was the surest dominion of all. "The Fulani . . . held their suzerainty by right of recent conquest," wrote Lugard in 1903, "and I can myself see no injustice in the transfer of the suzerainty thus acquired to the British Government by the same right of conquest."[101] In the end, military imperialism was but the imperialism of the official mind writ large.

The similarities and differences between French and British military expansion were mirrored in the administrative systems which the military attempted to elaborate during the initial stages of their occupation. Lugard came to Nigeria with deeply held convictions about the

97. Desbordes to Governor of Senegal, n.d. [December 10–15, 1881], cited in Desbordes, Rapport . . . 1881–82, n.d., Chap. 2, ANSOM Missions 50, Borgnis-Desbordes 1881–82; Archinard, Note, August 19, 1889, ANSOM Sénégal IV/93/a; Lugard to Onslow, December 23, 1902, Cd. 1433, *PP* [1903], *45,* 793.

98. Cf. Roland E. Robinson and John Gallagher, "The Partition of Africa," in *The New Cambridge Modern History, 11* (Cambridge, 1962), 609.

99. Desbordes, Rapport . . . 1880–81, July 6, 1881, pp. 507–10, ANSOM Sénégal IV/73 bis; Desbordes to Governor of Senegal, January 18, 1882, ANSOM Sénégal IV/75/b; Archinard to Governor of Senegal, January 9, 1890, ANSOM Sénégal IV/95/b; Lugard to Chamberlain, February 27, 1901, encl. in CO to FO, June 25, 1901, FO C.P. 7976, No. 13; *Annual Reports, Northern Nigeria,* 1901, Cd. 1388–81, *PP* [1903], *43,* 359.

100. Lugard to Flora Lugard, February 28, 1903, cited in Perham, *Lugard, 2,* 119.

101. *Annual Reports, Northern Nigeria,* 1902, Cd. 1768–14, *PP* [1904], *58,* 177.

nature of British imperial government. "The tradition of British rule," he wrote after the capture of Sokoto, "has ever been to arrest disintegration and to build up what is best in the social and political organisation of the conquered dynasties, and to develop on the lines of its own individuality each separate race of which our great empire consists."[102] From the start, the high commissioner and his government believed that "it is desirable to retain the native authority and to work through and by the native emirs."[103] The intention was to make the chiefs "an integral part of the machinery of the Administration" and to provide Nigeria with "a single Government, in which the Native Chiefs have clearly defined duties and an acknowledged status equally with the British officials."[104] The maintenance of the conquered dynasty was thus central to the system; it was in "the regeneration of the Fulani" that Lugard saw the future of his Protectorate.

But Lugard's system was not the product of ideological conviction alone. The conquest had left the structure of Fulani rule more or less intact and so enabled the British to make use of it; the size of the new empire left them no other choice. With their tiny complement of political officers—the Political Department had some sixty members in 1906—they simply could not have ruled the country on their own. The maintenance of the Fulani was itself an experiment, justified primarily by the need to avoid "a dislocation of methods which, however faulty, have the sanction of traditional usage and are acquiesced in by the people."[105] Their regeneration was a long-term objective. Lugard himself considered the emirs "unfit at present to exercise power except under supervision," nor did he "hope for any great success in the present generation."[106] Meanwhile, effective, power was to be kept in European hands, for the immediate objectives were to guarantee security and to provide the institutional framework for the exercise of British dominion. Having asserted suzerainty by right of conquest, the British assumed the rights of the

102. Ibid., p. 178.

103. Lugard, Memorandum, n.d., cited in Perham, *Lugard, 2,* 140. Onslow to Lugard, January 28, 1903, Cd. 1433, *PP* [1903], *45,* 801: "There is no desire on the part of His Majesty's Government to destroy the existing forms of administration or to govern the country otherwise than through its own rulers."

104. F. D. Lugard, *Instructions to Political and other Officers on Subjects chiefly Political and Administrative* (London, 1906), No. IX, para. 4.

105. Ibid., No. XVIII, para. 1.

106. *Annual Reports, Northern Nigeria,* 1902, Cd. 1768–14, *PP* [1904], *58,* 178.

conqueror. Most of the old emirs were deposed and replaced by more pliant successors who swore "to obey the laws of the Protectorate and the lawful commands of the High Commissioner and the Resident."[107] Although traditional electors retained some voice in the choice of new emirs, the government appointed them and warned them that efficiency and loyalty alone could guarantee the security of their tenure. Although the Fulani administration continued to be supported directly out of local revenue, British Residents assessed the taxes and supervised their collection. Although the validity of Muslim law was recognized, the verdicts of the Native Courts were subject to review by the Resident, and the more important Provincial Courts were placed directly under his control. The Fulani were disarmed, and the British tried to assume exclusive control over the military forces of the Protectorate. Lugard's objective, in a phrase, was to create "a little India in the Niger Sudan"; his model was the system adopted by Dalhousie in the states that were annexed during the 1850s; and the keynote of this system, as Lugard interpreted it, was "to vest all powers, judicial and executive, in a province in the hands of the Resident . . . in whose charge it was placed, subject to direct control and check by the Head of the Government."[108]

French officers were not bound by the same ideological considerations. Colonel Archinard was not an advocate of "indirect rule." On the contrary, he was convinced that "peu à peu . . . l'administration directe finira par s'imposer. Les chefs noirs n'ont pas assez de désintéressement pour que le peuple ne fasse vite la comparison entre eux et nos officiers, et pour qu'il ne cherche pas à nous obéir sans intermédiaire."[109] Nor was there any thought of ruling through the Tukulors. After the capture of Segu, Archinard restored the former Bambara dynasty and deported the Tukulors back to their homelands along the Senegal where they could be kept under stricter control. Kaarta was dismembered and placed under *commandants de cercle.* Its Tukulor population was confined to restricted areas and forbidden to travel without a pass. The commandants were ordered to exercise "la plus grande rigueur" in their surveillance, and to keep the people

107. Lugard, *Political Memoranda,* No. IX, para. 3.

108. Lugard to CO, September 22, 1900. I am indebted for this quotation to Professor E. T. Stokes of St. Catharine's College, Cambridge. I am also grateful to him for his help in the revision of this paper.

109. Archinard, Rapport . . . 1892–93, cited in J. Méniaud, *Les pionniers du Soudan, avant, avec et après Archinard, 1879–1894* (2 vols. Paris, 1931), *2,* 339.

weak by promoting rather than suppressing dissension between them.[110] Archinard, too, was more acutely concerned with the maintenance of security and European control. When restoring the Diara dynasty in Segu, he was careful to install a rival Massasi at Nango and to warn them both that their positions depended entirely upon the goodwill of their European masters. For good measure, Archinard reduced the boundaries of Segu in 1891 and made his most trusted Native Agent, Mademba Si, *fama* of Sansanding. The primacy of the European administrator was still more clearly established. Although the French also had their Native Courts and although the *commandants de cercle* were instructed not to waste their time "en intervenant dans toutes les petites questions d'intérêt particulier," there was little attempt to strike a balance between the European and African elements in the administration. "Vous êtes à peu près pour l'empire de Ségou un véritable commandant de cercle," Archinard told its Resident in 1891; "le fama . . . est là comme votre intermédiaire pour vous permettre de gouverner sans que nous soyons obligés d'imposer trop vite nos idées." [111]

Yet the French had to face the same discrepancy as the British between the size of the empire to be governed and the manpower available for its administration. Archinard's European personnel was just as severely overstretched; and to lighten the burdens "que l'administration directe nous impose," he too chose, when necessary, to rule through African intermediaries.[112] Loyalty and subservience, not religion or tribal background, were the chief qualifications for office.[113] Even Ahmadu's brother Aguibu, having shown his colors by surrendering Dinguiray to the French, was duly rewarded with the sultanate of Masina. Indeed, he and Mademba Si enjoyed far more extensive

110. Archinard to *commandants de poste,* December 2, 1890, cited in Archinard to Governor of Senegal, April 18, 1891, ANSOM Soudan II/2; Archinard to Commandant, Nioro, Instructions, January 1891, cited in Archinard, Rapport . . . 1890–91, Chap. 2, *JO,* October 14, 1891, pp. 4924–25.

111. Archinard, Rapport . . . 1890–91, Chap. 2, *JO,* October 13, 1891, p. 4903; Archinard to Briquelot, Instructions, March 9, 1891, cited in ibid. Chap. 3, *JO,* October 18, 1891, p. 5012.

112. Archinard, Rapport . . . 1892–93, cited in Méniaud, *Pionniers,* 2, 339: "Souvent, en reconnaissant l'autorité d'un Chef ou même en nommant un chef, j'ai cherché à alléger pour nous les devoirs et les obligations que l'administration directe nous impose, alors que notre personnel européen est si réduit et a un si lourde tâche."

113. E.g. Mademba Si to Archinard, February 7, 1891, Archinard papers: "Il est de mon devoir absolu de ne pas discuter, mais d'accepter tout ce que vous croyez bon de proposer."

powers than did the Nigerian emirs. Neither was deprived of his military forces; on the contrary, Mademba was supplied with a contingent of 2,000 Bambara warriors, and Aguibu was given permission to undertake, "sans même nous consulter, toute guerre que tu croiras nécessaire, pourvu que ce ne soit pas contre quelqu'un ayant signé des traités avec nous." [114] At the same time, the Resident at Bandiagara was ordered not to meddle in Masina's internal affairs and advised to turn a blind eye to the whole question of the slave trade, even if Aguibu raided the neighboring territories of Segu. The tradition of the razzia was so firmly entrenched, Archinard warned him, "que si vous interveniez une fois, vous serez absolumdent débordé et tout le pays en sera remué." [115] Thus French administration in the Western Sudan neatly bracketed its British counterpart. Whereas Lugard went for the middle ground, Archinard built his system on two opposing principles. Whereas Lugard wished to make his chiefs "an integral part . . . [of] a single Government," Archinard considered it wiser "ou que nous laissions toute l'autorité au chef indigène, ou que nous l'exercions nous-mêmes et en notre nom." [116]

There were good reasons for this divergence of approach to the basic common problem of maintaining security and establishing European dominion. Lugard himself wished to make his reputation as a great governor rather than as a brilliant military commander. He saw his conquests as no more than the necessary prelude to the accomplishment of a much more important task: the creation of a coherent, regulated, and permanent system of rule. His great ambition was to provide the Protectorate with an efficient government, to control the European impact upon the traditional political and social structure, and so "to bring the country all the gains of civilization by applied science . . . with as little interference as possible with Native customs and modes of thought." [117]

But Lugard had the opportunity as well as the desire to concentrate upon the short-term requirements of an efficient administration and to ponder upon the long-term objectives of indirect rule. When the military phase of British expansion in Northern Nigeria began, the

114. Archinard to Aguibu, Instructions, May 4, 1893, cited in *Bulletin du Comité de l'Afrique Française, Renseignements Coloniaux,* January 1896, pp. 27–28.

115. Archinard to Blachère, Instructions, May 4, 1893, Archinard papers.

116. Ibid.

117. Lugard, *Political Memoranda,* 1918 edition, No. I, para. 3, cited in A. H. M. Kirk-Greene, ed., *Principles of Native Administration in Nigeria* (London, 1965), p. 94.

European partition and occupation of West Africa was virtually complete. Since the international frontiers of the Protectorate had already been drawn, European rivalry was not a factor to be reckoned with, and the era of military expansion could be brought to a close with the effective assertion of British suzerainty. The very speed and comprehensiveness of his victory over the Fulani thus enabled Lugard to devote himself wholeheartedly to the elaboration of a settled and permanent administrative system. Although his Political Department was predominantly staffed by officers, British rule, even in its early stages, was not in the strictest sense military. From the start, a sharp distinction was drawn between the civilian and military branches of government. Residents, civilian or military, exercised exclusively political and administrative functions. Although they could call on the assistance of the Protectorate's military forces, they had no control over actual military operations. Nor was Lugard's description of his military Residents as less "militarist" than many civilians entirely disingenuous.[118] Most of the early Residents approached the problems of administration with as much passion as the high commissioner and showed little desire to abandon their administrative roles for the chance of participating in a major military campaign. After the conquest of Sokoto they were not even subject to the temptation. Political rather than military commands were the most attractive posts in Northern Nigeria, attractive enough for one Resident, Charles Orr, to resign his commission in order to become a full member of the Political Department.[119]

Lugard's policies, of course, were not translated into practice overnight. When he left Nigeria in 1906 the administrative system was still primitive and experimental; no more than the broad lines for future development had been laid down. Some of his objectives were already proving impossible to realize. Determined to maintain his personal control over all branches of the administration, Lugard ordered his Residents "to loyally carry out the policies of the High Commissioner" and to enforce the "laws and usages" of the Protectorate.[120] But how many political officers ever read his *Political Memoranda* or paid much attention to them if they did is a question well worth asking. The course of administration was already being

118. *Annual Reports, Northern Nigeria,* 1902, Cd. 1768–14, *PP* [1904], 58, 201–02.

119. Sir Charles Orr, *The Making of Northern Nigeria,* 2d ed., with a new introduction by A. H. M. Kirk-Greene (London, 1965), p. xv.

120. Lugard, *Political Memoranda,* No. I, paras. 2, 4.

determined more by the individual actions of Residents and Assistant Residents in response to the local situation that confronted them than by directives issued from Zungeru. "Anglo-African Government" was to evolve through the accumulation of experience at the local level and through the subtle interplay of personalities and circumstances beyond the control of the colonial or metropolitan capitals.[121] And this evolution was to be a long-term process. The capture of Sokoto was merely one stage in the extension of British rule. It took many more years for the new regime to make its impact felt in the remoter corners of the Protectorate, and effective power was never to be fully concentrated in European hands. Nevertheless, by 1906 the embryonic administration had achieved one of its major purposes: it had gained the loyalty and support of most emirs. The Satiru rebellion was the crucial test. Its sudden outbreak caught the British completely unprepared, with their troops engaged against the Munshi in the south and the northern Residents absent from their posts. Only the steadfastness of the emirs prevented an already serious military setback from turning into a catastrophe.

The French could not claim the same success. Their military established themselves in the Western Sudan when the era of the Partition was about to begin, and they operated throughout the most febrile period of European expansion in West Africa. The emphasis in their rule was on maintaining the impetus of the military advance; purely administrative considerations were secondary. The overriding objective in the frontier states was to create bases for continued expansion. Archinard did not install Mademba Si at Sansanding in the interests of good government but with the thought "que vous régnerez un jour à Bandiagara et nous donnerez ainsi le Niger jusqu'à Tombouctou et Tombouctou même."[122] Similarly, Aguibu's instructions contained nothing about administration, but they did authorize him to demand tribute from Timbuktu.[123] In these conditions, European control could not be effectively exercised. Taking advantage of his autonomy, Mademba instituted a minor reign of terror in Sansanding. "Il semble que jusqu'à présent vous ayez plutôt cherché à imiter

121. See Robert Heussler, *The British in Northern Nigeria* (London, 1968) and his chapter below. I am grateful to him for many helpful suggestions during the revision of this paper.

122. Archinard to Mademba, March 7, 1891, cited in Archinard, Rapport . . . 1890–91, Chap. 3, *JO*, October 17, 1891, p. 4998.

123. Archinard to Aguibu, Instructions, May 4, 1893, cited in *Bulletin du Comité de l'Afrique Française, Renseignements Coloniaux,* January 1896, pp. 27–28.

Ahmadou dans sa manière de gouverner que de vous inspirer de nos idées françaises," Archinard complained to him in 1893, "tout le monde a peur pour sa tête." But the *fama* was still a loyal collaborator, so only the boundaries of his kingdom were reduced; he was not deposed.[124] Aguibu's raids underlined the flimsiness of central control. In February 1894 the sultan attacked the town of Bossé. When he ran into trouble, the resident at Bandiagara, against instructions, marched to help him. When he in turn was beaten back, the commandant of Segu sent reinforcements without waiting for the permission of the governor, and the commander of the relief column then proceeded to raze the village of Kombori, acting once more against orders.[125]

The attempt to impose a more direct form of administration over Segu fared no better. As soon as the Bambaras recognized their restoration as a sham, they turned against their European allies. The first fama Mari Diara, began to plot against the French within weeks of his appointment and was summarily executed. His successor, Bodian Massasi, was more loyal but proved quite incapable of maintaining order. For three years after its conquest, Segu was rent by rebellions, and their suppression seriously complicated the campaigns against Samori. Indeed, Bambara unrest caused the French more trouble than the actual overthrow of the Tukulor empire.[126] In 1893 the experiment in Segu had to be abandoned: Bodian was pensioned off, and the province was turned into an administrative *cercle*.

French military rule in the Western Sudan had other drawbacks as well. During their twenty years of power, the *officiers soudanais* developed a proprietary interest in the colony which they were as anxious to defend against interference from above as against rebellion from below. As soon as Archinard took command, he systematically purged the administration of civilians, replacing them with his own officers.[127] But this merely added to the strain upon his manpower without providing him with a dedicated corps of administrators. For

124. Archinard to Mademba, n.d. [May 1893], Archinard papers; Archinard, Rapport . . . 1892–93, cited in Méniaud, *Pionniers, 2,* 442: "Le fama Mademba, toujours serviteur fidèle et dévoué de la cause française, . . . a rendu tant de services . . . que j'aurais été désolé d'avoir à prendre quelque mesure qui pût lui être réellement pénible."

125. For details of this incident, see Kanya-Forstner, *Conquest of the Western Sudan,* pp. 225–27.

126. The capture of Diéna in 1891, for example, was the most serious engagement, in terms of the losses incurred, that Archinard ever fought in the Sudan.

127. Archinard to Brière, n.d. [April 1889] [draft], Archinard papers.

as long as the era of conquest lasted, military campaigns remained the Sudan's chief attraction. The officers did not find their political roles congenial. They had come to the Sudan in the hope of seeing action, and the only way Archinard could persuade them to perform administrative duties was to make this service a prerequisite for participation in a campaign.[128]

The *commandant-supérieur,* however, could sympathize with his subordinates; conquest rather than government was his obsession too. Archinard wanted to go into the history books as the *conquérant du Soudan,* not as the author of some Gallic variation on the theme of indirect rule. He had little opportunity and no inclination to attempt more than the imposition of a semblance of order, "afin de ne pas être distrait du but principal, notre expansion en Afrique, par des questions de petite importance." [129] During the initial stages of European occupation, this was perhaps the fundamental contrast between French and British rule. To some extent it reflected a difference of personalities and backgrounds; but at a deeper level it also reflected the different conditions in which the military operated. As with the adoption of imperialist policies in Britain and France, the crucial difference between French and British expansion and administration in the Western Sudan was one of timing.

128. Archinard to Delcassé, September 1, 1893 [copy], ibid. Archinard claimed that the system functioned adequately, but he admitted that it had the serious defect of removing capable administrative officers from their posts just as they gained experience.

129. Archinard to Briquelot, Instructions, March 9, 1891, cited in Archinard, Rapport . . . 1890–91, Chap. 3, *JO,* October 18, 1891, p. 5012.

13. The African Factor in the Establishment of French Authority in West Africa 1880–1900

BONIFACE I. OBICHERE

La conquête de l'Ouest Africain est leur (tirailleur sénégalais) œuvre; elles ont donné à la France un territoire plus vaste que l'Europe et peuplé de 20 millions d'habitants; elle le lui gardent avec une effectif de 12,500 hommes, car dans toutes nos possessions de l'Afrique Occidentale et du Congo-Tchad, il n'existe comme troupe européenne qu'un seul bataillon d'infantérie coloniale de 3 compagnies (450 hommes) en garnison à Dakar pour la defense de ce point d'appui de la flotte.[1]

When in 1910 Lieutenant-Colonel Mangin wrote in this vein about the contributions made to French enterprise in West Africa by Senegalese sharpshooters, he was stressing a neglected theme in nineteenth-century European expansion in West Africa. It was not only the tirailleurs who contributed to the success of French colonization in West Africa. The aim of this chapter is to attempt an assessment of the totality of the role of Africans in, and their reaction to, the establishment of French authority in various regions of West Africa in the early years of the expansion of France into that part of the African continent. This will be done by the examination of several cases involving Africans and French agents from the 1880s onward. An effort will be made to survey the role in French expansion of both African political and religious leaders as well as that played by the common people.

We want to move away from the sensational. We want to explode some myths and platitudes—such as those involving Lat Dior, Samori Touré, Alpha Yaya, Rabeh, Glégié, and Behanzin[2]—and try to

1. Charles Mangin, *La Force Noire* (Paris, 1910), pp. 175–76.

2. G. Teullière, "Alpha Yaya et la politique indigène," *Revue Indigène* (1911), pp. 615–20. Henri Monet, *El Hadj Omar: L'Ambassadeur de Dieu* (Paris, 1857). Yves Person, *Samori, une revolution dyula* (Nîmes, 1968), vol. *1*. J. Lippert, "Rabah," *Mitteilungen des Seminars für orientalische Sprachen in Berlin, 1899, Afrikanische Studien*, pp. 246–50. P. Vigné, *Terre de Mort: Soudan et Dahomey* (Paris, 1892).

examine and evaluate the response of the African population in general to French imperialism in its early stages. Therefore, we will be concerned with several categories of Africans, from the flamboyant chiefs and pompous kings to the humble porters, patient *hamacaires,* timid auxiliaries, domestic and civil servants, astute guides, shrewd interpreters, and to passive housewives who often had to cook meals under duress for intruding hordes of armed strangers.

For convenience and to give focus to this study, initial African response to French colonisation has been subdivided into three broad categories. These are the factors of cooperation, of resistance, and of passivity. The most important factors are those of cooperation and resistance. The passivity factor would apply to those African communities which, like the chameleon, changed their attitude to serve the wishes of whoever was in control of their territories without reference to whether the occupying force was African or European. Those societies that remained passive did so because they had neither the military ability to resist nor the political organization and leadership to initiate opposition to a relatively well-organized and armed invading force. Let us then turn to the factors of cooperation and of resistance.

The nature of African cooperation with French authorities was complex. It depended in some cases on what African rulers hoped to gain by cooperating, and in other cases on the aims of French authorities in seeking the support of Africans in a given region or situation. The French had a long history of selective cooperation with Africans in their imperial experience. For instance, when it was realized that Abdel Kader would harass the French in Algeria, unsuccessful efforts were made to cooperate with him with a view to stiffling his rebellion, which was then imminent.[3] These efforts were immediately followed by vigorous attempts to enlist the goodwill and aid of the marabouts of the Tijani Brotherhood.[4] Earlier in the West African context,

3. S. Gsell, G. Marcais, and G. Yver, *Histoire d'Algérie* (Paris, 1929), p. 210. The Treaty of Tafna, May 30, 1837, concluded by Bugeaud, is a case in point. See Alexandre Bellemare, *Abd el-Kader, sa vie politique et militaire* (Paris, 1853). Maurice Wahl, *L'Algérie,* 5th ed. (Paris, 1908), pp. 121–30. P. Boyer, "Introduction à une histoire intérieure de la Régence d'Alger," *Revue Historique, 235,* no. 478 (1966), 297–316. M. Emerit, *L'Algérie à l'époque d'Abd el-Kader* (Paris, 1951), p. 148.

4. Jamil M. Abun-Nasr, *The Tijaniyya, A Sufi Order in the Modern World* (London, 1965), pp. 62–77. Paul Marty, *La Politique Indigène du Gouvérneur Général Ponty* (Paris, 1915).

General Faidherbe had resorted to the expedient of cooperation with established African polities. Governor Valière followed Faidherbe's footsteps and even recommended the avoidance of direct control as a means of securing the cooperation of African rulers.[5]

In the ebullient Tokolor Empire under Ahmadu of Ségou, French officials encouraged the Bambara in their recalcitrance against their Tokolor overloads. Captain J. S. Gallieni praised the virtue of quietly supporting the Bambara and other minorities in the Tokolor Empire while at the same time maintaining a façade of superficial friendship with Ahmadu of Ségou.[6] Such a policy, contended Gallieni, who was at that time in the Direction Politique of Senegal (1879–81), would hasten the collapse of the Tokolor Empire whose "decadence" Captain E. Mage had exaggerated earlier.[7] Gallieni selected the Bambara for special friendly treatment because they were not Muslim, for Gallieni asserted that Islam was the deadliest enemy of France's great work of penetrating into the heart of Africa. France's African work, he declared, "n'a pas de plus mortel ennemi que l'islamisme." [8] Islamophobia was an important factor in the development of the relations between French officials and Africans. It was generally believed by the French that the non-Moslem people were more receptive to French ideas than their Islamized counterparts.[9]

The making of treaties of protection, friendship, and commerce by French agents was motivated in some cases by reasons that were far from friendly. "C'est par nos traités de protectorat que nous devons combattre les entreprises des nations rivals," declared Gallieni.[10] This principle was put into practice whenever the necessity arose. The French thrust into Fouta Djallon in 1880 spearheaded by Dr. Jean

5. Archives Nationales Section Outre-Mer [ANSOM hereafter], Senegal I/56/v. Valière to Ministry of Marine and Colonies [MMC hereafter], October 31, 1869. Same to Same, April 14, 1870.

6. ANSOM, Sénégal I/70/b. Governor of Senegal to MMC, November 5, 1883. J. S. Gallieni, *Mission dans le Haut Niger et à Ségou* (Paris, 1883), p. 205. Gallieni, *Voyage au Soudan Française, 1879–1881* (Paris, 1885), p. 620. J. D. Hargreaves, *West Africa: The Former French States* (Englewood Cliffs, N.J., 1967), p. 98. For letters exchanged between Gallieni and Ahmadu see G. Grandidier, *Galliéni* (Paris, 1931), pp. 39–73.

7. E. Mage, *Voyage dans le Soudan Occidental (Sénégambie-Niger) 1863–1866* (Paris, 1868). Gallieni, *Voyage au Soudan Français,* p. 615. ". . . l'Empire fondé par El Hadj Oumar est actuellement dans une décadence complète."

8. Gallieni, *Voyage au Soudan Français,* pp. 616–18; Gallieni, *Mission dans le Haut Niger,* p. 205.

9. Maurice Delafosse, *Haut-Sénégal-Niger,* 3, 212.

10. Gallieni, *Deux Campagnes au Soudan Français* (Paris, 1891), p. 405.

Bayol[11] had the objective of forestalling any British designs in the area. Moreover, the news of Spanish officers winding their way from the Mauritanian coast toward Kaarta galvanized Gallieni into sustained action. He demanded that the French Foreign Office notify all the powers who were signatories of the General Act of the Berlin Conference (1885) of the Treaty of Gouri with Ahmadu on May 12, 1887.[12] This was not to say that Gallieni was interested in preserving the territorial integrity of the Tokolor Empire or that he was enamored with Ahmadu. On the contrary he saw the treaty with the Tokolor ruler as the small end of a wedge in the Tokolor body politic. He observed:

> Le Sultan nègre de Segou n'est assurément pas un souverain sur la simple parole duquel on puisse absolument faire fonds, et les stipulations du traité risqueront de rester lettre morte si nous n'en assurons nous-mêmes l'execution.[13]

Treaties were in most cases backed up with material gifts for the African rulers whose goodwill the French desired. In October 1886, the French government was persuaded that sending presents to Samori Touré could pave the way for better relations between this chief and France. It was decided to send Samori gifts befitting a monarch. The gifts were to be delivered by a special mission led by Captain Etienne Peroz. An impressive list of goods was compiled by Gallieni, and the estimated cost of the materials in the consignment was 29,329 francs. This was approved by A. de la Porte, the undersecretary of state for colonies, without question.[14] Similar, but less ambitious consignments of gifts were sent to Fama Tiéba of Sikasso, King Bantchande of Gurma, Aguibu of Dinguiraye, and even to King Glélé and King Behanzin of Dahomey whose relations with France were, to say the least, not cordial.[15] Ahmadu of Ségou was of

11. See Alain Quellien, *La Politique Musulmane dans l'Afrique Occidentale Française* (Paris, 1910). Gallieni, *Deux Campagnes au Soudan Français,* pp. 404–06. ANSOM Missions 16, Gallieni to Governor of Senegal, October 14, 1880.

12. ANSOM, Sénégal, IV/91/b. Gallieni to Etienne, October 20, 1887; Flourens to Barbey, November 21, 1887; MAE to Krantz, June 29, 1888; Flourens to Krantz, September 22, 1887. Hanotaux and Martineau, *Histoire des Colonies Françaises, 4,* 181.

13. Gallieni, *Voyage au Soudan Français,* p. 623.

14. ANSOM, Sénégal IV/88/c. "Rapport au Sous-Secrétaire d'Etat: Proposition d'autoriser l'achat de présents destinés à Samory" par la Sous-Directeur des Colonies chargé de la Sous-Direction Politique. October 8, 1886, R. 538.

15. ANSOM, Sénégal IV/88/e. "Rapport au Sous-Secrétaire d'Etat" par J. Haussman, September 8, 1887, Cadeaux pour Aguibou. Approved to Etienne.

the opinion that the French, like the Greeks, could not be trusted even when they gave gifts. He told Commandant Combes in September 1884 that he had no need for the gifts which the French said they would bring him because he knew that was a cover for other French designs against his kingdom, especially the introduction of the gunboat *Niger* on the waters between Ségou and Timbuktu.[16] It was reported by Captain Delanneau that Ahmadu's anger at the presence of a gunboat on the river arose from a forewarning by his father, El Hadj Omar, that when French gunboats sailed above Ségou the collapse of the Tokolor Empire would be at hand.[17]

In the mid-1890s when French presence in the Togo hinterland was threatened by both Germany and Britain, French officials not only gave lavish gifts to African rulers in the area but also paid them the annual salaries stated in previous treaties. For instance in 1895 King Nambema of the Chakosi not only saw his capital of Sansane-Mango graced with the presence of Administrator Alby and several loads of presents, but he also received the first payment of the annual salary promised him in an earlier treaty with Captain Baud in 1894.[18] This proved to King Nambema that the pieces of paper left with him by many a white man had other than decorative value.[19]

In order to win the friendship and cooperation of some powerful African rulers, free trips to Paris were also used by the French to condition their prospective allies and to enlist their support in the establishment of French authority in their respective regions. Shortly after their definitive establishment in Whydah in 1842, Victor Régis and Cyprien Fabre not only encouraged the development of the oil palm industry but ingratiated themselves with King Gezo by arranging the sending of two of his household to Marseille for the purpose

ANSOM Sénégal IV/82/a. "Rapport . . . 1884–1885" par Combes. Ibid. Sénégal IV/96/b. "Mission auprès de Tiéba roi de Kénédougou' par Quiquandon (Epreuves).

16. ANSOM, Sénégal IV/82/a. Ahmadu to Combes, September 22, 1884. Captain Delanneau to Combes, September 21, 1884, "Rapport sur le voyage du canonnière Le Niger de Bamako a Kouliokoro."

17. ANSOM, Sénégal IV/82/a. Rapport Complémentaire par Delanneau. Pièce No. 5.

18. ANSOM Sénégal I, 96, bis. Note au Président de la République, November 1895.

19. The British also fixed annual salaries for African rulers who made treaties with them. See Foreign Office Confidential Prints (1896) No. 6734, Foreign Office to Dufferin, February 7, 1896, No. 33 Africa Encl. 1. Treaty with Bussa signed at Kaware on November 12, 1885, 2. Treaty with Bussa signed January 20, 1890 at Bussa.

of education. This gave rise later to the erroneous belief in some quarters that Glégle was educated in France.[20]

Forced by the uneasy relation that existed between him and Tidjani, the Tokolor ruler of Macina,[21] the sultan of Timbuktu made overtures to the French for aid and protection. This gesture was received with enthusiasm in Saint-Louis where the envoys of Sheikh Khaer Hadj Ibrahim made a favorable impression.[22] A friendly state on the northeastern marches of the Tokolor Empire was desirable since it would mean overshooting Ahmadu's territory and hemming him in, in case of military action. Furthermore, the charming prospect of securing protection over the renowned city of Timbuktu[23] by a stroke of the pen could not but have been very tempting to the French officials in Saint-Louis. El Hadj Abdel Kader, who led the Timbuktu delegation to Saint-Louis, was filled with the idea of going to France to win support for his sultan's cause against the apparently fastidious Tokolors. Jules Ferry thought that a treaty of protection with Timbuktu would strengthen the French case at the Berlin Conference for the control of the Upper and Middle Niger.[24] El Hadj Abdel Kader went to Paris with the blessing of the governor of Senegal. He was accorded diplomatic dignity and had interviews with the leaders of the French government as well as with General Faidherbe.[25] Abdel Kader's luxury sojourn in Paris was crowned with loads of presents and gifts worth about 2,600 francs.[26] The illusion of the diplomatic

20. Le Père Eugène Chautard, *Le Dahomey* (Lyon, 1890), p. 6. It could not have been Glégle because heirs apparent and occupants of the Fon throne at Abomey were forbidden to see the ocean. A. Akindele and C. Aguessy, *Le Dahomey* (Paris, 1955), p. 25. See also Paul Mimande, *L'Héritage de Béhanzin* (Paris, 1898).

21. R. Cornevin, *Histoire des Peuples de l'Afrique Noire* (Paris, 1963), pp. 364–65. Tidjani ruled from 1864 to 1887. Delafosse, *Haut-Sénégal-Niger, 2*, 336.

22. ANSOM, Sénégal IV/82/b. Renseignements sur la ville de Tombouctou fournis par l'El Hadj Abdoul Laddou envoyé du Chief El Khaer Hadj Ibrahim, chef des Maures de Tombouctou vers M. le Gouverneur du Sénégal. September 22, 1884.

23. Réné Caillé, *Journal d'un voyage a Temboctou et à Jenné, dans l'Afrique Centrale* (Paris, 1830). See also Felix Dubois, *Tombouctou la Mystérieuse* (Paris, 1904).

24. ANSOM, Sénégal IV/82/b. Governor of Senegal to MMC, September 24, 1884. Ferry to Peyron, December 20, 1884. Peyron to Ferry, December 24, 1884.

25. See Roland Malric, "Les idées de Faidherbe en vue de la decouverte des voies d'accès et de pénétration au Soudan," *Memoire: Ecole Nationale de la France d'Outre-Mer* (Année Scholaire, 1936–37).

26. El Hadj Abdel Kader had rooms at the Grand Hotel du Louvre. Professor

victory scored by this visit could not be dispelled from the official French mind by the protests of Colonel H. Frey that Abdel Kader was a Moor and not a representative of the real ruler of Timbuktu. He represented traders of Timbuktu who were mainly foreigners of Djerma and Moorish origin and, Frey continued, "un grope de quelques marchands d'esclaves qui se partageaient le commerce de la cité." France was backing the wrong horse, contended Colonel Frey, since El Hadj Abdel Kader could neither speak for nor represent the indigenous ruling and landowning class of Timbuktu.[27]

This visit by an African envoy to the French capital was soon followed by another. This time it was the turn of the heir apparent to Samori. There was no question as to Prince Karamoko's qualifications to represent Samori. He was a prince and an officer in Samori's army. The origin of Karamoko's voyage to France is still obscure. It has been said that Samori asked that Karamoko be sent to Paris.[28] This is very unlikely in the light of Samori's whole attitude toward the French, and the attack Commandant Combes launched against Samori in 1884–85.[29] However, Frey's efforts to negotiate peacefully with Samori through a mission led by Captain Tournier[30] proved successful. The talks held at Samori's camp in Kenieba-Koura resulted in French recognition of Samori's rights over the auriferous regions of Bouró and Kangaba. As a token of his goodwill, it was reported, Samori agreed to send his favorite son Karamoko to France. The suggestion originated from the members of the French mission. The memory of the voyage to Paris of Abdel Kader of Timbuktu was still fresh in their minds.[31] In any case, Prince Karamoko made the journey to France. He sailed from Saint-Louis to Bordeaux, from where he went to Paris by train.

Angeli (professor of Arabic in Paris) was placed at his service as his interpreter. His hotel bill came to 2,451 francs, and was certified by Professor Angeli. Grand Hotel du Louvre, Facture March 19, 1885.

27. Colonel H. Frey, *Campagne dans le Haut Sénégal et dans le Haut Niger, 1885–1886* (Paris, 1888), pp. 190–92.

28. Abdel Kader Mademba, *Au Sénégal et au Soudan Français* (Paris, 1931), p. 25.

29. ANSOM, Sénégal IV/81/b. "Rapport au Ministre" du Lt.-Colonel Combes, Commandant Supérieur du Haut-Fleuve. Kayes, November 1, 1884. "Rapport . . . 1884–1885" par Combes. Chap. 3.

30. The mission sent to Samori by Frey comprised Captain Tournier, Captain Mahmadou Racine, Lieutenant Peroz, Interpreter Alassane Dia, 6 spahis, and 20 tirailleurs. ANSOM, Sénégal IV/85/b. Rapport Tournier July 6, 1886.

31. ANSOM, Sénégal IV/85/b. Frey to Governor of Senegal February 4, 1886. Frey, *Campagne*, pp. 183–88.

Accompanied by an impressive retinue of nine persons and two officers, Karamoko stayed in Paris from August 11 to September 9, 1886. He and his party were lodged at the Grand Hotel after initial efforts to secure accommodation for them at the Hotel Marillier proved unsuccessful.[32] The bill for this sojourn came to the astronomic total of 14,391.65 francs. Furthermore, Prince Karamoko's dental treatment cost 200 francs.[33]

On the diplomatic and social side Prince Karamoko's mission was very eventful. He was received by the president of the French Republic, by the minister of the navy and colonies, and by General Faidherbe. Above all, he was given a warm reception by General Boulanger, the minister of war, and his general staff. Karamoko was indelibly impressed by the military reviews he witnessed in Paris, especially the maneuvers of the cavalry. The *cuirassiers* fascinated and dazzled him by their uniforms and by the address and perfection of their charge.[34] With reference to the treaty that was concluded with Samori in March 1886, General Boulanger expressed the wish that relations between France and Samori would continue to be cordial in the spirit of this treaty.[35] This wish, like most of General Boulanger's other wishes, was never realized.[36] Samori fought against French forces until his surrender in 1898. Prince Karamoko was executed at Samori's orders for his Francophilism, which could be dated from his sojourn in Paris in 1886.[37]

Just as the French used means other than force to pave the way for the establishment of their authority in West Africa, so did some Africans resort to various forms of cooperation with French agents with a view to gaining certain advantages linked with their own political interests.[38] What each leader hoped to gain was particular to

32. Frey, "Rapport de la Mission, 1885–1886" in ANSOM, Sénégal IV/85/a. Rapport Frey, June 22, 1886. Frey, *Campagne,* pp. 117–80.

33. ANSOM, Sénégal IV/88/d. Hotel Marillier to MMC Tel., August 28, 1886.

34. Ibid., Sénégal IV/88/d. Voyage en France du Prince Karamoko, fils de Samory. M. Langronne (Grand Hotel) to MMC, September 10, 1886. Dr. James Neel to MMC, September 28, 1886.

35. Abdel Kader Mademba, *Au Sénégal et au Soudan Français,* p. 26. Prince Karamoko's reception in Paris may bear fruitful comparison with the red carpet treatment accorded to Cetewayo, the Zulu Chief, in London in 1880–83. I am indebted to Leonard Thompson for this view.

36. E. Rouard de Card, *Les Traités de protectorat conclus par la France en Afrique, 1870–1895* (Paris, 1897), pp. 230–31.

37. Carl Grimberg and Ragnar Svanström, *Histoire Universelle* (French edition by G. H. Dumont, Paris, 1965), *11,* 147–52.

38. Abdel Kader Mademba, *Au Sénégal et au Soudan Français,* p. 26.

him, and what he could do for the French depended on his political and economic circumstances. However, some general trends can be seen through an examination of several cases.

King Tièba of Sikasso was one of those African leaders who did not hesitate to ally himself with French agents in West Africa. The kingdom of Kénédugu was founded about the beginning of the nineteenth century by Tapri Taraore. By the 1880s it had developed considerably in size and strength, but its strength was offset by the gigantic military machines of its neighbors. The original capital of the kingdom was at Finkolo. It was Tièba who transferred the capital to Sikasso. Tièba succeeded his brother Molo, who died in the course of a fierce struggle with Fafa, chief of Kinian. Molo introduced Ahmadu's influence into Kénédugu by applying to him for military aid against Fafa. Ahmadu sent a battalion of his *talibés* under the command of Yahia to support Molo on condition that Molo would embrace Islam.[39] Tiéba moved the capital of Kénédugu to Sikasso, which was the birthplace of his mother. His policy was to build a Senufo empire strong enough to withstand and check the rapid expansion of the Mandingo Empire of Samori and the Tokolor Empire of Ahmadu. He conquered Ganadugu and Folona and used the captives of these wars in erecting a double wall of defense around Sikasso, which he turned into a veritable fortress.[40] From each conquered chieftaincy Tiéba took as hostage one of the sons of the ruler. He took these "princes" to Sikasso to ensure the loyalty of their fathers and to educate and train them in administrative and military matters. The stimulation of Senufo nationalism was also his objective. Eventually Tiéba defeated Fafa in March 1891 by the conjunction of the alliance of Sigmogo Kone, chief of Konseguela, and the aid of the French under Captain Quiquandon. This victory extended his influence farther and furthered his ambition for a Senufo Empire.[41]

Tiéba's relations with both Samori and Ahmadu were strained indeed. Tokolor and Mandingo expansion were inimical and detrimental to his avowed policy. The ferocity of the *sofas* struck terror into Tiéba, and early in 1886 he sent a delegation of ten to Bamako to propose a defensive and offensive alliance with France against their

39. See Jacques Meniaud, *Sikasso, ou l'Histoire Dramatique d'un Royaume Noir au XIXe Siècle* (Paris, 1935). This is a private publication of which only 1,125 copies were printed.

40. Delafosse, *Haut-Sénégal-Niger, 2,* 373–74. General Duboc, *Epopée Coloniale,* p. 112.

41. F. Petit, "Sikasso," in *Annales Afriçaines* (1958), pp. 309–12. Delafosse, *Haut-Sénégal-Niger, 2,* 375.

common enemies, and to ask for a cannon. Colonel Frey did not judge such an alliance opportune because of the proposed peace treaty with Samori which was actually concluded by Captain Peroz on March 23, 1887.[42]

In 1887 Samori marched against Kénédugu and laid siege on Sikasso. Tiéba's foresight and the fortification of Sikasso paid dividends. The sofas could not puncture the defenses of the Senufo capital.[43] Not even Captain Louis Gustave Binger with all his winsome and pacific attributes could reconcile the two warring rulers.[44] After sixteen months of campaigning and devastation, Samori withdrew his forces without having subdued Sikasso.[45] He lost many of his important generals in this unfruitful and protracted campaign, especially Fabou and Lankafali, his capable lieutenants.

Tiéba had had a foretaste of Mandingo militarism. He was more determined than ever to strengthen his position. He used the breathing space provided by the end of the siege of Sikasso to renew his overtures to the French in the autumn of 1888. More serious negotiations followed, and a treaty of friendship and protection was signed between France and Tiéba in July 1888. Henceforth Tiéba was to collaborate with the French forces in their struggles with both Samori and Ahmadu. The treaty provided for a French resident at Sikasso. Captain Quiquandon was stationed at Sikasso as resident and technical adviser to Tiéba, and after him Captain Marchand.[46] Captain Quiquandon taught Tiéba's men how to use modern precision rifles and ammunition. In short, giving military training to Tiéba's troops as well as procuring guns and weapons for them was an integral part of his functions at Sikasso. He won great popularity for himself.[47]

42. Capt. F. Quiquandon, "Dans la Boucle du Niger," in *Bulletin Societé de Géographie Commerciale de Bordeaux* (1891). Meniaud, *Sikasso,* pp. 29–33.

43. Frey, *Campagne,* p. 227. General Duboc, *Epopée Coloniale,* p. 127. Rouard de Card, *Les Traités . . . 1870–1895,* pp. 230–31. Commandant Combes had promised French help to Tiéba in 1885.

44. L.-G. Binger, *Du Niger au Golfe de Guinée par le pays de Kong et le Mossi, 1887–1889* (Paris, 1892), Vol. 1, pp. 69–108. Binger's expedition disquieted the governor of the Gold Coast, who feared that France would acquire all the territories to the interior including Ashanti. See CO96/172 Brandford Griffith to Stanley 5/2/86 No. 51. CO96/173 Brandford Griffith to Granville 22/4/86. But Sidney Webb of the Colonial Office thought it was not worth while to extend the Gold Coast Colony. CO96/188 Minutes by S. Webb 22/8/87.

45. G. Valbert, "Le Voyage du Capt. Binger dans la Boucle du Niger," *Revue des Deux Mondes* (February 1, 1890), p. 661.

46. ANSOM, Sénégal IV/96/b. "Rapport du Capitaine Quiquandon sur sa Mission auprès de Tiéba, roi de Kénédougou," 8/7/91. Delafosse, *Haut-Sénégal-Niger,* 2, 376, n. 1.

47. Meniaud, *Sikasso,* p. 31.

Tiéba had thus the best of both worlds. He had succeeded in his foreign policy in a limited manner. He used his temporary friendship with the French to preserve his kingdom from Tokolor or Mandingo conquest. The traditional Senufo pragmatism of having recourse to a stronger power for aid succeeded at least during his lifetime. He exploited his relationship with French agents to further his own interests. However, when he realized that Kénédugu was no longer threatened by any imminent danger, he lost interest in cooperating with the French. It is noteworthy that Tiéba furnished guides and auxiliaries for the French expedition against Ségou in the autumn of 1890.[48] In July 1891 the new French resident in Sikasso, Captain Marchand, asked Tiéba to contribute to the French campaign against Samori. Tiéba's hesitation was tantamount to refusal. Furthermore, Captain Etienne Peroz was sent to Sikasso by Colonel Humbert[49] to persuade Tiéba to fulfill his treaty obligations by joining the French in the fight against Samori. Peroz could not persuade Tiéba, who said he preferred to remain neutral.[50] His councillors, led by Ba Bemba, had pointed out to him that the French could not be trusted. They had been allies of Ahmadu and later turned against him and deposed him. Secondly, they made treaties of friendship with Samori, but soon started a war against him. After the disposal of Ahmadu and Samori, they speculated, Tiéba would be the next victim of the perfidious French.[51] This throws light on Tiéba's change of attitude. He had passed from cooperation to opposition. First of all, he entered into correspondence with both Ahmadu and Samori, as reported by Captain Marchand.[52] Second, he withdrew from active support of the French and claimed a neutralist stance. Third, he embarked on the erection of more fortifications around Sikasso at a time when his troops should have been fighting side by side with the French against Samori.

François Deloncle stated in the Chamber of Deputies that the

48. André Grassion, "La Pénétration française au Soudan dans ses rapports avec le Royaume de Sikasso," in *Memoires: Ecole Nationale de la France d'Outre-Mer,* Année Scholaire 1938–39 (Paris, 1939).

49. Captain S. P. Oliver, *The French Soudan Up to Date, January 1894.* Intelligence Division of the War Office (London, 1894), pp. 15–16. Lieutenant Colonel E. Peroz, *Par Vocation: Vie et Aventures d'un Soldat de Fortune, 1870–1895* (Paris, 1905). Lieutenant Colonel Humbert, "Le Soudan Français," in *Bulletin Société de Géog. 2e Trimestre* (1891). Delafosse, *Haut-Sénégal-Niger,* 2, 415.

50. Oliver, *The French Soudan,* p. 15.

51. Oliver, *The French Soudan,* p. 14. Abdel Kader Mademba, *Au Sénégal et au Soudan Français,* p. 101. ANSOM, Sénégal IV/96/b. Rapport Quiquandon, July 8, 1891.

52. Archives Nationales: 149AP, Papiers Mangin: "Missions Marchand."

efforts to discredit Tiéba as a slave dealer and as an enemy of France followed the usual pattern. First of all, pacific and sensible treaties are made with African rulers. Then residents are sent to them; and soon things take a turn for the worse and *galons et croix* follows.[53] Tiéba died in January 1893. His obsequies took place on 16 February 1893 at Bougoula, and according to Captain Quiquandon they befitted the first great monarch of Sikasso.[54]

Aguibou, son of El Hadj Omar and ruler of Dinguiraye, which was a province of the Tokolor Empire,[55] cooperated and collaborated with the French in the establishment of their authority in the Upper Niger basin. The experience of his father's struggles with the French may have been responsible for the resignation with which he reacted to their enterprise in his domain in the 1880s. In addition, the high-handedness with which Ahmadu treated his other brothers could not but have excited Aguibou's instincts of self-preservation. He signed a treaty of protection with the French in March 1887, and provided them with all the support he could in their expeditions further to the interior and to Segou.[56] In return for this cooperation, Aguibou was showered with gifts by France.[57] He, in return, furnished porters, guides, and laborers for the French forts and railways. After the conquest of Macina in 1893 by French forces, Archinard appointed Aguibou the ruler of this new French acquisition. This was Archinard's method of relegating the veteran Tokolor ruler to a position of powerlessness [58] from which he could never pose any threat to French authority. He was retired on pension in 1902.[59]

Banchande, king of Gurma, claimed to be the twenty-third successor of Diaba Lompo, the founder of the throne at Fada N'Gurma.[60] In the 1890s his right to the throne was challenged by the chiefs of Pama and Matiacuali. The Germans under von Carnap and Lieutenant

53. François Deloncle was one of the ardent imperialists of the "Group Coloniale" in the Chamber of Deputies. He disapproved of colonial expeditions. *Journal Officiel Chambre des Deputés: Débats Parlementaires,* April 8, 1892, p. 500.

54. Quinquandon to Archinard, February 28, 1893, quoted by Meniaud, *Sikasso,* p. 29.

55. Hanotaux and Martineau, *Histoire, 4,* 181.

56. ANSOM, Sénégal IV/91/b. Flourens to Krantz, September 22, 1887. The treaty with Aguibu was concluded on March 12, 1887.

57. Ibid., Sénégal IV/88/e. Cadeaux pour Aguibou. Rapport au Sous-Secretaire d'Etat par J. Haussmann, September 8, 1887.

58. Commandant Chailieu, "Archinard le Soudanais," in *Encyclopédie Mensuelle d'Outre-Mer, 1,* fasc. 19 (March, 1952), 79–81.

59. J. S. Trimmingham, *Islam in West Africa* (Oxford, 1962), p. 208.

60. See Davy, *Histoire du Pays Gourmantche* (Paris, 1952). Manuscript in Centre des Hautes Etudes d'Administration Musulmane, Paris.

Thierry lent their support to these dissident chiefs in the civil war that raged in Gurma from 1894 to 1897.[61] Banchande found a ready ally in the French under captains Baud and Vermeersch.[62] Within a short time after meeting the French officers, Banchande concluded a treaty of protection and friendship with them. Subsequent military aid from the French forces enabled him to defeat his rivals and secure his throne. He reigned as a French protégé from 1892 to 1911.[63] In return for French protection, Banchande provided carriers for French expeditions, provision for the columns that operated from Gurma to Say, and labor for the building of French military and administrative posts in his kingdom.[64]

On the Slave Coast, the French found an ally in King Toffa of Porto-Novo. Toffa's coronation and installation as king of Proto-Novo in 1874 changed the course of European enterprise in his unpretentious kingdom. He reversed the pro-British policy of his predecessor, King De Mikpon, by ratifying the treaty of protectorate signed by King De Sodji and French agents in 1863. Toffa was faced with hostility from both Britain and Dahomey. He therefore needed the prop provided him by his subservience to the French. Before 1883 Toffa enjoyed good relations with King Glegle of Dahomey, who even aided Toffa against his adversaries.[65] But when Toffa brought off the establishment of French authority in Porto-Novo in 1883 and thereby threatened Cotonou, Glegle took offense. From then on relations between the two monarchs were strained.

A chain of unpleasant events followed, aggravated by what Toffa called the arrogance of Prince Kondo, who was Glegle's favorite son and heir apparent.[66] Glegle declared war on Porto-Novo in March 1889. The involvement of Toffa in this unequal contest against the

61. On the political crisis in Gurma in the 1890s, see B. I. Obichere, *West African States and European Expansion: The Dahomey-Niger Hinterland, 1885–1898* (New Haven, 1971), Chap. 6.

62. ANSOM, Dahomey III/4/d. Rapport Baud, June 21, 1895. See Vermeersch, *Historique de la Mission Baud-Vermeersch: Le Dahomey, 1894–1895* (Paris, 1897).

63. R. Cornevin, *Histoire des Peuples de l'Afrique Noire* (Paris, 1963), pp. 308–11.

64. Jules Molex, "Le Gurma," in *Journal Officiel du Dahomey et Dépendances* (August 1, 1898), pp. 8–10. Von Carnap-Quernheimb, "Bericht uber den Marsch von Sansane-Mangu nach Pama und Gurma," in *Deutsche Kolonialzeitung* (June 22, 1895), pp. 195–97.

65. A. Akindele and C. Aguessy, *Contribution a l'Etude de l'Histoire de l'Ancien Royaume de Porto Novo* (Dakar, 1953), pp. 81–84, 106–08.

66. Akindele and Aguessy, *Le Dahomey*, pp. 26–29. Prince Kondo succeeded Glegle under the name of Behanzin.

military machine of Dahomey drew France into the vortex of local African politics. In the effort to protect their ally and his territory, France entered into a costly war with Dahomey from 1890 to 1894.[67]

All through the French war with Dahomey, Toffa cooperated with the agents of France. He provided auxiliaries for the French forces and procured spies and informants for them.[68] After the war when French expeditions into the interior followed in quick succession, Toffa collaborated with Governor Victor Ballot in recruiting porters and *hamacaires* for these expeditions.[69] Since Toffa was maintained in power by the French, he executed the orders of the governors of Dahomey without question. He remained faithful to France. He stayed within the limits prescribed to him and acquiesced in the gradual but steady loss of his political authority. When he died in 1908 he was succeeded by one of his sons who was given the title of "Chef Supérieur" and an annual pension of 25,000 francs.[70]

A striking illustration of African cooperation with French officials could be seen in the career of Mademba M'Baye Sy, alias Bougari Sega Demba Gnouman. The meteoric rise of Mademba Sy from the Ecole des Otages [71] in Saint-Louis and the rank of a postal clerk to the kingship of Sansanding was in the main the result of his submissiveness and his collaboration with the French.

Mademba Sy became a postal clerk in February 1869 as a *commis auxiliare.*[72] From this point till his death, he "served France with the greatest devotion and with unshakable loyalty," according to his son Abdel Kader Mademba. He earned the confidence of Faidherbe

67. R. Cornevin, "Les divers episodes de la lutte contre le royaume d'Abomey, 1887–1894," in *Rev. Fr. d'Histoire d'Outre-Mer,* 47 (1960), 161–212. MAE Afrique 126, Bayol to Etienne, January 11, 1890. Archives de la Marine BB4/1989, Cuverville to Marine, July 3, 1890, No. 63. ACM. BB4/1992. Rapport Dodds.

68. ANSOM, Dahomey V/2/a. "Journal de Marche de la Colonne Expeditionnaire: Campagne de 1890," par Lieutenant Colonel Terrillon. MAE Afrique 126. Governor of Senegal to Etienne, March 4, 1890, end. Terrillon to Governor of Senegal, March 4, 1890.

69. Archives Nationales, MI/214 "Journal du Dr. Alfred Bartet." See Captain Toutee, *Dahome Niger Touareg* (Paris, 1895), pp. 60–71.

70. Jean Suret-Canale, *Afrique Noire, l'ère coloniale, 1900–1945* (Paris, 1964), p. 100. Akindele and Aguessy, *Le Dahomey,* p. 31.

71. The Ecole des Otages in Saint-Louis was established by Faidherbe in 1855. Several schools of this type were established later on in French Sudan. See Denise Bouche, "Les Ecoles françaises au Soudan à l'Epoque de la conquête, 1884—1900," in *Cahiers d'Etudes Africaines, 6,* No. 22 (1966), 228–67.

72. Abdel Kader Mademba, *Au Sénégal et au Soudan Français,* pp. 8–14. Faidherbe, *Le Senegal: la France dans l'Afrique Occidentale* (Paris, 1889), pp. 258–76.

through the selfless service he rendered to the French during the expeditions against Lat Dior Ngone-Latir Diop, the damel of Kayor, from 1862 to 1882.[73]

Mademba's influence with the French waxed with the passage of time, and his prestige grew among the Africans in the service of France. He aided the agents of French expansion in the Sudan to the best of his ability. General Borgnis-Desbordes spoke very highly of him and advised his successors to seek out and rely on Francophiles like Mademba.

> L'exemple de M. Mademba est encouragement pour ceux qui veulent sérieusement s'appuyer sur l'élément indigène. Très devoué a son metier qu'il connait très bien, energique, très courageux bien élevé, instruit et modeste, ayant beaucoup d'autorité sur son personnel, sachant se servir des chefs des villages et obtenir d'eux ce dont il a besoin, M. Mademba m'a rendu, pendant les campagnes 1880–1881, 1881–1882, 1882–1883, les plus grands services. Il a dirigé effectivement, et avec plein succès, la construction de la ligne telegraphique qui va de Bafoulabe au Niger (427 km) et cela, dans les conditions les plus difficiles peut-être qui aient jamais été realisées.[74]

The unflinching support that Mademba Sy gave to the French was rewarded not only by rapid advancement in the civil service but also by elevation to the rank of a king. He was made the *fama* of Sansanding, a position specially created for him.[75] The installation ceremonies were held on March 15, 1891.[76] They were a strange admixture of the traditional rites, including the all-important sacrifice of a white sheep, with bizarre European usages such as the reading of an address declaring Sansanding a French city, declaring the obligations of the local population, and displaying the French letter of investiture as

73. General Faidherbe, "Notice historique sur le Cayor," in *Bulletin de la Société de Géographie de Paris, 4,* 527—64. El Hadj Assane Marokhaya, *Essai sur l'histoire du Cayor,* trans. from the Wolof by Samba Fall Samb (Dakar, 1963).

74. See Colonel Borgnis-Desbordes, *La France dans l'Afrique Occidentale Française* (Paris, 1884).

75. ANSOM, Soudan I/1/a. Archinard to Etienne, January 9, 1891. Jacques Meniaud, *Les Pionniers du Soudan,* (2 vols. Paris, 1931), 2, 79–82. "Instructions à M. le Commandant du cercle de Nioro" by Archinard in J. Meniaud, *Les Pionniers du Soudan, 2,* 58.

76. Archinard to Fama Mademba, March 7, 1891. Letter of Investiture in Meniaud, *Les Pionniers du Soudan, 2,* 117–20. See *Journal Officiel,* October 17, 1891, p. 4998.

the legitimizing factor of the new kingship. But to the Bambara, neither the superficial motion through the traditional rites nor the meaningless piece of paper brandished by Mademba was acceptable as the legitimization of his authority. In October 1891, the chiefs of Sokolo and Kolodougou barred Mademba's entry into their territory and revolted with their subjects against France and Mademba.[77] Sansanding was besieged for eight months before the Bambara were forced to retreat by French firepower.[78] Mademba hurdled over this first barrier to his new authority with French military aid. In like manner he was maintained in power by the French until he died of pulmonary congestion on July 25, 1918.[79]

These examples of African cooperation with the French show that both sides had interests which, most of the time, compelled them to work together. For instance, Archinard reported to Etienne in January 1891 that carving out three "kingdoms" in the Upper Niger was not merely putting into practice the textbook imperial theory of divide and rule. He contended that this would serve French interests best while installing powerful and devoted Africans as rulers:

> Avec ces trois royaumes: le Ségou rive droite, le Ségou rive gauche et celui de Tiéba, nour pouvons être maîtres de la situation sans établir d'autres postes que le residence de Ségou, rien ne pourra entraver notre action vers le Nord et l'Est.[80]

The French derived much needed support and supplies from the chiefs and people who cooperated with them. Provision for the French forces, horses, cattle and milk cows, sheep and beasts of burden were not only furnished but driven from place to place by those who furnished them.[81] In addition to these, mention must be made of the ubiquitous porters who were the veritable cement that bound together the various stages of French expansion. These porters not only

77. "Rapport sur la campagne de 1890–1891 au Soudan Français" by Archinard in *Journal Officiel,* October 10–20, 1891.

78. Commandant Bonnier, *Mission au pays de Ségou* (*Soudan Français*). *Campagne dans le Gueniè Kalary et le Sansanding en 1892* (Paris, 1897).

79. Abdel Kader Mademba, *Au Sénégal et au Soudan Français,* pp. 74–114.

80. ANSOM, Soudan I/1/a. Archinard to Etienne, January 9, 1891.

81. Detailed reports of the abundance of these animals in the Upper Niger, especially in the Ségou kingdom, were on file in both Paris and Saint-Louis. Archives du Sénégal, Dakar [henceforth ASD]. Governor Valière to MMC, July 20, 1874. 2 B/73 This detailed report relays information furnished by Ali Oumar, a notable from Ségou who visited Saint-Louis.

carried the necessary provisions, guns, powder, and cartridges, but also the French officers in hammocks.[82] It is in this regard that the masses appear more important than the few chiefs or French-created kings. One must not lose sight of the guides whose role was indispensable to foreigners in an unknown and strange country, where cartography was nonexistent and where regular astronomical observations were not always possible. If the chiefs and headmen of villages had refused to provide guides and porters for expeditions, and if the masses had not been coerced, the Africans would have thrown a real monkey wrench into the wheels of the progress of French penetration into the hinterland.

The forced recruitment of porters was one of the causes of African resistance to French, and for that matter European, expansion into the interior of Africa. Some porters never returned home.[83] They either died on the tedious journey or settled in a new distant community because they were too weak to return or afraid of a return journey for fear of being captured and sold as slaves.[84] In many cases, French officers encouraged this relocation of a part of the population by furnishing the male porters with wives from sacked and burned villages.[85] Furthermore, there were the villages of liberated slaves created by the French. These settlements became veritable reservoirs of manpower for French officials. Their inhabitants earned the pejorative epithet of "white man's slaves" among the local population.[86]

Most important in the contribution of the masses to French expansion was the military force of *tirailleurs*. The sharpshooters were indeed the business end of the chisel with which France carved out her West African empire. They were tough and rugged and, as General Mangin aptly put it, they gave France her West African colonies.[87] The first corps of Senegalese tirailleurs was formed in 1823 and was

82. AN MI/214 Journal du Dr. Alfred Bartet, 1897–98. AN 66/AP Papiers du Colonel Monteil Vol. 4.

83. H. R. Rudin, *Germans in the Cameroons, 1884–1914* (New Haven, 1938), p. 309. The Europeans were regarded in most places as awesome "messengers of death." Frey, *Campagne,* pp. 17–18.

84. There were many flourishing slave markets in the Niger basin by 1895, such as Bakel. ASD K25 Rapport de mission sur l'Esclavage en Afrique Occidentale Française par Deherme.

85. Paul Vigne d'Octon, *Au Pays des Fétiches* (Paris, 1890), pp. 70–76.

86. Robert Cuvillier-Fleury, *La Main-d'œuvre dans les colonies françaises de l'Afrique occidentale et du Congo* (Paris, 1907). Denise Bouche, "Les villages de Liberté en A.O.F.," in *Bulletin de l'I.F.A.N., 11,* No. 3–4 (1949), 491–540; *12,* No. 1 (1950), 135–215.

87. See note 1 above.

reconstituted into a battalion in 1857 by General Faidherbe. The tirailleurs were indispensable to the French in the campaigns against El Hadj Omar, in Kayor, Oualo, and in the Wolof territories.[88] The Senegalese tirailleurs were formed into a regiment in 1884 but were reorganized in June 1889 to meet the ever growing French involvement in the scramble for territory in West Africa. Among the main aims of the 1889 reorganization stated by Admiral Krantz, the minister of the navy, were "la création du'une 10ᵉ compagnie destinée à tenir garnison à Porto-Novo" and "l'augmentation du nombre des armuriers" to keep pace with the astronomic growth of French firepower in West Africa.[89]

In addition to the Senegalese tirailleurs, a corps of "tirailleurs haoussas" was established by a decree of June 23, 1891, for service in Dahomey. This corps was augmented and reorganized rather rapidly in response to the exigencies of the Franco-Dahomey wars. By June 1895 a battalion of Hausa tirailleurs was created "en vue de l'expedition de Madagascar." [90] The numbers of Africans in French military service continued to grow to meet the requirements of several expeditions and the enforcement of "the much-hated system known as the *indigénat,*" [91] which was established in West Africa by a decree of September 30, 1887. This repressive ordinance was not modified till November 21, 1904.[92]

Alongside the Senegalese and Hausa tirailleurs, the French created several units of spahis for action in the Sudan.[93] Senegalese were recruited for the navy to fill positions as cabinboys and mechanics and laptots.[94] The result of the recruiting and training program of France

88. A. Villard, *Histoire du Sénégal* (Dakar, 1943), pp. 137–70. ASD 1D/34 "Rapport de colonne du Cayor, janvier–février 1875" par Lieutenant-Colonel Begin. Lt. Col. Begin to Gov. Valière, February 11, 1875 (Tel.).

89. ANSOM, *Bulletin Official du Ministère de la Marine et des Colonies* [*B.O. Colonies* hereafter] (1889), pp. 726–48. *B.O. Colonies* (1895), p. 811. The date of 1887 given by Dimitrou in *Le Sénégal* (1967) is incorrect.

90. ANSOM, *B.O. Colonies* (1891), pp. 457–60. Ibid. (1895), pp. 90–93, 274–75.

91. Hargreaves, *West Africa: The Former French States,* p. 137.

92. G. François, *Le Gouvernement Général de l'Afrique Occidentale Française,* Exposition Franco-Britannique de Londres, 1908, pp. 28–29. See R. Ruyssen, *Le Code de l'indigénat en Algérie* (Alger, 1908).

93. Y. de Boisboissel, "Origine et historique sommaire des unites des tirailleurs et spahis sénégalais et soudanais," *Revue Internationale d'Histoire Militaire* (Dakar, 1956). See also Lieutenant Gatelet, *Histoire de la Conquête du Soudan français* (Paris, 1901).

94. ANSOM, *B.O. Colonies* (1891), pp. 455–56, "Décret du 25 août 1886 portant reorganisation des marins indigène du Sénégal" and "Decision Presidentielle modifiant l'article 10" of this decree, June 19, 1891.

was that she had the most formidable military force in West Africa during the peak of the scramble for territory by Europeans and Africans. The possession of this force led to the pyrrhic victory over African empire builders like Ahmadu of Ségou, Samori Touré, and King Behanzin of Dahomey. Britain was compelled to create a West African Frontier Force in 1897 in response to the military preponderance of France in West Africa.[95]

The French found among the African masses excellent material for their civil service. Just as they transformed rustic *talibés* and *sofas* into deadly sharpshooters, so they produced excellent interpreters, clerks, telegraph technicians, and artisans from their many schools. Famous among these were the Ecole des Otages and the Ecole d'apprentissage de Kayes, which opened on August 4, 1896, and another similar school at Koulikoro on January 1, 1897.[96] It was observed by French agents that the Wolofs enrolled mainly in the tirailleur corps whereas the Sarakole usually opted for the clerical and technical posts.[97] French missionaries increased the number of educated Africans by their teaching. They thus made available to the administrative and military agents a sizable eduated labor force. However, it should be noted that French missionaries were extremely slow in developing a native clergy. This might have been due to the Cham theory that influenced most of them.[98] More especially, official French policy must be taken into account in any consideration of the rather slow development of native clergy in this period. Anticlericalism was a trademark of the Third Republic.[99]

West Africa was by no means a bed of roses for the French. Their imperial enterprise there evoked stiff resistance from the original inhabitants and rulers of the land. The intensity of the resistance differed from place to place. Its organization and planning were not

95. PRO CO879/48, War Office to Colonial Office, May 8, 1897; Goldie to Chamberlain, May 28, 1897; Chamberlain to Goldie, July 1, 1897. University of Birmingham Library, Joseph Chamberlain papers, J.C. 11/6 Chamberlain to Salisbury, June 6, 1897. Chamberlain to Selbourne, September 29, 1897. CO875/51, *West African Frontier Force: Papers, July 23, 1897 to March 24, 1898.*

96. G. Deherme, *L'Afrique Occidentale Française: Action politique, économique et sociale* (Paris, 1908), p. 121. D. Bouche, "Les Ecoles françaises au Soudan," pp. 228–67.

97. Frey, *Campagne*, pp. 237–38.

98. Pierre Bouche, *La Côte des Esclaves et le Dahomey* (Paris, 1885). Abbé J. Lafitte, *Le Dahomey: Souvenir de Voyage et de Mission,* 5th ed. (Tours, 1880), p. 180.

99. Jean-Marie Sedes, *Le Clergé indigène de l'Empire Français* (2 vols. Paris, 1944). R. P. Joseph Bouchaud, *L'Eglise en Afrique Noire* (Paris, 1958).

uniform. Local circumstances played an important part in shaping the nature and intensity of the resistance wherever the French went in West Africa.

Theoretically, the nature of resistance in race relations comprises open opposition and repugnance. Opposition expresses itself in war, revolt, riots, mob violence, and other overt expressions of belligerence and pugnacity individually or collectively. Opposition has been defined as "the hostile co-habitation in enmity of two peoples in one territory."[100] Repugnance prevails in the absence of opposition and could be perceived even in cases of toleration, symbiosis, and acculturation. The causes of resistance may be reduced into two categories, the material and the spiritual. The spiritual causes of resistance are rooted in the acts of the ruler as well as in those of the ruled. They involve a man's subjective consciousness of the social relations in his community and any perceptions of the objective conditions that underlie those social relations. The material causes of resistance comprise all physical, economic, and technological differences that may be present in any given cases of race relations.[101]

The general results of resistance arising from race contact are extermination, absorption, or independence.[102] It is in the light of these theoretical constructs that we will examine African resistance to French expansion.[103]

The practical aspects of the resistance against the French included wars, guerrilla wars, pitched battles, and ambushes. Desertions of tirailleurs from French forces and gunrunning by European traders were ingredients. The tirailleurs usually joined the *talibés* or the *sofas* against the French.[104] An examination of some cases of resistance will show the stages and the development of anti-French movements in various parts of West Africa. The most important leaders of resistance against the agents of French imperialism in West Africa were Ahmadu, sultan of Ségou, Samori Touré of Kankan, Babemba of Sikasso, King Behanzin of Dahomey, Morgho Naba Boukari Koutou of Mossi, Rabeh

100. René Maunier, *The Sociology of Colonies* (English translation, London, 1948), 2, 469–77. Michael Banton, *Race Relations* (New York, 1968), pp. 55–100.

101. Thomas F. Gossett, *Race: The History of an Idea in America* (New York, 1965), p. 36. W. E. B. DuBois, *Dusk of Dawn: An Essay Toward an Autobiography of a Race Concept* (New York, 1968), pp. 97–133. Banton, *Race Relations*, pp. 193 ff.

102. Maunier, *The Sociology of Colonies*, 2, 473–77.

103. Samuel H. Beer, "Causal Explanation and Imaginative Reenactment," *History and Theory*, 3, No. 1 (1963) [Symposium: Uses of Theory in the Study of History], 6–29.

104. Frey, *Campagne*, pp. 83–84.

of the Chad basin, King Agoliagbo of Abomey, and Mahmadu Lamine of Senegal.

The picture Captain E. Mage painted of the Tokolor Empire after his travels in Senegambia was not only unbalanced but blurred by both anti-Muslim prejudices and military ambition. He stated that the empire founded by El Hadj Omar was on the verge of disaster and would collapse in no time because its restless subject peoples, especially the Mandingo and the Bambara, were about to splinter away. The Mandingo, who were imbued with a fierce sentiment of nationalism, were resistant to Tokolor domination. The case of the Mandingos typified what Mage described as the general trend in the tottering Tokolor Empire.[105] Later, in 1880, Gallieni could not but confess to the high degree of order and organization that reigned in the Tokolor Empire, especially in the vicinity of the district of Ségou. However, Gallieni also stated that Ahmadu's empire was in complete decadence and that the sultan was at loggerheads with his brothers.[106] The anti-Muslim prejudices of E. Mage were also shared by Gallieni who, as already reported, maintained that Islam was the worst enemy of France's work of penetrating into the heart of Africa.[107]

Joseph S. Gallieni began chipping away bits of territory from the Tokolor Empire in 1878 by taking Logo, Natiaga, and Saboucire. Bafoulabe came under French control the next year, and in January 1880 Gallieni led a mission into the Sudan with Ségou as its destination. This mission was ambushed at Dio and suffered serious losses. Ahmadu would not suffer the mission to come to Ségou. He caused the French to be detained at Nango, about twenty miles away from Ségou, where they were under close surveillance.[108] Gallieni had decided to ally with Ahmadu as an expedient. At the same time he was not to give up his support for the Mandingo and Bambara malcontents who were opposed to Tokolor domination.[109]

In any case, Ahmadu was not to be easily deceived. His lack of con-

105. See E. Mage, *Voyage dans le Soudan Occidentale.* L. Faidherbe, "Voyage de MM. Mage et Quintin: Progrès des Peuls," in *Nouv. Ann. des Voyages, 4,* No. 5.

106. Gallieni, *Voyage au Soudan Français,* pp. 615–16.

107. Ibid., pp. 616–18.

108. Hanotaux and Martineau, *Histoire, 4,* Afrique Occidentale, 175. G. Grandidier, *Galliéni,* pp. 39–73. Grandidier reproduces on these pages several letters which Gallieni wrote to Ahmadu from Nango. Gallieni, *Voyage,* pp. 370–407. Gallieni refers to his stay at Nango as a "long captivity," p. 502.

109. Gallieni, *Voyage,* p. 620. C. Pietri, *Les Français au Niger: Voyages et Combats* (Paris, 1885), p. 208.

fidence in the French seemed to have grown steadily since his encounter with Captain Mage, to whom he definitely stated that he would not allow French forts to be constructed in his dominion. He was therefore not in a hurry to enter into further negotiations with French officials. Gallieni and his entourage stayed at Nango for four months before Ahmadu dispatched his shrewd diplomat, Seidou Dieylia,[110] to open negotiations with them. Skillfully and firmly Seidou Dieylia pressed for the fulfillment of the obligations which the French undertook in the treaty concluded by Captain Mage. The French had not only failed to deliver the mountain guns to Ahmadu, but had also encroached on his territory in the Madingo region. Gallieni's demands that Ahmadu should accept French protection was unacceptable to the Tokolor diplomats. They would rather enter into friendly relations with France, since this would enhance Ahmadu's authority and even facilitate the expansion of his empire.[111]

France would benefit, on the other hand, from the expansion of Tokolor influence. "We shall open the road for you everywhere; you may follow us and profit from our efforts," Seidou Dieylia confidently announced to Gallieni.[112] Ahmadu would allow the construction of railways and forts as well as the free navigation of the Niger on the condition that the French were prepared for a quid pro quo. He demanded an annual pension of 25,000 francs, part of which was to be paid in kind by 200 flintlocks. Any resident that France might appoint to Ségou should be a Muslim African. Furthermore, the concession to France for railways and free navigation of the Niger, roads and *comptoirs,* was to be reciprocated by delivering one thousand flintlocks and four mountain guns to Ahmadu.[113]

While this hard bargaining was going on, Colonel Borgnis-Desbordes was given command of the new military district of the Upper Senegal. His arrival in the area quickened the release of Gallieni from Nango, where he had succeeded in concluding a treaty with Ahmadu.[114] Colonel Borgnis-Desbordes was a cantankerous and fastidious soldier. He was "a forthright and stubborn artillery man, whose professional

110. John D. Hargreaves, *Prelude to the Partition of West Africa* (London, 1963), pp. 260–62.

111. Gallieni, *Voyage,* p. 404.

112. Hargreaves, *Prelude,* p. 262.

113. Gallieni, *Voyage,* pp. 398–407. Negotiations with Seidou Dieylia: four sessions from October 31 to November 3, 1880.

114. The disparity that exists between the French text and the Arabic text of the Treaty of Nango has been pointed out by Hargreaves, *Prelude,* pp. 262 ff. Gallieni, *Voyage,* pp. 459–62.

instinct was to strike directly for the objective."[115] He differed with Gallieni and Governor Brière de L'Isle on the policy of alliance with Ahmadu. He attacked Colonel Frey for mismanagement in the Sudan. Orders from Paris and Saint-Louis stipulating that he should avoid armed conflict with the Tokolors drew his strong objections.[116] Borgnis-Desbordes ridiculed Gallieni's initial efforts in the Upper Senegal and derided his indecision.[117] Such a rugged character, who could neither agree with his own colleagues nor with his superiors, could not be expected to temporize with Ahmadu or to reach a peaceful settlement with him.

Colonel Borgnis-Desbordes attacked Goubanko, which was in Tokolor territory. He reasoned that the raids carried out by the people of Goubanko on the surrounding region were a threat to the security of Kita. Therefore, a preventive raid on Goubanko was justified.[118] This incursion into Tokolor territory so soon after the Treaty of Nango drew vehement protests from Ahmadu, whose distrust of the French continued to intensify.[119] It must be remarked that Brière de L'Isle was in favor of a policy of alliance with Ahmadu. He wanted the French government to fulfill the terms of the Treaty of Nango.[120] Unfortunately for Ahmadu, his official supporter was soon removed from office, and he had to contend with the hostile Borgnis-Desbordes unaided from the French side.

As a reprisal for the incursions of French troops into his dominion, Ahmadu decreed that none of his subjects should trade with them. Death was the penalty for those who would sell foodstuffs or supply workers or porters to the French.[121] Internal strife was on the increase in the Tokolor Empire, and Ahmadu's relations with his brothers who ruled different provinces of his empire were deteriorating rapidly. But he was in complete control in the central district of Ségou.

The news of the decision of the French to introduce the gunboat

115. Hargreaves, *Prelude,* p. 262.

116. A. S. Kanya-Fostner, "The Role of the Military and the Formulation of French Policy towards the western Sudan, 1879–1899" (Cambridge, Ph.D. thesis, 1965).

117. ANSOM, Sénégal IV/73/bis. Desbordes to Governor of Senegal, April 1, 1881, quoted by Hargreaves.

118. Ibid. Desbordes to Brière de L'Isle, February 20, 1881.

119. Ibid. Sénégal IV/73/c. Ahmadu to Governor of Senegal (received May 12, 1881).

120. Hargreaves, *Prelude,* p. 263. ANSOM, Sénégal IV/73/b. Brière de L'Isle to MMC, May 4, 1881.

121. ANSOM, Sénégal I/66/b. Canard to MMC, May 23, 1881.

Niger[122] to the river Niger in 1884 disquietened Ahmadu. Moreover, this French move came in the wake of the exchange of unfriendly letters between Ahmadu's brother and ruler of the Kaarta region, Mountaga, and the French officials. The sultan decided to leave Ségou because of its high vulnerability in case of bombardment from the river.[123] He appointed his son Madani[124] to be governor of Ségou and left for Nioro, a more sheltered headquarters. His journey would take him through Nyamina and across Beledugu and into Kaarta.

Colonel Frey replaced Borgnis-Desbordes as commandant of the Upper Senegal and Upper Niger in 1885. In November 1885 French troops dispersed the garrison which Ahmadu installed at Nyamina and concluded a treaty there.[125] This irritated Ahmadu and forced him to intensify his economic sanctions against the French. All caravan routes were closed to the Moors who continued to do business with the bothersome French. The sale of food to the French was forbidden. To keep the Nioro road under his control, he raised a force of 10,000 persons to guard it.[126] Ahmadu then announced retaliatory measures against the French, included among which were the various economic sanctions by which he intended to debilitate the effectives of France. This marks the commencement of the period of open hostility between both sides, and Ahmadu's vendetta with France had taken a turn for the worse.

> Don't forget that you have disrupted my states without authorization, without any rights, and in default of treaties which bind us together. I will reclaim, all my life, the possession of the very lands on which you have erected your forts.[127]

Ahmadu then proceeded to attain Nioro. He summoned his brother Mountaga, governor of Nioro, to his camp at Bassaka in the Bakounou country for a conference. Mountaga was accorded an amicable and fraternal welcome by Ahmadu, who had assured him of safe conduct

122. Ibid. Sénégal IV/82/a. Rapport Combes, 1884–85, Chap. 8: "Le Voyage du Niger."

123. ANSOM, *Conseil Supérieur des Colonies.* Generalité 1 bis: Séances 1883–97. Felix Faure, *Discours à l'ouverture de la Session du Conseil Supérieur des Colonies, 11 Fevrier 1885* (Paris, 1885), p. 3.

124. Madani was the favorite son of Ahmadu, not his brother as was wrongly stated by Oliver, *The French Soudan*, p. 8.

125. Frey, *Campagne*, p. 103. Hanotaux and Martineau, *Histoire, 4*, 180.

126. Frey, *Campagne*, pp. 105–06.

127. Ahmadu to Gallieni quoted by Frey, *Campagne*, pp. 20–21.

at the time of his invitation.[128] After discovering that Ahmadu's intention was to install himself at Nioro, Mountaga made a successful nocturnal flight from Bassaka and returned to Nioro. Ahmadu continued his journey to Nioro via Touroungoumbe and Yerere. He insistently sent messengers to Nioro to ask Mountaga to submit to his authority and to correspond with his plans. These overtures were not successful. It is not an easy thing to relinquish political and religious power when one has exercised them for several years, especially as an absolute despot. Therefore, after four months of unfruitful negotiations, Ahmadu decided to take Nioro by storm. He ordered his men to march against and besiege the city. They cut Nioro off from all its food and water supplies. After some resistance, famine constrained most of Mountaga's followers to surrender. When Nioro fell, Mountaga committed suicide rather than be captured alive by his brother's forces.[129]

Ahmadu had to stamp his authority on the Nioro district. Swift punishment was meted out to those who had cooperated with Mountaga in his resistance against Ahmadu. Mahmadou Kaya, the ringleader of an unsuccessful plot among Ahmadu's followers, was executed when the sultan learned that he had collaborated with Mountaga. Furthermore, Falibou, chief of the Fulani of Sambourou who revolted against Ahmadu, was executed by Boubakar Samba, one of Ahmadu's strong men.[130]

Franco-Tokolor relations continued to deteriorate rapidly. The governor of Senegal had counseled the authorities in Paris toward the end of 1883 that the best tactics to use against Ahmadu were to aggravate his internal difficulties while maintaining courteous external relations with him.[131] Thus Biolève was advised to incite the Bambara of Beledugu against Ahmadu during his march through the area on his way to Nioro.[132] On the other hand, Delanneau's treaty with Nyamina in October 1885 was rejected by Paris in order to appease Ahmadu and

128. This is evidence for the strained relations that existed between Ahmadu and his brothers.

129. Delafosse, *Haut-Sénégal-Niger*, 2, 333.

130. Frey, *Campagne*, pp. 99–102.

131. ANSOM, Sénégal I/70/b. Governor of Senegal to MMC, November 5, 1883.

132. ANSOM, Sénégal I/71/c. Sous-Secrétaire des Colonies to Bordiaux April 19, 1884. Ibid. Sénégal IV/82/a. "Note pour le Sous-Secrétaire d'Etat à la Marine par Col. Borgnis-Desbordes, January 2, 1884. Projet de voyage de Bamako à Tombouctou: Instructions concernant le Voyage à faire entreprendre par le chaloupe à vapeur."

to prepare the way for an alliance with the sultan against the redoutable Samori.[133]

The transfer of the seat of the Tokolor Empire from Ségou to Nioro by Ahmadu was undoubtedly a tactical move by the strongwilled sultan. Why did Ahmadu decide to adopt this line of action which he knew would embroil him in a serious dispute with Mountaga and exacerbate his already deplorable relations with his brothers? The explanation that Ahmadu moved his seat because of his unpopularity in Ségou is not satisfactory.[134] That the authority of his son and deputy Madani was never questioned in Ségou until the French defeated him on April 6, 1890 shows that the question of Tokolor unpopularity in Ségou is a baseless conjecture. It had been said that Ahmadu moved to Nioro to facilitate his control of the turbulent and recalcitrant Bambara in Beledugu.[135] There is no doubt that the sultan was disquietened by the news that the gunboat *Niger* was on the Niger River.[136] He protested vehemently against that move and described Combes as "an oppressor and an evil-doer."[137] The vulnerability of Ségou to shelling from a gunboat must have been very clear to Ahmadu. Since his distrust of the French was boundless at that time, he must have decided to transfer his seat to Nioro for strategic reasons.[138] Finally, Ahmadu did not wish to be succeeded by any of his brothers.[139] His move to Nioro furthered his plans of appointing his son Madani as his ultimate successor.

In order that Ahmadu's authority could be established at Nioro, Mountaga had to be vanquished. Ahmadu's relatives did not approve of his fratricidal campaign against Mountaga. Three of them, Daah, Alibou, and Bassirou, came out openly against him. Each in turn was defeated and died a victim of the very fratricidal forces they vehemently opposed. Disapproval of Ahmadu's policy also came from Macina where Tidjani, incensed by Ahmadu's proceedings, promised

133. ANSOM, Sénégal I/73/b. MMC to Governor of Senegal, November 4, 1885. ANSOM, Sénégal IV/84/a. MMC to Frey, *Instructions,* October 4, 1885.

134. Delafosse, *Haut-Sénégal-Niger,* 2, 331–32.

135. Frey, *Campagne,* pp. 98–99.

136. Requin, "Cannonnière sur le Niger" in *Tropiques* No. 381 (February, 1956), pp. 3–11.

137. ANSOM, Sénégal IV/82/a. *Rapport Combes . . . 1884–1885,* Chap. 8. General Duboc, *L'Epopée Coloniale,* p. 123.

138. G. Valbert, "Le Sultan Ahmadou et le campagne du Colonel Archinard dans le Soudan Francais" in *Revue de Deux Mondes, 102* (December 1, 1890), 678. Sénégal IV/82/a. *Rapport Delanneau: Rapport Complémentaire: Pièce No. 5.*

139. Frey, *Campagne,* p. 102.

to send reinforcements and supplies to Mountaga to help him in his resistance to Ahmadu. Unfortunately, Tidjani's promise was never fulfilled.[140]

These internecine dissensions constrained Ahmadu to temporize with the French. He cooperated with them in their struggle with Mahmadu Lamine because the defeat of Lamine was in his own interests.[141] Ahmadu concluded the Treaty of Gouri with France on May 12, 1887, by which a segment of his empire was placed under French protection. Even after this treaty Ahmadu did not alter his hostile attitude toward the French, however. Under his orders, the Tokolors of Ségou refused to deal with the French in any way. The ban on trade with French agents was not lifted after the Treaty of Gouri. French supplies were badly cut off at Ségou because Madani was cooperating actively with his father. When French officials complained to him, he replied that "il se moquait des Français comme de moustiques bourdonnant à ses oreilles."[142]

Ahmadu's search for a strong base from which to mount an assault on the French led him to seek an alliance with Samori. In one of his letters to Samori intercepted by Archinard he expounded the basis of his anti-French policy:

> C'est Dieu qui t'a donné l'idée de faire alliance avec moi . . . Les blancs veulent chasses tous les indigènes du pays. Il faut les tromper d'abord et dire que tu es leur ami. Celui qui ne sait pas tromper son ennemi est indigne de commander.[143]

Ahmadu was using, then, identical weapons with the French. Both were committed to a double-edged policy. The policy of France was not understandable among the Bambara as Captain Ruault reported after his fact-finding mission in Beledugu.[144] On the whole, Franco-Tokolor relations continued to deteriorate rather rapidly. Ahmadu rejected Archinard's offer to negotiate about frontiers early in 1890. The French occupied his territories, and he would not negotiate with

140. Ibid., pp. 99–103.

141. Duboc, *L'Epopée,* p. 123.

142. Valbert, "Le Sultan Ahmadou," p. 677. Letters seized from Ahmadu's messengers by French officials revealed that Ahmadu advised Madani on policy. He was to temporize with them until they could be defeated by the Tokolors. Archinard, "Rapport Militaire: Le Soudan Français en 1888–1889," in *Mem. de l'Artillerie de la Marine* (1890).

143. Valbert, "Le Sultan Ahmadou," p. 678.

144. Ibid., p. 679.

them because they were violating treaty engagements.[145] Archinard then decided to strike at Ségou in order to soften Ahmadu. Guided by envoys from Tiéba of Kénédugu, the French troops entered Ségou on April 6, 1890. Madani was not captured as Archinard had wished, however. He escaped and fled to Mopti.[146] Without loss of time the French expeditionary column headed for Nioro. Great difficulties had to be overcome by the column, which did not arrive in Nioro until January 1, 1891. Ahmadu had enough time to organize his men and move away from Nioro before the French expedition arrived there. His tactical gamble of 1884 had begun to pay dividends. He made his way to Macina despite the desperate efforts of the French to capture him.[147] Ahmadu continued to direct operations against the French from Macina. But since he had been reduced to a fugitive monarch, these operations did not have much effect. His resistance to the occupation of his empire by France was petering out painfully, and he knew it. His major concern then was not to be captured by French troops.

The showdown finally came during Colonel Archinard's second term of office as *commandant supérieur* of the Sudan, which began by the end of August 1892.[148] Hostilities were commenced against Ahmadu in Macina.[149] When he adjudged his position untenable in May 1893, he recommenced his retreat eastward to Hombori, Dori, Niamey, and Say. He always tried to reestablish himself, but the relentless hostility of French agents neutralized his haphazard efforts. As if by historical irony, Ahmadu finally retired into Sokoto, the place of his birth in 1833, where he died in 1898.[150]

Ma Lamine Demba Dibassi, who later was commonly known as Mahmadu Lamine, was born about 1840 at Goundiorou, a village in Khasso. His father was a marabout who taught the Koran and administered justice in the village. After a brief period of Koranic studies

145. Duboc, *L'Epopée,* p. 127.

146. Abdel Kader Mademba, *Au Sénégal et au Soudan Français,* pp. 40–41. Madani joined his father in Nioro and traveled via Vani, Mopti, Dia, and Sahel. Captain E. Peroz, "La tactique dans le Soudan: Quelques combats et épisodes de Guerre remarquables," in *Revue Maritime et Coloniale* (1890).

147. G. Hanotaux and A. Martineau, *Histoire des Colonies Françaises,* Vol. 4, *L'Afrique Occidentale Française* (Paris, 1934).

148. Commandant Chailieu, "Archinard le Soudanais," pp. 79–81.

149. Meniaud, *Les Pionniers du Soudan, 2,* 339.

150. Delafosse, *Haut-Sénégal-Niger, 2,* 306, 337. Yves Saint-Martin, "L'Artillerie d'El Hadj Omar et d'Ahmadou" in *Bull. IFAN, 27,* No. 3–4 (1965), 60–72.

under his father, Lamine was sent to Bakel to perfect his knowledge of Arabic. His adventurous spirit led him to participate in an expedition against Gamon during which he was captured, imprisoned, and punished. Like all other prisoners of war he was flogged several times. He never forgot it.[151]

Lamine grew in his knowledge of Islam and his devotion to his religion. After some time in the intensely religious Fouta,[152] he undertook a pilgrimage to Mecca. He spent seven years in Mecca deepening his knowledge of the Koran and of Islam. He was renowned for his piety and respected for his intelligence. "La persuasion de sa parole, son ardente foi, et la dignité de son attitude avaient déjà attiré sur lui l'attention et le respect de tous, lorsqu'il reprit le bâton de pèlerin pour retourner dans son village," observed Frey.[153] Several of the eleven African rulers with whom Lamine came into contact during his travels wished to retain his services, but he told them he must return to his home because Allah had assigned to him an important task which had to be carried out.

As it turned out, this messianic mission had for its chief aim the restoration of the political ascendancy of the Sarakoles over their neighbors. Lamine began his career by an appeal to the Sarakoles to unite so that they could resist foreign domination. The resurrection of the ancient Sarakole Empire of Ghana would be impossible unless the ruling foreigners were driven out. Therefore, both the Tokolors and the French were to be expelled. Lamine had already suffered the stings of Ahmadu's authority.[154] This worsened his distaste of Tokolor domination. "Les Sarakolais ont été assez humiliés, ont assez souffert de leurs maîtres. Il est temps qu'ils secouent le joug sous lequel ils sont courbés, et qu'ils reconquièrent leur indépendance," declared Mahmadu Lamine.[155]

In keeping with his policy, Lamine proffered his service to the French in their early incursions into Ahmadu's territory. But his growing influence deterred Colonel Frey from accepting this attractive offer.[156] Lamine then began his own wars of liberation and con-

151. Frey, *Campagne*, pp. 250 ff., on Lamine's biography.

152. Fouta Toro had produced many preachers and leaders including El Hadj Omar, Maba (1868), etc.

153. Frey, *Campagne*, p. 252.

154. Frey, *Campagne*, pp. 253–54. General Faidherbe, *Le Sénégal* (1889), pp. 420–21.

155. Frey, *Campagne*, p. 273.

156. ANSOM, Sénégal I/73/a. Governor of Senegal to MMC, December 12, 1885.

quest. The total success of his initial engagements enhanced his reputation as a prophet of liberation and spread farther the belief in his invincibility.[157] The death of Boubakar Saada, chief of Boundou on December 18, 1885, marked an entirely new phase of Lamine's policy. He forcibly removed Omar Penda, brother and successor of Boubakar Saada, and declared himself ruler of Boundou. Omar Penda had refused him permission to march through Boundou on his punitive expedition against Gamon.[158]

Omar Penda enlisted French support against Mahmadu Lamine. The latter then "enlarged the importance of his role and expanded the theatre of his operations." The professions of friendship with France which he had made to Frey in an interview in November, and to Houry at Bakel in early December 1885, were thrown overboard.[159]

> Il lui vint l'idée de mettre à profit cette surexcitation générale des esprits pour provoquer autour de lui une explosion de fantisme religieux, qui gagnerait successivement toutes les autres provinces de la Sénégambie et produirait une soulèvement générale *contre le domination étrangère.*[160]

First of all, Mahmadu Lamine, who had once claimed that he was the successor of El Hadj Omar, proclaimed himself the Mahdi of the West and whipped up more local support. He had around him by this time about 6,000 to 7,000 fighting men. Second, he proceeded with his plans of expelling the French. He cut telegraph lines, burned and sacked villages friendly to the French as object lessons to their neighbors, repelled Captain Joly's force, and besieged Bakel.[161] About this time it seemed that "l'ambition et l'audace de Mahmadou Lamine ne connurent plus de bornes." He organized an efficient chain of communication with all the Sarakole villages and communities. His messengers went into villages to warn them about the movements of the French, and to advise them on tactics to adopt. He bombarded them constantly with news of his successes, and assured them that "comme une vaine fumée dissipée par un vent d'orage, toutes les forces françaises s'etaient évanouies à [son] approche."[162]

157. Frey, *Campagne,* pp. 253–54.

158. Lamine had not forgiven the people of Gamon the cruel imprisonment he had suffered there in his youth, when he took part in an abortive attack on this rich town.

159. ANSOM, Sénégal IV/85/a. Rapport Frey, June 22, 1886.

160. Ibid., Frey, *Campagne,* p. 274. The emphasis is mine.

161. Frey to Governor of Senegal, February 2, 1886, and February 28, 1886. ANSOM, Sénégal IV/84/b.

162. Frey, *Campagne,* pp. 328–30, 386–87.

While Lamine was on the rampage, his village of Goundiourou was raided by the French forces led by Captain Ferrat and Lieutenant Rodot on March 13, 1886. His family was captured and taken to Médine. His favourite wife Mousso, who had accompanied him to Mecca, was among them. They were treated kindly.[163] So great was the respect and fear that the Sarakoles had for Lamine that the French could not secure guides to lead their forces to his village. Even those who were employed by the French remained loyal to him and acted as spies for him. They kept him well posted on French plans and movements. For instance, Alpha Sega, an interpreter at the French post of Bakel, collaborated with Lamine, his national hero. He furnished regular information to the Sarakole leader, enlisted false guides to lead the French columns astray from their Sarakole targets, and helped Lamine's war effort. When his double role was uncovered, Alpha Sega was shot in the public square in Bakel on April 6, 1886.[164]

Frey defeated the forces of Lamine at several battles.[165] But the defeat they suffered at Tambakano inflicted severe losses on them. There were also several desertions. These reduced appreciably the large following that Lamine had attracted. Lamine and his men retired into Diana near the Sierra Leone border.[166] This defeat did not crush his power. Gallioni had to continue the struggle with the Mahdi of the West[167] when he returned to the Sudan after his reappointment in October 1886 as Commandant Supérieur du Haut-Fleuve.[168] In the meantime Lamine had entrenched himself in the village of Toubakouta.[169] Gallieni sent a force against him under Captain Fortin. In December 1887 Toubakouta was stormed and sacked, but Lamine escaped. He was pursued and was finally defeated at Ngogo-Soukota. He was wounded in the thigh during the assault on his camp on December 9. Taken prisoner, he died on the way to Toubakouta on December 12, 1887. He was decapitated by a *griot*, and his head was taken to Captain Fortin to prove that he was dead! Thus ended the effort to resurrect the ancient Sarakole Empire.[170] By their victory over Mahmadu Lamine, the French acquired all the territory adjoining Gambia, and the Sarakole rebellion collapsed.

163. Ibid., pp. 283–84.
164. Ibid., p. 299.
165. Duboc, *Epopée*, pp. 114–15.
166. ANSOM, Sénégal IV/85/a. Frey, *Rapport*, June 22, 1886.
167. De la Porte to Governor of Senegal. *Instruction* (on French policy in the Sudan), October 20, 1886. ANSOM Sénégal IV/87/bis.
168. Duboc, *Epopée*, p. 115. Lt. Col. Frey left for France on July 7, 1886.
169. Galliéni had refused Lamine's offer to negotiate in July 1887.
170. Duboc, *Epopée*, p. 117. J. S. Gallieni, *Deux Campagnes*, pp. 19–37.

Samori Touré was born at Sanankoro near Bissandougou in (French) Guinea about 1835. His father, Lafia Touré, and his mother, Massorona Kamara, were both Mandingoes. After a short period of captivity during his adolescence, he became a Muslim and learned the art of war among his fellow Mandingo.[171] Unlike El Hadj Omar and Mahmadu Lamine, he was not a widely traveled man. However, he had the ambition of creating a vast empire under his sway. He declared himself chief of Bissandougou about 1870, and later took Sanankoro, where he erected his headquarters.[172]

By 1874 Samori had begun the systematic conquest of all the villages adjacent to his capital and between the Tingisso and the Milo, both affluents of the Niger. His confidence in himself grew apace, and in 1880 he proclaimed himself the Prince of the Faithful and declared a holy war against all unbelievers.[173] Samori's rapid advance soon took him to the right bank of the Niger, and he menaced Niagassole a short distance from the French post of Kita. Thus the French found themselves face to face with a virile and organized force, with which they would have to contend until 1898. Initial efforts by Borgnis-Desbordes to negotiate with Samori proved abortive, and Franco-Mandingo hostilities began early in 1882.[174]

Samori was not pleased with the barrier the French constituted against his expansion, and the French disliked the obstruction of their expansion by Samori's forces, whom they preferred to call bands. In addition, he made more complex the problems which Ahmadu created for the French. Sheer realism dictated the priorities for France. It was militarily inexpedient and unwise to involve her forces in wars on several fronts in a strange land whose physical conditions were very inhospitable to her soldiers. French efforts were to be concentrated against Ahmadu of Ségou, and Samori should be allowed to make incursions into Tokolor territory. Unfortunately, French attack on Kéniéra compelled Samori to deflect his movement against Ségou and to cross the Niger to confirm his authority on the left bank.[175] Even

171. E. Peroz, *Au Soudan Français* (Paris, 1889), pp. 382–88.

172. Y. Person, "La jeunesse de Samori" *Rev. Fr. d'Histoire d'Outre-Mer, 49* (1962), 151–80. The author includes sketch maps to illustrate the great extent of Samori's influence, and his local travels.

173. "Amir-el-moumenin" = Prince of the Faithful. Delafosse, *Haut-Sénégal-Niger, 2,* 343, n. 3. Among the Mandingo a short name carried little respect, and so the ambitious parvenu assumed a more impressive title.

174. A. Mévil, *Samori* (Paris, 1899).

175. ANSOM, Sénégal IV/77/b. *Rapport . . . , 1882–1883,* Desbordes. July 14, 1883. Chap. 20.

Commandant Combes' attack on Samori's forces in 1884–85 met with disapproval in Paris, and he explained that he had assumed that the ministerial instructions for an expedition against Ahmadu applied equally against Samori.[176] The *sofas* (Samori's soldiers) were brave warriors and gave the French forces a hard time in these campaigns.[177] After the battle of Nafadié the French forces began a march to Niagassola. The sofas accosted them for their apparent cowardice: "Allez vous soulager à Niagassolé!" they jeered.[178] In the negotiations that ensued, Lieutenant Peroz was sent to Samori along with the Senegalese Captain Mamadu Racine, Captain Tournier, and interpreter Alassane Dia. Colonel Frey directed the negotiations. Samori was stubborn in his demand that the French recognize his rights over Buré and Kangaba—his chief sources of gold.[179] A treaty was concluded at Kéniéba Koura (March 23, 1887), and at the suggestion of Colonel Frey, Samori, as already mentioned, allowed his favorite son to go on a trip to Paris as evidence of his good faith.[180]

The Franco-Samorian treaty of March 23, 1887, raised great expectations in the Mandingo camp but, disappointingly, produced none of the results expected by Samori. The acid test came during Samori's siege of Sikasso (1887–88). Despite the zeal and daring of the sofas and the valor and experience of the *sofa kele*, they could not penetrate the formidable *tata* which was Tiéba's greatest bulwark. Samori wished and asked in vain for a cannon from the French, which he said was all he needed to smash through the walls of Sikasso.[181] The tata of Sikasso was made up of three concentric walls, the outermost of which had a perimeter of nine kilometers and was about six meters thick. The height of this wall approximated four and a half meters.

Disappointed by the French, who had thrown in their weight on the side of Tiéba, and woefully unable to storm the impregnable tata of Sikasso, Samori called off the siege after having suffered the worst losses of his career. It is reported that Samori lost about seven thousand men in the sixteen months of the campaign, including his able officers Fabou and Lanakafali.[182] His cavalry lost over two thousand horses,

176. Ibid., IV/81/b. Combes, *Rapport 1884–1885,* Chap. 3.

177. Peroz, *Au Soudan Français,* pp. 225–318.

178. Delafosse, *Haut-Sénégal-Niger, 2,* 345.

179. Duboc, *L'Epopée,* p. 114. Delafosse, *Haut-Sénégal-Niger, 2,* 307.

180. Frey, *Campagne,* pp. 117–80, and *Rapport de la Mission 1885–1886* quoted p. 180.

181. Amadou Kouroubari, "Histoire de l'Imam Samori" *BIFAN, 21,* Série B, No. 3–4 (1959), 551.

182. See above, note 45.

for which he had to find replacements.[183] One of Samori's aims in trying to annex Kénédugu was to gain control of the Sikasso equine trade.[184] The notorious stigma left on Samori's career by the debacle of Sikasso did not dampen his ambition for empire, but sobered him to the realities of the times.[185] Samori realized that the French were not his friends but were out to conquer the Niger basin.

To strengthen his position vis-à-vis the French, Samori began to seek African allies. He scored a temporary success in this area by arranging an alliance with Aguibu of Dinguiraye. This enabled him to gain easy access to Fouta Djallon and to the coastal factories in Sierra Leone from which he acquired weapons.[186] Only Colonel Archinard's swift annexation of Dinguiraye in 1891 created a barrier between Samori and Sierra Leone. But as Colonel Barratier argued, the campaigns of 1892–93 against Samori's forces did not hurt them militarily to any appreciable degree. Kong and the Gold Coast replaced Sierra Leone as sources of supply for the sofas.[187] It was this sterling quality of Samori to move people and to keep supply lines open that earned him the admiration of his French opponents. He was a great strategist and tactician.

Samori's forces specialized in open battle and in guerrilla warfare. With no artillery comparable to that of the French forces sent against them, the sofas avoided fighting from fortified positions in order to avoid being caught in a siege or being overwhelmed and routed. Samori's effective forces were divided into three groups, each with special responsibilities. Troops armed with quick-firing rifles formed the crack force that was responsible for fighting the French and for general defense. The second group of soldiers were armed with breach loaders and chassepot rifles. They were responsible for guarding the civilian population and for evacuating populations threatened by the ever-advancing French forces from the west. The third group of

183. General Ingold, *Samory, Sanglant et Magnifique* (Paris, 1961), p. 92.

184. Robert R. Griffeth, "Varieties of African Resistance to French Conquest of the Western Sudan" (unpublished Ph.D. Thesis, Northwestern University, Evanston, Illinois, 1968), p. 139.

185. Kalil Fofana, "Almany Samori—L'Homme et son œuvre," *Recherches Africaines,* No. 7 (1963), p. 20; pp. 3–28.

186. Martin Legassik, "Firearms, Horses and Samorian Army Organisation, 1870–1898," *J.A.H., 8,* No. 1 (1966), 106. Christopher Fyfe, *A History of Sierra Leone* (London, 1962), pp. 240 ff. ANSOM, Sénégal IV/88/e. "Rapport au Sous-Secretaire d'Etat" par Jacques Haussmann, September 8, 1887. Cadeaux pour Aguibou. H. Labouret, "Les bandes de Samori," *Renseignements Coloniaux,* Comité d'Afrique Française (1925), pp. 348–52.

187. Lt. Col. Barratier, *A Travers l'Afrique* (Paris, 1912), pp. 71–73.

Samori's forces, charged with expansion eastward, were commanded by Sarankemory. By these arrangements, Samori was able to fight the French for a long time while assuring good government in all the territory conquered by his forces. One group of sofas constantly harried the French army and defended the rear and western frontier of the Samorian Empire while another group acquired new territories to the east to ensure new supplies of men and provision and other necessities. The third group policed the empire, maintained law and order, and assured the smooth functioning of the military workshops that played a very significant role in Samori's strategy. Thus the masses, whether as civilians or as soldiers (*sofa-kélé, sofas, bilakoro,* or *kélétigu*), were the backbone of the resistance of Samori to French imperialism.[188] Colonel Barratier observed:

> If he [Samori] lost in the west a section of his states, he only left us with ruins, and in the east he doubled his possessions. Such a defeat greatly resembles a victory; in any case, that defense in the west (while marching civilians east and conquering a replacement kingdom) would be called "strategy" in Europe.[189]

Samori was not only a military genius but was also versatile in diplomacy, as can be seen in his relations with other African rulers as well as with the French authorities prior to the advent of Colonel Archinard, "le Soudanais." Samori's diplomatic efforts to act in concert with Ahmadu of Ségou against the French were consistent with his policy of keeping the intruding Europeans out of the Upper Niger basin.[190] It was in the pursuit of this aim that a working relationship was established between Samori and Aguibu of Dinguiraye. When this tie was ruptured by the advancing French forces in 1892–93, Samori turned to the renowned kingdom of Kong for an alliance. Early in 1894, Samori's envoys arrived at Kong to negotiate the alliance. Samori assured the king of Kong that he desired nothing but good relations and commerce with the people of Kong. Samorian forces, he added, would never make war on other Muslims. Kong was strategically located and could furnish guns, rifles, and gunpowder from the coast and horses

188. Chistopher Fyfe, *Sierra Leone Inheritance* (London, 1964), pp. 196–240. Jean Suret-Canale, "Guinea Under the Colonial System," *Présence Africaine* (English edition), *1* (1960), 35 ff.

189. Barratier, p. 73.

190. A. H. Cann, *Le Pétaudière Coloniale* (Paris, 1894), p. 161. Suret-Canale, *Afrique noire, 1,* 268.

and provisions through her trade with Sikasso and Mossi.[191] The military weakness of the Watara princes and rulers of Kong coupled with Samori's appeal to Islam disposed them to an alliance with Samori. Considerations of Kong's treaty relations with the French were secondary in view of the reality of Samori's presence in the area and the fact that Colonel Monteil's expedition toward Kong in 1894 was forced back by Samorian forces, Agni warriors, and other obstacles such as malarial fever, inhospitable populations, and enervating weather conditions.[192]

Samori's relations with Kong remained friendly till 1897 when Samorian forces unleashed a ferocious attack against Kong.[193] The Watara princes of Kong were accused of bad faith because they provided refuge to Samori's enemies, and because a relative of one of the rulers intercepted horses destined for Samori's forces from Bobo Dioulasso, or from Sikasso. Samorian forces attacked Kong in the spring. The rulers of Kong fled to Bobo Dioulasso. Samori informed Captain Braulot of the French forces that he would launch a punitive expedition against Bobo Dioulasso because of the unfriendly actions of its inhabitants. However, the march on Bobo Dioulasso was called off after the Almany received the tribute of a large quantity of gold from the *marabout* of Bobo Dioulasso and a letter imploring Samori to spare the city.[194] Kong was destroyed by May 1897, after about three years of uneasy alliance with the all-conquering Samori, and Noumoudara was razed to the ground by August 1897.

Samori also tried to establish friendly relations with King Prempeh I of Ashanti. He knew that Ashanti was a richer source of gold than Buré. In the process of trying to cement his relations with Samori, Prempeh I sent him a gift of one hundred ounces of gold. Though Samori was pleased with this, he demanded one thousand ounces of gold as a price for assisting Ashanti forces in the proposed attack on Bondoukou. In the meantime, the sofas had overrun Gonja and had taken Buna and Wa. The British officials in the Gold Coast were thus drawn into the anti-Samori campaign because of the threat he posed

191. P. Herbert, "Samory en Haute-Volta," *Etudes Voltaiques* (1961) No. 2, pp. 32–36. Edmond Bernus, "Kong et sa Region," *Etudes Eburneennes, 8,* (1960), 270–75.

192. AN (Paris) 66/AP Papiers du Colonel Monteil, *10:* "Operation contre Samory. Rapports, cartes, bulletins des opérations, Fevrier 14 à mars 29, 1895."

193. Dominique Traoré, "Les relations de Samory et de l'Etat de Kong," *Notes Africaines,* No. 47 (1950), pp. 96–97.

194. P. Herbert, "Samory en Haute-Volta," *Etudes Voltaiques* (1961), No. 2, pp. 32–39.

to the Gold Coast hinterland.[195] However, it was the juggernautic military machine of French imperialism that crushed the Samorian state system and not British diplomatic rhetoric and the expatiation of the hinterland doctrine. Captain Francis B. Henderson who led a British force into Wa, Buna, and Lobi was taken prisoner by the sofas and sent to Samori's camp for interrogation in April 1897.[196]

By this period Samori had attained the optimum in eastward expansion, since he was unwilling to invade Ashanti territory. French forces pressed him from the south, north, and west. Sikasso had fallen in April 1898, and the troops tied down there were released to augment the total French effort against Samori. British action against Prempeh I of Kumasi precluded any collaboration or possible alliance between Ashanti and Samori. Populations could no longer be evacuated by the sofas into hitherto unoccupied areas. Samorian forces dug in north of the Ivory Coast and held out against the French until September 1898. Samori renewed his overtures to the French officials for a negotiated peace. He felt that the French were weary of the war and that they were ready to negotiate. While waiting for French officials with whom he would begin talks, Samori was surprised in his camp at Guélénou by a company of tirailleurs under Captain Gouraud on September 29, 1898. He surrendered. This marked the end of Samori's gallant and protracted resistance to French imperialism. His empire fell to the French and was incorporated into the French Sudan.[197]

Samori's reaction to the outcome of his war with France was marked by the same courage he displayed throughout his career. A few days

195. B. I. Obichere, "Britain, France and the Dahomey-Niger Hinterland, 1885–1898," pp. 399–406. William Tordoff, *Ashanti under the Prempehs, 1888–1935* (London, 1965), pp. 64–66. J. A. Braimah, *The Ashanti and the Gonja at War* (Accra, 1970), Pt. II, "The Sofa War," pp. 35–55. Jeff Holden, "The Samorian Impact on Buna: An Essay in Methodology," in *African Perspectives: Papers in the History, Politics, and Economics of Africa, Presented to Thomas Hodgkin*, ed. Christopher Allen and R. W. Johnson (Cambridge, 1970), pp. 83–108.

196. CO879/48. Leland to Governor Maxwell, April 15, 1897. Stewart to Maxwell, April 26, 1897. Maxwell to Chamberlain, April 26, 1897 (Tel.). Henderson to Maxwell, May 17, 1897. Francis B. Henderson, "West Africa and the Empire," *The Idler, 13* (April–June 1898).

197. Général Gouraud, *Au Soudan: Souvenirs d'un Africaine* (Paris, 1939), pp. 184–230. D. T. Niane and J. Suret-Canale, *Histoire de l'Afrique Occidentale* (Paris, 1965), pp. 126–28. J. B. Webster and A. A. Boahen, with H. O. Idowu, *The Growth of African Civilisation. The Revolutionary Years. West Africa since 1800* (London, 1967), pp. 46–59.

after his surrender, on October 3, 1898, he handed his prayer leaflets to Commandant Lartigue saying, "Allah made you the stronger. He abandoned me. I no longer have the need to pray. This prayerbook is for you." [198] While on his way by boat to exile in Gabon, a French officer asked Samori how he felt about the loss of his kingdom. With amazing nonchalance, Samori changed the subject to complain about the loss of his trousers. The prophecy of Samori that his progeny would fight on after his death came true, but within a different context. One of his sons, Adjutant Mandiou Touré was killed in 1915 on active service in the French army during World War I at the Dardanelles. Another son, Ahmadu Touré, was killed in the French action against Abdel Krim of Morocco.[199] Samori died in exile in the Ogooué region of Gabon on June 2, 1900. His spirit lived on in his successors and in his faithful followers. His rule over a wide area of the Sudan not only spread Islam among the African population, but inculcated in the people the attitude of opposition or repugnance to foreign domination. It may be pointed out that French conquest and the exile of Samori did not obliterate the memories of his valor and gallantry from the minds of the *sofas* or even from those of the *griots,* whose lives were dedicated to eulogizing Samori while he was in power. Traditions about Samori's power still prevail today in and around Kankan, Sikasso, Bobo Dioulasso, and other districts of the region.

Fama Babemba of Sikasso was one of the nineteenth-century African rulers who opposed the French. Babemba came to actual power in 1893 after the death of his brother Tiéba, whose relations with France had deteriorated by the time of his death in 1893. Before Babemba became fama at Sikasso, the French were aware of the development of friendly relations between Samori and the ruling family of Kénédugu. It was Captain Marchand who first reported the relations between the late Tiéba and Samori. Babemba preferred a rapprochement and an alliance with Samori to the French connection. This connection he would, however, maintain on his own terms and conditions and for his own advantage. This advantage was centered around the acquisition of firearms and artillery munitions. Babemba, it appears, was intent on making his famaship the most illustrious and prosperous that Kénédugu would ever experience. He had imperial ambitions which

198. Hanotaux and Martineau, *Histoire des Colonies Françaises, 4,* plate opp. 208. "Rapport par Commandant Latigue," in *Renseignements Coloniaux,* Comité d'Afrique Française (July 1899), p. 131.

199. Abdel Kader Mademba, *Au Sénégal et au Soudan Français,* pp. 102–03.

he hoped to fulfill by territorial expansion and by annexation of more subjects than his predecessor Tiéba.

Furthermore, Fama Babemba was a nationalist par excellence. His nationalism was not apparent but real. He gave vent to his nationalist sentiments in his correspondence with the French as well as with other African leaders. He was one of the first of the African resisters of European imperialism to inject racism into his policy. Colonel de Trentinian, who was in charge of the French Sudan at this time, made overtures to Babemba for the reestablishment of the French residency at Sikasso on a firm basis. Fama Babemba responded that he did not need any French resident at his court, and added that if de Tretinian was anxious to send a resident to Sikasso, he would only accept a black resident who should be a Muslim. In addition, Babemba demanded guns and cannons from the colonel.[200] Perplexed by the recalcitrant and intransigent attitude of the new ruler of Sikasso,[201] Colonel de Trentinian invited Babemba to Kayes for a conference so that his position could be explained and his demands examined. Babemba, who considered this invitation an insolence to his person, replied in the negative. The French officials then resorted to their old game of using Africans against Africans. This time they ordered their stooge, Mademba of Sansanding, to send a mission to Sikasso to explain France's "pacific intentions" to Babemba. These messengers of peace were ordered out of Sikasso as soon as their unwelcome message was received. Under French compulsion, Mademba of Sansanding dispatched a second mission to Sikasso. This time the leader of the delegation was put in chains for what Babemba considered the brazen effrontery of his master. He was soon released and sent home with the ominous warning for Mademba that his head would be the first black head to roll after the whites (Frenchman) would have been chased out of Kénédugu and the Sudan. Relations between Sikasso and France deteriorated so much that Babemba even refused to accept a French garrison. It was at this point that he served notice to the French officials that he was Samori's ally. The French knew this because Samori purchased horses and provisions from Babemba's territory.

The growing independence of Babemba alarmed French officials. His leaning toward France's arch opponent in the Sudan caused more consternation among the policy makers than his claims to indepen-

200. André Grassion, "La Pénétration française au Soudan dans ses rapports avec le Royaume de Sikasso," in *Mémoires: Ecole Nationale de la France d'Outre-Mer,* Année Scholaire 1938–39 (Paris, 1939).

201. F. Petot, "Sikasso," *Annales Africaines* (1958), pp. 312–14, 309–14.

dence. A coalition between these two African stalwarts and their forces would constitute a great barrier to French expansion in the Sudan. The prevention of such a coalition was therefore a cardinal priority in the Sudanic scheme of things. This explains why Captain Morrison was dispatched to Sikasso early in 1898. This show of force did not impress Babemba. He did not want whites in Sikasso. He did not want to see Senegalese and Sudanic tirailleurs in his capital.[202] He had vehemently told the French that his policy was not to accept any more whites there. Captain Morrison was given an ultimatum to leave Sikasso within twenty-four hours or be massacred with his escort. Morrison and his small force struck their tents and hurried away. The forces of Kénédugu were disappointed that Morrison and his men heeded the ultimatum. The *sofas* who were spoiling for a battle with the French pursued Morrison and his men, whom they ambushed and massacred on February 2, 1898. To the French officials, this was the last straw in the uneasy and very precarious relations with Babemba. A full expeditionary force was prepared and sent against him. The siege of Sikasso by the French began on April 18 and lasted until May 1, 1898, when the impenetrable *tata* of Sikasso, which had defied Samori almost ten years before, was breached by French cannons. The inner city was entered by the invading French forces. Furious fighting took place, and the palace guards of Sikasso fought against the overwhelming odds of French firepower and its barrage of bullets exuding from the inexorable rifled barrels of the *fussils à tir rapide*, which included Lebels.[203]

In the classical tradition of the valiant and defiant, and of noble souls, Fama Babemba resisted the French admirably and courageously. When it became clear to him that all was lost, he ordered Tiekoura Sanakoro, leader of his faithful guards, to kill him because he did not want to fall into the hands of his white enemies. Fama Babemba foresaw the debacle and the tragedy that was in store for Sikasso because of its relations with France. As early as 1892, he had counseled his brother Tiéba against any further involvement with the French, whom he believed could not be trusted. It was Babemba who pointed out that the French had been Ahmadu's allies at one point, but later overthrew him and chased him out of his capital. They made treaties with Samori and gave him gifts and took his son to France only to declare war against him a few years later. Sikasso, he argued, would be the

202. See Captain Marceau, *Les Tirailleurs Soudanais* (Nancy, 1911).

203. ANSOM (Bibliothèque) *Rapport d'ensemble pour l'année 1898* (Colonie du Soudan français) (Saint-Louis, 1898).

next victim of the French treachery after Samori and Ahmadu.[204] The irony of history is that Babemba lived to be the ruler who witnessed the fulfillment of his oracular analysis of the nature of French enterprise in the Sudan.

Like Babemba, King Behanzin of Dahomey (1890–94) was another African ruler who mobilized the masses against the French.[205] Behanzin resisted and resented French encroachment on the authority and the economy of Dahomey. This led to the first Franco-Dahomey war in 1890. The French underestimated the strength of Dahomey's forces and were quickly forced to seek a negotiated settlement, which was arrived at in October 1890. Chauvinists in France who could not accommodate the fact that France was to pay an indemnity of 20,000 francs annually to King Behanzin in exchange for trading rights at Cotonou clamored for another war with Dahomey. So did economic imperialists who wanted to tap the oil-palm and other resources of Dahomey. Even some missionaries pleaded for the conquest of the "pagan" kingdom of Dahomey, which they indicted for the annual customs at Abomey that involved human sacrifice among very many other rituals.

Because of their ethnocentric view of African culture and political systems, these missionaries could not see that the annual customs in Abomey had political, juridical, social, military, and economic functions as well as religious significance. It was at this annual festival that new laws were proclaimed and old ones amended. It was here that the troops were reviewed and new weapons displayed and demonstrated. It was at these festivals that good administrators were recognized and rewarded for their dedication. The annual ceremonies were also a festival of the arts of Dahomey. They served as a period of national renewal and rededication of the masses to the service of their nation and their king. Any European of the period who had an interest in institutions that were different from the normative structures of Europe could have perceived that in the absence of a regular parliamentary or consultative system, the annual festivals at Abomey were a necessary political event during which the king appointed new officers, promoted faithful and efficient officials of state, took care of the fiscal and other economic arrangements of his kingdom,

204. Oliver, *The French Sudan Up to Date,* pp. 14–15. P. Vigne d'Octon, *La gloire du sabre* (Paris, 1900).

205. For a full account of King Behanzin's resistance see Obichere, *West African States and European Expansion* Chaps. 3 and 4.

and defined general policy to his provincial, district, and village representatives.

When it became clear to King Behanzin that the French had not ratified the treaty they concluded with him on October 3, 1890, and that they were resolved to declare war on Dahomey, he wrote the French government a pungent letter in which he lucidly stated his political theory and what he thought should be the relations between the Whites and the Blacks.

Behanzin thus introduced the touchy issue of racism into his resistance to the French. Appealing to his cosmic view and to crude natural law, he declared that God made the earth and divided it between the Whites and the Blacks, keeping each in that part intended for its action and control. The Blacks have no right to seek to rule the white areas of the earth nor have the Whites any right to try to exercise control and authority in the black areas of the earth, Behanzin declared in this momentous letter of April 10, 1892.[206] He yielded, however, that he thought there could be commercial relations between the two races. The king insisted that the French were wrong in asserting that villages in the Porto-Novo area belonged to them and that they had rights over Cotonou. These areas naturally belonged to Dahomey, and Behanzin had no intentions whatsoever of parting with any piece of his patrimony.

Finally, he warned the French that when they attacked his forces in early 1890 he was ill-prepared, but that since then he and his forces had "learned to make war," and would fight the French to the bitter end if they attacked again. Behanzin was not indulging in any empty boast here. He had hired European mercenaries and had bought the latest weapons from the German company of Wolber and Broohm, who had comptoirs on the Dahomey coast. In order to preserve his prestige and his mystique, Behanzin learned how to operate these new weapons from the Europeans and then taught his officers and Amazons. This tedious process preserved the belief in the king's power and knowledge and authority. It was not until the onslaught by the French forces became unbearable that Behanzin was constrained to permit direct relations between his men and the European mercenaries he hired. At all events, it was the masses of the Dahomean people who mattered most in the conflict with France. Behanzin invoked well-entrenched Fon traditions such as the *dokpe* to keep local food production rolling. After the storming of Abomey in 1893, it was the support of his people that kept the fugitive king

206. ANSOM, Dahomey V/5/b. Behanzin to Ballot, April 10, 1892.

Bahanzin from being captured by the French troops, who always claimed that they were "sur le piste du Behanzin." Behanzin eluded them because his people rallied around him, and the guides whom the French officers constrained to lead the invading forces almost always led them away from where Behanzin was located. In the end, Behanzin, though vanquished in the field, obtained the terms he wanted. He nominated his brother, Prince Gouchili, to succeed him, for his greatest fear was that Toffa of Porto-Novo would be put on the throne of Abomey by the French. General Dodds accepted the nomination of Gouchili, and the princes and elders carried this news to Behanzin, who consequently gave himself up to General Dodds.[207] To Behanzin the preservation of the Fon dynasty at Abomey by the accession of King Agoliagbo (formerly Prince Gouchili) was a silver lining in the dark cloud of French occupation of his land.

The process of the occupation of Mossi and the Chad basin by the French was similar to the cases examined above. In their advance toward Ouagadougou the French troops under captains Voulet and Chanoine devastated the country and took hundreds of captives. They also took the cattle and sheep and goats belonging to their victims.

Captain Stewart of the British expeditionary forces to the hinterland of the Gold Coast in 1897 accused Captain Voulet of slave dealing and inhumanity after meeting him at Tenkedogo.[208]

The Morgho Naba of Mossi was so perplexed by the threatening French invasion of his kingdom that he ordered his high priest to consult the oracle to find out the best line of action to take in dealing with the imminent danger. The Delphic statement of the oracle did not help matters. Morgho Naba Wobogo offered sacrifices to the gods and to the ancestors of the Mossi to invoke their aid in the troubled times he had to face. The blood of the sacrificed animals had not dried on the shrines when the French forces fought their way into Ouagadougou on September 1, 1897.

Mossi resistance was fierce and spirited. In response to the call of their king, Mossi warriors and horsemen went all out to stop the belligerent French forces. But the effectives at the disposal of the king of Mossi had been diminished by the earlier French occupation

207. ANSOM, Dahomey V/10/a. Rapport Dodds: Campagne de 1893–1894. Ibid. Dahomey V/6/a. Rapport Dodds, 1892. For the memoirs of Behanzin, see H. Adolphe Lara, *Pour Behanzin* (Lyon, 1905).

208. CO879/48. Stewart to Governor Maxwell, February 18, 1897, enclosed in Maxwell to Chamberlain, March 31, 1897.

of the western provinces of his kingdom as well as the whole of Yatenga.[209] In addition, the Mossi, who lived in an inland kingdom far from the Atlantic coast of West Africa, had limited access to firearms compared with the states adjacent to the coast. Therefore, Mossi warriors had considerably less firepower than their enemies, even though they outnumbered the invading forces. There was also the cultural factor of the Mossi concept of bravery and valor and manhood. To them it was cowardly not to fight at close range and hand to hand. They rushed into action against the French forces hoping to confront them physically and man to man. The steady and deadly firepower of the tirailleurs soon put the Mossi to flight. It is reported that some of the horsemen galloped past their villages in their disorderly retreat. This should not be interpreted as an indication of their fright or indiscipline. They might have gone to regroup, as regroup they did, to escort Morgho Naba Wobogo out of Ouagadougou into the southeastern provinces of Mossi (Koumbi Siguiri) from where they harassed the French. The Mossi warriors who remained faithful to their fugitive king fought on his behalf until he was constrained to take refuge in Gambaga, a Mamprussi town in the Northern Territories of British Gold Coast.[210] Here again, we see the paramountcy of the role of the masses in the resistance of African rulers to French conquest. The Mossi continued to support their ruler even after the French occupied Ouagadougou.

There were discernible steps in the establishment of French authority in the interior of West Africa. From the well-established coastal headquarters like Dakar, Saint-Louis, Porto-Novo, and Bingerville, advances were made into the hinterland by the military whose backbone was the *Infantérie de la Marine* as Sydney Kanya-Forstner has demonstrated.[211] Military posts were established and local chiefs were made to accept French residents in their capitals. These residencies and military posts acted as launching pads for further advance into the interior. The residents collected information and submitted economic and political reports on the surrounding areas. The military officials

209. FO403/234. Gosselin to Salisbury, November 13, 1896, No. 96 Afr. See also Captain Voulet, *Mission au Mossi et au Gourounsi* (Paris, 1898); J. Chanoine, *Documents pour servir à l'Histoire de l'Afrique Occidentale Française de 1895 à 1899. Correspondance du Capitain Chanoine pendant l'expédition du Mossi et du Gourounsi* (Paris, 1905).

210. H. P. Northcott, *Report on the Northern Territories of the Gold Coast* (London, 1899).

211. A. S. Kanya-Forstner, *The Conquest of the Western Sudan: A Study in French Military Imperialism* (Cambridge, 1969), pp. 10–15.

surveyed the areas and reconnoitered the region. Their reports were used in the preparation of the tactical and logistical aspects of any further advances by military action. Regions occupied by Africans who were difficult to conquer or control were declared "military territories." In these *territoires militaires* the word of the commandant or *commandant supérieur* was law. He had the power of life and death over all the inhabitants, and he was the last court of appeal. This lack of accountability was probably intentional. The military officials in these areas were given such freedom of action to enable them to conquer and pacify the territories with ruthlessness and speed. Furthermore, the *indigénat* decreed in West Africa on September 30, 1887, remained in force until it was modified, only on November 21, 1904. Life under the *indigénat* meant that Africans should be suppressed by military action. They had no right to appeal to civil law in case of any disputes with French officials. This was the beginning of the system of political and social oppression and economic exploitation of the colonial period described in detail by Jean Suret-Canale.[212]

In the implantation of their authority in West Africa the French adopted the tactic and expedient of government by decrees. Decrees and *arrêtés* were issued by which the administrative structures in French West Africa were created. These decrees were very pragmatic in nature. Areas of special problems were left out in certain general decrees, such as the decree affecting the administrative structure of French West Africa. However, these areas would be decreed into the system as soon as the special problems were solved. An example would be Dahomey, which was left out of the system of the government general of French West Africa as defined by the decree of June 16, 1895, but was included in the system by another decree promulgated on October 17, 1899, after the conquest of the hinterland of Dahomey. The military territory of the Niger was also excluded from the general provisions of several decrees until it was completely conquered.[213]

From the foregoing examination of the African factor in the establishment of French authority in West Africa, we can see that the forces of cooperation were more successful in the achievement of their aims in the short run. Those African leaders who made common cause with the agents of French expansion gained only a temporary advantage over their neighbors. In many cases, these collaborators with the French lived to regret their action. Aguibu, for instance, was trans-

212. Suret-Canale, *Afrique noire, 2,* 93–154, 203–413.

213. *Annuaire du Gouvernement Général de l'Afrique Occidentale Française, 1917–1921* (Paris, 1921), pp. 77–79.

ferred out of his favorite capital of Dinguiraye and sent to Macina even against his will. Aguibu in his new station in Macina was no better perhaps than Ahmadu in exile in Sokoto. In reality Ahmadu enjoyed more freedom in Sokoto than Aguibu did in Macina under the close surveillance of French officials and their agents. Rulers like Tiéba, Bantchande, and Toffa, who collaborated with the French in order to obtain help and support against their African opponents, lived to witness the loss of their political power to the French. They were reduced to the same level in this case with their compatriots who resisted them and their French supporters.

In considering the question of resistance to the French, we see that the masses of the population were the most important factor to reckon with. It was the *talibé,* the *sofa,* and the *tirailleurs* who bore the brunt of the military action on both sides. African rulers recognized the role of the masses in times of emergency.

Another important factor we observe in the resistance movements is that migration was resorted to as part of the struggle. This underscores the principle that the people were valued more than the land in these African states. Both Samori and Ahmadu in the west and Rabeh [214] in the east migrated away from the French when the tough military conditions dictated such action. The French officers were perplexed to enter empty villages in their advance. This led them to the erroneous conclusion that Samori or Ahmadu devastated villages and left no survivors in these places. Samori, for instance, moved eastward with his followers and made them cultivate new land wherever they settled for a long time.[215] Authority was exercised over people not over land.

Religion played an important role in the resistance to French imperialism. Islam was central to the political thought of Ahmadu, Maba, Samori, and Rabeh. The faithful were exhorted to defend themselves from the invading Christians. Mahmadu Lamine used the mosque and the Friday prayer meeting to convert people to his point of view. He even performed magical acts in the mosque to convince

214. Elliot P. Skinner, *The Mossi of Upper Volta: The Political Development of a Sudanese People* (Stanford, 1964), p. 138. Georges Demanche, "Le Soudan Français et la Campagne contre Samory," *Revue Française de l'Etranger et des Colonies, 17* (April 1, 1893), 289–95. Trimmingham, *Islam in West Africa,* pp. 218–19. E. Gentil, *La Chute de l'Empire du Rabeh* (Paris, 1902). "Rabeh," *BCAF* (1898), p. 199. "Bismarch Africaine," *BCAF* (1898), p. 302. "La defaite et la mort de Rabeh: La combat de Koussari," *BCAF* (1900), pp. 266–69.

215. 1/G/202 Mission Le Filiatre et Nebout Auprès du Samory, July–Nov. 1897; 1/G/204 Rapport Braulot.

the masses that he was the real Mahdi of the West. Animism also played its part in the areas where it was the official religion, such as Mossi and Dahomey. "I am the king of the blacks, and the whites should stay at Porto-Novo and carry on commerce in peace and leave me alone," declared King Behanzin on April 10, 1892. Religious beliefs and practices in Dahomey were used as a pretext by the French in their invasion of Dahomey in 1892. In Mossi we see that faith in the gods and the ancestors of the people was quite alive at the time of the invasion of Ouagadougou in 1897. Religious considerations—Islam, Christianity, and Animism—were important in the conflict between Africans and the French during the scramble for and the partition of Africa. The masses and the warriors wore their gris-gris and their amulets for protection when they went into battles.

The leaders of the peoples of West Africa during this period came from a variety of backgrounds. This fact, in concert with others, was crucial in determining the attitudes adopted by these rulers toward the foreigners from France. Of course, we see a ruler like Babemba of Sikasso taking a hard racial line in his objections to French penetration of Kénédugu. This Senufo ruler explicitly declared that he did not want any white Christian resident at his court. He preferred black, Muslim residents should the French insist on sending a resident to Sikasso. The stream of correspondence between Victor Ballot, French resident at Porto-Novo, and King Behanzin brought out Behanzin's racial objections to French political ambition in Dahomey and its adjacent territories. This is an important point because many commentators of European origin have neglected it in their studies of this period. Colonel H. Frey who commanded the 1886–87 expedition against Samori, Ahmadu, and Lamine was surprised to discover that the people of the Sudan believed that the devil was white.[216]

Communication played a vital role in the resistance to French imperialism. Traditional channels of communication were employed to the fullest advantage. Markets served as nerve centers for the dissemination of information and for the forwarding of messages from one community to another. In this way, the movements of the French and their forces were closely followed. Horsemen were also used for the quick dispatch of messages from one area to the other. Unfortunately, some of these messages were intercepted when French officials captured the messengers. Africans in the service of the French communicated to their countrymen whatever information they could collect from their vantage points in French camps or forts. Samori purposely

216. Frey, *Campagne*, p. 152.

sent his trusted *bilakoro* to work as domestics for the French in order that they could keep him informed about the plans of his enemies. The kings of Dahomey had a highly developed intelligence system. King Behanzin even employed publicists who aired his views in European newspapers. He also sent his brother and other envoys to France in 1893 to put his case before the officials of the French government and the people of France.[217]

Finally, there is no question as to the politicizing effect of the resistance to or cooperation with the French in West Africa. The violent nature of French penetration alerted Africans to the new forces that entered their territories and their lives. The political and racial consciousness raised and sustained by colonial rule was perhaps by far the strongest single element in the struggle against imperialism that resulted in independence for French West Africa in 1960.

217. Gouraud, *Au Soudan: Souvenir d'un Africain* (Paris, 1939). Co96/278, Gov. to C.O., Nov. 6, 1896 (Gov. 24943 Minute Paper) (On Samory's farms, mines, industries, etc.).

☙ 14. *The French Colonial Service in French West Africa*

☙ WILLIAM B. COHEN

On board ship, on his way to Indochina in 1894, to the first assignment of a splendid colonial career, Captain Louis-Hubert Lyautey had occasion to compare his countrymen with the British who served as overseas officials. Deeply impressed by the gentlemanly qualities of his British companions, Lyautey was struck by the commonness and coarseness of the French officials.[1] Although Lyautey's observations were inspired by a cool, aloof disdain for the egalitarianism of the Third Republic, nevertheless they brought out salient differences between the British and French colonial services. Members of the British colonial service came from a very different social and educational background than their French counterparts. Although perhaps not sons of the most distinguished members of British society, nevertheless a very large number of British administrators could rightly identify themselves with the gentry. And their education confirmed them in their aristocratic pretensions; a very large proportion were graduates of Oxbridge. For instance, of the eighty-three members of the Sudan Political Service recruited from 1899 to 1914, thirty-six were graduates of Oxford, twenty of Cambridge, nine of Sandhurst, and six of Trinity College, Dublin.[2] Perhaps an even greater sign of their gentlemanly education was the large number who were graduates of public schools.[3]

The men who entered the French colonial service were of very different social background. Essentially they were middle class in origin. The aristocracy was violently opposed to the overseas expansion of the Republic; if its members entered government service, they

1. Lyautey cited in Hesketh Bell, *Foreign Colonial Administration in the Far East* (London, 1928), p. 163.

2. Prosser Gifford, "Indirect Rule: Touchstone or Tombstone for Colonial Policy?" in Prosser Gifford and Wm. Roger Louis, eds., *Britain and Germany in Africa* (New Haven, 1967), p. 356.

3. Ibid., p. 357.

chose a career either in the army or in the foreign service. The reluctance of the nobles to choose a colonial career was in part due to its low prestige. Georges Hardy, the director of the Ecole Coloniale, complained as late as 1929 that when a young man left for the colonies, his friends asked themselves, "What crime must he have committed? From what corpse is he fleeing?" [4] A couple of years later, a young administrator claimed that in 1931 the overseas official was still considered "a little bit the bad boy of the past, the gentleman of adventure, and his name evokes . . . the specter of the pirate . . . the sadistic bureaucrat, the professional liar, and the drunkard." [5] Many Frenchmen involved in the French overseas venture tended, obviously, to exaggerate the extent to which they were unappreciated at home; still, there was considerable truth to these complaints. The British colonial service enjoyed a much higher prestige; in part this seems to have been the result of the long tradition of civilian overseas service as exemplified in the Indian Civil Service. No such equivalent existed in France.

The problems of recruitment for the French overseas administration were extremely serious. In the early years, colonies such as Senegal were administered by naval officers. These men tended to stay for only a brief period before being reassigned to naval duty; in addition many seemed to be unduly harsh in their administration. By the 1860s J.-B. Jauréguiberry, a naval officer serving as governor, had suggested that it would be preferable to appoint civilians as administrators. This advice was followed and, for instance, by the 1880s, eight out of ten *commandants de cercles* in Senegal were civilians. These officials were subject to appointment by the local governors; the same was true in the other colonies.

The unhealthful and uncomfortable life in the colonies did not attract France's best men abroad. As the governor of Senegal noted in 1879, the colony drew "persons who if not compromised at home were at least incapable of making a livelihood in it." The only men attracted to the colonial administration, he wrote, were the "lost children of the mother country." [6]

Recruitment of the men was haphazard, depending to a large extent

4. Georges Hardy, *Ergaste, ou la vocation coloniale* (Paris, 1929), p. 9.

5. Hubert Deschamps, "La vocation coloniale et le métier d'administrateur," *Afrique française*, Supplément (September, 1931), p. 498.

6. Brière de L'Isle to Minister of Navy, April 7, 1879, in 2B52, Archives Nationales du Sénégal.

on political patronage. It is not surprising that until the late 1880s the French lacked any systematic method of recruiting their overseas service, for compared to the British, their empire was quite small and insignificant. It was only with its growth, the acquisition of Indochina, and the push into the interior of Africa that the French had to begin seriously to think about systematizing the recruitment and training of their overseas personnel.

In 1887, Eugène Etienne, the forceful undersecretary of colonies, unified all the administrators under his authority[7] into one service, the Corps of Colonial Administrators (except those serving in Indochina, who were formed into a separate corps). Although the Corps of Colonial Administrators included men serving in New Caledonia and in the French settlements in India, after the 1890s, when the French had carved out an empire in Africa, the corps became overwhelmingly an African service. The unification of the corps in 1887 did not bring immediate improvements: the only prerequisite for entering the service that Etienne had established was the possession of a government post either in France or overseas paying more than 2,000 francs a year. Two years later, Etienne found the old method of recruitment unsatisfactory: it had two alternative disadvantages. On the one hand, because the young administrators were ignorant about the colonial scene, they had to be given unimportant positions until they were sufficiently well acquainted with their regions, and by that time they had become so enervated by the climate that they had to be repatriated. On the other hand, Etienne claimed, when the young administrators had been given important posts immediately upon their arrival, "their inadequacy resulted in failures, [which] are sometimes deplorable for the work of colonization."[8] By giving the young men a formal training in the principles of colonial administration before appointing them, Etienne hoped he would be able to make a substantial improvement in the quality of the colonial administrators.

British officials sent to Africa were not given any specific training until the 1930s. Essentially the British seemed to believe that rulers were born, and in recruiting the colonial civil servants, the Colonial

7. Some French possessions were under the authority of other ministries than the Ministry of Colonies: Algeria was under the authority of the Ministry of Interior, Tunisia and Morocco under the Ministry of Foreign Affairs. Each one of these possessions had their own administrative corps.

8. Decree, November 23, 1889, *Journal officiel, République française, lois et décrets* (Paris, 1889), p. 5861.

Office attempted to find men possessing certain leadership qualities, more particularly character traits akin to those with which presumably the British gentry were endowed.[9] The French, on the other hand, believed that they could form, train, men fit to rule the empire.

Etienne established his training program at the Ecole Coloniale. This school had been founded in 1885 under the name of Ecole Cambodgienne to give sons of Indochinese dignitaries a French education. In 1888 the name of the school was changed to the Ecole Coloniale when the son of the king of Porto-Novo was enrolled. Since Indochina was the largest single French possession, it seemed natural to set up the training at the school to enable future administrators to use the Indochinese students as language informants. In 1892 a section to train administrators for service in Africa was established.

Originally it seems that Etienne intended to recruit all administrators from the school, but this procedure met with widespread resistance. Of particular importance was the opposition expressed by colonial officials attending the Colonial Congress of 1889 in Paris. They stressed the desirability of sending abroad only men with practical knowledge of the colonies; the congress as a whole attacked the notion of sending young men to the colonies whose comprehension of colonial affairs was limited to bookish learning.[10] The opponents of the school prevailed in 1892, and its graduates were denied a monopoly on recruitment into the corps; on the other hand, the school was not abolished, as some of the more entrenched critics had desired.

The failure of Etienne's plan to give the Ecole Coloniale students sole access to the corps meant that administrators henceforth would have to be selected from other sources as well. In trying to fill the corps, the undersecretariat, heeding the recommendations of its critics, returned essentially to the methods of recruitment employed in 1887; although Ecole Coloniale students were recruited, in addition, as under the decree of 1887, either metropolitan civil servants or men who had some form of government service in the colonies were appointed as administrators. By regulations adopted after 1892, the ministry could appoint into the corps graduates of the Ecole Coloniale, former colonial officers, or civil servants from the metropole of the colonies. The ministry's experience with the men coming from these various sources gradually, by 1912, shaped its recruitment policies.

The experience which the ministry of colonies gained in the alterna-

9. Robert Heussler, *Yesterday's Rulers* (Syracuse, 1963), passim.

10. *Récueils des délibérations du congrès colonial national, Paris, 1889–90* (Paris, 1890), passim.

tive methods of recruitment had, shortly after the turn of the century, by about 1905, decided it on appointing either agents (lower colonial officials serving as clerical aids to the administrators, or administering a subdistrict under an administrator's supervision), or Ecole Coloniale graduates. Both these sources, and especially the latter, proved to be satisfactory.

Except for the Ecole Coloniale graduates, most members of the corps were poorly educated before 1914. Of the administrators appointed prior to 1900, not even a third had had a secondary education. From 1900 to 1914, 52 percent were secondary school graduates. The proportion of university graduates was considerably less: prior to 1900, 20 percent; from 1900 to 1914, 30 percent. In spite of the leveling up of their education, clearly French administrators before World War I had not approached the high level of formal education of their British counterparts.

EVALUATION OF ADMINISTRATORS BY THEIR GOVERNORS

Year of recruitment	*Total files examined*	*Number of administrators considered capable*	*Number of administrators considered incapable*	*Files with insufficient information*
1887	18	3 (17%)	11 (61%)	4 (22%)
1888–99	85	40 (47%)	29 (34%)	16 (19%)
1900–09	345	172 (50%)	122 (35%)	51 (15%)
1910–14	249	148 (60%)	54 (22%)	47 (18%)

No one has systematically examined the personnel files of the British administrators in Africa. Lacking precise empirical data, one has to depend on the impressionistic judgment of contemporaries and historians who have been rather generous in speaking of the human qualities of the British administrators. Now, half a century later, one has to rely on the personnel files of the French functionaries in gauging the quality of the men who served in the French corps. Undoubtedly this is a hazardous venture; many higher officials were unfair and prejudiced toward their subordinates. Nevertheless, by checking reports of successive governors, one may arrive at a more exact picture of the administrators' achievements. Looking at the files of slightly more than half the men appointed before 1914, one discovers a rather large proportion of poor officials, although gradually better men were appointed. The governors' evaluations may be summarized by the accompanying table.

Roughly a third, then, of the men were found to be unsatisfactory by their superiors. And it should be noted that as a rule the latter were unusually thick-skinned and tolerant of their subordinates. The ministry in Paris and the governors in the colonies seem to have accepted with relative resignation the unreliability and brutality of many of the overseas functionaries. An administrator in the Congo in the 1890s, who had been certified by the colony's doctor as not being "in full possession of his mental faculties because of an overdose of certain drugs and alcohol," who had burned down two villages and whose favorite sport seems to have been taking pot shots at people imprudent enough to walk past his residence, was retained in the service, continuing to spread terror and misadministration.[11] An administrator in Senegal, noted as a chronic alcoholic in 1911, was allowed to serve fourteen more years until his death in 1925.[12]

Since most of the colonies were but recently conquered and "pacified," the administration did not consider that they required better functionaries than they had. When in 1909 the governor of Dahomey was asked to describe the morality of one of his administrators serving in what was then a remote area of the colony, he wrote, "Acceptable for Ouidah."[13]

Because so many of the administrators were of poor quality, the only thing a governor could do when he was dissatisfied with one of his subordinates was to recommend that he be transferred to another colony. This policy was baptized by one governor the "politique de débarras." No matter how bad, most administrators were considered good enough for service in the Congo. In effect that colony became, until 1914, the receptacle for administrators unwanted in the other French territories. When an administrator in Guinea was noted as having become "bizarre," he was transferred to the Congo,[14] while another was sent there when his governor discovered that he was a neurotic.[15] A dope addict and several alcoholics were banished to that colony.[16] To some extent this policy of transferring some of the worst functionaries to the Congo explains why French rule in that colony became a byword for colonial maladministration—just as did

11. Personnel file, EE II 140 (1) (1889), Archives Nationales, Section Outre-Mer [ANSOM hereafter], France.

12. Personnel file, 1C 612, Archives de l'AOF, Dakar [AAOF hereafter].

13. Personnel file, 1C 694, AAOF (1909).

14. Personnel file, 1C 56, AAOF (1907).

15. Personnel file, 1C 368, AAOF (1899).

16. For alcoholics see personnel files: EE II 140 (1) (1889); EE II 308 (14) (1890); EE II 1158 (4) (1910), ANSOM; 1C 598, AAOF (1905). An example of a dope addict is contained in personnel file EE II 859, ANSOM (1900).

King Leopold's rule in the Belgian Congo. Dismissal from the service was very rare; until 1910 only five men were dismissed.

Until 1914 many of the French administrators lacked that aristocratic concern with excellence, with incorruptibility, and with total integrity that supposedly had marked the British service. In their "native policy" the two services also acted quite differently. The British colonial service, which was imbued with traditions of the gentry, had a nostalgic sympathy for the local chiefs, whereas the French colonial administrators, most of whom came from the middle and lower middle classes, had a bourgeois disdain for feudalism or monarchism. The national traditions of the services were also quite different. In Britain the virtues of local rule were widely believed in—particularly by the class of men entering the colonial service. In France, a continental country threatened by its neighbors, local rule was considered a centrifugal force threatening the unity of the nation. In its history the French people found ample evidence to show that local rights were upheld by feudal and regressive forces, whereas progressive forces were represented by central authority. In France, until recently, centralization has been considered a good, and local rule has been thought of as a perilous system which gave the enemies of the state a base from which to challenge it. In effect, one can say that both colonial powers put into practice the policy of assimilation, for both powers attempted to establish overseas an administrative pattern similar to that existing, or thought to exist, in their homeland; the difference lay in their content.

Of course, the exigencies of the colonial situations had their own ironies, which sometimes required a French administrator of noble birth to crush a chief or unseat the local king, while on occasion putting a commoner in the position of defending traditional rule. Robert Delavignette described it best when he wrote:

> Cavalry Sergeant, de la Tour Saint-Ygest, who perhaps has left France because he suffers from the equality brought by the revolution, goes to Upper Senegal-Niger to destroy the Tuaregs—that is, the feudality, the principles and feelings of which are dear to him. On the other hand, the representative of the powers of the Republic in Dakar, a member of French Masonry and the Radical Socialist party, will, on the spot, in Africa, be an authoritarian governor, believing firmly in an hierarchical society, and he will use autocratic methods of rule in desiring to lead the natives toward progress.[17]

17. Robert Delavignette, *Service africain* (Paris, 1946), p. 38.

In general, however, most French administrators were suspicious of the local chiefs and regarded them as backward, feudal elements who were unreliable in their loyalty to France and who tended to exploit the local populations over which they ruled. In French West Africa (AOF), Governor-General William Ponty carried on an ambitious program to crush the chiefdoms. He advocated the need to "fight the influence of the local aristocracies in such a manner as to assure us of the sympathy of the multitudes, suppress the great native chiefs who are nearly always a barrier between us and the administered masses."[18] Ponty's attitudes had been formed in the Sudan: as an official he had found that the African military kingdoms established in the nineteenth century (for instance, Samori's) were extremely cruel and harsh in their treatment of the populations. Ponty wrote his governors in a circular of 1914,

> My long experience in West Africa among the black populations has permitted me to conclude in the clearest fashion, and you certainly have made the same observations, that the native intermediaries between the mass of the population and the administrators of the *cercles* or their subordinates are mostly nothing but parasites living on the population and existing without profit to the treasury.[19]

Ponty's policy was reflected in the reduction of several important chiefdoms in AOF; for instance, in Guinea the prestigious chiefs of Labé and the Fouta Djallon were removed.

For practical purposes of administration, the office of *chef de canton* was generally preserved everywhere. But the chiefs became creations of the French; the geographic limits of the canton, the powers of the chiefs, and the person who should occupy the position were decided by the administrators. Former kingdoms like the Fouta Djallon were carved up into several cantons; where the cantons were allowed to be coextensive with the former royal territory, the ruling house was dethroned, or at least an amenable member of the family put in the place of the former chief. In some cases, the administrator appointed his own houseboy or an interpreter as chief.[20] Village chiefs were usually not meddled with; they were allowed to stay on unless they were convicted of malfeasance.

It was obviously not only policy drawn up in the colonial capitals

18. Quoted by *Afrique française, 20* (July, 1910), 215.

19. Circular, January 30, 1914, 17G 38, AAOF.

20. Henri Labouret, *A la recherche d'une politique indigène dans l'Ouest africain* (Paris, 1931), p. 38.

or the different appointments and dismissals of chiefs by the administrators that had an influence on the evolution of the French policy toward the chiefs. More important were the attitudes exhibited by the administrators themselves in their daily contact with the chiefs. The administrators felt a keen pride in French culture, and they usually refused to show public respect or any special mark of deference or homage to the chiefs. Joost Van Vollenhoven noted that chiefs were sometimes made to wait for hours outside the French administrator's office, only to be received brusquely by the latter's subordinate.[21] In a number of cases the administrators did not hesitate to slap the chiefs publicly.[22]

In the face of the breakdown of the chief system, a number of colonial officials became worried and advised the preservation of the local hierarchies. But this advice was qualified in such a manner that its emphasis was always on the limited extent to which the chiefs could be trusted with authority and on the fact that they were to be considered only as auxiliaries of the French administration. Van Vollenhoven, who, as governor-general of French West Africa in 1917, did a great deal to encourage better treatment of the chiefs and the strengthening of the chieftain system, nevertheless concluded:

> There are not two authorities in the *cercle,* the French authority and the native authority. There is only one; the *Commandant de cercle* commands, only he is responsible. The native chief is only an instrument, an auxiliary.[23]

Until 1914 only a small proportion, 20 percent, of the corps originated from the Ecole Coloniale. Thereafter, however, all men appointed as administrators were either cadets who had undergone a two-year education at the school, or else agents who were required to spend one year there. In its organization and curriculum the school exhibited definite assimilationist traits. Until 1931 it was presided over by Paul Dislère, the well-known expert on colonial law who was an impassioned assimilationist. Both in its entrance examinations and in its curriculum the school emphasized the study of law, thus giving its graduates a training similar to that required by the upper civil service in France. The directors of the school trained the cadets in law because it was assumed that legal studies would transform the future

21. Comité d'initiative des amis de Vollenhoven, *Une Ame de chef, le gouverneur général J. Van Vollenhoven* (Paris, 1920), p. 203.
22. Personnel file, 1C 797, AAOF (1911).
23. *Ame de chef,* p. 208.

administrators into good civil servants who would respect government regulations and bureaucratic hierarchy. The study of law, it was also presumed, gave a certain sense of right and wrong and a respect for the rule of law. In addition, of course, since one of their main tasks was to administer and enforce the law, it was natural to demand that the future overseas functionaries know the law.

The teachers at the school viewed Roman law as having universal validity, the basic principles of which could be applied anywhere regardless of the human or physical particularities of a region. As M. J. Leveillé, a professor of colonial law at the Ecole, wrote:

> Law is . . . a universal language. . . . He who has studied it will immediately recognize [that there are] constant principles underlying [what are merely] superficial variations between different local laws. . . . There cannot be ten different ways to organize a family, to conceive of property or of a contract. For example, marriage, sales, borrowing, salaries are not a question of [local] customs but are, rather, basic to life.[24]

The formal structure of the curriculum at the Ecole Coloniale reflected the assimilationist trend. The curriculum not only ignored differences between France and its empire, but also the variations between the colonies themselves. Thus all administrators, regardless of where they were destined to serve, received a basically similar training; relatively few courses dealt with particularly Indochinese or African problems.

Although in its organization and curriculum the Ecole Coloniale was to retain many of its assimilationist attitudes, after the turn of the century the school ceased to be an advocate of pure assimilation and instead adopted part of the doctrine of association. This doctrine, developed as a result of increased knowledge of the colonies and the rise of racist anthropology, opposed the assimilation of the overseas possessions. Instead, it advocated that France associate itself with these societies and help them evolve within their own structures.[25] When practiced in its purest form the policy of association potentially could

24. "Rapport présenté au conseil d'administration de l'Ecole Coloniale, 1899–1900," polygraph copy (Paris, 1900).

25. For a discussion of the evolution of French colonial theory see Raymond F. Betts, *Assimilation and Association in French Colonial Theory* (New York, 1961); Hubert Deschamps, *Méthodes et doctrines coloniales de la France* (Paris, 1953).

have been similar to that of British Indirect Rule. But, with the exception of rare men such as Lyautey in Morocco, it had few sincere adherents. The goals of association and Indirect Rule were quite different; whereas Indirect Rule was seen as a way for the colonial societies to develop eventual self-government, association was considered the only way to ensure the evolution of the colonial societies and —in the end—their assimilation to France.

Many colonial officials taught at the Ecole Coloniale and through the doctrines they expounded in their classrooms they transformed the institution after 1900 into the main intellectual center advocating the policy of association and denouncing that of assimilation. The school was almost the only organ which, while advocating the policy of association, introduced the logical correlative to this doctrine, namely, a study of the colonial societies; for obviously if colonial institutions were to be respected, they would have to be understood.

After about 1905 the curriculum at the school underwent serious change; given the slim scientific resources then available, it began to give an impressive training in African customs, institutions, and history.

The French were far ahead of other colonial powers in realizing the usefulness of giving administrators training in ethnology and related subjects. It was not until thirty years later that the British instituted such courses for their colonial officials serving in Africa. Many of the professors at the school were former colonial officials. Drawing on their own experiences and personal research, they taught the courses dealing with methods of administration and with the history and institutions of the overseas empire. These teachers imbued the school with a new spirit, which along with the new curriculum, tended to give a more accurate picture of the colonial societies.

One of the best-known officials, whose course was later remembered as the highlight of every cadet's education at the Ecole Coloniale, was Maurice Delafosse. A former bush administrator and later a governor, he taught courses in African customs, language, and history. He was one of the greatest ethnologists of his times, and his teachings were far ahead of anything else then being taught in France. As Robert Delavignette has remarked:

> [While] Seignobos at the Sorbonne was declaring that the blacks were mere children and had never formed nations . . . Delafosse

at the Ecole Coloniale was teaching his students that they were men and in precolonial times had even founded empires.[26]

By teaching the future administrators that Africa had had a history of its own, and that it had its own particular political and social institutions, the teachers were imparting a certain respect for indigenous African institutions and a hesitancy to use methods of complete assimilation.

The Ecole Coloniale produced officials who were unquestionably superior in their sense of duty both to their superiors and to the peoples they ruled. After World War I all men entering the corps were either graduates of the school or agents who had been required to take a one-year training program. Beginning in the mid-1920s, with the appointment of Georges Hardy as director, the curriculum of the school was significantly reshaped. A former director of education in Morocco and AOF, Hardy brought to his post a good knowledge of colonial affairs and an intense faith in France's overseas mission. One of his most significant changes was an increased stress on ethnology while decreasing somewhat the emphasis on legal studies. When Delafosse died in 1928, Hardy replaced him with Henri Labouret, who trained a whole generation of administrators in ethnology, emphasizing to them the importance of local monographs. Hardy also changed the method of recruiting the students, by patterning it after the *grandes écoles;* as a result he raised the prestige of the school while at the same time significantly increasing the number of applicants. His successor, Robert Delavignette, was named in 1937. Delavignette's brilliant administrative career in Niger and Upper Volta made him well suited to head the school, and to impart to his students his faith in "humanist colonialism." [27]

The new men trained at the Ecole Coloniale gradually began to predominate in the corps; old age and illness were taking their toll of the older generation. By the end of the 1920s a fifth of those who had a decade earlier been in the corps had left the service; by 1939 only 14 percent of that generation remained. A majority of the corps' members in 1939, 52 percent, had been appointed during the last decade. Thus the corps on the eve of World War II consisted overwhelmingly of young men.

In view of this renovation of the corps, one must explain why, rather

26. Delavignette, *Christianity and Colonialism,* trans. J. R. Foster (New York, 1964), p. 33.

27. His favorite motto was "to command in order to serve better."

than bring change, the colonial service remained cautious, and in fact crystallized the status quo in the interwar period. Hubert Deschamps, who was one of the keenest observers of the French colonial scene and himself a member of the Corps of Colonial Administrators between the two world wars, has observed that French colonial rule, which at least partially had been characterized in the early period by an innovative spirit resulting from the original thought of men like Faidherbe, Gallieni, and Lyautey, became crystallized after World War I. Deschamps described the years 1919–39 as decisive, but "lost years." Of this period, he wrote: "We fell asleep somewhat from a political point of view, . . . when it would have been wise slowly and resolutely to lead an evolution."[28] It was because the French failed to take any initiative in the interwar years, Deschamps declares, that "From then on we could do nothing more than follow the developments without being able to guide them."[29]

The conservatism of the corps was due in part to the very way in which the young men were apprenticed to the overseas service. Regardless of the training at the school, they gained their most important experience from their elders, serving as bush administrators. This method of apprenticeship prepared the young men well for the daily tasks of administration, but at the same time it imbued them with methods and ideas of an older generation. Also, as with the British colonial service, which found it difficult to free itself from the authority of some of its early members, Lugard for instance, the members of the French colonial service held men like Gallieni, Lyautey, and Van Vollenhoven in high esteem. Their works were widely read, admired, and their doctrines followed, although circumstances had markedly changed.

In the early years, the administrators had as a rule left their families behind in France and had had much closer personal and social relations with the local populations. But as sanitary conditions were improved, the administrators took their families with them. By the 1920s white social groups had developed in nearly every administrative center, and the administrator was more likely to spend free evenings in these groups than with the people he ruled.

Probably the main factor preventing the administrators from maintaining close contact with the people was the chronic shortage of

28. Hubert Deschamps, "Les empires coloniaux et les nationalités d'outre-mer," mimeographed copy of course given at the Sorbonne in 1947–48, p. 45.

29. Deschamps, "La France d'outre-mer et la Communauté," mimeographed copy of course given at the Institut d'études politiques, 1958–59, p. 60.

personnel. During the interwar period the duties of the administrators had significantly increased. The administrators were required to spend an ever larger proportion of their time in interminable office work, filling out reports and sending statistics to the colonial capitals. The governor of Dahomey estimated in 1933 that since the time of the French occupation in the 1890s the work load of the administrators had quadrupled.[30] In spite of this increase in the administrators' duties, there was hardly any increase in personnel. The tight budgets of the colonial administrations limited their main expenditure, personnel costs. As a result, the administrations of the various colonies had scarcely more administrators than they had had before the war. In 1912 the administration of AOF had 341 administrators; in 1937 there were 385. In French Equatorial Africa (AEF) there were even fewer administrators in the 1920s than there had been prior to the war. In 1913 there had been 398; in 1928 there were only 366 (of whom only 250 were actually in AEF exercising their functions).[31] The governor-general of AOF pointed out in 1931 that his administration would require 200 more administrators in order to perform adequately.[32] Yet eight years later only thirty-three additional administrators had been added to AOF.

The constant turnover of the administrators also prevented them from getting into close contact with the people under their rule. The instability of the administrators was proverbial. In a *cercle* in Chad, a former administrator has noted, there were thirty-three different administrators between 1910 and 1952. Only seven of them remained for two years or longer, and some remained as briefly as four to six months.[33] In an extreme case in Senegal there were four different administrators who succeeded each other as *commandant de cercle* within five months.

The French tended to rotate their governors and especially their administrators for fear they might become too independent of superior authority or too partial to any one interest group in their administrative regions. Also, the furlough system tended to make it impossible for administrators to serve consecutively in the same cercle. After

30. Letter, Lieutenant-Governor of Dahomey to Governor-General, Porto-Novo, May 29, 1933, 18G67(17), AAOF.

31. Jean Suret-Canale, *Afrique noire, l'ère coloniale* (Paris, 1964), p. 392.

32. Letter, Governor-General to Minister of Colonies, Dakar, June 2, 1931, 18G63(17), AAOF.

33. P. Blondiaux, "Cinquante années d'administration française à Melfi," unpublished memoir, Centre des Hautes Etudes d'Administration (Musulmane, 1953), pp. 19–20.

serving two years in the colonies, the administrators were sent to France for a six months' leave. In the meantime their place was taken by other administrators, and upon their return they would be assigned to other regions. One of them bemoaned the bewildering variety of regions to which administrators successively had to adjust. He wrote:

> When we got to know the forest, they sent us to make our apprenticeship in the jungle, and then to the borders of the desert. We pass successively from fetishist people to Islamic tribes, from disorganized tribes to hierarchical kingdoms.[34]

The general tendency to move the administrators frequently had dire consequences for the colonies. As one administrator remarked shortly after World War II,

> As a result of frequent changes there is a lamentable lack of continuity, a number of praiseworthy initiatives without a future, and, in effect, after twenty years the country has not progressed more than in two, the efforts of some having reversed that of others, or at least not having continued their efforts.[35]

The frequent change in assignments generally meant that there was little incentive for the administrators to learn the local languages; for no sooner might they have mastered the language than they were assigned to another region where they had no use for that particular language. There really was no language which could serve as a lingua franca in either AOF or AEF. In the Ivory Coast alone there were over eighty different languages. Few administrators bothered to learn the indigenous tongues.

A study of the personnel files of approximately one-third of the men who served in the corps from 1887 until 1939 indicates that 12.5 percent of the administrators serving before World War I and 12.4 percent of those serving in the interwar period spoke an African language. This means that at some time this proportion of administrators was able to converse in the local language with the people living in their regions. But since the officials were so frequently moved around, their language abilities were of minimal use.

In general the colonial administration did little to encourage the study of the local languages. A colonial official expressed the concern

34. André Davesne, *Croquis de brousse* (Paris, 1946), p. 334.

35. René Grivot, "Problèmes d'Afrique noire, le beau métier d'administrateur colonial, essai de psychologie du commandement en brousse" mimeographed copy, n.d., p. 11.

of many of his contemporaries when he wrote in 1934 that it was admirable that some administrators were attempting to learn the local languages in the colonies, but

> Under the guise of advancing the natives within their traditions will we go through their school? . . . are we going to renounce the essential and fundamental principle of the access of the natives to the French language? [36]

The administrators were largely dependent on their interpreters. Traveling through AOF in the early 1930s, a young Englishman, Geoffrey Gorer, observed of the administrators that he had "never met one who was independent of an interpreter." [37]

The administrators, as Delavignette noted in a critical article in 1931, had lost contact with the indigenous populations and had failed to carry on research about the societies in which they were working. Delavignette remarked that missionaries and occasional travelers were contributing far more to an understanding of the local societies, while "the administrators live on the fruit of old works." [38]

In general the colonial administration as a whole did little to encourage the administrators to study the societies in which they were serving. An official who served in the interwar period has told of how, when he carried on ethnological research, he was called in by his superior, who told him, "I have to observe that you are not very serious. You, in effect, carry on completely superfluous ethnographic studies, and during your tours in the bush you take many photographs." It was only in secret that he was able to continue with his research.[39]

In the end, the administrators themselves, rather than the administrative system, must be blamed for the general lack of research on the colonial societies. The administrators had remarkably little interest in indigenous societies. It is nearly a mystery how a corps which after 1930 consisted of such a large proportion of graduates from the Ecole Coloniale (many of whom had also studied at the Institut des Langues Orientales) were so little concerned with the study of the customs and languages of the colonial societies. Of course, the administrators

36. XXX (pseud.) *Réalités coloniales* (Paris, 1934), p. 232.

37. Geoffrey Gorer, *Africa Dances* (London, 1935), p. 117.

38. Robert Delavignette, "Connaissance des mentalités indigènes en AOF," in *Congrèe International et Intercolonial de la société indigène* (Paris, 1931), Vol. 1, p. 561.

39. Jean Claude Froehlich, "De quelques anciens élèves de l'Ecole qui se sont illustrés dans les sciences humaines," *Latitudes* (1963), p. 10.

were heavily burdened with administrative tasks, which left them very little time for research. But Governor-General Marcel de Coppet was undoubtedly right when he accused the administrators, especially the young ones, of having fallen into "a certain inertia"[40] which prevented them from studying the colonial societies. The administrators had become seriously estranged from the local surroundings. They were unable to appreciate fully the evolution going on around them and therefore also had few, if any, proposals for a change in the colonial system. As Delavignette observed in his article of 1931, as a result of the failure of the administrators to keep in close touch with the developments of the colonial societies,

> It follows that the natives are evolving faster than the administrators or the administration. It follows that the natives are very far beyond the goals we have assigned for them from the official observatories in which the administrators are confined.[41]

The establishment of representative institutions would, to a great degree, have contributed to keeping the French abreast of the developments of the colonial societies. Furthermore, such institutions, by giving the indigenous populations a greater role in the process of governing their own societies, would have taken into account the new demands that were being raised by the local elites within the colonies.

In 1920 Albert Sarraut had called for the establishment of local assemblies in all the colonies, and an enlargement of their role where they existed. Beginning with a restricted electorate, the representative bodies, Sarraut wrote, should be gradually enlarged in order to become finally fully representative of the colonial populations.[42] The prerogatives of these assemblies were left somewhat vague, but evidently Sarraut envisaged that they would play an important role in voting the local budgets and in making decisions about the administration of each colony. In spite of the modesty of his proposal, Sarraut found it necessary to deny in advance, before any objections might be raised against it, that his plan, which would give the colonial populations experience in local rule, would lead to a demand for independence.[43] Rather than weaken the bonds of empire, this system would strengthen them, Sarraut claimed. Besides, Sarraut assured his readers, the colo-

40. Circular, October 27, 1937, unnumbered file, AAOF.

41. Delavignette, "Connaissance des mentalités indigènes," p. 561.

42. Albert Sarraut, *La mise en valeur des colonies françaises* (Paris, 1923), pp. 104–05.

43. Ibid., p. 115.

nial populations did not desire independence; too many of them were presumably aware of their incapacity to rule themselves and recognized the blessings of French rule.[44]

The local assemblies in the colonies never developed in the fashion Sarraut had hoped they would. In 1919–20 advisory councils were created at all administrative levels of AOF and Madagascar. (AEF, considered more backward, was given such institutions only in 1938.) During the interwar era they remained advisory, however, and were not permitted to develop into genuine legislative bodies.

The failure to found further representative political bodies, especially any that might have had an effective control over the administration, was attributable to the tendency of the administration to favor the preservation of a system in which its reign would continue to be untroubled and unhindered. Concerned mainly with administrative efficiency, the administrators could only regard with hostility the establishment of bodies that might question their acts. As an administrator who served in the interwar period noted,

> It would in effect be unnatural that functionaries holding in their hands the totality of power, should work for the establishment of local representative institutions which would have the effect of troubling the good harmony and the satisfactory serenity of their services.[45]

Most officials were basically interested in preserving a policy wedded to the status quo. If any kind of criticism of the French was voiced in the advisory councils, then the entire council system became suspect. In 1931 Governor-General Jules Carde noted that in the colonial councils the chiefs were appearing to be the representatives of the colonial peoples, for they were defending their interests by arguing for a tax cut. This situation, Carde wrote, proved that "one cannot be too prudent in the granting of political liberties to the natives." [46] When a more liberal official, like Jules Brevié, Carde's successor, suggested in 1934 a slight increase in the prerogatives of the colonial councils, he had to defend himself against a vehement charge by the Ministry of Colonies that he was advocating autonomy for the colonies and the liquidation of the French empire.[47]

44. Ibid., pp. 117–20.
45. Pierre Hugot, *Le Tchad* (Paris, 1965), p. 58.
46. "Rapports d'ensemble, AAOF, 1931, section B," p. 27, 2G31/18, AAOF.
47. Letter, Governor-General to Minister of Colonies, Dakar, June 13, 1934, 18G66/17, AAOF.

French colonization, by encouraging economic development, had created urban centers containing sizable urban populations. Through the spreading of education the French had created a restricted but educated elite. Both these groups were relatively new phenomena which first developed in the interwar period. The administrators, more used to serving in the bush, were ill fitted to handle the problems created by these new developments. In the bush, benevolent paternalism was still applicable, but in the urban centers that method of rule was becoming quickly outdated. Nevertheless, the administrators did not seem to find it necessary to establish new institutions which would give an outlet to these new elites. Brevié, in a circular to his subordinates in 1932, could only suggest that the administrators in their dealings with the new elite be just, kind, and patient.[48]

Since the administrators had mainly experienced bush administration, many felt that the elites developing in the cities were unrepresentative of the colonial societies in general; therefore, only a few officials recognized the need to give the African elites political and administrative responsibilities in their own societies.

A few officials like Marcel de Coppet, the liberal governor of Dahomey, sensed the political changes that were occurring. When in 1934 the governor-general of AOF suggested some minor reforms, de Coppet observed that they would not be sufficient to satisfy "the aspirations of Dahomean public opinion." "The Dahomean," de Coppet wrote, "aspires for neither more nor less than the status of a citizen and to enjoy the civic rights given the natives of Senegal in the four communes." [49] In a report to the Ministry of Colonies, Jules Reste, the governor-general of AOF, quoted de Coppet and added:

> The same tendencies are beginning to appear among the intellectuals in Soudan, Guinea, the Ivory Coast. They refuse to accept that their fellow Africans of the *communes de plein exercices* of Senegal, solely because of their birth, with no regard to their personal merit, even the lowest-born, can enjoy privileges from which they are excluded.[50]

These comments were unusually perceptive. In general, although the colonial administration repressed all nationalist demonstrations, it did

48. *Circulaires de M. le Gouverneur General J. Brevié sur la politique indigène en Afrique occidentale française* (Goree, 1935), pp. 22–23.

49. Letter, de Coppet to Governor-General, Porto-Novo, March 26, 1934, quoted in "AOF, Rapport politique annuel, 1934," 2G34/12, AAOF.

50. Ibid.

not recognize the existence of a nationalist sentiment. When in 1930 a serious nationalist uprising broke out in Indochina, the famous Yen Bay revolt, the Ministry of Colonies blamed the uprising on the lack of communications between the administrators and the colonial populations. Rather than understanding that the entire colonial system needed to be changed in order to give an outlet to the newly developed elites and to take into account, at least to some extent, the developing forces of nationalism, the minister of colonies recommended in a circular that the administrators both in Indochina and in Africa keep in more intimate contact with their people, that they increase their tours of the countryside, and that they take a more personal interest in the people under their rule.[51]

The entire imperial structure needed to be reshaped. Yet the very organization of the Ministry of Colonies prevented such a development. Because of parliamentary instability, no minister headed rue Oudinot long enough to impose his views on the colonial administration.[52] Formulation of policy remained in the hands of the top officials, the directors-general. These men had risen through the ranks within the ministry; by the time they arrived at the top of the hierarchy, Deschamps observes, they "were formed by tradition and they worked to preserve it." "One reaches thus more or less fossilization and a nearly total lack of vision for the future." In addition, Deschamps suggests, the legal education of these officials prevented them from conceiving the need for dynamic change; they lacked what Deschamps calls "historical sense." [53]

The ministry itself lacked close touch with developments overseas. There was very little interchange of personnel between the offices of rue Oudinot and the administrations in the colonies. Since the work in the central administration was considered dull, few good administrators served in its offices.[54] Usually only older and sickly adminis-

51. Circular, June 10, 1930, *Bulletin officiel des colonies* (Paris, 1930), pp. 907–10.

52. For the period 1871 to 1914 the ministers and undersecretaries of colonies averaged thirteen months of service; for the period from 1915 to 1929, eleven months of service; and for the years from 1930 to 1940, seven months of service. Of the seventy-four men in charge of colonial affairs from 1871 to 1940, only eleven served more than two years: five between eighteen and twenty-four months, twelve served between twelve and eighteen months, fifteen served between six and twelve months, nineteen served between one and six months, and twelve served a month or less.

53. Hubert Deschamps, "La France d'outre-mer," p. 69.

54. XXX, *Réalités coloniales,* pp. 112–14.

trators, who could not return to the colonies, served in the central administration. Supposedly there were so many of these in the ministry that one official facetiously suggested that the Ministry of Colonies, which was located a stone's throw from the Invalides, the home for aged and wounded war veterans, was itself the "invalides" of the French colonial service.[55]

Thus during the interwar period no satisfactory system was really established that brought the offices of rue Oudinot in close touch with developments overseas. As Delavignette has suggested, "a time lag" developed "between the highest level of the colonial administration and the fragmentary but valuable experience of the men on the spot." [56]

The imperviousness to change was best epitomized in the "native policy." In this field change was clearly indicated. Contact with European values was undermining the allegiance to traditionalism of segments of the colonial populations. The limited but increased tempo in establishing communications within the colonies and bringing them increasingly into a money economy partially led to the disintegration of the old social fabric within the colonial societies.

Faced by the possibility of the disintegration of entire indigenous societies, Van Vollenhoven had, during the 1914–18 war, addressed himself to that problem. He saw the populations of AOF as being composed of "a mass of natives" and of an elite group. The masses, Van Vollenhoven wrote in 1917, should evolve within their own environment. In order to assure them of security "in their families, their villages and their traditions," the indigenous society had to be consolidated. One had to prevent "a collapse" of the native society.[57] The elite Van Vollenhoven saw as having been formed by a small group of individuals who, because of their greater aptitudes and ambition, stood apart from the masses. "This elite," he wrote, "was ostracized from the native society because it no longer lived in the native manner, and could not return to it. Proud of their effort, presumptuous and sometimes unbearable in their vanity, this category represents the young, the avant garde, the example." while the masses were to develop along their own traditions, the elite, Van Vollenhoven stated, "must evolve more and more in our environment." [58]

55. Ibid., p. 116.
56. Delavignette, *Christianity and Colonialism,* p. 33.
57. *Ame de chef,* p. 48.
58. Ibid., pp. 48, 50.

After the war many officials regretted the degree to which the chief-system had been destroyed. In 1921, in a written report to the minister of colonies, the governor-general of AOF regretted the "inevitable errors that accompanied the beginnings of European occupation." These had occurred because the first generation of administrators had misunderstood the nature of the indigenous societies. Experience, the governor-general stated, had shown the value of respecting the traditional cohesion of these societies.[59] Labouret warned that the destruction of tribal organizations was producing a crisis of authority. And he called for a more careful study of the evolution of the colonies in order to stem the crisis.[60]

In the highest official circles concern was also expressed. The minister of colonies, Maginot, in a circular to the governors-general, expressed his misgivings in 1929 about the disappearing authority of the indigenous chiefs. The administrators alone, Maginot indicated, would be unable to keep order: the chiefs were an important element in making it possible for the administration to maintain its authority over the masses.[61] Governor-General Brevié, who had served as governor of Niger and had had experience dealing with the great Hausa emirs of that colony, stressed the need to preserve and strengthen the chiefs. In the past, Brevié indicated, French officials had been too impatient with the chiefs. They had been unrealistic, for

> To want to transform from one day to the next the *amenokal* of Ouillimède into a perfect collaborator of our administration would be equivalent to trying instantaneously to change the Sire de Coucy into a prefect of the Third Republic.[62]

The chiefs were treated with greater understanding and more was done to improve their lot and to strengthen their prestige. More responsibility and duties were transferred to them. Yet, in the final analysis, there still could be no doubt that all authority remained in French hands. Brevié quoted approvingly Van Vollenhoven's phrase, "Only the *commandant de cercle* commands; the native chief is only his instrument." He added, "This principle remains." [63]

If the aim of French policy had really been to strengthen the chiefs,

59. "Rapport politique," November, 1921, in 17G40, AAOF.

60. Henri Labouret, "Le noir et l'homme blanc en Afrique," *Le monde colonial illustré, 54* (1928), 147–48.

61. Circular, October 9, 1929, *Bulletin officiel des colonies* (Paris, 1929), pp. 1668–70.

62. Quoted in *Annales coloniales* (January 26, 1931).

63. Quoted in Anon., "Les administrateurs de la France d'outre-mer," *L'Economie, 451* (1954), 17.

then, as a former French administrator asks, "Why were they not given the power to levy taxes and to have their own budgets?" The real reason for the granting of greater authority to the chiefs, Pierre Hugot suggests, was, rather, motivated by the desire "to simplify the administration." The administrators, unable to handle the severely increased work load, turned to the chiefs, whom they transformed into something "like a police chief." [64]

French rule had emptied the traditional structures of their meaning, but it did not replace them. The French had destroyed the old structures in the name of liberty, equality, and fraternity, but once these societies were in the process of disintegration, they hesitated to transform their ideals into reality. The colonial system was in dire need of change, for it no longer corresponded to the needs of the African societies. These had undergone profound change, but the colonial system was virtually the same as it had been at its original inception in the 1880s. No basic reforms were introduced in the interwar period, except for palliatives, making the colonial rule somewhat less harsh than it had been prior to World War I; thus forced labor and application of the *indigénat,* the code giving the administrators special disciplinary powers, were curtailed.

On the eve of World War II the British and the French colonial systems had begun to resemble each other. Influenced by its tradition of Indirect Rule, the British system failed to introduce innovation. Although the British failure to innovate seems to have been the result of a continuation of revered traditions established before World War I, the French failure was due to short-term administrative expediency. The ideology and the class background of the French colonial service had prepared it admirably for the task of innovating, of laying the foundations of genuine assimilation—which, after all, was the stated goal of French colonization. Instead, ignoring the real extent of the political and social evolution overseas, the French colonial service was seriously out of step when war broke out in 1939.

In the midst of the war, a colonial inspector making a tour of West Africa observed that the French overseas system was suffering from "sclerosis." [65] The forces unleashed by the Second World War in the end could not be coped with. The very forces of change, which the colonial officials had helped set in motion at the end of the nineteenth century, in the end overwhelmed them. If Africans were the victims—so, ironically, were the imperial powers.

64. Hugot, *Le Tchad,* pp. 65–66.
65. Inspection report for Dahomey, 1940–41, 17G111, AAOF.

15. *Varieties of Trusteeship: African Territories under British and French Mandate, 1919–1939*

RALPH A. AUSTEN

At the Peace Conference that followed World War I, three former German colonies—Tanganyika, the Cameroons, and Togo—were given to Britain and France as Class B League of Nations Mandates. In neither their physical, human, nor administrative geography are these territories ideally matched for comparison nor, given the special circumstances of their acquisition, is their development typical of British and French Africa as a whole. But during the interwar period the particular pressures of publicity placed upon the mandates make them a useful basis for examining the relationship between British and French colonial ideas and their political application.

The mandates in fact suggest a serious reconsideration of long-standing conceptions about the roles of Britain and France in the colonial period of African history. First, it is commonly contended that British colonialism was essentially motivated by economic interests whereas France's overseas possessions served only to enhance the political prestige of the metropole.[1] In the administration of the African mandates, however, it was the British who gave priority to political considerations while the French concentrated their efforts upon economic development. Second, in the articulation of colonial policy, the British are often characterized as unsystematic pragmatists and the French were supposed to have imposed a well-formulated ideology upon Africa.[2] Yet British government of the mandates was accompanied by elaborate concepts of trusteeship and Indirect Rule whereas French policy here seemed to depend for the few ideas it expressed upon British stimulation. Finally, much debate has taken place in recent years as to whether Britain and France imposed different or

1. See Henri Brunschwig, "Anglophobia and French African Policy," above (chap. 1).

2. See Thomas L. Hodgkin, *Nationalism in Colonial Africa* (New York, 1957), pp. 33 ff., and Immanuel Wallerstein, *Africa: The Politics of Independence* (New York, 1961), pp. 64 ff.

essentially identical colonial experiences upon their respective African subjects.[3] From the perspective of the mandates, this issue seems to be wrongly posed. The British and French colonial experiences were extremely different, but it is the relevance of this difference to Africa that remains questionable.

The following discussion will concentrate upon the European dimensions of the mandate experience in Africa because available material makes those aspects more accessible to investigation than the African dimensions. Apart from tracing the differences between British and French African policy, a study of the mandates also indicates the extent to which both powers partook of what may be called the "paternalist consensus" involving the entire colonial establishment of the interwar period. To some extent the public discussions that created this consensus helped to overcome the consequences of varying British and French approaches to mandate rule and thus—together with African responses—offer some clues to the very similar progress toward independence that occurred in both sets of territories after World War II.

In tracing the divergence and convergence of British and French mandate policy, three arenas of comparison seem appropriate. The first is Europe where, in both metropoles as well as the Geneva chambers of the League of Nations Permanent Mandates Commission, policy toward Africa was formulated and debated. The second is the *pays officiel* of the mandated territories themselves, where European administrators executed colonial policies in collaboration with what they thought were the most politically relevant groups of Africans. Finally, there is the *pays reel* of Africans whose political responses proceeded from a perspective very alien to official colonial thinking.

The imperialist geography of the mandates, in its patent asymmetry, indicates the divergent basis upon which Britain and France began their mandate role. A standard map would indicate that Britain, with Tanganyika and slices of the Cameroons and Togoland, obtained by far the greater share of German colonial spoils. German East Africa, of which all but the relatively small Ruanda-Urundi was included in the Tanganyika mandate, exceeded in both size and population all of the Cameroons and Togoland put together. Moreover the British had here achieved their dream of an African territorial expanse running

3. See Hubert Deschamps, "Et maintenant, Lord Lugard?" *Africa,* 33 (1963), 293–306, and Michael Crowder, "Indirect Rule—French and British Style," *Africa,* 34 (1964), 197–205.

from "the Cape to Cairo." Both Tanganyika and the British West African mandates could, moreover, be integrated into the neighboring British colonies, thus strengthening what was already the most valuable block of dependencies in the entire continent.

The drawback of these new possessions was their limited economic value. Tanganyika, vast as it was, consisted largely of a semiarid plateau with more fertile areas strung out along its periphery. The British portions of the Cameroons and Togoland were cut off from the transport arteries constructed for the whole of these territories by the Germans. Although administered together with the adjacent provinces of, respectively, Nigeria and the Gold Coast, it took considerable effort to effect economic union between the mandates and their wealthy parent territories.

France, by contrast, had gained less politically and more economically. The Cameroons was of moderate size and Togoland tiny. Neither, for somewhat embarrassing reasons,[4] could be integrated into the large neighboring Federations of French Equatorial Africa (for the Cameroons) or French West Africa (for Togoland). Strategically, the gain of the two territories was important less as the achievement of major positive aims than as a compensation for previous French weaknesses. Part of the French Congo had earlier been lost to the German Cameroons and was now restored; the hitherto impoverished French Equatorial Africa and Dahomey could benefit from the fine ports and general prosperity of the Cameroons and Togo.

Recognition in German times that the West African colonies had more economic value than East Africa came only slowly and ambiguously. Partly because they were the scene of sensational uprisings, German East and South-West Africa received primary attention during the Dernburg reform era of 1906–10. Togo, however, with its balanced budget and total lack of political crises, gradually developed a reputation as German's "model colony," while the last colonial secretary, Wilhelm Solf, began to give attention to the rich potential of the hitherto badly administered Cameroons Protectorate.[5] Although valuable plantation areas were lost by France to the British Cameroons, in both West African mandates the French retained the economic

4. See André Kaspi, "French War Aims in Africa," above (chap. 10).

5. Robert Cornevin, *Histoire du Togo* (Paris, 1962), pp. 167–205; Colin Newbury, "Partition, Development, Trusteeship: Colonial Secretary Wilhelm Solf's West Journey, 1913," in Prosser Gifford and Wm. Roger Louis, eds., *Britain and Germany in Africa* (New Haven, 1967), pp. 455–77.

heart of the former German structures: railroads, harbors, and lands producing, particularly in the Cameroons, a happily varied assortment of tropical export crops.

Not only were Britain's imperial gains in the mandates system mainly political, but in justifying their administration of these new territories British spokesmen would initially give primacy to political rather than economic policies. The French, conversely, were to boast of the economic development they offered to their mandates.

The politically oriented ideology which Britain offered as the initial basis for its mandate role provided a distinct moral advantage in the international discussions that constituted the main sanctioning force of the mandates system. The close fit between British policies and the "sacred trust" ideals of mandate supervision is only to be expected since it was British, along with Commonwealth and United States, statesmen who at the end of World War I devised the mandates concept as a compromise between outright annexation and internationalization of the German colonies.[6] These ideals were also quite explicitly spelled out in the book which served as something like the Bible of interwar British colonial policy, Lord Lugard's *The Dual Mandate in British Tropical Africa* (1922). Far more than a moral tract, moreover, Lugard's work is a practical handbook based on the author's long and distinguished administrative career. The most famous idea to emerge from *The Dual Mandate* is thus a political-administrative one—the advocacy of Lugard's famous system of "Indirect Rule" whereby traditional African political organizations were to be preserved and adapted as the basic mediums for all colonial development.[7]

A corollary of Lugard's concern for rule through chiefs was his fear that unchecked European economic exploitation would undermine African institutions. The economics of British colonial ideology in this period is therefore somewhat negative, fearing disruption rather than urging development.

Even the arguments for the economic value to Britain of African colonies, by which Lugard tried to win a less idealistic segment of public opinion for his cause, remain loyal to the idea of an "open door," that is, free competition between British and foreign enterprises within British dependencies.[8] The survival of such classical liberal

6. Wm. Roger Louis, *Great Britain and Germany's Lost Colonies* (Oxford, 1967), pp. 117–60.

7. Prosser Gifford, "Indirect Rule: Touchstone or Tombstone for Colonial Policy?" *Britain and Germany in Africa*, pp. 351–92.

8. *Dual Mandate* (5th ed., Hamden, Conn., 1965), p. 611.

ideas among the servants of an etatist colonial regime in an era when free trade no longer gave Britain world commercial hegemony is of a piece with the other inconsistencies that made up the interwar British colonial "official mind." [9] But this liberalism was necessary in maintaining harmony between that mind and the "economic equality" demands of the mandate system.

The degree of British adherence to the "open door" can be seen in the easy access enjoyed by Germans who wished to return to their former colonies in a private capacity. Even before Germany's admission to the League of Nations, most of the plantations in the British Cameroons had been sold back to their previous owners, who became the largest nonofficial European group in that territory. After 1926, when Germany joined the League, Germans also returned in large numbers to Tanganyika, and German missionary societies played an educational role in all three British mandates.[10]

The British concept of mandates, compounded of conservative-sentimental beliefs in traditional institutions and liberal-rational advocacy of a free-market system, can therefore be summarized as one of "holding the ring"—that is, maintaining a system of order within which development might take place spontaneously.

The less articulate position of France in defending her rule over mandates may be traced in part to the fact that the French, rather than helping to formulate the ideal of mandates, virtually had the system forced upon them by the English-speaking statesmen at Versailles.[11] Far from addressing itself primarily to mandate ideals, the French book that is usually equated with Lugard's *Dual Mandate* is concerned, as its title suggests, with economic development of direct benefit to France. Albert Sarraut, author of *La mise en valeur des colonies françaises* (1923), had served as governor-general of Indochina, but in his interwar capacity as colonial minister he reflects the views of a domestic political leader rather than a professional colonial administrator. That the writings of career administrators like Joost

9. For a fuller exposition of this point in relation to Indirect Rule, see Ralph A. Austen "The Official Mind of Indirect Rule: British Policy in Tanganyika, 1916–1939," *Britain and Germany in Africa*, pp. 602–06.

10. Victor T. LeVine, *The Cameroons from Mandate to Independence* (Berkeley, 1964), pp. 119–25; Judith Listowel, *The Making of Tanganyika* (London, 1965), pp. 117–19; Hans W. Debrunner, *A Church Between Colonial Powers* (London, 1965), pp. 165–66. (Except for LeVine, these works are far from adequate accounts of German activity in the British mandates, documentation for which is scattered in numerous well-known sources.)

11. Louis, *Germany's Lost Colonies*, and Kaspi, "French War Aims."

Van Vollenhoven and Hubert Lyautey, also published during this period,[12] could have so little influence on mandates policy indicates both the weak position of such men as spokesmen for French colonial aims and also a certain confusion as to what system of administration in Africa would best fulfill these aims. Sarraut's work devotes a brief section to the policy of "association," defined mainly as something opposed to the naïve liberal "assimilation" of the past. More specifically, association was to consist of administrative and fiscal decentralization within the French sector of the colonial structure; but, apart from brief references to advisory councils, Sarraut gives almost no indication of the political role that African or Asian subjects were to play in relation to this structure.[13]

What the French concept of mandate trusteeship lacked in political inspiration it sought to compensate for in economic planning. The central argument of Sarraut's *Mise en valeur* is that a properly coordinated development program would assure both that France derived the maximum benefit from its colonies and that each individual colony received the guidance and assistance required to make the most of its particular resources. In an especially long chapter on the Cameroons, Sarraut further confessed that because of the high level of previous German development in this territory and the exposure of its present administration to League of Nations scrutiny, "the Cameroons is going to become the pivot of French policy in tropical Africa."[14]

Sarraut's book consists, in substance, of an actual project which, in his capacity as colonial minister, he had laid before the French Parliament. His proposals for major transportation, communications, and social welfare measures in the Cameroons and Togoland were designed to convince the governing forces at home of the necessity for more generous financial allocations than were actually forthcoming.[15] For the African territories, moreover, such plans also implied priorities and demands that contrast sharply with the British vision. This divergence

12. Comité d'initiative des amis de Vollenhoven, *Une Ame de chef, le gouverneur général J. Van Vollenhoven* (Paris, 1920); Hubert Lyautey, *Paroles d'Action* (Paris, 1927).

13. Albert Sarraut, *La Mise en valeur* (Paris, 1923), pp. 96–127; on assimilation and association in this period see also Hubert J. Deschamps, "French Colonial Policy" above, and Rudolf v. Albertini, *Dekolonisation* (Cologne and Opladen, 1966), pp. 323–57.

14. *Mise en valeur,* p. 441.

15. For a fuller discussion of the relationship between economic policy and the views of both Sarraut and Lugard, see D. K. Fieldhouse, "The Economic Exploitation of Africa," below (chap. 18).

can be seen most clearly in regard to the issue of forced labor, which the mandate agreements for all the former German African colonies explicitly restricted to "essential public works and services, and then only in return for adequate remuneration."[16] Lugard likewise condemned unpaid compulsory labor,[17] and the institution was limited in the British mandates to traditional services for chiefs, which were not to extend beyond the upkeep of minor local roads and paths.[18] Sarraut, on the other hand, speaks of the general laziness of "the native, especially in black countries" and claimed that compulsion was necessary to break the "vicious cycle" of undernourishment and inactivity.[19] Thus, despite mandate regulations, the French Cameroons and Togoland maintained the *prestation,* whereby Africans were forced to contribute ten days of free labor per year to the government.

While the French could not, as elsewhere in Africa, place protective tariffs upon their mandates, they revealed the limits of their adherence to the open door by the manner in which the government sequestered all German property not salable to French or local African buyers. German missionary societies likewise found it impossible to return to the French mandates.[20] Sarraut's constant denunciation of the ancient mercantilist *pacte coloniale,* like his attacks on assimilation, is thus in the nature of setting up a straw man to conceal the fact that the French had merely modified their old policies rather than evolving new ones consistent with their acceptance of the mandates system.

If the initial divergence between British and French interpretations of mandate trusteeship seems to place France in a somewhat unfavorable light, direct allegations to this effect were seldom made public during the actual period of mandate rule. Needless to say, official spokesmen for British and French colonial interests had every reason to shun such controversies, which could do the accuser little good in Europe and possibly undermine his position in Africa. These inhibitions were not restricted, however, to national colonial establishments; they also extended to the international body whose function it was to supervise mandate administration, the Permanent Mandates Commission of the League of Nations.

16. Mandates for Tanganyika and Ruanda-Urundi, Article 5 (3); Mandates for the Cameroons and Togoland, Article 6 (3).

17. *Dual Mandate,* pp. 410–15.

18. Lord Hailey, *An African Survey* (London, 1938), pp. 606–21.

19. Albert Sarraut, *Grandeur et Servitude Coloniale* (Paris, 1931), pp. 138–39.

20. See note 10 above. League of Nations Permanent Mandates Commission, *Minutes* [hereafter PMC], *19* (1930), 19.

The Mandates Commission in fact constituted the central institution of what might be considered an international colonial establishment of the interwar period. Of the ten more or less permanent commissioners, eight were nominated by states with colonial dependencies (Belgium, Britain, France, Italy, Japan, Netherlands, Portugal, Spain), and only one, the Swiss economist William Rappard, can be said to have exercised serious independent critical judgment, although even he was far from being an anticolonialist.[21] The members from colonialist countries, moreover, were almost inevitably former colonial administrators (Lugard served as British member from 1923 to 1936). Apart from the natural proclivity of such men not to rock the colonial boat, they seem to have been under some pressure from their own governments to refrain from criticism that might have diplomatic repercussions.[22]

In its actions the Mandates Commission was constitutionally limited to demanding annual printed reports and to interrogating accredited representatives from each mandated territory. The lack of independent information and initiative that such a procedure involved is admirably, and admiringly, summed up by Lugard in what he cited as the first principle of the commission's operation: "Abstention from direct advice or criticisms of administration or policy, either in advice to the accredited representative or by any attempt at local inspection." [23]

Within this constricted atmosphere, and with the additional widely ranging views of the members (especially the outspokenly reactionary Portugese), the Mandates Commission can hardly be said to have had a clear colonial policy, let alone the sanctions with which to enforce it. Nevertheless, the sophistication of the commission members did frequently give rise to questions that directly or indirectly put light

21. Rappard was only named a regular member of the commission after several years as an observer from the League of Nations Secretariat. Between 1927 and 1932 a German sat on the commission. In 1935 the Italian member (who had been chairman) resigned over the Ethiopian affair. A series of Scandinavian women commission members regularly restricted their concern to educational questions.

22. Margery Perham, *Lugard,* Vol 2, *The Years of Authority* (London, 1960), pp. 650–52.

23. H. Duncan Hall, *Mandates, Dependencies and Trusteeship* (Washington, D.C., 1948), p. 208. These restraints were circumvented in some cases, either by governors such as Sir Donald Cameron, who used his direct contacts with Lugard to build up pressure for reforms in Tanganyika, or by Rappard, whose private knowledge of petitions drawn up in the French mandates thwarted government efforts at keeping such documents from reaching the commission. (Margaret L. Bates, Private communication.) This entire side of the Permanent Mandates Commission's activities deserves further investigation.

on certain problems within the mandated territories; this publicity in turn had sufficient impact on informed British and French opinion so that policy changes were, in fact, effected. That portion of the commission which represented the Western democracies, therefore, asserted certain common standards that shaped the paternalist consensus of interwar African colonialism. British mandates policy generally met these standards from the beginning of the period, and the changes it underwent are not to any significant extent the result of Mandates Commission pressure. France received more severe criticism and consequently altered her policies, although the direction of change was, again, not directly guided by the commission.

Britain won the favor of the Mandates Commission by, first of all, complying more vigorously than France with the one explicit demand imposed by Geneva, the reporting of information. In the first years of the mandate system the commission did not hesitate to deliver direct reprimands to the British for turning in annual reports that were quite sparse compared to their French counterparts.[24] Even after this time the French reports, printed in Paris, were usually longer and contained more elaborate charts, graphs, maps, and illustrations. The British documents, however, give a livelier picture of actual developments within the territories, where they had been produced, and in the case of Tanganyika, were supplemented by annual reports from the provincial commissioners and the various technical departments. More significantly still, from the mid-1920s the accredited representatives of British African mandates were always administrative officers actually serving in the territory under discussion and thus able to convey a very immediate sense of local affairs. When they could manage it, the French sent the *commissaires* (i.e. governors) of the Cameroons and Togo to Geneva but when, more frequently, they could not, the mandates were represented by an official of the Colonial Ministry who had had no overseas experience.

These varying degrees of direct communication with the Mandates Commission had direct policy consequences in only one important case: the response to charges against both British and French mandate rule contained in the lengthy study by the American political scientist, Raymond Leslie Buell, *The Native Problem in Africa* (1928). Buell's allegations against British Tanganyika—not really severe or, it turned out, well-founded—were answered immediately and in full by the territorial administration. The French response was to attack Buell's gen-

24. PMC, *6* (1925), 114.

eral credibility (which was high) and to ignore his very serious charges against the Cameroons and Togo by shuttling responsibility for a reply back and forth between Paris and Africa.[25]

Along with demanding information generally, the Mandates Commission avidly and directly pursued any possibility that mandated territories were being absorbed beyond already agreed limits into the existing colonial possessions of either Britain or France. The British Cameroons and Togoland, which could hardly have been absorbed more into Nigeria and the Gold Coast, were constantly charged to maintain certain formal distinctions. To such interrogations British representatives could proudly reply that in effect they were willing to "make it necessary for the administration of the Gold Coast to conform with the principles of the mandate."[26] In East Africa, where plans to amalgamate Tanganyika, Kenya, and Uganda really threatened the mandate with white settler domination, the Mandates Commission showed more serious concern. But, characteristically, the proposed Closer Union was defeated at home by a coalition of missionaries and administrators (including Lugard) before the British government could even present the case formally to the League of Nations.[27] Although neither French Equatorial nor West Africa presented the French mandates with a political threat equal to that of Kenya, League scrutiny over customs links between the two sets of adjacent territories—as well as the very fact of their total administrative separation—helped recall that labor, military, and tariff regulations in French Africa generally did not meet mandate standards.[28]

From a contemporary perspective, the most significant item in the legal instruments creating the mandates system is their reference to former German colonial subjects as "populations not yet able to stand by themselves." In the orthodox, and British, interpretation of mandate trusteeship, this statement placed a prime responsibility upon mandatory powers to prepare their subjects for eventual self-government. The Permanent Mandates Commission, unlike its successor, the United Nations Trusteeship Commission, did not, however, direct its most strenuous inquiries toward this somewhat embarrassing subject. Although the contrast between British and French policy comes out most directly in regard to the manner in which they promoted African par-

25. PMC, *15* (1929), 20–22, 143, 147, 241–49.

26. PMC, *3* (1923), 149; also *12* (1927), 84 for similar statements on Nigeria as a system which had "guided those who were responsible for drawing up the mandate."

27. Perham, *Lugard, 2,* 677–91.

28. PMC, *3* (1923), 26–27.

ticipation in mandate government, with regard to long-range political aims the paternalist consensus very quickly took precedence over any critical comparisons.

Despite these inhibitions, the frequent statements by British mandate representatives of the manner in which they were applying the policy of Indirect Rule undoubtedly contributed to the great reputation which this doctrine achieved throughout the interwar colonial world. With their particular brand of benevolent conservatism, the Mandates Commission members were generally enthusiastic about reports on Indirect Rule, raising questions only in regard to the protection of subjects from chiefs, but never about the limitations this policy placed upon more modern forms of political development.

The French, on the other hand, were allowed in both their printed reports and oral testimony to give only cursory attention to questions of political development. Lugard represented the most intense concern of the commission when he questioned the commissaires of both Togo and the Cameroons as to the possibility of the Councils of Notables established in these territories foreshadowing a Western parliamentary form of representative government. The apparently satisfactory reply in both cases was that no political advance of any kind had yet been planned.[29] By the 1930s the French were, in fact, to adopt a degree of Indirect Rule in West and Equatorial Africa generally and the two mandated territories particularly, but this would emerge only ambiguously before the Mandates Commission.[30]

In contrast to its cautious approach to political affairs, the Mandates Commission made very forthright inquiries into the economic status of the territories under its supervision. Questions were thus asked about the constant deficits of the British West African mandates as opposed to the impressive prosperity of French Togoland and especially the French Cameroons. Rappard neatly caught the problems which "holding the ring" presented for development by commenting that the cautious economic behavior of British administrators in the Cameroons "would undoubtedly have pleased Adam Smith." [31] British observers themselves admired the development of the Cameroons, which were to show a profit even during the darkest years of the Depression.[32]

The budgetary surpluses displayed throughout the 1920s by both

29. PMC, *6* (1925), 27; *9* (1926), 78.

30. PMC, *30* (1936), 33–34.

31. PMC, *7* (1925), 42.

32. Margery Perham, "France in the Cameroons," *The Times,* May 15, 1936, pp. 15–16.

French mandates also became a target of criticism, since they indicated a higher rate of taxation than was apparently warranted by development investments.[33] The combination of these surpluses with the large-scale use of compulsory labor and the unwillingness of the metropolitan French government to lend the mandates money was unfavorably compared with the generous grants by Britain to Tanganyika, as well as Nigerian and Gold Coast subsidies to the West African British mandates.[34]

This double pressure from the Mandates Commission again helped bring British and French policy closer together. By the 1930s the first British Colonial Development Act (along with the Commonwealth Preferences of the Ottowa Agreements—which did not affect the mandates) signaled a break with Lugardian liberal economic caution. At the same time France was beginning to offer at least small loans to support Sarraut's original grandiose plans.[35]

On other aspects of colonial development—particularly education—the Mandates Commission had a great deal to say but little of substance to offer either Britain or France by endorsing their programs for "adapting" school curricula to African needs.[36] Here, as elsewhere, the commission seemed to favor a benevolent yet gradualist style that fitted especially well with British ideology but did not directly challenge the less defined French position.

Therefore in the European arena, consensus on mandate policy was achieved through a combination of public confrontation and mutual conservatism. In the African territories, where little direct confrontation between British and French officials took place, policy was initially formulated on premises even more distinct from one another than the domestic colonial ideologies of the two powers. But here also a concensus came about, partially through feedback from the League of Nations, but perhaps more importantly through separate comprehension by each colonial government of certain common practical realities. These realities were mainly economic and social in nature, but here they will form a background for a discussion focusing on politics.

Politics in the normal sense of competition for power among various groups was of course virtually absent in the pax colonialia of interwar

33. PMC, 9 (1926), 79–82, 90.

34. PMC, 3 (1923), 34–38.

35. J. M. Lee, *Colonial Development and Good Government* (Oxford, 1967), pp. 44–45, 72–74; Albertini, *Dekolonisation,* pp. 122 ff.

36. PMC, passim, and see Gifford and Weiskel, "African Education," below (chap. 19).

Africa. The general history of all the mandated territories during this period was punctuated by a rhythm of reorganization, upsurge, depression, and recovery largely determined by factors that are non-political, non-African, or both. The distinction between the British and French mandate regimes, however, is best seen in terms of their respective efforts to legitimize themselves in relation to subjects who really had no choice as to their rulers. Policy of this kind not only summarizes the attitude of European administrators to their own function in Africa; it also indicates what role they intended Africans to play in the colonial system. That Africans failed to confirm either British or French conceptions of their development indicates both an ambivalence in the way such conceptions were finally applied and an inability of the colonial system as a whole to withstand the kind of external pressures that finally brought about decolonization. Although a broader and more penetrating perspective is therefore needed to determine what colonial rulers actually accomplished, the study of political policy offers indispensable indications of what colonial rulers were at least attempting to do.

If all efforts at legitimizing colonial rule resulted in ultimate failures, the British as opposed to the French undertaking in the African mandates emerges as a more noble failure. Britain in general put a higher social value upon colonial endeavors than did France, and the more impressive quality of its African administrators is explained first of all by the fact that they were recruited from among the best educated and most highly regarded social groups at home.[37] Elitism was, of course, a universal attitude among colonial officials in Africa itself; the fact that the British officers felt they were elites even before entering the colonial service possibly added a certain extra element of conservatism to their outlook but more probably compelled them to maintain a stricter and more effective sense of values.

In the confusion of wartime the newly conquered German territories were not always staffed with the best men that the British system had to offer. The Cameroons and Togoland, as somewhat impoverished appendages of Nigeria and the Gold Coast, probably never attracted a particularly outstanding group of administrators, although in such small territories staffing did not require any extreme compromises

37. Sir Ralph Furse, *Aucuparius* (London, 1962), passim, and Robert Heussler, *Yesterday's Rulers* (Syracuse, 1963), passim. There is a sense in which British colonial officers represented a country gentry manqué rather than a functioning twentieth-century elite. Nonetheless, they were mainly graduates of the exclusive public school system and Oxford or Cambridge universities.

with usual standards either. It was in Tanganyika that the first years of British rule witnessed numerous examples of ineffectual administration, rapid turnover of personnel, and even minor scandals of illegal ivory trading. But by the middle 1920s this territory, large, salubrious, and the site of ambitious political programs, had attracted an administrative staff noted even within the British service for its high degree of talent and spirit.[38]

A serious study of the French colonial service during this same period still remains to be written.[39] Enough is already known, however, to suggest that its representatives in Africa were recruited from a far less prestigious domestic social group than British administrators: in the interwar years only half seem to have been products of the prescribed Ecole Coloniale–Law School program, the others being men with only secondary school degrees who began their African careers as lower level "*Agents Civiles*" and were promoted later to the senior *Corps d'Administration.* Senior officers were paid lower salaries than their British equivalents, but with the combination of *agents* and *administrateurs,* the total European staff of French territories was proportionally larger than its counterpart in British Africa.[40]

The difficulties experienced in Tanganyika during the early mandate years are paralleled in somewhat different fashion by the French Cameroons and Togo. Actual procurement of staff was no problem in the latter territories since all of French West and Equatorial Africa (including, for this purpose, the mandates) drew its administrators from a common pool which readily shifted individual officers across territorial lines. However, far from escaping disorder and corruption, the French mandates were, throughout the 1920s, notorious for ir-

38. These observations are based upon a general perusal of the Tanganyika personnel files in the National Archives, Dar es Salaam, Tanzania.

39. The comments that follow are based to a large extent on information supplied by William B. Cohen of Indiana University; see his "French Colonial Service in West Africa," above (chap. 14), and also Deschamps, "French Colonial Policy in Tropical Africa Between the Two World Wars, below (chap. 16).

40. According to the respective 1938 reports the French Cameroons had 2.6 million inhabitants governed by 207 *administrateurs* and 43 *agents.* Tanganyika's population was exactly double this (5.2 million) under only 165 senior administrators and 12 subordinate European political staff. The gap was made up by African administrators whose numbers are difficult to compare precisely. French Cameroons had 346 Africans (including chiefs and clerks) on its political staff. The 1938 Tanganyika territorial budget shows a proportionately smaller number of Africans (548, mostly clerks), but in addition at least as many administrative staff (including all the chiefs) were paid from local Native Administration budgets which are not collated anywhere.

regular occurrences, the most sensational case being that of Alfred Lewis Woefel, the second commissaire of Togo, who in 1922 was dismissed for graft in the disposal of former German landholdings.[41]

In the better years that followed, the administrators of the Cameroons at least are said to have developed a unique esprit de corps which even allowed some of them to serve with a degree of continuity in the same territory.[42] However, neither the collective nor the individual personality of this body emerges from any published documents of the Cameroons, nor did any of the officers produce private writings on their experiences. By contrast, reports from Tanganyika are full of memorandums from individual administrators—during the 1930s their ethnographic and other unofficial writings were appearing in *Tanganyika Notes and Records*—and no less than four senior officers of this period ultimately published their memoirs.[43]

All the above having been said, it remains true that the middle and latter 1920s represent, in both the British and French mandates, a period when the personalities of at least territorial governors emerge along remakably parallel lines. It is perhaps wrong to identify Sir Hugh Clifford of Nigeria and Sir Gordon Guggisberg of the Gold Coast with the British Cameroons and Togoland, since neither governor saw fit to represent his portion of these territories before the Permanent Mandates Commission.[44] In Tanganyika, however, 1925 to 1931 are the years of Sir Donald Cameron, one of the key figures in all British interwar African policy. In the French Cameroons Governor Theodore Marchand was commissaire from 1923 to 1931, and in French Togo Governor Auguste Bonnecarrère served in the same capacity from 1922 to 1931. Both appeared before the Mandates Commission several times and lent a very definite stamp to the administration of their respective territories.

41. R. L. Buell, *The Native Problem in Africa* (New York, 1928), Vol. 2, pp. 297–300; also William Cohen, private communication.

42. PMC, *30* (1936), 29; Cohen cites complaints from the Togo government to the French Colonial Ministry about the lack of continuity in local staffing; private communication.

43. Sir Donald Cameron, *My Tanganyika Service and Some Nigeria* (London, 1939), Sir Stewart Symes, *Tour of Duty* (London, 1946), Sir Charles C. F. Dundas, *African Crossroads* (London, 1955), Sir Philip Mitchell, *African Afterthoughts* (London, 1955); see also *Tanganyika Notes and Records*, 1936 et seq., and Gordon C. Brown and Alexander M. Bruce Hutt, *Anthropology in Action* (London, 1935).

44. Sir Donald Cameron, as governor of Nigeria, did so represent the British Cameroons in 1932; see PMC, *22* (1932), 160.

The governorships of all these men are identified with programs of political reform and economic development, whereas the succeeding period, characterized by a series of brief governorships in all the mandates, shows a definite flagging of élan. The 1920s are also the years in which differing British and French concepts of administrative-political legitimacy show the greatest contrast; in the 1930s the two systems begin, both consciously and unconsciously, to imitate one another.

Enough has been written about Indirect Rule generally as well as its Tanganyika, Cameroons, and Togoland applications so that no detailed summary is required here.[45] For present purposes it is only necessary to note the basic administrative essentials of the system: research to discern the legitimate traditional African rulers of a given area, their recognition (or reorganization) as a "Native Authority," and the devolution of judicial and fiscal functions upon the same institutions as a "Native Court" and "Native Treasury." In this form Indirect Rule came to the Northern Cameroons almost as soon as they were taken over by the British; to the Southern Cameroons beginning in 1922; to Tanganyika beginning in 1925; and to Togoland (not always with Native Treasuries) during the 1930s.

Whatever must ultimately be said about the positive contribution of Indirect Rule to political development, the ideology linking its application in these three territories is clear, the administrative effort involved was extensive, and the sense of accomplishment in terms of preparing Africans for eventual, if very gradual, self-government was great. In the French mandates no comparable program existed.

One reason for the failure of French mandate administrators to clarify their aims in regard to African political development has already been cited: the Permanent Mandates Commission put no pressure upon them to do so, and the Colonial Ministry, as exemplified by the commitment of Sarraut to "association," seemed almost opposed to any steps toward self-government. But in Africa, where French no less than British administrators had to come to some kind of systematic terms with their native charges, mandate officials did have a rich doctrinal heritage to draw upon: their problem was that the message of this doctrine had become ambiguous.

Before World War I, Lugard's Indirect Rule, which so well suited the British temperament, had been matched by the "politique des

45. Austen, "Official Mind"; David E. Gardinier, "The British in the Cameroons, 1919–1939," *Britain and Germany*, pp. 538–47; F. M. Bourret, *Ghana: the Road to Independence* (London, 1960), pp. 92–107.

races" of West African Governor-General William Ponty, who urged, if not literally "direct rule," maximal French intervention in traditional African politics to achieve "une contacte plus directe entre l'administrateur et l'administratée." [46] The war, however, with its particularly harsh demands upon both Frenchmen and Africans in French Africa, had produced a series of minor uprisings which demonstrated the dangers of relying upon such direct efforts to maintain a smoothly working colonial system.[47] In 1917, therefore, the then governor-general, Joost Van Vollenhoven, issued a circular in which he insisted that his subordinate seek by whatever means possible to approach Africans through the medium of their traditional chiefs. Dismayed at French military recruitment policies in West Africa, Van Vollenhoven resigned his post in 1918 and met a heroic battlefield death in Europe. This action made the administrator into a legend, but it also prevented any systematic execution of his policies or even a clear ideology for the interwar period.[48]

For the purposes of examining the operation of this ambiguous political heritage in the mandates, it is perhaps best to restrict analysis to the French Cameroons, a territory that has some features in common with the two areas where the British most assiduously applied Indirect Rule, Tanganyika and the British Cameroons. The first distinction to be noted between French and British native policy in this period is the relative inarticulateness of the former. The most elaborate statements concerning political development in the French Cameroons occurred during the period of the first commissaire, Jules Carde (later governor-general of French West Africa). Carde's reports make occasional reference to the term "association," but it was never used to impose a common definition on what appears to be a highly contradictory series of policies. Thus, in a manner very reminiscent of Indirect Rule, French practice in the Cameroons was described as essentially an effort to "conserve the local [indigenous] political organization while suppressing what is unavoidable." [49] At the same time, following the tradition of the "politique des races," Carde began

46. Cited in C. W. Newbury, *The Western Slave Coast and Its Rulers* (Oxford, 1961), p. 203.

47. Jacques Lombard, *Autorités Traditionnelles et Pouvoirs Europeens en Afrique Noire* (Paris, 1967), p. 121 f.

48. *Ame du chef,* pp. 189–211; Robert Cornevin, "Evolution des Chefferies traditionnelles en Afrique Noire d'expression française," *Recueil Penant,* 1961, pp. 248–49.

49. *Rapport Annuel du Gouvernement Français sur l'administration du Cameroun pour l'annee* [hereafter *Rapport Cameroun*] 1921, p. 43.

breaking the hold of Muslim Fulani emirs over their pagan subjects.[50] Finally, in a policy that many commentators have interpreted as "direct rule," Carde sanctioned the creation of new "regional chiefs" who were to have "no authority of their own; above all else they are administrative organs." Even where he recognized the practical impossibility of direct administration, Carde instructed his administrative officers that "your political function is summed up in two words: direction-control . . . make him [the local traditional ruler] understand that he is only an executive arm . . . make sure that he acts only within the outline of instructions which you will have traced for him." [51]

Carde's successor, the long-tenured Marchand, indicated no departure from any of these policies, but brought the Cameroons into line with established French concepts of association by establishing "Councils of Notables" in each district of the territory. These bodies, drawn from various types of local African leadership circles (excluding salaried government employees), met twice a year with the French district administrator to discuss a broad range of policy matters.

It is difficult to say, from the sparse reports of Marchand's intentions and the even more limited information on the functioning of the councils, whether they represent a principle of replacing or adapting traditional African political institutions.[52] Although it constitutes the most substantial French political reform of the entire mandate period, the establishment of the notables' councils seems simply not to have been viewed by the French administrators involved with the same degree of seriousness as parallel efforts in the British mandates. Often the chiefs recognized by the French as somehow representative "notables" were the same individuals who had been chosen on an admittedly haphazard basis to help collect taxes in the early years of the mandate.

Contemporary and more recent critics have made much of the artificiality and corruption of these African collaborators, particularly the notorious Charles Atangana of Yaoundé, who became one of the two African members of the territorial Administrative Council.[53] There is,

50. *Rapport Cameroun*, 1922, p. 60.

51. Ibid., pp. 59, 61.

52. LeVine (*The Cameroons*, pp. 91–98), who relies heavily on Buell, Vol. 2, pp. 308–11, for his argument, seems to oversimplify French policy somewhat by characterizing it as a systematic and insensitive attack upon chiefs.

53. LeVine, pp. 95–96, 102–03, 107, based largely on Buell.

on the other hand, evidence of French efforts to straighten out ethnic boundaries and seek general knowledge that would help them adjust their policies to African concerns.[54] Their opposition to more thorough reforms along this line seems to have become, by the late 1920s, less a matter of principle than one of disinterest. Similarly, neither the chiefs in their administrative capacity nor the councils as representative bodies were given any regular and recognized judicial or fiscal powers. The resulting monopolization of *indigenat* jurisdiction by French administrators represents a real variation from British practice. It should be remembered, however, that Cameron fought vigorously in Tanganyika to take the review of Native Court judgments away from the territorial High Court and place it in the hands of the Provincial Administration.[55] The absence of Native Treasuries or their equivalent in French territories reflects less the difference between British and French policies toward traditional chiefs than the trust placed by the respective colonial governments in their own civil servants. In Tanganyika it was not chiefs but British administrators or African clerks who controlled most Native Treasury budgets, thereby achieving bureaucratic flexibility if not real political devolution. In French Africa, however, neither administrative nor political concern for decentralization could overcome the fear that, given an opportunity to evade supervision, local officials would embezzle funds—something they seem to have managed frequently even within the prevailing system, according to William B. Cohen (personal communication).

It is common to balance British achievements in Indirect Rule with French propensities to "assimilate" educated African classes. Officially, as already indicated, the doctrine of assimilation was not applied to mandates. The immediate policy of the governments of both the Cameroons and Togo in the 1920s was also opposed to promoting educated Africans to high positions in local government or in the central civil service.[56] Insofar as political development in either of the mandate systems was glad to be gradual, the British idea of working through traditional elites did, therefore, seem both more realistic and idealistic.

By the 1930s this truth had also struck French policy planners and

54. See sections marked "Organization Administrative" and "Situation Politique" in *Rapport Cameroun,* 1923 et seq.; also Jacques Kuoh Moukouri, *Doigts Noirs* (Montreal, 1963), p. 36.

55. Austen, "Official Mind," p. 589.

56. *Rapport Cameroun, 1925,* pp. 34–35.

the era was marked—at least at the level of stated intentions—by "un lugardisme moderé" (or perhaps a neo-Vollenhovenism), most notably expressed in the 1932 West African circulars of Governor-General Brévié.[57] In the Cameroons this new mood is reflected in the governorship of Bonnecarrère, promoted from his successful Togo tenure, who proceeded to denounce the anarchistic tendencies of the "politique des races" and reform the council system so as to make it more representative of traditional ruling groups.[58] The same period is also characterized by a new emphasis on administrative ethnography, inspired by Henri Labouret, a professor at the Ecole Coloniale who worked closely with British Indirect Rule theorists through the London-based International Institute for African Languages and Cultures (today the International African Institute).[59]

It is perhaps symbolic that in 1934, as an austerity measure, Bonnecarrère was forcibly retired. The demands of the Depression were to reveal other harsh truths about the authoritarian realities that underlay all colonial administrative arrangements.

The contradiction between economic priorities and African political development had been recognized by both British and French administrators well before the 1930s. The British position, expressed frequently by Lugard in his writings and at the Mandates Commission, and by Sir Hugh Clifford and Cameron in Nigeria and Tanganyika, was to give deliberate priority to the protection and fostering of African governing institutions over the production of exports. As Cameron put it, in stifling an effort to improve forcibly one of Tanganyika's most valuable crops, "The native is, after all, greater than his coffee."[60] The result was to slow down the output of the African sector in all the British territories, most notably in Tanganyika where peasant exports actually declined during the generally prosperous years of Cameron's governorship.[61] By the same token the British mandates in this period enjoyed an almost perfect record of freedom from scandal of any kind. Even Buell's list of peccadilloes

57. See Deschamps, below, p. 558.

58. *Rapport Cameroun,* 1933, pp. 147–50.

59. See Labouret, *A la recherche d'une politique indigène dans l'Ouest africain* (Paris, 1931), passim, and Labouret, *Le Cameroun* (Paris, 1937), esp. pp. 14–24. The programs of ethnographic research by administrators promoted (and described) by Labouret in these works did not, for the most part, materialize during the interwar period; Cohen, private communication.

60. Memorandum, November 4, 1930, Secretariat Minute Papers, 11969, Dar es Salaam.

61. Austen, "Official Mind," p. 596.

was added as an appendage to his judgment that "the future of native policy in Tanganyika looks bright." [62]

French mandate policy during the 1920s took a line almost diametrically opposed to the British notion of political priorities, and it produced logically consequent results. Just as *la mise en valeur* had been the key theme of Sarraut's manifesto, economic development was stressed in all the official pronouncements of the Cameroons and Togo regimes. In the former territory, particularly, infrastructure was expanded in accordance with Sarraut's program, and revenue from commodity exports managed to keep well ahead of import expenditures. At the same time serious charges were leveled against the Cameroons government for the high mortality of forced laborers on its main railroad project. The accusations also extended to African collaborators of the government, particularly Atangana, who found numerous methods of exploiting their subjects.[63]

As with Indirect Rule, the French reacted during the 1930s to the invidious comparisons with British mandates by making greater efforts to supervise labor conditions and local authorities. The system of direct rule, however modified, was in fact well suited to such efforts, and the impressive economic performance of the Cameroons continued up to World War II without further report of major abuses.

But for the British mandates, the 1930s revealed the incompatibility of traditional African political structures and accelerated economic development. Tanganyika particularly experienced during the depression years a successful response to crop production demands at a considerable cost to the dynamism of political reform.[64] Throughout the territory experiments with centralizing acephalous societies were abandoned, legitimate but uncooperative chiefs were deposed, and ever more reliance came to be placed upon African collaborators with little claim to traditional status. Just as Atangana in the Cameroons could be forced into sufficient respectibility to earn a memorial statue from the postcolonial government, so Mgei bin Hema of Singida, like Atangana a former German appointee, became the man to whom the British sent recalcitrant legitimate chiefs for lessons in rulership.[65]

62. Buell, Vol. 2, p. 464.

63. Ibid., pp. 327, 344–46; LeVine, pp. 102–03, 106–07.

64. Austen "Official Mind," pp. 598–602.

65. J. Gus Liebenow, "The Establishment of Legitimacy in a Dependency Situation: A Case Study of the Nyatura of Tanganyika," Indiana University, mimeograph, n.d.; Mwanza Provincial Minute Paper 816, National Archives, Dar es Salaam, Tanzania.

In protest against regulations for improved agricultural methods, the very natives whom Cameron had found greater than their coffee engaged in 1937 in widespread antigovernment riots.[66]

Despite such incidents British East and West African policy during the 1930s maintained its reputation for greater adherence than the French to mandate ideals. This feeling was shared not only among European observers of the colonial scene but also among Africans subject to mandate regimes. A brief comparison of African responses to British and French rule indicates that there were differences, although not always along the lines predicated by administrative theory, but that the political relevance of such distinctions, like that of administrative policy, tends to disappear in the face of larger common pressures.

In considering the very widespread display of pro-British attitudes among Africans throughout the mandated territories, it is important to note that both before, and even to a large extent during, the occupation of these territories by Germany, all had lain within a British commercial and missionary "sphere of influence." Thus, despite first German and then French education policies, the major lingua franca of the Cameroons was and has remained pidgen English. The German language, similarly, had little impact on Tanganyika Swahili, whereas this language had, even before World War I, borrowed vast numbers of words from English. Although the origins of the influence lie in the "informal empire" maintained by Britain in both West and East Africa before the late nineteenth-century colonial partition, its continuation up to and after World War I must be explained by the thriving British colonies of Nigeria, the Gold Coast, Kenya, Uganda, and (to a lesser extent) Northern Rhodesia and Nyasaland which surrounded the German colonies geographically, dominated them commercially, and even exercised cultural influence through missions and British mission-trained Africans.

The greater employment opportunities and higher wages in British Africa account for a labor migration out of German Africa before the war and out of the French Cameroons and Togo during the mandate period. But, despite French explanations to this effect before the Mandates Commission, some of the labor movement must be seen as a conscious African response to differences in administrative policy. The fact that laborers stopped going from Tanganyika to Kenya after

66. Ralph A. Austen, *Northwest Tanzania Under German and British Rule* (New Haven, 1968), pp. 224–27.

the British took over the former territory is not without significance here.[67] In West Africa French demands for both paid and unpaid public labor account for migration from the Cameroons, and French insistence on individual taxation at relatively high rates helps explain movements into British Togoland, where no such levy existed.[68]

For reasons that also have their roots in premandate developments, the French likewise experienced difficulty in winning over those more sophisticated Africans in the Cameroons and Togo who might have been expected to form a gallicized elite. A small number of subjects in these territories did, in fact, take on French citizenship during the mandate period, but their statistical and political insignificance is a logical result of France's declared disinterest in practicing here the kind of assimilation policy earlier established in the communes of Senegal. In the Cameroons, moreover, the most advanced commercial group of the precolonial period, the Duala, had suffered an economic eclipse under the German regime and simply continued their quarrels over land and political prerogatives with the French.[69] In Togo the highly sophisticated Creole elites of the coast were able to establish more numerous and egalitarian social contacts with the French than might have been possible under a British regime.[70] But it is precisely these groups whom the French colonialist historian of Togo has described as particularly marked by British influences, and their leading figure, the later Togo premier, Sylvanus Olympio, received his higher education at the London School of Economics and returned to his homeland as a representative of the British United Africa Company.[71]

Among what may be considered a middle level of educated African elites in Togo and, to a lesser extent, the Cameroons, the French were consistently embarrassed by expressions of pro-German sentiment. The vociferous Deutsch-Togo Bund can at least partly be explained away by the displacement of German-speaking Togolese from government jobs, which now demanded a knowledge of French. Again, however,

67. Compare reports in Reichskolonialamt File 118 (Deutsche Zentralarchiv, Potsdam) on labor problems with *Annual Reports, Tanganyika Labor Department.*

68. PMC, *24* (1938), 121.

69. Harry Rudin, *Germans in the Cameroons, 1884–1914* (New Haven, 1938), pp. 408–13; reports of Franco-Duala conflict are found in almost every year of the *Rapport Cameroun* as well as many PMC sessions.

70. PMC, *24* (1938), 118–21.

71. Cornevin, *Histoire du Togo,* p. 266.

the failure of such movements to surface in the British mandates suggests that they indicate real hostility to the French.[72]

If the character and distribution of popular protest expressions in the mandates point to widespread African awareness of the distinctions between British and French rule, their translation into meaningful political action cannot be so readily differentiated. According to the tenets of Indirect Rule, political development in British Africa should have followed ethnic lines, while in the French mandates, where tribal organizations were undermined, the specter of mass political agitation would have made its appearance. In a superficial sense this analysis did hold true for the 1920s. In Tanganyika, at least, Africans responded enthusiastically to the restoration of their traditional political structures, and even in the French Cameroons, where administrators took an interest in applied ethnography, they seem to have gained popularity.[73] But the unwillingness or inability of the colonial regimes to direct their development programs through traditionalist channels ultimately nullified the effect of such reforms. Similarly a religiously inspired uprising among the Baya on the western border of the Cameroons in 1929 may be typical of the kind of unrest common to socially disrupted colonial dependencies; nevertheless, the movement was minor in scope, marginal to the main centers of French mandate impact (its inspiration came from the far more disrupted French Equatorial Africa), and not repeated elsewhere in the history of the mandate.[74]

Tribal politics with serious territorial implications appeared only in the French mandates but more as a result of specific local conditions than of direct or indirect administrative policies. The case of the Duala in the Cameroons has already been cited. Apart from their efforts to protect specific interests from the local French administrators, this group also made appeals on a protonationalist basis to the League of Nations; but exposure of the particularist ethnic backing for these various front organizations served the French in convincing the Mandates Commission to ignore them.[75] A more formidable movement developed during the same period among the Ewe of Togo, a group spurred on by pride in the success of individual Europeanized

72. Robert Cornevin, *Le Togo: Nation Pilote* (Paris, 1963), p. 92. See frequent petitions of this group in PMC, passim.

73. Austen, "Official Mind," p. 593; Moukouri, *Doigts Noirs,* p. 36.

74. *Rapport Cameroun,* 1929, pp. 71–72; PMC, *19* (1930), 109–10.

75. LeVine, pp. 113–16.

members under the mandate regime. The growth of an independent Ewe Protestant Church resulted partly from French unwillingness to allow German missionaries back into Togo; but the more purely political side of the Ewe movement cannot be attributed to any specific colonial policy particularly when, after World War II, the Ewe demanded tribal reunification through elimination of the boundaries between both Togolands and the Gold Coast.[76]

It is a mark of the common authoritarianism of both British and French mandate regimes that neither viewed sympathetically the development of territorial politics on a Western (or Indian) nationalist model. The British, whose Indirect Rule system was designed precisely to provide an alternative to such a model, nevertheless laid the ground more directly for nationalism by the establishment of territorial legislative councils in Nigeria, the Gold Coast, and Tanganyika. During the interwar years, however, no Africans from any of the British mandates participated in these bodies: Cameroonians and Togolese because representation was not extended to their areas, Tanganyikans because only Europeans and Asians were considered sufficiently proficient in English to participate in the local legislative council.

France, without the tradition of decolonization which the British unavoidably brought from the white dominions to tropical Africa, explicitly denied that the system of notables' councils should imply "any form, however vague and distant it might appear, of a representative regime." [77] At both the local and territorial level, the councils of both the Cameroons and Togo resembled less political bodies than professional or technical pressure groups (there were parallel agricultural, health, and commercial councils) whose function was cooperation with the administration rather than representation of the populace.

But just as significant as the restrictions placed by both regimes on territorial politics was the limited perspective of those Africans in a position to act on a territorial basis. Perhaps the only group ready to do so in any of the mandates was the corps of African junior civil servants. A Tanganyika Civil Servants Association was formed in 1924 and five years later sought to establish itself on a wider base as the Tanganyika African Association. Despite the formation (or

76. Jean-Claude Pauvert, "L'evolution politique des Ewe," *Cahiers Africaines*, 2 (1958), 161–91; Claude E. Welch, *Dream of Unity* (Ithaca, 1966), pp. 37–81.

77. Marchand in *Rapport Cameroun*, 1923, cited in LeVine, pp. 92–93.

recognition) of branches in various provincial centers, the TAA depended for survival upon various forms of government sponsorship, and the advent of World War II found it virtually moribund.[78]

In the Cameroons the more stringent French regime forbade the formation of a civil servants union in 1931.[79] With the threat of German propaganda in the late 1930s, however, the government here also saw fit to sponsor organizations of educated Africans, one, the Union Camerounaises, having begun life as a Duala protest body and the other, Jeunesses Camerounaises Françaises, created especially for the occasion. Although, like the Tanganyika African Association, Jeucafra (as it was later known) ultimately provided a basis for post-World War II nationalism, during its brief prewar life it effectively helped rally Cameroons sentiment behind retention of the French mandate.[80]

In summing up the meaning of the mandates experience for Britain and France it is necessary to turn back from the inconclusive spectacle of African politics to more defined questions of European aims. Because of their broad efforts at controlling the evolution of African society, the British in this period appear to have been far more ambitious than the French. For this reason also the failure of African society to conform to the pattern set out for it appears more severe in the British mandates. The French, with their desire merely to keep order and foster the maximal economic and social development consonent with their limited means, were more in tune with the realities of the interwar situation, however shabby their regime may have seemed in its moments of failure.

The one solid advantage of the British regime from its own viewpoint was its built-in anticipation of African self-assertion, unprepared as the architects of Indirect Rule may have been for the form this self-assertion would take. Had France continued with her interwar political outlook, it is conceivable that the tropical African empire might have undergone the same bloody decolonization as French North Africa or Indochina. Along with the special events of World War II and its immediate aftermath, it is perhaps the sensitivity of the French to British precedents in black Africa generally and in the

78. Ralph A. Austen, "Notes on the Pre-History of TANU," *Makerere Journal*, 9 (1964), 1–6; for a more optimistic view of these developments, see J. M. Lonsdale, "Some Origins of Nationalism in East Africa," *Journal of African History* 9 (1968), 133–35.

79. Moukouri, p. 32, fn. 1.

80. LeVine, p. 117; Moukouri, p. 74.

mandates particularly which helped bring about the reforms allowing such a smooth transition to independence here. This is not a formulation that would please the man who presided over both the Brazzaville reforms of 1944 and steps leading to emancipation from 1958 onward. But for France to achieve a worthy destiny in her African mandates, it was necessary to borrow a degree of inspiration from the British.

16. *French Colonial Policy in Tropical Africa Between the Two World Wars*

HUBERT DESCHAMPS

There is no comprehensive study of French colonial policy and practice in tropical Africa from 1919 to 1939; it is as if between the conquest and the formation of the French Union nothing of importance took place.[1] Doubtless this period of respite "in the shadow of the swords" offers no material for heroic history. But its duration, and the presence of a twentieth-century administration in a traditional Africa, brought about a slow evolution that paved the way for the future. Further, the period permits one to appreciate the particular characteristics of French actions.

The time has not yet come for a vast and complete work on the subject. The archives still cannot be consulted for the period since 1918. They alone, and above all the ones of the posts in the bush, completed by the African oral traditions, would provide a precise picture of reality. In default one can utilize the rather conformist specialized reviews and some books appearing at that time, notably those of certain great masters—Sarraut, Brévié, Olivier—whose experience tempers somewhat the official optimism. Freer in their expression are the writings, theoretical but inspired by practice, of administrators like Delafosse, Labouret, Delavignette, Geismar, and myself.

I was, in effect, one of those humble "kings of the bush" that Delavignette has called "the true chiefs of the Empire." Student of the Colonial School from 1923 to 1926, administrator in Madagascar from 1926 to 1936, member of the cabinet of the president of the Council of Ministers in 1936–37, governor in Africa (Somaliland, the

1. The large work of Jean Suret-Canale, *Afrique noire, l'ère coloniale, 1900–1945* (Paris, 1964), thoroughly covers the period and constitutes an indictment from a Communist perspective, putting in relief the scandals and the abuses. The author has nonetheless undertaken careful research, both in the printed materials of the period and in the Guinea archives. This picture in dark tones offers a useful contrast to the uniformly rosy hues of the official statements. A complete and impartial history remains to be established.

Ivory Coast, Senegal beginning in 1938), I participated in different capacities in the colonial life of this period. I can, therefore, in this short historical essay, bring the impressions of an actor, although a very secondary one, and of a witness.

With the Treaty of Versailles, France reached its greatest extent as a colonial power. To the Maghreb, Indochina, and the little colonies dispersed over all the seas were added the mandates for Syria and Lebanon. For tropical Africa alone, there came to be joined to the three great governments-general of French West Africa (A.O.F.), French Equatorial Africa (A.E.F.), and Madagascar, the mandates for the former German Cameroons and Togoland. In addition, it is necessary to cite two little colonies, French Somaliland and Réunion.[2]

This enormous empire[3] (which in Africa alone occupied nearly a third of the continent) was acquired by France more through political pride than through economic interest. It was a revenge for Waterloo and Sedan, a field of action for military glory and an affirmation of grandeur. From thence came the spiritedness of the colonial rivalries with England and Germany. In 1919 everything was resolved. No longer was the national sentiment at stake; there remained no more than a passive vanity in contemplating the world map widely tinted with French colors. The Frenchman, *terrien* and European above all, showed little interest in these distant countries. In the Parliament they held only an insignificant place: twenty deputies out of six hundred, of which only one, elected by the four assimilated communes of Senegal, came from tropical Africa. The Parliament rarely intervened except for the discussion of the budget (which was very modest) of the Ministry of the Colonies, for the guarantees for loans, and at long intervals in order to denounce a scandal, which was a simple, ephemeral pretext for the opposition to attack the government. The *senatus-consulte* of May 3, 1854, a law of the Second Empire, laid down the principle of exception (*spécialité*) for colonial

2. It is about this African whole that the present study will speak. I am excluding Réunion from it. This "old colony" was in fact assimilated after 1848 with a local assembly and representatives in the French Parliament; all of its inhabitants were citizens. Its status was therefore entirely different from that of the other African colonies and much closer to the Metropolitan departments, to which it was legally assimilated in 1946.

3. The term "empire" was not officially used, doubtless through a republican sentiment that preserved its hostility to the Second Empire. One spoke of "the French colonies" or "the French colonial domain."

legislation: the colonies shall be ruled by decree. The Republic never abolished this text. The colonies remained, therefore, abandoned to the specialists, that is, to the bureaucrats.[4]

At the head, the minister of the colonies was a member of Parliament who often considered this secondary post as a steppingstone to more grandiose positions; in addition, the ministers did not last long in office; a minister just had time to get accustomed to his job before he disappeared from the scene. It was, therefore, the *fonctionnaires* (civil servants) of the Ministry who assured continuity. They formed a body apart, which but rarely ventured overseas. This bizarre system was justified by the independence of judgment that it insured. At the same time a few overseas administrators were temporarily assigned to the Ministry. In addition, the minister was kept informed by the inspectors of the colonies, whom he sent on missions in order to control the finances or give an account of happenings.

On a day-to-day basis there was little room, in such a system of administration, for large doctrinal constructs.[5] "Assimilation," a concept of simplifying universalism, simultaneously Latin, Christian, and Cartesian, was the natural bent of the French: men are alike; "reason is the most widely apportioned thing in the world"; laws recognized as rational are valid for all. The Old Regime had, it is true, admitted the huge exception of slavery. The Revolution had proclaimed the liberation of the slaves, their accession to the function of French citizens, and the division of the colonies into Departments (*départements*), all measures that war and revolts kept from being applied. After this failure, which was followed in 1830 by the annexation of Algeria, and then by the progress of the human sciences (especially geography and ethnology), the nineteenth century thence had come to admit the diversity of men and of their civilizations and to respect the latter while at the same time dominating them. Bonaparte in

4. The French colonial system is set forth in detail and with great clarity in the classic work of a professor of law, Arthur Girault, *Principes de colonisation et de Législation coloniale,* which first appeared in 1894 and which went through four revisions (1903, 1907, 1921, 1927), each containing careful updating and many additions, passing little by little from one volume to five. This uninterrupted success shows the interest of this work, which has shaped and inspired generations of colonials. Republican, and even at the beginning mildly assimilationist, Girault sees in colonization an educative mission. His judgment sticks closely to the facts. He sets forth different opinions at length and tries to present sensible solutions. He evolves with his times.

5. See my work, *Les Méthodes et les Doctrines coloniales de la France du XVIème siècle à nos jours* (Paris, 1953).

Egypt had shown the way for this practical policy by invoking the Prophet and utilizing the *ulemas* (Muslim scholars). The Republicans, however, faithful to their slogan of brotherhood, preserved assimilation, if not as an immediate practice at least as an ultimate goal. But the assimilationist party became divided, bourgeoisified, and was satisfied at the parliamentary level with waving the flag of the ideal in the peroration of its speeches.

The intellectuals who belonged to the Right, however—among others Jules Harmand, who was qualified by Indochinese experience—extolled a policy of "Association" founded on respect for customs, indirect administration, and economic development to the advantage of the two parties. More and more, people accepted their slogan, which had the advantage of changing nothing already acquired while at the same time appearing wise, scientific, and humane. Therefore, it coincided very well with the most recent and stylish practice, that of Lyautey in Morocco, which was enriched by a princely allure and a dazzling literary style. In his doctrine, only the distant possibility of autonomy and of secession was suppressed.

The Frenchman, peasant and thrifty petty bourgeois, does not easily abandon what he has, especially if it does not cost him dearly. In addition, as heir of the Latins, adding to the frontiers of a great whole seemed to him a generous extension of French civilization and at the same time flattered his national pride. Such had indeed already been seen in the case of the "liberation of peoples" by the French Revolution and then in Napoleonic Europe. "Association," stripped of meaning (as was the case with the old "*Pacte Colonial*") was thus a useful word for maintaining the status quo. In fact, there was scarcely more genuine "Association" in it than there had been "Pact." And the assimilationist tendencies had not, for all this, disappeared. The natives were, at one and the same time in this terminology, those associated with France and its "children," who ought to be unswervingly grateful to her for this double title. All that was mixed together in the speeches, nay even in the minds.

The obscurity of brilliant intentions once again covered an absence of real interest on the part of the Metropole. All real action therefore lay with the local governments, that is, with the fonctionnaires possessing delegated authority in the colonies—the governors and administrators.

The governor was at the same time the representative of the central government and the head of the colony. The governors of Madagascar (who had the title of governor-general), Somaliland, the Cameroons, and Togo corresponded directly with the minister of the colonies. Those of the colonies of French West Africa and French Equatorial Africa were subordinate in each federation to a governor-general, who alone was responsible in relation to Paris. The governor simultaneously directed the administrators of the technical services, but in the federations the latter were largely dependent upon their directors, who were directly responsible to the governor-general. The post of governors-general was sometimes given to an influential member of Parliament. But the governors, and more and more the governors-general, were chosen from the ranks of the administrators.

Each colony was divided into *circonscriptions* ("*cercles*" in Africa, provinces in Madagascar), each one often split up further into "subdivisions" or "districts." The administrator was responsible for his *cercle* vis-à-vis the governor, and the heads of subdivisions (subadministrators) were his subordinates. His role was totalitarian: responsible for order, head of the militia, judge, census taker, tax collector, bookkeeper, supervisor of labor, constructor of roads and buildings, organizer of markets, urban planner, nurseryman, in charge of the progress of the economy and of public health, protector of the forests, inspector of education, chief of the Europeans, representative of the native collectivities. He had to see all, rule all, conceive all, accomplish all. Besides, theoretically, he had to supervise the application of an enormous mass of regulations contained in the official journals, and which constantly varied.

He had all the powers. Nothing could be done without his aid or his authorization. Ten days each month at least he was on tour over the roads in order to insure contacts, explain instructions to the villagers, receive their complaints, arbitrate, activate, and, if need be, punish. The order and progress of the country depended upon him. As a result, there were sometimes abuses or oversights the governor had to sanction, but also in general there was a pride, a stimulation to activity, an emulation that counted for much in the transformation of the country. The peasant fiber is never far from a Frenchman; as his ancestors used to say "my land," the administrator said "my *cercle*," "my roads," "my natives," and wished that they might be the first and the best.

All therefore lay with him, except for several truly very specialized services: medicine and railroads. Later, and little by little, technical services were developed. The administrator could then devote himself more fully to his proper role: political and financial. But this transformation would be achieved only much later, after the Second World

War when the administrator himself would be close to disappearing.

In 1919 his role, inherited simultaneously from the officers of the conquest (in Africa the administrator was called "*commandant*") and from the declining or vanished native kings, was at the maximum. It was very necessary to count on his authority and his ability to untangle and clear up things. The petty-bourgeois Frenchman of the Republic, as well as of the Old Regime, was willing to have colonies on condition that they cost him nothing. A 1900 law on finances laid down the principle that the colonies had to be self-sufficient, with self-sufficiency including the salaries of the European personnel, which were greater than in the Metropole in order to encourage them to go abroad. From this came rather heavy direct taxes, the duties on products exported still being insufficient to furnish the resources.

A good part of the working time of the administrators was used up in collecting taxes in the form of currency. A tax in kind, the "*prestations*," which also existed in France but on a lesser scale, consisted of ten days of public labor each year: and it was with the prestations that the roads were built. The "code of the *indigénat*" offered another means of action. It was the right of the administrator directly to inflict five days in prison upon anyone who had not paid his taxes, done his prestations, obeyed the hygienic regulations, or raised enough produce. These prisoners, with others sentenced by the courts, constituted an urban labor force used to construct buildings. Poverty led to such primitive procedures, which were rather easily accepted in the areas where *corvées* were owed to the former chiefs; but the anarchic populations, the so-called "segmentary societies," became resigned to them but slowly, and not without revolts.

The segmentary societies posed a much more difficult problem since in these cases the administrator was in direct contact with the population, and needed the cooperation of his "*gardes-cercles*" (local police) or "*gardes-indigènes*" (native police), that is to say his armed and uniformed policemen. Although the police were few in numbers, they often abused this situation. Elsewhere the native chiefs intervened, though not without dangers.

This bureaucratic, hierarchic, and authoritarian system had no counterweight. The "government councils" were only the private councils of the governors, in the majority of cases composed of high *fonctionnaires* who were the governors' subordinates. Only the four original communes of Senegal had been provided with a General Council (*conseil-général*) elected on the model of the French departments. Their inhabitants in effect were citizens. All the other natives were "French subjects," without political rights, subject to the *in-*

digénat, the *prestations,* and to a special system of justice—the native tribunals, presided over by the administrator assisted by two native notables charged with saying what local custom was. Local custom continued to rule them, for the French laws applied only to citizens.

The influence of French settlers and businessmen was not negligible. They were organized into Chambers of Commerce and Chambers of Agriculture, and they did not hesitate to make their voices heard by the governor, even by Paris where they often had influential supporters among big businessmen and members of Parliament. It was sometimes possible for them to secure the transfer of governors or administrators who opposed their interests too vigorously. "The administration" and "the settlers" were frequently at odds. Despite everything, there existed in the cities a white "colonial society" which extended social invitations to its own members but did not invite the natives, whose ways of life were different. There was no official racism and, in practice, the French were on rather familiar terms with the Africans. But each of the two groups lived to itself, especially after white women, who had been few in earlier periods, came to the colony.

Such a system, functioning in a self-contained fashion, had few opportunities for evolving. The decrees of the minister were in effect prepared by the governors, who took the pulse of the bush through the administrators, and to whom the settlers did not hesitate to point out their views. Thus some suggestions for change would arise, either in the decrees or in official writings, and even more rarely, some plans or some perspectives for the future.

The year 1919 marked the end of the conquests and opened the era of peaceful achievements. There no longer was any armed opposition and as yet almost no native nationalism. It seemed that, taken as a whole, the Africans, despite taxes and dependence, appreciated the cessation of domestic wars and *razzias* (slave raids) and local tyrannies; they were grateful for the enlarging of horizons, the opening of roadways, and a certain liberty for the individual. The French might be tempted to give in to their natural tendency to make everything uniform, to a return to the "Night of August Fourth," to rational construction on a tabula rasa. But we have seen how these tendencies had been held in check in the area of doctrine and nearly abandoned in practice. The fact is that there was no tabula rasa. The colonials knew this very well. However much a jurist and geometrician the Frenchman might be, he was also a peasant who took account of realities. And the African realities were obviously not only different from French realities but different one from the others. Geography, ethnic groups, history, religions, customs revealed several Africas to which the colonizer was obliged to adapt his action. One must not, therefore, without serious error, imagine that there was a uniform French colonial practice. It proceeded from this that it could not be the same practice in Indochina, in North Africa, and in tropical Africa. This fact had been understood in creating cadres of different *fonctionnaires*. But, further, the administrators of the African colonies, all specialists in tropical Africa, were finding themselves placed in some very diverse positions according to country.

In French West Africa the native political institutions were very varied, going from "anarchies" (resting on the equilibrium of lineages and secret societies) to "chiefdoms" and to "states." The utilization of the chiefs had appeared from the beginning (since Faidherbe) as a convenient means of pacification, then of administration. Hostile chiefs were replaced (not always according to customs) and often overly large states were dismantled. The chief, reduced the most often to a canton, became a subordinate of the *commandant* of the *cercle*, an instrument of the administration, drawing his strength from it as much as from tradition but obliged from this fact to an obedience that weakened his prestige. There was nothing in the soul of the Republican French comparable to the respect for hierarchies and the past that was natural for the British. The canton chief, and beneath him the village chief, were administrative agents, charged with securing the observance of regulations and collecting taxes. But their position remained ambiguous; they were not paid as much as the civil servants and, if they defended their *administrés* too vigorously, they were replaced. One can say that the administration was three-quarters direct, the interposition of the chief and his traditional, even religious, aspect making up the rest.

The proportion was different in certain cases, either where it was a question of states that had been strongly constituted for centuries, or where the personality of the ruler maintained a certain luster in his post. Such was the case of the Mossi Empire during the long reign of Naba Kom II (1905–42); his administration was maintained, doubtless at a subordinate level but with a certain efficiency.

The utilization of the chiefs facilitated the task of the administrators to such a degree that attempts were made to impose canton chiefs in regions of anarchy, most often with a total lack of success. It would therefore be erroneous to believe that the French sought systematically to impose direct rule. It was not possible for one man to command alone, and directly, 100,000 persons. The chiefs were necessary, but the French transformed these kings into civil servants who were subordinated to the Republic.

The situation was almost the same in the Cameroons and French Equatorial Africa, but the latter presented, in addition, populations so sparse and so dispersed over immense steppes, savannas, and forests that the authority of the chiefs scarcely extended beyond a village or a tribal fraction. Furthermore the administrators, besides being few in number, had directly to administer immense areas without roads, which took much effort and often resulted in low efficiency. Among certain of them abuses of power occurred that the literary figures denounced and that caused much scandal.[6]

French Somaliland had scarcely any administration other than at Djibouti. It was only between the two wars that a rudimentary rule was installed in several interior centers in order to prevent internal wars among the tribes. In 1935 the administrator, Bernard, was killed while pursuing a *razzia* (raid) that had come from the Ethiopian frontiers. There was no question of trying to impose taxes on the desert nomads, who were always on the edge of famine. Here France bore the expenses, helped a bit by the receipts of the port.

Madagascar, a little continent apart, had a political past that went beyond African perspectives. The Merina Kingdom in the Nineteenth century had conquered and colonized the other peoples of the island, installing garrisons and governors among them. The local chiefs had thus declined, and when the French arrived not much remained of them except in some marginal regions that had stayed independent. The French administrators therefore succeeded the Merina governors and were able to utilize as subordinates Malagasy peoples of every origin educated in the mission schools, then in the public schools. Secretaries or canton chiefs were the most common; they were not hereditary chiefs as in Africa but veritable civil servants. It was a blessing for direct administration and a bounty for the development of red tape, which proliferated. Taxes, collected in a lump sum by the chiefs in Africa, were paid on an individual basis as in France. The administrator remained the source of power, but he took on some characteristics of a subprefect at the same time that the African "commander" kept a military allure.

The difference was further revealed in the domain of education.[7]

6. René Maran, *Batouala* (Prix Goncourt, 1922); André Gide, *Voyage au Congo* (1927) and *Retour du Tchad* (1928); Albert Londres, *Terre d'Ebène* (1929); Denise Moran, *Tchad* (1934).

7. The following figures are those of the year 1921 given by Albert Sarraut in

In French West Africa, which had 13,000,000 inhabitants, there were only 22,000 students, of whom 20,000 were at the primary level, 500 at the post-primary, 120 at the William Ponty School being trained to teach in the primary schools, and 60 at the medical school. In French Equatorial Africa, with 2,800,000 inhabitants, there were 4,000 primary-level pupils. In Madagascar, with 3,400,000 people, there were 177,000 primary-level pupils (in the government and mission schools), and 1,000 students in the post-primary; Le Myre de Vilers school trained primary teachers and administration employees and prepared students for entrance to the medical school.

Madagascar, where education had begun on a large scale from the period of the Merina dominance, therefore possessed native literate elements in sufficient number for the subordinate ranks of the administration and of the economy: secretaries, canton chiefs (certain ones, who supervised several cantons, even kept the title of "governor"), teachers, physicians (few with the Doctor of Medicine degree), and clerks. There was among the Merina an old bourgeoisie, which was rather rich and had a tradition of public service and commerce. Nothing like that existed in French West Africa, except for some of the citizens of the four Senegalese communes. Because of this situation, there occurred in Africa a proliferation of Frenchmen from Europe in the jobs which, on the big island, were entrusted to the Malagasy: primary teachers, clerks in the administration or in the stores.

Assimilation manifested itself in one area: everywhere and at every level, education was given exclusively in French. It was not only the convenience (for those in charge) which determined this choice, but especially the idea that by speaking French the natives would end by thinking in French and feeling French. If this view was in a large part illusory (for the masses did not leave their environment), at least the small educated elite would be partially assimilated. But France did not know how to draw political conclusions from this situation in time. Education prolonged Republican Assimilation in a period that no longer believed in it, and did so, moreover, in an abusively rigid manner.

1919–1930

From 1920 to 1924 the post of minister of the colonies was occupied by Albert Sarraut. This rare longevity was the result of competence.

---

his book of 1923, *La mise en valeur des colonies françaises,* which will be discussed below.

Sarraut, an important man in the Radical Party, had been governor-general of Indochina. His first concern at the Ministry would be to aid the colonies to escape from their misery by devising a plan that was to be implemented through loans guaranteed by the Metropole. His bill was introduced into Parliament in April 1921. He knew that in a France ruined by the war it would encounter the mistrust of the Chambers for distant financial obligations. In order to launch a movement of opinion that would carry off the vote in the Chambers, he published a project in 1923 containing ample statements of his intentions.[8]

The war, he said, had shaken "the weakness of public opinion" in regard to the colonies. The latter had contributed to the struggle by the dispatch of combatants (French West Africa, 170,000; French Equatorial Africa, 18,000; Somaliland 2,500; Madagascar, 41,000) and of products (vegetable oils from Africa; graphite, manioc, preserves, and leathers from Madagascar). We must recognize this effort and bind tightly this solidarity, he said. The part of all the colonies in French commerce does not reach 13 percent; we must increase their potential for production in order to replace a large number of foreign imports that bring a deficit in our commercial balance. Thus followed the entire plan, involving above all the economic infrastructure (railroads, roads, port facilities, irrigation projects), but also social projects (hospitals, school buildings, urbanism).

A part of the preliminary considerations was devoted to colonial policy. It was streaming with eloquence. It spoke of the "value of humanity" of the colonized peoples, of the "right of the strongest to aid the weakest," of the virtue of the Association practiced by France: "it does not oppress, it liberates; it does not exhaust, it makes fertile; it does not exploit, it shares." It brings "order, security, health, justice, hope for a better future. It wishes progressively to call them to the management of their country, to qualify them by its administration to this collaboration. In the shapeless clay of the primitive multitudes, it models the face of a new humanity." [9]

This moral conforms with the ideal defended by the Allies. It is necessary to develop medical assistance "in order to preserve and increase human capital." Education "made general in the French language must have above all a practical and realistic character." One must, however, form a "native elite . . . the faculties of access to the higher domains of science," but avoid creating dangerous classless

8. Albert Sarraut, *La mise en valeur des colonies françaises* (Paris, 1923), 670 pp. with maps.

9. Ibid., pp. 88–89.

persons (*déclassés*). It is necessary "to open the door of the French city to whoever merits to pass over to it" and not attempt mass naturalization which would be a disastrous error. One cannot "let pass, on a large scale, all the political power into the hands of a crowd incapable of using it reasonably." It is proper, therefore, on the one hand to enlarge French naturalization, and on the other to accord to the noncitizens "a perceptible extension of their political rights in the native city . . . , within the scheme of their civilization" It will be necessary to increase native representation in the existing local assemblies, to create assemblies where there are none, and to enlarge the number of electors.[10]

The evolution of the colonies is "the enigma of future times"; even if it were to be terminated by independence, it would remain for France the result "of having knotted, with its adult children, by noble bonds of gratitude and interest, economic and political relations of which the Metropole would remain the privileged beneficiary, without bearing the charges or the responsibilities" of earlier times.[11]

This was a prophetic view, doubtless inspired by his Indochinese experience with precolonial states, that is, with preexisting nations. For the remainder, it was an able mixture of association and assimilation with its immediate perspectives very limited, capable of disturbing nobody, while allowing one to have a good conscience. There was no innovation on the doctrine of the status quo reigning since 1900, but there was an outline of several political measures and a plan of economic development.

The application was deceiving: the government councils, purely consultative, were augmented with a handful of native members named by the governor. The General Council of Senegal, limited to those elected from the four communes, became a "Colonial Council," enlarged to the whole colony by the addition of the native chiefs, who were agents of the administration. Some "Councils of Notables," created in each *circonscription* and convened annually under the presidency of the administrator, were to give their advice on taxes, *prestations,* the program of public works; in fact, as docile and intimidated subordinates, they limited themselves to approving the administration's proposals.

The principal novelty was the creation in Madagascar in 1924, of the "Economic and Financial Delegations" on the Algerian model. This representation had been requested by the French settlers, who

10. Ibid., pp. 98, 101, 103, 104.
11. Ibid., p. 127.

were rather numerous on the island (10,000) and who dominated the economy. The delegations included an elected French section and a native section designated by the notables. They were convened annually to give their advice (purely consultative) on the budget, taxes, public works, and economic development. The sections deliberated separately; the French section was very much in sight, followed by the press, chiding the government; the Malagasy section was humble, obscure, and almost unknown.

The political opportunities of the postwar period were thus lost through ministerial conceptions, which were generous but ambiguous, and above all by a wretched application.

Native opinion therefore, remained indifferent. The traditional masses were not moved by the ideas and inefficient creations of Paris. The French Communists, with Jacques Doriot, were calling for the "struggle against imperialism and colonialism" but were finding only a few responses—those in North Africa and especially in Indochina. The Senegalese Blaise Diagne, the only African deputy, had presided during the war over the recruitment of black troops and above all thought about his electors in the four communes, who were already French citizens. He was to become undersecretary of state a bit later.

The opposition was very limited in its effects. It came from two persons belonging to the demi-elite of the primary-school intellectuals, people with simple convictions, students who admired the Revolution of 1789 and the emancipation of France and who wished to have them pass from the verbal domain into that of facts. The Malagasy schoolteacher Ralaimongo, who had voluntarily enlisted during the First World War, having frequented the parties of the Left in France, returned to Madagascar and created a newspaper. He demanded the transformation of the island into a French department and of the Malagasies into citizens; he denounced the abuses of the administration and the settlers. In 1929, with the assistance of a few Frenchmen, some Malagasies dared to engage in a demonstration before the government-general. Ralaimongo was interned, and the movement went underground again; but several demonstrations were produced here and there in the bush on the occasion of land acquisitions by settlers or over questions of manpower.

A Congolese bookkeeper, André Matsoua, who was an army veteran, had created a club (*amicale*) in Paris. The *amicalists* spread in the Congo, protesting against the *indigénat* and demanding the right to vote. In 1930 Matsoua was condemned to three years in prison and the demonstrations that followed his arrest were dispersed by some hundreds of arrests.

The political opening was therefore illusory. The economic consequences of the Sarraut plan were happier. The colonies were authorized little by little to float loans on the French market with the guarantee of the state. In this way several large projects were completed, including railroads, ports, buildings, and urban development. But outside the towns and several rare major crossroads, the order and development of the bush continued to rest upon the administrators.

The recruitment of the latter had been improvised from the start, drawing chiefly on explorers, officers, and settlers. In 1894 the Colonial School had been created and opened to students at the level of the *licence* who passed a competitive examination. Alongside this regular recruitment, the school also admitted some *fonctionnaires* from the Civil Service (the lower level taken among the military men or *lycée* graduates) having a certain number of years in colonial positions. In addition, some former combat officers were enrolled after the war. The amalgam of these diverse elements was made without difficulty at the school, which had become the melting pot of the "kings of the bush."

Before 1914 colonial careers had a bad reputation in French opinion. It was generally agreed that only second-raters were sent there. This was a myth, but it is certain that the number of student candidates for the Colonial School did not exceed by many the number of places. There existed two sections, one for Indochina, another for Africa. The latter each year included from twelve to fifteen students, plus an equal number from the "Civil Service." The courses lasted for two years, plus one preparatory year for the competitive examination, which likewise took place at the school. The orientation was in large part juridical and financial, but with important elements of colonial history and African geography. In my time languages and local ethnology were taught by two great specialists, administrators of long experience, who had ended their career as governors; Maurice Delafosse for black Africa, Gustave Julien for Madagascar.

The students often belonged to colonial families; there were in nearly every graduating class one or two Negroes from the West Indies. But the majority came from the provincial petty bourgeoisie, that very numerous middle class, often of peasant origin, which kept to the tradition of work, order, and reason. It was a class generally favorable to the Republic, which had given it the possibility of advancing itself and having its say in the affairs of the nation. But this class was also strict in its rules of conduct, limiting its sights to questions of money and of comfort. From such a situation there resulted among certain young people, after their classical studies, a desire to escape toward a freer life and a higher ideal. These petty bourgeois were in semirevolt, eager for distant horizons, strange lands, primitive and unforseen life, for leading and transforming new worlds. Such, it seems to me, were the majority of my colleagues. At the congress of administrators, at the time of the Colonial Exposition of 1931, I thought I had interpreted well the sentiments of my colleagues on the sense and the honor of our craft when I declared that the administrator must be "native-phile," "for in order to do one's job well, it is necessary to like it. And our job is the native. . . . To us has fallen a decisive moment in the planet: the task of *mise en valeur* in the still fallow spaces and the unification of humanity." [12] I received acclamations.

The outstanding personality of Delafosse and his course in colonial policy had contributed to forming us. I produce from it some maxims taken from my classnotes: "In colonial matters, à-priorism is an error. Colonial policy must be objective, founded on the facts, thus varied, for if countries differ, methods must differ. There are colonial *policies*." "Colonization would not be able to justify itself if it did not lead to a better existence for both the colonized and the colonizer . . ." "It is necessary to determine our duties, without which colonization would only be exploitation. . . . Colonial policy is therefore essentially a native policy." "The human races are equal—not similar—as to their possibilities, but the environment makes civilizations different."

From the examination of local situations, he drew five general principles: increase of the race; its amelioration; safeguard of local institutions; preservation of native administration (there he cited Lugard); and intellectual training: to adapt to the needs in preparing the masses to evolve and in forming an elite, but not a classless, group of persons. He put forth the rules for a sound indirect administration: "leave the native free in the matters where he alone is interested"; intervene discreetly and indirectly in the public affairs of the natives; "intervene openly and firmly in case of open rebellion" (he himself, in the early days of the Ivory Coast, had gone through some tragic situations); "in economic affairs, for the introduction of new crops or new procedures, intervene directly with the chiefs, taking account of their advice"; "in financial matters, intervene the least possible" except in case of

12. "La Vocation coloniale et le métier d'administrateur," *L'Afrique Française—Renseignements Coloniaux* (Supplément, 1931), pp. 497–500.

provocation. It is necessary to "improve the environment," "improve the diet," expand medical care and health ("the largest part of the budget must be consecrated to them"), "arouse the needs which are creative of civilization," satisfy them by developing communications, commerce, export crops, local crafts, and increased prosperity. The white man must be an example: "dignity, never harshness, never fly into a passion; never despise; always be interested."[13]

Delafosse died in October 1926, just as we were leaving the school to go to our respective fields of application. I learned of his death while at sea. He had raised our enthusiasms, incarnated for us the "king of the bush" and the "colonial faith." At least for general inspiration we were to find them again on the spot, in action, if not always in the procedures, for those of Delafosse were drawn above all from his Ivory Coast and Sudanese experience.

Twenty years of Sudanese experience had also inspired the work of Jules Brévié, then governor of Niger, later governor-general of French West Africa.[14] French liberalism and the needs of pacification had led us to "use Muslim clericalism." Brévié, formed in the militant French laicism of the pre-1914 period, disliked this commitment and foresaw instead an evolution from *naturisme* toward laicism by eliminating "the religious phase." While waiting we must defend naturisme and teach it to persevere. The inspiration is simultaneously that of defense of native cultures and that of intellectual assimilation in the long run.

Marcel Olivier gave an account later of his six years' experience (1923–29) as governor-general of Madagascar.[15] He revealed the motives, modalities, and the results of his principal achievements: settlement of the agrarian question (in trying to state precisely the rights, often very vague, of the natives, which was not always to their liking); labor charter (labor record, verification of the freedom of employment, jurisdiction); utilization of the second contingent of the military recruitment for large works (the "Smotig"); struggle against the chief endemic diseases. In matters of education, Olivier thought that "the essential goal of a primary school is to give to the child the sum of useful knowledge which will permit him later to hold con-

13. One can find an outline of this teaching in an article by Delafosse, "L'Orientation de la politique indigène dans l'Afrique noire," *L'Afrique Française* (1921), pp. 145–52.

14. Jules Brévié, *Islamisme contre Naturisme au Soudan français* (1923). Brévié calls *naturisme* the traditional African paganism, baptized by others as "fetishism" or "animism."

15. Marcel Olivier, *Six ans de politique sociale à Madagascar* (1931), 279 pp.

veniently and usefully his place in the environment where he was born and where he is called to spend his existence." To devote the best efforts of the bush school to the teaching of French would result only in an effort of absurd memorization, because the language would not be used and would be quickly forgotten. In 1929 Oliver decided, therefore, that primary education at the lower levels would take place in Malagasy, with the exception of certain elements of useful French. At the upper levels, which were intended for future *fonctionnaires* and clerks, the use of French would in contrast be intensified.

"A good native policy," wrote Olivier, "is that which, without upsetting anything, permits the sane and normal evolution of the native societies toward a form of civilization as close as possible to *Western* civilization." He repudiated, however, "the chimera of assimilation . . . whoever says assimilation, says destruction." Also distrusting "a vain business of resurrection" of dead institutions, he extolled a compromise: maintain the old cadres wherever they exist; open upper-level positions to the natives; confer on them the presidency of the civil tribunals of the first degree; perfect the Councils of Notables and the native section of the Delegations. "The essential is to furnish to native society the bridge which will make it pass without danger from the old order of things to the new." There was always the illusion of the virtue of compromise and of peaceful economic and social evolution during unlimited periods toward undefined political ends.

1931–1939

The world-wide economic crisis of 1931–39 seriously hit the French economy and still more that of the colonies, which was very fragile because it was founded on several luxury crops with an almost exclusively French outlet. The crisis was overcome slowly by reinforcing autarky and by granting subsidies to colonial products upon their entrance into France. The subsidies were financed by taxes on similar products coming from foreign sources. The groundnuts of Senegal, the cocoa of the Ivory Coast and of the Cameroons, the bananas from Guinea, the oils of Dahomey, the precious woods of Gabon, the coffee of Madagascar, were saved and could pursue their upward climb. The colonies' portion of total French commerce passed to a quarter.

The Colonial Exposition of 1931 in the Bois de Vincennes, a suburb of Paris, was grandiose, in the style of its organizer, Lyautey, who was assisted by Olivier. All France came to admire "Overseas France" (*France d'Outre-mer*) and took notice of it. Georges Hardy, former director of education in Morocco (who was then in French

West Africa), colonial historian, a man of initiative and of a vast culture, who had been named director of the Colonial School (renamed "the School of Overseas France"), profited from this vogue in order to organize preparations for the entrance competition in a certain number of lycées in France. The number of candidates passed from thirty to six hundred, recruitment from twenty to eighty.

The Ministry had also become the Minister of Overseas France. This assimilationist title was only a label of good republicanism. Nothing in fact had changed, but the specialists asked questions of themselves.

Henri Labouret, administrator and ethnologist of French West Africa, tried to define a native policy.[16] "Association" has been correctly chosen; it is necessary to reinforce the two native structures that were still solid—the village and the canton—and to teach the administrators how to use local institutions. Labouret replaced Delafosse at the school.

Léon Geismar, an Alsatian who had passed heroically from the German army into the French army during the war, the brilliant collaborator of Olivier and a specialist in comparative colonization, passed in review the French and English solutions for the same practical problems.[17] The Frenchman, "democrat," was basically authoritarian. The Englishman, monarchist, remained a Celtic individualist, respecting nature and customs. The indirect administration advocated by Lugard was repugnant to the French temperament. Geismar advocated, without being specific, "a mixture of the system of Madagascar and the British methods."

Robert Delavignette, an administrator from French West Africa, having become a regular collaborator of *Afrique Française,* declared there, "we have renounced assimilation and the idea that the natives were not perfectible." [18] He published a novel, *The Black Peasants,* in which he showed in this "native labor force" some men who are ingenious, hardworking, thoughtful, suffering, and sensitive to the aid of the "*commandant.*" Into a colonization that was turned more and more toward the economic, he brought a gust of humanity.[19]

16. Henri Labouret, *A la recherche d'une politique indigène dans l'Ouest africain.* This work was originally a long series of articles appearing in *L'Afrique Française* in 1930 and 1931, which was then edited into a separate volume.

17. Léon Geismar, "La colonisation européenne en Afrique," *Revue Politique et Parlementaire, 10* (1930), and "Du rôle comparé des administrateurs dans les possessions africaines de la France et de l'Angleterre," *L'Afrique Française—Renseignements Coloniaux* (1931), p. 574.

18. *L'Afrique Française* (1931), p. 632.

19. Robert Delavignette, *Les Paysans Noirs* (1931), 224 pp.

Sarraut, the same year of the Exposition, where the current of opinion he launched had triumphed, expressed simultaneously his satisfaction and his worries. He evoked Valéry, Lothrop Stoddard, and the "surf of European colonization." "France cannot have two faces, the one of liberty, turned toward the Metropole, and the one of tyranny, extended toward the colonies." Must one, after the "great and profound uprooting provoked by colonization, abandon to disorder these peoples who are unprepared? Europe cannot wish that." He saw the remedy in the "power of a federated Europe." [20]

Why had these peoples not been "prepared"? And prepared for what? The question of the goal, constantly raised and avoided with fear and pessimism by Sarraut, I posed then in claiming, with the boldness and brutality of youth, to resolve it. "Native society," I said, "has collapsed under the blows of the European rush. Religion, customs, the authority of the chiefs have been ripped into shreds. The elements of a new society are forming according to the practical necessities of the new world. But they are still very insufficient and unadapted . . . It is here that education intervenes. Its role will consist in preparing the building of new native societies adapted to the new conditions of life." [21]

As for the goal, I condemned our so-called "Association" enriched by the system of Lugard and his French followers. These tendencies, I said, ultimately have for their support and perspective the "separation of the races." Therefore, the latter, as well as the policy based on the reconstitution of the chiefdoms, go against the tides of evolution. "To the degree that Africa is incorporated more closely into the general economy of the world, the material facts draw the natives closer to us and it does not depend on us to hold them apart."

I concluded with a resumption of Assimilation on the basis of a real evolution, which would be accelerated by the diffusion of education. "Among the natives, those whom we can receive tomorrow as citizens are already French in fact before being so in law. We would be unpardonable if in the name of a foreign doctrine we refused to cement French unity." [22]

My revolutionary blows against Association encountered only the wind. The review that had published my article was mostly dissemi-

20. Albert Sarraut, *Grandeur et Servitude Coloniales* (1931), pp. 18, 102, 277, and 282.

21. "Education et Colonisation," *La Grande Revue* (October 1932), pp. 635–49.

22. Ibid.

nated in university circles and was not read by the colonials. The only result was an exchange of letters, after three months delay, between Geismar, then in Senegal, and me, in the extreme south of Madagascar.

The orientation of the real policy was defined, at this time, in French West Africa by the circulars of Governor-General Brévié. "We have come here to accomplish a duty of humanity, not to look for testimonials of recognition." If the native no longer has for the European "the almost superstitious respect of former days," it is because "the eyes which are open are observing . . . whence the necessity for frank and clear explanations, especially when it is a question of innovating." The native must be "in apprenticeship until the day when emancipation will permit him to be made an associate." It is necessary "to remove him as little as possible from tradition," to consolidate the chiefs, to select and instruct their legitimate heirs, to study the customs, to organize village and canton committees composed of notables, to have only exceptional recourse to the *indigénat.* "In the social order, all precipitateness is hazardous, and experience must condition the rhythm of the progress." [23]

It was Lugardism that was moderate, anemic, preached to the veritable "kings of the bush" with the mirage, vague and indefinitely retreating, of the famous "Association."

The coming to power of the Popular Front in June 1936 was, in the colonies, a total surprise, inspiring fear in some and hope in others. The native masses of the bush, who were not yet reached by the radio, were doubtless ignorant of it. At that moment new times appeared possible to the *évolués.* Ravoahangy, Malagasy first lieutenant and successor of Ralaimongo, who like him had been interned, resumed believing in France and enrolled in the Socialist party.

Léon Blum, on the sixth of June, declared in the Chamber: "A great hope and a great expectation are attached to our work; they are attached here on French soil; they are attached on the soil of the territories of North Africa and of our colonies." [24] Not knowing colonial questions, and having difficult battles to lead in other areas, both

23. "Circulaires de M. le Gouverneur-Général J. Brévié sur la Politique et l'Administration Indigènes en Afrique Occidentale Française" (1935), pp. 20, 22–23, 29, 33, and 57.

24. Cf. the colloquium *Léon Blum, chef de gouvernement 1936–37* (Fondation Nationale des Sciences Politiques, 1967), especially pages 377–403.

domestic and foreign, he entrusted these problems to his friend, Marius Moutet, with the certainty that he would know how "to extract from the colonial regime all that it can contain that is humane." Moutet, a Socialist and a well-known lawyer, had passionately defended, in the name of the "League of the Rights of Man," several important native causes in Indochina and in Africa. He took into his cabinet Delavignette and Inspector General Barthes, a man of a brilliant and solid intelligence who was well known for his leftist opinions. Brévié was placed at the head of Indochina, and Governor Marcel de Coppet, a Socialist, was named in his place.

Such a concern to call upon men who were members of the traditional cadres and who were both competent and sympathetic to the reforms, immediately motivated the action of Moutet. He did not claim to be doing a revolutionary work but to be changing what, in the view of a moderate leftist and jurist of the League of the Rights of Man, appeared to him to be blameable. In this sense, he brought several measures to completion: the battle against famine, inspection of labor, diminution of the *prestations,* numerous exemptions from the *indigénat,* creation of the Institut d'Afrique Noire and of the Musée de l'Homme. Above all, in the line of *The Black Peasants* he launched the idea of a "big program of small works" destined to improve the lot of the villagers: mechanization, irrigation, and wells.

This was little in relation to the hopes of the évolués: the system remained and the main lines of the evolution were once more avoided. However, the same obstacles were not encountered here as in North Africa where the efforts of the Ministers Violette and Vienot, energetically supported by the secretary-general of the Mediterranean High Committee, the Socialist Charles-André Julien, ran up against the reactionary vehemence of the settlers and the passivity, more or less accessory, of certain high fonctionnaires. Settlers and merchants in the tropical colonies did not represent, as in Algeria, a great number, and they thought less about fighting than adapting themselves. As for the administrators of the colonies, their syndicate was of a clearly leftist tendency; formed in July 1936, it soon included the majority of the corps. Thus it seemed posssible to carry out the bigger initiatives and at the same time to announce and prepare for the future.

It was there, doubtless, that the major difficulty presented itself. France, since the beginning of the century, no longer had one colonial policy but the weak beginnings of several contradictory and bizarrely mixed ones. The Opposition of the Right favored the status quo. The government of the Popular Front was supported by three parties: the

Communist party preached independence; the Radical party, which had been anticolonial in its early days and later assimilationist, had become among the most insipid of reformers, and its leader, Sarraut, who was the most involved in colonial activities, preached a liberal Association; the Socialist party, which for a long time had been defiant in regard to "colonialism," had ended by envisioning a certain rapproachment with Metropolitan institutions in the traditional republican line but without great interest and in very narrowly juridical perspectives.

It was necessary to take account of all these opinions and especially not to engage in revolutionary experiments which would have led, at the domestic level, to an increase in criticisms and opposition to a government that was already much disputed and threatened at every instant with civil war.

The main proposals of Moutet were therefore blocked by the Senate, which was dominated by hostile Radicals in coalition with the Right. The Colonial Fund, which was to finance the "big program of little works," was rejected. Similarly, the Senate suppressed the very tiny credits for the large "Committee of Inquiry on the Colonies" convoked by Moutet. Alongside sympathetic administrators on the committee sat a large number of diverse personalities like André Gide and Cardinal Verdier.

The circumstances were thus not very favorable if one wished to maintain oneself in constitutional legality. One had not been able, even with the best intentions in the world, to get out of the stagnation. "When in 1946 we came back into the Government," said Moutet, "we were able to do what we wished." One can regret that it had not been sooner and more durable.

A year after its formation, in June 1937, the Senate overthrew the Blum ministry. The Popular Front did not disappear entirely, but its direction passed to the Radicals in April 1938. Georges Mandel succeeded Moutet as minister of the colonies. Certain measures marked this period. Admission to the status of citizen was enlarged and become automatic in numerous cases simply upon application; several thousand Malagasies profited from it. The application of French legislation on labor unions, collective agreements, and associations was followed by strikes and disorders on the railroads of Senegal; they unleashed a campaign by the Right against Marcel de Coppet, who was transferred to Madagascar.

A precious testimony was then given to French policy by two Englishmen in a book with the significant title, *Africans Learn to be*

French.[25] The authors found the natives "well-nourished and happy." "The happiest and friendliest relations between Frenchmen and natives were everywhere evident." Nowhere was there a fortress. Education tended toward assimilation; Africans and Frenchmen went side by side to school. The graduates of the William Ponty School were "entirely French." The authors quoted Inspector General Albert Charton, director of education in French West Africa, who was the animating force for the rural schools and for the adaptation of the programs to African realities, as saying: "Assimilation can not be taken as a point of departure, but . . . as a result, that it is necessary to pursue, win, and consolidate. For this final assimilation, the prior condition is adaptation." [26]

Delavignette, having become director of the School of Overseas France, taught the practice and the ideal of his craft. He drew from it a beautiful book, which appeared at the start of the war and was immediately censured for certain pages that were judged "nonconformist." [27] The craft of administrator, he said, is "a matter of courageous good sense," plus that of regulation. "He commands only on condition of engaging his personality." "It is necessary to believe and act" in having "faith in the human value of the natives . . . and in the new world that he builds with them." His method is experimental. "He observes; he verifies his action in the country and the reaction of the country." Colonization is "the heroic organization of the world by a superior and sacrificing personnel." "It is in the vocation that resides the famous liberty of colonial life." "The administrator personifies the responsibility of France. . . . He is the chief only if he remains alone. . . . The *commandant* is at the top of his command only on the strength of his internal life." [28]

"Assimilation has value only by the assimilable substance that it brings, and Association has value only if it gives them a community with the Metropole. . . . Reality escapes from categories." "Rather than the theoretical conceptions of the Metropole, it is the evolution

25. W. Bryant Mumford and Orde Brown, *Africans Learn to Be French* (London, 1937). Earlier books in English are rather critical, such as the one of the Australian Stephen Roberts, *History of French Colonial Policy 1870–1925* (2 vols. London, 1929), and that of the American Raymond Leslie Buell, *The Native Problem in Africa* (2 vols. New York, 1928).

26. Mumford and Brown, pp. 16 and 104.

27. Robert Delavignette, *Les vrais chefs de l'Empire* (1939). Reedited after the war with the title *Service Africain,* it has been translated into English as *Freedom and Authority in French West Africa* (London, 1950).

28. *Les vrais chefs,* pp. 19, 25, 29, 30, 50, 60, 62, and 63.

of the natives in a new African world that determines colonial institutions." "The countries shall do for themselves, by successive improvements, in an air of freedom." "There exists a new African world. And it is we who have given birth to it. It is our native policy that has been the instrument delivering it." [29]

The end was an invocation to Leopold Sédar Senghor, prophet of "négritude" and the first African to receive the *agrégation*. "We therefore," Delavignette says to him, "wish to save African civilizations; we wish to give the blacks to themselves, but in order to render them at the same time to the human person. And it is there that the spirit of peace resides." "Brotherhood is the difference—is it thus so difficult to understand?" [30]

Results

In relation to the relative weakness of the financial assistance given by the Metropole, the economic progress of the colonies between the two wars can appear honorable.[31] The loans contracted by the colonies, the burden of which had been happily reduced by devaluations, had permitted the extension of the railroad network and the construction of ports: completion of the Dakar-Bamako line; extension of the railroads of the Ivory Coast, Dahomey, and the Cameroons; the ports of Dakar, Pointe-Noire, Tamatave; the beginning of the port of Abidjan. The hardest work had been the Congo-Ocean Railroad (C.F.C.O.) from Brazzaville to the sea across a mountainous region covered with forests. The local population being very sparse, Governor-General Antonetti had called upon forced recruitment throughout French Equatorial Africa; 10 percent of the workers, coming from the dry lands of the North, died, having been unable to adapt themselves to the climate; revolts broke out. Only after strict medical measures were adopted was the railroad completed in 1934. By contrast, the surroundings and good working conditions of the second portion of the contingent, organized by Olivier, permitted the completion, without losses, of the southern Madagascar railroad (F.C.E.) which was built at the same time and in a region just as difficult.

The roads had been built for the most part by the administrators thanks to *prestations*, and 70,000 kilometers of track were thus opened for French West Africa alone. The bush was penetrated, and travel

29. Ibid., pp. 89, 92, 123, 250.

30. Ibid., pp. 252, 260.

31. One can consult J. Ganiage, H. Deschamps, and O. Guitard, *L'Afrique* (collection entitled *L'Histoire du XXème siècle*, Paris, Sirey, 1966), 908 pp.

over the roadways entered into the people's customs. Connections with the Metropole thereafter became more rapid; there was regular automobile service across the Sahara; planes linked Paris to Abidjan in four days.

The extension of food crops was one of the preoccupations of the administrators. The last great famine took place in 1931 in Niger and in the extreme south of Madagascar. At his departure, Governor Poiret left 6,000 ploughs in Guinea to replace the hoe.

The crops for export, either introduced or developed, had attained their first vigor. A total of 600,000 tons of groundnuts were produced in Senegal, where the creation of the Provident Societies (*Sociétés de Prevoyance*) had permitted the accumulation of reserves, the organization of sales, and the regularization of prices. In the Ivory Coast, 50,000 tons of cocoa and 10,000 tons of coffee were produced. Guinea grew bananas. Dahomey produced 100,000 tons of oil and palm kernels; and 150,000 tons of cocoa, bananas, oily products, and woods were exported from the Cameroons. In Gabon, okoumé wood was exploited and beginnings made in the production of cocoa. Authoritarian planting of cotton in Ubangi-Shari and in Chad resulted in exports of 70,000 tons. Madagascar surpassed 40,000 tons of coffee; its production of vanilla had become the first in the world and that of cloves the second; and Maryland tobacco and sisal had been introduced.

To the heavy exports of the early period had been added such products as cocoa, coffee, vanilla, and shelled groundnuts. But the economic autarchy and the domination of the commerce by the big French houses, which were interested in metropolitan affairs, braked industrialization. European agricultural undertakings were on the wane, and the big concessions in the Congo had disappeared. The French plantations, notably in the Ivory Coast, the Cameroons, and Madagascar, had seen their local working force set themselves up on their own. European activity often subsisted only thanks to the support of administration recruitment, often conducted at great distances; for example, recruits for the lower Ivory Coast were brought from as far away as Upper Volta. The Popular Front reacted against this forced labor, which the League of Nations had condemned. Now more than 95 percent of the products exported derived exclusively from the native planters.

The battle against diseases and for the increase of the population had been undertaken. Governor-General Carde had launched the slogan, "More Negroes!" (*Faire du nègre*). The dispensaries in the bush were multiplied. The fight against the important endemic diseases brought some spectacular victories: sleeping sickness snuffed out by Dr. Jamot in the Camcroons and in French Equatorial Africa; a vaccine against the plague discovered by Drs. Girard and Robic in Madagascar. The results were still weak, and the population stagnated in Gabon and in the south of French Equatorial Africa. In French West Africa it dropped to 16,000,000, and in Madagascar to 4,000,000.

Native society evolved; European products transformed tools and clothing; the new communications and security permitted migrations: a part of the young people went to work at a distance and escaped from the influence of traditions. Paganism lost ground to the profit of Christianity and Islam. The towns grew: Dakar reached 100,000 inhabitants; Tananarive 150,000; Brazzaville 60,000; Abidjan, Pointe-Noire, sprang forth from nothing. A mixed population inhabited these cities, less encumbered by traditions and partially Westernized.

Education had made uncontestable progress but was still very far from the people's needs. In Madagascar there were 200,000 pupils; 20,000 in French Equatorial Africa; 70,000 in French West Africa, with very variable proportions: 10 percent of school-age children in Senegal, 1.5 percent in the Upper Volta. The natives did not pass the primary level; the elite of the *fonctionnaires* was at the post-primary level. The wish to create auxiliaries, not competitors, was obvious despite the "generosity" and the "brotherhood" boasted of in official writings. Secondary education was represented in all by two *lycées* in Senegal and two in Madagascar, where the whites were in the majority. No university existed; it was necessary to go to France for advanced studies, and black African or Malagasy students were still a rarity there. One can count on one's fingers those who graduated with positions in view: there were several physicians in Madagascar; in Senegal, Lamine Gueye was a counselor at the Court of Appeals and Sédar Senghor a teacher with the *agrégation* the diploma allowing one to teach in the French lycées. These were the men who soon would play an essential role in the formation of the French Union.

There had been no progress in policy since the abandonment of Assimilation around 1880. No colonial doctrine had been elaborated, save for the appearance of Association, which had furnished a good conscience cheaply. Admixed were the restraints of Lugardism without its real practice. Therefore there remained in the style of the relations and in education a good dose of assimilationist tendencies. People seemed to imagine that this Empire, which they dared not name but which gave France a considerable place on the planisphere, would be eternal, like France in the verses of Victor Hugo. Like parents who refuse to see their children grow up, one administered from day to day without thinking about the evolution that one ought to be conducting. When maturity came in 1945, one would improvise in a whirlwind of eloquence and a vertigo of policy; one would institute Assimilation and Association together—and they would founder, the one after the other.

However, at the time France entered the Second World War, the enlightened despotism of the "kings of the bush" had borne its fruits. The populations were calm and often even confident and friendly. To imagine a police state, founded on force, would be to be totally deceived. In my last district, which contained 100,000 inhabitants dispersed in the bush, forty policemen, recruited in the same area, largely sufficed to ensure order and the observance of regulations. I always went about, from ten to fifteen days per month, without escort and unarmed, and everywhere I was well received, without servility and with dignity. When I returned twenty years later, as a simple scientific inquirer, I was received like a prince. And I am conscious of not having been an exception. Many former clerks of the administration, having become prefects of the new republics and therefore of the bush natives, spoke to me later with emotion of such and such former administrator who had trained them or whose efficiency they had appreciated. These Frenchmen were "the true chiefs of the Empire" (which is the title of Delavignettes' book), and it is through them and their colleagues of the other services—teachers, physicians, engineers, agronomists, some missionaries, and even certain settlers—that France was manifested authentically. It was through all these Frenchmen, working on the ground level, that the incoherent whole of the French possessions had been upheld and had been able to give the impression of a solid bloc, despite the absence of doctrine from Paris, despite its unkept promises and its horror of the future.

On November 8, 1939, Georges Mandel, minister of the colonies, declared that from all places there were Africans asking to enlist, saying: "France is good and just. Germany is the enemy of the blacks." I had known a similar reward when Mussolini claimed French Somaliland. All the peoples of Djibouti, so often violently divided among themselves—Afars, Issa Somalis, Arabs—came to march in front of me with posters: "We wish to live." "We wish to remain French." Must one think that for lack of attention, will, and doctrine, France between the two wars let a great historical opportunity escape? In the epoch when one perceives the necessity for regroupings and for large units, one can ask oneself if the Balkanization of Africa was not an avoidable accident.

❧ 17. *British Rule in Africa*

❧ ROBERT HEUSSLER

During the first half of the present century there were ten territories on the mainland of Africa that had roughly comparable relationships with London and shared a common administrative system: Nigeria, the Gold Coast, Sierra Leone, and the Gambia in West Africa; Somaliland, Uganda, Kenya, and Tanganyika in the East; and Northern Rhodesia and Nyasaland in Central Africa.[1] Their governors were in effect appointed by the Colonial Office, were responsible to it, and held office at its pleasure. The Colonial Office also recruited the remainder of their services, administrative, professional, and technical. Social and educational backgrounds shared by the officers gave a binding force of sorts, as did the training courses that were started in the 1920s. There was the "drill"—"the same Secretariat system, the same ritual at Government House, the same service structure, and largely the same problems of education, agriculture and all the many facets of native life." [2] Generally speaking, communications, both with Britain and internally, were primitive. Everywhere budgets were small and dependent on local revenue.

Like the rest in these respects, each territory was otherwise autonomous and unique. No two were acquired in exactly the same way or in circumstances that showed the same interplay of relationships on the world diplomatic stage. They were added to the imperial collection one by one over a period of more than a century. Chartered com-

1. The island groups, Mauritius and the Seychelles, were governed similarly to the mainland colonies, as was Zanzibar, although her ruler, like the kabaka of Buganda, had a special relationship to Britain. The High Commission Territories were also administered in the usual way, but their particular ties to South Africa caused them to be put under the Dominions Office. Southern Rhodesia enjoyed dominion status in all but name. The Sudan was under its own office in London, while, again, being administered in a manner more like than unlike that of the colonial territories.

2. A. N. Strong, letter of July 17, 1960. Mr. Strong, former president of the Colonial Civil Servants Association, served in Ceylon and Burma.

panies or missionary bodies gave the main impetus in some places. Strategic considerations were important elsewhere. A number of quite different and discordant voices made up the chorus of overseas interests in London: those of party faction, of humanitarian and religious grouping, of journalism, geography, adventure, and military thought. Differences in the fields of investment, shipping, and trade alone serve to frustrate the social thinker of orderly mind who looks for underlying laws, for certainty, neatness, and simplicity. Starting out separately and with ad hoc arrangements about help or control from London and about aims and type of government locally, each unit naturally developed in its own groove. Precedent and momentum being what they are, it was not long before the special characteristics of a dependency's first few years had become ingrained in political procedure and solidified by the force of time. The counterpart of original British initiative here was the stubborn fact of each territory's special ecology and its particular combination of peoples. The Colonial Empire presented from earliest times a spectacle of almost infinite variety in ethnic stock and natural resources. Some lands were possessed of considerable tribal unity. Most were not. European settlement was a strong influence on government and economy in a few countries but was negligible or nonexistent in others. Foreign business firms played a big role in some parts, whereas elsewhere the economy remained largely unaffected by the advent of European administration.

As individualism and autonomy were the basic facts of colonial life, and administrative style was the only source of unity worth mentioning, it may be asked whether cohesion could have been achieved by means of a grand scheme, articulated in England and put to work in coordinated ways throughout the dependencies. Parliament was sovereign, and governors were the legates of its ministerial apparatus. London had the freedom and the resources that would have been needed to get a plan into operation. That nothing of the sort was done requires some explanation.

Before the Scramble, as everyone knows, there was Little Englandism and an understandable concern to hold onto a place only if it had a strategic worth or was paying its way commercially.[3] It is true that antislavery measures and competition with other European powers drew England forward in Africa and elsewhere. But this came about in response to particular events and not according to an overarching, long-term rationale.[4] Then in the nineties, rather suddenly, an extraor-

3. Cf. J. A. Froude, *The English in the West Indies,* 1888.

4. Ibid., pp. 352 ff. And see A. Sandison, *The Wheel of Empire,* 1967, p. 190,

dinarily massive forward push, generated by French competition, coincided with the arrival in office of Chamberlain, a secretary of state who had ideas, home-based power, and an extended tenure, none of which characterized typical colonial secretaries of the nineteenth century.[5]

Chamberlain spoke of imperial estates that would benefit both England and the territories. He saw to the raising of a military force and wrung sums from the Treasury that could not have been got, even considering the international power demands of the Scramble, by an ordinary minister who lacked domestic influence and was serving his time as a junior. Yet in West Africa there would be no radical departure from time-worn colonial ways. Even before Chamberlain left office, things had relapsed into a pattern and tempo that would not have seemed unfamiliar to administrators with West Indian or Southeast Asian experience. New places had been taken over. But mechanisms and systems were the usual ones. As for London's intent, the wife of the first head of Northern Nigeria's administration accurately summed it up in two words: "Go slow."[6]

That Lugard and other governors in the first two decades had to do just that was made certain by lack of money beyond what could be raised by local taxation on a singularly benign and modest scale. England neither subsidized heavily from the center nor allowed taxes to be burdensome.[7] African peoples were among the world's poorest. Unless and until some new factor appeared, colonial government would continue as always: just and minimal.

In Westminster and Whitehall people thought about what ought to

---

on Buchan's views; E. A. Cunningham, "The Future Commonwealth," *The Christian Science Monitor,* January 18, 1961, p. 14. Captain Cunningham's opinions are those of a Uganda D.C. in the post-1945 period. They may be compared with what a Tanganyika D.C. wrote somewhat earlier, from his posting in the Northern Province: "There is no long range policy which we . . . carry out year after year." G. A. Tomlinson to his mother, August 31, 1941, Colonial Records Project, Oxford University.

5. On the Scramble in general and on the continuity of nineteenth-century expansion in Africa, see J. Gallagher and R. Robinson, "Imperialism of Free Trade," *Economic History Review,* 2nd series, *6* (1963), No. 1; D. Fieldhouse, "Imperialism: An Historiographical Revision," *Economic History Review,* 2nd series, *14* (1961); C. Newbury, "Victorians, Republicans and the Partition of Africa," *Journal of African History, 3* (1962).

6. Lady Lugard, *A Tropical Dependency* (London, 1906), p. 419.

7. It is true that the pump was primed a bit at first; see Margery Perham, *Lugard,* vol. 2, *The Years of Authority* (London, 1960), Chapter 3. But the era of welfare spending and overseas aid was not yet.

be done, and their views are not lacking in interest as indications of political sentiment during the time when colonial rule had settled into the rhythm of its core period. Milner, whose African experience was greater than that of any other twentieth-century minister, saw England's role as being one of leadership.[8] Less favored races needed supervision by advanced peoples in order to proceed to higher levels of civilization. There were obvious advantages in the kind of cooperation achieved by England and the Dominions. Even though Africans were not of the same racial stock as Canadians and New Zealanders, their best hope lay in going forward under the imperial umbrella. What could they hope to gain on their own in a world of cutthroat military and economic competition among giants? A flexible association with a benevolent overlord would be in the best interests of ruler and ruled alike.

Churchill and Amery were of similar minds to Milner on the philosophical plane, the former drawing his ideas of what the Empire ought to be from his own substantial acquaintanceship with actual conditions in parts of India and Africa. But Milner and Churchill did not remain many years in office, and Amery, who was secretary of state for the colonies for the longest period of anyone in this century, found that philosophy was one thing and the imperial system another. The Treasury would not spend money on the colonies; Parliament was not interested in them; and the minister in Downing Street was by no means a free agent.[9] Long before Amery's time the habit of autochthony, as Ormsby-Gor called it, was deeply entrenched. Governors might be appointed by the Colonial Office, but once they had left Tilbury Dock there was little that anyone in London could do about daily administration. When he called a conference of governors and proposed a form of economic cooperation that would have cost each colony 1 percent of its annual income, Amery was frustrated by the same "local particularism" that had impressed itself on so many of his predecessors.[10]

In the twenties steps were taken to tighten up the system in ways that would contribute to a more unified and prosperous empire. Aspects of unity were brought to branches of the Colonial Service. Train-

8. Although much has been written by and about Milner, perhaps the clearest and most down-to-earth presentation of his thought is in his early book, *England in Egypt*, 1893.

9. L. S. Amery, *My Political Life*, Vol 2, 1953, pp. 339 and 346.

10. Ibid., p. 346. And see Perham, *Lugard*, *2*, 267, for Lugard's statement on the relationship between the C.O.'s power and that of governors.

ing courses already in existence were improved and new ones begun. Research and development schemes were initiated. The first Governors' Conference met in 1927. If secretaries of state still could not dictate to colonies, perhaps a coherence of sorts could be attained through the men who ran the territories. In seeking to influence the direction of colonial government in this way the Colonial Office was facing up to the essential difference between domestic policy and the overseas kind. At home one dealt with the familiar, time-honored trappings of liberal democracy: a comparatively large and informed electorate, the plural strands of power that go with industrial society, the cut and thrust of party politics, the constant bending and adapting of institutions and officeholders in response to pressures from diverse sources. Policy in such a milieu had to try for a wide appeal to many interests. Yet at the same time, and once it had passed through the stages of conception and refining, it could be implemented with the force and efficiency that characterize modern statecraft. For all their complexity, English society and government allowed for relatively strong, sure action by the central authority. In dealing with overseas dependencies, however, that same authority was operating in a vastly different situation. Instead of a single body politic in one small country, there were several dozen of them scattered over the face of the earth. If the center did not hand out largesse, neither did it control local expenditure. Indeed the splintering of power did not stop at colonial capitals. Though there was no democracy to inhibit them, the autocracies that ran the territories independently of London lacked the money and the manpower to come anywhere near the control and effectiveness of government in industrial countries. In these circumstances any realistic policy would have to be of local derivation and would face internal obstacles more formidable than those that confronted European governments.[11]

Although it is possible to point to certain broad premises vouchsafed in England from time to time, it would be too much to say that any of these constituted a compelling idea that could be applied generally in all of the dependent territories. Given the nature of the system,

11. In 1943 a senior member of the C.O. staff drew up a memorandum for the secretary of state defining the role of the colonial civil servant as a maker of policy and not a mere carrier out of London's instructions or those of governors. (I am not at liberty to name the author of this paper.) One of its many counterparts at the other end, i.e. the colonial end, is the comment of Sir Colville Deverell to the effect that he never remembers having had any policy guidance worth mentioning. (Interview June 15, 1965.) Sir Colville was a D.C. in Kenya for some twenty years and afterward governed the Windwards and Mauritius.

moreover, it is clear that if such an idea had existed, its transportation from England to particular units of the Colonial Empire would have been fortuitous. At the start of each colony's association with England policy was important, for there had to be a reason to move forward. At the end of the colonial time, similarly, there was a rationale of going away. In between, the landscape was dominated by a system, not a policy.

The first characteristic of that system, again, was its limited scope and therefore its inability to be as pervasively effective as European governments could be. This is not to say that colonial governments were incapable of presiding over considerable social change, but only that their resources were far smaller than those of metropolitan regimes. The directly administered areas of colonial society were usually not as large as those that felt the pressure of the alien government less forcefully or saw it as a distant authority that hardly touched their daily lives. As late as the 1940s there were assistant district officers who rode into hamlets on the great plain of the western sudan where a white man had never been seen before or had been seen only at intervals of several years. Other communities that received annual or seasonal visits thought of the European officer as a man who talked with chiefs or listened to complaints and rode off again in the morning. In Northern Nigeria during the average interwar year more than ten million people were served by some 250 administrative officers.

The job of colonial governments was to hold the ring. Par excellence they brought and maintained order and thereby acted as stewards to the opening up of whole new contexts of social development. In every case enough discipline, uniformity, and regularity were imposed to drastically reduce or bridle ancient egotism, localism, and destructiveness. The new stabilities, at first unfamiliar and unloved, meant taxation that was reasonable, continuous, and of visible benefit to everyone. Roads and bridges, fanatically maintained, broadened horizons and helped trade. Justice, though deferential in the beginning, became steadily more insistent and more useful in interracial brokerage. Bit by bit there emerged a new atmosphere that was conducive to economic progress and that tended everywhere to throw up self-conscious, semi-Europeanized youths who rejected their own past with a vehemence that was at least equal to their enthusiasm for a future that would be controlled by them and not by aliens. While those concerned with policy in colonies could of course address themselves to these trends and could lay down official lines, the trends themselves were subjected less to a priori planning than to adjustment and partial control in each situation. No matter how he rationalized it all, the most policy-minded governor was always well behind events. His own hand was not very strong, and his tenure was short.

It is interesting in this regard to look at the pronouncements of colonial secretaries and governors on the subject of ultimate aims, and to compare these with what actually took place. Self-government in Tanganyika, thought Sir Donald Cameron, was unlikely to come "within the next few generations." [12] Amery assumed that the African colonies would stay in the Empire indefinitely, and Lugard, still exercising considerable influence on policy and on the selection of governors after his retirement from the Colonial Service in 1918, held that "representative institutions and legislative councils are . . . unsuited to African peoples." [13] Most highly placed British officials wanted a gradual devolution of local power onto traditional elites that would retain their own ways and add just enough Europeanism to help them adjust to the modern world. Increased competence on the part of such people would not mean cutting their countries adrift from the Empire. Negatively the aim was to avoid babu government of the kind that was thought to be evolving in India and elsewhere, a slow surrender of power to self-selected leaders who despised tradition and had taken on a veneer of European civilization. Yet with the wisdom of hindsight we can see that in many places it was precisely these people who took over from the British, and much earlier than interwar policy makers had expected. In Accra and Dar es Salaam, as in Colombo and Kingston before, the new chief ministers appealed to the masses. They lacked the support of traditionalists and climbed to power on the backs of organized minorities. In rather fewer places—Kaduna and Kampala—"natural rulers" did succeed; but even there the pace of events was

12. To Lugard, June 29, 1928, privately held. C. Whybrow, a Tanganyika Education Officer, wrote in 1926 of the British leaving the country in "fifty or a hundred years." Diaries, Colonial Records Project, Oxford.

13. Amery's views are set out quite fully in his own apologia, note 9 supra. They are also commented on by Cameron in his letter of November 8, 1925, to Lugard, privately held. See also Lugards' paper, "Note on the Present Position of Indirect Rule in Nigeria," December 17, 1928, sent by Lugard on January 9, 1933, to G. J. (later Sir Gordon) Lethem, then serving in Northern Nigeria. Colonial Records Project, Oxford. And see Lethem, Secretary Northern Provinces, to Residents, Northern Nigeria, circular of January 24, 1928, National Archives, Kaduna. Also Cameron to Lugard September 12, 1925, June 22, 1930, August 14, 1930, and November 11, 1930, and Cameron to Oldham July 26, 1925, privately held.

set from outside, with both the British and hereditary authorities struggling to keep up.

The main theme of colonial government in fact was the interaction of tradition and imported ways. One focuses on what happened when Europeans and Africans met in the myriad social, economic, and political situations of the era between the Scramble and nationalism. Here in the last analysis is the bedrock reality, the partly planned, mainly spontaneous surge of African life in the time when it reached and crossed the greatest watershed in its modern history. It is appropriate to look at this vast phenomenon through the eyes of provincial administrators, for if they could not always control it or, in many instances, even take action with respect to it, they nonetheless saw it close up. Because of the gray silence of Africans on the subject we stand to learn uniquely from officers in charge of Nigerian divisions and East African districts, the men so centrally placed to see and listen and do. Year in and year out they lived the lives of little kings in an epoch when their home-based brothers had exchanged kingship for bourgeois democracy. Their rule did not last long. The stamp of what they were and what they did is on Africa still.

These general comments may be illustrated by reference to British experience in two African territories that can be called typical or representative of the whole group in certain essentials. Northern Nigeria had the largest population of all. It was the most important of the units added as a consequence of the Scramble. Although millions of its people were primitive in cultural attainment, social organization, and economy, the Fulani chiefdoms of the loose-jointed Sokoto Empire were among the most advanced and best organized native regimes in sub-Sahara Africa. The high savanna of the North was rich in arable land, in pasture, and in minerals. Tanganyika by contrast, though it was the largest of the British territories, had less than half the population of Northern Nigeria and nothing approaching even the ramshackle religious and political unity of Sokoto. Though it was eventually to lead the world in sisal production, Tanganyika at the time Britain took it over was poor and getting poorer. The 1914 war had brought more suffering and disruption to her than to any other African territory. Lastly, Tanganyika was an important area of European settlement, an economic and social factor of major importance in East and Central Africa, but virtually unknown in the West. And it was European missionaries who took the primary responsibility for education in Tanganyika, a task that was left mainly to the government in Northern Nigeria.

It has been remarked that French steeplechasers were the prime movers in bringing Britain to Northern Nigeria, that the early administration was hampered by lack of money, and that from the outset Lugard and his small staff confronted strong local polities. The character of rule would therefore depend on the men who staffed the provincial administration and on the relationship they worked out with Fulani and other chiefs. The residents were partly new men from other tropical countries and from the military, and partly former officers of Sir George Goldie's Niger Company. The procedures of the whole group would reflect the traditions of British rule overseas and also the experienced assumptions of ex-Company men on how to deal with Moslem chiefs and pagan tribes. In the period 1900 to 1903 the job was one of pushing garrisons northward and posting political officers at the towns of major chiefs so as to cover the Protectorate with a skeletal administration. Residents were then occupied with a combination of military intelligence and anthropology, the complicated and seemingly endless business of "assessment." Slowly the hand of government was strengthened by imposing tolls on caravans and taking a percentage of chiefs' taxes. Punitive expeditions continued to be sent against recalcitrant groups, with the gradual result of substantially pacifying the whole region. Yet by the end of Lugard's time, 1906, there remained wide variation in the actual amount of ruling being done by residents and, overall, African systems still predominated.

Individual residents groped for solutions to each separate problem of power and hand-tailored a modus operandi in each place according to circumstances. For the first seventeen years Hadejia had no resident at all because there were not enough British officers to go around.[14] When he visited its emir in 1904, Larymore was received courteously and with the deference that Islamic potentates accord to acknowledged overlords.[15] But British sovereignty had by then made small difference in the life of the emirate. Two years later the emir was to lose his life resisting a British attack made necessary by his having ignored an authority that he naturally saw as distant and incomprehensible. By contrast Bornu, the largest emirate, received strong, direct British management from the start. The early giants, Hewby, Thomson, McClintock, and Benton, worked amid the shambles left by Rabeh, a Sudanese raider of the nineties. They built a new head-

14. See Confidential Reports on Emirs (of Hadejia and Gumel) and Secret File on Emirs, Northern Division Office, Kano Province, 1907 ff. And files on Hadejia Emirate, Kano Province, National Archives, Kaduna.

15. C. Larymore, *A Resident's Wife in Nigeria* (London, 1908), pp. 99 ff.

quarters town from nothing, founded courts, regulated tax collections, hired, fired, and supervised members of the shehu's administration, and sometimes told their own superiors and the chief what they were doing as they went along.[16] Hewby, an ex-Company man, was every inch an empiricist. As Resident Bornu he ran the place according to his own ideas of reasonable efficiency and according to the performance of the native officeholders. If things were going well and the populace seemed generally content, the British could confine themselves mainly to supervision. If not, interference was called for, and vigorous, direct methods would be used.[17]

To the south in riverain provinces such as Bassa there were no strong chiefs, no binding cultural force comparable to Islam, and therefore no possibility of ruling in tandem with an existing authority. Atomized pagan tribes had to be grouped together and placed under "warrant chiefs" recruited from farther north. British officers played an intimate role in such areas faute de mieux, and the power of native clerks from other parts of British West Africa rose similarly.[18]

More typical was the situation in which a resident worked closely with an emir who headed an old and well-established Moslem chiefdom. Following the short-lived disruption of the Occupation, affairs settled down rather quickly in Sokoto, Kano, Zaria, Bauchi, and the other major units. Chiefs swore loyalty to the government in Zungeru. Slave raiding and interemirate warfare were stopped. Part of the revenue went to the British. Otherwise life went on much as it had before, while the British proceeded with the herculean task of gathering demographic information on which eventual administrative reforms would be based. A few chiefs were so unsatisfactory that they were deposed —the emir of Katsina in 1906—but in most places residents concentrated on influencing their chiefs in the direction of good government

16. At one point during Lugards' high commissionership Hewby wrote laconically to Zungeru, "I never appoint a District Head without having consulted the Shehu," and was genuinely surprised to get back a rocket informing him that it was the shehu who should do the appointing, with the resident acting in an advisory role. This exchange was noted in a Maiduguri file by a later Resident Bornu, T. E. Letchworth, who was good enough to pass it on to me.

17. See undated note on this, by Hewby, written as he was leaving Kano to take over Bornu again, about 1908. "Confidential Notes on Indirect Rule," 1907 ff., National Archives, Kaduna.

18. Audu dan Afoda, Hewby's Yoruba groom, later became a political agent and ended as headman of Makurdi. On warrant chiefs, see the diaries of C. M. Woodhouse, especially on his service in Kabba and Bassa, 1908 ff. Colonial Records Project, Oxford.

as Europeans defined it. At Kano, Cargill tried to bring progress without undercutting the emir who, as head of the richest and most populous emirate, was a man whom the British, with their miniscule staff, could not help taking seriously. It was not easy.

> I have never been able to effect reforms after consultation with and with the concurrence of the Emir . . . because he has invariably adopted an attitude of *non possumus* towards all proposals, although always intimating his willingness to accept a direct order . . . [the] frame of mind which Major Festing describes as passive resistance. . . . I am afraid I have got into the habit of giving him direct orders . . . and it is likely that this has tended to upset his sense of the dignity due to his position.[19]

In regretting the need for direct orders Cargill had reference to the wishes of headquarters, especially in the Lugard years, that residents defer where possible to native tradition and to the residual power of chiefs. In fact, however, these wishes remained in the realm of general policy, on a high enough plane to be almost useless as a guide in practical situations.[20] In Katsina, shortly after he had removed the emir and put in his own man, Palmer laid it on the line:

> Whether we wish to be so or not we are the rulers. We must be either above or below the rank and file. . . . the Protectorate has its laws and ordinances, and our functions have long been far in excess of mere Residential Advisors . . . a native can no more understand the idea of joint rule by Emirs and Residents than he can understand the doctrine of the Trinity and where the Resident does exercise a fairly strong influence, he is bound to be recognized as a big [man], if not . . . bigger than the Emir.[21]

Orr and Fremantle at Zaria a few years earlier had emphasized how individualistic administration had become as they discussed "to what extent [the] systems [of the various officers] could or should dovetail

19. Penciled draft of a note to accompany Major Festing's annual report, Kano, 1907, National Archives, Kaduna.

20. See the entry of May 2, 1908, Woodhouse diaries, note 18 supra. Sir Richmond Palmer, whose Northern Nigerian service began in 1904, wrote to Margery Perham, December 17, 1949, "I don't remember myself doing more than glancing at [Lugard's Political Memoranda]." Sir William Gowers, who arrived in the North in 1902, wrote to Margery Perham, November 26, 1949, that the Memoranda had not made "much difference one way or another."

21. "Confidential Notes on Indirect Rule," National Archives, Kaduna. Palmer's letter containing this passage is dated November 9, 1908, Katsina.

into each other." [22] And when Byng-Hall completely reversed his predecessor's policy in Bassa, the new governor, Girouard, gave him "a freer hand than he had ever dreamed of." [23] Governors were remote. They were much occupied with staff matters and with their duties as liaison officers between the residents and London.[24] Being birds of passage it was only natural that they would be unable to compete in the long run with the career officers who ran provinces and divisions. Very soon individualism, precedent, and momentum were dominant in fact if not in law.

During the interwar period the tension between policy and administration became at bottom an undeclared competition: on the one hand were hard-driving officers who dragged their emirates forward, and on the other a composite group of men who for one reason or another—laziness, literal-mindedness about policy, lack of imagination, timidity—failed to keep up the pressure for progress, honesty, and efficiency. The relationship between either kind of officer and his superiors in the regional headquarters at Kaduna or in Lagos, now the capital of a unified Nigeria, was so circumstantial as to virtually defeat generalization. In 1920 the emir of Zaria was deposed after an agonizingly long campaign on the part of several residents. Emir Aliyu had been put in by the British in 1903 after the deposition of his predecessor, who had intrigued against them. His services while the railway was being built and during the 1914 war had given him a privileged position at a time when British weakness made it necessary to

22. A. F. Fremantle, ed., *Two African Journals and Other Papers of the Late John Morton Fremantle, C.M.G., M.B.E.* (London, 1938, printed for private circulation), p. 38.

23. Woodhouse to his sister, from Itobe, April 19, 1909, Colonial Records Project, Oxford. Lacking instructions from headquarters Ruxton, Resident Muri, wrote his own "Instructions for the Guidance of Newly Joined Officers." Copied at the Provincial Office by H. M. Brice-Smith, 1909, Colonial Records Project, Oxford.

24. In 1913 when he was in charge of all Nigeria, Lugard wrote gloomily that local officers were carrying all before them and "The Governor is left out." Perham, *Lugard 2,* 479. The distance between residents and headquarters is underscored by Sir William Gowers in a letter to Margery Perham of September 4, 1950: "I never saw Lugard till 1906," i.e. the last year of Lugard's high commissionship. That the independence of provincial administrators in West Africa was not confined to the early years alone is shown in the experience of D. A. Anderson who entered the Gold Coast Service in 1941; a famous officer under whom Anderson served in the Northern Territories posted a government circular in the usual place outside his office and wrote across the top, "This circular does not apply in my district."

depend on able chiefs regardless of their shortcomings. The easygoing ways of Fremantle, Grier, and other residents had encouraged the emir to think that he was indispensable and therefore invulnerable.[25] With the war over and the period of regularized administration and economic development well advanced, however, Aliyu's corruption and oppression could no longer be rationalized. For several years Arnett, Browne, and Byng-Hall maneuvered to build a solid case against him, gathering concrete information and native testimony on the worst of the emir's crimes. Strangely, the governor, a man remembered as a progressive and an enemy of Lugard's supposed overemphasis on ruling through native chiefs, acted in such a way as to obstruct their best efforts. While Aliyu was busily planning to arrange the murder of the local resident, Sir Hugh Clifford wrote:

> I regard it as improper and inexpedient that the Government should attempt, in the absence of any complaint by persons believing themselves to have suffered injury, to press inquisitorial investigations into the personnel of the harem of a Muhammaden Chief.[26]

So unanswerable was the case against Aliyu however, and so well organized was the cooperation of senior Northern administrators, that the emir was at last brought down.

Yet two years later in the still more important emirate of Sokoto a similar case ended differently. Again the trouble grew out of a combination of indigenous evil and British laxity. Webster, Resident Sokoto for almost all of the 1920s, was a notorious *mai lafiya,* or easygoing man, who felt that British interference in native administration was a violation of the policy of indirect rule. Sultan Muhammadu Mai Turare, therefore, had a free hand to milk his subjects and perpetuate injustice behind the backs of the British staff. During Webster's absence on leave in 1921–22 the acting resident, Edwardes, tried to move against the sultan as his brother officers had done in the Zaria case. But his preparations were not as careful or as thorough as those at Zaria had been; he was too junior and too isolated to be able to count on support in Kaduna, which naturally saw his charges as reflecting badly on Webster and on the regime as well as on the sultan. After a visit by Clifford and the lieutenant governor of the Northern Region,

25. Fremantle papers, note 22 supra, pp. 81 ff. And see the Zaria-Zungeru and Zaria-Kaduna correspondence on the case, 1909–20, National Archives, Kaduna.

26. To the Lieutenant Governor, October 16, 1920, National Archives, Kaduna. The emir's crimes included child raiding and taking slave concubines as young as fourteen years of age.

it was Edwardes and not the chief who fell from grace. The result was to cover up a diseased situation which then erupted again later on and not only ruined the next sultan but exposed British administration to international ridicule.

The accumulation of similar incidents as time went on shows in the aggregate a bewildering galaxy of variables with both good and bad results.[27] Sokoto in the 1930s under Carrow and a new sultan, Hassan, was a model of progressive, energetic, and enlightened administration, this being achieved without reference to the extraordinary meanderings of policy in Lagos and Kaduna during the period.[28] District officers in charge of the minor emirate of Jema's south of Zaria tried for a decade to improve its administration by removing a hopeless emir, but they were consistently frustrated. On one occasion a district officer's nemesis in Kaduna was none other than Palmer, who had been ruthless with an equally bad and far more powerful emir in Katsina two decades before. The farther they moved from bush administration, it seemed, the more some officers tended to take a rigid, theoretical stand in matters of policy. In Zaria during the mid-1930s a vigorous and self-reliant D.O. personally brought about the selection of an able and enlightened emir despite the ineligibility of his candidate by tradition and even though the D.O.'s methods were frowned on by his superior, the resident. Shortly afterward the same D.O., now Resident Niger, reformed the administration of a minor emirate in that province in the face of Kaduna's disapproval. Refused permission

27. My archival work on these cases has been balanced by talks and correspondence with officers who were involved and in some instances by examination of their papers, some of which were deposited in the collections of the Colonial Records Project, Oxford. Notably among such officers are Sir Bryan Sharwood Smith, who served in the North from 1927 to 1957, and Commander J. H. Carrow, 1919 to 1946. In Northern Nigeria itself I have been greatly helped by the late Sir Ahmadu Bello, first premier of independent Northern Nigeria, and by the emirs of Gwandu and Yauri.

28. During his governorship of Nigeria, 1931–35, Cameron fought a running battle with the Northern administration on both policy and power questions. Although on balance the Northerners prevailed, the governor did succeed in downgrading the lieutenant governorship to a chief commissionionership and putting into that position in 1933 an officer of his own choosing, G. S. Browne. The result was more uncomfortable for Browne than debilitating for the North. Although Browne's successor was from Malaya and therefore not identified with Northern sensibilities, he found himself opposing the new governor, Bourdillon, on many of the same issues that had divided Cameron and the old Northern group.

to depose the chief, the Resident packed him off on the Pilgrimage to Mecca and then quietly effected the needed reforms during the emir's absence. A D.O. in Kano Province sought the resident's approval to put on an emir's council a man who was not of the ruling class but was competent and was wanted by the emir himself. Permission was denied and progress held up on the grounds that the candidate was a former slave. Zaria Province, as late as the 1950s, slipped backward in administrative efficiency because its once progressive emir had grown old and conservative, and the resident of the time was a traditionalist—a situation full of irony in that the D.O. who had dictated the emir's selection in the first place was now governor of the region. Yet in the same years happier results were obtained in Bornu, where the governor had never served, because he personally intervened to ram through a series of long-overdue reforms.

In so individualistic a set of circumstances it will be clear that policy was often irrelevant and that it became important mainly when a senior officer took it seriously enough to act on it. Even in such cases, however, the totality of separate actions by lieutenant governors and their provincial subordinates during the interwar years shows that policy was whatever strong men were willing and able to make of it. Put differently: by the time any overall policy got down to the divisional level it no longer had enough cutting edge to make much difference and could then become the plaything of individual officers. The system, together with financial stringency and poor communications, gave great personal discretion to district officers and residents. The character of government and its net effects are thus to be found in the sum total of what was done with that discretion and how the Africans were affected in the process.

From earliest times the most energetic officers characteristically thought of making things more European. Little could be done at first, but prospects improved with every passing year. Forbidding the Africans their old habits of violence and waste and disciplining them toward the rudiments of European bureaucracy, finance, and justice were bound to have their effect in time. Native Authorities, at first nothing more than chiefs and their traditional Islamic coteries of slaves, relatives, and supporters, were gradually remade into quasi-modern agencies of local government. Students trained in British-run schools were given jobs in N.A.'s. British officers toured the countryside training and supervising rural officeholders in the petty but regularized and uniform duties of tax collecting and justice and later on of agricultural and communications improvements. Traditional ways took a steady battering as the younger generation looked more and more to Europeans for inspiration. An education officer recalls:

> At the time of the First War and after, schoolboys absorbed western ideas in the classroom but remained African in habits and outlook and did not apparently want to be anything else. But during the last war I was conscious of a steady pull between the ultraconservative ideas of some of my African staff and a desire among boys for non-African standards—wearing shoes indoors and out, a decided preference during the holidays for clothes of European style, abandonment of traditional salutations, discarding of old Hausa names . . . all these things spoke of a revulsion against what must have appeared as the marks of servitude and a determination to rise above them.[29]

It was the mere presence of the white man and his natural inclination to do things his own way that lay at the heart of British rule. The other side of the coin in Northern Nigeria was the changing but still essential hold of native cultures. Systems found in existence when the British arrived had roots deep in the soil, and it was on these systems that the British built. What slowly evolved during the colonial years was a hybrid that was all the stronger for having taken a half century to grow.

Britain's experience in Tanganyika was shorter and in many ways more straightforward. While scholars still argue the reasons for the Scramble, there can be no dispute over Tanganyika. It fell into Britain's lap as a simple consequence of the wartime need to destroy German forces that happened to be there. Conquest has a logic of its own. There was no reasonable alternative to British management once the Germans had gone. Although her role was the subject of an agreement with the League of Nations, Britain controlled the Territory before the League was born and after it died, and her conduct of government in the interim was in no important way affected by the League.

Although in Tanganyika the British were fighting other Europeans rather than Africans, the occupation of the country was piecemeal as in Northern Nigeria. There were additional similarities: the length of time needed to complete the conquest was comparable, the territory

29. E. L. Mort, letter of June 4, 1966.

was large, and communications were generally primitive. Many of the first political officers had had previous experience of tropical countries, especially while in military service. The central ethos and system of government were certain to be roughly the same as in the rest of British Africa. This was true not only because the first head of the administration was an experienced colonial civil servant, but because the full weight of precedent and tradition was bound to fall, unthinkingly and with irresistible force, on this last major addition to Britain's overseas domains. The essentials were all there: lack of money from London, local discretion, the ring-holding function, and, whether adorned with high rationalizations or not, the cultural assurance of the men on the ground, despite their small numbers, that they would lead and the natives follow.[30]

At the grassroots there was a basic difference of varying importance according to area, and it gave the first rulers an advantage over their brothers of two decades earlier in Northern Nigeria: Tanganyika had been under Europeans for a considerable period before the British arrived. With the 1914 war still raging a few valleys away, political officers were already receiving Africans who advanced claims to local authority, many presenting German documents in support of their claims. British officers made efforts to find German records so that they would have some way of sorting out the various allegations and preparing the ground for taxation and the wider business of reestablishing a shattered order. Even in this sphere, however, there were similarities to the Nigerian and other cases. Everywhere one's common-sense aim was to learn what local society was like and how it worked so that the European superstructure could be solidly based. In the war years this was sometimes a matter of life and death, for one could have no illusions about what the chiefs or akidas would do if a German column reappeared. Later it was a question of differentiating between what would respond to the minimum demands of the new administration and what would not. Morality and legitimacy aside, the British had to find leaders whom the tribes would follow, since there was no possibility of importing enough Europeans to do the whole job unaided. Methods varied. At Tunduru in 1918 Barnes held a baraza and

30. A factor of somewhat unsettling effect, especially at the secretariat level in the first years, was the uncertainty in Europe as to Tanganyika's ultimate fate. This cropped up again in the 1930s when there was talk of turning the country over to Germany once more. But its effect on district administration was negligible.

made the various claimants to authority stand together before the whole crowd.[31] Tribesmen were then told to queue up behind the man they recognized as their leader. Others used German files, which in some cases were almost current, and at Kasulu a bit later Longland read Stanley for information about the Waha.[32] In the absence of any practical lead from headquarters—just as well, as headquarters had little knowledge of the districts—empiricism was the order of the day. Individual officers had the only authority worth talking about in their areas, and the governor was not at pains to deny it: "You know, Longland, that you have far more power than I have." [33]

Throughout the short period of time remaining before the 1939 war, the provincial administration ran Tanganyika in the time-honored way. D.O.'s could smile at the Golden Rule—"Thou shalt collect thy tax, thou shalt not worry thy Government"—and agree that this was the essence.[34] But they would then proceed to explain what else the day was full of. Everyone had his special assignment or pet project: Wyatt's road in Mahenge in the time when Lettow was still at large: Jumbe Baker's schools in the Lake Province; Longland's field engineering; Malcolm's land-development scheme in Sukumaland; Leechman on tsetse control; Rooke Johnston on markets; Culwick on rice; Savory on casava; Page-Jones on the right way to bring development to the Masai; and a long line of clarified butter men in the Central Province. Some D.O.'s—Hignell comes to mind—were so jealous of native rights that they opposed all schemes involving untraditional activity by the local people, especially any suggestion of compulsory labor. One officer went so far in this direction that he advised his people not to pay tax. But most worked instinctively for improvements as Europeans would define them. Though this was done mainly in the economic area, there was always the bureaucratic side as well. Bagshawe built up the administrative and judicial functions of tribal authorities in the Kondoa

31. Interview, W. S. G. Barnes, January 13, 1965.

32. Interview, Frank Longland, February 2, 1965. See also the diaries of F. J. Bagshawe, Colonial Records Project, Oxford, e.g. the entries of June 23, 1920 referring to his barazas in Kondoa.

33. Interview, Longland, April 29, 1965, referring to Sir H. Byatt's visit to his boma at Urambo Kilimani in 1918.

34. Interview, J. F. R. Hill, April 19 and 21, 1965. For information on the work of administrative officers in these years I depend on extensive talks and correspondence with former officers and on written materials, notably the papers of the National Archives, Dar es Salaam; district books in a selection of bomas throughout the country; and the collections of the Colonial Records Project, Oxford, which are especially rich in Tanganyika papers.

area in 1920 as other D.O.'s were doing in their districts and for similar reasons. Few Englishmen could put up with the spectacle of exploitation and abuse within a context of anarchy. Yet European resources were hopelessly inadequate. Therefore, coach the locals in basic techniques and maintain a watching brief on their progress. German-trained akidas were plentiful and if given strong supervision were well suited to intermediary or noncommissioned officer roles.[35]

By the mid-20s the foundations had been securely built, the patterns established, and the whole country habituated to workable and working interracial procedures. There was plenty of room for further improvement, which did come in the fullness of time. Minor and major adjustments could still be made and were made. University graduates replaced the soldiers of the first years and went forward to new achievements without always being aware of their debts to pioneer predecessors. But the coordinates of the whole Anglo-African situa-

35. The akidas, mainly Swahilis, had a long history, going back before the Germans, of service to the sultans of Zanzibar and to Arabs operating well inland of the sultan's territories. Large numbers of them were employed by the Germans. Many were kept on by the British, some of them seeing their influence rise during the interwar period. One, for example, was made a wakili in Bagamoyo in 1940; see the Bagamoyo District Book. Further details may be found in the Mwanza and Arusha District Books, the former covering all of the East Lake Districts. The career of a Central Province akida, K. H. Alimasi, is instructive: he was hired as an akida in 1917 and served as such until 1926 when he became an instructor to chiefs in Manyoni while the Cameron reforms were being carried out there. He then became a boma clerk. In effect his functions from 1917 to 1931 had not changed in essence; see African civil service file, Manyoni, March 12, 1931. See also D.O. Moshi to P.C., May 29, 1946, on a Somali whose service began in 1916 and who was still serving as headman of Boma la Ngombe in 1946. Cameron himself was reconciled to the continuation of akida help, and occasionally to its reinstitution, in places where chieftaincy was nonexistent or hopelessly weak, e.g. in Kibondo, Kasulu, and Kilwa. After Cameron's departure it became more difficult for some administrative officers to go on covering up the inadequacies of the N.A.'s. In July 1939 the D.O. Mwanza abolished several subchieftaincies in order to be able to hire a wakili: "The Chiefs of this District, with few exceptions, are lazy and given to over indulgence in liquor . . . they are inclined to lean on the D.O. and rely on him . . . to assert their authority." Gilbert to P.C., January 4, 1940. In Iringa it was much the same: "Before the baraza an old man stood up . . . and stated that the time had now come for an outsider to govern Pawaga . . . his words were applauded. Averse as I am to appointing what can only be called a wakili . . . I am convinced that the people of this . . . area want it." D.O. Robinson, to P.C., December 19, 1939. In Bukoba, often cited as an area of strong chiefs and N.A.'s, everything depended not on the chiefs but on the D.O. and "Mwami" Lwamgira. Interview, W. F. Page, April 7, 1965.

tion in 1939 were still essentially the same as they had been in 1919: there was no money in Dar es Salaam; many D.O.'s were out of touch for weeks or months with their own provincial commissioners, not to mention the Secretariat, and they were masters in their own houses.[36] The weakness of indigenous political institutions compared with those in Northern Nigeria was pronounced, which could only mean that D.O.'s would rule. Depending on circumstances, they could and did make use of particular chiefs, headmen, elders, and especially akidas and liwalis. But a truly cooperative relationship and procedure on the Northern Nigerian model, albeit with the British as senior partners, was never on the cards. German East Africa had had no Sokoto.

During his governorship, 1925–31, Sir Donald Cameron articulated policy in a much more self-conscious and closely reasoned way than his predecessor had done. He and his one-man inspectorate, P. E. Mitchell, issued the well-remembered "little brown books" to all administrative officers and saw to it that almost every district on the big territorial map in the governor's office was colored red to signify the gazetting of Native Authorities. Cameron's instructions involved the provincial administration in considerable additional paper work and ultimately resulted in a good deal of training being given to office-holders and employees of N.A.'s. This would stand independent Tanganyika in good stead even though its government abolished N.A.'s, for experienced bureaucrats would be one of Africa's most glaring needs in the 1960s. Nevertheless Cameron's notion of what had been accomplished as a result of his policy stood in marked contrast to the facts as D.O.'s saw them and lived them in the Cameron years and later.

The new governor's assumption before he arrived was that native political structures and leaders clearly existed, and that it would only be necessary to find these and endow them with local power while the British played an advisory role. D.O.'s, he thought, knew nothing of local traditions and must be made to study the tribes so as to understand what it was they were to revive and prop up. The gradual modernization of the country would then go forward on the lines of authentic tradition rather than being subject to district officer whim.

A few officers, knowing the shortcomings of tribal institutions, had difficulty suppressing their doubts about what the governor wanted to

36. E. G. Rowe, who began his Tanganyika career in 1928, first saw the capital, Dar es Salaam, twelve years later.

do.[37] Others, notably some who inclined to abstractions or to the bureaucratic aspect of administration, looked on Cameron as a savior. Newly arrived juniors, fresh from university, tended to be impressed with the way the governor appeared to be tidying up in the wake of a lackadaisical and aimless administration that had conquered the country and then sat down to wait. It would probably be right to say that the majority belonged to neither group. The average D.O. of the twenties and thirties knew full well how little could be expected of most chiefs in Tanganyika. It was of doubtful use to give them back powers and functions they had never really had, especially since the D.O. would go right on ruling anyway and would now have to carry extra burdens of tuition as he did so.[38] But it was neither necessary nor expedient to oppose Cameron and Mitchell openly.

In retrospect there is a certain similarity between Cameron's experiences in Tanganyika and in Northern Nigeria. His own comprehension of the personality and character of district administration was at best spotty and superficial in both places. The 1929 Depression had an arresting effect on all colonial government and served to blunt the edges of Cameronian instructions along with everything else. In neither territory could the governor's innovations and prescriptions hope to compete over the long pull with the way the system and native

37. A. M. D. Turnbull, in charge of Mwanza when Cameron arrived, was soon transferred to Lindi, notoriously the dustbin post of Tanganyika. Turnbull was said to have disagreed openly with Cameron. At Lindi he wrote to his D.O.'s on April 7, 1926, that they could start N.A.'s if they wanted to, but, since the people seemed happy, they might like to leave well enough alone and go on ruling directly. F. H. Page-Jones, D. O. Mikindani, replied on May 7 that the villages were under their own elders and that there was no central authority except the D.O. himself. If there was to be an N.A. it should be "a grouping of villages with an Akida or Jumbe primus inter pares." Bagshawe (diary, February 20, 1926) in Iringa called indirect rule a "farce." Scupham wrote (Mwanza Book, June 1932) that after 1926 the Sukuma Federation disintegrated, the officer who set it up having left the province. Rooke Johnston in 1934 got the chief secretary's permission to recognize an accomplished fact, that the Ujiji N.A. was hopeless; and the D.O. Moshi (Hutt, Annual Report, 1941) referred with unusual frankness to the policy as "so-called indirect rule."

38. Some of Cameron's successors such as Young and Jackson understood what the real situation was and saw D.O. rule as unexceptionable. Many former D.O.'s would accept the views of J. F. R. Hill, who ended his Tanganyika career as minister for Communications, Works and Development, that the best aim in the 1920s would have been economic development. Faster Europeanization would have followed naturally. N.A.'s were seen as a waste of the D.O.'s time and a retrograde or irrelevant step for the natives.

life meshed. A secretariat's powers of enforcement were not great in any case. And governors, as always, were soon gone.[39]

It would be too much to say that policy, or official intent, was utterly lacking in importance during the first half of this century in British Africa. There were great issues that occupied the Colonial Office, prompted parliamentary questions, and drew considerable public attention. The extended fight over East African Union was no local matter; the vivid contrasts between developments in the two Rhodesias were cause for substantial concern in Britain, as was settler domination in Kenya and resistance to it in Tanganyika. Large-scale agricultural, mineral, and social development in such places as the Gold Coast and Malaya were discussed in London circles that extended beyond the purely colonial. Humanitarian and religious considerations went on playing an important part long after the demise of the slavery issue and well before anyone gave much thought to nationalism. And in the diplomatic sphere such questions as the possibility of giving Germany back her former colonies could and did make colonial civil servants feel small and helpless by comparison with their counterparts in Whitehall.

But taken as a whole, all this was a kaleidoscope of widely disparate impulses, elaborations, and playings out. There was no overall theme that London stuck to decade by decade, exhorting all of the territories in a uniform way. Often, moreover, it seemed that the influence of colonies on the mother country was more substantial than hers on them.

A lack of vital and sustained inspiration from the center left initiative to the men on the spot, especially to administrative, educational, and agricultural officers and to other local Europeans such as businessmen and missionaries. All of them did what came naturally, pushing on according to their own standards. There were never enough staff and money to remake society, although over the years African peoples did become aware of options different from those their fathers had known. They experienced great changes in style and condition of life. It was Britain's presence in Africa rather than her voice in London that acted as the prime mover.

39. Cf. the remark of Lady Tomlinson, the wife of an assistant undersecretary of state, "Governors don't matter," in a letter to her son, G. A. Tomlinson, a D.O. in Tanganyika. Quoted by him in his letter of August 17, 1941, Colonial Records Project, Oxford.

18. *The Economic Exploitation of Africa: Some British and French Comparisons*

DAVID K. FIELDHOUSE

Exploitation, like imperialism, is no word for scholars because it has long been confused by ideological concepts. Semantics apart, two usages must be distinguished. The original French meaning can best be translated as "use" or "development." In English, however, "exploitation" is pejorative, suggesting unfair or unrequited advantage obtained. In Marxist thought it implied extraction of surplus value from variable capital; and in contemporary neo-Marxist terminology it may indicate imperialist superprofit from a dependent economy. Since this chapter is concerned with the actual policies followed by Britain and France and their economic consequences rather than with theoretical questions, "exploitation" will be understood as "development," though some attempt will be made to assess the validity of Marxist assumptions.

Even so restricted, the economic development of British and French Africa after about 1880 is too vast a subject to be comprehended in a single chapter.[1] It must also be said that the materials now available are an insufficient basis for answering most questions with confidence. More work has been done and published on the British than on the French side, but even there the gaps remain large. For both it is possible to describe with some precision what may be called the imperial factor as it affected economic development—metropolitan policy on tariffs and currency, governmental intervention in Africa in such basic fields as law, land, and labor. But the actual working of the colonial economies, more particularly in the private sector, remains largely unknown. Public investment can be measured with some accuracy, but private direct investment and its profitability remain speculative at

1. Since this is a general survey of a vast subject, it would be impracticable moreover to document every statement. Specific references are given for quotations, statistics, and attributable points of view. Otherwise a note on the main sources used is given for each main section.

all periods. A leading economic role was taken by British and French trading, shipping, investment, and plantation companies, yet there are no detailed studies of any of these after about 1900. On the African side very little is known about the activities of merchants or entrepreneurs or about the response of producers to the stimulus of overseas markets. It need hardly be added that sophisticated data on production does not exist. The present chapter is therefore more a chart of areas requiring further study than an effective account of British and French achievements. Starting with the relatively certain, it points to the unknown. First a survey of contrasting Anglo-French attitudes to the basic aims of the *mise en valeur;* then an estimate of the economic significance of official policy in various fields; finally a survey of available evidence on trade, investment, and the positive achievements of the colonial period.

Behind most discussion of British and French development policies lies the assumption that colonies had economic functions and that development was therefore inevitable. This is paradoxical because, as earlier chapters have suggested, strictly economic factors often played little part in the partition of Africa. Some territories had obvious economic potential: but why expect to develop or gain economic advantage from regions acquired primarily to exclude a rival from some "strategic" area or to round off a frontier? An answer can be found by examining characteristic British and French assumptions during each of three periods—before 1914, between the two world wars, and after 1945.

The origins of modern thought about African economics lie in the years after about 1880, and they derived from the urgent need to justify expensive and politically dangerous expansionist policies before suspicious publics and parsimonious legislatures. Political necessity, strategic advantage, and national honor served up to a point; but, as the bills mounted, more substantial benefits had to be projected. The common solution was to revive elements of the old concept of the *pacte colonial* as against the ethic of mid-Victorian free trade. Conditions, it was said, had changed with the adoption of protective tariffs by most states from the 1870s on. In a world of closing markets and growing autarky it was no longer safe to rely on free competition. Colonies were necessary to safeguard markets, provide raw materials, and absorb capital looking for profitable openings. Not to compete for colonies offering such opportunities was to mortgage the nation's future. However expensive to annex and govern, colonies would and must provide an economic return.[2]

Such arguments were common currency in Britain and France, though the emphasis naturally differed. Free-trading British statesmen and publicists underlined the need to annex in order to hold the doors open in Africa against the assumed intentions of protectionist rivals to monopolize African trade. The French, being protectionist, proposed to enclose new colonies within their metropolitan tariff walls in order to exclude more efficient competitors. Such contrasts remained characteristic until the 1930s; but they must not obscure the extent of common ground in the early period. The British also assumed that commercial enterprise would ensure them a virtual monopoly of trade in their own colonies, despite the open door. Like the French they were excessively optimistic about the economic possibilities of territories of which they were largely ignorant. Determination to discover the pot of gold led both countries into similar practices. Because governments lacked experience and money, they left development to private concerns under minimal public control—the chartered British companies, the French land concessionary companies, individual settlers and prospectors. Little attempt was made to provide an infrastructure of communications or other public works. Except in British West Africa there was little concern on either side for the interests of Africans. Indeed exploitation in the pejorative sense was more typical of British and French Africa in this first period than at any later stage precisely because excessive economic expectations were matched by ignorance of the economic and social problems involved in extracting wealth from Africa.

Well before 1914 the consequences were economically disappointing and morally disturbing. No new Rand was discovered, investors showed marked reluctance to risk their capital, and colonial governments were too poor and inexperienced to undertake essential public works. Clearly Africa was no treasure trove offering easy fortunes. Conversely, the attempts of private concessionary companies to squeeze profits out of wild rubber and other indigenous products requiring minimal investment, and to obtain African land and labor, proved unacceptable to the humanitarian conscience in Europe. The

2. Such views were expressed by many French or British statesmen and publicists. For the main examples see George Bennett, ed., *The Concept of Empire* (2nd ed. London, 1962) and Henri Brunschwig, *Mythes et Réalités de l'Impérialisme colonial français, 1871–1914* (Paris, 1960).

outcome was a serious reappraisal of African policies on both sides of the Channel which began about 1900 and continued to 1914 and beyond, providing the basis for new experiments between the two world wars.

During this second phase, neither France nor Britain discarded belief in the economic potential of Africa.[3] The new factor was recognition that the state must play a more positive role. The metropolis must take stock of its own needs and stimulate production in Africa to meet them. Colonial governments must become the agents of development by developing communications, stimulating all forms of economic activity, and planning for the future. Conversely, governments must balance European needs against African interests, acting, if necessary, as protector of Africans against expatriate pressures. Development would thus be undertaken systematically to the benefit of European and African alike.

So much was common ground between Britain and France. Beyond, there were inevitably differences of emphasis and method. It is always tempting to overstate these; yet there were undoubtedly certain divergencies which may be exemplified briefly from the ideas of those two great colonial administrators and publicists, Frederick Lugard and Albert Sarraut, whose best-known works, *The Dual Mandate in British Tropical Africa* and *La Mise en Valeur des Colonies Françaises,* were published in 1922 and 1923 respectively.

To Lugard it seemed fundamental, if economic development in Africa was to be morally justifiable, that it should not be planned in relation to the selfish interests of any one imperial power. He accused France of "preserving the products and markets of her colonies for the exclusive use of France by every means in her power." This was wrong.

> The tropics are the heritage of mankind, and neither, on the one hand, has the suzerain Power a right to their exclusive exploitation, nor, on the other hand, have the race which inhabit them a right to deny their bounties to those who need them. The responsibility for adequate development rests on the custodian on behalf of civilisation—and not on behalf of civilisation alone, for much of these

3. For discussion of post-1914 attitudes see W. Keith Hancock, *Survey of British Commonwealth Affairs* (2 vols. London, 1940–42), 2 (2 parts), *Problems of Economic Policy, 1918–39;* Stephen H. Roberts, *History of French Colonial Policy, 1870–1925* (2 vols. London, 1929); Henri Brunschwig, *La Colonisation française* (Paris, 1949).

products is returned to the tropics converted into articles for the use and comfort of its peoples.[4]

Any of these premises might be challenged, but in this passage Lugard effectively homogenized the best in current British thought deriving variously from free-trade theory, humanitarianism, and more recent internationalist arguments by men like J. A. Hobson.[5] Lugard had no doubt that Britain would benefit from development of her own colonies, but it must be incidental to the greater interest of Africa and the world.

> Our present task is clear. It is to promote the commercial and industrial progress of Africa, without too careful a scrutiny of the material gains to ourselves, that we may not incur the accusation of having inflicted upon Africa "the grave economic wrong" for which our commercial policy in India is alleged to have been responsible in that country.[6]

Such concepts were alien to French thought. Few Frenchmen were more liberal in their attitudes to colonial development than Albert Sarraut, former governor-general of Indochina and minister of colonies in 1923. In *La Mise en Valeur* he explicitly rejected the extreme protectionist doctrine that France should monopolize colonial markets and discourage colonial exports that competed with metropolitan products.[7] Denouncing what he called "l'ancienne conception mercantile ou 'impérialiste,'" he propounded a universalist approach.

> La France qui colonise va organiser l'exploitation pour son avantage sans doute, *mais aussi pour l'avantage général du monde* [sic], de territoires et de ressources que les races autochtones de ces pays arriérés ne pouvaient à elles seules ou ne savaient mettre en valeur, et dont le profit était ainsi perdu pour elles, comme pour la collectivité universelle.[8]

4. Frederick D. Lugard, *The Dual Mandate in British Tropical Africa* (3rd ed. London, 1926), p. 61.
5. John A. Hobson, *Imperialism: A Study* (London, 1902). See also Wm. Roger Louis, *Great Britain and Germany's Lost Colonies, 1914–19* (Oxford, 1967), pp. 77–116.
6. *Dual Mandate,* p. 509.
7. Albert Sarraut, *La Mise en Valeur des Colonies Françaises* (Paris, 1923), p. 114. The same criticism of metropolitan protectionism was expressed by many supporters of colonial interests, notably Arthur Girault in *The Colonial Tariff Policy of France* (Oxford, 1916).
8. *La Mise en Valeur,* p. 87.

But he did not maintain this lofty approach. Almost immediately he reverted to a liberalized form of the classic French concept of the *pacte colonial:*

> L'opération n'est plus unilatérale: elle est conçue pour l'avantage et le bien des deux parties. Il n'y a plus spoilation d'une race par une autre, mais *association,* suivant la formule heureuse qui est devenue la devise de notre politique coloniale. . . . Les colonies ne sont pas que des "marchés": ce sont des entités vivantes, des créations d'humanité, des parties solidaires de l'Etat français dont on va, par le progrès scientifique, économique, moral et politique, favoriser l'accès à de plus hauts destins, au même titre que les autres parties du territoire national.[9]

Obviously the key words were "integral parts of the French state." Mutuality of interests between metropolis and colonies replaced both French unilateralism and British multilateralism. Much of Sarraut's book in fact constituted an inventory of the economic condition and potential of the colonies together with a detailed prescription—based on his own abortive *projet de loi* of 1921—for planned development. Planning, indeed, was fundamental. In the past matters had been left to chance. Now, after the destructive effects of the war, all imperial resources must be used methodically. "Fournir, dans le moindre délai, aux besoins de la vie nationale la plus grande somme des produits principaux qu'elle réclame, tel est le but." [10]

How characteristic were Lugard and Sarraut of British and French attitudes to African development between the wars and after? On the French side, at least, there was no substantive change of view. Up to 1939, and even more after 1945, metropolis and colonies were seen as complementary parts of a single economy whose integration must be promoted by tariffs, administrative regulation, and eventually currency controls.[11] On the British side there was less consistency. In one sense Lugard's ideas remained dominant. There was never an integrated imperial economic plan relating African development to British needs. African colonies remained virtually free-trading, part of a multilateral world commercial system rather than satellites of Britain. As against

9. Ibid., p. 88.
10. Ibid., p. 339.
11. E.g. Guy Lacam, *Inventaire Economique de l'Empire* (Paris, n.d. 1938?); Pierre Moussa, *Les Chances Economiques de la Communauté Franco-Africaine* (Paris, 1957).

this there was undoubtedly a trend in favor of a French approach. The theme of imperial self-sufficiency, originating in the 1900s with Joseph Chamberlain and other tariff reformers, received a new strength during the First World War and after. In an environment of state control and raw material shortages, "development" acquired mercantilist overtones. Thus, in its final report of 1917, the Dominions Royal Commission recommended planned integration of all imperial economic activity; and in the same year an unofficial body—the Empire Resources Development Committee—put out propaganda in favor of treating the dependent empire as a source of wealth which could be used to pay off the war debt and provide a basis for postwar British prosperity. In the 1920s little came of these proposals; but under slump conditions after 1930 they became central to the British approach. The return to protectionism in 1932, the use of quotas against Japanese textiles, wartime control of trade and currency, and postwar bulk-purchasing and trade controls were evidence that Britain was adopting an imperial interpretation of African development. In the later 1940s it was, indeed, difficult to see much difference between British and French economic policy in dependent Africa. But in the 1950s the trend again turned from close imperial integration as the British and colonial economies emerged from wartime controls. By the time of decolonization, British Africa was working free of the imperial economy, and British aid was much less related to metropolitan needs than that of France. After independence the once British states were economically far less tied to Britain than those of Francophone Africa. In the end Lugard's concepts won out.

But in the period after 1945 the very concept of development in any earlier form suffered eclipse and was replaced by that of "growth." Earlier Anglo-French concepts had assumed that economic growth was best achieved through specialization within an imperial or international trading system, since this would maximize production in line with comparative advantage. Technical progress would result from influx of capital and transference of European technology.[12] After 1945 these assumptions were challenged. With increased emphasis in Europe and North America on planned overall economic development, it now seemed unsatisfactory to leave "growth" in the colonies to the chance that market forces would operate in the right way. Indeed evidence suggested that the classical formula was not producing

12. For a useful discussion of this concept see Hla Myint, "The Classical Theory of International Trade and the Underdeveloped Countries," *Economic Journal, 68* (1968), 316–37.

"growth" in many dependencies.[13] After 1945 attempts were therefore made to plan for "growth" in Africa. Five- and ten-year plans treated each region as an entity rather than as part of an imperial or international system. Particularly in British Africa, policy aimed to make African territories autonomous economies controlling their own instruments of economic policy. Metropolitan "aid" on essentially noncommercial terms was provided as a substitute for prewar colonial loans and to augment private investment. It would be an exaggeration to say that these policies were necessarily inconsistent with continued close economic relations between Britain and France and their African territories, but the change of emphasis is nonetheless significant.

It is not proposed in this chapter to consider British and French economic policy in Africa during the age of "growth" except as an epilogue to the classical period of colonial "development." It has been mentioned to emphasize by contrast the special features of the earlier two periods.

The distinctive feature of an imperial economic system was that the metropolis could, within limits, create the formal framework for economic activity and in some degree determine the character of development. This capacity, indeed, differentiated "formal" from "informal" empire in the economic sphere. To ignore it is to misunderstand the character of Anglo-French policies in Africa. Some critics and historians have treated formal and informal control as merely points along the same spectrum, differing in degree rather than kind.[14] This is a dangerous half-truth. It is, of course, true that European states could exercise considerable economic control over weaker sovereign states. In China, for example, treaty rights between 1842 and 1928 gave such

13. On the concept of "growth" there is now a very large literature. See in particular Gunnar Mydal, *Economic Theory and Under-Developed Regions* (London, 1957); Arthur Lewis, *The Theory of Economic Growth* (London, 1955); Walt W. Rostow, *The Stages of Economic Growth* (Cambridge, 1960); Ragnar Nurkse, *Patterns of Trade and Development* (Stockholm, 1959); Alexander K. Cairncross, *Factors in Economic Development* (London, 1962); Hla Myint, *The Economics of the Developing Countries* (New York, 1965); S. Daniel Neumark, *Foreign Trade and Economic Development in Africa: A Historical Perspective* (Stanford, 1964).

14. E.g. Vladimir I. Lenin, *Imperialism, The Highest Stage of Capitalism* (1917); Charles R. Fay, *The Cambridge History of the British Empire* [*CHBE* hereafter] (Cambridge, Vol 2, 1940), p. 414; John Gallagher and Ronald E. Robinson, "The Imperialism of Free Trade," *Economic History Review*, 2nd Series, 6, No. 1 (1953).

extensive commercial rights to foreigners that Europeans could operate almost as freely as in formal colonies. But there, and also in Siam, the Ottoman Empire, and Latin America absence of political sovereignty imposed substantial limitations on the type and scale of expatriate activities. In the last resort the depth of economic and social penetration was limited by the political factor.[15] No such obstacle existed in formal British and French possessions. In Africa, Britain and France possessed the power to determine the character of economic development to a degree inconceivable in "informal" dependencies; and this power was expressed above all in the formal framework set up to regulate economic activity. This framework not only expressed contrasting metropolitan objectives in Africa, but very largely determined the character of the development that took place.

The imperial factor in Africa operated in many ways, not all of which can be considered here. Metropolitan policies that affected economic development fell into two main overlapping categories: external policies relating the colonies to the metropolitan or imperial economy; and internal policies concerned primarily with the economic and social affairs of the colonies. The first category included control of external trade and currency, the second such matters as colonial law, land usage, labor, and direct governmental economic intervention.

Control of trade was one of the oldest devices for exploiting colonies, in the pejorative sense, during the three and a half centuries before about 1850. In common with other colonial powers, Britain and France had imposed metropolitan monopoly of trade in both directions, excluded foreign ships, and given companies exclusive commercial rights in some territories. Were these or similar controls used by Britain and France in Africa in the modern period to ensure that "development" was closely related to the needs of the metropolitan economy?

British commercial policy in Africa was simple and can be outlined briefly.[16] Long before 1880 Britain had committed herself to "free trade" at home and in her colonies. With very few exceptions she preserved this policy in tropical Africa throughout the colonial period,

15. See George C. Allen and Audrey G. Donnithorne, *Western Enterprise in Far Eastern Economic Development: China and Japan* (London, 1954), for analysis of this question.

16. See Charles R. Fay, *Great Britain from Adam Smith to the Present Day* (London, 1928); Hancock, Survey, 2, 1; F. V. Meyer, *Britain's Colonies in World Trade* (London, 1948); The Economist Intelligence Unit, *The Commonwealth and Europe* (London, 1960).

although she modified it in other dependent territories. The navigation acts had been repealed in 1849, and thereafter there was never any formal control of shipping entering or leaving African ports in peacetime. From 1846 all colonies were free to abolish surviving preferences on imported British goods, and by 1860 all preferences on colonial products entering Britain had disappeared. During the next decade British commercial treaties barred differential tariffs at home or in the colonies. African trade had been open to all British subjects since the late seventeenth century, and none of the chartered companies formed in the later nineteenth century to operate in Africa had a commercial monopoly or the right to differentiate between British and foreign traders. All this amounted to the "open door" and an absence of discrimination throughout British Africa, which remained British policy throughout the partition period and largely influenced British attitudes to foreign ambitions in Africa. Hence British agreement to the Berlin Act of 1885 and the Brussels Agreement of 1890, which together banned protective or differential duties and guaranteed freedom of access on equal terms in much of West Africa and in the conventional basin of the Congo, including British East Africa and Northern Rhodesia. Hence, also, later acceptance of the 1898 French treaty on West African trade, the 1918 Convention of St. Germain, and the commercial conditions attached to the mandates in 1919. Since the bulk of British Africa—excluding only Sierra Leone, Gambia, South Africa, Southern Rhodesia, and Nyasaland—fell within the scope of these or other treaties, the British were willing prisoners of their own free-trade theories before 1914.

During the twentieth century, however, British tropical Africa became an exception to the increasingly protectionist trend of British tariff policy. The Belgian and Zollverein treaties were abrogated in 1898, leaving Britain and her colonies free, unless tied by other agreements, to create a discriminatory tariff system. Britain herself gradually moved to protection and discrimination, first in giving colonies exemption from certain wartime and postwar import duties, then in obtaining limited preferences in colonial markets in the 1920s, finally adopting full protection and multilateral imperial preference in 1931–32. But in Africa the swing to imperial economy had minimal effect. South Africa, Rhodesia, Sierra Leone, and Gambia gave small preferences, but the rest of British Africa remained predominantly free-trading. In Nigeria and the Gold Coast this was voluntarily maintained, since France abrogated the 1898 treaty in 1936, leaving Britain free to impose discrimination; but for broad political reasons the chance was rejected, though discriminatory export duties on palm kernels were imposed from 1919–22 and on tin ore until 1938, in each case to canalize these raw materials to Britain rather than to Germany or America. In most other areas, however, whatever British inclinations might have been, the "open door" was imposed by surviving treaties and the conditions attached to "B" class mandates. The only significant exception was the imposition of textile quotas, effectively, though not ostensibly, against Japan after 1934. During the Second World War all colonial trade and shipping were controlled; but after 1945 there was a gradual return to free conditions which was virtually complete by the 1950s.

It is clear, then, that in British tropical Africa tariffs or other physical controls on trade or shipping played a minimal part in economic development. If Britain obtained a large proportion of the trade and raw materials of her African dependencies, it was due to other causes.[17]

The French case was different on two main counts.[18] First, it happened that a relatively small part of French Africa was committed to the "open door" by treaty: the eventual French Equatorial Africa (A.E.F.), excluding Gabon; Dahomey and the Ivory Coast; and the mandates, the Cameroons and Togo. Second, France was an intensely protectionist country which deliberately organized her African empire to conform to the concepts of "national economy."

The basic French assumption after about 1880 was that the African territories should be made to serve the economic interests of the metropolis first, of themselves second, and of the rest of the world last. So much was clearly implicit in Sarraut's argument. Free trade along British lines had few supporters. It had been adopted in the 1860s, following the Cobden Treaty, for political rather than economic reasons, and it became an anachronism in the colonies after the metropolis returned effectively to protection in 1883. In the later period the main relic of this free-trading interlude was the fact that the ports and carrying trade of the colonies were open to foreign ships and that France accepted free trade in the conventional basin of the Congo in 1885. For the rest, the question was not whether colonies should be reserved for metropolitan trade but how this could best be done. On the one side there was the Republican tradition of the 1790s that colonies should be incorporated into the metropolitan tariff and ultimately assimilated; on the other the practice of *l'ancien régime* and the

17. See Table 5.
18. See Girault, *The Colonial Tariff Policy;* Roberts, *History of French Colonial Policy;* François Bloch-Lainé, *La Zone Franc* (Paris, 1956).

two Empires which pointed to a distinct colonial tariff "personality" but also to strong imperial preference. After 1883 policy alternated between these possibilities, neither winning complete victory. With the Méline tariff of 1892 the Republican tradition seemed dominant. Where possible, colonies were incorporated into the new metropolitan tariff. Algeria was already assimilated, Gabon was assimilated in 1891–92, and Madagascar in 1897. The West African colonies, excluding Dahomey and the Ivory Coast, were given preferential tariffs which were consolidated, on their incorporation into French West Africa (A.O.F.) in 1905, into an average tariff of 25 per cent with a 7 per cent surcharge on foreign goods. The remaining colonies and protectorates (except for Somali which had no tariff) had revenue-producing tariffs. All, however, received either free entry or preference on goods imported to France, and French ships were exempt from the *droit de pavillon* and *surtaxe d'entrepôt* charged on foreigners.

These arrangements marked the high-water mark of the policy on tariff assimilation in French Africa. By the time the next major modification was undertaken in 1928, the tide was flowing toward greater fiscal autonomy for the colonies and federations and in favor of imperial preference rather than full assimilation to the metropolis. In that year a general reclassification took place. Algeria was fully incorporated as a metropolitan department. Madagascar and Gabon were unassimilated, the former with a preferential tariff, the latter incorporated into the "free-trade" federation of A.E.F. Tunis and Morocco as protectorates with treaties remained nonpreferential. A.O.F. retained its preferential tariff into which Dahomey and the Ivory Coast were incorporated in 1936, when France abrogated the relevant treaties of 1890 and 1898 with Britain. The Cameroons and Togo, as mandates, necessarily had nondiscriminatory tariffs. All these territories, however, continued to receive preferences for their exports to France, French-owned ships were favored against foreign, and quotas were applied to foreign imports to the colonies and on colonial exports to France.

This broadly preferential system was inevitably disrupted by the Second World War, but the French Union of 1946 attempted to revive the same principles and to extend them. By 1954 Algeria was a fully assimilated metropolitan department; A.O.F., Madagascar, and Somali were preferential, giving French virtual free entry; A.E.F. and the mandates—now Trust Territories—retained the open door. Tunisia and Morocco, however, as Associated States of the Union, were now free to give as well as to receive moderate preferences. In all areas tariffs were heavily buttressed by quotas, bulk buying, control of shipping, and currency allocation. The result was that, within a short period after the war, France had once again become the chief market for all these territories and herself supplied a very large proportion of their imports.[19] The dissolution of the Union and the entry of France into the European Economic Community in 1958 made remarkably little difference to these arrangements. Apart from Somali, all French Africa was independent by 1962, yet all but Guinea made special tariff arrangements with France and became Associate Members of E.E.C. The result was gradually to transmute the special economic relationship between French Africa and France into one between French Africa and the Six. The Associate Members of E.E.C. gave other members of E.E.C. the same tariff preferences as France, and quotas for French imports were gradually shared out among the Six. Conversely African imports to France were exempt from the common external tariff of E.E.C., and duties on reexport of these goods to other member states were run down over a period. Thus the French imperial system became integrated with the new political order in Africa and Europe.

If one reviews the general trend of British and French tariff policy between 1880 and 1960 as part of the formal structure of economic "exploitation" in Africa, a pattern can be discerned. Down to about 1932 policies diverged—France moving toward assimilation or severe preference, Britain remaining loyal to free trade and the open door in both directions. But thereafter policies tended to converge. The French dropped tariff assimilation except for Algeria, whereas the British imposed preference on some of their African territories and gave preference to all of them. Thereafter both countries used quotas, bulk buying, and bounties to stimulate colonial production and guide it to the metropolis. In the end, after decolonization, both countries attempted to preserve special economic relationships with the former colonies, Britain within the framework of Commonwealth preferences, France within E.E.C. Contrasts, therefore, became matters of degree rather than of kind. In symbolic terms, Sarraut rather than Lugard became the text of Anglo-French commercial policy.

Which country, finally, was more successful in its tariff policy? The question is difficult to answer correctly, for under free-trade conditions success was not necessarily measured by the proportion of trade between colony and metropolis. If, however, we adopt the French standpoint and measure the proportion of colonial imports that came from the metropolis and the proportion of colonial exports sent to metropoli-

19. See Tables 1 and 2.

tan markets, the results can be seen in Tables 1–6 in the appendix to this chapter and will be discussed below.

Metropolitan control of colonial currency,[20] though easily overlooked, was an important element in the formal structure of imperial economy in Africa. In terms of "development" the creation of a European currency system in African colonies closely linked with the metropolitan currency performed two main functions. First, it was a means of intensifying European penetration of an indigenous economy, especially in the conditions of sub-Saharan societies which lacked monetary systems comparable with those of Europe. Up to a point trade could be carried on in such places, as had been done in West Africa for centuries, by means of barter and credit. But such devices usually caused friction and were in any case inadequate once Europeans attempted to penetrate beyond the coasts and to shape the character of the colonial economy. To establish complex buying and selling organizations, employ wage labor, invest in productive enterprizes—in short, to transform what Marxists called "natural economy" into "cash economy"—a proper monetary system was vital. In Islamic African territories, more or less efficient currencies already existed, and there the need was to assure stability through links with the metropolitan currency. In other territories, where cowries, copper bars, or other measures of value were found, the work had to be done from the beginning as a prerequisite of effective development.

The other main function of currency in a dependency was to link it with the metropolis, and so tie it to the imperial economy. Development as such only demanded sound currency, whatever its relationship with that of the metropolis. If, however, the colonial monetary supply was intimately tied to that of the metropolis and was only convertible into foreign currencies through Paris or London, then it necessarily intensified the economic links of empire. Even during the period before 1939, when currencies were freely convertible, currency alignment encouraged trade with other parts of the same monetary system. After 1939 exchange restrictions enabled the metropolis virtually to force

20. For British colonial currency policy, see Robert Chalmers, *A History of Currency* (London, 1893); G. L. M. Clauson, "The British Colonial Currency System," *Economic Journal, 54* (1944–45), 1–25; W. T. Newlyn and D. C. Rowan, *Money and Banking in Colonial Africa* (Oxford, 1954); A. R. Conan, *The Sterling Area* (London, 1952). For French policy see Arthur Girault, *Principes de Colonisation et de Législation coloniale* (Paris, 5th ed. 3 vols. 1927–30, 4th vol. [6th ed.] 1933); Albert Duchêne, *Histoire des Finance coloniales de la France* (Paris, 1938); Bloch-Lainé, *La Zone Franc;* Michel Leduc, *Les Institutions Monétaires Africaines, Pays Francophones* (Paris, 1965).

dependencies to buy within their own currency area and to surrender the bullion and foreign currency they earned as support for the metropolitan currency as a whole. Such advantages were the direct reward of political empire, though they might be sustained after decolonization on different conditions.

These broad aims were common to Britain and France in the modern period, but their methods, and also the attitudes they adopted in the period of decolonization, differed considerably.

Provision of currency in colonies that did not already possess one was a novel feature of British and French policy alike in the nineteenth century, for in the past both countries had attempted little more than to impose their own denominations for accounting purposes, leaving the colonies to attract a money supply by trade. The result was confusion and inadequate currency in all American colonies. After 1816, however, the old bullionist objection to exporting currency to colonies ceased to be important, and in 1825 the British adopted the policy of making the pound sterling the normal colonial denomination (except where a local currency—the dollar in America, the rupee in India, etc.—was too strong to replace) and of exporting British silver token coins to meet demand. Thus, when African territories were annexed, the pound sterling automatically became the local denomination except in the East African Protectorate and Somaliland, where the Indian rupee was used. In this way most British possessions had identical currencies with that of Britain; and even the silver-based rupee territories were closely related to the gold-based pound through the established Indian rupee exchange rate.[21]

But to establish the imperial denomination was not to provide a money supply; and in this the British were dilatory. Paper money was then—as throughout the colonial period—supplied by private banks, none of which had a monopoly or was directly controlled by government. Coin was imported by banks to meet local demand. Little attempt was made to eliminate indigenous "currencies" or to provide coins in small denominations suitable for non-European needs. More serious, trading balances with the metropolis had to be settled ultimately by moving currency, and from the British point of view it was inconvenient that large sums of British coin—not legal tender at home—might be repatriated and embarrass the Bank of England. These problems did not apply to South Africa, which had its own

21. The Indian rupee was an autonomous silver currency until 1893 when it was related to the pound sterling at a fixed exchange rate as a result of fluctuations in the silver values.

currency and mint, nor to Southern Rhodesia and the South African protectorates, which formed part of the same monetary system. But by the early twentieth century there was an urgent need for properly managed local currencies in other parts of British Africa.

An answer was found in that characteristic device of the modern British Empire—the Colonial Sterling Exchange Standard. The essentials of the system, which was contrived for West Africa in 1912 and extended to East Africa in 1919 and to the Rhodesias and Nyasaland in 1940, were as follows. A Currency Board was set up in London to manage the currency of each of these areas, with agents in each colonial territory. A supply of special coins was minted in London for each area. These had British denominations and were convertible into sterling at face value but had legal currency only in the colonies. Until 1920 these coins had intrinsic value based on current silver prices in relation to gold. Thereafter, as token coinage replaced silver in Britain, colonial currency followed suit. The value of this token currency was assured by a device that remained the fundamental feature of the Colonial Exchange Standard until decolonization, and eventually provoked much controversy. Every newly issued alloy coin had to be covered in full by securities held by the Currency Board in London. Ninety per cent of the cover could be in gild-edged British securities, whose interest was credited to the territories concerned, and 10 percent in bullion to provide liquidity. New coins were issued against repatriated silver coin or commercial credits, so that the volume of colonial coin in circulation at any time exactly represented the value of silver coin, goods, or credit transferred to London.

The aim and achievement of this system was to give the African colonies an absolutely sound currency freely convertible into sterling at face value. This was of great value for colonies that traded primarily with Britain or other sterling areas, and it gave them impeccable standing in the rest of the world. Other advantages were that colonial governments were spared the problems of currency management, and domestic inflation could not be induced by currency manipulation. Criticism of the system, which became strong after about 1940 as economists developed techniques for using money supply as an economic regulator, centered on the fact that the colonies were now being bound by orthodox monetary principles which Britain and Europe had discarded. By 1939 British currency ceased to have gold cover and was a fiduciary issue, partially covered by British government securities. Government could therefore use both notes and coin as instruments of economic policy. The colonies, however, were left in the position of countries that did not produce gold but retained a 100 percent gold cover for their currency. They received minimum interest on the securities held in London, whereas these capital sums would have assisted economic growth if invested in the colonies. Every increase in currency involved unrequited exports and so tended toward inflation, whereas an adverse trade balance automatically reduced the coin circulating and so tended to disinflation. Above all, the system was automatic, beyond control by the colonies. There were no central banks in these African territories other than in South Africa, and commercial banks were strictly limited as sources of paper money by their statutes and by metropolitan control. If Britain devalued, as she did in 1931 and 1949, colonial currencies followed suit, whether or not this was in their best interests. During and after World War II the apparent injustice and inconvenience of the system increased. After 1939, when the pound sterling ceased to be freely convertible, colonies found their overseas trade controlled in the interests of British gold and dollar reserves. In effect, this meant that colonial earnings of hard currency were pooled in London, and that the colonies could only import goods from outside the sterling area with specific permission from British authorities. For the first time, therefore, imperial control of colonial currency also involved effective control of the pattern of colonial trade, reinforcing tariffs, quotas, and shipping controls, and tending to isolate the colonies within an imperial economic enclosure.

It is very difficult to assess these arguments for and against the Colonial Sterling Exchange Standard. On the one hand the system was probably beneficial to the colonies in that it gave them an absolutely sound currency which small independent states with limited reserves, no domestic money market, and little financial expertise invariably find difficult to sustain. Moreover, as long as they were politically dependent, it was probably best that monetary policy, which was potentially a source of debate, should be protected from pressures in the colony or metropolis. Like free trade, monetary orthodoxy was a priori evidence that the colony was not being deliberately exploited in the interests of the metropolis. On the other hand the British system was ill-adapted to flexible use of money in the post-1945 world of "growth" economics and was conceptually incompatible with political independence. Free states wanted the tools and symbols of economic sovereignty—central bank, government control of monetary policy, local use of currency cover. Monetary autonomy seemed more important than stable currencies or convertibility. The result was that, although most one-time British colonies in Africa remained within the sterling area after independence, they quickly dismantled the old monetary system. Each new state had its own currency, more or less closely tied to the pound sterling through credits held in London and through use of the London money market for buying foreign exchange. In sharp contrast with French West Africa, the British government now took no responsibility for the currency of the former colonies; and the fact that only three African states followed the British devaluation of 1967 indicated how far monetary independence had proceeded in the decade after the first British tropical territory in Africa achieved independence.

The general aims of French monetary policy in Africa were the same as those of Britain—to impose the metropolitan franc as a common currency throughout the Empire, with free convertibility and, as far as possible, common coinage. This, it can be said briefly, was achieved by 1914 in all French colonies in Africa, whereas Tunisia and Morocco, as protectorates, retained their own currency denominations which were strictly tied to the franc. Elsewhere the French imposed the franc by the simple expedient of refusing to accept any other coin or quasicoin as legal tender, even though until 1908 no positive effort was made to supply coins, which had to be minted in France. Colonial currency was identical with that in the metropolis and automatically devalued with the metropolitan franc (FM) between 1914 and 1938. Thus currency filled precisely the same role in French and British Africa as an instrument linking the African colonies with the metropolis and providing the basis for Western penetration of the colonial economy. Between 1939 and 1958 metropolitan control of foreign currency exchange and the pooling of all hard currency reserves within the French Empire tied French Africa to the French economy in the same way that British colonies were tied to Britain.

Beyond these similarities, however, there were contrasts in method that ultimately produced very different monetary relations between one-time African dependencies and their previous masters. Paradoxically, given the general trend of French imperial policy, France permitted her colonies more monetary autonomy within this general framework than the British colonies received. The key to the system was the chartered bank with a monopoly of note-issue in a colony or group of colonies. The model for such banks was created in the Antilles, where chartered banks were set up in the mid-nineteenth century with the right of note-issue. Control was exercised by governmental agencies, but essentially these banks were free to determine their note-issue—and thus the volume of credit in the colony—provided note-issue did not exceed three times the metallic reserves. With some differences this model was applied in Africa. The Bank of Algeria was created in 1851. Its director was nominated by the French minister of Finance, and part of the capital was subscribed by the Treasury; but it was an autonomous profit-making institution, issuing paper money and giving credit within limits similar to those imposed on the Bank of France. Unlike the Caribbean chartered banks, it was permitted to operate branches in other French African territories, and in 1904 became the bank of issue for Tunisia. Senegal, meantime, had been given a chartered bank similar to those in the Antilles. In 1901 it was reconstituted as the Bank of West Africa, now with entirely private capital and under control only by a commission in Paris and local government censors. Its headquarters were in Paris, and it opened branches and provided paper money in all the then French West African colonies. In 1925 a similar bank was set up for Madagascar, which hitherto had been provided with French bank notes. Morocco had its own national bank beginning in 1924, after a long struggle between the Bank of Algeria and the State Bank of Morocco over the issue of currency.

The significance of this system of chartered banks in French Africa was, perhaps, less obvious before 1945 than it later became. The banks had considerable freedom, and note-issue was restricted by the reserve requirements of their charters rather than by direct governmental control. But the fact that these were metropolitan banks under state supervision, which was steadily tightened between the two world wars, meant that no colonial government could use money supply as an instrument of economic policy. Colonial economy was, in fact, as strictly tied to orthodox monetary policy and the fortunes of the metropolitan franc as under the British Sterling Exchange Standard. During and after the Second World War, however, changes occurred that eventually produced a monetary system in French Africa very different from that in the British colonies, and one that proved well adapted to the postindependence era.

The first effect of the war was to destroy the unity of the franc. In 1941 the Free French Committee arranged for a sterling exchange rate for francs in territories under their control of 176.625 francs to the pound. This applied to French Equatorial Africa and the Ivory Coast. In 1942–43, however, a rate of 220 francs to the pound was adopted in French North Africa and French West Africa. All territories were reunited at the 200 francs per pound rate in 1944, but in 1945, when the metropolitan franc (FM) was devalued, it was decided to give all

African territories a special franc (CFA) worth 1.70 of the new FM. In October 1948 the CFA was again appreciated to 2 FM, and in March 1949 the Somali franc was detached from the franc altogether and tied to the United States dollar. Thereafter the CFA remained fixed to the FM; but the exchange unity of the French imperial currency had been broken and replaced by free convertibility at fixed rates of exchange. This was a significant step toward the postindependence system of separate currencies similarly linked to the French franc by agreed exchange rates.

Parallel with this process went the creation of new monetary institutions in place of the chartered banks, which led ultimately to a system of central banks. In 1942 the *Caisse Centrale* of Free France took over note issue in Equatorial Africa and the Cameroons. In 1946 the Bank of Algeria was nationalized, giving the government full control over note-issue. In 1950 the government acquired a majority of shares in the Bank of Madagascar to achieve the same end with less expense. The Bank of West Africa, however, retained its monetary powers in A.O.F. until 1955, when a major new policy was adopted in French tropical Africa. Both A.E.F. and A.O.F. were then given institutions resembling central banks, whose councils represented the French and colonial governments, financial agencies, and local experts. These had no commercial banking functions, but controlled all currency and exchange matters. In other French territories the chartered banks continued to control money, but now, under state control, operated in much the same way as these institutes. More important, the colonial currencies were now given a new basis. Up to then convertibility of colonial into metropolitan francs had been ensured by each colonial bank of issue maintaining deposits amounting to one-third of the local note issue in Paris and paying all their metropolitan francs and foreign currency earnings into an account at the French treasury. In 1952, however, a new system was established. Each colonial bank or institute of issue was given a *compte d'opérations* at the Treasury into which it paid all its holding of metropolitan or foreign currencies. Apart from this the new monetary institutions were freed from the obligation to keep money or securities in Paris as cover for the local currency, yet the French government guaranteed full convertibility of colonial into metropolitan francs, and thence into foreign currencies if required. In effect this meant that, in return for receiving foreign exchange earnings, France guaranteed her colonial currencies, and allowed the colonies to use the capital that would otherwise have been required to provide cover for the fiduciary issue to be used for investment or imports.

In the colonial context this system of the 1950s was a device for maintaining the unity of the franc zone under effective French control at minimum cost to the colonies. Yet for many French African states it proved equally attractive after independence. The French aim was undoubtedly to preserve the commercial and monetary unity of the franc zone despite political decolonization. This proved unacceptable to new states, and in its old form the unity of the zone ceased to exist in 1960. Thereafter French Africa divided into two groups according to whether they did or did not maintain full convertibility at fixed ratios with the metropolitan franc, with Guinea as the only new state that retained no connection at all with the franc. In the first category were Tunisia, Morocco, and, from 1962–67, Mali, which retained loose monetary connections with Paris, which they used for buying and selling foreign currency. By contrast the states of West and Equatorial Africa, together with Madagascar and (after 1962) Algeria, tied themselves to the French franc while setting up nominally autonomous curriencies. Conventions were signed with each state or group that bound themselves to operate their currencies along "sound" lines, with a minority of French representatives on councils of their central banks. Madagascar and Algeria had their own central banks, but the small states of West and Equatorial Africa were persuaded to preserve the monetary unity of the colonial period by having joint currencies and central banks. In return, each of these states or groups was given a *compte d'opérations* in Paris with unlimited rights of converting local currency into FMs. Even Somali had a similar account in Paris, though this had always to be in credit.

The significance of these developments in the postdecolonization world was considerable. Alone among the one-time metropolitan powers France had succeeded in preserving a substantial monetary control over her former colonies in Africa. Together with tariff preferences, Associate Membership in the E.E.C., and import quotas, currency convertibility based on French guarantees ensured that they would remain for the time being at least within the economic orbit of France.

Apart from metropolitan control of external trade, shipping, and currency, the economic development of formal colonies in Africa was most strongly affected by the policies adopted by colonial governments. The character of British and French government in Africa is discussed elsewhere in this book;[22] but some attempt must be made to assess their economic role.

In the broadest context the fact of alien rule was more significant for economic development in Africa than in any other part of the

22. See in particular Chapters 16 and 17.

modern colonial empires because there the pre-European environment was at once relatively unsatisfactory for European enterprise and relatively easy for Europeans to mold. If Africa had not been partitioned between the powers and if, under a general "hands off" policy, indigenous regimes had survived, there would certainly have been European economic penetration, but of a very different sort.[23] First, in order of importance, was the fact of total political penetration—the "pacification" of new colonies and protectorates by the destruction or subordination of all indigenous political units. Pacification had no necessary connection with desire to develop economically: often it reflected political or military preoccupations, personal ambition on the part of soldiers or administrators, or the need to raise taxes. But the economic consequences were incalcuable. By 1914 most of British and French Africa was physically wide open to Western enterprise, and Africa had been tamed for development.

If the role of government had stopped with pacification and the maintenance of order, the result would have been merely to hand over now defenseless Africans to abuse by Europeans. In the early years of the twentieth century this was indeed how it appeared in many places. Land concessions in the French Congo, the virtually unlimited powers of the British South Africa Company in Central Africa, settler land grabbing in Kenya and elsewhere, forced African labor almost everywhere, all suggested that colonial rule was merely a tool of exploiting European capitalism. Fortunately for the European conscience this proved a false start. Except where the settler ruled—in Southern and Central Africa and to some extent also in Algeria—colonial governments, influenced by enlightened opinion at home and themselves increasingly professional in character, evolved responsible attitudes and adopted the stance of umpire rather than protagonist. During the "classical" period of African colonization it was they who defined the terms for African development through policies on taxation, law, land, and labor.

Fiscal policy was necessarily critical for potential investors, settlers, planters, and traders; and here colonial governments normally adopted tax systems which favored alien enterprise. Most revenue came from import duties and hut or head taxes, which were regressive in that they fell on Africans more heavily than on Europeans. Income tax was rare and low where used. Company taxation was almost always

23. It would be interesting to construct a counterfactual proposition on this question. Patterns of development would obviously have been very different, but a projection could be based on the ample evidence of trends before about 1880.

paid in the metropolis rather than in the colony. There were few attempts to tax undeveloped concessions. Export duties, when adopted, were designed to canalize exports to the metropolis rather than raise revenue. Thus fiscal policy generally favored European enterprise in that the cost of providing the security and social infrastructure European investors required was borne by African taxpayers and the metropolitan government through subsidies rather than by expatriate enterprises.

The legal systems of British and French Africa were too complex to be described adequately here, but they may be said to have served economic interests well enough.[24] Before the partition period both countries applied simplified versions of metropolitan law to small coastal possessions such as Lagos and Senegal, but such assimilation of Africans to alien legal systems was clearly impracticable once vast hinterlands were acquired. The solution lay in legal pluralism such as already existed in Algeria. Modified versions of British and French courts, enforcing something like metropolitan law, were set up in all dependencies with jurisdiction over Europeans and "assimilated" Africans. Conversely special courts, commonly run by administrators rather than lawyers, were provided for Africans in which indigenous custom was the rule in civil cases and European principles in criminal matters. The British made no clear juridical distinction between categories of people, but the French distinguished precisely between "citizens" and "subjects." The latter were under a special administrative jurisdiction in criminal matters—the *indigénat*—which permitted summary imprisonment without appeal for up to two weeks. French subjects were also liable to *prestation*—forced labor on public works without pay—and to military conscription. Few French subjects became citizens, but after 1924 African notables and others with certain qualifications were exempt from these disabilities.

These legal principles and institutions served European economic interests well enough. Expatriates could operate within a familiar framework of civil and commercial law and benefited from the substitution of single legal systems covering vast areas for the multiplicity of indigenous jurisdictions of precolonial Africa. The extralegal powers of administrators were often used to help expatriates, for example by persuading chiefs to stimulate "voluntary" labor or to grow cash crops

24. For South Africa see *CHBE,* Vol. 8, Chap. 31. For British tropical Africa see Lord Hailey, *An African Survey* (rev. ed. London, 1957), and works on individual colonies. For French Africa see Girault, *Principes;* P. F. Gonidec, *Droit d'Outre-Mer* (2 vols. Paris, 1959).

for export. Conversely legal pluralism was potentially an obstacle to some forms of development because indigenous custom, especially on land ownership, prevented free alienation. Hence the great importance of governmental policy on African land and labor.

The question of land raised a fundamental policy issue.[25] Should the government treat land primarily in relation to maximum economic efficiency or in terms of African social stability? The problem was particularly acute in Africa because on the one hand most European enterprises, even perhaps effective development, involved radical changes in existing methods of land use; while on the other hand such changes normally had serious repercussions on African society. Broadly, colonial governments had to choose between two lines of policy. At one extreme they might treat all land that was not immediately and demonstrably "used" by Africans at a particular time as "crown" or "public" property and feel free to alienate it to Europeans. Alternatively they might regard all land as African property, or as held in trust on behalf of Africans, refuse to alienate any land to Europeans in perpetuity, but grant leases for limited periods in special cases. Within these limits there were many possible variations: for example, should Africans be allowed or encouraged to individualize communal tenures? In practice, policies varied immensely, not only between Britain and France but also within each imperial system. It is therefore impossible to summarize contrasting systems briefly, but some indication of the broad patterns is essential since these very largely determined the character of economic development in different regions.

Land policy in British territories ran the entire gamut of possibilities, determined in each case by three main factors. First, the chronology of annexation and occupation—the earlier this occurred the more likely that large areas would be alienated to Europeans. Second, geography and climate—the more attractive for permanent European settlement the more alienation. Third, the degree of self-government—the more white settlers and autonomy, the more land alienation. On this basis British African territories fell into three main groups, though land policy in fact shaded off from one to another.

South Africa stood alone as the only territory in which it was de-

25. For British territories there is a useful summary in Lucy P. Mair, *Native Policies in Africa* (London, 1936). See also Lord Hailey, *Native Administration in the British African Territories* (5 vols. London, 1950–53), and Margery Perham, *Native Administration in Nigeria* (London, 1937). For French territories see Girault, *Principes;* Gonidec, *Droit;* Jean Suret-Canale, *Afrique noire: l'ère Coloniale, 1900–1945* (Paris, 1964).

liberately held that Europeans were the best users of land and where Africans retained land only on sufferance. In 1931 some 6,000,000 Africans occupied reserves totaling about 34,000 square miles, and 1,800,000 Europeans occupied 440,000 square miles. The second group of colonies, in Central and East Africa, ranged from Southern Rhodesia, which had much in common with South Africa, to Tanganyika, which more closely resembled the West African colonies. In the Rhodesias and Nyasaland large areas were originally acquired by the British South Africa Company, which encouraged white settlement. Hence, under the Southern Rhodesian Land Apportionment Act of 1930, Europeans, who already owned 31,000,000 acres, were free to purchase half the balance of 34,000,000 acres of crown lands, while Africans, with reserves of 21,000,000 acres, were assigned a further 7,000,000. In Northern Rhodesia 8,750,000 acres had been alienated to Europeans by the 1930s, and large areas were held by Europeans in Nyasaland. In Tanganyika 1,750,000 acres had been alienated by the Germans and could not be resumed; but from 1923 all unalienated land was vested in the governor as trustee for African interests, and thereafter only restricted leases were given to Europeans in line with West African practice. In Uganda also there was little alienation, for by the Uganda Agreement of 1900 most land in Buganda had been individualized in the hands of the king and aristocracy, and after 1920 Africans were unable to alienate land to Europeans. In 1930 only 300 square miles out of a total area of 94,131 had been alienated. In Kenya, however, large areas were sold to European settlers under the 1902 Crown Lands Ordinance, primarily to make the railway a paying concern, and a system of native reserves was set up on the South African model. From about 1930 the government increasingly protected African land occupation, and the balance in the 1930s was some 53,000 square miles of African reserves to 16,700 square miles of European property and 99,000 square miles of crown lands.

The general pattern in British Southern, Central, and East Africa, with the exceptions of Uganda and Tanganyika, was therefore that ample land was initially available for European occupation, either by small settlers and farmers or large plantations. In West Africa things were very different. From the 1890s governments adopted the principle that African interests were primary and that large European settlement or land ownership were undesirable. In Nigeria all land was deemed to belong to indigenous occupiers: in Northern Nigeria it was vested in the governor as trustee and in Southern Nigeria in the native tribes, so that permanent alienation was virtually barred. To prevent Africans from alienating their land, an ordinance of 1916 provided that in Northern Nigeria no title was valid without the governor's consent. As a result very little land was ever alienated to Europeans, and leases were normally granted only for mining or timber-felling. A similar policy was adopted in the Gold Coast. An attempt in 1896 to empower the governor to control alienation by Africans was defeated by African protests, but in 1900 an ordinance limited each concession to 5 square miles, with valid title only if approved by the courts. This excluded agricultural land; and in 1916 an Order in Council made consent by the governor obligatory for alienation of more than 1 square mile by Africans. As a result valid concessions in 1925 were only 1 percent of the colony, and much of this was not actually occupied by Europeans. The general result in both colonies, as in Sierra Leone, was that there was very little scope for direct European economic activity, except in mining and trade. The case of William Lever, who was refused permission to acquire land for palm oil plantations after 1902 and had to go to the Congo Free State instead, symbolized the situation.[26]

Similar contrasts existed for analogous historical and environmental reasons in French Africa. Everywhere the Roman Law principle that vacant land belonged to the state was adopted, but the use made of it varied greatly. In Algeria—the oldest effective colony—nineteenth-century policy was settlement of small French peasant farmers in consolidated villages under official control. There were some 200,000 of them in 1891 and about the same number in the 1920s. Very little land was available for large "capitalist" agricultural concerns. To make land available for settlers, Algerians were driven off vast areas before 1863 and a system of *cantonnements*—amounting to reserves—created for them. From 1873 Algerians were encouraged to individualize tenures in the reserved areas in order to release more land for European use. The consequences of these policies were, however, so terrible that France never again resorted to them in full.[27] In Tunisia there was no

26. Lever's reaction to the offer of a twenty-one-year lease in Sierra Leone was: "If the Government had offered us a twenty-one days' lease we might have been wise in buying a wheelbarrow or two. . . . On a twenty-one years' lease we could go further, but, after all, it would be comparatively a very small amount of money that we would be justified in expending . . . I can never understand why a black man should be allowed . . . neither . . . [to] develop his own land nor allow other people to do so." Charles Wilson, *The History of Unilever* (2 vols. London, 1954), 2, 166–67.

27. It was later alleged by V. Piquet that Algerian natives lost 40 percent of their remaining lands between 1883–89 as a result of individualization of tenures and forced judicial sales. See Roberts, *History of French Colonial Policy*, p. 201.

peasant or village settlement and no expropriation. Instead large land investment companies were encouraged and land obtained for them from public *habous* (religious endowments not still occupied by the original owners). Individualization of communal holdings was also stimulated. As a result there were few French settlers but many large estates owned by absentees, which were commonly worked by Tunisian or Sicilian tenant farmers. In Morocco foreigners were entitled to hold land under agreements made by the 1880 Madrid Congress, but land was always in short supply. The French encouraged individualization of tenures but alienated land only de facto, through the traditional association between a Moroccan landowner, who worked the land, and a European capitalist who advanced money in return for part of the crop. In addition certain unoccupied tribal lands were let on pereptual leases. In the 1920s Europeans owned only about 290,000 hectares, and there were only about two hundred genuine colonists.

In black Africa French land policy varied equally widely. It was at its most responsible in A.O.F. where, from 1904, communal land could be alienated only with the consent of the governor-general in council, though Africans could individualize tenures on the Torrens system. "Vacant" land belonged to the state and could be alienated, but title depended on improvement; and from 1925–35 courts had to investigate African claims based on custom before such claims were ratified. In 1955 African customary rights took precedence over the state's claim to "vacancy." The result was that few Africans individualized tenures and that little land was alienated to Europeans. Despite large concessions made in the Ivory Coast before 1904, Europeans held only 75,000 hectares on permanent title in 1938 and some 80,000 hectares on provisional titles. A.O.F. remained, like British West Africa, a region of African peasants, with very few large European estates.

In the Congo region—later A.E.F.—conditions were very different. Mainly because initially there was no established trade, few communications, and no possibility of a West African economic system based on peasant production, the government used its claim to "vacant" land to make large concessions to French companies on the Congo Free State model. In 1899, forty companies were given concessions for thirty years covering some 70 percent of the Congo, with ownership of land actually improved. The results were so notoriously bad that after 1906 some concessions were reduced in return for full ownership of smaller areas. When all concessions lapsed in 1930, the concessionaires were given substantial blocks of land in full ownership. A.E.F. therefore emerged as a region of vast estates owned by absentee companies. Here was scope for intensive capitalist activity; but poor communications and lack of enterprise prevented much constructive development until after 1945.

In Madagascar, finally, the French adopted the same basic policies as in A.O.F. after an early attempt to encourage both French peasant settlement and investment by large concessionaires. Few early concessions were taken up and few settlers came. Madagascar remained essentially a country of peasant cultivators.

Surveying the general field of land usage, it is therefore obvious that possible lines of development were greatly affected by contrasting governmental policies. In Algeria, Kenya, Southern Rhodesia, and South Africa there was ample scope for small and medium settlers and farmers. In Southern and Central Africa, Morocco, Tunisia, Tanganyika, the Cameroons, and A.E.F. there were opportunities for large-scale plantations or farms and considerable capital investment in production of tropical or subtropical raw materials. In A.O.F., British West Africa, and Uganda European enterprises requiring land were deliberately restricted in varying degrees. Although not all the reasons lay in British and French policy, there are few clearer examples of the economic significance of the imperial factor in Africa.

The question of African labor was equally important to economic development, whether working under European employers or producing commercial crops on their own account.[28] From the first it was assumed that ample cheap labor was a major asset in Africa. Marx, for example, assumed that capital invested in colonies would yield a higher rate of profit because of "backward development" and because "slaves, coolies etc., permit a better exploitation of labor." [29] Practical experience soon showed, however, that Africans did not, as a rule, approximate to Indian coolies. Few in sub-Saharan Africa had experience of working for pay or outside the traditional subsistence economy, and few had any real need to do so. In course of time monetary incentives might generate a voluntary labor force, but during the first decades after pacification neither governments nor private investors could afford to wait indefinitely for the market to work this revolution. In addition the European ethic underlined the virtue of work as a means to social regeneration. How, then, could Africans be induced to work in order to improve themselves and develop Africa?

Broadly five main devices were used, individually or in conjunction; and official policy on these largely determined the economic possibili-

28. For labor policies see the general works listed in n. 25 and studies of individual territories.

29. Karl Marx, *Capital* (3 vols. Chicago, 1909) *3*, 279.

ties of particular regions. First, governments might claim specified periods of work, with or without pay, for public purposes, or even for approved private concerns. Second, administrative pressure might be placed on chiefs to put forward "volunteers" for expatriate enterprises, or to produce specified commercial crops. Third, Africans might be induced to take paid work or produce commercial crops by obligation to pay taxes. Fourth, land policy might squeeze labor from inadequate reserves to take paid work or work for Europeans in lieu of rent. Finally, a system of contracts, often with penal sanctions, might increase the value of all "voluntary" labor. The use made of these devices varied substantially between French and British territories and within each imperial system.

Considering British Africa in these terms, there was a striking absence of nominally forced labor, with the partial exception of Uganda (until 1922) and Kenya. On the other hand administrative pressures were very generally placed on African chiefs and officials to "get them out to work," though this tended to decrease over time. Thus in Tanganyika the government ceased to encourage Africans to work on plantations after 1927, and in Kenya the notorious circular of 1919 ordering officials to "use every lawful influence" to stimulate paid labor was denounced by London in 1921. Eventually a broad distinction emerged between South and Central Africa, where governments always supported private labor recruiters, and other colonies, where policy was to stimulate African production without positively forbidding recruitment for paid work. Taxation of Africans was, however, universal. Outside South Africa it was seldom admitted that taxation was intended to force Africans to take paid work or to produce for the market, but that was the invariable result.[30] Land alienation operated to produce labor in South and Central Africa and to some extent in Kenya, but not in other territories. Contracts were common where African labor was most used in European enterprises, and breach of contract was a penal offense in South Africa, the Rhodesias, East Africa, and until 1928 in Tanganyika. Finally, there was no formal restriction on the formation of trade unions except in South Africa.

30. Lugard, for example, defended a direct tax on various grounds other than stimulating labor: that it would produce a revenue, finance autonomous native authorities, constitute African recognition of imperial authority, and provide close contact between British collectors and Africans. He admitted, however, that "in so far as a tax stimulates productive industry, and compels a man, as in England, to provide an extra margin . . . its effect can only be good." *Dual Mandate,* p. 235.

The distinctive feature of French labor policy in sub-Saharan (though not in North) Africa was the system of *prestation*—forced labor—for public works. This was universal, though the period required and conditions varied widely. In addition, obligatory military service in Madagascar and A.O.F. (it never existed in A.E.F.) could be commuted for labor on public works. In the 1930s paid labor gradually replaced *prestation* in A.O.F., and it was abolished everywhere in 1946. Military conscription ceased to be used for public works from 1950. *Prestation* was not normally used to help private concerns, though forced labor was sometimes directed to private contractors building public works. Administrative pressures were used, as in British Africa, and were grossly abused during the concessionary period in A.E.F. Government insisted on cultivation of commercial crops in many regions, and from 1930 had legal authority for doing so. Taxation was explicitly intended to stimulate paid work and cash crops in all regions, and it seems to have been effective. But, apart from Algeria, land shortage was not a significant incentive for Africans to take paid work in French Africa. Finally, trade unions were illegal for noncitizens wherever the *indigénat* was in force until they were legitimized, under strict limitations, in A.O.F. in 1937. After 1944 more liberal regulations were evolved, until in 1952 they were brought into line with those of the metropolis.

Cursorily reviewing Anglo-French policies on taxation, law, land, and labor, certain obvious patterns emerge. Although the imperial factor made all African territories more open to development and attractive for European enterprise than they would otherwise have been, in many places governments substantially restricted potential lines of economic developmest. West Africa and Uganda were virtually closed to large-scale direct European production, apart from mining, and development there necessarily meant stimulation of peasant production on commercial lines. Algeria and Kenya were conditioned for white settlers aided by indigenous labor, but they were virtually barred to large capitalist land concerns. These were encouraged or tolerated in A.E.F., the Cameroons, Tanganyika, Tunisia, Madagascar, and much of Central Africa; but South Africa offered the widest range of opportunities for European land use of all kinds. Mining was possible wherever minerals were discovered; and enterpreneurs could afford to attract African labor by relatively high wages and other attractions. Even so governmental policy sometimes checked mining development and limited the benefits it might have had for the local economy: for example by preventing permanent relocation of migrant laborers and their families in order to prevent destruction of the tribal societies from which they came. This was particularly significant in Northern Rhodesia after 1932 but also affected other territories.

In general, therefore, governmental policies tended to cut across "natural" lines of economic development. Although often beneficial to African welfare in the short term, such interference was often based on a very limited grasp by the metropolitan authorities or local officials of the complex economic and social issues involved. In the long term it is arguable that state paternalism, particularly in British territories, proved an obstacle to those sorts of economic and social change connected with European enterprise that were necessary for true economic "growth."

To this point the various forms of imperial action influencing economic development have been environmental rather than direct. They defined conditions for economic activity but did not involve direct governmental action. Did the state play a more positive role, as was envisaged by Sarraut and many others? The answer is that, until after 1939, state initiative was on a much smaller scale than enthusiasts for the *mise en valeur* would have liked, but that the trend was toward ever greater state action over time, and the total achievement during the colonial period was substantial.

The incentive for such action was the obvious inadequacy of private enterprise in certain fields; and it was here that the state took the lead. First in point of time were communications. Partly for strategic reasons, but also because private concerns were not prepared to act, colonial governments built and operated most of the railways, ports, and roads. Whatever their original purpose, these were crucial for economic development. Thus peanut production in Northern Nigeria and the French Sudan, white settlement in Kenya, the cotton industry of Uganda, and plantations in the French Congo were all direct products of railway construction undertaken by the state. The Rhodesian railway system was the only significant privately owned and operated transport system in French or British Africa. Another specifically governmental field was improvement of potentially productive land by irrigation, for example the French Niger scheme and the British Gezira project, both too expensive for private enterprise to consider worthwhile. Governments also took the initiative in scientific research into problems of tropical agriculture and pest control. In addition they provided many social services essential to economic development above the simplest levels—education, medicine, and so on.

The scale of these and other public initiatives was, however, always limited by finance. African colonies were poor, revenues small. Until perhaps the 1930s it was assumed that colonial improvements must be financed from local resources, which in practice normally meant floating loans in the metropolis or contracting with a private concern to provide and work public utilities such as electricity or docks. But the lesson of the period between the wars was that most colonies could not afford to pay for effective development, and that the metropolis must give help. Until 1939 such help was minimal. The British Colonial Development Act of 1929 set aside public funds for loans and grants to the poorer colonies, and grants-in-aid were given on occasion. The French set up a similar fund—*Fonds d'Investissement pour le Développment Economique et Social* (F.I.D.E.S.)—in 1938, but had subsidized the colonies through concealed civil and military appropriations before then. It is difficult to measure the total sums involved, but one estimate places the British contribution to all colonies (excluding Iraq) between 1918 and 1939 at an annual average of only about £2,000,000; [31] and a comparable rough estimate for all French colonies gives an annual average of civil expenditure between 1918–20 of £1,370,000.[32] These sums were small by comparison with post-1945 "aid," though in their context they were often of considerable importance because, unlike colonial loans, they did not constitute a burden on local revenues. Yet the general conclusion must be that before 1939 neither the British nor the French government was prepared to make any substantial effort to accelerate development in Africa from metropolitan funds; the initiative and burden were left to colonial governments and private enterprise. The results are clearly reflected in the patterns of investment and production.

The test of development, however interpreted, lies ultimately in hard statistics. A satisfactory assessment of British and French achievements in Africa would require detailed analysis of more fields of activity than can be considered here, but three obvious tests can be applied. First, from a metropolitan viewpoint, what proportion of British and French overseas trade was conducted with their African territories and, conversely, what share of African overseas trade lay with the metropolis? Second, concentrating on the actual economic achievement

31. Kenneth E. Robinson, *The Dilemmas of Trusteeship* (London, 1965), p. 33.

32. Taken from data in Constant Southworth, *The French Colonial Venture* (London, 1931), Table II.

in Africa, how much capital, public or private, was invested there? Finally, what were the broad achievements of development in the colonial period, and on which side did the balance of advantage lie? It is, of course, easier to pose such questions than to provide satisfactory answers, but the attempt must be made.

To consider the commercial statistics for each empire before making comparisons, the French data is shown in Tables 1–3.[33] Three points stand out. First, whereas French Africa was of relatively very small commercial importance to France before 1914, its share of French trade rose dramatically after 1930, until in 1935 it took over 25 percent of French exports and supplied over 20 percent of French imports. These proportions remained remarkably stable thereafter, and there was no evidence that independence had any marked effect. Second, in terms of total French overseas trade, French Africa was always more significant as a market for French exports than as a source of her imports. The disproportion was greatest after 1945, when French "aid" enabled the colonies to run a very large trading deficit with her, while exchange controls forced them to import from France. Paradoxically, however, in almost all cases the colonies sent a higher proportion of their exports to the metropolis than they imported from her. Third, in terms of African overseas trade, the relative importance of the French market increased dramatically (except in North Africa) with the system of *surprix* for colonial products entering France; and in 1949 France took over 75 percent of exports from all black Africa and Algeria. This represented the ultimate victory of the French protectionist ideal and the concept of economic interdependence. The fact that most French territories became members of E.E.C. and remained in the franc zone after 1958 reflected their dependence on the French market. Conversely the *surprix* system had less effect on the metropolitan share of imports into Africa in the 1930s, but after 1945, supported by French currency controls, the French proportion of imports rose higher than ever before in most territories, and remained very high in 1963.

33. There are variations in the data resulting from the sources used. I could find no reliable figures for A.E.F. exports in the early period; but those given by Roberts, p. 362, for the French Congo suggest that the trade was too small to have had much effect on these percentages. Poquin's figures are for trade with the franc zone and not only with France; but before 1939 the difference was small. Bloch-Lainé's figures relate only to trade with France. Small variations should therefore be discounted.

The British experience, reflected in Tables 4 and 5 was very different.[34] First, both as a proportion of total British trade and of British intraimperial trade, Africa was always relatively unimportant. Excluding South Africa it would have been almost negligible. From very low proportionate levels at the end of the nineteenth century[35] British Africa's share of United Kingdom imports and exports rose to a rough plateau before 1914, taking between 5 and 6 percent of British exports and supplying about 8 percent of her imports. Between the wars these patterns changed. Africa became a relatively important consumer of British products, whereas, in value at least (reflecting changes in the terms of trade) African exports to Britain declined in importance. The significance of African markets continued until the mid-1950s, and then declined, running in parallel with imports in the early 1960s. In 1966 African trade was about as important for Britain as it had been in 1914. These tendencies were markedly different from those in the French Empire. Before 1914 French and British Africa were of similar relative commercial importance to the metropolitan states, especially on the export side. But although Africa's share of British exports was remarkably constant between 1928 and 1956, French Africa's share of French exports rose from 12.2 percent in 1926 to 26.9 percent in 1935 and was just under 30 percent in the 1950s. Given the far greater population and resources of British Africa, these trends were remarkable evidence of the efficacy of French protectionist policies.

If the statistics are considered from the side of British Africa, the picture is again very different from French Africa. Whereas in the latter (excluding Algeria, which was fully assimilated into the French tariff by the 1890s) trade with France showed a marked secular increase throughout the period, reaching a peak in the period after 1945, Britain was most important to her African dependencies before 1914. Thereafter the proportion of African exports going to Britain decreased steadily throughout the period, though reviving in the 1950s slightly. The significance of these secular trends must not be overstated. Britain remained the largest single market for most British African territories at all times, and even in 1962 accounted for more than a third of their overseas trade. The downward trend reflected the

34. Groupings of African territories vary because the basis of statistical returns changed during this period. They are consistent to 1937 and from 1947 onward. As with the French trade figures, too much emphasis should not be placed on precise percentages.

35. See J. A. Hobson's wise comment on the relatively small value of trade with tropical territories in *Imperialism,* pp. 34–44.

relative decline of Britain as manufacturer, consumer, and entrepôt and indicated that, under virtually free-trade conditions, the African territories were naturally and increasingly drawn into multilateral world trade.

Ignoring trends and contrasts in individual African territories, which are clearly reflected in the tables, the dominant fact was therefore that the secular trends of British and French trade with Africa during the colonial period were directly contradictory. The consequences were clearly reflected in divergent relationships between them and their one-time dependencies in the 1960s.

Whereas statistics on the direction of African overseas trade relate primarily to the theme of imperial autarky, capital investment is the true measure of the efforts made by the imperial powers to use and develop these dependencies. It is therefore extremely unfortunate that reliable evidence on investment is scarce. Domestic capital formation and investment within the colonies is virtually unmeasurable until after 1945, but it must in any case have been very small, since no tropical African territory possessed resources capable of being converted into substantial fixed investment. Even South Africa and French North Africa depended almost entirely on imported capital. Yet the size of this capital inflow remains highly dubious, though some forms are more measurable than others. Metropolitan expenditure on colonies, though small, can be assessed from budgetary appropriations. Public loans raised in Europe by the colonies can also be estimated with some accuracy. The real difficulty comes with direct private investment. Capital brought by small settlers or traders is unrecorded. Even the far more important investment by large commercial, industrial, and utility companies is speculative, except in South Africa, where publication of company accounts was obligatory. One can therefore only present available estimates as evidence of approximate orders of magnitude and admit that no precise calculation of capital employed in the *mise en valeur* is possible.

In examining this limited data a dividing line must be drawn at 1939. To this point virtually all capital invested in Africa came either from colonial public loans raised in Europe, with or without metropolitan guarantee, or from direct private investment. After 1945 an increasing proportion of new capital came as "aid" from Europe or North America in the form of grants or loans on noncommercial terms. Before 1939 the determinant of all investment was the capacity of a colony to pay interest or of an enterprise dividends. In the second period, while private investors retained the same commercial criteria, the bulk of public investment was related to planning for "growth" by the metropolitan and colonial governments rather than to colonial revenues. Two main questions are, however, relevant in each period. First, how much private and public capital was invested? Second, how significant was this capital outflow to Britain and France in relation to their total overseas investments?

Various calculations of public investments have been made which differ quite substantially. Bloch-Lainé's estimate for the whole French Empire are set out in Table 6. For black Africa the total (in current values) was 5,480 million francs. For the same area Poquin calculated that 2657.1 million francs was actually realized from loans of 3,234 million francs contracted for.[36] Frankel's total for 1936 was £43,031,-000, equivalent to 3,316.5 million francs at current rates.[37] That was higher than an estimate made for the Vichy government in 1943,[38] but will serve for comparison with British Africa. Frankel's total for all British Africa in 1936 was £448,836,000, of which £285.8 million was in South and Central Africa, £50.8 million in West Africa, and £112.2 million in East Africa, including the Anglo-Egyptian Sudan.[39]

Estimates of private direct investment vary more widely. For British Africa the best data was compiled by Frankel and is reproduced in Table 8. Frankel also gave figures for other African territories, but his estimate for sub-Saharan French Africa was much lower than that made for the Vichy government in 1943 on the basis of returns from companies and individuals—26.9 milliard francs (1940) as against Frankel's adjusted and converted figure of 7.8 milliard francs.[40] A third estimate, made by a French committee in 1940, was also 26.9 milliard francs.[41] Such discrepancies are significant because they suggest that Frankel may have understated French private investments, even if the French overstated them; so that his relative figures for British and French investment per capita (Table 10) may be too unfavorable to France.

How did these African investments relate to total British and French overseas investment: that is, how attractive was Africa to metropolitan

36. Jean-Jacques Poquin, *Les Relations Economiques Extérieures des Pays d'Afrique Noire de l'Union Française, 1925–1955* (Paris, 1957), p. 188.

37. See Table 8, based on S. Herbert Frankel, *Capital Investment in Africa* (London, 1938), Table 28.

38. Suret-Canale, *Afrique noire,* pp. 206–07.

39. See Table 8.

40. Suret-Canale, p. 206, n. 2.

41. Poquin, p. 190.

investors? Total French overseas investment in 1939 is uncertain. But if Staley's figure of about £719 million for 1929[42] is related to Frankel's 1936 total of £66.7 million in sub-Saharan Africa, the proportion was 9.3 percent. One rough estimate for British overseas investment in 1938 is £4,500 million.[43] Frankel's figure of £941 million for all British Africa represented 21 percent. Of this, £657 million was in South Africa (15 percent of the total) and only £273 million in other territories—6 percent. British West Africa, directly comparable with French tropical Africa, had £116.7 million or 2.6 percent. The conclusion is important. Tropical Africa was neither a leading or necessary field for Anglo-French investment. Certainly the figures give no support to Marxist theories of surplus European capital urgently seeking outlets. Conversely the attraction of gold, copper, or diamonds, when coupled with white settler societies and favorable political conditions in South and Central Africa, was irresistible.

Selectivity, based on expected profitability, was therefore the main feature of direct private investment, and this is clearly reflected in the distribution of capital in different sectors of colonial economies. French private capital in A.O.F. and A.E.F. in 1940 was employed as follows: 39 percent in trade, 6 percent in banks, 3.6 percent in private transport (excluding trading capital used for transport), and only 47 percent for production—industry, plantations, mines, forestry, and stockbreeding.[44] No comparable figures are available for British tropical Africa; but in Nigeria the 1938 Cocoa Commission stated that trading firms had invested £13 million, of which £9.4 million was used in the export of produce, as against Frankel's total of £36.8 million private investment there. In the Gold Coast comparable figures were £9.5 million invested in trade out of a total of £20.2 million.[45] In 1936 tin mining employed estimated aggregate issued capital of £4.6 million in Nigeria, and gold mining in the Gold Coast £2.7 million in 1936–37.[46] Clearly trade rather than production dominated investment in West Africa. But in South and Central Africa mining was far more important. In a recent study[47] Frankel put accumulated total capital

42. Quoted in Frankel, *Capital Investment,* p. 18.

43. Conan, *The Sterling Area,* p. 180.

44. Suret-Canale, p. 207.

45. Margery Perham, ed., *Mining, Commerce, and Finance in Nigeria* (London, 1948), p. 206.

46. Ibid., pp. 21 and 304.

47. S. Herbert Frankel, *Investment and the Return of Equity Capital in the South African Gold Mining Industry, 1887–1965* (Oxford, 1967), p. 116.

in large South African gold mines, with vendors at par, at about £167 million—66.5 percent of the £251 million private capital invested there in 1936.

Some other important patterns may be noticed. With few exceptions, capital was invested in African colonies by nationals of the metropolis rather than by foreigners. Private portfolio investors were attracted either by the slightly higher yield on colonial loans than on gilt-edged securities at home, or by the speculative possibilities of mines, plantations, or land investment companies. Commercial and other companies invested as little as they found necessary to achieve their limited objectives. Governments were left to provide unremunerative public services, with the result that public investment constituted 71.6 percent of the total in British East Africa, 47.7 percent in all British Africa, and perhaps 61.2 percent in French tropical Africa.[48] The collective results are seen in Tables 9 and 10. The contrast in capital investment per capita is startling: £55.8 a head in South Africa, £38.4 in the Rhodesias, and under £10 in all other British and French sub-Saharan territories. This suggests the ironical conclusion that capital investment—and therefore to a large extent economic development—were in inverse ratio to the concern shown in particular colonies for African welfare as conceived in the interwar period. This, in a nutshell, was the central problem of developing Africa before 1939, reflecting the inexorable economic law that private capital went where it might operate most effectively rather than where social need was greatest. Post-1945 metropolitan planning and "aid" were conceived as a means of avoiding this economic straitjacket.

The obvious fact of postwar French public investment in Africa was that the vast concepts of men like Sarraut were at last to some extent realized. Partly for the political aim of strengthening the Union of 1946, partly to strengthen the franc zone at a time of acute shortage of exchange, the metropolis was prepared to invest heavily in basic development.[49] Since development was seen in terms of the whole Union, planning and finance were centralized in specialized agencies set up in Paris, notably the C.C.F.O.M. as a department of the Treasury, F.I.D.E.S. which did the planning for tropical Africa, and F.D.E.S. which dealt with North Africa. Hopes that colonies would bear a substantial part—45 percent in 1946—of development costs from local budgets proved false. By 1955 this was reduced to 10 percent, amounting to about 3 percent of total F.I.D.E.S. investments. In

48. Frankel, *Capital Investment in Africa,* Table 29.

49. For a reasoned defense of this policy see Bloch-Lainé, pp. 10–12.

addition there were less obvious forms of financial assistance amounting to investment: French Treasury "advances," budgetary subsidies, *surprix* on colonial imports to France, etc.

How much capital investment this produced depends on how it is calculated. For the period 1947–55, Bloch-Lainé gave a total of 758.5 milliard francs (1955)—$2,167.2 million—of which 358 milliards went to sub-Saharan Africa, including 271.4 milliards to A.O.F., A.E.F., Togo, and the Cameroons.[50] For these last four territories Poquin gave a total of 245 milliards,[51] which suggests that Block-Lainé's figures are right. For the period 1956–64 D.A.C. statistics give total French aid as $7,629 million,[52] of which, on the 1962 distribution, about $6,126 million would have gone to French Africa. The total public investment in Africa from 1946–64 may therefore have amounted to about $8,293 million, or £2,961 sterling. These figures leave no doubt that after 1945 France at last made great efforts to develop French Africa, and in 1962 total French aid represented 1.76 percent of national income.[53] How much of these vast sums represented a constructive addition to African resources is more debatable. Much was spent on salaries of French technicians and advisers—a third of total aid in 1965—and more flowed back to France through repatriation of salaries and profits of French firms undertaking projects in Africa. It is also arguable that, because virtually all materials and men were drawn from within the franc zone, the monetary value of aid was inflated by high price levels. Again, an obvious result of aid was to enable African dependencies to run a very large visible trade deficit with France, as seen in Table 3. Finally, it has been held that far too much "aid" was placed in nonproductive sectors of African economies, though the proportion spent on "infrastructure" declined over the period.[54]

It is therefore difficult to assess the real value of French "aid" to Africa, but at least there is no doubt that in sheer volume it was far greater than comparable British public investment there. After 1945 the British preserved the basic features of the 1929 Colonial Development Act and the 1940 Colonial Development and Welfare Act: that is, colonies were expected to take the initiative and put up their own development plants for consideration by the Colonial Office and other

50. Bloch-Lainé, pp. 117 and 136. These totals include a proportion of the "general" (nonterritorial) aid administered by F.I.D.E.S.

51. Poquin, pp. 195–96.

52. Quoted in Teresa Hayter, *French Aid* (London, 1966), p. 45.

53. Ibid.

54. Ibid., pp. 38 and 167.

agencies in London. There was little overall imperial planning. But the scale of grants and loans increased substantially. Between 1929 and 1945 British Africa received £8,875,000, of which £3,000,000 was in loans, the rest in outright grants.[55] From 1946–55 total C.D. & W. grants were about £43 million; [56] and if loans for this period were in the same ratio to grants as in 1955–64 (for which statistics are available), loans to Africa would have been about £52 million. Between 1955 and 1964 total grants (including money from other British public sources) were £243 million and loans were £168 million.[57] On these calculations British public grants and loans to British Africa for 1946–64 were thus about £506 million, or $1,417 million, as against $8,293 million French aid. But this may be too low. A rough calculation for 1950–63 based on O.E.C.D. data (taking the African share of aid in 1960–63 and applying this to total British aid 1950–63) gives a total of about $1,940 million for this shorter period.[58] As in the French case relatively little "aid" was used for production as against communications and social services, though the emphasis shifted more to production after 1959. The Colonial Development Corporation, however, put 45 percent of its loans into primary production, processing, commerce, and industry.[59]

The size of postwar direct private investment in Africa is frankly unknown in the absence of official statistics or detailed study. In the French case Poquin used new public issues by companies primarily involved in A.O.F., A.E.F., Togo, and the Cameroons to obtain a total of at least 63.5 milliard francs (1955), equal to $182 million, or about $20 million a year.[60] For 1956–63 O.E.C.D. figures give total French private direct investment in all developing countries at $3,205 million, or $2,583 million excluding export credits.[61] Applying the African share of the 1962 and 1963 totals (88.6 percent) [62] to 1956–63 would make French private investment in Africa some $2,288.5 million. To arrive at a total for all French Africa for the postwar period involves guess-

55. Overseas Development Institute [O.D.I. hereafter], *British Aid,* Vol. 5, *Colonial Development* (London, 1964), pp. 28–30.

56. O.D.I., *British Aid,* Vol. 2, *Government Finance* (London, 1964), p. 96.

57. Central Statistical Office, *Annual Abstract of Statistics,* Vol. 100 (London, 1963), p. 227, and Vol. 102 (London, 1965), 244.

58. O.E.C.D., *The Flow of Financial Resources to Less-developed Countries, 1956–1963* (Paris, 1964), pp. 148 and 168.

59. O.D.I., *British Aid, 5,* 57, and *2,* 30.

60. Poquin, *Les Relations Economiques,* p. 195.

61. O.E.C.D., *Flow, 1956–63,* p. 139.

62. Ibid., pp. 75–76.

work. If the proportion invested in black Africa in 1962–63—28 percent—is applied to Poquin's figures for 1945–53, French North Africa would have received about $648 million in these years. Added to the 1956–63 figures, the total is $3,119 million (£1,224 million). Taking an average of this for the years 1954 and 1955 gives a total for 1945–63 of about $3,486 million; and if the 1962–63 distribution was constant, about $976 million (£348 million) was in black Africa, including Madagascar, and $2,510 million (£896 million) in North Africa.

Such figures are too conjectural to be of value except as a rough indication of order of magnitude and for comparison with comparable estimates for British Africa. During 1959–62 total new British direct overseas investment was £838.3 million, of which £138.6 million (16.5 percent) was in British Africa. Of this £97.6 million was in South and Central Africa, leaving only £41 million for the rest of tropical Africa—4.9 percent of total British overseas private investment in these years. Table 11 shows the Board of Trade's figures for private investment at the end of 1962. The essential points are that the African share was only £693 million out of £4,496.9 million—15.4 percent; and that tropical Africa had only £247.8 million—5.5 percent.[63]

These figures invite three comparisons: with official British "aid," with British private investment in Africa before 1939, and with postwar French private investment in Africa. First, O.E.C.D. figures for 1956–63 suggest that, whereas British "aid" and private investment in all areas were running at similar levels—$2,867 million and $2,791 million—French official "aid" was more than twice private investment, $6,811 million to $2,853 million.[64] Second, a comparison of the 1962 figures for British private investment in Africa with Frankel's figures for 1936 shows that the total had increased only from £413.5 million to £693 million—£280 million in twenty-six years, or an average increase of £10.7 million a year. Even so this does not allow for declining money values. In real terms there must have been a substantial disinvestment. There was also a change in the regional distribution of private investment, or at least in capital directly controlled by British firms. The South Africa share declined from 62.3 percent to 46.1 percent, though this probably conceals the fact that many companies in South Africa were now locally registered and were therefore excluded from the Board of Trade's figures. In fact there was a substantial flow

63. *Board of Trade Journal,* Vol. 187 (London, 1964), p. 293, and Vol. 189 (London, 1965), p. 230.

64. O.E.C.D., *Flow, 1956–63,* pp. 139 and 148.

of British capital to South Africa after 1945. The Central African share had risen from 13.7 percent to 18.1 percent. But, although black Africa's share of total investment had also risen, postwar private investment there was not impressive. In Nigeria and the Gold Coast, the totals in 1962 were about three times those of 1936, thus merely keeping pace with declining money values; and the most impressive increase was in Kenya and Uganda, which increased their joint total from £8.5 million to about £52 million. In general it is clear that relatively little postwar British private investment went to Africa, whose share of total overseas direct investment had dropped from 21 percent in 1936 to 15.4 percent in 1962. The tropical African share was roughly constant—5.5 percent of private investment in 1962 as against 6 percent of all British overseas investment in 1936.

Finally, how did post-1945 British private investment in Africa compare with that of France? In 1962 French sub-Saharan Africa received £25.6 million and British Africa, excluding South and Central Africa, £12.3 million. In the same year all French Africa received £83.3 million as against £21.7 million for all British Africa. Between 1956–63 the annual average for French Africa was £102 million—£28.5 million in black Africa—against a 1959–62 annual average of £39.5 million for all British Africa and £10.2 million for identified black Africa. Total net postwar British private investment in Africa was calculated at £280 million, as against an estimate figure of £1,224 million in French Africa. These rough estimates confirm the general impression that Africa proved a much less attractive field for investment to Britain than to France after 1945. The British clearly preferred other regions; and in 1962 Australia and New Zealand between them had more direct private British capital than all British Africa.

The reasons behind these contrasting attitudes toward Africa of British and French private direct investors can only be conjectured. On the British side Reddaway has shown that there was no correlation between the absolute or proportionate addition to the net overseas operating assets and the average pretax profitability of investment in particular countries for the British companies whose statistics he used. This suggests that relatively low African returns on capital may not have been decisive,[65] though Board of Trade figures for 1962 "earnings" in Africa were in fact low: South Africa 9.8 percent, Central Africa 8.1 percent, Ghana 7.9 percent, Kenya 7.1 percent, Nigeria 1.9

65. W. B. Reddaway, *Effects of U.K. Direct Investment Overseas: an Interim Report* (Cambridge, 1967), p. 44.

percent, Uganda 1.0 percent.[66] The crucial factors were, however, more likely to have been the relative advantage of investing in other parts of the world as against political uncertainties and technical problems of expanding existing lines of activity in Africa. Conversely the scale of French private investment in Africa may have reflected governmental control of investment outside the franc zone, the stimulus of high profits within the area of French tariff protection, and the demand for capital to develop petroleum and natural gas resources in Algeria. Beyond this no firm conclusions are possible.

What, then, was the extent and quality of British and French economic achievements in Africa, and how should these be measured? A convincing answer would necessarily be based on a comparison between the size of the national product of each African country in, say, 1900 and 1960, for this was the true measure of development. But no such calculation is possible. No data are available on national products in the early period, and even contemporary calculations are normally too hypothetical to be useful. Audit, therefore, must be based on circumstantial evidence and will be impressionistic rather than conclusive. Emphasis has so far been placed on trade and capital investment as evidence of metropolitan objectives and achievements; but other factors, such as production of all kinds, population trends, communications, education, medical and other social services, would have to be quantified in any fair assessment. Tables 12 to 15 provide limited data on certain general trends. Tables 12 and 13 are intended to give some indication of the expansion of colonial exports and shipping as a partial substitute for data on the national product. Export figures are given in current values, despite changing money values and terms of trade, because no indexes are available to convert these into constant values over the whole period. Thus the data on British colonial shipping (Table 12.1) and on the tonnage of French tropical African exports (Table 13.2) provide some check on the relevance of export values to production in the export sector. In the second case it is significant that the quinquennial averages in tons of French tropical African exports changed remarkably little between 1935–39 and 1946–50, though values fluctuated widely; and that the volume of exports in the early 1950s was in most cases not much more than twice the 1925–29 figure. This does not suggest very substantial development in the export sector of these economies over a quarter of a century. Tables 14 and 15 give an indication of population growth and railway communi-

66. *Board of Trade Journal, 187,* 290 and 293.

cations. Population increased substantially in all territories, and provides at least an a priori reason for thinking that economic and social conditions improved. Railway mileages are ambiguous. They can either be seen as a substantial achievement in creating an economic infrastructure, or as evidence that far too little had been done to open up African hinterlands to commercial production. More detailed analysis would show that a large proportion of the eventual total had been built before 1914, and that thereafter the effort partially lapsed.

Did these achievements add up to satisfactory development during the colonial period? The answer depends, of course, on the criteria adopted. For the present inquiry the problem can best be approached from three different angles. Did Britain and France reap the economic reward they expected from Africa? In doing so did they "exploit" Africans in the pejorative sense? Did economic development of this sort provide a satisfactory basis for "growth" after independence?

The first question is the simplest to answer. Generally speaking Britain and France obtained a much smaller economic reward from most parts of Africa than their more optimistic early enthusiasts predicted; but conversely they received as much advantage as was compatible with African endowment factors and the effort Europeans made to use them. The real lesson of the seventy years after 1890 was that economic return was in direct proportion to effort made. Sarraut and others demanded heroic metropolitan efforts to develop Africa, but until after 1945 the Anglo-French effort can only be described as comparatively puny. With the exception of mineral production and communications, far too little capital was invested to translate potential into production. Why was this? The main answer—ignoring the significant effects of two world wars and an international slump—lies in those factors that discouraged further effort in many regions. Within Africa, governmental policies were often a deterrent insofar as they obstructed "natural" economic trends. How could agriculture be capitalized and improved in West Africa when governments forbade Europeans to acquire land and preserved African communal land tenures? How could plantations in other regions be made profitable if no adequate voluntary labor supply existed and coercion was barred? How could commercial development take place before road, rail, and port facilities were created? Outside Africa there were other equally important deterrents. Development, as understood before 1945, implied an overseas demand for African products at remunerative prices. By and large, however, international demand for tropical raw materials was smaller and less consistent between the wars than before 1914, and for many products there was little elasticity of demand. Why, then, invest in production for a saturated market? Most metropolitan concerns settled readily for limited investment and restricted turnover to avoid gambling on the market. The result was partial and very uneven economic development which seldom fulfilled early expectations.

Within these limits, however, Britain and France received a fair reward for limited enterprise. In terms of imperial autarky, both countries obtained secure supplies of raw materials and a remarkably large share of African markets. Only a myopic mercantilist could have complained when the metropolis controlled more than half the trade of its African dependencies. If both export production and markets remained relatively small, this was due to lack of development through investment. Capital, like trade, followed national lines very closely; for, by contrast with Portuguese and Belgian possessions, British and French Africa received little foreign capital beyond portfolio investment in mining. If, therefore, as predicted by early theorists of imperialism, colonies were necessary as outlets for surplus capital in Europe, Africa offered ample opportunities for the parent states. Shipping lines also observed imperial limits very closely, largely as a result of the conference system. It was almost as if the navigation laws had not been repealed.[67] Finally, currency and trade restrictions after 1939 ensured that Africa's bullion and hard currency earnings were available to each metropolis to bolster the sterling and franc currency pools. These economic advantages were substantial, even if Africa did not prove the economic salvation of Britain and France.

The problem of exploitation in the pejorative sense is more difficult to handle because it cannot be defined in measurable economic terms. The case against Britain and France, in a nutshell, is that through their political and economic power they took more out of Africa than they put in: that the *mise en valeur* was a cover for piracy. Evidence supporting this hypothesis is easy to produce but is often misleading. Least impressive is the accusation that, due to favorable conditions produced by colonialism, metropolitan investment in colonial Africa obtained "superprofit." There is insufficient data to prove or disprove this generally; but there is no reason to think that over a long period profits of capital in Africa were higher than those in Europe or elsewhere, though profits in extractive industries (such as wild rubber)

67. See Charlotte Leubuscher, *The West African Shipping Trade 1909–1959* (Leyden, 1963) for an excellent treatment of shipping conferences.

might be very large for short periods.[68] Much has also been made of the high profit margins made by European trading concerns, especially in West Africa, due to quasimonopolistic or monopsonistic conditions there. From the viewpoint of the African producer there was a priori justification for this belief,[69] since margins between what he received and the f.o.b. price at the port of shipment were large, as were margins between what he paid for imports and their c.i.f. price. Part of these margins undoubtedly reflected the disparate bargaining positions of big expatriate trading concerns and peasant producers or consumers. But in fact high inland transport costs, handling charges, middleman profits, and customs were more significant than company profits. Conversely the net profitability of capital employed by these large companies seems generally to have been low; and their constant tendency to form rings or to amalgamate was due to financial weakness and the risks inherent in speculative commodity trading rather than the character of "finance capitalism." The equation is in fact balanced by the inefficiencies of African trade and their marginal character. The African suffered from both, but his loss did not reflect vast imperialist gain.

A stronger case can be made for saying that the apparent benefits resulting from an inflow of European capital were substantially diminished by a "drain" of real resources from Africa. Because companies registered in Britain or France paid little or no tax in the colonies and often reinvested as little of their retained profits there as possible, Africa obtained only minimal advantages from development. By contrast, independent states could impose taxation and control repatriation of profits; so this element in the "drain" from Africa was directly attributable to colonial status. In principle these facts are undeniable, but it is important to distinguish primarily economic from political causes. Favorable tax conditions and freedom to repatriate profits were a precondition of European investment in the dependencies; and if they were subsequently refused by successor states, some compensating advantages—guaranteed profit margins, monopoly, etc.—were normally required. The real significance of this "drain" was not that

68. For interest rates on pre-1930 colonial loans, see Southworth, *French Colonial Venture*, Appendix Tables 3, 5, 6; and for pre-1914 British loans, Alexander K. Cairncross, *Home and Foreign Investment, 1870–1913* (Cambridge, 1953). For the return on private capital see Frankel, *Capital Investment in Africa*, pp. 89 and 91, and *The Return of Equity Capital*, passim; Reddaway, pp. 43 and 44.

69. See, for example, Hancock, *Survey, 2*, Pt. 2, pp. 220–36; Suret-Canale, *Afrique noire*, pp. 237–38, 239; Poquin, *Les Relations Economiques*, pp. 102–03, 104; P. T. Bauer, *West African Trade* (Cambridge, 1954), pp. 232–40.

it demonstrated the unique injustice of colonialism, but that it substantially reduced the real value of the apparent flow of capital resources from Europe to Africa and hence the benefits of empire. It is impossible to say how this operated in the long term, but very recent figures illustrate the tendency. In 1961 $61.6 million out of $266 million British private investment in all developing countries consisted of reinvested local profits. In 1962 it was $91.3 million out of $200.2 million.[70] In 1962 $117.2 million of the $172.4 million privately invested by France in Algeria consisted of reinvested local profits.[71] Between 1959 and 1962 British investment in the overseas sterling area was £483.6 million, compared with £179.3 million unremitted profits of British subsidiaries and £158.4 million in dividends distributed in Britain.[72] Obviously the net flow of capital and resources to Africa was much less than nominal new investment; and in the French case there may actually have been a net reverse flow in the late 1950s due to repatriation of salaries, savings, profits, and capital at a time of political uncertainty.[73]

Other elements in the "drain" may be mentioned very briefly. Currency control, especially in post-1945 French Africa, may have transferred wealth to France by forcing Africans to buy from the metropolis at artificially high prices while having to transfer their hard currency earnings to the central monetary pool.[74] In the British case it has been claimed that the 100 percent sterling security cover required for colonial currencies implied that the colonies had to lend the metropolis large sums at low interest rates and were thus deprived of funds needed for productive local investment. In both cases, however, African territories received the substantial benefits of stable and internationally convertible currencies, and many Francophone African states chose to preserve their monetary relations with France after independence. As regards tariffs, the question turns on the relative advantage to the metropolis or dependency of preferential duties. In the British case this can be disregarded, since there were virtually no tariff preferences in British tropical Africa, and the dependencies gained a slight benefit from preferences on their exports entering Britain. The French case is more debatable. Poquin calculated that in 1954 it cost France some 8 milliard francs to buy from French tropical Africa

70. O.E.C.D., *Flow, 1956–63,* pp. 130–31.
71. Ibid., p. 75.
72. *Board of Trade Journal, 187,* 287 and 289.
73. Hayter, *French Aid,* p. 59.
74. Poquin, pp. 94–100.

rather than from cheaper foreign sources; but that it cost French tropical Africa 26 milliard francs to import from France rather than elsewhere.[75] This large "drain" reflected a short-run deficit on visible trade, but was nonetheless substantial. Another calculation for the same year gave France a favorable balance on the *surprix* with all overseas territories of 20 milliards.[76] Thereafter, however, as the trading balance was partially redressed, the advantage came to lie with the dependencies. In 1962 all overseas regions of the franc zone had a net *surprix* advantage of 877 million francs, or 520 million without Algeria.[77] With such variations in the volume and value of trade, it is impossible to say which party gained a secular advantage from French preferential tariffs.

The evidence on the "drain" theory is therefore inconclusive. All that can be said with any certainty is that the transfer of real resources from Britain and France to Africa was much smaller than the gross totals of public and private investment; and that the positive achievements of Britain and France in creating the basis for a Western economy in Africa was to a large extent paid for by African labor and resources. In this the experience of British and French colonial Africa was identical with that of all relatively underdeveloped countries in other parts of the world, whether sovereign states or colonial dependencies.

Finally, the evidence must be reviewed from the postindependence viewpoint of African territories as autonomous economies rather than as components of an imperial economy. Did the economic patterns and policies of the colonial period lay sound foundations, by design or accident, to "growth" as understood after 1945? The subject is, of course, too controversial to be disposed of briefly. The evidence of this chapter suggests that the answer varied from one region to another. By the 1960s South Africa was the only territory where "growth" had clearly reached the point at which an economy could be called "developed." In varying degrees all others were still heavily dependent on imported capital and skills. Why was this? The time factor was obviously crucial. South Africa had been developing a "Western" economy for several centuries, while other territories had been receiving capital and skills for much less than a century. A second factor was the deliberate preservation of indigenous social and economic forms by colonial governments. Outside Africa no "advanced" econ-

75. Ibid., p. 116.
76. Moussa, *Les Chances Economiques*, pp. 76–84.
77. Hayter, p. 54.

omy preserved precapitalist social patterns, and to the extent that these were artificially protected in colonial Africa by Britain and France, they obstructed economic development.

Fundamentally, however, it must be concluded that while the typical patterns of colonial economy and the objectives of European entrepreneurs did not prevent "growth," equally they were not calculated to promote it, and did so largely by accident. The British, following the classical economists, might think of comparative advantage within the world economy, the French of a mercantilist *pacte colonial,* but it came to much the same thing. African colonies, like other parts of the world, were developed in order to produce raw materials while importing manufactures and capital. The result was inevitably a high degree of commercial metrocentrism, intense specialization in a few raw materials, and uneven development. By the 1950s much of French Africa was so tied to France by high price levels and dependence on a protected market that independence brought little freedom to choose future economic policy. British Africa was far less tied to Britain by these factors, but in other respects the same problems had to be faced. Only where a fortuitous coincidence of factors had occurred (such as mineral deposits, adequate labor supply, and communications, resulting in large capital inflow, transfer of skills to Africans, and the growth of a substantial local market) was this pattern likely to be broken in the colonial period.

A perspective view of British and French exploitation in Africa from the late nineteenth century onward is therefore dominated by half tints and qualifications. Development was neither as heroic as early enthusiasts for the *mise en valeur* wanted, nor as negative and disastrous for African interests as critics have commonly alleged. Under ideal conditions it might have been done better and with less pain to Africans without imperial control, though in the historical context it is difficult to see any practicable alternative. Tropical Africa was not like Japan. One thing at least is certain. Alien rule brought Africa forcibly into the world economy and ensured that future development would be in the direction of Western economic systems, whether capitalist, socialist, or mixed. This was the substantive product of exploitation.

APPENDIX

TABLE 1

RELATIVE IMPORTANCE OF FRENCH AFRICAN TERRITORIES AS PROPORTION OF TOTAL FRENCH OVERSEAS TRADE

1. *Percentage of Total French Exports* (excluding Togo and the Cameroons to 1920 and A.E.F. and Morocco to 1910)		2. *Percentage of Total French Imports* (excluding Togo and the Cameroons to 1920 and A.E.F. and Morocco to 1910)	
	Percent		*Percent*
1900	8.9	1900	5.0
1910	9.8	1910	9.1
1914	13.7	1914	7.5
1920	13.6	1920	5.0
(All French Africa)		(All French Africa)	
1926	12.2	1926	9.3
1928	14.5	1928	10.4
1935	26.9	1935	20.9
1938	22.5	1938	20.9
1951	29.6	1951	14.5
1954	29.0	1954	18.8
1959	28.2	1959	20.3

Sources: 1900 and 1910, Constant Southworth, *The French Colonial Venture,* Tables II and IV; 1928–38, League of Nations, *The Network of World Trade* (Geneva, 1942); 1951–54, François Bloch-Lainé, *Le Zone Franc,* pp. 486–87; 1914, 1920, 1926, 1959, *Annuaire Statistique de la France* (Paris, 1966).

TABLE 2

SHARE OF FRANCE IN THE TRADE OF FRENCH AFRICA

1. *Percentage of Imports to French African Territories from France*

Year	*Algeria*	*Tunisia*	*Morocco*	*A.O.F.*	*Cameroons*	*Togo*	*A.E.F.*	*Madagascar*
1895	79.5	51.0	—	45.0	—	—	—	66.4
1905	85.0	65.0	—	44.5	—	—	—	90.0
1913	82.5	65.0	52.6	37.5	—	—	—	85.7
1920	74.5	54.8	64.8	36.4	—	—	—	52.4
1926	82.6	79.7	68.7	56.7	—	—	—	86.5
1925	—	—	—	49.0	32.5	14.8	56.0	—
1928	80.0	63.4	52.2	—	—	—	—	44.8
1929	—	—	—	50.0	35.4	30.0	52.5	—
1935	80.4	64.6	39.5	47.0	22.0	11.2	50.5	55.5
1938	76.2	60.0	34.4	69.0	30.0	20.0	37.0	62.1
1939	77.5	65.7	40.1	64.4	30.6	16.3	44.8	75.0
1945	25.4	21.5	20.3	22.9	5.5	18.0	4.2	10.8
1947	65.0	61.7	55.8	51.2	47.4	53.7	53.1	50.2
1949	77.9	75.1	58.5	68.7	72.7	69.2	64.2	74.4

2. *Percentage of Exports of French African Territories to France*

Year	*Algeria*	*Tunisia*	*Morocco*	*A.O.F.*	*Cameroons*	*Togo*	*A.E.F.*	*Madagascar*
1895	86.5	76.7	—	50.3	—	—	—	42.2
1905	75.1	60.2	—	60.2	—	—	—	54.6
1913	67.7	45.6	51.9	60.8	—	—	—	51.9
1920	71.5	66.6	62.4	82.9	—	—	—	83.1
1926	81.4	53.9	44.3	62.9	—	—	—	83.9
1925	—	—	—	62.0	36.6	46.4	23.0	—
1928	71.1	48.8	35.3	—	—	—	—	46.1
1929	—	—	—	57.0	38.0	56.8	35.0	—
1935	85.6	54.9	46.3	80.0	62.0	59.0	75.7	71.4
1938	83.3	71.2	46.5	82.0	56.4	67.5	72.0	78.1
1939	82.5	62.2	39.7	85.3	63.4	73.0	74.3	76.2
1945	49.8	60.5	44.4	56.0	66.1	63.2	47.2	52.6
1947	82.8	52.2	63.6	73.2	67.8	62.6	71.8	72.0
1949	76.2	47.3	49.7	78.5	77.2	79.0	76.0	80.1

(*Continued*)

TABLE 2—*Continued*

3. *Share of France in Trade of Overseas Countries, 1959 and 1963*

	Percentage 1959	*Imports: from France: 1963*	*Percentage 1959*	*Exports: to France: 1963*
Algeria	83	75	82	74
Morocco	47	43	45	41
Tunisia	66	48	51	50
Ivory Coast	58	66	51	47
Dahomey	63	62	76	71
Upper Volta	75	50	16	27
Mali	(68)	35	(23)	21
Mauritania	(81)	68	(15)	41
Niger	64	52	85	71
Senegal	(66)	63	(76)	86
Togo	47	33	76	52
Central African Republique	62	60	76	47
Congo-Brazzaville	63	61	29	16
Gabon	64	60	55	50
Chad	55	53	73	53
Cameroons	61	57	53	57
Madagascar	72	74	57	52
Comoros	43	54	51	46

Note: The figures in parentheses are 1961 percentages.

Sources: For parts 1 and 2: 1895–1926, Southworth, Table III; 1925–38, League of Nations, *The Network of World Trade,* and Jean-Jacques Poquin, *Les Relations économiques extérieures des pays d'Afrique Noire et l'Union Française, 1925–1955,* pp. 275, 277, 279, 281; 1939–49, Bloch-Lainé, pp. 351, 355. For part 3: Teresa Hayter, *French Aid,* p. 60.

TABLE 3

BALANCE OF PAYMENTS BETWEEN FRANCE AND THE OVERSEAS COUNTRIES OF THE FRANC ZONE
(In million francs)

	1952	*1953*	*1954*	*1955*	*1956*	*1957*	*1958*	*1959*	*1960*	*1961*	*1962*	*1963*	*1964*
1. Public transfers (balance)	*2,875*	*2,546*	*2,738*	*3,525*	*5,267*	*5,975*	*6,237*	*6,710*	*7,557*	*8,902*	*9,348*	*4,438*	*3,308*
2. Private transfers (balance) of which:	2,578	2,414	2,498	2,946	5,091	4,884	5,758	6,823	8,103	9,139	9,544	4,696	3,554
Trade balance with the overseas countries	2,417	1,762	1,723	1,924	1,836	2,492	2,963	4,080	4,224	2,992	935	1,620	1,396
Counterpart of foreign exchange transactions on the Paris market	23	119	*112*	*7*	*323*	513	401	*296*	257	*318*	*531*	*651*	*1,289*
Invisible operations	138	533	887	1,029	2,932	1,879	2,394	3,039	3,662	6,465	9,140	3,727	3,447
3. General balance	*297*	*132*	*240*	*579*	*176*	*1,091*	*479*	113	546	237	196	258	246

Note: Figures in italics indicate an outflow from France, figures in roman are inflows to France.
Source: Hayter, p. 57, compiled from *Comité Monétaire de la Zone Franc* annual reports.

TABLE 4

Relative Importance of British Africa for United Kingdom Overseas Trade

1. As a Market for U.K. Exports

Date	(1) Total U.K. Exports (£000)	(2) Percentage of Exports to Empire/Commonwealth	(3) Total Exports to British Africa (£000)	(4) Percentage of Exports to British Africa
1900	416,524	32.4	20,681	5.0
1905	492,375	34.4	24,701	5.0
1910	573,087	34.2	33,230	5.8
1914	537,481	39.8	33,362	6.2
1920	459,296	34.3	101,785	22.2
1928	556,526	42.5	63,173	11.3
1933	363,159	41.3	37,777	10.4
1937	521,000	48.4	69,154	13.3
1947	1,138,276	52.7	150,435	13.2
1950	2,174,000	52.1	272,905	12.5
1956	3,172,000	49.2	406,278	12.8
1962	3,949,000	37.5	381,791	9.7
1966	5,236,000	33.3	463,461 [a]	8.8

2. As a Source of U.K. Imports

Date	(1) Total U.K. Imports (£000)	(2) Percentage of Imports from Empire/Commonwealth	(3) Total Imports from British Africa (£000)	(4) Percentage of Imports from British Africa
1900	617,491	21.0	8,768	1.4
1905	656,620	22.6	35,672	5.4
1910	686,980	25.1	55,402	8.1
1914	691,660	26.9	60,519	8.7
1920	671,615	25.3	90,936	13.5
1928	878,510	27.5	40,617	4.6
1933	825,719	35.0	18,655	2.2
1937	1,028,000	39.4	39,238	3.8
1947	1,794,540	45.2	113,749	6.3
1950	2,609,000	44.4	325,323	12.5
1956	3,886,000	47.1	381,159	9.8

TABLE 4—*Continued*

2. *As a Source of U.K. Imports*

Date	(1) *Total U.K. Imports (£000)*	(2) *Percentage of Imports from Empire/Commonwealth*	(3) *Total Imports from British Africa (£000)*	(4) *Percentage of Imports from British Africa*
1962	4,487,000	36.0	387,863	8.6
1966	5,954,000	33.3	475,118 [a]	8.0

a. Excluding Rhodesia.

Sources: Cols. (1) and (2), W. Schlote, *British Overseas Trade* (Oxford, 1952), to 1933; thereafter Commonwealth Economic Committee, *Commonwealth Trade 1950 to 57* (London, 1959) and Commonwealth Secretariat, *Commonwealth Trade, 1966* (London, 1967). Col. (3), *Statistical Abstract for the British Empire* [Commonwealth] (London), Nos. 5, 51, 57, 70, 71, 81.

TABLE 5

Relative Importance of the United Kingdom for British African Overseas Trade

1. *Origins of Imports into British Africa*

a. *South Africa* (including the Rhodesias to 1937, thereafter the Union of South Africa only)

	From U.K. (£000)	*Total (£000)*	*Percentage from U.K.*
1900	17,232	26,373	65.3
1905	20,165	35,017	57.6
1910	24,724	40,105	61.6
1914	22,946	39,372	58.3
1920	62,780	111,667	56.2
1928	39,513	88,463	44.7
1933	27,518	55,503	49.6
1937	49,456	115,753	42.7
1947	93,919	299,703	31.3
1950	126,625	306,870	41.3
1956	156,518	494,884	31.6
1962	155,567	512,916	30.3

(*Continued*)

TABLE 5—(*Continued*)

b. *Nyasaland and the Rhodesias* (Nyasaland only to 1937, thereafter with the Rhodesias)

	From U.K. (£000)	*Total* (£000)	*Percentage from U.K.*
1900	156	156	100.0
1905	182	253	71.9
1910	169	230	73.5
1914	156	203	76.8
1920	335	517	64.8
1928	375	906	41.4
1933	341	629	54.2
1937	313	747	41.9
1947	14,260	47,671	29.9
1950	41,809	93,014	44.9
1956	65,239	159,266	41.0
1962	47,334	142,995	33.1

c. *British East Africa* (Kenya, Uganda, Zanzibar, Somaliland to 1937, and Tanganyika from 1947)

	From U.K. (£000)	*Total* (£000)	*Percentage from U.K.*
1900	224	844	26.5
1905	463	1,162	39.8
1910	531	1,823	29.1
1914	775	3,687	21.0
1920	3,976	12,905	30.8
1928	4,781	12,381	38.6
1933	1,998	5,893	33.9
1937	3,912	11,409	34.3
1947	14,196	47,861	29.7
1950	39,963	74,948	53.3
1956	60,036	139,866	42.9
1962	49,062	140,804	34.8

TABLE 5—(*Continued*)

d. *British West Africa* (Nigeria, Gold Coast, Sierra Leone, Gambia)

	From U.K. (*£000*)	*Total* (*£000*)	*Percentage from U.K.*
1900	3,069	4,071	75.4
1905	3,891	5,470	71.1
1910	7,806	11,039	70.7
1914	9,485	13,451	70.5
1920	34,694	43,773	79.2
1928	18,504	29,858	62.0
1933	7,920	12,688	62.4
1937	15,473	29,328	52.7
1947	28,060	60,553	46.3
1950	64,508	119,514	54.0
1956	124,485	268,369	46.4
1962	129,828	357,009	36.4

e. *All British Africa*

	From U.K. (*£000*)	*Total* (*£000*)	*Percentage from U.K.*
1900	20,681	31,444	65.8
1905	24,701	41,902	58.9
1910	33,230	53,197	62.5
1914	33,362	56,713	58.8
1920	101,785	168,862	60.3
1928	63,173	131,608	48.0
1933	37,777	74,713	50.6
1937	69,154	157,237	44.0
1947	150,435	455,788	33.0
1950	272,905	594,346	45.9
1956	406,278	1,062,385	38.2
1962	381,791	1,153,724	33.1

(*Continued*)

TABLE 5—(*Continued*)

2. *Destination of Exports from British Africa*

a. *South Africa* (including the Rhodesias to 1937, thereafter the Union of South Africa only)

	To U.K. (£000)	*Total* (£000)	*Percentage to U.K.*
1900	7,053 [a]	9,273 [b]	76.0
1905	32,791 [a]	35,759 [c]	91.7
1910	50,193 [d]	55,429	90.5
1914	51,619	63,061	81.8
1920	63,062	89,924	70.1
1928	25,283	51,608	49.0
1933	10,691	28,463	37.6
1937	22,452	55,476	40.5
1947	26,767	99,635	26.9
1950	64,783	215,622	30.0
1956	127,877	363,918	35.1
1962	145,410	432,224	33.6

b. *Nyasaland and the Rhodesias* (Nyasaland only to 1937, thereafter with the Rhodesias)

	To U.K. (£000)	*Total* (£000)	*Percentage to U.K.*
1900	38	39	97.4
1905	40	87	46.0
1910	146	190	76.8
1914	162	235	68.9
1920	616	748	82.3
1928	672	676	99.4
1933	500	514	97.3
1937	821	887	92.5
1947	22,770	43,049	52.9
1950	43,294	96,885	44.7
1956	105,872	181,748	58.2
1962	87,758	209,516	41.9

TABLE 5—(*Continued*)

c. *British East Africa* (Uganda, Kenya, Zanzibar, Somaliland to 1937, and Tanganyika from 1947)

	To U.K. (*£000*)	*Total* (*£000*)	*Percentage to U.K.*
1900	17 [e]	435	3.9
1905	39	645	6.0
1910	421	2,313	18.2
1914	679	1,932	35.1
1920	3,385	9,127	37.0
1928	3,119	8,214	38.0
1933	2,034	6,407	31.7
1937	2,079	10,025	20.7
1947	11,191	38,641	29.0
1950	25,505	75,800	33.6
1956	30,875	123,538	25.0
1962	36,765	139,658	26.3

d. *British West Africa* (Nigeria, Gold Coast, Sierra Leone, Gambia)

	To U.K. (*£000*)	*Total* (*£000*)	*Percentage to U.K.*
1900	1,660	3,549	46.8
1905	2,802	5,340	52.5
1910	4,642	9,787	47.4
1914	8,059	13,729	58.7
1920	24,873	34,697	71.7
1928	11,543	32,593	35.4
1933	5,430	15,594	34.8
1937	13,886	34,308	40.5
1947	53,021	78,007	68.0
1950	101,741	168,190	60.5
1956	116,535	228,445	51.0
1962	108,697	293,028	37.1

(*Continued*)

TABLE 5—(*Continued*)

e. *All British Africa*

	To U.K. (£000)	*Total* (£000)	*Percentage to U.K.*
1900	8,768	13,296	65.9
1905	35,672	41,831	85.3
1910	55,402	67,719	81.8
1914	60,519	78,957	76.6
1920	90,936	134,496	67.6
1928	40,617	93,091	43.6
1933	18,655	50,978	36.6
1937	39,238	100,696	39.0
1947	113,749	259,332	43.9
1950	325,323	556,497	58.4
1956	381,159	897,649	42.5
1962	387,863	1,074,426	36.1

a. Cape and Natal only.

b. Cape, Natal, and Basutoland only.

c. Excludes Northern Rhodesia and Bechuanaland.

d. Excludes Northern Rhodesia.

e. Excludes Somaliland and Uganda, as data are too incomplete to be significant.

Source: Statistical Abstract for the British Empire [*Commonwealth*], Nos. 5, 51, 57, 70, 71, 81.

TABLE 6

Public Loans Raised by French African Territories with Metropolitan Guarantees

'000 Francs	Before 1914 Current Francs	Before 1914 Revalued in 1955 Francs[a]	From 1919 to 1930 Current Francs	From 1919 to 1930 Revalued in 1955 Francs[a]	From 1931 to 1939 Current Francs	From 1931 to 1939 Revalued in 1955 Francs[a]
North Africa						
Algeria	200	33,600	890	31,150	3,316	116,060
Tunisia	339	56,952	255	8,925	263	9,205
Morocco	74	12,432	1,345	47,075	2,050	71,750
Total	613	102,984	2,490	87,150	5,629	197,015
Sub-Saharan Africa						
French West Africa	176	29,568	100	3,500	3,120	109,200
French Equatorial Africa	10	1,680	393	13,755	1,513	52,955
Madagascar	90	15,120			752	26,320
The Cameroons					25	875
Togo					73	2,555
Somali					44	1,540
Total	276	46,368	493	17,255	5,527	193,445
Total All French Africa	889	149,352	2,983	104,405	11,156	390,460

a. Based on an average between the wholesale and retail price indexes in Paris, the average conversion coefficients applied are: for loans before 1914, 168; for loans authorized after 1914, 35.

Source: Bloch-Lainé, p. 109.

TABLE 7

INVESTMENTS IN A.O.F., A.E.F., THE CAMEROONS, AND TOGO 1900–40 [a]

Type of Activity	*Investments by Companies*	*Investments by Individuals*	*Total Investments*	*By type (or group of types) of Investment*	
	'000 francs (1940)				
Trade	8,751,962	1,752,392	10,514,354	39%	48.5%
Real estate companies	814,953	81,495	896,448	3.5%	
Banks	1,556,732		1,556,732	6%	
Industries	2,176,801	435,460	2,612,161	9.6%	17.1%
Mines	1,860,304	186,030	2,046,334	7.5%	
Transport	879,150	87,915	967,065	3.6%	3.6%
Plantations	2,451,848	2,451,848	4,903,696	18%	30.8%
Stock farming	71,450	14,290	85,740	0.3%	
Forests	1,933,236	1,449,927	3,383,163	12.5%	
Total of private investments	20,506,436	6,459,357	26,965,693	100%	
Public investments (loans)	7,033,014	—	7,033,014		
Grand Total	27,539,450	6,459,357	33,998,707		

a. Drawn up by the minister of colonies in 1943 from published company balance sheets and replies to a questionnaire.

Source: Jean Suret-Canale, *Afrique noire: l'ère Coloniale* (Paris, 1964), p. 207.

TABLE 8

THE AMOUNT OF THE CAPITAL INVESTED IN AFRICA FROM ABROAD BY INDIVIDUAL TERRITORIES, 1870–1936

	Listed Capital			*Non-Listed Capital*		*Total Capital*
	Public Listed Capital	*Private Listed Capital*	*Total Listed Capital*	*Estimated Percentage to Total Listed Capital*	*Amount*	*Listed + Non-Listed*
a. *British Territories*						
	(£000)	*(£000)*	*(£000)*	*%*	*(£000)*	*(£000)*
Union of S. Africa	224,089	250,835	475,470	10	47,547	523,017
Basutoland and Swaziland	546					
South-West Africa	21,557	7,228	28,785	10	2,879	31,664
Bechuanaland	886	53,484	93,094	10	9,309	102,403
Southern Rhodesia	35,993					
Northern Rhodesia	2,731					
Total	285,802	311,547	597,349	—	59,735	657,084
Nigeria	34,721	36,790	71,511	5	3,576	75,087
Gold Coast	13,462	20,160	33,622	5	1,681	35,303
Sierra Leone	2,454	750	3,204	5	160	3,364
Gambia	234		234	5	12	246
Sundry West African Issues	—	2,730	2,730	—	—	2,730
Total West Africa	50,871	60,430	111,301	—	5,429	116,730
Anglo-Egyptian Sudan	36,143	5,145	41,288	5	2,064	43,352
British Somaliland	2,840	—	2,840	5	142	2,982
Kenya and Uganda	31,542	8,583	40,125	15	6,019	46,144
Tanganyika	31,211	15,841	47,181	10	4,718	51,899
Zanzibar	129					
Nyasaland	10,298	1,000	11,298	7.5	848	12,146
Total	112,163	30,569	142,732	—	13,791	156,523
Miscellaneous	—	10,970	10,970	—	—	10,970
Total all British Territories	448,836	413,516	862,352	—	74,955	941,307
b. *French Territories*						
French Equatorial Africa	15,248	5,000	20,248	5	1,012	21,260
French West Africa	16,477	12,500	28,977	5	1,449	30,426
Togo and the Cameroons	11,306	6,431	17,737	5	887	18,624
Total French	43,031	23,931	66,962	—	3,348	70,310

Source: S. Herbert Frankel, *Capital Investment in Africa* (London, 1938), pp. 158–59.

TABLE 9

Summary Percentages of Capital, Trade, Exports, Area, and Population in Sub-Saharan Africa, 1936

	Capital Invested in Each African Territory as Percentage of Total Capital Invested in Africa	*Trade of Each African Territory as Percentage of Total Trade of Africa*		*Domestic Exports of Each African Territory as Percentage of Total Domestic Exports of Africa*		*Area of Each African Territory as Percentage of Total Area of Africa*	*White Population of Each African Territory as Percentage of Total White Population of Africa*	*Total Population of Each African Territory as Percentage of Total Population of Africa*
		1928	*1935*	*1928*	*1935*			
All British Territories	77.05	83.42	84.76	85.65	85.04	43.68	96.02	57.71
All Non-British Territories	22.95	16.58	15.24	14.35	14.96	56.32	3.78	42.29
All British Territories excluding the Union of South Africa and South-West Africa	34.24	34.28	28.83	33.50	28.78	33.66	5.19	48.75
Union of South Africa	42.81	47.38	54.69	50.29	54.87	5.95	89.51	8.61
Southern Rhodesia, Northern Rhodesia, Bechuanaland	8.38	4.81	6.74	4.16	7.15	8.94	2.99	2.91
British West Africa	9.56	18.08	12.43	18.80	12.53	5.66	.38	24.29
British East Africa	12.81	11.39	9.66	10.54	9.10	22.48	1.63	19.72
French West Africa	2.49	5.95	5.87	5.22	5.28	22.88	.85	14.63
French Equatorial Africa	1.74	.87	1.48	.68	1.32	10.98	.19	3.37
All French Territories	5.76	8.08	8.34	7.01	7.62	34.54	1.15	21.08

Source: Frankel, pp. 202–03.

TABLE 10

Total Overseas Capital per Head of the Population of Each African Territory, 1936

	Total Capital Invested (£000)	*Estimated Total Population (000,000)*	*Capital per Head of the Population (£)*
Union of South Africa South-West Africa	554,681	9.9	55.8
Northern Rhodesia Southern Rhodesia	102,403	2.7	38.4
Nigeria	75,087	19.1	3.9
British West Africa	116,730	24.4	4.8
Anglo-Egyptian Sudan	43,352	5.8	—
Kenya and Uganda	46,144	6.7	6.8
Total Kenya, Uganda, Tanganyika, and Nyasaland	110,189	13.5	8.1
French West Africa	30,426	14.7	2.1
French Equatorial Africa Togo and the Cameroons	39,884	6.5	6.1
Total French Colonies	70,310	21.2	3.3
Belgian Congo	143,337	11.0	13.0
Angola and Mozambique	66,732	6.8	9.8

Source: Frankel, p. 170.

TABLE 11

TOTAL BRITISH DIRECT INVESTMENT OVERSEAS, 1962
(excluding oil, insurance, and banks)

Area		*Value (£m)* [a]
North America		1,333.1
Latin America		206.4
Western Europe		474.4
Other nonsterling areas		103.0
Overseas sterling areas		2,379.8
Of which:		
South Africa	319.6	
Central Africa	125.6	
Nigeria	102.2	
Sierra Leone	22.0	
Ghana	68.0	
Kenya	22.6	
Uganda and other East Africa	30.0 [b]	
Tanzania	2.0 [b]	
Other British Africa	1.0 [b]	
	693.0	
Total		4,496.7

a. Calculated at book values (total net asset value plus depreciation provision), and therefore substantially below replacement value. Only companies registered in the U.K. are included. Since many South African companies were locally registered, the actual British private investment there (and elsewhere) is undervalued.

b. Excluding depreciation provision, which was not stated.

Source: Board of Trade Journal, 187 (July–December 1964), 293, and *189* (July–December 1965), 230.

TABLE 12

The Growing Trade of British Africa

1. *Net Tonnage of Vessels Entered in the Foreign Trade, 1901 and 1946*

Country	*All Nationalities*		*British*			
	1901	*1946*	*1901*	*%*	*1946*	*%*
British East Africa	65,478	2,886,000	13,453	20.5	2,361,000	81.8
British West Africa	1,097,687	7,020,000	603,611	54.9	5,301,000	75.5
British South Africa	1,370,068	5,882,000	872,599	63.7	3,714,000	63.1

2. *Value of Exports in Current Prices, 1902–60* (*£000*)

Country	*1902*	*1913*	*1921*	*1938*	*1947*	*1960*
South Africa	1,548 [a]	66,659.5	62,381	28,074	99,635	383,968
Nyasaland	6	248	427	960	2,709	205,870 (Nyasaland and The Rhodesias combined)
The Rhodesias	—	3,737	5,380	14,850	37,075	
British East Africa [b]	20	2,116	5,022	8,473	21,843	86,708
Nigeria	1,337	7,352	9,690	9,286	37,052	164,818
Gold Coast	381	5,427	6,942	6,235	16,586	104,893
Sierra Leone	207	1,731	1,625	2,136	3,732	26,139
Gambia	228	867	793	256	1,100	2,760
Total	3,727	88,137.5	92,260	70,270	219,738	975,162

a. Including the Rhodesias.

b. Uganda, Kenya, and Zanzibar.

Source: Statistical Abstract for the British Empire [*Commonwealth*], Nos. 5, 51, 57, 70, 71, 81.

TABLE 13

The Growing Trade of French Africa

1. *Value of Exports (at current prices) ($m. U.S.)*

	1902	*1913*	*1928*	*1938*	*1948*	*1953*
Algeria	58.7	93.9	280.0	161.2	420.4	396.6
Tunisia	7.9	34.4	82.0	38.7	61.0	103.6
Morocco	—	7.5	85.0	43.2	174.5	268.0
A.O.F. (incl. Togo)	13.1	29.2	88.0	40.5	151.9	267.2
A.E.F.	1.6 (Congo)	—	{ 20.0	7.5	54.7	57.3
Cameroons	—	—		7.2	35.9	74.8
Madagascar	1.8	9.4	—	23.5	48.6	84.7

2. *The Volume of Exports from French West Africa, French East Africa, the Cameroons, and Togo, 1925–55* (in tons)

Period	*A.O.F.*	*A.E.F.*	*Cameroons*	*Togo*
1925–29	717,723	331,019	97,932	26,660
1930–34	719,383	335,823	105,937	26,533
1935–39	1,064,290	361,444	152,647	52,134
1946–50	701,573	267,681	180,386	31,297
1951–55	1,620,583	519,818	264,915	45,988

Sources: For part 1: 1902 and 1913: Southworth, Table IV, and Suret-Canale, p. 60; 1928: League of Nations, *The Network of World Trade.* 1938, 1948, 1953: O.E.E.C., *Foreign Trade Statistical Bulletin,* Series 1, 1928, 1937–53 (Paris, 1954). For part 2: Poquin, p. 13.

TABLE 14

Population Growth in Colonial Africa

1. *Population of British African Territories, 1901 and 1961*

	1901		*1961*
South Africa	4,992,188		16,122,000
Swaziland	85,491		266,000
Basutoland	348,848		697,000
Bechuanaland	120,776		288,000
The Rhodesias	1,250,000	1,956,000	8,510,000
Nyasaland	706,000		
Uganda	4,500,000		6,845,000
Kenya and Zanzibar	2,960,000		7,602,000
Nigeria	13,606,093		35,752,000
Gold Coast	1,486,433		6,943,000
Sierra Leone	1,027,000		2,450,000
Gambia	90,354		267,000

2. *Population of French African Territories*

	1911 (unless otherwise indicated)		*1959*
Algeria	5,563,800		10,930,000
Tunisia	1,939,087		3,935,000
Morocco	3,533,786	(1921)	10,550,000
Madagascar	2,966,000	(1909)	5,287,000
French West Africa	11,343,000		20,884,000
French Equatorial Africa	2,851,000	(1921)	5,000,000
The Cameroons	2,110,000	(1924)	3,225,000
Togo	731,000	(1922)	1,442,000

Sources: For part 1: *Statistical Abstract for the British Empire,* No. 5 (1909); *Statistical Abstract for the Commonwealth and the Sterling Area,* No. 83 (1962). For part 2: UNO, *Demographic Yearbook, 1948, 1960* (New York, 1949, 1960).

TABLE 15

COMMUNICATIONS

1. *Railways in British Africa, 1946*

Country	*Miles*
South Africa (incl. South-West Africa)	13,483
Nigeria	1,903
Gold Coast	500
Sierra Leone	311
Rhodesian System [a]	2,514
Tanganyika	1,355
Kenya and Uganda	1,625
Nyasaland	316
Total	22,007

2. *Railways in French Africa*

Country	*Kilometers*	*Date*
French West Africa	3,878	1946
French Equatorial Africa	511	1960
Algeria	4,491	1955
Tunisia	938	1955
Morocco	1,612	1956
Madagascar	210	1955
Total	11,540	

a. Including some mileage in South Africa and Bechuanaland.

Sources: For part 1: *Statistical Abstract for the British Commonwealth,* No. 70 (1950). For part 2: for French West Africa, Thompson and Adolf, *French West Africa* (London, 1958), p. 295; for French Equatorial Africa and Madagascar, Thompson and Adloff, *The Emerging States of French Equatorial Africa* (Stanford, 1960), p. 142; for Algeria, Tunisia, and Morocco, the *Encyclopaedia Britannica,* 1964 ed.

19. *African Education in a Colonial Context: French and British Styles*

PROSSER GIFFORD AND TIMOTHY C. WEISKEL

Few aspects of colonial policy seem in retrospect so dated in intent, so parochial in scope, and so contradictory in result as certain features of the colonial systems of education maintained in Africa by both the French and the British. Using the sharp edge of ideology, Abdou Moumouni wrote that colonial education was cut-rate, designed to secure subordinate officials by impoverishing their spiritual life and detaching them completely from their own people, and that it produced an anti-national, bureaucratic neo-bourgeoisie.[1] Julius Nyerere characteristically cast his criticism in gentler, more homespun speech: "Our young men and women must have an African-oriented education. That is an education which is not only given in Africa but also directed at meeting the present needs of Africa. For, while other people can aim at reaching the moon . . . our present plans must be directed at reaching the villages."[2] At a later time he enumerated the basic elements in the system of education derived from colonial Tanganyika, which encouraged in students "attitudes of inequality, intellectual arrogance and intense individualism."[3] The system was elitist; it divorced its participants from their society, overstressed book learning, and removed from productive work some of the country's healthiest and strongest young men and women.[4]

In seeking to understand the interplay between colonial conditions and the development of formal education in French and British African territories, we will emphasize both the motivating ideas and the varying practices of those concerned with education during the colonial years. We will try to thresh the seminal matter from the husks of dry controversy. For despite many welcome changes in teachers and

1. Abdou Moumouni, *Education in Africa* (New York, 1968), pp. 46–62.

2. Julius K. Nyerere, *Freedom and Unity* (London, 1967), pp. 130–31.

3. Julius K. Nyerere, "Education for Self-Reliance," in *Freedom and Socialism* (Dares Salaam, 1968), p. 275.

4. Ibid., pp. 275–78. For a critique, see Philip Foster, "Education for self reliance," in R. Jolly, ed., *Education in Africa* (Nairobi, 1969), pp. 81–101.

subjects taught, in goals and structure, there remains a discouraging, almost desperate continuity between some of the current debates over educational strategy in Africa and those which filled colonial committee rooms and reports. What, for instance, should be the relationship between the educational and agricultural sectors of the society?

> It is interesting to recall that in 1897 a committee of the Privy Council in London sat to consider the form of education desirable in rural Africa, and decided that one of the main requirements was for schools that would prepare students for a more effective life on the land. The Phelps Stokes Commission that sat between 1922–26 came to a similar conclusion. But all along parents thought otherwise, and they still do. Countries like Nigeria may make their living off the land, but the individuals who make the best living are those who get off the land. The experience of independent Nigeria confirms that of the colonial governments—primary education alone cannot change the social pattern, the social pattern determines the shape of education. Education will remain an urban-orientated activity until work on the land is sufficiently attractive, prestige-conferring and rewarding to make it a desired goal for an intelligent young man.[5]

One reason for the apparent confirmation of colonial experience is that the colonial skeleton still gives shape to the structure of Nigerian education, although it has grown greatly in size. In addition, educational reward is and must be tied to the job structure within the society. Although colonial requirements setting academic standards for entry to certain jobs can and have been altered, the capacity of the society at large to absorb and use highly-trained manpower is much less tractable. A marked acceleration of the numbers graduating from universities cannot of itself alter the rate at which scientists, engineers, and technicians can raise the technological level of a country. The result of an enlarged group of graduates may simply be migration, or "brain drain." "Rapidly expanding university systems in many countries have produced high-level manpower in much larger quantity than was thought possible even a decade ago. . . . It has become evident that it is easier to produce high-level manpower than bring

5. "Does 'Universal' Education Work in Nigeria?" *West Africa*, February 24, 1968, pp. 225–26, reprinted in C. Legum and J. Drysdale, *Africa Contemporary Record, 1968–69* (London, 1969), pp. 877–79.

into being the organization—and to marshal the resources—to utilize it." [6]

The relationship between higher education and the society's capacity to absorb graduates has long been a concern in colonial Africa. When Cromer wrote in 1902 that he wished to restrict the enrollment of Egyptians in the Westernized government schools to those who could be absorbed by the economy and the administration, he was worried by the experience of Indian universities and the political explosiveness of a group of dissatisfied intellectuals.[7] Cromer's paternalism and his Anglocentric superiority now seem offensive, but the problem with which he struggled remains disturbingly real and highly charged with emotion. Is it possible to reconcile the great aspirations for individual betterment through enlarged educational opportunity with the manpower needs and the fiscal health of a developing nation?

The debate is unending between those who would free intelligence to serve the ends it defines and those who would harness intelligence to serve ends already defined by the society. Both sides were represented—sporadically and inconsistently—in the educational controversies of French and British Africa. And advocates of both elicited sympathetic responses. In Egypt, at the turn of the century, Muhammad Abduh expressed his resentment of the British restriction of higher education to strictly professional preparation for the law, medicine, and engineering:

> The result is that we possess judges and lawyers, physicians and engineers more or less capable of exercising their professions; but amongst the educated classes one looks in vain for the investigator, the thinker, the philosopher, the scholar, the man in fact of open mind, fine spirit, generous sentiments, whose whole life is found devoted to the ideal.[8]

Rooted in the nineteenth-century liberal tradition, Abduh sought a deep and rigorous exposure to Western culture, seeing no contradiction between such knowledge and the future of a free Islamic Egypt.[9]

6. *Modernization and the Migration of Talent,* A Report from Education and World Affairs (New York, 1970), p. 37.

7. Robert L. Tignor, *Modernization and British Colonial Rule in Egypt, 1882–1914* (Princeton, 1966), pp. 322–23.

8. Ibid., p. 337.

9. For the relationships among national education, reformist Islam, and the adoption of European liberal ideas in the thought of Muhammad Abduh, see Charles C. Adams, *Islam and Modernism in Egypt* (London, 1933), pp. 68–82; Albert

He believed that the study of Western intellectual history could free men to see Western as well as Eastern inconsistencies. Real education would prove, he argued, incompatible with colonialism as well as inhospitable to much traditional lore.

We, like Abduh, can condemn the fear of free intelligence that informed the cautious temporizing in colonial education. We can assert the importance of African subject matter taught in accord with African priorities. But what should be the language of instruction? How can the experience of the primary school be made satisfying to those who do not proceed to secondary school? How can able teachers be kept in rural areas? Ought practical skills and applicable knowledge be stressed, rather than fundamental inquiry? How many students should go to universities? to which sorts of universities? These questions retain a pithy pertinence, and we will try to suggest the partial, often abortive answers attempted during the colonial period.

Ever since the publication in 1937 of *Africans Learn to be French,* [10] English-speaking observers of French Africa have felt comfortable in understanding French colonial education as a transplant of French metropolitan education into African soil. In the absence of any substantial historical studies to date on French African education, this point of view remains largely unchallenged.[11] Adhering to this inter-

---

Hourani, *Arabic Thought in the Liberal Age* (London, 1962), pp. 130–92; H.A.R. Gibb, *Modern Trends in Islam* (Chicago, 1947), pp. 33–47; Gibb, "Studies in Contemporary Arabic Literature," reprinted in *Studies in the Civilization of Islam* (Boston, 1962), pp. 245–319; Nadan Safran, *Egypt in Search of Political Community* (Cambridge, Mass., 1961), pp. 62–84; J. M. Ahmed, *The Intellectual Origins of Egyptian Nationalism* (Oxford, 1960), pp. 35–57; and J. N. D. Anderson, "Law Reform in Egypt: 1850–1950," in P. M. Holt, ed., *Political and Social Change in Modern Egypt* (London, 1968), pp. 209–30. For Abduh the conflict between European secular positivism and the principles of Islam gave a special, focused urgency to questions of educational content, morality, style, and authority.

10. W. Bryant Mumford and Major G. St. J. Orde-Brown, *Africans Learn To Be French: A Review of Educational Activities in the Seven Federated Colonies of French West Africa, Based upon a Tour of French West Africa and Algiers Undertaken in 1935* (London, 1936). In addition to containing evaluations by the authors of French educational efforts, the volume includes English translations of several policy statements by French officials themselves. The book has been out of print for several years, but a reprinting is expected to appear on the market shortly. It is hoped that new readers will not accept it as uncritically as the previous generation seems to have accepted the first edition of the work.

11. The only published scholarly study to date that refutes this point of view is a short article by Denise Bouche, " 'Autrefois, notre pays s'appelait la Gaule . . .'

pretation as a basic assumption, scholars have suggested ever since the interwar years that French educational policy in West Africa held unswervingly to the goal of assimilating African subjects into French cultural and political life.

Recent scholarship still reflects an uncritical acceptance of this interpretation. Guy de Lusignan, for example, in his *French-Speaking Africa Since Independence*, stated quite baldly:

> The French . . . naively convinced that their own system was perfect, dreamed of reshaping Africa on the model of France, and just as any little boy from Toulouse, Brittany or Flanders learned to say "Our forefathers, the Gauls . . . " so did the little African. . . . The French educational system, free, secular and republican, was to create black Frenchmen.[12]

Similarly Jerry Bolibaugh, an American scholar, characterized this approach in his study of educational development by concluding that "the history of French educational strategies for sub-Saharan Africa at the intentional or policy level reveals a remarkable consistency of purposes." [13] He further asserted that the turbulent debate in French colonial theory at the turn of the century did not alter French educational intentions: "shifts in the general colonial policy from assimilation to association had little effect upon the fundamental objectives of French educational strategies in sub-Saharan Africa." [14]

In reality, however, the debate over colonial policy at the turn of the century profoundly altered the aims of colonial education, and historical evidence indicates that the purposes reflected in the changing policies were far from consistent. Furthermore, during the period of colonial rule from 1890 to 1945, educational policy defined itself in specific opposition to the earlier doctrine of assimilation. It may well be true that Africans learned to be French, but this was not the funda-

---

Remarques sur l'adaptation de l'enseignement au Sénégal de 1817 à 1960," *Cahiers d'études africaines*, 8, no. 29 (1968), 110–22. In addition, an unpublished thesis by Timothy C. Weiskel entitled "Education and Colonial Rule in French West Africa, 1890–1945" (Yale University, Scholar of the House Program, 1969) challenges this assumption. This chapter draws heavily upon the research undertaken in Paris, Dakar, and Abidjan for the completion of the thesis.

12. Guy de Lusigan, *French-Speaking Africa Since Independence* (London, 1969), p. 47.

13. Jerry Bolibaugh and Paul Hanna, *French Educational Strategies for Sub-Saharan Africa: Their Intent, Derivation, and Development* (Stanford, Calif., 1964), p. 68.

14. Ibid., p. 73.

mental intent of the educational policy makers between 1903 and 1945. Indeed, educators and administrators alike attempted to frame policy during this period expressly to discourage such an outcome, and they were bewildered when attempts failed.[15]

A careful reading of the colonial documentation reveals that the French educational effort in West Africa from 1890 to 1945 was by no means a transplanted version of the metropolitan system. The structure, programs, and procedures which emerged were neither wholly French nor wholly African. Although educational policy formulation did remain exclusively a French prerogative, the terms of the policy decisions were not within the control of those alien administrators. Officials found themselves framing policy in response to colonial conditions which they could rarely anticipate, let alone direct. The French administrators recognized this at least implicitly, and by the end of the interwar years few had any illusions of being able to transfer metropolitan practices to the colonies. Robert Delavignette, a former administrator, expressed this realization when he wrote in 1947:

> The time has come when African principles are no longer intrinsically native, nor European methods purely metropolitan, but both are closely mingled and profoundly modified. A new fact has come into existence—an African world which has reacted to Europe and

15. The discussion of French policy in this chapter refers only to efforts in French West Africa—that is, in the territories under the former administrative designation of "Afrique Occidentale Française" (A.O.F.). French policy in the North and Equatorial African possessions as well as in Madagascar had many similarities with that in French West Africa, but there were in each of these cases important differences in timing and content. For example, missionaries played a central role in French Equatorial Africa (A.E.F.), where formal government policy did not emerge until the 1920s, and in North Africa the Muslim schools achieved far more importance than they ever did in French West Africa.

Those interested in French policy for Equatorial Africa should begin with Gerard Lucas's study, "Formal Education in the Congo-Brazzaville: A Study of Educational Policy and Practice," (Ph.D. diss., Stanford University, n.d.).

Finally, this chapter does not deal with Africans educated in the metropole, for in the few instances in which Africans studied directly in France between 1903 and 1945, they did so independently and usually in spite of French colonial education policy. The only exception to this was a brief period in the 1920s when a few selected graduates of the William Ponty School were given scholarships to Aix-en-Provence. This program, however, was discontinued as a matter of policy by 1930. For the most thorough examination yet undertaken of the African students in France during the colonial period, scholars can look forward to the publication of James Spiegler's "Aspects of Nationalist Thought among French-speaking West Africans, 1921–1939" (Ph.D. diss., Oxford University, 1968).

> which is creating a regime proper to itself. . . . Colonial institutions are determined by the evolution of the natives in a new African world, rather than by the theoretical conceptions of the home country.[16]

The evolution of education, then, is best understood not as a process of institutional transfer, but rather as a patterned series of decisions designed on the spot in response to the exigencies of the colonial situation.

There are three different phases in the history of the French presence in French West Africa.[17] The first is the precolonial phase, lasting until about 1890. During these years the influence of the French on the coast and in the interior was increased by means of informal empire, based largely upon the activities of a coastal commercial community and an energetic military contingent. The creation of the Ministry of the Colonies in 1894 signaled the beginning of the second phase, that of colonial rule. Extending until 1945, this period witnessed the creation of formal structures and procedures in colonial administration, finance, and education; and it is the phase which forms the subject matter for students of comparative colonialism. The postwar era of decolonization marked the final period of formal French presence. During this time the structures of colonial administration, finance, and education were reshaped for political independence in 1960. Although the second period is our central concern in studying French colonial rule, the two surrounding periods need to be placed in perspective as well. Misunderstandings of French educational policy have resulted most often from a failure to keep these three phases analytically separate; generalizations from information in one period or another have been extended to the history of French colonial education as a whole. Proceeding chronologically, we hoped to clarify some of these confusions.

The first phase of French presence can be understood in terms of

16. Robert Delavignette, *Freedom and Authority in French West Africa*, (London, 1950), p. 51. A vivid example of this fusion is the strike by African workers on the Dakar-Koulikoro railroad during 1947–48, as imaginatively recreated by Sembene Ousmane in *Les bouts de bois de Dieu* (Paris, 1960); the English translation by Francis Price is entitled *God's Bits of Wood* (New York, 1962).

17. These three phases correspond roughly to those distinguished by Michael Crowder in the introduction to his *West Africa Under Colonial Rule* (Evanston, Ill., 1968), p. 19.

two major developments: first, the growth of a coastal commercial community from 1815 on; and second, the thrust of imperial expansion into the interior, leading in the later decades of the nineteenth century to French participation in the European scramble for African territory. With the return of the Senegalese possessions to France in 1815 at the conclusion of the Napoleonic wars, France launched a brief and unsuccessful scheme of colonial settlement. The attempt was to encourage French emigrants to establish themselves along the coast in productive agricultural communities, cultivating indigo and cotton for export to France. In undertaking the venture the French government hoped to induce the African populations to follow suit and contribute in this fashion to the reconstruction of a vital commerce which might once again reach the profitable level of the former slave trade. The settlement scheme ultimately failed for a series of reasons, stemming from inaccurate assessments of agricultural potential, insufficient planning and financing, and difficulties in attracting French settlers. By the middle of the nineteenth century it became apparent to French officials that the best prospects for commerce lay in the revival of trading links to the interior, and the coastal commercial enclave of Saint-Louis undertook a series of retrenchments.

The optimism which accompanied attempts of the French government to foster profitable settlement was reflected as well in a positive educational program, although it too ended in disappointment. In 1816 the government established a school at Saint-Louis under the directorship of Jean Dard. This "Ecole Mutuelle de Saint-Louis" prospered in the early years of its operation, largely because Dard was willing both to learn and to teach in Wolof, the local language. The attempt at this stage seemed less an effort to imbue Africans with the elements of French culture than an effort to encourage the indigenous population to join the French in what was expected to be a mutually profitable venture.

As it became apparent that the settlement schemes were a failure, government interest in education waned. Dard himself left the colony in 1820, and although the school carried on under Dominique Daspres and then Baüyn de Perreuse until the late 1820s, it was subjected to increased criticism, especially in reference to the continued use of Wolof as the language of instruction. Throughout the 1830s the French government welcomed the increased educational activities of the missionary groups in Senegal, and by 1841, discouraged with the costly failure of the settlement efforts, the government cut its expenses even further by signing an agreement with the Frères de Ploermel, handing over the direction of education in the colony to Catholic instructors. Similarly, the instruction of girls was entrusted to the two orders of French nuns present in Senegal.[18]

In summary, then, in the first half of the nineteenth century the failure of the settlement scheme and the corresponding rejection of Dard's programs of Wolof instruction dampened French governmental interest in education. In retrenching to the position of a commercial enclave in an alien country rather than that of an expanding settlement community, the French were in a defensive position. Their continued security depended upon the indulgence of interior tribes and cooperative métis. In this context their educational efforts were designed to entice rather than to compel Africans into increasing participation in the exchange economy. Cultural superiority was assumed, particularly by the missionaries, but it was not aggressively asserted, for to do so would have offended African rulers in the interior whom the French could not afford to antagonize. The role of education in this period was perhaps best summarized by Anne Raffenel when she emphasized in 1856 that the school could be expanded as an agent of assimilation to minimize potential antagonisms between the French and the local populations: "That which matters above all else is to attack the antagonism which separates the two races . . . in a word to foster assimilation."[19] As used in this context, the concept of assimilation was understood to be a relatively passive process of incorporating cooperative Africans into the business of the commercial coastal communities. Nevertheless, in common with the more doctrinaire statements which were to emerge in the second half of the century, this early concept of assimilation affirmed that Africans both could and should be converted into Frenchmen.

The second chapter in the precolonial phase of the French presence begins with the administration of L. L. Faidherbe from 1854 to 1861. Faidherbe realized that without a substantial settler population, the continued security of the coastal commercial interests depended upon the relationships with political forces of the interior. Merchants in Saint-Louis urged the French government to reinforce their position

18. For a more detailed account of this period and specifically the shift from government to missionary education, see Georges Hardy, *L'enseignement au Sénégal de 1817–1854* (Paris, 1920). In addition, Joseph Gaucher's study, *Les débuts de l'enseignement en Afrique francophone: Jean Dard et l'école mutuelle de Saint-Louis du Sénégal* (Paris, 1968), provides a useful analysis and an admirable compilation of documents pertaining to the period.

19. A. Raffenel, *Nouveau voyage au pays des nègres* (Paris, 1856).

in trade with the interior, and through a series of skillful political maneuvers and successful military campaigns, Faidherbe was able to accomplish this.

In education, as in administration and politics, Faidherbe introduced significant innovations to accompany his efforts to ensure coastal security. Realizing that in the long run France's continued presence depended upon at least a partial accommodation with the Islamic rulers of the interior, Faidherbe was not anxious to extend missionary education. Nevertheless, he recognized the functional value of French training for the African leaders with whom he increasingly had to deal. To resolve the dilemma, Faidherbe resumed direct government interest in African education by creating a secular government school in Saint-Louis in 1855. The students at the school were to be the sons of chiefs and notables who had been brought back from Faidherbe's military campaigns and political negotiations in the interior. As a result it became known as the "School of Hostages" (L'Ecole des Otages). Its curriculum emphasized French language training, but beyond this Faidherbe tried to focus the study upon local conditions. By the end of his second term of administration in Senegal from 1863 to 1865, it was clear that Faidherbe considered education not the exclusive preserve of the Europeanized coastal community but an effective means of extending and preserving French influence among traditional hierarchies in the interior.

Faidherbe's military successors, Generals Joseph Gallièni and Louis Archinard, shared his attitude toward the strategic value of education, and following his example they continued to recruit students for the school in Saint-Louis from the sons of chiefs. In addition, as they marched further into the continent they created schools in the interior to train translators. Schools followed on the heels of conquest, and, since many of the initial instructors were in fact army officers, the discipline and procedures of early education in the interior were decidedly military in flavor.[20]

As the era of aggressive imperial expansion progressed, colonial educational issues became the cause célèbre of cultural chauvanist groups in the metropole such as the Alliance Française. Founded on July 21, 1868, this organization grouped together both government

20. For the role of the schools in the process of military expansion, see Denise Bouche, "Les écoles françaises au Soudan à l'époque de la conquête, 1884–1900," *Cahiers d'études africaines,* 6, no. 22 (1966), 228–67; also a contemporary article written by Pierre Foncin, "Les écoles françaises du Sénégal et du Soudan," *Revue internationale de l'enseignement,* 19 (April 15, 1890), 361–77.

officials and members of missionary and colonial societies to mobilize support for overseas education. The Alliance provided an explicit program of cultural imperialism to accompany the military and economic expansion in the late 1880s and 1890s, and in the western Sudan it soon provided annual allocations to finance the schools suffering from a lack of sufficient government money. Faced with the financial restrictions on colonial budgets, the government was content to leave the major portion of the task to private groups, providing occasional subsidies when they were most urgently needed. Once again the development of educational structures went from government initiative to private operation, and toward the end of the century the Alliance and Catholic missionary societies dominated educational efforts.

There is no doubt that the rhetoric of assimilation permeated virtually every educational program during this period. Missionaries, government officials, military officers, and enthusiastic "armchair imperialists" all shared a common faith in the emerging "greater France," and education was commonly believed to be the means through which alien territories could be assimilated into the expanding empire. By the end of the century assimilation had become a doctrine of cultural imperialism, generated to accompany rapid military expansion.

It would be a fundamental mistake, however, to conclude that assimilation became the governmental policy in the period of colonial rule that followed. Although the French government had provided sporadic financial assistance to educational efforts in Africa prior to 1890, there was no systematic means of regulating standards, no organized group of teaching personnel, and no standing budgetary allocations, much less a well-articulated policy. As the administrative apparatus of empire emerged after the creation of an autonomous Ministry of the Colonies in 1894, the beginnings of a formal educational policy took shape in response to two immediate problems.

The first problem was the need for subordinate administrative personnel on a scale previously unknown in West Africa. With the acquisition of extensive territory by military conquest, the French confronted the problem of imposing their control over the areas of the interior. The task required far more personnel than the French community alone could provide. Furthermore, even if the needed administrators could be recruited in France, the expense of hiring enough French personnel from the metropole was far greater than the meager colonial budgets could bear. The cheapest solution clearly was to train African personnel to undertake all but the top administrative tasks and to hire them on a much reduced salary scale. The existing schools in the coastal communities and the interior, dominated by the Alliance Française and the missions, might have been able to produce the increased number of trained Africans with only an incremental expansion of their facilities if the government had provided supplementary financial assistance to them. This alternative was swiftly eliminated, however, by a second problem: the radical break between church and state precipitated in metropolitan France by the Dreyfus affair.

Anticlerical sentiment in the French Third Republic had been evident ever since the 1880s, when republican leaders in France had succeeded in establishing lay instruction in public primary schools. The sentiment reached renewed heights as it became clear that the Catholic Church was implicated in the mistrial of Captain Dreyfus, a Jewish army officer who had been unjustly accused of treason. The crisis in metropolitan France had its repercussions in the colonies, and the era of cooperative arrangements between the French government and the missions in African education ended abruptly with a resolution passed by the French parliament on January 22, 1903, calling for the secularization of all Church-directed schools in West Africa.

Faced, then, with the growing need for personnel, and deprived of future missionary assistance in the task of training such personnel, the administration was forced to create its own schools and develop its first formal educational policy. In two ordinances dated November 24, 1903, Governor-General Ernest Roume outlined the structures and the procedures which were to form the basis for government policy in education for the next forty years.[21] These ordinances firmly established the four distinctive features of the French educational system in West Africa. First, all instruction was in the French language, reflecting the earlier enthusiasm of the Alliance Française for the extension of the mother tongue. Although many scholars have interpreted this insistence upon French language training as evidence of the assimilative concept of education which dominated much of nineteenth-century educational development, the other part of the

21. Governor-General Roume issued these decrees following the recommendations of the Lieutenant Governor of Sénégal, Camile Guy, contained in a report on education in West Africa presented to the Conseil Du Gouvernement in November 1903. The ordinances were published in the *Journal officiel du Sénégal et dépendances,* 152 (November 28, 1903), 678–81.

story is that the French language was retained as the medium of instruction primarily for practical reasons. In the absence of a single dominant language community throughout their possessions, the French could not use a local language to achieve the kind of universality of communication they desired.

The second feature of the new education policy was that it was free; no school fees were charged at any level. This policy partially paralleled the republican enthusiasm for the extension of free education in the metropole, and in addition it reflected a concern to eliminate all obstacles which might have discouraged African response to educational programs. Even minimal fees, it was thought, would inhibit African enrollment. Third, education was secular. Anticlericism had forced the termination of much of the missionary activity in education, and the educational ordinances were framed with no provision for support or endorsement of missionary education. And fourth, education was closely tied to the need for administrative personnel. The structures were expressly designed at all levels to facilitate French administration. Graduates of the "écoles de villages" would be the literate go-betweens needed by the local administrators to interpret to the natives; graduates of the "écoles régionales" (and, later, of the upper primary schools) could become subordinate clerks in each individual territory; and those who reached the federal schools in Dakar would emerge as teachers or "commis d'administration," able to assist the French administration throughout the federation.

The French in Dakar were anxious to avoid what they felt had been the mistakes of French education in other colonial areas, particularly in the French possessions in the West Indies. The feeling was that education modeled strictly upon French domestic patterns would be useless for the training of a subordinate African administrative personnel. Worse yet, it might be dangerous, for it would probably lead to the same kind of political dissension among the educated elite which was becoming the pattern in other colonial possessions. In 1866, positions on the municipal councils in the Senegalese Communes had become elective posts, and thereafter Europeans had been obliged to compete with the métis and African population for support from the electorate. Fearing the development of a politically volatile educated elite, the French commercial community opposed the rapid extension of European education.

In addition, government administrators began to doubt the efficacy of purely European institutions in the colonial context. Experience had taught government officers in the coastal towns as well as in the interior bush stations that no matter how well conceived policy had been in Paris, it needed to be substantially modified in Africa. The writings of Generals Joseph Simon Gallièni and Louis Hubert Lyautey on the necessity for pragmatic administrative procedures in the colonies encouraged other administrators to affirm what they knew from their own experience to be true. In the realm of general colonial theory, administrators began to emphasize the need to adjust procedures and regulations to local exigencies. In educational efforts as well, immediate problems called for pragmatic solutions, and "l'adaptation" soon replaced "l'assimilation" as the guiding principle for educational programs.

The case for adapted education in West Africa received support in Paris from the proponents of new social and pedagogical theories. The writings of Gustave Le Bon and Léopold de Saussure were particularly influential in this respect. In his major theoretical piece, *Les lois psychologiques de l'évolution des peuples,* Le Bon reflected the predominant racial theories of the late nineteenth century. He asserted that it would be fruitless to assimilate Africans to French civilization because the racial characteristics of the Africans made them incapable of even the simple thoughts of ordinary Europeans:

> One easily makes a school graduate or a lawyer of a Negro or of a Japanese; but one only gives him a simple veneer, altogether superficial, without acting on his mental constitution, and without his knowing how to take any part in it. That which no instruction can give him, because only heredity creates them, are the forms of thought, the logic, and especially the character of Western man. This Negro or this Japanese will accumulate all the diplomas possible without ever arriving at the level of an ordinary European.[22]

Léopold de Saussure applied many of Le Bon's theories directly to colonial conditions in *Le psychologie de la colonisation française dans ses rapports avec les sociétés indigènes.*[23] This book and the works of Le Bon were well circulated in France around the turn of the century, and the architects of colonial educational policy began to see in these theories a "scientific" justification for adapting education in the colonies to the "native mentality." In effect, they made a virtue out of what had already become a necessity in West Africa for other reasons.

22. Gustave Le Bon, *Les lois psychologiques de l'évolution des peuples* (Paris, 1894), p. 35.

23. Léopold de Saussure, *La psychologie de la colonisation française dans ses rapports avec les sociétés indigènes* (Paris, 1899).

By the turn of the century the Ministry of the Colonies officially embraced these theories. Armed with what it regarded as intellectually respectable justifications, the Ministry boldly cast aside the earlier doctrines of assimilation and sought a new approach to colonial educational policy. In a publication prepared for the Colonial Exposition in 1900 on behalf of the Ministry of the Colonies, Henri Froidevaux stated the new position emphatically:

> Without any doubt, this instruction should not be given everywhere, in the same fashion. . . . There cannot and there should not be any assimilation here (in the former sense of the word) between the programs elaborated for usage of our indigenous peoples and those that are applied in the metropole; it is necessary to reflect maturely, and to study long and carefully the ideas and the needs of the indigenous peoples of the country before one would fall back into the former errors, and into the faults analogous to those that M. Léopold de Saussure has so properly and energetically pointed out following M. Gustave Le Bon in his *Psychologie de la colonisation française*.[24]

When translated into specific policy in West Africa, the new approach meant that education would come to be regarded as a long and deliberate process through which the natives could expect to acquire skills and techniques which would enable them to make incremental improvements in their traditional patterns of living. Summarizing the Governor-General's intent in 1906, A. Mairot, Inspector of Education in Senegal, expressed the new policy in these words:

> Respectful of the beliefs, the customs, the habits and the traditions of the African peoples submitted to this authority, the Governor-General wants in no way *to assimilate the indigenous peoples* nor to orient in this direction the education given to them.
>
> Leaving the native in his surroundings, in his usual life we hope to ameliorate his well being, to surround him with security; to inculcate in the black Africans the ideas of justice and equality, to give to them a *practical French education, appropriate to their mentality*.[25]

24. Henri Froidevaux, *L'oeuvre scolaire de la France dans nos colonies* (Paris, 1900), pp. 199–200.

25. A. Mairot, "Rapport sur les écoles," January 1, 1906, Archives de la République du Sénégal,, J–10–#52, p. 45 (italics in original).

As we shall explore later, the strongest impetus for the elaboration of adapted education came after 1914 from Georges Hardy, Inspector General of Education in French West Africa.

The sources of educational activity in English-speaking West Africa lay in trade, in the commitment to provide opportunity for liberated Africans in Sierra Leone, and in the missionary movement. In each instance the crucial and, from a colonial viewpoint, surprising fact is that educational activities were sustained before 1890 largely by Africans. This point deserves emphasis because it puts into perspective both the increased British racial arrogance that permeated the missions after 1890 and the relatively temporary nature of much colonial thought about African problems.

The half-century between 1840 and 1890 was a period of experiment and growth for the schools and churches in West Africa. During these years the complex Creole culture flourishing in Freetown contributed directly to the surge of commercial, educational, and missionary energies that flowed into Abeokuta, Lagos, Calabar, and the delta areas of what was to become southern Nigeria. There was much going and coming, not only between Sierra Leone, Cape Coast, and Lagos but between West Africa and Jamaica, Cuba, and Brazil. The optimistic sense of African possibilities combined with the difficulties of cultural symbiosis apparent in these years provide in many ways better clues to the nature of African thought after independence than do the intervening seventy years of colonial rule.

The Portuguese had introduced to the Gold Coast and to Benin that blend of religious, commercial, and military enterprise symbolized by the fortified entrepot with resident priests. By the eighteenth century, British, Dutch, and Danish castletowns had displaced those of the Portuguese, but the intermingling of trade with strategic and "improving" missions continued.[26] From the trade in commodities and slaves there emerged along the Gold Coast a small salient group of

26. There is considerable literature concerning the coastal forts and the communities that grew around them. Most useful are J. W. Blake, *Europeans in West Africa, 1450–1560* (2 vols. London, 1942); K. G. Davies, *The Royal African Company* (London, 1957); A. W. Lawrence, *Trade Castles and Forts of West Africa* (London, 1963); E. C. Martin, *The British West African Settlements, 1750–1821* (London, 1927); G. E. Metcalfe, *Maclean of the Gold Coast* (London, 1962); G. Norregaard, *Danish Settlements in West Africa, 1658–1850* (Boston, 1966). Alan Ryder deals fully with the Portuguese and Dutch eras in *Benin and the Europeans, 1485–1897* (London, 1969), and Margaret Priestley traces the Brew family from its fountainhead in Ireland to the various Fanti Brews in *West African Trade and Coast Society, A Family Study* (London, 1969).

wealthy African traders whose opulence, inheritance, haughtiness, and social standing is noted as early as 1701–02 by Bosman.[27] These coastal entrepreneurial families mixed and intermarried with the small number of resident Europeans in the castle townships. The communities thus created gave rise to the first organized efforts at European-style education. The sons and relatives of powerful trader-intermediaries like Eno Basie Kurentsi of Anomabu and Birempon Cudjo of Cape Coast were educated overseas under European sponsorship.[28] This group—the tiny minority of literate Africans—linked in their own lives a Western education and its Christian foundations to the lively African and mulatto trading families of the coastal towns. It was not an easy role: their achievements brought grudging recognition from Europeans and often suspicion from those who wished to preserve African social patterns unchanged. But the achievements were real, as is made clear by the examples of William Ansah, linguist and writer at Anomabu Castle, and Philip Quaque, chaplain and teacher at Cape Coast.[29]

This small group of literate pioneers educated the children and influenced the families of the innovating, trading, emergent "middle class." These families formed communities that antedated the establishment of formal mission churches and schools and, in fact, sustained the churches on the Gold Coast before and after the frequent deaths of the pioneering European missionaries during the 1820s and 1830s.[30] In the same manner, these communities had evolved a set of expectations for European education before mission schools began. The desire for training in European modes of thought was clearly tied to the limited number of positions in trade, merchant offices, schoolteaching, and the ministry that offered the possibility of paid em-

27. In his fourth and ninth letters. William Bosman, *A New and Accurate Description of the Coast of Guinea,* ed. J. C. Willis,, J. D. Fage, and R. E. Bradbury (new ed., London, 1967), pp. 56–57, 135–36.

28. Priestley, *West African Trade,* pp. 20–24. An analogous role was preformed on the upper Guinea coast by the few *filhos da terra* who were literate in Portuguese and related to the local ruling class. See Walter Rodney, *A History of the Upper Guinea Coast, 1545 to 1800* (Oxford, 1970), esp. pp. 204–13.

29. Priestley, *West African Trade,* pp. 20–24; also Margaret Priestley, "Philip Quaque of Cape Coast," in *Africa Remembered,* ed. P. Curtin (Madison, Wis., 1967), pp. 99–139. Miss Priestley's chapter is based on ten of Quaque's letters to the S.P.G.

30. See, e.g., F. L. Bartels, *The Roots of Ghana Methodism* (Cambridge, 1965), p. 13: "As [Dunwell] walked through the town on the morning after his arrival [1834], a young African approached him and handed him a letter congratulating him on his safe arrival. The letter was signed by members of the 'Meeting,' thirteen of them. They had long waited for a teacher."

ployment outside traditional African society.[31] To understand the origin of the modest demand for Western education in the early nineteenth century is to understand why those who sought it wanted training in English suitable for a business or clerical career in the coastal towns of the Gold Coast. This is the principal reason for the close parallel between the curricula of the Cape Coast and Wesleyan mission schools and that of their contemporary counterparts in England.[32]

Philip Foster's thorough study of *Education and Social Change in Ghana* follows the development of the African demand for education in coastal, and later in the Ashanti, areas, pointing out that missionary schools largely succeeded or failed in response to the different demands evident in African communities. The basic conditions of access to commercial and clerical opportunity, not missionary predilection, linked education to the occupational and prestige categories illustrated and practiced by the mulatto and European trading elites. By the 1840s on the Gold Coast it was already clear that the age and scope of a community's mercantile activities with Europe was the most reliable index to its inhabitants' desire for a European education, and that the educated, mission-related African was in the best position to create schools responsive to those desires. The great period of missionary expansion was summarized in the Educationists' Committee Report of 1920:

> The Basel missionary Society founded in the year 1815 began work in this country twelve years later, and one of their first missionaries was employed in a school started by the Government. Every year saw the extension of the educational work of this Society, and in the year 1881 there were nearly fifty Basel Mission Schools throughout the Colony. During the first 60 years of its establishment in this country 100 of the European missionaries died.
>
> In 1834 the Wesleyan Mission started educational work in the Gold Coast and before the passing of the first Educational Ordinance in 1882 it had over 80 schools in the country. During the first eight years of the establishment of this Mission, it sustained the loss of 14 missionaries.[33]

31. Philip Foster, *Education and Social Change in Ghana* (Chicago, 1965), pp. 45, 59.

32. Ibid., p. 53; see also Bartels, *Ghana Mehodism*, appendix B, "Curriculum and Time Table of Theological Seminary (1842)," p. 350.

33. G. E. Metcalfe, ed., *Great Britain and Ghana. Documents of Ghana History, 1807–1957* (London, 1964), no. 459, "Report of the Educationists' Committee

These few statistics indicate the importance of the African teachers on whom the expansion depended and make vivid the reluctance of the Company of Merchants (until 1821) and thereafter of the colonial governments of the Gold Coast to limit the spread of education. African teachers were responding to parents' awareness of the real income advantages of clerical employment and to their own desire for educational parity with the Europeans whom they saw as traders and missionaries. These factors established the pattern of education well before the renewed imperial scramble of the 1880s. Both the character of the curriculum and the unequal distribution of the schools, with their heavy concentration in the coastal areas, were features of the African demand for education, and as such they proved very resistant to colonial attempts to alter them.[34]

The enthusiasm for education displayed during the first half of the nineteenth century on the Gold Coast was equaled or exceeded in intensity by the liberated African communities of Sierra Leone. Evangelization and training had been considered from the outset inseparable aspects of the process of liberation. After the Crown assumed the government of Sierra Leone, Governor Charles MacCarthy (in office 1814–24) effected a division of responsibility with the missionary societies, so that the years before 1827 were marked by "great cooperation" between the missions and the government concerning education.[35] Although cooperation gave way to government direction of the Freetown schools after 1827, the missions continued to expand their elementary schools in the environs. By 1840 the Church Missionary Society was maintaining 18 schools in the region of Freetown and the Wesleyan Mission 14, a pattern comparable with that of the Gold Coast.

The rise of a prosperous, commerically-oriented, Creole elite showing both initiative in self-government and strong acculturative desires was the factor that induced educational expansion. The fast-growing recaptive population was heterogeneous in origin, language, and custom; this heterogeneity, along with the group's uprootedness, probably created incentives to innovation and to learning. The increasing size

. . . appointed on 5 March, 1920, to Advise the Government on Educational Matters . . . ," pp. 578–81.

34. Foster, *Education and Social Change,* Chap. 3; and Bartels, *Methodism,* Chap. 3, appendixes C and D.

35. Gladys Harding, "Education in Freetown," in *Freetown,* ed. C. Fyfe and E. Jones (Freetown, 1968), p. 143.

of Freetown and its continued importance to the West Africa squadron occasioned a substantial investment of British commercial and maritime capital, and this in turn gave opportunity to Creole merchants for investment in African coastal trade as well as in Freetown real estate.[36] Liberated Africans showed initiative in local politics, in opening relations with the Sierra Leone hinterland, and in cultural innovation. "The wide range of institutions developed by the Colony villagers for mutual aid, social control and the regulation of disputes grew from authentically African roots; the diversity and tolerance of religious life represented an effective exercise of personal freedom; the Krio language and the fufu-based cuisine symbolized the 'cultural fusion' which by 1870 had produced a mature and original Creole society." [37] The Creole community developed a characteristically Protestant blend of virtues. "The successful businessmen who emerged in Freetown in the fourth and fifth decades of the nineteenth century went their own way in trade and religion, outsmarting their trading competitors by their personal initiative, and then retiring to pray and read the Bible in privacy." [38]

These were the families who supported the C.M.S. Grammar School for Boys, which opened in 1845 with a curriculum including English grammar and composition, Greek, Latin, mathematics, geography, the Bible, English history, astronomy, and music. More surprisingly they also supported the Female Institution; this opened in 1849 to give post-primary instruction to girls.[39] The result of missionary endeavor and local demand was "the structure of an educational progression from elementary to secondary school and college which probably gave bright children of the poor greater opportunities than in contemporary England." [40]

The confluence of commerce and Christianity led through education to renewed missionary purpose; the desire was to bring the good news from Sierra Leone back to one's land of origin, particularly to the Yoruba or Aku areas. The first group of "repatriates" left Freetown in 1839; by 1844 Shodeke, the ruler of the new Yoruba city of Abeokuta,

36. J. D. Hargreaves, "Liberia and Sierra Leone," in *Boston University Papers in African History*, ed. J. Butler, *1* (Boston, 1966), pp. 55–76.

37. J. D. Hargreaves, *Journal of African History, 11* (1970), 284–85, reviewing John Peterson's *Province of Freedom. A History of Sierra Leone, 1787–1870* (London, 1969).

38. C. Fyfe, "The Foundation of Freetown," in Fyfe and Jones, *Freetown*, p. 5.

39. Harding, "Education in Freetown," p. 144.

40. George Shepperson, introduction to James Africanus Horton, *West African Countries and Peoples* (London, 1868; reprinted Edinburgh, 1969), p. viii.

was writing to Governor Macdonald of Sierra Leone to explain why he welcomed Egba returning from Freetown:

> I wish that not only my own people may return but that the English missionary and Merchant may settle among us. And if the Queen of England would assist me in building a Fort for the protection of my people she would confer a great favour upon us.[41]

Thus the liberated Africans of Sierra Leone helped to sustain in the Yoruba hinterland the mixture of motives—trade, conversion, and protection—that characterized the early European castle-factories on the Gold Coast.

Samuel Ajayi Crowther symbolized the forceful outpouring of Christian precept and example that spread into Yoruba country and then to the interior missions on the Niger. Crowther was one of the first Yoruba to land at Freetown (in 1822), and he made a career as teacher and missionary, opening the Abeokuta mission in 1845. He participated in three Niger expeditions (1841, 1854, 1857), the last for the express purpose of establishing interior missions, and was consecrated in 1864 as bishop of the territories of West Africa beyond the British dominions. This circumlocution was based upon the belief of men like Thomas Fowell Buxton and Reverend Henry Venn that educated Africans must bear the burden of spreading Christianity in the African interior. Bishop Crowther was the preeminent example of the African agency in the Anglican church, and during the 1870s his example drew many after him.[42]

The Creole contribution to the educational aspirations of the Nigerian peoples, and indeed to the peoples of the Gold Coast as well, was varied and continuous. Thomas Babington Macaulay, son-in-law of Bishop Crowther, founded and became the first principal of the C.M.S. Grammar School in Lagos. Samuel Johnson served as a schoolteacher in Ibadan while collecting the materials for his massive *History of the Yorubas*. One of his brothers, Henry, after studying Arabic in Palestine,

41. Jean H. Kopytoff, *A Preface to Modern Nigeria* (Madison, Wis., 1965), p. 52, quoting from Shodeke to Macdonald, Abeokuta, Jan. 7, 1844, CO267/187.

42. For Crowther's career, see J. F. A. Ajayi, *Christian Missions in Nigeria, 1841–91* (Evanston, Ill., 1965), esp. chap. 7; R. W. July, *The Origins of Modern African Thought* (New York, 1967), chap. 9; E. A. Ayandele, *The Missionary Impact on Modern Nigeria, 1842–1914* (London, 1966), pp. 205–26. Crowther's own works deal chiefly with his contributions to the Niger expeditions of 1854 and 1857 (published in London, 1855 and 1959) and his pioneering vocabularies and grammars of Nupe (London, 1864), of Yoruba (London, 1870), and of Ibo (London, 1882).

was an archdeacon on the upper Niger; another brother, Obadiah, qualified in England as a doctor. James Johnson served for tweny years as pastor of St. Paul's Breadfruit Church in Lagos, attempting during his intellectual ministry to give more African forms to his parishioners' Christianity.[43] Dr. James Africanus Horton (M.R.C.S. King's College, London, 1858; M.D. Edinburgh, 1859) wrote widely on medical, social, and political questions during his arduous West African service in the 1860s and 1870s. In 1861 he proposed to the Secretary of State for War that "a small Government Medical Establishment" be created in Sierra Leone to offer under an African master a two-year course in the preclinical aspects of medicine. Horton returned frequently and with realistic plans to the idea that "Fourah Bay College should henceforth be made the University of West Africa."[44] He attained the rank of Surgeon-Major in 1875 and five years later retired on half-pay to Freetown, where he promoted commercial and educational ventures. Samuel Lewis (Sir Samuel after 1893)—lawyer, legislative council member, judge, and mayor of Freetown—argued that the most effective education was practical participation in local self-government, to which his own career was consistent testimony. In the next generation the Creole line of intellectual descent continued in Nigeria with men like Herbert Macaulay, publicist and politician, and his opponent Henry Rawlinson Carr, inspector of schools and professional educator.[45]

One final instance of the intellectual complexity and stature of Freetown is the arrival at Fourah Bay College in 1871 of Edward W. Blyden as a teacher of Arabic. Blyden had left Liberia largely for political reasons, hoping to establish a University of West Africa, in Sierra Leone; this scheme had proved abortive in Liberia. Blyden recommended his plan to Governor Pope Hennessy in 1872, and prob-

43. On the Johnsons, see Ajayi, *Christian Missions,* chaps. 5, 8; July, *Origins,* chaps. 7, 14; E. A. Ayandele, *Holy Johnson, Pioneer of African Nationalism, 1836–1917* (London, 1970).

44. Horton, *West African Countries.* His letter of July 13, 1861, to the Secretary of State for War is quoted in a footnote on pp. 42–45; the remarks about Fourah Bay are made in chap. 14, "Requirements of Sierra Leone," p. 183 (Edinburgh edition). Davidson Nicol has edited a selection of Horton's writings entitled *Africanus Horton* (London, 1969) that illustrates the variety of his interests.

45. J. D. Hargreaves, *A Life of Sir Samuel Lewis* (London, 1958); R. W. July, "The Sierra Leone Legacy in Nigeria," in Fyfe and Jones, *Freetown,* pp. 212–24 also *Origins,* chaps. 18, 20.

ably his and Horton's arguments helped achieve the partial result of affiliating Fourah Bay to the University of Durham in 1876. Blyden did not remain a teacher of Arabic for long, but he stayed on in Freetown as a government agent to the Muslim tribes of the interior, acting out his increasingly strong conviction that Islam was the religion genuinely suited to the African genius. Although he hated mixed blood and what he took to be Creole subservience to British culture, Blyden developed in Freetown his trenchant views about the renascence of a purely African culture. Born on a Danish island in the West Indies; raised for a few years in Venezuela; educated largely in Liberia after attempting to attend college in the United States; literate in Spanish, English, Latin, Greek, Hebrew, and Arabic; traveled in Egypt and the Near East—Blyden represented the universal West African. He was familiar with black life on both sides of the Atlantic, knew both Christianity and Islam, announced the need for a self-confident African culture, and urged the creation of an independent African church.[46]

Ironically, the achievements of these men did not serve to open the way for other West Africans to attain advanced education. European officers and professionals serving in West Africa did not view African competition kindly: they nipped Horton's suggestion for local medical training in the bud and succeeded in terminating medical education in Britain for any more Africans.[47] By the mid-1880s the whole climate of "informed" opinion had become hostile to African advance. Imperial acquisition and social Darwinism (prodded by physical anthropology) encouraged "scientific" racial theories that touted white superiority and allowed few capabilities to Africans. Quinine and the

46. July, *Origins,* chap. 11; H. R. Lynch, *Edward Wilmot Blyden* (London, 1966). Blyden's most powerful statement about his ideas for an African university is his inaugural address as President of Liberia College in Monrovia (1881), quoted in his *Christianity, Islam, and the Negro Race* (London, 1887; reprinted Edinburgh, 1968), pp. 71–93. His call for "the Christian natives along the coast to establish a Church of their own" is discussed in July, *Origins,* pp. 230–32; and in J. B. Webster, *The African Churches among the Yoruba, 1888–1922* (Oxford 1964), pp. 65–66.

47. Horton received a curt note from Edward Lugard (Permanent Undersecretary of State for War) dated June 19, 1862, to the effect that "it is not intended for the present to train any further candidates natives of Africa for Army surgeonries" (Nicol, *Horton,* p. 108). Horton himself indicates that his idea was circulated to the principal Medical Officer and to the Officer Commanding on the Gold Coast, from whom it received "a combined and warm opposition, which nipped it in the bud" (*West African Countries,* p. 45).

steamship made possible more heavily European, larger scale, and more direct enterprise in coastal and riverain areas, requiring capital investment beyond the scope of even successful African enterpreneurs in Freetown or Lagos. Empire builders like George Taubman Goldie called independent African traders "disreputable coloured men" when they failed to go along with the monopoly he wished to create on the Niger.[48] British army officers and administrators, now beginning to appear in numbers, expressed preference for the "unspoiled" tribesmen and peasants of the interior and for (Muslim) "natural rulers" over the educated groups in the eclectic Euro-African coastal towns.

The most dramatic indication of the changed perspective was G. W. Brooke's purge of Bishop Crowther's Niger mission in 1890, which discredited the work of African missionaries without substantial evidence and virtually destroyed in one year the work of the previous quarter century to establish an African agency in the Anglican missions. Although a minority of the C.M.S. parent committee in England believed that English racial arrogance was responsible for the decisions concerning the Niger, its views could not prevail against the new orthodoxy.[49] As J. B. Webster, the most thorough historian of these sordid events, states:

> The story of the Niger mission simply cannot be comprehended without a clear understanding of the deep racist feeling of the English embodied in almost all communications to and from the C.M.S. This is the only explanation for the credence which the C.M.S. gave to reports so contradictory, so incomplete, so defamatory to a whole race.[50]

The result of these actions of 1890 was to place the Anglican episcopate in Africa firmly in white hands, to occasion the creation of independent African churches under lay leadership, and to destroy the image of the established church as a place congenial to African social and political advancement. "To discredit Crowther was to discredit the Sierra Leonians. To discredit the Sierra Leonians was to say in effect that Africans, given the benefit of education and Christianity, would never fully rise to the status of the English." [51] This chill and

48. Ajayi, *Christian Missions,* pp. 242–43.
49. Webster, *African Churches,* part 1.
50. Ibid., p. 8. This sad and unjustified conclusion to Bishop Crowther's career is also discussed in Ajayi, pp. 250–54; Ayandele, *Missionary Impact,* pp. 220–26.
51. Webster, pp. 40–41.

arrogant message also emanated from government circles. By the turn of the century the administrations of both the Gold Coast and Sierra Leone had become steadily whiter; there was less candor in recognizing the ability of Africans, and whites overtly expressed their dislike of serving under African superiors, be they bishops or chief secretaries.

Heightened British racial exclusiveness produced two trends in educational practice that were of fundamental importance during the colonial years. First, the newly formed departments of education (Gold Coast, 1887; Southern Nigeria, 1903; Sierra Leone, 1911) showed marked skepticism toward any extension of secondary or specialized education and thought mainly in terms of adapted curricula and avoidance of the mistakes made by the mission schools. In the first decade of the twentieth century the forceful personalities of two British proconsuls, Cromer in Egypt and Lugard in Nigeria, had much to do with making the language of education department circulars reflect the assumptions and vocabulary of aristocratic paternalism—whether direct or indirect. The similarity was not coincidental: both were alarmed by what they had seen of the educational pattern in British India; both formulated policy in areas where an established Muslim educational system sustained traditional learning; both were anxious (Cromer for the Sudan, Lugard for Northern Nigeria), for political reasons, to limit the impact of Christian missionary education on a population which valued Islam; both sought to confine the indigenous educated group to a small, employable handful in order to avoid the creation of a restless nationalist movement.[52] James Currie, appointed Director of Education in the Sudan in 1900, summarized the aims of educational policy in 1901 as: "1. The creation of a competent artisan class. . . . 2. The diffusion among the masses of the people of education sufficient to enable them to understand the merest elements of the machinery of government. . . . 3. The creation of a small native administrative class." [53]

52. For the background of Cromer's policy in the Sudan, see M. O. Beshir, *Educational Development in the Sudan, 1898 to 1956* (Oxford, 1969), chap. 2. Sir Eric Ashby's *Universities: British, Indian, and African* (Cambridge, Mass., 1966) makes clear the fear of Indian example. The development of Lugard's educational policy in Northern Nigeria is best set out by Sonia Graham in *Government and Mission Education in Northern Nigeria, 1900–19* (Ibadan, 1966).

53. Sir James Currie, "The Educational Experiment in the Anglo-Egyptian Sudan, 1900–33, Part I," *African Society Journal, 33* (1934), 364.

The process of stamping these purposes upon educational policy began before 1914 and continued unabated into the 1920s. By 1925 official language read as if the careers of several generations of Sierra Leonians had never taken place. The perspective of Indirect Rule had effaced the earlier West African experience, and in that year the Advisory Committee on Native Education in the British Tropical Dependencies recommended:

> Education should be adapted to the mentality, aptitudes, occupations and traditions of the various peoples, conserving as far as possible all sound and healthy elements in the fabric of their social life; adapting them where necessary to changed circumstances and progressive ideas as an agent of natural growth and evolution. . . . The first task of education is to raise the standard alike of character and efficiency of the bulk of the people, but provisions must also be made for the training of those who are required to fill posts in the administrative and technical services, as well as those who as chiefs will occupy positions of exceptional trust and responsibility.[54]

The second trend produced by heightened British racial expression was directly opposed to the first. Whereas the turn-of-the-century paternalist view was skeptical of a literary education for Africans, the demand for such an education was greater than ever. The imposition of colonial rule, whether direct or indirect, made still more apparent the class and income advantages for those who received a metropolitan-style education. Africans felt more keenly than ever the need to demonstrate, as had Horton and Blyden, that in mastering European culture they were not abandoning their own. For those who lived in the older coastal cities, imperial rule gave a new edge to learning: it could open doors for them into the rulers' employment while giving them the knowledge to prove that the rulers abjured their own best traditions.

Because colonial governments did not recognize the increased African demand for a literary education as legitimate, and because before the mid-1920s few governments had the resources to undertake significant expansion of educational staff or facilities,[55] much helter-skelter expansion occurred under mission, or even under private-ven-

54. Advisory Committee on Native Education in the British Tropical Dependencies, *Education in British Tropical Africa* (London, 1925), pp. 4–5.

55. For illustrative purposes, the following figures indicate government expenditure on education in the years 1922 and 1928 and (in parentheses) the percentage that education comprises of the colonial governments' total expenditure in each

ture, auspices. This growth served to further differentiate areas of early mission influence from those which had only recently come under European control. Where missions and missionary staffs were already present, schools (of whatever quality) grew in number; in newly acquired areas missions were often discouraged and government primary schools were few. This regional variation in school facilities, often accentuated by variations in policy between Muslim and non-Muslim areas, created a divisive legacy.[56] In 1912, for example, two years before the amalgamation of Southern and Northern Nigeria, 35,700 pupils attended primary school in the south. These were concentrated largely in areas of early missionary activity, even though the government had opened fifty primary schools in the "educationally deprived" non-Yoruba provinces. By contrast, 950 pupils attended similar schools in the north, and approximately 250,000 pursued some form of traditional Koranic education.[57]

---

year. Figures are in thousands of pounds, except for the Sudan, where they are in Egyptian pounds.

	1922	*1928*
Sierra Leone		48.3 (5.7)
Gold Coast	100.0 (2.9)	
Togo (mandate)		8.5 (11.1)
Nigeria		
Cameroon (mandate)		7.0 (5.2)
Sudan	99.5 (2.8)	157.9 (2.3)
Uganda	9.5 (1.0)	51.4 (3.6)
Kenya (African education 1930)		84.0
Tanganyika (mandate)	8.0 (0.5)	59.7 (3.5)
N. Rhodesia (African education 1930)		15.3 (2.3)

SOURCES: Colonial Office, *Annual Reports; African Education in Kenya* (Nairobi, 1949), p. 2; D. L. Sumner, *Education in Sierra Leone* (Freetown, 1963), p. 329; Coombe, "Secondary Education in Zambia," *African Social Research* 3 (1967), 174.

56. The extent and seriousness of the regional differentiations in the Gold Coast are made clear in David Kimble, *A Political History of Ghana* (Oxford, 1963), esp. pp. 70–124; and in Foster, *Education and Social Change.* For Nigeria they are discussed in James Coleman, *Nigeria, Background to Nationalism* (Berkeley, 1958); and in D. B. Abernethy, "Nigeria" (1966), in *Church, State, and Education in Africa,* ed. D. G. Scanlon (New York, 1969), pp. 197–244. For the Sudan these differentiations are examined in Beshir, *Educational Development;* D. L. Sumner, *Education in Sierra Leone,* statistics p. 228; and R. Clignet and P. Foster, *The Fortunate Few . . . Students in the Ivory Coast* (Evanston, 1966), Chap. 3, reveal similar serious differentiations.

57. Abernethy, pp. 205–06.

By the time World War I disoriented colonial governments, French and British pronouncements concerning education in West Africa had a similiar ring. Two ideas shaped educational policy: curricula adapted to local circumstances, and a limited access to secondary school. The latter was designed to restrict graduates of secondary schools to the small number immediately employable by the government and by commercial firms. These ideas appeared at the time to have emerged from the colonial situation, despite differences between French and British policy on such other matters, as the role of chiefs. But the element they really had in common was not the similarity of conditions in Africa (which, in fact, varied widely); it was the heightened sense of European racial superiority and the resulting distrust of African capacities. The lenses through which Europeans viewed the image of Africa had clouded considerably between 1870 and 1910.[58] Many Europeans had grown to believe that educated Africans were tiresome imitators at best or, more likely, meddlesome agitators. This perspective was as much the basis of educational policy as were objective conditions, and it distorted European assessments of African potential for more than a generation.

The First World War aggravated the shortage of French administrative officers, and the increased output of trained African personnel was designed to counteract this shortage and fill the vacated administrative posts. Governor-General William Ponty appointed Georges Hardy to the post of Inspector General of Education for French West Africa at the outset of the war in 1914. Hardy began immediately to expand enrollment in the French schools located in Dakar. To accomplish this he placed renewed emphasis upon the practical content of education, overhauling the curriculum in the rural schools and publishing a series of textbooks and teacher guides designed specifically for African conditions. In addition he published a journal, *Le bulletin de l'enseignement de l'Afrique Occidentale Française,* through which he communi-

58. The now standard study of the change in attitude brought about by the slave trade in an earlier period (up to ca. 1840) is Philip D. Curtin's *The Image of Africa* (Madison, Wis., 1964). Nothing of comparable scope exists for the Victorian era, although individual African responses of frustration and rage show plainly that prejudice hardened, or perhaps that more people who were prejudiced ventured to go to Africa. See Horton's lament to the Rev. Henry Venn (Feb. 3, 1860) about "the unbearable treatment I have received from one of Her Majesty's officers" (Nicol, *Horton,* pp. 112–13). Novels and autobiographies are perhaps still the best guide to the continual humiliations caused by European racial attitudes.

cated his pedagogical theories and practical advice to the corps of European and African teaching personnel throughout the French West African colonies. Hardy's version of adapted education reflects undisguisable racist assumptions, as do many of his articles in the *Bulletin.* Furthermore, he made no secret of the fact that the education which he intended to offer to the Africans would be in no way equivalent to that of metropolitan France. As he stated quite unabashedly,

> we have put much water in the wine of African programs. . . . One day perhaps, the great light that shines from the north will provide illumination that does not blind; for the time being let us remain in the cave of which Plato speaks so beautifully, and let us look at the overly bright sun only through its reflection in the muddy waters of African streams.[59]

With Hardy's explicit emphasis upon curricular adaptation to the African conditions, a de facto two-track educational system became well established. As events proved, the education reserved for Europeans and a few elite métis and Africans was markedly different from that offered to the mass of Africans. This principle was never written into legislation or ordinances, but the loose wording of the initial educational decrees of 1903 made it possible for European families in the urban centers to assure their children of an education modeled on that available in France. Article 12 of the 1903 ordinance provided for the organization of urban schools, guaranteeing metropolitan examinations and diplomas:

> Article 12:
>
> Schools opened or to be opened in all towns with a sufficient European or assimilated element to justify their establishment will receive the name of "urban schools."
>
> In principle, the personnel of these schools are to be exclusively European. The course of study is to be that of the primary schools of the Metropole although certain modifications may be permitted to meet local needs.[60]

Although no racial restrictions were officially spelled out for admission to these schools, it became increasingly apparent that Europeans were assured admittance and Africans were encouraged instead to attend

59. *Bulletin de l'Enseignement de l'A.O.F., 21* (February 1916), 73,

60. Arrêté No. 806, *Journal officiel du Sénégal et dépendances* (November 28, 1903).

rural or regional schools. By 1908, despite vociferous African protest over this evolving pattern, the practice was quite common, and Acting Governor-General Martial Merlin summed up the situation in a government publication: "As for the urban schools, they constitute . . . special schools, or more properly exceptional schools, because they are in principle reserved for the European or assimilated population."[61] Hardy's policies, then, did not initiate a two-track system; rather, they merely gave official reinforcement to the tendency toward a dual system which resident French families had sought to develop ever since the 1903 ordinances.

The African elite in Dakar reacted strongly to the general drift toward a two-track system and specifically toward Hardy's policies of adapted education. They held Hardy responsible for what they felt to be a dramatic decline in the quality of African education, and they began to attack him early in 1919 in editorials published in *La Démocratie* and its successor *l'Ouest Africaine Française.* Until the time of Hardy's appointment, one article declared, "our Normal School . . . had provided us with black teachers equal in learning to their European colleagues," but after Hardy took charge, "they wish to form only some young people speaking 'petit-nègre' [pidgin French]." The editorial continued:

> THIS WAS TO THROW THE MACHINE IN REVERSE
>
> . . . Thus instead of advancing, we slide back 50 years, in the midst of the century of secularization, steam and electricity!
>
> This might have been comic if it were not tragic.
>
> They hope, O faithful people of Senegal, that tomorrow the people, whose only merit (if it is one!) consists in having "*white skin*" possess forever the superiority over you children, sons and nephews of the World War, with whom the rivalry might become uneasy.
>
> "Nigger. You are inferior to the European, you will always remain so whatever might be your capacities."

61. Circulaire du Governeur Général, February 27, 1908, in *Journal Officiel del l'Afrique Occidentale Française* (March 7, 1908), pp. 116–17. The same practice of a dual system, with effective segregation the result, was followed in Morocco from 1912 to 1944, despite the obligations of the Treaty of Fez. In 1939 the director of primary education in Morocco wrote, "The admission of a native into a European school is to be regarded as a great favor." A small number did succeed in surmounting the barriers to attaining a French education, and they played an important part in the nationalist movement. For an excellent dicussion of the actual effects of French education policy in Morocco, see John P. Halstead, *Rebirth of a Nation. The Origins and Rise of Moroccan Nationalism, 1912–44* (Cambridge, Mass., 1967), esp. chaps. 6 and 7.

> We say NO! to Mr. Hardy. . . .
>
> . . . Leave; but leave quickly. If not, the voice of the people will purely and simply throw you out from French West Africa.[62]
>
> Amadou l'Artilleur

Using slogans like "Down with the Saboteurs of African Education," the elite continued their campaign against Hardy and his educational programs throughout the spring of 1919, and the effort was at least partially successful. The administration kept a close eye on African criticism, and as the pressure mounted the Governor-General granted Hardy leave to go to France for what was described officially as a "congé de convalescence."

Despite Hardy's departure, the principles of adapted education which he had championed remained dominant throughout the interwar period, even in the face of persistent criticism. The policy statements of other educational officers rarely exhibited the same unbridled confidence that had characterized Hardy's pronouncements, but his central principle endured: that African education should reject metropolitan norms and tailor itself to African necessities. This is not to suggest that Hardy's successors were copies of him—far from it. Charles Béart, for instance, director of the William Ponty School from 1939 to 1945, stands out in marked contrast. There are some parallels that can be drawn between the two men, but the mere suggestion that they were comparable is enough to enrage graduates of the Ponty school who knew Béart; the affection which these men express toward him is equaled only by their disdain for Hardy. Whereas Hardy advocated adapted education because he felt that the native mentality and colonial conditions would not support a full dose of metropolitan learning, Béart championed it because he valued the study of African tradition and culture far more than the standard French curriculum; thus each man's emphasis was markedly different. Nonetheless, both rejected the use of French metropolitan education in the colonies, and in his own fashion Béart remained as strong an advocate for adapted education until the end of the Second World War as Hardy had been throughout the First World War.[63]

The period of genuine colonial rule ended with World War II. In the era of decolonization after 1945, metropolitan policy was directed

62. *La Démocratie,* February 9, 1919.

63. For a more thorough discussion of the impact which Charles Béart had upon colonial education and the characteristics which distinguished him from Georges Hardy, see Weiskel, "Education and Colonial Rule," chap. 5.

toward granting the colonies increased autonomy through administrative devolution. The period of decolonization is not our central concern here, but it is important to realize that after 1945 the policy of adapted education characteristic of the period of colonial rule was eclipsed swiftly by the resurgence of assimilation. Not only Hardy's programs but those of Béart as well were cast aside in a full-scale effort to transplant French institutions to West Africa.

Only after 1945 did African political pressure begin to effectively shape educational policy in French areas. The demands articulated by the nascent political parties stressed the desire for immediate parity with the French system in examinations and degrees, and in each territory African political leaders gained support among local populations by promising the rapid extension of educational facilities. In the postwar political context the French administration could not afford to resist African demands for long, and despite considerable reluctance on the part of the local administrators and educators, the French government began to create in West Africa strict copies of French metropolitan schools. Between 1946 and 1949 a series of ordinances were enacted both to expand and to improve the quality of post-primary education. Graduates of the William Ponty School were allowed for the first time to present themselves for the French *Brevet Elémentaire.* Scholarships for study in French institutions of higher learning were rapidly expanded; and within the colonies the French aid money voted by the metropolitan parliament went principally toward financing post-primary education, with responsibility for primary level expansion assumed by individual territories. The upper primary schools in each territory were converted to "collèges modernes" modeled directly upon French counterparts. By 1949 the administration had created an "Institut des Hautes Etudes" in Dakar theoretically capable of giving instruction equivalent to that of the Universities of Paris and Bordeaux.[64] As political independence became imminent, African demands for strict educational parity with the French were increasingly met. By 1960 African students could feel confident that their schools offered the same curriculum available in any French town.

Given the pace of events after 1945, it is not difficult to see why scholars have frequently misinterpreted French educational policy during the colonial years. They have viewed the colonial period through the lens of decolonization, assuming that the institutional transfers characteristic of decolonization must have been anticipated

64. For a review of the postwar reforms, see J. Capelle, "Education in French West Africa," *Overseas Education, 21* (October 1949), 956–72.

by a nascent form of the same process. In a similar fashion scholars have confused the statements of military officers and cultural chauvanists of the period of military expansion before 1890 with subsequent government policy. In fact, study of the period of colonial rule in French Africa has been remarkably limited, largely because much of the archival material remains restricted.

Texts from the colonial era itself have also been misunderstood. For example, songs such as the one that follows are often taken as evidence of the French desire to make Africans into complete Frenchmen:

> Salut à toi, terre dahoméene
> Terre sacrée où dorment nos aieux,
> La France un jour t'adopte comme sienne
> Et d'être ses enfants soyons heureux.
> Depuis ce jour nous avons l'espérance
> De mériter ce qu'elle a fait pour nous
> Et de grand coeur nous te disons, ô France,
> Dès maintenant (bis), tu peux compter sur nous.
>
> [Refrain]
> Enfants du Dahomey, de la brousse ou des villes,
> Souvenons-nous toujours que nous sommes Français
> Quel que soit l'avenir, confiants et tranquilles
> Nous resterons français, toujours français.[65]

This song and others like it were composed by Georges Hardy during the First World War, at a time when France was terrified of losing African allegiance. The fear stemmed from a feeling that Africans might respond to the war as Muslims, uniting with their Ottoman brothers to defeat France in Europe and expel her from the colonies. The songs, then, were designed with a specific and limited purpose in mind—that of inculcating a strong sense of allegiance to the French cause in the war. From this perspective the most significant line of the song just quoted is: "Dès maintenant, tu peux compter sur nous." Texts composed to inspire such a response in the face of war should not be read as an overall program for the colonial period.

As we have seen, the purpose of French educational policy from 1890 to 1945 was to avoid making Africans into Frenchmen. Yet scholars are correct to point out that the colonial period was in fact highly

65. Cited in Albert Tevoedjre, *L'Afrique revoltée* (Paris, 1958), p. 71. For more examples of similar songs, see Georges Hardy, *La chant à l'école indigène* (Gorée, 1916).

assimilatory. However, results should not be confused with intentions, and the significant question is, Why did French attempts to foster adapted education fail?

It is clear that, in formulating policy, officials in West Africa consciously sought other models than that of the French metropolitan system in order to frame their programs. In 1906 A. Mairot, Director of Education in Senegal, returned to Dakar with a plan for the reorganization of the Ecole Normale after visiting the Madras Presidency Normal School in Saidapeth, India. Again in 1934 Albert Charton, Director of Education for French West Africa, remodeled the Ecole Normale William Ponty with specific reference to Achimota, near Accra, and to British accomplishments in Ibadan and Lagos. Further, interdepartmental memoranda indicate that in the 1930s the American Negro colleges provided inspiration for French policy.[66] But there was nearly always a gap between policy articulated in official circles and the way in which programs were implemented locally. As Robert Delavignette observed after years of service in French West Africa, "there is no administrative problem, however well-conceived the departmental instructions on it, which does not change its nature when it comes down to earth somewhere."[67] Despite official reference to other systems, it is undoubtedly true that the French metropolitan system continued to operate as a subconscious model, particularly for the individual schoolteacher subject to local conditions. Often prone to follow their own educational experience, French teachers fell back upon metropolitan models through sheer economy of effort in conditions of uncertainty. When formal policy provided no solution for immediate problems, they tended to draw upon the system they knew best.

It is illuminating, moreover, to examine the texts that the teachers were using. Some of the first French texts tried to deal with specifically African conditions. By 1826 Dard had published a Wolof-French dictionary and a Wolof grammar for use in Senegal. Similarly, General Faidherbe, frustrated by the lack of relevant teaching materials, pub-

66. See, for example, the allusion to the American Negro College as a model for French programs at William Ponty in "L'Ecole William Ponty," *Bulletin d'information et de renseignements du gouvernement general de l'A.O.F.*, 196 (July 4, 1938), 237. Recent scholarship has revealed substantial links between American Negro education and efforts in the British colonies. See Kenneth J. King, "Africa and the Southern States of the U.S.A.: Notes on J. H. Oldham and American Negro Education for Africans," *Journal of African History*, 10 (1969), 659–77.

67. Delavignette, *Freedom and Authority*, p. 11.

lished a geography text, *Chapitres de géographie sur le Nord-Ouest de l'Afrique à l'usage des écoles de Sénégambie* (Saint-Louis, 1868). Hardy's texts provided additional material, and with his encouragement a whole series of history texts and readers were published in Paris and Dakar for use in the African village and regional schools. Although all texts after Dard's were published in French, they tried to focus on local conditions and steer African students away from the French literary education which seemed so generally preferred. The French were more aware of this need than were other colonial powers. As Raymond Leslie Buell noted in 1928:

> Despite the use of the French language, the French education system has adapted courses of instruction to the needs of the African much more successfully than has been done in any other territory in Africa. There is no teaching of Latin or of detailed French history in the French colonial schools. Texts and courses have been designed to fit native needs.[68]

Although these adapted texts were in use throughout the colonial period, their actual impact upon African students is hard to assess. They were adapted with reference to local events, places, problems, and geography, but their underlying intent was to inculcate a deep and abiding respect for French civilization and its accomplishments in West Africa. The texts were written in such a way as to encourage Africans to deny the validity of their own cultural traditions and to admire instead those of the French. Thus they could be considered more assimilative in their overall effect than a straightforward metropolitan curriculum might have been, because they encouraged Africans to measure all experience against the norm of French culture. In short, while the adapted curriculum began to teach the African about his own milieu, it reminded him continuously that everything about his environment was inferior to France and the French way of life.

Extracts from history textbooks clearly illustrate this effect. In a booklet entitled *Histoire de l'Afrique Occidentale Française,* published in 1913, André Leguillette includes a section under the heading "The Prophets and the Conquerors" about such African political leaders as El Hadj Omar and Samory who resisted French penetration in West Africa. After discussing briefly the old kingdoms of the interior prior to the European arrival, he explains that "towards the middle of the

68. Raymond Leslie Buell, *The Native Problem in Africa* (2 vols. New York, 1928), 2, 61.

nineteenth century, almost nothing remained in Africa of the States which existed there for a long time. Then opened the era of the prophets and the adventurers: El Hadj Omar, Mahmadou Lamine, Samory, Rabah." [69] The image is one of false prophets and exploiters possessing none of the traditional dignity associated with the ancient Sudanese empires. After conceding that El Hadj Omar had ascended to a position of considerable authority over large parts of the Sudan, Leguillette was quick to assure his readers that

> this splendor was only ephemeral. On the ruins of conquered states El Hadj Omar and his Toucouleurs did not know how to create any stable organization, resting on the prosperity of agriculture and the development of commerce. In addition, the conquered people only accepted the foreign domination with repugnance.[70]

Having thus condemned El Hadj Omar as a "foreign" conqueror, the text concluded by portraying France not as another foreign intruder but as the force that liberated the African people from the tryanny of her own leaders:

> In less than half a century France has transformed the country that extends between the Sahara, the Atlantic and Tchad. In the place of violence and continual warfare, she has substituted peace and security; thanks to her, order has replaced anarchy, and the exertions of the little tyrannic powers have given way to the good works of regular and stable administration. Abandoned country is repopulated, and some desert regions have been developed. The inhabitants, protected against famine, pillage and sickness, have seen their liberty and their property guaranteed. Also they are beginning to put themselves to the task and to draw out part of the riches of their soil. Little by little, they enter into the advantages of civilized life and advance in the way of progress.
>
> France has the right to be proud of her African accomplishment and merits the graditude and the affection of her black children.[71]

If African students learned their lessons well from these adapted texts, it is hard to imagine how they could have avoided internalizing the assumptions and standards and prejudices of French culture and society.

69. André Leguillette, *Histoire de l'Afrique Occidentale Française* (Dakar, 1913), p. 26.
70. Ibid., p. 22.
71. Ibid., p. 103.

Whereas a struggle with the inconsistencies of adapted texts and curricula marked French educational policy in West Africa during the colonial period, educational policy in British colonial Africa between 1920 and 1939 grew largely from a slow and grudging realization that educational advance and Indirect Rule were incompatible. The organization of the Colonial Office during the interwar years encouraged comparison among British territories in Africa, and the official doctrine of Indirect Rule was widely promoted.[72] Although its precepts may have been disregarded or found irrelevant by some district officers, the doctrine certainly influenced the language of educational policy: "the central difficulty lies in finding ways to improve what is sound in indigenous tradition."[73] The desire was to reduce the disintegrating and unsettling effects of education. We can see in retrospect that the long-term result of Indirect Rule on African education was to alter the perspective upon which policy was based from a very low estimate of African capabilities to toleration of a qualified local autonomy. Although this change might very well have occurred in any case, Indirect Rule provided the framework for thought and the justification for action. A few of its effects were positive, some were quixotic, and many were harmful.

In the southern Sudan a combination of missionary self-interest and dedicated administrative indirection led to disastrous results. Arabic was discarded as an educational medium in favor of the local vernaculars, and heavy reliance was placed upon grants-in-aid to inadequate mission schools. The chief aim of policy appeared to be to provide an education that guarded against "the destruction of native social institutions and the diversion of the African from his natural background."[74] That the attempt to eradicate Arabic—one of the principal international languages of Africa—and to substitute Dinka, Bari, Nuer, Lotuka, Shilluk, and Zande—in which no textbooks existed and which few teachers could speak—was made in the name of educational advance is hard to believe. The reasons underlying this substitution were the government's fear of northern Sudanese and Egyptian nationalism and the missions' hatred of Islam. At the Rejaf Conference in 1928 to

72. See P. Gifford , "Indirect Rule," in *Britain and Germany in Africa,* ed. P. Gifford and W. R. Louis (New Haven, 1967), pp. 351–91.

73. Advisory Committee on Native Education in the British Tropical African Dependencies, *Education Policy in British Tropical Africa* (London, 1925), p. 4.

74. Beshir, *Educational Development,* p. 75, quoting minutes of Sixth Educational Conference of Mongalla Province, Juba, April 16, 1932; chaps. 4 and 5 deal with the 1920–32 period.

consider educational problems, Arabic was rejected on the grounds that "it would open the door to the spread of Islam, Arabicize the south, and introduce the northern Sudanese outlook which differed from that of the southern people." [75] Indirect Rule provided the apparent justification for an emphasis upon local languages and local initiative, but the policy did not work: the process of Arabicization continued in the southern Sudan. This only made the south's educational deficit in comparison to the north more acute and widened the division between the two parts of the country. "The final outcome was stagnation in education." [76] It is probably not a coincidence that Sir James Currie, who began his career in 1900 as Director of Education in the Sudan, had by 1930 become an advocate of accelerated higher education in Africa and increased central government responsibility.[77] He had seen the results of the opposite approach in a region that he knew well.

The anti-educational attitudes that informed southern Sudanese policy were shared by administrative officers in other parts of British Africa. It was believed that one must "strengthen the solid elements in the country—sheiks, merchants, etc.—before the irresponsible body of half-educated officials, students and town riff-raff takes control of the public mind." [78] An unintended result of this cultivation of chiefs and "natural rulers" was that European settlers could support an educational policy for Africans emphasizing village schools and solid elements. Such a policy did not threaten to train skilled Africans who could compete for European jobs. Although administrative officers

75. Ibid., p. 70.

76. Ibid., p. 76.

77. After a return visit to the Sudan in 1932, Currie's opinions hardened. By 1934 he was objecting in print to "the romanticists of indirect administration" and their policies, which he thought "an unmitigated evil." "This policy of indirect rule, as interpreted by many of its devotees, is having such mischievous reactions, both on native sentiment and on educational progress in Africa, that the writer feels it necessary to criticise it freely" (Sir James Currie, "The Educational Experiment in the Anglo-Egyptian Sudan, 1900–33, Part II," *African Society Journal, 34* (1935), 53–54). He served as chairman of the subcommittee formed by the Advisory Committee on Education in the Colonies to study the question of higher education in Africa and wrote the report of the subcommittee (December 1933) that recommended the elevation of Makerere, Gordon, Yaba, Achimota, and Fourah Bay Colleges to real university standard. See Trevor Coombe, "The Origins of Secondary Education in Zambia," *African Social Research,* 3 (1966), 191–92 and n. 28. The Currie Report is printed in full in Ashby, *Universities,* pp. 476–81.

78. Beshir, *Education Development,* p. 76. quoting the Governor of Berber Province.

sometimes found such allies embarrassing, there is no doubt that facing up to the contradictions inherent in Indirect Rule was made more difficult by the settler support of village-centered primary education. In northern Rhodesia, for example, considerable outside pressure from the Colonial Office and the De La Warr Report (1937) as well as internal protest from African students was required before a full course of secondary education for Africans was instituted at Munali in 1939,[79] more than ninety years after secondary schools began in Freetown.

In color-bar economies (and to some degree in both the Ivory Coast and Senegal), representatives of settler agricultural and extractive industries supported a policy designed to create an African educational pyramid that was relatively wide at the bottom and very restricted at the secondary level. A similar structure was often desired by administrative officers acting on a contradictory premise—a fear not of competition but of unemployable school leavers. When such a conjunction of restrictive interests occurred, it made an African's progress to higher education extraordinarily difficult, necessitating a long period of residence overseas.[80]

During the interwar years the chief instrument of British educational control in Africa became the grant-in-aid. Its underlying purpose was to make the missions a partner of the government in improving the quality and limiting the quantity of the schools available to African children. A quid pro quo evolved into a formal system in all territories by 1940: in return for annual government grants and a voice in the central councils which formulated educational policy, the missions would subject their schools to regular inspection by the Education

79. See Coombe, "Origins of Secondary Education," p. 192–99, 388–97.

80. We know of no comprehensive essay discussing the experience of African students overseas during the interwar years. Most of the information must be culled from autobiographies and biographies. Aspects of a general study exist for the post-1945 period; see, for example, Presence Africaine, *Les étudiants noirs parlent* (Paris, 1953); and the two studies by Jeanne-Pierre N'Diaye, *Enquête sur les étudiants noirs en France* (Paris, 1962) and *Elites africaines et culture occidentale* (Paris, 1969). The importance of French-educated leadership in African nationalist movements is demonstrated in several analyses for different countries. John Halstead shows that the majority of the inner executive group of the Moroccan nationalist movement, the majority of the theoreticians, and all the external propagandists received a French education (*Rebirth of a Nation,* appendix D). Ruth S. Morgenthau, *Political Parties in French-Speaking West Africa* (Oxford, 1964), shows in appendix 8 the educational backgrounds of members of the territorial assemblies in the Ivory Coast, Mali, Upper Volta, Niger, Senegal and Guinea after 1947.

Department and prepare their pupils to meet established secular standards for certificates and diplomas.

The grant-in-aid helped to maintain a varied school system at a minimum cost to the government during the financial stringency of the 1930–35 period, when world depression induced in British Africa attitudes of extreme caution in public finance. This resulted in a relatively large primary school population (when compared, for instance, with that in French areas); it also augmented both the pressure for and the possibility of a substantial increase in the number of secondary schools, which came in many countries soon after the conclusion of the Second World War.[81]

But the grant-in-aid had its disadvantages. It entrenched missionary influence at the headquarters of educational policy and thus perpetu-

81. One has only to compare the provision of secondary schools in 1949 with that in 1938 to see the magnitude of the change. Where the data permit I have tried to show only secondary schools that have at least one class going to School Certificate level. The data for both schools and students are surprisingly difficult to obtain and miscellaneous in their descriptive categories.

	1938		*1949*	
	A	B	A	B
Gambia	2 asst	57(?) boys 101(?) girls	4	184 boys 175 girls
Sierra Leone	1 govt 7 asst	258 boys 168 girls	12 govt and asst	2092 boys 220 girls
Gold Coast	1 govt 3 asst		11 govt and asst	2091 boys 451 girls
Togo (mandate and trust)	no secondary school		one "to be opened in Jan. 1950"	
Nigeria *			25	c. 5800
Cameroon (mandate and trust)	no secondary school		2	237
Uganda	Makerere 153		6	c. 300
Kenya	no full secondary course for Africans		2	324
Tanganyika (mandate and trust)	junior secondary only		10 govt 15 asst	2001 boys 81 girls
N. Rhodesia	no African secondary		2	c. 250
Nyasaland	no secondary school		2	140

NOTE: Col. A = number of assisted or government schools.
Col. B = number of pupils in those schools.

* Figures are for 1943.

SOURCES: Colonial Office, *Annual Reports; Higher Education in East Africa* (Col. No. 142, 1937); *Higher Education in West Africa* (Cmd. 6655, 1945).

ated an ambiguity of purpose in the schools. In some cases (such as eastern Nigeria) sectarian rivalries greatly complicated planning for educational expansion; in others (such as the southern Sudan and Tanganyika) they led to a policy prejudicial to Muslim schools or even to missionary intransigence toward the expansion of government schools into areas over which they believed that they had staked spiritual claims.[82] Africans viewed with sardonic amusement and irritation the parochial battles that resulted from the union of God and literacy. The schools grew, but often (as in *The Arrow of God*[83]) it was not clear whether hope of gaining new knowledge and opportunity or fear of the white God's malevolence was the compelling force.

Neither the inducements of grants-in-aid nor the cautious policies of Education Departments succeeded in preventing the opening of marginal unaided schools in response to African demand. In southern Nigeria up to the 1940s, these bush schools "probably accounted for over two-thirds of the South's primary school enrollment."[84] In Northern Rhodesia in 1938 more than twice as many pupils were in unaided schools (86,495) as were in government and aided schools combined (35,197); and in the same year in Uganda the ratio of unaided to aided on the primary level was more than 5 to 1 (258,537 to 50,102).[85] By contrast, in 1938 there were in the Gold Coast twice as many primary- and middle-school pupils in government and aided schools (60,569) as in unaided ones (25,951).[86] This reflected the determination of Governor Guggisberg to build a strong government school system and the relatively buoyant cocoa economy that made his policy possible.[87] Although the instruction in unaided schools was often rudimentary and the percentage of pupils who finished more than several years of schooling very small, the bush schools served to spread widely the idea of education as the path to opportunities outside the village. They were undoubtedly a factor in the widespread support for universal primary education which became a political rallying cry in the

82. For the conflicts on Nigeria, see Abernethy, "Nigeria," esp. pp. 220–37; for the Sudan see Beshir, *Educational Development*, chap. 8; for Tanzania see J. Cameron and W. A. Dodd, *Society, Schools, and Progress in Tanzania* (Oxford, 1970), chap. 5; for Zambia see Coombe, "Origins of Secondary Education," p. 380.

83. Chinua Achebe, *Arrow of God* (London, 1966).

84. Abernethy, p. 208.

85. Coombe, Table facing p. 174; R. Jolly, *Planning Education for African Development* (Nairobi, 1969), Table III-3, p. 58.

86. Jolly, Table IV-3, p. 108.

87. R. E. Wraith, *Guggisberg* (London, 1967), chaps. 5, 6.

1950s, first in West Africa and toward the end of the decade in East Africa.[88]

On the secondary school level the characteristic result of British policy before 1945 was the residential boarding school. Originally made necessary by the small numbers of qualified students drawn from an enormous geographical area, these schools were favored by the Advisory Committee as "the most effective means of training character." [89] The model of the British Public School hovered latent in their minds. In Africa these schools were few, but they achieved an influence out of all proportion to their size. It is necessary to realize how selective secondary education was. In 1937, for example, the only school offering a full secondary course for African students in the whole of British East and Central Africa was Makerere. Six students had taken the Cambridge School Certificate examinations there in 1935.[90]

> Junior secondary education was given at five mission schools in Uganda in 1937, two of which, Budo and Kisubi, had in the previous year opened courses leading to the Cambridge School Certificate. Kenya likewise had five mission junior secondary schools of which two (Alliance and Kabaa) were about to begin the full course. In Tanganyika one government school (Tabora) and four mission schools offered junior secondary education, though none as yet contemplated going to school certificate. Zanzibar's sole secondary school had been opened in 1935. . . . Nyasaland and Northern Rhodesia had not yet introduced secondary education.[91]

In this context it is easy to understand both the importance of the grant-in-aid to mission schools and Makerere's preeminence.[92]

Set against the background of the longer tradition of secondary education in West Africa, the rise to prominence of Achimota (outside Accra) and The Higher College, Yaba (near Lagos), reflects the money and energy poured into them by respective colonial governments. Achimota, opened in January 1927, was almost a personal triumph for Sir Gordon Guggisberg; during his term as governor (1919–

88. On bush schools in general, see A. Victor Murray, *The Schools in the Bush: A Critical Study of Native Education in Africa* (2d ed. London, 1938; reprint 1967).

89. *Education Policy in British Tropical Africa*, p. 5.

90. Coombe, "Origins of Secondary Education," p. 368.

91. Ibid., p. 369.

92. For Makerere, see M. Macpherson, *They Built for the Future* (Cambridge, 1964).

27) he voiced official aspirations for an autonomous African university in West Africa,[93] and he planned for Achimota to be its basis.

> From the very beginning, Achimota will be entirely independent, and will be organised in such a manner that it can, when the time comes, be transferred to the control of whatever board or authority that by then may be considered the most suitable to take charge of the university into which it will blossom.[94]

Guggisberg's faith in African advance and the timetable he laid down for the Africanization of the senior civil service were outspokenly ahead of his official colleagues. In addition, he secured the help of J. E. Kwegjir Aggrey, a Fanti from Anomabu who had taught for twenty years in the United States and gained firsthand knowledge of the Negro colleges of the American south. As a member of the Phelps-Stokes Commission, Aggrey had brought his personal experience to bear in interpreting black life on both sides of the Atlantic, and he made a very considerable contribution to the success of Achimota.[95]

The Higher College, Yaba, was designed with less elevated purposes in mind. No one held for it the vision that Guggisberg had for Achimota. When it opened in temporary buildings in 1932, Yaba was to be a postsecondary institution for students "seeking to become Assistant Agricultural, Forestry, Medical, Survey and Veterinary Officers." Nigerians have been quick to point out that the "operative word is 'Assistant.' "[96] They resented the direct connection between Yaba and government employment. After four years of study graduates of Yaba received a diploma; they were not allowed to take the London Univer-

93. Wraith, *Guggisberg*, p. 158.

94. From Guggisberg's address to the Legislative Council, March 6, 1924, in Metcalfe, *Great Britian and Ghana*, p. 559. The African leaders of the Gold Coast (Ghana) went back to Guggisberg's vision to support their own convictions that a university college should be established in the Gold Coast. See *Report of the Commission on Higher Education* (Accra, 1946), p. 3. They were furious that Creech Jones, as Secretary of State, had accepted the minority view of the Elliot Commission (that only one university college be established in West Africa, at Ibadan). In the event, the Secretary reversed himself. See *Secretary of State's Despatch of 6th August 1947 and the Inter-University Council Memorandum on Higher Education in West Africa* (Accra, 1947).

95. Edwin W. Smith, *Aggrey of Africa: A Study in Black and White* (New York, 1930); J. Kingsley Williams, *Achimota—the Early Years* (London, 1962); W. E. F. Ward, *Fraser of Trinity and Achimota* (Accra, 1965); Wriath, *Guggisberg*.

96. O. Ikejiani and J. O. Anowi, "Nigerian Universities," in *Nigerian Education*, ed. O. Ikejiani (Ikeja, 1964), p. 130.

sity external examinations. The numbers entering the school were very small: an average of fewer than 40 annually (1932–44). Although in fact students from Yaba formed the nucleus of the undergraduate body of the University College at Ibadan when it opened in January 1948, Yaba never caught the imagination of Nigerians. The conception behind it seemed less generous and more technical than they believed the situation warranted. But together with Fourah Bay, Achimota, Gordon Memorial College (Khartoum), and Makerere, Yaba formed the foundation for higher education in British Africa.

At the secondary level these schools were directly analogous to the British system, and they soon made use of external examinations—first at the school certificate level and then at the level of university entrance, the higher certificate. The external examination was a powerful tool of educational assimilation. Because of it, curricula tended to follow the well-established tracks of the metropolitan system with the incentive that a good performance might make possible continued education overseas. At a time when university education was almost unobtainable in Africa, the external examination was negotiable coinage.[97]

Inevitably, full-time residence in the ethos of character and leadership emphasized by these schools underlined the elite nature of secondary education. To add esprit and to inculcate a sense of responsibility had certainly been Guggisberg's intent with Achimota. Its success made it the focus for visiting groups and a model for institutions as distant as Tabora (Tanganyika), Munali (Northern Rhodesia), and the Ecole Normale William Ponty (Senegal).[98] The stimulus of elite status established for staff and students alike expectation about the quality of university education. The manner added a certain cachet to the fact that numbers alone made unambiguous—very few African students could attain a secondary education before the Second World War.

Many of the participants have written their versions of the creation

97. J. D. Hargreaves made some perceptive remarks about external examinations during the course of the Yale conference discussions. Ashby's *Universities* deals with them incidentally (pp. 236–49), but there is no thorough study of their effect upon African curricula. Michalina Vaughan, in "The *Grandes Ecoles,*" in *Governing Elites,* ed. R. Wilkinson (New York, 1969), p. 75, demonstrates that in France competitive examinations are "both democratic as a means of selection and elitist as a method of classification." In the colonies, however, selection by examination reinforced those who already had a strong identification with metropolitan culture and thus reduced the open or representative aspect of recruitment.

98. See Coombe, "Origins of Secondary Education"; also p. 696 above.

and endowment of a university system in British Africa.[99] The Elliot Commission, appointed in June 1943 in the midst of war, was the first to establish officially the need for degree-granting universities in West Africa. We will not rehearse here the succession of commissions, reports, and plans for African higher education that attempted to match the accelerated pace of political devolution,[100] but three points about this enormous effort remain significant. First, it reasserted for a decade the direct applicability of metropolitan models. The new university colleges drew heavily upon existing British universities for their staffs, in constitution making, and in curriculum design. The frequent reference to "standards" reflected a metropolitan perspective. In British West Africa, as in French, the decade 1950–60 meant renewed educational assimilation during a period of growing political independence. Second, the heavy concentration of expatriates or Europeans employed by African universities during this period tended to push salaries to levels equivalent with those of Britain. This had two unfortunate effects: it created an enormous gap between the pay of a primary school teacher and a university teacher, and it meant that salaries were a much greater proportionate cost in Africa than in Western Europe. "A

99. K. Mellanby, *The Birth of Nigeria's University* (London, 1958); J. T. Saunders, *University College, Ibadan* (Cambridge, 1960); A. M. Carr-Saunders, *New Universities Overseas* (London, 1961); Sir Eric Ashby, *African Universities and the Western Tradition* (Cambridge, Mass., 1964); idem., *Universities.*

100. *Report of the Commission on Higher Education in the Colonies* [Asquith Commission], Cmd. 6647 (London, 1945); *Report of the Commission on Higher Education in West Africa* [Elliot Commission], Cmd, 6655 (London, 1945); Gold Coast, *Report of Commission on Higher Education* (Accra, 1946); *Inter-University Council for Higher Education in the Colonies: Second Report,* 1947–49, Cmd. 7801 (London, 1949); *University of Nigeria* (Eastern Region Doc. No. 4 of 1958); Nigeria, Federal Ministry of Education, *Investment in Education* [Ashby Commission] (Lagos, 1960); East African Governments, *Report of the Quinquennial Advisory Committee* (on higher education in East Africa) (Nairobi, 1960); *Report of Inter-University Council Delegation—University of Northern Nigeria* (April 1961); UNESCO, *Draft Report of Advisory Commission for the Establishment of the University of Lagos* (Paris, 1961); UNESCO, *Development of Higher Education in Africa* (Tananarive Conference) (Paris, 1963).

In East Africa the concept of a federal university was evolved as a compromise between costly educational duplication and political reality. There is reason to believe that one of the important stimuli for the federal idea was the desire to placate the donors (chiefly American and British foundations) who had put millions of pounds into Makerere during the 1950's. Even at its inception, some of the architects of the federal university believed it to be a temporary expedient. Political independence did not seem to them compatible with the use of a university in another country.

senior secondary school teacher starts at less than two and a half times *per capita* income in England, at seven times in Ghana and at 27 times in Uganda." [101] At Ibadan, for instance, the Nigerian members of the academic staff succeeded in instituting the principle of equal pay for equal work,[102] which is both desirable and appropriate within the university. But the larger effect is that teachers, like many employed persons on civil service scales, earn a disproportionate share of the existing national wealth and thus contribute to the continued slowness with which total employment expands.[103] Third, the rate of increase in investment in education during the decade 1950–60 was enormous, but it masked the very low levels from which the increase began. "In spite of the rapid increases, public expenditure on education still averaged little more than three per cent of gross domestic product in 1962—2.8% in 13 French-speaking countries and 3.4% in 11 English." [104] This was a measure of the educational deficit remaining from the colonial years.

In the long run the most intractable aspect of the colonial legacy may prove to be the wage structure of higher education and, more broadly, the very high premium paid to the educated. Without a full-scale revision of the wage structure on a national scale, many African countries will be caught in the apparent paradox of having educated unemployed and a simultaneous shortage of high skilled manpower. During the colonial period—as well as today—many have urged that the problem would be ameliorated if only people could be taught different things, if they could be trained to meet the needs of the country. This approach has, in general, failed, because the real incentives for individuals—financial return, status, and future opportunity—were, and continue to be, in the civil service and the professions. If one is to invest twenty years of one's life in education, one wants to aim at maximum returns.

Some argue that the best course is for African nations to produce graduates of secondary schools and universities at a rate beyond the capacity of the society to absorb them in the belief that they will help to bring about a revision of the wage scale.[105] This policy is hazardous:

101. Jolly, *Planning Education*, p. 116. In *Education in Africa* (Nairobi, 1969), pp. 47–62, Jolly emphasizes that rapid increases in wages and salaries since 1960 continue to aggravate this problem and to consume much of the increased educational budgets.

102. Ikejiani and Anowi, "Nigerian Universities," pp. 149–55.

103. Jolly, *Educational Planning*, chap. 4, and p. 116 n. 1.

104. Ibid., p. 115.

105. Jolly suggests this (p. 139), following W. A. Lewis's arguments of 1961.

instability, perhaps revolution, is a real risk; and it may not succeed in changing "entrenched interests and attitudes."[106] We mention it here because it is an integral part of the educational heritage of British and French Africa. The high standards of construction and appointment for a few secondary schools and universities, the high cost and frequently large return of an overseas education, and the high expectations established for the generation in school during the 1950s all stood in the way of a genuine domestication of higher education in Africa. From this perspective the 1970s will be the decade of disassimilation.

For the African child schooling was a long process: "I began by attending the Moslem school, and a little later I was enrolled in the French school. Neither my mother nor I had any notion how long I would be a student at the latter."[107] If he did well, the student moved physically and psychically further and further from his village (although he sought the help of the marabouts in passing his examinations): "Yes, she must have guessed at the workings of the inner wheels which, from the school in Kouroussa, led me to Conakry and would finally take me to France . . . my destiny was to go away from home."[108] Paris (or London or Bordeaux or Edinburgh) brought new acquaintances, new humiliations, new hopes. It occasioned new insight; reaffirmation of negritude,[109] alienation ("A Senegalese learns Creole in order to pass as an Antilles native: I call this alienation."[110]), and real knowledge of the metropole:

> In the evenings, exhausted, he returned home, his head stuffed with crude jokes and insults heard all day long. His mouth dry, without appetite, he bolted a sandwich and forced himself to go to Trade School. . . . For a whole year he dragged his poor body from the champagne wholesaler to the Trade School.[111]

106. Ibid., p. 156.

107. Camara Laye, *L'enfant noir* (Paris, 1954); trans. James Kirkup, *The African Child* (London, 1959), p. 63.

108. Kirkup, p. 157.

109. The literature of and about negritude is enormous. Perhaps the most useful analysis is that by the Nigerian Abiola Irele in two articles: "Negritude or Black Cultural Nationalism" and "Negritude—Literature and Ideology," both in *Journal of Modern African Studies,* 3 (1965), 321–48, 499–526.

110. Franz Fanon, *Peau noire, masques blancs* (Paris, 1952); trans. C. L. Markman, *Black Skin, White Masks* (New York, 1967), p. 38.

111. Aké Loba, *Kocoumbo, l'étudiant noir* (Paris, 1960), trans. P. Gifford, from the selection in A. C. Brench, *Writing in French from Senegal to Cameroon* (London, 1967), p. 95.

And perhaps then the student returned with a wider vision of Africa:

> And we shall be steeped my dear in the presence of
> Africa.
> Furniture from Guinea and Congo, heavy and
> polished, sombre and serene.
> On the walls, pure primordial masks distant and yet
> present.
> Stools of honour for hereditary guests, for the
> Princes of the High Lands.[112]

Both in imagination and in fact, the colonial period brought into being a *civilisation métisse:* a jostling, a juxtaposition of values. The indelible education, imbedded in the mind and felt through the senses, was a blend of contrasts.

> Abdou, born a Muslim and a man of the east, had been educated in French schools. His mind thrived upon European ideas and logic. His sensibility was formed upon the curious combination of the Senegalese guitar (Khalam), French poetry and European music. Great contrasts existed within him. He could dance a tango as well as a *tam-tam;* he loved African music and African girls, but also dreamed about Deauville and Paris.[113]

What the novelist sensed in 1935, the sociologist confirmed thirty years later. The experience in France enriched certain ideas for African students and impoverished or isolated others.[114] Living in France, the idea of nation took on new dimensions and new particularity; the experience "had the effect of mobilizing in these African students a stronger determination to build an African nation."[115] On the other hand, they found the experience of European religion nugatory; it had little effect on their aspirations or cultural attitudes.[116] Upon returning to Africa most of them took up again the religious practices they had left behind. The syntheses that men make are their real education.

The most enduring legacy is the colonial language itself. French and English have become rooted in Africa as means of international

112. Leopold Sedar Senghor, *Nocturnes* (Paris, 1961); trans. John Reed and Clive Wake, *Nocturnes* (London, 1969), p. 12.

113. Ousmane Socé Diop, *Karim: Roman senegalais* (Paris, 1935), trans. J. D. Hargreaves, *France and West Africa* (London, 1969), p. 246.

114. N'Diaye develops this thesis in *Élites africaines.*

115. Ibid., p. 209, trans. P. Gifford.

116. Ibid., pp. 204–05.

communication, as modes of analysis. Literature is written, government conducted, and universities organized through what were once foreign and are now national languages. This is a result of the whole weight of colonialism—its potent result. Through the intimacy and estrangement that comes with mastery of another's language, Africans have achieved the power to assimilate what they wish.

> Lord, you have made me Master-of-language
> Me, son of a trader, puny and grey at birth
> My mother called me Shame, I gave such offence to
> the beauty of the day.
> You in the unfairness of your justice have given me
> the power of speech
> Lord, harken to my voice.[117]

This bittersweet legacy of language, reinforced by education, means that African peoples must present themselves to the world largely through the words, the metaphors, the concepts of the Western intellectual tradition. To speak through another's mask and to preserve the self within is a constraining art. In this sense the colonial struggle continues still: Africans must wrest from French and English the power to enhance rather than efface themselves.

117. Senghor, *Nocturnes*, p. 50.

☙ 20. *Free France in Africa: Gaullism and Colonialism*

☙ D. BRUCE MARSHALL

World War II worked many lasting changes on the colonial systems of both Britain and France. At best, most of the colonies found themselves cut off from their respective metropole, forced to survive on their own resources without economic support, with diminished personnel and uncertain leadership. At worst, some, such as the territories of the Maghreb, became part of the battlezone.

In retrospect, the effects of World War II seem at first glance to have been much the same for France and for Britain, weakening the hold of the metropolitan bureaucracy over the colonial administration and sharply reducing the control the latter could in turn exercise over the indigenous peoples of the colonies; reducing drastically the means available for promoting economic and social development; and strongly stimulating the emotional and political movement of the colonial peoples toward independence.

In fact, however, the impact of World War II on French colonial politics in Africa was neither as unambiguous nor as consistent as these first impressions suggest. The shocks imparted by the war were especially damaging to France, whose authority overseas as well as her capacity to perform the functions of an imperial power were deeply undermined by the military defeat of her armies and the political surrender of the metropole. France's position after June 1940 was quite different from that of Britain, and far more desperate. The men who led her wartime government were of a different sort, whose ideas and expectations reflected a different tradition from that which inspired British statesmen. Most important of all, perhaps, France's role in the wartime alliance, and consequently her access to the military, economic, and political support necessary to any colonial program, was much more limited than that of Britain. Hence, although it is true that both the two great European imperial states found themselves confronted with pressing demands for independence from their African colonies during the two decades after World War II, it would be a mistake to assume that the war affected both countries in the same manner.

The immediate effect of World War II on French African policy seems to have been to alter the political system, and particularly the institutional framework within which change was later to occur, rather than to transform French policies or the guiding ideas that underlay them. By generating new expectations on the part of the indigenous African elites and by providing the African colonies with a rudimentary political system within which new demands, once legitimized, could be made politically effective, the wartime reforms set the stage for the eventual emergence of native nationalist movements throughout the French territories. Such was not the intention of the Gaullist wartime leadership, however, even though some French writers have asserted that the policies of decolonization later implemented by the Fifth Republic received their initial impetus from reforms drafted during this period, notably at the Conference of Brazzaville convened by General de Gaulle in January 1944. The attention lavished upon the Brazzaville Conference in particular appears all the more ironical when one considers that the primary aim of that meeting, as of all the rest of Gaullist policy during the wartime period, was to tie the overseas territories more securely to France.

The pervasive irony that characterizes Gaullist policy toward the African territories can best be understood by examining two actions taken by the Gaullist Provisional Government: the Brazzaville Conference in January 1944 and the *Ordonnance* of March 7, 1944, which conferred French citizenship on tens of thousands of Algerian Muslims. The former brought together the principal threads of Gaullist political thought regarding the colonies and sought to apply them to the problems of sub-Saharan Africa. The latter expanded on some of the same themes in the very different context of the rising movement of Muslim self-consciousness in Algeria and throughout the Maghreb. Central to both actions was de Gaulle's determination to hold the colonies close to the metropole as a guarantee of France's world status and grandeur. In both cases, too, the actions taken had unanticipated consequences which were to vitiate and eventually to confound those intentions.

The first occasion on which the disparate elements of Gaullist colonial doctrine were brought face to face with the realities of colonial life was the Brazzaville Conference of January–February 1944. This important meeting assembled the governors of all French Africa, now once again united under Free French control, together with members of the Consultative Assembly at Algiers and the ranking members of the Gaullist provisional regime. Its primary purpose was to formulate a plan to coordinate the economic and political development of the African territories. The results of the conference, although difficult to assess in detail, must be accounted impressive by any reasonable standard. For not only did the conference advance a comprehensive program of economic and social improvement, but for the first—and, indeed, the only time in recent history—the men who were directly responsible for the execution of French policy were given the opportunity to lay out a program of political action as well. This effort at shaping the process of political change, and the attempt to maintain a close relationship between political, economic, and social developments within the vast area of French Africa was truly a monumental undertaking.

The grand scope of these purposes was dramatically presented by de Gaulle in his opening speech. After stressing the urgent need for coordinated planning and hailing "the centuries-old civilizing mission of the Republic" that had been carried out by France's great colonial administrators, de Gaulle analyzed the changing position of the colonies in French strategy and urged his listeners to take careful account of the enormously accelerated pace that the war had given to the political evolution of the colonies. Such rapid changes created many problems which, he said, France was determined to confront in a generous spirit, for,

> if there is one imperial power that has been led by recent events to heed its lessons, to choose nobly, liberally, the way of a new era in which to direct the 60 million people who find themselves associated with the destiny of her own 42 million children, that country is France.[1]

As one would expect on such an occasion, the familiar themes of Gaullist colonial doctrine were prominently displayed. Special emphasis was placed upon "the immortal genius of France . . . for raising men toward the summits of dignity and fraternity where . . . they may all unite" and upon the "definitive bond" between France and the colonies formed by the heavy sacrifices of blood and treasure on the part of colonial populations "who had not for a moment altered

1. The Ministry of the Colonies published a transcript of the Brazzaville Conference under the title: *Conférence Africaine Française de Brazzaville, 30 janvier–8 fevrier 1944* (Paris, 1945). It is cited here as *Conférence de Brazzaville.*

their loyalties." But such ideas were not mere decoration; neither were they invoked to justify inaction. It was change and radical innovation that de Gaulle clearly intended to inspire, for he repeatedly stressed the need for France to look forward to the day when Africa would come of age politically as well as economically, and to prepare the way for increased economic wealth, improved standards of living, and much larger measures of political autonomy. He told the conference:

> There will be no real progress if men in their native lands do not profit by it morally and materially; if they cannot raise themselves little by little to the level where they will be capable of participating directly in the management of their own affairs. It is France's duty to see to it that it shall be so.[2]

If these admonitions are considered in conjunction with his other statements of policy, however, it becomes clear that de Gaulle conceived of political change in Africa as part of a larger strategic plan whose ultimate purpose lay outside the realm of colonial problems altogether. In his view, the African colonies like the rest of the colonial empire were but a means to a greater end, an end which was embodied in de Gaulle's own strategic vision of France's national purposes. Initially, he had been concerned to rally the colonies to the side of Free France both to legitimate the political claims made by the French National Liberation Committee (CFLN) in the name of the French people and to secure Allied recognition of the CFLN as the official spokesman for France within the wartime coalition. Thus, in June 1940 it was the allegiance of the overseas empire that de Gaulle sought when he declared: "France is not alone. She has a vast empire behind her. Together with the British Empire, she can form a bloc that controls the seas and continues the struggle."[3]

Later, as the war was drawing to a close, de Gaulle became concerned with the political fate of France, which he saw as intimately linked to France's role in the postwar world. He regarded the unity of the Empire as essential to France in order to restore a sufficient sense of self-confidence to prevent the various political factions within France from returning once again to "the savory games of illusion and denigration" rather than attending to the hard realities that lay ahead. Moreover, it seemed to de Gaulle that the Empire alone could restore to France the needed prestige with the victorious allies to guarantee

2. *Conférence de Brazzaville*, p. 28.
3. Charles de Gaulle, *Discours et Messages 1940–1946* (Paris, 1947), p. 1.

her a proper role in the postwar European system. As he told a gathering in Algiers in 1943:

> For the future, France, by her genius, by her experience, will be one of the best artisans of universal peace. Integrated into the old Europe . . . but spread out over the entire world by its territories and its humanitarian influence, the France of tomorrow will be among the front rank of the nations who are great.[4]

And again, de Gaulle insisted to the Consultative Assembly that, "In the refound unity of the nation and the Empire, we will be sure enough of ourselves to be able to contribute powerfully to the maintenance of peace." [5]

Finally, looking toward the more distant future, de Gaulle posited a central role for France in the creation of a new European power balance; a role that could be effectively filled only if France and the colonies remained united in a coherent, mutual association. As he later explained:

> It is perfectly clear to me that in order to conduct such a policy in Europe, we must have our hands free beyond the seas. If the overseas territories detach themselves from the metropole, or if we allow our forces to become hung up there, how much will we count for between the North Sea and the Mediterranean? Should they, on the contrary, remain associated with us, why then the way would be open for our action on the continent—secular destiny of France! [6]

Unity between the metropole and the colonies was, consequently, a primary prerequisite to the achievement of the most basic goals of Gaullist foreign policy: the restoration of France's "rank" among the nations of the world and the preservation of that "grandeur" which de Gaulle had always considered essential to France's destiny and which had formed such an important part of his own "certain idea of France."

The amount of innovation that the Brazzaville Conference could accomplish was limited by two important factors, one constitutional and the other economic. Primarily an assembly of civil servants, the conference was empowered only to recommend action to the Consultative Assembly and the Provisional Government, and even these organs had no constituent powers; therefore, any structural changes which the

4. De Gaulle, *Mémoires de Guerre* (3 vols. Paris, 1955–60), *2*, 516.
5. Ibid., *3*, 90, 130.
6. Ibid., *3*, 223.

conference proposed had to await action by a competent national assembly. This meant that structural reforms were to be excluded because, "it is for the French nation, and for her alone, to proceed when the time comes, to the reforms . . . which she, in her sovereignty, will decide." Meantime the conference was asked:

> to study what social, political, economic and other conditions seem to you to be capable of progressively being applied in each of our territories in order that, through their own development and the progress of their populations, they will integrate themselves into the French community with their interests, their aspirations, their future.[7]

It would be a mistake, however, to underestimate the extent to which plans adopted to meet immediate problems tended effectively to shape the future. It had happened before in the course of French history, most notably under the National Government of M. Thiers in 1870, and de Gaulle was fully aware of this possibility: "en attendant il faut vivre, et vivre c'est chaque jour entamer l'avenir." [8]

A second important limitation stemmed from the conditions under which it was necessary to operate and the poverty of the means available. Hence, de Gaulle advised against trying to conceal how long and slow development was bound to be.

At the heart of the problem of colonial reform lay the tangled web of political and administrative institutions that linked the prewar colonial empire. These were substantially the same ones created by Napoleon III in 1854, although the *Senatus-Consulte* of 1854 no longer possessed constitutional force and hence could be altered by ordinary law. Since no general law was ever adopted during the Third Republic, the *Senatus-Consulte* amounted to a broad grant of power under which the executive governed the colonies by administrative decrees except for the Antilles and Réunion, Algeria, Tunisia, and Morocco, each of which enjoyed special legislative arrangements. Occasionally metropolitan laws had been extended by the government to meet particular colonial problems. Generally, however, these had been treated by ministerial decree or by special local regulations issued by the colonial governor.

As long as colonial interests were confined to the local European community, this system worked reasonably well, since it was usually possible to shape policy in consultation with commercial groups in

7. *Conférence de Brazzaville,* pp. 29–30.
8. Ibid., p. 30.

the colony or, in the case of parliamentary acts, through the auspices of ministers and deputies who were indirectly interested in colonial questions. With the rapid expansion of economic life and a consequent increase in the importance of non-Europeans within the colonies, a more effective system of policy making was essential. Such a system had to be based upon four broad groups of existing institutions: the predominantly European economic organizations such as the *Chambres de commerce,* producers' syndicates, employers organizations, etc.; traditional local authorities, including religious leaders, tribal chiefs, local notables, occasional intellectuals, or indigenous farmers or workers organizations; the colonial administration, which traditionally operated to coordinate and balance the influence of the first two groups as well as to take charge of most local policy making; and, finally, the representative institutions of metropolitan France, which traditionally had remained apart from any direct role in colonial affairs.

The Gaullist provisional regime approached the problem in a manner consistent with the French colonial tradition. Unlike the British, who tended to seek to establish responsible local governments by integrating local elites into the civil administration and by emphasizing its responsibility to locally designated legislatures, the French stressed the need for community-wide political representation and administrative centralization. By putting the issue in such terms, they raised a number of exceedingly difficult problems, such as the nature of French citizenship and the related questions of participation in local and metropolitan assemblies, as well as the thorny problems of civil rights in regard both to the executive and judiciary, and the distribution of power between the central and local government bodies. Characteristically, it was assumed that there existed sufficient underlying consensus—an effective "general will"—to prevent conflict between the people and the policy-making elite, provided sufficient opportunity for local expression could be provided. One writer notes:

> The politicians of that period did not conceive of the Empire, even under the more liberal and egalitarian form of the French Union, as an association of autonomous peoples or Dominions. Convinced of the rightness of her cause and of the utility of her presence, France did not believe that a single one of the colonial peoples was sufficiently advanced to govern itself without her protection. Lacking any sort of powerful dynastic bond such as England and the dominions possess in the King, France and her possessions, in order that their association or their union be durable, needed to develop

between them a bond as strong if not stronger, but a Republican bond.[9]

In confronting the problem of political change, the Brazzaville Conference followed the lead given several years earlier by Félix Eboué in a report entitled, *La nouvelle politique indigène pour l'Afrique Equatoriale Française*.[10] The substance of Eboué's position was that "assimilation," which in Central Africa had never been more than the official facade behind which traditional chiefs continued to rule under the formal authority of the *commandant de cercle*, should be abandoned in favor of a regime that would recognize openly the important role played by the local elites both European and non-European.

Eboué insisted that French policy explicitly renounce any intention "to remake native society according to our image or our mental habits." He argued that the French administration should strive "not to disturb any tradition nor change any habits." Rather, they should remember the secret of successful colonial rule enunciated by L. H. G. Lyautey, who once had written that in every society there exists a ruling class [*class dirigeante*] born to command, without which nothing can be done: "Let us get it on our side." Following the example of Lyautey, Eboué hoped to induce the traditional African elite to cooperate with the colonial administration in its efforts to improve economic and social conditions. He proposed political and administrative changes calculated to give the educated elite—the *notables évolués*—an active role in the administration of the larger towns. More important, however, it freed this group from the penalties commonly imposed under the *indigénat*, or native code, which permitted local officials to impose punishment for infractions of discipline, and from compulsory labor service which was required of most non-Europeans. The purpose of such liberality toward the African elite was to associate them with the colonial administration in order to encourage them to assume more responsibility for local affairs. It was not aimed, however, at developing the sort of autonomy that would replace French administration with local self-government.

Similarly, the Brazzaville Conference in the preamble to its "recommendations" pointedly observed that no such move, even in the long run, was to be considered.

9. Michel Devèze, *La France d'outre-mer* (Paris, 1948), p. 216.

10. The report is reprinted as an annex in Jean Laroche and Jean Gottman, *La Fédération française* (Montreal, 1945), pp. 586–627.

The goals of the task of civilization accomplished by France in her colonies rule out any idea of autonomy, any possibility of evolution outside the French bloc of the empire; the eventual creation, even in the distant future, of *self-government* [sic] for the colonies is to be set aside.[11]

It was within this rather narrow, traditional framework that the conference took up the questions of greater autonomy for the colonies and increased political participation for non-Europeans both in the colonies and in the metropole. The recommendations it offered on these matters, although not entirely unprecedented, nevertheless went a considerable distance in the direction of recognizing the political personality of the colonies. And despite a general lack of precision in the choice of language, it is evident that what was intended was a substantial change from existing practices.[12]

Within the colonies, the conference sought to gain the support of indigenous leaders by encouraging progressive development toward a system of effective representation: "It is indispensable to create the means for political expression which will permit the governors . . . to rely, on the side of both Europeans and Natives, upon a perfectly balanced and legitimate representative system."[13] Specifically, it recommended that existing consultative bodies be abolished and replaced by a set of new organs. At the lower administrative levels, the subdivision and region, councils were to be formed from existing indigenous organizations, supplemented by other members, and were to enjoy the right to consult with the administration. At the territorial level, representative assemblies were to be instituted in which both Europeans and Africans participated. Members of the territorial assemblies were to be elected "by universal suffrage everywhere and under all conditions where the possibility will have been recognized."[14] Where election was impracticable, members might be chosen by co-

11. The recommendations of the Brazzaville Conference are summarized in H. Michel and B. Mirkine-Guetzevitch, *Les Idées politiques et sociales de la Résistance* (Paris, 1945), pp. 339 ff., and are briefly reviewed in "L'Evolution recente des institutions politiques dans les territoires d'Outre-Mer et Territoires Associés," *La Documentation française, Notes et Etudes Documentaires,* No. 1847, March 11, 1954.

12. For an enlightening contemporary critique of the conference, see Henry Solus, "La Conférence de Brazzaville," in *Le Monde français* (October 1945), pp. 54 ff.

13. *Idées politiques . . . de la Résistance,* p. 340.

14. Ibid., p. 341.

optation or, in exceptional cases, appointed. The powers of the territorial assemblies were primarily consultative, but they were to have the right to deliberate on the budget of the territory.[15] The Conseils d'Administration, which were composed entirely of civil servants, were to assist the governor only in matters relating to the application of regulations, and all other representative bodies within the colonies were to be disbanded.

At the metropolitan level too, the link between France and the colonies was to be strengthened by increasing the role of non-Europeans in the development of colonial policy. The most important step taken by the Brazzaville Conference was to call for the inclusion of overseas representatives in the Constitutional Assembly that was expected to follow the end of the war. It was assumed by everyone in the Free French movement that extensive constitutional reforms would be required in order both to wipe out the repressive legislation of Vichy and to strengthen the feeble institutions of the Third Republic. The precise role of the African and other colonial peoples in such a Constituent Assembly would, of necessity, have to be determined by a higher political authority. Therefore, the Brazzaville Conference sought merely to lay down general guides for government action. Although the conference did not ignore the choice of means, it was much more explicit about the ends to be sought.

That such participation was "desirable and even indispensable" appeared beyond question in view of "the importance of the colonies in the French community, an importance which should no longer need discussion after the service they have rendered to the nation during the course of this war." [16] In an effort to assure that colonial representation would be more effective than it had been in the past, the conference declared that, "a priori any reform is to be rejected that would tend merely to ameliorate the system of representation existing on 1 September 1939 (colonial deputies and senators in the Metropolitan Parliament with new seats being granted to those colonies not

15. The budget was always prepared by the colonial administration and customarily contained two parts: the budget for existing expenses, which were primarily costs of administration, and the budget for new programs, including most economic development projects. The only area in which any freedom of choice could be said to exist was the second of these. See P. F. Gonidec, *Droit d'Outre-Mer* (Paris, Ed. Montchrestien, 1959–60), pp. 185–91. All decisions required administrative endorsement.

16. *Idées politiques . . . de la Résistance,* p. 349.

presently represented)."[17] Instead, a new representative body was recommended.

This new organ, the "Colonial Parliament" or, preferably, "Federal Assembly," was intended to meet several specific needs: "to affirm and guarantee the infrangible unity of the French world" and to "respect the life and the local freedom of each of the territories that constitute the bloc France-Colonies—or if one may use the term, in spite of the objections it may raise, *La Fédération française.*" Exactly what powers were to be exercised by this new body could not be determined, since they would reflect the division of authority between the central (metropolitan) government and the colonies. Similarly, the separation of powers between the legislature, the executive, and the local administration would depend on the exact form of the federal system, but the conference wanted it clearly noted that "it is desirable to see the colonies make their way by stages from administrative decentralization toward a political personality."[18]

By these actions, the Brazzaville Conference explicitly recognized the need for the colonies to establish their own political identity. It sought a new institutional framework for the Empire which would permit such a development, thereby breaking out of the traditional mold of "assimilation" and "association" and carrying the debate over France's colonial relationship far beyond the point reached by any prewar government. In this regard, Brazzaville is rightly considered as a major turning point in French colonial politics. Nevertheless, in order to understand subsequent controversies, it is essential to take note of the deep ambivalence which marked the conference's recommendations on several levels.

First, on the political level, the Brazzaville Conference assumed that by encouraging the political development of the colonies those indigenous forces working for a political change could be controlled and channeled into constructive economic and social fields with results that would be mutually beneficial to France and the colonies. At the same time, the criterion by which political reforms were to be judged was explicitly understood to be the reestablishment of French national grandeur, and where metropolitan interests and colonial interests might conflict, the interests of the metropole took precedence. Thus, what began as a concern for local autonomy ended with the reassertion of metropolitan predominance.

17. Ibid., p. 340.
18. Ibid., p. 349.

It is to be emphasized that the only criterion to be adopted is the necessity, *from the national point of view,* of forming strong, coherent groupings which can be compared with other important foreign colonies in Africa and *bring to the Metropole their aid and their economic and political strength.* . . .

France places not only her honor but her interests in having the colonies endowed with their own prosperity, and access to the riches of all that bears the French name is the most certain measure of our country's return to grandeur.[19]

On the administrative level, too, there was ambivalence. On one hand, the conference emphasized the need to involve larger numbers of Africans in local administrative positions as a step toward effective local government. On the other hand, it called for strengthening the financial controls of individual colonies and urged the "modernization of the administration in the domain of material installations and methods as well as the re-valuation of the civil service." [20] Lateral recruitment, which would be necessary if Africans were to be brought into the local administration in any numbers, was approved, subject to "reasonable limitations." Given the vagueness of the language employed, it remained unclear which took precedence: the Africanization of cadres or the modernization of the existing services?

A similar ambivalence characterized the treatment of economic questions. For example, the conference stressed the need for raising standards of living for the masses of Africans and hence for increasing economic productivity. To this end, it proposed to break with established patterns of colonial agriculture by promoting industrialization in areas where resources were available. Yet this departure, which certainly constituted a major step in the direction of economic self-sufficiency, was hedged about with conditions and limitations. It was to be carried out, "by steps, with method and prudence, within the strict limits resulting from the application of a general plan of production." [21] It was taken for granted that the colonial administration would control the plan.

Any lingering doubts about whose interests were controlling in the economic sphere were removed by the recommendations concerning the closely related issue of customs regulations—customs duties being one of the principal sources of revenue for the local treasuries and a

19. Ibid., pp. 349, 353. Italics added.
20. *Notes et Etudes Documentaires,* No. 1847, p. 4.
21. Ibid.

prime factor in determining economic growth. After first objecting to the inflexibility of the existing customs regime, the conference recommended that individual colonies exercise greater control over customs duties and import and export licenses in order to promote more stable and rapid economic growth. Hence, they urged that initial decisions on these matters be taken by local representative bodies. However, such decisions had to be approved by a decree signed by the minister of the colonies after consultation with the other ministerial departments concerned; thus, there was no danger that metropolitan interests would be endangered in the process. Only if the central government failed to act within a delay of three months did local decisions become operative directly. Obviously, then, the thrust toward local economic self-sufficiency stopped well short of a complete transformation of traditional economic relationships between the metropole and the colonies.

A somewhat different sort of ambivalence was evident in the recommendations relating to social and cultural matters. Here the conference found itself caught between the desire not to change African customs and values or attempt to make over Africans in the image of Frenchmen, and the necessity for social change as a prerequisite to economic and political modernization. Furthermore, since modernization meant developing the capacity to function in the world of Western bureaucracy, it was inevitable that it should have recommended the introduction of French values in many areas of civil and private life. Hence, there appears to be a direct conflict in the conference recommendations between the desire to preserve and strengthen the role of African customary law and the need to introduce more modern concepts and practices derived from French civil law.

Three examples will illustrate these difficulties.[22] The conference adopted the general principle that "the development of the indigenous population" should guide social policy. In line with this view, it was recommended that Africans become more directly involved in the adjudication of local conflicts, and that the system of administrative punishments prescribed by the native code (the *indigénat*) be "progressively abolished, as soon as hostilities are ended." Civil and commercial conflicts would continue to be decided locally, in accordance with customary law as interpreted in the first instance by African judges. At the same time, however, the conference called on administrators "to intervene constantly in the domain of public law and of

22. All are from ibid., pp. 4 and 5.

the family in order that the evolution of customary law may be controlled and guided according to the principles [of women's rights and freedom of marriage] which were set forth at the time of marriage."

In relation to labor practices, too, the conference envisioned reforms that would eliminate the system of forced labor, "conditionally maintained in force by reason of the war effort." It was to be replaced with a "free labor market" which, however, was to be "really effectively controlled" by the creation of a body of "labor inspectors" dependent on the Ministry of the Colonies. The inspectors would be charged with applying a comprehensive labor code which would extend to the colonies many of the rights and practices that had become established in French labor law: the right to organize unions and professional organizations, wages and hours limitations, vacations, working conditions, etc. Thus, the changes which were proposed as a means of "ameliorating the condition of the native worker" carried with them the prospect of greater personal liberty and security, but also of closer conformity to French standards of work and more elaborate supervision by the colonial administration.

Finally, in the area of education, the conference recommended a dual approach that would provide a general education that would both "reach and penetrate the masses and teach them to live better," and "result in a rapid and reliable selection of elites." The possibility of conflict between these aims was not examined, and most emphasis was devoted to plans for training primary school teachers and organizing professional training programs. On one point, however, the conference was unequivocal: "Instruction is to be given in the French language; the use of local spoken dialects in teaching being absolutely forbidden, in private schools as well as in the public schools." Thus, while education was clearly seen as the necessary means toward the further progress of the African peoples, there was no disposition to relinquish control over any phase of it to local, indigenous authorities or to permit local interests to influence its methods or direction. Nothing was even mentioned about the content of basic education in the recommendations.

Looking back at the record of the Brazzaville Conference, it is clear that its members were for the most part unaware of the ambivalence inherent in their recommendations, probably because it was concealed by the tone of paternalism that pervaded both the discussions and the final report. This paternalistic attitude, which French writers seldom seem to recognize, reflected a set of underlying assumptions and experiences. Most obviously, it coincided with the long-standing French tradition of bureaucratic centralism that tended to reduce all problems to questions of administrative procedure capable of direction from the center according to a common plan. Similarly, the spirit of *dirigisme,* which is inherent in all modern economic planning, also was conducive to a paternalistic approach to public issues.

The peculiarities of the French political style may also have encouraged paternalistic attitudes. Traditional patterns of authority, particularly the desire to avoid face-to-face relationships,[23] produce a need to discover authoritative answers to matters affecting the public interest and help to explain the French penchant for seeking global solutions to complex policy questions. Furthermore, the French political tradition encourages paternalism by legitimizing the appeal to superior authority in times of crisis or in the absence of a workable political consensus. The political doctrines of French republicanism also provide the basis for a conception of public policy as a set of abstract questions demanding formal, logical responses, in contrast to the common Anglo-American notion of policy making as a matter of devising pragmatic solutions to immediate conflicts.

All these explanations of the Gaullists' paternalistic attitude, although necessarily speculative, make it possible to understand the implicit assumption that specific policies for reform would remain more or less indefinitely within the control of the colonial administration. Political, social, and economic change, from their point of view, was seen as the consequence of French generosity and liberality, or at least as means of fulfilling enlightened self-interest. In no case was change regarded as the outcome of political struggle. Perhaps most important of all, the assumptions and attitudes that underlay the recommendations of the conference were consistent with the strategic goals of the Free French at that moment: to promote the development of the African colonies within a political and administrative framework that contributed to the restoration of French grandeur.

Symptomatic of the contrast between the overt and latent dimensions of the Brazzaville Conference was the spirit of optimism and the romantic aura of unity that pervaded its recommendations, largely obscuring the seriousness of the underlying political conflicts. Because of its location and timing, the conference met with no organized political opposition from any groups either in the colonies or in the metropole. In such an atmosphere, it was possible for the participants to confront the prospect of political change with considerable confidence

23. See Michel Crozier, *The Bureaucratic Phenomenon* (Chicago, 1964).

in the outcome, and whatever lingering doubts may have existed were outweighed by the hope that the enunciation of general principles of reform would satisfy all existing discontent.[24] A vivid example of the "spirit of Brazzaville" generated by the conference was offered by Félix Gouin, veteran Socialist parliamentarian and president of the Consultative Assembly, who declared:

> more and more there emerges among Frenchmen of the Metropole a very keen feeling of increased and reinforced responsibility toward our colonies; those creations of our own flesh and blood which we owe it to ourselves to protect, to aid and to assist more each day in order to bring them slowly toward a better future. . . .
>
> We are deeply convinced that after the gigantic tidal wave of the war, the relations between the Metropole and the colonies should be based on a policy that is realistic but disinterested. . . .
>
> Let us, therefore, be careful in the period that we have now reached not to aggravate the sense of right which is awakening nor the susceptibility to insult on the part of those spirits newly promoted to civilization.
>
> I know already that along this general line, your thoughts and ours are the same and that like all of us you have the feeling—I should say, the certainty—that the best civilizer is he who knows how to find the words that join hands and unite hearts.[25]

More than words were required, however, to bring unity between the metropole and the colonies. During the course of 1944 a number of decrees were issued putting into effect some of the most important recommendations of the conference, including the suppression of forced labor,[26] the promulgation of a uniform penal code to replace

24. Devèze, *La France d'outre-mer*, p. 181; Laroche and Gottman, *La Fédération française*, pp. 536 ff.

25. *Conférence de Brazzaville*, p. 21. See also de Gaulle, *Mémoires de guerre*, 2, 184–86.

26. Probably the best overview of the prewar, wartime, and postwar labor conditions in the overseas territories is offered by P. F. Gonidec and M. Kirsch, *Droit du Travail des territoires d'Outre-Mer* (Paris, 1958). On wartime effects of forced labor, see pp. 40–48; 472–79; 539–44; 691–96.

It should be noted that elimination of the excess of the native labor practices in force during the interwar period was an important part of the programs advanced by the Popular Front government in 1936, and that the first concrete steps in that direction had been taken by the Socialist minister of the colonies, Marius Moutet. Most important of all was the Decree of March 11, 1937, applying the metropolitan laws regarding the organization of trade unions to all of French West Africa. This effort at reform remained incomplete, however, and other as-the *indigénat,* the reestablishment of trade unions, and a wholesale reorganization of the educational system.

The most important questions of political organization remained to be decided by the Constituent Assembly, but these partial reforms, together with the decision that Africans should be represented in the Constituent Assembly, changed both the context and the content of the political discussions when they were reopened in 1946. They are also important because in the interim they gave rise to two sets of conflicting expectations. De Gaulle, like many other Frenchmen, seems to have regarded the recommendations of Brazzaville as a maximum concession to local interests in the form of a limited federal system which left the essential constitutional unity of the Republic unaltered. Many Africans, however, soon began to look upon Brazzaville as but a short step in the direction of complete local autonomy. These expectations, although not sufficiently at odds to openly disturb the unity of the colonies and the metropole, were to make it much more difficult to find a workable formula for unity in 1946 than was the case at Brazzaville.

The efforts of the Free French to build colonial unity by timely reforms were not confined to Tropical Africa. In North Africa, too, they sought, under very different conditions, to promote political changes that would encourage close relations between the local populations and metropolitan France. As at Brazzaville, the preferred avenue of approach was that of enlarged representation. The most noteworthy example is the decree of March 7, 1944, which extended considerably the voting rights of Algerian Muslims.

General de Gaulle had been deeply impressed by the support given to the Free French by the colonial populations, but he was well aware that he could continue to hold their confidence during the crucial period of the Liberation and the difficult months that would follow only if the colonial territories were not forced to remain in their former roles.[27] Summing up his attitude in a speech to a large crowd of Muslims in the Place de la Breche in Constantine on December 12, 1943, he declared:

> By proving their profound unity throughout these last four agonizing years, all the territories of the French imperial community have

pects of the labor system, particularly the recruitment of African workers, was left largely unaltered until after the Second World War.

27. De Gaulle, *Mémoires de guerre,* 2, 182.

been a credit to France. To France—that is, to the evangelist of racial brotherhood, equality of opportunity, and the vigilant maintenance of order to assure the liberty of all. . . .

All the peoples have lavished upon France the proof of a fidelity to which the extent of her own suffering gives a decisive character that is not only deeply moving, but that places her under obligation from now on.

Yes, it places her under obligation; and especially toward the Muslims of North Africa. . . . What better occasion could I find to announce that the Government . . . has just adopted a number of important resolutions concerning Algeria? The Liberation Committee has decided to extend immediately to several tens of thousands of French Muslims their full rights as citizens without allowing the exercise of these rights to be interfered with or limited by objections based on personal status [i.e. the retention of their rights under Koranic law].[28]

These declarations were given official form in the decree of March 7, 1944, which enlarged the noncitizens' electoral college by extending voting rights to all Muslims twenty-one years of age or older (about 1.6 million) who were not French citizens and by increasing the number of seats apportioned to noncitizens in the selected assemblies of Algeria to two-fifths of the total. It further abrogated all special administrative measures applicable to Muslims who were assured "equal rights and equal responsibilities" with non-Muslim French citizens. Finally, the decree granted French citizenship to a number of specified categories of Muslims (about 50,000 to 60,000) in recognition of their individual achievements. This grant was limited to voting rights and it was strictly personal in its scope. These changes, which were not contingent on the renunciation of any existing rights under Koranic law, were substantially those that had been proposed in the rejected Blum-Violette plan of 1936.

The clear intent of the decree was to maintain unity by providing a larger outlet within the French community for the expression of local Muslim opinion. But its real significance can be seen only after examining some of the circumstances surrounding its adoption, for Algeria enjoyed a very special role in the French colonial system.

Algeria was regarded by most Frenchmen as an extension of metropolitan France, and it had been described as such even in the nineteenth century, despite the fact of its large Muslim population and

28. De Gaulle, *Discours et Messages,* pp. 383–84.

the special political institutions that were provided for it. The large urban areas were governed in much the same way as metropolitan departments, whereas the rural sections were under various forms of colonial administration. Algeria was very different from other colonies in Africa because of the size of its resident European community and the extent of European land ownership and commercial activity. It was also distinguishable from other North African territories because it lacked an indigenous, Muslim political authority. The Algerian Muslim community, nevertheless, had developed a degree of political self-consciousness during the years before 1940 that gave its local politics a flavor very different from that of Tropical Africa.

During the war, Algeria had been, first, a center of pro-Vichy, anti-Gaullist sentiment among the European population, and, later, the temporary capitol of the Free French Provisional Government. More important, it had been for a time part of the war zone, and during that period French authority was overshadowed by the military might of the American armed forces and undermined by the political maneuvers of American diplomacy. President Franklin D. Roosevelt's personal representative in North Africa, Robert Murphy, was said to have been instrumental in consolidating the efforts of the several Muslim nationalist organizations which up to that time had remained divided into opposing factions. With encouragement from the American authorities, a group of Algerian Muslims under the leadership of Ferhat Abbas drafted a "Manifesto" urging drastic revision of the relations between France and Algeria and recognition for the predominant interest of the Muslim population in Algeria. Its issuance, on February 12, 1943, according to Charles-André Julien, marked, "the beginning of a new era of nationalist activity," [29] for it was the first occasion on which anyone had demanded explicit autonomy for Algeria in a form that commanded public attention.

The Gaullist response to the Manifesto was one of total opposition. In an effort to counter its effects, General Georges Catroux, who had been named by de Gaulle in June 1943 to be governor-general of Algeria and Commissaire d'Etat for Muslim Affairs in the Provisional Government, issued a series of decrees aimed at integrating Muslims and Europeans still more closely. These decrees were bitterly resented by the Algerian Muslim leadership, and they elicited massive opposition on the part of the Muslim elite, many of whom threatened to cease all participation in public bodies unless consideration was given

29. Charles-André Julien, *L'Afrique du Nord en Marche* (Paris, 1952), pp. 281, 284, 290–94.

to the issues raised by the Manifesto. This time the Gaullists responded even more vigorously, placing Ferhat Abbas and a number of other nationalist leaders under house arrest or compelling them to issue public apologies.[30] Yet the seriousness of these events, especially the threat of public demonstrations, led the Gaullists to reconsider their policies, and ultimately to take the steps embodied in the decree of March 7.

That decree, like the Brazzaville recommendations, seems to reflect the same political frame of reference, and to have been inspired by many of the same calculations. Although conditions in Algeria were drastically different, the Gaullists clearly assumed that increased representation would allay the resentments and capture the imagination of Muslim leaders bringing them and their followers into line behind a new French regime. As at Brazzaville, de Gaulle was prepared to consider new local institutions and to grant a wider range of personal rights. By removing the stigma of colonial subjection, he hoped both to restore confidence in French administration and to encourage economic and even military support.

Yet some of the same ambivalence was also present in the decree, for more liberal institutions were again considered only as a reflection of French generosity, in response to acts of heroism on her behalf. Greater political participation was not intended to open the way to separation, rather it was supposed to unify the Muslim and European populations within the same political system. In the case of Algeria, however, the Free French reforms were instituted among peoples who had already entered a phase of national self-consciousness, whose leaders were fairly well established, ready and willing to organize resistance to continued French domination.

Consequently, both in sub-Saharan Africa and in the Maghreb, Gaullist Free French policies encountered a variety of unintended consequences. Greater administrative autonomy and enlarged representation were permitted to function only as unifying structures within the French community. Wherever political consensus was inadequate, in practice, to sustain continued cooperation, the Gaullists quickly asserted the rigorous administrative controls of the past. The result was that the Gaullist Free French frequently sought to affirm a new ideal of unity between the colonies and the metropole, but when reforms proved ineffective they resorted to repressive methods that generated deeper hostilities and provoked greater antagonism. Both in the Maghreb and in the sub-Saharan colonies, the consequences of Guallist reforms were often the opposite from what was intended or desired.

30. Ibid., pp. 295–96.

Free French colonial policy in Africa, as elsewhere, was dominated by the determination to safeguard French sovereignty and to restore national prestige. Many of the actions taken by de Gaulle, however, bore little relationship to the real grievances or the political demands of the indigenous population. In North Africa, particularly, the conflict was severe, for there, as Ferhat Abbas later wrote, "France was late not by a war but by a revolution."

Muslim nationalism, grounded in the social and economic impoverishment of the great mass of the indigenous population, made most of the Gaullist reforms empty gestures. On the other hand, the Free French determination to maintain full control over the colonial territories led directly to violent conflicts that quickly reduced the credibility of the government's liberal declarations. The end result, as the past twenty years have demonstrated, was to create hostility and encourage mounting violence on both sides. This was particularly the case in Morocco and Tunisia, and most tragically in Algeria.

French rule in Morocco operated through the authority of the sultan, the traditional sovereign. In January 1943, at the Casablanca Conference, Sultan Sidi ben Youssef discussed the future of his country with President Roosevelt and was reported to be encouraged by Roosevelt's criticism of France's colonial claims and by his suggestion that the United States would support the efforts of colonial countries to gain full independence.[31]

Sultan ben Youssef later cooperated with the Moroccan nationalist party, the Istiqlal, which was organized during December 1943. The Istiqlal program demanded that France immediately recognize Morocco's independence and grant political autonomy to the traditional governmental institutions of the sultanate. It denounced the French administration for infringing on the sultan's authority in violation of the protectorate agreements, proclaimed the need for a number of social and economic reforms, and promised to use every legal means to achieve these ends.[32]

The French responded to the Istiqlal demands with repression. The party's leader, Ahmed Balafrej, was arrested and deported to Corsica, an act that provoked major disorders in Rabat and Fez in which more than forty lives were lost and hundreds were injured or imprisoned.

31. On the Casablanca Conference, in addition to the relevant memoirs, see A. L. Funk, *Charles De Gaulle, The Crucial Years* (Norman, Oklahoma, 1959), Chap. 2, especially pp. 83–88. Roosevelt's remarks were reported by Elliott Roosevelt, *As He Saw It* (New York, 1946), pp. 115–16.

32. See Robert Rezette, *Les Partis Politiques Marocains* (Paris, 1955), pp. 140–62, 173–88, and Robert Montagne, *Révolution au Maroc* (Paris, 1953).

Throughout most of 1944 French troops patrolled much of the country.

In Tunisia there was also strong nationalist feeling expressed by the Neo Destour party which evoked similarly repressive reactions from the French authorities. General Alphonse Juin, acting under orders from General Henri Giraud, deposed Moncef Bey on May 13, 1943, on charges of conspiring with the Axis. The bey was forced into exile, and a number of administrative changes were introduced that effectively subordinated the nominally sovereign Tunisian government to the French authorities.[33] These hasty and ill-considered acts not only violated the terms of the treaty of May 12, 1881, which guaranteed the bey's authority, they also created new sympathy for the nationalist movement, and provided it with a powerful impetus toward unity.[34]

Throughout the war, the attitude of the Tunisian elite had remained generally tolerant toward France and favorable to the Allies. Despite its antipathy to French colonial administration, and some pro-Nazi sentiment among the young intellectuals of the Neo Destour, the ruling group in Tunisia was conscious of the threat to Tunisian independence posed by Italian ambitions, and most of them assumed a neutral stance, awaiting an Allied victory. Habib Bourguiba urged the Neo Destour leaders to cooperate actively with the Gaullist Resistance in 1942, and in a declaration to the people of Tunisia in May 1943 he proclaimed the need to "form a bloc today together with France: without France there is no salvation."[35]

33. Julien, *L'Afrique du Nord,* pp. 95–97, 100–01. General Juin in his *Mémoires* (*I,* 188), declared that he regretted having been forced into "an impolitic act to the detriment of a sovereign against whom there was nothing serious to reproach and who had always been loyal." According to Roger Le Tourneau, the real reasons behind his removal had nothing to do with collaboration: "The Bey who was being deposed was the same one who stood up to the Resident General of France, whoever he was, who had formed a Government on his own initiative (January 1943) contrary to all the accepted usages and without prior negotiations, who on many occasions affirmed his desire to profoundly change the political habits acquired during sixty years of the protectorate. In sum, the French authorities jumped on the opportunity to rid themselves of an extremely inconvenient partner." *Evolution politique de l'Afrique du Nord musulmane, 1920–1961* (Paris, 1962), p. 105.

34. Julien, *L'Afrique du Nord,* pp. 175–77. See also, Habib Bourguiba, *La Tunisie et la France* (Paris, 1954), pp. 184–87.

35. Bourguiba, *La Tunisie et la France,* p. 186. The 1942 statement appears in a secret letter to Habib Thamer, chief of the clandestine political bureau of the Neo Destour, dated August 8 and smuggled to him from prison. Ibid., pp. 177–82. Cf. Julien, *L'Afrique du Nord,* pp. 92–97. The social composition of the Neo

The removal of Moncef Bey and the attempt to reassert control over the affairs of Tunisia had the principal effect of creating a powerful new movement of nationalist opposition. Rather than capitalizing on the personal influence of Moncef and the realism of Bourguiba in an effort to arrive at a compromise that would ensure French interests in Tunisia, de Gaulle installed a puppet who could not command respect from any segment of Tunisian opinion. Lacking any valid spokesman with whom to carry on negotiations, the French administration was forced to confront strikes, demonstrations, and public manifestations of discontent. Once the nationalists took to the streets, however, repression was swift and severe. Hence, the pattern of disorder and recourse to force was repeated in Tunisia, much as it had appeared in Morocco. The last chance for a peaceful resolution of Franco-Tunisian conflicts thus passed even before the Free French had established their authority in North Africa. From 1943 on, feelings grew more hostile on both sides.

The limited reforms proposed by the Gaullists in 1945 and 1946 failed to meet the demands of the Tunisian nationalists. In an effort to bring pressure on France, their spokesmen, especially the Neo-Destour leader, Habib Bourguiba, presented the Tunisian case to various agencies of the United Nations, to the Arab League, and to many official and unofficial figures in the United States. At the same time, greater freedom to conduct internal affairs permitted the nationalists to organize popular support through trade unions, particularly the Confédération Générale du Travail Tunisien, and to develop an institutional base from which to press for further changes. Reflecting on his experiences at this critical period, Bourguiba later testified that he now knew that nothing was to be expected from France.

> Nothing more from Free France than from the other one, and nothing more from the Fourth Republic than from the Third. Relying on the good sense of the French for the liberation of Tunisia was a waste of time. . . . Between France and us, it has become a question of force.[36]

Destour is examined by Clement Henry Moore in Charles Micaud, *Tunisia, the Politics of Modernization* (New York, 1964), pp. 79–88. See also, F. Garas, *Bourguiba, et la naissance d'une nation* (Paris, 1956).

36. Bourguiba, *La Tunisie et la France,* pp. 188, 192. In a revealing letter to Ferhat Abbas written from exile in Cairo, July 29, 1946, Bourguiba set forth the details of his strategy to gain international support for Tunisian independence, and emphasized the common links between his experience and that of the Algerian nationalists. Even in the face of French intransigence, however, he was not

In Algeria, the unintended consequences of Gaullist policy were even more tragic. The Muslim population reacted to the decree of March 7 with derision. Only the moderate, urbanized *évolués* endorsed it because, like the Blum-Violette plan of the thirties, it recognized their long-standing claims to greater participation in local government. The Communist Party, a group which included a number of Europeans and Algerian Jews as well as Muslims, took a more qualified position because it saw possibilities for political propaganda and electoral support.

As if in response to the assimilationist intent of the decree, Ferhat Abbas announced on March 14 the formation of a single, unified nationalist organization, the Amis du Manifeste, which brought together the three major factions within the Algerian nationalist movement: the Islamic reformers of the 'Ulemas association,[37] the impoverished urban working-class supporters of Messali Hadj's clandestine Parti du People Algérien (PPA), and the middle-class supporters of the Manifesto. The Amis du Manifeste took advantage of the newly restored liberties to organize a campaign among the *évolués* enfranchised by the decree of March 7 aimed at discouraging them from registering on the electoral lists of French citizens in order to demonstrate Algerian determination to refuse assimilation. Membership in the Amis

---

vindictive, and if he was convinced that conflict was unavoidable it was more out of despair than anger. "If only France made an effort to understand us! If only she got around in time to changing her policy, we would hold out our hands to her with genuine relief, and we would form a real bloc with her against whatever sorts of foreign undertakings. But where is the French statesman who is able to make the French colony listen to reason in Tunisia (or Algeria) and make them understand and accept the necessary concessions? The only time a French minister wanted to do something in Tunisia (Vienot), he was swept away like a wisp of straw before he could even begin to put his policy into action. It's unfortunate, but that's the way it is." Ibid., pp. 195–96. See also, Le Tourneau, *Evolution . . . de L'Afrique du Nord musulmane,* pp. 105–16.

37. The "Association of the Reformist 'Ulema of Algeria" was a group of Muslims connected with the Salafiya movement that sought to promote a reformed, puritan version of Islam, which left room for modern technological developments. As David Gordon noted, "The reformers wanted the best of two worlds. They were adamant in rejecting all the superstitions and saint-worship that in Algeria came under the rubric of *maraboutisme,* and they insisted on a strict, puritan pattern of behavior, the revival of Arabic as the official language of the nation, and its purification (according to the standards of the language of the Koran)."—*The Passing of French Algeria* (London, 1966), pp. 31–33. In 1945 the 'Ulemas strongly supported the founding in Algeria of an independent Islamic state aligned with other Islamic communities in North Africa.

du Manifeste grew rapidly; by September 1944 it claimed 500,000 adherents, and in December, Ferhat Abbas's newspaper, *Egalité,* attained a circulation of 30,000 copies.

As agitation continued to spread the Muslim population became more and more restless, stirred on by the excitement generated by the founding of the Arab League as well as by the emotional speeches of their own leaders. At its first national congress in March 1945, the party, by then under the influence of Messali's PPA, adopted a program that called for "an Algerian Parliament and Algerian Government," abandoning the more cautious language of Ferhat Abbas who earlier advocated autonomy for Algeria within "a French federation of nations." The consequence, as Roger Le Tourneau observed, was that:

> The young people, scouts, high school and university students, and pupils at the reformist [Koranic] schools, followed the activities of their political chiefs with passionate interest and egged them on to intransigence. In short, the political climate was like nothing Algeria had ever known.[38]

Tension was further increased during the spring of 1945 by the shift of military operations from North Africa to Western Europe, which deprived Algeria of important economic resources and drastically reduced the strength of French garrisons, leaving the country's internal security in the hands of the police and the local militia. In this highly explosive atmosphere it required very slight provocation to evoke the worst fears and the most bitter hatreds among both French and Muslim Algerians. The first intimations of serious disorder occurred on May Day when the PPA sought to turn the CGT's traditional workers' parade into a nationalist rally in the large cities of Algiers, Oran, Bone, and Bougie. The police intervened and order was restored, but not before several dozen casualties had occurred, including three or more killed.

During the week of May 8, 1945, a major uprising began as a result of riots that occurred when groups of Muslims attempted to demonstrate in favor of Algerian independence during V-E Day ceremonies. The worst of these occurred in the small, provincial cities of Sétif and Guelma, as well as in the surrounding Constantine region. In a semi-organized outburst, set off by a policeman in Sétif, thousands of armed Muslims roamed the towns and countryside indiscriminately killing Europeans. The French authorities, urged on by terrified, outraged

38. *Evolution . . . de L'Afrique du Nord,* p. 347.

colonists, launched a vicious repression that lasted until the middle of June, and in which the armed forces were used, including naval bombardment of the coastal villages and aerial attacks on the interior towns, in addition to administrative and judicial executions.

Losses on both sides were heavy. French sources list 97 killed and more than 100 wounded among the Europeans in the region, and 1,500 Muslims killed. Nationalist sources have estimated that as many as 50,000 Muslims may have died. The true number will never be known, but the bitterness engendered by these events became evident in 1954.

An official investigation failed to discover any direct connection between the nationalist parties and the uprisings, but there was strong public pressure from European *colons* and in the metropolitan press for their suppression and a demand for the recall of Governor-General Yves Chataigneau, a socialist criticized for dealing too leniently with the nationalists. De Gaulle refused to replace Chataigneau and went ahead with the municipal elections scheduled for July 1945. Ferhat Abbas and most of the leaders of the Amis du Manifeste were arrested and convicted, together with about 2,000 other participants in the uprisings. Forty-eight persons were executed, and most of the rest remained in prison until March 1946 when they were liberated under an amnesty voted by the First Constituent Assembly. A number of the nationalist leaders, including Abbas, were elected to the Second Constituent Assembly under the banner of the Union Démocratique du Manifeste Algérien.[39]

Most authorities agree that May 1945 marked a critical turning point in the relations between France and Algeria. To cite just one example, Le Tourneau has concluded that:

> From May 1945 on, there developed a profound break between the two communities who, nevertheless, had lived together for a century. The scope and severity of the repression and the fact that it was only a very small proportion of the Muslim population that took up arms, made it unlikely thereafter that a new explosion would occur right away. But if the two communities did not confront each other again immediately, each remained deeply distrustful of the

39. The events summarized above have been documented by many writers, including Robert Aron, *Les Origines de la guerre d'Algerie* (Paris, 1962); Julien, *L'Afrique du Nord* (who cites the casualty figures), p. 303; Th. Oppermann, *Le Problème algérien* (Paris, 1961); Charles Gallagher, *The United States and North Africa* (Cambridge, Mass., 1963); Gordon, *The Passing of French Algeria;* and Le Tourneau, *Evolution . . . de l'Afrique du Nord musulmane,* pp. 348–54.

The texts of the various programs are reprinted in *La Documentation française, Notes et Etudes Documentaires,* No. 333, p. 678.

other. The Muslims feared that any political decisions taken by the Metropole were inspired by the French Algerians or would strengthen their domination; while these same Frenchmen were convinced, especially after the uprisings of 1945, that force alone would protect them and they put all their confidence in it.[40]

The situation in the two colonial federations of West and Central Africa was less tense than in Algeria, but even in relatively remote areas like Guinea and the Ivory Coast, new movements were developing in the aftermath of the wartime reforms. There was very little discussion of "independence" anywhere in French West Africa, but demands for social, economic, and administrative changes emerged quickly after the announcement of the "Recommendations" of Brazzaville. Until then, Africans had been divided into two groups: those born in the "four communes" of Senegal who enjoyed civil and political rights granted by metropolitan legislation during the Third Republic; and the rest, who were without any guarantees of civil or political liberty. The vast majority of the African population was ruled by the *indigénat* or native code, which gave the local administrative officer general authority to maintain discipline, define offenses, and prescribe punishment. In practice, the local *commandant de cercle* exercised virtually total discretion over the lives of Africans in his district.

In matters of military service and forced labor, the ordinary African was subject to special liabilities not imposed on French citizens, whether African or European. In addition to a longer period of military service, noncitizens were subject, as part of their military obligation, to assignment to the *deuxième contingent* which was employed to provide labor for the maintenance of roads and construction of public works. The administration also had the power to requisition labor for use on European plantations and to establish wage scales which would assure a profit.

On the other hand, the personal lives of the subjects in regard to matters such as marriage, divorce, and inheritance were left to local tradition and, where applicable, to Koranic law rather than to French civil law. Hence, political liberties were available only to a tiny fraction, about 80,000 out of a total population of roughly 14.5 million in West Africa, prior to World War II.[41] Explicitly political organizations

40. *Evolution . . . de l'Afrique du Nord,* p. 353.

41. For a detailed discussion of prewar administrative arrangements in French West Africa, see R. L. Buell, *The Native Problem in Africa* (New York, 1928), Lord Hailey, *An African Survey* (London, 1938), and Robert Delavignette, *Free-*

were almost totally lacking until 1945. During the interwar period an assortment of economic and cultural groups had emerged whose activities, though primarily directed at other goals, often verged on the political. The most important among these were trade unions, veterans' organizations, and school alumni associations (the "Anciens de l'Ecole Normale William Ponty" in Dakar included many of the most dynamic leaders of the African elite from all of French West Africa), youth groups, tribal societies formed to aid those who had migrated, sometimes from great distances, to the growing towns, and cultural societies of many types. These quasipolitical groups, as Hodgkin and Schachter have noted,[42] provided a basis for the subsequent development of organized political movements. They were not mass organizations, but they provided a source of experienced militants for the rich assortment of political movements and parties that sprang up after the Second World War.

Beginning during the Popular Front period, more explicit political education was provided for some of the elite by missionaries or teachers with connections among the Leftist parties—Socialists or Communists—of the metropole. The French Communist Party in 1943 established an organization known as the Groupes d'Etudes Communistes, (GEC), with centers in several large towns of West Africa. Although they produced few orthodox Marxists, the GECs afforded access to Marxist language and modes of analysis.[43] The emotional shock that followed the French military defeat in 1940 was felt even in the most remote corners of French Africa. Yet, it did not precipitate any overt opposition to France among the African elite. This tiny group tended, for the most part, to show great sympathy for France and, initially at least, to echo the sentiments of the colonial administration with which

---

dom and Authority in French West Africa (London, 1950). A useful summary is offered by K. E. Robinson, "Political Development in French West Africa," in C. W. Stillman, ed., *Africa in the Modern World* (Chicago, 1955), pp. 142–51.

42. Thomas Hodgkin and Ruth Schachter, *French-speaking West Africa in Transition* ("International Conciliation," No. 528, May 1960; New York, 1961), p. 386. In addition, other writers have pointed to the appearance of quite specific interest groups, such as the Syndicat des Chefs Supérieurs et de Canton, and regional organizations with broad programs of social and political reform. See Amon d'Aby, *La Côte d'Ivoire dans la cité africaine* (Paris, 1951), pp. 36–37; also Thomas Hodgkin, *Nationalism in Colonial Africa* (New York, 1957), pp. 142–46, and his "Political Parties in British and French West Africa" (*Information Digest*, Africa Bureau, No. 10, London, 1953) cited by Robinson, in *Africa and the Modern World*, pp. 170–71.

43. Hodgkin and Schachter, *French-speaking West Africa*, p. 387.

a substantial proportion had very close ties of economic or professional interest. However, the announcement of the Armistice produced a wave of sympathy for the dissident Gaullists, with the result that a greater degree of political awareness began to emerge, and some Africans openly opposed the local administration. Admiration for the venerable Marshal Petain and the Vichy officials diminished rapidly as it became clear to Africans that "restoring the authority of the state" provided the basis for a new, brutal policy of exploitation and repression. What was not accomplished by racial discrimination and forced labor was achieved by the anti-Negro, racist propaganda of the Nazis.

The impact of the disputes among Vichy and Gaullist colonists is difficult to estimate, although it did create an impression of administrative confusion. Where Vichy officials were in firm control, that is, in nearly all of West Africa, Africans who took part in pro-Gaullist activities were treated as subversives and some who were caught were subjected to torture and imprisonment. Nevertheless, some Africans did participate in the Gaullist resistance groups, and in a few instances whole tribes or villages fled into neighboring British colonies until the end of the war.[44] The most dramatic gestures of resistance were those of Ora Ashedi, chief of Porto-Novo in Dahomey, who committed suicide for fear his subjects would be turned over to German authorities, and of the Mogho Naba, ruler of the Mossi kingdom and the most powerful traditional chief in French Africa, who ended his life in an elaborate ceremonial at his capitol of Ouagadougou. Such gestures generated considerable emotion among the masses of Africans who had remained generally impassive.[45] For the peoples of West Africa as a whole, however, the decline in French authority was far less dramatic than in North Africa.

During the closing phase of World War II, Free French policy in Africa suffered as a consequence of the diminished role which the African region came to occupy in the military strategy of the Allied powers. As the centers of conflict shifted to Western Europe and the Far East, the Gaullist regime was forced to realign its strategic concerns. Particularly after 1944, the Free French found themselves con-

44. Amon d'Aby, *La Côte d'Ivoire,* pp. 41–44. In the Ivory Coast, Prince Kouamé Adingra led about 10,000 of his followers, together with his aged father, Kouadio Adjoumani, king of Bondoukou, into exile in Gold Coast.

45. Devéze, *La France d'outre-mer,* pp. 157–58. De Gaulle mentions this incident in his *Mémoires, 2,* 31. See also Laroche and Gottman, *La Fédération française,* p. 533.

fronted both in the Levant and in Indochina with acute threats to the political unity of the French Empire and to its grandeur.

The collapse of German power in North Africa brought British and French forces into a bitter confrontation over the control of the Levant. That crisis, which was almost simultaneous with the end of the war in Europe, found the troops of the two allies on the verge of open conflict. While the issues at stake in the French claims to a predominant position in Lebanon and Syria had little to do with the African policies of the Free French, the outcome of the crisis was an added factor in undermining the legitimacy of the French position, especially in North Africa.

The attempt to restore French authority in the Levant, in opposition to the express desires of the local authorities and in the face of the effective destruction of French rule by the wartime struggles, was bitterly resented not only by all the Arab peoples, but also by the United States, which by then had become the chief supplier of French military equipment. Such unilateral actions on the part of the Free French served further to antagonize all those groups in North Africa who were beginning to look favorably upon appeals for Arab unity.

The failure of intervention in Lebanon also appears to have confirmed de Gaulle's suspicions about the long-run intentions of the Arabs and the anti-French bias of his Anglo-Saxon allies. At a critical moment of the war, the Free French in effect cut themselves off from their principal sources of economic assistance, seriously weakening their position within the diplomatic and military coalition that was to determine the fate of Western Europe in the immediate postwar period.

Similarly, de Gaulle's decision during the closing days of the war to proceed with plans to reoccupy French Indochina, even after all French forces there had been interned by the Japanese and later replaced by Indochinese nationalists under the leadership of Ho Chi Minh, produced shock waves that affected even the Gaullists' African policies. The commitment to Indochina greatly diminished the already critically short supplies of goods and materials available to meet the promises of Brazzaville. It seriously reduced the chances of finding an acceptable political solution to growing nationalist demands in Africa. Thus the involvement in Indochina, which was only dimly perceived at the time by most French leaders, including de Gaulle, had a doubly destructive influence on the fate of the wartime reforms in Africa. Confronted with mounting costs of military intervention, the Gaullists and their successors were compelled to defer badly needed and repeatedly promised plans for educational improvements, economic development, and social changes that formed a vital part of the Brazzaville recommendations.

Perhaps more important in the longer run, however, was the fact that the defeat suffered in the Levant and the bitter struggle with the Viet Minh in Indochina generated deep anxieties both within the metropolitan French political elite and among the general public. As a result, the spirit of optimism that characterized the Brazzaville Conference was replaced in the constituent assemblies by a deep sense of distrust on the part of many metropolitan deputies. On the other hand, those nationalist groups within the colonies that had viewed Brazzaville as a sign of hope and a promise of further change were progressively disillusioned by these evidences of French determination to preserve every shred of French authority.

The absence of integrated, modern political communities in most of French Africa and the lack of an effective political consensus among the small, indigenous, modernizing elite in those countries tended to obscure these developments, while economic dependency further discouraged interest in radical political change. Nevertheless, local self-consciousness had been aroused throughout French Africa, and the need for internal reforms was clearly felt by a growing African elite which waited impatiently for an extensive reform of the French colonial system.

Gaullist wartime efforts to restore France's grandeur by assuring the unity of the colonies and the metropole take on an aspect of mounting paradox when viewed from the perspective of the postwar period. The Gaullists always thought of themselves as preserving and developing the heritage of republican colonialism, yet their policies of reform and repression contributed significantly to its transformation. The myths of French colonialism supplied the Gaullists with a framework of ideas so familiar that they could be taken for granted in shaping policy, even if the ideal of a reborn Republic that was "one and indivisible" with its colonies did not correspond very closely to the desires of important segments of the colonial population. In drafting a series of electoral reforms for choosing the National Constituent Assembly, the Gaullists completed their last major act of the wartime period, and this innovation, like the political changes discussed earlier, provides a sharp insight into the paradoxical character of Gaullist colonialism.

The electoral reforms of 1945 were in large part the culmination of the policy that began at the Conference of Brazzaville, and that aimed to encourage unity with the colonies by giving the peoples of the overseas areas a direct and substantial voice in the making of French policy. The Conference of Brazzaville had reached a decision in principle to permit the colonial population to participate in the eventual reorganization of the institutions of the Republic; but it had been unable to agree on the implementation of this policy. The events leading up to the liberation of the metropole and the transfer of the Gaullist government from Algiers to Paris prevented further action on the question during the ensuing year. By the spring of 1945, with the war in Europe nearly over and elections scheduled for fall, decisions on the matter of colonial participation could wait no longer.

The decisions that had to be made were, nevertheless, exceedingly complicated because of the great variety of conditions existing in the colonies, the short amount of time available for the preparation of voting lists, the lack of administrative personnel, and the enormous distances and difficulty of communications. The continuation of hostilities in Indochina made it impossible even to attempt to hold elections there. As a first step, the Ministry of the Colonies appointed a committee under the direction of Gaston Monnerville to study the problem of colonial representation and to present specific proposals.

Under existing laws, the so-called "old colonies" (French Guiana, Guadeloupe, Réunion, Martinique, and St. Pierre et Miquelon) were fully represented in the National Assembly. The "four communes" of Senegal had been represented by African deputies since 1914, but the rest of West Africa had no representation, and the Senegalese seat had remained vacant following the death of the incumbent Galandou Diouf in 1942. The only other colony to send a deputy to the last parliament in 1936 was composed of the tiny French enclaves in India. In addition, ten deputies represented the French colonists in Algeria.

The principle of colonial representation having been established, the Monnerville Commission had to determine what proportion of the seats in the Constituent Assembly were to be allocated to the overseas areas and how the seats were to be filled in each case. Since no decision had been reached by the late spring of 1945 on the form of the Constituent Assembly—whether it was to be bicameral, like the parliaments of the Third Republic, or a new unicameral assembly specially chosen to draft the Constitution—the commission had to formulate alternative plans to fit both possibilities. Its composition assured that the recommendations of the commission would represent primarily the opinion of the ministries concerned. An additional factor that may also have exerted some influence was the pressure generated by a group of African students in Paris who resented what they took to be governmental indifference toward the sacrifices made by the colonies for the war effort, and repeatedly intervened to demand enlarged representation.[46]

The Monnerville Commission completed its report on July 5, 1945, while de Gaulle was still seeking agreement among the various metropolitan parties on a plan for the forthcoming elections. The commission proposed that, in the case of a bicameral parliament, the colonies should be represented in the lower house by sixty-six members and in the upper house by twenty-nine. The members of the lower house were to be allocated approximately according to population whereas each colony was to have a single member in the upper chamber. In the event of a unicameral parliament, the colonies were to have ninety-five seats out of a total of six hundred. These totals did not include any seats for Algeria because that area was considered part of metropolitan France, but they did provide for representation of the mandated territories of Togoland and Cameroons, despite the fact that these areas were not, strictly speaking, "French territory." No provision was made for representing those French citizens residing in the protectorates of Morocco and Tunisia for fear of alienating the sovereigns of those countries.

A second proposal, stemming from a conference of Resistance groups called the Etats Généraux de la Renaissance Française, and largely influenced by Communist and Socialist opinion, urged more extensive assimilation of the colonies, and proposed to set aside one-fifth of the seats in the Constituent Assembly for overseas representatives.[47] On the whole, however, there was little public comment in Paris on either of these proposals. In fact, their importance seemed to be generally ignored in the midst of more urgent and dramatic incidents concerning the fate of the new economic program, the bloody struggle in Indochina, the bitter incidents in the Levant, and the deepening governmental crisis over the constitution.

In characteristic fashion, the Provisional Government, after deciding to leave the form of the Constituent Assembly to be determined by a referendum, resolved the problem of colonial representation in a manner different from both the Monnerville Proposal and the plans of the Resistance groups. De Gaulle's plan, set forth in a series of decrees during August and September 1945,[48] was significantly more modest than either of the other two proposals. It provided for twenty-nine

46. Amon d'Aby, *La Côte d'Ivoire,* p. 54.

47. *Le Monde,* July 14, 1945, *Année Politique,* 1944–45, pp. 245–48.

48. Procedures for the elections of 1945 were set forth in the following decrees: *No. 45–1837* (August 17, 1945) relative to elections in the Metropole and Algeria (*Journal Officiel,* August 19, p. 5155 [*JO* hereafter]).

deputies to represent Algeria, sixteen of whom were to be chosen by noncitizens, while in Morocco and Tunisia French citizens were permitted to select three and two deputies respectively. In most of the other colonies French citizens and native subjects voted in separate colleges. Thus, the French citizens in the colonies (not more than about 10 percent of whom were non-Europeans, apart from the four communes of Senegal and the Antilles) controlled better than half the overseas seats. Noncitizens held twenty-three seats out of a total of sixty-four provided for overseas areas. In some very small colonies like New Caledonia, the islands of Oceania, and the Indian enclaves, both citizens and noncitizens voted together in a single, mixed college. It is clear from the figures in the accompanying table, that substantial inequalities existed within both electoral colleges as well as between citizens and noncitizens.

These decisions of the Provisional Government concerning the electoral system make it clear that, although the "spirit of Brazzaville" was still part of the prevailing doctrine, General de Gaulle was not prepared to expose the fragile unity of the recently liberated metropole and the colonies to serious threat from overseas. Most of the outspoken opponents of colonial unity were excluded from the First Constituent Assembly since the nationalist groups in Morocco and Tunisia were not represented, nor were the sovereigns of these states involved in any direct way in the reorganization of the French colonial system. Indochina, although on the minds of many people, was not directly represented either. The Algerian leaders of the Amis du Manifeste were still in prison following the Sétif uprising. Thus the only possible organized opposition to the policy of a continuing union to be found was among the two deputies from Madagascar who represented a growing movement in favor of greater autonomy for their island col-

---

No. 45-2112 (September 13, 1945) and No. 45-2119 (September 15, 1945) modifying the foregoing (*JO*, September 16, 1945, pp. 5811, 5816).

No. 45-1874 (August 22, 1945) concerning representation of the territories under the authority of the Ministry of the Colonies (*JO*, August 23, 1945, p. 5266).

Nos. 45-2114, 45-2117 (September 15, 1945) completing the foregoing in relation to Tunisia and Morocco (*JO*, September 16, 1945, pp. 5813, 5814).

The general features of the electoral procedure are discussed in R. Husson, *Elections et referendums des 21 Octobre 1945, 5 Mai et 2 Juin 1946* (Paris, 1946), which provides a complete statistical analysis of the results. In the table below, compiled from these statistics, the figures in the column "voters" are those given for the number of registered voters (*inscrits*) in the election of October 21, 1945.

Overseas Representation in the First Constituent Assembly, 1945–46

Constituency (No. of seats in 1936)	*Citizens' College*		*Non-citizens' College*		*Mixed College*	
	Voters	*Seats*	*Voters*	*Seats*	*Voters*	*Seats*
Algeria [a]	(501,724)	(13)	(1,341,978)	(13)		
Algiers (4)	209,222	5	460,826	4		
Constantine (3)	103,026	3	586,322	6		
Oran (3) [b]	189,576	5	294,830	3		
Morocco	91,451	3				
Tunisia	75,526	2				
Martinique (2)	114,543	2				
Guadeloupe (2)	106,528	2				
Réunion (2)	107,120	2				
Guiana (1)	12,309	1				
St. Pierre et Miquelon	2,487	1				
Oceania					19,294	1
New Caledonia					9,829	1
Indian Establishments (1)					3,141	1
Somalia (Djibouti)					620	1
Senegal Mauritania (1) [c]	44,292	1	25,188	1		
Ivory Coast	3,646	1	31,384	1		
Soudan-Niger	3,243	1	33,626	1		
Guinea	1,944	1	16,233	1		
Dahomey-Togo	1,279	1	11,599	1		
Cameroons	1,991	1	12,468	1		
AEF						
Gabon-Moyen Congo	2,803	1	5,873	1		
Oubangui-Chad	1,361	1	6,858	1		
Madagascar	(16,604)	(2)	(72,473)	(2)	(4,447)	(1)
1st District	11,271	1	46,426	1		
2nd District	5,333	1	26,047	1		
3rd District					4,447	1
Totals (64 seats)	1,088,941	36	1,557,680	23	37,331	5

a. Algeria was represented in 1936 by 10 deputies elected by French citizens only.

b. Three deputies from Oran were never seated.

c. Africans born in the four communes of Dakar, Rufisque, Gorée, and St. Louis were citizens.

ony. While a few such isolated individuals might exert some personal influence within the Assembly, it was certainly not expected that the colonial deputies as a group would wield very much power. On the contrary, it was hoped that by their presence the colonial peoples would be brought to identify themselves more fully with the new political system that was to be created.

By their doctrines and their policies the Gaullists had largely succeeded in preserving the forms of France's colonial system, and by important reforms in sub-Saharan Africa and the Maghreb they had maintained and possibly increased somewhat the political consensus that supported a strong, renovated French community. But none of the wartime Gaullist reforms was either very novel or very precise, and most important of all, none was able to resolve the crucial issue of political structure. What was needed above all by 1945 was not a more complete set of doctrines, but a new pattern of political institutions that could assure further, and more liberal, changes.

The problem was put very concisely by Governor Henri Laurentie in an address at the Palais de Chaillot:

> The Colonies having passed through the test of war—their war—are not quite the same as before. They have grown up. . . . They have confidence in the intentions of France, but now it is necessary that those intentions be carried into actions.[49]

The reforms adopted by the Gaullist Free French regime guaranteed that when those actions were determined, the opinions of African and Muslim groups would, at least in part, be taken into account. However, the policies pursued by the Gaullists in applying the reforms frequently served to divide rather than unite the new politically conscious elites overseas from the metropolitan leadership, and hence tended to defeat the underlying goal of unity. In the end, the reforms of Brazzaville did indeed contribute both to the desire for independence within the colonies and to the creation of a political system that tended to legitimate the pursuit of that aim. Yet nothing could have been further from the intentions of those responsible for Free French policy, especially Charles de Gaulle. To him, the unity of the Empire and the metropole appeared, in that prenuclear era, to hold the key to the restoration of French grandeur and to provide tangible evidence of her rank as a world power.

49. *Le Monde,* July 11, 1945.

☙§ 21. *Algeria, 1962–1967: An Essay on Dependence in Independence*

☙§ DAVID C. GORDON

France is hard,
France is hard
For those who are not able;
One leaves very young
And he returns old.

France is easy,
France is easy
For those who are able;
One must be courageous
To support its pains.

France is good,
France is good.
It is she who nourishes us;
One leaves broke,
One comes home with many *sous*.

Leave, do not be afraid.
But to the young, I advise
Do not go.
For you France will be hard!

Berber Song of Exile
from Pierre Savignac
Poésie populaire de Kabyle
(Paris, 1964)

The new "developing" nations of the Third World, in almost all cases, are dependent economically and culturally upon either the Communist or the Western bloc. In many cases, because of relationships developed over the years of colonization, they are dependent, in particular, on the power that once colonized them. This is obviously true of the new African states whose economies are significantly dependent upon external aid and whose working, if not official, languages are English or French. It is also true of a large state like India whose functioning language is still English, and of a small state like Lebanon whose ruling elite is still largely French educated. Algeria, the subject of the present essay, is one of the most extreme cases of such dependence.

This was evident, in 1967, in the areas of oil production, wine distribution, and technical and educational assistance. In the case of oil, Algerian production and research was a joint Franco-Algerian enterprise, and Algerian oil was marketed in France at prices higher than those of the world market. In the case of wine production, a heritage of the colonial era, because there was no domestic market in Muslim Algeria, and because the Algerians had to compete with other countries throughout the Mediterranean, Algeria needed the French market —even if Russia did absorb some of her surplus in 1967. In the interests of cooperation, the French government periodically allowed part of Algeria's wine surplus to enter France, but only in the face of bitter opposition from the winegrowers of the Midi. In the field of technical and educational assistance, France provided Algeria with about 6,500 "*coopérants*" (a neologism in the age of the Third World), and, in 1964 at least, about 30 percent of the personnel at the top level of administration and about 40 percent of the personnel at the next highest level. Indicative of the importance of these coopérants (and of Algeria's deeper psychic dependence on France) were remarks made by *Le Monde*'s Gerard Viratelle: "When Colonel Boumedienne travels by helicopter, he is piloted by a coopérant. The officials in control of air security are, also, often, technical assistants (*fonctionnaires de la coopération*). One Algerian administrator takes pride in running his program exclusively with French cadres; a director of a lycée boasts that most of his professors are coopérants. In the Sahara, almost all of the doctors belong to the French medical mission." [1]

Algeria's continuing dependence was in large part the result of the inability of her leaders to cooperate with one another and to lead effectively, as Hervé Bourges demonstrated for the period 1962–67 in his *L'Algérie à l'épreuve du pouvoir* (Paris, 1967). Bourges' testimony is of particular interest because he was the last Frenchman to occupy a senior post in the Algerian government. Less pessimistic was Robert Buron, vice-president of the Association France-Algérie and an old

1. *Le Monde*, August 17, 1966. See also, on Algerian dependence upon France, the special issue of *Europe-France-Outremer*, January 1968, entitled "L'Economie Algérienne et les relations avec la France."

Algerian hand, after a trip he took to Algeria in December 1967.[2] Nevertheless, he observed that Algeria's technocrats (Belaid Abdessalam, the Minister of Industry, in particular), by opting for a concentration upon export crops and heavy industry (rather than upon small-scale industry with a variegation of products for the internal market) were tying Algeria's economy to Europe's for many years to come. In an interview given to *Jeune Afrique*,[3] Buron repeated his concern and observed, as many others have, the deep anxiety of the Algerian rulers over the fate of "cooperation" after de Gaulle—another indication of Algeria's dependence, in spite of its militant pride, after seven years of valiant struggle.

In a volume that treats imperialism comparatively, the inclusion of the present essay may seem strange. Not that Algeria's experience as a newly independent nation as yet unable to fend for itself is unique, or that the particular case of dependence to be considered—that of migrant labor as a link and source of needed revenue—is peculiar only to Algeria, but because one might have expected a comparison to a parallel British case of "neocolonialism" or "decolonization" (to use two recently coined, fashionable terms). The author's explanation, if not justification, is that as a historian he prefers to emphasize the unique he is familiar with, rather than the general, although this does not mean, of course, that he denies the dialectical relationship, both methodological and substantial, of the unique and general in social studies. He hopes that by implication he can suggest comparisons with British cases of dependence, as well as other cases, and perhaps also encourage a consideration of the general phenomenon of dependence itself.

It would seem, for example, that the previous colonies of Kenya and Northern Rhodesia (and perhaps someday of Southern Rhodesia and even South Africa), where significant colon populations have, as in Algeria, dominated the social and economic life of their communities, might be fruitfully compared to the Algerian case, or that the problem Great Britain faced in 1967 with respect to colored migrant peoples in her midst, could be compared to the case considered in this chapter. More generally, the particular drama of Algerian migrant labor may be of comparative value since so many of the new nations help to support their weak economies through migrant labor in the more developed countries of Europe. This is true of some Black African, Arab, and Asian countries as well as of the less developed areas of Europe

2. Open letter to *Le Monde*, January 31, 1968.

3. *Jeune Afrique*, February 5–11, pp. 28–29.

itself such as, for example Turkey, Greece, southern Italy, and Iberia.[4] The Algerian case, then, if unusual, is so only in a quantitative sense. And perhaps the very fact of its relatively greater dependence makes Algeria a convenient model for students of other cases of dependence in independence.

As stated, the case being considered is only one particular case of dependence after independence, but it concerns over half a million Algerians who worked in France five years after Algerian independence, and who, by so doing, provided subsistence for about two million Algerians at home. This pathetic and sometimes dramatic relationship between the former colonizer and the former colonized had its origin on the eve of World War I, forty years before the Revolution began in 1954, and it not only survived independence in 1962, but did so on a larger and more significant scale than ever before.

The history of this movement is an important part of the story of Algeria's awakening to national self-consciousness, to her rejection of France in revolution, and now to her "cooperation" with France, in respect to which the link of migration has been both pledge and irritant. And beyond economics and politics lies a human drama that is not only Algeria's but also France's. To Algeria, the problem to be discussed is an ordeal; to France, the major partner, it is a test of her values. The period discussed covers the five years since independence. Changes will occur, but short of a cataclysm, changes in regard to this migration are likely for some time to be only variations on the same theme.

By way of background to the postindependence period, a brief historical introduction might be given.[5] Until the eve of World War I,

4. It is estimated that there are in the whole world about fifty million "economic migrants." In 1966, three million foreign workers, 6 percent of her population, were present in France. See Pascale Courbot in *Exchanges*, January 1967, pp. 2–5. The largest group were the Italians, who numbered about 700,000. The second largest group were the Algerians.

5. The most useful sources on the period before 1962 are: Jean Jacques Rager, *Les Musulmans algériens en France et dans les pays islamiques* (Paris, 1950); the demographic study issued jointly by Etudes Sociales Nord-Africaines and the Institut National d'Etudes Démographiques, which is entitled *Les Algériens en France: étude démographique et sociale* (Paris, 1955); Pierre Bourdieu, et al., *Travail et Travailleurs en Algérie* (Paris, 1962); and André Michel, *Les Travailleurs algériens en France* (Paris, 1956). The most comprehensive bibliography is *Connaissance de l'immigration nord-africaine en France,* published in mimeographed form in February 1964 by the Centre Africain des Sciences Humaines Appliquées in Aix-en-Provence. Many statistical data appear in the mimeographed studies prepared by Robert Montagne but not completed before his death. They

Muslim Algerian migration was internal to Algeria (from the poorer regions to areas like the Mitidja valley), or to other Muslim Arab countries (at times in reaction against the French Christian presence). On the eve of the war, recruitment began to obtain manpower for industry and the army. It was only after the war that migration became spontaneous as Algerians, tempted by wages three to four times higher than those paid in Algeria, shed their suspicion and fear of life in France. During World War I there had been about 78,566 Algerian workers in France. By 1948 the figure was about 230,000, and on the eve of the Revolution, in 1954, the figure was 280,000. For the most part this migration was temporary, seasonal, male, young, and almost wholly urban (agriculture has never attracted the Algerians in France). In general, the migrants worked on the lowest levels of French industry and government service. Most of them lived in *bidonvilles,* most often with covillagers. In 1954, about 5 percent were qualified workers, 25 percent specialized, and 70 percent manual laborers. They came from the poorest areas of Algeria, the Kabyle mountains in particular. In 1949, 29 percent of the men between 20 and 50 years of age in the area of Tizi-Ouzou were migrants in France. The figure for the commune of Djudjura was 50 percent. They usually settled where friends and relatives were. In 1950, for example, of the 1,224 Algerians in the 5th arrondissement of Paris, 70 percent came from the Soumman valley. The need to migrate was the result of two factors: the sequestration by European colons (who numbered about one million by 1954) of the best lands of Algeria, and the rapid demographic increase of the population of Muslim Arabs (from three million in 1830 to about ten million in 1954), in large part the result of improved hygiene that came with the French presence.

The flow of migration was discouraged at periods, originally because of colon reluctance to part with cheap labor, on later occasions because of depression in France (in the thirties in particular) or because of the German occupation of France. Migration was encouraged at other periods by factors such as France's need for manpower (during and after World War I, for example), famine (in Kabylia in 1945, for example), and when in 1947 all Algerians received French citizenship and could migrate freely to the metropole.

During the Revolution, particularly after the dramatic march of several thousand Algerians in central Paris in October 1961, which

---

are available at the Ministry of Labor in Paris. These "cahiers" are entitled *Etude sociologique de la Migration des travailleurs musulmans d'Algérie en Métropole* (1957).

was followed by savage repression, the migrant society, now molded into a political force, proved its loyalty to the Algerians' struggle for independence. They had (although not always without constraints) provided as much as 60 percent of the budget of the Front for National Liberation. It was with hope that they looked forward to the triumph of the cause that had started in their midst when, in 1925, the *North African Star* was founded to reject assimilation in France, and finally, under Messali Hedj's leadership, to demand full independence.

But with the first flush of victory gone, with the mass exodus of the colons and the disintegration of the FLN into varying factions, the pride of independence gave way for many to disillusionment. The political chaos in Algeria and the appalling economic problems it faced found reflection, of course, among the migrants, although it could be expressed only discreetly in France, now a foreign country to them. Nevertheless, with independence the mutual hostilities between nationalist and collaborationist; between Messali's new small Algerian National Movement (MNA) and the Front for National Liberation (FLN); Ben Bellist and Ben Kheddist; the supporters of Ait Ahmed, the dissident kabyle leader, and those of Ben Bella; and, finally, the supporters of Ben Bella and Boumedienne—all were there, and Paris, in particular, was to remain a hotbed of intrigue of Algerian against Algerian. Also, because of both economic disruption at home and the massive exodus of the colon population with its trained cadres, as well as to a lesser degree the disillusionment with Algerian politics, the number of Algerians who came to France (some even becoming French citizens, which, according to the Evian agreements, they could opt for until 1965) rose to figures greater than in the past history of migration—ironically and pathetically. In the spring of 1962 there were about 380,000 Muslim Algerians in France; in September 1963, there were 484,000; and by 1965, the figure had risen to over one-half million.[6]

6. Many of the statistical data in this essay are derived from the following sources: the bulletins of the Etudes Sociales Nord-Africaines entitled *Hommes et Migrations; Maghreb: Documents* (Paris, La Documentation Française); the Annuaires de l'Afrique du Nord whose publication, started with the issue of 1962, by the Centre National de la Recherche Scientifique, is prepared by the Center for North African Studies in Aix-en-Provence; *Esprit* (Paris), especially its special issue on migration of April 1966; and Pierre Moreau's long essay on the subject in *Lettre aux Communautés de la Mission de France* (April, 1966). For current events of a political or social nature, I have used, inter alia, *Le Monde, L'Express, Jeune Afrique, El-Moudjahid* (Algiers), *L'Algérien en Europe*

The Revolution over, the administrative framework of the Algerian community in France had to be refashioned. Understandably, the Federation of France, the leading wartime body of the FLN in France, now a foreign political organization, had to be abolished. It had already, in any case—having been controlled by the political opponents of President Ben Bella—become suspect. The Amicale des Algériens en France (ADAF) took its place as the overall organizing institution of the Algerian migrant workers, and the Amicale, except for a period of confusion in the summer of 1965, when Ben Bella was overthrown, remained under the control of the Algerian government.

The Amicale des Algériens en France (later "et en Europe" was added), was set up in November 1962 under the leadership of Ait El Hocine and Mohammed Lebjaoui. According to a semiofficial source, the majority of migrant workers had already rejected the leadership of the Comité Fédéral, a group opposing Ben Bella's Political Bureau, which in turn had, by force, taken over power from the provisional government of Ben Khedda. El Hocine's organization, the Comité de Soutien de l'Action du Bureau Politique, its task completed, had dissolved itself to make way for the ADAF.

The ADAF, directed by a Direction Centrale, considered itself a nonpolitical organization whose function was to coordinate the Algerian workers and help them with their problems. It represented a request to the French Prefecture of Police, asking to be considered a "foreign association" under a French law of 1901. It was only in February 1964 that it received implicit, though not explicit, recognition under curious circumstances described below. On January 16, 1964, it began to publish a French language newspaper called *al-Djazairi* (*l'Algérien*), which was later changed to *L'Algérien en Europe*.

The ADAF established a number of branches, the most important of which was the Amicale Générale des Travailleurs Algériens (AGTA). Others were the Amicale Générale des Femmes Algériennes (AGFA, related to the UNFA in Algeria); the Amicale Générale des Commerçants Algériens (AGCA, representing the Algerian merchants in France); the Amicale Générale de la Jeunesse Algérienne (AGJA).

The AGTA had a rival in an organization by the same name—one that opposed Ben Bella's Bureau Politique and then his government for at least two years after independence. This rival AGTA claimed to be the only legal representative of the migrant workers with continuity

---

(Paris), and *Révolution Africaine.* For purposes of brevity citations are limited mainly to direct quotations. Translations, unless otherwise indicated, are my own.

from 1957, when it was founded as a clandestine organization. In April 1964 the official AGTA repudiated it on the grounds that its own directors (that is, the directors of the ADAF's AGTA) had been legally elected in March 1963 to represent the Union Générale des Travailleurs Algériens (the UGTA) in France. This repudiation of the "pseudo" AGTA followed publication of a study by the latter stating that the exodus of Algerian workers had risen above 620,000 because of "unemployment, hunger and misery"; that 10 percent of them, out of disillusionment, had opted for French citizenship; and that the Algerian government encouraged the exodus of the very people who were needed to "build socialism" because, unable to provide work, it feared their opposition.[7]

Whether the reasons for the exodus of Muslim Algerians after independence given by the "pseudo" AGTA were correct or not, the exodus itself was only too evident, and most who came, even up to 1964, stated that they wished to avoid "unemployment and misery."[8] Between independence and the end of 1963, the migrant population increased by at least 60,000, and it continued to grow at a fast rate until controls were first established in April 1964 (see below), when the figure was somewhere in the region of half a million.

With independence, the legal status of the individual Algerian migrant and of his organizations became an important issue, particularly in respect to his rights to French citizenship, the status of the ADAF, and the conditions under which an Algerian could work in France. In regard to these, three precedents—the Evian agreements of 1962, a judicial case, and the protocol of April 10, 1964—set the legal framework.

According to the Evian agreements, an Algerian resident in France continued for three years to enjoy the civil—though not the political—rights of French citizens. In other words, an Algerian could neither vote in France nor engage in political activity of any sort. After three years, he had either to choose French citizenship or be considered a foreigner. A later law provided that, except for various provisions in regard to minors, any Algerian "de statut civil de droit local" who, three months after adoption of the law (adopted December 9, 1966), had not registered as a French citizen, would be considered to have lost his French nationality, retroactively, on January 1, 1963. Until this loss of citizenship was final, Algerians had the right to circulate freely between France and Algeria, and to enjoy all benefits, other than political, that they had enjoyed to date.

7. *Le Monde,* April 18, 1964.
8. *Le Monde,* February 29, 1967.

In regard to the legal status of the ADAF, which, as indicated, had applied for recognition as a "foreign association" upon its founding, it was not until February 1964 that any recognition of it at all was given, and this only implicitly. The recognition came in a court decision of the Tribunal de la 16e Chambre Correctionelle de la Seine in regard to a case involving the head of the Paris section of the Amicale (Ahmed Farès) and a group of his associates involved in an affair which had taken place at Créteil (on the outskirts of Paris) on January 12, 1963. At a meeting of the local Amicale, a former *harki* (an Algerian in the French army), named Ali Lakhdar, fired shots at a group of militants, killing one named Belaid. Some of the members of the Amicale gave chase and captured two of the assailants, locking them up and doubtlessly roughing them up. They were *not* turned over to the police. The French police then intervened, seizing twenty-two members of the Amicale indiscriminately. Twelve others who had taken their wounded associate, Belaid, to the hospital, were also arrested. Of the latter, eight were freed and four held for "*violences volontaires*" (with premeditation). The judge of the tribunal indicated that he intended to hold the Amicale, as such, responsible, and implicate its head, Ahmed Farès, presumably for running an illegal organization. At this point, a group of prominent Frenchmen, interested in defending and extending Franco-Algerian cooperation, intervened as witnesses. These were Edmond Michelet, and other members of the Association France-Algérie, and René Soyer, of the Association de Sauvegarde des Français d'Algérie. They all defended the legitimacy and value of the Amicale as a link between Algeria and France. Finally, the four Algerians held guilty of an open violation of French law were given three-year prison sentences, but Farès and an associate were released. Thus, the French court waived its contention that the Amicale, as opposed to certain individuals, had behaved illegally, and by so doing gave it tacit recognition.

The large incidence of Algerians coming to France caused consternation among Frenchmen and raised a host of problems. In March 1964 the French press expressed alarm over the influx of over 1,000 arrivals a day, and already the Algerians had been angered by the unilateral refusal to admit migrants in poor physical health to Marseille. Both governments agreed that the problem of migration could be negotiated. Earlier attempts in 1962 and 1963 to resolve these difficulties had come to nothing, but the issue had become too sensitive a matter by March 1964 to postpone any longer. Finally, after negotiations between Dr. Mohamed Seghir Nekkache, Algerian minister of social affairs, Gilbert Grandval, French minister of labor, Jean de Broglie, secretary of state to the prime minister, in charge of Algerian affairs, agreement was reached on the Protocol of April 10, 1964. This agreement was to set the basis for controls of immigration for at least the next three years. It did *not* modify the Evian agreements, but only provided regulations to implement them. The major terms of the protocol provided that beginning July 1, 1964:

1. To enter France, an Algerian must have the approval of the Office National Algérien de la Main-d'Œuvre (ONAMO); must be between 19 and 55 years of age; must have a medical certificate issued in Algeria by a mixed board of French and Algerian doctors.
2. The incidence of entry would be determined by the French Ministry of Work which would advise the Algerian government of French labor needs and possibilities every three months. The Algerian government would determine the number of permits it issued, accordingly.
3. France would provide professional training to Algerian workers.
4. A commission would be established to study problems arising from the migration.
5. Among those unaffected by these conditions would be the following categories:
    a. Students sent by the Algerian government to study;
    b. Government officials and their families;
    c. Workers already registered under Social Security, and with a notice of salary received, in France, covering at least three months;
    d. Families of workers already installed in France, provided accessibility of lodging could be provided;
    e. Members of learned professions duly registered as such;
    f. Algerians invited by some administrative branch of the French government;
    g. Tourists with a return ticket and a sum of 200 francs (the police having the right to decide if such people appeared to be genuine rather than pseudo tourists).[9]

Almost immediately, anxieties were expressed as to the repercussions the protocol would have. In Kabylia, the main source of immigration, there was talk of tensions that might arise from a "*claustrophobie col-*

9. The protocol is discussed in *Maghreb*, May–June 1964, and the *Annuaire* for 1965, p. 273. Tayeb Belloula presents an Algerian point of view in *Les Algériens en France* (Algiers, 1965), pp. 67 ff.

lective" if too many Algerians were debarred.[10] Complaints, when the protocol was implemented, became increasingly vociferous in Algeria as some migrants were sent home after arriving in France; their amour propre and that of their country was often bruised; the ONAMO worked inefficiently for lack of trained personnel; and Algerians were unhappy with the numbers the French government told ONAMO France needed. Tourists (the sum they were required to have was unilaterally raised by France from 200 to 500 francs) had to go through special checkpoints and, if they were legitimate tourists, felt insulted when they were rebuffed.

The French, on the other hand, complained that many Algerians, turned down by the ONAMO, were entering France illegally as pretended tourists. One ruse was for a village to raise the 500 francs to send an immigrant to France. Upon arrival, he would send the sum back for another migrant to come, again as a "tourist," and the new migrant would then do the same for someone else. The tension produced by these illegal devices continued to plague Franco-Algerian cooperation.

In August and then October 1966, two conferences were held to consider these pressing problems. The first, sponsored by the Algerian government, took place at the Club des Pins, in Algiers, August 8–15; the second, sponsored by sympathetic Frenchmen in Paris, was held at the Centre des Conférences Internationales, avenue Klébers, October 13–15.[11] In both, the problems, the hopes, and the tensions involved in Algerian migration to France were dealt with openly and frankly. The discussions and talks underlined the main issues clearly, as they appeared then and would most likely appear for a long time to come.

In anticipation of the opening of the first conference, it was evident, as Abdelkrem Gheraieb, a vice-president of the *Amicale*, told the French journalist, Ania Francos, that "the ideal solution, obviously, is for there not to be any migration, for all Algerians to find work at home. But this will be a dream for at least twenty years. Therefore, since it is a matter of a necessary evil. . . . [one must] define and apply an emigration policy.[12] The statistical realities, he said, showed that the increase in the Algerian birthrate was 3 percent a year (it

10. *Le Monde,* April 11, 1967.

11. Material on these two conferences appears in *Révolution Africaine,* August issues; *Maghreb,* September–October 1966, pp. 11–12; and *Le Monde,* October 18, 1966.

12. *Jeune Afrique,* September 18, 1966, p. 12.

might rise to 4 percent; if so, Algeria would have 48 million in the year 2000). A million and a half were then unemployed in Algeria; 50,000 new jobs a year were needed to meet the growing population pressure; and 200,000 new jobs a year would be needed to absorb unemployment in ten years.

The August conference, which consisted of some 150 delegates representing the FLN, various ministries, and the *Amicale,* was opened by Colonel Boumedienne. The goal, he stated, was to "elaborate a national program in regard to emigration, to direct it into channels, coordinate it with the national economy, make it pay." Three major aspects of the problem were treated at the conference: the economic needs of Algeria that were making emigration necessary; the difficulties created by the French; and the weaknesses in the way emigration was being handled by the Algerian government. Proposals as to a "national policy" were then made. Only the main speeches were published, much of the debate being held in camera.

In regard to Algerian needs, the facts of Algerian unemployment were readily admitted, though some of the figures given were lower than most nonofficial sources give. Thus Lahbib Djafari, a member of the Central Directorate of the Party and the seminar's coordinator, stated in a major speech that only *one million* Algerians were unemployed, and that 100,000 new permanent jobs would be needed to absorb Algeria's unemployed by 1977. He added, as did others, that "the imperatives of organized and planned development oblige us to consider emigration, for some time to come, as a necessity."

French policies that evoked criticism included limiting the free circulation of persons and the free access to residence, in violation of the Evian agreements (particular concern being expressed as to the "*notice individuelle*" by which Algerians—but not others—could be legally evicted from their residences by landlords); the racist press campaigns against Algerians; bad housing in bidonvilles; the unilateral limitation by France of the number of migrants allowed to enter (only 12,000 for 1965); the "hypocritical" provisions that families could only come if decent housing was assured (an effective way of excluding women and children); and the exclusion of many tourists by obliging them to bear a minimum of 500 francs on their persons. Veiled and vague hints were made by some speakers that if "cooperation" between France and Algeria was not revised, to become genuine, Algeria would look for "new solutions."

In self-criticism, the major complaint voiced was that the consular facilities available to Algerian migrants were inadequate both in amount and quality. Efforts were needed, it was also stated, to encourage Algerian merchants living in France to invest in Algeria, and to encourage Algerian doctors to return home. (It was stated that 300 Algerian doctors were working in the Paris area alone.)

The conclusions and concrete proposals to emanate from the conference, as Djafari summarized the recommendations of the commissions, were as follows:

1. *Sanitary and Social Commissions:* The recommendation was made that facilities for informing and advising emigrants be organized at points of departure from Algeria and arrival and settlement in France.

2. *Juridical and Administrative Commission:* Algeria should insist that France respect the principles of the free circulation of persons and of freedom of residence; should suppress the "notice individuelle" as applied only to Algerians; and should respect her own procedures for expulsion (the law of 1945). It also recommended that new outlets be found for Algerian workers, and that action be taken against the journalistic disparagement of the Algerian community. Administratively, it recommended an improvement, both qualitative and quantitative, of consular service to the emigrants.

3. *Economic and Demographic Commissions:* A three-stage program should be implemented to enable: (1) highly trained technicians, members of learned professions, and well-off merchants (the latter with their capital) to return as rapidly as possible to Algeria; (2) the progressive return of qualified workers; and (3) the eventual reflux of all categories to Algeria. In the meantime, Algeria should seek outlets outside France for emigrants in the third category, and should seek training for them in conformity with the needs of Algeria as well as the host country.

The conference was closed by Cherif Belkacem, coordinator of the Executive Secretariat of the Party, who stated: "History shows us that the current of migration must be seen as a result of constraint, a purely political one, during World War I, with the forced departure of Algerians to Europe, and then the economic and demographic constraint afterward . . . The main cause of every migration is the disequilibrium (*rupture d'équilibre*) between demographic increase and the resources of a country." He insisted that Algeria's migration was beneficial for France as well as necessary for Algeria.

The second conference was sponsored by the Association France-Algérie under the auspices of Edmond Michelet, Algeria's most faithful defender among the French, and Reda Malek, Algeria's ambassador to France. Discussions were led by distinguished Algerians as well as

Frenchmen in an atmosphere of mutual friendliness and frankness. Among the outstanding problems posed at the conference were these: the problem of adaptation to urban industrial conditions of a people of rural background; the social segregation, for racist reasons, in part, of many of these people, which made their assimilation that much more difficult; and the poor reception and the inadequacy of lodging offered the migrants.

Alain Girard, technical counselor to the National Institute of Demographic Studies, emphasized that France, as Algeria, benefited from migration. J. Fernand-Laurent, *chef du Service des Affaires Etrangères,* answered Algerian objections to the limits placed on the influx of workers by observing that the number of workers could be doubled if "tourists" would only return to Algeria after three months, according to international custom. Thus all was not flattering to the Algerian position. Fernand-Laurent was answered by Ben Ameur, member of Algeria's Ministry of Foreign Affairs, who argued that if France stuck to its Evian commitment on the free circulation of persons, Algeria would impose a strict control over its emigration. And the social counselor to the Algerian embassy, Sedoun, argued that French barriers against Algerian immigration were more severe than those affecting other ethnic groups.

Sympathetic French deplored the misery of Algerian migrant housing, and Ronald Nungesser, secretary of the Etat au Logement, said everything possible was being done to house Algerians decently. A French health official observed that the argument that Algerians were tubercular could be countered by statistics showing that the number of Algerians who were victims of tuberculosis, relative to the total in France, had diminished from 20 percent (five years before) to 8.7 percent. A French economist, after pointing out that in the final analysis of the total picture the Algerian migrants were not crucial to France, nevertheless agreed that France derived some benefit from this immigration, which, he said, was good, because "in a policy (*politique*) of cooperation, disinterestedness was suspect." Pierre Le Brun, a trade-union leader, insisted that Algerians be given preference in France's Five Year Plan in regard to immigration policy. The Algerian ambassador praised the value of the conference, and Michelet, after admitting to being somewhat overwhelmed by the problems involved in the whole issue, and recommending that France abandon her "*mentalité de belle-mère,*" closed the proceedings.

As might be expected in a conference gathering Algerians and Frenchmen of goodwill, among the points widely agreed upon were that French fears for themselves (in regard to employment, security, and health) caused by the Algerian presence, were unfounded, and that it was unfortunate that French prejudices were so strong in regard to North Africans in particular. But no concrete solutions resulted from the conference, and at the end of 1966 the tension over the crisis of migration became even more acute than it had been, and it continued to be serious through 1967. In December 1966 efforts to revise the 1964 protocol came to nothing—the Algerians arguing in favor of free circulation (with controls in Algeria), the French declaring that France had to impose controls, however hard, to stop the clandestine entrance of Algerian workers as tourists. *El Moudjahid* continued to denounce the "*mesures vexatoires*" of the French officials, and Algerian pressure on France took the form of demanding that French residents (not tourists) in Algeria only be allowed to leave Algeria if they presented a "*quitus fiscal*" proving they had paid all their taxes. Their word of honor would no longer be acceptable as before. *Jeune Afrique* referred to the battle of "*quitus contre quota.*" (France had already unilaterally limited Algerian tourists to 250 a week.)

The social anatomy of the Algerian migrant community during the first five years of independence resembled, in essentials, its anatomy on the eve of the Revolution. Differences, however, were apparent. The migrants, now no longer colonized subjects, had the backing of a sovereign government, but they suffered from the vulnerability of being foreigners in a country whose government, inevitably, now had less of a conscience in their regard than before. New also, was the fact that, as France had entered into the European community, so also Algerian migrant labor was entering the European scene as a whole, and, in this larger context, France had to compete for these workers. In 1966 there were perhaps 100,000 Algerians in Belgium and Germany, where wages were higher than in France. Finally, as France developed economically and the standard of living of its people rose, it was more apparent than before that the trend was for the largely illiterate migrants to become a sort of subproletariat—performing functions in the European economy undesirable to the now more finicky, since more prosperous, Europeans.

In general, the Algerians who migrated to France continued to do so essentially to find work where there was none in Algeria; in 1967, unemployment there was still in the area of two million. The political refugees who opposed the military rule of Colonel Boumedienne, and the intellectuals who preferred to live in Paris rather than in the dreary atmosphere of an Algeria still in search of itself both economically and socially, were a small minority. The bulk of laborers were divided, as before independence, into those who had virtually settled in France and those who came seasonally. The rhythm increased at the end of summer, then fell again. Sometimes more came than returned and sometimes (for example at the end of 1965) more left France than immigrated. Some came through regular channels, others as genuine or fake tourists (twenty to twenty-five thousand Algerians came to France as "tourists" in 1965).

Figures were very hard to be certain of because of the factor of clandestine entries, but a fair guess, for the end of 1966, was that there were 500,000 Algerians in France (probably 600,000 in Europe). The main sources of this exodus were the traditionally poorest regions of Algeria (the Kabylia and, to a lesser extent, Nedronia-Marnia), areas of emigration since 1945, and the Hauts Plateaux. The big cities, Constantine, Algiers, and Oran, provided a more recent source. Origins from them were roughly 60 percent Constantinois, 30 percent Algérois, and 10 percent Oranie. Before independence, 80 percent of the Algerian workers were of Kabylia or Constantine origin. An estimate for 1960 of families having members working in France was that of 96 percent of the families living in the major cities, 2.4 percent had one family member in France; of 92.7 percent living in other cities (not including the Kabylia), 8.4 percent had one member in France; from the Kabyle cities, of 80 percent, 16 percent had one; of rural, non-Kabyle communes of grouped population, no family; of scattered populations, of 96.9 percent, 2.5 percent had one member in France, while of 75.7 percent of rural Kabyle families, 17.8 percent had one member, and 4.9 percent had two family members in France.[13] By 1967, the percentages had changed, but in proportion to its population, at least, Berber Kabylia, whose population is about two million, remained the main source of emigration.

Although the numbers of immigrants had increased, the patterns of settlement and types of employment in France had remained the same since 1954. In 1963, estimates were: Paris region, 207,000; department of Seine, 180,000; Bouches-du-Rhône, 30,000; Moselle, 28,000; and Nord, 28,000. Migrants, as before the Revolution, tended to seek employment where their families and fellow-villagers had already settled.

As for occupations, these were, in the main, on the lowest levels of pay and routine, as the most casual observer in Paris could easily see. As to the kind of work they did, of 217,466 salaried workers, in 1963, in enterprises employing more than ten people, 50 percent (94,135)

13. *Maghreb*, May–June 1964, p. 43.

worked on public road gangs and the like; 25 percent (44,046) in the mechanical and electrical industry; the rest in other industries, mines, etc.[14] Only 2,150 were in agriculture, the least well paid and hence least popular occupation among the Algerians. Of the half-million in France, in 1967, about 280,000 were regularly employed, about 100,000 were women and children, and the remaining 120,000 were either unemployed or only partly employed. Roughly 10,000 were merchants working on their own, wooed in vain to invest their capital in Algeria, whose unpredictable policies of nationalization frightened them.

Other than finding gainful employment, the major problem for the Algerian migrant, as for other migrant groups, was finding lodging—a problem for Frenchmen themselves. "Only ten percent of the Algerian emigrants in France have decent lodging," declared Mahmoud Guennez, coordinator of the Amicale des Algériens en Europe, in March 1966; [15] but, he added, "the French authorities are making a decided effort in the field of lodging, which is in a state of crisis, one suffered by the French themselves."

The terrible conditions of all too many Algerians were portrayed in Algeria's publications. A representative description appeared in 1966 accompanied by distressing photographs.[16] It was of the bidonville of Gennevilliers on the outskirts of Paris. The correspondent wrote: "human shadows . . . pass us by and disappear as they have come. Furtively, with eyes cast down and hunched shoulders. Go elsewhere? (You ask them), Paris? It's far—another world—why go there unless to arrange for some administrative matter at the consulate? And there, one must wait, stand in line, hours and hours without speaking, and lose a day of work." A typical bidonville shack "is little more than two meters by one and a half. Facing the entrance, to the right, a camp bed and two old blankets; a tiny table by the side. This constitutes all the furniture. I was forgetting a petrol lamp which has a double function: to illuminate and to heat. Asked if Gennevilliers was their Casbah, a worker answered: No, no . . . Gennevilliers is as different from the Casbah as the latter is from Hydra [a fashionable Algiers quarter]. This is another world."

14. Ibid., pp. 42–43. *Europe-France-Outremer*, June 1966, pp. 26–27, indicates proportions for 1966 were the same as for 1963.

15. *Le Monde*, March 15, 1966.

16. Mustapha Sihimi in *Révolution Africaine*, January 29–February 4, 1966, pp. 13–15. Such descriptions abound in this publication and in *L'Algérien en Europe*. They suggest the sad world of the disinherited fictionalized in Driss Chraibi's *Les Boucs* (Paris, 1955).

Such testimonies could be multiplied indefinitely. To allay the suspicion that such accounts by Algerians in Algerian periodicals were only propaganda, one might cite several French sources. According to a report in *Le Monde,* a few steps away from the new Faculty of Letters, "eight North Africans live like troglodytes in one of the newest areas of Montpellier" in an abandoned *chantier* of an apartment house, only the subsoil cellar rooms of which had been built. "The inhabitants have only . . . a camp bed or boards, straw mats, a stone; a frying pan is a luxury. Lighting is by candle. No water: one can only obtain water by pail at the Saint-Eloi hospital, 500 meters away. . . . In another industrial area, 60 North Africans are piled into a dilapidated house recently largely destroyed by fire. Others in hotels, six to a room . . . but these are perhaps the privileged ones." [17]

Why such misery? Some of the main answers have already been suggested: France as a whole was poor in lodging; Algerians who supported families in Algeria deliberately lived as simply as possible to save as much as they could. But there were also factors of a sociological and psychological nature. Racism on the part of French landlords and communities, as discussed below, was a factor as was the desire of many Algerians to live together with fellow-citizens and also fellow-villagers.

Of course, in the bidonville, "the phoenix which is reborn of its ashes," as Denuzière has put it, "each shack abandoned by its inhabitants is immediately reoccupied by new arrivals. . . . each terrain evacuated by Frenchmen is immediately *bidonvillisé.*" [18] The problem the French government faced was formidable. Nevertheless, both on a private and a public basis, the French had taken measures to ameliorate the lives of those people who were worst off and expunge this shame of the cities, the bidonville.

Under state auspices, in the Paris region in 1966, 4,380 people were relocated from bidonvilles to healthier quarters, and a plan inaugurated in 1966 extended this effort. Some of the improvements were made in areas described above—La Corneuve and Gennevilliers, for example. The legal basis for erasing bidonvilles was the "loi Debré" of December 14, 1964, which allowed the government to take over slum areas. The chief organizations involved in clearances were the Fonds d'Action Sociale pour les Travailleurs Etrangers (supplied with a million francs in 1966); le Ministère de l'Equipement (60 million in

17. *Le Monde,* January 4, 1967.
18. *Le Monde,* February 3, 1967.

1966); and the Société Nationale de Construction pour les Travailleurs (SONOCTRA) and its affiliate, and the Habitation à Loyer Modéré (HLM) (for Paris called Logement et Gestion Immobilière pour la Région Parisienne [LOGIPEP]). Public and private collaboration contributed to improvements in cities like Marseille and Lyon. Efforts in the latter have been unusually effective; 90 percent of the slums, it is reported, have been eliminated.

The task of clearing bidonvilles and providing decent alternative housing was enormous. Among the difficulties were the reluctance of mayors of towns where Frenchmen themselves were not properly lodged to cooperate; the problem of relocating all the inhabitants of a razed slum; and the problem of educating usually illiterate foreigners in upkeep and cleanliness. Conversely, the problem needed to be solved not only for moral reasons and because slums breed disease and crime, but because by 1966–67 other European countries were beginning to compete for Algerian workers, as they were already competing for workers from countries like Spain, Portugal, Italy, Turkey, and Greece.

Housing, though perhaps the major problem presented by migration to France, was not, of course, the exclusive problem. Most of the Algerians who came to France were illiterates, knew little or no French, were often discriminated against, and, in short, were difficult to assimilate to French metropolitan life and a modern economic complex, which now required considerable training for a worker to rise above the level of a simple manual laborer.

Social assistance and some training were provided by both the French government and private individuals. To give some examples: in Marseille, in 1967, private and church groups provided social assistance and medical treatment in the bidonvilles; in Montpellier, a private organization provided facilities for studying French, offered counseling, and helped pressure the public authorities to take action on behalf of the migrants; in Lyon, an organization named Accueil et Rencontres did the same. The Régie Renault at Billancourt provided its foreign employees with facilities for training to prepare them for more advanced jobs. In the area of education and professional training (to which France committed itself in 1964 in regard to the Algerians), a variety of organizations, some partly private, offered help. Foreigners received government-sponsored training in building and metallurgy, aimed toward specialization. In 1966, 1,546 Algerians were taking advantage of this latter opportunity, the largest group (43.5 percent) of all foreign workers. The most important source of funds for such aid was Fonds d'Action Sociale pour les Travailleurs Etrangers (FAS), established in April 1964.

By 1967, the French language was taught by a variety of organizations with the usual bewildering French initials (CIMADE, ANARF, AMANA, ASFA, SSAFNA, and CREDIF). The Direction de la Coopération, which collaborated with private groups, provided free courses in factories and in Muslim sections of cities. In 1967, it had 273 centers for men (about 500 classes) serving 20,000 foreign workers; 70 classes in Paris and the Provence were open to women. The French teachers were both public and voluntary. Hygiene, reading, and other topics were taught.

Serious problems confronted this French effort to enculturate Algerian, as well as other, migrants into a modern society. Workers were often too tired after work to be successful students: they often had to travel long distances to attend classes; teachers had to cope with considerable variations of knowledge of the French language even in the same class. A more fundamental problem, from the Algerian point of view, was that workers, and particularly their children attending French schools, assimilated to one degree or another to French culture, would have a difficult time reintegrating into their homeland whose policy, however half-hearted to date, was to reject the French cultural legacy and resurrect the Arabic language and culture. Significantly, Edmond Michelet, later minister of civil service, when on a goodwill mission to Algeria in November 1967, was asked that migrant children in France be taught Arabic as well as French.[19] France's record in regard to the Algerian workers, though partial and often spotty, was in any case not discreditable. Both the government and private individuals had shown that conscience operated in regard to the Algerians in the face of enormous difficulties. But one of the principal difficulties that hampered and blocked the social assimilation of the Algerians was racist prejudice among many Frenchmen, in regard to Algerians in particular.

France boasts of a good record in regard to racial toleration, and Frenchmen have been proud that their great Revolution was universalist in its inspiration, a revolution for the Rights of Man. This is the

19. *Le Monde,* November 23 and 28, 1967. In return for this visit, Algeria's minister of the interior, Ahmed Medeghri, visited France in March 1968. It appears that he succeeded in persuading the French government that because Algeria was tightening its control of Algerians going to France as tourists, France should waive its limitation on the number of Algerian tourists allowed into France and abolish the special corridor for Algerian entries. *Le Monde,* March 2–4, 1968.

ideal. A good test of the reality has been the attitude and behavior of Frenchmen toward the some half-million Algerians in their midst—a group that from the start has had disadvantages other ethnic groups have not had. They were a people of a different religion, who had only recently been "the enemy" both overseas and in France itself for more than seven years, and they were citizens of a nation that had rejected its "Frenchness" and, both in spite of and because of narrow ties of "cooperation," that continued to experience moments of hostility and tension with France, often exacerbated by the former *pieds noirs,* the colons, who brought with them to France their natural racist attitude, compounded by the loss of what they considered to be their homeland. On the other hand, newly independent, vulnerable, unsure of themselves, it was not strange that Algerians should be unduly sensitive to seeming slights, to tend to interpret as racist what might be the enforcement of regulations, to inflate minor incidents into major issues. In addition, one must remember that to most Frenchmen, Algerians, once independent, were simply foreigners, to whom they owed no special responsibility. But to many Algerians—dependent upon jobs in France and often suffering from a love-hate complex in regard to France, their former ruler—France would for a long time be more than just another country.

It would be impossible to sort out all these factors in analyzing the relationship of Algerian to Frenchman, and vice versa, in terms of attitudes. Some studies of a qualitative sort have, however, been made, which do point to certain tendencies during the first five years of independence.[20] All of these studies indicate that the average Frenchman is indeed prejudiced in regard to the Algerian and more prejudiced against him than toward any other foreign migrant group in France including the Black African; and one of the studies indicates that Algerians are aware of the stereotype held of them; this was a study in which the Algerians consulted stated that the clichés applied to them by the French were: "beasts of burden"; "always playing with

20. Four such studies are described in Paul-Marie de La Gorce, *La France pauvre* (Paris, 1965), pp. 241 ff.; Paul Maucorps, Albert Memmi, Jean-François Held, *Les Français et le racisme* (Paris, 1965); and Jacques Mesnil, "Quelques Opinions et attitudes de Français à l'égard des travailleurs africaines" in *Esprit* (April 1966), pp. 745–57. The study that probed stereotypes referred to immediately below was done on the eve of the Revolution and is described in La Gorce. In this context, it is interesting that as early as 1955 an American, David McLelland, wrote an article entitled "The North African in France: a French racial problem," *Yale Review* (March 1955), pp. 421–88. His conclusions are implicit in his subtitle.

knives"; "men of no dignity"; "men from another planet with no culture"; and "one never knows with those people." (This prejudice was not based, it might be noted, on color, but, it would seem, upon a historical legacy.)

It is not strange that in face of a real prejudice that exists in regard to them, Algerians should react strongly, perhaps sometimes paranoiacally, to a number of incidents since independence, which they interpreted as the external manifestation of this prejudice.

Ironically, one of the first "incidents" of a racist sort that occurred after independence and that received some press coverage involved not the Algerian nationalists, but their enemies and France's allies, the *harkis.*

In early 1963, the government ordered that some land in the commune of Conflans (Seine-et-Oise), be requisitioned for the purpose of constructing some seventy homes for former harkis. In horror, the citizens of Conflans, led by their mayor, rose in indignant revolt.[21] "I have nothing against them," said the mayor to the correspondent of *L'Express* (Michel Vianey). "I even married one off . . . with huge moustaches. . . . Shortly after, he killed his wife. A sad story." He went on to explain that Algerians had many children (as they had many wives also, he suggested), and that it would cost the commune a good deal to educate them. Too many Muslims together would "provoke indicidents" with the local population and among themselves. Old accounts would be settled. One citizen virtually told Vianey that the harkis must be kept away to avoid turning a nonracist community into a racist one! An Algerian, long resident in Conflans, observed to Vianey that the harkis, for whom he had little use himself, suffered from a reputation for criminality, for crimes, ironically, they had committed only at the order of French officers. The community really objected to them, he claimed, because of the color of their skins. This was an opinion the studies discussed above did not confirm.

Another affair that received publicity in 1964 was the refusal of the municipality of Saint-Claude (Jura) to allow Algerians to enter the public swimming pool without medical certificates, asked of no other ethnic group. Many groups protested, including trade unions, and Michelet, honorary president of the Association France-Algérie, cited Saint-Claude as a dangerous indication of what might become, even if only unconsciously, a campaign of "racial and xenophobic hatred," reminiscent of Nazi and Vichy days.[22] He compared the swimming-pool incident to the expulsion of a number of Algerians from their

21. *L'Express,* March 7, 1963.
22. *Le Monde,* May 28 and June 1, 1964; *Jeune Afrique,* June 8, 1964.

apartments and the refusals to rent lodgings to others in the Paris area.

In June 1964, at Meudon (Seine-et-Oise), one hundred and fifty Moroccans and Algerians were expelled from an apartment building at 38, avenue du Chateau, by one hundred and twenty agents of the "corps urbains." No incidents occurred. The workers were taken to different points of the city (métro stops, etc.), from which they were encouraged to disperse. Madame Rosy Wolimer, member of a committee to defend these Algerians legally, protested that the defense committee had not been allowed to present its case properly, and that the workers had been expelled before a new development in Meudon had been completed, one that could have housed them.

As in many other cities of the world, "police brutality" is a problem in France. On occasions, the Algerians, as might be expected, claimed to have been the victims. And they, and their French liberal sympathizers, naturally tended to attribute such incidents to racism. On one such occasion, two murders that occurred in the 19th arrondissement of Paris were assumed by the police to be by the same man, most probably an Algerian. One of the victims, before dying, had identified his assailant as a North African. A witness also claimed to have seen a North African run away. With excessive ferocity, one hundred and twenty Algerians and forty Frenchmen were taken to police stations to be questioned in the Algerian sections of the 18th and 19th arrondissements of Paris. Twenty of those arrested were charged with carrying prohibited weapons, for thefts, and so forth. On June 5, 1964, an Algerian arrested for exhibitionism was put into Fresnes, where he died, perhaps as a result of beatings by the police.[23] *Le Monde* stated in its story that such behavior on the part of the police revealed a mentality reminiscent "of the tragic days of October, 1961."

A final case that might be cited is that of Kaddour Mehyaoui, an Algerian found guilty, on the basis of considerable circumstantial evidence, of the brutal murder of four people at the end of June 1967.[24] Because of the feeling, perhaps, that some of the circumstantial evidence may have been inspired by racism, the prisoner, on the grounds of unspecified "extenuating circumstances" was not sentenced to death. One of Mehyaoui's French lawyers, Emile Pollack, was quoted as having said: "I have the horrible feeling that if this man were not an Arab, he would not be here now. But because he was an Arab, he became suspect and then he became the probable killer."

Whether or not Algerians were really more prone to crime than

23. *Le Monde,* June 27, 1964.

24. *Le Monde,* issues of June 25 and July 2, 1967. James Goldsborough summarizes the case in the *International Herald Tribune,* July 3, 1967.

other nationalities, segregation made them seem so, and prejudices against them made them seem more suspect than others.

In fact, the proportion of crimes committed by foreigners in France compared to the total number of foreigners was larger than the same figures for Frenchmen. In 1963, of 415,085 people arrested in France, 52,411 were foreigners, or 12.6 percent of the foreign population as compared to 4.16 percent of French citizens. In the Paris-Seine region, 26.4 percent of those arrested were foreigners. But, as La Gorce has observed, the world of the migrants was largely one of young, male, segregated people, living on a low and depressed standard of living. Taking the same age-group among Frenchmen, the proportion of French crimes would be about the same as those committed by Algerians, he concluded, which is a higher proportion than those committed by the Spanish, Portuguese, and Africans.[25]

There were, during the Revolution and after, newspapers and periodicals (particularly those sympathetic to "Algérie Française" and reflecting colon and rightist opinions of various shades) who fanned racist feelings. This was especially true in the spring of 1964, when articles that particularly angered the Algerians asked Algeria to "keep its criminals." In a speech to the FLN congress of 1964, Ben Bella retorted that Algerians were only in France because of an economic situation that was the legacy of "132 years of colonialism." The coincidence of this press campaign and the first rejection of Algerians at airports and ports (following the April protocol) seriously intensified Algerian indignation (Algerian entrants were processed through a "*couloir réservé aux passagers de nationalité algérienne*") and attacks on the Algerian minority appeared in, among other papers: *Minuit, Le Démocrate, Riom, Rivarol, Fraternité Française, Réforme,* and *Aux Ecoutes.*[26] In the last mentioned, Pierre Poujade talked of the "Arab Invasion," and *Riom* accused the Algerians of getting ready to "avenge Poitiers"! *Rivarol* accused the Algerians of a crime wave, and of monopolizing French hospital beds, because most of them, it said, were sick. The Algerians continued to protest against similar attacks. In November 1966 the Algerian embassy objected to the pejorative use of the cliché "*individu du type 'nord africain'*" during a fresh press campaign against Algerian "criminality," and on behalf of the Algerians, the liberal French journalist, Marc Valle argued: "It is not their origin, nor their temperament which causes some Algerians to violate our laws, but the moral isolation in which they find themselves, and the

25. *La France pauvre,* pp. 240 ff.

26. The attacks are described in Belloula, *Les Algériens en France,* pp. 207 ff.

grave difficulties they face. . . . They live among themselves with nostalgia for a land they have had to abandon and with the persisting temptation to rebel against a brilliant civilization which fascinates them but which they cannot understand." But those who took to crime, he observed, were only a small minority.[27] *Révolution Africaine,* an organ of the FLN, denounced the French racist press for whipping up racist feelings over even the most minor incidents involving Algerians, and protested: "It is current practice that every time an assault occurs anywhere in France without the author being discovered, the assailant is always described as a North African." [28] It also took the occasion to protest against discrimination in public places, cafés, restaurants, and hotels, which helped to give rise to bidonvilles by making it difficult for Algerians to find decent or normal lodging.

Reflecting on some of the attitudinal tendencies among Frenchmen in regard to the Algerians, as well as other foreign minorities, the editor of the leftist Christian journal, *Esprit,* at the conclusion of a long, special issue on migrant laborers in France, observed a paradox. Although few nations had been as receptive to foreigners as France, few people were as xenophobic or as culturally provincial. Thus in France, a traditional land of asylum, administrators and policemen were particularly hard on those who spoke French badly; "few societies are as closed and distrustful as our own," the editorialist concluded, and saw the migrants being segregated as a new proletariat of inferior people to occupy the unwanted and menial tasks of a modern society.[29]

The Algerians were among the contemporary victims of this paradox of French cultural exclusiveness, if not racism, but, by way of compensation, Algerians enjoyed the sympathy and support of the Michelets, the Germaine Tillions, and writers for *Esprit,* also a part of the French paradox.

In any case, Algeria's dependence on France in 1967, five years after independence, was clear. The figure of employment in 1967 remained in the area of two million. The Algerian economy, plagued by a lack of Algerian cadres, with what private enterprise it had frustrated by precipitous but often ill-conceived "socialist" measures, seemed unable to take off. It is not strange that the Algerians should migrate to France; that, however reluctantly, its poorer communities should send their sons abroad to make money; that the Algerian government should accept the inevitability, if only temporarily, of this

27. *Le Monde,* November 18, 1967.
28. December 30, 1965–January 5, 1966, pp. 12–13.
29. April 1966.

migration, hoping that, someday, those trained by policy or by occasion, only in France, would develop into an army of trained workers whom the Algerian economy would eventually be able to absorb and use. It was understandable that Algerians should both resent this dependence and at the same time denounce restrictions to the easy flow of their sons to France. It was also understandable that the French should look with alarm on the new proletariat in their midst, not wholly employable, a dangerous problem in the event of economic recession, but at the same time feel the moral responsibility for their erstwhile wards, as well as the importance of continuing to employ Algerians as a part of total French strategy, to maintain France's role as a leader of the Third World, to protect her oil investments in Algeria, and to preserve her cultural *presence* abroad.

The statistics of the migration show the importance of this migration to Algeria eloquently enough. In 1962, 480 million francs, and in 1966, 800 million francs (i.e. roughly $200,000,000) kept about one to two million Algerians alive through remittances. This sum represented about half of the salaries made by Algerians in France. About 20 percent of Algeria's population lived off these remittances. What was unique about the Algerian situation in contrast to other countries sending migrants to Europe was the degree of national dependence it involved, and the fact that, because of habit, tradition, and language, Algerians depended so heavily on only one nation and one economy. (The proportion of Algerian migrant workers in France to those elsewhere, mainly in Belgium and West Germany, was about 5 to 1 in 1967.)

Did the French need these workers? Was the link represented by the migrants of only one-way advantage economically, or was it reciprocal?

According to Plan V, for 1965–70, it was projected that for France to sustain her economic expansion, she needed 325,000 more immigrants to begin with and more to follow. Why so many? Mainly because the lower and more arduous manual jobs were avoided by the now relatively well-off French workers, and so areas of the economy were undermanned. As early as 1955, it was observed that the foreigner would work at jobs Frenchmen avoided, that France's postwar "*politique de peuplement*" had turned into a "*politique de main-d'œuvre.*" [30] To France's advantage, young migrant workers arrived

30. *Les Algériens en France: étude démographique et sociale* (Paris, 1955), pp. 576–77. For the important role of migrant labor in Europe's postwar boom, see Charles P. Kindleberger, *Europe's Postwar Growth: The Role of Labor Supply* (Cambridge, Mass., 1967).

already trained (for such menial jobs) and cost France nothing to bring them up as adults; family allocations, if the worker's family was not in France, were lower than for the French, the same rate as in the country of origin; and, also, Algerians were more mobile than Frenchmen, who like to stay put in their own communities. Frenchmen, seeing only the petty hawker rather than the factory worker, failed to realize that they needed these migrants to sustain a relatively prosperous economy, that France, now in the Common Market, had to compete with countries like Belgium, where conditions were relatively better for manual workers. In addition, it was not inconceivable that Portugal, Spain, and Italy, as they developed, would dry up as sources of manual workers.

But there were problems. The projection of Plan V assumed economic expansion would be continuous, yet in 1966–67 there was a recession in France (more than 300,000 were unemployed in December 1966). In a depression, it would be, of course, the migrants who would first suffer.[31] Again, if pay should rise in certain areas where it was then low, French distaste might change. (In the United States the building trade is lucrative and attractive.) The French birthrate might increase more rapidly than expected, and technological modernization might alter the need for cheap labor. (It has been suggested that reliance on cheap foreign migrant labor might retard French technological development by discouraging innovation.)

Whether these eventualities would materialize or not, it appeared in 1967 that France did have use for the Algerian migrant workers, as for workers from elsewhere, but it was not evident that France's dependence on any particular group of workers was crucial. And certainly France did not need as many Algerians as would come if all controls were eliminated. But whether in France, on the periphery of the French economy and on the lowest levels of occupation, or, in any emergency, forced to return to Algeria, these workers would continue to constitute, like millions of their brothers in the underdeveloped world, an ominous problem for the world. A Christian monthly recently wondered if the presence of foreign migrants in Europe, a "subproletariat being fashioned under our eyes," did not constitute "a new social revolution?" [32] The implication of this question, presumably, was

31. In this connection, my colleague, Frank Harris, was told by a French official in 1967: "We would get no thanks from anyone for having tried to assist Algeria by admitting large numbers of its unemployed for training and for humanitarian purposes in 1967, if we were forced to expel them in several years to deprivation in Algeria in order to save French or other European workers from unemployment in France."

32. *Exchanges,* January 1967, p. 1.

that the significant division in the world in formation, in the second part of the twentieth century, might be between the usually colored *have-nots* and the white *haves*, and that, so to speak, Frantz Fanon was replacing Marx as the prophet for the oppressed of the new era. As in the United States the Negro population constituted the most alarming case of this division along racist lines, so the migrant workers, the Algerians in particular, defined France's most immediate responsibility in regard to the "damned of the earth."

Tensions resulting from Algerian immigration to France will undoubtedly rise and fall; prejudices, or worse, perhaps, indifference, will continue among most Frenchmen. But France, both publicly and privately, has shown that the qualities that are among the best the French can boast of—enlightened realism and humanism—do operate, even in the midst of prosperity. As for the Algerians, there are many who feel that where these qualities operated among the French in regard to them, dependence was not wholly either humiliation or frustration. One could only hope that other qualities, less fortunate ones, might not lead to a rupture between the two nations that could only end in tragedy for many of the migrants and their dependents, and that the "*bicots*," as the memory of the Revolution faded, might be treated as one Algerian speaker at the Conference on Migrants in Paris put it, "like other human beings."

This would remain France's challenge until Algeria could meet her own proper challenge, of developing her economy to the point where she could absorb the migrant workers and so, finally, end the song of exile. And, more broadly, Algeria's success in this regard might provide hope, as its Revolution once did, or disillusionment, as the bitter aftermath of the Revolution has, to many peoples of Africa, the Arab world, and perhaps further.

22. *France and Britain in Africa: A Perspective*

LEONARD THOMPSON

Now that the era of French and British rule in Africa is receding into the past, we can begin to see it in historical perspective. The second part of this book is a contribution to the resultant reappraisal. During the colonial era itself, the fact that Africa was divided among rival European powers gave white observers of the African scene an analytical framework for their commentaries. Thus, Buell wrote successively of British Africa, French Africa, and so on; and although Lord Hailey's organizing principle was thematic ("Political and Social Objectives," "Systems of Government," etc.), within each chapter he highlighted the differences among the British, French, Belgian, and Portuguese territories.[1] In this book, several contributors have reconsidered some of these differences. In my judgment, they have demonstrated that the differences were in fact much less significant than they seemed to white observers at the time.

Kanya-Forstner shows that during their respective phases of territorial expansion in West Africa the French and British agents of expansion acted under similar assumptions, had similar expectations, and employed similar means. Moreover, when Obichere's chapter on African reactions to French expansion in West Africa is compared with what we know of African reactions to British expansion in various parts of the continent, we find an essentially similar story of Europeans making the utmost use of the internal cleavages and conflicts in African societies—state versus state and faction versus faction.

In the era of colonial rule itself, we can now see that the policies argued about in Paris or London, or even in Dakar or Kaduna, played a much smaller part in determining the major processes of change than was assumed by white observers at the time. The great French debate between the advocates of assimilation and those of association, as well as the contemporaneous British elaborations of indirect rule, now ap-

1. Lord Hailey, *An African Survey* (London, 1938; rev. ed. London, 1957); Raymond Leslie Buell, *The Native Problem in Africa*, 2 vols. (New York, 1928).

pear to have been somewhat sterile exercises; it was, rather, the specific ecological and cultural situations within colonial Africa that had the greatest effects upon the trend of events in each area. Consequently, we may expect the emphasis among historians of French and British rule in Africa to shift from theory to practice and from the metropole to the colony—especially to the cercle or district—where each local white administrator formed part of a unique network of human relationships.

The authors of several chapters in this book have raised the question of whether the French and British district officers (or their equivalents) handled these problems in significantly different ways. Deschamps explains that the majority of the French colonial officials were drawn from the provincial petite bourgeoisie and were culturally not far removed from the French peasantry; their British counterparts, Heussler shows, came mainly from the middle class and, as a result of their public-school and Oxbridge education, regarded themselves as members of the ruling elite in British society. In addition, France itself was already comparatively egalitarian and centralized, whereas Britain was still comparatively aristocratic and decentralized. The result was that French colonial officials were subjectively less inclined to respect and support the claims of traditional African political and religious leaders than were their British counterparts. Nevertheless, French and British colonial administrators had a great deal in common. Most members of both groups were imbued with the assumption prevalent throughout the West in the first half of the twentieth century—that Western culture was absolutely superior to African cultures, and that it would take many generations before Africans could catch up with Europeans in what was viewed as a unilinear route to "civilization." Most members of both groups adopted a paternalistic attitude in their dealings with African chiefs as well as commoners. Both groups also worked under similar material limitations. Until very late in the colonial period, all European colonies were expected to balance their budgets, and the administrators had to manage their districts with meager resources in money and technical personnel. Moreover, during the 1920s and 1930s there was a trend toward convergence in both theory and practice in the two major colonial empires in Africa. Deschamps remarks upon this in the administrative sphere; Fieldhouse in the economic sphere. Austen shows that the Permanent Mandates Commission of the League of Nations was one of the influences that promoted this convergence. There was conscious borrowing, too, as when French educationalists applied some of the ideas that they found at Achimota to their William Ponty school near Dakar.

It is often assumed that the constitutional structures of the two empires were sufficiently different to have made the decolonization process revolutionary in the French case and evolutionary in the British case. Even this contrast seems to diminish with the lapse of time. Marshall's chapter does indeed show us that as late as 1944 Charles de Gaulle was trying to preserve French control over a centralized empire—that the essential purpose of the Brazzaville Conference and the contemporaneous reforms in Algeria was to elicit cooperation from the educated elites of tropical Africa and the Maghreb. It took military disasters in Indochina, diplomatic pressures from the West as well as the East, and British precedents in India and the Gold Coast to cause de Gaulle to relinquish France's overt political power in tropical Africa; and it took further military failures in Algeria itself to cause him to abandon the claim that Algeria was French. But is it accurate to view British decolonization in tropical Africa as an essentially evolutionary process—a logical extension of an age-old policy of creating colonial legislatures, making them first partly and later predominantly elective, increasing the size of their electorates, and giving them powers over the local executive governments? Did not British disengagement from the tropical empire involve a change as radical, in British terms, as French disengagement did in French terms? In promoting Indian independence, the Attlee Cabinet was the first British government to extend to an indigenous colonial society the full autonomy that had previously been confined to white-settler communities, and it did so in the face of bitter opposition from Winston Churchill. That was as revolutionary a step as French decolonization. Only after that step had been taken in 1947 was the decolonization of British tropical Africa a logical extension of an established policy.

I am not, of course, contending that there were no differences between the French and the British methods of expansion, control, and disengagement. What I do believe is that our predecessors who were assessing the French and British empires while they were still flourishing tended to assume that these differences were fundamental; that assumption still seems to be in the minds of some of the contributors to this volume. In fact, the state of society in the French Ivory Coast was not so very different from that in the contiguous British Gold Coast, and French Algeria with its pied noirs had points of similarity with British Kenya and its white settlers. Imperial historians may therefore find a fruitful field for research if they identify similar phenomena within the different empires in Africa and rigorously compare them, with a view to distinguishing the changes produced by policies that were specifically French or specifically British.

This leads me to my second theme. The enduring significance of imperialism lies in the changes that took place among the colonized peoples. The major question for historians to pose concerning France and Britain in Africa is, What effects did they have upon indigenous African societies?

For the most part this book reflects the older European historical tradition in focusing on questions concerning French and British motives and methods in Africa. It tells us more about what the French and the British thought they were doing in Africa than what they were actually doing there. All the chapters except Obichere's are written by white scholars, and with that same exception all of them begin to lose their perspicacity and intellectual thrust just at the point where they probe the African side of the colonial situation. For example, in his substantial and important chapter on "The economic exploitation of Africa," Fieldhouse says that "on the African side very little is known about the activities of merchants or about the response of producers to the stimulus of overseas markets";[2] he leaves it at that. Heussler, after asserting that "the bedrock reality" of the colonial situation was "the partly planned, mainly spontaneous surge of African life," goes on to declare that we can only learn about this from the evidence of the white administrators, "because of the grey silence of Africans on the subject."[3]

First, on the question of evidence, it is true that the bulk of the official archives left by the colonial regimes consists of documents written by white officials. It is also fruitful to do as Huessler himself has done—to amplify that evidence by obtaining further information from surviving colonial officials.[4] But it is by no means impossible to correlate the white evidence with evidence from the African side. In many colonies there were vigorous African newspapers long before the end of the colonial period. Since independence, African politicians have written a spate of autobiographies that contain a great deal of subjective information from the African side about the colonial era. There is also a mass of unpublished African evidence, which is less accessible to Western historians who are accustomed to working in European archives and libraries and interrogating white informants and who are not familiar with African languages. Most of the documents written by Africans during the colonial period are still in private hands, and most African participants in the events of the colonial pe-

2. See above, p. 594.
3. See above, p. 578.
4. Robert Heussler, *The British in Northern Nigeria* (London, 1968).

riod are to be sought out in their own countries. African evidence is available—in published books and articles, in unpublished documents, and in the minds of men; it is the historian's task to seek it out, to record it where necessary, and above all to understand it.

A fruitful start has already been made. Thomas Hodgkin's brief but perceptive sketch of the background of nationalism in tropical Africa, in which he identified some of the major processes of change in the colonial period, was published as long ago as 1956.[5] By now, most of the principal landmarks of, for example, the political changes among the Akan peoples during the colonial period have been clarified.[6] This is, perhaps, an exceptional case, but it is almost matched by work in many other parts of the continent.

The second half of this book might leave the reader with the impression that, once the indigenous political systems had been subdued at the turn of the century, there ensued a period of about fifty years in which the social situation in tropical Africa was somewhat static and such change as did take place was entirely the result of European initiative. That was how the European officials tended to see it at the time (except when they were involved in suppressing rebellions), but it was not the whole picture. In a recent essay Jacob Ajayi, professor of history at the University of Ibadan, has looked back at the colonial period in the context of African history as a whole; he claims not only that Africans continued to take initiatives at all stages but also that not all those initiatives were mere responses to the activities of Europeans. Indeed, Ajayi labels colonialism in Africa "An Episode in African History"—a brief period in the history of peoples who, like all others—have experienced countless other changes over the centuries.[7]

Nevertheless, fundamental changes certainly took place in African

5. Thomas Hodgkin, *Nationalism in Colonial Africa* (London, 1956).

6. E.g., David Apter, *The Gold Coast in Transition* (Princeton, 1955); Dennis Austin, *Politics in Ghana, 1946–60* (London, 1964); K. A. Busia, *The Position of the Chief in the Modern Political System of Ashanti* (London, 1951); J. B. Danquah, *The Akim Abuakwa Handbook* (London, 1928); David Kimble, *A Political History of Ghana, 1850–1928* (Oxford, 1963); Kwame Nkrumah, *Ghana* (London, 1957); William Tordoff, *Ashanti under the Prempehs, 1888–1935* (London, 1965); United Kingdom, *Report of the Commission of Enquiry into the Disturbances in the Gold Coast*, cmd. 231 (1948); Martin Wright, *The Gold Coast Legislative Council* (London, 1947).

7. J. F. A. Ajayi, "Colonialism: an Episode in African History," in L. H. Gann and Peter Duignan, eds., *Colonialism in Africa: 1870–1960* (Cambridge, 1969), 1: 497–509.

societies during the colonial period. Even though Europeans were largely responsible for initiating such changes, they did not control the consequential chains of events. Changes did not stop at points willed or even envisaged by white rulers. Rather, they were the cumulative effects of complex processes of interaction between white rulers and African subjects, each operating within the range of his specific powers, interests, opportunities, and limitations. By transforming African chiefs from heads of autonomous political systems, legitimized by custom and disciplined by popular sanctions, into agents of alien rule, Europeans initiated a process that was to undermine the hereditary aristocracies, hardly any of which survive as ruling groups in former colonial territories.[8] By transmitting Western norms and modern literary skills in mission and public schools, Europeans nourished a new African elite who eventually won political power for themselves on the ruins of chiefly power as well as white power. By setting a wide social and economic gulf between themselves and their subjects, Europeans provided an example of a living style and standard for the African elite to follow when they gained power, thereby creating a serious cleavage in postcolonial African society.[9] In short, the most profound effects of British and French rule were changes in the systems of values and in the distribution of power, wealth, and skills in African societies. These cannot be explored in depth by historians who decline to search beyond the evidence provided by members of the ruling caste in colonial societies. Yet they are the changes that warrant the attention of historians who now aspire to assess the significance of European imperialism.[10]

We can, for example, pose a battery of questions about white racism and its consequences. How did Europeans perceive Africans in the colonial situation? What were the differences among the perceptions of the French and the British, the administrators, the soldiers, the missionaries, the traders, and the settlers? In what ways did diverse types of Europeans distinguish and relate to diverse types of Africans—chiefs and commoners, peasants and townsmen, the educated and the illiterate, Muslims, Christians, and animists? Did their perceptions be-

8. The main exceptions are in Ethiopia, Morocco, Northern Nigeria, and Swaziland.

9. The government of Tanzania has thus far been the most successful in tackling this heritage from the colonial era.

10. So far, anthropologists have paid more attention to these problems than historians. P. C. Lloyd's *Africa in Social Change* (Baltimore and Harmondsworth: Penguin Books, 1967) is a good introduction to the subject.

come more realistic or more stereotypic over time? How did different categories of Africans, in turn, perceive and distinguish among Europeans? What, finally, were the links that connected white racism with concepts such as negritude, pan-Africanism, neocolonialism, and African humanism? These questions have been considered only indirectly in this book, and they raise interesting possibilities for further research.

One would also expect the colonial historian to examine the process that has been called "institutional transfer." This very phrase is misleading; it implies that Western institutions such as parliamentary government are capable of being transplanted from the societies within which they germinated and grew as integral elements into societies with different political and legal traditions and needs. The actual process that is being referred to is more complex. Institutions are not simply transplanted. When an institution graft takes, the receiving society adapts the borrowed institution to the totality of its own social system and in so doing transforms it. Time after time African societies, like societies elsewhere, have incorporated and transformed alien institutions. The idea of kingship may have spread into some African societies from others, but in each case it became a very distinct institution.[11] Islam spread from North Africa into the Sudanic belt, but there it made diverse accommodations with preexisting religious beliefs and institutions.[12] It is therefore not surprising that major political changes have taken place in the African states since they were launched into independence with constitutions drafted on French and British models.[13]

Nevertheless, postcolonial Africans have accepted and (thus far) preserved two legacies designed by their former rulers. One is the territorial framework that the Western powers created in the partition period and modified after World War I. This survives, with few modifications, in spite of many illogicalities. It does so because African vested interests have been built up around it. The strength of those interests has been demonstrated in the catastrophic Nigerian civil war of the late 1960s. The other legacy is the linguistic division within Africa. The Europeans implanted the French and English languages as the media of communication of the new elites beyond the range of

11. See, for example, Daryll Forde and P. M. Kaberry, eds., *West African Kingdoms in the Nineteenth Century* (London, 1967); and the review article by P. C. Lloyd, "The political development of West African Kingdoms," *Journal of African History*, vol. 9, no. 2 (1968), pp. 319–29.

12. I. M. Lewis, ed., *Islam in Tropical Africa* (London, 1966).

13. Aristide R. Zolberg, *Creating Political Order: The Party-States of West Africa* (Chicago, 1966).

their local vernaculars, which in most cases was a very short range. These languages have promoted intercourse and understanding and cultural, economic, and political affiliations among all the French-speaking countries in tropical Africa and, to a lesser extent, among all the English-speaking countries as well. At the same time, they have created a barrier to intercourse, understanding, and affiliation between the two groups of states. In this sense, too, the European partition of Africa endures.

Though the French and British empires in North and tropical Africa have now passed away, the argument of empire continues. But I believe that the terms of the argument should shift away from reconsideration of the policies and methods of the individual colonial powers toward a deeper analysis of the interactions of the French and the British with the indigenous societites of Africa, for that is where the imprint of imperialism remains.

PART III

Bibliography

☙§ 23. *French Colonial Rule in Africa: A Bibliographical Essay*

☙§ DAVID E. GARDINIER

This essay discusses the most important literature on French colonial rule in Africa between 1914 and 1960. Its sections on the Maghrib and Black Africa were written originally to be integrated with another author's sections covering imperial rivalry and the period before 1914. Although an integrated treatment of the whole literature of French expansion and rule has not proved possible, it is hoped that the publication of these sections alone will nevertheless contribute to an understanding of French colonial rule during the twentieth century.*

THE MAGHRIB

French colonial rule existed in Algeria from 1830 to 1962, in Tunisia from 1881 to 1956, and Morocco from 1912 to 1956. French control involved the settlement of considerable numbers of Europeans in each country. In the early 1950s there were 1,026,587 settlers in Algeria, 255,000 in Tunisia, and 330,000 in Morocco. The presence of the settlers led to the establishment of many secondary schools and several institutions of higher education. Their professors have produced a large number of historical works as have historians in France itself and elsewhere. Most of the historical writing has concerned the individual countries rather than French North Africa as a whole. E. Albertini, G. Marçais, and G. Yver's *L'Afrique du Nord Française dans l'histoire* (1937) is the best-executed example of one kind of historical study which appeared in the interwar period. It deals with the whole of North African history, placing the French conquest and colonization in perspective. For the period of French rule, it stresses French achievements. It deals with various aspects of French rule such as military pacification in Algeria and Morocco, settlers and their activities,

* The author wishes to express his appreciation to the Marquette University Graduate School for its support of this project and to Raymond Betts for reading the manuscript.

political and administrative organization, and status of the natives. Another type of older work is exemplified by Victor Picquet's *La Colonisation française dans l'Afrique du Nord* (1912), which concentrates on the period of European activity, in this case in Algeria and Tunisia. A recent example of this type of study is an Italian work by Enrico de Leone, *La Colonizzazione dell'Africa del Nord (Algeria, Tunisia, Morocco, Libia)* (2 vols., 1957–60). Unlike the Picquet work, it treats the history of European colonization in each country without showing common influences and interrelationships. It also contains errors.

Another kind of work typical of the interwar period treated the North African countries within the framework of the French Empire as a whole. Stephen H. Roberts, an Australian scholar, in *The History of French Colonial Policy 1870–1925* (1929) presents sections on North Africa which concentrate on the political, economic, and military aspects of French rule from the birth of the Third Republic through the mid-1920s. It is still the most detailed and most readable account of French administrative theory and practice in North Africa. More general is the later work of a historian from the University of California, Herbert I. Priestly, *France Overseas: A Study of Modern Imperialism* (1938), which deals with the entire nineteenth century and the first thirty-five years of the twentieth.

The most comprehensive and up-to-date account of French rule in the Maghrib during the present century is found in the sections of *L'Afrique au XXe siècle* (1966) which were written by Professor Jean Ganiage of the Sorbonne. After an excellent summary of the internal history of each country at the beginning of the twentieth century, Ganiage turns to the French takeover of Morocco, military conquest and pacification, and administrative reorganization. Thereafter follows a discussion of the interwar period in the three countries. Especially valuable is the analysis of economic and social change, including urbanization, and its relation to the development of nationalism in the 1930s. The final two-fifths of Ganiage's 268-page essay cover the period 1942–65, including the emancipation of the Muslims from French control, the economic evolution of the three countries, and their course since independence.

Marcel Peyrouton, who served for many years as an administrator in the three countries and was Vichy's last governor-general in Algeria, could have written a highly interesting work if he had chosen to draw upon his rich personal experiences. Instead, his *Histoire générale du Maghreb: Algérie, Maroc, Tunisie* (1966) rests on secondary works and allegedly on archival sources which he does not document. Thus his work remains a competent text but one without distinction. General Georges Spillmann is a career officer who served for twenty-four years in Morocco, where he became a scholar of the Draa people and of Berber Islam. At the beginning of the Algerian insurrection, he was commanding the French army division at Constantine. His *Souvenirs d'un colonialiste* (1968) contain his views of the evolution of North African life under French colonialism between 1912 and the present.

A short volume by Richard Brace, *Morocco, Algeria, and Tunisia* (1964), has the merit of reviewing the whole of the colonial period in the three countries in about one hundred pages. Regrettably, it shows little depth of understanding of the Muslim society, its earlier history and institutions, upon which the French imposed their rule. Therefore, it is strongest in its analysis of political evolution toward independence after the Second World War. Resting on recent French- and English-language scholarship and personal study in Algeria, it is still by far the best historical account in English and the most objective in a field filled with polemical literature. *A Survey of North West Africa* (1959), edited by Nevill Barbour, supplements Brace by providing data on Muslim society which his work lacks. Charles Gallagher (1963), resident in North Africa for a number of years as an American Universities Field Staff representative, provides a good introduction to the recent history of the three countries. He includes an analysis of the political development and the economic and social problems of each country from a historical perspective. A somewhat similar work published earlier (1959) by a onetime German foreign service officer turned correspondent is Friedrich-Wilhelm Fernau's *Arabischer Westen: Der Maghrib in Bewegung*. After examining the historical reasons for the distinctive character of each country, he investigates the roots, shapes, and directions of the conflicts between French colonialism and local nationalism after 1945. In 1947 Georges Spillmann published *L'Afrique du Nord et la France*, in which he reviewed French policies and achievements and took a liberal view toward the aspirations of the Muslims. His work contains many insights into the economic development of North Africa and its social consequences, as well as into the social effects of the political and administrative organization instituted by the French.

Three works on the Berbers of North Africa contain information on their evolution under French rule. Georges-Henri Bousquet's *Les Berbères: histoire et institutions* (2d ed., 1961) is the only good brief but comprehensive work on the Berbers. Eugene Guernier's *La Berbérie, L'Islam, et la France* (2 vols., 1950) is a detailed cultural history which discusses French and Arab influences on the Berbers. Lhoussine Mtouggui's *Vue générale de l'histoire berbère* (1950) is a brilliant but biased account of the Berbers which looks at their relations with the French from a Muslim viewpoint.

Samir Amin's *L'Economie du Maghreb* (2 vols., 1966) is an economic and social history of North Africa that describes the development of Algeria after 1880, Tunisia after 1910, and Morocco after 1920. The first volume, *La colonisation et la décolonisation,* deals with population growth, urbanization, the transformation of the economic and social structures during the colonial period, and the conditions of decolonization. There is some evaluation of the overall impact of French colonial rule from a non-French, anticapitalist view. The brief work of René Gallisot, *L'Economie de l'Afrique du Nord* (1961), deals mainly with French activities during the colonial period and since independence. André Tiano's *Le Maghreb entre les mythes* (1967), though primarily concerned with economic policies since independence, casts light on colonial structures and concepts, including their influence since 1956. A German work by Margaret and Eberhard Wohlfahrt, *Nordafrika: Tunisien, Algerien, Marokko* (1955), is an extensive economic and social survey that emphasizes the twentieth century. Charles Celier et al., *Industrialisation de l'Afrique du Nord* (1952), is a collection by specialists on all aspects of industrialization. Lucien Golvin's *Aspects de l'artisanat en Afrique du Nord* (1957) is a solid study on artisanry. The study of Pierre Moussa (1960) has much data on the economic relationship between France and the North African countries.

Jean Despois's *L'Afrique du Nord* (1949) is a reliable older work by an economic geographer which discusses the effects of European colonization on the indigenous population through the years right after the Second World War. Pierre Birot and Jean Dresch in *La Méditerranée et le Moyen-Orient* (1953), pp. 391–525, deal with much the same topic from a Marxist viewpoint. An article by the American economist Melvin M. Knight, "Economic Space for Europeans in North Africa," (*Economic Development and Social Change,* February 1953) deals with North African demography and land utilization. It contains a critical evaluation of most French thinking on those matters at the time. Louis Chevalier, *Le Problème démographique nord-africain* (1947) discusses population growth and its economic and social consequences. La Documentation Française, "L'Enseignement des musulmans en Afrique du Nord," *Notes et études documentaires,* no. 344 (July 5, 1946) is a good brief account of the education of Muslims right after World War II. Henri-François Marchand's *Les Mariages franco-musulmans* (1955) is a detailed sociological study of mixed marriages in French North Africa.

A study by the Algerian-born French sociologist Jacques Berque, *French North Africa: The Maghrib between Two World Wars* (1967 trans. of the 1962 French ed.), deals with the economic and social transformations of the interwar period and their political implications. Berque's work is in some ways analagous to that of Balandier on Equatorial Africa, although he is dealing with a different society under the impact of French colonial rule. Berque's long residence in North Africa and his rich knowledge of Egypt and Islam result in a volume filled with insights on the changes that were occurring in tribal organization, rural and urban life, and cultural values in the period. His approach is neither chronological nor country-by-country; he is not strictly analytical according to any explicit comprehensive themes. His method is often impressionistic as he paints a brilliant mosaic of North African life between 1919 and 1939 by tackling such apparently discrete subjects as land tenure, the arts and literature, urbanization, Islam, the impact of the French Socialist Party, and changing customs and dress styles. He shows how French colonization in Northwest Africa, where settlers were 10 percent of the population in Algeria and roughly 6 percent in Tunisia and Morocco, gave that part of the Arab world a different orientation from Arab lands to the east while at the same time not altering the distinctive features of the Maghrib.

A work which concentrates on the political evolution of the three countries from 1920 to 1961 is Roger Le Tourneau's *L'Evolution politique de l'Afrique du Nord musulmane, 1920–1961* (1962). A historian who lived and taught in Morocco, Tunisia, and Algeria for more than a quarter-century, Le Tourneau writes dispassionately from a French administrator's viewpoint of the developing conflicts between French colonialism and Maghrib nationalism. Despite its lack of sympathy for Arab Muslim nationalism, his is still the best political history yet written of the area and the period. It is better in the narration of events than on the analysis of institutions. It reveals greater understanding of Morocco and Algeria than of Tunisia, but is rather weak in its analysis of Algerian nationalism. Le Tourneau's study shows that despite geographic proximity, religio-cultural similarity, and a common French colonial rule, the three countries developed politically in different ways. It implicitly reveals the existence by 1961 of three nations, and not the artificial creations of French colonialism found in some parts of Black Africa. A work in English which deals with the same subject is Lorna Hahn, *North Africa: Nationalism to Nationhood* (1960). While Miss Hahn's book does not reflect the same depth of understanding of traditional Muslim society, it does a better job than Le Tourneau's of making the nationalist movements come alive for the reader. Louis-Jean Duclos, Jean Leca, and Jean Duvignaud's *Les Nationalismes maghrébins* (1966) is an attempt to analyze the historical development and synthesize the major characteristics of national consciousness in Morocco, Algeria, and Tunisia. The authors conclude that different types of nationalism result from different historical experiences, even when countries have basically the same traditional religio-cultural background and the same European colonial ruler in a similar geographic setting. Clement Henry Moore, *Politics in North Africa: Algeria, Morocco, and Tunisia* (1970) compares the political development of the three countries from precolonial times to the late 1960s. His analyses of the impact of the colonial experience upon postindependence politics are particularly insightful.

Professor von Albertini's work on decolonization (1966) has useful data on French policies and Muslim reactions in the three countries, especially for the interwar period in Morocco and Algeria. Also useful on French rule and Muslim responses between 1918 and 1938 are two long articles in the Royal Institute of International Affairs' *Survey of International Affairs,* edited by Arnold Toynbee. Volume 1 (1925) includes the section "The Islamic World since the Peace Settlement," of which part 2 deals with the Maghrib. Volume 1 (1937) has long sections on "Unrest in the Northwest African Territories under French Rule, 1927–1937."

The symposium *Léon Blum, Chef de Gouvernement, 1936–1937* (1967) contains three short pieces on the efforts of the Popular Front government to liberalize the situation of North African Muslims. Charles-André Julien discusses the Blum-Viollette reforms in "Léon Blum et les pays d'outre-mer," pp. 377–90. Governor Robert Delavignette presents "La Politique de Marius Moutet au ministère des colonies," pp. 391–95, which is followed by an intervention by the one-time Socialist minister himself. A short work by Herbert Liebesny, *The Government of French North Africa* (1943) contains a good analysis of the administrative and legal systems, including the position of the Muslims, up to 1942.

World War II in North Africa has produced a large literature. The war served to undermine French colonial rule both politically and ideologically. The struggle between Vichy and Free France undermined French prestige. The American landing in Morocco and Algeria in November 1942 and the subsequent warfare in Tunisia until May 1943 further weakened French military prestige, already damaged by the armistice of 1940. Elliott Roosevelt presents a vivid portrait of the Anfa encounter between his father, the President, and the sultan of Morocco (1946). Kenneth Pendar's *Adventure in Diplomacy: Our French Dilemma* (1944), by one of Ambassador Robert Murphy's consuls in North Africa in the early part of World War II, describes the situation there during the war and its effect on the people.

Yves Maxime Danan, *La Vie politique à Alger de 1940 à 1944* (1963) is based on *mémoirs* and *témoignages,* mainly of provisional government figures. Danan shows that the Allied debarcation was the work of only a very few men and discusses settler attitudes toward the changes brought by the Vichy and Free French regimes. His work presents very biased evaluations of the roles of Darlan, Giraud, and other wartime figures who ended up on the wrong side in various conflicts.

Some of the major French participants have written about the Vichy–Free French struggle and later the struggles within the Free French movement. *Mémoires, vol. 1, Alger, Tunis, Rome* (1950), by Maréchal Alphonse-Pierre Juin, the Algerian-born (1888) commander of the French expeditionary forces in North Africa and Italy (1941–44), throws much light on the political history in French North Africa before and after the Allied debarcation. Another Algerian-born general, Georges Catroux, *Dans la bataille de la Méditerranée: Egypte, Levant, Afrique du Nord, 1940–1944* (1949) recounts his role and impressions of the same period. Also useful are the accounts by Generals Charles de Gaulle, *L'Appel* (vol. 1 of his *War Memoirs,* 1954), Henri Giraud, *Un Seul But, la victoire: Alger, 1942–1944;* and Marshal Maxime Weygand. All of them throw light indirectly on the evolution of the relations between France and its colonial subjects. Peyrouton (p. 788 above) has a chapter on Weygand and the war. André Truchet (1955) holds the thesis, based on abundant documentation, that it was possible to defend North Africa against the Axis in June 1940 at the time of the armistice.

Among the most important political studies which touch the entire Maghrib is Charles-André Julien's *L'Afrique du Nord en marche: nationalismes musulmans et souveraineté française* (1952). Julien analyzes the rise of Muslim nationalist movements in the three North African countries under French rule. The work places the evolution of these movements within the larger historical context of the centuries-long resistance of indigenous North African peoples to foreign rule and shows how twentieth-century nationalisms came to be inseparable from orthodox reformist Islam. According to Julien, the problems of the French in governing these areas after 1945 resulted from a combination of two factors: the shortsighted attitude of the local settler interests and the paralysis of the Paris government; together they gave rise to proconsulships in North Africa under the domination of the *colons* and failed to satisfy the legitimate aspirations of the Muslim majorities to govern themselves. The work of René Schaefer, *Drame et chances de l'Afrique du Nord* (1953) is primarily a discussion of the economic and socio-cultural backgrounds of the conflict between the French and various nationalists. Henri Benazet's *L'Afrique française en danger* (1947), by a French radio commentator, contains perceptive analysis of the development of Maghrib nationalism. The issue of *International Conciliation* (November 1953) on the problem of the French Union by General Georges Catroux is the work of a liberal officer, Algerian-born, with long experience in the area and many insights. Articles by Julien, "From the French Empire to the French Union" (*International Affairs,* October 1950) and "Crisis and Reform in French North Africa" (*Foreign Affairs,* 1951) have perceptive comments on North Africa not entirely repeated in his book of 1952. The latter article concerns the evolution of Morocco and Tunisia. An article by Roger Le Tourneau, "Causes des mouvements d'autonomie en Afrique du Nord," (1954) deals primarily with Morocco and Tunisia also.

Maréchal Alphonse-Pierre Juin, *Le Maghreb en feu* (1957) is an important eyewitness account by the Algerian-born general who served as resident-general in Morocco. It makes clear that the deposal of Mohammed V was contemplated and was not accidental. In criticizing the North African policy of the various Fourth Republic governments, Juin omits the fact that he was with Mendès at Carthage in 1954 when the latter sought to settle the Tunisian question by granting increased self-government.

De l'impérialisme à la décolonisation (1965), a collection of essays on colonial rule in North Africa edited by Jean-Paul Charnay, is essentially useful for French agricultural colonization, Berber emigration to the new cities, and decolonization.

Odette Guitard in *Bandoeng et le réveil des anciens peuples colonisés* (1961) traces the anticolonialist themes enunciated at Bandung in 1955 and elaborated upon at subsequent conferences at Cairo, Accra, and Tunis, in particular as they pertained to French policy in North and Black Africa.

David Gordon's *North Africa's French Legacy, 1954–1962* (1962) is a significant short study of the evolution of the place of French culture in the life of the three Maghrib countries during the era of decolonization. It discusses French policies and Muslim Arab reactions to them. It concludes that the French language, administrative methods, tastes, and values will remain an intrinsic part of North African life. But there will be a trend towards increased Arabization, involving a recovery of Arabic as a bearer of traditional Islamic values and a diminution of the French presence. Gordon's study includes excellent short accounts of French educational efforts among Muslims and of literature in French by Muslims that is critical of French policies. The critical work "Regards sur la littérature maghrébine d'expression française" (*Cahiers nord-africains 61* [October–November 1957]) shows the evolution of Muslim thinking about French culture.

There are many works on Islam in the Maghrib which touch on the impact of and the response to French policies. Georges-Henri Bousquet's *L'Islam maghrébin: Introduction à l'étude générale de l'Islam* (2d ed., 1949) is a good study from a sociological approach. Roger Le Tourneau's "North Africa: Rigorism and Bewilderment," in Gustav von Grunebaum, *Unity and Variety of Muslim Civilization* (1955), pp. 231–60, deals with twentieth-century Islam in the Maghrib from a historical approach.

There are several important works on the relation of the religious brotherhoods to French rule. Jamil M. Abun-Nasr's *The Tijaniyya: A Sufi Order in the Modern World* (1965) discusses the order's cooperation with the French in the Maghrib from the beginning of the occupation and pacification in the nineteenth century. The social and religious exclusiveness of the order led its chiefs to see their interests as different from the Muslim community at large. Their belief that their members were predestined for paradise removed the obligation to battle the infidel and allowed them in good conscience to enlist French assistance against their opponents in the Qadiriyya order led in the 1830s and 1840s by the Amir 'Abdul Qadir. The services of the Tijani sheikhs against him made the Tijanis dependent on the French for protection and French rule a necessity for the welfare of their order.

An older work by Octave Depont and Xavier Coppolani, *Les Confréries religieuses musulmanes* (1897) is the most comprehensive study of the sufist orders throughout Northwest Africa at the end of the nineteenth century. This work is updated by General Pierre J. André, *Confréries religieuses musulmanes* (1956). It provides data on the conservatism of the brotherhoods and their relations with the French authorities in the twentieth century prior to the rebellion.

André Chouraqui's study of the Jews of North Africa (1952) contributes to our understanding of the transformations of the life of the Maghrib Jews under French rule. In Algeria the Jews acquired their place in French society only at the price of an almost complete adoption of Western ways. In Tunisia, too, the Jews abandoned many of their religious and ancestral characteristics in contact with the French, while acquiring a new economic and social dynamism. In the 1950s the Jews numbered 160,000 in Algeria (1.75 percent of the population), 105,000 in Tunisia (3.73 percent), and 255,000 in Morocco (2.5 percent). This work on Maghrib Judaism rests on Arabic and Hebrew materials not customarily employed by European scholars. In 1965 Chouraqui supplemented his orginial work with two completely new chapters on the exodus of the Maghrib Jews and their emigration to Israel, which was published as *Etudes maghrébines* (no. 5, 1965). Between 1948 and 1964 80 percent of the Jews left the Maghrib and 280,000 of them went to Israel. The role of French policies which assimilated the Jews and awakened nationalism among the Muslim Arabs in this exodus and emigration are discussed in this short study. Also useful for an understanding of the Maghrib Jews under French rule is a more general work by Haim Z. Hirschberg (1965).

ALGERIA

Historical writing on Algeria tended until the last two decades to be concerned mainly with French colonization—either with its achievements or with its shortcomings. Algeria was viewed in its relation to French politics and affairs. There was little attention devoted to the indigenous populations—Arab, Berber, or Jewish—except within the context of French interaction with them in the military pacification and administrative organization of the country after 1830.

Further, Douglas Johnson in his article "Algeria: Some Problems of Modern History" (1964) points out that historians have been influenced in their approach to North Africa by the domination of two successive modes of thought. One, first expressed by certain French officers and then by settler representatives, emphasized the *mise en valeur* of the area and its production. Economic and human geographers led the way in this type of study. A second and more recent school of thought emphasized that colonization is a contact of peoples, and stressed the need to study the changes experienced by indigenous populations subjected to foreign influences. In this type of work, sociologists, ethnologists, and students of institutions from a juridical or legal viewpoint tended to predominate.

Among the older works on Algeria which are still useful are the semiofficial *L'Algérie* (1930) by Augustin Bernard, which is the second volume of G. Hanotaux and A. Martineau's *Histoire des colonies françaises et de l'expansion de la France dans le monde;* Stephen Gsell, Georges Marçais, and Georges Yver's *Histoire de l'Algérie* (1927); and Victor Picquet's *L'Algérie française: Un siècle de colonisation, 1830–1930* (1930). Typical of older works which present French accomplishments up to the time of the centenary is Emile F. Gautier's *L'Evolution de l'Algérie de 1830 à 1930* (1931). More recent historical works include a short but excellent volume in the *Que sais-je* series by Gabriel Esquer, *Histoire de l'Algérie, 1830–1960* (1960), which was edited and brought up to the year 1966 by Charles-Robert Ageron, a specialist in nineteenth-century Algeria (2d ed., 1966). Claude Martin, a good historian who is pro-settler, sees the French Communist Party, left-wing intellectuals, General de Gaulle, the Soviet Union, and the United States in different ways as responsible for the demise of Algérie française, in his detailed volume *Histoire de l'Algérie française 1830–1962* (1963).

Several older volumes, not primarily historical, have useful historical sections. Marcel Larnaude's *Algérie* (1950), is an excellent general introduction by a geographer. J. Alazard et al., *Initiation à l'Algérie* (1957), is a collection of articles by specialists on peoples and demography, religious life, social life, the economy, and administrative and political organization that purposely omits contemporary political problems. Two volumes, *Algérie* and *Sahara,* in the *Encyclopédie coloniale et maritime,* edited by Eugène Guernier and G. Froment-Guiyesse, present a comprehensive set of essays on every aspect of Algerian life, including its history. Originally issued between the two world wars, these volumes were extensively revised and reissued (1948) after World War II.

Pierre Nora in *Les Français d'Algérie* (1961) presents a good account of the settlers—their history, society, and psychology. Nora's work is complemented by the law thesis of Bruno Etienne (Aix, 1965), which is not merely a juridical study, but the most complete study on the consequences of independence for the one million Europeans in Algeria. It contains 125 pages of documents, some complete and others excerpted, and the best bibliography on the subject. Pierre Bourdieu in *The Algerians* (1961, a translation of *Sociologie de l'Algérie,* 1958), discusses the different types of traditional Berber and Arab societies in Algeria and their evolution under the impact of French colonial rule from the perspective of the late 1950s.

Among the older works on the economic development of Algeria under the French are several volumes by Victor Demontès, *L'Algérie économique* 5 vols., 1922–30); *L'Algérie agricole* (1930); and *L'Algérie industrielle et commerçante* (1930). The geographer Hildebert Isnard undertook a detailed study of what was solely a European enterprise, the wine industry: *La vigne en Algérie: Etude géographique* (2 vols., 1951–54). At about the same time Henri Rebour (1950) studied the production of vegetables, Ghislaine Mollard (1950) wheat production from 1830 to 1939, and Michel-François Auquebon (1953) the mechanization of agriculture. Jean Despois's *La Hodna* (1954) is a regional geography of the semiarid area near Constantine where various irrigation and modernization projects were undertaken after the Second World War. In another book, *Le Djebel amour: Algérie* (1957), Despois studies one area in depth prior to the rebellion, emphasizing geography, demography, economics, and sociology. A similar study for another area during the entire period of French rule is P. Boyer's *L'Evolution de l'Algérie médiane: ancien département d'Alger de 1830 à 1956.*

After World War II also, a number of French scholars turned their attention to the social consequences of economic development. Xavier Yacono's *La Colonisation des plaines du Chélif, de Lavigerie au confluence de la Mina* (2 vols., 1955–56) is a history of French colonization in the valley of Algeria's longest river, between Algiers and Oran. Yacono describes and analyzes the valley in 1830, the origins of the settlers (French, Spanish, Jewish), the different forms of colonization (official or private, civil or military), the factors of transformation (capital invested, roads and railroads, health, security), and then gives an overall economic and social evaluation.

Despite its Marxist suppositions, the study of André Nouschi (1961) on the living standards of the populations of the Constantine region between the French conquest and the end of World War I is a valuable contribution to the economic and social history of French rule. Nouschi sees the European capitalist economy, which was established most fully in the Constantinois between 1881 and 1901, as producing severe shocks and dislocations for the socio-economic structures of the traditional society. He also links world economic crises with the social evolution of Algeria.

Michel Launay's *Paysans algériens: la terre, la vigne, et les hommes* (1963) is a study in depth of the *arrondissement* of Ain Temochent in the Oranie, an area that contains one-quarter of Algerian viticulture. It analyzes the problem of the vineyards, landholding and credit systems, division of lands between Europeans and Muslims, and resulting tensions.

Pierre Bourdieu and Abdelmalek Sayad's *Le Déracinement: la crise de l'agriculture traditionnelle* (1964) deals with the effects of European colonization in Algeria, which removed the Muslim peasant from the land and despoiled him of his crops, putting him in a new situation in which he lacks the financial means to modernize. Alain Darbel, Jean-Paul Rivet, Claude Seibel, and Pierre Bourdieu in *Travail et travailleurs en Algérie,* vol. 1, *Données statistiques;* vol. 2, *Enquête sociologique* (1964) offer a statistical and sociological study of workers in Algeria in the last years of French rule. Through analysis of data on migrations, employment, professional qualifications, and incomes of European and Algerian families, one can see the social differentiation that results from the economic and social transformation of an evolving society.

Germaine Tillion's *L'Algérie en 1957* (1957, trans. 1958), is an impressionistic but incisive work of a Marxist ethnologist who observed rural Muslims in the 1930s and the again in the late 1950s. She analyzes the economic and cultural foundering of populations not adapted to the modern industrial world and sees their present fate as *clochardisation,* that is, proletarian pauperization. Jean Morizot in *L'Algérie kabylisée* (1962) discusses the evolution of Berber village life under the impact of French colonial rule. Morizot shows that the eventual peace brought by the French permitted the expansion of village business activities throughout a much wider geographic area, encompassing the whole of Algeria. The sons of Berber villagers, in addition, were among the first to obtain a French education and to enter French business and administrative service, but without abandoning their customs, dialects, and institutions.

Xavier Yacono's *Les Bureaux arabes et l'évolution des genres de vie indigènes dans l'Ouest du Tell algérien* (1953) is a work on the Arab bureaux which Bugeaud established in 1844 and which functioned during the Second Republic and the Second Empire. It discusses the attempts of French officers to promote Muslim agriculture within the framework of the Arab kingdom policy of Napoléon III. The officers failed because of insufficient means, the absence of overall policy, and an excessive confidence in assimilation.

The best introductions to the Algerian economy in the period between World War II and the outbreak of the rebellion are the chapter by Xavier Yacono, "L'économie algérienne" (in J. Alazard et al., 1957, pp. 371–416); J. Saint-Germès, *Economie algérienne* (1950) and *La Réforme agraire algérienne* (1957); and Jean Blanchard, *Le Problème algérien: Réalités et perspectives* (1955). Several works deal with the industrialization of Algeria in the same period: Aimé Baldacci's *L'Algérie et la société de l'Ouenza* (1947) on a mining company; Pierre Fontaneau's (1952) on the problem of electrification; and Yves Laye's richly documented study of the port of Algiers (1953).

The financial relations between France and Algeria are the subject of the so-called Maspetiol Report of June 1955. A study of the entire Algerian economy, undertaken at the height of the Algerian war at a time when France was seeking to promote economic and social advancement in order to hold Algeria, is the detailed work of René Gendarme, *L'Economie de l'Algérie: Sous-développement et politique de croissance* (1959). Roger Dumoulin's *La Structure asymétrique de l'économie algérienne: D'après une analyse de la région de Bône* (1959) is a study in depth of one area in the east which contrasts with Gendarme's comprehensive study of the same year.

As early as World War I, writings were appearing on the so-called *question indigène*. Chérif Benhabiles's *L'Algérie française vue par un indigène* (1914), Emir Khaled's *La Situation des musulmans d'Algérie* (1924), and R. Zenati's *Le Problème algérien vu par un indigène* (1938) present the views of three Algerians on the situation created by French colonization. Malek Bennabi's *Vocation de l'Islam* (1954) deals with the consequences of French cultural assimilation and political domination for the Muslim elite who have received a French education. Belkacem Saadallah's "Rise of the Algerian Elite" (*Journal of Modern African Studies,* 1967) deals with the gallicized elite that emerged in the late nineteenth and early twentieth centuries. Despised by the settlers and alienated from the masses, its members sought equality with the French. *De la colonie vers la province: le Jeune Algérien* (1931) is a collection of newspaper articles and writings by young Ferhat Abbas, a French-educated pharmacist from Sétif. His work shows a love of France and its culture, but bitterness about its failure to bring freedom and equality for the Muslims. At that time he still favored advancement within a French framework. Ramdane Bouazzouni in *Du réformisme au nationalisme en Algérie à travers Ferhat Abbas* (Thesis, 1963) traces the evolution of Algerian thinking on relations with France as exemplified by Ferhat Abbas, who originally favored integration, then federalism involving association, and became finally a nationalist desiring independence. While primarily concerned with the political elite from 1954 to 1968, William Quandt (1969) has useful analyses of the different types of political socialization which its members experienced during the previous decades under colonial rule.

In *La Naissance du nationalisme algérien, 1914–1954,* André Nouschi (1962) places the origins of modern Algerian nationalism in the period between the two world wars and traces its development within a general framework which relates it to economic, social, and religious evolution. He rejects the notion that Muslim resistance to European colonization in the period 1871 to 1919, that is, after the Muslims realized its permanence, can be termed "nationalist" in the modern sense of the word, for such resistance took place in relation to the tribes and the religious brotherhoods. He contends that growing misery among the rapidly increasing Muslim population spurred the nationalist awakening in the interwar period. His sections on the period 1939 to 1954 are too brief to be very useful. Articles by Robert Ageron treat the *Jeune Algérien* movement (1964) and the role of Emir Khaled in the development of nationalism (1966). An article by Jacques Carret (1957) discusses the relationship of the reformist ulema to the rise of nationalism.

Nouschi is also the author of the historical sections on Algeria between 1830 and 1919 in the revisionist work *L'Algérie passé et présent: Le Cadre et les étapes de la constitution de l'Algérie actuelle* (1960). (In a sense his nationalism study forms the sequel to these sections.) Especially useful is the discussion of the economic and political impact of World War I on Algeria. The war saw 155,000 Frenchmen and Jews and 173,000 Muslims mobilized, of whom 22,000 Europeans and 25,000 Muslims were killed. 119,000 Muslim workers were drawn into industrial service, marking the large-scale beginning of the exodus of workers to France and exposing them to socialist and Communist influences there.

C. Vincent Confer in *France and Algeria: The Problem of Civil and Political Reform, 1870–1920* (1966) reviews the discussions in the early 1900s on the degree to which the non-Europeans should be brought into the political process by civil and political concessions. The proposed reforms were largely scuttled by the Algerian deputies and senators in Paris. The outstanding reform, embodied in the Jonnart Law of 1919, introduced the dubious principle of a double electoral college, an institution that further separated the European and Muslim communities.

Wolfgang Ohneck's *Die Französische Algerienpolitik von 1919–1939* (1967) is a detailed history of administrative reform during the interwar period, including the 1919 law, the Blum-Viollette proposals of the Popular Front era, and the reactions of various settler and Muslim groups to them. Marie-Renée Mouton's "L'Algérie devant le Parlement français de 1935 à 1938" (*Revue Française de Science Politique,* March 1962, pp. 93–128) discusses the fate of the proposed reforms. Maurice Viollette in *L'Algérie: vivra-t-elle? Notes d'un gouverneur-général* (1931) gives a personal account of his administration and his proposals for reforms. R. C. V. Bodley's *Algeria from Within* (1927) contains a useful sketch of French administration in the twenties. Bodley grew up in Algeria and served as a military attaché at the Versailles Conference.

Quite a number of works deal with the status of the Muslims in the interwar period. Paul Hutin's *La Doctrine d'association des indigènes et des Français en Algérie* (1935) reflects long experience in the Algerian administration; Paul Viard's *Les Droits politiques des indigènes d'Algérie* (1937) includes a discussion of the attempted reforms of the Popular Front. An older work by the noted colonial sociologist René Maunier, *Loi française et coutume indigène en Algérie* (1932), dealt with the problem of acculturation from a socio-juridical viewpoint. J. P. Charnay's *La vie musulmane en Algérie d'après la jurisprudence de la première moitié du XXe siècle* (1965) is a socio-juridical study that uses the operations of Muslim justice in the period 1892–1945 as a focal point for evaluating the impact of colonial society upon Muslim society and the Muslim reactions. Areas studied are the family, land, usury, Muslim religious life, and relations between Muslims and Europeans. An official publication, "Evolution du statut politique des Français musulmans d'Algérie," (La Documentation française, *Notes et études documentaires,* no. 678 [1947]) contains a discussion of de Gaulle's reforms of 1944 and background data on the status of Muslims prior to the reforms embodied in the Statute of 1947.

A short article by Manfred Halpern, "The Algerian Uprising of 1945" (*Middle East Journal* [1948]: 191–202), is an American political scientist's account of the Sétif rebellion of 1945 and the French response, as well as a discussion of the Statute of 1947. *Origines de la guerre algérienne,* by Robert Aron et al. (1962), is a collection of essays dealing chiefly with the period 1945–54. It is based upon *témoignages,* both printed and oral, plus unpublished administrative documents such as the famous *Rapport Tubert* on the Sétif incidents of 1945. It is in the form of a dossier, rather than a history of Algerian nationalism.

The article by L. Gray Cowan (1951) is a thorough discussion of the Algerian Statute of 1947, which attempted to reconcile the demands of the indigenous population for more political rights and their unwillingness to abandon their personal status under Islamic law. Two

French works on the same subject are Henri Pellegrin's *Le Statut de l'Algérie* (1948) and Pierre Lampué's "Le Statut de l'Algérie" (*Revue Juridique et Politique de l'Union Française,* 1947). Ivo Rens in *L'Assemblée algérienne* (1957) presents the history of the Algerian assembly established by the Statute and includes many documents on its structure and functioning.

The juridical and political status of Algeria resulting from the Statute of 1947 and the reforms embodied in the Constitution of the Fourth Republic the previous year led to a large literature. Jacques Lambert's *Cours de législation algérienne, tunisienne, et marocaine,* vol. 1, *Législation algérienne* (1949, rev. ed. 1952) is the classic work on the subject from a conservative viewpoint. It covers the sources of Algerian legislation, political and administrative organization, the legal position of the individual, citizen and foreigner, the financial regime, judiciary, colonization and land laws, all in historical perspective. Other useful works on this subject include: René Passeron, *Cours de droit algérien* (1947) and "La structure administrative de l'Algérie" (*Revue juridique et politique de l'Union Française* [1951]: 449–465); Paul-Emile Viard, *Les caractères politiques et le régime législatif de l'Algérie* (1949); Manuel Merlo, *Organisation administrative de l'Algérie* (1951); Louis Milliot, *Le Statut organique de l'Algérie* (1948); F. Dulout, *Traité de legislation algérienne* (2 vols., 1951); Charles Ettori, *Le régime législatif de l'Algérie: Textes, documents, et étude juridique* (1948); Pierre Lampué, "Les Lois applicables en Algérie" (*Revue juridique et politique de l'Union Française* [1950]: 1–23).

Sylvain Wisner's *L'Algérie dans l'impasse: démission de la France* (1948) is a sharp criticism of official French policy in Algeria. A scholarly and mildly antinationalist work on Algerian nationalism in the late 1940s, Paul-Emile Sarrasin's *La Crise algérienne* (1949), analyzes principal groupings and presents in sixteen annexes the significant documents of the 1930s and 1940s on the question. The personal recollections of two governors-general provide additional light for the period between the end of World War II and the start of the rebellion. Marcel Naegelen, author of *Mission en Algérie* (1962), served from February 1948 to April 1951, being succeeded by Roger Leonard, author of *Quartre ans en Algérie,* from 1951 to 1955.

The Algerian rebellion of 1954–62 against French colonial rule has become one of the most thoroughgoing social revolutions of our time. What began as a rebellion had by 1958 clearly become a revolution; it cost one million lives and displaced more than three million persons, including the 900,000 Europeans who fled the country. It led to sweeping dislocations in the economy and society and to restructurings that are still going on. The literature on the subject is immense and only some of the major works can be described here. Mostefa Lacheraf's *L'Algérie: nation et société* (1965) is a collection of essays on the period 1830–1965, written between 1954 and 1964, which take a sociocultural approach to the history and politics of Algeria. Lacheraf's work contains two theses relevant to the Algerian revolution. The first is that indigenous opposition to the French from 1830 through the 1954 rebellion was basically peasant in character. He contends that the bourgeoisie and "feudal" elements came to terms with the French, but the rural Algerians resisted them. His analysis of the Constantinois insurrection of 1871 supports this thesis; but he fails to prove that the 1954 rebels are basically rural in origin. His other thesis is that the Algerian revolution is far less a Muslim resistance to the French than a national and social movement. Jacques Chevallier's *Nous, Algériens* (1958), by the liberal mayor of Algiers, contains large excerpts from documents on the Algerian situation, including prefectoral reports from the spring of 1950 giving disturbing details on the organization of the rebellion. René Schaefer, *Révolution en Algérie* (1956) is a good analysis of the background and early course of the revolution, emphasizing its economic, social, cultural, and psychological aspects. Schaefer contends that the continued terrorism after the initial insurrection in November 1954 was inspired and directed from Cairo.

Colette and Francis Jeanson (1955) deal poorly with the background and first year of the rebellion. Their work is interesting only as a reflection of a Communist viewpoint. Jean Servier's *Dans L'Aurès sur les pas des rebelles* (1955) is the work of an ethnologist who lived in the Aurès for seven years prior to the rebellion. His observations help to enlighten some of the deeper causes of the rebellion.

Le Peuple algérien et sa révolution (1956), written by the FLN, presents the FLN positions on the Algerian question, while *Action du gouvernement en Algérie: Mesures de pacification et réformes* (1957), a publication of the Algerian Ministry, gives in detail the official view of the problem. Jacques Soustelle's *Aimée et souffrante Algérie* (1956) is the account of the noted anthropologist's Algerian mission, January 20, 1955 to January 31, 1956. Chosen by Mendès-France to represent the French government in Algeria and made governor-general by Edgar Faure, Soustelle subsequently came to oppose Algerian nationalism and to support the French presence there. He advocated complete integration of the country and its peoples into the French

Republic as the only political solution, buttressing his case with many references. A second booklet, *Le Drame algérien et la décadence française: Réponse à Raymond Aron* (1957) develops the thesis enunciated in the first work with more vehemence than precision. Raymond Aron, the liberal sociologist and writer for *Le Figaro,* wrote two booklets, *La Tragédie algérienne* (1957) and *L'Algérie et la république* (1958), contending that the integration which Soustelle advocates is feasible neither politically nor economically, without himself setting forth any clear alternative. *La Question algérienne* (1958), by Jean Dresch, Charles-André Julien, et al., is a clearly written work by several specialists that treats various aspects of the Algerian problem—ideological and historical, juridical, geographic, and economic.

Thomas Oppermann's *Algerische Frage: Rechtlich-Politische Studie* (1959) (French trans. 1961, *Le Problème algérien, donnés historiques, juridiques, politiques*) is an objective historical and legal study of the developments that led to the Algerian conflict, with good analyses of the political, legal, and international issues and the economic and social structures. It has all the official texts on the status of Algeria and the Algerians since 1830 and is rich in its documentation of bibliographical and legal materials.

Serge Bromberger, correspondent for *Le Figaro* in the Maghrib, in *Les Rebelles algériens* (1958) gives an eyewitness account of the rebellion between November 1954 and the Sakhiet incident in early 1958. He describes the origins of the rebellion, its actions in the Aurès and the Kabylia, French actions against it in the city of Algiers, and the role of Tunisia. Behind the internal quarrels within the FLN he sees an Arab-Berber conflict. Saadi Yacef's *Souvenirs de la bataille d'Alger, décembre 1956–septembre 1957* (1963) is not in any sense a complete history of the French army's successful campaign against the FLN within Algiers, but it presents useful data and interpretations by an eyewitness.

In May 1958 settler and army elements in Algiers made a revolution against the government of the Fourth Republic which they feared was about to negotiate with the rebels and abandon Algeria to them. The Algerian question thus ceased to be merely a colonial question and became the most important issue in French national life. Some works written before May 1958, like those of Raymond Aron, gave attention to the relation of the Algerian problem to French political life, but nearly all those written after that time consider this dimension. (There is need for studies which would show the influence of the Algerian problem on French colonial policy in Black Africa.)

Les Treize Complots du 13 mai, ou la délivrance de Gulliver (1959), by Serge and Merry Bromberger, is an account of the various plots and counterplots which ultimately brought General de Gaulle to power in the wake of the May 1958 army revolt in Algeria. It throws light on the role the Algerian issue played in French politics in the period from 1954 until September 1958. Alain de Sérigny's *La Révolution du 13 mai, avec les témoignages de ses principaux acteurs* is a penetrating work on the events of May and June 1958 in Algiers by a newspaper owner and politician. P. Gerin's *L'Algérie du 13 mai* (1958) is a work done by a French journalist with much useful data from interviews that would contribute to a history of the May revolution.

Michael Clark, a British journalist for the *New York Times,* wrote the polemical pro-settler *Algeria in Turmoil* (1959). It nevertheless has a quite complete chronology of events through May 1959 and useful data on the internal struggles within the nationalist movement. *Algeria: Rebellion and Revolution* (1961) by the late Joan Gillespie, a onetime Foreign Service officer, deals perspicaciously with the forces and events that produced the rebellion and its changing structure and strategy from October 1954 to January 1960. She makes a good analysis of the revolution that was taking place in the structure and outlook in Algerian society. Gerard Mansell's *Tragedy in Algeria* (1961) is an excellent brief and honest account of the origins, development, and consequences of the Algerian rebellion through January 1961.

Richard and Joan Brace, in *Ordeal in Algeria* (1960), present the best documented and most complete account of the impact of the Algerian problem on French political life and the resulting official policies in the period 1954–60. More than half of their study deals with the period 1958–59. Their discussion of the impact of the rebellion on North Africa shows less familiarity with Algerian society. But their cautious analysis and honesty make this volume one of the least partisan written.

Two other works by professional journalists, Joseph Kraft's *Struggle for Algeria* (1961) and Edward Behr's *The Algerian Problem* (1961) are very competent discussions of the question. Kraft has some fine insights into the impact of the rebellion upon French development. Behr had firsthand experience with both sides in the war in Algeria itself and approaches his subject historically.

One of the most objective accounts of the revolution is the work of a Swiss journalist, Charles Favrod's *La Révolution algérienne* (1959), which he revised under the title, *Le FLN et l'Algérie* (1962). The original work, which contained one hundred pages of basic documents and one hundred of text, saw the roots of the rebellion in French conquest and in the ethnic diversity of the country. It put forth the thesis that the rebellion was becoming a revolution. The revised work developed this thesis by showing how the FLN was led gradually to deal with the entire Algerian problem and not just its political aspects. Jacques C. Duchemin's *Histoire du FLN* (1962) rests on a personal acquaintance with the FLN leaders but is not always clear or convincing. André Mandouze's *La Révolution algérienne par les textes: documents du FLN* (1961) is a useful collection of FLN documents. Edgar O'Ballance's *The Algerian Insurrection, 1954–1961* (1967) is largely a military history that analyzes FLN tactics.

The view that the 1954 rebellion was inspired by Egypt and was being conducted to promote the goals of Nasserian foreign policy was expressed by Jacques Soustelle (1956) and elaborated upon by Jacques Baulin (pseudonym of Youssef el Masry) in *The Arab Role in Africa* (1962). The influence of the myth of Egyptian origins of the rebellion upon French statesmen at the time of the Suez invasion of 1956 is treated in a well-documented study by Herbert Luethy and David Rodnick, *French Motivations in the Suez Crisis* (1956). General André Beaufré's *L'Expédition de Suez* (1967) is the work of the commander of the French expeditionary force in the Suez invasion of 1956. He tries to fix responsibility for the affair and to see the political and strategic causes of the failure as well as the consequences for the French army and for Arab-Israeli relations.

The internationalization of the Algerian question is the subject of two important works. Mohammed Alwan's *Algeria before the United Nations* (1959), though weak on balance and analysis, provides much data on the UN discussions of the Algerian question through 1958. Jean-Claude Revol, in *La Question algérienne et l'ONU* (Thesis, 1962), supplements Alwan by carrying the examination of the Algerian question by the UN into its final stages.

The question of the use of torture in the Algerian war is the subject of several works. Henry Alleg's *The Question* (trans. 1958) is by a Communist and director of the *Alger Républicain* who was arrested, detained, and tortured in 1957. The French edition was seized by the government. Pierre Vidal-Naquet wrote *Torture, Cancer of Democracy: France and Algeria, 1954–1962* (trans. 1963). An accompanying volume gives some of the evidence: *La Raison d'état: textes publiées par le comité Maurice Audin* (1962).

Several works by officers, journalists in civilian life, give their views about being asked to implement war policies with which they disagreed. Jacques Servan-Schreiber's *Lieutenant in Algeria* (trans. 1957) is the work of the writer for the left-wing *L'Express.* Jules Roy's *The War in Algeria* (trans. 1961) and *Autour du drame* (1961), a collection of articles from *Le Monde* and *L'Express,* 1955–61, reflect the war experience of the Algerian-born colonel and friend of Albert Camus. Camus, the novelist and philosopher who was born in Oran, returned to Algeria after living abroad and described vividly the miserable existence of the Muslims in the Kabylia on the eve of the Second World War. *Actuelles 3: Chroniques algériennes, 1939–1958* (1958) is a collection of his writings over two decades, including his views on the early years of the Algerian revolution. They show the dilemma posed by the revolution for the Algerian-born French democrats.

The last years of the war saw the appearance of several works which have value less for the new information presented than for the viewpoints and the interpretations. Germaine Tillion in *Les Ennemis complementaires* (1960, trans. *France and Algeria: Complementary Enemies,* 1961) discusses Franco-Algerian relations and the evolution of French thinking about them, and emphasizes the interdependence of the two peoples. The account of this Marxist ethnologist contains many documents. Francis Jeanson's *La Révolution algérienne: Problèmes et perspectives* (1961) is a pro-FLN analysis of the problems and perspectives of the Algerian Revolution by a noted French Communist. Alain Savary in *Nationalisme algérien et grandeur française* (1960) argues against the integration of Algeria into the French nation. Savary, a onetime secretary of state for foreign affairs in the Mollet government, quit the Socialist Party after the kidnap-arrest of Ben Bella and became a PSA leader. Jules Moch's *En 1961, paix en Algérie* (1961) is the work of a longtime Socialist minister and anti-Gaullist. It discusses the Algerian policy of the Fourth and Fifth Republics and the UN debates on the question. It provides much data on the cost of the war: 15,000 French and 160,000 Muslims dead at the time of writing and 750 billion francs a year. Jacques Soustelle, *L'Espérance trahie, 1958–1961* (1962) is an attack on de Gaulle's Algerian policies by the onetime governor-general and former Gaullist, interesting because of the personal involvement of the author in the plots against the Gaullist regime.

Louis Terrenoire in *De Gaulle et l'Algérie* (1964) presents a quite objective account of General de Gaulle's policies towards Algeria in the period 1958–62. Christian Purtshet and André Valentino's *Sociologie électorale en Afrique du Nord* (1966) contains a section by Purtshet on the French legislative elections in Algeria on November 30, 1958, held without FLN participation at a time when France was still seeking to retain Algeria. Amar Naroun's *Ferhat Abbas, ou les chemins de la souveraineté* (1961) is a personal account of the career of Ferhat Abbas, with good portraits of two of his chief collaborators, Ahmed Francis and Ahmed Boumendjel, and some annexes containing letters and important articles. *La Nuit coloniale* (1962), by Ferhat Abbas, contains the personal recollections of the nationalist leader, including the 1931 centenary. Hocine Ait Ahmed's *La Guerre et l'après-guerre* (1964) is a collection of the FLN leader's writings, 1957–63, which show the evolution of the thinking that made him one of the main opponents of Ben Bella's regime. Alain Jacob's *D'une Algérie à l'autre* (1963) is the enlightening work of a *Le Monde* correspondent in Algeria between 1958 and 1962 which contains valuable portraits of military and political leaders on both sides of the conflict. Albert-Paul Lentin's *Le dernier quart d'heure* (*L'Algerie entre deux mondes*) (1963) is the work of a *pied-noir* journalist who favored the Algerian revolution. In a readable account of the period November 1960 to April 1961, one finds good portraits both of important (e.g. Dr. Bernard Lefevre) and of ordinary settlers. Pierre Houart's *L'Attitude de l'église dans la guerre d'Algérie, 1954–1960* (1960) is a study of the texts of the ecclesiastical authorities concerning the war in Algeria. Arslan Ben Kritly in *Le Parti communiste et la question algérienne* (Thesis, 1962) studies the evolution of the French Communist Party's position on the Algerian question.

The policies of General de Gaulle provoked many violent reactions, especially as it became clear that the president would not support integration and was willing to negotiate with the FLN. *Barricades et colonels, 24 janvier 1960* (1960), by Serge Bromberger et al., is the best and most impartial book on the insurrection. It shows that the insurgents found much support among the European population of Algiers and that the army, even the top echelons, tried to arbitrate between them and the Paris government. The Bromberger team had access to official sources and held numerous interviews with the personalities involved, but they do not cite their sources. Jean-André Faucher's *Les Barricades d'Alger, janvier 1960* (1960) is an error-laden apologia for the insurgents, who were provoked, he claims, by government policy.

Jacques Fauvet and Jean Planchais in *La Fronde des généraux* (1961) deal with the military revolt led by generals Salan, Challe, Zeller, and Jouhaud in April 1961 in the aftermath of the referendum of January 8, 1961, which gave de Gaulle *carte blanche* to find a solution to the Algerian problem. It throws light on both the military and civilian origins of the revolt. On the same subject is Henri Azeau's *Révolte militaire Alger, 22 avril 1961* (1961).

Settler and military opposition also gave rise to the Organisation de l'Armée Secrète (OAS) in the summer of 1961. A good introduction to the OAS is found in *La Nef,* the special issue "Histoire de la guerre d'Algérie suivie d'une histoire de l'OAS," (October 1962–January 1963), especially the article by Paul-Marie de la Gorce, "Histoire de l'OAS en Algérie." Morland, Barangé, and Martinez (pseudonyms), *Histoire de l'Organisation de l'Armée Secrète* (1964) is a collection of eighty-five documents on the movement chronologically arranged. They show that there never was any real unity within the OAS, but only disparate parts in Algiers, Madrid, and Paris. Robert Buchard's *Organisation Armée Secrète, vol. 1, Février–Décembre 1961* (1963), is a generally poor work by a journalist which has the merit of showing the rivalries and cross purposes among the different groups within the OAS, including those of Salan and Susini. Fernand Carreras in *L'Accord FLN–OAS: Des négotiations secrètes au cessez-le-feu* (1967) presents a good account of the negotiations between the Algerian and European rebels from April 20, 1962 (the arrest of Salan) to June 25, 1962 (Colonel Dufour's order ending the *attentats* in Oran). He indicates that there was no real dialogue within, and that marginal actors like Jacques Chevallier, Jean-Jacques Susini, and Abderrahmane Farès still hoped for a reconciliation between the two communities. The two secret *dossiers Paillat* on the Algerian war, the first covering the period May 1958 to April 1961 and the second the period from autumn 1954 until the May revolution, make no references to sources and, though useful for the sequence of events, must be used with great caution in making judgments. Brian Crozier's study *The Morning After* (1963) contains a discussion of the *colon* reaction to the ceasefire between the FLN and the OAS.

Serge Mourreaux's *Les Accords d'Evian et l'avenir de la révolution algérienne* (1962) contains the text of the Evian agreement and an account of the discussions that led to its conclusion. Maurice Allais in *Les Accords d'Evian: Le référendum et la résistance algérienne, L'autorité, la majorité, le droit* (1962) offers a bitter critique of the agreement, correctly charging that it held no real guarantees for the *colons* or pro-French Muslims. Robert Buron's *Carnets politiques de la guerre d'Algérie, par un signataire des accords d'Evian* (1965) is the account of an MRP politician who served in the governments of both the Fourth and Fifth Republics. In April 1961 he was a prisoner of the

OAS. Based on his notes at the Evian negotiations, he draws good portraits of the Algerian and French representatives. He describes the way in which the French government tried to safeguard the interests of the settlers and blames the OAS for what happened to them ultimately. He reveals that France thought it would have to repatriate no more than 200,000 to 300,000 of the settlers prior to the OAS insurrection.

William Andrews in *French Politics and Algeria* (1962) studies the impact of the Algerian question on domestic French politics. Dorothy Pickles, a longtime English specialist in French politics, discusses the Algerian problem in similar fashion in *Algeria and France: From Colonialism to Cooperation* (1963), but also takes up the changing relationship between the two countries as a result of the Algerian revolution. Jacques Goutor's *Algeria and France, 1830–1963* (1965) is the most complete brief account in English of the entire period of French rule that concentrates on the period 1954–62. Its French counterparts for the revolutionary period are the special issue of *La Nef* already cited, and the sections of Ganiage.

Arslan Humbaraci's *Algeria: A Revolution That Failed* (1966) is the work of a journalist for the *Economist* and the *Observer* in North Africa. It is excellent for the last stages of the rebellion which brought Ben Bella to power and for the first three years of independence until his fall. It shows how many of the tensions within the FLN during the rebellion period were fatal to progress once independence was won.

David Gordon in *The Passing of French Algeria* (1966) analyzes both Algeria's struggle for its identity from the 1930s until the fall of Ben Bella in July 1965 and France's gradual acceptance of that identity. It further examines the role that the French language and cultural values were playing in Algeria during the first three years of independence. The work is an important contribution to the cultural history of Algeria as it emerges from a century and a third of French colonialism. The work also contains valuable biographical sketches of the revolutionary leaders.

Frantz Fanon, the Martinique-born black psychiatrist (1925–61), served in Blida, Algeria, during the early years of the rebellion (1953–56), became an FLN supporter, and spent his last years based at Tunis as editor of the FLN paper and representative of the movement to Ghana. A fine intellectual biography by David Caute (1970) places Fanon in a global political setting while a concise introduction to his writings is found in Gordon (1966), pp. 121–34. Fanon's first book, *Peau noire, masques blancs* (1952, trans. 1957), reflects his early life in

Martinique in a racist situation. His concern in it was to diagnose the psychological dependence of the Antilles black in regard to the French white and to metropolitan French culture, and then to prescribe ways in which the Negro might transcend his situation to discover self-possession and authenticity.

L'An V de la révolution algérienne (1959) (trans. 1965 as *Studies in a Dying Colonialism*) discusses the Algerian revolution as a process through which dignity and liberty are created. The revolution in his opinion produced a transformation of the structure of Algerian society and a psychological transformation of the individual Algerian. Regardless of whether there was an Algeria before the French came, the Algerian nation has now created itself by choosing revolution. The work contains a perceptive essay on the European settler minority and their relation to the revolutionary forces in the 1950s.

Les Damnés de la terre (1961, trans. 1963) reiterates some of the themes of the two earlier works and then projects them onto a universal plane. In a book that shows much hostility to European whites and Western culture, Fanon projects his experiences from the colonial situation in the Antilles and Algeria to the whole Third World. He concludes that only through violence can colonialism be defeated and the native overcome his complex of dependence. The revolution must also eliminate the rule of the local bourgeoisie that is financially and culturally dependent upon the West and replace it with a party that serves the downtrodden peasant masses. *Pour la révolution africaine* (1964, trans. 1967) is a posthumous collection of various articles by Fanon including many from the FLN paper *El-Moudjahid* and excerpts from his diaries containing his impressions of various black African revolutionary leaders like Felix Moumié of Cameroon.

One of the consequences of the French control of Algeria was the migration of Algerian workers, in particular from the impoverished Berber areas of the Kabylia and the Nord Constantinois, to France. At the beginning of the Algerian rebellion in 1954 there were 380,000 Algerians in France and by the end of 1962 there were 620,000. An early work on the Algerians in France was Jean-Jacques Rager's *Les Musulmans algériens en France et dans les pays islamiques* (1950). He concluded that at that time Berbers outnumbered Arabs by a ratio of six to four, just about the opposite of the ratio in Algeria. David S. McLellan, in "The North Africans in France: a French Racial Problem" (*The Yale Review*, 1955) deals with the North African industrial workers in France, most of them Algerian, in the period before the rebellion. André Michel's *Les Travailleurs algériens en France* (1956) is a well-documented account of the Algerian workers' adjustment to industrial life in France. It shows the durability of their Islamic and family ties but has nothing on their political or syndicalist life. Joseph Leriche in *Les Algériens parmi nous: Essai psycho-sociologique d'après les enquêtes et travaux des études nord-africaines* (1959) studies North African immigration into France and the problems of integrating the Muslims into French life. Tayeb Belloula's *Algériens en France* (1965) is the first work on the Algerians in France since independence by an Algerian diplomat in Paris who has observed the situation at first hand. (Also on Algerians in France: *Les Algériens en France: étude démographique et sociale* [1955]). A comprehensive bibliography on Algerian workers is found in *Connaissance de l'immigration nord-africaine en France* (mimeographed, Aix: Centre Africain des Sciences Humaines Appliquées, Feb. 1964).

The study of Pierre Bourdieu et al., *Travail et travailleurs en Algérie* (1963), deals with the Algerian workers in Algeria itself. Bourdieu sees as a sign of greater modernization among the Berbers compared with the Arabs the fact that the Berbers know when they are only partially employed. *L'Algérie de Demain* (1962), edited by François Perroux, is a collection of well-documented essays on Algeria at the close of the colonial period, dealing with such subjects as migration and focusing on the choices and possible methods of development.

L'Algérie des Bidonvilles (1961), by Robert Descloitres, Jean-Claude Reverdy, and Claudine Descloitres, is a sociological study of the city of Algiers, where the influx of the pauperized rural masses produced a Muslim majority by 1954. Between 1936 and 1954, the Muslim urban population doubled from 700,000 to 1,400,000 creating a new subproletariat among the older Muslim bourgeois and European elements.

TUNISIA

The period of French colonial rule in Tunisia lasted from 1881 to 1956. By that time there were 233,000 Europeans and 22,000 Jews with French nationality settled in the country. The French had not only established a protectorate but had assumed control of much of the internal administration of the country. It is the political and economic aspects of French rule and the nationalist response that have received the most attention from scholars.

A number of general surveys of Tunisia, some of them written since 1956, have useful historical sections or are historically oriented. Charles Gallagher's "Tunisia," in Gwendolen Carter, ed., *African One-Party States* (1962) is the only one by a non-Frenchman and in English.

Although the seventy-five page essay concentrates on the Neo Destour regime since independence, it provides a good brief account of the protectorate regime and the development of nationalism during the colonial period. The small volume in the *Que sais-je* series by André Raymond (1961) provides an excellent introduction to the country and its recent history. Among older works still of use are: Paul Sebag, *La Tunisie: essai de monographie* (1951), a competent economic, social, and political survey from a Marxist-Leninist viewpoint; Pierre Hubac, *Tunisie* (2d ed., 1954), a good introductory survey written from a historical perspective; and Jean Despois, *La Tunisie: aperçu historique, races, religion, moeurs et coutumes, organisation administrative, avenir économique* (1930), which is an important reference work for the period of colonial rule. It has excellent sections on political and administrative organization, economic activity, demography, settlers, Muslims, Jews, and religious life.

One fairly comprehensive study of the entire period of French rule is Dwight Ling's *Tunisia: From Protectorate to Republic* (1967). It provides a more complete examination of many events than any French work does through use of American consular reports and the French press in addition to the usual French sources. It is best for the political and economic impact of French rule and clearly synthesizes existing literature on the rise of Tunisian nationalism. Older French histories which are still useful but which cover only parts of the French colonial period are those of J. L. de Lanessan (2d ed., 1917), Arthur Pellegrin (4th ed., 1948), Georges Hardy (1931), and Henri Cambon (1948). Cambon is the son of Paul Cambon, the diplomat who as resident-general in Tunis in the 1880s formulated many of France's protectorate policies. Despite an official viewpoint that is generally unsympathetic to Tunisian nationalism, he treats well the period from 1881 until the Axis defeat in 1943.

The second volume of Elie Fitoussi and Aristide Benozet's *L'Etat tunisien et le protectorat français: histoire et organisation, 1881–1931* (1931) provides a detailed description and analysis of the establishment and functioning of the protectorate regime. Another study written about the same time by W. Basil Worsfold (1930) compares French colonial administration in Tunisia and Algeria. Albert Memmi (1957), a Jewish Tunisian, provides many psychological insights into the status and relationships of Europeans and Muslims in the colonial society. His work might have had even greater depth if he had given more attention to the historical background of colonization, especially its socio-economic aspects.

The response of Tunisians to French rule in the form of nationalism is the theme of many works. C. Kheirallah's *Le Mouvement jeune-tunisien: essai d'histoire et de synthèse des mouvements nationalistes tunisiens* (1957) is an effort to identify some of the origins of the nationalist movement in the mid-nineteenth century before the protectorate. Nicola A. Ziadeh's *Origins of Nationalism in Tunisia* (1962), which utilizes Arabic sources not employed by Western historians, is the most important work on early Tunisian nationalism. It throws much light on the period 1897–1907 in particular by showing the links between Tunisian political evolution and developments in the Arab and Muslim worlds in general, such as the influence of Muhammad Abduh (which he concludes has been much overrated), the Pan-Islam of Abdul Hamid, and the Young Turks. What the work fails to do, however, is to show the precise relationship between the economic and educational work of France, which it carefully analyzes for the period 1896–1925, and the nationalist movement which arose in the decade before the First World War. Modern nationalism was the creation of the Young Tunisians in the period 1907–11. They enlisted the masses against the protectorate for the first time in 1911–12 at a moment when the latter were reacting strongly against the Italian invasion of neighboring Libya. *La Tunisie après la guerre (1919–1921): Problèmes politiques* (2d ed., 1922), by Rodd Balek (Charles Monchicourt), is a collection of articles that appeared in *L'Afrique Française* from 1920 to 1922 on the founding of the Destour Party and the reform establishing the Grand Council. The classics of Abdelaziz Taalbi, *La Tunisie martyre, ses revendications* (1920) and Habib Bourguiba, *Le Destour et la France* (1937), are important for the thinking of the nationalists in the interwar period.

The most complete work on the nationalist movement is that of Ling, already cited. Leon Carl Brown's *Tunisia under the French Protectorate: A History of Ideological Change* (Ph.D. dissertation, Harvard University, 1962) provides insights into the process of modernization that included the rise of nationalism. In a volume primarily concerned with Tunisia since independence, Clement Moore (1965), a political scientist, discusses the historical development of Tunisian society that permitted the Neo-Destour (founded in 1934) to come to power. He shows how the party arose from a traditional society that was severely disrupted and further diversified by colonial rule. The French recruited their junior administrators not from the heirs of old bourgeois families but from the sons of well-to-do peasants in the Sahel whom they educated in their schools. This new group pursued its goals of self-government and ultimate independence by seeking support from French opinion and by mobilizing the peasant and worker masses.

Two recent theses have dealt with the Tunisian trade union movement which European colonization called into being, including its relation to the nationalist movement. Pierre Mamet in *Les expériences syndicales en Tunisie de 1881 à 1956* (1966) deals with the entire protectorate period. A. Hermassi in *Le mouvement ouvrier en société coloniale: la Tunisie entre deux guerres* (1966) concentrates on the interwar period. Willard Beling's study (1965) shows the influences of the French CGT and the Neo Destour on the Tunisian syndicalist movement. In a discussion of the international relations of the labor movement, he concludes that its international policies before 1956 were a product of the needs of Tunisian nationalism and anticolonialism. Ziadeh also has an interesting summary of trade unionism prior to the 1930s. Leon Laitman (1954) deals primarily with the economic aspects of French colonialism, which he views as the main source of Franco-Tunisian tensions.

Félix Garas's *Bourguiba et la naissance d'une nation* (1956) offers a reliable narrative of the Tunisian struggle for emancipation with special emphasis on the role of the Neo-Destour leader through independence on March 20, 1956. Habib Bourguiba (1954) presents a collection of his writings from 1930 to 1954 on the problem of Franco-Tunisian relations, together with commentary that provides the setting and continuity. Jean Lacouture, a longtime correspondent in North Africa, gives interesting portraits of Bourguiba, Ferhat Abbas, and Mohammed V in his *Cinq Hommes et la France* (1961). Jean Rous, *Tunisie . . . Attention* (1952) is a sympathetic account by another correspondent with long experience in Tunisia which presents more than a hundred pages of Neo Destour documents and letters. In addition to presenting the nationalist movement from a Tunisian viewpoint, the officially published (1965) *Min Sigill al-Kifah—al Ma'raka-l-hásima* (*Du dossier de la lutte—la Bataille décisive*) presents excerpts from important party documents in Arabic from the colonial period. Of the many articles on the nationalist movement, two interpretative ones on the development of the Neo Destour by Hedi Nouira (1954) and Benjamin Rivlin, "The Tunisian Nationalist Movement: Four Decades of Evolution" (1952), should be noted.

There is quite an extensive literature on French reaction to Tunisian nationalism, including proposals for reform and actual enactments, and on the internationalization of the Tunisian question in the early 1950s. Most of the writings on French policies support, at least implicitly,

Julien's thesis that lack of clear policies and firm action by the Paris government allowed proconsuls to govern and, together with the settlers, to scuttle any real reforms. An issue of *La Nef* (1952) devoted to the problems of the two protectorates, Tunisia and Morocco, contains an article by foreign minister Robert Schuman which reveals official attitudes towards reform. It advocates reform of the French administration more than a basic change in the protectorate relationship.

Alexander Werth in *The Strange History of Pierre Mendès-France and the Great Conflict over French North Africa* (1957) describes Mendès's policies towards North Africa and his efforts to disengage France there. The work contains well-chosen excerpts from his speeches and articles and is generally favorable to his policies. Pierre Boyer de la Tour (1956) served as resident-general both in Tunisia and in Morocco during the final stages of French rule in 1954–55. For the loss of these countries he is critical of Mendès and Faure, as well as Bourguiba and Mohammed V.

A work by Victor Silvéra, *La Réforme des assemblées locales en Tunisie: conseils municipaux et conseils de caidats* (1953) deals with the 1952 reforms which did not touch the essence of the dispute between France and Tunisia. Three of his articles, published in 1948, 1951, and 1954, analyze the various reforms in which the French tinkered with the internal administration of the country while retaining most of their power. The Conventions of June 3, 1955, which granted internal self-government to Tunisia, are reproduced and analyzed by Noë Ladhari (1955) and also briefly by Roger Pinto (1955). Victor Silvéra in two articles published in 1956 and 1957 also provides the best analysis of the transition from autonomy to independence on March 20, 1956.

The internationalization of the Tunisian question is the subject of two studies. Georges Day, *Les Affaires de la Tunisie et du Maroc devant les Nations Unies* (1953), takes the position that under Article 2, Section 7 of the UN Charter, the Tunisian and Moroccan questions are internal French matters and cannot be considered by the international organization. Paul Sigaud (Thesis, 1962) supplements Day by bringing the account of the Tunisian and Moroccan questions before the UN through independence in 1956.

The economic aspects of French colonization and rule in general have been the subject of many studies. *La Tunisie orientale, Sahel et Basse Steppe, étude géographique* (1st ed. 1940, 2d ed. 1955), by Jean Despois, is a study in depth which contributes much to an understanding of French economic activities and their repercussions in diverse parts of eastern Tunisia. Jean Poncet's *La Colonisation et l'agriculture européenne en Tunisie depuis 1881: étude de géographie historique et économique* (1962) is a highly detailed study of European agriculture in Tunisia. It describes the process by which, especially after 1891, French commercial agriculture produced wheat, wine, and olive oil, mostly for export, using Tunisian labor. At the same time it shows how most of the Tunisian farmers were pushed out to the poorest land or were forced into a rural proletariat. A second study by Poncet, *Paysages et problèmes ruraux en Tunisie* (1963), takes up, region by region, the transformations introduced into agriculture by European colonization. It shows clearly in what ways the European settlement profoundly altered the pre-1881 juridical, social, and demographic structures. Articles by John Clarke (1952 and 1955) examine some of the consequences of European presence on summer nomads and for demographic growth. The detailed work of André Martel, *Les Confins saharo-tripolitains de la Tunisie, 1881–1911* (2 vols., 1965), examines the economic, social, and political structures of tribes on the edge of the Sahara and the impact of French rule upon them during the two decades prior to the establishment of Italian rule in neighboring Tripolitania.

Dealing with still another area of economic life, P. Pennec, (Thesis, 1964), studies the impact of European capitalism upon Muslim artisan groups in the city of Tunis during the Protectorate. He analyzes their position in mid-nineteenth-century society and the factors which hindered them from modernizing or resisting the encroachments of European industrial capitalism. Their close links with the sufist brotherhoods cut them off from the reformist Islam which might have aided their adjustment to the new economic competition. Their particular socio-economic situation also prevented them from becoming a bourgeoisie that could play a political role in the state. Gabriel Ardant in *La Tunisie d'aujourd'hui et de demain: Une expérience de développement économique* (1961) stresses the importance of the bourgeoisie for Tunisian economic development in the pre-independence period.

An older work by a Muslim which deals with economic trends during the first four decades of French rule is Mohammed Mzali's *L'Evolution économique de la Tunisie* (Tunis, 1921). *L'Economie tunisienne depuis la fin de la guerre* (1955), by Jules Lépidi, is an overall survey of the Tunisian economy that is nicely complemented by the *Tableau de l'économie tunisienne* (1956) of Jean Vibert, who for seven years served as director of foreign commerce in the Residency administration.

Henri de Montety's *Les Femmes de Tunisie* (1958) is a sociological study of the situation of women in the Tunisia of the 1950s. It is one of the very few works that are predominantly social in focus.

MOROCCO

Few general surveys of Morocco exist that are of use to the historian. The sections on Morocco in the Northwest Africa survey edited by Nevill Barbour (1959) are satisfactory for the colonial period but brief. Jean Célérier's *Maroc* (1948) is a simple and authoritative survey that emphasizes the benefits to Morocco of the French administration and economic development in the first three decades of the protectorate. *Initiation au Maroc* (1952) is a reissue of a collection edited in 1945 that has good articles on the economy before 1939.

Two recent brief histories cover the entire period of the protectorate: those of Vincent Monteil (1962) and Jean-Louis Miège (1962). A more detailed work, Henri Cambon's *Histoire du Maroc* (1952), devotes most of its last half to French activities and achievements during the protectorate. Cambon, son of the first Resident in Tunisia and nephew of a governor of Algeria, himself served as an official in Morocco and favored the French presence there. *Histoire du Maroc* (Casablanca, 1967), by Jean Brignon et al., is a text for secondary school students which has several useful chapters on the protectorate period from a Moroccan perspective. It provides a counterweight to the previous work.

A standard two-volume work by Henri Terrasse (1949–50) on the history of Morocco before 1912 provides background to the French takeover but contains some questionable views about the nature of Moroccan institutions. Eugène Aubin's *Morocco of Today* (1906) has one of the best descriptions of preprotectorate Morocco, especially of political institutions. Georges Surdon's *La France en Afrique du Nord* (1945) is by far the most thorough and authoritative work on political institutions, both Moroccan and French, before and after 1912. Walter Harris, the London *Times* correspondent based at Tangier, has written two good eyewitness accounts. *Morocco That Was, 1887–1912* (1921) reflects his early experiences. *France, Spain, and the Rif* (1927) deals with the periods from the establishment of the protectorate through the French campaign against Abdel Krim in 1925–26. Cecil V. Usborne's *Conquest of Morocco* (1936), is a British vice-admiral's personal experiences; he gives a historical account of French penetration before 1912 and the pacification under Lyautey.

There is a large number of French works on the French penetration and pacification of the country. Jean Caloni in *La France au Maroc* (1937) provides the historical background of the French conquest. A joint work by J. Ladreit de Lacharrière, M. Bernard, and H. Simon, *La Pacification du Maroc, 1907–1934* (1936), deals with the military pacification during more than a quarter of a century, while the works of René Pinon (1935) and Antoine Huré (1952) are concerned with the final stages.

There are several good biographies of Lyautey, including those of André Maurois (1931) and Sonia Howe (1931) in English. General Georges Catroux, one of the greatest French specialists on colonial questions, was present during the 1912 occupation and served Lyautey as commander at Marrakech. His biography, *Lyautey, le Marocain* (1952), emphasizes the great proconsul's desire for peaceful construction and modernization while respecting Morocco's originality. It is the best general account of Lyautey in the period 1907–25. Pierre Esperandieu in *Lyautey et le protectorat* (1947) treats the origins and application of Lyautey's ideas on the protectorate. Alan Scham's *Lyautey in Morocco: Protectorate Administration, 1912–1925* (1970) concentrates upon the changes which were effected under Lyautey in central, municipal, and tribal government, property administration, education, and the judiciary, and their significance both for the Berber and Arab populations and for French colonization. Guillaume de Tarde's *Lyautey, le chef en action* (1959) is a biography which concentrates upon Lyautey's administration. Lyautey himself published *Paroles d'action* (1927) on his policy. His nephew, Pierre Lyautey, has edited his writings and correspondence for the years 1912–25 in *Lyautey, l'Africain* (4 vol., 1953–57). Frank Trout's study of Morocco's Saharan frontiers from 1845 to the present (1969) shows a conflict in objectives and policy on the nomadic tribes between Lyautey and the French Algerian administration. The protectorate regime extended administrative control and laid claim to territory with repercussions for future Moroccan-Algerian relations. Lyautey wrote a short article, "Les origines du conflit," on the Rif War (1926), the French involvement in which helped to terminate his service in Morocco. Lt. Col. Auguste Laure's *La Victoire franco-espagnole dans le Rif* (1927) was a contemporary account of Franco-Spanish operations against the rebel forces.

Two recent works have dealt with Abdel Krim and the Rif War. Rupert Furneaux's *Abdel Krim, Emir of the Rif* (1967) is based on interviews with Krim's family and survivors of the war. It has a good chapter on the organization of the independent Rifian state, which was a kind of tribal federation. David S. Woolman, *Abdel Krim and the Rif Rebellion* (1968) contains an account of France's involvement in the Rif rebellion, including the Franco-Spanish cooperation. It tries to show the links between the uprisings and the later Moroccan nationalist liberation movement in the mid-1950s. Woolman emphasizes that in resisting colonialism, Krim did not seek to form a modern state. But by replacing Berber customary law with Koranic law, he aided national unification.

There were a half-dozen or so works, mainly historical, which appeared around 1930 and evaluated French efforts up to that point. Among them are the histories of Georges Hardy (1931) in the Hanotaux series, Auguste Terrier (1931), and Augustin Bernard (7th ed., 1931), which is reliable for Moroccan life and social institutions both before and after 1912. André Colliez in *Notre protectorat marocain: La première étape, 1912–1930* (1930) and J. Ladreit de Lacharrière in *La Création marocaine* (1930) both analyze the French actions, including the economic, in the first years of the protectorate. A postwar examination of governmental institutions is André de Laubadère, *Les Réformes des Pouvoirs Publiques: le Gouvernement; l'Administration; La Justice* (1949). Work of the same period by Frédéric Bremard treats the problems of regional and local government (1949). Brémard (1950) deals with the grant of special privileges and powers to the settlers. André Chouraqui's *La Condition juridique de l'israélite marocain* (1950) contains annexes with all the legislative texts and regulations on the juridical situation of Moroccan Jews. Two important works concern the city of Tangier. Graham Stuart's *The International City of Tangier* (rev. ed., 1955) is a significant history of international rivalry before and after World I, and of the settlement embodied in the Statute of 1923 providing for international control. Jacques Bonjean's *Tanger* (1967) is a discussion of the international status of the city, 1925–56, and its economic activity during that period.

There is a large and varied literature on French rule and Moroccan reactions to it, including the rise of nationalism. Albert Ayache's *Le Maroc: Bilan d'une colonisation* (1956) is a valuable work by a Marxist teacher and syndicalist who starts from the premise that all colonization is a moral evil that can lead only to evil results. He gives a detailed description of the economic and financial aspects of French colonization and an excellent analysis of the economic and social transformations wrought by French rule. But his thesis that Moroccan nationalism is a workers' movement is debatable. Georges Spillmann's *Du Protectorat à l'Indépendance: Maroc, 1912–1955* (1967) is the account of a liberal French officer who witnessed events between 1920 and 1955 and who knew all the Residents. He sees French efforts under the protectorate as ultimately happy for all, despite the regime's deterioration after 1940. Rom Landau's *Moroccan Drama, 1900–1955* (1956) is a book based on long experience in Morocco and personal contacts with the royal family and leading nationalists. When written it was the most complete work on the period of the protectorate and the nationalist movement. It does an especially good job of analyzing those aspects of French rule which most provoked Moroccan resentment and gave rise to nationalism. Forthrightly pronationalist but honest, it complements such pro-French works as those of Robert Montagne. Pierre Corval's *Le Maroc en révolution* (1956) is a brief account of French rule in Morocco from the Treaty of Fez to the La Celle agreements. It is critical of the direct rule and domination introduced after Lyautey's departure. An American doctoral dissertation by Rashid Kabbani, *Morocco: From Protectorate to Independence, 1912–1956* (Ph.D. dissertation, American University, 1957), deals primarily with the origins and subsequent development of the international problem of Morocco and the world status of Morocco, but also analyzes nationalism as a response to French rule. John P. Halstead in *Rebirth of a Nation: The Origins and Rise of Moroccan Nationalism, 1912–1944* (1967) deals with nationalism in the period when nationalists sought mainly to reform the protectorate system rather than to terminate it as they did after 1944. He shows that French colonial rule triggered the nationalist reaction, but that the response was in terms of Morocco's own particular history and was first couched in forms taken from the Salafiyya movement of reformist Islam. Nationalism was first spurred not by foreign control but by the threat of cultural assimilation, which menaced Arab and Islamic values as well as Morocco's traditional institutions. The nationalist movement was led primarily by the young French-educated elite. Its program, as it moved from reformism to separatism, came more and more from European sources—as did its organization. The nationalitists ultimately assimilated on their own terms much that was French in order to have a modern state. An article by John Damis (1970) interprets the emergence of nationalism in the period 1925–43.

An important article by Jamil Abun-Nasr (1963) on the Salafiyya movement in Morocco shows the religious bases for the nationalist movement. Albert Hourani in *Arabic Thought in the Liberal Age, 1798–1939* (1962) deals with the intellectual background for the Salafiyya in the Arab world. Henri Laoust's "Le Réformisme orthodoxe des 'Salafiyya' et les caractères généraux de son orientation actuelle" (*Revue des Etudes Islamiques* 6 [1932]: 175–224), is an older study which treats Morocco specifically. Federico S. Vidal's "Religious Brotherhoods in Moroccan Politics" (*Middle East Journal,* October 1950, pp. 427–46) is the work of an official of the Spanish Service of Native Affairs from 1940 to 1947. Among older works Georges Drague's *Esquisse d'histoire religieuse du Maroc: Confréries et Zaouias* (1951) is a good history of the religious brotherhoods through 1939, showing the interrelationships of religious, social, and political life. It contains essays on six individual brotherhoods based in large part on firsthand data. Octave Depont and Xavier Coppolani's *Les Confréries religieuses musulmanes* (1897) is the most comprehensive work on the Sufi orders of North Africa and provides data on them as they existed two decades before the French takeover.

Two perceptive articles in the 1930s by Louis Jalabert in *Etudes* deal with the relationships between religion and nationalism (1938) and with nationalism itself sympathetically and discerningly (1934). A paper by Omar El Maki, "Le Nationalisme dan la littérature marocaine de langue arabe de 1925 à 1955" (1965) is a contribution to the history of the ideas of nationalism during the days after Lyautey's departure. Fulbert Taillard's *Le Nationalisme marocain* (1947), though based on some questionable premises, is a quite objective account of the development of nationalism in the period 1944–46. Allal al-Fasi's *The Independence Movements in Arab North Africa* (trans. 1954 from the 1948 Arabic original), concerns the nationalist movements in all three Maghrib nations. But it is most valuable as an account of the Istiqlal leader's experiences and impressions in the years 1944–48, including Moroccan relations with the Arab League and activity at the United Nations. It is unreliable, however, on many controversial matters.

Two works by liberal Catholics are Ignace Lepp's *Midi sonne au Maroc* (1954), one of the most objective and perceptive works on Moroccan nationalism, which unfortunately is not documented, and Paul Buttin's *Le Drame du Maroc* (1955), the account of a French lawyer long resident in Morocco who is sympathetic to Moroccan nationalism. Robert Montagne's *Révolution au Maroc* (1953) is an undocumented portrait of the transformations of Moroccan life under French rule by an official sociologist who is hostile to the nationalists but has long experience in the country. Through a series of impressionistic but penetrating tableaux of the crises affecting the urban proletariat, youth, and the state, we get an excellent picture of the revolutionary currents shaking the country.

Robert Rézette's *Les Partis politiques marocains* (1955) is a detailed history of the Moroccan political parties formed in response to French colonialism, with special emphasis on their structure. It examines the juridical, political, and social frameworks within which the parties arose and had to act. Because of the authoritarian and professional character of the institutions which the French erected after 1912, there was little scope for political action within them by the nationalists, nor were there any real civil liberties. Moroccan parties had to evolve outside these institutions and work for the end of the protectorate as the only means of obtaining genuine reforms. A second important work on parties is Douglas Ashford's *Political Change in Morocco* (1961). It focuses on the first three years after independence, but presents a great deal of useful data, sometimes ill-digested, on Istiqlal in the postwar period, its local organization, its relation to the labor movement, and attempts at representative government.

Stéphane Bernard's *The Franco-Moroccan Conflict, 1943–1956* is an English translation (1968) of two volumes of the three-volume French original (1963). It is part of a series on international conflicts and attempts to formulate a theory of decolonization of a political system. The research was undertaken by a team headed by a Belgian sociologist without personal experience with Morocco. While the study is somewhat sympathetic to Moroccan nationalism, its sources (many of them unpublished) are almost exclusively French. Thus it tells the story from a French viewpoint that severely minimizes the roles of the main Moroccan actors, even decisive ones like Prince Hasan, Balafrej, and al-Fasi. Even more serious, the work barely mentions the French usurpations and impositions of inferiority upon Moroccans that are at the root of many Moroccan nationalist reactions. The most valuable sections for the historian are volume one, which is the best detailed history of the period 1943–56 yet available in English, telling the story of the conflict Resident by Resident, and in the French edition, volume 3, which is a mine of information about institutions and social groups. Ladislav Cerych in *Européens et Marocains, 1930–1956: Sociologie d'une décolonisation* (1964) discusses the main political, economic, and social problems after the French passed to direct rule and official encouragement of colonization. Its most original sections deal with the social aspects of French rule. Margaret Hamilton's *French Policy Towards Morocco: 1944–1956* (Ph.D dissertation, Columbia University, 1959) is a useful account of the final stages of French rule. Jean and Simone Lacouture in *Le Maroc à l'épreuve* (1958) give an excellent evaluation of the protectorate period as a prelude to their main discussions of the first two years of independence. Jean Cassaigne's *La Situation des Français au Maroc depuis l'indépendance, 1956–1964* (1964) in the course of treating the settlers since 1956 provides data on their position under the protectorate as well. Doris Bensimon Donath (1968) discusses the evolution of Moroccan Jews during the protectorate.

Many works deal with different aspects of the last decade of French rule and the transition to independence. Gavin Maxwell's *Lords of the Atlas: The Rise and Fall of the House of Glaoua, 1893–1956* (1966) presents a somewhat simplified but useful account of the family that produced al-Glawi of Marrakech and of its relations with the monarchy and the French. Marvine Howe's *The Prince and I* (1955) is the personal account of an American woman's life at Fez, 1950–53, where she knew the royal family. She contends that the Moroccans resented the racial and cultural snobbery of the French far more than their economic exploitation. Rom Landau in *The Sultan of Morocco* (1951) presents a valuable portrait of Sidi Mohammed ibn Yusuf, Mohammed V, who became sultan in 1927, which is complemented by one a decade later by Jean Lacouture in *Cinq hommes et la France* (1961). Two volumes present writings and speeches of Mohammed V during the transition to independence, 1955–57: Mohammed V, *Le Maroc à l'heure de l'indépendance* (vol. 1, 1957), and Maroc, Ministère de l'Information et Tourisme, *Réalisations et perspectives, 16 novembre 1955–18 novembre 1957: Recueil de textes et de discours* (1957).

Three works deal with the international aspects of the Moroccan question. They include those by Georges Day and Paul Sigaud already cited in the section on Tunisia, and one by Khaled el Saghieh (Ph.D. dissertation, American University, 1955), which treats the Moroccan question in the United Nations from a non-French viewpoint.

Two of the residents-general in 1955 have recorded accounts of their service. Pierre Boyer de la Tour's work is mentioned above. Gilbert Grandval in *Ma mission au Maroc* (1956), deals with the events of July 7 to August 26, 1955, and justifies his own role as Resident. The two books show the lack of decisive leadership in the Fourth Republic. They point up the fundamental problem of the centralized control in the French Union, which did not permit any real local autonomy and was consequently unprepared to deal with local nationalisms within the framework of the existing relationship with France. *La Nef*, Cahier no. 2, *Maroc et Tunisie: Le Problème du protectorat* (March 1953), discusses the problem of the French relationship with the two protectorates and shows how little even progressive thinking on the questions had evolved in the direction of independence. Most of the suggestions for reform advocated tinkering with the administration to give Moroccans a larger role while safeguarding the essence of the French position. M. S. Agwani's "Morocco: From Protectorate to Independence" (*International Studies,* July 1959, pp. 51–70) is a good account of the transition to independence. Henri Marchat in "Vie et morts du statut de Tanger" (*Revue politique et parlementaire,* August–September 1960, pp. 124–33), takes up the termination of international control in Tangier.

The economic development of Morocco by the French has been the subject of many studies. Several important articles by Pierre Guillen (e.g. 1963) have dealt with French economic penetration prior to the establishment of the protectorate. The most general and yet interpretative study of the protectorate period is Charles F. Stewart's *The Economy of Morocco, 1912–1962* (1964), which is nicely complemented by the International Bank of Reconstruction and Development's report *The Economic Development of Morocco* (1966) and the doctoral thesis of Abdelassis Belal, *L'Investissement au Maroc (1912–1964) et ses enseignements en matière de développement économique.* Among older studies still of value are those of the French economist and civil servant René Hoffherr, *L'Economie Marocaine* (1932), and of an American economist, Melvin M. Knight, *Morocco as a French Economic Venture* (1937). Knight studied the first twenty-five years of the French protectorate, including the consequences of the world depression and French protectionist measures. Yves Famchon in *Le Maroc d'Algéciras à la souveraineté économique* (1957) deals with the juridical aspects of the Moroccan economy by studying the bases of the economic, financial, and customs relationships between Morocco and France under the protectorate and their consequences.

Two works have dealt with agriculture. Marc Bonnefous in *Perspectives de l'agriculture marocaine* (1949) treats the transformations of rural—and primarily subsistence—agriculture. *La modernisation rurale au Maroc* (1948) by Yves Barennes, is a monograph on the measures that the Paysannat Marocain undertook to develop agriculture after the Second World War, including the encouragement of cooperatives. A more general work which also treats agriculture is Albert Guillaume's *L'Evolution économique de la société rurale marocaine* (1956).

René Gallisot's *Le Patronat européen au Maroc, 1931–1942* (1964) examines one sector of French colonization in depth. He looks at the social and political activities of the *patronat* after the period of its installation (1926–30) until the American landing of November 1942, which opened the period of national affirmation leading to independence. Gallisot excludes from his study the entrepreneurs in banking and commerce, concentrating on the segments of the bourgeoisie which have charge of mining, industry, and workshops. More powerful than the agricultural capitalists, they became the dominant element within the settler community through their financial power, variety of activities, and multiplicity of relations. Looking at the social and political activities of the *patronat,* Gallisot sees its members moving in 1937 from a liberalism in principle to a preventive paternalism. His history is a fundamental contribution to the understanding of Moroccan social problems and an important analysis of the origins of the Moroccan syndicalist movement under the protectorate.

French educational policies under the protectorate have been the subject of two important studies. Roger Gaudefroy-Demombynes's *L'Oeuvre française en matière d'enseignement au Maroc* (1928) is the only thorough nonofficial study of French education in Morocco prior to Paye (1957). It has a strong colonialist and assimilationist bias. Lucien Paye's *Enseignement et société musulmane: introduction et évolution de l'enseignement moderne au Maroc* (Thesis, Paris, 1957) is an excellent history of education that is thoroughly assimilationist in its views.

There have been quite a few studies of the social transformations brought about by the French protectorate policies and economic development both in the urban and rural settings. Robert Montagne, ed., *Naissance du prolétariat marocain: enquête collective exécutée de 1948 à 1950* (1952) is a collection of studies by French experts on the consequences of emigration of rural southern Moroccans toward the north and coastal cities, especially in the period after 1939, and of demographic growth. It ignores, however, the real origins of the rise of an urban proletariat in the sequestration by French authorities of the land of 500,000 Moroccan families in the period 1926–29 for the benefit of Frenchmen. It also ignores the fact that thousands of Moroccans left home to escape the rapacity of the caids and pashas (e.g. al-Glawi) installed or supported by the French. Thus the reader is left almost completely in the dark as to the fundamental causes of the proletarianization of the Moroccan peasants. André Adam's *Le 'Bidonville' de Ben Msik à Casablanca: Contribution à l'étude du prolétariat musulman au Maroc* (1950) is a study in depth of one of the shantytowns that arose at Casablanca during the aftermath of the Second World War and was inhabited by rural immigrants. Adam's history of Casablanca from its origins to 1914 provides an excellent background to his detailed two-volume *Casablanca: Essai sur la transformation de la Société Marocaine au Contact de l'Occident* (1968). Jean-Paul Trystram's *L'Ouvrier mineur au Maroc: Contribution statistique à une étude sociologique* (1957) is a study of Moroccan miners working for European concerns. Jean d'Etienne, Louis Villème, and Stéphane Delisle in *L'Evolution sociale du Maroc* (1950) study the cities of Casablanca, Fès, and Port Lyautey in the postwar period.

There are several studies of the transformations of rural peoples during the period of the protectorate. Robert Montagne's *Les Berbères et le makhzen dans le sud du Maroc: Essai sur les transformations politiques des Berbères sedentaires* (*groupe chleuh*) (1930) deals with the changed relationships between some Berber groups and the Sherifian government as a result of the French conquest. Jacques Berque's *Structures sociales du Haut-Atlas* (1955) provides deep insights into rural society through a study of the Seksawa tribe and its institutions as they have evolved in recent decades. André Adam in *La Maison et le village dans quelques tribus de l'Anti-Atlas* (1951) deals with the evolution of rural society. Marcel Lesne's *Evolution d'un groupe berbère: les Zemmours* (1959) examines the transformations of a Berber group from the nineteenth to the twentieth centuries. *Plaines et piedmonts du Bassin de la Moulouya* (1961) and "La terre et l'homme en Haut Moulouya" (*Bulletin économique et social du Maroc*, November 1960–February 1961, pp. 281–346), by René Raynal, both concern northeastern Morocco. Marvin Micklesell's *Northern Morocco: A Cultural Geography* (1961) provides useful information for the historian about a little-studied part of the country. P. Flamant's *Les Communautés israélites du Sud-Marocain: Essai de description et d'analyse de la juive en milieu berbère* (1959), treats the evolution of Jewish communities in predominantly Berber areas during the protectorate.

BLACK AFRICA AND MADAGASCAR

We begin the discussion of the literature of Black Africa and Madagascar with the years 1914–19, the period of World War I and its immediate aftermath.

During World War I French troops with Belgian assistance occupied the parts of French Equatorial Africa that had been ceded to Germany in the treaty of November 4, 1911. Then the French forces undertook joint military operations with the British to occupy the pre-1911 Cameroons and Togoland. The campaign in Togoland ended late in August 1914 and the one in the Cameroons in February 1916.

Most of the writing on the military aspects of the war took place at the time or during the period between the two world wars. Among the most important are the accounts of the forces coming from Equatorial Africa, such as that of the commander, General J. Aymerich, *La Conquête du Cameroun: Ier août 1914–20 février 1916* (1933); and of Henri Mailier, "Le Rôle des colonies françaises dans la campagne du Cameroun" (*Afrique française*, June 1916, pp. 209–15); Captain J. Ferrandi, *Conquête du Nord Cameroun, 1914–1915* (1928); Captain Lemoine, "Les Pays conquis du Cameroun Nord" (*Afrique française*, July–August 1918); M. L. J. E. Weithas, *La Conquête du Cameroun et du Togo* (1931). A detailed account of the military operations and occupation of the Cameroons is found in the *Journal Officiel de la République Française*, September 7, 1921, Annex, 415–92. This source also describes the establishment of French provisional administration in the years between the end of the fighting and the League approval of the mandates. The Belgian role in the Equatorial Africa campaigns is located in the official Belgian history, *Les Campagnes coloniales belges: 1914–1918* (1927 and after).

An eyewitness account by the British officer who took Yaoundé is Colonel E. H. Gorges's *The Great War in West Africa* (1930), which also covers Togo. The most comprehensive account in English is a history based on official documents by F. J. Moberly, *Military Operations: Togoland and the Cameroons, 1914–1916* (1930). General Maroix, the French military commander in the Togoland campaign and in the first partition, later described these events in *Le Togo, pays d'influence française* (1938). Contemporary French accounts appeared in *Afrique française:* "La Conquête du Togoland" (in *Renseignements Coloniaux*, supplement to *Afrique française*, May 1915, pp. 82–102) and Henri d'Arboussier's "La Conquête du Togoland: l'action des partisans mossi" (April 1915); and in the *Revue des Deux Mondes* (Charles Stienon, "La campagne coloniale des alliés en 1914 et 1915: le Togo," November 1, 1915). An official British account concerning the Togoland campaign is *Correspondence Relating to the Military Operations in Togoland* (Cmd. 7872, Parliamentary Paper 1915, Accounts and Papers, vol. 46). A detailed account of the French occupation of Togoland and the two partitions, comparable to the one already cited for the Cameroons, is found in the *Journal Officiel de la République Française*, August 25, 1921, p. 9868.

The most important German works on the fighting in the two colonies are: Erich Student, *Kameruns Kampf* (1937); H. Mentzel, *Die Kampf in Kamerun, 1914–1916* (1936); and M. Schwarte et al., *Der Grosse Kriege* (8 vols., 1921–25). Georges Bruel, well-known for his work on French Equatorial Africa, compiled a "Bibliographie de la conquête du Cameroun, 1914–1916" (*Afrique française*, June 1934).

Two post–World War II French authors have provided convenient summaries of the military operations in the course of their works. Surgeon-General A. Sicé in *L'Afrique équatoriale française et le Cameroun au service de la France, 26–27–28, août 1940* (1946), chapter 4, summarizes French operations in those countries, 1914–16. Robert Cornevin's *Le Togo* (1959) does the same for that country in 1914, pp. 207–17. In English, W. O. Henderson's *Studies in German Colonial History* (1962), chapter 8, provides a good brief introduction to the conquest of the German colonies and a bibliography of the major French, British, and German accounts.

Immediately after the war, Sir Charles Lucas in *The Gold Coast and the War* (1920) examined the effects of the war, in particular its economic and military consequences, on a British territory adjacent to Togoland. But the impact of the war on the peoples of the German territories or those of the neighboring French and British colonies has received scholarly attention only recently. The article by David Gardinier, "The British in the Cameroons, 1919–1939" (1967), discusses the consequences of the partition of 1916 and the repartition of 1919 for some of the African populations who were affected as well as for the British and French administrations. Charles Pelham Groves (1958) in the fourth volume of his history of Christian missions examines the impact of the war on the Africans under missionary influence throughout West and Equatorial Africa. Maurice Gontard (1969) discusses the impact of the war on Madagascar.

The opening of the British archives for the period of the war made possible the article by P. H. S. Hatton, "The Gambia, the Colonial Office, and the Opening Months of the First World War" (1966). Hatton examines the economic results of the French failure to purchase their usual share of the Gambian groundnut crop in 1914. His article also reveals the important links between the British enclave and the adjacent French colony of Senegal. Michael Crowder in "West Africa and the 1914–1918 War" (1968) treats the significance of the war in the British colonies. This same material is incorporated in summary into an excellent chapter in his *West Africa under Colonial Rule* (1968). There, drawing on the Dakar archives, he also discusses the French policies in West Africa during World War I. The French policy of recruiting two hundred thousand Africans for military service from a population of eleven millions conflicted with the concurrent policy of increased agricultural production for the French war effort. It also led to a large-scale exodus to neighboring British territories, where only thirty thousand troops were recruited.

French use of African troops has been a subject of recurrent interest. Arguments for the recruitment of black Africans were presented in the book of General Mangin, *La Force noire* (1910), even before the war. French use of black troops in the nineteenth century and in World War I is the subject of a work (1934) by an American economist, Shelby Cullum Davis. Recruitment by the French during the two World Wars is covered in the highly critical short study by the Senegalese economist and politician Abdoulaye Ly, *Mercenaires noirs: Notes sur une forme d'exploitation des Africains* (1957). Crowder and G. Wesley Johnson are presently studying the question of recruitment, particularly the role of the Senegalese deputy, Blaise Diagne, in recruiting blacks for the French armies.

The effects of military recruitment and increased economic requirements, both of which put heavy demands on already scarce African labor, contributed to numerous revolts against French rule in Dahomey, Sudan, Upper Volta, and Niger. These revolts are described, within the context of a discussion of the impact of the war upon French West Africa, in the general work by Chailley (1968), himself a longtime military officer there. Useful for the Sanusi-inspired revolts among the Tuareg is the official history, *Les Troupes coloniales pendant la guerre, 1914–1918* (1931). The Niger uprisings, which were the most serious and which led the French to seek assistance of British-led Nigerian troops, are recounted in the detailed work of Séré de Rivières on that territory (1965). Recent studies of the Dahomeyan uprisings by Robert Cornevin (1962) and Luc Garcia (1970) have drawn upon archival materials in Africa. Garcia has published a section of his Paris doctoral dissertation on Dahomeyan resistance between 1914 and 1917.

While the wartime military operations in the colonies have been well documented, much less is known about the colonial war aims of the French government and the measures used to achieve them. The lack of memoirs and studies by the leading officials in Paris and in Africa poses a permanent handicap to the understanding of the question. Until the French archives are opened for the period of the First World War, no definitive answers can be attempted. In this volume André Kaspi uses the available sources to discuss French war aims in Africa as they emerged in the course of the war, especially during its last year. It is clear from his study that African questions played a very minor part in French thinking and at the Versailles Conference. Only the work of an American advisor, George Louis Beer's *African Questions at the Paris Peace Conference* (1923) throws light on French diplomacy at the conference. The article by Roger Louis (1963) discusses Beer's scheme for an American mandate in the Cameroons and the opposition to the idea from the French colonial minister, Henry Simon. The article is based on the diary Beer kept at the conference, with his observations of the French participants. E. Rouard de Card (1924) discusses the public statements of Simon and his successor between 1919 and 1922 on the status of the Cameroons and Togo. He asserts that Simon's position that these territories would not become mandates was due to his ignorance of the provisions of the Versailles Treaty.

American and British sources, and works based upon them, have been able to reveal some further information about French goals. In 1943 the U. S. Department of State published the minutes of the meetings of the Council of Ten in the series *Papers Relating to the Foreign Relations of the United States.* Several articles and a recent book (1967) by Wm. Roger Louis drawing upon recently opened British archives shed light on Franco-British diplomacy concerning African matters and on the origins of the French mandates in the Cameroons and Togoland. Some British government circles feared that the elimination of Germany from Africa might make France once more the rival of Britain. Louis shows that the Colonial Office and the Foreign Office pursued different policies towards the occupied portions of the Cameroons and Togo. The Colonial Office wanted to keep the strategic port of Duala and portions of the hinterland while the Foreign Office saw the Cameroons and, to an even greater extent Togoland, as pawns that could be used to secure British goals elsewhere. Louis demonstrates that British willingness to cede nearly all of the Cameroons and more than half of Togoland to France resulted from the greater priority assigned to securing British control elsewhere in Africa, particularly German East Africa, and in the world. The prime consideration was the security of the Empire and not acquisition of more colonial territory.

THE MANDATES

The bibliographical essay in this book's companion volume, *Britain and Germany in Africa,* contained a section on the mandates (pp. 742–

44), including works on the historical origins of the mandates system and on its general functioning. It is interesting that not one volume in the French language is cited there. This situation shows how very little French colonial experience and thinking contributed to the development of the ideas of trusteeship and international accountability for colonial administration.

After France acquired parts of the Cameroons and Togoland, French authors turned their attention to the application of the mandates system in those territories. The works of Costedoat (1930), Chazelas (1931), Wilbois (1934), and Labouret (1937) on French administration of the Cameroons discuss various aspects of the mandate in passing. But only the study of Roger Franceschi (1929) deals in any detail with the historical origins of the mandate for the Cameroons, its operation in the twenties, and the supervision of the Permanent Mandates Commission. In 1953 a French scholar who was at first interested in the trusteeship in the Cameroons turned his attention to a systematic study of the application of the mandate in the Cameroons. The doctoral dissertation of Paul Blanc is an excellent piece of scholarship which examines the juridical and legal structure and functioning of the mandate within the French colonial system and within the League of Nations. Blanc's detailed analysis shows that the French introduced policies previously developed in their Black African colonies with only minor modifications to meet the requirements of the mandates system. His study also illustrates how little influence the League supervision exerted on the formulation and execution of French policies.

In the religious sphere, the French permanently excluded all German missionaries, both Protestant and Catholic, from the Cameroons and Togo, and facilitated their replacement by French missionaries. By contrast, some German missionaries, mainly Protestant, were allowed after 1924 to resume their work in the British zones of those territories. The French policy and its implementation are recounted by a German Catholic, Joseph Schmidlin, in *Das Deutsche Missionswerk der Gegenwart* (1929), and by a British Protestant, Charles Pelham Groves, in his history of Christian missions (1958).

At the time France acquired part of the Cameroons, colonial circles, as shown in Kaspi's article, objected to the proposal for economic equality for all League members and desired preference for Frenchmen. Late in the mandate era G. Lawless (1937) undertook a study of the application of the principle of economic equality in the Cameroons. His investigations show in detail, as do those of Blanc, how French policies sought to erode the principle to the advantage of

France. In 1933 when France gave special subsidies to products transported in French ships, there were protests in the Cameroons to the League.

France, as Austen's article points out, emphasized economic development rather than political advancement in the mandates. Costedoat's study (1930) is rich in economic data for the decade of French administration prior to the world depression, in particular on the extensions of the midlands railroad northeast to Yaoundé and southeast to Mbalmayo. A section of Victor T. LeVine's *The Cameroons from Mandate to Independence* (1964), pp. 104–10, deals with the forced labor employed to build the railroad and the discussion in the Permanent Mandates Commission on this issue. LeVine's book is the only detailed discussion in English of the French administration during the mandate period. Though sketchy in places and impressionistic, it is full of insights on the transformations of Cameroonian society before the Second World War. The chapter on the mandate period in the general history of Father Mveng (1963) does not reach the high standards of some of his sections on precolonial periods.

Several other works provide useful information about French administration in the mandate period. Jacques Kuoh-Moukouri, a Duala who became Cameroonian ambassador to the United States in the early 1960s, described his many years of service in the French administration in *Doigts Noirs* (1963). Pastor H. Endresen (1954), a Norwegian Lutheran stationed at N'Gaoundéré from the late 1920s until after independence, recounts his efforts to secure the liberation of the Dourou people from their Fulani overlords. Maurice Farelly (1967), a Swiss pastor, gives a vivid picture of Cameroonians and Europeans in Duala and the Mungo Valley prior to the Second World War. Also helpful for the early 1920s are the contemporary works of Buell and Roberts. Buell touches upon the Duala opposition to French rule, of which no systematic study has yet been made. Two articles published in the London *Times* by Margery Perham after a visit in 1933 have been reprinted (1967). She compares French accomplishments favorably with British in neighboring territories.

For Togoland in the mandate period, the best studies are the doctoral dissertation of Ralph J. Bunche (1934), which compared French administration with that in neighboring Dahomey; the work of Chazelas (1931), which compared Togo and the Cameroons; and that of Ferjus (1926). The most complete study of French administration is *Le Mandat français sur le Togo* (1939) by the longtime colonial official and post–World War II governor of the Ivory Coast, Laurent

Péchoux. He makes some effort to compare French efforts with German, which is difficult because France administered less of Togolese territory than Germany did. It is noteworthy that Péchoux did not choose to compare the French administration with that in British Togoland or in neighboring Dahomey. His short section on League supervision is very general and takes up none of the issues that developed before the Permanent Mandates Commission. Péchoux presents detailed factual descriptions of the administrative and legislative regimes, economic development and commerce, education, missions, and health. The general *Histoire du Togo* (1959) by Robert Cornevin has a useful fifty-page chapter on the period between the two world wars. Like most of the other works of this longtime colonial administrator in Togo and Dahomey, it is heavily factual without very much interpretation and synthesis. In the 1920s R. L. Buell visited Togoland and reported on the early years of French administration. In the course of a chapter on Ewe nationalism, Claude Welch (1966) provides the only recent information in English on the French mandate. A more detailed account of the Ewe movement during the mandate era is found in Jean-Claude Pauvert, "L'Evolution politique des Ewe" (1960). Aspects of the Ewe question in the British zone are examined by D. E. K. Amenumey, "The Pre-1917 Background to the Ewe Unification Question" (1969).

ADMINISTRATION BETWEEN THE WARS 1919–1939.

Most of the historical writing on the period between the two World Wars has occurred since the Second World War, especially during the past decade, from the perspective of the decolonization of the overseas territories. The period tends to be seen both as the heyday of colonial rule and as the seedtime of the movements for emancipation that would sprout forth during and after World War II.

There are several general histories in French which include sections on Black Africa in the interwar period. Hubert Deschamps has written the sections on the French territories in *Afrique au XXe Siècle*. Taking a country-by-country approach, the former colonial governor gives attention primarily to administrative organization, political evolution, and economic development. In these topics he has achieved a good balance between general developments and details. He also discusses briefly the overall transformations of African society under colonial rule. The short bibliographies appended to his section of the book contain few of the important English-language works on these countries. Deschamps has also discussed French Administration in his essay

"France in Black Africa and Madagascar between 1920 and 1945" (1970).

Also useful are the works of Robert Cornevin, despite their lack of synthesis, and the second volume of Jean Suret-Canale (1964) despite its Marxist bias. The latter work treats French territories in Black Africa in the period 1900–1945, which Suret-Canale sees as "the colonial era" par excellence. His work provides an antidote to works by semi-official historians and former administrators which gloss over the seamy side of French colonialism. The detailed studies of French capital invested, commercial houses and banks, and the construction of the economic infrastructure result in a vivid picture of the French economic activities and of their social consequences. Suret-Canale pictures the period 1919–45 as one of *immobilisme* and economic stagnation with very few accomplishments. He concludes that despite all the theories of administration—assimilation, association, etc.—empiricism dominated French actions. A final merit of his work is the sections on Equatorial Africa, which are the most up-to-date and complete in any language.

The history of Black Africa by another Marxist, the Hungarian scholar Endre Sik, is now available in English translation (1966). The long chapter on the French colonies in the period 1918–39 relies on scanty and outdated secondary sources. It presents its very incomplete data in unadulterated Marxist-Leninist terms.

The best short accounts in English are found in the text of Robert I. Rotberg (1965) where the interwar period in Black Africa is set forth systematically though briefly on the basis of nearly all the sources available at that time. Since then works covering the former French territories in West Africa have appeared. John Hargreaves's study (1967) contains a brilliant chapter on colonial rule including some comparisons with British rule in neighboring territories. It takes up the entire period of colonial rule as a whole and discusses the manifold changes wrought by French colonialism as they occurred between the late 1800s and 1940.

Michael Crowder's work (1968) on all the countries of West Africa (except Portuguese Guinea and French Togoland) between the late nineteenth-century partition and the close of the Second World War is a monumental piece of scholarship. It rests on a very wide range of sources and some archival research at Dakar. It contains the best detailed treatment of French rule yet to appear in English and perhaps in any language. It has excellent sections on French administration, economic development and social change, as well as the beginnings of African politics, 1919–39. It presents many provocative comparisons with policies and practices in the British territories. Crowder contends that colonial rule in general retarded Africa's entrance into the modern world.

Among other studies of importance is the history of the French in West Africa by Chailley (1968). He presents a long factual chapter on the interwar period which is largely devoted to administrative organization, military operations to effect pacification, and economic and social development. An analogous section in the history of Niger by Séré de Rivières (1965) gives a detailed account of administrative organization and the constant reorganizations, and of the effort at pacification. In neither work does one find very much that is explicit on French policy. In contrast, the thesis of Pierre Dufournet (1967) studies French penetration and organization of Niger between 1898 and 1932, and the evolution of its peoples under French rule. Two recent theses on Chad provide information on the establishment of French rule there. Pierre Gentil (1967) deals with French exploration and occupation between 1894 and 1914 while Odda Nodiigoto (1960) treats the beginnings of French administration between 1900 and 1920. A small work by Pierre Hugot (1965) on Chad has a chapter that interprets the policies and practices of the interwar period and defends his fellow commandants against the critics of our own times.

The work of Madame Désiré-Veuillemin on Mauritania covers the period of French penetration and pacification, 1900–1934. It shows how the French expansion was influenced by relations with Spain, which had interests there and in neighboring Morocco. It sheds light on French policies towards the Moorish emirs and the various religious brotherhoods which loomed so large in Moorish society.

Governor Deschamps's history of Madagascar (2d ed., 1961) has a brief chapter on the period 1905–39 which contains suggestive vignettes of the various governors, some of whom he served under personally, and of their accomplishments. He also gives a useful account of the rise of Malagasy nationalism. Almost all other works on Madagascar, including those of Kent (1962) and Thompson and Adloff (1965), draw on Deschamps for their sections on this period. The Adloffs also have a useful discussion of the growth of settler influence on policies. A work by a Communist scholar, Pierre Boiteau, (1958) contains a detailed examination of French activities from a Marxist-Leninist approach. Its mass of factual data on land alienation, French investments, commerce, and forced labor provides the basis for a careful examination of economic development in the interwar period and a discussion of the rise of new classes.

There is a good deal of other writing, much of it nonhistorical, from the interwar period itself which is useful for the understanding of French colonial rule. The five-volume work of Arthur Girault, *Principes de colonisation et de législation coloniale,* of which the first three volumes concern Black Africa either generally or specifically, appeared in its fifth edition, 1927–30. Girault presents a summary of events and of colonial legislation together with useful bibliographies. His work is less a history or an analysis than a painstaking collection and a valuable sourcebook. More analytical and interpretive but briefer is the *Précis de législation coloniale* (1931) by Louis Rolland and Pierre Lampué. Later editions of this work, under the title *Précis de droit des pays d'outre-mer,* in 1949 and 1959, give a historical perspective to the evolution of ideas and institutions, as do the perspicacious works of Professor P. F. Gonidec, *Droit d'Outre-Mer,* vol. 1, *De l'Empire colonial de la France à la communauté* (1959), and Rudolph von Albertini, *Dekolonisation* (1966). A study by L. Gray Cowan (1958) includes chapters comparing government and administration in French West Africa and Nigeria before 1939.

As the chapters in this volume by Austen and Deschamps illustrate, France during the interwar period stressed economic development rather than political advancement. Henri Cosnier, a longtime colonial civil servant, then a deputy, and finally a senator and member of the Higher Council for Agriculture, toured West Africa in 1918–19 and wrote a detailed report on its agricultural and commercial potential, *L'Ouest africain français: ses ressources agricoles, son organisation économique* (1921). (Cosnier was also highly critical of the instability of government personnel at every level of administration.) The colonial minister shortly thereafter advocated a policy of association for Black Africa, including economic development assisted by the metropole. In the volume which treats the programs presented to Parliament, Albert Sarraut (1923) presents an economic survey, territory-by-territory, and a description of the projects envisioned.

Several studies since World War II have provided detailed views of the transformations wrought by French rule in particular territories during the interwar period. A French sociologist, Georges Balandier (2d ed., 1963, trans. 1970), using an approach that is historically sound, has examined the reactions of the Fang of Gabon and the Bakongo of the French Congo to colonial rule between the 1890s and the 1950s. Based on field work between 1948 and 1951 and on archives of Equatorial Africa, his study compares the reorganization of practically every aspect of life in the two societies within what Balandier calls the "colonial situation." Gilles Sautter (1967) has published an account of the construction of the Congo-Ocean Railroad, 1921–34, in the Congo colony. The enterprise involved forced labor and led to the deaths of seventeen thousand African workers. Jacques Serre (1963) has written an economic and social history of the Grimari district of central Oubangui-Chari from 1907 to 1948. Between 1907 and 1921 the administration forced the Africans to collect rubber in order to pay taxes, and, after that, introduced cotton as a cash crop that could provide the revenue from taxes. For the Haut-Oubangui district within the same colony, Eric de Dampierre's "Coton noir, café blanc" (1960) shows how the administrator Félix Eboué in the 1920s encouraged cotton as a cash crop among the blacks. He encountered opposition from the European rubber companies and from the local sultans who saw their interests threatened. In the same district in the 1930s European planters introduced coffee for export.

Roughly one-third of de Dampierre's massive *Un Ancien Royaume Bandia du Haut-Oubangui* (1967) treats the drastic consequences for Abandia society of European economic exploitation and colonial rule, especially before the Second World War. In detailed sections on French treatment of traditional rulers between 1890 and 1960, he shows that Governor Martial Merlin in 1909 launched a policy of dismembering the three powerful sultanates among the Zande and Nzakara peoples, which led to confusing fragmentation and ineffective administration. Brian Weinstein (1970) has studied Félix Eboué's relations with chiefs while an administrator in the Kouango subdivision of the Oubangui-Chari, 1914–17. While the colonial administration regarded a particular canton chief as Eboué's auxiliary in executing its policies, the ordinary Africans looked upon this chief as the main actor in the situation and viewed his actions primarily in terms of local rivalries and problems.

In his study of neighboring Chad, Jacques Le Cornec (1963) examined different types of traditional authorities—those of the small acephalous groups in Sara country, the strongly centralized and hierarchized sultanate of Ouaddai, and the intermediate sultanates of Baguirmi and Kanem. He describes how the French from 1900 on transformed the chiefs from independent rulers into subordinates and functionaries, everywhere cutting down the powers and territory of the sultans, thus ultimately creating both customary and administrative *chefferies.* Frederick C. Thomas (1959) studied the Juhaina Arabs of Chad during the interwar period. He describes how the French tried to invest certain chiefs with considerable authority, but without much success. In 1932–33 they dismissed several of them, and after World War II passed to direct administration.

A number of works by colonial officials and administrators of the interwar period contain reflections on their overseas experiences and programs and prescriptions for the future. Several of these writings are discussed in some detail in Governor Deschamps's chapter in this volume. Among them are those of Olivier (1931), who served as governor-general of Madagascar in the 1920s, Brévié (1923 and 1935), Delavignette (1931 and 1939), who had extensive experience in West Africa, and Labouret (1930–31), who served in both West Africa and Cameroons. What is common to all of them is the assumption that French colonial rule is to continue for the foreseeable future, and a concern for finding the most effective methods of administration. All of them implicitly reject any à priori or doctrinaire solutions, whether under the rubrics of "assimilation" or "association," and they all adopt a basically empirical approach to the problems they face. An evaluation of the tenure of Marius Moutet as colonial minister by Governor Delavignette, followed by some comments by Moutet himself (1965) is found in a colloquium on Leon Blum as head of the French government in 1936–37. Also useful for understanding the problems faced by colonial administrators and their reactions to them are works by Reste, who was governor in Dahomey from 1929–31 (1934) and then governor-general in Equatorial Africa from 1936–38 (1938); De Santi (1945), who served in Dahomey in the 1930s; and Gaston Joseph (1944), who served in the Ivory Coast. Of further value is the account of the military officer who helped to bring many of the hinterland tribes of the Somali Coast under French administration, Alphonse Lippmann (1953). A comparable work by Henri J. E. Gouraud (1943) is the account of French penetration and pacification of the desert tribes.

A further category of writing is what one might call *exposé.* Nearly all of these appeared in the interwar period and concerned Equatorial Africa, where the abuses of colonial rule seem to have been the greatest. Among the most important are the fictionalized account of Oubangui-Chari by the West-Indian-born administrator, René Maran, *Batouala* (1921), and that of Denise Moran, *Tchad* (1934), based on three years' residence there. The abuses of the concessionaires and the administration are the subject of the works of André Gide (1927 and

1928), Albert Londres (1929), and Pierre Fontaine (1943). A work by Marcel Homet (1934) deals with the abuses that occurred in the building of the Pointe-Noire–Brazzaville railroad, including the death of seventeen thousand laborers.

A number of other works by Frenchmen from the interwar period itself are helpful for an understanding of French rule. A study by Jean Runner (1927) discusses the political rights of the subjects of the French colonies, including the application of the *indigénat.* René Mercier (1933) takes up the juridical and legal aspects of forced labor. Albert Duchêne (1938) deals with the finances of the overseas territories. Georges Spitz, a onetime governor in Niger, provides an account of the Niger irrigation project at Sansanding in his study published shortly after the war (1949). Also important are nine volumes prepared by the Direction des Troupes Coloniales of the War Ministry for the international colonial exposition of 1931. Among them are military histories of French forces in West Africa, Equatorial Africa, Madagascar, the Cameroons, and Togo. Other volumes describe the colonial troops during the First World War and give biographies of important French colonial officers.

During the 1920s two works appeared in English which still have value. Stephen Roberts, an Australian, made a detailed analysis and an overall assessment of French rule from the beginning of the Third Republic through 1925. An American scholar, Raymond Leslie Buell (1928), visited most of the French territories and reported on their administration in detail in his massive two-volume work. In a chapter on the Empire since 1914, Roberts discusses the French realization of the economic and military importance of Africa to their war effort and the resulting need for economic planning and development in the overseas areas. He also contends that the circumstances of the war, in which the Allies condemned the Germans as morally unfit to rule colonies, gave new importance to the *moral* aspect of French rule and tended to give support to the policy of association, which was already in the ascendance. Buell also discusses the evolution of colonial theory and policy, in particular the association advocated by Vignon and Sarraut. Buell is a vigorous critic of the policy of assimilation, both in theory and in practice. He further provides useful comparative data on expenditures in the 1920s by French, British, and Belgian territories, and on African opposition to French policies, in particular in the two mandates.

One additional work by an American scholar, Herbert Ingram Priestly's *France Overseas: A Study of Modern Imperialism* (1938), has the merit of presenting the evolution of the French Empire from the Restoration through the mid-1930s and thereby placing the interwar period in a longer perspective than Roberts. But it lacks the detailed analyses of Roberts and Buell on individual territories.

Finally, the beginnings of African politics both in Africa and in France during the interwar period have been the subject of recent studies. G. Wesley Johnson's *The Emergence of Black Politics in Senegal* (1971) deals with Senegalese politics between 1900 and 1920. In an article (1966) Johnson has examined the parliamentary career of Blaise Diagne, Senegal's black deputy between 1914 and 1934. Charles Cros (1961) has reproduced many of Diagne's speeches and parliamentary interventions. Robert W. July in his study of West African thought (1968) treats the Senegalese situation and Diagne's career. In a brief article Irving L. Markovitz (1969) discusses the political thought of Diagne and the jurist and Socialist politician Lamine Gueye (1891–1968). Gueye has recorded his personal recollections of politics during the interwar period (1955 and 1966).

Although Diagne attended the Paris session of the Second Pan-African Conference in 1921, he declared that his loyalty to France came ahead of his loyalty to other blacks. Professor Rayford W. Logan of Howard University has preserved his reminiscences of the meetings in "The Historical Aspects of Pan-Africanism, 1900–1945" in the AMSAC's *Pan-Africanism Reconsidered* (1962). Jabez Ayodele Langley has published an article, "Pan-Africanism in Paris, 1924–1936" (1969), which describes the activities of militant anticolonialists, mainly from Senegal and Dahomey, in Paris. Hostile to Diagne for his accommodations with colonialism, they had ties with both Garveyists and the Marxist Pan-Africanist George Padmore. Langley has drawn a second article "Garveyism and African Nationalism" (1969) from his Edinburgh thesis (1968), which examines the interaction of French and Senegalese politics between 1900 and 1945 as part of a study of Pan-Africanism. The Oxford doctoral dissertation of James S. Spiegler (1968) treats African politics in Paris between 1921 and 1939.

John Ballard in "The Porto-Novo Incidents of 1923: Politics in the Colonial Era" (1966) treats African politics in the Dahomeyan port. Ruth Schachter-Morgenthau (1964) shows the extension of politics to the gallicized elite throughout West Africa during the Popular Front era. Michael Crowder (1968) has synthesized much of the existing literature on interwar African politics and protests against French rule.

For Equatorial Africa, Comé Manckasa's *troisième cycle* thesis (1966) treats the activities of André Matsoua and his followers and their relationship with the colonial administration. Marc Michel (1966) has studied the origins of the 1928 revolt in the Haute-Sangha.

THE PERIOD OF WORLD WAR II, 1939–1945.

World War II weakened the political and ideological foundations of French rule in Africa. Free French recognition of this situation led to the government-sponsored conference at Brazzaville in January–February 1944 to discuss colonial reforms. But most of the literature which appeared during and shortly after the war gives little attention to the effects of the war upon the Africans or to colonial rule during the conflict. Contemporary works more often concerned the impact of the war in Europe upon the colonies, the Free French–Vichy struggle, the British role and intervention, and the military operations in Africa. For the most part it was left to studies undertaken in the 1950s, concerned with the postwar evolution of the various territories, to examine the decolonizing forces set in motion by the war.

The novelist Maurice Martin du Gard in *La Carte impériale: Histoire de la France outre-mer, 1940–1945* (1949) provides a vivid account of the French in Africa between the armistice of June 1940 and the close of the war in September 1945. He presents chapters on all the French territories, taking up the Free French–Vichy conflict and relations with the British. There are lively portraits of the personalities involved in the rallying of Equatorial Africa, including René Pleven and Félix Eboué, and a detailed analysis of the motives for their actions. Although largely undocumented, the work rests on many interviews and makes an important contribution to an understanding of the period. The history of Vichy, 1940–44, by Robert Aron (1954) discusses events in Africa in the European context.

There are also works on Free French activities, both in general and in individual territories. *The Complete War Memoirs of General de Gaulle* (1968; French originals 1950, 1954, 1959) presents the general's views of his own role, while the memoirs of Generals Henri Giraud (1949) and Maxime Weygand (1950 and after) look at events from different perspectives. One of the most detailed accounts of the Free French movement is the two-volume work (1947 and 1950) by the anthropologist and Fourth Republic politician, Jacques Soustelle. The first volume, which covers the period 1940–42, has much useful data on Africa. A recent two-volume work by the journalist Claude Paillat (1966) throws light on the factional struggles within the French war effort at Algiers after 1942, including the African aspects.

For Equatorial Africa and the Cameroons Surgeon-General Adolphe

Sicé (1946) provides a clear but not entirely objective narrative of the Free French movement. René Labat (1941) tells of the Free French takeover in Gabon as does the pro-Vichy author, Jacques Mordal, in an article a decade later (1951). Pierre O. Lapie (1943), a wartime governor of Chad, discusses Free French activities there and the formation of General Leclerc's army. The campaigns of Leclerc, who led the French forces into Libya and Tunisia from their base in Chad, are recounted by General F. J. J. Ingold, *L'Epopée Leclerc au Sahara, 1940–1943* (1945). In 1946 Ingold published a good general work on the Free French during the war with emphasis on the military aspects, including African participation. The rallying of Equatorial Africa to Free France and the campaigns of Leclerc are the subject of a recent eyewitness account by Raymond Dronne, *Le Serment de Koufra* (1965).

There are several contemporary accounts of the war in French West Africa. Paul M. Atkins, an American who was there, published two articles in 1942 on the effects of the war throughout the federation. In the second he described the reactions of the Dakar population to the British bombardment of their city in September 1940 and to the subsequent blockade. An official Vichy account of the events is found in the Haut-Commissariat de l'Afrique Française, *L'Agression de Dakar* (1940). Ernest Louveau, head of the Upper Volta, relates his unsuccessful attempts to convince Vichy's Governor-General Pierre Boisson to rally to the side of de Gaulle in *"Au Bagne": Entre les griffes de Vichy et de la milice* (1947). Pro-Vichy accounts of the battle of Dakar and Vichy policies in West Africa are found in Daniel Chenet's *Qui a sauvé l'Afrique* (1949) and Jacques Mordal's *La Bataille de Dakar* (1956). Abdel-Kader Diagne describes Free French underground activities in Senegal and neighboring areas of French West Africa in his unpublished study, *La Résistance française au Sénégal et en A.O.F. pendant la guerre, 1939–1945* (1949). Michael Crowder (1968) has provided an excellent brief account of the war in French West Africa, including the economic impact of the conflict.

The British occupation of Madagascar is the subject of a long chapter (pp. 208–41) in the official work of Lord Rennell of Rodd, *British Military Administration of Occupied Territories in Africa, 1941–1947* (1948). Armand Annet, a Vichy official in Madagascar, has provided information on the Free-French–Vichy struggle there and in Gabon in his *Aux heures troublées de l'Afrique française, 1939–1943* (1952). Both Jacques Mordal (1951) and Henry de Monfried (1958) have written accounts of the war at Djibouti. The latter examines the effects of

French relations with Italy and Ethiopia in the thirties on the internal history of Somaliland.

French rule of Africa during the war and the changes in French thinking and practice influenced by the war have been the subjects of several contemporary and many later works. The Vichy regime in West Africa abolished the representative institutions for Africans and reduced the black citizens of the four communes of Senegal to the status of subjects. The Vichy governor-general, Pierre Boisson, issued three directives on these matters in August 1941, which are quoted by Governor Deschamps in his study of doctrine (1953, p. 177). Little special material has so far been written about the African policies of the Vichy regime.

On the Free French side, the wartime study by Jean de la Roche and Jean Gottmann (1945) of the Empire at war contains the complete text of Governor-General Félix Eboué's circular of November 8, 1941, "La Nouvelle Politique indigène pour l'A.E.F." (pp. 581–627). (An English translation was published at Lagos in 1942.) A speech of Eboué, published at Brazzaville in 1943, throws further light on his thinking concerning reforms as well as the wartime situation. De la Roche and Gottman also provide detailed information on Eboué's role in formulating a new native policy for France as does the study by Michel Devèze (1948) on the transformation of the French Empire into the French Union. Additional information on Eboué's wartime career and role in policy formulation can be found in the biographies by de la Roche (1957), René Maran (1957), and Elrich Sophie (1950). The recent biography of Eboué by Brian Weinstein provides even fuller data on the background of Eboué's policies. The *Mémoires* of Edgard de Larminat (1962), a Free French official at Brazzaville, give further insights into the period.

Details on the Brazzaville Conference can be found in de la Roche and Gottman, and in Devèze. The texts of the conference were published in several places, by the French government at Brazzaville and Algiers (1944) under the title *La Conférence africaine française,* and in *Renaissances* (Algiers, October 1944, pp. 209–35). Devèze discusses the evolution of the colonial policy of Free France from 1941 to 1945, taking in the North African countries as well as those in Black Africa. The most incisive and comprehensive brief account of French colonial policies during World War II is found in the volume of Rudolph von Albertini on decolonization (1966).

CONSTITUTIONAL AND POLITICAL ASPECTS, 1945–1960.

World War II led to a new relationship between France and Black Africa which was institutionalized in the French Union of 1946. The colonies became Overseas Territories of the Fourth Republic and the mandates, which became trust territories in December 1946, Associated Territories of the French Union. Both types of territories acquired representation in the legislative organs of the Republic and Union. Local assemblies, comparable to the departmental *conseils-généraux*, were established in each territory and municipal government was further extended.

The constitutional framework for African advancement erected in 1946 lasted without significant reforms until April 1957, when decrees implementing the *Loi-Cadre* of June 23, 1956 established a degree of genuine self-government at the territorial level in the Overseas Territories. (The reforms for the Associated Territories were embodied in separate measures). The reformed territorial institutions lasted only until September 1958 because the May 1958 revolution led to the subsequent collapse of the Fourth Republic. The French Community which was established under the Fifth Republic never became fully functional as the African territories moved towards independence during 1960.

There is a sizable contemporary literature on the transformation of the French Empire into the French Union. The works of Michel Devèze (1948) and Henri Brunschwig (1949) and an article by Charles-André Julien (1950) provide interpretive accounts of this period from an historical perspective. A historical study by an American scholar, Gordon Wright, *The Reshaping of French Democracy* (1948), reveals what a small percentage of attention was given to colonial matters in the two Constituent Assemblies of 1945–46.

Among the best works on Black Africa within the French Union written by French scholars prior to the *Loi-Cadre* are the clear, incisive study by Henri Culmann (1950), the long article by the jurist Pierre Lampué (1947), the collection by Daniel Boisdon et al. (1949), the textbook of Hubert Deschamps (1952), and the booklet in English by the liberal General Georges Catroux (1953). All of them benefit from the government service of their authors. The British political scientist Kenneth Robinson published a fine brief study of the 1946 Constitution, *The Public Law of Overseas France since the War* (rev. ed. 1954), and two important articles on the political evolution, "Political Development in French West Africa" (1953) and "French Africa and the French Union" (1955). Articles by the Senegalese deputy

Léopold Senghor on the need to reform the Union along federal lines are instructive for African thinking throughout the period. The personal reminiscences of the Senegalese socialist deputy, Lamine Guèye (1955 and 1966) give another African view of the entire era.

There are several important studies of the constitutional and political evolution of the French Union or its Black African components published prior to the May 1958 revolution but covering nearly the entire period of the Fourth Republic. Among the most important is that of François Borella, *L'Evolution juridique et politique de l'Union Française* (1958), which examines the evolution of the entire French Union in relation to the legal texts by which it was instituted. In Borella's view many of the provisions were inspired more by a desire to design a facade that masked the continuation of the colonial relationship than by a determination to create a framework for decolonization. As an involuntary association not based on mutual confidence and merely placing French domination in a new setting, it could not endure. Borella's study has the special merit of showing the influence of developments in other parts of the French Union upon the evolution of Black Africa, and within Black Africa, of the trust territories upon the Overseas Territories. P. F. Gonidec's *L'Evolution des territoires d'outre-mer depuis 1946* (1957–58) discusses Black Africa in the same period as Borella. Gonidec contends that the *Loi-Cadre* represents an abandonment of the policies of centralization and assimilation and the adoption of forms of autonomy in the Overseas Territories. In *Les Institutions politiques et administratives des territoires d'outre-mer après la loi-cadre* (1958) François Luchaire describes the institutions established by the decrees of April 1957, showing how they established a kind of self-government at the territorial level for the first time.

The Associated Territories of the French Union, the Cameroons, and Togoland, were also United Nations trust territories. Thus there is a body of literature on their status and evolution within both the United Nations and the French systems. A brief but excellent article by Richard J. Kozicki, "The United Nations and Colonialism" (1958), and the study by Emil Sady, *The United Nations and Dependent Peoples* (1956), provide the general setting for international supervision of French administration. The most detailed account of the making of the trusteeship agreements is found in R. N. Chowdhuri's *International Mandates and Trusteeship Systems: A Comparative Study* (1955), with briefer accounts in James N. Murray, Jr., *The United Nations Trusteeship System* (1957) and Charmian E. Toussaint, *The Trusteeship System of the United Nations* (1956).

The status of the two territories within the French Union is treated by the jurist Pierre Lampué (1951). The international status of the territories and criticism in the UN of the French policy of treating them as if they were parts of the French Republic are examined by several French scholars: Pierre O. Lapie (1950), André Homont (1952), A. Mathiot (1948–49 and 2 vols., 1950). At the request of the General Assembly, the Trusteeship Council studied the trust territories' inclusion in the French Union. The report has been published as United Nations, General Assembly, *Official Records: Seventh Session, Supplement No. 12* (A/2151). *Special Report of the Trusteeship Council on Administrative Unions Affecting Trust Territories and on the Status of the Cameroons and Togoland under French Administration Arising out of Their Membership in the French Union* (New York, 1952). The Council concluded that there was no evidence to indicate that the practical operation of the administrative arrangements of the Cameroons and Togo was incompatible with the UN Charter and the Trusteeship Agreements. But it stated that their separate status should be maintained with a view to final self-government or independence.

The application of the trusteeship system to the Cameroons and the first years of UN supervision are treated in the Montpellier thesis of Paul Blanc (1953). UN supervision of French administration of the Cameroons, 1946–59, is recounted in the doctoral dissertation of David E. Gardinier (Yale University, 1960) and in summary in his book (1963).

There are no comparable studies of UN supervision of Togoland. But the studies by James Coleman (1956) and Claude Welch (1966) describe United Nations' involvement in the Ewe and Togoland unification issues. The reports of several UN visiting missions (1949, 1952, 1955) and *Special Report on the Ewe and Togoland Unification Problem* (1950) provide further information on these matters and on supervision in general.

The structure and functioning of French African territorial assemblies and municipal institutions between 1946 and 1956, including the participation of Africans, is the subject of several studies. The Paris thesis of Albert Béville (1950) examined the assemblies in all Black African territories during the 1940s as did P. F. Gonidec through the early 1950s (1952–53). Bernard Jouvin (1949) studied the territorial assembly of the Cameroons during its first three years of operation. All these scholars found that the territorial assemblies, though endowed with decision-making powers primarily in the area of the territorial budgets, actually exerted great practical influence in areas where their powers were only advisory. An article by J. Ravenal (1951) treated the

French Conseil d'Etat's supervision of the assemblies. The Paris thesis of André Heurot (1948) compared the composition of the first assemblies in French territories with that of comparable bodies in British territories, including non-African ones. L. Gray Cowan (1958) compares the political systems, including territorial and municipal government, of French West Africa and Nigeria. Charles Cros (1956) has examined the status of African and Malagasy municipalities prior to the November 1955 municipal reforms. David Gardinier (1966) has studied Duala opposition between 1944 and 1955 to municipal reforms which threatened their hegemony in the Douala city government.

The Paris thesis of S. K. Diagne (1950) deals with the first *grands conseils* of West and Equatorial Africa, that is, the federation-level bodies elected by the territorial assemblies to represent them in Dakar and Brazzaville respectively. Robert Bourcart in 1956 published his study of the functioning of the *grand conseil* of French West Africa.

While the Africans in 1946 acquired majority representation in the territorial and municipal institutions which voted local budgets, legislative power remained in the hands of Frenchmen who dominated the parliament in Paris. Similarly, executive power both in Paris and in the territories remained in the hands of Frenchmen until the reforms of April 1957 placed some executive power in African hands at the territorial level. The Paris thesis of Yves Blin (1954) treated the structure and functioning of the Overseas Ministry during almost the first decade after World War II. Alain Gandolfi in *L'Administration territoriale en Afrique Noire de langue française* (1959) presents a good analysis of the administrative system at the territorial and local levels, including their relations with the territorial assemblies and their members as they existed prior to the 1957 reforms. For all aspects of the French system of government and administration in Black Africa, the best works with excellent bibliographies are those of Pierre Lampué, *Précis de droit des pays d'outre-mer;* P. F. Gonidec, *Droit d'Outre-Mer,* vol. 1 (1959); François Luchaire (1949 and 1951 supplement) and Borella (1958).

With the advantage of hindsight, historians who have turned their attention to French Black Africa in the period 1945–60 have been able to view it as the age of decolonization. As yet no historian has attempted to look at the totality of colonial rule or to synthesize the existing literature on the scale which Michael Crowder has done for all of West Africa, 1885–1945, or which Jean Suret-Canale has attempted, with less detail, for all of French Black Africa. Those who have studied various aspects of colonial rule have in some instances obtained access to archival materials in Africa, but the archival records in France are still unavailable. Therefore, historians have had to rely upon published documents, unpublished studies by administrators, and interviews with the actors of the period, as well as a great variety of published secondary sources.

The aspect of colonial rule receiving the most attention has been the political evolution which led to self-government and independence for all territories except the Somali Coast between 1958 and 1961. Franz Ansprenger in *Politik im Schwarzen Afrika* (1961) presents the political and constitutional evolution of French Black Africa between the Second World War and independence from a historical perspective. He supplies clear accounts of the rise of the large interterritorial movements like the RDA, MSA, and PRA, as well as of the relations between the African and metropolitan parties. He furnishes a good account of Guinea's secession from the French framework. René Viard in *La Fin de l'empire colonial français* (1963) interprets the history of the entire French Union from the Brazzaville Conference to independence and *coopération* in the early 1960s. He examines the relationship of the Algerian war to Black African developments.

Ruth Schachter Morgenthau's *Political Parties in French-Speaking West Africa* (1964) covers the entire period of decolonization but is most detailed for 1944–56, that is, prior to the *Loi-Cadre*. She treats the development of political parties at the territorial, federation, and metropolitan (French) levels. Her coverage is especially detailed for Senegal, Mali, Guinea, and the Ivory Coast. She shows how modern politics began with the Popular Front's encouragement of African activity. In her view the French concept of a permanent union between France and Africa led to an institutional framework that provided a political education in organization and tactics for the Africans. African representatives were legitimately able also to form ties with metropolitan parties and federation-wide movements which foundered one after the other in the face of pressures for genuine self-government at the territorial level. Michael Crowder in "Independence as a Goal in French West African Politics, 1944–1960" (1965) contends that French assimilation policy, involving extension of French culture to the elite and African participation in the central organs of the Republic, delayed demands for independence until the crises of 1958–60.

Edward Mortimer's *France and the Africans, 1944–1960* (1969) is a fuller development of the studies of Morgenthau and Ansprenger, with the benefit of more hindsight and the papers of several important political figures, including Dr. Louis-Paul Aujoulat, who represented the

Cameroons in the French National Assembly. Mortimer focuses upon the politics of the relationship between France and its Black African territories between the end of the Second World War and complete independence in 1960. (He omits Madagascar.) He discusses the consequences of the political assimilation of the African territories into the French Republic with African participation in the central institutions. Taking up the development of politics in each individual territory and in the two federations in relation to the center, he tries to show why the idea of independence took the forms that it ultimately did. This very readable work is a good place to start for understanding the evolution that led from integration to independence. A good brief account in French for the same period is Jean Debay's *Evolutions en Afrique noire* (1962).

Two works on decolonization in the twentieth century include sections on Afrique Noire after the Second World War. Henri Grimal in *La Décolonisation, 1919–1963* (1966) deals with Asia as well as Africa and thereby shows the global setting for French African developments. Rudolph von Albertini (1966) examines the relationships that the colonial powers sought to establish with their colonies, and the administrative systems employed to implement their goals, and then analyzes various concepts of decolonization which challenged them.

The liberal Catholic journalist, Ernest Milcent, who was based in Togo and Senegal during the postwar period, published a work rich in personal observations, *L'A.O.F. entre en scène* (1958). He deals with the political evolution of French West Africa, and particularly Senegal, from the Brazzaville Conference to the *Loi-Cadre* of June 23, 1956. He shows that the emancipation on the level of local institutions, envisioned at Brazzaville but really implemented with the *Loi-Cadre,* was paralleled by the emancipation of local parties and trade unions from the metropolitan ones. A booklet by Thomas Hodgkin and Ruth Schachter Morgenthau (dated May 1960, published in 1961) deals succinctly with the entire postwar period in French West Africa through the formation of the French Community. Philip Neres's *French-Speaking Africa: From Colonial Status to Independence* (1964) is a brief account of French colonial policy and the events leading to independence.

The works of Virginia Thompson and Richard Adloff on *French West Africa* (1957), *French Equatorial Africa* (1960), *The Malagasy Republic* (1965), and *Djibouti and the Horn* (1968) are important for understanding the postwar political evolution of French Black Africa. The first was written prior to the *Loi-Cadre,* the second prior to the independence of the Equatorial states; but they have the merit of providing detailed accounts of political evolution in the individual territories and in the federations based upon interviews and nearly all of the published sources at the time.

Robert Delavignette's *L'Afrique Noire Française et son destin* (1962) is an insider's account of the evolution of Black Africa from 1920 to 1962. A longtime colonial administrator and governor, Delavignette provides a good discussion of the constitutional changes and major political decisions. He criticizes the decisions of 1945–46 which made French West Africa and French Equatorial Africa integral parts of the Fourth Republic. He preferred the extension of the system of the Third Republic, which left the colonies outside the Republic and gave colonial administrators who were in direct contact with Africans greater leeway in making decisions. He criticizes the manner of decolonization, which had its roots in an ignoble *cartierisme* and has reduced African to the state of a *clochard.* He favors aid to restore French honor and African well-being. Delavignette's essay "French Colonial Policy in Black Africa, 1945–1960" authoritatively interprets the postwar period while giving more specific data than the longer work. The journalist George Chaffard in *Les Carnets secrets de la décolonisation* (1965) presents many of the behind-the-scenes and backstairs details of the political decisions that led to independence. While his reports seem reliable, they are not usually the kind that can be documented.

There are quite a number of accounts which concentrate on political evolution from the implementation of the *Loi-Cadre* to the demise of the French Community. Gil Dugué's *Vers les Etats-Unis d'Afrique* (1960) contains a history of the French territories from the 1956 reforms to the formation of the Mali Federation with much detail on the political forces at work for and against supraterritorial unions. Part of the same period is covered in the work of *Le Monde's* correspondent, André Blanchet, *L'Itinéraire des partis africains depuis Bamako* (1958). He treats the political evolution of French Black Africa from the RDA conference of September 1957 at Bamako, where the future of French West Africa as a unit and relations with France were discussed, through the May 1958 revolution, which made a rapid and radical reorientation in Franco-African relations possible. W. A. E. Skurnik's "France and Fragmentation in West Africa, 1945–1960" (1967) shows the forces that acted against the maintenance of the federation or its revival between 1956 and 1960. A Cameroon scholar, Meinrad Hegba (1968), looks at the political and economic evolution of all the French territories after 1945 from the point of view of the attempted and successful regroupings that have occurred in the decade since independence. Léo Hamon's *Introduction à l'étude des partis politiques de l'Afrique française* (1959 and 1961) deals primarily with the periods between 1956 and 1961 which gave rise to new interterritorial groupings in an attempt to offset the "balkanization" institutionalized by the *Loi-Cadre* reforms. An important article by Marcel Merle, "La Constitution et les problèmes d'outre-mer" (March 1959), treats the Franco-African politics that led to the constitutional arrangements for the French Community in the Fifth Republic.

There are two detailed works which concentrate upon the origins of the Community. Frédéric Dumon's *La Communauté franco-afro-malgache: Ses origines, ses institutions, son évolution, octobre 1958-juin 1960* (1960) deals with the evolution of the French Union from 1946 to 1958 as a background for the birth and evolution of the French Community. It presents the positions of the African leaders before and during the elaboration of the constitution of the Fifth Republic. Another study by the Belgian P. Pierson-Mathy, published the following year, *L'Evolution politique de l'Afrique*, concentrates upon the evolution of the new states of French Africa from the formation of the Community through its disintegration, and thus nicely complements Dumon. Léopold Senghor's "Nationhood: Report on the Doctrine and Program of the Party of African Federation" (1964) reveals the Senegalese president's thinking on these matters as of July 1959.

Within Africa itself William Foltz, *From French West Africa to Mali Federation* (1965) studies the forces in the former administrative federation that gave rise to the Mali Federation and led to its breakup. He contends that the federation between Senegal and the Sudan failed above all because the political elites of each territory saw greater advantages in separation than in continued union. The Paris thesis of Michel Fatoux (1959) dealt with the birth of Mali and that of Pierre Gam (1965) with its breakup.

A thesis by André Angsthelm (1965) studies the changing political role of the civil service in French Africa. Under colonial rule until 1956 the bureaucracy supported French dominance. Between 1956 and 1960, it aided the political emancipation of the African countries. After 1960 it served as an instrument of national development. Angsthelm noted that the civil service has always had a political character which pushes it to intervene in every sector of economic and social activity in the overseas territories.

There is a large number of works that deal with decolonization in one country, not always as the main subject of the book. Alfred Gerteiny's *Mauritania* (1967) has several good chapters on the postwar political evolution of Mauritania, insufficiently related to the federation and metropolitan levels. Francis G. Snyder in *One-Party Government in Mali: Transition towards Control* (1965) describes the formation of the Union Soudanaise and its rise to power. In his view the party's success resulted from good organization, a common aim, and a well-defined political ideology. For the Upper Volta, Elliott Skinner (1964) discusses the post-1945 changes that ended the isolation of the Mossi people and weakened the power of their chiefs, profoundly disorienting a society that had remained cohesive for centuries. The rise to power of the Western-educated elite and the transition to independence are described in the final chapter. François Djoby Bassolet (1968) has written on the entire period 1898–1966. For Niger, the final chapter of Edmond Séré de Rivière's history discusses the postwar political evolution briefly. Much more detailed and analytical is "Niger" by Virginia Thompson (1966). There are useful personal reminiscences in Pierre Bonardi's *La République du Niger: Naissance d'un état* (1960). A thesis by Finr Fuglestad (Aix, 1967) examines the origins of anti-colonialism and the movements for self-government and independence.

The literature on the political evolution of the coastal territories is much larger than that on the interior ones. Michael Crowder in *Senegal: A Study in French Assimilation Policy* (2d ed., 1967) discusses the policy of assimilation and the Senegalese intellectual and political reactions to it, in particular after the Second World War. He presents an excellent analysis of the French and Levantine settlers as social groups in an African society. Ernest Milcent's "Senegal," in G. Carter, ed., *African One-Party States* (1962) gives a brief account of the postwar period. In *Au carrefour des options africaines: le Sénégal* (1965) Milcent discusses the transition from colonial rule to independence. Dimitri Georges Lavroff's *La République du Sénégal* (1966) concentrates upon the period of independence but provides interpretive background on the colonial era, especially the post-1945 period. Kenneth E. Robinson's "Senegal: The Elections to the Territorial Assembly, March 1957" (1960) traces the postwar evolution of political parties. Paul Mercier, a French sociologist, relates political developments to social change in two articles, "Evolution of Senegalese Elites" (1956) and "Political Life in the Urban Centers of Senegal: A Study of a Period of Transition" (1960).

Bakary Traoré analyzed the evolution of political parties since 1946 and Mamadou Lo examined the development of Léopold Senghor's

Union Progressiste Sénégalaise in Bakary Traoré, Mamadou Lo, and Jean-Louis Alibert's *Forces politiques en Afrique Noire* (1966). M. G. Devez (1960) compares the political evolution of Senegal, Ivory Coast, and Guinea between 1944 and 1959. The Paris thesis of Jack Louis Hymans (1964) discusses the intellectual development of President Senghor and in the process throws much light on his political leadership. Irving L. Markovitz in *Léopold Sédar Senghor and the Politics of Negritude* (1969) discusses the changing social functions of negritude as an ideology, which Senghor helped to elaborate, after 1931. Markovitz contends that negritude became an instrument for furthering collaboration between French and African elites. In an article (1969) Markovitz analyzes the political thought and actions of Blaise Diagne and Lamine Guèye in Franco-Senegalese life. He contends that Senghor incorporated into his own political style the former's accommodation with traditionalist groups and colonialism, and the latter's willingness to accept French rule as the framework for reform and advancement.

Finally, two mainly historical works should be mentioned. Hubert Deschamps's *Le Sénégal et la Gambie* (1964) is a stimulating interpretive account based on firsthand experience. Deschamps was governor of Senegal in 1943 after the fall of Vichy and led the battle to increase groundnut production. The *Histoire moderne et contemporaine du Sénégal* (1966) by Félix Brigaud treats the entire period of French rule, but adds little that cannot be found in Villard (1943).

L. Gray Cowan's "Guinea" in G. Carter, ed. *African One-Party States* (1962), contains a good account of the postwar period and the transition to independence. More detailed are the unpublished doctoral dissertations of Victor D. DuBois (1962) and John W. Ryan (1966). DuBois draws upon his thesis for two articles (1962) on Guinea's postwar political evolution and the September 1958 referendum. Diabate Boubacar, *Porte ouverte sur la Communauté Franco-Africaine* (1961) reproduces many of the documents in Sékou Touré's confrontation with de Gaulle on the issue of independence. A short work by a Swiss journalist, Fernand Gigon, *Guinée, état pilote* (1959) gives the immediate background and consequences of the break with France.

A recent work by the Marxist historian Jean Suret-Canale, *La République de Guinée* (1970), incorporates and expands upon his earlier article "La Guinée dans le système colonial" (1959–60). His accounts provide good antidotes to official histories. Suret-Canale's article, "La Fin de la Chefferie en Guinée" (1966) presents the thesis that the first Guinean government's abolition of the chiefs, instituted by the French administration, resulted from a profound popular movement to which the Parti Démocratique de Guinée responded. Its suppression, in turn, helped to make possible the "no" vote in the September 1958 referendum.

Two documentary collections by the PDG have much value for revealing Guinean views of the political evolution of the country in the 1950s. *Guinée, Prélude à l'indépendance* (1959) contains the debates in July 1957 at the conference of *commandants de cercle* with the new *conseil d'administration* on various questions, including suppression of the canton chiefs, local customary justice, and taxes. *L'Expérience guinéenne et l'unité africaine* (1959) contains speeches and statements of Sékou Touré, including data on the entire postwar period. Bernard Charles (1962) has written an important article on the organization and ideas of the PDG in the late 1950s as well as a general work on the country (1963) which contains much of the same data. The University of Denver dissertation of W. J. Le Melle (1963) analyzes the political philosophy of Sékou Touré.

An appraisal of French colonial rule in the Ivory Coast including the postwar period is found in the *mémoire* of Cragbe-Gnagbe, *Réflexions sur la colonisation française en Côte d'Ivoire* (1967). Virginia Thompson's "The Ivory Coast," in G. Carter, ed., *African One-Party States* (1962) contains a good brief account of the country's postwar evolution. An African scholar, F. J. Amon d'Aby, in *La Côte d'Ivoire dans la Cité Africaine* (1951) gives a firsthand account of the political scene in the early postwar years, including the changes brought by Brazzaville and formation of the French Union; but his descriptions of political affairs reveal a strong anti-RDA bias. An important article by M. Vignaud deals with the January 1956 elections (1956). Aristide Zolberg's *One-Party Government in the Ivory Coast* (1964) provides a political history of the postwar period based on little known and hard-to-get documents. He concentrates upon the Parti Democratique de la Côte d'Ivoire, showing how it originated in 1945 as a "congress" of affiliated associations, how subsequently it was remodeled to withstand the assault of the colonial administration, how in 1952–55 it became a political machine concerned with winning elections, and how finally it turned into an instrument of government. Zolberg relates political events to ethnic and social tensions. In an interesting comparative study of Ghana and the Ivory Coast (1964) Immanuel Wallerstein examines the role of voluntary associations and modern elites in the social and political transformations of the postwar period, and in particular their relations to the nationalist movement.

A recent work by a Dahomeyan, Maurice A. Glélé's *Naissance d'un état noir: L'évolution politique et constitutionnelle du Dahomey, de la colonisation à nos jours* (1969), is essentially a history of politics and political parties from 1944 to 1965. It includes valuable party documents and constitutional texts for the period 1944–59. Also in French, the sections of Robert Cornevin's history of Dahomey on the period after 1939 (1962) are detailed and useful. In English the postwar political evolution is treated in detail by Virginia Thompson's "Dahomey," in G. Carter, ed., *Five African States* (1963), and in Martin Staniland's unpublished thesis at the University of Ghana, which concerns political history, 1945–57.

Souran M. Apithy's speeches and reports have been published as *Au service de mon pays* (1957). They reflect his long service as deputy in Paris and as a territorial leader. Albert Tevoedjré's *L'Afrique révoltée* (1958) is a young Catholic Dahomeyan's attack on French colonialism, which he sees as having few achievements and even fewer benefits for Africans. Although concerned with Black Africa in general, it has valuable material on Dahomey. René Grivot's *Réactions dahoméennes* (1954) deals with Dahomeyan responses to postwar reforms and modernization, and *Dahomey*, by A. Akindélé and C. Aguessy, (1955) contains useful contemporary data though from a semi-official viewpoint.

The trusteeship territory of Togoland received attention from scholars throughout the postwar period because of the appearance soon after the war of the Ewe and Togoland unification movements. A brief study by James S. Coleman, *Togoland* (1956), analyzes those movements, which involved British Togoland and the Gold Coast as well, through May 1956, and is especially good on the subject of United Nations involvement. The story is carried to a conclusion by Claude E. Welch in *Dream of Unity: Pan-Africanism and Political Unification in West Africa* (1966). His account focuses on the role of Ewe nationalism in the evolution of the two Togolands, as does an article by the sociologist Jean-Claude Pauvert, "L'Evolution politique des Ewé" (1960). The reports of several UN Visiting Missions (1949, 1952, 1955) and *Special Report on the Ewe and Togoland Unification Problem* (1950) provide data on the movements as well as on the political evolution of French Togoland. The *Annual Reports of France to the United Nations, 1947–57,* tended to underplay political questions and to give much factual data on economic and social advances.

Edmond-Pierre Luce in *Le Référendum du Togo, 28 octobre 1956* (1958) analyzes the juridical and political status of Togo before and after the referendum which established the trust territory as an "autonomous republic" within the French Union as well as reporting the course and results of the referendum itself. François Luchaire, "Le Togo français de la tutelle à l'autonomie" (1957), is a detailed account of the political and constitutional evolution of Togoland within the French system. The last chapter of Robert Cornevin's history of Togo (1959) and sections in his short general work on Togo (1963) introduce the postwar political evolution of the French territory and carry the story through independence in 1960. Two *mémoires* written by Africans studying in France on the political evolution are Mensah Kodjo's study of Togolese political sociology (1967) and Nicholas Nomedji's comparative study of political parties in Togo and the Cameroons (1966).

The most complete and comprehensive study of the political evolution of the Cameroons from World War II until 1960 is Victor T. LeVine's *The Cameroons from Mandate to Independence* (1964). Modeled after James Coleman's study of Nigerian nationalism, it shows the various historical influences which helped to shape the course of decolonization. Much of the same data, plus some new material on the British Cameroons and the unification of its southern sections with the French Cameroons is found in LeVine's "The Cameroun Federal Republic" in G. Carter, ed., *Five African States* (1963). David E. Gardinier's *Cameroon: United Nations' Challenge to French Policy* (1963) employs archival materials to present an account of the political evolution from 1944 to 1962. It supports the thesis that UN trusteeship both spurred the Cameroons' political advancement and tied it more closely to France. It also presents a brief account of the movement to unify or "reunify" the two Cameroons. The most detailed account of the unification movement and its relation to political emancipation is contained in two chapters in Claude Welch's *Dream of Unity* (1966). Willard R. Johnson's *The Cameroon Federation: Political Integration in a Fragmentary Society* (1970) focuses on unification while also throwing light on the movement prior to independence.

The first Cameroonian to receive a French doctorate in political science, Joseph-Marie Zang-Atangana, devoted his attention to the development of political parties (1963). A portion of his work was summarized in "Les Partis politiques camerounais" (December 1960). The Paris thesis of Abel Eyinga deals with political power in the periods both before and after independence. An article by Paul Blanc (writing under the pseudonym of M. D.) and one by Paul Marie Gaudemet (1958) both deal with the regime of limited self-government established by the Statute of 1957 and the workings of the Mbida and Ahidjo governments prior to the May 1958 Algiers revolution. Another article by Blanc discusses the Statute of January 1, 1959, which established complete internal self-government. P. F. Gonidec, "De la dépendance à l'indépendance" (1957) is a political and constitutional study on the period 1944–57. A monograph by David Gardinier treats Duala resistance to the establishment of democratic municipal government which threatened to diminish their influence in the port city of Douala (1966).

Paul Blanc's *Les Régimes du mandat et de tutelle: leur application au Cameroun* (1953) contains a juridical and legal study of the UN trusteeship. Marcel Nguini (1956) examines the first decade of trusteeship and is highly critical of France's failure to promote greater economic and social advancement and genuine self-government. The Paris thesis of Françoise Pain (1959) gives a clear picture of the economic and social evolution from 1947 to 1959. The *Annual Reports of France to the United Nations, 1947–58,* on administration, provide much factual data, especially on economic and social advances. The reports of several UN Visiting Missions (1949, 1952, 1955, 1958) complement them with data on political questions, including unification

Jacques Lestringant in *Les Pays de Guider au Cameroun, essai d'histoire régionale* (1964) shows how untouched the northern Cameroons was by the political evolution in the south. By contrast, developments in the overpopulated Bamiléké highlands in the west produced an explosive situation that erupted in the wake of the 1955 UPC revolt. Works by Victor Kanga (1959) and Enock Katté Kwayeb (1960) take up the impact of European rule on traditional Bamiléké institutions. Kwayeb in particular perceptively analyzes their modification, including the rapid transformation of family structures and the status of women, the disaggregation of political institutions such as tribal consultative and judicial bodies, and the resistance to the introduction of French land law. Two other works by Europeans, those of Claude Tardits (1960) and J. Hurault (1962), deal with the same material from somewhat different perspectives. Hurault focuses upon the *chefferies,* which lie at the center of the Bamiléké political and social system. The French administration contributed to the deterioration of the traditional system by their policies, which regarded this institution as only transitory. Also basic to the disintegration of the *chefferies* is overpopulation, which forced Bamiléké to emigrate by the thousands to the Mungo Valley and the coast, exposing them to influences that were subversive to the traditional society. Tardits examines the crisis produced by the introduction of representative institutions in 1946. He contends that at the same time the traditional political framework was in a state of disaggregation, the Bamiléké were adjusting to the new economic situation and prospering from it. He shows that the UPC used the agrarian and chiefs' quarrels to its advantage.

The master's thesis of Harold S. Gray (American University, 1967) pulls together many sources on the UPC rebellion with special attention to Chinese Communist involvement. An article by Willard Johnson (1970) provides the best brief account of the *Upéciste* rebellion.

Only a small number of studies deal with the political evolution of the former units of French Equatorial Africa. In addition to the work of Thompson and Adloff (1960) already cited, John Ballard's unpublished doctoral dissertation deals with the development of political parties in the four territories and at the federation level. Ballard utilizes some of this material in "Four Equatorial States," in G. Carter, ed. (1966), which contains the most recent summaries of political developments available in English.

Brian Weinstein in *Gabon: Nation-Building on the Ogooué* (1966) examines the creation of a nation-state in Gabon. An unpublished study by Alain Mauric (1959) deals with political evolution from the *Loi-Cadre* of 1956 to the referendum of September 1958. The *mémoires* of Michel Anchoucy (1965) on politics after 1960 and of Jean-Michel Filippi (1967) on post-1958 politics both have useful data on the period before independence.

Jean-Michel Wagret's *Histoire et sociologie politique de la République du Congo (Brazzaville)* (1963) discusses the political parties and forces that arose in postwar Congo and the course of advancement toward self-government and independence. The unpublished studies of two Congolese—the Catholic journalist Côme Manckasa (1966) and Julien Matongo (1966)—though concerned primarily with the period since independence, also have useful data on the period of decolonization.

Pierre Kalck's *Réalités oubanguiennes* (1959) is a general work which has information on postwar political developments, while his recent Sorbonne thesis concentrates on history alone. The work of Jacques Le Cornec (1963), though primarily concerned with the evolution of the *chefferies,* also has information on development of Chadian political life after 1945. Also useful is the article by Pierre Gentil, "Le Tchad: décolonisation et indépendance" (1969).

The basic work in English for the postwar evolution of Madagascar is the detailed yet interpretive study by Virginia Thompson and Richard Adloff, *The Malagasy Republic* (1965). It contains useful data on the postwar nationalist movement and the 1947 revolt as well as other developments which brought Philippe Tsiranana's regime to power. The last half of Raymond Kent's short work (1962) deals with the postwar period. The general histories by Hubert Deschamps (1960) and Roger Pascal (1965) also have useful accounts from a French viewpoint. A work by a French Communist who was active in Malagasy politics in the late 1940s, Pierre Boiteau's *Contribution à l'histoire de la nation malgache* (1958), has sections on political evolution from a still different perspective. R. Boudry, former secretary-general in the Madagascar administration in the 1940s, who was sympathetic to the nationalist aspirations, has written two articles in *Esprit* (1948 and 1949) on the Malagasy revolt and the trial of the three MDRM deputies. Dominique Otare Mannoni, *La Psychologie de la colonisation* (1950), translated into English as *Prospero and Caliban* (1956), is a French psychologist's explanation of the 1947–48 revolt which he attributes basically to a Malagasy fear of abandonment by the French.

A different viewpoint is presented by leaders of the Mouvement Démocratique de la Rénovation Malgache, the Merina-led nationalist movement which was crushed in the wake of the 1947 revolt. Jacques Rabemananjara is a poet and one of the three MDRM deputies exiled after the rebellion. His *Témoignage malgache et colonialisme* (1956) and *Nationalisme et problèmes malgaches* (1959) give many insights into the period. His brother, Raymond W. Rabemananjara, has written *Madagascar: Histoire de la nation malgache* (1952) and *Madagascar sous la rénovation malgache* (1953) on postwar nationalism and the revolt. Pierre Gentil's *Sur les sentiers malgaches* (1956) is an administrator's view of the French administration and postwar Franco-Malagasy relations.

The most recent work on Madagascar's political evolution is the doctoral thesis of Alain Spacensky, *Les Partis et la vie politique à Madagascar, 1945–1965* (1965), some parts of which have been published in article form, "Regards sur l'évolution politique malgache, 1945–1966" (1967).

In 1967 the tiny territory of French Somaliland became the "French Territory of the Afars and the Issas." The change in name reflected political tensions in the territory that have surfaced mainly since the rest of French Africa became independent. An Overseas Territory during the Fourth Republic, Somaliland became an Overseas Department within the Fifth Republic, which involved a greater degree of integration. In 1967 it received a special status which provided for local self-government within the Republic. *Mémoires* by two French students,

Antoine Noel (1963) and Louis Chapuisat (1967), and an article by R. Chiroux (1968) constitute the chief French studies of the territory's political evolution since 1945. The last of these discusses the department's status after the March 1967 referendum which led to the end of direct administration and the granting of local autonomy. In 1968 Virginia Thompson and Richard Adloff published their *Djibouti and the Horn of Africa,* a general work which includes a long chapter on political developments in the territory.

One aspect of the postwar political evolution which has received special attention from scholars is the situation of the chiefs and traditional structures in general. The French instituted direct rule wherever they could. In the process they turned traditional chiefs into auxiliaries and in many areas established nontraditional canton chiefs. French policy never involved long-range plans for retaining or reforming traditional structures, and those which survived did so largely in spite of official policy.

After the Second World War, the French established representative institutions in Africa—territorial assemblies and municipal and rural councils with expanded powers. While some chiefs were elected to these bodies, and thereby acquired a new basis for their authority, the new system in general set up rivals to the chiefs and further weakened their influence.

There have been a few general studies of the evolution of the *chefferies* during the entire period of colonial rule, of which Jacques Lombard's *Autorités traditionnelles et pouvoirs européens en Afrique Noire* (1967) is probably the most detailed and analytical. Also important are two shorter studies which emphasize developments in the post-1945 era, including the competition of new Western-educated elites: Robert Cornevin's "Evolution des chefferies traditionnelles dans l'Afrique Noire d'expression française," which includes a bibliography of unpublished sources and *mémoires,* and Pierre Alexandre's "Le problème des chefferies en Afrique noire française" (1959). In addition, Alain Gandolfi (1959) in his study of territorial administration discusses the changing situation of the chiefs in local administration in the post-1945 period.

The majority of studies on the evolution of traditional political structures concern only one territory or a particular area or people within it. Many of them are short unpublished studies by French administrators or by Africans studying in France to become administrators. They thus draw upon personal experience and often expertise.

For Chad, where chiefs retained much power and influence, the work of Le Cornec (1963) is the starting point for a study of the postwar evolution of the *chefferies.* Charles Schweisguth (1957) and Jean Duriez (1960) studied the sultanate of Ouaddai in the east, Jean Catala (1954) the Mao area of Kanem, and B. Lopinot the Gambayes of the Logone River Valley. M. La Truffe (1949) has written on the sultanates of Chad.

Jacques Serre has made a general study of the *chefferies* of the Central African Republic. Georges Balandier's study (2d ed. 1963) contains data on the evolution of *chefferies* in Gabon and the Congo.

There is a large literature on the chiefs in the Cameroons, where chiefs in the west and north remained important throughout the postwar period. The studies of Delarozière, Kwayeb, Tardits, and Hurault all deal in various ways with the Bamiléké. The power of the Bamiléké chiefs was weakened and in some cases destroyed in the disorders of the late 1950s and early 1960s. Articles by J. C. Froelich dealt with the Fali and Fulbe of the Adamaoua area of the north during the 1950s. F. Tougeri (1959) discussed the *lamidos* of the north in the face of the country's political evolution while R. Essama (1967) and A. Onana (1959) dealt with the evolution of traditional *chefferies* in the Beti area of the central South. Right after the Second World War H. Auclair (1948) wrote about the deterioration of the *chefferies* in the southern Cameroons. An article by Tchernogog (1953) treated the juridical aspects of the *chefferies.* In 1959 Benôit Balla treated the traditional *chefferies* throughout the entire country.

In West Africa, Mossi areas, where chiefs retained much power, have been studied. Elliott Skinner has treated this aspect of Mossi life in his study of Ouagadougou (1964), while V. Kabore (1966) concentrated upon the evolution of the traditional political organization, including the chiefs. Earlier in 1952 M. Reuillard analyzed Yatenga and in 1956 P. Garreau studied one particular *cercle.*

For Dahomey, Jacques Lombard (1965) has studied the reactions of the Bariba to the colonial situation, including the subject of the chiefs. Oke Finagnon (1967) has concentrated specifically upon the traditional chiefs in relation to the post-1945 political evolution. Immediately after World War II, P. Antoine (1948) studied the customary chiefs in lower Dahomey as did A. Kinde in the same area in 1957. In 1958 F. J. Amon d'Aby published a short study on the problem of the *chefferies* in the Ivory Coast, while J. Barthélémy (1957) studied the *cercle* of Abengourou. In 1955 François Fournier discussed the new tensions in the Soudan connected with the postwar reforms. In 1960 Yves Person in "Soixante Ans d'évolution en pays kissi" dealt with the entire period of French rule, including the post-1945 tensions, in a district of Guinea.

In 1955 André Robert examined the evolution of customary law in the face of economic and social changes, expecially after 1945. He also dealt with the impact of French legislation upon customary law in West Africa. In 1956 a Leiden symposium compared the evolution of customary law in French, British, and Belgian territories. A Cameroonian jurist, Victor Kanga, studied the evolution of Bamiléké law in the face of European influence. Robert Pageard (1969) undertook a detailed study of Mossi private law and its evolution during the colonial period and since 1960.

ECONOMIC ASPECTS OF FRENCH RULE

The essence of colonialism is the colonial power's exploitation of the resources and labor of the colony. French policy after the colonial occupation treated any land not actually inhabited or used by Africans as "vacant and ownerless." It became the property of the state and could be alienated for the benefit of European interests. Such a policy ignored both traditional African customs of communal ownership as well as agricultural practices which left large areas uncultivated each season. The registration of individual property for Africans as well as Europeans further helped to destroy traditional tenure patterns. Land policy developed originally in French West Africa was soon extended to Equatorial Africa and, after the First World War, to the mandates of Togoland and the Cameroons.

The basic French land policy is described by P. Dareste in *Le Régime de la propriété française en A.O.F.* (1908). A convenient summary of French practices prior to World War II is found in Lord Hailey, ed., *An African Survey* (1938, pp. 782–89, 858–62), and in P. Dareste, *Traité de droit colonial* (1931).

In French West Africa there was not the widespread alienation of land to Europeans, either individually or corporately, that occurred in Equatorial Africa where concessionaires in 1899 acquired 70 percent of the land. In 1936 Robert Lenoir studied land concessions in both West and Equatorial Africa. The Equatorial companies' abuses of Africans are the subject of a large literature by eyewitnesses, among which the most useful are those of Jules Saintoyant (1960), Jules Lefébure (1904), and Félicien Challaye (1909). The last of these contains extracts from the report of Savorgnan de Brazza, who investigated the abuses in 1905.

Despite some official attempts at reforms, the abuses continued until World War II, as evidenced by the exposés of André Gide (1927), Albert Londrès (1929), and Marcel Homet (1934). R. Jeaugeon (1961) has examined the reactions of French public opinion to the concession scandals, and S. J. S. Cookey has examined British reactions (1966); Marc Michel (1968) has studied the 1928 rebellion in the Haute Sangha that resulted in part from concession abuses. Jean Suret-Canale (1964) has synthesized the existing literature for the period 1900–1945 and analyzed the relationship of the companies with French financial and economic interests.

An article by Hubert Fréchou (1955) dealt with European plantations in the Ivory Coast. At that time 220–30 European planters on thirty thousand hectares produced 5 percent of the cocoa, 7 percent of the coffee, and nearly all of the bananas exported. The Europeans first arrived in 1925, setting in his opinion a strong example for the blacks.

With the granting of representation to Africans in and after 1945 and the giving of advisory powers on land matters to the territorial assemblies, Africans for the first time gained a voice in the granting of concessions. But the basic French system remained. It was not reformed until May 1955 for West and Equatorial Africa and July 1956 for the trust territories. The new regulations took account both of African custom and the evolution of that custom under colonial rule. The reforms are recounted by Paul Blanc [P. B.] (1957) for all territories, B. De Maison (1956), J. Chabas (1958), and Pierre Drouet (1958) for French West Africa.

After World War II France gave attention to economic development which would benefit the overseas peoples as well as the French. At the same time the French government undertook a program of public investments, more in the form of grants than of loans. A large literature on economic and financial matters during the age of decolonization reflects these policies of public investment and development. Right after the war Charles Robequain (1949) surveyed the economic structure and status of the overseas territories and their potential for development in terms of benefits for the indigenous populations. René Hoffherr, a longtime administrator in Morocco and Black Africa, discussed the public investment policy in Black Africa during the Fourth Republic in his work, *Coopération économique franco-africaine* (1958), while the Paris doctoral dissertation of Rémy Lévi (1960) is a more systematic treatment of the same subject. An official booklet, *French Africa: A Decade of Progress, 1948–1958* (1958) discusses the activities of the FIDES in West and Equatorial Africa. W. A. E. Skurnik (1967) contends that French investment policy after 1945 weakened and ultimately contributed to the disintegration of the federation of French West Africa. The Paris thesis of Mamadou Touré (1960) discusses the economic and financial relations between France and French West Africa from 1945 to 1958. H. Korner's *Kolonialpolitik und Wirtschaftsentwicklung: Das Beispiel Franzosisch Westafrikas* (1965) analyzes French policy with emphasis on the origins, typology, and realization of the plans of modernization and equipment in French West Africa. He examines the effects of various plans under the FIDES on the internal economic situation and on the development of external economic relations. Teresa Hayter (1966) deals with French aid to Africa both before and after independence.

Pierre Moussa has written two works on the economic relationships between France and French Africa, including their financial aspects, which view the problems more from the French side than from the African. His brief *L'Economie de la zone franc* (1960) draws on the more detailed *Les Chances économique de la communauté franco-africaine* (1957). He shows that some sectors of the French economy, in particular textiles and iron-steel products, depended heavily on African markets, and that French Africa was producing for the franc zone a hard currency surplus of $200 to $300 millions annually. Jean Ehrhard in *Le Destin du colonialisme* (1958) evaluates postwar economic policy in Black Africa, in particular the impact of public investments, primarily from the French side. France associated her Black African territories to the European Economic Community, formed in 1957. P. B. Couste explored the initial consequences of this relationship in *L'Association des pays d'outre-mer à la Communauté Economique Européenne* (1959).

The financial relationship alone is explored in a number of works. Albert Duchêne's *Histoire des finances coloniales de la France* (1938) presents a detailed view of colonial finances on the eve of World War II. A number of essays in F. Bloch-Laine's *La Zone franc* (1956) treat the monetary relationships with the franc zone. Michèle Saint Marc in *Zone franc et décolonisation* (1964) complements and extends the previous work. She treats the organization of monetary emission and credit, its effects on public finances, and the role of currency in development.

Two works treat financial arrangements during the Fourth Republic. J. C. Haumant's *Initiation aux finances publiques des territoires d'outremer* (1953) treats the financial regime within the overseas territories, including the territorial budgets which were voted by local assemblies, and the execution of services in material and personnel. Jean Ehrhard's study (1960) is a textbook on overseas public finances more than an account of any particular operations. It does not examine the political aspects of finances as Haumant does.

Quite a large number of works have concentrated upon economic development during the postwar era. Professor Gaston Le Duc (1955) gave lectures at the Law Faculty in Paris which placed the postwar economic development of Black Africa in perspective. The Senegalese economist and statesman Mamadou Dia in 1957 discussed briefly the evolution of economic institutions in all of sub-Saharan Africa and compared French methods with British and Belgian. In addition, he examined the economic relations between France and its African territories. In 1961 he updated and expanded his work in the light of formal independence.

Marcel Capet (1958) in his study of the economy of the federation of FWA discussed the consequences of the system of production and consumption introduced by the French. He focuses upon the village and the impact of a money economy based on cash crops upon it. He also analyzes the urban economy, including the action of the French state in investments and the building of an infrastructure. Scrutinizing the results of all these activities, he sees a nonintegration of local activities in the overall economy of the Federation. He also sees five veritable geographic economies within the Federation: (1) Senegal and Mauritania; (2) Guinea; (3) Ivory Coast and Upper Volta; (4) Dahomey and Niger; (5) the Sudan, which is an extension of both (1) and (3). In each of the first four, the economy is centered about a port. Capet also treats the social consequences of the colonial economy.

Richard J. Peterec's *Dakar and West African Economic Development* (1967) deals with the development of the port of Dakar and its economic hinterland during the period of the Federation, 1904–57, and of the reorientations which occurred in the subsequent decade. A Senegalese scholar, Abdoulaye Ly, in *Les Masses africaines et l'actuelle condition humaine* (1956) attacked French rule, and in particular foreign commercial exploitation of French West Africa. Another Senegalese, Abdoulaye Wade (1964), though concerned with the French West African economy after independence as well as before, has useful discussions of agricultural production, industrialization, problems of investment, capital formation, and growth during the colonial period.

J. J. Poquin (1957) has studied the commercial relations (prices, exchange of goods) and financial relations of French Africa with the rest of the world from 1925 to 1955. He concludes that the close relationship between France and the African territories led to a failure to develop indigenous agriculture and to encourage inter-African trade. He advocated increasing peasant revenue and establishing light industry as a means of raising the capital necessary to industrialize Africa. J. Chemery (1960) has written the history of the French mining industry in all Black African territories and Madagascar.

Two works, when taken together, give a good look at French economic development of Equatorial Africa between 1914 and 1956. In 1913 the government-general of A.E.F. published *L'Evolution économique des possessions françaises d'Afrique Equatoriale.* In 1956 a special 358-page issue of *Réalités Africaines* was entitled "La Mise en valeur de l'Afrique Equatoriale Française." Jean and René Charbonneau (1961) made an informal study of trade and traders in Equatorial Africa in which they included comments on the European merchant firms and traders as well as African merchants.

There has been a lack of research and study of the large European firms that have played such a significant role in the export-import business in all French territories. Only the general surveys of colonial rule by Jean Suret-Canale and Michael Crowder touch upon them.

The Lebanese and Syrian traders who along with some Greeks became retailers in French West Africa and the Cameroons in the 1920s and after have been the subject of several studies. Jean-Gabriel Desbordes (1938) studies Lebanese and Syrian immigration into French West Africa prior to World War II. An important article by R. Bayly Windor (1962) updates this study through independence. Fuad I. Khuri is a Levantine who published "Kinship, Emigration, and Trade Partners among the Lebanese of West Africa" (1965).

A rather large literature exists on particular aspects of economic development in various territories. A longtime administrator, Henri Labouret, discusses the attempts to create a viable economy based on rural communities in French West Africa (1941). R. Portères (1952) presents a history of groundnut production in Senegal. Abdoulaye Ly in *L'Etat et la production paysanne, ou l'état et la révolution au Sénégal* (1963) attacks the economic policies and practices of the French administration, particularly in the rural agricultural sector. A section of volume 3 of *Le Développement rural dans les pays d'Afrique noire d'expression française* (1965) treats the activities of the Compagnie Générale des Oléagineux Tropicaux en Casamance from 1948 to 1964.

The prolific Samir Amin in *Trois expériences africaines de développement: le Mali, la Guinée, et le Ghana* (1965) discusses and compares the colonial economic structure of each country and its evolution since independence, with the most attention being given to Mali. René Dumont (1961) discusses agricultural development in Mali, Guinea, and the Ivory Coast. In *Le Développement du capitalisme en Côte d'Ivoire* (1967) Amin deals with the economic development of the Ivory Coast since 1950. He contends that the economy is dominated by French interests and that there has been growth benefiting foreigners without real development. French rule created an administrative bourgeoisie which is potentially parasitical rather than an effective economic bourgeoisie. He also contends that Houphouet-Boigny and the RDA strengthened the hold of the traditional chiefs on the fruits of the land and that rural development primarily has benefited this class.

The Lyon thesis of Emile Randolph (1967) has dealt with the industrialization of the Ivory Coast since 1900. The Brasseurs (1953) studied the economy of the Dahomeyan port of Porto Novo and the neighboring palm-oil producing districts. The Izards (1959) studied the impact of colonial rule on the economic and social life of the Yatenga Mossi in the Upper Volta, including the impact of emigration of Mossi laborers to Ghana and the Ivory Coast.

There have been quite few economic studies of the territories that formed the federation of French Equatorial Africa. Guy Lasserre's study of Libreville, Gabon (1958), treats historically the growth of the city and the development of its economic activities as communications center and exporter of forest products. Lasserre also dealt with the development of okoumé wood exploitation (1955) from 1889 on. The Montpellier thesis of R. Prats (1955) deals with the economic development of Gabon. In "Le Régime des terres et ses modifications récentes aux environs de Brazzaville et au Woleu N'Tem," Gilles Sautter (1954) shows the effects of the introduction of cash crops on the traditional landowning patterns. In the N'Tem district of Gabon, the raising of cacao led to individual property among the Fang; but in the Brazzaville area, the raising of manioc on a large scale for the Brazzaville market did not change the Bacongo-Balali collective patterns. Sautter has also written the monumental economic geographic work *De L'Atlantique au Fleuve Congo: Une géographie de sous-peuplement* (1966). It deals with the economic transformation of Gabon and the Congo, particularly in the same areas discussed in the article. An essay by Cathérine Coquéry-Vidrovitch (1969) on French economic activities in the Congo from 1890 to 1920 provides a background to later developments. André Teulières (1953) focuses upon the economic development of Oubangui-Chari as does the longtime settler Jean Romeuf (1958) in his long essay. Samir Amin has discussed the economic development of the Congo after 1914 in a volume in which Cathérine Coquéry-Vidrovitch has written the sections on Congolese economic history from 1880 to 1914 (1969).

Jean Cabot's *Le Bassin du Moyen Logone* (1965) is a work of economic geography which discusses the economic and social consequences of French rule in the twentieth century in the most densely populated areas of Chad. The conditions under which cotton was developed as an export crop impoverished the soil and brought few real benefits to peasant producers in the middle Logone area. A large section of the work *Le Développement rural dans les pays d'Afrique noire d'expression française* (1965) treats an experimental modernization sector in the Central Cameroons (the work of SEMAC and SEMCENTRES). The thesis of Serge Lacquemond (1959) examines public investments in the Northern Cameroons during the postwar period. Philippe Hugon (1968) has studied the economy of the Federal Republic of Cameroon, including the colonial background, as has Reginald Green (1968). The International Monetary Fund's *Survey of African Economics,* volume 1 (1968) deals with Cameroons and the former Equatorial African countries primarily since 1960. Thompson and Adloff's works *Equatorial Africa* (1960) and *French West Africa* (1955) also contain detailed economic sections on each territory during the postwar period. The best account of economic development in French Somaliland is found in Thompson and Adloff (1968), while a French government study in 1954 discussed the economic and social evolution of the territory during the postwar decade.

The Second World War saw the abandonment of forced labor and the *prestation* in French Africa. In 1944 it became possible for the masses to join labor unions, and strikes became legal. But it was not until the so-called Lamine Guèye Law of 1950, which placed African civil servants on an equal footing with metropolitan ones, that the French Parliament regulated general labor conditions. Then in 1952 the Labor Code for the Overseas Territories applied the Lamine Guèye provisions to all territories and occupations and established machinery for wage negotiations and work inspection.

Pierre F. Gonidec and M. Kirsch, *Droit de travail des territoires d'outre-mer* (1958) discuss labor legislation, including the amendments of 1955 to the 1952 Labor Code. Two older works by P. Huguet (1953) and Pierre Chauleur (1958) also treat the Labor Code. Several works deal with labor problems in general. John A. Noon, *Labor Problems of Africa* (1944) discusses the rise of a class of wage earners during the Second World War. *Présence Africaine* in 1953 issued *Le Travail en Afrique Noire,* a collection of articles by leftist French economists and sociologists on labor questions. The work was updated and reissued in 1965. In 1958 the International Labor Office issued the massive *African Labor Survey,* which dealt with all aspects of labor throughout Africa. The same year the same body published *Les Problèmes du travail en Afrique Noire,* by J. Poirier.

Three works published since African independence have dealt with black labor migration into France itself: a special issue of the magazine *Hommes et Migrations* (1965); G. Bassane-N'Diaye, *Les Travailleurs noirs en France: Pourquoi les migrations?* (1963); and Souleymane Diarra, "Les Travailleurs africains noirs en France" (1968).

There is a rather large literature on the development of labor unions during the Second World War and thereafter. The unions at first, like many African political parties, were affiliates of the large metropolitan syndicalist federations—CGT, CGT-FO, CFTC. But in the mid-1950s, especially after the *Loi-Cadre,* they began to disaffiliate and to regroup on national and inter-African bases.

Works which deal with the labor movement in all of Africa and therefore provide comparisons between French and British territories are those of Jean Meynaud and Anisse Saleh-Bey (1963), Imanuel Geiss (1965), Ioan Davies (1966), Andras November (1965), and Georges Fischer (1961). Fischer's "Trade Unions and Decolonization" presents pioneering essays on French and British colonial labor policies. Meynaud and Saleh-Bey do better with North Africa than with Black Africa, but their book is useful for showing the relation of the unions to political movements. Davies also does this, placing the development of the unions within the historical context of the postwar period as well. November discusses the relationship of the metropolitan unions to West African ones and the evolution of independent unions. An article by Guy Pfefferman (1967) discusses the relationship of the trade unions and political parties during the Fourth Republic. The work of Elliott Berg, "French West Africa" (1959), is a study of labor and economic development while his essay with Jeffrey Butler, "Trade Unions" (1964), provides the most complete discussion in English of French West Africa.

The Abbé L. Bovy (1965) has also dealt with the historical evolution of the syndicalist movement in French West Africa and Togo from before the Second World War until after independence, examining the ideological and juridical aspects in particular. A brief study by Michel Rézeau (1962) discusses the role of syndicalism in the evolution of Black Africa. The work of M. Abdou N'Diaye (1964) has special value for its treatment of the formation of the Union Générale des Travailleurs de l'Afrique Noire under Guinean auspices at the time the African unions separated from the metropolitan ones. An article by P. F. Gonidec (1962) also concentrates on the disaffiliation of the African unions from the metropolitan ones. The study by Gérard Bedos (1959) treats this process through the end of the Fourth Republic. An article by Raymond Delval (1965) treat unions in Madagascar, and one by Audrey Wipper (1964) compares union development in French West Africa and the Philippines.

EDUCATION, THE MISSIONS, AND SOCIAL CHANGE

Education is a very important aspect of French policy, for the French sought to assimilate Africans by the extension of the metropolitan educational system into Black Africa. The great French cultural influence which persists among the African political elite has resulted from assimilationist instruction. There is no detailed history of education in Black Africa; but the study by Jerry B. Bolibaugh (1964) provides an excellent introduction to French policy and practice from 1815 to 1962. Bolibaugh emphasizes the continuity in objectives as well as the disparity between objectives and results throughout the entire period. The two surveys edited by Lord Hailey (1938 and 1957) also introduce French education in the twentieth century and give useful statistics. (They omit Madagascar). The volumes by Thompson and Adloff on West Africa (1957), Equatorial Africa (1960), Madagascar (1965), and French Somaliland (1968) provide a fuller treatment of educational practice and the historical evolution of Western education.

A reference book edited by Helen Kitchen, *The Educated African: A Country-by-Country Survey of Educational Development in Africa* (1962), has detailed factual accounts concerning all of the individual countries under French rule with very complete statistical information. Education in the trust territories of the Cameroons and Togoland was reviewed on the basis of French Annual Reports to the United Nations and studied by both the Trusteeship Council and the Economic and Social Council. The doctoral dissertation of Richard I. Miller (Columbia University, 1958) deals with the trusteeship system and educational advancement. A three-part *World Survey of Education* (1955–61) published by UNESCO provides data on all countries.

A work by a longtime colonial administrator, Georges Hardy, examined French education in West Africa in 1917. In 1928 the Harvard scholar Raymond Leslie Buell in his monumental study devoted attention to French education in the colonies and in the two mandates. He was highly critical of assimilation and the practices connected with it. P. Crouzet's "Education in the French Colonies" (in the International Institute of Teachers' College, Columbia University, *Education Yearbook*, 1931, pp. 267–566) provides one of the most detailed studies of education during the interwar period. In the same year Georges Hardy reported on the education of Africans in all African territories. Ralph J. Bunche (1934) in an article compared French educational policy in Dahomey and Togo. William Bryant Mumford and G. St. J. Orde-Brown's *Africans Learn to be French: A Review of Educational Activities in the Seven Federated Colonies of French West Africa Based on a Tour of French West Africa Undertaken in 1935* (1937) is the product of two British officials, one a specialist in colonial education and the other on African labor. It is the best single account of the educational system that produced most of the political leaders of the post–World War II period. It analyzes both policy and practice and compares French approaches with British. Appendixes contain translations of educational policy statements by French colonial officials.

Other documents on French policies, including post-1940 ones, are found in David Scanlon, ed., *Traditions of African Education* (1964). The Phelps-Stokes Commission published *Education in Africa* (1922), which included French territories in West and Equatorial Africa within its purview. In 1931 the Government-General of French Equatorial Africa published *Histoire et organisation generale de l'enseignement en A.E.F.*, covering both government and mission education. In 1938 the review *Enseignement Publique* contained "Rapport sur l'enseignement en A.E.F. 1936–1937" (pp. 398–423), which gave a good summary for the federation on the eve of the Second World War.

As early as 1930 a British Protestant missionary, James W. C. Dougall, published the general work *Religious Education in Africa,* which discussed the sometimes conflicting aims of government and mission education. In 1957 Thomas M. J. Burke published an edition of four papal encyclicals, 1919–57, which dealt with mission education, and provided a historical introduction to them.

There seems to be a gap in interest in education between the 1930s and the 1960s if the published results are any indication. During the Fourth Republic there were important articles but no systematic studies on policies and practices in France itself as far as can be learned. Even when the political struggles were finished and self-government and independence in view, some of the most important studies were undertaken not in France but in the United States.

Jean de la Roche (1946), Durand-Reveille (1948 and 1950), Jean Capelle (1949), and Albert Charton (1950), all French administrators, discussed in articles the postwar changes and expansion of education in Africa. In articles in *Présence Africaine* Ray Autra (1956) criticized education in French West Africa from a historical perspective, and Bernard Dadié (1956–57) discussed its inadequacies in all French African territories. In other articles Guy Devernois (1958 and 1959) and Robert Cornevin (1961) reviewed education at the close of the Fourth Republic while the black historian Rayford W. Logan (1961) surveyed French education in Black Africa during the colonial period.

The Harvard doctoral thesis of Jane Kessler (1958) dealt with primary education of Africans in Dakar. Abdou Moumouni's *L'Education en Afrique* (1964, trans. 1968) includes a historical sketch of education under colonial rule since 1816 but is primarily concerned with the adaptation of the French legacy to the new conditions of independence. Many of the detailed statistics have been omitted from the English translation. Moumouni accuses France of limiting education in order to prevent African independence. An article by Michel Debeauvais in James S. Coleman, ed., *Education and Political Development* (1965) summarizes French educational policy in relation to political goals during the post-1945 period. He discusses why the teaching training institutions were the major source of recruitment for the political leaders of the states formed from colonies.

Since independence there have been detailed studies of education in specific territories. By far the most complete is Gerard Lucas's *Formal Education in the Congo-Brazzaville: A Study of Educational Policy and Practice* (1965). This doctoral dissertation contains a historical account of the development of the educational system since 1883, including both public and private schools. He shows that the institutions established were almost identical with those in France and tended to become more so as secondary and higher levels were expanded. The entire educational system has been geared to produce an elite that would enter the secondary system and become the leaders of the country. Its failure to have any other goals for the bulk of the students has turned them away from agriculture and industry where they are badly needed, thus both injuring the economy and creating a *lumpen-bourgeoisie* that cannot find jobs in the civil service.

Marc Botti and Paul Venizet studied education in Gabon, which at independence had one of the highest percentages of school-age children in school in Africa. In *Enseignement au Gabon* (1965) they show that the beneficial effects of this high enrollment are mitigated by the poor training of teachers, the overcrowding of classes, and the brevity of the average pupil's total stay in years. The study is not a historical one, but it shows the cumulative effects of the transfer of the French system of education without adaptation to an African context. Another work by the same authors, *Scolarisation au Tchad* (1961), earlier gave a good picture of education in Chad at independence and showed poignantly how ill-suited for that country an unadapted French curriculum was.

The short study of H. B. Mbarga (1962) discusses education in the Cameroons prior to independence. An essay by Hugh O. H. Vernon-Jackson (1967) deals with the history of language policy in education in the two Cameroons during the colonial period, with emphasis on the British sector.

A study of development in Senegal (1960) by the Reverend Louis-Joseph Lebret, O.P., at the close of the colonial period provides a detailed examination of the French system of education there. In 1966 Rémi Clignet and Philip Foster published a study of secondary schools and their students in the Ivory Coast that threw light on education during the colonial period.

French assimilation policy led to the education of hundreds of Africans in France itself. One of the most noted students during the interwar period was Léopold Senghor, whose intellectual development in the French cultural setting is studied by Jack Louis Hymans (1964). In the preface to *Présence Africaine's Les Etudiants noirs parlent* (1953) Alioune Diop explored the implication of French education of Africans in Europe. In the essays which make up the volume the student authors subordinated racial issues to political and cultural relationships. In 1962 a Senegalese scholar, Jean-Pierre N'Diaye, undertook a study of the black students in France, including their responses to France and their views of Africa. The volumes by Thompson and Adloff also have brief sections on the gallicized student elite in France.

In a brief article (1962) Joseph Ki-Zerbo analyzed the transformation of the elite's attitudes, from cultural dependence upon France before World War II to assertion of the Negro-African personality during the postwar period.

The concept of the African personality and the African reactions to French assimilation policy embodied in the negritude movement have led to a very large literature, some of which only can be mentioned here. Lilyan Kesteloot in *Les Ecrivains noirs de langue française: nais-*

sance d'une littérature (1963) and *Négritude et situation coloniale* (1968) presents a literary history and critical analysis of the negritude movement from the 1930s on. Her work shows the relationships of Antilleans with Black Africans. Several works provide further information about the critical analysis of the writings of French Black Africans: Thomas Melone's *De la négritude dans la littérature négro-africaine* (1963); Claude Wauthier's *L'Afrique des Africains, Inventaire de la négritude* (1964) (Eng. trans., *The Literature and Thought of Modern Africa: A Survey*, 1967); Robert Pageard's *Littérature négro-africaine* (1966); and Judith I. Gleason's *This Africa: Novels by West Africans in English and French* (1965). The essay of G. E. von Grunebaum (1964) explores some of the cultural implications of literature in French by Black Africans and North Africans. Robert W. July in *The Origins of Modern African Thought* (1967) devotes several chapters to Senegal from the nineteenth century until World War II.

African reactions to French rule, and especially to the assimilation policy, led to the founding in Paris in 1947 of *Présence Africaine* by Alioune Diop, then a member of the upper house of the parliament, as "a cultural review of the Negro world." In 1956 in Paris and in 1959 in Rome the review organized international congresses of Negro writers and artists. During these meetings it became evident that the cultural reaction reflected in the negritude movement was becoming as well a political reaction that would produce demands for independence. The proceedings have been published as issues of *Présence Africaine* (nos. 8–10, 1956; and nos. 24–25, 1959).

With the end of the colonial period, there have been comparisons of the French and British systems of education in Africa. Michael Crowder devotes a substantial chapter of his *West Africa under Colonial Rule* (1968) to Western education. L. Gray Cowan has considered all of Africa in his essay "British and French Education in Africa: A Critical Approach" (1964). The study by John Wilson, a longtime teacher and school administrator in Ghana, *Education and Changing West African Culture* (1963), deals with British West Africa and especially the Gold Coast; but Wilson has much to say about Western education in the African context that is of wider application. Since independence, there has been research in the historical development of education in French West Africa. Denise Bouche has written on the adaptation of French education in Senegal between 1816 and 1960 and on French schools in the Sudan between 1884 and 1900 (1966).

Because the Christian missions touched every aspect of African life, including education, it is not surprising that there is a large literature on them. Two works by Protestant scholars are the most comprehensive and rest on practically all the printed sources. Volume 4 of Charles Pelham Groves's *The Planting of Christianity in Africa* (1958) deals with the period 1914–54 in all of Africa. It is especially good for the impact of the two world wars, the decolonization of the missions and the establishment of African-directed churches, and the effects of political events upon Christian institutions. Kenneth Scott Latourette's *The Twentieth Century outside Europe* (1962) includes Black Africa and Madagascar from 1914 until independence.

Two works on French Roman Catholic missions throughout the world, including Africa, are Georges Goyau's *La France missionnaire dans les cinq parties du monde* (vol. 2, 1948), which is very detailed for the nineteenth and twentieth centuries, and Bernard de Vaulx's *Histoire des missions catholiques françaises* (1951). Both carefully relate the missionary expansion overseas to the situation in France and conditions in Africa. A second shorter work by de Vaulx, *History of the Missions* (translated in 1961 from the original French edition of 1960) has a good brief account of Africa. A long chapter by the Holy Spirit priest and historian, Joseph Bouchaud, in volume 3 of the semi-official *Histoire universelle des missions catholiques,* edited by Monsignor Simon Delacroix (1958), covers all African missions. The Irish priest Martin Bane has written a good account of French Catholic missionary efforts in West Africa through the mid-1950s (1956). An American Holy Spirit Father, Henry J. Koren (1959), published a history of his congregation that contains accounts of its work in Equatorial Africa and the Cameroons. Joseph Bouchaud (1969) has written a brief biography of the French Spiritan Monsignor Pierre Bonneau, who served as bishop of Duala.

On the French Protestant side, Jean Bianquis in *Les Origines de la Société des Missions Evangéliques* (vol. 3, 1935) described the work of the Paris-based Huguenots in the former German territories after the First World War. Gustave Mondain (1948) has dealt with French Protestant missionary efforts in Madagascar.

A large number of unpublished theses has dealt with the history of missions. Two American Protestant missionaries have written detailed histories of Equatorial Africa and the Cameroons. A Presbyterian, Norman A. Horner, has described the development of both Roman Catholic and Protestant Missions among the Bantu-speaking Cameroonians (1956). He recounts the developments that led to the establishment of the Cameroonian Presbyterian Church in 1957. Benjamin A. Hamilton, a Church of the Brethren minister who served in Oubangui-Chari, has written (1959) the most detailed account of the many Protestant mission organizations in the four territories of Equatorial Africa. Both works discuss the official French hostility toward non-French missions. French pressures upon American Congregationalists and Presbyterians in Gabon to teach only in French led to the transfer of that field to French Protestants and the transfer of the missionaries to the German Cameroons, where after the First World War they encountered the same French policy.

Roman Catholic hostility towards the Protestant missions in Equatorial Africa and the pressures applied upon the French government are described by Hamilton and Gérard Lucas (1965). Monsignor Augouard, the Bishop of Brazzaville, regarded Catholic missions as promoting both French and Catholic interests. His life and work are recounted by Jehan de Witte (1924) and Canon Augouard (1934). Although the Berlin Act and the Act of St. Germain-en-Laye of 1919 prevented the French administration from excluding foreign missionaries, the administration took measures in practice which hindered their establishment and expansion. O. D. Jobson (1957) touched upon relations with the administration in his history of the Church of the Brethren mission in Oubangui-Chari from 1921 on.

Edmond Marquier de Villemagne has written a detailed thesis on the work of the Holy Spirit Fathers in French Equatorial Africa between 1839 and 1940. This order was most active in all territories but Chad, where the Jesuits became active only after the Second World War. Sister Joan Wheeler has written a Paris thesis on the Holy Spirit Fathers in the Cameroons, where they replaced German priests after the First World War. Raphael Onombélé's thesis deals with Roman Catholic expansion in the Cameroons from 1890 to 1945 while Louis Ngongo's (1967) treats the political role of religious forces in the Cameroons, 1939–65. J. Gobbe's *mémoire* (1948) gives a French view of the American Presbyterian Mission in the Cameroons. Dominique Goyi (1967) discusses the development of the missions and their social effects in Congo-Brazzaville between 1880 and 1930. The thesis of Geneviève Davérat (1967) deals with the Roman Catholic missions in Gabon, 1844–1914. There is a large literature, ranging from the pictorial to the polemical, on the individual work of Dr. Albert Schweitzer at Lambaréné, Gabon, including his own writings: *On the Edge of the Primeval Forest* (1922), *Forest Hospital at Lambaréné* (1931), and *African Notebook* (1939). In his essay "Our Colonial Task," in R. Joy and Melvin Arnold, *The Africa of Albert Schweitzer* (1949), Dr. Schweitzer gave his views on the desired evolution of the Gabonese, which would include their assimilation of the best in world civilization.

A quite different type of study on the Equatorial African area is Efraim Andersson's *Churches at the Grass-roots: A Study in Congo-Brazzaville* (1968). Andersson studies from historical and sociological perspectives the development of the Protestant Chuch of the Congo from the work of the Swedish Evangelical Mission. Just as Balandier looks at the transformation of life in Equatorial Africa under the impact of colonial rule, Andersson examines the formation of Christians in the African setting and the establishment of an indigenous Christian church. Included in the work are data on French policy toward the mission and Roman Catholic attitudes.

In French West Africa, mission activity was far more restricted because of the presence of Islam and official reluctance to allow Christian missionaries to enter Muslim areas. Except where Protestant missionaries entered before the establishment of French rule, the missions were largely Roman Catholic. Lila Santarelli's thesis (1968) treats the Catholic missions in Senegal between 1848 and 1914 and Michel Bée's (1967) both Catholic and Protestant in the lower Ivory Coast from 1895 to 1939. Georges Hardy has written a biography (1949) of the Catholic missionary in Dahomey, Monsignor Francis Aupiais, who represented Black Africans in the French National Assembly in 1945.

Jean Faure's *Togo, champ de missions* (1948) deals with French Protestant efforts between the wars as successors to German missionaries. H. W. Debrunner in *A Church between Colonial Powers: A Study of the Church in Togo* (1965) treats the development of the Evangelical Church among the Ewe under French mission guidance. The Strasbourg thesis of Alphonse Dietman (1946) discusses the role of missions in French colonization and their legal status in Black Africa. In 1944 Jean-Marie Sédès published a study of the indigenous clergy througout the French Empire. The thesis of Michel Robert (1958) dealt with the status of the secular clergy in Black Africa. The French administration gave subsidies to the missions for that part of their educational work that met official standards. Joseph Delpech's *Des subventions à l'enseignement confessionnel et missionnaire dans les territoires d'outre-mer* (1956) deals with this subject.

Whereas up to this point this essay has looked at French policy toward the missions, mission attitudes toward French rule became important during the period of decolonization. A richly documented study by the Huguenot jurist François Mejan, *Le Vatican contre la France d'outre-mer* (1957) presents the thesis that the Vatican in the 1950s adopted a policy hostile to French rule and Western civilization in the nonwhite world in order to try to preserve Catholic influence. René-Pierre Millot's *Missions in the World Today* (1961; French original, 1960), discusses papal teaching on missions and analyzes the four major missionary encyclicals between 1919 and 1959, as does T. B. J. Burke in *Catholic Missions: Four Great Encyclicals* (1959).

The policy of africanization of the church formalized by Pope Pius XII in 1953 and after, which involved the expansion of an episcopal hierarchy and the appointment of many more African bishops in 1955, is discussed in the work of Joseph Bouchaud, *L'Eglise en Afrique Noire* (1958). Alexis Kagame in *Le Colonialisme face à la doctrine missionnaire à l'heure de Vatican II* (1964) updates Bouchaud through the era of independence.

There have been several studies of the missions in relation to decolonization. *L'Eglise catholique face au monde no chrétien* (1959), which is volume 4 of the *Histoire universelle des missions catholiques,* looks at the changing colonial situation from a French Catholic perspective. "Catholicism's Problems in French Black Africa: The Historical Aspect" (1962) by Victor D. Du Bois looks at the mission church and its problems in the light of independence. Robert Delavignette in *Christianisme et colonialisme* (1960) presents a Catholic view of decolonization in the light of the encyclical *Fidei Donum.* An article by M. Ekwa, S.J., (1965) treats the role of Catholic mission education in the light of John XXIII's encyclical *Pacem in Terris.* R. Mehl (1964) has dealt with the problems of the Protestant missions in the face of decolonization. The collection edited by Marcel Merle, *Les Eglises chrétiennes et la décolonisation* (1967) has important articles and documents on the Vatican and decolonization, French Catholics, French Protestants, and non-French Protestants and decolonization. The report of the *Présence Africaine* colloquium held at Abidjan in 1961, *Religions en Afrique noire aujourd'hui: Bilan et perspectives,* contains various African views of decolonization.

V. Martin in *La Chrétienté africaine de Dakar* (1964) has studied the Christian minority of Dakar, 7 percent of its population, which during the age of decolonization often gave rise to African churches of various kinds. Among the earliest and most important was the revival movement led by the Wesleyan prophet William Wade Harris in the Ivory Coast at the time of the First World War. G. van Bulck's "Le Prophète Harris vu par lui-même" (1961) presents Harris's own account with commentary by a Catholic missionary. A number of contemporary accounts, most of them by European missionaries, on Harris and the movement he created include those by Jean Bianquis (1924),

W. J. Platt (1934), F. Deauville Walker (3d ed. 1938) and J. J. Cooksey and A. McLeish (1931). Harris's evangelical preaching had a lasting influence on lower Ivory Coast Christianity as a base on which European Protestant missionaries built further. Bohumil Holas reported on the later Harris influence in a brief article in 1954 and in his book *Le Séparatisme religieux en Afrique Noire: l'exemple de la Côte d'Ivoire* (1965). In the later work he studies the sociological aspects of a variety of syncretist sects that have arisen in Protestant areas. Although African churches and syncretist movements have grown out of Catholic influences, most of them in French Africa have arisen in areas where Protestants have been active. Ernest Amos-Djoro (1966) reported on the relationship of the Harrisite churches and Ivoirian nationalism. Finally, the London doctoral dissertation of G. N. Haliburton, *The Prophet Harris and His Work in the Ivory Coast and Western Ghana* (1968) represents the latest scholarship on the Harris movement.

For the Cameroons, Pastor J. R. Brutsch (1954) has studied the Native Baptist Church, which grew out of German attempts to control the former English missions. But no one has done a detailed study of the Ngumba Independent Church, which split off from the American Presbyterian mission over questions of church discipline. In neighboring Equatorial Africa, important syncretist movements have been studied. Efraim Andersson, a Swedish Evangelical missionary long resident in the French Congo, treats prophetic movements including the Kimbanguist movement of the 1920s and after among the Bakongo of both Congos in *Messianic Popular Movements in the Lower Congo* (1958). An article by Willy Béguin extends the account of Kimbanguish influence through the independence era.

Georges Balandier in a now famous article, "Messianismes et nationalismes en Afrique Noire" (1953), discusses the relationship of religious and political factors in various movements, especially in the Congo and Gabon. He discusses these movements, including Kimbanguism, Kakaism, and Matsouanism, in detail in his *Sociologie Actuelle de l'Afrique Noire* (2d ed., 1963). The Abbé Fulbert Youlou (1955) analyzed Matsouanism, and *Le Monde Non Chrétien* (1953) reproduced important documents on the movement. A Balali student, Martial Sinda, wrote his Paris doctoral dissertation on *Le Messianisme congolais et ses incidences politiques depuis son apparition jusqu'à l'époque de l'indépendance, 1921–1961.* James Fernandez (1970) examines Alar Ayong and Bwiti as movements of protest in central and northern Gabon.

The French fought against Islamic chiefs during their expansion into the interior of French West and Equatorial Africa. They therefore were concerned about Islam as a political force during their "pacification" and occupation. They had to develop a policy towards Islam thereafter, for Muslims formed important parts of the population in all the interior territories except the Upper Volta as well as in the coastal countries of Senegal and Guinea. Donal Cruise O'Brien (1967) has shown that the French aimed after 1900 to secure the loyalty of the Muslim notables and to use them as intermediaries and instruments in their administration. The loyalty of most of the Muslim elite during World War I reassured the French of the soundness of their policy. In its implementation the administration sponsored the studies of Robert Arnaud and Paul Marty, which were published during and after World War I. But the government of French West Africa under Governor William Ponty from 1908 on also sought to end policies that might encourage the spread of Islam, and instituted a *politique des races,* which protected indigenous animisms. The work of Jules Brévié, later governor-general from 1930 to 1936, reflected a shift in official thinking. In *L'Islamisme contre "Naturisme" au Soudan Français* (1923) he contended that French expansion had facilitated the spread of Islam, which was destructive of society. He felt that the administration should restrict Muslim activities which were harmful to animist society.

The bulk of writing on Islam in Black Africa since the 1920s has dealt with its development and expansion from different perspectives and has touched on official policy only in this setting. Two classics by J. Spencer Trimingham, *Islam in West Africa* (1959) and *A History of Islam in West Africa* (1962), treat Islam from sociological and historical perspectives. The first work contains a short chapter on the influence of westernism and the second treats briefly the period of European rule, including the spread of Islam. Vincent Monteil's *L'Islam noir* (1964) is mostly on French Africa and is concerned primarily with the economic and social implications of Islam. Monteil discusses the adaptation of a religion born in an Arabian setting to animistic Black Africa. He sees no uniformity in the varieties of Islam that have taken root in different places. J. C. Froelich (1963) also shows the diversity of Islam in sub-Saharan Africa but emphasizes the relation of religion to politics more than to the society or economy. The work of Alphonse Gouilly, *L'Islam dans l'Afrique Occidentale Française* (1952) also treats the impact of Islam on Black African life and the new Islamic forms and practices arising from African soil. His study deals with French policy toward Islam and has good sections on the various brotherhoods, particularly those of Senegal and the sudanic areas. Also useful for all these subjects are two works by Marcel Cardaire (1949 and 1954) and a brief official one by Jean Chapelle (1949). In his second work Cardaire treats the development of Islamic thought in the sudanic belt, including the brotherhoods and the impact of Wahhabism and reformism.

There is a substantial literature on the various brotherhoods dating from before World War I to the postindependence era. Alfred Le Chatelier (1899) studied them in West Africa and Octave Depont and Xavier Coppolani (1897) in both West and North Africa. Between 1916 and 1926, under official auspices, Paul Marty studied Islam, including the brotherhoods in Mauritania, Senegal, Sudan, Ivory Coast, and Dahomey. P. J. André (1924) studied the brotherhoods throughout West Africa and Islam in Dahomey. A. Leriche (1949) devotes a good part of his study of Islam in Mauritania to them, as does Governor J. Beyries in his work on Islam in Chad (1957). Jamal M. Abun-Nasr has devoted two chapters of *The Tijaniyya* (1965) to the confraternity in West Africa, including the period of European rule. He discusses its relations with the French, its involvement in Senegalese politics from 1934 on, and its relations with other confraternities.

Fernand Quesnot has done unpublished studies of the influence of Mouridism on Tijanism (1951) and on the evolution of the Tijaniyya in Senegal after 1921 (1958). He has published two essays on these subjects in the collection by M. Chailley et al., *Notes et études sur l'Islam en Afrique Noire* (1962). He contended that Muridism is unlikely to satisfy the religious needs of young Senegalese intellectuals. He studied various revival movements, including Hamallism, and presented much data on the personalities who are so important in these movements. In the same collection is an essay by A. Bourbon on the Muridiyya in Senegal. Vincent Monteil has also published (1962) an important article on the same brotherhood, including data on its leader Ahmadu Bamba. Amadou Hampate Ba and M. Cardaire have written (1957) a biography of the distinguished Hamallist chief and Fulani mystic Tierno Bokar (1875–1940) and his religious and political role. Pierre Alexandre (1970) treats Hamallism, and Ba, a disciple of Tierno Bokar, has written about the effects of Islam upon the African personality and social organization in *Présence Africaine* volume from the Abidjan colloquium of 1961. In the same collection is an article by

Vincent Monteil on Black Islam. Lucy C. Behrmann (1970) has written on the relationship of the brotherhoods to political development in Senegal as has Irving Markovitz (1970) in far less detail.

The Chailley collection cited above has articles on Islam in particular areas: Mali, Ivory Coast, and the Mossi lands of the Upper Volta. Other recent data on specific countries and on Islam in Black Africa is found in two collections in English: James Kritzeck and William H. Lewis, eds., *Islam in Africa* (1969); and Ioan Lewis, ed., *Islam in Tropical Africa* (1966). The Kritzeck volume has valuable articles by Pierre Alexandre on Cameroons, John Ballard on Chad, and Alfred Gerteiny on Mauritania, and the Ioan Lewis volume one by Elliott Skinner on Mossi society. General articles in I. Lewis's book by J. C. Froelich on the Islamicization of West Africa and in Kritzeck by Vincent Monteil on marabouts and Humphrey Fisher on separatist movements in West Africa also represent the latest scholarship. A recent French thesis by Picciola has dealt with both Christian and Muslim penetration of northern Ivory Coast peoples since 1918.

A good introduction to the general aspects of social change in the new societies which arose in Africa largely because of colonial rule is Guy Hunter's *The New Societies of Tropical Africa* (1962). The collection of essays edited by Immanuel Wallerstein, *Social Change: The Colonial Situation* (1966), includes a translation of some theoretical writings of Georges Balandier on the colonial situation. The volume by Peter C. Lloyd, *Africa in Social Change: Changing Traditional Societies in the Modern World* (1967), despite the title deals with West Africa. More detailed for the former British territories, it is also useful for the French. Skinner has also published "Labour Migration and its Relationship to Socio-Cultural Change in Mossi Society" (1961). Jean Rouch studied (1956) migrations from French territories into the Gold Coast. M. Dupire and Edmond Bernus examined (1960) relations between native planters and migrant laborers in the coffee and cacao-producing Kong area of lower eastern Ivory Coast and the effects on the culture and society of both groups. J. B. Boutillier studied (1960) the immigrant communities at Bongouanou among the Agni people and the transformation of a largely self-sufficient rural society into a money economy based on cacao, coffee, and kola plantations. Georges Balandier has dealt with the Fang migrations in his studies of Gabon and Congo (1963). Suzanne Bernus has studied (1966) the immigrant groups and their impact upon Niamey, Niger.

In two pioneer studies J.-P. Lebeuf studied the demographic growth of Bangui (1954) and Fort-Lamy (1954). At about the same time

Georges Balandier in *Sociologie des Brazzavilles noires* (1955) studied two immigrant towns that grew up around the European administrative capital of A.E.F. They are Poto-Poto, whose population is drawn from the northeast of the country and southern Oubangui-Chari, and Bacongo, inhabited by Lari people. Balandier analyzes the process of urbanization and the phenomena of acculturation in its sharpest conflicts. He shows the profound psychological, social, and political malaise that arose from the installation of a new economic structure and by the transmission of civic responsibilities to blacks. Concurrently, Marcel Soret examined (1954) urban problems in these same towns and at Dolisie on the Congo-Ocean Railroad.

The immigration of black African workers to France itself was the subject of a study shortly after independence in *Etudes sociales nord-africaines: Africains noirs en France* (1961).

The study of the new social classes resulting from the colonial situation, and especially of the westernized elites, has received much attention, above all recently. The French Communist leader Raymond Barbé in *Les Classes sociales en Afrique Noire* (1964) deals with the transformation of traditional structures under the impact of colonial rule, the factors of social differentiation, and the rise of the bourgeoisie. During the postwar period Jean Pauvert pursued the subject of social classes in French Equatorial Africa (1955). Jean-Louis Seurin studied (1958) the relationship of the social elites to political parties in French West Africa. The sociologist Claude Tardits studied (1958) the new African generations in the Dahomeyan coastal city of Porto Novo in relation to traditional society and the new society. He found that the segmentary lineage was threatened as an economic unit by the fragmentation of landed property and the reduction of available manpower, which was attracted by nonagricultural employment. It was found that within a lineage, traditional practices and innovations are juxtaposed, rather than syncretized.

The status of women has been the subject of frequent study. *La Femme noire en Afrique occidentale* (1939), by Sister M. André du Sacré Coeur, is based on rural study in Mali, Upper Volta, and inland Guinea. It deals with the effects of Islam, Christianity, and Europeans on social organization, including the family. A second work by the same author (1953) deals with the social problems arising from the rapid evolution of African society after the Second World War, including problems relating to women such as marriage, bride wealth, and customary law. Denise Paulme edited (1960) a collection of six essays on women in Black Africa that contains the most complete bibliography of publications on women up to that time (pp. 219–78). The essay by Anne Laurentin treats the changing status of women in Nzakara society in the Central African Republic. Jacques Binet discussed (1956) the situation of women in the cacao-producing areas of the southern Cameroons; Jacques Lombard treats (1954) the evolution of family life and women's status in the Dahomeyan city of Cotonu. Massata Ndiaye discussed (1960) social problems as they existed in the late 1950s and the extension of legal protection and benefits under the postwar French governments.

Race relations is the subject of an older work on colonial society by René Maunier (1932). He discusses contacts between the races and the psychological reactions of both races. He treats the problem of transforming white domination into collaboration.

CONCLUSION

As archives in France are opened for the period after 1914 and as more records in Africa are organized for scholarly use, it is becoming possible to reexamine many aspects of colonial rule and to look at others in detail for the first time. From the inquiries being undertaken in the middle and late sixties, one can already see some of the new interests and perspectives from which the sources are likely to be approached.

Studies which see Africans in the colonial situation as actors and not just reactors have already appeared. An excellent example is Brian Weinstein's article (1970) on Oubangui-Chari. It shows that Africans viewed events involving Félix Eboué and several chiefs from a very different perspective than did European writers. Further collection of the impressions of elderly Africans who lived under colonial rule may offer different perspectives and thereby contribute to a more balanced view of events than is presently available.

During the late 1960s several African and European scholars studied the Christian missions during the colonial period, generally using the archives of the societies and congregations of priests involved. Regrettably, the archives of the congregations of sisters either have not been made available or have not been utilized. Studies of European economic institutions such as concession companies and trading firms are just beginning, though sometimes without the use of the analytical tools of contemporary economics.

Within the colonial period much greater attention is being given to the beginnings of modern African politics between the two world wars and the origins of nationalism. The studies of Adalbert Owona on

Cameroon, Côme Manckasa on Congo-Brazzaville, Jean Domenichini on Madagascar, and G. Wesley Johnson on Senegal illustrate these types of interest. Some of their findings suggest that the links between interwar protest and activities and post-1945 politics may be difficult to establish.

Recent works of synthesis and comparison on colonial rule in West Africa, one by Michael Crowder on British and French territories, another by Jean Suret-Canale on French West and Equatorial Africa, have not included the final period of colonial rule from 1945 to 1960. Failure to do so may give a distorted view of colonial rule, for the way in which the colonial regime acted under stress and was transformed reveals much about its basic structure and processes.

Comparative and synthetic studies like those of Crowder and Suret-Canale, which rely mainly upon secondary works, are very difficult to undertake successfully because of the sheer bulk of the data and the varied conceptual approaches and terminologies in the works being utilized. Despite these obstacles, future works comparing French, Belgian, and Portuguese rule in Equatorial and Central Africa might prove instructive as would comparisons of French, Italian, and British rule in North Africa or of French rule in Black Africa and the Maghrib.

In such publications as the *Bulletin de l'IFAN,* the *Abbia,* and the *Hespéris-Tamuda,* one can see the greatly increased attention which is being given within Africa to the precolonial period. Greater knowledge of the precolonial era has thrown more light on the continuities and changes of the colonial period. This is one of the reasons why the colonial period is increasingly being treated as but one segment in a centuries-long contact between Africa and western nations. Examples of this tendency are the history of Cameroon by Engelbert Mveng (1963) and the history of Morocco by Jean Brignon et al. (1967).

That a team of scholars in Morocco headed by a Frenchman prepared the first really national history of that country indicates the large role which French scholars continue to play within Africa in writing the history of colonial rule. The presence of French scholars resulted in this case from the continued French aid to secondary and higher education in the Maghrib since independence.

In Black Africa a large part of the historical research since independence has been the work of French scholars commissioned by the Office de la Recherche Scientifique et Technique Outre-Mer (ORSTOM) in Paris. Their investigations have been facilitated by the agreements on cultural and educational cooperation which Madagascar and all of the Black African countries except Guinea made with France in 1960 and after. Those agreements also ensured a large French role in the curriculum and personnel of secondary and higher education.[1] In 1967 the fourteen countries of Francophone Africa (again without Guinea) adopted for their secondary schools a common history curriculum which gives a larger place to Africa and Madagascar within the context of world history than did the metropolitan French one previously employed. The new curriculum was the work of a team of nine French scholars and only two Africans. While the establishment of new postsecondary institutions in Cameroon, Congo-Brazzaville, Ivory Coast, Madagascar, Dahomey, and Togo has led to greater attention to the colonial period within national contexts, French scholars are involved at least as much as Africans in this type of research.

As the 1970s began, nearly all of the African historians of colonial rule from formerly French territories and almost all of those pursuing advanced studies had their training in French universities or in African universities using French curricula and largely staffed by Frenchmen. In these countries the number of Africans trained as historians lags behind that in former British territories and necessitates the aid of expatriate staff for a long time to come. Thus despite the new interests and perspectives on the colonial period which appeared during the 1960s, the traditions of French historical scholarship and the role of French scholars remained strong. Under present conditions this situation is likely to persist.

GUIDES TO THE SOURCES

The International Council for Archives, which is affiliated with UNESCO, has planned a series called *Guide to the Sources of the History of Africa*. The first volume, *Quellen zur Geschichte Afrikas sudlich der Sahara in den Archiven der Bundesrepublic Deutschland* (Zug, Switzerland, 1970, 126 pp.) appeared in 1970. The staff of the Overseas Section of the French National Archives has completed the two-volume *Guide des sources archivistiques de l'histoire de l'Afrique au Sud du Sahara*, which is as yet unpublished. It surveys both public and private archives in France as well as the archives of the former

1. Detailed information on cooperation agreements and French aid are found in two official government publications: La Documentation Française, "La Coopération entre la France, l'Afrique Noire d'Expression Française, et Madagascar," *Notes et Etudes Documentaires*, no. 3330 (October 25, 1966), 47 pp; and "Le Service de la Coopération Culturelle, Scientifique, et Technique avec les Etats Francophones Africains et Malgache: bilan et perspectives," *Notes et Etudes Documentaires*, no. 3787 (May 4, 1971), 34 pp.

French territories in West and Equatorial Africa.[2] The series will also include two volumes from Italy and one from the Holy Sea, Spain, Scandinavia, Belgium, the United Kingdom, and the United States. Inter Documentation AG of Zug, Switzerland, is publishing all but the last three volumes, which will appear with other publishers.

Until these volumes appear, an annotated bibliography by Helen F. Conover (*African Libraries, Book Production, and Archives: A List of References,* Library of Congress, 1962, 64 pp.) and a bibliographical article by Peter Duignan ("Library and Archive Collections in Sub-Saharan Africa: A Bibliography," *A Current Bibliography of African Affairs,* parts 1 and 2, July and August 1969) continue to have value. Conover cites both published guides and articles about archival holdings in Africa. Her citations for North Africa reveal a lack of guides for the archives of the Residency in Tunisia. Duignan's references on library and archival collections supplement and update the Conover work for Black Africa.[3] Articles by Jean Valette on the Madagascar archives (*Africana Newsletter,* Fall 1964, pp. 70–72), by David E. Gardinier on those in Yaounde, Cameroon (*Africana Newsletter,* Summer 1963, pp. 37–38), and G. Wesley Johnson on the archives of the countries of French West Africa ("The Archival System of Former French West Africa," *African Studies Bulletin,* April 1965, pp. 48–58) are among the most important cited. A continuing source of information about the Senegal Archives is its *Bulletin bibliographique des archives du Sénégal.* Laurence Porges's bibliography (*Bibliographie des régions du Sénégal* (Dakar, 1969, 707 pp.) lists the archival holdings on each of the seven regions of Senegal, including the annual administrative reports for the years 1945 to 1958.

Although some of the materials at Brazzaville have been transferred to Aix, the article by Jean Glénisson ("Les archives de l'A.E.F.: Lettre de Brazzaville," *Gazette des Archives,* n.s. 22 [July 1957]: 23–30) still gives the best indication of holdings on the Equatorial Africa federation. Hubert Deschamps in *Traditions orales et archives au Gabon* (Paris, 1962, pp. 143–58), reported on the archives at Libreville and at several regional centers of Gabon. When David Gardinier visited Libreville in July 1969, the archives were not yet organized for use by researchers, nor were the ones at Bangui, the Central African Republic. It was not possible to enter Brazzaville to make inquiries about

2. A report on the archives of the former French North African countries will be included in a volume on the Arab countries of Africa distinct from this series.

3. Duignan and Conover have collaborated on a *Guide to African Research Materials,* to be published by the Hoover Institution of Stanford University in 1971.

the Congo archives. In Fort Lamy the Institut National Tchadien pour les Sciences Humaines held copies of many administrative reports from the periods before 1945. But the holdings of the Chad Archives have not been catalogued and nothing definite could be learned about the possibilities of using them.

For West African materials in European archives there have been several guides compiled by the Institute of Historical Research of the University of London (Patricia Carson, *Materials for West African History in the Archives of Belgium and Holland* [London, 1962]; which is supplemented by H. M. Feinberg, "Further Additions to *Materials* . . . by Patricia Carson", *African Studies Bulletin,* April 1969, pp. 81–89; A. F. C. Ryder, *Materials for West African History in Portuguese Archives* [London, 1965]; J. R. Gray and D. S. Chambers, *Materials for West African History in Italian Archives* [London, 1965]; Patricia Carson, *Materials for West African History in French Archives* [London, 1968]). The volume on French materials includes archives and library collections in the provinces as well as Paris. Additional information on French provincial centers is provided by Joanne Coyle Dauphin in "French Provincial Centers of Documentation and Research on Africa" (*African Studies Bulletin,* December 1966, pp. 48–65. The *Répertoire des bibliothèques d'étude et organismes de documentation* (Paris, 1963) lists 2,382 research collections and libraries in France, 30 of them dealing specifically with Africa and others having Africana. In 1969 there was issued an *Inventaire des Ressources Documentaires Africanistes à Paris,*[4] which contains information on archives and library collections. At present the Groupe de Recherches sur l'Histoire de l'Afrique Noire du Centre d'Etudes Africaines, Ecole Pratique des Hautes Etudes, Sorbonne, 6e Section: Sciences Economiques et Sociales, is undertaking inventories of several Paris collections and private papers of colonial figures.

The Carson volume on French materials for West Africa cites the main guides (pp. 2–3) to French holdings, which can also be used for locating materials on North Africa. A very important article by Vincent Confer, "The Dépot in Aix and Archival Sources for France Outre-Mer" (*French Historical Studies,* Spring 1969, pp. 120–26), describes the organization of a branch of the National Archives at Aix and lists the registers of its holdings. Included are materials brought

4. *Bulletin d'information et de liaison: Recherche, enseignement, documentation africaniste francophone* (Centre d'Analyse et de Recherche Documentation pour l'Afrique Noire [CARDAN], Paris), *1,* no. 1, (1969).

from Algeria, the Sahara, Madagascar, and Equatorial Africa, with the North African holdings being the most numerous. There are as well microfilms of materials left at Dakar. Archivist Pierre Boyer, "Présentation des archives d'Outre-Mer d'Aix-en-Provence", (*Bulletin d'Histoire des Pays d'Outre-Mer* 5 [1968–69]: 10–19) provides further details. The same journal also published F. Rebuffat's "Ressources des services historiques (Archives, bibliothèques, et musée) de la Chambre de commerce et d'industrie de Marseille pour l'histoire des pays d'Outre-Mer" *3* [1968–69]: 34–38).

The Institute of Historical Research of the University of London is currently preparing a fifth volume on materials for West African history, this one including the British archival sources. Much of the data is being drawn from a volume on the British sources for African history, compiled by Noel Matthews and M. Doreen Wainwright on behalf of the School of Oriental and African Studies, which has been accepted for publication by the Oxford University Press. Unlike the German and French volumes in the ICA series, this guide includes documents on northern Africa. In 1967 the Standing Committee on Library Materials on Africa (SCOLMA) issued a revised directory of libraries and special collections on Africa in Great Britain. In the same year Donald D. Leopard in "African-Related Materials in European Missionary Archives" (*African Studies Bulletin,* September 1967, pp. 1–5) described the holdings of four Protestant mission societies which were active in Madagascar, three in London and the Société des Missions Evangéliques de Paris.

The *Annuaire d'Afrique du Nord* has published two important articles on archives for North Africa. Pierre Guillen in "Les Sources Allemandes sur le Maroc (fin du XIXe-debut du XXe siècle)" (*2* [1963]: 1023–38) discusses German sources on the eve of the French penetration of Morocco. V. Aumeunier and Jean-Louis Miège in "Sources italiennes sur l'Afrique du Nord" (*3* [1964]: 713–26; and *5* [1966]: 793–812) report upon Italian government, provincial, and Vatican archives in the nineteenth century, as well as those of the independent polities such as the Two Sicilies which existed until the 1860s.

Peter Duignan's *Handbook of American Resources for African Studies* (Stanford, 1966) is a monumental contribution to library and manuscript collections, church and missionary libraries and archives, and business archives. It includes a long section (pp. 59–99) by Morris Rieger on the holdings of the United States National Archives. Rieger is preparing the United States volume in the ICA series. The American volume encompasses North African materials as well as sub-Saharan ones. Details of the project are found in the *African Studies Bulletin* (April 1965, pp. 80–82).

Archivum: Revue Internationale des Archives (Paris), the review of the International Council for Archives; *Gazette des Archives,* the quarterly organ of the Association Amicale Professionnelle des Archivistes Français; and *Library Materials on Africa* (London), publication of SCOLMA, can be expected to report further archival activities.

OFFICIAL PUBLICATIONS

The African section of the reference department of the Library of Congress has pioneered in the production of guides to official documents. It has published *Official Publications of French West Africa, 1946–1958: A Guide* (1960, 88 pp.); *Official Publications of French Equatorial Africa, French Cameroons, and Togo, 1946–1958: A Guide* (1964, 78 pp.); *Madagascar and Adjacent Islands: A Guide to Official Publications* (1965, 58 pp.); *French-Speaking West Africa: A Guide to Official Publications* (1967, 201 pp.). The last two volumes cover the entire period of French rule and the very last one incorporates Togoland along with the eight countries of the French West African Federation. Julian W. Witherell, the compiler of the last three of these excellent guides, cites the French bibliographical guides to official publications. They include the *Bibliographie de France* and its *Suppléments* A and F, published in Paris since 1911, and the *Bibliographie sélective des publications officielles françaises* published semimonthly from 1952. Both publications contain many references to official documents on North Africa. But there are no guides for French North Africa comparable to the Congressional Library volumes for Sub-Saharan Africa. *Official Publications of Somaliland, 1941–1959: A Guide* (Library of Congress, 1960), compiled by Helen F. Conover, has two pages of references to French Somaliland.

The publications of the United Nations and the League of Nations have been carefully indexed. In addition, Hans Aufricht's *Guide to League of Nations Publications: A Bibliographical Survey of the Work of the League, 1920–1947* (New York, 1951, 682 pp.) gives references to the materials on the mandates of Togoland and the Cameroons.

SERIALS

In 1970 the African section of the Library of Congress completed *Sub-Saharan Africa: A Guide to Serials,* which includes over 4,600 entries. The Near East section of the library is preparing a list of serials for the Middle East, including the Maghrib. Until it appears, the Library's earlier volume *Serials for African Studies* (1961) can be consulted for periodicals dealing with French North Africa. In 1965 SCOLMA issued a list of periodicals published in Algeria, Tunisia, and Morocco as supplement to the November 1965 issue of *Library Materials on Africa.* In 1969 there appeared a *Liste de périodiques africanistes édités en France* [5] and a *Liste mondiale des périodiques spécialises: études africaines* (Paris: Maison des Sciences de l'Homme, 1969, 214 pp.), the latter an annotated list of social studies serials for Sub-Saharan Africa.

The Press in Africa, edited by Helen Kitchen (Washington, 1956) provides tabulated indexes for the principal newspapers which existed in the post–World War II era. It gives special emphasis to the African press. "Cameroon Newspapers: Before and After Independence" (*Africana Newsletter,* Spring 1963, pp. 8–12) gives additional information on the press of that country. The Library of Congress, *African Newspapers in Selected American Libraries* (3d ed. 1965, 135 pp.) provides a union list of holdings in thirty-three American libraries.

DISSERTATIONS AND THESES

1. United States. In 1962 the Library of Congress published *A List of American Doctoral Dissertations on Africa* (69 pp.) which cited those completed through 1960. There is no volume which cites dissertations between 1961 and 1964. Only in the 1965 volume of *United States and Canadian Publications on Africa* did coverage of dissertations reported in *Dissertation Abstracts* begin. In 1970 the Library of Congress issued *American Doctoral Dissertations on the Arab World, 1883–1968* (103 pp.), which includes those on the Maghrib.

2. Great Britain. In 1964 a list of theses on Africa accepted by United Kingdom and Irish universities up to 1962 was published by SCOLMA. Beginning in the year 1963 SCOLMA has issued an annual volume of all United Kingdom publications and theses on Africa (1963 through 1966 so far). The Institute of Historical Research of the University of London annually issues a bibliography of British dissertations. In 1970 there appeared lists of dissertations in African history completed in 1969 and those still in progress at the beginning of 1970.

3. France. The periodicals *Penant* and *Revue Française de Science Politique* for many years have carried annual lists of doctoral dissertations and often *mémoires* presented for diplomas at various institutes

5. *Bulletin d'information et de Liaison, Recherche, enseignement, documentation africanistes francophones, 1,* no. 4, (1969): 114–43.

in the social sciences and law. Marion Dinstel has compiled *List of French Doctoral Dissertations on Africa, 1884–1961* (Boston, 1966, 336 pp.). The Centre d'Analyse et de Recherche Documentaires pour l'Afrique Noire in Paris has announced plans for an annual compilation of all dissertations, theses, and *mémoires* completed and in progress in French-speaking countries, including Belgium and Canada. Britta Rupp and A. Rosset compiled *Inventaire de thèses et mémoires africanistes de langue française soutenus depuis 1966,* which is volume 1 (no. 2, 1969) of the *BIL, REDAF* (93 pp.) (full citation footnote 4 above). The same periodical listed twelve hundred studies in progress in French-language institutions in volume 1 (no. 3, 1969) and volume 2 (no. 1, 1970).

BOOKS AND ARTICLES

Though incomplete and sparsely annotated, *Afrique noire d'expression française, sciences sociales et humaines: guide de lecture* (Paris: CARDAN, 1969, 301 pp.) is the best general recent bibliographical guide to Sub-Saharan Africa. It omits Madagascar and the French Territory of the Afars and Issas. The first three pages list twenty important bibliographies. Completed and to be published under the auspices of the University of Dakar is Paule Brasseur and Jean-François Maurel's *Les sources bibliographiques de l'Afrique de l'ouest et de l'Afrique équatoriale d'expression française.*

Among the most important older bibliographies are those prepared by Helen M. Conover of the Library of Congress. *Africa South of the Sahara: A Selected, Annotated List of Writings* (1963) is a valuable compilation of three thousand titles. It too lists the bibliographies existing at the time. Three pre-World War II bibliographies still have much value: Monroe N. Work, *A Bibliography of the Negro in Africa and America* (New York, 1928; reprinted 1965); Georges Bruel, *Bibliographie de l'A.E.F.* (Paris, 1914, 330 pp.); Edmond Joucla, *Bibliographie l'A.O.F.* (Paris, 1937, 704 pp.). Unfortunately, there is no comparable volume for North Africa. The North African sections of *Introduction to Africa* (1952) and *North and Northeast Africa: A Selected, Annotated List of Writings, 1951–1957* (1957) cover writings available in the Library of Congress through 1957.

For North Africa, some additional guides should be cited. Since 1962 the *Annuaire de l'Afrique du Nord,* edited at Aix, has contained a two-part bibliography (alphabetical and systematic) of articles and book reviews. While most complete for works in French, it cites a great many items published in English-speaking lands. Benjamin Rivlin's

"Selective Survey of the Literature in the Social Sciences and Related Fields on Modern North Africa" (*American Political Science Review*, September 1954, pp. 826–48), is an excellent introduction. Maurice Flory, Roger Le Tourneau, and Jean-Paul Trystram's "L'Afrique du Nord: état des travaux" (*Revue Française de Science Politique*, June 1959, pp. 410–53) is a comparable effort but almost exclusively of works in French. Paul E. A. Romeril's "Tunisian Nationalism: A Bibliographical Outline" (*Middle East Journal*, Spring 1960, pp. 206–15) updates the Tunisia section of Rivlin, while Jean-Louis Miège and Viviane Michel's "Le Maroc, 1959–1962: état de travaux" (*Revue Française de Science Politique* [1964]: 885–910) performs a similar function in relation to Flory et al. André Martel's "Le Maghreb" (*Revue Française d'Histoire d'Outre-Mer 206* [1970]) discusses historical literature of the late 1960s, in particular that treating Morocco.

For Black Africa in general, Kenneth Robinson's "Survey of the Background Material for the Study of Government in French Tropical Africa" (*American Political Science Review 50* [1956]: 179–98) is supplemented by John A. Ballard's "Politics and Government in Former French West and Equatorial Africa: A Critical Bibliography (*Journal of Modern African Studies 3* [1965]: 589–605). Together they cover most of the materials on the political evolution of Black Africa from 1945 to 1960. Guy Feuer's "Madagascar: état des travaux" (*Revue Française de Science Politique*, December 1962, pp. 920–62) adds the Malagasy dimension, especially on politics and history. Finally, Roger Pasquier's "Chronique de l'histoire coloniale: l'Afrique Noire d'expression française" (*Revue Française d'Histoire d'Outre-Mer* [1961]: 438–57; and [1963]: 74–129, 382–535) is a detailed essay on works in French from the entire colonial period.

Two publications of the Oxford University Press provide a Soviet view of French Africa. Mary Holdsworth's *Soviet African Studies, 1918–1959* (1961) is supplemented by a more detailed annotated bibliography, *Soviet Writing on Africa, 1959–1961* (1963). R. Lowenthal has compiled "Russian Materials on Africa: A Selective Bibliography" (*Der Islam*, October 1960, pp. 128–51). Samir Zoghby of the Library of Congress is compiling *Islam in Africa South of the Sahara: An Annotated Guide*. A bibliography on West Africa compiled by Ruth Jones for the International African Institute (1958) is very complete for ethnography, sociology, and linguistics.[6]

6. Ruth Jones, comp, *African Bibliographical Series, West Africa: General, Ethnography, Sociology, Linguistics* (London: *International African Institute*, 1958, 116 pp.).

A number of bibliographical guides published in the 1960s on individual countries of Sub-Saharan Africa have value for the historian of the colonial period. They include: Charles Toupet, "Orientation bibliographique sur la Mauritanie" (*Bulletin de L'IFAN*, ser. B [1959]: 201–35; and [1962]: 594–613); Laurence Porgès, *Bibliographie des régions du Sénégal* (Dakar, 1969, 707 pp.); Paule Brasseur, *Bibliographie générale du Mali* (Dakar, 1964, 462 pp.). Françoise Izard, *Bibliographie générale de la Haute-Volta, 1956–1965* (Paris and Ouagadougou, 1967, 300 pp.); Guillaume da Silva, "Contribution à la bibliographie du Dahomey" (*Etudes Dahoméennes,* June 1968 and January 1969, 4,286 items); André Jacquot, *Catalogue des publications et rapports du service des sciences humaines, 1949–1967* (Brazzaville, 1968, 91 pp.), which lists the studies, both published and unpublished, of twenty-five researchers at the ORSTOM; Françoise Perrois, *Gabon: répertoire bibliographique des études de sciences humaines, 1960–1967* (Libreville, 1969, 58 pp.); Jean-Paul Lebeuf, *Bibliographie du Tchad* (*sciences humaines*) (Fort Lamy, 1968, 2,044 items). Hans E. Panofsky has prepared a manuscript on national libraries and bibliographies in Africa (34 pp.), which is deposited in the Africana section of the Northwestern University Library.

From 1960 there have been annual bibliographies of all U. S. and Canadian publications on Africa. The Library of Congress published the volume for 1960 and the Hoover Institution has published the volumes from 1961 to 1966 so far.[7] The volume for 1967, which was completed in 1970, is as yet unpublished. Beginning with the year 1963 SCOLMA has issued an annual volume of all *United Kingdom Publications and Theses on Africa* (1963–66 to date). For German-speaking Europe for the years since 1960 there has been published *Afrika: Bibliographie: Verzeichnis der wissenschaftlichen Literatur aus Deutschland, Osterreich, Der Schweiz* (Bonn: Schroeder für Deutsche Afrika-Gesellschaft). For France the Comité Inter-Bibliothèques de Documentation Africaine (CIDA), located at the Bibliothèque Nationale, issued its first annual bibliography of French books and articles on Sub-Saharan Africa for 1968, published by CARDAN in 1969. The Ivory Coast Government began the annual publication of *Bibliographie de la Côte d'Ivoire* for the year 1968 (1970).

Many periodicals carry bibliographies of use to the historian. *The Middle East Journal* (Washington) includes North Africa in its bib-

7. From 1960 to 1964 the title was *United States and Canadian Publications on Africa in 1960,* etc., and from 1965, *United States and Canadian Publications and Theses on Africa in 1965,* etc.

liographical coverage and has references to book reviews. The *American Historical Review* has a bibliography of articles on the Near East by Sidney Glazer which includes citations on North Africa. Since 1964 the same review has published a bibliography of articles on African history prepared by David Gardinier. Ruth Jones's "Survey of Bibliographical Services Covering Current Publications on Africa," in J. D. Pearson and Ruth Jones, ed., *The Bibliography of Africa* (New York, 1970, 301–48), provides a guide to current bibliographies of both books and articles, while in the same volume Julian Witherell's "Appendix 2: Bibliographical Control of Periodical Literature on Africa" (pp. 355–59) lists periodicals which contain bibliographies.

OFFICIALS

RESPONSIBILITY FOR COLONIAL AFFAIRS IN FRANCE

Responsibility for French possessions in Africa was divided between the Ministry of the Interior (Algeria), the Ministry of Foreign Affairs (Morocco and Tunisia), and the Ministry of the Colonies. Responsibility for Algerian affairs between 1830 and 1871 under the July Monarchy, the Second Republic, and the Second Empire is a complicated story, best set out in tableau 1, pp. 501–02 of Charles-André Julien's *Histoire de l'Algérie contemporaine,* volume 1, *La Conquête et les debuts de la colonisation, 1827–1871,* (Paris, 1964). In appendix 2 of the English edition of Henri Brunschwig's *French Colonialism, 1871–1914* (London, 1966, pp. 194–98) there is a note on the central administration of the colonies. The Directions des Colonies evolved gradually to full departmental status, beginning as part of the Ministry of the Navy (from 1815), becoming for one year (1881) a Ministry of Commerce and the Colonies, then an undersecretaryship of state from 1882 to 1894, and finally in that year a Ministry of the Colonies.

Political Heads of French Colonial Administration 1871–1940 [8]

Minister of the Navy and the Colonies

Louis Pothuau, vice-admiral	February 15, 1871
Charles de Dampierre d'Hornoy, vice-admiral	May 25, 1873
Marquis Louis de Montaignac de Chauvange, rear-admiral	May 22, 1874
Martin Fourichon, vice-admiral and senator	
Berthault, general (May 17–22, 1877)	March 5, 1875

8. Sources: Henri Brunschwig, *French Colonialism 1871–1914,* pp. 195–98 and William Cohen, *Rulers of Empire: The French Colonial Service in Africa* (Stanford, 1971), p. 204.

Albert Gicquet des Touches, vice-admiral	May 23, 1877
Albert Roussin, vice-admiral	November 23, 1877
Louis Pothuau, vice-admiral and now also senator	December 13, 1877
Jean Jauréguiberry, vice-admiral and senator	February 4, 1879
Louis Pothuau, vice-admiral and senator	September 23, 1880

Minister of Commerce and the Colonies

Pierre Rouvier, deputy	November 14, 1881

Under-Secretary of State for the Colonies

Albert Berlet, deputy	January 30, 1882
Félix Faure, deputy	September 22, 1883
Armand Rousseau, deputy	April 28, 1885
Jean de La Porte, deputy	January 15, 1886
Eugène Etienne, deputy	June 7, 1887
Félix Faure, deputy	January 5, 1888
Jean de La Porte, deputy	February 19, 1888
Eugène Etienne, deputy	March 14, 1889
Emile Jamais, deputy	March 8, 1892
Théophile Delcassé, deputy	January 18, 1893
Maurice Lebon, deputy	December 3, 1893

Minister for the Colonies

Ernest Boulanger, senator	March 20, 1894
Théophile Delcassé, deputy	May 30, 1894
André Chautemps, deputy	January 26, 1895
Pierre Guieyesse, deputy	November 4, 1896
André Lebon, deputy	April 29, 1896
Georges Trouillot, deputy	June 29, 1898
Antoine Guillain, deputy	November 1, 1898
Albert Decrais, deputy	June 22, 1899
Gaston Doumergue, deputy	June 7, 1902
Etienne Clémentel, deputy	June 24, 1905
Georges Leygues, deputy	March 18, 1906
Raphaël Milliès-Lacroix, senator	October 25, 1906
Georges Trouillot, deputy	July 25, 1909
Jean Morel, deputy	November 3, 1910
Adolphe Messimy, deputy	March 2, 1911
Albert Lebrun, deputy	June 27, 1911
René Besnard, deputy	January 12, 1913
Jean Morel, deputy	January 21, 1913
Albert Lebrun, deputy	December 9, 1913
Maurice Maunoury, deputy	June 3, 1914
Maurice Raynaud, deputy	June 13, 1914
Gaston Doumergue, senator	August 26, 1914

André Maginot, deputy	March 21, 1917
René Besnard	September 13, 1917
Henri Simon (Clemenceau Ministry)	November 17, 1917
Albert Sarraut	January 20, 1920
Jean Fabry	March 29, 1924
Edouard Daladier	June 14, 1924
André Hesse	April 17, 1925
Léon Perier	October 29, 1925
Dariac	July 19, 1926
Léon Perier	July 23, 1926
André Maginot	November 11, 1928
François Piétri	March 2, 1930
Théodore Steeg	December 13, 1930
Paul Reynaud	January 27, 1931
Louis de Chappedelaine	February 20, 1932
Albert Sarraut	June 3, 1932
Albert Dalimier	September 6, 1933
François Piétri	October 26, 1933
Albert Dalimier	November 26, 1933
Henry de Jouvenel [9]	January 30, 1934
Pierre Laval	February 9, 1934
Louis Rollin	October 13, 1934
Jacques Stern	January 24, 1936
Marius Moutet	June 4, 1936
Théodore Steeg	January 18, 1938
Marius Moutet	March 13, 1938
Georges Mandel	April 10, 1938
Louis Rollin	May 18, 1940

After the fall of France in 1940, there was great confusion in the direction of colonial affairs. Following the lead of Chad in August 1940, the four colonies of A.E.F. reentered the war on the side of Great Britain, repudiating the Vichy regime. De Gaulle toured A.E.F. in October 1940 and established a High Commissariat for the Free French at Brazzaville. The administration in French West Africa under Governor General Boisson, however, remained loyal to the Vichy government of Pétain until the Allied landing in North Africa in November 1942. Relations between the Vichy government and many of the West and North African colonies had by this time seriously deteriorated. In June of 1943 a provisional government formed in Algiers by de Gaulle took over the direction and planning of colonial affairs. The accompanying table indicates for the major French governments of

9. Only one to use the title of "Ministre de la France d'Outre-Mer" before World War II.

GOVERNMENTS AND MINISTRIES PERTAINING TO AFRICA

The French Committee for National Liberation (CFLN) and the Provisional Governments

Dates	*Premiers*	*Foreign Minister*	*Overseas Minister*
CFLN June 3, 1943–June 2, 1944	Charles de Gaulle Henri Giraud	René Massigli	
First provisional government June 3, 1944–Nov. 9, 1945	Charles de Gaulle	René Massigli later Georges Bidault (MRP)	René Pleven Giacobbi
Second provisional government Nov. 13, 1945–Jan. 20, 1946	Charles de Gaulle resigned on Jan. 20, 1946	Georges Bidault (MRP)	Jacques Soustelle (UDSR)
Third provisional government Jan. 23–June 11, 1946	Félix Gouin (SFIO)	Georges Bidault (MRP)	Marius Moutet (SFIO)
Fourth provisional government June 19–Nov. 28, 1946	Georges Bidault (MRP)	Georges Bidault (MRP)	Marius Moutet (SFIO)
Fifth provisional government Dec. 12, 1946–Jan. 16, 1947	Léon Blum (SFIO)	Léon Blum (SFIO)	Marius Moutet (in CR)
The Fourth Republic Jan. 21–Nov. 19, 1947 + 2 cabinet reshuffles (May and Oct. 1947)	Paul Ramaudier (SFIO)	Georges Bidault (MRP)	Marius Moutet (in CR)
Nov. 22, 1947–July 19, 1948	Robert Schuman (MRP)	Georges Bidault (MRP)	Paul Coste-Floret (MRP)
July 24–Aug. 28, 1948	André Marie (Rad.)	Robert Schuman (MRP)	Paul Coste-Floret (MRP)
Sept. 10, 1948–Oct. 6, 1949	Henri Queuille (Rad.)	Robert Schuman (MRP)	Paul Coste-Floret (MRP)

Oct. 27, 1949–June 24, 1950	Georges Bidault (MRP)	Robert Schuman (MRP)	Jean Letourneau (MRP)
July 11, 1950–Feb. 28, 1951	René Pleven (UDSR)	Robert Schuman (MRP)	François Mitterrand (UDSR)
Mar. 9–July 10, 1951	Henri Queuille (Rad.)	Robert Schuman (MRP)	François Mitterrand (UDSR)
Aug. 8, 1951–Jan. 7, 1952	René Pleven (UDSR)	Robert Schuman (MRP)	Louis Jacquinot (Ind. Rep.)
Jan. 18–Feb. 29, 1952	Edgar Faure (Rad.)	Robert Schuman (MRP)	Louis Jacquinot (Ind. Rep.)
Mar. 6–Dec. 23, 1952	Antoine Pinay (Ind.)	Robert Schuman (MRP)	Pierre Pflimlin (MRP)
Jan. 7–May 21, 1953	René Mayer (Rad.)	Georges Bidault (MRP)	Louis Jacquinot (Ind. Rep.)
June 26, 1953–June 12, 1954	Joseph Laniel (Ind.)	Georges Bidault (MRP)	Louis Jacquinot (Ind. Rep.)
June 18, 1954–Feb. 5, 1955 *	Pierre Mendès-France (Rad.)	Pierre Mendès-France (Rad.) Edgar Faure (Rad.)	Robert Buron (MRP)
Feb. 23, 1955–Jan. 24, 1956 * + 1 cabinet reshuffle (Oct. 6, 1955)	Edgar Faure (Rad.)	Antoine Pinay (Ind.)	Pierre-Henri Teitgen (MRP)
Jan. 31, 1956–May 21, 1957 *	Guy Mollet (SFIO)	Christian Pineau (SFIO)	Gaston Defferre (SFIO)

* In the governments of Mendès-France and Faure a special cabinet post of Minister for Moroccan and Tunisian Affairs existed (from June 19, 1954 to Oct. 20, 1955), and it was held respectively by Christian Fouchet (Soc. Rep.) and Pierre July (ARS, then RGR). The ministry was then dissolved and its powers reassumed by th Quai d'Orsay. In the Mollet cabinet, Alain Savary (SFIO) was the Secretary of State for Foreign Affairs in charge of Moroccan and Tunisian Affairs until he resigned on Nov. 4, 1956.

the provisional period and of the Fourth Republic (omitting a few caretaker governments which lasted a matter of days) the premier, the minister of foreign affairs, and the overseas minister. Party affiliations, if any, are given in parentheses.[10]

RESPONSIBILITY FOR COLONIAL AFFAIRS IN BRITAIN

A full discussion of the devolution of responsibility for British colonial territories in Africa is given in Gifford and Louis, eds., *Britain and Germany in Africa* (New Haven, 1967, pp. 768–70), together with lists of Secretaries of State for Foreign Affairs, Secretaries of State for Colonies, and Permanent Colonial Undersecretaries. The disposition of each official's papers is also indicated, so far as it is known.

ARCHIVES DIPLOMATIQUES FRANÇAISES

The most recent information from the Archives Diplomatiques Françaises is that "the Archives prior to May 31, 1918 are actually open to the public (with the exception of Private Papers and Personal Files subject to special regulations). . . . Reconstitution and reconstruction of the Archives [following destruction during the last war] has progressed so that the files for the period from June 1918–1929 will be opened in early 1973. The necessary reorganization of the files for the period from 1929–1945 before they can be opened for research has now begun. By 1976 it may be possible to apply normally the so-called rule of thirty years."

We do not yet know whether a similar rule will be applied to colonial materials.

OFFICIALS LOCALLY RESPONSIBLE FOR FRENCH AND BRITISH COLONIES IN AFRICA

David P. Henige in *Colonial Governors from the Fifteenth Century to the Present* (Madison, 1970) sets out comprehensive lists of governors and chief administrators for all European colonies, territories and dependencies in Africa. There is no need to repeat here his most useful and clearly presented information. The colonies are listed alphabetically under France (twenty-seven entries for Africa and Madagascar) and Great Britain (thirty-three entries for Africa).

10. Sources: Ruth Schachter Morgenthau, *Political Parties in French-Speaking West Africa* (Oxford, 1964), appendix 1, p. 378; Stéphane Bernard, *The Franco-Moroccan Conflict 1943–1956* (New Haven, 1968), annex 2, 656–58.

☙ LIST OF TITLES

Those titles marked with an asterisk have been discussed in the preceding essay, and are followed by the numbers of the pages on which they are mentioned.

*Abbas, Ferhat, *De la Colonie vers la province: le Jeune Algérien.* Paris, 1931. P. 800.

*———, *La Nuit Coloniale,* Paris, 1962. P. 809.

Abbou, Isaac D., *Musulmans andalous et judéo-espagnols,* Casablanca, 1953.

*Abun-Nasr, Jamil M., "The Salafiyya Movement in Morocco: The Religious Bases of the Moroccan Nationalist Movement," *St. Antony's Papers, 16* (London, 1963), 90–105. P. 822.

*———, *The Tijaniyya: A Sufi Order in the Modern World,* London, 1965. Pp. 795, 883.

*Adam, André, *Le "Bidonville" de Ben Msik à Casablanca. Contribution à l'étude du prolétariat musulman au Maroc,* Algiers, 1950. P. 827.

*———, *La Maison et le village dans quelques tribus de l'Anti-Atlas,* Paris, 1951. P. 828.

*———, *Casablanca: Essai sur la transformation de la Société Marocaine au Contact de l'Occident,* 2 vols., Paris, 1968. P. 828.

*———, *Histoire de Casablanca (des origines à 1914),* Aix, 1968. P. 828.

Afrika-Institut (Pays-Bas), *L'Avenir du droit coutumier en Afrique, Symposium-Colloque,* Amsterdam, 1955. Leiden, 1956.

Agblemagnon, Ferdinand N., "Masses et élites en Afrique Noire: le cas du Togo," *The New Elites of Tropical Africa,* ed. P. C. Lloyd (1966), 118–25.

*Ageron, Charles-Robert, "L'Emir Khaled, petit-fils d'Abdelkhader, fut-il le premier nationaliste algérien?, *Revue de l'occident musulman, 2* (1966), 9–49. P. 801.

———, *Histoire de l'Algérie contemporaine,* Paris, 1966.

*———, "Le mouvement *jeune-algérien,*" *Etudes maghrébines,* Paris, 1964, 217–43. P. 801.

*Agwani, M. S., "Morocco: From Protectorate to Independence," *International Studies* (July 1959), 51–70. P. 826.

*Ahmed, Hocine Ait, *La Guerre et l'après-guerre,* Paris, 1964. P. 809.

Akindélé, Adolphe, and Cyrille Aguessy, *Contribution à l'étude de l'histoire de l'ancien royaume de Porto-Novo,* Dakar, 1953.

*Akindélé, Adolphe, and Cyrille Aguessy, *Le Dahomey*, Paris, 1955. P. 857.
*Alazard, J., et al., *Initiation à l'Algérie*, Paris, 1957. P. 797.
*Albertini, Eugène, G. Marçais, and G. Yver, *L'Afrique du Nord Française dans l'histoire*, Paris, 1937. P. 787.
*Albertini, Rudolf von, *Dekolonisation, Die Diskussion über Verwaltung und Zukunft der Kolonien, 1919–1960*, Cologne and Opladen, 1966. Pp. 792, 838, 845, 851.
*Alexandre, Pierre, "Le Problème des chefferies en Afrique noire française," *La Documentation Française*, No. 2508 (Feb. 10, 1959). P. 862.
*———, "A West African Islamic Movement: Hamallism in French West Africa," *Protest and Power in Black Africa*, ed. R. I. Rotberg and A. A. Mazrui, New York, 1970, 497–512. P. 883.
*al-Fasi, Allal, *The Independent Movements in Arab North Africa*, Washington, 1954 (trans. from 1948 Arabic original). P. 823.
*Algérie, Cabinet du Ministre, *Action du gouvernement en Algérie. Mesures de pacification et réformes*, Algiers, 1957. P. 804.
*"Les Algériens en France: étude démographique et sociale," in *Etudes sociales nord-africaines, Cahiers nord-africains*, Paris, 1955. P. 813.
*Allais, Maurice, *Les Accords d'Évian. Le réferendum et la résistance algérienne. L'autorité, la majorité, le droit*, Paris, 1962. P. 810.
*Alleg, Henri, *The Question*, New York, 1958. P. 807.
Alwan, Mohammed, *Algeria before the United Nations*, New York, 1959. P. 807.
*Amenumey, D. E. K., "The Pre-1947 Background of the Ewe Unification Question," *Transactions of the Historical Society of Ghana, 10* (1969), 65–84. P. 835.
*Amin, Samir, *Trois expériences africaines de développement: le Mali, la Guinée, et le Ghana*, Paris, 1965. P. 868.
*———, *L'Economie du Maghreb*, 2 vols., Paris, 1966. P. 790.
*———, *Le Développement du capitalisme en Côte d'Ivoire*, Paris, 1967. P. 869.
*———, and Catherine Coquery-Vidrovitch, *Histoire économique du Congo, 1880–1968. Du Congo français à l'Union douanière de l'Afrique centrale*, Paris, 1969. P. 870.
*Amon d'Aby, F. J., *Le problème des chefferies traditionnelles en Côte d'Ivoire*, Paris, 1949. P. 863.
*———, *La Côte d'Ivoire dans la Cité Africaine*, Paris, 1951. P. 856.
Amos-Djoro, Ernest, *Les Mouvements marginaux du protestantisme africain: les Harristes en Côte d'Ivoire*, Mémoire, University of Paris, 1956.
*———, "Les Eglises harristes et le nationalisme ivoirien," *Mois en Afrique* (May 1966). P. 881.
*Anchouey, Michel, *La vie politique du Gabon de 1960 à 1965*, Mémoire, University of Poitiers, 1965. P. 860.
*Andersson, Efraim, *Messianic Popular Movements in the Lower Congo*, Uppsala, 1958. P. 881.
*———, *Churches at the Grass-Roots: A Study in Congo-Brazzaville*, London, 1968. P. 879.
Andrain, Charles F., "The Political Thought of Sékou Touré," *African Polit-*

ical Thought: Lumumba, Nkrumah, and Touré, ed. W. A. E. Skurnik, Denver, 1968, 101–47.

*André, Pierre J., *L'Islam noir. Contribution à l'étude des confréries religieuses islamiques en Afrique occidentale, suivie d'une étude sur l'Islam au Dahomey,* Paris, 1924. P. 883.

*———, *Confréries religieuses musulmanes,* Algiers, 1956. P. 795.

*André du Sacre Coeur, Sister Marie, *La Femme noire en Afrique occidentale,* Paris, 1939. P. 885.

*———, *La condition humaine en Afrique Noire,* Paris, 1953. P. 885.

*Andrews, William, *French Politics and Algeria,* New York, 1962. P. 811.

*Angsthelm, André, *Le Service public africain. La contribution des services publics à l'évolution politique et à la modernisation de l'Afrique Occidentale d'expression française,* 4 vols., Thesis, University of Grenoble, 1965. P. 853.

*Annet, Armand, *Aux Heures troublées de l'Afrique française, 1939–1943,* Paris, 1952. P. 844.

*Ansprenger, Franz, *Politik im Schwarzen Afrika,* Cologne, 1961. P. 850.

*Antoine, P., *Les Chefs coutumiers dans le Bas-Dahomey,* Mémoire, E.N.F.O.M., 1948. P. 863.

Antonelli, Etienne, *L'Afrique et la paix de Versailles,* Paris, 1921.

*Apithy, Souran M., *Au Service de mon pays,* Montrouge, 1957. P. 857.

*d'Arboussier, Henri, "La Conquête du Togoland; l'action des partisans mossi," *Renseignements Coloniaux,* supplement to *Afrique française,* April 1915. P. 829.

*Ardant, Gabriel, *La Tunisie d'aujourd'hui et de demain: une expérience de développement économique,* Paris, 1961. P. 818.

*Aron, Robert, *Histoire de Vichy,* Paris, 1954. P. 843.

*———, *La Tragédie Algérienne,* Paris, 1957. P. 805.

*———, *L'Algérie et la République,* Paris, 1962. P. 805.

*———, et al., *Origines de la guerre Algérienne,* Paris, 1962, P. 802.

*Ashford, Douglas, *Political Change in Morocco,* Princeton, 1961. P. 824.

Asso, Bernard, *Le Dahomey à l'aube de l'indépendance (1960),* Mémoire, University of Lyon, 1969.

Atger, Paul, *La France en Côte-d'Ivoire de 1843 à 1893,* Dakar, 1962.

*Atkins, Paul M., "French West Africa in Wartime," *National Geographic, 81* (1942), 370–408. P. 844.

*———, "Dakar and the Strategy of West Africa," *Foreign Affairs, 20* (1942), 358–66. P. 844.

*Aubin, Eugène, *Morocco of Today,* London, 1906. Trans. of *Le Maroc d'aujourdhui,* Paris, 1904. P. 819.

*Auclair, H., *Décadence des cadres sociaux et politiques indigènes dans le Sud Cameroun,* Mémoire, E.N.F.O.M., 1948. P. 863.

*Augouard, Canon, *Physionomie documentaire ou vie inconnue de Monseigneur Augouard,* Evreux, 1934. P. 878.

*Auquebon, Michel-François, *La Mécanisation de l'agriculture algérienne. Aspects agricoles demographiques et economiques,* Constantine, 1953. P. 798.

*Autra, Ray, "Histoire de l'enseignement en A.O.F.," *Presénce Africaine, 6* (1956), 68–86. P. 874.

*Ayache, Albert, *Le Maroc. Bilan d'une colonisation,* Paris, 1956. P. 821.
*Aymerich, General Joseph G., *La Conquête du Cameroun: Ier août 1914, 20 février 1916,* Paris, 1933. P. 829.
*Azeau, Henri, *Révolte militaire Alger, 22 avril 1961,* Paris, 1961. P. 810.
*Ba, Amadou Hampate and M. Cardaire, *Tierno Bokar, le sage de Bandiagara,* Paris, 1957. P. 883.
*———, "L'Islam et l'Afrique noire", Présence Africaine, *Les Religions en Afrique Noire aujourdhui,* Paris, 1961, 101–18. P. 883.
Ba, Mamadou Hamidou, "L'Emirat de l'Adrar mauritanien de 1872 à 1908," *Bulletin Société geographique et archeologique de la province d'Oran,* Oran, 1932) 85–119, and 263–98.
*Balandier, Georges, "Messianismes et nationalismes en Afrique Noire," *Cahiers Internationaux de Sociologie, 14* (1953), 41–65. P. 881.
*———, *Sociologie des Brazzavilles noirs,* Paris, 1955; 2d ed., *Sociologie actuelle de l'Afrique noire,* Paris, 1963; trans. *The Sociology of Black Africa,* London, 1970. Pp. 838, 863, 879, 881, 885.
———, "Les mythes politiques de colonisation et de décolonisation en Afrique." *Cahiers Internationaux de Sociologie, 33* (1962), 85–96.
*———, "The Colonial Situation: a theoretical approach," *Social Change,* Immanuel Wallerstein, ed., New York, 1966, 34–61. P. 884.
*Baldacci, Aimé, *L'Algérie et la société de l'Ouenza,* Algiers, 1947. P. 800.
*Balek, Rodd (Charles Monchicourt), *La Tunisie après la guerre (1919–1921). Problèmes politiques,* Paris, 2d ed., 1922. P. 815.
*Balla, Benoit, *La Chefferie traditionnelle face à l'émancipation politique au Cameroun,* Mémoire, E.N.F.O.M., 1959. P. 863.
*Ballard, John, *The Development of Political Parties in French Equatorial Africa,* Thesis, Fletcher School of Law and Diplomacy, 1964. P. 860.
*———, "Les incidents de 1923 à Porto Novo: La politique à l'epoque coloniale," *Études dahoméenes,* May 1965. P. 842.
*———, "Four Equatorial States," *National Unity and Regionalism in Eight African States,* Gwendolen Carter, ed., Ithaca, 1966, 231–335. P. 860.
*Bane, Martin, *Catholic Pioneers in West Africa,* Dublin, 1956. P. 877.
*Barbé, Raymond, *Les Classes sociales en Afrique Noire,* Paris, 1964. P. 885.
*Barbour, Nevill, *A Survey of Northwest Africa (the Maghrib),* London, 1959. Pp. 789, 819.
*Barennes, Yves, *La Modernisation rurale au Maroc,* Paris, 1948. P. 826.
*Barthelemy, J., *Monographie du cercle d'Abengourou (Côte d'Ivoire),* Mémoire, C.H.E.A.M., 1957. P. 863.
*Bassane-N'Diaye, G., *Les travailleurs noirs en France. Pourquoi les migrations,* Paris, 1963. P. 871.
Basset, A., et al., *Initiation à la Tunisie,* Paris, 1950.
*Bassolet, François Djoby, *Evolution de la Haute Volta de 1898 au 31 janvier 1966,* Ouagadougou, 1968. P. 854.
*Baulin, Jacques (pseudonym for Youssef el Masry), *The Arab Role in Africa,* Baltimore, 1962. P. 807.
Baumont, Maurice, *L'Essor Industriel et l'Impérialisme Colonial,* Paris, 1937.
*Beaufré, General André, *L'Expédition de Suez,* Paris, 1967. P. 807.

*Bedos, Gerard, *Le syndicalisme en Afrique noire,* Paris, 1959 (mimeographed). P. 872.

*Bée, Michel, *Les Missions en basse Côte d'Ivoire de 1895 à 1939,* Thesis, University of Paris, 1967. P. 879.

*Beer, George L., *African Questions at the Paris Peace Conference,* ed. L. H. Gray, New York, 1923. P. 832.

*Béguin, Willy, "Découverte du Kimbanguisme: son actualité, son histoire," *Le Monde non Chrétien,* Jan.–June 1969, 4–37. P. 881.

*Behr, Edward, *The Algerian Problem,* London, 1961. P. 806.

*Behrmann, Lucy, *Muslim Brotherhoods and Politics in Senegal,* Cambridge, Mass., 1970. P. 884.

*Belal, Abdelassis, *L'Investissement au Maroc (1912–1964) et ses enseignements en matière de développement économique,* Paris, 1968. P. 826.

*Belgium, *Les Campagnes Coloniales Belges: 1914–1918,* Bruxelles, 1927. P. 829.

*Beling, Willard, *Modernization of African Labor: a Tunisian Case Study,* New York, 1965. P. 816.

Belkacem, Saadallah, *The Rise of Algerian Nationalism: 1900–1930,* Ph.D. Dissertation, University of Minnesota, 1965.

*Belloula, Tayeb, *Algériens en France,* Algiers, 1965. P. 813.

*Benazet, Henri, *L'Afrique française en danger,* Paris, 1947. P. 794.

*Benhabiles, Chérif, *L'Algérie française vue par un indigène,* Algiers, 1914. P. 800.

*Ben Kritly, Arslan, *Le Parti Communiste et la question algérienne,* Mémoire, University of Paris, 1962. P. 809.

*Bennabi, Malek, *Vocation de l'Islam,* Paris, 1954. P. 800.

*Berg, Elliott, "French West Africa," *Labor and Economic Development,* ed. Walter Galenson, New York, 1959. P. 871.

*———, and Jeffrey Butler, "Trade Unions," *Political Parties and National Integration in Tropical Africa,* ed. James S. Coleman and Carl G. Rosberg, Jr., Berkeley and Los Angeles, 1964, 340–81. P. 871.

*Bernard, Augustin, *L'Algérie,* Paris, 1930. P. 797.

*———, *Le Maroc,* 7th ed., Paris, 1931. P. 821.

*Bernard, Stéphane, *The Franco-Moroccan Conflict, 1943–1956,* New Haven, 1968. P. 824.

*Bernus, Suzanne, *Particularismes ethniques en milieu urbain: l'exemple de Niamey,* Thesis, University of Paris, 1966. P. 884.

*Berque, Jacques, *Structures sociales du Haut-Atlas,* Paris, 1955. P. 828.

———, *Histoire Sociale d'un village Égyptien au xxe siècle,* The Hague, 1957.

*———, *Le Maghreb entre deux guerres,* Paris, 1962, trans. *French North Africa: The Maghrib between Two World Wars,* London, 1967. P. 791.

———, et al., *De l'Impérialisme et la Décolonisation,* Paris, 1965.

Betts, Raymond F., *Assimilation and Association in French Colonial Policy, 1890–1914,* New York, 1961.

*Béville, Albert, *Les Assemblées représentatives dans les Territoires d'outre-mer et les Territoires sous tutelle de l'Union Française,* Thesis, University of Paris, 1950. P. 848.

*Beyries, J., *L'Islam au Tchad,* Mémoire, C.H.E.A.M., 1957. P. 883.

*Bianquis, Jean, *Le Prophète Harris ou dix ans d'histoire religieuse à la Côte d'Ivoire, 1914–1924,* Paris, 1924. P. 880.

*———, *Les Origines de la Société des Missions Evangeliques,* vol. 3, Paris, 1935. P. 877.

Bidwell, R. L., *The French Administration of Tribal Areas of Morocco,* Thesis, Cambridge University, 1969.

*Binet, Jacques, "Condition des femmes dans la région cacaoyère du Cameroun," *Cahiers internationaux de Sociologie, 20* (1956), 109–23. P. 886.

*Birot, Pierre, and Jean Dresch, *La Méditerranée et le Moyen-Orient,* vol. 1, Paris, 1953. P. 790.

*Blanc, Paul, *Les Régimes du mandat et de tutelle: leur application au Cameroun,* Thesis, University of Montpellier, 1953. Pp. 833, 848, 859.

*———, "La Réorganisation foncière en A.O.F., en A.E.F., au Togo et au Cameroun," *Revue juridique et politique de l'Union française,* Jan.–Mar. 1957, 101–14. P. 865.

*———, (pseudonym M.D.), "Le Statut du Cameroun," *Recueil Penant* (July 1958). P. 858.

*———, (pseudonym M.D.), "Les Nouveaux Statuts du Togo et du Cameroun," *Recueil Penant* (April 1959). P. 859.

Blanc, René, Jacques Blocher, and Étienne Kruger, *Histoire des Missions Protestantes Françaises,* Belgium, 1970.

*Blanchard, Jean, *Le Problème algérien. Réalités et perspectives,* Paris, 1955. P. 799.

Blanchard, Marcel, "Administrateurs d'Afrique Noire," *Revue d'Histoire des Colonies, 140* (1953), 377–430.

*Blanchet, André, *L'Itinéraire des partis africains depuis Bamako,* Paris, 1958. P. 852.

*Blin, Yves, *L'Organisation du ministère de la France d'Outre-Mer,* Thesis, University of Paris, 1954. P. 849.

*Bloch-Laine, F., et al., *La Zone franc,* Paris, 1956. P. 866.

*Bodley, R. C. V., *Algeria from Within,* Indianapolis, 1927. P. 802.

*Boisdon, Daniel, et al., *Les Institutions de l'Union Française,* Paris, 1949. P. 846.

*Boiteau, Pierre, *Contribution à l'histoire de la nation malgache,* Paris, 1958. Pp. 837, 861.

*Bolibaugh, Jerry B., *French Educational Strategies for Sub-Saharan Africa: Their Intent, Derivation, and Development,* Stanford, 1964. P. 872.

*Bonardi, Pierre, *La Republique du Niger: Naissance d'un état,* Paris, 1960. P. 854.

*Bonjean, Jacques, "Tanger," *Etudes Maghrebines, 8,* 1967. P. 821.

*Bonnefous, Marc, *Perspectives de l'agriculture marocaine,* Bordeaux, 1949. P. 826.

*Borella, François, *L'Evolution juridique et politique de l'Union Française depuis 1946,* Paris, 1958. Pp. 847, 849.

*Botti, Marc, and Paul Venizet, *Scolarisation au Tchad,* Paris, 1961. P. 875.

*———, *Enseignement au Gabon,* 2 vols., Paris, 1965. P. 875.

*Bouazzouni, Ramdane, *Du Réformisme au nationalisme en Algérie à travers Ferhat Abbas,* Mémoire, University of Aix. 1963. P. 800.

*Boubacar, Diabate, *Porte ouverte sur la Communauté Franco-Africaine,* Brussels, 1961. P. 855.
Bouchard, Robert, *Organisation Armée Secrète,* vol. 1, *Février–Décembre 1961,* Paris, 1963.
*Bouchaud, Joseph, C.S.Sp., "Les Missions d'Afrique," *Histoire Universelle des Missions Catholiques,* Msgr. Simon Delacroix, ed., Paris, 1958, *3,* 297–354. P. 877.
*———, *L'Église en Afrique noire,* Paris, 1958. P. 880.
*———, *Monseigneur Pierre Bonneau, Évêque de Douala,* Douala, 1969. P. 877.
*Bouche, Denise, "Les ecoles françaises au Soudan à l'époque de la conquête, 1884–1900," *Cahiers d'études africaines, 6* (1966), 228–67. P. 876.
*———, "Autrefois, notre pays s'appelait la Gaule—Remarques sur l'adaptation de l'enseignement au Sénegal de 1817 à 1860," *Cahiers d'études africaines, 8* (1968), 110–22. P. 876.
———, *Les villages de liberté en Afrique noire française, 1887–1910,* Paris, 1968.
*Boudry, R., "Le Problème Malgache," *Esprit,* Feb. 1948, 189–226. P. 861.
*———, "K'ai Témoigné au Procès de Madagascar," *Esprit,* Jan. 1949, 125–40. P. 861.
Bouquerel, Jacqueline, *Le Gabon,* Paris, 1970.
*Bourbon, A., "Mourides et Mouridisme 1953," *Notes et études sur l'Islam en Afrique Noire,* M. Chailley, ed., Paris, 1962. P. 883.
*Bourcart, Robert, *Le Grand Conseil de l'A. O. F.,* 2d ed., Paris, 1956. P. 849.
*Bourdieu, Pierre, *Sociologie de l'Algérie,* Paris, 1958; trans. *The Algerians,* Boston, 1961. P. 797.
*———, et al., *Travail et travailleurs en Algérie,* Paris, 1963. P. 813.
*———, and Abdelmalek Sayad, *Le déracinement: la crise de l'agriculture traditionelle,* Paris, 1964. P. 799.
*Bourguiba, Habib, *Le Destour et la France,* Tunis, 1937. P. 815.
*———, *La Tunisie et la France: vingt-cinq ans de lutte pour une coopération libre,* Paris, 1954. P. 816.
———, *Histoire du mouvement national,* Centre de Documentation Nationale, Articles de Presses, 1929–1934, Paris, 1967.
*Bousquet, Georges-Henri, *L'Islam maghrébin. Introduction à l'étude generale de l'Islam,* 2d ed., Paris, 1949. P. 795.
———, "Les élites gouvernantes en Afrique du Nord depuis le conquête française," *Welt des Islam, 1,* Leiden, 1953.
*———, *Les Berbères: histoire et institutions,* 2d ed., Paris, 1961. P. 789.
*Boutillier J. L., *Bongouanou, Côte d'Ivoire: étude socio-économique d'une subdivision,* Paris, 1960. P. 884.
Bouvier, J., "Les intérêts financiers et la question d'Egypte," *Revue Historique* (1960).
Bovy, Abbe L., "Aspects historiques et idéologiques du mouvement syndical en Afrique d'expression française," *Penant,* 1964, 383–401.
*———, *Le mouvement syndical ouest-africain d'expression française,* Brussels, 1965. P. 871.

*Boyer, P., *L'Evolution de l'Algérie médiane: ancien department d'Alger de 1830 à 1956,* Paris, 1960. P. 798.

*Brace, Richard, *Morocco, Algeria, Tunisia,* Englewood Cliffs, N.J., 1964. P. 789.

*Brace, Richard and Joan, *Ordeal in Algeria,* New York, 1960. P. 806.

*Brasseur-Marion, Paule and G. Brasseur, *Porto-Novo et sa palmeraie,* Dakar, 1953. P. 869.

*Brémard, Frédéric, *L'Organisation régionale du Maroc,* Paris, 1949. P. 821.

*———, *Les Droits publics et politiques des français au Maroc,* Paris, 1950. P. 821.

Brench, A. C., *Writing in French from Senegal to Cameroon,* London, 1967.

*Brévié, Jules, *Islamisme contre "Naturisme" au Soudan français,* Paris, 1923. Pp. 840, 882.

*———, Circulaire de M. le Gouverneur-Général J. Brévié sur la Politique et l'administration indigenes en Afrique Occidentale Française, Dakar, 1935. P. 840.

*Brigaud, Félix, *Histoire moderne et contemporaine du Sénégal,* Senegal, 1966. P. 855.

*Brignon, Jean, et al., *Histoire au Maroc,* Casablanca, 1967. Pp. 819, 887.

Broadley, Alexander M., *The Last Punic War: Tunis, Past and Present,* London, 1882.

*Bromberger, Serge, *Les Rebelles algériens,* Paris, 1958. P. 805.

*———, and Merry Brombérger, *Les Treize Complots du 13 Mai,* Paris, 1959. P. 806.

*———, et al., *Barricades et colonels, 24 janvier 1960,* Paris, 1960. P. 809.

*Brown, Leon Carl, *Tunisia under the French Protectorate: A History of Ideological Change,* Ph.D. Thesis, Harvard University, 1962. P. 815.

———, "Tunisia," in *Education and Political Development,* ed. James S. Coleman, Princeton, 1965.

*Bruel, Georges, "Bibliographie de la conquête du Cameroun, 1914–1916," *Afrique française,* June 1934. P. 830.

*Brunschwig, Henri, *La colonisation française,* Paris, 1949. P. 846.

———, *L'Expansion allemande outre-mer du XVe siècle à nos jours,* Paris, 1957.

———, *Mythes et Réalités de l'Impérialisme colonial français 1871–1914,* Paris, 1960, trans. *French Colonialism 1871–1914,* London, 1966.

———, *L'avènement de l'Afrique noire der XIXe siècle à nos jours,* Paris, 1963.

*Brutsch, J. R., "Origines et développement d'une église indépendante africaine: L'Eglise baptiste camerounaise," *Monde non-chrétien,* Oct.–Dec. 1954, 408–24. P. 881.

*Buchard, Robert, *Organisation Armée Secrète, vol. 1, Février–Décembre 1961,* Paris, 1963. P. 810.

*Buell, Raymond Leslie, *The Native Problem in Africa,* 2 vols., New York, 1928. Pp. 834, 841, 873.

*Bunche, Ralph J., *French Administration in Togoland and Dahomey,* Thesis, Harvard University, 1934. P. 834.

*———, "French Educational Policy in Togo and Dahomey," *Journal of Negro Education, 3* (1934), 69–97. P. 873.

*Burke, Thomas M. J., ed., *Catholic Missions, Four Great Missionary Encyclicals,* New York, 1957. Pp. 873, 880.

*Buron, Robert, *Carnets politiques de la guerre d'Algérie. Par un signataire des accords d'Evian,* Paris, 1965. P. 810.

*Buttin, Paul, *Le drame du Maroc,* Paris, 1955. P. 823.

*Cabot, Jean, *Le Bassin du Moyen Logone,* Paris, 1965. P. 870.

Cahnman, Werner J., "France in Algeria—A Problem of Culture Contact," *Review of Politics, 7* (1945), 343–57.

———, "North Africa in Transition: The Jews of North Africa," *Jewish Frontier, 14* (1947), 13–18.

*Caloni, Jean, *La France au Maroc,* Paris, 1937. P. 820.

Camara, Camille, *Saint-Louis du Sénégal: évolution d'une ville en milieu africain,* Dakar, IFAN, 1968.

*Cambon, Henri, *Histoire de la Régence de Tunis,* Paris, 1948. P. 814.

*———, *Histoire du Maroc,* Paris, 1952. P. 819.

*Camus, Albert, *Actuelles 3: Chroniques algériennes, 1930–1958,* Paris, 1958. P. 808.

*Capelle, Jean, "Education in French West Africa," *Overseas Education, 21* (1949). P. 874.

*Capet, Marcel, *Traité d'économie tropicale; Les Economies d'A.O.F.,* Paris, 1958. P. 867.

*Card, E. Rouard de, *Les Mandats français sur le Togoland et le Caméroun,* Paris, 1924. P. 832.

*Cardaire, Marcel, *Contribution à l'étude de l'Islam noir,* Paris, 1949. P. 883.

*———, *L'Islam et le terroir africain,* Paris and Koulouba, 1954. P. 883.

*Carreras, Fernand, *L'Accord F.L.N.-O.A.S.: Des négotiations secrètes au cessez-le-feu,* Paris, 1967. P. 810.

Carret, Jacques, "Le Problème de l'indépendance du culte musulman en Algerie," *Afrique et Asie, 37* (1957), 53–78.

Carroll, E. Malcolm, *French Public Opinion and Foreign Affairs, 1870–1914,* New York, 1941.

*Cassaigne, Jean, *La Situation des Français au Maroc depuis l'indépendance, 1956–1964,* Paris, 1964. P. 825.

*Catala, Jean, *L'Évolution des chefferies africaines du district de Mao de 1899 à 1953,* Mémoire, C.H.E.A.M., 1954. P. 863.

*Catroux, Georges, *Dans la Bataille de la Méditerranée: Egypte, Levant, Afrique du Nord, 1940–1944,* Paris, 1949. P. 793.

*———, *Lyautey, le marocain,* Paris, 1952. P. 820.

*———, "The French Union," *International Conciliation* (November 1953). Pp. 794, 846.

*Caute, David, *Frantz Fanon,* New York, 1970. P. 811.

*Célérier, Jean, *Maroc,* Paris, 1948. P. 819.

*———, et al., *Initiation au Maroc,* Paris, 1952. P. 819.

*Celier, Charles, et al., *Industrialisation de l'Afrique du Nord,* Paris, 1952. P. 790.

Centre of African Studies, University of Edinburgh, *The Theory of Im-*

perialism and the European Partition of Africa, Edinburgh, 1967.
*Cerych, Ladislav, *Européens et Marocains, 1930–1956. Sociologie d'une décolonisation,* Bruges, 1964. P. 824.
Chabas, J., "La Justice Indigène en A.O.F.," *Annales Africaines* (1954).
*———, "La Réforme foncière et le régime des concessions en Afrique Occidentale Française," *Annales Africaines* (1958), 37–51. P. 865.
*Chaffard, George, *Les Carnets secrets de la décolonisation,* Paris, 1965. P. 852.
*Chailley, Marcel, et al., *Notes et études sur l'Islam en Afrique Noire,* Paris, 1962. Pp. 883, 884.
*———, *Histoire de l'Afrique occidentale française,* Paris, 1968. Pp. 831, 837.
*Challaye, Félicien, *Le Congo français: la question internationale du Congo,* Paris, 1909. P. 864.
*Chapelle, Jean, *L'Islam en Afrique Noire, La Documentation Française Notes et Etudes documentaires,* no. 1152, June 1949. P. 883.
———, *Documents d'archives I. Tchad, Cameroun, Nigéria, Niger,* Paris, 1968.
*Chapuisat, Louis, *La Côte française des Somalis,* Mémoire, University of Paris, 1967. P. 862.
*Charbonneau, Jean and René, *Marchés et marchands de l'Afrique noire,* Paris, 1961. P. 868.
*Charles, Bernard, "Un Parti politique africain: le Parti Démocratique de Guinée," *Revue Française de Science Politique,* June 1962, 312–59. P. 856.
*———, *Guinée,* Lausanne, 1963. P. 856.
*Charnay, Jean-Paul, ed., *De l'Impérialisme à la décolonisation,* Paris, 1965. P. 794.
*———, *La Vie musulmane en Algérie d'après la jurisprudence de la première moitié du XXe siècle,* Paris, 1965. P. 802.
*Charton, Albert, "French Tropical and Equatorial Africa: The Birth of African-French Culture," *Year Book of Education,* 1950, 366–79. P. 874.
*Chauleur, Pierre, "La Condition du travail en Afrique noire française," *Etudes, 1992* (May 1958), 159–73. P. 870.
*Chazelas, V., *Territoires africains sous mandat de la France,* Paris, 1931. Pp. 833, 834.
*Chemery, J., *Histoire de la mise en valeur minière des territoires d'Afrique central,* Paris, 1960. P. 868.
*Chenet, Daniel, *Qui a sauvé l'Afrique, Témoignages contemporains,* Paris, 1949. P. 844.
*Chevalier, Louis, *Le problème démographique nord-africain,* Paris, 1947. P. 790.
*Chevallier, Jacques, *Nous, Algériens,* Paris, 1958. P. 804.
Chevans, Henry, *La Mise en valeur de l'Afrique occidentale française,* Paris, 1907.
Chiala, Luigi, *Pagine di storia contemporanea,* Turin, 1892.
*Chiroux, R., "Le Nouveau Statut du Territoire français des Afars et des Issas," *Penant,* Jan.–Mar. 1968, 1–47. P. 862.
*Chouraqui, André, *La Condition Juridique de l'Israélite marocain,* Paris, 1950. P. 821.

*———, *Les Juifs d'Afrique du nord,* Paris, 1952. P. 795.
*———, "Les Juifs d'Afrique du nord entre l'orient et l'occident," *Etudes maghrébines* 5 (Paris, 1965). P. 796.
*Chowdhuri, R. N., *International Mandates and Trusteeship Systems, A Comparative Study,* The Hague, 1955. P. 847.
Clapham J. W., *John Olley, Pioneer Missionary to the Chad,* Glasgow, 1966.
*Clarke, John I., "The Population of Tunisia: An Example of Contact between Modern Civilization and the Moslem World," *Economic Geography, 28* (1952), 364–71. P. 818.
*———, "Summer Nomadism in Tunisia," *Economic Geography, 31* (1955), 157–67. P. 818.
*Clark, Michael, *Algeria in Turmoil,* New York, 1959. P. 806.
Clignet, Remi, "Ethnicity, Social Differentiation, and Secondary Schooling in West Africa," *Cahiers d'études africaines, 7* (1967), 360–78.
*———, and Philip Foster, *The Fortunate Few: A Study of Secondary Schools and Students in the Ivory Coast,* Evanston, Ill., 1966. P. 875.
Clough, Shepard Bancroft, *France: A History of National Economics 1789–1939,* New York, 1939.
Cohen, Amnon, "Allal al-Fasi: His Ideas and His Contribution towards Morocco's Independence," *Asian and African Studies, 3* (1967), 121–64.
Cohen, William B., *Rulers of Empire: The French Colonial Service in Africa,* Stanford, 1971.
*Coleman, James S., "Togoland," *International Conciliation, 509* (Sept. 1956). Pp. 848, 857.
———, *Nigeria: Background to Nationalism,* Berkeley and Los Angeles, 1958.
*Colliez, André, *Notre Protectorat marocain. La première étape, 1912–1930,* Paris, 1930. P. 821.
*Confer, C. Vincent, *France and Algeria: The Problem of Civil and Political Reform, 1870–1920,* Syracuse, 1966. P. 801.
**Connaissance de l'immigration nord-africaine en France,* mimeographed, Centre Africain des Sciences Humaines Appliqués, Aix, Feb. 1964. P. 813.
*"La Conquête du Togoland," *Renseignements Coloniaux,* supplement to *Afrique française,* May 1915, pp. 82–102. P. 829.
*Cookey, S.J.S., "The Concession Policy in French Congo and the British Reaction, 1896–1906," *Journal of African History, 7* (1966), 263–78. P. 865.
*Cooksey, Joseph J., and Alexander McLeish, *Religions and Civilization in West Africa: A Missionary Survey of French, British, Spanish, and Portuguese West Africa with Liberia,* London, 1931. P. 881.
Coquéry-Vidrovitch, Cathérine, "L'Échec d'une tentative économique: l'impôt de capitation au service des compagnies concessionaires du 'Congo français,' 1900–1909," *Cahiers d'études africaines, 8* (1968), 96–109.
———, "Quelques problèmes posés par le choix économique des grandes compagnies concessionnaires au Congo français, 1900–1920," *Bulletin de la Société d'Histoire Moderne, 1* (1968), 2–13.

Coquéry-Vidrovitch, Cathérine, "French Colonization in Africa to 1920: Administration and Economic Development," *The History and Politics of Colonialism,* ed. L. H. Gann and P. Duignan, 2 vols., Cambridge, 1969–70, 1: *1,* 165–98. P. 869.

*Cornevin, Robert, *Histoire du Togo,* Paris, 1959. Pp. 830, 835, 858.

*———, "Evolution des chefferies traditionnelles dans l'Afrique Noire d'expression française," *Penant,* April, July, October, 1961, 235–50, 379–88, 539–56. P. 862.

*———, "Problèmes de l'enseignement en Afrique Noire d'expression française," *Revue de Défense Nationale* (July 1961), 1216–31. P. 874.

*———, *Le Dahomey,* Paris, 1962. Pp. 831, 857.

*———, *Le Togo, nation-pilote,* Paris, 1963. P. 858.

*Corval, Pierre, *Le Maroc en révolution,* Paris, 1956. P. 822.

*Cosnier, Henri, *L'Ouest Africain Français: ses ressources agricoles—son organisation économique,* Paris, 1921. P. 838.

*Costedoat, Rene, *L'Effort français au Cameroun. Le mandat français et la Réorganisation des Territoires du Cameroun,* Paris, 1930. Pp. 833, 834.

*Couste, Pierre B., *L'Association des pays d'outre-mer à la Communaute Économique Européenne,* Paris, 1959. P. 866.

*Cowan, L. Gray, "The New Face of Algeria," *Political Science Quarterly, 66* (1951), 340–65, 507–31. P. 802.

*———, *Local Government in West Africa,* New York, 1958, Pp. 838, 849.

*———, "Guinea," *African One-Party States,* ed. Gwendolen Carter, Ithaca 1962, 149–236. P. 855.

*———, "British and French Education in Africa: a Critical Appraisal," *Post-Primary Education and Economic Development, ed.* D. C. Piper and T. Cole, Durham, N.C., 1964. P. 876.

*Cragbe-Gnagbe, *Réflexions sur la colonisation française en Côte d'Ivoire,* Mémoire, C.H.E.A.M., 1967. P. 856.

Cromer, Lord, *Modern Egypt,* London, 1908.

*Cros, Charles, *Le Statut des Municipalités Africaines et Malgaches,* Paris, 1956. P. 849.

*———, *La Parole est à M. Blaise Diagne: premier homme d'Etat africain,* Paris, 1961. P. 842.

*Crouset, P., "Education in the French Colonies," in the International Institute of Teachers' College, Columbia University, *Education Yearbook,* 1931, 267–566. P. 873.

*Crowder, Michael, "Independence as a Goal in French West African Politics: 1944–60," in W. H. Lewis, ed., *French-Speaking Africa: The Search for Identity,* New York, 1965, 15–41. P. 850.

*———, *Senegal—a Study in French Assimilation Policy,* 2d edition, London, 1967. P. 854.

*———, "West Africa and the 1914–1918 War," *Bulletin de l'I.F.A.N.,* Jan. 1968, 227–47. P. 830.

*———, *West Africa under Colonial Rule,* Evanston, Ill., 1968. Pp. 830, 836, 842, 844, 849, 868, 876, 887.

———, ed., *West African Resistance: The Military Response to Colonial Occupation,* New York, 1970.

———, and Otaro Ikime, eds., *West African Chiefs: Their Changing Status under Colonial Rule and Independence,* New York, 1970.

Crowe, S. E., *The Berlin West African Conference,* London, 1942.

*Crozier, Brian, *The Morning After: A Study of Independence,* London, 1963. P. 810.

*Culman, Henri, L'Union Française, Paris, 1950. P. 846.

*Dadié Bernard, "Misère de l'enseignement en A.O.F.," *Presénce Africaine, 11* (Dec. 1956–Jan. 1957), 57–70. P. 874.

*Damis, John, "Developments in Morocco under the French Protectorate, 1925–1943," *Middle East Journal,* Winter 1970. P. 822.

*Danan, Yves Maxime, *La Vie politique à Alger de 1940 à 1944,* Paris, 1963. P. 793.

*Darbel, Alain, Jean-Paul Rivet, Claude Seibel, and Pierre Bourdieu, *Travail et travailleurs en Algérie. I. Données statistiques. II. Enquête sociologique.,* Paris and The Hague, 1964. P. 799.

*Dareste, Pierre, *Le Régime de la propriété française en A.O.F.,* Paris, 1908. P. 864.

*———, *Traité de droit colonial,* 2 vols., Paris, 1931–32. P. 864.

*Davérat, Geneviève, *Les Missions catholiques au Gabon de 1844 au debut du XXe siècle,* Thesis, University of Paris, 1967. P. 878.

*Davies, Ioan, *African Trade Unions,* Harmondsworth, 1966. P. 871.

Davies, K. G., *The Royal African Company,* London, 1957.

*Davis, Shelby Cullum, *Reservoirs of Men: A History of the Black Troops of French West Africa,* Geneva, 1934. P. 831.

*Day, Georges, *Les Affaires de la Tunisie et du Maroc devant les Nations Unies,* Paris, 1953. Pp. 817, 825.

*Debay, Jean, *Evolutions en Afrique Noire,* Paris, 1962. P. 851.

*Debeauvais, Michael, "Education in Former French Africa," *Education and Political Development,* ed. James S. Coleman, Princeton, 1965, 75–91. P. 874.

*Debrunner, H. W., *A Church between Colonial Powers: A Study of the Church in Togo,* London, 1965. P. 879.

De Courcel, Geoffroy, *L'Influence de la Conférence de Berlin de 1885 sur le droit colonial international,* Paris, 1935.

*de Dempierre, Eric, "Coton noir, cafe blanc," *Cahiers d'études africaines,* 1960, 128–43. P. 839.

*———, *Un ancien royaume Bandia du Haut-Oubangui,* Paris, 1967. P. 839.

*de Gaulle, Charles, *The Complete War Memoirs of General de Gaulle,* New York, 1968. Pp. 793, 843.

Delafosse, Maurice, *Haut-Sénégal-Niger,* 3 vols., Paris, 1912.

*de Larminat, Edgard, *Chroniques irrévérencieuses,* Paris, 1962. P. 845.

*de la Roche, Jean, and Jean Gottmann, *La Fédération Française,* Montréal, 1945. P. 845.

*———, *Le Gouverneur-Général Félix Eboué, 1884–1944,* Paris, 1957. P. 845.

*Delarozière, R., "Les Institutions politiques et sociales des populations dites Bamiléké," *Etudes camerounaises, 25–26* (1949), 5–68, and *27–28* (1949), 127–75. P. 863.

*de la Tour, Pierre Boyer, *Vérités sur l'Afrique du Nord,* Paris, 1956. P. 817.
*Delavignette, Robert, *Les paysans noirs,* Paris, 1931. P. 840.
*———, *Les vrais chefs de l'Empire,* Paris, 1939. P. 840.
*———, *Christianisme et Colonialisme,* Paris, 1960. P. 880.
*———, *L'Afrique noire française et son destin,* Paris, 1962. P. 852.
*———, "La politique de Marius Moutet au Ministère des Colonies," in *Léon Blum, Chef de Gouvernement, 1936–1937, Cahiers de la Fondation Nationale des Sciences Politiques, 155* (1967), 391–95. Pp. 792, 840.
*———, "French Colonial Policy in Black Africa, 1945 to 1960," *Colonialism in Africa 1870–1960,* ed. L. H. Gann and P. Duignan, vol. 2, Cambridge, 1970, 251–85. P. 852.
*Delpech, Joseph, *Des Subventions à l'enseignement confessional et missionnaire dans les territoires d'outre-mer,* Paris, 1956. P. 879.
De Lusignan, Guy, *French-Speaking Africa since Independence,* London, 1969.
*Delval, Raymond, "Le Syndicalisme à Madagascar," *Recueil Penant,* Oct.–Nov. 1965. P. 872.
DeMaison, B., "Le problème de l'immatriculation foncière en A.O.F.," *Revue juridique et politique de l'Union française, 3* (July–Sept. 1956), 421–78. P. 865.
*Demontés, Victor, *L'Algérie economique,* 5 vols., Algiers, 1922–30. P. 797.
*———, *L'Algérie agricole,* Paris, 1930. P. 798.
*———, *L'Algérie industrielle et commerçante,* Paris, 1930. P. 798.
*Depont, Octave, and Xavier Coppolani, *Les Confréries religieuses musulmanes,* Algiers, 1897. Pp. 795, 823, 883.
*De Santi, H., *Du Dahomé au Benin-Niger,* Paris, 1945. P. 840.
*Desbordes, Jean-Gabriel, *L'Immigration Libano-Syrienne en Afrique Occidentale Française,* Poitiers, 1938. P. 868.
*Deschamps, Hubert, *L'Union Française: histoire, institutions, réalités,* Paris, 1952. P. 846.
*———, *Les Méthodes et les doctrines coloniales de la France du XV*[e] *siècle à nos jours,* Paris, 1953. P. 845.
*———, *Histoire de Madagascar,* Paris, 1960, 2d ed. 1961. Pp. 837, 861.
———, "Et maintenant, Lord Lugard," *Africa,* 1963.
*———, *Le Sénégal et la Gambie,* Paris, 1964. P. 855.
*———, with Jean Ganiage and Odette Guitard, *Afrique au XX*[e] *siècle, 1900–1965,* Paris, 1966. P. 835.
———, *L'Europe découvre l'Afrique: Afrique occidentale, 1794–1900,* Paris, 1967.
———, et al., "Hommage à Robert Delavignette," *Revue française d'histoire d'outre-mer, 54* (1967), 5–84.
*———, "France in Black Africa and Madagascar between 1920 and 1945," *Colonialism in Africa 1870–1960,* ed. L. H. Gann and P. Duignan, 2 (1970), 226–50. P. 836.
*Descloitres, Robert, Jean-Claude Reverdy and Claudine Descloitres, *L'Algérie des Bidonvilles,* Paris, 1961. P. 813.
*Désiré-Vuillemin, Geneviève, *Contribution à l'histoire de la Mauritanie de 1900 à 1934,* Dakar, 1962. P. 837.
*Despois, Jean, *La Tunisie,* Paris, 1930. P. 814.

*———, *La Tunisie orientale, Sahel et Basse Steppe. Études géographiques,* Paris, 1940, 2d ed. 1955. P. 817.

*———, *L'Afrique du Nord,* Paris, 1949. P. 790.

*———, *La Hodna,* Paris, 1954. P. 798.

*———, *Le Djebel Amour (Algérie)*, Paris, 1957. P. 798.

*de Vaulx, Bernard, *Histoire des Missions Catholiques Françaises,* Paris, 1951. P. 877.

*———, *History of the Missions,* New York, 1961. P. 877.

*Devernois, Guy, "Social Evolution in the Franco-African Community," *Civilizations* 8 (1958), 585–610. P. 874.

*Devez, M. G., *L'Evolution de la vie politique au Sénégal, en Côte d'Ivoire, et en Guinée de 1944 à 1959. Essai de comparaison.* Thesis, University of Paris, 1960. P. 855.

*Devèze, Michel, *La France d'Outre-Mer de l'Empire Colonial à l'Union Française, 1938–1947,* Paris, 1948. Pp. 845, 846.

*Dia, Mamadou, *L'Economie africaine, études et problemes nouveaux,* Paris, 1957, revised 1961. P. 867.

*Diagne, Abdel-Kader, *La Résistance française au Sénégal et en A.O.F. pendant la guerre, 1939–1945,* mimeographed, Dakar, 1949. P. 844.

*Diagne, S. K., *Les Assemblées de groupe ou grands conseils d'A.O.F. et d'A.E.F.*, Thesis, University of Paris, 1950. P. 849.

*Diarra, Souleymane, "Les Travailleurs africains noirs en France," *Bulletin de L'I.F.A.N.*, 1968. P. 871.

*Dietman, Alphonse, *Le Rôle des missions religieuses dans la colonisation française et leur statut legal en Afrique noire,* Strasbourg, Doctorat d'Etat in Law, 1946. P. 879.

Diké, K. O., *Trade and Politics in the Niger Delta, 1830–1885,* Oxford, 1956.

*Documentation Française, La, "L'Enseignement des musulmans en Afrique du Nord," *Notes et études documentaires,* no. 344 (July 5, 1946). P. 790.

*Documentation française, La, "Evolution du statut politique des Français musulmans d'Algérie," *Notes et études documentaires, 678,* 1947. P. 802.

*Domenichini, J. P., "Jean Ralaimongo (1884–1943) ou Madagascar au seuil du nationalisme," *Revue Française d'histoire d'outre-mer,* 1969, 236–87. P. 887.

*Donath, Doris Bensimon, *Evolution du Judaisme marocain sous le protectorat français, 1912–1956,* The Hague, 1968. P. 825.

*Dougall, James W. C., *Religious Education in Africa,* London, 1930. P. 873.

*Drague, Georges, *Esquisse d'Histoire Religieuse du Maroc: Confréries et Zaouias,* Paris, 1951. P. 823.

*Dresch, Jean, Charles-André Julien, et al., *La Question algérienne,* Paris, 1959. P. 805.

*Dronne, Raymond, *Le Serment de Koufra,* Paris, 1965. P. 844.

*Drouet, Pierre, "L'Immatriculation foncière en A.O.F. depuis le décrêt du 20 mai 1955," *Annales Africaines,* (1958), 207–17. P. 865.

*DuBois, Victor D., "Catholicism's Problems in French Black Africa: The

Historical Aspect," *American Universities Field Staff Reports, West African Series,* 5 (3), 1962. P. 880.

*———, "Guinea's Prelude to Independence: Political Activity, 1945–58," *American University Field Staff Reports, West Africa Series,* 5 (6), 1962. P. 855.

*———, "The Guinean Vote for Independence," *American University Field Staff Reports, West Africa Series,* 5 (7), 1962. P. 855.

*Duchemin, Jacques C., *Histoire du F.L.N.*, Paris, 1962. P. 807.

*Duchêne, Albert, *Histoire des finances coloniales de la France,* Paris, 1938. Pp. 841, 866.

*Duclos, Louis-Jean, Jean Leca, and Jean Duvignaud, *Les Nationalismes maghrébins,* Paris, 1966. P. 792.

*Dufournet, Pierre, *Les Populations du Niger et la colonisation du Niger, 1898–1932,* Thesis, University of Paris, 1967. P. 837.

*Dugué, Gil, *Vers les Etats-Unis d'Afrique,* Dakar, 1960. P. 852.

*Dulout, Fernand, *Traité de législation algérienne,* 2 vols., Algiers, 1951. P. 803.

*Dumon, Frédéric, *La Communauté franco-afro-malgache: Ses origines, ses institutions, son évolution, octobre 1958–juin 1960,* Bruxelles, 1960. P. 853.

*Dumont, René, *Afrique noire, développement agricole; reconversion de l'économie agricole: Guinée, Côte d'Ivoire, Mali,* Paris, 1961. P. 869.

———, *L'Afrique Noire est mal partie,* Paris, 1962, trans. *False Start in Africa,* London, 1966.

*Dumoulin, Roger, *La Structure asymétrique de l'économie algérienne. D'Après une analyse de la région de Bone,* Paris, 1959. P. 800.

*Dupire, Marguerite, and Edmund Bernus, *Planteurs autochtones et étrangers en basse Côte d'Ivoire orientale . . . Kong et sa région,* Abidjan, 1960. P. 884.

*Durand-Reveille, "Le problème de l'enseignement en Afrique Noire Française," *Académie des Sciences Coloniaux comptes-rendus mémoires,* 8 (1948), 391–410. P. 874.

*———, "Aspects du problème de l'enseignement dans les territoires françaises d'outre-mer," *Cahiers Institut Solvay,* (1950), 88–108. P. 874.

*Duriez, Jean, *La monarchie ouadienne,* Mémoire, C.H.E.A.M., Dec. 5, 1960. P. 863.

*Eboué, Félix, *Native Policy in French Equatorial Africa.* Trans. of a memorandum by M. Eboué, Governor-General, French Equatorial Africa, Nov., 1941. P. 845.

*———, *L'A.E.F. et la guerre. Discours du 1er décembre, 1943,* Brazzaville, 1943. P. 845.

*Ehrhard, Jean, *Le Destin du colonialisme,* Paris, 1958. P. 866.

———, *Communauté ou sécession?*, Paris, 1959.

*———, *Finances publiques d'outre-mer,* Paris, 1960. P. 867.

*Ekwa, M., S. J., "Catholic Education in the Mind of the Church," *Catholic Education in the Service of Africa,* Tournai, (1965), 150–72. P. 880.

el-Fassi, Allal, *The Independence Movements in Arab North Africa,* Washington, 1954. (trans. from the Arabic original, Cairo, 1948).

*El Maki, Omar, *Le Nationalisme dans la littérature marocaine de langue arabe de 1925 à 1955*, Mémoire, University of Paris, 1965. P. 823.

*Endressen, Pastor H., *Slavekâr I Dagens Afrika,* Oslo, 1954. P. 834.

*Espérandieu, Pierre, *Lyautey et le Protectorat,* Paris, 1947. P. 820.

*Esquer, Gabriel, *Histoire de l'Algérie, 1830–1960,* Paris, 1960; 2d ed. *Histoire de l'Algérie contemporaine,* Paris, 1966. P. 797.

*Essama, R., *Evolution de la chefferie traditionnelle en Pays Beti (Sud-(Cameroun)*, Mémoire, University of Paris, 1967. P. 863.

*Etienne, Bruno, *Les Européens d'Algérie et l'Indépendance algérienne,* Thesis, University of Aix, 1965. P. 797.

*d'Etienne, Jean, Louis Villème, Stephane Delisle, *L'Evolution sociale du Maroc,* Paris, 1950. P. 828.

*Ettori, Charles, *Le Régime legislatif de l'Algérie. Textes, documents, et études juridiques,* Algiers, 1948. P. 803.

*Etudes sociales nord-africaines, *Africains noirs en France,* Cahiers Nord-Africains, no. 86, 1961. P. 885.

*Etudes sociales nord-africaines, *Hommes et Migrations,* "Approche des problèmes de la migration noire en France," Paris, 1965. P. 871.

*Eyinga, Abel, *Le Pouvoir de décision au cameroun,* Thesis, University of Paris, 1969. P. 858.

*F.L.N., *Le Peuple algérien et sa révolution,* Algiers, 1956. P. 804.

*Famchon, Yves, *Le Maroc d'Algéciras à la souveraineté économique,* Paris, 1957. P. 826.

*Fanon, Frantz, *Peau Noire, masques blancs,* Paris, 1952, trans. *Black Skin, White Masks,* New York, 1967. P. 811.

*———, *L'An V de la Révolution algérienne,* Paris, 1959, trans. *Studies in a Dying Colonialism,* New York, 1965. P. 812.

*———, *Les Damnés de la terre,* Paris, 1961, trans. *The Wretched of the Earth,* New York, 1966. P. 812.

*———, *Pour la Révolution africaine: écrits politiques,* Paris, 1964, trans. *For the African Revolution,* New York, 1967. P. 812.

*Farelly, Maurice, *Africains d'hier et de demain,* Neuchâtel, 1967. P. 834.

*Fatoux, Michel, *La Fédération du Mali: naissance et perspectives,* Thesis, University of Paris, 1959. P. 853.

*Faucher, Jean-Andre, *Les barricades d'Alger, janvier, 1960,* Paris, 1960. P. 809.

*Faure, Jean, *Togo: champ de mission,* Paris, 1943. P. 879.

*Fauvet, Jacques, and Jean Planchais, *La Fronde des généraux,* Paris, 1961. P. 809.

*Favrod, Charles-Henri, *Le F.L.N. et l'Algérie,* Paris, 1962. P. 806.

*Ferjus, *La Mise en valeur du Togo sous mandat français,* Paris, 1926. P. 834.

*Fernandez, James W., "The Affirmation of Things Past: Alar Ayong and Bwiti as Movements of Protest in Central and Northern Gabon," *Protest and Power in Black Africa,* ed. R. I. Rotberg and A. A. Mazrui, New York, 1970, 427–57. P. 881.

*Fernau, Friedrich Wilhelm, *Arabischer Westen: Der Maghrib in Bewegung,* Stuttgart, 1969. P. 789.

*Ferrandi, Captain, *Conquête du Nord-Cameroun,* Paris, 1928. P. 829.

Fidel, Camille, *La Paix coloniale française,* Paris, 1918.

*Filippi, Jean-Michel, *L'Evolution politique du Gabon depuis 1958,* Mémoire, University of Nice, 1967. P. 860.

*Finagnon, Oke, *La Chefferie traditionnelle et l'évolution politique du Dahomey,* Thesis, University of Paris, 1967. P. 863.

Fischer, Georges, "Trade Unions and Decolonization," *Présence Africaine,* 6–7 (Oct. 1960–Jan. 1961), 121–69. P. 871.

*Fitoussi, Elie, and Aristide Benezet, *L'État Tunisien et le Protectorat francais.* Vol. 2: *Histoire et organisation, 1881–1931,* Paris, 1931. P. 814.

*Flamant, P., *Les Communautes israélites du Sud-Marocain: Essai de description et d'analyse de la vie juive en milieu berbère,* Thesis, University of Paris, 1959. P. 828.

Flint, John E., *Sir George Goldie and the Making of Nigeria,* London, 1960.

*Foltz, William J., *From West Africa to the Mali Federation,* New Haven, 1965. P. 853.

*Fontaine, Pierre, *La Mort mystérieuse du Gouverneur-Général Renard,* Paris, 1943. P. 841.

*Fontaneau, Pierre, *L'Electrification de l'Algérie,* Paris, 1952. P. 800.

*Fournier, François, "Aspects politiques du problème des chefferies au Soudan présahelien," *Revue juridique et politique de l'Union française,* 1955, 147–82. P. 863.

*France, Ambassade, U.S., Service de presse et d'information, *French Africa: A Decade of Progress, 1948–1958, Achievements of F.I.D.E.S.,* New York, 1958. P. 865.

*France, Documentation, "Evolution économique et sociale de la Côte Française des Somalis," *Notes et Etudes documentaires, 1854* (1954). P. 870.

*France, Groupe d'Etudes des Relations Financières entre la Métropole et l'Algérie. [Maspétiol, Président] Rapport Général, Algiers, June 1955. P. 800.

*Franceschi, Roger, *Le Mandat Français au Cameroun,* Paris, 1929. P. 833.

*Fréchou, Hubert, "Les Plantations européennes en Côte d'Ivoire," *Cahiers d'Outre-Mer,* Jan.–March 1955, 56–83. P. 865.

*Froelich, J. C., "Le Commandement et l'organisation sociale chez les Foulbé de l'Adamoua," *Etudes Camerounaises, 45–46* (Sept.–Dec. 1954), 5–90. P. 863.

*———, "Le commandement et l'organisation sociale chez les Fali du Nord-Cameroun," *Etudes camerounaises, 53–54* (Oct.–Dec. 1956), 20–60. P. 863.

*———, "L'Importance et l'influence de l'Islam, du Christianisme, et des sectes en Afrique noire," *Europe-France-Outre-Mer, 396* (1963), 36–40. P. 882.

*Fuglestad, Finr, *Les origines du nationalisme du Niger,* Thesis, Aix-en-Provence, 1967. P. 854.

*Furneaux, Rupert, *Abdel Krim, Emir of the Rif,* London, 1967. P. 820.

*Gallagher, Charles, "Tunisia," *African One-Party States,* ed. Gwendolen Carter, Ithaca, 1962, 11–86. P. 813.

*———, *The United States and North Africa*, Cambridge, Mass., 1963. P. 789.

*Gallisot, René, *L'Economie de l'Afrique du Nord*, Paris, 1961. P. 790.

*———, *La Patronat européen au Maroc (1931–1942)*, Rabat, 1964. P. 826.

*Gam, Pierre, *Les Causes de l'éclatement de la Fédération du Mali*, Thesis, University of Paris, 1962. P. 853.

*Gandolfi, Alain, *L'Administration territoriale en Afrique Noire de langue française*, Aix-en-Provence, 1959. Pp. 849, 862.

Ganiage, Jean, *Les origines du protectorat français en Tunisie, 1861–1881*, Paris, 1959.

———, *L'Expansion coloniale de la France sous la Troisième République*, Paris, 1968.

*———, Hubert Deschamps, and Odette Guitard, *L'Afrique au XXᵉ siècle*, Paris, 1966. Pp. 788, 835.

Gann, Lewis H., and Peter Duignan, *Burden of Empire: An Appraisal of Western Colonialism in Africa South of the Sahara*, New York, 1967.

———, eds., *Colonialism in Africa 1870–1960*, vol. 1, *1870–1914*, vol. 2, *1914–1960*, Cambridge, 1969, 1970.

*Garas, Félix, *Bourguiba et la naissance d'une nation*, Paris, 1956. P. 816.

*Garcia, Luc, "Les mouvements de résistance au Dahomey (1914–1917)," *Cahiers d'études africaines*, no. 1 (1970), 144–78. P. 831.

*Gardiner, David, *French Policy in the Cameroons, 1945–1959*, Ph.D. Dissertation, Yale University, 1960. P. 848.

*———, *Cameroon: United Nations Challenge to French Policy*, London, 1963. Pp. 848, 858.

*———, "Political Behavior in the Community of Douala, Cameroon: Reactions of the Duala People to Loss of Hegemony, 1944–1955," *Ohio University Papers in International Studies, 3* (1966). Pp. 849, 859.

*———, "The British in the Cameroons, 1919–1939, *Britain and Germany in African*, ed. P. Gifford and W. R. Louis, New Haven, 1967, 513–55. P. 830.

*Gaudefroy-Demombynes, Roger, *L'Oeuvre française en matière d'enseignement au Maroc*, Paris, 1928. P. 827.

*Gaudemet, Paul Marie, "L'Autonomie camerounaise," *Revue Française de science politique*, March 1958. P. 858.

Gaudio, Attilio, *Contribution à l'étude de la pensée sociale et politique d'Allal El-Fassi*, Mémoire, University of Paris, 1969.

*Gautier, Emile F., *L'Evolution de l'Algérie de 1830 à 1930*, Algiers, 1931. P. 797.

*Geiss, Imanuel, *Gewerkschaften in Afrika*, Bonn, 1965. P. 871.

Gellner, Ernest, "The Struggle for Morocco's Past," *Middle East Journal, 1* (1961), 79–90.

*Gendarme, René, *L'Economie de l'Algérie: Sous-développement et politique de croissance*, Paris, 1959. P. 800.

*Gentil, Pierre, *Sur les sentiers malgaches*, Paris, 1956, P. 861.

*———, *Histoire du Tchad de 1894 à 1914 (exploration et occupation)*, Thesis, University of Paris, 1967. P. 837.

*Gentil, Pierre, "Le Tchad: décolonisation et independance," *C. R. mens. Acad. Sci. Outre-Mer,* 29 (1969), 1–24. P. 860.

*Gerin, P., *L'Algerie du 13 mai,* Paris, 1958. P. 806.

*Gerteiny, Alfred, *Mauritania,* New York, 1967. P. 854.

*Gide, André, *Voyage au Congo,* Paris, 1927, and *Retour du Tchad,* Paris, 1928, both trans. as *Travels in the Congo,* New York, 1929. Pp. 840, 865.

*Gifford, Prosser, and Louis, Wm. Roger, eds. *Britain and Germany in Africa: Imperial Rivalry and Colonial Rule,* New Haven, 1967. P. 832.

*Gigon, Fernand, *Guinée, état Pilote,* Paris, 1959. P. 855.

*Gillespie, Joan, *Algeria: Rebellion and Revolution,* New York, 1961. P. 806.

Giraud, Henri, *Mes Évasions,* Paris, 1946.

*———, *Un Seul But, la victoire, Alger, 1942–1944,* Paris, 1949. Pp. 793, 843.

Girault, Arthur, *The Colonial Tariff Policy of France,* ed. John Bates Clark, Oxford, 1916.

*———, *Principes de colonisation et de législation coloniale,* 3 vols., Paris, 1927. P. 838.

*Gleason, Judith I., *This Africa: Novels by West Africans in English and French,* Evanston, 1965. P. 876.

*Glélé, Maurice A., *Naissance d'un état noire. L'évolution politique et constitutionnelle du Dahomey, de la colonisation à nos jours,* Paris, 1969. P. 857

*Gobbe, J., "La Mission presbytérienne américaine: son activité au Cameroun," Unpub. paper at Institute des Hautes Etudes d'Outer-Mer, Paris, S.A.C. 41, 1948. P. 878.

*Golvin, Lucien, *Aspects de l'artisanat en afrique du Nord,* Paris, 1952. P. 790.

*Gonidec, P. F., "Les assemblées locales des territoires d'Outre-Mer," *Revue juridique et politique de l'Union française,* July–Sept. 1952, 317–55, and Oct.–Dec. 1953, 443–91. P. 848.

*———, "De la Dépendance à l'indépendance. L'État sous tutelle du Cameroun," *Annuaire Français de Droit International,* 1957, 507–626. P. 859.

*———, *L'Evolution des territoires d'outre-mer depuis 1946,* Paris, 1958. P. 847.

*———, and M. Kirsch, *Droit de travail des territoires d'outre-mer,* Paris, 1958. P. 870.

*———, *Droit d'outre-mer.* Vol. 1, *De l'Empire colonial de la France à la Communauté,* Paris, 1959. Pp. 838, 849.

*———, "L'Evolution du syndicalisme en Afrique Noire," *Penant,* 1962, 167–92. P. 872.

*Gontard, Maurice, *Madagascar pendant la première guerre mondiale,* Tananarive, 1969. P. 830.

*Gorce, Paul-Marie de la, "Histoire de L'O.A.S. en Algérie," in *La Nef,* special issue, "Histoire de la guerre d'Algérie suivie d'une histoire de l'O.A.S." (Oct. 1962–Jan. 1963), 139–92. P. 810.

*Gordon, David, *North Africa's French Legacy, 1954–1962,* Cambridge, Mass., 1962. P. 794.

———, "Frantz Fanon: Voice of the Algerian Revolution," *Middle East Forum,* 1963.

*———, *The Passing of French Algeria,* London, 1966. P. 811.

*Gorges, Edmund Howard, *The Great War in West Africa,* London, 1930. P. 829.

*Gouilly, Alphonse, *L'Islam dans l'Afrique Occidentale Française,* Paris, 1952. P. 882.

*Gouraud, Henry J. E., *Mauritanie, Adrar; souvenirs d'un Africain,* Paris, 1945. P. 840.

*Goutor, Jacques R., *Algeria and France, 1830–1963,* Ball State Monograph no. 3, Muncie, Ind., 1965. P. 811.

*Gouvenement-Général de l'A.E.F., *L'Évolution economique des possessions françaises d'Afrique Equatoriale,* Brazzaville, 1913. P. 868.

*———, *Histoire et Organisation générale de l'enseignement en A.E.F.,* Brazzaville, 1931. P. 873.

*Goyau, Georges, *La France missionnaire dans les cinq parties du monde,* vol. 2, Paris, 1948. P. 877.

*Goyi, Dominique, *Les Missions et l'évolution sociale au Congo-Brazzaville de 1880 à 1930,* Thesis, University of Bordeaux, 1967. P. 878.

*Grandval, Gilbert, *Ma Mission au Maroc,* Paris, 1956. P. 825.

*Gray, Harold S., *A Study of Cameroon's U. P. C. Rebellion and Chinese Communist Involvement,* M.A. Thesis, American University, 1967. P. 860.

*Great Britain, *Correspondence Relating to the Military Operations in Togoland,* Cmd. 7872, Parliamentary Paper 1915, Account and Papers, vol. 46. P. 829.

*Green, Reginald, *L'Economie de la République-Fédérale du Cameroun,* Paris, 1968. P. 870.

*Grimal, Henri, *La Decolonisation, 1919–1963,* Paris, 1966. P. 851.

*Grivot, René, *Reactions dahoméennes,* Paris, 1954. P. 857.

*Groves, Charles Pelham, *The Planting of Christianity in Africa,* vol. 4, *1914–1954,* London, 1958. Pp. 830, 833, 877.

*Gsell, Stéphane, Georges Marçais, and Georges Yver, *Histoire de l'Algérie,* Paris, 1927. P. 797.

*Guernier, Eugène, *La Berbérie, L'Islam et la France,* 2 vols., Paris, 1950. P. 789.

———, *Afrique équatoriale française,* Paris, 1950.

*Guernier, Eugène, and G. Froment-Guiyesse, *Algerie et Sahara* in *Encyclopédie coloniale et maritime,* 2 vols., Paris, 1948. P. 797.

Gueye, Lamine, *De la Situation politique des Sénégalais originaires des communes de plein exercice,* Paris, Doctorat d'Etat, 1921.

*———, *Étapes et perspectives de l'Union française,* Paris, 1955. Pp. 842, 847.

*———, *Itinéraire africain,* Paris, 1966. Pp. 842, 847.

*Guillaume, Albert, *L'Evolution économique de la société rurale marocaine,* Paris, 1956. P. 826.

*Guillen, Pierre, "L'Implantation de Schneider au Maroc—Les débuts de la XXe siècle: La fondation de la Compagnie marocaine," *Revue d'histoire* (Apr.–June 1963). P. 826.

*Guillen, Pierre, "L'Implantation de Schneider au Maroc—Les débuts de la Compagnie marocaine (1902–1906)," *Revue d'histoire diplomatique,* April 1965.

———, *L'Allemagne et le Maroc de 1870 à 1905,* Paris, 1967.

———, *Finance et diplomatie. Les emprunts marocains de 1902–1904* (in press).

*Guitard, Odette, *Bandoeng et le reveil des anciens peuples colonisés,* Paris, 1961. P. 794.

*Hahn, Lorna, *North Africa: Nationalism to Nationhood,* Washington, 1960. P. 792.

*Hailey, Lord, *An African Survey,* London, 1938. Pp. 864, 872.

*———, *An African Survey, Revised 1956,* London, 1957, P. 872.

Hale, Oron James, *Publicity and Diplomacy,* New York, 1940.

*Haliburton, G. N., *The Prophet Harris and His Work in the Ivory Coast and Western Ghana,* Thesis, University of London, 1968. P. 881.

*Halpern, Manfred, "Algerian Uprising of 1945," *Middle East Journal,* 2 (1948), 191–202. P. 802.

Halstead, John P., *The Origins of Moroccan Nationalism, 1919–1934,* Ph.D. Dissertation, Harvard, 1960.

*———, *Rebirth of a Nation: The Origins and Rise of Moroccan Nationalism, 1912–1944,* Cambridge, Mass., 1967. P. 822.

*Hamilton, Benjamin A., *The Environment, Establishment and Expansion of Protestant Missions in French Equatorial Africa,* Th.D. Dissertation, Grace Theological Seminary, 1959. Pp. 877, 878.

*Hamilton, Margaret L., *French Policy toward Morocco: 1944–1956,* Ph.D. Dissertation, Columbia, 1959. P. 824.

*Hamon, Léo, *Introduction à l'étude des partis politiques de l'Afrique française,* Paris, 1959. P. 853.

*Hanotaux, G., and A. Martineau, eds., *Histoire des colonies françaises et de l'expansion de la France dans le monde,* Paris, 1931. P. 797.

*Hardy, Georges, *Une Conquête morale: L'enseignement en Afrique Occidentale Française,* Paris, 1917. P. 872.

*———, "L'Enseignement aux Indigènes dans les possessions françaises d'Afrique," in Institut Colonial International, *L'Enseignement aux Indigènes,* Paris, 1931, 239–472. P. 873.

*———, et al., *Le Maroc, la Tunisie, la Syrie, l'oeuvre scientifique française en Syrie et en Perse,* Paris, 1931. Pp. 814, 821.

*———, *Le Reverend Père F. Aupiais,* Paris, 1949. P. 879.

Hargreaves, John D., "*Entente Manquée:* Anglo–French Relations, 1895–1896," *Cambridge Historical Journal, 11* (1953)

———, *Prelude to the Partition of West Africa,* London, 1963.

*———, *West Africa, the Former French States,* Englewood Cliffs, 1967. P. 836.

*Harris, Walter B., *Morocco That Was, 1887–1912,* London, 1921. P. 819.

*———, *France, Spain, and the Rif,* New York, 1927. P. 819.

*Hatton, P. H. S., "The Gambia, the Colonial Office, and the Opening Months of the First World War," *Journal of African History,* 7 (1966), 123–32. P. 830.

*Haumant, J. C., *Initiation aux finances publiques des territoires d'Outre-Mer,* Paris, 1953. P. 866.

Hauser, Henri, *Le Problème colonial,* Paris, 1915.
*Haut-Commissariat de l'Afrique Française, *L'Agression de Dakar,* Dakar, 1940. P. 844.
*Hayter, Teresa, *French Aid,* Overseas Development Institute, London, 1966. P. 866.
*Hegba, Meinrad, "Les Etapes des regroupements africains (1945–1965)," *Afrique documents, 98–99,* 108–268. P. 852.
*Henderson, W. O., *Studies in German Colonial History,* London, 1962. P. 830.
*Hermassi, A., *Le Mouvement ouvrier en société coloniale: la Tunisie entre deux guerres,* Thesis, University of Paris, 1966. P. 816.
*Heurot, André, *La Composition des assemblées locales dans les départements et territoires d'Outre-Mer français et dans les territoires du Commonwealth britannique, Étude comparee,* Thesis, University of Paris, 1948. P. 849.
*Hirschberg, Hayyim Ze'eb, *Toledoth Hay-Yehudim Be-Afrikah Has-Sefonith. A History of the Jews of North Africa from Antiquity to Our Times,* 2 vols., Jerusalem, 1965. P. 796.
*Hodgkin, Thomas and Ruth Schachter (Morgenthau), "French-Speaking West Africa in Transition" *International Conciliation, 528,* May 1960. P. 851.
*Hoffherr, René, *L'Économie Marocaine,* Paris, 1932. P. 826.
*———, *Coopération économique franco-africaine,* Paris, 1958. P. 865.
*Holas, Bohumil, "Bref aperçu sur les principaux cultes syncrétiques de la Basse Côte d'Ivoire," *Africa, 24* (1954), 55–61. P. 881.
*———, *Le Séparatisme religieux en Afrique Noire: l'example de la Côte d'Ivoire,* Paris, 1965. P. 881.
*Homet, Marcel, *Congo: terres de souffrances,* Paris, 1934. Pp. 841, 865.
*Homont, André, "L'Application du régime de tutelle aux territoires sous mandat," *Revue juridique et politique de l'Union française,* Apr.–June 1952, 149–88. P. 848.
*Horner, Norman A., *Protestant and Roman Catholic Missions among the Bantu of Cameroun,* Ph.D. Dissertation, Hartford Seminary Foundation, 1956. P. 877.
*Houart, Pierre, *L'Attitude de l'Eglise dans le guerre d'Algérie, 1954–1960,* Brussels, 1960. P. 809.
*Hourani, Albert, *Arabic Thought in the Liberal Age, 1798–1939,* London, 1962. P. 822.
*Howe, Marvine, *The Prince and I,* New York, 1955. P. 825.
———, "The Birth of the Moroccan Nation," *Middle East Journal, 10* (1956), 1–16.
*Howe, Sonia E., *Lyautey of Morocco: An Authorized Biography,* London, 1931. P. 820.
*Hubac, Pierre, *Tunisie,* Paris, 1948. P. 814.
*Hugon, Philippe, *Analyse de sous-développement en Afrique Noire. L'exemple de l'économie du Cameroun,* Paris, 1968. P. 870.
*Hugot, Pierre, *Le Tchad,* Paris, 1965. P. 837.
*Huguet, P., *Code du Travail Outre-Mer,* Paris, 1953. P. 870.
*Humbaraci, Arslan, *Algeria: A Revolution That Failed,* New York, 1966. P. 811.

*Hunter, Guy, *The New Societies of Tropical Africa,* London, 1962. P. 884.

*Hurault, Jean, *La Structure sociale des Bamiléké,* Paris, 1962. Pp. 859, 863.

*Huré, Antoine, *La Pacification du Maroc: Dernière étude: 1931–1934,* Paris, 1952. P. 820.

*Hutin, Paul, *La Doctrine d'association des indigènes et des Français en Algérie,* Paris, 1935. P. 802.

*Hymans, Jack Louis, *L'Élaboration de la pensée de Léopold Sédar Senghor: Esquisse d'un itinéraire intellectuel,* Thesis, University of Paris, 1964. Pp. 855, 875.

Ingold, General F. J. J., *Oeux de Leclerc en Tunisie,* Ebolowa, Cameroun, 1943.

*———, *L'Epopée Leclerc au Sahara, 1940–1943,* Paris, 1945. P. 844.

*———, *La France et son Empire dans la Guerre,* Paris, 1946. P. 844.

*International Bank of Reconstruction and Development, *The Economic Development of Morocco,* Baltimore, 1966. P. 826.

*International Labor Office, *African Labor Survey,* Geneva, 1958. P. 871.

*International Monetary Fund, *Survey of African Economies, Vol. I, Cameroon, Central African Republic, Chad, Congo (Brazzaville), and Gabon,* Washington, 1968. P. 870.

*Isnard, Hildebart, *La Vigne en Algérie: Etude géographique,* 2 vols., Gap, 1951–1954. P. 798.

*Izard, Françoise and Michel, *Les Mossi du Yatenga. Étude de la vie economique et sociale,* Bordeaux, 1959. P. 869.

*Jacob, Alain, *D'une Algérie à l'autre,* Paris, 1963. P. 809.

*Jalabert, Louis, "Le Nationalisme marocaine," *Etudes* (Aug. and Sept. 1934), 433–48, 625–37, 758–67. P. 823.

———, "La Turbulence de l'Islam arabe: du arabisme aux nationalismes," *Etudes, 234* (1938), 170–84.

*———, "Dans le Maghreb qui bouge. I. Tendances generales religieuses. II. Les Reactions politiques et religieuses," *Etudes* (1938), 164–78, 342–60. P. 823.

*Jeanson, Colette and Francis, *L'Algérie hors la loi,* Paris, 1955. P. 804.

*Jeanson, Francis, *La Révolution algérienne. Problèmes et perspectives,* Milan, 1961. P. 808.

*Jeaugeon, R., "Les Sociétés d'exploitation au Congo et l'opinion française de 1890 à 1906," *Revue française d'histoire d'outre-mer, 48* (1961), 353–437. P. 865.

*Jobson, O. D., *Conquering Oubangui-Chari for Christ,* Winona Lake, Indiana, 1957. P. 878.

*Johnson, Douglas, "Algeria: Some Problems of Modern History," *Journal of African History, 5* (1964), 221–42. P. 796.

Johnson, G. Wesley, *The Diffusion of Nationalism in French West Africa,* Thesis, Columbia University, 1966.

*———, "The Ascendancy of Blaise Diagne and the Beginning of African Politics in Senegal, *Africa,* July, 1966. P. 842.

*———, *The Emergence of Black Politics in Senegal: The Struggle for Power in the Four Communes,* Stanford, 1971. Pp. 831, 842, 887.

*Johnson, Willard R., *The Cameroon Federation: Political Integration in a Fragmentary Society,* Princeton, 1970. Pp. 858, 860.

*Jones, T. J., (Phelps-Stokes Foundation), *Education in Africa,* New York, 1922. P. 873.

*Joseph, Gaston, *Côte d'Ivoire,* Paris, 1944. P. 840.

**Journal Officiel de la République Française,* August 25, 1921, p. 9868. *Rapport au ministre des colonies sur l'administration des territoires occupés du Togo de la conquête du I*[er] *juillet 1921.* P. 829.

**Journal Officiel de la République Française,* September 7, 1921, Annex, 415–92. P. 829.

*Jouvin, Bernard, "Les Debuts d'une assemblée locale d'outre-mer," Conseil d'Etat, *Etudes et Documents, 3* (1949). P. 848.

*Joy, R., and Melvin Arnold, *The Africa of Albert Schweitzer,* London, 1949. P. 878.

*Juin, Maréchal Alphonse-Pierre, *Le Maghreb en feu,* Paris, 1957, P. 794.

*———, *Mémoires,* 2 vols., Paris, 1959. P. 793.

Julien, Charles-André, *Les Techniciens de la colonisation,* Paris, 1946.

———, *Les Politiques d'expansion imperialiste,* Paris, 1949.

*———, "From the French Empire to the French Union," *International Affairs,* Oct. 1950, 487–502. Pp. 794, 846.

*———, "Crisis and Reform in French North Africa," *Foreign Affairs, 29* (1951), 445–55. P. 794.

*———, *L'Afrique du nord en marche. Nationalismes musulmans et souveraineté francaise,* Paris, 1952. P. 793.

———, *Histoire de l'Afrique du nord,* 2d ed., revised by C. Courtois and R. Le Tourneau, 2 vols., Paris, 1953.

*———, "Léon Blum et les pays d'outre-mer," in *Léon Blum, Chef de Gouvernment, 1936–1937, Cahiers de la Fondation Nationale des Sciences Politiques, 155* (Paris, 1967), 377–90. P. 792.

*July, Robert W., *The Origins of Modern African Thought,* New York, 1968. Pp. 842, 876.

*Kabbani, Rashid, *Morocco: From Protectorate to Independence, 1912–1956,* Ph.D. Dissertation, American University, 1957. P. 822.

*Kabore, V., *Organisation politique traditionnelle et évolution politique des Mossi de Ouagadougou,* Paris and Ouagadougou, 1966. P. 863.

Kaddache, Mahfoud, "La Question nationale algérienne et le parti communiste entre 1919 et 1939," *Revue d'Histoire et de Civilisation du Maghreb,* Jan. 1967, 95–104.

———, *La Vie politique à Alger de 1919 à 1939,* Thesis, University of Algiers, 1968, 2 vols.

*Kagame, Alexis, *Le Colonialisme face à la doctrine missionnaire à l'heure de Vatican II,* Butare, Rwanda, 1964. P. 880.

*Kalck, Pierre, *Réalités oubanguiennes,* Paris, 1959. P. 860.

*Kanga, Victor Jean-Claude, *Le Droit coutumier Bamiléké au contact des droits européens,* Yaoundé, 1959. Pp. 859, 864.

Kanya-Forstner, A. Sydney, *The Conquest of the Western Sudan: A Study in French Military Imperialism,* Cambridge, 1969.

———, "French African Policy and the Anglo-French Agreement of 5 August 1890," *Historical Journal, 12* (1969).

Keith, Arthur Berridale, *The Belgian Congo and the Berlin Act,* Oxford, 1919.

*Kent, Raymond, *From Madagascar to the Malagasy Republic,* New York, 1962. Pp. 837, 861.

*Kessler, Jane S., *Educating the Black Frenchmen,* Ph.D. Dissertation, Harvard University, 1958. P. 874.

*Kesteloot, Lilyan, *Les Ecrivains noirs de langue française: naissance d'une littérature,* Brussels, 1963. P. 875.

*———, *Negritude et situation coloniale,* Yaoundé, 1968. P. 876.

*Khaled, Emir, *La Situation des musulmans d'Algérie,* Algiers, 1924. P. 800.

*Kheirrallah, C., *Le Mouvement jeune-tunisien. Essai d'histoire et de synthèse des mouvements nationalistes tunisiens,* Tunis, 1957. P. 815.

*Khuri, Fuad I., "Kinship, Emigration, and Trade Partners among the Lebanese of West Africa," *Africa,* Oct. 1965, 385–95. P. 868.

*Kinde, A., *La Chefferie dans le Bas-Dahomey,* Mémoire, E.N.F.O.M., 1957. P. 863.

*Kitchen, Helen, *The Educated African: A Country by Country Survey of Educational Development in Africa,* New York, 1962. P. 872.

*Ki-Zerbo, Joseph, "La personnalité négro-africaine," *Présence africaine,* no. 41 (1962), 137–43. P. 875.

Klein, Martin A., *Islam and Imperialism in Senegal: Siné-Saloum, 1847–1914,* Edinburgh, 1968.

*Knight, Melvin M., *Morocco as a French Economic Venture: A Study of Open Door Imperialism,* New York, 1937. P. 826.

*———, "Economic Space for Europeans in North Africa," *Economic Development and Cultural Change, 1* (1952), 360–75. P. 790.

*Kodjo, Mensah, *Eléments pour une sociologie politique de la vie togolaise,* Mémoire, University of Paris, 1967. P. 858.

*Koren, Henry J., C. S. Sp., *The Spiritans: A History of the Congregation of the Holy Ghost,* Pittsburgh, 1959. P. 877.

*Korner, H., *Kolonialpolitik und Wirtschaftsentwicklung. Das Beispiel Französisch Westafrikas,* Stuttgart, 1965. P. 866.

*Kozicki, Richard J., "The United Nations and Colonialism," *The Idea of Colonialism,* ed. R. Strausz-Hupé and N. Hazard, New York, 1958. P. 847.

*Kraft, Joseph, *Struggle for Algeria,* New York, 1961. P. 806.

*Kritzeck, James, and William H. Lewis, eds., *Islam in Africa,* New York, 1969. P. 884.

*Kuoh-Moukouri, Jacques, *Doigts Noirs,* Montreal, 1963. P. 834.

Kuper, Hilda, ed., *Urbanization and Migration in West Africa,* Berkeley and Los Angeles, 1965.

*Kwayeb, Enoch Katté, *Les Institutions de droit public au pays Bamiléké (Cameroun): Evolution et Régime Actuel,* Paris, 1960. P. 859, 863.

*Labat, René, *Le Gabon devant le Gaullisme,* Bordeaux, 1941. P. 844.

*Labouret, Henri, *À la Recherche d'une politique indigène dans l'Ouest africaine,* Paris, 1931. (Originally published in *Afrique francaise,* 1930–1931.) P. 840.

*———, *Le Cameroun,* Paris, 1937. P. 833.

*———, *Paysans d'Afrique occidentale,* Paris, 1941. P. 868.

*Lacharrière, J. Landreit de, *La Création marocaine,* Paris, 1930. P. 821.

*———, M. Bernard, and Simon, *La Pacification du Maroc, 1907–1934,* Paris, 1936. P. 820.
*Lacheraf, Mostefa, *L'Algérie: nation et société,* Paris, 1965. P. 804.
*Lacouture, Jean and Simonne, *Le Maroc à l'Epreuve,* Paris, 1958. P. 825.
*Lacouture, Jean, *Cinq Hommes et la France,* Paris, 1961. Pp. 816, 825.
*Lacquemond, Serge, *Les Investissements publics metropolitains et le développement économique du Nord-Cameroun pendant le régime de Tutelle (1947–1959),* Paris, Doctorat d'Etat, 1959. P. 870.
*Ladhari, Noë, *Les Conventions franco-tunisiennes du 3 juin 1955,* Tunis, 1955. P. 817.
*Laitman, Leon, *Tunisia Today,* New York, 1954. P. 816.
*Lambert, Jacques, *Manuel de législation algérienne,* Alger, 1952. P. 803.
*Lampué, Pierre, "L'Union francaise d'après la Constitution," *Revue juridique et politique de l'Union française,* Jan. and June 1947, 1–39, 149–97. P. 846.
*———, "Le Statut de l'Algérie," *Revue juridique et politique de l'Union Française,* Oct.–Dec. 1947, 477–525. P. 803.
*———, *Précis de droit du pays d'outre-mer,* Paris, 1949. P. 849.
*———, "Les Lois Applicables en Algérie," *Revue juridique et politique l'Union Française, 4* (1950), 1–23. P. 803.
*———, "Le territoire associé et l'état associé suivant la constitution," *Recueil Dalloz,* 1951.
Landau, Rom, *Invitation to Morocco,* London, 1950.
*———, *The Sultan of Morocco,* London, 1951. P. 825.
*———, *Moroccan Drama, 1900–1955,* San Francisco, 1956. P. 822.
Landes, David S., *Bankers and Pachas,* Cambridge, Mass., 1958.
*Lanessan, J. L. de, *La Tunisie,* 2d ed., Paris, 1917. P. 814.
Langer, William L., "The European Powers and the French Occupation of Tunis," *American Historical Review, 31* (1925–26).
*Langley, Jabez Ayodele, *West African Aspects of the Pan-African Movement, 1900–1945,* Thesis, University of Edinburgh, 1968. P. 842.
*———, "Pan-Africanism in Paris, 1924–1936," *Journal of Modern African Studies,* April 1969, 69–94. P. 842.
*———, "Garveyism and African Nationalism," *Race,* Oct. 1969, 157–72. P. 842.
*Laoust, Henri, "Le Réformisme orthodoxe des 'Salafiya' et les caractères généraux de son orientation actuelle," *Revue des études islamiques, 6* (1932), 175–224. P. 823.
*Lapie, Pierre O., *Mes Tournées au Tchad,* Paris, 1943. P. 844.
———, *Le Tchad fait la guerre,* Paris, 1945.
*———, "La tutelle française devant l'O.N.U.," *Revue Politique et Parlementaire,* Apr. 1950, 11–16. P. 848.
*Larnaude, Marcel, *Algérie,* Paris, 1950. P. 797.
*Lasserre, Guy, "Okoumé et chantiers forestiers au Gabon," *Cahiers d'outre-mer,* April–June 1955, 119–60.
*———, *Libreville et sa région (Gabon, A.E.F.): étude de géographie humaine,* Paris, 1958. P. 869.
*Latourette, Kenneth Scott, *The Twentieth Century outside Europe,* New York, 1962. P. 877.

*La Truffe, M., *Les Sultanats du Tchad,* Mémoire, C.H.E.A.M., May 6, 1949. P. 863.

*Laubadère, André de, *Les Réformes des pouvoirs publiques: le gouvernement; l'administration; la justice,* Paris, 1949. P. 821.

*Launay, Michel, *Paysans algériens: la terre, la vigne, et les hommes,* Paris, 1963. P. 798.

*Laure, Lt. Col. Auguste, *La Victoire franco-espagnole dans le Rif,* Paris, 1927. P. 820.

*Laurentin, Anne, "Femmes Nzakara," *Femmes d'Afrique Noire,* ed. Denise Paulme, Paris, 1960, 121–72. P. 886.

*Lavroff, Dimitri Georges, *La République du Senegal,* Paris, 1966. P. 854.

*Lawless, G., *Le Principe de l'égalité économique au Cameroun,* Paris, 1937. P. 833.

*Laye, Yves, *Le Port d'Alger,* Algiers, 1953. P. 800.

*Lebeuf, J.-P., *Rapport d'une enquete preliminaire dans les milieux urbains de la Federation,* vol. 2, (Oubangui-Chari, A.E.F.), Paris, 1954. P. 884.

*———, *Fort Lamy, Tchad, A.E.F.*, Paris, 1956. P. 884.

Lebon, André, *La Politique de la France en Africa, 1896–1898,* Paris, 1901.

*Lebret, Rev. Louis-Joseph, O.P., *Rapport Générale sur les Perspectives de Développement du Sénegal,* vol. 1, Dakar, 1960. P. 875.

*Le Chatelier, Alfred, *L'Islam dans l'Afrique occidentale,* Paris, 1899. P. 883.

*Le Cornec, Jacques, *Histoire politique du Tchad de 1900 à 1962,* Paris, 1963. Pp. 839, 860, 863.

*Le Duc, Gaston, *Le Développement économique de l'Afrique noire,* Paris, 1955. P. 867.

Lee, Dwight E., *Great Britain and the Cyprus Convention of 1878,* Cambridge, Mass., 1934.

*Lefébure, Jules, *Le Régime des concessions au Congo,* Paris, 1904. P. 864.

**L'Eglise Catholique face au monde non Chrétien,* vol. 4 of the *Histoire Universelle des Missions Catholiques,* Paris, 1959. P. 880.

*Le Melle, W. J., *A Concept of the Modern African State: A Critique of the Political Philosophy of Sékou Touré,* Thesis, University of Denver, 1963. P. 856.

*Lemoine, Captain, "Les Pays conquis du Cameroun Nord," *Afrique française,* 28 (1918). P. 829.

*Lenoir, Robert, *Les Concessions foncières en A.O.F. et équatoriale,* Paris, 1936. P. 864.

*Lentin, Albert-Paul, *Le Dernier Quart d'heure* (*L'Algerie entre deux mondes*), Paris, 1963. P. 809.

*Leonard, Roger, *Quatre Ans en Algérie,* Algiers, 1955. P. 803.

Leonard, Roger, and Maurice Cuttoli, *Les Territoires du Sud de l'Algérie; compte rendu de l'oeuvre accomplie de 1947 à 1952,* Alger, 1953.

*Leone, Enrico de, *La Colonizzazione dell'Africa del Nord* (*Algeria, Tunisia, Morocco, Libia*) 2 vols., Padua, 1957–60. P. 788.

*Lépidi, Jules, *L'Eonomie tunisienne depuis la fin de la guerre,* Tunis, 1955. P. 818.

Le Pointe, Henri, *La Colonisation Française au Pays des Somalis,* Paris, 1914.

*Lepp, Ignace, *Midi sonne au Maroc,* Paris, 1954. P. 823.

*Leriche A., "L'Islam en Maritanie," *Bulletin de L'I.F.A.N.*, 1949. P. 883.

*Leriche, Joseph, *Les Algériens parmi nous. Essai psycho-sociologique d'après les enquêtes et travaux des Etudes nord-africaines,* Paris, 1959. P. 813.

*Lesne, Marcel, *L'Evolution d'un groupe berbère: les Zemmours,* Rabat, 1959. P. 828.

*Lestringant, Jacques, *Les pays des Guider au Cameroun: essai d'histoire régionale,* Paris, 1964. P. 859.

*Le Tourneau, Roger, "Causes des mouvements d'autonomie en Afrique du Nord," in Portugal, Ministerio do ultramar, Centro de estudios politicos e sociais, *Estudios de ciencas politicas e sociais, 2* (Porto, 1954). P. 794.

*———, "North Africa: Rigorism and Bewilderment," *Unity and Variety of Muslim Civilization,* ed. Gustave Edmund von Grunebaum, Chicago, 1955, 231–60. P. 795.

*———, *L'Evolution politique de l'Afrique du Nord musulmane, 1920–1961,* Paris, 1962. P. 791.

LeVine, Victor T., "The Cameroun Federal Republic," *Five African States,* ed. Gwendolen Carter, Ithaca, 1963. P. 858.

*———, *The Cameroons from Mandate to Independence,* Berkeley and Los Angeles, 1964. Pp. 834, 858.

*Lewis, Ioan, ed., *Islam in Tropical Africa,* London, 1966. P. 884.

*Liebesny, Herbert J., *The Government of French North Africa,* Philadelphia, 1943. P. 792.

Ling, Dwight, "Paul Cambon, Coordinator of Tunisia," *Historian,* Aug. 1957.

———, *Tunisia: From Protectorate to Republic,* Bloomington, 1967. P. 814.

*Lippmann, Alphonse, *Guerriers et sorciers en Somalie,* Paris, 1953. P. 840.

*Lloyd, Peter C., ed., *Africa in Social Change: Changing Traditional Societies in the Modern World,* Baltimore, 1967. P. 884.

*Logan, Rayford Whittingham, "Education in Former French West and Equatorial Africa and Madagascar," *The Journal of Negro Education, 30* (1961), 277–85. P. 874.

*———, "The Historical Aspects of Pan-Africanism, 1900–1945," *Pan-Africanism Reconsidered,* A.M.S.A.C., Berkeley and Los Angeles, 1962, 37–52. P. 842.

*Lombard, Jacques, "Cotonou, ville africaine. Tendances évolutives et réaction des coutumes traditionnelles," *Bulletin de l'I.F.A.N.*, 3 (1954), 341–77. P. 886.

*———, *Structures de type "féodal" en Afrique Noire. Etude des dynamismes internes et de relations sociales chez les Bariba du Dahomey,* Paris, 1965. P. 863.

*———, *Autorités traditionelles et pouvoirs européens en Afrique Noire. Le declin d'une aristocratic sous le régime colonial,* Paris, 1967. P. 862.

*Londres, Albert, *Terre d'ébène,* Paris, 1929. Pp. 841, 865.

*Lopinot, B., *Aspects particuliers du problème des chefferies chez une population anarchique: les Gambayes du Logone,* Document C.H.E.A.M., 1954. P. 863.

*Louis, William Roger, "The U. S. and the African Peace Settlement of 1919: The Pilgrimage of George Louis Beer," *Journal of African History, 4* (1963), 413–33. P. 832.
*———, *Great Britain and Germany's Lost Colonies, 1914–1919,* Oxford, 1967. P. 832.
*Louveau, Ernest, *"Au Bagne": Entre les griffes de Vichy et de la milice,* Bamako, 1947. P. 844.
*Lucas, Sir Charles, *The Gold Coast and the War,* London, 1920. P. 830.
*Lucas, Gerard, *Formal Education in the Congo-Brazzaville: A Study of Educational Policy and Practice,* Thesis, Stanford University, 1965. Pp. 874, 878.
———, "Congo-Brazzaville," *Church, State, and Education in Africa,* ed. David G. Scanlon, New York, 1966, 111–34.
*Luce, Edmond-Pierre, *Le Référendum du Togo, 28 Octobre 1956,* Paris, 1958. P. 857.
*Luchaire, François, *Manuel de droit d'Outre-Mer,* Paris, 1949, *Supplément,* 1951. P. 849.
*———, "Le Togo français de la tutelle a l'autonomie," *Revue juridique et politique de l'Union française, 11* (1957), 1–46, 501–87. P. 858.
*———, *Les Institutions politiques et administratives des territoires d'outre-mer après la loi-cadre,* Paris, 1958. P. 847.
Luethy, Herbert, *France Against Herself,* New York, 1955.
*———, and David Rodnick, *French Motivations in the Suez Crisis,* Princeton, 1956. P. 807.
*Ly, Abdoulaye, *Les Masses africaines et l'actuelle condition humaine,* Paris, 1956. P. 867.
*———, *Mercenaires noires: noteo sur une forme de l'exploitation des Africains,* Paris, 1957. P. 831.
———, *La Compagnie du Sénégal,* Paris, 1958.
*———, *L'Etat et la production paysanne, on l'état et la révolution au Sénégal,* Paris, 1963. P. 868.
*Lyautey, Marshal Louis Hubert, "Les origines du conflit," *Les Cahiers des Droits de l'Homme,* June 10, 1926, 267–73. P. 820.
*———, *Paroles d'action,* Paris, 1927. P. 820.
*———, *Textes et Lettres (1912–1925),* ed. Pierre Lyautey, 4 vols., Paris, 1953–57. P. 820.
M. D. (Paul Blanc), "Les nouveaux statuts du Togo et du Cameroun," *Penant,* April, 1959.
*Mailier, Henri, "Le Rôle des colonies françaises dans la campagne du Cameroun, 1914–1916," *Afrique française* (June 1916), 209–15. P. 829.
Mameri, Khalfa, *Les Nations Unies face à la question algérienne (1954–1962).* Mémoire, University of Paris, 1969.
*Mamet, Pierre, *Les Expériences syndicales en Tunisie de 1881 à 1956,* Mémoire, University of Paris, 1966. P. 816.
*Manckasa, Côme, *Mutations politiques au Congo, Brazzaville,* Mémoire, University of Paris, 1966. Pp. 842, 860, 887.
*Mandouze, André, *La Révolution algérienne par les textes: documents du F.L.N.,* Paris, 1961. P. 807.
*Mangin, Charles, *La Force noire,* Paris, 1911. P. 831.
*Mannoni, Otare Dominique, *La Psychologie de la colonisation,* Paris, 1950,

trans. *Prospero and Caliban: The Psychology of Colonization,* New York, 1956. P. 861.
*Mansell, Gerard, *Tragedy in Algeria,* London, 1961. P. 806.
*Maran, René, *Batouala,* Paris, 1921. P. 840.
*———, *Félix Eboué, grand commis et loyal serviteur, 1885–1944,* Paris, 1957. P. 845.
*Marchand, Henri-François, *Les Mariages franco-musulmans,* Algiers, 1955. P. 791.
*Marchat, Henri, "Vie et morts du statut de Tanger," *Revue politique et parlementaire,* (Aug.–Sept., 1960), 124–33. P. 826.
*Markovitz, Irving L., *Leopold Sedar Senghor and the Politics of Negritude,* New York, 1969. P. 855.
*———, "The Political Thought of Blaise Diagne and Lamine Gueye: Some Aspects of Social Structure and Ideology in Senegal," *Presence Africaine,* 72 (1969), 21–38. Pp. 842, 855.
*———, "Traditional Social Structure, the Islamic Brotherhoods, and Political Development in Senegal," *Journal of Modern African Studies, 8* (1970), 73–96. P. 884.
*"Maroc et Tunisie: Le Problème du protectorat," *La Nef,* Cahier No. 2 (March 1953). P. 826.
*Maroc. Ministère de l'Information et Tourism. *Réalisations et perspectives. 16 novembre 1955–18 novembre 1957. Recueil de textes et de discours,* Rabat, 1957. P. 825.
*Maroix, General, *Le Togo, pays d'influence française,* Paris, 1938. P. 829.
*Martel, André, *Les confins saharo-tripolitains de la Tunisie, 1881–1911,* 2 vols., Paris, 1965. P. 818.
*Martin, Claude, *Histoire de l'Algérie française, 1830–1962,* Paris, 1963. P. 797.
*Martin, V., *La Chrétienté africaine de Dakar,* Dakar, 1964. P. 880.
———, *Notes d'introduction à une étude socio-religieuse des populations de Dakar et du Sénégal,* Dakar, 1964.
*Martin du Gard, Maurice, *La Carte impériale: Histoire de la France outremer, 1940–1945,* Paris, 1949. P. 843.
Marty, Paul, *La Politique indigène du Gouverneur—général Ponty,* Paris, 1915.
*———, *Etudes sur l'Islam maure,* Paris, 1916. P. 882.
*———, *Etudes sur l'Islam au Sénégal,* 2d ed., Paris, 1917. P. 882.
*———, *Etudes sur l'Islam et les tribus du Soudan,* 4 vols., Paris, 1920–1921. P. 882.
*———, *L'Islam en Guinée.* Fouta Djalon, Paris, 1921. P. 882.
*———, *L'Islam en Côte d'Ivoire,* Paris, 1922. P. 882.
*Mathiot, A., "Le Contrôle de l'O.N.U. sur l'administration des territoires non autonomes," *Revue juridique et politique de l'Union française,* Oct–Dec. 1948 and Jan.–Mar. 1949, pp. 405 ff. and 26–59. P. 848.
*———, "Les Territoires sous tutelle et le problème des Unions administratives," in *Principes et Techniques du Droit Public,* 2 vols., Mélanges G. Scelle, Paris, 1950. P. 848.
*Matongo, Julien, *L'Evolution constitutionnelle et politique du Congo (Brazzaville) depuis l'indépendance,* Mémoire, University of Paris, 1966. P. 860.

"Matswa," *Monde non-Chrétien,* June 1953, 202–210 (extract of "Le Problème le plus délicat du XXe siècle en A.E.F.").
*Maunier, René, *Sociologie coloniale,* Paris, 1932. P. 886.
*———, *Loi française et coutume indigène en Algérie,* Paris, 1932. P. 802.
*Mauric, Alain, *Le Gabon de la Loi-Cadre au Référendum,* unpublished study, Institut des Hautes Etudes d'Outre-Mer, 1959. P. 860.
*Maurois, André, *Lyautey,* New York, 1931. P. 820.
*Maxwell, Gavin, *Lord of the Atlas: The Rise and Fall of the House of Glaoua, 1893–1956,* London, 1966. P. 825.
*Mbarga, H. B., *Problèmes africains de l'éducation. Précéde de l'étude du cas du Cameroun,* Paris, 1962. P. 875.
*McLellan, David S., "The North Africans in France: A French Racial Problem," *Yale Review,* March 1955, 421–88. P. 812.
McPhee, Allan, *The Economic Revolution in British West Africa,* London, 1926.
*Mehl, R., *Décolonisation et missions protestantes,* Paris, 1964. P. 880.
*Méjan, François, *Le Vatican contre la France d'outre-mer,* Paris, 1957. P. 879.
*Melone, Thomas, *De la Négritude dans la littérature negro-africaine,* Paris, 1963. P. 876.
*Memmi, Albert, *Portrait du colonisé précédé du portrait du colonisateur,* Paris, 1957. P. 814.
Mendouze, Andre, *La Révolution algérienne par les textes: documents du F.L.N.,* Paris, 1961.
Ménier, M.-A., "La Marche au Tchad de 1887 à 1891," *Bulletin d'Etudes Centrafricaines, 5* (1953).
*Mentzel, H., *Die Kampf in Kamerun, 1914–1916,* Berlin, 1936. P. 830.
*Mercier, Paul, "Evolution of Senegalese Elites," *International Social Science Bulletin 8* (1956), 441–52. P. 854.
*———, "Political Life in the Urban Centers of Senegal: A Study of the Period of Transition," *P.R.O.D.* (Princeton), *3* (1960), 3–20. P. 854.
*Mercier, René, *Le Travail obligatoire dans les Colonies francaises,* Paris, 1949. P. 841.
*Merle, Marcel, "La Constitution et les problèmes d'outre-mer," *Revue Française de science politique,* March 1959. P. 853.
*———, *Les Eglises Chrétiennes et la Décolonisation,* Paris, 1967. P. 880.
*Merlo, Manuel, *L'Organisation administrative de l'Algérie,* Algiers, 1951. P. 803.
*Meynaud, Jean, and Anisse Saleh-Bey, *Trade Unions in Africa,* London, 1967. P. 871.
*Michel, André, *Les Travailleurs algériens en France,* Paris, 1956. P. 812.
*Michel, Marc, "Les Debuts du soulèvement de la Haute Sangha en 1928," *Annales Centre Enseignement Superieur Brazzaville,* 2 (1966), 33–48. Pp. 843, 865.
———, *La Mission Marchand,* Thesis, Paris, 1968.
*Micklesell, Marvin, *Northern Morocco: A Cultural Geography,* Berkeley and Los Angeles, 1961. P. 828.
*Miège, Jean-Louis, *Le Maroc,* Paris, 1962. P. 819.
*Milcent, Ernest, *L'A.O.F. entre en scène,* Paris, 1958. P. 851.

*———, "Senegal," *African One-Party States,* ed. Gwendolen Carter, Ithaca, 1962, 87–148. P. 854.

*———, *Au carrefour des options africaines: le Senegal,* Paris, 1965. P. 854.

Mille, Pierre, "The Black Vote in Senegal," *Journal of the African Society, 1* (1901), 64–79.

*Miller, Richard I., *United Nations' Trusteeship System and Educational Advancement,* Thesis, Columbia University, 1958. P. 872.

*Milliot, Louis, *Le Statut organique de l'Algérie,* Paris, 1948. P. 803.

*Millot, René-Pierre, *Missions in the World Today,* New York, 1961. (French original, Paris, 1960.) P. 880.

**Min Sigill al-Kifah—al Ma'raka-l-hasima* (*Du dossier de la lutte: la Bataille decisive*), Tunis, 1965. P. 816.

Mitchell, Pearl B., *The Bismarckian Policy of Conciliation with France, 1875–1885,* Philadelphia, 1935.

*Moberly, Frederick J., *Military Operations in Togoland and the Cameroons,* London, 1931. P. 829.

*Moch, Jules, *En 1961, paix en Algérie,* Paris, 1961. P. 808.

*Mohammed V, *Le Maroc à l'heure de l'indépendance. Tome I,* Rabat, 1957. P. 825.

*Mollard, Ghislaine, *L'Evolution de la culture et de la production du blé en Algérie de 1830 à 1939,* Paris, 1950. P. 798.

*Mondain, Gustave, *Un siècle de Mission à Madagascar,* Paris, 1948. P. 877.

*Monfreid, Henri de, *Le Radeau de la Méduse ou comment fut sauvé Djibouti,* Paris, 1958. P. 844.

Monger, G. W., *The End of Isolation: British Foreign Policy, 1900–1907,* London, 1963.

*Montagne, Robert, *Les Berbères et le Makhzen dans le Sud du Maroc,* Paris, 1930. P. 828.

———, "Morocco between East and West," *Foreign Affairs, 26* (1948), 360–72.

*———, ed., *Naissance du prolétariat marocain, enquête collective executée de 1948 à 1950,* Paris, 1952. P. 827.

*———, *Révolution au Maroc,* Paris, 1954. P. 823.

Monteil, P.-L., *Souvenirs Vécus: Quelques Feuillets de l'Histoire Coloniale,* Paris, 1924.

Monteil, Vincent, "Une Confrérie Musulmane: Les Mourides du Sénégal," *Archives de Sociologie des Religions,* July–Dec. 1962, 77–112.

*———, *Le Maroc,* Paris, 1962. P. 819.

*———, *L'Islam noir,* Paris, 1964. P. 882.

*———, "Contribution à l'étude de l'Islam en Afrique Noire," *Notes et etudes sur l'Islam en Afrique Noire,* ed. M. Chailley, Paris, 1962. P. 883.

*Montety, Henri de, *Femmes de Tunisie,* Paris, 1958. P. 818.

Moon, Parker T., *Imperialism and World Politics,* New York, 1938.

*Moore, Clement Henry, *Tunisia since Independence,* Berkeley and Los Angeles, 1965. P. 815.

*———, *Politics in North Africa: Algeria, Morocco and Tunisia,* New York, 1970. P. 792.

*Moran, Denise, *Tchad,* Paris, 1934. P. 840.

*Mordal, Jacques, "Le Blocus de Djibouti," *Ecrits de Paris,* Oct. 1951, 78–94. P. 844.

*———, "La Campagne du Gabon," *Ecrits de Paris,* Dec. 1951, 94–105. P. 844.

*———, *La Bataille de Dakar,* Paris, 1956. P. 844.

Morgenthau, Ruth Schachter, "Single-Party Systems in West Africa," *American Political Science Review,* 55 (1961), 294–303.

*———, *Political Parties in French-Speaking West Africa,* Oxford, 1964. Pp. 842, 850.

*Morizot, Jean, *L'Algérie kabylisée,* Paris, 1962. P. 799.

*Morland, Barangé and Martinez (pseudonyms), *Histoire de l'Organization de l'Armée Secrète,* Paris, 1964. P. 810.

*Mortimer, Edward, *France and the Africans, 1944–1960: A Political History,* London, 1969. P. 850.

*Moumouni, Abdou, *L'Education en Afrique,* Paris, 1964, trans., *Education in Africa,* New York, 1968. P. 874.

*Mourreaux, Serge, *Les Accords d'Evian et l'avenir de la révolution algérienne,* Paris, 1962. P. 810.

*Moussa, Pierre, *Les Chances économiques de la communauté franco-africaine,* Paris, 1957. P. 866.

*———, *L'Economie de la zone franc,* Paris, 1960. Pp. 790, 866.

*Mouton, Marie-Renée, "L'Algérie devant le Parlement français de 1935 à 1938," *Revue Francaise de Science Politique,* March 1962, 93–128. P. 801.

*Mtouggui, Lloussine, *Vue générale de l'histoire berbère,* Algiers, 1950. P. 790.

*Mumford, William Bryant, and G. St. J. Orde-Brown, *Africans Learn to be French: A Review of Educational Activities in the Seven Federated Colonies of French West Africa Based on a Tour of French West Africa Undertaken in 1935,* London, 1937. P. 873.

Murphy, Agnes, *The Ideology of French Imperialism,* Washington, 1948.

*Murray, James N., Jr., *The United Nations Trusteeship System,* Urbana, Ill., 1957. P. 847.

Murray, Victor, "Education under Indirect Rule," *Journal of the Royal African Society* (1935).

*Mveng, Father Engelbert, *Histoire du Cameroun,* Paris, 1963. Pp. 834, 887.

*Mzali, Mohammed, *L'Evolution économique de la Tunisie,* Tunis, 1921. P. 818.

*Naegelen, Marcel, *Mission en Algérie,* Paris, 1962. P. 803.

*Naroun, Amar, *Ferhat Abbas ou les chemins de la souverainété,* Paris, 1961. P. 809.

*N'Diaye, Jean-Pierre, *Enquête sur les étudiants noirs en France,* Paris, 1962. P. 875.

*N'Diaye, M. Abdou, *Le Mouvement syndical africain devant ses responsabilites,* Conakry, 1964. P. 872.

*Ndiaye, Massata, *Aspects sociaux africains,* Paris, 1960. P. 886.

*Neres, Philip, *French-Speaking West Africa: From Colonial Status to Independence.* London, 1964. P. 851.

*Ngongo, Louis, *Le Rôle politique des forces religieuses au Cameroun de 1939 à 1965,* Thesis, University of Paris, 1970. P. 878.
*Nguini, Marcel, *La Valeur politique et sociale de la tutelle française au Cameroun,* Aix-en-Provence, 1956. P. 859.
Newbury, Colin W., "The Development of French Policy on the Lower and Upper Niger, 1880–1898," *Journal of Modern History, 31* (1959).
———, "The Formation of the Government General of French West Africa," *Journal of African History, 1* (1960), 111–28.
———, "The Government General and Political Change in French West Africa," *St. Antony's Papers, 10* (1961), 41–59.
———, "Victorians, Republicans, and the Partition of West Africa," *Journal of African History, 3* (1962), 493–501.
———, *British Policy toward West Africa,* vol. 1, *Select Documents 1786–1874,* Oxford, 1965.
———, "North African and Western Sudan Trade in the Nineteenth Century: A Re-evaluation," *Journal of African History, 7* (1966), 233–46.
———, *The Western Slave Coast and Its Rulers,* 2d ed., Oxford, 1966.
———, "Military Intervention and Political Change in West Africa," *African Quarterly, 7* (1967), 215–21.
———, "The Protectionist Revival in French Colonial Trade: The Case of Senegal," *Economic History Review, 21* (1968), 337–48.
———, and A. S. Kanya-Forstner, "French Policy and the Origins of the Scramble for West Africa," *Journal of African History, 10* (1969).
*Nodiigoto, Odda, *La Genèse de l'administration française au Tchad, 1900–1920,* Thesis, University of Paris, 1969. P. 837.
*Noel, Antoine, *La Côte française des Somalis, vie économique, sociale, et politique,* Mémoire, University of Aix, 1963. P. 862.
*Nomedji, Nicholas, *Les partis politiques au Togo et au Cameroun,* Mémoire, Poitiers, 1966. P. 858.
*Noon, John A., *Labor Problems of Africa,* Philadelphia, 1944. P. 870.
*Nora, Pierre, *Les Français d'Algérie,* Paris, 1961. P. 797.
*Nouira, Hedi, "Le Néo-Destour," *Politique étrangère* (June 1954), 317–34. P. 816.
*Nouschi, André, *Enquête sur le niveau de vie des populations rurales constantinoises de la conquête jusqu'en 1919, essai d'histoire économique et sociale,* Doctorate d'État, Paris, 1961. P. 798.
*———, *La Naissance du nationalisme algérien, 1914–1954,* Paris, 1962. P. 801.
———, "North Africa in the Period of Colonization," *The Cambridge History of Islam,* 2 vols., Cambridge, 1970, 2, 299–326.
*———, Yves Lacoste, and André Prenant, *L'Algérie passé et présent,* Paris, 1960. P. 801.
*November, Andras, *L'Evolution du mouvement syndical en Afrique occidentale,* Paris, 1965. P. 871.
*O'Ballance, Edgar, *The Algerian Insurrection, 1954–62,* Hamden, Conn., 1967. P. 807.
Obichere, Boniface I., *West African States and European Expansion: The Dahomey-Niger Hinterland, 1885–1898,* New Haven, 1971.
*O'Brien, Donal Cruise, "Towards an 'Islamic' policy in French West Af-

rica, 1854–1914," *Journal of African History, 8* (1967), 303–16. P. 882.
———, *The Mourides of Senegal: The Political and Economic Organization of an Islamic Brotherhood,* London, 1970.
*Ohneck, Wolfgang, *Die Französische Algerienpolitik von 1919–1939,* Cologne and Opladen, 1967. P. 801.
Oliver, Roland, *Sir Harry Johnston and the Scramble for Africa,* London, 1957.
*Olivier, Marcel, *Six Ans de Politique Sociale à Madagascar,* Paris, 1931. P. 840.
Onambele, Raphael, *L'Expansion catholique au Cameroun, 1890–1945,* Thesis, University of Paris, 1967. P. 878.
*Onana, A., *Evolution de la chefferie traditionnelle en Pays Beti,* Mémoire, E.N.F.O.M., 1959. P. 863.
*Oppermann, Thomas, *Algerische Frage: Rechtlich-Politische Studie,* Stuttgart, 1959 (French trans., Paris, 1961, *Le Problème algérien, données historiques, juridiques, politiques*). P. 805.
*Owona, Adalbert, "À l'aube du nationalisme camerounais: la curieuse figure de Vincent Ganty," *Revue Française d'histoire d'outre mer, 204* (1969), 199–235. P. 886.
*Pageard, Robert, *Littérature negro-africain,* Paris, 1966. P. 876.
*———, *Le Droit privé des Mossi. Tradition et évolution,* 2 vols., Paris, 1969. P. 864.
Paillat, Claude, *Dossier secret de l'Algérie,* Paris, 1961.
———, *Deuxième dossier secret de l'Algérie,* Paris, 1962.
*———, *L'Echiquier d'Alger,* 2 vols., Paris, 1966. P. 843.
*Pain, Françoise, *Evolution économique et sociale du Cameroun depuis 1947,* Paris, Doctorat d'Etat, 1959. P. 859.
*Parti Démocratique de Guinée, *Guinée. Prelude à l'indépendence,* Paris, 1959. P. 856.
*———, *L'Expérience guinéenne et l'unité africaine,* Paris, 1959. P. 856.
*Pascal, Roger, *La République Malgache,* Paris, 1965. P. 861.
*Passeron, René, *Cours de droit algérien,* Algiers, 1947. P. 803.
*———, "La Structure administrative de l'Algérie," *Revue juridique et politique de l'Union Française* (1951), 449–65. P. 803.
*Paulme, Denise, ed., *Femmes d'Afrique Noire,* Paris, 1960. P. 885.
*Pauvert, Jean-Claude, "Le Problème des classes sociales en Afrique Equatoriale," *Cahiers Internationaux de Sociologie, 19* (1955), 76–91. P. 885.
*———, "L'Evolution politique des Ewé," *Cahiers d'études africaines, 2* (1960), 161–92. Pp. 835, 857.
*Paye, Lucien, *Enseignement et société musulmane: introduction et évolution de l'enseignement moderne au Maroc,* Thesis, University of Paris, 1957. P. 827.
*Péchoux, Laurent, *Le Mandat français sur le Togo,* Paris, 1939. P. 834.
*Pellegrin, Arthur, *Histoire de la Tunisie depuis les origines jusqu'à nos jours,* 4th ed, Tunis, 1948. P. 814.
*Pellegrin, Henri, *Le Statut de l'Algérie,* Algiers, 1948. P. 803.
*Pendar, Kenneth, *Adventure in Diplomacy: Our French Dilemma,* New York, 1944. P. 793.
*Pennec, Pierre, *Les Transformations des corps de métiers de Tunis sous*

l'influence d'une économie de type capitaliste, Thesis, University of Tunis, 1964. P. 818.

*Perham, Margery, *Colonial Sequence 1930 to 1949: A Chronological Commentary upon British Colonial Policy Especially in Africa,* London, 1967. P. 834.

*Perroux, Francois, et al., *L'Algérie de Demain,* Paris, 1962. P. 813.

*Person, Yves, "Soixante ans d'évolution en pays kissi," *Cahiers d'études 1* (1960), 86–112. P. 863.

*Peterec, Richard J., *Dakar and West African Economic Development,* New York, 1967. P. 867.

*Peyrouton, Marcel, *Histoire Générale du Maghreb: Algérie–Maroc–Tunisie; des Origines à Nos Jours,* Paris, 1966. P. 788.

*Pfefferman, Guy, "Trade Unions and Politics in French West Africa during the Fourth Republic," *African Affairs,* July 1967. P. 871.

*Pickles, Dorothy, *Algeria and France: From Colonialism to Cooperation,* New York, 1963. P. 811.

*Picquet, Victor, *La Colonisation française dans l'Afrique du Nord,* Paris, 1912. P. 788.

*———, *L'Algérie française: un siècle de colonisation, 1830–1930,* Paris, 1930. P. 797.

Pierre-Alype, François, *La Provocation allemande aux colonies,* Paris, 1915.

*Pierson Mathy, Madame P., "L'Evolution politique de l'Afrique," *Chronique de politique étrangère, 14* (1961). P. 853.

*Pinon, René, *Au Maroc: Fin des Temps Héroiques,* Paris, 1935. P. 820.

*Pinto, Roger, "Les Conventions du 3 juin 1955 entre la France et la Tunisie," *Annuaire francais de droit international, no. 1,* 1955, 53–66. P. 817.

*Platt, W. J., *An African Prophet: The Ivory Coast Movement and What Came of It,* London, 1934. P. 881.

*Poirier, J., *Les Problèmes du travail en Afrique Noire,* Geneva, 1958. P. 871.

*Poncet, Jean, *La Colonisation et l'agriculture Européennes en Tunisie depuis 1881: Étude de Géographie Historique et Économique,* Paris, 1962. P. 818.

*———, *Paysages et problèmes rurant en Tunisie,* Paris, 1963. P. 818.

*Poquin, J. J., *Les Relations économiques extérieures des pays d'Afrique Noire de l'Union Française 1925–1955,* Paris, 1957. P. 867.

*Portères, Roland, *Aménagement de l'économie agricole et rurale du Sénégal,* Dakar, 1952, 3 vols., mimeographed. P. 868.

Power, Thomas F., Jr., *Jules Ferry and the Renaissance of French Imperialism,* New York, 1966.

*Prats, R., *Le Gabon: La mise en valeur et ses problèmes,* Montpellier, Doctorat d'État in Law, 1955. P. 869.

**Présence Africaine, Le Travail en Afrique Noire,* Paris, 1953. P. 871.

*———, *Les Etudiants noirs parlent,* Paris, 1953. P. 875.

*———, *Le Ier Congrès International des Écrivains et Artistes Noire* (Paris and Sorbonne, September 19–22, 1956), Compte Rendu Complet, nos. 8–9–10 (June–Nov. 1956). P. 876.

*Présence Africaine, Deuxième Congrès des Ecrivains et Artistes Noire (Rome: 26 mars–Ier avril 1959), nos. 24–25 Feb.–May 1959. P. 876.

*———, *Religions en Afrique noire aujourd'hui. Bilan et perspectives,* Paris, 1961. P. 880.

*Priestly, Herbert Ingram, *France Overseas: A Study of Modern Imperialism,* New York, 1938. Pp. 788, 841.

*Purtshet, Christian, and André Valentino, *Sociologie électorale en Afrique du Nord,* Paris, 1966. P. 808.

*Quandt, William, *Revolution and Political Leadership: Algeria, 1954–1968,* Cambridge, Mass., 1969. P. 800.

*Quesnot, Fernand, "Influence du Mouridisme sur le Tidjanisme," *Notes et études sur l'Islam en Afrique Noire,* ed. M. Chailley, Paris, 1962. P. 883.

*———, "Les Cadres maraboutiques de l'Islam sénégalais," *ibid.* P. 883.

*Rabemananjara, Jacques, *Nationalisme et problèmes malgaches,* Paris, 1959. P. 861.

*Rabemanjara, Raymond, *Madagascar, sous la Rénovation malgache,* Paris and Tananarive, 1953. P. 861.

*Rager, Jean-Jacques, *Les Musulmans algériens en France et dans les pays islamiques,* Paris, 1950. P. 812.

Ramm, Agatha, ed., *The Political Correspondence of Mr. Gladstone and Lord Granville, 1876–1886,* 2 vols., Oxford, 1962.

*Randolph, Emile, *L'Industrialisation de la Côte d'Ivoire au XXe siècle,* Thesis, University of Lyon, 1967. P. 869.

*"Rapport sur l'enseignement en A.E.F. 1936–1937," *Enseignement Publique* (1938), 398–423. P. 873.

*Ravenal, "Le Conseil d'État et les assemblées d'Outre-Mer," *Penant,* 1951. P. 848.

*Raymond, André, *La Tunisie,* Paris, 1961. P. 814.

*Raynal, René, "La terre et l'homme en Haut Moulouya," *Bulletin économique et sociale du Maroc* (Nov. 1960–Feb. 1961), 281–346. P. 828.

*———, *Plaines et piedmonts du Bassin de la Moulouya,* Rabat, 1961. P. 828.

**Réalités Africaines,* "La mise en valeur de l'A.E.F.," Casablanca, 1956. P. 868.

*Rebour, Henri, *Les Agrumes en Afrique du Nord,* 3d ed., Algiers, 1950. P. 798.

*"Regards sur la littérature maghrébine d'expression française," *Cahiers, nord-africains, 61* (Oct.–Nov. 1957). P. 795.

Renouvin, P. "Les Origines de l'Expédition de Fachoda," *Revue Historique, 200* (1948).

*Rens, Ivo, *L'Assemblée algérienne,* Paris, 1957. P. 803.

*Republique française, Ministère des Colonies, *La Conference Africaine Française, 30 Janvier 1944–8 Février 1944,* Algiers, 1944. P. 845.

———, in *Renaissances,* Algiers, October 1944, 209–35.

*Reste, Joseph F., *Le Dahomey, Réalisations et Perspectives d'avenir,* Paris, 1934. P. 840.

*———, *Action politique, économique, et sociale en A.E.F., 1936–1938,* Brazzaville, 1938. P. 840.

*Reuillard, M., *Un Royaume africain, le Yatenga,* Mémoire, E.N.F.O. M., 1952. P. 863.

*Revol, Jean-Claude, *La Question algérienne et l'O.N.U.*, Memoire, University of Grenoble, 1962. P. 807.

*Rézeau, Michael, *Le Rôle du syndicalisme africaine dans l'évolution de l'Afrique noire française,* Mémoire, University of Paris, 1962. P. 871.

*Rézette, Robert, *Les Partis politiques marocains,* Paris, 1955. P. 824.

*Rivières, Edmond Séré de, *Histoire du Niger,* Paris, 1965. Pp. 831, 837, 854.

*Rivlin, Benjamin, "The Tunisian Nationalist Movement: Four Decades of Evolution," *Middle East Journal,* Spring 1952, 167–93. P. 816.

*Robequain, Charles, *Les Richesses de la France d'outre-mer: structure économique et problèmes humains,* Paris, 1949. P. 865.

*Robert, André, *L'Evolution des coutumes de l'ouest africain et la législation française,* Paris, 1955. P. 864.

*Robert, Michel, *Les Statuts du clergé, seculier d'Afrique noire,* Paris, Doctorat d'Etat in Law, 1958. P. 879.

*Roberts, Stephen H., *The History of French Colonial Policy, 1870–1925,* London, 1929. Pp. 788, 834, 841.

*Robinson, Kenneth E., *The Public Law of Overseas France since the War,* Oxford Institute of Colonial Studies, rev. ed. 1954. P. 846.

*———, "French Africa and the French Union," *Africa Today,* ed. C. Grove Haines, Baltimore, 1955, 311–31. P. 846.

*———, "Political Developments in French West Africa," *Africa in the Modern World,* ed. Calvin Stillman, Chicago, 1955. P. 846.

*———, "Senegal: the Elections to the Territorial Assembly, March, 1957," *Five Elections in Africa,* ed. K. E. Robinson and W. J. M. Mackenzie, Oxford, 1960, 281–390. P. 854.

Robinson, Ronald, and John Gallagher, with Alice Denny, *Africa and the Victorians: The Official Mind of Imperialism,* London, 1961.

Robinson, Ronald E., and John Gallagher, "The Partition of Africa," *New Cambridge Modern History, 11,* Cambridge, 1962.

*Roche, Jean de la, "Education in French Equatorial Africa and French West Africa," *Journal of Negro Education, 15,* no. 3 (1946), 396–410. P. 874.

*Rodd, Francis J. Rennell, *British Military Administration of Occupied Territories in Africa, 1941–1947,* London, 1948. P. 844.

Rolland, Georges, *Le Trans-Saharien: Un an après,* Paris, 1891.

*Rolland, Louis, and Pierre Lampué, *Précis de législation coloniale,* Paris, 1931. P. 838.

*———, *Précis de droit des pays d'outre-mer,* Paris, 1949 and 1959. P. 838.

*Romeuf, Jean, *Vues sur l'économie de l'Oubangui (Essai dur une économie sous-développée),* Paris, 1958. P. 870.

*Roosevelt, Elliott, *As He Saw It,* New York, 1946. P. 793.

*Rotberg, Robert I., *A Political History of Tropical Africa,* New York, 1965. P. 836.

*Rouch, Jean, "Migrations au Ghana," *Journal de la Société des Africanistes, 26* (1956), 33–196. P. 884.

Rouget, Fernand, *L'Expansion coloniale au Congo français,* Paris, 1906.

*Rous, Jean, *Tunisie . . . attention!* Paris, 1952. P. 816.
*Roy, Jules, *The War in Algeria,* New York, 1961. P. 808.
*———, *Autour du drame,* Paris, 1961. P. 808.
Ruedy, John, *Land Policy in Colonial Algeria: The Origins of the Rural Public Domain,* Los Angeles, 1967.
*Runner, Jean, *Les Droits politiques des indigènes des colonies,* Paris, 1927. P. 841.
*Ryan, John W., *The Emergence of the Republic of Guinea, 1946–1962,* Ph.D. Dissertation, St. John's University, 1966. P. 855.
Saadallah, Belckacem, *The Rise of Algerian Nationalism, 1900–1930,* Ph.D. Dissertation, University of Minnesota, 1965–66.
*———, "Rise of the Algerian Elite," *Journal of Modern African Studies,* 5 (1967), 69–77. P. 800.
*Sady, Emil, *The United Nations and Dependent Peoples,* London, 1956. P. 847.
*Saghieh, Khaled el-, *Nationalism in Morocco: A Study of Recent Developments with Special Reference to the Moroccan Question in the United Nations,* Ph.D. Dissertation, American University, 1955. P. 825.
*Saint-Germès, J., *Economie algérienne,* Algiers, 1950. P. 799.
*———, *La Réforme agraire algérienne,* Algiers, 1957. P. 799.
*Saint Marc, Michèle, *Zone franc et décolonisation,* Paris, 1964. P. 866.
*Saintoyant, Jules F., *L'Affaire du Congo, 1905,* Paris, 1960. P. 864.
Sanderson, G. N., "Contributions from African Sources to the History of the European Competition in the Upper Valley of the Nile," *Journal of African History,* 3 (1962).
———, *England, Europe, and the Upper Nile, 1882–1899,* Edinburgh, 1965.
*Santarelli, Lila, *Les Missions catholiques au Sénégal de 1848 à 1914,* Thesis, University of Paris, 1968. P. 879.
*Sarrasin, Paul-Émile, *La Crise algérienne,* Paris, 1949. P. 803.
*Sarraut, Albert, *La Mise en valeur des colonies françaises,* Paris, 1923. P. 838.
*Sautter, Gilles, "Le Régime des terres et ses modifications récentes aux environs de Brazzaville et au Woleu N'Tem," *Bulletin de l'Institut d'Études Centrafricaines,* 7 and 8 (1954), 201–09. P. 869.
*———, *De l'Atlantique au Fleuve Congo. Une géographie de sous-puplement,* 2 vols., Paris, 1966. P. 869.
*———, "Notes sur la construction du Chemin de fer Congo-Océan (1921–1934)," *Cahiers d'études africaines, 26* (1967). P. 839.
*Savary, Alain, *Nationalisme algérien et grandeur française,* Paris, 1960. P. 808.
*Scanlon, David, ed., *Traditions of African Education,* New York, 1964. P. 873.
*Schaefer, René, *Drame et Chances de l'Afrique du Nord,* Paris, 1953. P. 794.
*———, *Révolution en Algérie,* Paris, 1956. P. 804.
*Scham, Alan, *Lyautey in Morocco: Protectorate Administration, 1912–1925,* Berkeley and Los Angeles, 1970. P. 820.

*Schmidlin, Joseph, *Das Deutsche Missionswork der Gegenwart,* Münster, 1929. P. 833.

Schnapper, Bernard, "La Fin du régime de l'exclusif: le commerce étranger dans les possessions françaises d'Afrique tropicale (1817–1870)," *Annales Africaines* (1959).

———, *La Politique et le commerce français dans le Golfe de Guinée de 1838 à 1871,* Paris, 1961.

Schultz, L., "William Wade Harris und seine Massenbewegung," *Evangelisches Missions-magazin,* May 1942, 83–92.

*Schuman, Robert, "Nécessité d'une Politique" in *La Nef,* issue "Maroc et Tunisie. Le Problème du Protectorat," March 1953, 7–9. P. 817.

Schwarte, M., et al., *Der Grosse Krieg,* 8 vols., Berlin, 1921–1925.

*Schweisguth, Charles, *Le Sultanat du Ouaddai: Evolution Politique, Economique, et Sociale,* Unpublished study, Institut des Hautes Études d'Outre-Mer, Paris, 1957. P. 863.

*Schweitzer, Albert. *On the Edge of the Primeval Forest,* New York, 1922. P. 878.

*———, *Forest Hospital at Lambaréné,* New York, 1931. P. 878.

*———, *African Notebook,* New York, 1939. P. 878.

*Sebag, Paul, *La Tunisie: essai de monographie,* Paris, 1951. P. 814.

———, *La Hara de Tunis: l'Évolution d'un Ghetto Nord-Africain,* Paris, 1959.

Sébillot, Amédée, *Le Transfricain,* Paris, 1893.

*Sédès, Jean-Marie, *Le Clergé indigène de l'Empire français,* 2 vols., Paris, 1944. P. 879.

*Senghor, Léopold, "Pour une solution fédéraliste," in *La Nef,* issue "Où va l'Union Française?" June 1955, 148–61. P. 847.

*———, "Nationhood: Report on the Doctrine and Program of the Party of African Federation," *On African Socialism,* New York, 1964, 7–65. P. 853.

*"Les Sénoussistes pendant la guerre 1914–1918," *Les Troupes coloniales pendant la guerre 1914–1918,* Paris, 1931. P. 831.

*Sérigny, Alain de, *La Révolution du 13 mai; Avec les témiognages de ses principaux acteurs,* Paris, 1958. P. 806.

*Serre, Jacques, *Histoire économique et sociale du District de Grimari,* Thesis, University of Paris, 1963. Pp. 839, 863.

*Servan-Schreiber, Jean-Jacques, *Lieutenant in Algeria,* New York, 1957. P. 808.

*Servier, Jean, *Dans L'Aurès sur les pas des rebelles,* Paris, 1955. P. 804.

*Seurin, Jean-Louis, "Elites sociales et partis politiques en A.O.F.," *Annales Africaines* (1958), 123–57. P. 885.

*Sicé, Surgeon-General Adolphe, *L'Afrique équatoriale française et le cameroun au service de la France,* Paris, 1946. Pp. 830, 844.

*Sigaud, Paul, *Le Nationalisme musulman dans les affaires tunisiennes et marocaines et la position de la France devant l'O.N.U.,* Mémoire, University of Grenoble, 1962. Pp. 817, 825.

*Sík, Endre, *The History of Black Africa,* vol. 2, Budapest, 1966. P. 836.

*Silvera, Victor, "La Récente Réforme gouvernementale tunisienne," *Revue* *juridique et politique de l'Union française,* April–June 1948, 175–212. P. 817.

*———, "De l'administration directe et du controle dans le régime du protectorat français en Tunisie," *Revue juridique et politique de l'Union française,* March 1952. P. 817.

*———, *La Réforme des Assemblées locales en Tunisie; Conseils municipaux et conseils de caidats,* Paris, 1953. P. 817.

*———, "Les réformes tunisiennes de février 1951," *Revue tunisienne de droit,* Jan.–March 1954, 22–39. P. 817.

*———, "De l'autonomie interne à l'indépendance de la Tunisie," *Revue juridique et politique de l'Union française,* Oct.–Dec. 1956, 687–704. P. 817.

*———, "Du Régime beylical à la République tunisienne," *Politique Etrangère, 5* (1957), 594–611. P. 817.

*Sinda, Martial, *Les Messianisme congolais et ses incidences politiques depuis son apparition jusqu'à l'epoque de l'indépendance (1921–1961),* Doctorat in Letters, University of Paris, 1961. P. 881.

*Skinner, Elliott, "Labor Migration and Its Relationship to Solid-Cultural Change in Mossi Society," *Africa 30* (1961), 375–401. P. 884.

*———, *The Mossi of the Upper Volta,* Stanford, 1964. Pp. 854, 863.

*Skurnik, W. A. E., "France and Fragmentation in West Africa: 1945–1960," *Journal of African History, 8* (1967), 317–33. Pp. 852, 865.

*Snyder, Francis G., *One-Party Government in Mali: Transition Towards Control,* New Haven, 1965. P. 854.

*Société d'Études pour le développement économique, *Le Développement rural dans les pays d'Afrique noire d'expression française,* vol. 3, Paris, 1965. Pp. 868, 870.

*Sophie, Ulrich, *Le Gouverneur-général Félix Eboué,* Paris, 1950. P. 845.

*Soret, Marcel, *Démographie et problèmes urbains en A.E.F.: Poto-Poto, Bacongo-Dolisie,* Brazzaville, 1954. P. 885.

*Soustelle, Jacques, *Envers et Contre Tout,* vol. 1, *De Londres à Alger. Souvenirs et documents sur la France Libre 1940–1942,* Paris, 1947. P. 843.

*———, *Aimée et souffrante Algérie,* Paris, 1956. Pp. 804, 807.

*———, *Le Drame Algérien et la décadence française. Réponse à Raymond Aron,* Paris, 1957. P. 805.

*———, *L'Espérance trahie (1958–1961),* Paris, 1962. P. 808.

*Spacensky, Alain, *Les Partis et la vie politique à Madagascar (1945–1965),* Thesis, University of Paris, 1965. P. 861.

*———, "Regards sur l'évolution politique malgache, 1945–1966," *Revue Française de Science Politique,* April and July 1967, 263–85, 668–88. P. 861.

*Spiegler, James S., *Aspects of Nationalist Thought among French-Speaking West Africans, 1921–1939,* Thesis, Oxford University, 1968. P. 842.

*Spillman, Georges, *L'Afrique du Nord et la France,* Paris, 1947. P. 789.

———, *Souvenirs d'un colonialiste,* Paris, 1968. P. 789.

*———, *Du Protectorat à l'indépendance. Maroc, 1912–1955,* Paris, 1967. P. 821.

*———, *Souvenirs d'un colonialiste,* Paris, 1968. P. 789.

*Spitz, Georges, *Sansanding: les irrigations du Niger,* Paris, 1949. P. 841.

*Staniland, Martin, *Regionalism and Political Parties of Dahomey,* Thesis, University of Ghana, 1965. P. 857.

Stengers, Jean, "La Première Tentative de reprise du Congo par la Belgique, 1894–1895," *Bulletin de la Société Royale Belge de Géographie, 73* (1949).

———, "A propos de l'Acte de Berlin, ou comment nâit une légende," *Zaïre, 8* (1953).

———, ed., *Textes inédits d'Emile Banning,* Brussels, 1955.

———, "Aux Origines de Fashoda: l'Expédition Monteil," *Revue Belge de Philologie et d'Histoire, 36* (1958), *38* (1960).

———, "L'Impérialisme colonial de la fin du XIXe siècle: mythe ou réalité," *Journal of African History, 3* (1962).

———, "Léopold II et la fixation des frontières du Congo," *Le Flambeau* (1963).

Stevens, Edmund, *North African Power Keg,* New York, 1955.

*Stewart, Charles F., *The Economy of Morocco, 1912–1962,* Cambridge, Mass., 1964. P. 826.

*Stienon, Charles, "La Campagne coloniale des alliés en 1914 et 1915: le Togo," *Revue des Deux Mondes,* November 1, 1915. P. 829.

*Stuart, Graham H., *The International City of Tangier,* 2d ed., Stanford, 1955. P. 821.

*Student, Erich, *Kameruns Kampf,* Berlin, 1937. P. 830.

*Surdon, Georges, *La France en Afrique du Nord,* Algiers, 1955. P. 819.

*Suret-Canale, Jean, "La Guinée dans le système colonial," *Présence Africaine, 29* (1959), 21–62. P. 855.

———, *Afrique Noire: Occidentale et Centrale,* Paris, 1961.

*———, *L'Afrique Noire: L'ère coloniale, 1900–1945,* Paris, 1964. Pp. 836, 849, 865, 887.

*———, "La Fin de la Chefferie en Guinée," *Journal of African History, 7* (1966), 459–93. P. 855.

*———, *La République de Guinée,* Paris, 1970. P. 855.

Sy, Cheikh Tidiana, *La Confrérie sénégalaise des Mourides. Un essai sur l'Islam au Sénégal,* Paris, 1969.

*Taalbi, Abdelaziz, *La Tunisie martyre, ses revendications,* Paris, 1920. P. 815.

*Taillard, Fulbert, *Le Nationalisme marocain,* Paris, 1947. P. 823.

*Tarde, Guillaume de, *Lyautey, le chef en action,* Paris, 5th ed., 1959. P. 820.

*Tardits, Claude, *Porto-Novo: les nouvelles générations africaines entre leurs traditions et l'Occident,* Paris, 1958. P. 885.

*———, *Les Bamiléké de l'Ouest Cameroun,* Paris, 1960. Pp. 859, 863.

Taylor, A. J. P., "British Policy in Morocco, 1886–1902," *English Historical Review, 66* (1951).

———, *Germany's First Bid for Colonies, 1884–1885,* London, 1938.

Tchaidjè, Abdurrahman, *La Question tunisienne et la politique ottomane (1181–1913),* Erzeroum, 1963.

*Tchernonog, "La Nature juridique des chefferies au Cameroun," *Revue juridique et politique de l'Union Française,* April–June 1953, 197–203. P. 863.

*Terrasse, Henri, *Histoire du Maroc des origines à l'établissement du Protectorat français,* 2 vols., Casablanca, 1949. P. 819.

*Terrenoire, Louis, *De Gaulle et l'Algérie, témoignage pour l'histoire,* Paris, 1964. P. 808.

*Terrier, Auguste, *Le Maroc,* Paris, 1931. P. 821.

*Teulières, André, *L'Oubangui Face à l'Avenir,* Paris, 1953. P. 869.

*Tevoedjré, Albert, *L'Afrique révoltée,* Paris, 1958. P. 857.

*Thomas, Frederick C., Jr., "The Juhaina Arabs of Chad," *Middle East Journal,* Spring 1959, 143–55. P. 840.

Thompson, Robert Stanley, *Fondation de l'Etat Indépendant du Congo,* Brussels, 1933.

*Thompson, Virginia M., "The Ivory Coast," *African One-Party States,* ed. Gwendolen Carter, Ithaca, 1962, 237–324. P. 856.

*———, "Dahomey," *Five African States,* ed. Gwendolen Carter, Ithaca, 1963, 161–232. P. 857.

*———, "Niger," *National Unity and Regionalism in Eight African States,* ed. Gwendolen Carter, Ithaca, 1966, 151–230. P. 854.

*Thompson, Virginia M., and Richard Adloff, *French West Africa,* Stanford, 1957, Pp. 851, 870, 872.

*———, *French Equatorial Africa,* Stanford, 1960. Pp. 851, 860, 870, 872.

*———, *The Malagasy Republic: Madagascar Today.* Stanford, 1965. Pp. 837, 851, 860, 872.

*———, *Djibouti and the Horn of Africa,* Stanford, 1968. Pp. 851, 862, 870, 872.

*Tiano, André, *Le Maghreb entre les mythes,* Paris, 1967. P. 790.

*Tillion, Germaine, *L'Algérie en 1957,* Paris, 1957; trans., *Algeria: The Realities,* New York, 1958. P. 799.

*———, *Les Ennemis complementaires,* Paris, 1960; trans., *France and Algeria: Complementary Enemies,* New York, 1961. P. 808.

*Tougeri, F., *Les Grands Lamibé devant le développement politique de l'Adamoua,* Mémoire, E.N.F.O.M., 1959. P. 863.

*Touré, Mamoudou, *Les Rapports économiques et financiers entre la France et l'Afrique occidentale de 1945 à 1958,* Paris, Doctorat d'État, 1960. P. 866.

*Toussaint, Charmian E., *The Trusteeship System of the United Nations,* London, 1956. P. 847.

*Toynbee, Arnold, ed., "The Islamic World since the Peace Settlement," *Survey of International Affairs,* vol. 1, London, Royal Institute of International Affairs, 1925. P. 792.

*———, "Unrest in the Northwest African Territories under French Rule, 1927–1937," *Survey of International Affairs,* vol. 1, London, Royal Institute of International Affairs, 1937.

*Traoré, Bakary, Mamadou Lo, and Jean-Louis Alibert, *Forces politiques en Afrique Noire,* Paris, 1966. P. 855.

*Trimingham, J. Spencer, *Islam in West Africa,* New York, 1959. P. 882.

*———, *History of Islam in West Africa,* Oxford, 1962. P. 882.

*Trout, Frank, *Morocco's Saharan Frontiers,* Geneva, 1969. P. 820.
*Truchet, André, *L'Armistice de 1940 et L'Afrique du Nord,* Paris, 1955. P. 793.
*Trystram, Jean-Paul, *L'Ouvrier mineur au Maroc. Contribution statistique à une étude sociologique,* Paris, 1957. P. 828.
Tucker, Spencer C., *The Fourth Republic and Algeria,* Thesis, University of North Carolina, 1966.
*UNESCO, *World Survey of Education,* 3 vols., Paris, 1955–61. P. 872.
plement No. 12 (A/2151), *Special Report of the Trusteeship Council on Administrative Unions Affecting Trust Territories and on the Status of the Cameroons and Togoland under French Administration Arising out of Their Membership in the French Union,* New York, 1952. P. 848.
United Nations, Trusteeship Council, Official Records: Seventh Session, 1950, Supplement No. 2 (T/498), *Reports of the United Nations Visiting Mission to Trust Territories in West Africa,* 1949.
———: Seventh Session, Supplement No. 2, 1951 (T/798), *Reports of the United Nations Visiting Mission to Trust Territories in West Africa, Together with Related Documents,* 1949.
United Nations, Trusteeship Council, Official Records: Eleventh Session, Special Supplement Nos. 1–2 (T/1034), *Special Report of the United Nations Visiting Mission to Trust Territories in West Africa, 1952, on the Ewe and Togoland Unification Problem,* November 7, 1952. P. 857.
*United Nations, Trusteeship Council, Official Records: Thirteenth Session, 1954, Supplement No. 3 (T/1108), United Nations Visiting Mission to Trust Territories in West Africa, 1952, *Report on Togoland under French Administration.* P. 848.
*United Nations, Trusteeship Council, Official Records: Thirteenth Session, 1954, Supplement No. 5 (T/1110), United Nations Visiting Mission to Trust Territories in West Africa, 1952, *Report on the Cameroons under French Administration.* P. 848.
United Nations, Trusteeship Council, Official Records: Seventeenth Session, 1956, Supplement No. 2 (T/1238), United Nations Visiting Mission to the Trust Territories of Togoland under British Administration and Togoland under French Administration, 1955, *Report on Togoland under French Administration.*
United Nations, Trusteeship Council, Official Records: Seventeenth Session, 1956, Supplement No. 4 (T/1240), United Nations Visiting Mission to the Trust Territories of the Cameroons under British Administration and the Cameroons under French Administration, 1955, *Report on the Cameroons under French Administration.*
United Nations, Trusteeship Council, Official Records: Seventh Special Session, 1957, Supplement No. 2 (T/1343), *Report of the United Nations Commission on Togoland under French Administration,* 1957.
United Nations (T/1441), Trusteeship Council, Official Records: Twenty-Third Session, 1959, Supplement No. 3. United Nations Visiting Mission to Trust Territories in West Africa, 1958, *Report on the Cameroons under French Administration.*
United Nations, Trusteeship Council, Official Records: Eleventh Special

Session, 1961 (T/1556), *Report of the United Nations Commissioner for the Supervision of the Plebiscites in the Southern and Northern Parts of the Trust Territory of the Cameroons under United Kingdom Administration,* April 3, 1961, Dhalal Abdoh, Commissioner.

*United States, Department of State, *Papers Relating to the Foreign Relations of the United States,* Washington, 1943. P. 832.

*Usborne, Cecil V., *Conquest of Morocco,* London, 1936. P. 819.

*van Bulck, G., "Le Prophète Harris vu par lui-meme," *Devant les sectes, non chrétiennes. Rapports et compte rendu de la XXXIe siècle semaine de Missiologie,* Louvain, 1961, 120–24. P. 880.

*Vernon-Jackson, Hugh O. H., *Language, Schools and Government in Cameroon,* New York, 1967. P. 875.

*Viard, Paul-Emile, *Les Caractères politiques et le régime législatif de l'Algérie,* Paris, 1949. P. 803.

*———, *Les Droits politiques des indigènes d'Algérie,* Paris, 1937. P. 802.

*Viard, René, *La Fin de l'empire colonial français,* Paris, 1963. P. 850.

*Vibert, Jean, *L'Economie Tunisienne à la Fin de 1955. Notes et Études Documentaires,* Tunis, 1955. P. 818.

*Vidal, Federico S., "Religious Brotherhoods in Moroccan Politics," *Middle East Journal,* October 1950, 427–46. P. 823.

*Vidal-Naquet, Pierre, *La Raison d'Etat: textes publiées par le comité Maurice Audin,* Paris, 1962. P. 807.

*———, *Torture, Cancer of Democracy: France and Algeria, 1954–1962,* London, 1963. P. 807.

*Vignaud, M., "Les Elections du 2 janvier 1956 en Côte d'Ivoire," *Revue Française de Science Politique,* July–Sept., 1956, 570–82. P. 856.

Vignes, K., "Etude sur la rivalité d'influence entre les puissances européenes en Afrique équatoriale et occidentale depuis l'acte général de Berlin jusqu'au seuil du XXe siècle," *Revue française d'histoire d'outre-mer, 48* (1961).

———, "Etude sur les relations franco-britanniques qui conduisirent à la convention du 14 juin 1898," ibid., 52 (1965).

*Villard, André, *Histoire du Sénégal,* Dakar, 1943. P. 855.

*Villemagne, Edmond Marquier de, *La Congrégation du Saint Esprit et l'oeuvre des missions catholiques en A.E.F. (1839–1939–1940),* Thesis, University of Paris, 1965. P. 878.

*Violette, Maurice, *L'Algérie: vivra-t-elle? Notes d'un gouverneur-général,* Paris, 1931. P. 802.

*von Grunebaum, Gustav E., *French African Literature: Some Cultural Implications,* The Hague, 1964. P. 876.

*Wade, Abdoulaye, *Economie de l'ouest-africain: unité et croissance,* Doctorat d'Etat in Law, Grenoble, 1959. P. 867.

*Wagret, Jean-Michel, *Histoire et sociologie politique de la République du Congo (Brazzaville),* Paris, 1963. P. 860.

*Walker, Frank Deauville, *The Story of the Ivory Coast,* London, 1926. P. 881.

*Wallerstein, Immanuel, *The Road to Independence: Ghana and the Ivory Coast,* The Hague, 1964. P. 856.

*———, *Social Change: The Colonial Situation,* New York, 1966. P. 884.

*Wauthier, Claude, *L'Afrique des Africains. Inventaire de la négritude*, Paris, 1964, trans., *The Literature and Thought of Modern Africa: A Survey*, New York, 1967. P. 876.

*Weinstein, Brian, *Gabon: Nation-Building on the Ogooué*, Cambridge, Mass., 1966. P. 860.

*———, "Felix Eboué and the Chiefs: Perception of Power in Early Oubangui-Chari," *Journal of African History, 11* (1970), 107–26. Pp. 839, 886.

*———, *Eboué*, New York, 1971. P. 845.

Weiss, Herbert, "Comparisons in the Evolution of Pre-Independence Elites in French-Speaking West Africa and the Congo," in *French-Speaking Africa: The Search for Identity*, ed. W. H. Lewis, New York, 1965.

*Weithas, M. L. J. E., *La Conquête du Cameroun et du Togo*, Paris, 1931. P. 829.

*Welch, Claude, *Dream of Unity: Pan-Africanism and Political Unification in West Africa*, Ithaca, 1966. Pp. 835, 848, 857, 858.

*Werth, Alexander, *The Strange History of Pierre Mendès-France and the Great Conflict over French North Africa*, London, 1957. P. 817.

*Weygand, Maxime, *Mémoires: Rappelé au service*, Paris, 1950. Pp. 793, 843.

*Wheeler, Sister Joan, *L'Action missionnaire de la Congrégation du Saint-Esprit au Cameroun, 1919–1939*, Thesis, University of Paris, 1964. P. 878.

*Wilbois, Joseph, *Le Cameroun*, Paris, 1934. P. 833.

*Wilson, John, *Education and Changing West African Culture*, New York, 1963. P. 876.

*Winder, R. Bayley, "The Lebanese in West Africa," *Comparative Studies in Society and History*, April 1962. P. 868.

*Wipper, Audrey, "A Comparative Study of Nascent Unionism in French West Africa and the Philippines," *Economic Development and Cultural Change*, Oct. 1964, 20–55. P. 872.

*Wisner, Sylvain, *L'Algérie dans l'impasse: démission de la France*, Paris, 1948. P. 803.

*Witte, Johan de, *Un Explorateur et un apôtre en Congo française, Monseigneur Augouard—Vicaire Apostolique du Congo française; sa vie—ses notes de voyage et sa correspondance*, Paris, 1924. P. 878.

Wodie, Francis, "La Vie politique en Côte d'Ivoire de 1945 à 1969," *Revue Algérienne des Sciences Juridiques, Economiques, et Politiques*, June 1969.

*Wohlfahrt, Margaret and Eberhard, *Nordafrika: Tunisien, Algerien, Marokko*, Stuttgart, 1955. P. 790.

*Woolman, David S., *Abd el Krim and the Rif Rebellion*, Stanford, 1968. P. 821.

*Worsfold, W. Basil, *France in Tunis and Algeria: Studies of Colonial Administration*, London, 1930. P. 814.

*Wright, Gordon, *The Reshaping of French Democracy*, New York, 1948. P. 846.

*Yacef, Saadi, *Souvenirs de la bataille d'Alger, décembre 1956–septembre 1957*, Paris, 1962. P. 805.

*Yacono, Xavier, *Les Bureaux arabes at l'évolution des genres de vie indigènes dans l'Ouest du Tell algérien,* Paris, 1953. P. 799.

*———, *La Colonisation des plaines du Chélif, de Lavigerie au conference de la Mina,* 2 vols., Paris, 1955–56. P. 798.

*———, "L'Economie algérienne," in J. Alazard et al., *Initiation à l'Algérie,* Paris, 1957. P. 799.

———, "A propos d'un grand livre d'Histoire de l'Algérie," *Revue d'histoire moderne et contemporaine,* Oct.–Dec., 1965.

———, *Un Siècle de Franc-Maçonnerie Algérienne,* Paris, 1969.

*Youlou, Abbé Fulbert, *Le Matsouanisme,* Brazzaville, 1955. P. 881.

*Zang-Atangana, Joseph-Marie, "Les Partis politiques camerounais," *Recueil Penant,* December 1960. P. 858.

*———, *Les Forces politiques du cameroun réunifié,* Thesis, Paris, 1963. P. 858.

*Zenati, R., *Le Problème algérien vu par un indigène,* Alençon, 1938. P. 800.

*Ziadeh, Nicola A., *The Origins of Nationalism in Tunisia,* Beirut, 1962. Pp. 815, 816.

*Zolberg, Aristide, *One-Party Government in the Ivory Coast,* Princeton, 1964. P. 856.

CONTRIBUTORS

RALPH A. AUSTEN (Ph.D. Harvard University) is an assistant professor at the University of Chicago, where he teaches African history. He is the author of *Northwest Tanzania under German and British Rule: Colonial Policy and Tribal Politics, 1889–1939* (New Haven, 1968); and *Modern Imperialism: Western Overseas Expansion and Its Aftermath, 1776–1965* (New York, 1969). Together with Wm. Roger Louis he is writing a textbook on European Imperialism.

HENRI BRUNSCHWIG (Agrégé d'histoire, Docteur ès lettres, Strasbourg) is director, Ecole pratique des hautes études, Paris, and professor at the Institut des sciences politiques. He is the author of *Mythes et réalités de l'impérialisme colonial français, 1871–1914* (Paris, 1960), *L'Avènement de l'Afrique noire du XIXe siècle à nos jours* (Paris, 1963), and numerous articles on De Brazza and French expansion in colonial Africa.

WILLIAM B. COHEN (Ph.D. Stanford University) is the author of *Rulers of Empire: The French Colonial Service in Africa* (Hoover Institution Press, 1971). His interests include European imperialism, French history, and modern Europe. He is assistant professor at Indiana University.

HUBERT J. DESCHAMPS (Licencié en droit, Docteur ès lettres, Paris), a former colonial governor (1938–50), is the author of thirty works, among which the best known are *Les Méthodes et doctrines coloniales de la France* (Paris, 1953), *Histoire de Madagascar* (Paris, 1960), and *L'Europe découvre l'Afrique* (Paris, 1967). Editor of a general history of black Africa (1970), he has in preparation a history of the slave trade. He is professor of modern African history at the University of Paris.

DAVID K. FIELDHOUSE (M.A. Oxford University) is Beit Lecturer in Commonwealth History and a Fellow of Nuffield College, Oxford. His written work includes *The Colonial Empires* (London, 1966) and *The Theory of Capitalist Imperialism* (London, 1967).

JEAN GANIAGE (Agrégé de l'Université, Docteur ès lettres, Paris) is the author of *Les Origines du protectorat français en Tunisie, 1861–1881* (Paris, 1959), *Histoire de l'Afrique au XXe siècle* (Paris, 1966), *L'Expansion coloniale de la France sous la IIIe République* (Paris, 1968) and other works. He is professor of contemporary history at the Sorbonne, where he teaches courses in European imperialism and historical demography.

DAVID E. GARDINIER (Ph.D. Yale University) is the author of *Cameroon: United Nations Challenge to French Policy* (London, 1963) and is currently completing a history of the states of former French Equatorial Africa. He serves as subeditor for the African history section of the *American Historical Review* and is professor and chairman at Marquette University.

PROSSER GIFFORD (Ph.D. Yale University) teaches African history at Amherst College, where he is also dean of the faculty. He edited (with Wm. Roger Louis) *Britain and Germany in Africa* (New Haven, 1967) and has in preparation a collection of documents from African history before 1800 and a series of essays interrelating African literature and history.

DAVID C. GORDON (Ph.D. Princeton University) is the author of *The Passing of French Algeria* (Oxford, 1966) among other studies. He is a professor of history at the American University of Beirut.

PIERRE GUILLEN (Agrégé de l'Université, Docteur ès lettres) is the author of *Germany and Morocco from 1870 to 1905* (Paris, 1967) and of numerous articles on North African problems. Having been for several years professor of contemporary history at the University of Rabat (Morocco), he now teaches at the University of Grenoble.

JOHN D. HARGREAVES (M.A. University of Manchester) is professor of history at the University of Aberdeen. He has taught in Sierra Leone and Nigeria. His books include *A Life of Sir Samuel Lewis* (London, 1958); *Prelude to the Partition of West Africa* (London, 1963); and *West Africa: The Former French States* (Englewood Cliffs, N.J., 1967).

ROBERT HEUSSLER (Ph.D., Princeton University) is a visiting Fellow in the Center of International Studies, Princeton University. Author of

Yesterday's Rulers (Syracuse, 1963) and *The British in Northern Nigeria* (London, 1968), his latest book is *British Tanganyika* (Durham, N.C., 1971).

A. S. KANYA-FORSTNER (Ph.D. Cambridge University) is the author of *The Conquest of the Western Sudan: A Study in French Military Imperialism* (Cambridge, 1969) and several articles on the history of French Africa. He is a Fellow of Gonville and Caius College, Cambridge, where he teaches European expansion and African history.

ANDRÉ KASPI (Doctorat de Troisième Cycle, Université de Paris) has written "The United States and the French question in 1943." He is now at work on a book concerning French-American relations in 1917–18. He is *maître-assistant* at the Sorbonne, where he teaches the history of the United States.

WM. ROGER LOUIS (D.Phil. Oxford University) is the author of *Ruanda-Urundi 1884–1919* (Oxford, 1963), *Germany's Lost Colonies* (Oxford, 1967), *E. D. Morel's History of the Congo Reform Association* (with Jean Stengers; Oxford, 1968) and *British Strategy in the Far East, 1919–1939* (Oxford, 1971). He is professor of history at the University of Texas.

D. BRUCE MARSHALL (Ph.D. Yale University) is a specialist in international relations with a particular interest in French politics. He is preparing a major study, *The French Colonial Myth and Constitution-making in the Fourth Republic,* to be published by Yale University Press. At present, he is assistant professor of international studies at the University of South Carolina.

COLIN W. NEWBURY (Ph.D. Australian National University) is the author of *The Western Slave Coast and Its Rulers* (Oxford, 1961) and *British Policy Towards West Africa,* vol. 1, *Select Documents, 1786–1874* (Oxford, 1965), among other studies. He is a Senior Research Officer at the Institute of Commonwealth Studies and a Fellow of Linacre College and is presently engaged in an extensive study of immigration policies.

BONIFACE OBICHERE (D.Phil. Oxford University) is associate professor of history at the University of California, Los Angeles, and is the author of *West African States and European Expansion: The Dahomey-Niger Hinterland, 1885–1898* (New Haven, 1971). He spent the year 1970–71 doing research in Nigeria.

AGATHA RAMM (M.A. Oxford University) is editor of *The Political Correspondence of Mr. Gladstone and Lord Granville* (2 vols., Royal

Historical Society, 1952; 2 vols., Oxford University Press, 1962) and author of "The Crimean War" in *New Cambridge Modern History*, vol. 10, and *Germany, 1789–1919* (London, 1967). She is a Fellow of Somerville College, Oxford, and university lecturer in nineteenth-century history.

HARRY R. RUDIN (Ph.D. Yale University) is professor emeritus of history, Yale University. He is the author of *Germans in the Cameroons, 1884–1914: A Case Study in Modern Imperialism* (New Haven, 1938) and *Armistice, 1918* (New Haven, 1944). He is presently completing a manuscript on international security and writing a book on the Congo.

G. N. SANDERSON (Ph.D. University of London) is the author of *England, Europe, and the Upper Nile, 1882–1899* (Edinburgh, 1965) and numerous articles. He taught at the University of Khartoum and is now professor of modern history, Royal Holloway College, University of London. His main interests are in the partition of Africa and the modern history of the Sudan.

JEAN STENGERS (Ph.D. University of Brussels) is chairman of the Department of History at the University of Brussels. His books include *Combien le Congo a-t-il coûte à la Belgique?* (Brussels, 1957), *Belgique et Congo: l'élaboration de la Charte coloniale* (Brussels, 1963), and, with Wm. Roger Louis, *E. D. Morel's History of the Congo Reform Association* (Oxford, 1968).

LEONARD M. THOMPSON (M.A. Oxford University, D.Litt. Rhodes University) now teaches African history at Yale. His books include *The Unification of South Africa* (Oxford, 1960) and *Politics in the Republic of South Africa* (Boston, 1966) and he is co-editor of *The Oxford History of South Africa* (vol. 1, 1969; vol. 2, 1970).

TIMOTHY C. WEISKEL (B.A. Yale University) is a student of French-speaking West Africa. He is undertaking research at the Institute of Social Anthropology and Balliol College, Oxford, under a Rhodes Scholarship. His current work focuses upon African responses to colonial administration.

INDEX